THE POEMS OF SEAMUS HEANEY

by the same author

poetry
DEATH OF A NATURALIST
DOOR INTO THE DARK
WINTERING OUT
NORTH
FIELD WORK
SELECTED POEMS 1965–1975
STATION ISLAND
SWEENEY ASTRAY
SWEENEY'S FLIGHT
(*with photographs by Rachel Giese*)
THE HAW LANTERN
NEW SELECTED POEMS 1966–1987
SEEING THINGS
LAMENTS BY JAN KOCHANOWSKI
(*translated with Stanisław Barańczak*)
THE SPIRIT LEVEL
OPENED GROUND: POEMS 1966–1996
BEOWULF
ELECTRIC LIGHT
DISTRICT AND CIRCLE
THE TESTAMENT OF CRESSEID & SEVEN FABLES
HUMAN CHAIN
NEW SELECTED POEMS 1988–2013
AENEID BOOK VI
100 POEMS
THE TRANSLATIONS OF SEAMUS HEANEY
(*edited by Marco Sonzogni*)

THE RATTLE BAG
(*edited with Ted Hughes*)
THE SCHOOL BAG
(*edited with Ted Hughes*)

prose
PREOCCUPATIONS: SELECTED PROSE 1968–1978
THE GOVERNMENT OF THE TONGUE
THE REDRESS OF POETRY: OXFORD LECTURES
FINDERS KEEPERS: SELECTED PROSE 1971–2001
STEPPING STONES
(*with Dennis O'Driscoll*)
THE LETTERS OF SEAMUS HEANEY
(*edited by Christopher Reid*)

plays
THE CURE AT TROY
THE BURIAL AT THEBES

The Poems of

SEAMUS HEANEY

edited with an introduction and commentary by

ROSIE LAVAN *and* BERNARD O'DONOGHUE
with MATTHEW HOLLIS

faber

First published in 2025
by Faber & Faber Ltd
The Bindery, 51 Hatton Garden
London EC1N 8HN

Typeset by Sam Matthews
Printed by CPI Group UK Ltd, Croydon CR0 4YY

All rights reserved
© The Estate of Seamus Heaney, 2025
Introduction and editorial matter © Rosie Lavan, Bernard O'Donoghue and Matthew Hollis, 2025

The right of Rosie Lavan, Bernard O'Donoghue and Matthew Hollis to be identified as editors of this work has been asserted in accordance with Section 77 of the Copyright, Designs and Patents Act 1988

A CIP record for this book is available from the British Library

ISBN 978–0–571–34038–5

Printed and bound in the UK on FSC® certified paper in line with our continuing commitment to ethical business practices, sustainability and the environment.
For further information see faber.co.uk/environmental-policy

Our authorised representative in the EU for product safety is
Easy Access System Europe, Mustamäe tee 50, 10621 Tallinn, Estonia
gpsr.requests@easproject.com

10 9 8 7 6 5 4

Contents

Acknowledgements xxvii
Abbreviations xxx
Archives xxxii
Introduction xxxiii
A Note on the Text xli

POEMS

UNCOLLECTED POEMS (1959–1966)

Reaping in Heat 5
October Thought 5
Nostalgia in the Afternoon 6
Aran 6
Lines to Myself 7
Song of My Man-Alive 7
Her Home 8
Tractors 9
Scotch Fir in City Cemetery 9
Going In 10
Essences 10
Welfare State 11
Poor Man's Death 11
MacKenna's Saturday Night 12
Fair 12
Fisher 13
The Indomitable Irishry 13
Easter Son 14
Such Men Are Dangerous 14
Writer and Teacher 15
Young Bachelor 15
Soliloquy for an Old Resident 16
Taking Stock 17
On Hogarth's Engraving 'Pit Ticket for the Royal Sport' 18
Saint Patrick's Stone 19
Peter Street at Bankside 20
Lint Water 20
Gate 21
For a Young Nun 21

DEATH OF A NATURALIST (1966)

Digging 25
Death of a Naturalist 26
The Barn 27
An Advancement of Learning 27
Blackberry-Picking 28
Churning Day 29
The Early Purges 30
Follower 31
Ancestral Photograph 31
Mid-Term Break 32
Dawn Shoot 33
At a Potato Digging 34
For the Commander of the 'Eliza' 36
The Diviner 37
Turkeys Observed 37
Cow in Calf 38
Trout 38
Waterfall 39
Docker 39
Poor Women in a City Church 40
Gravities 40
Twice Shy 41
Valediction 42
Lovers on Aran 42
Poem 42
Honeymoon Flight 43
Scaffolding 44
Storm on the Island 44
Synge on Aran 45
Saint Francis and the Birds 45
In Small Townlands 46
The Folk Singers 46
The Play Way 47
Personal Helicon 47

UNCOLLECTED POEMS (1966–1969)

Thaw 51
Aries 51
Rookery 51
Aubade 52
Triptych for the Easter Battlers 52

Boy Driving His Father to Confession 54
South Derry Evening 55
Corncrake 56
Chestnut Time 56
Last Look 56
Child Lost 57
The Survivor 57
The Evening Land 58
Ceili on the Deck 58
Inisheer 59
The Oarsmen's Song 59
The Basket-Maker 60
The Basket-Maker's Song 60
Michael 61
Neddy 61
The Dealing Man 62
The Dealer 62
The Cargo 63
Lullaby 63
Bachelor Deceased 64
Frogman 65
Driving in the Small Hours 66
Birdwatcher 67
In an Airport Coach 67

DOOR INTO THE DARK (1969)

Night-Piece 71
Gone 71
Dream 71
The Outlaw 72
The Salmon Fisher to the Salmon 73
The Forge 73
Thatcher 74
The Peninsula 74
In Gallarus Oratory 75
Girls Bathing, Galway, 1965 75
Requiem for the Croppies 76
Rite of Spring 76
Undine 77
The Wife's Tale 77
Mother 78
Cana Revisited 79

Elegy for a Still-born Child 79
Victorian Guitar 80
Night Drive 80
At Ardboe Point 81
Relic of Memory 82
A Lough Neagh Sequence 83
  1 *Up the Shore* 83
  2 *Beyond Sargasso* 83
  3 *Bait* 84
  4 *Setting* 85
  5 *Lifting* 85
  6 *The Return* 86
  7 *Vision* 87
The Given Note 87
Whinlands 88
The Plantation 89
Shoreline 90
Bann Clay 91
Bogland 91

UNCOLLECTED POEMS (1969–1972)

Medallion 95
Icon 95
Idyll 96
Offerings 97
  1 *Turnip Man* 97
  2 *High Street, 1786* 97
  3 *From Cave Hill* 98
  4 *September Song* 98
An Evening at Killard 99
Their Brother 99
Crowing Man 100
Lictor 100
A Twilight 101
Yank 101
Elegy for a Postman 102
Rags 103
Third Degree 103
Retort 104
Last Camp 104
Intimidation 105
Rubric 106

Museum Pieces 106
Craig's Dragoons 107
Letter to an Editor 108
Slieve Gallon's Brae 109
Woodcut 109
Father of the Bride 110
Baptism 110
The Blinker 111
Scullions 111
January God 112
Sile na Gig 112

WINTERING OUT (1972)
For David Hammond and Michael Longley 117
Fodder 117
Bog Oak 118
Anahorish 119
Servant Boy 119
The Last Mummer 120
Land 121
Gifts of Rain 122
Toome 124
Broagh 125
Oracle 125
The Backward Look 126
Traditions 127
A New Song 128
The Other Side 128
The Wool Trade 130
Linen Town 131
A Northern Hoard 132
  1 *Roots* 132
  2 *No Man's Land* 132
  3 *Stump* 133
  4 *No Sanctuary* 133
  5 *Tinder* 133
Midnight 134
The Tollund Man 135
Nerthus 136
Cairn-Maker 136
Navvy 137
Veteran's Dream 137

Augury 138
Wedding Day 139
Mother of the Groom 139
Summer Home 140
Serenades 141
Somnambulist 142
A Winter's Tale 142
Shore Woman 143
Maighdean Mara 144
Limbo 146
Bye-Child 146
Good-night 147
First Calf 147
May 148
Fireside 149
Dawn 149
Travel 150
Westering 150

UNCOLLECTED POEMS (1973–1975)

A New Life 155
A Flourish for the Prince of Denmark 156
The Belfast Harp Festival 1792 157
John Field 157
The Poet Crowned 158

STATIONS (1975)

Cauled 161
Branded 161
Hedge-School 161
Nesting Ground 162
Sinking the Shaft 162
Waterbabies 163
Patrick and Oisin 163
Sweet William 164
The Discharged Soldier 164
The Sabbath-Breakers 164
Kernes 165
July 166
England's Difficulty 166
Visitant 167
Trial Runs 167
The Wanderer 168

Cloistered 168
Ballad 169
The Stations of the West 169
Inquisition 170
Incertus 170

NORTH (1975)

Mossbawn: Two Poems in Dedication 173
  1 *Sunlight* 173
  2 *The Seed Cutters* 174
Antaeus 174
Belderg 175
Funeral Rites 176
North 178
Viking Dublin: Trial Pieces 180
The Digging Skeleton 183
Bone Dreams 184
Come to the Bower 187
Bog Queen 187
The Grauballe Man 189
Punishment 190
Strange Fruit 191
Kinship 192
Ocean's Love to Ireland 196
Aisling 197
Act of Union 197
The Betrothal of Cavehill 198
Hercules and Antaeus 198
The Unacknowledged Legislator's Dream 199
Whatever You Say Say Nothing 200
Freedman 203
Singing School 203
  1 *The Ministry of Fear* 204
  2 *A Constable Calls* 205
  3 *Orange Drums, Tyrone, 1966* 206
  4 *Summer 1969* 207
  5 *Fosterage* 208
  6 *Exposure* 208

UNCOLLECTED POEMS (1975–1979)

A Strange House 213
The Pleasures of the Day 213
A Toy for Catherine 214

FIELD WORK (1979)

  Oysters 217
  Triptych 217
    I *After a Killing* 217
    II *Sibyl* 218
    III *At the Water's Edge* 219
  The Toome Road 219
  A Drink of Water 220
  The Strand at Lough Beg 220
  A Postcard from North Antrim 221
  Casualty 223
  The Badgers 226
  The Singer's House 227
  The Guttural Muse 228
  In Memoriam Sean Ó Riada 229
  Elegy 230
  Glanmore Sonnets 231
  September Song 235
  An Afterwards 236
  High Summer 237
  The Otter 238
  The Skunk 239
  Homecomings 240
  A Dream of Jealousy 240
  Polder 241
  Field Work 241
  Song 243
  Leavings 243
  The Harvest Bow 244
  In Memoriam Francis Ledwidge 245
  Ugolino 246

UNCOLLECTED POEMS (1979–1984)

  A Cart for Edward Gallagher 253
  A Hank of Wool 254
  A Villanelle for Marie 255
  The Well at New Place 256
  A Lighting Plot 256
  An Open Letter 257
  A Summer Night 263
  Among the Whins 264
  Anniversary Verse 265

Verses for a Fordham Commencement 267
Ulster Quatrains 275
  1 *Sectarian Water* 275
  2 *Sectarian Latin* 275
  3 *Sectarian Alphabet* 276
Pastoral 276
Expectant 276
Station Island III 277
Shelf Life 279
  I *Old Perfume Bottle* 279
  II *Pussy Willow* 279
  III *Pewters* 280
Station Island IV 280
A Night Piece for Tom Flanagan 282
The Hag 285
A Paved Text 285
The Easter House 286
Tremor 287

STATION ISLAND (1984)

The Underground 291
La Toilette 291
Sloe Gin 292
Away from it All 292
Chekhov on Sakhalin 293
Sandstone Keepsake 294
Shelf Life 295
  1 *Granite Chip* 295
  2 *Old Smoothing Iron* 295
  3 *Old Pewter* 296
  4 *Iron Spike* 296
  5 *Stone from Delphi* 297
  6 *A Snowshoe* 297
A Migration 298
Last Look 300
Remembering Malibu 301
Making Strange 302
The Birthplace 303
Changes 304
An Ulster Twilight 305
A Bat on the Road 306
A Hazel Stick for Catherine Ann 307

A Kite for Michael and Christopher 308
The Railway Children 308
Sweetpea 309
An Aisling in the Burren 309
Widgeon 310
Sheelagh na Gig 310
The Loaning 312
The Sandpit 313
  1 *1946* 313
  2 *The Demobbed Bricklayer* 313
  3 *The Sand Boom* 314
  4 *What the Brick Keeps* 315
The King of the Ditchbacks 315
Station Island 317
The First Gloss 337
Sweeney Redivivus 337
Unwinding 338
In the Beech 338
The First Kingdom 339
The First Flight 339
Drifting Off 340
Alerted 341
The Cleric 342
The Hermit 342
The Master 343
The Scribes 344
A Waking Dream 344
In the Chestnut Tree 345
Sweeney's Returns 345
Holly 346
An Artist 346
The Old Icons 347
In Illo Tempore 347
On the Road 348

UNCOLLECTED POEMS (1985–1987)

  The Late Paul Cézanne 353
  Lenten Stuff 353
  Villanelle for an Anniversary 354
  Birthday Tribute to Marie Bullock 354

THE HAW LANTERN (1987)

   Alphabets 357
   Terminus 359
   From the Frontier of Writing 359
   The Haw Lantern 360
   The Stone Grinder 361
   A Daylight Art 361
   Parable Island 362
   From the Republic of Conscience 363
   Hailstones 365
   Two Quick Notes 366
   The Stone Verdict 366
   From the Land of the Unspoken 367
   A Ship of Death 368
   The Spoonbait 369
   In Memoriam: Robert Fitzgerald 369
   The Old Team 370
   Clearances 370
   The Milk Factory 374
   The Summer of Lost Rachel 374
   The Wishing Tree 375
   A Postcard from Iceland 375
   A Peacock's Feather 376
   Grotus and Coventina 377
   Holding Course 377
   The Song of the Bullets 378
   Wolfe Tone 379
   A Shooting Script 380
   From the Canton of Expectation 380
   The Mud Vision 382
   The Disappearing Island 383
   The Riddle 384

UNCOLLECTED POEMS (1988–1989)

   Valedictory Verses 387
   Dublin 4 387
   New Worlds 387
   The Strand Hotel 388
   Resin 388
   from Holdings 389
   Five Derry Glosses 390

THE CURE AT TROY (1990)

from Voices from Lemnos: IV 395

UNCOLLECTED POEMS (1990–1991)

Grove Hill 399
The Stirling Stanzas 399

SEEING THINGS (1991)

The Golden Bough 403
The Journey Back 404
Markings 405
Three Drawings 406
  1 *The Point* 406
  2 *The Pulse* 407
  3 *A Haul* 407
Casting and Gathering 408
Man and Boy 409
Seeing Things 410
The Ash Plant 411
1.1.87 412
An August Night 412
Field of Vision 412
The Pitchfork 413
A Basket of Chestnuts 414
The Biretta 414
The Settle Bed 416
The Schoolbag 417
Glanmore Revisited 417
  1 *Scrabble* 417
  2 *The Cot* 418
  3 *Scene Shifts* 418
  4 *1973* 418
  5 *Lustral Sonnet* 419
  6 *Bedside Reading* 419
  7 *The Skylight* 420
A Pillowed Head 420
A Royal Prospect 421
A Retrospect 422
The Rescue 424
Wheels within Wheels 424
The Sounds of Rain 425
Fosterling 426

Squarings 427
  1 *Lightenings* 427
  2 *Settings* 432
  3 *Crossings* 437
  4 *Squarings* 442
The Crossing 448

UNCOLLECTED POEMS (1992–1996)

To Sorley MacLean 453
The Villanelle of Northwest Orient Flight 4 454
Skims and Glances 455
More River Rhymes 456
A Landfall 457
Cheers 458
In Bellaghy Graveyard 458
A Transgression 458

THE SPIRIT LEVEL (1996)

The Rain Stick 463
To a Dutch Potter in Ireland 463
  2 *After Liberation* 465
A Brigid's Girdle 465
Mint 466
A Sofa in the Forties 467
Keeping Going 468
Two Lorries 470
Damson 472
Weighing In 473
St Kevin and the Blackbird 474
The Flight Path 475
An Invocation 478
Mycenae Lookout 480
  1 *The Watchman's War* 480
  2 *Cassandra* 481
  3 *His Dawn Vision* 483
  4 *The Nights* 483
  5 *His Reverie of Water* 485
The First Words 486
The Gravel Walks 486
Whitby-sur-Moyola 487
The Thimble 488
The Butter-Print 489

Remembered Columns 489
'Poet's Chair' 490
The Swing 491
The Poplar 493
Two Stick Drawings 493
A Call 494
The Errand 494
A Dog Was Crying Tonight in Wicklow Also 495
M. 495
An Architect 496
The Sharping Stone 496
The Strand 498
The Walk 498
At the Wellhead 499
At Banagher 500
Tollund 501
Postscript 502

UNCOLLECTED POEMS (1996–2001)

A Grace Note for Michael 505
The Road to Derry 505
Three-Piece 505
  1 *A Suit* 505
  2 *A Tie* 506
  3 *A Coat* 507
Carlo 508
Two Paintings by Le Douanier Rousseau 509
  1 *La muse inspirant le poète* 509
  2 *'L'enfant aux rochers'* 510
Sonnets from the Peloponnese 510
  Bassae 510
  Mycenae 511
The Stick 511
Non-U 513
Our Lady of Guadalupe 514
Willow, Ophelia, Moyola 514
A Dream of Solstice 515
Screenplay 516
An Empty Surfboard on a Flat Sea 517
Úrlár 518
The Dearest Freshness 518
Postscript to St Lucia 519

Sally Rod 520
Trea 521
A Present from Mr Pause 521
No Harm 522
Natura Naturans 522
Brother Stalk 522
The Boiling House 523

ELECTRIC LIGHT (2001)

At Toomebridge 527
Perch 527
Lupins 527
Out of the Bag 528
Bann Valley Eclogue 531
Montana 532
The Loose Box 533
Turpin Song 535
The Border Campaign 536
Known World 536
The Little Canticles of Asturias 539
Ballynahinch Lake 541
The Clothes Shrine 541
Red, White and Blue 542
  1 *Red* 542
  2 *White* 542
  3 *Blue* 543
Virgil: Eclogue IX 544
Glanmore Eclogue 547
Sonnets from Hellas 549
  1 *Into Arcadia* 549
  2 *Conkers* 549
  3 *Pylos* 550
  4 *The Augean Stables* 550
  5 *Castalian Spring* 550
  6 *Desfina* 551
The Gaeltacht 551
The Real Names 552
The Bookcase 556
Vitruviana 557
Ten Glosses 558
  1 *The Marching Season* 558
  2 *The Catechism* 558

   3 *The Bridge* 559
   4 *A Suit* 559
   5 *The Party* 559
   6 *W. H. Auden, 1907–73* 559
   7 *The Lesson* 559
   8 *Moling's Gloss* 560
   9 *Colly* 560
  10 *A Norman Simile* 560
The Fragment 560
On His Work in the English Tongue 561
Audenesque 563
To the Shade of Zbigniew Herbert 565
'Would They Had Stay'd' 565
Late in the Day 566
Arion 567
Bodies and Souls 567
   1 *In the Afterlife* 567
   2 *Nights of '57* 568
   3 *The Bereaved* 568
Clonmany to Ahascragh 568
Sruth 569
Seeing the Sick 570
Electric Light 571

UNCOLLECTED POEMS (2001–2005)

  Le Brocquy's *Táin* 575
  The Snowball 576
  A Present from Old Ardboe 577
  In Memory of Bill Cole 577
  For Alma Mater 578
  A Keen for the Coins 578
  A Snapshot 579
  Sister Clare 579
  Watercolour 579
  Santiago de Compostela 580
  An Epithalamium 581
  The Big Wiper 583
  Sophoclean 583
  Pit Stop Near Castletown 584
  The Comet at Lullwater 585
  Beacons at Bealtaine 585
  An Iridescence 586

Confirmation Day 586
After Dark 587
Lauds and Gauds for a Laureate 587

DISTRICT AND CIRCLE (2006)

The Turnip-Snedder 593
A Shiver 593
Polish Sleepers 594
Anahorish 1944 594
To Mick Joyce in Heaven 595
The Aerodrome 597
Anything Can Happen 598
Helmet 598
Out of Shot 599
Rilke: After the Fire 599
District and Circle 600
To George Seferis in the Underworld 602
Wordsworth's Skates 603
The Harrow-Pin 603
Poet to Blacksmith 604
Midnight Anvil 605
Súgán 605
Senior Infants 606
  1 *The Sally Rod* 606
  2 *A Chow* 606
  3 *One Christmas Day in the Morning* 607
The Nod 608
A Clip 608
Edward Thomas on the Lagans Road 608
Found Prose 609
  1 *The Lagans Road* 609
  2 *Tall Dames* 610
  3 *Boarders* 611
The Lift 611
Nonce Words 612
Stern 613
Out of This World 614
  1 *'Like everybody else . . .'* 614
  2 *Brancardier* 614
  3 *Saw Music* 615
In Iowa 616
Höfn 617

On the Spot 617
The Tollund Man in Springtime 617
Moyulla 620
Planting the Alder 621
Tate's Avenue 622
A Hagging Match 622
Fiddleheads 622
To Pablo Neruda in Tamlaghtduff 623
Home Help 624
  1 *Helping Sarah* 624
  2 *Chairing Mary* 624
Rilke: The Apple Orchard 625
Quitting Time 625
Home Fires 626
  1 *A Scuttle for Dorothy Wordsworth* 626
  2 *A Stove Lid for W. H. Auden* 626
The Birch Grove 627
Cavafy: 'The rest I'll speak of to the ones below in Hades' 627
In a Loaning 628
The Blackbird of Glanmore 628

UNCOLLECTED POEMS (2006–2010)

  A Toast for Rand 633
  Our Mystery 633
  Fragment: 'Nairn in darkness and in light' 634
  Who Is Billy? 634
  Cutaways 635
  A Birl for Burns 637
  Centenary Stanza 638
  The City 638
  With Hindsight 639

HUMAN CHAIN (2010)

  'Had I not been awake' 643
  Album 643
  The Conway Stewart 645
  Uncoupled 646
  The Butts 646
  Chanson d'Aventure 648
  Miracle 649
  Human Chain 649

A Mite-Box 650
An Old Refrain 650
The Wood Road 651
The Baler 652
Derry Derry Down 653
Eelworks 654
Slack 656
A Herbal 657
Canopy 663
The Riverbank Field 664
Route 110 665
Death of a Painter 669
Loughanure 670
Wraiths 672
  I *Sidhe* 672
  II *Parking Lot* 672
  III *White Nights* 673
Sweeney Out-Takes 673
  I *Otterboy* 673
  II *He Remembers Lynchechaun* 674
  III *The Pattern* 674
Colum Cille Cecinit 674
  I *Is scíth mo chrob ón scríbainn* 674
  II *Is aire charaim Doire* 675
  III *Fil súil nglais* 675
Hermit Songs 675
'Lick the Pencil' 679
'The door was open and the house was dark' 680
In the Attic 680
A Kite for Aibhín 682

UNCOLLECTED POEMS (2010–2014)

'Of all those starting out' 685
Actaeon 685
On the Gift of a Fountain Pen 686
Lauds for Loretta 686
In a Field 687
In Time 688
The Latecomers 688
Banks of a Canal 689

COMMENTARY

Uncollected Poems (1959–1966) 693
Death of a Naturalist (1966) 701
Uncollected Poems (1966–1969) 721
Door into the Dark (1969) 727
Uncollected Poems (1969–1972) 743
Wintering Out (1972) 751
Uncollected Poems (1973–1975) 777
Stations (1975) 781
North (1975) 795
Uncollected Poems (1975–1979) 823
Field Work (1979) 825
Uncollected Poems (1979–1984) 855
Station Island (1984) 865
Uncollected Poems (1985–1987) 913
The Haw Lantern (1987) 915
Uncollected Poems (1988–1989) 947
The Cure at Troy (1990) 951
Uncollected Poems (1990–1991) 953
Seeing Things (1991) 955
Uncollected Poems (1992–1996) 999
The Spirit Level (1996) 1003
Uncollected Poems (1996–2001) 1037
Electric Light (2001) 1049
Uncollected Poems (2001–2005) 1087
District and Circle (2006) 1095
Uncollected Poems (2006–2010) 1131
Human Chain (2010) 1137
Uncollected Poems (2010–2014) 1165

APPENDICES

I: UNPUBLISHED POEMS 1175

At Yeats's Grave 1177
Lighting the Lamp 1177
Mirror 1178
Omen and Plan 1178
Hawthorns 1179
In a Yard 1180
The Dirraghs 1180
Twins 1181
Oral English 1181

Grief in North Antrim 1182
The Discovery of the Eel 1183
'Chestnut was the whitest wood veneer' 1183
An Education 1184
Ribbons 1185
The Whirligig 1186
The Race 1186
Arkansas 1187
Sweeney as Lyre 1188
Chair, Pocket Knife, Guitar 1189
Working the Head 1189
  1 *Plasterseed* 1189
  2 *Plaster Cast* 1190
The Cassette 1190
In the Loft 1191
Swallow 1191
Black Walnuts 1192
Those Winter Evenings 1192

COMMENTARY 1195

II: UNPUBLISHED COLLECTIONS IN TYPESCRIPT 1207
III: SELECTED EDITIONS AND RECORDINGS 1209

Bibliography 1221
Index of First Lines 1227
Index of Titles 1244

Acknowledgements

Our profound thanks are due to a great many people and institutions who have helped and advised us in our research for this edition.

Our deepest debt of all is to the Heaney family – Seamus's widow Marie, and his three children, Catherine, Christopher and Michael – for their indefatigable contribution to the work of this volume over many years, from commission to delivery. Their knowledge and advice have been invaluable, their trust and support enabling, and we cannot repay profoundly enough the patient and tireless way in which they have worked with us to engage and shape all elements of this edition. We would also like to thank warmly the wider Heaney family – especially Seamus and Marie's siblings and their families – for their support and encouragement throughout the process.

Our second debt is to Rand Brandes, whose bibliographic expertise and personal kindness are a fundamental presence in this edition. His tireless reception of editorial queries and his generous sharing of his own research materials have been to the immeasurable benefit of this publication.

Christopher Reid and Marco Sonzogni have been founts of information and advice, and we are indebted to them for their collegiate support throughout the publishing of Seamus Heaney's editions.

Our profound thanks are due also to the publishers of this edition, Faber & Faber in London, and Farrar, Straus and Giroux in New York, and also to the Gallery Press in Co. Meath, imprints with whom the author worked and published throughout his writing life: to Peter Fallon, Jane Feaver, Jonathan Galassi and Lavinia Greenlaw we are especially grateful; and to Samantha Matthews, also, for her textual expertise and care.

We are enduringly grateful to Eugene and Gerardine Kielt for their hospitality during our visits to Co. Derry, and to Eugene for the generosity with which he has shared his unparalleled knowledge of Heaney country.

In addition, our thanks are due to the following institutions (and individuals) who have aided us immeasurably in our research: Aidan Heavey Library, Athlone (especially Edel Scally); Amherst College Archives and Special Collections (Margaret R. Dakin); Bellaghy-Ballyscullion Parish, Co. Derry; the Bodleian Library; the British Library; the College of St Benedict and St John's University Archive

(Peggy Roske); Department of Special Collections, Stanford University; Drumragh Parish, Omagh, Co. Tyrone; Faber & Faber Archives (Leigh Haddix); Harvard University Library; *Harvard Review* (Chloe Garcia Roberts); Ireland Funds America; the Linen Hall Library, Belfast (Samantha McCombe); the London Library; Morris Library, Southern Illinois University (Matthew J. Gorzalski); National Irish Visual Arts Library at the National College of Arts and Design, Dublin; National Library of Ireland (Eoghan Ó Carragáin, Gerard Kavanagh and Ger Wilson); National Library of Scotland (Ciara Colthart); National Poetry Library, London; Pembroke College, Cambridge; the School of English, Trinity College Dublin; Senate House Library; Special Collections and Archives in the McClay Library, Queen's University Belfast; Special Collections and Archives, Z. Smith Reynolds Library, Wake Forest University (Megan Mulder); Special Collections Centre at the Sir Duncan Rice Library, University of Aberdeen; Special Collections Department, University of Memphis Libraries (Gerald Chaudron); St John's College, Oxford (Petra Hofmann and Angharad Jones); the staff of the Library of Trinity College Dublin (Tony Carey, Lydia Ferguson, Isolde Harpur, Maria Kelly, Simon Lang, Helen McGinley, Shane Mawe, Shona Nolan and Margaret Rooney); Stuart A. Rose Manuscripts, Archives and Rare Book Library, Emory University (Kathy Shoemaker); Thomas Fisher Rare Book Library, University of Toronto; University Archives and Special Collections, Fordham University (Gabriella DiMeglio and Vivian Shen); UC Berkeley Library; Special Collections, University College Cork Library (Crónán Ó Doibhlin); University College Dublin Special Collections; University of Galway Library; University of Notre Dame Archives; University of York Library; Wadham College, Oxford; War Memorial Library and College Archive, Trinity College, Oxford (Clare Hopkins).

We would also like to thank the following individuals for their personal and professional assistance with this edition: Rachel Alexander, Nicholas Allen, Alex Alonso, John Barnard, Jean Barry, William Bedford, Alex Bowler, Fran Brearton, Cathy Brown, Paddy Bushe, Jim Campbell, Mary Cannam, Moya Cannon, Eileen Carney, Ian Cathrow, Mike Cherry, Rali Chorbadzhiyska, David Clark, Sheila Clarke, Sophie Clarke, Mary Clayton, Brian Cliff, Harry Clifton, Catriona Clutterbuck, Ciara Colthart, Claire Connolly, Helen Conrad O'Briain, Neil Corcoran, Patricia Coughlan, Patrick Crotty, Tony Crowley, Caitriona Curtis, Julie Curtis, Anna Davidson, Gerald Dawe, Laura Degnan, Paul Delaney, Monsignor Andrew Dolan, Aileen Douglas, Gwendoline Dyar, Martin Dyar, Paddy Dyar, Terry Eagleton, Hans van Eijk, Martin Enright, Martina Evans, Mark Everett, Rachel

Falconer, Gabriel Fitzmaurice, Andrew Fitzsimons, Brendan Flynn, Tadhg Foley, Roy Foster, John Fuller, Sinead Garrigan, Luke Gibbons, Geoff Gould, Nicholas Grene, Jane Griffiths, Adolphe Haberer, Keith Hanley, Joe Hassett, Hugh Haughton, Nick Havely, Michael Henry, Ellen Hewings, Geraldine Higgins, Jefferson Holdridge, Alan Hollinghurst, Rose Hollis, Christopher Howell, Jodie Hyatt, Hamish Ironside, Darryl Jones, Des and Mary Kavanagh, Margaret Kelleher, Christine Kelly, John Kelly, Tom Kenny, Jarlath Killeen, Cormac Kinsella, Vera Kreilkamp, Catherine La Farge, Desmond Lally, Anne Lavan, Seamus Lavan, Hermione Lee, Cecilia Lybeck, Eleanor Lybeck, Eric Lybeck, Marianne Lybeck, Kathryn McCance, Joe McCann, Máirín MacCarron, Tom McCarthy, Gail McConnell, Lucy McDiarmid, Tara McEvoy, Iggy McGovern, Patrick McGuinness, Jamie McKendrick, Jim MacMahon, Joe McMinn, Niall MacMonagle, Andrew McNeillie, Kathryn McSharry, Deirdre Madden, Charbel Mattar, Julian May, John Minihan, Michael Moloney, Christopher Morash, Andrew Motion, Ankhi Mukherjee, Andrew Murphy, Bernice Murphy, Hayden Murphy, Fíona Ní Chinnéalaigh, Ailbhe Ní Ghearbhuigh, Cliona Ní Riordáin, David Norbrook, John O'Connor, Séamus Ó Cróinín, Cormac Ó Cuilleanáin, John O'Donnell, Heather O'Donoghue, Josie O'Donoghue, Tom O'Donoghue, Paul O'Donovan, Maura O'Leary, Stephen O'Neill, Edward O'Shea, Fintan O'Toole, Ray Ockenden, Jane Ohlmeyer, Ellen Orchard, Anne Owen, Michael Parker, Eve Patten, Brian Pattinson, Giti Paulin, Tom Paulin, Rosamund Pike, James Pinder, Amy Prendergast, John Purser, Stephen Regan, Marilynn Richtarik, John Rigby, Maurice Riordan, Margaret Robson, Steven Rose, Beaty Rubens, Richard Rankin Russell, Declan Ryan, Ray Ryan, Claire Sands, Antonio Raúl de Toro Santos, Ronald and Keith Schuchard, Frank Shovlin, Lavinia Singer, Peter Sirr, Ann-Marie Smith, Gerard Smyth, Martin Spoor, Fiona Stafford, Oliver Taplin, Hazel Thompson, Alice Troy-Donovan, Tom Walker, Thijs Weststrate, Michael Whitworth, David Williams, Ita Williams, Jonathan Williams, Mark Wormald, Enda Wyley, Robert Young.

Abbreviations

100P	*100 Poems* (2018)
ABVIa	*Aeneid Book VI* (2016)
ABVIb	*Aeneid Book VI* (FSG, 2016)
Beowulf	*Beowulf* (1999)
Beowulf BE	*Beowulf: Bilingual Edition* (FSG, 2000; Norton, 2001; Faber & Faber, 2007)
BP	*Bog Poems* (Rainbow Press, 1975)
BTa	*The Burial at Thebes* (2004)
BTb	*The Burial at Thebes* (FSG, 2004)
CP	*Crediting Poetry* (Gallery Press, 1995)
CTa	*The Cure at Troy* (Field Day/Faber & Faber, 1990)
CTb	*The Cure at Troy* (FSG, 1991)
DC	*District and Circle* (2006)
DD	*Door into the Dark* (1969)
DN	*Death of a Naturalist* (1966)
DOWV	*Diary of One Who Vanished* (1999)
EL	*Electric Light* (2001)
EP	*Eleven Poems* (Queen's University Belfast, 1965)
FA	*A Family Album* (Byron Press, 1979)
FK	*Finders Keepers: Selected Prose 1971–2001* (2002)
FP	*Four Poems* (Crannog Press, 1976)
FW	*Field Work* (1979)
Gravities	*Gravities: A Collection of Poems and Drawings* (with Noel Connor, Charlotte Press, 1979)
GS	*Glanmore Sonnets* (Edition Monika Beck, 1977)
GT	*The Government of the Tongue* (1988)
Hailstones	*Hailstones* (Gallery Press, 1984)
HC	*Human Chain* (2010)
HL	*The Haw Lantern* (1987)
KG	*Keeping Going* (Bow & Arrow Press, 1993)
Laments	*Jan Kochanowski: Laments* (1995)
LL	*The Light of the Leaves* (with Jan Hendrix, Bonnefant Press, 1999)
LSH	*The Letters of Seamus Heaney* (2023)
LW	*The Last Walk* (Gallery Press, 2013)
MV	*The Midnight Verdict* (Gallery Press, 1993, 2000)
ND	*Night Drive* (Richard Gilbertson, 1970)

North	North (1975)
NSP1990	New Selected Poems 1966–1987 (1990)
NSP2014	New Selected Poems 1988–2013 (2014)
OG	Opened Ground: Poems 1966–1996 (1998)
P1980	Poems 1965–1975 (1980)
PM	Poems and a Memoir (Limited Editions Club, 1982)
Preoccupations	Preoccupations: Selected Prose 1968–1978 (1980)
RP	The Redress of Poetry (1995)
PSH	The Poems of Seamus Heaney (2025)
RF	The Riverbank Field (Gallery Press, 2007)
SA	Sweeney Astray (Field Day, 1983; Faber & Faber, 1984)
SD	Stone from Delphi: Poems with Classical References, ed. Helen Vendler (Arion Press, 2012)
SF	Sweeney's Flight (1992)
SI	Station Island (1984)
SL	The Spirit Level (1996)
SP	Selected Poems 1965–1975 (1980)
Squarings12	Squarings: Twelve Poems (Hieroglyph, 1991)
Squarings48	Squarings: A Sequence of Forty-eight Poems (Arion, 2003)
SS	Stepping Stones (with Dennis O'Driscoll, 2008)
ST	Seeing Things (1991)
Stations	Stations (Ulsterman Publications, 1975)
TC	The Tree Clock (Linen Hall Library, 1990)
TCSF	The Testament of Cresseid & Seven Fables (2009)
Toome	Toome (National College of Art and Design, 1980)
TSH	The Translations of Seamus Heaney (2022)
WO	Wintering Out (1972)

(The publisher is Faber & Faber unless stated otherwise.)

Archives

BC	The Barrie Cooke Archive, Pembroke College Cambridge, MS 1280725, 1280758
EU	Emory University, Stuart A. Rose Manuscript, Archives, and Rare Book Library: MS Collection 644, Ted Hughes Papers MS Collection 653, Seamus Heaney Collection MS Collection 1420, Dennis O'Driscoll Papers
FF	Faber & Faber Archives, London: E/16, E/18; L7; ME104; N50; P/Rdlm/547, P/Rdlm/604, P/Rdlm/667, P/Rdlm/716, P/Rdlm/759, P/Rdlm/778
HFC	Heaney family collection
NLI	National Library of Ireland, Dept. of Manuscripts: MS 49,493, Seamus Heaney Literary Papers MS 49,602, McCabe Heaney Collection
NLS	National Library of Scotland, Archives and Manuscripts, Papers concerning *Broadsheet*, poetry magazine, containing manuscripts and typescripts of poems, with related correspondence, art work and press cuttings, Acc.8845

Introduction

This volume collects the poems that Seamus Heaney published in a final form in his lifetime, beginning during his days as an undergraduate at Queen's University Belfast in 1959, and concluding with those pieces he completed in the weeks immediately before his death in 2013. It constitutes a record of international and personal significance: from the violence and conflict of Northern Ireland, Afghanistan, Iraq, Kosovo and the attacks of 9/11 and 7/7, to some of the most intimate and memorable domestic portraits written over the past century of poetry in English. It traces a literary career marked by a rare combination of a readership that is both critical and popular: a poet who sold a million books within a lifetime, while garnering the most prestigious accolade of all, the Nobel Prize in Literature.

The qualities that define a life of such literary achievement are not easily summarised. Heaney's work covers such range and distance in poems, in prose and in interview, and does so with such vibrant articulacy, that a full exploration of its characteristics falls beyond the scope of this introduction. Nevertheless, certain strands running throughout his commentary and prosody can be woven together to offer insight. In an interview with friend and bibliographer Rand Brandes in 1988, Heaney said this:

> Fundamentally, what I want from poetry is the preciousness and foundedness of wise feeling become eternally posthumous in perfect cadence. Good poetry reminds you that writing is writing, it's not just expectoration or self-regard or a semaphore for self's sake. You want it to touch you at the melting point below the breastbone and the beginning of the solar plexus. You want something sweetening and at the same time something unexpected, something that has come through constraint into felicity. (Brandes 1988, 17)

If the aim of a poem is to achieve a state that is 'eternally posthumous in perfect cadence' – to transcend, to become metaphysical – then what characterises Heaney's thinking on poetry throughout his life is a clear-eyed sense of the necessity for grounding that experience in everyday life. In 1997, he wrote:

> A poem is, among other things, a process of coming to for the first time in a place which nevertheless feels like home ground. (*Metre*, 3, Autumn 1997, 15)

This process of 'coming to' – of achieving new consciousness – and then inhabiting that experience as if it were commonly day-to-day, encapsulates something at the core of Heaney's approach to writing: what he calls finding *home ground*. The work that would bring together in a poem these twin ideals – of an eternally posthumous life on home ground – was not in the least rarefied. It didn't wait politely on the muse to 'transmit', or on the poet's patience to 'receive'. Instead it relied on blazing graft with the sleeves rolled high, arduously mining for matter that could prove elusive. In this, Heaney was a skilled engineer: he would work the grounds of copious drafts until he had reached a desired level of attainment, and would strip-for-parts those pieces that he considered least successful in order that they might grant the chance of life to others. New creations would arise from old, and one of the truly exciting paths that can be traced in this edition is Heaney's extraordinary navigation of disparate parts in his assembly of resolute poems.

Endeavour in itself is not enough, however, and Heaney believed that, for all a poet's art of making, if a poem is to succeed it must arrive in a place where technical accomplishment alone will never be able to take it. In a Royal Society of Literature lecture of 1974, Heaney made a much-quoted distinction between two words that are often given interchangeably, 'craft' and 'technique':

> I think technique is different from craft. Craft is what you can learn from other verse. Craft is the skill of making. It wins competitions in the *Irish Times* or the *New Statesman*. It can be deployed without reference to the feelings or the self. It knows how to keep up a capable verbal athletic display; it can be content to be *vox et praeterea nihil* – all voice and nothing else – but not voice as in 'finding a voice'. Learning the craft is learning to turn the windlass at the well of poetry. Usually you begin by dropping the bucket halfway down the shaft and winding up a taking of air. You are miming the real thing until one day the chain draws unexpectedly tight and you have dipped into waters that will continue to entice you back. You'll have broken the skin on the pool of yourself. (*Preoccupations*, 47; FK, 19)

It is at that moment, Heaney continues, that it becomes appropriate to speak of 'technique': above and beyond the skill of making, technique involves a definition of the writer's whole reality, and, memorably, of their 'stance towards life'.

In his own life, Heaney grasped the dramatic opportunities that opened up for his writing, moving with his family from the north of Ireland to the Republic in 1972, and trading a lecturing job for one of full-time writing. And while the writing life ahead would see constant evolution, the practical mechanics with which Heaney would draft his poems would remain essentially unchanged. Invariably, his first thoughts came in manuscript: at times fragmentary, frequently in line-form, and often captured in a body of stanzas, but almost always in a way that might be considered a 'rough' or 'sketch', sometimes in a notebook, sometimes loose leaf, occasionally on the headed paper of an airline or hotel, and even on the back of an envelope. Of all the stages of drafting that survive in the author's archives, these formative moments are generally the only occasions that Heaney dates, and where such a date is given in this edition it usually marks a beginning of a composition, rarely its end. At these times, Heaney often marks his calendar with the place of composition, and not infrequently with the time of day or night, which, revealingly for a hard-working poet, tutor and father in his early years, was often well into the small hours ('3:00 a.m.' appears in Heaney's hand on a number of manuscripts).* Mostly, these primary drafts are pressing and progressive: urged forward by their author on to captured ground, without the hesitancy in that moment of a paralysing backward glance. Despite the pace of such moments, these 'roughs' possess a formal sense of themselves from the outset, and are often gathered in tercets or quatrains or the received form of the moment, showing that the shape and breath of a poem was instrumental to Heaney in its first steps.

'Roughs' were swiftly worked into a second stage resembling a first full manuscript draft. Sometimes this occurs in the same moment as the initial sketch, but more commonly it comes at a later, reflective moment that Heaney frequently acknowledges through the use of differing inks to distinguish revisions from original markings. Often these pages come without title or carry one that will be replaced, and may be one draft or many, at times refined until something akin to a fair copy is achieved by hand.

More usually, it is at this moment that Heaney transfers his efforts to type, a third stage in his process which, from the 1950s until the 1990s, was undertaken on a series of typewriters in Belfast, Berkeley, Glanmore, Dublin and Harvard that are sometimes so distinctive in their impression that with careful examination it is possible to identify with reasonable assurance on which of his machines a draft was made, which in turn can offer a window into a place and time of production. Typed drafts are corrected by hand and then retyped in a process that Heaney not only finds formally clarifying (a sonnet would transpose

---

* Among manuscripts from 1978–83 time-stamped '3:00 a.m.' by Heaney are 'Song' (NLI 49,493/49), 'Sweeney Redresses the Artist' (NLI 49,493/69), 'Sweeney Infans [Alerted]' (NLI 49,493/70), 'The Discovery of the Eel' (NLI 49,493/70).

into tercets occasionally, or couplets into a sonnet) but one that would often lengthen the poem, as he pursues the development that he believes his piece is chasing. When in the 1990s Heaney embraces word processing, tracks become harder to follow: manuscript directives by hand continue to be made, but some traces are lost in electronic revision.

Typescripts in all their eras – manual and electric, by young poet and mature – would be shared with trusted readers for comment before they went out for publication. Print life for these typescripts was active, and not exclusive, with some poems seeing print in three or four places, and in different versions (which we record here in variants), before their settlement in a collection. But once this last process had been achieved – a printing between covers in a full-length collection – the developmental life of a poem would be essentially complete. Heaney said that he would never 'interfere' with contents of a volume once this stage had been achieved, at least rarely beyond the level of occasional punctuation (*SS*, 86). If this were a working rule then the one exception to it would be the author's debut, *Death of a Naturalist*, to which Heaney would make meaningful amendments when an opportunity came to reset the book in 1991 twenty-five years after its first outing, the changes to which we record here.

Titles for poems came bountifully to Heaney, but not always with immediate fit. Frequently, a poem would try out numerous different headings until the correct note was struck. Usually, titles followed after the poems; for some manuscript 'roughs', titles trigger the formative sketch, but on such occasions, more often than not, those triggering titles rarely survive into print. Even in print life, and often in preparation for a volume, titles would be revised, as Rand Brandes (2008) has expertly documented; but as with the body text of the poems, once they were collected in a single volume, titles remained largely unaltered.

The seniority of standing which Heaney assigned to the texts of his single volumes has been the central point of guidance in this edition. We have preserved the twelve volumes of lyric verse in the order that Heaney gave them, and adopted for our edition the latest book printings that he supervised. To the dozen canonical volumes published by Faber & Faber that comprise Heaney's career, we have added *Stations*, his 1975 chapbook by Ulsterman Publications, because it was the sole pamphlet that Heaney chose to see represented in his later selected editions. The care with which Heaney prepared his canonical volumes is documented throughout this edition, and provides the volume's majority content of some 550 or so poems.

The same attention that brought the twelve books such rigour and coherence meant that, inevitably, whenever Heaney came to review his materials for a prospective volume, there would be casualties among his printed poems of the period. Some 200 or so poems that Heaney published in journals and magazines were not collected by him into his single volumes. Some, such as 'Villanelle for an Anniversary', maintained an independent readership or were returned to view by a decision to revive the poem outside of the twelve books, in a later selection such as *Opened Ground* (1998). For the most part, however, the body of uncollected work has remained out of the sight of anyone but scholars, librarians and the collectors of back catalogues, an absence that Heaney himself appeared to acknowledge as regrettable, when, late in his career, he reflected on some of the omissions from an early volume as being poems 'that I still like' (*SS*, 89).

In this edition, we collect for the first time those individual poems to which Heaney gave his imprimatur through his decision to publish them in newspapers, journals, magazines, anthologies and with small presses. We have gathered these poems into chronological groups between the twelve collected volumes and have printed them in the order and in the textual version in which they made their initial appearance. Where an uncollected poem is published more than once, we have wherever possible recorded its variant printings so that readers can follow its development, and have, for the sake of clarity, identified our copy-text when there is more than one version of the poem.

If the dominance of the twelve volumes marginalises these uncollected poems, it also undervalues the contribution of pamphlets and booklets, beginning with *Eleven Poems* (1965) and continuing with a series of shorter books published throughout Heaney's writing life. Mostly, the poems published in those smaller books were subsequently incorporated into the author's main volumes: only one piece in *Eleven Poems* and two each in *Hailstones* (1984) and *The Tree Clock* (1990) were not collected later. Even so, some of those shorter publications, such as *Bog Poems* (1975), are of great significance in the historical development of the oeuvre, in exemplifying how in some cases dominant thematic concerns are divided across two volumes, in the way that the bog poems, characteristic formally as well as thematically, are distributed between *Wintering Out* and *North*. But to have seen those shorter books as volumes in their own right, and to have reprinted their contents discretely, would have involved a duplication that Heaney himself took great care to avoid within his twelve collections.

If the place of some pamphlet poems risks marginalisation, then, conversely, the re-collecting of other poems in the author's later selected volumes risks granting those choices further predominance. Selections appeared at a relatively early stage in Heaney's career, beginning after four books in 1980, with another made after six books in 1990, another after eight in 1998, with a further gathering from the author's final five books released posthumously in 2014 based on his preferences. Taken together, they comprise a substantial body of selected work, and account for around half of all the poems that Heaney gathered in his volumes between 1966 and 2010 (Appendix III, 1209). That these poems merit their privileged place in the author's regard is not in question; Marianne Moore said 'Omissions are not accidents', and this is even more true of inclusions. But the relative spotlight on selected poems leaves an enormous body of work comparatively in the shade. Preserving the full contents of the individual volumes brings back into view the original poems, their contexts and the decision-making of the poet.

Beyond the collected and uncollected poems of this edition, there exists, also, a third category of poems of which there are a great many examples in archives: namely, poems that the author did not progress into the public space of print. A selection of twenty-five poems made from the author's papers, chosen by the Heaney family, has been included in an appendix to this edition and is published here for the first time (Appendix I, 1175).

One kind of poem that this edition does not represent exhaustively is the significant body of translated work made by Heaney throughout his career. These pieces have been comprehensively published in a sibling volume, *The Translations of Seamus Heaney*, edited by Marco Sonzogni (Faber & Faber, 2022; FSG, 2023), thereby collecting the uncollected translations that had been published throughout Heaney's career. Because we wish to preserve the sanctity of the twelve lyric collections, the only exceptions here are translations that Heaney included in those volumes, such as 'The Golden Bough' from Book 6 of the *Aeneid* at the start of *Seeing Things*, or 'A Ship of Death' from *Beowulf* in *The Haw Lantern*. In any such common cases we cross-reference our edition with the *Translations*.

Another kind of poem that this edition does not reproduce is the small number of verse letters that have been published in *The Letters of Seamus Heaney*, edited by Christopher Reid (Faber & Faber, 2023; FSG, 2024); that volume seemed a more natural home for them than this edition might offer. Occasionally there are points of overlap, such as 'An Open Letter' to Blake Morrison and Andrew Motion, the editors of *The Penguin Book of Contemporary British Poetry*, a poem of popular renown in its own right as much as a personal letter to its recipients, which is therefore reproduced in each volume (*LSH*, 218–25). In any such common cases we cross-reference our edition with the *Letters*.

Deciding on the ordering of an author's poems is not a simple matter; there are several ways of assembling a poet's work and the method appropriate for one poet is not entirely the same as for another. The most obvious decision to be made is whether to organise the poems individually as far as possible on chronological grounds (the feasibility of this varies greatly from case to case), or whether instead to preserve the unity of the major publications. Reflecting on this question for himself, Samuel Taylor Coleridge wrote, at a time when the 'collection' of poems was just becoming a publishing convention:

> After all you can say, I think the chronological order is the better for arranging a poet's work. All your divisions are in particular instances inadequate, and they destroy the interest which arises from watching the progress, the maturity, and even the decay of genius. (*Collected Works*, 14: 1, 453)

But did Coleridge have in mind the chronology of individual poems or their books, for which the latter might be taken to be another kind of 'division'?

In Heaney's case, an argument can be made for beginning with *Death of a Naturalist*, the first major volume, published in May 1966, rather than what could be judgementally termed 'the juvenilia' that preceded it. It is an argument that might follow accordingly: that, as well as giving priority to the poet's own publishing choices, it would allow this edition to begin with a familiar bang: namely, 'Digging', the poem that would be placed first by Heaney in every volume throughout his career in which it was included. ('Where else could it be placed?' he reflected some years later. 'It decided its position for itself' (SS, 82).) Furthermore, Heaney said of the early Incertus poems that 'those verses were what we might call "trial-pieces", little stiff inept designs in imitation of the master's fluent interlacing patterns, heavy-handed clues to the whole craft' (*Preoccupations*, 45). This hardly gives us the poet's imprimatur to begin with the earliest recorded poems as we have done here. However, *Death of a Naturalist* itself had a less insignificant predecessor than those 'trial-pieces', the short collection, *Eleven Poems*, published by Queen's University in November 1965; it also had a forebear in the markedly different collection of poems that Heaney sent to the Dolmen Press in Dublin (Appendix II, 1207) that seemingly would have become a full debut had the offer from Faber & Faber not arrived in the interim.

And what of chronology when an author chooses to revise? Should priority be given to the writer's last word, or to their first word, or to something else again? In considering Heaney's own appraisal of his poems and the choices that he made, we might recall the famous W. B. Yeats quatrain prefaced to a projected edition of his *Collected Poetry and Prose* in 1908:

> The friends that have it I do wrong
> Whenever I remake a song
> Should know what issue is at stake,
> It is myself that I remake.

Is Heaney at any stage 'remaking' himself chronologically in the Yeats sense? Might we talk about him 'becoming Seamus Heaney' at some point in his career? And has Heaney in his observations about his early poems given us an indication of what Ian Jack called 'the poems by which the poet wishes to be judged' (Jack 1985, 266), in keeping with what Wordsworth said was the charge of any great and original author: 'the task of *creating* the taste by which he is to be enjoyed'? (Wordsworth, *Poems*, 1, 1815, 368). There were occasions throughout his career when Heaney described and passed judgement on his own decision-making: occasions when he paused to evaluate his progress. One result is that there are a few instances where the text of this edition departs from what is printed in later selected volumes, notably when Heaney makes changes to existing poems in the preparation of the 1998 *Opened Ground*, and we have recorded those incidents as variant readings of our text.

But these few changes are the exception rather than the rule. From inaugural printings to these final amendments, through journals and collections and retrospective selections, from undergraduate stages to the platform of the Nobel Prize, it is Heaney's own guidance that we have attempted to follow in this edition, as a torchlight brighter and more far-seeing than our own: illumination, in words from 'Squarings' in *Seeing Things*, by 'The virtue of an art that knows its mind'.

A Note on the Text

The edition presents the collected and uncollected POEMS of Seamus Heaney in a primary section, and, in a secondary section, an editorial COMMENTARY to accompany those poems. A selection of unpublished poems, chosen by the poet's family, appears as a third-section APPENDIX together with a commentary by the editors.

For the twelve full-length volumes and *Stations* that comprise the author's collected poems, copy-texts are those that were the last text to pass through the author's hands with approval or amendment. These are indicated below the headnote of the respective volume using a short-form reference for distinction: in the case of *Death of a Naturalist* (*DN*), for example, the appearance of *DN1966* specifically indicates the first edition of that book in 1966, while *DN1991* is the text that was personally revised by Heaney for the reset edition of 1991, which in turn became the basis of the corrected (of literals) text *DN2016*, which in this example is the copy-text for our edition.

For uncollected poems, the copy-text is the first publication unless otherwise stated.

For the unpublished poems in the Appendix, copy-texts are given in the commentary that follows them.

Errors in the copy-text are silently corrected, and are noted in the commentary after the variant source as '(error)'.

Poems reproduce the layout of their copy-text, although the following elements of uniformity have been imposed for the sake of consistency: they are ranged left throughout the edition, are punctuated in house style in regard to quotation marks, dashes, ellipses and relative placement of punctuation marks. Poems are typeset to run on consecutively within their sections in order to minimise the edition's extent. In the case of sequenced or 'part' poems, it has not been possible to preserve the distinction that Heaney sometimes made between sequences that should flow continuously on a page from one poem to another, and those that should be printed each time on a new page.

Epigraphs and dedications reflect the original layout of the copy-text; as with the poems, for the typographical purposes of this edition they have been left-aligned as standard.

Partition numbers within poems have been retained in the Roman or Arabic style of their original printing.

In the footers, the verso indicates the edition section, and the recto gives a cross-reference to the poems or commentary relevant to that spread.

Subsequent to the poems, the edition presents an editorial commentary that proceeds in the following order: (i) a POEM TITLE; (ii) a TEXTUAL HISTORY of the published life of a poem; (iii) a COPY-TEXT source, if relevant; (iv) a record of published VARIANTS if a poem appears in print in more than one version, and (v) a COMMENTARY with LINE NOTES contextualising the poem:

Poem Title

Textual history.

[text: *source*]

1 lemma] variant *source*

Commentary.
  1 *lemma*: line note.

A textual history attempts to trace, as fully as possible, and through the original materials, the published life of a poem, from its first printing and collection by Heaney, through to any reselection of it made by the author for a later edition of his poems. In this work, we have benefitted greatly from the efforts of a number of archives and archivists in our efforts to locate and consult the primary texts; we have also been aided incalculably by the bibliographic collation made by Rand Brandes and Michael J. Durkan in *Seamus Heaney: A Bibliography 1959–2003* (Faber & Faber, 2008), and by Rand Brandes' generous and collegiate sharing of his work-in-progress towards a revised edition, which will be published after this edition of the poems.

Where the textual history carries a single source, such as in the example of the edition's first poem, 'Reaping in Heat' (*PSH*, 5), the textual history simultaneously serves to indicate the copy-text for the poem without need of further clarification.

Where a poem has more than one printing, such as in the example of the second poem, 'October Thought' (*PSH*, 5), the copy-text is acknowledged below the history in the following form:

[text: *source*]

which, in the example of 'October Thought', reads:

[text: *Q*]

indicating that the copy-text is taken from the journal *Q* rather than from the subsequent text, given there as *First Lines*.

On such occasions as these, where a poem has been published in more than one version, we record the variant printings in the following sequence: line-number in bold, lemma from the copy-text, square bracket, variant, *source*. So that, staying with the example of 'October Thought':

2 shoots] breaks *First Lines*

indicates that in line 2 of the poem, the copy-text reads 'shoots', while the variant text from *First Lines* reads 'breaks'.

Where a line carries more than one variant reading, a second lemma is given spaced after the first. To use the example of 'October Thought':

10 heaven-hue plum-blue] heaven-hue, plum-blue *First Lines*   gorse pricked] gorse-pricked *First Lines*

Where multiple versions produce different readings of the same lemma, the subsequent variants are separated by a pipe, as in an example from 'Fisher' (*PSH*, 13):

7 of the river-bed;] of riverbed *Interest* | of river-bed *PM*

indicating that in line 7 of that poem, the copy-text reads 'of the river-bed', while variant texts in *Interest* magazine and *PM* (*Poems and a Memoir*) read 'of riverbed' and 'of river-bed' respectively.

Where a variant reading extends to a complete line, the lemma is not used and the variant version alone is given following its emboldened line cue and square bracket. In 'Fisher', for example:

16] Than good luck, and skill more than fun: *Interest* | Than good luck and skill more than fun *PM*

In recording variants, line breaks are indicated by / and stanza breaks by //, while variants of four lines and longer are printed in verse form for clarity.

A caret between line numbers refers to an insertion between those lines. In 'October Thought', for example:

8^9] [stanza break] *First Lines*

denotes that a stanza space appears in the variant text between lines 8–9 in the copy-text.

All variant and commentary line numbers refer to the text of the poem as it appears in *PSH*.

In the commentary and line notes, the lemma is given in italics and followed by a colon in order to distinguish it readily from a variant, such as in the following example from 'October Thought':

6 *Haystalks straw-broken*: A curious linking since hay and straw [etc.]

A NOTE ON THE TEXT | xliii

In order to distinguish between titles that are used commonly by Heaney for more than one format, poem titles appear in single quotes (for example, the poem entitled 'Station Island'), part titles appear in small caps (part II of *SI* entitled STATION ISLAND) and book titles in italics (the full-length volume *Station Island*). The titles of unpublished typescript collections are underlined (e.g. Winter Seeds).

References to Heaney's primary works appear in long-form in the headnotes (e.g. *Death of a Naturalist*), and in abbreviation in references and line notes (e.g. *DN*), for which a legend appears at *PSH*, xxx.

Secondary references appear in short form in the commentary (e.g. Brandes 2008), and in full-length form in the bibliography (*PSH*, 1221).

POEMS

UNCOLLECTED POEMS (1959–1966)

     new and naked
  Upon the open roadside of time,
And when you gathered me up, tenderness bloomed
Like billowing smoke, and the milk-silver moon sang
    and cold tingling stars rang
     at the gentle anvil-ding
of your kiss. We stood at the centre, our world
Rippled and rayed away from us, and golden life
    Pumped through dark pulses
    of trees and houses and clouds.
This night was all sun-sparkle spume, splashed
From the sea of ourselves, it was lightning that licked us
    and seared us to burning beauty,
    and I could wish
That the shrill skirl and mountain-power of the moment
which has passed would swell, swelter and crash
    Into a life-time symphony,
    Resonant through all days to come.

Her Home

Sudden, stunted, crooked-cross
  Of a village,
Hunched, bunched,
  And hiccuping houses.

I have bolted, unheeding,
  Under the Sunday
Frown of your dour windows,
  Neglecting to notice

These unique intricacies,
  Of humped street,
Bumped bridge on lean stream,
  And uneven gallop of roof.

But as I shuttle-shoot
  In a late rush
Round your warped and windy
  Corners, I hush

With an old happiness,
  For here I found

Fishing the muscular, swallowing acres of sea
And thanking God if he comes back safely.

The knifing wind shivers, but no tree rustles
No sedge whispers; only the numb rocks,
The dumb squat houses acknowledge it with indifference.
Around the shore, the breakers constantly rush
With a slow snow-smash explosion, and overhead
A slush of grey cloud is forever melting
And running to the edge of the sky.

Lines to Myself

In poetry I wish you would
Avoid the lilting platitude.
Give us poems humped and strong,
Laced tight with thongs of song,
Poems that explode in silence
Without forcing, without violence,
Whose music is sharp and clear and good
Like a saw zooming in seasoned wood.
You should attempt concrete pression,
Half guessing, half expression.

Song of My Man-Alive

At first, in oil-swirls of shadow, in whirlpools of sound,
We were a giddy eddying; it was all tune-tumbling
      Hill-happy and wine-wonderful,
        The lithe liquid spurts
Of the dancing thrush-girls and hawk-boys spat round us,
    Yet hooded in the soft music of your presence
      I wandered away
      and swam in the gush of my joy.
Then all along the wide grey smile of the street
And choir-echoing up in the boom of the night-sky
    It was life leaping wild in the womb
        of my young spring
And bursting headlong from the dead belly of twenty-one years
I suddenly found myself, chestnut-ripe-round, pitched

Nostalgia in the Afternoon

Great blue-scooped sky, arching above me,
Breeze-winnowed, shell-sounding and bubbling white
  With the smooth soap-slip caressing of pot-bellied clouds,
I leap towards your high intangible blueness
        With Gothic agility.

Up above now, widely wheeling in free cool curvings,
The sky is talking to me, and soft whorls of feathery
    cloud-cream lick over my skin:
Now I am all days spent close to the warm breathing earth,
Here in a firm rounded moment, suspended in swaying space,

    And I live times distilled from time past.

Times when the cuckoo curled lobes of smooth music
      Over sunny acres of hay
And larks were spilling light pebbles of all coloured sound
      Sand falling, tumbling, tinkling,
Sound torn ragged and open with a corn-crake's
      Jagged-edge noise,
Rasping backwards and forwards
      As metal through gravel.

Upsurging into the blue scoop of the sky
This rich translucent music, coming through
The lovely objective slant of hot sunlight,
Until the grey billows of night unfurl and roll down,
Leaving me low on black hard rocks.

Aran

The rock breaks out like bone from a skinned elbow
And the island coughs itself into high cliffs
That drop straight down to goose-flesh waves on the winter sea.

Here the people live the necessary life.
They feed and worship, lancing the wizened veins
Of scanty soil, trying to draw life from the stones.
But as he digs, the islander's spade spangs off rock
And stops, even to-day, he must fight for life,

Reaping in Heat

Hushed
And lulled
   Lay the field, under a high-sky sun.
Pushed
And pulled
   Came the rasp of steel on stone,
For, slashing the drowsiness,
   The mower was whetting his scythe . . .
And the sycamores heaved a sleepless sigh.
Close hills
Shimmered
   Liquidly, fascinating the mower,
Lark's trills
Shimmered
   Down the thin burnt air. Lower
And deeper and cooler sinks now
The sycamore's shade, and naked sheaves
Are whitening on the empty stubble.

October Thought

Starling thatch watches, and sudden swallow
Straight shoots to its mud-nest, home-rest rafter,
Up through dry, dust-drunk cobwebs, like laughter
Flitting the roof of black-oak, bog-sod and rods of willow;
And twittering flirtings in the eaves as sparrows quarrel.
Haystalks straw-broken and strewn
Hide, hear mice mealing the grain, gnawing strong
The iron-bound, swollen and ripe-round corn-barrel.
Minute movement millionfold whispers twilight
Under heaven-hue plum-blue and gorse pricked with gold,
And through the knuckle-gnarl of branches, poking the night
Comes the trickling tinkle of bells, well in the fold.

The jolted, certain joy
    Of my sudden love. 20

Tractors

Grey as slugs,
Blue or red as lug-worms,
The tractors lumber in fields.
Their hopelessness hurts thought.

On roadways, 5
    Broad-bottomed and embarrassed;
On land, impassive before
Ruthless, rooting ploughs or morose trailers.

They cannot sweat in summer
Though their bonnets burn. In winter 10
They ache across mud; or gargle
    Sadly, astraddle unfolding furrows.

Do not ignore then
The melancholy spouts of tractors
That never have been broken in 15
And inspire no fear.

Scotch Fir in City Cemetery

Tufted cranium
topping
charred bone
that stiffens
up from bone-veined clay. 5

Bleak mote
in the horizon's eye,

propping open
eyelid clouds that smart
cold-rimmed flint-gold 10
in morning sun.

Flak-plop frozen
and skewered,

15 bleaching the grave stones
    with a black contrast.

Going In

The dark swooned and flung out a shower
As I came round from the gable.
A gust from the fields cuffed my hat
And bullied hail down my collar.

5   With gooseflesh trousers tugging hard
I took three backdoor steps at one leap
When a soft thick kiss on the foot
Punctuated my hurrying.

Fingers hesitated towards the knob.
10 The cold cat flattened along the door,
Eyes keen as a judge's, waiting,
Erect tail exclaiming. It lived

With my step into the swampy heat
Of the kitchen and rubbed twice
15 Round my shins. My father shouted:
'Keep that bloody cat out in the yard.'

And I had a crumpled handful
Of furred skin, and hard thin neck-bones
Under my knuckles. As always,
20 It landed outside on all fours.

Behind the door there I waited,
Domestic Judas. No paw-scrape,
No mew of protest came from the yard;
So I sat, listening to the wind.

Essences

Sunlight twitches on leaves,
Belly-flaps on puddles;
Between tall gables
Stalks cautiously; angles.

5   Darkness has no distinctions.

The wind will struggle
In a twig-webbed beech-net;
Muddle through night alleys,
Helter-skelter on hillsides.

Stillness we cannot classify.

And these two whet anger
To a thin blade; or jaunt
Reckless in lust's chariot.
Then sit, hopeless as twin statues.

Does love admit these variations?

Welfare State

Old men in distant country summers
Who bent fierce backs among the cracked black peat
Would straighten up to fire sour clay pipes,
Gaunt as Celtic crosses in the sky; listen
To silent hills strumming the horizon.

Eyes that could appraise the efficiency
Of a plough's ravishing and relish
The flash of a billhook through a spring hedge
Swivelled and probed the heavens. That straight-backed lull
From stooping pillared them into majesty.

To-day I only meet that questing stare
Under the mitred and condemning brows
Of a plaster Patrick. Old pensioners
Turn their archaic eyes away from screens,
Or daily watch the hopeless clash of chessmen.

Poor Man's Death

          Neighbours collected
Money for a coffin; he was buried
Without the dubious meed of duteous tears,
Sunk in the dirt, 'Gone to rest at last.'
Then cattle bedded on his mattress straw
And the bedhead made a gate for our back garden.
Still, one does not lament; one just observes

Clay, conscripted and identified, now
Demobbed. Epitaphs are irrelevant
To a grassy grave that boasts no headstone.

MacKenna's Saturday Night

Mouth loose like an open waistband
On a porter belly, to-night
He argues loud, sleek pint in hand.
Stout loosens the limbs for a fight
And hate, sparked long ago from the cold
Flint of farming jealousies, scorches
The bar and flames into the yard.
From the drunk dark a crowd watches
Frothing mouths, bloody fists, the hard
Final trip on the clubbing stones.
MacKenna returns to his drink;
Hate has fathered a new feud.
He gets drunk; in a sharp porter stink
Reels home as a good husband should.

Fair

(A Progress Report)

In this cobbled gabled village under
The raw-jawed mountain hill farmers dander
Among trailers to drive hard grudged bargains.
Sheep stuff slitted cribs. Bark of arguing

Crystallizes on wind. Hands rough and warm
As ram's horn smack money in clustered storms
Of protest or support; notes are crumpled
And crammed deep, the deal sealed with porter and grumbles.

Men gaunt as ancestral photographs reflect
That horse-fairs have died out; on the humped street
Tractor fumes have not killed the sheep-reek,
And among these shepherds cheques are suspect.

Fisher

Elbows snugged on the low bridge-wall,
He would stare ravenously down
Into the deep pool where the brown
Spine-wobbling trout hung, all

Poised on a silent slur of fin.
He watched happily as they fed
In that dark swoon of the river-bed;
And once, with green thread and bent pin,

Tried to hook one. He hoped to land
A lithe oil-spurt of gill and tail,
Hoist it slapping like a silver flail
And hold it cold in his thrilled hand.

But the worm plopped, the trout were gone
Sudden as swallows off wires.
Which taught him that angling is more
Than good luck, that skill is not fun;

So he contemplated again
And never disturbed the smooth stream.
I think of him much. I, too, seem
To be snatching at life that has lain

In memory's pool. A thought jumps.
I cast a line baited with metre
And images ripple, words scatter.
I hook verse, dead as an old stump.

The Indomitable Irishry

Slept (with a boast) on the parquet floor beneath
A liquor-lurched couch at a Hampstead Heath
Party. Conformed to the blarney-bloated
Image, blasphemed against bishops, quoted
The Proclamation. Court cases never disturbed
And critics were answered when Guinness burped.
Reduced rebellion to slapstick and slick cracks –
Played to full houses, came out in paperbacks.

Easter Son

The air here, laundered as a nurse's apron,
Rinses all casual suds out of his head.
Thought is sterilized: suddenly a son
Has burst, all chestnut-ripe, into her bed

To rivet – or to wedge between – their love.
On other beds, under drifts of sheet
And counterpane, more new lives bud or move;
Shrill on frail concertina lungs; feed

Seedling blood and milky curd of bone.
A glass-walled corridor windows on the ward:
They watch with numb surprise as nurses run
A bulging, shrouded trolley towards the morgue.

And outside, in the dancing bugling sun,
A tangle of bells maintains the Resurrection.

Such Men Are Dangerous

Even now at twenty-five
Shortness of breath, a double-chin,
Self-consciousness when I have to jive,
And creases in the abdomen
Have stolen on me gradually
To put heavy stress on mortality.

The waistline that was thirty-two
Takes one size larger, though at that
The buttons strain. My collars, too,
Are overlaid with nascent fat
And as taut seams burst with this expansion
Conscience stretches for looser action.

There's a school of thought who would maintain
That soul is inscaped in the flesh.
If so, my recent heavy gain
Would indicate a moral mess –
A verdict, admittedly, hard to refute
Since I cast off my better, straiter suit.

I feel no longer bound to give
Generously at Sunday Mass;   20
I neglect neglected relatives,
Allow perhaps six weeks to pass
Without a letter home. Small things? Why bother?
I would not tell the real things to another.

And that's just it – I mind my step,   25
Walk with knowing circumspection,
Beware of any verbal slip
That might just lead to the detection
Of the lean and hungry fox who goes
Stalking round in the easy fat man's clothes.   30

Writer and Teacher

A humble master of two trades
Who keeps to his own room, evades
The market-place and the headline;
Teaching each child to use his eyes,
To tell small truths instead of lies   5
In big words that sound fine.

He hatches talent with his own;
Can breed a tenderness in bone-
heads, always helping them to look
With love at movement in the street,   10
To celebrate each joy they meet.
Reads every boy like a new book.

A week's a chapter in the tale
Where thirty boys drive towards the gale
Of living – once his lessons cease.   15
'His work says little that is new'
According to one slick review.
But the pupils are his masterpiece.

Young Bachelor

From the mantelpiece my lecture program stares,
Five days all neatly chopped up into squares.

This timetable dictates the way I spend
Five nights a week and much of the weekend.

5   This single room I keep means that I cook,
Sleep and feed in one place. Here, too, I read my book.

I pad around the room as round a cage,
I fit the timetable as words a page:

Each moment regulated by a typed space,
10   Each day and night crammed in a single place.

And though these masters cramp my every move
I need the stricter discipline of love.

Soliloquy for an Old Resident

The place has gone down badly. Not like then.

Then it was all so very right, each room
Furnished so lovingly and in good taste
According to its function. All of us
5   Had a real weakness for good solid oak:
The loaded sideboard stood, a great carved bulwark,
In the dining-room; mirrors, plates, and trays
Glinting in candlelight like silver shields.
And maids sailed in, tureens gulping like tides,
10   And thick delph rattled curtly as they served.
Father would say the grace with eyes cast down
Upon the stiff white cloth and then would nod
Permission to begin. The maids cleared off
Very punctually until the final course
15   When we withdrew into the drawing room.
They had prepared a grate of sputtering logs
And as we talked till ash began to fall
Grandfather, in oils, stared steady from the wall.

And it was all so thoughtfully arranged.
20   The scullery commodious, the larder deep,
Running water in the big enamelled sink.
Bedrooms were never shared – except for maids
Who had an attic room, a wide brass bed
And two hotwater bottles, if they wished:
25   Father insisted that maids know their place

But treated good ones as if they were his own.
And after dark the house would settle gently.
We lay and listened to the shunting trains.

But the place has gone down badly.
We never thought, when the young men dealt with us,
Of things like this: the good room downstairs
Fitted with a foul electric stove, beds
In the kitchen, and other stoves reeking
On landings. There is a dull smell of grease
In father's room, the paper has been torn
And left hanging. Instead of hunting prints
They hang these ugly photographs of girls
Curling their naked bodies like she-cats.
No maids, no order, and no silent nights.
They come for one year, cook their wretched meals,
Swill beer from cans and in the noisy dark
Perhaps bring bad girls to our crumbling walls.
They come and go, each year they come and go,
Bringing no family, leaving only stains.

The place has gone down badly. Not like then.
Agents have no care: for them houses are
Houses, never homes. And birds of passage
Will dirty the nest, then just fly off again.
No neighbours, no respect, and no good name.

These new proprietors are much to blame.

Taking Stock

A year has gone, twelve salaries have been spent
And not a penny saved; each month pounds went
To landlord, grocer, barmen, waitresses,
To girls at petrol-pumps and in payboxes.
Bed, meals, journeys, entertainments – there's how
The whole thing slipped away. It's April now
Again, and still no earthly treasure stored.
No heed paid to the canny unjust steward;
Just one year older, with no child, no poem
That will endure, no shape in paint or stone
Shored up against the ruins. The diary

Makes depressing reading. I can't tell why
I noted meals and meetings that now look
As useless as the stubs of old cheque-books –
'Dined with Joan' or 'Wild night with Donal. Booze.'
Rise like ghost hangovers to accuse
And puncture resolutions of amendment.
I'll bridge no future from a quicksand present
Where necessary routine buries guilt
And time's blade sinks in surely to the hilt.

On Hogarth's Engraving 'Pit Ticket for the Royal Sport'

A shadow lurches on the sandy ring,
The crowd elbows and grunts. Coarse bodies sweat
All round the pit, obscenely twisting
For a better view: one thin veined hand claws
At the sand where it has flung a bet.
The yells burst loud as amplified applause.

And in the sun where shadows flick and blur,
Two crested cocks, like hammers drawn back
On trigger legs, crouch low to spring: each spur
Fixed deadly, each beak honed as a saw's tooth.
A lust that's bred during the squawked attack
Freezes the eyes, contorts the bawling mouth

Of every sporty punter hunkered there.
A blind-eyed noble arbitrates. He rubs
A folded knee, ignores the surly bear
Who clutches at his ruff, the thugs who shout
And threaten with a crutch, or whips, or clubs.
The trapped hag gapes and chokes; a man with gout

Is howling to the air and two old rakes
Are pinching at their snuff excitedly.
Now the cocks rear up to kill. The ringside aches.
Battling furiously as a hot stud:
The blind, the maimed, the deaf dementedly
Easing the daily pain with daily blood.

Saint Patrick's Stone

The legend tells how Patrick
Waded the shallow water
To pray seven days and nights
On this island among stones
And water-hens that spluttered   5
Dirtily in the sedge.
Came with eyes blazing and knees
Hard as his staff for prayer,
Fasts and penance and knelt there
Continuously one week   10
Branding Christ into the bone.
Then rose and staggered away
Leaving knee-marks in the stone.
Rain collects in these holy
Cups, sanctified where it falls,   15
To be soaked in faithful rags,
Dabbed on blisters, warts, and boils
With prayers that the island saint
May cleanse such corrupting flesh.
The wet cloths are hung to dry   20
On twigs of stunted hawthorn
Spiking out of a dead trunk:
A multiform crucifix
Decked with streamers of pain
That celebrate Saint Patrick's   25
Benediction of the rain.
And pilgrims never bother
To find if the legend's true;
It serves their end by being
What pilgrims would like to do.   30

Peter Street at Bankside

In December, 1598, Peter Street, the builder, and a dozen armed workmen began to dismantle the old Theatre, and on 28th December 'did then alsoe in most forcible and ryotous manner take and carrye awaye from thence all the wood and timber thereof unto the Banckside . . . and did there erect a new playhouse with the same timber and wood.' This was to be the Globe Theatre.

Upon soft ground I found a mortal church.
These twelve who sink the piles are laying down
My one defence against the seeping water:
Even the Thames that undermines the town
Must never undermine my theatre.
My theatre will tower from the marsh.

My twelve, you see, are armed. These knives and swords
Guard the quick transfer from old ground to new
Of players' rites, the liturgy of mirth
And sorrow. And though an ignorant crew,
Their crude traffic with plaster, lath and earth
Provides an altar for your sacred words.

I dedicate to speech, to pomp and show,
This house that I erect for poets, actors.
I set my saw and chisel in the wood
To joint and panel solid metaphors:
The walls a circle, the stage under a hood.
I fit the players thus with cowl and halo.

Lint Water

The flax was pulled by hand once it ripened,
Bound into tall green pillars with rush bands
And buried underwater, roots upwards.
When the dam was full they loaded stones and sods
On top, then left the whole thing for three weeks
To rot, to stink: a pit of rotten eggs
Could not have generated such a fug
As flax decaying, steaming like a bog,
Wafting its heavy, nauseating fall-out.
As soon as stems had turned to slime and smut

The dam was emptied: men stood waist deep
In the fouled water, with fork and four-pronged graip
Pitching out sheaves like half-gone carcasses.
They spread it dripping, then, flat on the grass
To crisp and dry hard in the summer sun   15
Until it could be stooked up, stiff as broom
And whistling in the wind. Toughened to sticks,
The stems were milled, spun, woven into fabrics.
The dam was cleared, poured down into the river
Its poisonous bellyful. 'Lint water'   20
It was called. Across the stream it swirled brown froth
That scummed clean stone and sickened fish to death;
And if the drains were blocked, it still seeped down,
Filtering unseen contamination.
Putrid currents floated trout to the loch,   25
Their bellies white as linen tablecloths.

Gate

What has the end of an ancestral bed
To do with stopping gaps and cattle?
Now on its last legs, the old brass head
Trails open awkwardly on wire hinges,
Entrance and exit every morning and night   5
For cudding maters, udders swinging full.
Such necessary traffic seems its plight,
Bracketing departure and arrival:
Think of the labour pains, shudders, whinges,
The hectic round of birth cry and death rattle.   10

For a Young Nun

A wave of Christ's love blood has washed
The selfishness all out of you.
Christ, the dove-thighed groom, has veiled you.
Between close brick walls, deeply gashed

With spearhead windows of stained glass,   5
Down bead-clicked corridors, alone,
You meditate. The blood-shot sun
Sprays linen crimson as you pass.

Cloistered from traffic, queues and dins,
From anger in the market-place,
You draw down veils and turn your face
Where noises end and love begins.

DEATH OF A NATURALIST (1966)

Digging

Between my finger and my thumb
The squat pen rests; snug as a gun.

Under my window, a clean rasping sound
When the spade sinks into gravelly ground:
My father, digging. I look down

Till his straining rump among the flowerbeds
Bends low, comes up twenty years away
Stooping in rhythm through potato drills
Where he was digging.

The coarse boot nestled on the lug, the shaft
Against the inside knee was levered firmly.
He rooted out tall tops, buried the bright edge deep
To scatter new potatoes that we picked,
Loving their cool hardness in our hands.

By God, the old man could handle a spade.
Just like his old man.

My grandfather cut more turf in a day
Than any other man on Toner's bog.
Once I carried him milk in a bottle
Corked sloppily with paper. He straightened up
To drink it, then fell to right away
Nicking and slicing neatly, heaving sods
Over his shoulder, going down and down
For the good turf. Digging.

The cold smell of potato mould, the squelch and slap
Of soggy peat, the curt cuts of an edge
Through living roots awaken in my head.
But I've no spade to follow men like them.

Between my finger and my thumb
The squat pen rests.
I'll dig with it.

Death of a Naturalist

All year the flax-dam festered in the heart
Of the townland; green and heavy headed
Flax had rotted there, weighted down by huge sods.
Daily it sweltered in the punishing sun.
Bubbles gargled delicately, bluebottles
Wove a strong gauze of sound around the smell.
There were dragon-flies, spotted butterflies,
But best of all was the warm thick slobber
Of frogspawn that grew like clotted water
In the shade of the banks. Here, every spring,
I would fill jampotfuls of the jellied
Specks to range on window-sills at home,
On shelves at school, and wait and watch until
The fattening dots burst into nimble-
Swimming tadpoles. Miss Walls would tell us how
The daddy frog was called a bullfrog,
And how he croaked, and how the mammy frog
Laid hundreds of little eggs and this was
Frogspawn. You could tell the weather by frogs too
For they were yellow in the sun and brown
In rain.

    Then one hot day when fields were rank
With cowdung in the grass, the angry frogs
Invaded the flax-dam; I ducked through hedges
To a coarse croaking that I had not heard
Before. The air was thick with a bass chorus.
Right down the dam, gross-bellied frogs were cocked
On sods; their loose necks pulsed like sails. Some hopped:
The slap and plop were obscene threats. Some sat
Poised like mud grenades, their blunt heads farting.
I sickened, turned, and ran. The great slime kings
Were gathered there for vengeance, and I knew
That if I dipped my hand the spawn would clutch it.

The Barn

Threshed corn lay piled like grit of ivory
Or solid as cement in two-lugged sacks.
The musty dark hoarded an armoury
Of farmyard implements, harness, plough-socks.

The floor was mouse-grey, smooth, chilly concrete. 5
There were no windows, just two narrow shafts
Of gilded motes, crossing, from air-holes slit
High in each gable. The one door meant no draughts

All summer when the zinc burned like an oven.
A scythe's edge, a clean spade, a pitch-fork's prongs: 10
Slowly bright objects formed when you went in.
Then you felt cobwebs clogging up your lungs

And scuttled fast into the sunlit yard –
And into nights when bats were on the wing
Over the rafters of sleep, where bright eyes stared 15
From piles of grain in corners, fierce, unblinking.

The dark gulfed like a roof-space. I was chaff
To be pecked up when birds shot through the air-slits.
I lay face-down to shun the fear above.
The two-lugged sacks moved in like great blind rats. 20

An Advancement of Learning

I took the embankment path
(As always, deferring
The bridge). The river nosed past,
Pliable, oil-skinned, wearing

A transfer of gables and sky. 5
Hunched over the railing,
Well away from the road now, I
Considered the dirty-keeled swans.

Something slobbered curtly, close,
Smudging the silence: a rat 10
Slimed out of the water and
My throat sickened so quickly that

　　　　I turned down the path in cold sweat
　　　　But God, another was nimbling
15　　　Up the far bank, tracing its wet
　　　　Arcs on the stones. Incredibly then

　　　　I established a dreaded
　　　　Bridgehead. I turned to stare
　　　　With deliberate, thrilled care
20　　　At my hitherto snubbed rodent.

　　　　He clockworked aimlessly a while,
　　　　Stopped, back bunched and glistening,
　　　　Ears plastered down on his knobbled skull,
　　　　Insidiously listening.

25　　　The tapered tail that followed him,
　　　　The raindrop eye, the old snout:
　　　　One by one I took all in.
　　　　He trained on me. I stared him out

　　　　Forgetting how I used to panic
30　　　When his grey brothers scraped and fed
　　　　Behind the hen-coop in our yard,
　　　　On ceiling boards above my bed.

　　　　This terror, cold, wet-furred, small-clawed,
　　　　Retreated up a pipe for sewage.
35　　　I stared a minute after him.
　　　　Then I walked on and crossed the bridge.

Blackberry-Picking

for Philip Hobsbaum

　　　　Late August, given heavy rain and sun
　　　　For a full week, the blackberries would ripen.
　　　　At first, just one, a glossy purple clot
　　　　Among others, red, green, hard as a knot.
5　　　　You ate that first one and its flesh was sweet
　　　　Like thickened wine: summer's blood was in it
　　　　Leaving stains upon the tongue and lust for
　　　　Picking. Then red ones inked up, and that hunger
　　　　Sent us out with milk-cans, pea-tins, jam-pots
10　　　Where briars scratched and wet grass bleached our boots.

Round hayfields, cornfields and potato-drills,
We trekked and picked until the cans were full,
Until the tinkling bottom had been covered
With green ones, and on top big dark blobs burned
Like a plate of eyes. Our hands were peppered
With thorn pricks, our palms sticky as Bluebeard's.

We hoarded the fresh berries in the byre.
But when the bath was filled we found a fur,
A rat-grey fungus, glutting on our cache.
The juice was stinking too. Once off the bush,
The fruit fermented, the sweet flesh would turn sour.
I always felt like crying. It wasn't fair
That all the lovely canfuls smelt of rot.
Each year I hoped they'd keep, knew they would not.

Churning Day

A thick crust, coarse-grained as limestone rough-cast,
hardened gradually on top of the four crocks
that stood, large pottery bombs, in the small pantry.
After the hot brewery of gland, cud and udder,
cool porous earthenware fermented the buttermilk
for churning day, when the hooped churn was scoured
with plumping kettles and the busy scrubber
echoed daintily on the seasoned wood.
It stood then, purified, on the flagged kitchen floor.

Out came the four crocks, spilled their heavy lip
of cream, their white insides, into the sterile churn.
The staff, like a great whisky muddler fashioned
in deal wood, was plunged in, the lid fitted.
My mother took first turn, set up rhythms
that slugged and thumped for hours. Arms ached.
Hands blistered. Cheeks and clothes were spattered
with flabby milk.

              Where finally gold flecks
began to dance. They poured hot water then,
sterilized a birchwood-bowl
and little corrugated butter-spades.
Their short stroke quickened, suddenly

a yellow curd was weighting the churned up white,
heavy and rich, coagulated sunlight
that they fished, dripping, in a wide tin strainer,
heaped up like gilded gravel in the bowl.

The house would stink long after churning day,
acrid as a sulphur mine. The empty crocks
were ranged along the wall again, the butter
in soft printed slabs was piled on pantry shelves.
And in the house we moved with gravid ease,
our brains turned crystals full of clean deal churns,
the plash and gurgle of the sour-breathed milk,
the pat and slap of small spades on wet lumps.

The Early Purges

I was six when I first saw kittens drown.
Dan Taggart pitched them, 'the scraggy wee shits',
Into a bucket; a frail metal sound,

Soft paws scraping like mad. But their tiny din
Was soon soused. They were slung on the snout
Of the pump and the water pumped in.

'Sure isn't it better for them now?' Dan said.
Like wet gloves they bobbed and shone till he sluiced
Them out on the dunghill, glossy and dead.

Suddenly frightened, for days I sadly hung
Round the yard, watching the three sogged remains
Turn mealy and crisp as old summer dung

Until I forgot them. But the fear came back
When Dan trapped big rats, snared rabbits, shot crows
Or, with a sickening tug, pulled old hens' necks.

Still, living displaces false sentiments
And now, when shrill pups are prodded to drown,
I just shrug, 'Bloody pups'. It makes sense:

'Prevention of cruelty' talk cuts ice in town
Where they consider death unnatural,
But on well-run farms pests have to be kept down.

Follower

My father worked with a horse-plough,
His shoulders globed like a full sail strung
Between the shafts and the furrow.
The horses strained at his clicking tongue.

An expert. He would set the wing
And fit the bright steel-pointed sock.
The sod rolled over without breaking.
At the headrig, with a single pluck

Of reins, the sweating team turned round
And back into the land. His eye
Narrowed and angled at the ground,
Mapping the furrow exactly.

I stumbled in his hob-nailed wake,
Fell sometimes on the polished sod;
Sometimes he rode me on his back,
Dipping and rising to his plod.

I wanted to grow up and plough,
To close one eye, stiffen my arm.
All I ever did was follow
In his broad shadow round the farm.

I was a nuisance, tripping, falling,
Yapping always. But today
It is my father who keeps stumbling
Behind me, and will not go away.

Ancestral Photograph

Jaws puff round and solid as a turnip,
Dead eyes are statue's and the upper lip
Bullies the heavy mouth down to a droop.
A bowler suggests the stage Irishman
Whose look has two parts scorn, two parts dead pan.
His silver watch chain girds him like a hoop.

My father's uncle, from whom he learnt the trade,
Long fixed in sepia tints, begins to fade

And must come down. Now on the bedroom wall
There is a faded patch where he has been –
As if a bandage had been ripped from skin –
Empty plaque to a house's rise and fall.

Twenty years ago I herded cattle
Into pens or held them against a wall
Until my father won at arguing
His own price on a crowd of cattlemen
Who handled rumps, groped teats, stood, paused and then
Bought a round of drinks to clinch the bargain.

Uncle and nephew, fifty years ago,
Heckled and herded through the fair days too.
This barrel of a man penned in the frame:
I see him with the jaunty hat pushed back
Draw thumbs out of his waistcoat, curtly smack
Hands and sell. Father, I've watched you do the same

And watched you sadden when the fairs were stopped.
No room for dealers if the farmers shopped
Like housewives at an auction ring. Your stick
Was parked behind the door and stands there still.
Closing this chapter of our chronicle,
I take your uncle's portrait to the attic.

Mid-Term Break

I sat all morning in the college sick bay,
Counting bells knelling classes to a close.
At two o'clock our neighbours drove me home.

In the porch I met my father crying –
He had always taken funerals in his stride –
And Big Jim Evans saying it was a hard blow.

The baby cooed and laughed and rocked the pram
When I came in, and I was embarrassed
By old men standing up to shake my hand

And tell me they were 'sorry for my trouble'.
Whispers informed strangers I was the eldest,
Away at school, as my mother held my hand

In hers and coughed out angry tearless sighs.
At ten o'clock the ambulance arrived
With the corpse, stanched and bandaged by the nurses.

Next morning I went up into the room. Snowdrops
And candles soothed the bedside; I saw him
For the first time in six weeks. Paler now,

Wearing a poppy bruise on his left temple,
He lay in the four foot box as in his cot.
No gaudy scars, the bumper knocked him clear.

A four foot box, a foot for every year.

Dawn Shoot

Clouds ran their wet mortar, plastered the daybreak
Grey. The stones clicked tartly
If we missed the sleepers, but mostly
Silent we headed up the railway
Where now the only steam was funnelling from cows
Ditched on their rumps beyond hedges,
Cudding, watching, and knowing.
The rails scored a bull's-eye into the eye
Of a bridge. A corncrake challenged
Unexpectedly like a hoarse sentry
And a snipe rocketed away on reconnaissance.
Rubber-booted, belted, tense as two parachutists,
We climbed the iron gate and dropped
Into the meadow's six acres of broom, gorse and dew.

A sandy bank, reinforced with coiling roots,
Faced you, two hundred yards from the track.
Snug on our bellies behind a rise of dead whins,
Our ravenous eyes getting used to the greyness,
We settled, soon had the holes under cover.
This was the den they all would be heading for now,
Loping under ferns in dry drains, flashing
Brown orbits across ploughlands and grazing.

The plaster thinned at the skyline, the whitewash
Was bleaching on houses and stables,
The cock would be sounding reveille
In seconds.

And there was one breaking
In from the gap in the corner.

Donnelly's left hand came up
30 And came down on my barrel. This one was his.
'For Christ's sake,' I spat, 'Take your time, there'll be more.'
There was the playboy trotting up to the hole
By the ash tree, 'Wild rover no more,'
Said Donnelly and emptied two barrels
35 And got him.

Another snipe catapulted into the light,
A mare whinnied and shivered her haunches
Up on a hill. The others would not be back
After three shots like that. We dandered off
40 To the railway; the prices were small at that time
So we did not bother to cut out the tongue.
The ones that slipped back when the all clear got round
Would be first to examine him.

At a Potato Digging

I

A mechanical digger wrecks the drill,
Spins up a dark shower of roots and mould.
Labourers swarm in behind, stoop to fill
Wicker creels. Fingers go dead in the cold.

5 Like crows attacking crow-black fields, they stretch
A higgledy line from hedge to headland;
Some pairs keep breaking ragged ranks to fetch
A full creel to the pit and straighten, stand

Tall for a moment but soon stumble back
10 To fish a new load from the crumbled surf.
Heads bow, trunks bend, hands fumble towards the black
Mother. Processional stooping through the turf

Recurs mindlessly as autumn. Centuries
Of fear and homage to the famine god
15 Toughen the muscles behind their humbled knees,
Make a seasonal altar of the sod.

II

Flint-white, purple. They lie scattered
like inflated pebbles. Native
to the black hutch of clay
where the halved seed shot and clotted,
these knobbed and slit-eyed tubers seem
the petrified hearts of drills. Split
by the spade, they show white as cream.

Good smells exude from crumbled earth.
The rough bark of humus erupts
knots of potatoes (a clean birth)
whose solid feel, whose wet insides
promise taste of ground and root.
To be piled in pits; live skulls, blind-eyed.

III

Live skulls, blind-eyed, balanced on
wild higgledy skeletons,
scoured the land in 'forty-five,
wolfed the blighted root and died.

The new potato, sound as stone,
putrefied when it had lain
three days in the long clay pit.
Millions rotted along with it.

Mouths tightened in, eyes died hard,
faces chilled to a plucked bird.
In a million wicker huts,
beaks of famine snipped at guts.

A people hungering from birth,
grubbing, like plants, in the earth,
were grafted with a great sorrow.
Hope rotted like a marrow.

Stinking potatoes fouled the land,
pits turned pus into filthy mounds:
and where potato diggers are,
you still smell the running sore.

IV

Under a gay flotilla of gulls
The rhythm deadens, the workers stop.
Brown bread and tea in bright canfuls
Are served for lunch. Dead-beat, they flop

5   Down in the ditch and take their fill,
Thankfully breaking timeless fasts;
Then, stretched on the faithless ground, spill
Libations of cold tea, scatter crusts.

For the Commander of the 'Eliza'

> . . . the others, with emaciated faces and prominent, staring eyeballs, were evidently in an advanced state of starvation. The officer reported to Sir James Dombrain . . . and Sir James, 'very inconveniently', wrote Routh, 'interfered'.
>   CECIL WOODHAM-SMITH, *The Great Hunger*

Routine patrol off West Mayo; sighting
A rowboat heading unusually far
Beyond the creek, I tacked and hailed the crew
In Gaelic. Their stroke had clearly weakened
5   As they pulled to, from guilt or bashfulness
I was conjecturing when, O my sweet Christ,
We saw piled in the bottom of their craft
Six grown men with gaping mouths and eyes
Bursting the sockets like spring onions in drills.
10   Six wrecks of bone and pallid, tautened skin.
'Bia, bia,
Bia'. In whines and snarls their desperation
Rose and fell like a flock of starving gulls.
We'd known about the shortage, but on board
15   They always kept us right with flour and beef
So understand my feelings, and the men's,
Who had no mandate to relieve distress
Since relief was then available in Westport –
Though clearly these poor brutes would never make it.
20   I had to refuse food: they cursed and howled
Like dogs that had been kicked hard in the privates.
When they drove at me with their starboard oar
(Risking capsize themselves) I saw they were

Violent and without hope. I hoisted
And cleared off. Less incidents the better.   25

Next day, like six bad smells, those living skulls
Drifted through the dark of bunks and hatches
And once in port I exorcised my ship,
Reporting all to the Inspector General.
Sir James, I understand, urged free relief   30
For famine victims in the Westport Sector
And earned tart reprimand from good Whitehall.
Let natives prosper by their own exertions;
Who could not swim might go ahead and sink.
'The Coast Guard with their zeal and activity   35
Are too lavish' were the words, I think.

The Diviner

Cut from the green hedge a forked hazel stick
That he held tight by the arms of the V:
Circling the terrain, hunting the pluck
Of water, nervous, but professionally

Unfussed. The pluck came sharp as a sting.   5
The rod jerked with precise convulsions,
Spring water suddenly broadcasting
Through a green hazel its secret stations.

The bystanders would ask to have a try.
He handed them the rod without a word.   10
It lay dead in their grasp till, nonchalantly,
He gripped expectant wrists. The hazel stirred.

Turkeys Observed

One observes them, one expects them;
Blue-breasted in their indifferent mortuary,
Beached bare on the cold marble slabs
In immodest underwear frills of feather.

The red sides of beef retain   5
Some of the smelly majesty of living:
A half-cow slung from a hook maintains

That blood and flesh are not ignored.

But a turkey cowers in death.
10 Pull his neck, pluck him, and look –
He is just another poor forked thing,
A skin bag plumped with inky putty.

He once complained extravagantly
In an overture of gobbles;
15 He lorded it on the claw-flecked mud
With a grey flick of his Confucian eye.

Now, as I pass the bleak Christmas dazzle,
I find him ranged with his cold squadrons:
The fuselage is bare, the proud wings snapped,
20 The tail-fan stripped down to a shameful rudder.

Cow in Calf

It seems she has swallowed a barrel.
From forelegs to haunches,
her belly is slung like a hammock.

Slapping her out of the byre is like slapping
5 a great bag of seed. My hand
tingled as if strapped, but I had to
hit her again and again and
heard the blows plump like a depth-charge
far in her gut.

10 The udder grows. Windbags
of bagpipes are crammed there
to drone in her lowing.
Her cud and her milk, her heats and her calves
keep coming and going.

Trout

Hangs, a fat gun-barrel,
deep under arched bridges
or slips like butter down
the throat of the river.

From depths smooth-skinned as plums,
his muzzle gets bull's eye;
picks off grass-seed and moths
that vanish, torpedoed.

Where water unravels
over gravel-beds he
is fired from the shallows,
white belly reporting

flat; darts like a tracer-
bullet back between stones
and is never burnt out.
A volley of cold blood

ramrodding the current.

Waterfall

The burn drowns steadily in its own downpour,
A helter-skelter of muslin and glass
That skids to a halt, crashing up suds.

Simultaneous acceleration
And sudden braking; water goes over
Like villains dropped screaming to justice.

It appears an athletic glacier
Has reared into reverse: is swallowed up
And regurgitated through this long throat.

My eye rides over and downwards, falls with
Hurtling tons that slabber and spill,
Falls, yet records the tumult thus standing still.

Docker

There, in the corner, staring at his drink.
The cap juts like a gantry's crossbeam,
Cowling plated forehead and sledgehead jaw.
Speech is clamped in the lips' vice.

That fist would drop a hammer on a Catholic –
Oh yes, that kind of thing could start again.

The only Roman collar he tolerates
Smiles all round his sleek pint of porter.

Mosaic imperatives bang home like rivets;
10   God is a foreman with certain definite views
Who orders life in shifts of work and leisure.
A factory horn will blare the Resurrection.

He sits, strong and blunt as a Celtic cross,
Clearly used to silence and an armchair:
15   Tonight the wife and children will be quiet
At slammed door and smoker's cough in the hall.

Poor Women in a City Church

The small wax candles melt to light,
Flicker in marble, reflect bright
Asterisks on brass candlesticks:
At the Virgin's altar on the right,
5   Blue flames are jerking on wicks.

Old dough-faced women with black shawls
Drawn down tight kneel in the stalls.
Cold yellow candle-tongues, blue flame
Mince and caper as whispered calls
10   Take wing up to the Holy Name.

Thus each day in the sacred place
They kneel. Golden shrines, altar lace,
Marble columns and cool shadows
Still them. In the gloom you cannot trace
15   A wrinkle on their beeswax brows.

Gravities

High-riding kites appear to range quite freely,
Though reined by strings, strict and invisible.
The pigeon that deserts you suddenly
Is heading home, instinctively faithful.

5   Lovers with barrages of hot insult
Often cut off their nose to spite their face,

Endure a hopeless day, declare their guilt,
Re-enter the native port of their embrace.

Blinding in Paris, for his party-piece
Joyce named the shops along O'Connell Street 10
And on Iona Colmcille sought ease
By wearing Irish mould next to his feet.

Twice Shy

Her scarf *à la* Bardot,
In suede flats for the walk,
She came with me one evening
For air and friendly talk.
We crossed the quiet river, 5
Took the embankment walk.

Traffic holding its breath,
Sky a tense diaphragm:
Dusk hung like a backcloth
That shook where a swan swam, 10
Tremulous as a hawk
Hanging deadly, calm.

A vacuum of need
Collapsed each hunting heart
But tremulously we held 15
As hawk and prey apart,
Preserved classic decorum,
Deployed our talk with art.

Our juvenilia
Had taught us both to wait, 20
Not to publish feeling
And regret it all too late –
Mushroom loves already
Had puffed and burst in hate.

So, chary and excited 25
As a thrush linked on a hawk,
We thrilled to the March twilight
With nervous childish talk:
Still waters running deep
Along the embankment walk. 30

Valediction

Lady with the frilled blouse
And simple tartan skirt,
Since you left the house
Its emptiness has hurt
All thought. In your presence
Time rode easy, anchored
On a smile; but absence
Rocked love's balance, unmoored
The days. They buck and bound
Across the calendar,
Pitched from the quiet sound
Of your flower-tender
Voice. Need breaks on my strand;
You've gone, I am at sea.
Until you resume command,
Self is in mutiny.

Lovers on Aran

The timeless waves, bright, sifting, broken glass,
Came dazzling around, into the rocks,
Came glinting, sifting from the Americas

To possess Aran. Or did Aran rush
To throw wide arms of rock around a tide
That yielded with an ebb, with a soft crash?

Did sea define the land or land the sea?
Each drew new meaning from the waves' collision.
Sea broke on land to full identity.

Poem

for Marie

Love, I shall perfect for you the child
Who diligently potters in my brain

Digging with heavy spade till sods were piled
Or puddling through muck in a deep drain.

Yearly I would sow my yard-long garden.
I'd strip a layer of sods to build the wall
That was to exclude sow and pecking hen.
Yearly, admitting these, the sods would fall.

Or in the sucking clabber I would splash
Delightedly and dam the flowing drain,
But always my bastions of clay and mush
Would burst before the rising autumn rain.

Love, you shall perfect for me this child
Whose small imperfect limits would keep breaking:
Within new limits now, arrange the world
Within our walls, within our golden ring.

Honeymoon Flight

Below, the patchwork earth, dark hems of hedge,
The long grey tapes of road that bind and loose
Villages and fields in casual marriage:
We bank above the small lough and farmhouse

And the sure green world goes topsy-turvy
As we climb out of our familiar landscape.
The engine noises change. You look at me.
The coastline slips away beneath the wing-tip.

And launched right off the earth by force of fire,
We hang, miraculous, above the water,
Dependent on the invisible air
To keep us airborne and to bring us further.

Ahead of us the sky's a geyser now.
A calm voice talks of cloud yet we feel lost.
Air-pockets jolt our fears and down we go.
Travellers, at this point, can only trust.

Scaffolding

Masons, when they start upon a building,
Are careful to test out the scaffolding;

Make sure that planks won't slip at busy points,
Secure all ladders, tighten bolted joints.

And yet all this comes down when the job's done,
Showing off walls of sure and solid stone.

So if, my dear, there sometimes seem to be
Old bridges breaking between you and me,

Never fear. We may let the scaffolds fall,
Confident that we have built our wall.

Storm on the Island

We are prepared: we build our houses squat,
Sink walls in rock and roof them with good slate.
This wizened earth has never troubled us
With hay, so, as you see, there are no stacks
Or stooks that can be lost. Nor are there trees
Which might prove company when it blows full
Blast: you know what I mean – leaves and branches
Can raise a tragic chorus in a gale
So that you listen to the thing you fear
Forgetting that it pummels your house too.
But there are no trees, no natural shelter.
You might think that the sea is company,
Exploding comfortably down on the cliffs,
But no: when it begins, the flung spray hits
The very windows, spits like a tame cat
Turned savage. We just sit tight while wind dives
And strafes invisibly. Space is a salvo,
We are bombarded by the empty air.
Strange, it is a huge nothing that we fear.

Synge on Aran

Salt off the sea whets
the blades of four winds.
They peel acres
of locked rock, pare down
a rind of shrivelled ground;
bull-noses are chiselled
on cliffs.
        Islanders too
are for sculpting. Note
the pointed scowl, the mouth
carved as upturned anchor
and the polished head
full of drownings.
            There
he comes now, a hard pen
scraping in his head;
the nib filed on a salt wind
and dipped in the keening sea.

Saint Francis and the Birds

When Francis preached love to the birds,
They listened, fluttered, throttled up
Into the blue like a flock of words

Released for fun from his holy lips.
Then wheeled back, whirred about his head,
Pirouetted on brothers' capes,

Danced on the wing, for sheer joy played
And sang, like images took flight.
Which was the best poem Francis made,

His argument true, his tone light.

In Small Townlands

for Colin Middleton

In small townlands his hogshair wedge
Will split the granite from the clay
Till crystal in the rock is bared:
Loaded brushes hone an edge
On mountain blue and heather grey.
Outcrops of stone contract, outstared.

The spectrum bursts, a bright grenade,
When he unlocks the safety catch
On morning dew, on cloud, on rain.
The splintered lights slice like a spade
That strips the land of fuzz and blotch,
Pares clean as bone, cruel as the pain

That strikes in a wild heart attack.
His eyes, thick, greedy lenses, fire
This bare bald earth with white and red,
Incinerate it till it's black
And brilliant as a funeral pyre:
A new world cools out of his head.

The Folk Singers

Re-turning time-turned words,
Fitting each weathered song
To a new-grooved harmony,
They pluck slick strings and swing
A sad heart's equilibrium.

Numb passion, pearled in the shy
Shell of a country love
And strung on a frail tune,
Looks sharp now, strikes a pose
Like any rustic new to the bright town.

Their pre-packed tale will sell
Ten thousand times: pale love
Rouged for the streets. Humming

Solders all broken hearts. Death's edge
Blunts on the narcotic strumming.

The Play Way

Sunlight pillars through glass, probes each desk
For milk-tops, drinking straws and old dry crusts.
The music strides to challenge it,
Mixing memory and desire with chalk dust.

My lesson notes read: *Teacher will play*
Beethoven's Concerto Number Five
And class will express themselves freely
In writing. One said 'Can we jive?'

When I produced the record, but now
The big sound has silenced them. Higher
And firmer, each authoritative note
Pumps the classroom up tight as a tyre,

Working its private spell behind eyes
That stare wide. They have forgotten me
For once. The pens are busy, the tongues mime
Their blundering embrace of the free

Word. A silence charged with sweetness
Breaks short on lost faces where I see
New looks. Then notes stretch taut as snares. They trip
To fall into themselves unknowingly.

Personal Helicon

for Michael Longley

As a child, they could not keep me from wells
And old pumps with buckets and windlasses.
I loved the dark drop, the trapped sky, the smells
Of waterweed, fungus and dank moss.

One, in a brickyard, with a rotted board top.
I savoured the rich crash when a bucket
Plummeted down at the end of a rope.
So deep you saw no reflection in it.

A shallow one under a dry stone ditch
10 Fructified like any aquarium.
When you dragged out long roots from the soft mulch,
A white face hovered over the bottom.

Others had echoes, gave back your own call
With a clean new music in it. And one
15 Was scaresome for there, out of ferns and tall
Foxgloves, a rat slapped across my reflection.

Now, to pry into roots, to finger slime,
To stare, big-eyed Narcissus, into some spring
Is beneath all adult dignity. I rhyme
20 To see myself, to set the darkness echoing.

UNCOLLECTED POEMS (1966–1969)

Thaw

Last snow remaindered everywhere on ditches,
Thaw filtering black into all the drains,
We drove through watery air and fog patches,
Past swimming water-hens, great flopping cranes
And children playing at the ends of lanes.

Our summer's freak storm, too, was melting clear.
Wafers only remained of that ice-floe.
All corroding black drained out of the year,
Our currents overtook their old clear flow.
Why such freeze-ups must come, we'll never know.

Remember that walk on the harbour wall?
The seal showed his head like an ocean god,
Dived to come up closer, his regal skull
Shining. And going home, swans flew above the road,
Each neck strained forward, stiff as a ramrod.

Aries

The ram, my sign, wheels into his own now
Gallivanting at the year's circumference,
Influential if indifferent to
The new season's anachronistic dance.

As ever, sun hoses grass, ploughland and flowers
And something begins to lilt a green rhythm,
Restores the pigment, retraces contours.
Even I retrieve my origin

For I am a spoke the old ram turns up,
Following myself, like his horn's tight whorl,
Grateful to re-enter this April landscape.
It is the solid felloe of my world.

Rookery

Here they come, freckling the sunset,
The slow big sailers bearing down

On the plantation. They have flown
Their sorties and are now well met.

5   The upper twigs dip and wobble
With each almost two-point landing,
Then ride to rest. There is nothing
Else to do now only settle.

But they keep up a guttural chat
10 As stragglers knock the roost see-saw.
Something's satisfied in that caw.
Who wouldn't come to rest like that?

Aubade

From Cork to Malin the rummaging tide
Sluices, spends itself round promontory,
Lighthouse, harbour and swallowing haven,
A bag of waters at whose centre I
5   Stay wide-eyed as an early wakened bride.

Late May, with bud, bird and light opening fire
Early, leaves so long from dawn to rising!
I lie still under my mound and the drift
Of white linen, finger my gold ring,
10 Knowing this fellow in me will not tire

For he works relentlessly day and dark
Prospecting light, making me his tunnel.
I finger the ring that has anchored me –
Stowed with a cargo eager to embark –
15 And feel my baby moving like a sea.

Triptych for the Easter Battlers

I

It drew them compulsively as a lover:
A word whispered between mouthfuls of stout
Or a wink when they were standing around
After chapel summoned this new passover.

5   And birds fed up like kings of the yard

Were gathered and starved into condition;
Five counties prepared themselves with caution.
The spurs were brought down, all ragged claws pared

For this circus of wild pulse and death leap
When the new year sought its underground passion: 10
Old hungers wakening in the dancing sun,
The law melting, irrelevant, in their heat.

2

The shuttered eye is his least brilliant part,
Efficient, pebbly, busy as radar,
Cool arbiter of his so flashy art.
A dead star

Among his enamelled constellations.   5
Copper and golden like some Saxon grail
The nebula of wing, a sheen of oiled guns
From his comet tail.

He is the centre of his own system.
All gravities tending toward claw and beak;   10
Generating his own cataclysm
When all those worlds must strike.

3

One eye matched his. Here is Hogarth's cockpit:
The crowd elbows and grunts, the cripples sweat.
A trapped hag gapes and chokes, obscenely twisted
To keep her view. As in a Way of the Cross
Eyes are glutting, armpits and hair wet.   5
The yells burst loud as amplified applause.

For in the sun, their shadows a quick blur,
Two crested cocks, like hammers drawn back
On trigger legs, crouch low to spring: each spur
Fixed deadly, each beak honed as a saw's tooth.   10
Look at the blind man's mouth, opening black,
And, flailing his crutch, the man with gout –

All set down as for a crucifixion.
His eye maintains it all in ecstasy,
Bird and man extinguished in communion: 15
The battling ringside, hot as a hot stud

(This is the Easter battlers' Calvary)
And airborne cocks, buoyant on their own blood.

Boy Driving His Father to Confession

Four times now I have seen you as another
Man, a grown-up friend, less than a father;
Four times found chinks in the paternal mail
To find you lost like me, quite vulnerable.
Twice it was your incredible distress,
Once your adult laughter, now your weakness.
There was the time when my child-brother died
And in the porch, among the men, you cried.
Again, last year, I was shocked at your tears
When my mother's plane took off: in twelve years
You had not been apart for one whole day
Until this long-threatened, two-week holiday.
I left you lonely at the barrier,
Was embarrassed later when you stood a beer.
The third time you made a man of me
By telling me an almost smutty story
In a restaurant toilet; we both knew
This was an unprecedented breakthrough.

Today, a sinner, and shy about it,
You asked me to drive up to church, and sit
Morose as ever, telling me to slow
On corners or at pot-holes that I know
As well as you do. What is going on
Beneath that thick grey hair? What confession
Are you preparing? Do you tell sins as I would?
Does the same hectic rage in our one blood?
Here at the churchyard I am slowing down
To meet you, the fourth time, on common ground.
You grunt and slam the door. I watch another
Who gropes as awkwardly to know his father.

South Derry Evening

The rain smouldered,
any far hedge a horizon,
birch trunks ghosting the edge
of every ploughed acre.

Somewhere under its hug
a tractor gargled down
its own tracks. The grazing
would be slicing neatly as soap.

A man was out there
opening lea. I thought of him
cowled like a monk, twisting to watch
three furrows screw flat on their back,

rain censing his progress.
I was soaked to the socks
knowing my feet small
and the road incredibly solid

as his acrid greeting
welcomed and followed each step,
insisting on some conjunction
across open country,

declaring here was a world
of more than the moment,
promising the land
to old lags and junkies.

The rain had stopped
and ahead, the road steamed –
a real sign of spring.
I walked on a hotbed of tarmac

towards a marked headland
of carparks and chimneys,
past birches glowing with wet
at the skirts of the clouds.

Corncrake

In the wet catacombs of the grass
A loner with a breaking note
Prays tenebrae.

He is the mendicant of these dark acres
And makes his own responses:
Solace and reproach, his nightly office.

My window's open for the cool
So he takes advantage.
All night his beads go ratcheting.

Chestnut Time

His boots would bruise the crackling detritus.
He would pitch brick-bats and posts through branches
Disarming them of their splitting clusters.
They fell, spikes blunt, on last year's leaves and husks.

To rupture cleanly then the sectioned shell
Tighten the fist on it for the gentle
Cluck. Chestnuts. Remember his cold handfuls?
Glossy bellies and such pale whorled navels.

He still parades his autumn under trees
Scenting old trails of littered pith, retrieves
Notions of conquest after seasoning:
The years fly, shattered, off the loaded string.

Last Look

He was standing like a milestone
With his back to the road, in November
Frost, the scraggy fields.

Bare hedges, shoots of ash tipped
Black, the cobwebbed silent weeds
Were poor fare for starving eyes

That never even turned as we raced by,

Only a dwindling interruption now.
Tousled smoke stood up off the country.

When I think of his plinth back, black coat,   10
The grey eaves on the skull –
And those flat acres laid out under rime –

He could have been ghost already.

Child Lost

He's run away from rocking-horse and toys
To crouch out of the light of common day,
Escaped like a giant fieldmouse between drills
In rods, green shoots and pods, and cold, cold clay.
His anxious parents raise a distant noise.   5
His eyes turn green, his fingers hook up tendrils.

The Survivor

That dull land was ringed
With such: drums in the evening
Scourged beyond the hills;
From a slaughterhouse miles
Away, amplified under zinc,   5
Pigs' squeals ripped like lightning.
In unseen quarries, rock rifted
Away from the dynamite –
Men turned on their carts
At its curt thunder.   10
Down far sidings, at dawn and all day,
A train was shunting, shunting
And sometimes a whistle
Pursued a V of wild geese
Discordant and travelling   15
Fast as despatch riders
Across the cold, shook air.

The Evening Land

From Connemara, or the Moher clifftop,
Where the land ends with a sheer drop,
You can see three stepping-stones out of Europe,

Anchored like hulls at the dim horizon
Against the winds' and the waves' explosion.

The Aran Islands are all awash.
East coastline's furled in the foam's white sash.
The clouds melt over them like slush.

And on Galway Bay, between shore and shore,
The ferry plunges to Aranmore.

Ceili on the Deck

1

The dance floor rocks the wind frocks,
The fiddles fool the seagulls;
From the minute we leave the Galway docks
We're footing it in circles.
They play the Sailor on the Rock
And the Girl I Left Behind Me
And foot-taps answer the engine's knock
On the decks of the Aran ferry.

2

Says a New York girl, her head in a swirl,
'I just love your Irish dancing',
To a Cork boy, as they do their twirl,
Retiring and advancing.
The very boat takes up the air,
Starts pitching on the rollers,
And keeps good time off the coast of Clare
With her crew of swinging sailors.

3

Until we reach the frothing beach
And pass the winking shorelight,

Tin whistles shrill and fiddles screech –
With jigs and reels and hornpipes;
> They play the Sailor on the Rock
> And the Girl I Left Behind Me
> And foot-taps answer the engine's knock
> On the decks of the Aran ferry.

Inisheer

We first drop anchor, beyond the pier,
Off the first island called Inisheer,
Where all the islandmen and women
Wear bright-knit shawls and well-patched homespun,
The women with rainbows round their shoulders,	5
The oarsmen strong and grey as boulders.
The currachs that lie along the strand
Are hoisted up. Black new moons walk the sand
Down where the breakers scatter white lace.
The flotilla puts out – like a race –	10
To row right under the steamer's bows.
Then back they ride with their homely cargoes.

The Oarsmen's Song

1

It's only twice a week she comes –
How we look forward to that day.
Like some good omen to our homes
She blows her note across the bay.
There's bread in chests and oil in drums,	5
A wardrobe and a mattress
A box of nibs, a card of combs,
And a mail bag full of letters.

2

And black and hollow, as huge pods,
The currachs dandle on the wave,
Wild winch and pulley lower the goods,
The sailors shout, the seagulls rave.
There's whitewash brushes, bags of nails,	5

With bottled gas and liquor,
Long iron gates, enamel pails,
And a hamper made of wicker.

   3

What we can't load we float behind –
Slim planks for rafters, boards for floors,
Back from the steamer to the land
We're lying heavy on the oars:
5 With tins of polish, panes of glass,
And shafts for scythes and shafts for spades,
A pram, a cot, a plastic bath,
And shaving soap and razor blades.

The Basket-Maker

My shed is full of long green willow shoots.
On each good day I roam the hedge for more,
Climbing stone ditches, tripping on bared roots,
Combing Aran from hilltop to the shore.

5 But, when a grey rain smoulders on the sea,
I'm on my stool and at my proper trade:
Inside my shed, the children gather round me
To hear my song and see the baskets made.

The Basket-Maker's Song

   1

The uprights are sharpen'd, pegged straight in the ground.
I pick forty rods, here's how they're stuck round.
The uprights are sharpen'd, pegged straight in the ground:
I pick forty rods, here's how they're stuck round –
5   *Four twos for each side, three twos for each end.*
    Four threes for the corners where all the rods bend.

   2

Then I twist and I stitch, I weave, nick and peel
At a basket for eggs or dainty turf creel –
Then I twist and I stitch, I weave, nick and peel

At a basket for eggs or dainty turf creel –
  Four twos for each side, three twos for each end.
  Four threes at the corners where all the rods bend.

  3

So wicker, like waves, criss-crosses uprights.
The children are wide-eyed and each child recites –
So wicker, like waves, criss-crosses uprights.
The children are wide-eyed and each child recites –
  Four twos for each side, three twos for each end.
  Four threes at the corners where all the rods bend.

  4

And forty it is, for jobs big or small.
The sizes may differ, the song not at all –
And forty it is, for jobs big or small.
The sizes may differ, the song not at all –
  Four twos for each side, three twos for each end.
  Four threes at the corners where all the rods bend.

Michael

Now, from the basket-maker's door
Michael runs along the shore
Up the paved lane and through a gate.
The larks, that nest at his donkey's feet,
Go up in song at his quick approach.
The donkey brays at his well known touch
And down they go along the same track;
Michael fits new creels on his donkey's back.

Neddy

  1

Go easy, now, go steady
It's just a new yoke Neddy,
Don't panic and strike sparks with your shod heel
For your back's well tried and tough
And your small feet sure enough
To bear a hundred weight in either creel.

    2

My old Neddy's aged a score
And I'll have him ten years more
For trotting and for work he has no match,
But he's cute as any fox,
Knows each path across the rocks,
Can knock stones off a wall, can lift a latch.

    3

Well harnessed and firm-shod,
He clip-clops brightly on the road,
Brays sweetly as a 'cello tuning up.
But my heart drops to my boots
Every time the ferry hoots.
There's a dealer with his pound notes and his rope.

The Dealing Man

He comes to Aran's scanty grass
Surprised again that beasts can thrive
On the thin acres of the place,
He knows the islandmen will drive
The hardest bargain in the West
But offers them the most he can
For Aaron donkeys are the best
And the best attracts your dealing-man.

The Dealer

    1

I am the dealer from Tipperary,
I bargain hard I bargain fairly,
I buy whatever I get my hands on
But mostly donkeys I ask on Aran.

    2

In my laced brown boots, with my sharp ash plant
And my dealer's hat at a jaunty slant
It's not for nothing I've crossed the water
A wad of notes I have to scatter.

3

So come all you rascals, trot those asses
And when I bid, don't pull sour faces.
I can't waste time with each greedy fool
I need ten beasts for the strand at Blackpool.

4

When I drive them off the mothers will sigh
The boys will hide and the girls will cry
Until I feel like a cruel pirate
But can I swop tears for ready profit?

The Cargo

Now, the currachs put out again
With cargo of regret and pain.
The donkeys on their backs in the stern,
Their four legs tied, their eyes forlorn.

Braying in panic as the sea 5
Weeps at the gunwale furiously
White tears of froth hiss at Michael's feet.
Neddy lies trussed like a side of meat.

And the busy oarsmen take the strain
Of tug-of-war with the bay again. 10
Under the ferry the pulley hook
Is lowered like a thread – and look!

Neddy's lifted into the air
Above the deck, then lower,
Lower, down, down to the hold. 15
It's Michael's heart that they have sold.

Lullaby

1

Oh young boy sad upon the strand,
Oh, basket maker happy at your trade,
Oh, weary oarsman with your blister'd hand

Let this day drown beneath the rising tide,
And leave its mem'ries on the sand.

2

The dark is blotting up the day,
From cloud to cloud down to the ocean rim;
The ferry is black smoke upon a black sky,
The mainland's shrouded and the islands swim
Into the ink swell of the bay.

3

O dews that gleam and rains that weep,
O west wind from the far Americas,
O lighthouse beam that blazes on the deep,
O wandering fishes and all birds that pass,
Bless, bless these islands in their sleep.

Bachelor Deceased

in memoriam Pat McGuckin

Discovered rigid as an abandoned plough
That lies by broken ground a whole season –
He was on his back in the muck and straw

For hours. The sow he never got to see,
Disposed beneath the infra heater, grunted
For him and the dog barked in the small hours

According to the neighbours. But his tilt
Was quiet and steady as the bicycle
Stood up to the windowsill at eight o'clock.

I took my last look at him on a dry day
When the cobbles in the yard looked scrubbed as eggs.
And I heard he'd left by the back again

Leaving the door open as ever, the light
Blazing out all night in the empty house.

Frogman

I

Unsettling silt
In the holds of liners,

Nudging about
Under greasy piers, wrench,

File and crowbar
Remotely in contact –

Cantilevers
Coming and going on

The strength of bolts
He had better locate –

He bargained for
All that. It was a job.

II

Now after hours
In the dirtiest reach

He tries old tyres,
Petrol drums, carcasses

And pokes about
In the slimiest clefts.

His bubbling plume
Surrenders to currents,

No one watches
Its sud on the surface.

III

He's slipped away
Beyond blueprints and planned dives.

When he rises
There's no audience or foreman

Owns or tells him.
He's nobody's feeler

        For drownings or
        Sinkings or loose bridges –

        It's come to be
10   He just loves the water.

            IV

        The straitjacket
        Of clock and calendar

        Dissolves, the bed
        Of the river is soft –

5   It's not overtime
        Keeps him here at all.

        The air's a slap
        In the face. He always

        Walks home late now
10   In his rubber and goggles.

Driving in the Small Hours

            I

        A time for confidences,
        Man to man,
        Wife to husband.

        Between the party and home
5   A recap on possibility,
        Obituaries on chances missed.

        The babysitter waits
        Beside a dead fire; wives
        Grope out to the empty place.

            II

        One foot on the dip-switch,
        The tail of an eye in the mirror
        Take care of dazzling trucks

        And fast passers-out.
5   A match burns up the mood.
        'Would you light one for me?'

And two coals glow
In their hoods of ash, two wasting points,
Glimpsed portholes of limbo.

III

Under wires
Live with demands for *Enquiries*
And operators trying to connect,

Zipping up puddles,
Humbled to a halt									5
By the obstinate amber . . .

It is never a journey,
Hardly a coming or going.
Mirage as motion. Hiatus.

Birdwatcher

When he died a congregation of owls
Dropped out of the air and the shires about:
The gables, the dormers, the ridge tiles
By the end of that day were feathered and capped.

Mourners making their way late up the drive						5
Were screened by eyes, unblinking and foreign.
All night then occasionally one would leave
For its deserted copse or empty barn.

In an Airport Coach

The mouths of tunnels
Fanged with icicles,
Toll-gates spiking
The roads, we entered the grey
Badlands of New Jersey.								5
I remember spring

Seed-beds covered
With soot, manured
Black on black:
In this steel-fenced rink								10

Of fallout and waste stink,
The chemical muck

Ridged, the tainted snow
Packed like a garden row –
Winter tempered earth
And air to a barren
Anti-sun.
Un-joy, dearth

Ghosted the dumps, drains,
Feed-pipes and power-lines
Linked to Manhattan.
Behind us we presume
That placid, phantom
Pile-up of a town.

And in a subway station
The rushing businessman
Muttering through his stare.
The siren's wail.
A bum on the Bowery, pale
And blank as a soothsayer.

DOOR INTO THE DARK (1969)

for my father and mother

Night-Piece

Must you know it again?
Dull pounding through hay,
The uneasy whinny.

A sponge lip drawn off each separate tooth.
Opalescent haunch,
Muscle and hoof

Bundled under the roof.

Gone

Green froth that lathered each end
Of the shining bit
Is a cobweb of grass-dust.
The sweaty twist of the bellyband
Has stiffened, cold in the hand,
And pads of the blinkers
Bulge through the ticking.
Reins, chains and traces
Droop in a tangle.

His hot reek is lost.
The place is old in his must.

He cleared in a hurry
Clad only in shods
Leaving this stable unmade.

Dream

With a billhook
Whose head was hand-forged and heavy
I was hacking a stalk
Thick as a telegraph pole.
My sleeves were rolled
And the air fanned cool past my arms
As I swung and buried the blade,
Then laboured to work it unstuck.

    The next stroke
10 Found a man's head under the hook.
    Before I woke
    I heard the steel stop
    In the bone of the brow.

The Outlaw

Kelly's kept an unlicensed bull, well away
From the road: you risked a fine but had to pay

The normal fee if cows were serviced there.
Once I dragged a nervous Friesian on a tether

5 Down a lane of alder, shaggy with catkin,
Down to the shed the bull was kept in.

I gave Old Kelly the clammy silver, though why
I could not guess. He grunted a curt 'Go by.

Get up on that gate'. And from my lofty station
10 I watched the business-like conception.

The door, unbolted, whacked back against the wall.
The illegal sire fumbled from his stall

Unhurried as an old steam engine shunting.
He circled, snored and nosed. No hectic panting,

15 Just the unfussy ease of a good tradesman;
Then an awkward, unexpected jump, and,

His knobbled forelegs straddling her flank,
He slammed life home, impassive as a tank,

Dropping off like a tipped-up load of sand.
20 'She'll do,' said Kelly and tapped his ash-plant

Across her hindquarters. 'If not, bring her back.'
I walked ahead of her, the rope now slack,

While Kelly whooped and prodded his outlaw
Who, in his own time, resumed the dark, the straw.

The Salmon Fisher to the Salmon

      The ridged lip set upstream, you flail
Inland again, your exile in the sea
Unconditionally cancelled by the pull
      Of your home water's gravity.

      And I stand in the centre, casting.   5
The river cramming under me reflects
Slung gaff and net and a white wrist flicking
      Flies well-dressed with tint and fleck.

      Walton thought garden worms, perfumed
By oil crushed from dark ivy berries   10
The lure that took you best, but here you come
      To grief through hunger in your eyes.

      Ripples arrowing beyond me,
The current strumming water up my leg,
Involved in water's choreography   15
      I go, like you, by gleam and drag.

      And will strike when you strike, to kill.
We're both annihilated on the fly.
You can't resist a gullet full of steel.
      I will turn home, fish-smelling, scaly.   20

The Forge

All I know is a door into the dark.
Outside, old axles and iron hoops rusting;
Inside, the hammered anvil's short-pitched ring,
The unpredictable fantail of sparks
Or hiss when a new shoe toughens in water.   5
The anvil must be somewhere in the centre,
Horned as a unicorn, at one end square,
Set there immovable: an altar
Where he expends himself in shape and music.
Sometimes, leather-aproned, hairs in his nose,   10
He leans out on the jamb, recalls a clatter
Of hoofs where traffic is flashing in rows;

Then grunts and goes in, with a slam and flick
To beat real iron out, to work the bellows.

Thatcher

Bespoke for weeks, he turned up some morning
Unexpectedly, his bicycle slung
With a light ladder and a bag of knives.
He eyed the old rigging, poked at the eaves,

5 Opened and handled sheaves of lashed wheat-straw.
Next, the bundled rods: hazel and willow
Were flicked for weight, twisted in case they'd snap.
It seemed he spent the morning warming up:

Then fixed the ladder, laid out well-honed blades
10 And snipped at straw and sharpened ends of rods
That, bent in two, made a white-pronged staple
For pinning down his world, handful by handful.

Couchant for days on sods above the rafters,
He shaved and flushed the butts, stitched all together
15 Into a sloped honeycomb, a stubble patch,
And left them gaping at his Midas touch.

The Peninsula

When you have nothing more to say, just drive
For a day all round the peninsula.
The sky is tall as over a runway,
The land without marks so you will not arrive

5 But pass through, though always skirting landfall.
At dusk, horizons drink down sea and hill,
The ploughed field swallows the whitewashed gable
And you're in the dark again. Now recall

The glazed foreshore and silhouetted log,
10 That rock where breakers shredded into rags,
The leggy birds stilted on their own legs,
Islands riding themselves out into the fog

And drive back home, still with nothing to say
Except that now you will uncode all landscapes
By this: things founded clean upon their own shapes, 15
Water and ground in their extremity.

In Gallarus Oratory

You can still feel the community pack
This place: it's like going into a turfstack,
A core of old dark walled up with stone
A yard thick. When you're in it alone,
You might have dropped, a reduced creature, 5
To the heart of the globe. No worshipper
Would leap up to his God off this floor.

Founded there like heroes in a barrow,
They sought themselves in the eye of their King
Under the black weight of their own breathing. 10
And how he smiled on them as out they came,
The sea a censer and the grass a flame.

Girls Bathing, Galway, 1965

The swell foams where they float and crawl,
A catherine-wheel of arm and hand;
Each head bobs curtly as a football.
The yelps are faint here on the strand.

No milk-limbed Venus ever rose 5
Miraculous on this western shore.
A pirate queen in battle clothes
Is our sterner myth. The breakers pour

Themselves into themselves, the years
Shuttle through space invisibly. 10
Where crests unfurl like creamy beer
The queen's clothes melt into the sea

And generations sighing in
The salt suds where the wave has crashed
Labour in fear of flesh and sin 15
For the time has been accomplished

As through the shallows in swimsuits,
Bare-legged, smooth-shouldered and long-backed,
They wade ashore with skips and shouts.
So Venus comes, matter-of-fact.

Requiem for the Croppies

The pockets of our great coats full of barley –
No kitchens on the run, no striking camp –
We moved quick and sudden in our own country.
The priest lay behind ditches with the tramp.
A people, hardly marching – on the hike –
We found new tactics happening each day:
We'd cut through reins and rider with the pike
And stampede cattle into infantry,
Then retreat through hedges where cavalry must be thrown.
Until, on Vinegar Hill, the fatal conclave.
Terraced thousands died, shaking scythes at cannon.
The hillside blushed, soaked in our broken wave.
They buried us without shroud or coffin
And in August the barley grew up out of the grave.

Rite of Spring

So winter closed its fist
And got it stuck in the pump.
The plunger froze up a lump

In its throat, ice founding itself
Upon iron. The handle
Paralysed at an angle.

Then the twisting of wheat straw
Into ropes, lapping them tight
Round stem and snout, then a light

That sent the pump up in flame.
It cooled, we lifted her latch,
Her entrance was wet, and she came.

Undine

He slashed the briars, shovelled up grey silt
To give me right of way in my own drains
And I ran quick for him, cleaned out my rust.

He halted, saw me finally disrobed,
Running clear, with apparent unconcern.   5
Then he walked by me. I rippled and I churned

Where ditches intersected near the river
Until he dug a spade deep in my flank
And took me to him. I swallowed his trench

Gratefully, dispersing myself for love   10
Down in his roots, climbing his brassy grain –
But once he knew my welcome, I alone

Could give him subtle increase and reflection.
He explored me so completely, each limb
Lost its cold freedom. Human, warmed to him.   15

The Wife's Tale

When I had spread it all on linen cloth
Under the hedge, I called them over.
The hum and gulp of the thresher ran down
And the big belt slewed to a standstill, straw
Hanging undelivered in the jaws.   5
There was such quiet that I heard their boots
Crunching the stubble twenty yards away.

He lay down and said 'Give these fellows theirs,
I'm in no hurry,' plucking grass in handfuls
And tossing it in the air. 'That looks well.'   10
(He nodded at my white cloth on the grass.)
'I declare a woman could lay out a field
Though boys like us have little call for cloths.'
He winked, then watched me as I poured a cup
And buttered the thick slices that he likes.   15
'It's threshing better than I thought, and mind
It's good clean seed. Away over there and look.'

Always this inspection has to be made
Even when I don't know what to look for.

20 But I ran my hand in the half-filled bags
Hooked to the slots. It was hard as shot,
Innumerable and cool. The bags gaped
Where the chutes ran back to the stilled drum
And forks were stuck at angles in the ground
25 As javelins might mark lost battlefields.
I moved between them back across the stubble.

They lay in the ring of their own crusts and dregs
Smoking and saying nothing. 'There's good yield,
Isn't there?' – as proud as if he were the land itself –
30 'Enough for crushing and for sowing both.'
And that was it. I'd come and he had shown me
So I belonged no further to the work.
I gathered cups and folded up the cloth
And went. But they still kept their ease
35 Spread out, unbuttoned, grateful, under the trees.

Mother

As I work at the pump, the wind heavy
With spits of rain is fraying
The rope of water I'm pumping.
It pays itself out like air's afterbirth
5 At each gulp of the plunger.

I am tired of the feeding of stock.
Each evening I labour this handle
Half an hour at a time, the cows
Guzzling at bowls in the byre.
10 Before I have topped up the level
They lower it down.

They've trailed in again by the ready-made gate
He stuck into the fence: a jingling bedhead
Wired up between posts. It's on its last legs.
15 It does not jingle for joy any more.

I am tired of walking about with this plunger
Inside me. God, he plays like a young calf

Gone wild on a rope.
Lying or standing won't settle these capers,
This gulp in my well. 20

O when I am a gate for myself
Let such wind fray my waters
As scarfs my skirt through my thighs.
Stuffs air down my throat.

Cana Revisited

No round-shouldered pitchers here, no stewards
To supervise consumption or supplies
And water locked behind the taps implies
No expectation of miraculous words.

But in the bone-hooped womb, rising like yeast, 5
Virtue intact is waiting to be shown,
The consecration wondrous (being their own)
As when the water reddened at the feast.

Elegy for a Still-born Child

I

Your mother walks light as an empty creel
Unlearning the intimate nudge and pull

Your trussed-up weight of seed-flesh and bone-curd
Had insisted on. That evicted world

Contracts round its history, its scar. 5
Doomsday struck when your collapsed sphere

Extinguished itself in our atmosphere,
Your mother heavy with the lightness in her.

II

For six months you stayed cartographer.
Charting my friend from husband towards father.

He guessed a globe behind your steady mound.
Then the pole fell, shooting star, into the ground.

III

On lonely journeys I think of it all,
Birth of death, exhumation for burial,

A wreath of small clothes, a memorial pram,
And parents reaching for a phantom limb.

5   I drive by remote control on this bare road
Under a drizzling sky, a circling rook,

Past mountain fields, full to the brim with cloud,
White waves riding home on a wintry lough.

Victorian Guitar

for David Hammond

Inscribed 'Belonged to Louisa Catherine Coe before her marriage to John Charles Smith, March 1852.'

I expected the lettering to carry
The date of the gift, a kind of christening:
This is more like the plate on a coffin.

Louisa Catherine Smith could not be light.
5   Far more than a maiden name
Was cancelled by him on the first night.

I believe he cannot have known your touch
Like this instrument – for clearly
John Charles did not hold with fingering –

10   Which is obviously a lady's:
The sound-box trim as a girl in stays,
The neck right for the smallest span.

Did you even keep track of it as a wife?
Do you know the man who has it now
15   Is giving it the time of its life?

Night Drive

The smells of ordinariness
Were new on the night drive through France:

Rain and hay and woods on the air
Made warm draughts in the open car.

Signposts whitened relentlessly.
Montreuil, Abbéville, Beauvais
Were promised, promised, came and went,
Each place granting its name's fulfilment.

A combine groaning its way late
Bled seeds across its work-light.
A forest fire smouldered out.
One by one small cafés shut.

I thought of you continuously
A thousand miles south where Italy
Laid its loin to France on the darkened sphere.
Your ordinariness was renewed there.

At Ardboe Point

Right along the lough shore
A smoke of flies
Drifts thick in the sunset.

They come shattering daintily
Against the windscreen,
The grill and bonnet whisper

At their million collisions:
It is to drive through
A hail of fine chaff.

Yet we leave no clear wake
For they open and close on us
As the air opens and closes.

Tonight when we put out our light
To kiss between sheets
Their just audible siren will go

Outside the window,
Their invisible veil
Weakening the moonlight still further,

And the walls will carry a rash

20 Of them, a green pollen.
They'll have infiltrated our clothes by morning.

If you put one under a lens
You'd be looking at a pumping body
With such outsize beaters for wings
25 That this visitation would seem
More drastic than Pharaoh's.
I'm told they're mosquitoes

But I'd need forests and swamps
To believe it
30 For these are our innocent, shuttling

Choirs, dying through
Their own live empyrean, troublesome only
As the last veil on a dancer.

Relic of Memory

The lough waters
Can petrify wood:
Old oars and posts
Over the years
5 Harden their grain,
Incarcerate ghosts

Of sap and season.
The shallows lap
And give and take:
10 Constant ablutions,
Such drowning love
Stun a stake

To stalagmite.
Dead lava,
15 The cooling star,
Coal and diamond
Or sudden birth
Of burnt meteor

Are too simple,
20 Without the lure

That relic stored –
A piece of stone
On the shelf at school,
Oatmeal coloured.

A Lough Neagh Sequence

for the fishermen

1 *Up the Shore*

I

The lough will claim a victim every year.
It has virtue that hardens wood to stone.
There is a town sunk beneath its water.
It is the scar left by the Isle of Man.

II

At Toomebridge where it sluices towards the sea
They've set new gates and tanks against the flow.
From time to time they break the eels' journey
And lift five hundred stones in one go.

III

But up the shore in Antrim and Tyrone
There is a sense of fair play in the game.
The fishermen confront them one by one
And sail miles out and never learn to swim.

IV

'We'll be the quicker going down,' they say.
And when you argue there are no storms here,
That one hour floating's sure to land them safely –
'The lough will claim a victim every year.'

2 *Beyond Sargasso*

A gland agitating
mud two hundred miles in-
land, a scale of water
on water working up

5   estuaries, he drifted
       into motion half-way
       across the Atlantic,
       sure as the satellite's
       insinuating pull
10   in the ocean, as true
       to his orbit.
                   Against
       ebb, current, rock, rapids,
       a muscled icicle
15   that melts itself longer
       and fatter, he buries
       his arrival beyond
       light and tidal water,
       investing silt and sand
20   with a sleek root. By day,
       only the drainmaker's
       spade or the mud paddler
       can make him abort. Dark
       delivers him hungering
25   down each undulation.

3 Bait

Lamps dawdle in the field at midnight.
Three men follow their nose in the grass,
The lamp's beam their prow and compass.

The bucket's handle better not clatter now:
5   Silence and curious light gather bait.
Nab him, but wait

For the first shrinking, tacky on the thumb.
Let him re-settle backwards in his tunnel.
Then draw steady and he'll come.

10   Among the millions whorling their mud coronas
       Under dew-lapped leaf and bowed blades,
       A few are bound to be rustled in these night raids,

       Innocent ventilators of the ground,
       Making the globe a perfect fit,
15   A few are bound to be cheated of it

When lamps dawdle in the field at midnight,
When fishers need a garland for the bay
And have him, where he needs to come, out of the clay.

4 Setting

I

A line goes out of sight and out of mind
Down to the soft bottom of silt and sand
Past the indifferent skill of the hunting hand.

A bouquet of small hooks coiled in the stern
Is being paid out, back to its true form,   5
Until the bouquet's hidden in the worm.

The boat rides forward where the line slants back.
The oars in their locks go round and round.
The eel describes his arcs without a sound.

II

The gulls fly and umbrella overhead,
Treading air as soon as the line runs out,
Responsive acolytes above the boat.

Not sensible of any *kyrie*,
The fishers, who don't know and never try,   5
Pursue the work in hand as destiny.

They clear the bucket of the last chopped worms,
Pitching them high, good riddance, earthy shower.
The gulls encompass them before the water.

5 Lifting

They're busy in a high boat
That stalks towards Antrim, the power cut.
The line's a filament of smut

Drawn hand over fist
Where every three yards a hook's missed   5
Or taken (and the smut thickens, wrist-

Thick, a flail
Lashed into the barrel
With one swing). Each eel

10 Comes aboard to this welcome:
The hook left in gill or gum,
It's slapped into the barrel numb

But knits itself, four-ply,
With the furling, slippy
15 Haul, a knot of back and pewter belly

That stays continuously one
For each catch they fling in
Is sucked home like lubrication.

And wakes are enwound as the catch
20 On the morning water: which
Boat was which?

And when did this begin?
This morning, last year, when the lough first spawned?
The crews will answer, 'Once the season's in.'

6 *The Return*

In ponds, drains, dead canals,
she turns her head back,
older now, following
whim deliberately
5   till she's at sea in grass
and damned if she'll turn so
it's new trenches, sunk pipes,
swamps, running streams, the lough,
the river. Her stomach
10 shrunk, she exhilarates
in mid-water. Its throbbing
is speed through days and weeks.

Who knows now if she knows
her depth or direction?
15 She's passed Malin and
Tory, silent, wakeless,
a wisp, a wick that is
its own taper and light
through the weltering dark.
20 Where she's lost once she lays
ten thousand feet down in

her origins. The current
carries slicks of orphaned spawn.

7 Vision

Unless his hair was fine-combed,
The lice, they said, would gang up
Into a mealy rope
And drag him, small, dirty, doomed,

Down to the water. He was
Cautious then in riverbank
Fields. Thick as a birch trunk,
That cable flexed in the grass

Every time the wind passed. Years
Later in the same fields
He stood at night when eels
Moved through the grass like hatched fears

Towards the water. To stand
In one place as the field flowed
Past, a jellied road,
To watch the eels crossing land

Re-wound his world's live girdle.
Phosphorescent, sinewed slime
Continued at his feet. Time
Confirmed the horrid cable.

The Given Note

On the most westerly Blasket
In a dry-stone hut
He got this air out of the night.

Strange noises were heard
By others who followed, bits of a tune
Coming in on loud weather

Though nothing like melody.
He blamed their fingers and ear
As unpractised, their fiddling easy,

10 For he had gone alone into the island
    And brought back the whole thing.
    The house throbbed like his full violin.

    So whether he calls it spirit music
    Or not, I don't care. He took it
15 Out of wind off mid-Atlantic.

    Still he maintains, from nowhere.
    It comes off the bow gravely,
    Rephrases itself into the air.

Whinlands

    All year round the whin
    Can show a blossom or two
    But it's in full bloom now.
    As if the small yolk stain

5   From all the birds' eggs in
    All the nests of the spring
    Were spiked and hung
    Everywhere on bushes to ripen.

    Hills oxidize gold.
10 Above the smoulder of green shoot
    And dross of dead thorns underfoot
    The blossoms scald.

    Put a match under
    Whins, they go up of a sudden.
15 They make no flame in the sun
    But a fierce heat tremor

    Yet incineration like that
    Only takes the thorn –
    The tough sticks don't burn,
20 Remain like bone, charred horn.

    Gilt, jaggy, springy, frilled,
    This stunted, dry richness
    Persists on hills, near stone ditches,
    Over flintbed and battlefield.

The Plantation

Any point in that wood
Was a centre, birch trunks
Ghosting your bearings,
Improvising charmed rings

Wherever you stopped.
Though you walked a straight line,
It might be a circle you travelled
With toadstools and stumps

Always repeating themselves.
Or did you re-pass them?
Here were bleyberries quilting the floor,
The black char of a fire,

And having found them once
You were sure to find them again.
Someone had always been there
Though always you were alone.

Lovers, birdwatchers,
Campers, gipsies and tramps
Left some trace of their trades
Or their excrement.

Hedging the road so,
It invited all comers
To the hush and the mush
Of its whispering treadmill,

Its limits defined,
So they thought, from outside.
They must have been thankful
For the hum of the traffic

If they ventured in
Past the picnickers' belt
Or began to recall
Tales of fog on the mountains.

You had to come back
To learn how to lose yourself,

35   To be pilot and stray – witch,
        Hansel and Gretel in one.

Shoreline

   Turning a corner, taking a hill
   In County Down, there's the sea
   Sidling and settling to
   The back of a hedge. Or else

5 A grey foreshore with puddles
   Dead-eyed as fish.
   Haphazard tidal craters march
   The corn and the grazing.

   All round Antrim and westward
10 Two hundred miles at Moher
   Basalt stands to.
   Both ocean and channel

   Froth at the black locks
   On Ireland. And strands
15 Take hissing submissions
   Off Wicklow and Mayo.

   Take any minute. A tide
   Is rummaging in
   At the foot of all fields,
20 All cliffs and shingles.

   Listen. Is it the Danes,
   A black hawk bent on the sail?
   Or the chinking Normans?
   Or currachs hopping high

25 On to the sand?
   Strangford, Arklow, Carrickfergus,
   Belmullet and Ventry
   Stay, forgotten like sentries.

Bann Clay

Labourers pedalling at ease
Past the end of the lane
Were white with it. Dungarees
And boots wore its powdery stain.

All day in open pits   5
They loaded on to the bank
Slabs like the squared-off clots
Of a blue cream. Sunk

For centuries under the grass,
It baked white in the sun,   10
Relieved its hoarded waters
And began to ripen.

It underruns the valley,
The first slow residue
Of a river finding its way.   15
Above it, the webbed marsh is new,

Even the clutch of Mesolithic
Flints. Once, cleaning a drain,
I shovelled up livery slicks
Till the water gradually ran   20

Clear on its old floor.
Under the hummus and roots
This smooth weight. I labour
Towards it still. It holds and gluts.

Bogland

for T. P. Flanagan

We have no prairies
To slice a big sun at evening –
Everywhere the eye concedes to
Encroaching horizon,

Is wooed into the cyclops' eye   5
Of a tarn. Our unfenced country

Is bog that keeps crusting
Between the sights of the sun.

They've taken the skeleton
Of the Great Irish Elk
Out of the peat, set it up
An astounding crate full of air.

Butter sunk under
More than a hundred years
Was recovered salty and white.
The ground itself is kind, black butter

Melting and opening underfoot,
Missing its last definition
By millions of years.
They'll never dig coal here,

Only the waterlogged trunks
Of great firs, soft as pulp.
Our pioneers keep striking
Inwards and downwards,

Every layer they strip
Seems camped on before.
The bogholes might be Atlantic seepage.
The wet centre is bottomless.

UNCOLLECTED POEMS (1969–1972)

Medallion

*struck to commemorate the Reverend George Walker,
our inspiration during the late siege*

The head like a death-mask
Bogged deep in the silver:
Just looking
Loads your eye.

This is the hero
Who started it all,
Besieged forever
In the raised thick rim.

It lies on its obverse –
Gates shut on the enemy –
Like a ring-fort thrown up
On the baize.

We have an aerial view
But under the glass
He holds out, impervious
To arguments, sit-downs and bombs.

Icon

Here is Patrick
Banishing the serpents,
The gold nostrils flared
On his crozier.

He has staked a cluster
One of which slithers
Its head up the staff.
Still from low swamps

And secret drains,
The drenched grasslands,
Luxuriant growths
Beside dunghills and wells,

Their sphincters quietly
Rippling, snakes point

15 And pass to the sea.
    Crusty with sand

    They dirty and fatten
    The lip of the wave.
    The whole island
20 Writhes at the edges.

    Here is Patrick
    Ridding the country,
    A celtic worm-clot
    Paralysed round his staff.

Idyll

    That's a shooting range.
    In the cool of the evening
    Attentive herds are well used
    To reports and short volleys

5   That die barking on the slopes.
    Do they recognise those characters
    Peaked, buckled and hitched
    To traditions, unstacking the poles

    Of a stile or so expertly
10 Unbushing and bushing the gaps?
    Their boots spattered with raindrops,
    Rigid and sparbled, are ripping

    The grass in their wedges.
    Their hands on barrel and butt
15 Are polished as these. Lately
    When pigs squealed under

    The sixteen-pound hammer and gully,
    When the lame horse was destroyed
    In the yard and the carcass winched away,
20 These troopers were just warming up.

    Look at the palings they sharpened
    And drove. And the stretch they can put
    On barbed wire. Target practice
    Is child's play to these boys.

Offerings

(*In memoriam Patrick Rooney*)

1 *Turnip Man*

My Aunt Jane, she's awful smart,
She bakes a ring in an apple tart
And when Hallowe'en comes round
Fornenst that tart I'm always found.

At Hallowe'en they rapped the doors, 5
Lifted yard gates off the hinges
Or climbed the slates and stuffed the flues.
Chaos ruled in the year's young darkness.

A head only, squat on the ground,
His eyes blazed green through bottle glass. 10
The scooped-out inside charred and burned
Swimming with smoke and candle grease.

He sat there grinning. The kids ran home
To crowd the lighted window, stare
Doubtful at his blazing eye 15
And slit mouth wide as an open razor.

He sat there grinning. The kids at home
Looked for the ring baked in the tart.
He ruled the backs, a guttering totem.
He would upset the applecart. 20

2 *High Street, 1786*

Here are men in tricorn hats
And lownecked belles, all full of chat,
Blocking the vista to the docks;

The loosed-out carts
And panniered horse, the dogs 5
At random.

It's twenty to four
By the public clock. A cloaked rider
Clops off into an entry

10 Coming perhaps from the Linen Hall
    Or Cornmarket
    Where (this civic print unfrozen)

    In twelve years time
    They hanged young MacCracken –
15 And this man with a crutch

    And the tricorned fop
    Never again set in such communion.
    Pen and ink, water tint

    Fence and fetch us in
20 Under bracketed tavern signs,
    The edged gloom of arcades.

    It's twenty to four
    On one of the last afternoons
    Of reasonable light.

25 Smell the tidal Lagan:
    Take a last turn with citizens
    In the tang of possibility.

3 *From Cave Hill*

    Some evenings the city smokes
    Up through the dead damp aftermath
    Of rain, a grimy steam
    Roofing the lough and tower flats;
5   A smouldering hill-ringed-pit
    Placid and shrunk on itself
    Like a compost heap.

4 *September Song*

    And still the youngsters commandeer the trolleys
    At four o'clock, like scattering dwarfed armies

    TELE EARLY! HALLELUJAH!
    CURSE THE POPE AND FIRE AWAY!

5   But a thick line through the roll book blanks his name,
    His half-filled jotter's hidden in the storeroom

TELE EARLY! HALLELUJAH!
CURSE THE POPE AND FIRE AWAY!

For he, when Hallowe'en again comes round,
Among the rites of misrule won't be found   10

TELE EARLY! HALLELUJAH!
CURSE THE POPE AND FIRE AWAY!

Nor safe in the shining chip shop after dark
From the lost voice, calling him to homework

TELE EARLY! HALLELUJAH!   15
CURSE THE POPE AND FIRE AWAY!

An Evening at Killard

for Michael McLaverty

You told me how cattle breasted the sound
Across to the island; how herring fry
Made inlet and pool flex like a muscle.

Herring gull, crane and sandhopper came near
For your phrase. Plovers were blessed in their absence.   5
The oyster-catcher heard talk of his 'neb'.

St Patrick's Rock with its twin black pillars
Horning the swell had its own story too:
It split open like that to let Patrick sail through.

It's this water and cliff that ballast   10
Your books. 'So look for the intimate thing,'
(Cliff and horizon shutting like covers

Around us as we step the firm margin)
'And go your own way,' you say, 'and do your own work.'
Your bay's loved voices follow us into the dark.   15

Their Brother

He's a trouble to them.
Supposing they leave him a loaf

And a knife on the board,
He'll not know how to use it

5 And will have starved while they fished.
They both need to go,
One rowing, one paying or lifting.
Their billy smokes in the bow.

As they feed, they know him
10 Hutched under the table at home,
His man's hands flying like bats.
They think that's him running a line.

He'll be in there
Until they arrive on the floor.
15 Then he'll bump out croaking and
Clapping at the sight of a fish.

Crowing Man

A tramp whom parents made crow
Like a cock for his victuals.
His head re-appearing now
Tilts disembodied and falls
5 Wide open in a bellow

That for years the lower jaw
Gagged into performances
For frightened youngsters below
Kitchen tables. He wants his
10 Revenge. All right then. Bellow.

Lictor

The gully flashes
At the shins of marrowstem
That skip off their stumps.
The plied brims

5 Dislocate, squeaking
Faintly, and plash
To the ground. Pale,
Ranked stalks on the field

Wait like casualties
Until they are bundled.　　　　　　　　　　　　　　　　　　10
He hitches them and heads off,
The gully sheathed up the butts.

A Twilight

Slowly into his whispering pad
A man arrives with horse and cart
Gathering wrack. The skimmed sand
Pubescent with browning lien and wort

Bruises under them. They approach　　　　　　　　　　　　5
With creakings, a laboured snore,
And pass, heading their dark tracks
Where the strand curves off to nowhere.

I saw the solid felloe turn,
The cleansed hoop sink clean to its rut　　　　　　　　　10
And the hoofs' upheld slow motion.
On bared sand their inscriptions wait.

Yank

Kennedy thought he'd test him from the start
And never slackened, but the old arm shot out
Imperiously. 'There you are. You land
Across the sandy bottom. Good God, man,
Is this your first time in upon the island?'　　　　　　　5
And Kennedy, well shocked that sixty years
Unsettled neither certainty nor sand,
Headed the currach in to the bare shore.
The green land bulked up and blocked the sky.

'That hill was never steep as that before,'　　　　　　　10
The old man said, standing in wet shoes
Between the silent land and lashing breaker,
Hearing his voice diminished in his ear.
Kennedy wondered if he knew the house
But said nothing, letting the heaped shingle,　　　　　15
Anonymous acres, deserted right-of-ways

Divest their undisturbed green desolation
To close with the ghost world that had lured them there.

'God O God, man, eighteen when I left!
20   They were every one lined up there to convey me
And when I walked over the shoe mouth in the tide
The youngsters cried but the old ones watched my back.'
They climbed up the cart track to his house
Where he knelt down outside the rotten door
25   To pray. 'God bless and God rest my father.'
The door ripped off its hinges when he pushed.
He stooped himself under the mildewed roof,
Put out his arms almost from wall to wall
As if to shoulder an antique yoke, called
30   Kennedy. 'Our house was a bigger house
Than this house; there never were five children
Reared on this floor. I guess it's caving in.'
When they came out he reckoned it too dull
For photographs so Kennedy produced
35   The whiskey and they drank a lot quickly
On the doorstep, leaving the door collapsed.

'No wonder they all left. There's no life here.
I'm sorry, fellow, to have dragged you out
To a place like this.' He never looked back
40   Going down to the currach. At his back
The marked shore sloped vacant to the tide;
The unpictured hill reflected and diminished
In Kennedy's unwatching oarsman's eye.

Elegy for a Postman

Who rowed out between islands one evening
Before Christmas, with a white mist censing
The clunk of the boat, the guttural oars
And noise of children playing round the shores.

5   Silent, lumpy as a berg, the mailbag
Lay at his feet. Under the swathing fog
Perhaps he is content to drift a while:
Those scattered homesteads won't expect his call.

He seals quietly on the lough. The lamps

Are desultory markers as he gazes.   10
A child's called in. The opened door blazes
On to the water. His old head nods. He dozes.

At one in the morning the lough was black.
Fathers awoke to far shouts, the crack
Of an oar on ice and calling of their names   15
By a late postman, locked out from all their homes.

His voice wailed out the roll-call of his beat.
The water would not open to his knock.
They reached him the next day by ten o'clock
Clad in hard frost, the bag stiff at his feet.   20

Rags

at a Holy Well in Ulster

The stripped and bitten flags
Of a last camp –
They moved on from here,

Wart, blain and chancre
Wiped clean as a bead,   5
Their touched cloths knotted in the wind.

This is our device:
Reduced insignia whipping
On a stunted bush,

Tough and cold   10
As a sheep's head in winter dawn.
The gules and green fields

Of our heraldry all faded,
Our rinsed-out purposes
Shrivelling like dulse.   15

Third Degree

A salmon sunk on the stiff tines of his fork
Beats a wild morse along the springy shaft
That seesaws from his fulcrum armpit.

He studies his come-back a second and catapults
5　　The fish over his head, a pocked ingot.
　　　Again his fine nibs doodle through the water.

Retort

　　　Inside sleek satin cribs
　　　The whited inky hands
　　　Hasped on the breast bone
　　　And glistening eyelids

5　　Sealed cold as the coins:
　　　All my dead relatives
　　　Lay in tainted rooms
　　　For a couple of days.

　　　And I'll be shouldered out
10　　Topped and tailed
　　　With the brown scapulars
　　　Bibbing me,

　　　Like the cousin
　　　I myself shouldered,
15　　A weighty boy in his shroud
　　　Put down so early.

　　　In future, thought-out hurt
　　　Must survive my test:
　　　Would you want such a man
20　　Stepping out of the crowd

　　　For a lift with your coffin?
　　　If not, he's the one
　　　Who falls in late and
　　　Smokes over the unclosed grave.

Last Camp

I

　　　Our Lars always at stud –
　　　Battering out a spore
　　　Of fouled whitewash and tar –

Now haunts the charred gables,
Poison curd on the walls, 5
Abandoned urinals.

II

Here in the tundra we
Trot among our icons,
Old dung scattered like brains

Hardening underfoot.
We gather and burn it, 5
Reeking our lives.

III

Purses shrivelled like figs,
Cast-offs, spent cartridges –
God, we will defend these

Scraps with nails and canines.
Our bonded detritus, 5
Pieties, rare droppings.

Intimidation

Their bonfire scorched his gable.
He comes home to kick through
A tumulus of ash,
A hot stour in the moonlight.

Each year this reek 5
Of their midsummer madness
Troubles him, a nest of pismires
At his drystone walls.

Ghetto rats! Are they the ones
To do the smoking out? 10
They'll come streaming past
To taste their ashes yet.

He sits long after bedtime
With the light out.
Moondust drifts down the street 15
And soot, off his blackened gable.

Rubric

*An ill-disposed person could, merely by looking at it,
'blink' a cow so that its milk would yield no butter.*
E. ESTYN EVANS, *Irish Folk Ways*

Leave a holed flint on the shelf,
A good eye among our delph.

Ring salt on the churn lid,
Drive coffin nails in the hooped wood.

Hoop it again with a twisted
Rowan twig. And stud

The wall once butter breaks
With butter lumps, smear streaks

Of it on your cupboards
And fear before all bad words.

For the blinker, peering through hedges
In a buzz of dung-flies and midges,

Can steer venom from his rimmed eye,
Sour and curd your white pantry

Until the milk is bile and gall
And whitewash blisters on the wall.

He'll be swishing through the aftergrass
To-night, blazing at our windows.

Museum Pieces

for Michael S. Harper

I

They have grafted his nightmares
to the palace wall –
a dark cyclone

hosting, breaking.
In old age, Goya
painting with his fists and elbows

watched history charge and
swept the gored linings of his heart
in a desperate veronica.

   II

The fluid wrist is struck,
is earthed, conducts.

I turn a stair
in the Musée des Impressionistes,
a sulphurous Van Gogh 5
fumes in my eyes.

   III

Conjure among
their adept bayonets
oppose your phial
to the phalanxes.

Craig's Dragoons

Air: 'Dolly's Brae'

Come all ye Ulster loyalists and in full chorus join,
Think on the deeds of Craig's Dragoons who strike below the groin,
And drink a toast to the truncheon and the armoured water-hose
That mowed a swathe through Civil Rights and spat on Papish clothes.

We've gerrymandered Derry but Croppy won't lie down, 5
He calls himself a citizen and wants votes in the town.
But that Saturday in Duke Street we slipped the velvet glove –
The iron hand of Craig's Dragoons soon crunched a croppy dove.

Big McAteer and Currie, Gerry Fitt and others too,
Were fool enough to lead the van, expecting to get through, 10
But our hero commandos, let loose at last to play,
Did annihilate the rights of man in the noontime of a day.

They downed women with children, for Teagues all over-breed,
They used the baton on men's heads, for Craig would pay no heed,
And then the boys placed in plain clothes, they lent a loyal hand 15
To massacre those Derry ligs behind a Crossley van.

O William Craig, you are our love, our lily and our sash,
You have the boys who fear no noise, who'll batter and who'll bash.

Letter to an Editor

Michael, you know I'm expert with the spade
and get official backing for each action:
then stand back, for this folk-museum blade
can choose to lop off handshake or erection.

I warn you, your wee fly bedsetter-king
sweats in the palm of this Rachmann of the arts
who comes with fake concern and a Claddagh ring
to evict him from the reek of his own farts.

(God but his H.U. stuff, so sweet and sour
is easy going as the turnip-snedder –
I'd say at least twelve quatrains to the hour,
including tea-breaks, which gives us a newsletter

eight times a day, going at minimum rate.
There's a vocation lost, but what's the use?
I should have read, I realize too late,
not 'The Great Hunger' but 'Collected Pruse'.)

Now didn't you learn it all from Kavanagh,
the slapdash truth and the well-meaning lie?
Distrust your solemn man. Go for the ba.
And ironically don't care – spit in their eye.

Your prose style, I must say, is excellent,
fit instrument for cheek-slash and death-blow
but is all that courage at the sticking point
screwed up by the real thing or some dildo?

Official gadflies are co-opted. Then beware.
You too might lunge and find your angry stick
is dunlopillo. Who do you think you are?
Rare Ben Jonson? Swift? Dryden? Or Ulick?

We both know the Big Study and Pre Par,
the half-day syndrome and the day-boy lunch.
It would be a pity to spoil things as they are
with a clip on the ear or rabbit punch

so instead I write to say I am fed up
finding myself too much in gossip columns.
Show proper respect, you editorial dope. 35
You're dealing with a prefect from St Columb's.

Slieve Gallon's Brae

I was thinking of your flowers
                all a-going to decay

All the times I have heard you sing it
with your eyes closed, the cairns of your body
stilled:
        as your voice coupling with
air wears to a shape for air to carry, 5
the familiar slope of the mountain loads
itself
        between the dressed flanks of two stacks
where I stood at sunset, listening.
When we are dead on borrowed time and breath, 10
absence
        palpable as love in the first days
can be assigned to a hollow under stones;
and they can name Slieve Gallon cairn our bed.

Woodcut

Words are scarfing
Out of his mouth
In blackletter latin.

His stumpy legs,
The curls at his shoulders, 5
His buckles

Are no less heavily
Cut. The art of the emblem
Is so hard-edged.

Is he a loom or a spool 10
For his speech? Is he force-fed
Or finding these words?

Father of the Bride

He has given her away
Wound like a silkworm
From damasked foot
To the crown of flowers

5   And now everyone meets goodbye
At the cool pane of her kiss
But he is wandering
Towards the loop on the drive

To be the last to wave,
10   A cut spray on his breast,
A tendril loosed off
His arm and flickering past.

Baptism

for Ellen and Kate Flanagan

I came from water through the hoop of bone
Into this cold pool in the womb of stone.

I drowned my first mind in the font's small well,
A new world breaking on my fontanel.

5   Again I broke the waters and again I came
Wet and glistening, into my name

Drowning, my life passed through me in a flash
And I emerged, marked secretly, my sign the fish.

Now I have known my origin and my end
10   And swim towards myself in a new element,

Marvellously single and, marvellously, a shoal
Of all those washed in that water, salt and oil.

17th December 1971

The Blinker

Leave a holed flint on the shelf,
A good eye among our delph.

Ring salt on the churn lid,
Drive coffin nails in the hooped wood.

Hoop it again with a twisted   5
Rowan twig. And stud

The wall once butter breaks
With butter lumps, smear streaks

Of it on your cupboards
And fear above all bad words.   10

For this one, peering through hedges
In a buzz of dung flies and midges,

Can steer venom from his rimmed eye,
Sour and curd your white pantry

Until the milk is bile and gall   15
And whitewash blisters on the wall.

He'll be swishing through the aftergrass
To-night, blazing at our windows.

Scullions

Big-voiced ancestors,
squires of the cockpit,
misers of tender words,
arbitrators of the burying grounds

where their kingdom   5
is a legend on mossed stones:
Ballyscullion, mat sacking
spread at the demesne gates,

a name like a device
of shouldered fork and rake,   10
a key to open
byres and museums.

Found in a bog
at Ballyscullion:
15 I see them straggling towards
well-spoken power, with finds

or forms badged X *His Mark*
and stand for a last time
where misery and love
20 grunt behind the thickets

of a hedge. I part thorns
and there is the mongol
dragging his burden of riches,
a graipful of manure.

January God

Then I found a two-faced stone
    On burial ground,
God-eyed, sex-mouthed, its brain
    A watery wound.

5   In the wet gap of the year,
    Daubed with fresh lake mud,
I faltered near his power –
    January god

Who broke the water, the hymen
10   With his great antlers –
There reigned upon each ghost tine
    His familiars,

The mothering earth, the stones
    Taken by each wave,
15 The fleshy aftergrass, the bones
    Subsoil in each grave.

Sile na Gig

Downpours overhead.
And I move into
the marrow of currents,
the river's long nerve

and natural contractions,
a muscle system
turning on its bed.
At the source,

under tufted levels
of upland bog,
the accouchement of water
is neverending:

contortionist water,
double-jointed, shameless,
flaunter on gravel,
lipper of bridges.

Hushed madam
among reed-beds,
the masseuse
of somnolent farms,

her skirts rumple
at the stepping-stones,
she opens her legs
for bushy islands

and shocks the faithful
by pissing high
off the church gable.
She leaps gargoyles

a tergo
and squats giggling
under a long mare's tail
from the spout.

WINTERING OUT (1972)

For David Hammond and Michael Longley

This morning from a dewy motorway
I saw the new camp for the internees:
a bomb had left a crater of fresh clay
in the roadside, and over in the trees

machine-gun posts defined a real stockade.
There was that white mist you get on a low ground
and it was déjà-vu, some film made
of Stalag 17, a bad dream with no sound.

Is there a life before death? That's chalked up
on a wall downtown. Competence with pain,
coherent miseries, a bite and sup,
we hug our little destiny again.

PART ONE

Fodder

Or, as we said,
fother, I open
my arms for it
again. But first

to draw from the tight
vise of a stack
the weathered eaves
of the stack itself

falling at your feet,
last summer's tumbled
swathes of grass
and meadowsweet

multiple as loaves
and fishes, a bundle
tossed over half-doors
or into mucky gaps.

These long nights
I would pull hay
for comfort, anything
to bed the stall.

Bog Oak

A carter's trophy
Split for rafters,
a cobwebbed, black,
long-seasoned rib

under the first thatch.
I might tarry
with the moustached
dead, the creel-fillers,

or eavesdrop on
their hopeless wisdom
as a blow-down of smoke
struggles over the half-door

and mizzling rain
blurs the far end
of the cart track.
The softening ruts

lead back to no
'oak groves', no
cutters of mistletoe
in the green clearings.

Perhaps I just make out
Edmund Spenser,
dreaming sunlight,
encroached upon by

geniuses who creep
'out of every corner
of the woodes and glennes'
towards watercress and carrion.

Anahorish

My 'place of clear water',
the first hill in the world
where springs washed into
the shiny grass

and darkened cobbles
in the bed of the lane.
Anahorish, soft gradient
of consonant, vowel-meadow,

after-image of lamps
swung through the yards
on winter evenings.
With pails and barrows

those mound-dwellers
go waist-deep in mist
to break the light ice
at wells and dunghills.

Servant Boy

He is wintering out
the back-end of a bad year,
swinging a hurricane-lamp
through some outhouse;

a jobber among shadows.
Old work-whore, slave-
blood, who stepped fair-hills
under each bidder's eye

and kept your patience
and your counsel, how
you draw me into
your trail. Your trail

broken from haggard to stable,
a straggle of fodder
stiffened on snow,
comes first-footing

the back doors of the little
barons: resentful
and impenitent,
carrying the warm eggs.

The Last Mummer

I

Carries a stone in his pocket,
an ash-plant under his arm.

Moves out of the fog
on the lawn, pads up the terrace.

The luminous screen in the corner
has them charmed in a ring

so he stands a long time behind them.
St George, Beelzebub and Jack Straw

can't be conjured from mist.
He catches the stick in his fist

and, shrouded, starts beating
the bars of the gate.

His boots crack the road. The stone
clatters down off the slates.

II

He came trammelled
in the taboos of the country

picking a nice way through
the long toils of blood

and feuding.
His tongue went whoring

among the civil tongues,
he had an eye for weather-eyes

at cross-roads and lane-ends
and could don manners

at a flutter of curtains.

His straw mask and hunch were fabulous

disappearing beyond the lamplit
slabs of a yard.

III

You dream a cricket in the hearth
and cockroach on the floor,

a line of mummers
marching out the door

as the lamp flares in the draught. 5
Melted snow off their feet

leaves you in peace.
Again an old year dies

on your hearthstone, for good luck.
The moon's host elevated 10

in a monstrance of holly trees,
he makes dark tracks, who had

untousled a first dewy path
into the summer grazing.

Land

I

I stepped it, perch by perch.
Unbraiding rushes and grass
I opened my right-of-way
through old bottoms and sowed-out ground
and gathered stones off the ploughing 5
to raise a small cairn.
Cleaned out the drains, faced the hedges
often got up at dawn
to walk the outlying fields.

I composed habits for those acres 10
so that my last look would be
neither gluttonous nor starved.
I was ready to go anywhere.

II

This is in place of what I would leave
plaited and branchy
on a long slope of stubble:

a woman of old wet leaves,
rush-bands and thatcher's scollops,
stooked loosely, her breasts an open-work

of new straw and harvest bows.
Gazing out past
the shifting hares.

III

I sense the pads
unfurling under grass and clover:

if I lie with my ear
in this loop of silence

long enough, thigh-bone
and shoulder against the phantom ground,

I expect to pick up
a small drumming

and must not be surprised
in bursting air

to find myself snared, swinging
an ear-ring of sharp wire.

Gifts of Rain

I

Cloudburst and steady downpour now
for days.
       Still mammal,
straw-footed on the mud,
he begins to sense weather
by his skin.

A nimble snout of flood
licks over stepping stones
and goes uprooting.

                He fords
his life by sounding.
          Soundings.

II

A man wading lost fields
breaks the pane of flood:

a flower of mud-
water blooms up to his reflection

like a cut swaying
its red spoors through a basin.

His hands grub
where the spade has uncastled

sunken drills, an atlantis
he depends on. So

he is hooped to where he planted
and sky and ground

are running naturally among his arms
that grope the cropping land.

III

When rains were gathering
there would be an all-night
roaring off the ford.
Their world-schooled ear

could monitor the usual
confabulations, the race
slabbering past the gable,
the Moyola harping on

its gravel beds:
all spouts by daylight
brimmed with their own airs
and overflowed each barrel

in long tresses.
I cock my ear
at an absence –
in the shared calling of blood

arrives my need
for antediluvian lore.
Soft voices of the dead
are whispering by the shore

that I would question
(and for my children's sake)
about crops rotted, river mud
glazing the baked clay floor.

   IV

The tawny guttural water
spells itself: Moyola
is its own score and consort,

bedding the locale
in the utterance,
reed music, an old chanter

breathing its mists
through vowels and history.
A swollen river,

a mating call of sound
rises to pleasure me, Dives,
hoarder of common ground.

Toome

My mouth holds round
the soft blastings,
Toome, Toome,
as under the dislodged

slab of the tongue
I push into a souterrain
prospecting what new
in a hundred centuries'

loam, flints, musket-balls,
fragmented ware,
torcs and fish-bones
till I am sleeved in

alluvial mud that shelves
suddenly under
bogwater and tributaries,   15
and elvers tail my hair.

Broagh

Riverbank, the long rigs
ending in broad docken
and a canopied pad
down to the ford.

The garden mould   5
bruised easily, the shower
gathering in your heelmark
was the black O

in *Broagh*,
its low tattoo   10
among the windy boortrees
and rhubarb-blades

ended almost
suddenly, like that last
gh the strangers found   15
difficult to manage.

Oracle

Hide in the hollow trunk
of the willow tree,
its listening familiar,
until, as usual, they
cuckoo your name   5
across the fields.
You can hear them
draw the poles of stiles
as they approach
calling you out: 10
small mouth and ear

in a woody cleft,
lobe and larynx
of the mossy places.

The Backward Look

A stagger in air
as if a language
failed, a sleight
of wing.

5 A snipe's bleat is fleeing
its nesting ground
into dialect,
into variants,

transliterations whirr
10 on the nature reserves –
little goat of the air,
of the evening,

little goat of the frost.
It is his tail-feathers
15 drumming elegies
in the slipstream

of wild goose
and yellow bittern
as he corkscrews away
20 into the vaults

that we live off, his flight
through the sniper's eyrie,
over twilit earthworks
and wall-steads,

25 disappearing among
gleanings and leavings
in the combs
of a fieldworker's archive.

Traditions

for Tom Flanagan

I

Our guttural muse
was bulled long ago
by the alliterative tradition,
her uvula grows

vestigial, forgotten
like the coccyx
or a Brigid's Cross
yellowing in some outhouse

while custom, that 'most
sovereign mistress',
beds us down into
the British isles.

II

We are to be proud
of our Elizabethan English:
'varsity', for example,
is grass-roots stuff with us;

we 'deem' or we 'allow'
when we suppose
and some cherished archaisms
are correct Shakespearean.

Not to speak of the furled
consonants of lowlanders
shuttling obstinately
between bawn and mossland.

III

MacMorris, gallivanting
round the Globe, whinged
to courtier and groundling
who had heard tell of us

as going very bare
of learning, as wild hares,

       as anatomies of death:
       'What ish my nation?'

       And sensibly, though so much
10   later, the wandering Bloom
       replied, 'Ireland,' said Bloom,
       'I was born here. Ireland.'

A New Song

       I met a girl from Derrygarve
       And the name, a lost potent musk,
       Recalled the river's long swerve,
       A kingfisher's blue bolt at dusk

5   And stepping stones like black molars
       Sunk in the ford, the shifty glaze
       Of the whirlpool, the Moyola
       Pleasuring beneath alder trees.

       And Derrygarve, I thought, was just,
10   Vanished music, twilit water,
       A smooth libation of the past
       Poured by this chance vestal daughter.

       But now our river tongues must rise
       From licking deep in native haunts
15   To flood, with vowelling embrace,
       Demesnes staked out in consonants.

       And Castledawson we'll enlist
       And Upperlands, each planted bawn –
       Like bleaching-greens resumed by grass –
20   A vocable, as rath and bullaun.

The Other Side

       I

       Thigh-deep in sedge and marigolds
       a neighbour laid his shadow
       on the stream, vouching

'It's poor as Lazarus, that ground,'
and brushed away
among the shaken leafage:

I lay where his lea sloped
to meet our fallow,
nested on moss and rushes,

my ear swallowing
his fabulous, biblical dismissal,
that tongue of chosen people.

When he would stand like that
on the other side, white-haired,
swinging his blackthorn

at the marsh weeds,
he prophesied above our scraggy acres,
then turned away

towards his promised furrows
on the hill, a wake of pollen
drifting to our bank, next season's tares.

II

For days we would rehearse
each patriarchal dictum:
Lazarus, the Pharaoh, Solomon

and David and Goliath rolled
magnificently, like loads of hay
too big for our small lanes,

or faltered on a rut –
'Your side of the house, I believe,
hardly rule by the book at all.'

His brain was a whitewashed kitchen
hung with texts, swept tidy
as the body o' the kirk.

III

Then sometimes when the rosary was dragging
mournfully on in the kitchen
we would hear his step round the gable

though not until after the litany
would the knock come to the door
and the casual whistle strike up

on the doorstep. 'A right-looking night,'
he might say, 'I was dandering by
and says I, I might as well call.'

But now I stand behind him
in the dark yard, in the moan of prayers.
He puts a hand in a pocket

or taps a little tune with the blackthorn
shyly, as if he were party to
lovemaking or a stranger's weeping.

Should I slip away, I wonder,
or go up and touch his shoulder
and talk about the weather

or the price of grass-seed?

The Wool Trade

> *'How different are the words "home",
> "Christ", "ale", "master", on his
> lips and on mine.'*
> STEPHEN DEDALUS

'The wool trade' – the phrase
Rambled warm as a fleece

Out of his hoard.
To shear, to bale and bleach and card

Unwound from the spools
Of his vowels

And square-set men in tunics
Who plied soft names like Bruges

In their talk, merchants
Back from the Netherlands:

O all the hamlets where
Hills and flocks and streams conspired

To a language of waterwheels,
A lost syntax of looms and spindles,

How they hang
Fading, in the gallery of the tongue!

And I must talk of tweed,
A stiff cloth with flecks like blood.

Linen Town

High Street, Belfast, 1786

It's twenty to four
By the public clock. A cloaked rider
Clops off into an entry

Coming perhaps from the Linen Hall
Or Cornmarket
Where, the civic print unfrozen,

In twelve years' time
They hanged young McCracken –
This lownecked belle and tricorned fop's

Still flourish undisturbed
By the swinging tongue of his body.
Pen and ink, water tint

Fence and fetch us in
Under bracketed tavern signs,
The edged gloom of arcades.

It's twenty to four
On one of the last afternoons
Of reasonable light.

Smell the tidal Lagan:
Take a last turn
In the tang of possibility.

A Northern Hoard

And some in dreams assured were
Of the Spirit that plagued us so

1 Roots

Leaf membranes lid the window.
In the streetlamp's glow
Your body's moonstruck
To drifted barrow, sunk glacial rock.

And all shifts dreamily as you keen
Far off, turning from the din
Of gunshot, siren and clucking gas
Out there beyond each curtained terrace

Where the fault is opening. The touch of love,
Your warmth heaving to the first move,
Grows helpless in our old Gomorrah.
We petrify or uproot now.

I'll dream it for us before dawn
When the pale sniper steps down
And I approach the shrub.
I've soaked by moonlight in tidal blood

A mandrake, lodged human fork,
Earth sac, limb of the dark;
And I wound its damp smelly loam
And stop my ears against the scream.

2 No Man's Land

I deserted, shut out
their wounds' fierce awning,
those palms like streaming webs.

Must I crawl back now,
spirochete, abroad between
shred-hung wire and thorn,
to confront my smeared doorstep
and what lumpy dead?
Why do I unceasingly

arrive late to condone
infected sutures
and ill-knit bone?

3 *Stump*

I am riding to plague again.
Sometimes under a sooty wash
From the grate in the burnt-out gable
I see the needy in a small pow-wow.
What do I say if they wheel out their dead?
I'm cauterized, a black stump of home.

4 *No Sanctuary*

It's Hallowe'en. The turnip-man's lopped head
Blazes at us through split bottle glass
And fumes and swims up like a wrecker's lantern.

Death mask of harvest, mocker at All Souls
With scorching smells, red dog's eyes in the night –
We ring and stare into unhallowed light.

5 *Tinder*

We picked flints,
Pale and dirt-veined,

So small finger and thumb
Ached around them;

Cold beads of history and home
We fingered, a cave-mouth flame

Of leaf and stick
Trembling at the mind's wick.

We clicked stone on stone
That sparked a weak flame-pollen

And failed, our knuckle joints
Striking as often as the flints.

What did we know then
Of tinder, charred linen and iron,

15 Huddled at dusk in a ring,
    Our fists shut, our hope shrunken?

    What could strike a blaze
    From our dead igneous days?

    Now we squat on cold cinder,
20 Red-eyed, after the flames' soft thunder

    And our thoughts settle like ash.
    We face the tundra's whistling brush

    With new history, flint and iron,
    Cast-offs, scraps, nail, canine.

Midnight

Since the professional wars –
Corpse and carrion
Paling in rain –
The wolf has died out

5   In Ireland. The packs
Scoured parkland and moor
Till a Quaker buck and his dogs
Killed the last one

In some scraggy waste of Kildare.
10 The wolfhound was crossed
With inferior strains,
Forests coopered to wine casks.

Rain on the roof to-night
Sogs turf-banks and heather,
15 Sets glinting outcrops
Of basalt and granite,

Drips to the moss of bare boughs.
The old dens are soaking.
The pads are lost or
20 Retrieved by small vermin

That glisten and scut.
Nothing is panting, lolling,
Vapouring. The tongue's
Leashed in my throat.

The Tollund Man

I

Some day I will go to Aarhus
To see his peat-brown head,
The mild pods of his eye-lids,
His pointed skin cap.

In the flat country nearby
Where they dug him out,
His last gruel of winter seeds
Caked in his stomach,

Naked except for
The cap, noose and girdle,
I will stand a long time.
Bridegroom to the goddess,

She tightened her torc on him
And opened her fen,
Those dark juices working
Him to a saint's kept body,

Trove of the turfcutters'
Honeycombed workings.
Now his stained face
Reposes at Aarhus.

II

I could risk blasphemy,
Consecrate the cauldron bog
Our holy ground and pray
Him to make germinate

The scattered, ambushed
Flesh of labourers,
Stockinged corpses
Laid out in the farmyards,

Tell-tale skin and teeth
Flecking the sleepers
Of four young brothers, trailed
For miles along the lines.

III

Something of his sad freedom
As he rode the tumbril
Should come to me, driving,
Saying the names

5   Tollund, Grauballe, Nebelgard,
Watching the pointing hands
Of country people,
Not knowing their tongue.

Out there in Jutland
10 In the old man-killing parishes
I will feel lost,
Unhappy and at home.

Nerthus

For beauty, say an ash-fork staked in peat,
Its long grains gathering to the gouged split;

A seasoned, unsleeved taker of the weather,
Where kesh and loaning finger out to heather.

Cairn-Maker

for Barrie Cooke

He robbed the stones' nests, uncradled
As he orphaned and betrothed rock
To rock: his unaccustomed hand
Went chambering upon hillock

5   And bogland. Clamping, balancing,
That whole day spent in the Burren,
He did not find and add to them
But piled up small cairn after cairn

And dressed some stones with his own mark.
10 Which he tells of with almost fear;
And of strange affiliation
To what was touched and handled there,

Unexpected hives and castlings
Pennanted now, claimed by no hand:
Rush and ladysmock, heather-bells
Blowing in each aftermath of wind.

Navvy

The moleskins stiff as bark,
the drill grafting his wrists
to the shale:
where the surface is weavy

and the camber tilts
in the slow lane, he stands
waving you down. The morass
the macadam snakes over

swallowed his yellow bulldozer
four years ago, laying it down
with lake-dwellings and dug-outs,
pike-shafts, axe-heads, bone pins,

all he is indifferent to.
He has not relented
under weather or insults,
my brother and keeper

plugged to the hard-core,
picking along
the welted, stretchmarked
curve of the world.

Veteran's Dream

Mr Dickson, my neighbour,
Who saw the last cavalry charge
Of the war and got the first gas
Walks with a limp

Into his helmet and khaki.
He notices indifferently

The gas has yellowed his buttons
And near his head

Horses plant their shods.
His real fear is gangrene.
He wakes with his hand to the scar
And they do their white magic

Where he lies
On cankered ground,
A scatter of maggots, busy
In the trench of his wound.

Augury

The fish faced into the current,
Its mouth agape,
Its whole head opened like a valve.
You said 'It's diseased.'

A pale crusted sore
Turned like a coin
And wound to the bottom,
Unsettling silt off a weed.

We hang charmed
On the trembling catwalk:
What can fend us now
Can soothe the hurt eye

Of the sun,
Unpoison great lakes,
Turn back
The rat on the road.

PART TWO

Wedding Day

I am afraid.
Sound has stopped in the day
And the images reel over
And over. Why all those tears,

The wild grief on his face   5
Outside the taxi? The sap
Of mourning rises
In our waving guests.

You sing behind the tall cake
Like a deserted bride   10
Who persists, demented,
And goes through the ritual.

When I went to the gents
There was a skewered heart
And a legend of love. Let me   15
Sleep on your breast to the airport.

Mother of the Groom

What she remembers
Is his glistening back
In the bath, his small boots
In the ring of boots at her feet.

Hands in her voided lap,   5
She hears a daughter welcomed.
It's as if he kicked when lifted
And slipped her soapy hold.

Once soap would ease off
The wedding ring   10
That's bedded forever now
In her clapping hand.

Summer Home

I

Was it wind off the dumps
or something in heat

dogging us, the summer gone sour,
a fouled nest incubating somewhere?

Whose fault, I wondered, inquisitor
of the possessed air.

To realize suddenly,
whip off the mat

that was larval, moving –
and scald, scald, scald.

II

Bushing the door, my arms full
of wild cherry and rhododendron,
I hear her small lost weeping
through the hall, that bells and hoarsens
on my name, my name.

O love, here is the blame.

The loosened flowers between us
gather in, compose
for a May altar of sorts.
These frank and falling blooms
soon taint to a sweet chrism.

Attend. Anoint the wound.

III

O we tented our wound all right
under the homely sheet

and lay as if the cold flat of a blade
had winded us.

More and more I postulate
thick healings, like now

as you bend in the shower
water lives down the tilting stoups of your breasts.

IV

With a final
unmusical drive
long grains begin
to open and split

ahead and once more 5
we sap
the white, trodden
path to the heart.

V

My children weep out the hot foreign night.
We walk the floor, my foul mouth takes it out
On you and we lie stiff till dawn
Attends the pillow, and the maize, and vine

That holds its filling burden to the light. 5
Yesterday rocks sang when we tapped
Stalactites in the cave's old, dripping dark –
Our love calls tiny as a tuning fork.

Serenades

The Irish nightingale
Is a sedge-warbler,
A little bird with a big voice
Kicking up a racket all night.

Not what you'd expect 5
From the musical nation.
I haven't even heard one –
Nor an owl, for that matter.

My serenades have been
The broken voice of a crow 10
In a draught or a dream,
The wheeze of bats

Or the ack-ack
Of the tramp corncrake

15 Lost in a no man's land
    Between combines and chemicals.

    So fill the bottles, love,
    Leave them inside their cots.
    And if they do wake us, well,
20 So would the sedge-warbler.

Somnambulist

Nestrobber's hands
and a face in its net of gossamer;

he came back weeping
to unstarch the pillow

5   and freckle her sheets
with tiny yolk.

A Winter's Tale

A pallor in the headlights'
Range wavered and disappeared.
Weeping, blood bright from her cuts
Where she'd fled the hedged and wired
5   Road, they eyed her nakedness
Astray among the cattle
At first light. Lanterns, torches
And the searchers' gay babble
She eluded earlier:
10 Now her own people only
Closed around her dazed whimper
With rugs, dressings and brandy –
Conveying maiden daughter
Back to family hearth and floor.
15 Why run, our lovely daughter,
Bare-breasted from our door?

    Still, like good luck, she returned.
    Some nights, crossing the thresholds
    Of empty homes, she warmed
20 Her dewy roundings and folds

To sleep in the chimney nook.
After all, they were neighbours.
As neighbours, when they came back
Surprised but unmalicious
Greetings passed   25
Between them. She was there first
And so appeared no haunter
But, making all comers guests,
She stirred as from a winter
Sleep. Smiled. Uncradled her breasts.   30

Shore Woman

> *Man to the hills, woman to the shore.*
> GAELIC PROVERB

I have crossed the dunes with their whistling bent
Where dry loose sand was riddling round the air
And I'm walking the firm margin. White pocks
Of cockle, blanched roofs of clam and oyster
Hoard the moonlight, woven and unwoven   5
Off the bay. At the far rocks
A pale sud comes and goes.

Under boards the mackerel slapped to death
Yet still we took them in at every cast,
Stiff flails of cold convulsed with their first breath.   10
My line plumbed certainly the undertow,
Loaded against me once I went to draw
And flashed and fattened up towards the light.
He was all business in the stern. I called
'This is so easy that it's hardly right,'   15
But he unhooked and coped with frantic fish
Without speaking. Then suddenly it lulled,
We'd crossed where they were running, the line rose
Like a let-down and I was conscious
How far we'd drifted out beyond the head.   20
'Count them up at your end,' was all he said
Before I saw the porpoises' thick backs
Cartwheeling like the flywheels of the tide,
Soapy and shining. To have seen a hill
Splitting the water could not have numbed me more   25

　　　　Than the close irruption of that school,
　　　　Tight viscous muscle, hooped from tail to snout,
　　　　Each one revealed complete as it bowled out
　　　　And under.
30　　　　　　　They will attack a boat.
　　　　I knew it and I asked him to put in
　　　　But he would not, declared it was a yarn
　　　　My people had been fooled by far too long
　　　　And he would prove it now and settle it.
35　　　　Maybe he shrank when those sloped oily backs
　　　　Propelled towards us: I lay and screamed
　　　　Under splashed brine in an open rocking boat
　　　　Feeling each dunt and slither through the timber,
　　　　Sick at their huge pleasures in the water.

40　　　　I sometimes walk this strand for thanksgiving
　　　　Or maybe it's to get away from him
　　　　Skittering his spit across the stove. Here
　　　　Is the taste of safety, the shelving sand
　　　　Harbours no worse than razor-shell or crab –
45　　　　Though my father recalls carcasses of whales
　　　　Collapsed and gasping, right up to the dunes.
　　　　But to-night such moving sinewed dreams lie out
　　　　In darker fathoms, far beyond the head.
　　　　Astray upon a debris of scrubbed shells
50　　　　Between parched dunes and salivating wave,
　　　　I have rights on this fallow avenue,
　　　　A membrane between moonlight and my shadow.

Maighdean Mara

for Seán Oh-Eocha

I

　　　　She sleeps now, her cold breasts
　　　　Dandled by undertow,
　　　　Her hair lifted and laid.
　　　　Undulant slow seawracks
5　　　　Cast about shin and thigh,
　　　　Bangles of wort, drifting
　　　　Liens catch, dislodge gently.

This is the great first sleep
Of homecoming, eight
Land years between hearth and 10
Bed steeped and dishevelled.
Her magic garment al-
most ocean-tinctured still.

II

He stole her garments as
She combed her hair: follow
Was all that she could do.
He hid it in the eaves
And charmed her there, four walls, 5
Warm floor, man-love nightly
In earshot of the waves.

She suffered milk and birth –
She had no choice – conjured
Patterns of home and drained 10
The tidesong from her voice.
Then the thatcher came and stuck
Her garment in a stack.
Children carried tales back.

III

In night air, entering
Foam, she wrapped herself
With smoke-reeks from his thatch,
Straw-musts and films of mildew.
She dipped his secret there 5
Forever and uncharmed

Accents of fisher wives,
The dead hold of bedrooms,
Dread of the night and morrow,
Her children's brush and combs. 10
She sleeps now, her cold breasts
Dandled by undertow.

Limbo

Fishermen at Ballyshannon
Netted an infant last night
Along with the salmon.
An illegitimate spawning,

5   A small one thrown back
To the waters. But I'm sure
As she stood in the shallows
Ducking him tenderly

Till the frozen knobs of her wrists
10   Were dead as the gravel,
He was a minnow with hooks
Tearing her open.

She waded in under
The sign of her cross.
15   He was hauled in with the fish.
Now limbo will be

A cold glitter of souls
Through some far briny zone.
Even Christ's palms, unhealed,
20   Smart and cannot fish there.

Bye-Child

He was discovered in the henhouse
where she had confined him. He was
incapable of saying anything.

When the lamp glowed,
A yolk of light
In their back window,
The child in the outhouse
5   Put his eye to a chink –

Little henhouse boy,
Sharp-faced as new moons
Remembered, your photo still
Glimpsed like a rodent

On the floor of my mind,

Little moon man,
Kennelled and faithful
At the foot of the yard,
Your frail shape, luminous,
Weightless, is stirring the dust,

The cobwebs, old droppings
Under the roosts
And dry smells from scraps
She put through your trapdoor
Morning and evening.

After those footsteps, silence;
Vigils, solitudes, fasts,
Unchristened tears,
A puzzled love of the light.
But now you speak at last

With a remote mime
Of something beyond patience,
Your gaping wordless proof
Of lunar distances
Travelled beyond love.

Good-night

A latch lifting, an edged den of light
Opens across the yard. Out of the low door
They stoop into the honeyed corridor,
Then walk straight through the wall of the dark.

A puddle, cobble-stones, jambs and doorstep
Are set steady in a block of brightness.
Till she strides in again beyond her shadows
And cancels everything behind her.

First Calf

It's a long time since I saw
The afterbirth strung on the hedge

    As if the wind smarted
    And streamed bloodshot tears.

5   Somewhere about the cow stands
    With her head almost outweighing
    Her tense sloped neck,
    The calf hard at her udder.

    The shallow bowls of her eyes
10 Tilt membrane and fluid.
    The warm plaque of her snout gathers
    A growth round moist nostrils.

    Her hide stays warm in the wind.
    Her wide eyes read nothing.
15 The semaphores of hurt
    Swaddle and flap on a bush.

May

    When I looked down from the bridge
    Trout were flipping the sky
    Into smithereens, the stones
    Of the wall warmed me.

5   Wading green stems, lugs of leaf
    That untangle and bruise
    (Their tiny gushers of juice)
    My toecaps sparkle now

    Over the soft fontanel
10 Of Ireland. I should wear
    Hide shoes, the hair next my skin,
    For walking this ground:

    Wasn't there a spa-well,
    Its coping grassy, pendent?
15 And then the spring issuing
    Right across the tarmac.

    I'm out to find that village,
    Its low sills fragrant
    With ladysmock and celandine,
20 Marshlights in the summer dark.

Fireside

Always there would be stories of lights
hovering among bushes or at the foot
of a meadow; maybe a goat with cold horns
pluming into the moon; a tingle of chains

on the midnight road. And then maybe
word would come round of that watery
art, the lamping of fishes, and I'd be
mooning my flashlamp on the licked black pelt

of the stream, my left arm splayed to take
a heavy pour and run of the current
occluding the net. Was that the beam
buckling over an eddy or a gleam

of the fabulous? Steady the light
and come to your senses, they're saying good-night.

Dawn

Somebody lets up a blind.
The shrub at the window
Glitters, a mint of green leaves
Pitched and tossed.

When we stopped for lights
In the centre, pigeons were down
On the street, a scatter
Of cobbles, clucking and settling.

We went at five miles an hour.
A tut-tutting colloquy
Was in session, scholars
Arguing through until morning

In a Pompeian silence.
The dummies watched from the window
Displays as we slipped to the sea.
I got away out by myself

On a scurf of winkles and cockles
And found myself suddenly

Unable to move without crunching
Acres of their crisp delicate turrets.

Travel

Oxen supporting their heads
into the afternoon sun,
melons studding the hill like brass:

who reads into distance reads
beyond us, our sleeping children
and the dust settling in scorched grass.

Westering

In California

I sit under Rand McNally's
'Official Map of the Moon' –
The colour of frogskin,
Its enlarged pores held

Open and one called
'Pitiscus' at eye level –
Recalling the last night
In Donegal, my shadow

Neat upon the whitewash
From her bony shine,
The cobbles of the yard
Lit pale as eggs.

Summer had been a free fall
Ending there,
The empty amphitheatre
Of the west. Good Friday

We had started out
Past shopblinds drawn on the afternoon,
Cars stilled outside still churches,
Bikes tilting to a wall;

We drove by,
A dwindling interruption
As clappers smacked
On a bare altar

And congregations bent
To the studded crucifix.
What nails dropped out that hour?
Roads unreeled, unreeled

Falling light as casts
Laid down
On shining waters.
Under the moon's stigmata

Six thousand miles away,
I imagine untroubled dust,
A loosening gravity,
Christ weighing by his hands.

UNCOLLECTED POEMS (1973–1975)

A New Life

Tonight, my love, a first movement, a pulse,
As if the rains of bogland gathered head
To preface small landslides, to slip and burst
And crack the banks and flood the ferny beds.

Your back is a firm line of eastern coast.
Your arms and legs like bony headlands thrown
Beyond your pastures make a barren west
To the heave of counties where our past has grown.

I, the tall kingdom over your shoulder,
Whom you would neither cajole nor ignore,
Unlearn the lie of conquest and grow older,
Concede the independence of your shore

Within whose borders now my legacy
Is culminating inexorably.

    When I came among your loughs and bushes,
    Your soft levels between gradual hills,
    Your hide-outs among ferns and webbing ivies,
    Your mounds and ring-forts, secret grassy wells,

    I came determined upon occupation.
    You were a wood-kerne that I would uncover.
    I'd bring you past the wood's skirts where my bawn
    Stood on the planted ground, in crops and clover.

    Advances that I made over the years
    Ended in skirmishes by hedge and stream.
    When our union did come, the night before
    Was memorable for tear and bite and scream.

    Regularly since then the fit comes on
    Your blood beats wild against my condescension.

Our dual citizen's a blood-sucker –
My swimming fleets have turned into your lamprey.
When I withdrew from you by pass and harbour
I left within you more than memory.

Your mouth is fluent with my language now,
My dark deeds have become your bitter cud

And as my secret papers come on show
You rightly drag my name into the mud.

But now this civil strife inside the compound
That was reserved in you for my love's sake
Will leave you raw again, like broken ground.
O we foreknow it all, how you will take

The weeping issue, bloody, unwashed, blind
And find my name re-uttered through your wound.

    My tone is still imperial, you say.
    Too reasonably I leave you with your pain,
    The rending process in the colony,
    The battering ram, the boom burst from within.

    My seed sprouted an obstinate fifth column
    Whose stance is growing unilateral.
    His heart beneath your heart is a war-drum
    Mustering force. His parasitical

    And ignorant little fists already
    Beat at your borders and I know they're cocked
    At me across the water. Reasonably,
    I must anticipate deadlocks unlocked,

    His fury cradled, us two hand in glove,
    The triangle of forces solved in love.

A Flourish for the Prince of Denmark

Ease him towards the strict arrest of bone,
this handler of beloved skulls. Let him
follow the worm of his thought
into the mound.

Set the ring-hoard's whorls like leeches
to his poison, borrow
the longship's swimming tongue
to carry his weight in words

for he must prove most royally.
Out of the silence a prow emerges
elaborate as a language
bursting its runes,

outrunning shed alphabets
and oral harbourings:
a northerly migration, a southern breeze,   15
an English landfall.

The Belfast Harp Festival 1792

Edward Bunting, organist of St Anne's
Cathedral, Belfast, transcribes ancient airs.
His drying manuscript contains the banns
Of a forced marriage between the heirs

Of the harp and the piano's *nouveau*   5
Riche. A bored revolutionary writes,
'All go to the Harpers at one . . . no
New musical discovery', and bites

His lip and taps his toe to a planxty.
'Ten performers, seven execrable'.   10
Thus Mr Tone, on the academy
Of the north. 'Strum, strum, and be hanged'. He will
Cut his own jugular. Mr Bunting
Saves a lament, dips his pen, sits humming.

John Field

Technique is vehicular: the slow pains
Of making his hands do what they were bid –
Not unsettle Master Clementi's coins,
Swallowing apprenticeship as he played

To demonstrate Clementi's instruments –   5
Strung his mind for right hand and left hand,
Conferred on him the postures of silence.
He sat upright, stiff as a music stand,

An intermediary, while his touch
Exfoliated and his Dublin tongue   10
Budded with venom. Among the rich
His dissipated melody and drank

His reputation, like champagne, in Moscow
Under its somnolent nocturnes of snow.

The Poet Crowned

I rode south through the petty kingdoms
(Belfast to Dublin on *The Enterprise*)
Resplendent in my emperor's new bays.
Gods make their own importance! Metronomes
And metres, tattoos on the sacral drums
Of memory, etymologies
Superb as nations risen off their knees:
Our name is shouted and the influence comes.
While somewhere in the monotonous fields
The herdsman and his wife who kept the boy
Unawares through all his marvellous growing.
Bewildered now by this new name,
Think themselves forgotten and grow lonely.

STATIONS (1975)

Cauled

They thought he was lost. For years they talked about it
until he found himself at the root of their kindly tongues,
sitting like a big fieldmouse in the middle of the rig. Their
voices were far-off now, searching something.
    Green air trawled over his arms and legs, the pods and 5
stalks wore a fuzz of light. He caught a rod in each hand
and jerked the whole tangle into life. Little tendrils unsprung,
new veins lit in the shifting leaves, a caul of shadows stretched
and netted round his head again. He sat listening, grateful
as the calls encroached. 10
    They had found him at the first onset of sobbing.

Branded

He draws four of five straws from the stack that stands in
the haggard like a gold apple bitten round and climbs the
warm bars of the gate into the grazing. The straws are so
light, his fist tightens on them till it aches. They hang
broken, gleaming and riffling at the swing of his arm. His 5
eye comes level with the horse's chest, that twitches. A fly
rises from a glossy eddy and away down between the legs, the
tail is lazy in the air. As he lifts the straws towards the
muzzle his small head hits the ground like a pod splitting
open to the faraway acreage of the sky. 10
    Now he is curled on the sofa, sucking, weeping. Fust in
sunlight swirls like filings to the sun's magnet. Slowly motes
compose the opening of a hairy canopy as the pastern unclouds
its moon and again the shod hoof strikes and brands him.
Pain still flutters against the trap of his ribs, under the 15
inflamed crescent on his breast.

Hedge-School

The tan clay between the stones in the foot of the hedge was cool
and wet. Nettles and ivy and moss and docken flourished in the
ditchback. The whitethorn was green as the blackthorn.
    Their skirts brushed away over the headrig, their voices

humble and familiar as pads across grazing. How the big air
of the evening was saddened by them, as if it lay over utensils
on a back window-sill, as if it might begin to whisper,
'Pray for us, pray for us, pray for us.'
  Primroses grew in a damp single bunch out of the bank,
imploding pallors, star plasm, nebula of May. He stared himself
into an absence.
  'Pull them for the May altar and hurry up.' He knelt and
reached the stems. Pod ridges. Legs of nestlings. 'Hurry up.'
  Patiently, deliberately, they retraced their steps. 'What
are you crying about now, son? What is it next? Come on, come
on, come on, we have to go. There's a good boy.' He walked
behind them, homesick, going home.

Nesting Ground

The sandmartins' nests were loopholes of darkness in the
riverbank. He could imagine his arm going in to the armpit,
sleeved and straitened, but because he once felt the cold
prick of a dead robin's claw and the surprising density of
its tiny beak he only gazed.
  He heard cheeping far in but because the men had once
shown him a rat's nest in the butt of a stack where chaff
and powdered cornstalks adhered to the moist pink necks and
backs he only listened.
  As he stood sentry, gazing, waiting, he thought of
putting his ear to one of the abandoned holes and listening
for the silence under the ground.

Sinking the Shaft

Once he woke late, the sun already warm on the linoleum,
strange voices in the yard and insistently as if prolonged
from underneath his sleep, a contralto metal note, the
flinty bite of spades at gravel. The men had come to sink
the pump.
  It was a big wound in front of the back door. Backs
and elbows skylined at ground level but by the afternoon,
nothing but a light spray of sand that dribbled gold and

capped the dark heap at the rim. Some of it fell back in
as he climbed and looked over.   10
    'Are you not for coming down, young Heaney?'
    A stirabout, a gleam, a wet bronze puddled by their
wellingtons.
    'We're not a mile off it. Would you not come down?'
    Snouted, helmeted, the plunger like an active gizzard,   15
the handle dressed to a clean swoop, set on a pediment
inscribed by the points of their trowels, I suppose we thought
it never could be toppled.

Waterbabies

We were busy in the fetid corner we christened Botany Bay.
You pumped, I dammed. We opened sluice-gates, flooded mucky
runnels and set sails by the black marina, penning white
feathers into old potatoes. Sometimes a bomber warbled far
beyond us, sometimes a train ran through the fields and small   5
ripples quivered silently across our delta.
        Perversely I once fouled a gift there and sank my new
kaleidoscope in the puddle. Its bright prisms that offered
incomprehensible satisfactions were messed and silted: instead
of a marvellous lightship, I salvaged a dirty hulk.   10

Patrick and Oisin

Aside from their tenebrous conversation, I sat learning my catechism
with its woodcut mysteries and polysyllabic runs, its 'clandestine
solemnizations', its 'morose delectation and concupiscence'. In
the stove-warmed kitchen, neighbours' names seeded and uncurled
upon their tongues, a back-biting undergrowth mantling the hard   5
stones of 'calumny and detraction'.
    Father Hughes had clapped the frost out of his gloves and
clappered the silenced room. 'Hands up who said their morning
prayers this morning.' My hand was a tendril reaching with the
others. 'Who'll say their catechism?'   10
    The night wore on. The phrases that had sapped my concentration
atrophied, incised tablets mossed and camouflaged by parasites
and creeping greenery.

Sweet William

In the gloomy damp of an old garden with its gooseberry bushes,
strawberry plants and shot leeks, their blooms infused themselves
into the eye like blood in snow, as if the clumped growth had
been spattered with grapeshot and bled from underneath.
     Sweet William: the words had the silky lift of a banner
on the wind, where that king with crinkling feminine black
curls reached after the unsheathed flare of his sword – and
that was heraldry I could not assent to. And the many men
so beautiful called after him, and the very flowers, their
aura could be and would be resisted.

The Discharged Soldier

Flanders. It sounded heavy as an old tarpaulin being dragged
off a wet load. Their big voices that conceded nothing
to pity or wonder moulded it over so that it was years
before I could stare long and sadly into its gules. Flanders.
Once again the yarn was rehearsed, inflated and kicked
between them like the pig's bladder they declared an
infallible diversion of their youth.
     'Drunk again, full as the Boyne, staggering home on
the old club foot like a good one, and letting the big squeals
out of him like a stuck pig. Aye they all went down, they all
went down but Danny.'
     'Oh, a bad old rip, the same Danny, a bad-tongued godless
old bastard. Him and his Flanders.'
     I dreaded the twilit road. Once or twice a month his
artesian and desolate wailing lifted over the fields.
     'Oh there's badness there for sure.'
     My shell-shocked Pew, stamping the parish with his
built-up hoof, proffering the black spot of his mouth.

The Sabbath-Breakers

Call it a pattern. We called it a tournament. Two pavilions
in the corner of the field, meal-sacks nailed across birch
poles, whitewashed GENTS and LADIES. And the summer grass

marked out with sawdust: touchline, square, the 'twenty-one'
line and the 'fifty'. The goalposts were whitewashed, the
loudspeakers wired and pouting from the hedge like iron
honeysuckles. To-morrow night, before the final, the pitch
would be pegged out with players at attention, the spectators
bare-headed, children held at bay for a strict moment before
the amplified rasping and then the record of 'The Soldier's
Song', brusque and husky, flung like a gauntlet in the
Sabbath air. So we walked home late by the concrete road,
a band of brothers high with anticipation; when a dog barked
from an outlying farm we thought of Setanta's feats at hurling
and our steps trampolined along the glimmer.

    Call it a pattern. We can hardly call it a pogrom. The
next morning the goalposts had been felled by what roundhead
elders, what maypole hackers, what choristers of law and
liberty. Undaunted we threw in the ball, manned the gap of
danger match after match, raised a tricolour in the chestnut
tree and faced it proudly for the anthem. We lived there too.
We stared into the pennanted branches and held the tableau.
IN SPITE OF DUNGEON, FIRE AND SWORD. Implacable.

Kernes

Candystriped red, white and blue, ringed with influence
like a fairy thorn, the newly painted flagpole cut the wind.
With his hand to its true wood, Dixon balanced upright on
the bicycle, a saddled, declamatory king of the castle.
    'I could beat every fucking papish in the school!'
    We piled our schoolbags at a distance, defied from
sanctuary, and began to tear a small arsenal of sods from
the green verge. The bicycle, with its chrome insignia
and rivetted breastplate of Sir Walter Raleigh in his
inflated knickers, motioned.
    'No surrender! Up King Billy every time!'
    He came through us with his head sunk and the pedals
flying and further down the road was standing to on the
first bar of their yard gate, singing 'God Save the King'.
    One by one we melted down lanes and over pads, behind
a glib he hadn't even ruffled.

July

The drumming started in the cool of the evening, as if the
dome of air were lightly hailed on. But no. The drumming
murmured from beneath that drum.
    The drumming didn't murmur, rather hammered. Soundsmiths
found a rhythm gradually. On the far bench of the hills tuns
and ingots were being beaten thin.
    The hills were a bellied sound-box resonating, a low
dyke against diurnal roar, a tidal wave that stayed, that
still might open.
    Through red seas of July the Orange drummers led a chosen
people through their dream. Dilations and engorgings, contra-
puntal; slashers in shirt-sleeves, collared in the sunset,
policemen flanking them like anthracite.
    The air grew dark, cloud-barred, a butcher's apron. The
night hushed like a white-mothed reach of water, miles down-
stream from the battle, skeins of blood still lazing in the
channel.
    And so my ear was winnowed annually.

England's Difficulty

I moved like a double agent among the big concepts.
    The word 'enemy' had the toothed efficiency of a
mowing machine. It was a mechanical and distant noise
beyond that opaque security, that autonomous ignorance.
    'When the Germans bombed Belfast it was the bitter
Orange parts were hit the worst.'
    I was on somebody's shoulder, conveyed through the
starlit yard to see the sky glowing over Anahorish. Grown-ups
lowered their voices and resettled in the kitchen as if
tired-out after an excursion.
    Behind the blackout, Germany called to lamplit kitchens
through fretted baize, dry battery, wet battery, capillary
wires, domed valves that squeaked and burbled as
the dial-hand absolved Stuttgart and Leipzig.
    'He's an artist, this Haw Haw. He can fairly leave
it into them.'

I lodged with 'the enemies of Ulster', the scullions
outside the walls. Squires of the cockpit, barkers of
auction notices, arbitrators of the burial grounds.
An adept at banter, I crossed the lines with carefully   20
enunciated passwords, manned every speech with checkpoints
and reported back to nobody.

Visitant

It kept treading air, as if it were a ghost with claims
on us, precipitating in the heat tremor. Then, released
from its distorting mirror, up the fields there comes
this awkwardly smiling foreigner, awkwardly received,
who gentled the long Sunday afternoon just by sitting with us.   5
   Where are you now, real visitant, who vivified 'parole'
and 'POW'? Where are the rings garnetted with toothbrush,
the ships in bottles, the Tyrol landscapes globed in
electric bulbs?
   'They've hands for anything, these Germans.'   10
   He walked back into the refining lick of the grass,
behind the particular judgements of captor and harbourer.
As he walks yet, feeling our eyes on his back, treading
the air of the image he achieved, released to his fatigues.

Trial Runs

WELCOME HOME YE LADS OF THE EIGHTH ARMY
   There must be some defiance in it because it was
painted along the demesne wall, a banner headline over
the old news of REMEMBER 1690 and NO SURRENDER, a great
wingspan of letting I hurried under with the messages.   5
   In a khaki shirt and brass-buckled belt, a demobbed
neighbour leaned against our jamb. My father jingled silver
deep in both pockets and laughed when the big clicking
rosary beads were produced.
   'Did they make a papish of you over there?'   10
   'O damn the fear! I stole them for you, Paddy, off
the pope's dresser when his back was turned.'
   'You could harness a donkey with them.'
   Their laughter sailed above my head, a hoarse clamour,

15 two big nervous birds dipping and lifting, making trial runs
over a territory.

The Wanderer

In a semi-circle we toed the line chalked round the master's
desk and on a day when the sun was incubating milktops and
warming the side of the jamjar where the bean had split its
stitches, he called me forward and crossed my palm with silver.
5 'At the end of the holidays this man's going away to Derry,
so this is for him winning the scholarship . . . We all wish
him good luck. Now, back to your places.'
   I have wandered far from that ring-giver and would not
renegue on this migrant solitude. I have seen halls in flames,
10 hearts in cinders, the benches filled and emptied, the
circles of companions called and broken. That day I was a
rich young man, who could tell you now of flittings, night-vigils,
let-downs, women's cried-out eyes.

Cloistered

Light was calloused in the leaded panes of the college chapel
and shafted into the terrazzo rink of the sanctuary. The duty
priest tested his diction against pillar and plaster, we tested
our elbows on the hard bevel of the benches or split the gold-
5 barred thickness of our missals.
   I could make a book of hours of those six years, a Flemish
calendar of rite and pastime set on a walled hill. Look:
there is a hillside cemetery behind us and across the river the
plough going in a field and in between, the gated town. Here,
10 an obedient clerk kissing a bishop's ring, here a frieze of
seasonal games, and here the assiduous illuminator himself,
bowed to his desk in a corner.
   In the study hall my hand was cold as a scribe's in winter.
The supervisor rustled past, sibilant, vapouring into his
15 breviary, his welted brogues unexpectedly secular under the
soutane. Now I bisected the line AB, now found my foothold
in a main verb in Livy. From my dormer after lights out I
revised the constellations and in the morning broke the ice
on an enamelled water-jug with exhilarated self-regard.

I was champion of the examination halls, scalding with
lust inside my daunting visor.

Ballad

Blood ran a jewelled delta down the back of the lorry, the
ascetic boy screamed for relief, the riddled lorry hammered
on for the border. And with the constabulary closing on them
they left him dying there on the cold floor of a barn.
    When exhaustion had been nominated peace, I went to
ceilidhes where his name was a host on the singer's tongue,
his tale an insubstantial wound we dipped in beyond question
and doubting.
    We sat on benches round the hall that was dark and close
as a gravewatcher's hut. The band was backstage at their tea,
the dancefloor an area cleared before his honoured tomb. It
was there, when the song and the anthem of applause had sowed
us all with quiet, I grew to love the manifold griefs of
chanters and assuaging bows.

The Stations of the West

On my first night in the Gaeltacht the old woman spoke to me
in English: 'You will be all right.' I sat on a twilit bedside
listening through the wall to fluent Irish, homesick for a
speech I was to extirpate.
    I had come west to inhale the absolute weather. The
visionaries breathed on my face a smell of soup-kitchens, they
mixed the dust of croppies' graves with the fasting spittle of
our creed and anointed my lips. EPHETE, they urged. I blushed
but only managed a few words.
    Neither did any gift of tongues descend in my days in that
upper room when all around me seemed to prophesy. But
still I would recall the stations of the west, white sand,
hard rock, light ascending like its definition over Rannafast
and Errigal, Annaghry and Kincasslagh: names portable as altar
stones, unleavened elements.

Inquisition

'That's what three women could never do – piss in the same po!'
   Porter drinkers' laughter in the jakes. Back-thumping.
Close-up testing eyes.
   'Do you come here often, brother?'
   What combination should have slipped open to that proffered
'brother'? One barred the door, the other caught my hand in
a grip alive with some pincer alphabet.
   'I don't know what you are brother, but would you believe
me if I told you I was christened in Boyne water?'
   I thought he was going to ask me to curse the pope. Instead,
he thumped my back again.
   'Ah, live and let live, that's my motto, brother. What
does it matter where we go on Sundays as long as we can still
enjoy ourselves. Isn't that right, brother?'
   The door was unexpectedly open and I showed them the face
in the back of my head.

Incertus

I went disguised in it, pronouncing it with a soft
church-latin c, tagging it under my efforts like a damp
fuse. Uncertain. A shy soul fretting and all that.
Expert obeisance.
   Oh yes, I crept before I walked. The old pseudonym
lies there like a mouldering tegument.

NORTH (1975)

Mossbawn: Two Poems in Dedication

for Mary Heaney

1 *Sunlight*

There was a sunlit absence.
The helmeted pump in the yard
heated its iron,
water honeyed

in the slung bucket
and the sun stood
like a griddle cooling
against the wall

of each long afternoon.
So, her hands scuffled
over the bakeboard,
the reddening stove

sent its plaque of heat
against her where she stood
in a floury apron
by the window.

Now she dusts the board
with a goose's wing,
now sits, broad-lapped,
with whitened nails

and measling shins:
here is a space
again, the scone rising
to the tick of two clocks.

And here is love
like a tinsmith's scoop
sunk past its gleam
in the meal-bin.

2 The Seed Cutters

They seem hundreds of years away. Breughel,
You'll know them if I can get them true.
They kneel under the hedge in a half-circle
Behind a windbreak wind is breaking through.
They are the seed cutters. The tuck and frill
Of leaf-sprout is on the seed potatoes
Buried under that straw. With time to kill,
They are taking their time. Each sharp knife goes
Lazily halving each root that falls apart
In the palm of the hand: a milky gleam,
And, at the centre, a dark watermark.
Oh, calendar customs! Under the broom
Yellowing over them, compose the frieze
With all of us there, our anonymities.

PART I

Antaeus

    When I lie on the ground
I rise flushed as a rose in the morning.
In fights I arrange a fall on the ring
    To rub myself with sand

    That is operative
As an elixir. I cannot be weaned
Off the earth's long contour, her river-veins.
    Down here in my cave,

    Girded with root and rock,
I am cradled in the dark that wombed me
And nurtured in every artery
    Like a small hillock.

    Let each new hero come
Seeking the golden apples and Atlas.
He must wrestle with me before he pass
    Into that realm of fame

Among sky-born and royal:
He may well throw me and renew my birth
But let him not plan, lifting me off the earth,
　　　My elevation, my fall.

　　　1966

Belderg

'They just kept turning up
And were thought of as foreign' –
One-eyed and benign,
They lie about his house,
Quernstones out of a bog.

To lift the lid of the peat
And find this pupil dreaming
Of neolithic wheat!
When he stripped off blanket bog
The soft-piled centuries

Fell open like a glib:
There were the first plough-marks,
The stone-age fields, the tomb
Corbelled, turfed and chambered,
Floored with dry turf-coomb.

A landscape fossilized,
Its stone-wall patternings
Repeated before our eyes
In the stone walls of Mayo.
Before I turned to go

He talked about persistence,
A congruence of lives,
How, stubbed and cleared of stones,
His home accrued growth rings
Of iron, flint and bronze.

So I talked of Mossbawn,
A bogland name. 'But *moss*?'
He crossed my old home's music
With older strains of Norse.
I'd told how its foundation

Was mutable as sound
And how I could derive
A forked root from that ground,
Make *bawn* an English fort,
A planter's walled-in mound,

Or else find sanctuary
And think of it as Irish,
Persistent if outworn.
'But the Norse ring on your tree?'
I passed through the eye of the quern,

Grist to an ancient mill,
And in my mind's eye saw
A world-tree of balanced stones,
Querns piled like vertebrae,
The marrow crushed to grounds.

Funeral Rites

I

I shouldered a kind of manhood,
stepping in to lift the coffins
of dead relations.
They had been laid out

in tainted rooms,
their eyelids glistening,
their dough-white hands
shackled in rosary beads.

Their puffed knuckles
had unwrinkled, the nails
were darkened, the wrists
obediently sloped.

The dulse-brown shroud,
the quilted satin cribs:
I knelt courteously,
admiring it all,

as wax melted down
and veined the candles,

the flames hovering
to the women hovering

behind me.
And always, in a corner,
the coffin lid,
its nail-heads dressed

with little gleaming crosses.
Dear soapstone masks,
kissing their igloo brows
had to suffice

before the nails were sunk
and the black glacier
of each funeral
pushed away.

II

Now as news comes in
of each neighbourly murder
we pine for ceremony,
customary rhythms:

the temperate footsteps
of a cortège, winding past
each blinded home.
I would restore

the great chambers of Boyne,
prepare a sepulchre
under the cup-marked stones.
Out of side-streets and bye-roads

purring family cars
nose into line,
the whole country tunes
to the muffled drumming

of ten thousand engines.
Somnambulant women,
left behind, move
through emptied kitchens

imagining our slow triumph
towards the mounds.

            Quiet as a serpent
            in its grassy boulevard,
25   the procession drags its tail
            out of the Gap of the North
            as its head already enters
            the megalithic doorway.

            III
            When they have put the stone
            back in its mouth
            we will drive north again
            past Strang and Carling fjords,

5   the cud of memory
            allayed for once, arbitration
            of the feud placated,
            imagining those under the hill

            disposed like Gunnar
10   who lay beautiful
            inside his burial mound,
            though dead by violence

            and unavenged.
            Men said that he was chanting
15   verses about honour
            and that four lights burned

            in corners of the chamber:
            which opened then, as he turned
            with a joyful face
20   to look at the moon.

North

            I returned to a long strand,
            the hammered shod of a bay,
            and found only the secular
            powers of the Atlantic thundering.

5   I faced the unmagical
            invitations of Iceland,

the pathetic colonies
of Greenland, and suddenly

those fabulous raiders,
those lying in Orkney and Dublin
measured against
their long swords rusting,

those in the solid
belly of stone ships,
those hacked and glinting
in the gravel of thawed streams

were ocean-deafened voices
warning me, lifted again
in violence and epiphany.
The longship's swimming tongue

was buoyant with hindsight –
it said Thor's hammer swung
to geography and trade,
thick-witted couplings and revenges,

the hatreds and behindbacks
of the althing, lies and women,
exhaustions nominated peace,
memory incubating the spilled blood.

It said, 'Lie down
in the word-hoard, burrow
the coil and gleam
of your furrowed brain.

Compose in darkness.
Expect aurora borealis
in the long foray
but no cascade of light.

Keep your eye clear
as the bleb of the icicle,
trust the feel of what nubbed treasure
your hands have known.'

Viking Dublin: Trial Pieces

I

It could be a jaw-bone
or a rib or a portion cut
from something sturdier:
anyhow, a small outline

was incised, a cage
or trellis to conjure in.
Like a child's tongue
following the toils

of his calligraphy,
like an eel swallowed
in a basket of eels,
the line amazes itself,

eluding the hand
that fed it,
a bill in flight,
a swimming nostril.

II

These are trial pieces,
the craft's mystery
improvised on bone:
foliage, bestiaries,

interlacings elaborate
as the netted routes
of ancestry and trade.
That have to be

magnified on display
so that the nostril
is a migrant prow
sniffing the Liffey,

swanning it up to the ford,
dissembling itself
in antler combs, bone pins,
coins, weights, scale-pans.

III

Like a long sword
sheathed in its moisting
burial clays,
the keel stuck fast

in the slip of the bank,
its clinker-built hull
spined and plosive
as *Dublin*.

And now we reach in
for shards of the vertebrae,
the ribs of hurdle,
the mother-wet caches –

and for this trial piece
incised by a child,
a longship, a buoyant
migrant line.

IV

That enters my longhand,
turns cursive, unscarfing
a zoomorphic wake,
a worm of thought

I follow into the mud.
I am Hamlet the Dane,
skull-handler, parablist,
smeller of rot

in the state, infused
with its poisons,
pinioned by ghosts
and affections,

murders and pieties,
coming to consciousness
by jumping in graves,
dithering, blathering.

V

Come fly with me,
come sniff the wind

with the expertise
of the Vikings –

5   neighbourly, scoretaking
killers, haggers
and hagglers, gombeen-men,
hoarders of grudges and gain.

With a butcher's aplomb
10   they spread out your lungs
and made you warm wings
for your shoulders.

Old fathers, be with us.
Old cunning assessors
15   of feuds and of sites
for ambush or town.

VI

'Did you ever hear tell,'
said Jimmy Farrell,
'of the skulls they have
in the city of Dublin?

5   White skulls and black skulls
and yellow skulls, and some
with full teeth, and some
haven't only but one,'

and compounded history
10   in the pan of 'an old Dane,
maybe, was drowned
in the Flood.'

My words lick around
cobbled quays, go hunting
15   lightly as pampooties
over the skull-capped ground.

The Digging Skeleton

after Baudelaire

I

You find anatomical plates
Buried along these dusty quays
Among books yellowed like mummies
Slumbering in forgotten crates,

Drawings touched with an odd beauty   5
As if the illustrator had
Responded gravely to the sad
Mementoes of anatomy –

Mysterious candid studies
Of red slobland around the bones.   10
Like this one: flayed men and skeletons
Digging the earth like navvies.

II

Sad gang of apparitions,
Your skinned muscles like plaited sedge
And your spines hooped towards the sunk edge
Of the spade, my patient ones,

Tell me, as you labour hard   5
To break this unrelenting soil,
What barns are there for you to fill?
What farmer dragged you from the boneyard?

Or are you emblems of the truth,
Death's lifers, hauled from the narrow cell   10
And stripped of night-shirt shrouds, to tell:
'This is the reward of faith

In rest eternal. Even death
Lies. The void deceives.
We do not fall like autumn leaves   15
To sleep in peace. Some traitor breath

Revives our clay, sends us abroad
And by the sweat of our stripped brows

We earn our deaths; our one repose
When the bleeding instep finds its spade.'

Bone Dreams

I

White bone found
on the grazing:
the rough, porous
language of touch

and its yellowing, ribbed
impression in the grass –
a small ship-burial.
As dead as stone,

flint-find, nugget
of chalk,
I touch it again,
I wind it in

the sling of mind
to pitch it at England
and follow its drop
to strange fields.

II

Bone-house:
a skeleton
in the tongue's
old dungeons.

I push back
through dictions,
Elizabethan canopies.
Norman devices,

the erotic mayflowers
of Provence
and the ivied Latins
of churchmen

to the scop's
twang, the iron

flash of consonants
cleaving the line.

III

In the coffered
riches of grammar
and declensions
I found *ban hus*,

its fire, benches,
wattle and rafters,
where the soul
fluttered a while

in the roofspace.
There was a small crock
for the brain,
and a cauldron

of generation
swung at the centre:
love-den, blood-holt,
dream-bower.

IV

Come back past
philology and kennings,
re-enter memory
where the bone's lair

is a love-nest
in the grass.
I hold my lady's head
like a crystal

and ossify myself
by gazing: I am screes
on her escarpments,
a chalk giant

carved upon her downs.
Soon my hands, on the sunken
fosse of her spine
move towards the passes.

V

And we end up
cradling each other
between the lips
of an earthwork.

As I estimate
for pleasure
her knuckles' paving,
the turning stiles

of the elbows,
the vallum of her brow
and the long wicket
of collar-bone,

I have begun to pace
the Hadrian's Wall
of her shoulder, dreaming
of Maiden Castle.

VI

One morning in Devon
I found a dead mole
with the dew still beading it.
I had thought the mole

a big-boned coulter
but there it was,
small and cold
as the thick of a chisel.

I was told, 'Blow,
blow back the fur on his head.
Those little points
were the eyes.

And feel the shoulders.'
I touched small distant Pennines,
a pelt of grass and grain
running south.

Come to the Bower

My hands come, touched
By sweetbriar and tangled vetch,
Foraging past the burst gizzards
Of coin-hoards

To where the dark-bowered queen, 5
Whom I unpin,
Is waiting. Out of the black maw
Of the peat, sharpened willow

Withdraws gently.
I unwrap skins and see 10
The pot of the skull,
The damp tuck of each curl

Reddish as a fox's brush,
A mark of a gorget in the flesh
Of her throat. And spring water 15
Starts to rise around her.

I reach past
The riverbed's washed
Dream of gold to the bullion
Of her Venus bone. 20

Bog Queen

I lay waiting
between turf-face and demesne wall,
between heathery levels
and glass-toothed stone.

My body was braille 5
for the creeping influences:
dawn suns groped over my head
and cooled at my feet,

through my fabrics and skins
the seeps of winter 10
digested me,
the illiterate roots

pondered and died
in the cavings
of stomach and socket.
I lay waiting

on the gravel bottom,
my brain darkening,
a jar of spawn
fermenting underground

dreams of Baltic amber.
Bruised berries under my nails,
the vital hoard reducing
in the crock of the pelvis.

My diadem grew carious,
gemstones dropped
in the peat floe
like the bearings of history.

My sash was a black glacier
wrinkling, dyed weaves
and phoenician stitchwork
retted on my breasts'

soft moraines.
I knew winter cold
like the nuzzle of fjords
at my thighs –

the soaked fledge, the heavy
swaddle of hides.
My skull hibernated
in the wet nest of my hair.

Which they robbed.
I was barbered
and stripped
by a turfcutter's spade

who veiled me again
and packed coomb softly
between the stone jambs
at my head and my feet.

Till a peer's wife bribed him.
The plait of my hair,

a slimy birth-cord
of bog, had been cut

and I rose from the dark,
hacked bone, skull-ware,
frayed stitches, tufts,
small gleams on the bank.

The Grauballe Man

As if he had been poured
in tar, he lies
on a pillow of turf
and seems to weep

the black river of himself.
The grain of his wrists
is like bog oak,
the ball of his heel

like a basalt egg.
His instep has shrunk
cold as a swan's foot
or a wet swamp root.

His hips are the ridge
and purse of a mussel,
his spine an eel arrested
under a glisten of mud.

The head lifts,
the chin is a visor
raised above the vent
of his slashed throat

that has tanned and toughened.
The cured wound
opens inwards to a dark
elderberry place.

Who will say 'corpse'
to his vivid cast?
Who will say 'body'
to his opaque repose?

And his rusted hair,
a mat unlikely
as a foetus's.
I first saw his twisted face

in a photograph,
a head and shoulder
out of the peat,
bruised like a forceps baby,

but now he lies
perfected in my memory,
down to the red horn
of his nails,

hung in the scales
with beauty and atrocity:
with the Dying Gaul
too strictly compassed

on his shield,
with the actual weight
of each hooded victim,
slashed and dumped.

Punishment

I can feel the tug
of the halter at the nape
of her neck, the wind
on her naked front.

It blows her nipples
to amber beads,
it shakes the frail rigging
of her ribs.

I can see her drowned
body in the bog,
the weighing stone,
the floating rods and boughs.

Under which at first
she was a barked sapling

that is dug up
oak-bone, brain-firkin:

her shaved head
like a stubble of black corn,
her blindfold a soiled bandage,
her noose a ring

to store
the memories of love.
Little adulteress,
before they punished you

you were flaxen-haired,
undernourished, and your
tar-black face was beautiful.
My poor scapegoat,

I almost love you
but would have cast, I know,
the stones of silence.
I am the artful voyeur

of your brain's exposed
and darkened combs,
your muscles' webbing
and all your numbered bones:

I who have stood dumb
when your betraying sisters,
cauled in tar,
wept by the railings,

who would connive
in civilized outrage
yet understand the exact
and tribal, intimate revenge.

Strange Fruit

Here is the girl's head like an exhumed gourd.
Oval-faced, prune-skinned, prune-stones for teeth.
They unswaddled the wet fern of her hair
And made an exhibition of its coil,

5 Let the air at her leathery beauty.
      Pash of tallow, perishable treasure:
      Her broken nose is dark as a turf clod,
      Her eyeholes blank as pools in the old workings.
      Diodorus Siculus confessed
  10 His gradual ease among the likes of this:
      Murdered, forgotten, nameless, terrible
      Beheaded girl, outstaring axe
      And beatification, outstaring
      What had begun to feel like reverence.

Kinship

I

Kinned by hieroglyphic
peat on a spreadfield
to the strangled victim,
the love-nest in the bracken,

5   I step through origins
like a dog turning
its memories of wilderness
on the kitchen mat:

the bog floor shakes,
10 water cheeps and lisps
as I walk down
rushes and heather.

I love this turf-face,
its black incisions,
15 the cooped secrets
of process and ritual;

I love the spring
off the ground,
each bank a gallows drop,
20 each open pool

the unstopped mouth
of an urn, a moon-drinker,
not to be sounded
by the naked eye.

II

Quagmire, swampland, morass:
the slime kingdoms,
domains of the cold-blooded,
of mud pads and dirtied eggs.

But *bog* 5
meaning soft,
the fall of windless rain,
pupil of amber.

Ruminant ground,
digestion of mollusc 10
and seed-pod,
deep pollen-bin.

Earth-pantry, bone-vault,
sun-bank, embalmer
of votive goods 15
and sabred fugitives.

Insatiable bride.
Sword-swallower,
casket, midden,
floe of history. 20

Ground that will strip
its dark side,
nesting ground,
outback of my mind.

III

I found a turf-spade
hidden under bracken,
laid flat, and overgrown
with a green fog.

As I raised it 5
the soft lips of the growth
muttered and split,
a tawny rut

opening at my feet
like a shed skin, 10

       the shaft wettish
       as I sank it upright

       and beginning to
       steam in the sun.
15   And now they have twinned
       that obelisk:

       among the stones,
       under a bearded cairn
       a love-nest is disturbed,
20   catkin and bog-cotton tremble

       as they raise up
       the cloven oak-limb:
       I stand at the edge of centuries
       facing a goddess.

           IV
       This centre holds
       and spreads,
       sump and seedbed,
       a bag of waters

5   and a melting grave.
       The mothers of autumn
       sour and sink,
       ferments of husk and leaf

       deepen their ochres.
10   Mosses come to a head,
       heather unseeds,
       brackens deposit

       their bronze.
       This is the vowel of earth
15   dreaming its root
       in flowers and snow,

       mutation of weathers
       and seasons,
       a windfall composing
20   the floor it rots into.

       I grew out of all this
       like a weeping willow

inclined to
the appetites of gravity.

V

The hand-carved felloes
of the turf-cart wheels
buried in a litter
of turf mould,

the cupid's bow
of the tail-board,
the socketed lips
of the cribs:

I deified the man
who rode there,
god of the waggon,
the hearth-feeder.

I was his privileged
attendant, a bearer
of bread and drink,
the squire of his circuits.

When summer died
and wives forsook the fields
we were abroad,
saluted, given right-of-way.

Watch our progress
down the haw-lit hedges,
my manly pride
when he speaks to me.

VI

And you, Tacitus,
observe how I make my grove
on an old crannog
piled by the fearful dead:

a desolate peace.
Our mother ground
is sour with the blood
of her faithful,

they lie gargling
in her sacred heart
as the legions stare
from the ramparts.

Come back to this
'island of the ocean'
where nothing will suffice.
Read the inhumed faces

of casualty and victim;
report us fairly,
how we slaughter
for the common good

and shave the heads
of the notorious,
how the goddess swallows
our love and terror.

Ocean's Love to Ireland

I

Speaking broad Devonshire,
Ralegh has backed the maid to a tree
As Ireland is backed to England

And drives inland
Till all her strands are breathless:
'Sweesir, Swatter! Sweesir, Swatter!'

He is water, he is ocean, lifting
Her farthingale like a scarf of weed lifting
In the front of a wave.

II

Yet his superb crest inclines to Cynthia
Even while it runs its bent
In the rivers of Lee and Blackwater.

Those are the plashy spots where he would lay
His cape before her. In London, his name
Will rise on water, and on these dark seepings:

Smerwick sowed with the mouthing corpses
Of six hundred papists, 'as gallant and good
Personages as ever were beheld.'

III

The ruined maid complains in Irish,
Ocean has scattered her dream of fleets,
The Spanish prince has spilled his gold

And failed her. Iambic drums
Of English beat the woods where her poets   5
Sink like Onan. Rush-light, mushroom-flesh,

She fades from their somnolent clasp
Into ringlet-breath and dew,
The ground possessed and repossessed.

Aisling

He courted her
With a decadent sweet art
Like the wind's vowel
Blowing through the hazels:

'Are you Diana . . . ?'   5
And was he Actaeon,
His high lament
The stag's exhausted belling?

Act of Union

I

To-night, a first movement, a pulse,
As if the rain in bogland gathered head
To slip and flood: a bog-burst,
A gash breaking open the ferny bed.
Your back is a firm line of eastern coast   5
And arms and legs are thrown
Beyond your gradual hills. I caress
The heaving province where our past has grown.
I am the tall kingdom over your shoulder

That you would neither cajole nor ignore.
Conquest is a lie. I grow older
Conceding your half-independent shore
Within whose borders now my legacy
Culminates inexorably.

II

And I am still imperially
Male, leaving you with the pain,
The rending process in the colony,
The battering ram, the boom burst from within.
The act sprouted an obstinate fifth column
Whose stance is growing unilateral.
His heart beneath your heart is a wardrum
Mustering force. His parasitical
And ignorant little fists already
Beat at your borders and I know they're cocked
At me across the water. No treaty
I foresee will salve completely your tracked
And stretchmarked body, the big pain
That leaves you raw, like opened ground, again.

The Betrothal of Cavehill

Gunfire barks its questions off Cavehill
And the profiled basalt maintains its stare
South: proud, protestant and northern, and male.
Adam untouched, before the shock of gender.

They still shoot here for luck over a bridegroom.
The morning I drove out to bed me down
Among my love's hideouts, her pods and broom,
They fired above my car the ritual gun.

Hercules and Antaeus

Sky-born and royal,
snake-choker, dung-heaver,
his mind big with golden apples,
his future hung with trophies,

Hercules has the measure
of resistance and black powers
feeding off the territory.
Antaeus, the mould-hugger,

is weaned at last:
a fall was a renewal
but now he is raised up –
the challenger's intelligence

is a spur of light,
a blue prong graiping him
out of his element
into a dream of loss

and origins – the cradling dark,
the river-veins, the secret gullies
of his strength,
the hatching grounds

of cave and souterrain,
he has bequeathed it all
to elegists. Balor will die
and Byrthnoth and Sitting Bull.

Hercules lifts his arms
in a remorseless V,
his triumph unassailed
by the powers he has shaken,

and lifts and banks Antaeus
high as a profiled ridge,
a sleeping giant,
pap for the dispossessed.

PART II

The Unacknowledged Legislator's Dream

Archimedes thought he could move the world if he could find the right place to position his lever. Billy Hunter said Tarzan shook the world when he jumped down out of a tree.

I sink my crowbar in a chink I know under the masonry
of state and statute, I swing on a creeper of secrets into the
Bastille. My wronged people cheer from their cages. The
guard-dogs are unmuzzled, a soldier pivots a muzzle at the
butt of my ear, I am stood blindfolded with my hands above
my head until I seem to be swinging from a strappado.

  The commandant motions me to be seated. 'I am honoured
to add a poet to our list.' He is amused and genuine. 'You'll
be safer here, anyhow.'

  In the cell, I wedge myself with outstretched arms in the
corner and heave, I jump on the concrete flags to test them.
Were those your eyes just now at the hatch?

Whatever You Say Say Nothing

I

I'm writing this just after an encounter
With an English journalist in search of 'views
On the Irish thing'. I'm back in winter
Quarters where bad news is no longer news,

Where media-men and stringers sniff and point,
Where zoom lenses, recorders and coiled leads
Litter the hotels. The times are out of joint
But I incline as much to rosary beads

As to the jottings and analyses
Of politicians and newspapermen
Who've scribbled down the long campaign from gas
And protest to gelignite and sten,

Who proved upon their pulses 'escalate',
'Backlash' and 'crack down', 'the provisional wing',
'Polarization' and 'long-standing hate'.
Yet I live here, I live here too, I sing,

Expertly civil-tongued with civil neighbours
On the high wires of first wireless reports,
Sucking the fake taste, the stony flavours
Of those sanctioned, old, elaborate retorts:

'Oh, it's disgraceful, surely, I agree.'
'Where's it going to end?' 'It's getting worse.'
'They're murderers.' 'Internment, understandably . . .'
The 'voice of sanity' is getting hoarse.

II

Men die at hand. In blasted street and home
The gelignite's a common sound effect:
As the man said when Celtic won, 'The Pope of Rome
's a happy man this night.' His flock suspect

In their deepest heart of hearts the heretic   5
Has come at last to heel and to the stake.
We tremble near the flames but want no truck
With the actual firing. We're on the make

As ever. Long sucking the hind tit,
Cold as a witch's and as hard to swallow,   10
Still leaves us fork-tongued on the border bit:
The liberal papist note sounds hollow

When amplified and mixed in with the bangs
That shake all hearts and windows day and night.
(It's tempting here to rhyme on 'labour pangs'   15
And diagnose a rebirth in our plight

But that would be to ignore other symptoms.
Last night you didn't need a stethoscope
To hear the eructation of Orange drums
Allergic equally to Pearse and Pope.)   20

On all sides 'little platoons' are mustering –
The phrase is Cruise O'Brien's via that great
Backlash, Burke – while I sit here with a pestering
Drouth for words at once both gaff and bait

To lure the tribal shoals to epigram   25
And order. I believe any of us
Could draw the line through bigotry and sham,
Given the right line, *aere perennius*.

III

'Religion's never mentioned here,' of course.
'You know them by their eyes,' and hold your tongue.

'One side's as bad as the other,' never worse.
Christ, it's near time that some small leak was sprung

In the great dykes the Dutchman made
To dam the dangerous tide that followed Seamus.
Yet for all this art and sedentary trade
I am incapable. The famous

Northern reticence, the tight gag of place
And times: yes, yes. Of the 'wee six' I sing
Where to be saved you only must save face
And whatever you say, you say nothing.

Smoke-signals are loud-mouthed compared with us:
Manoeuvrings to find out name and school,
Subtle discrimination by addresses
With hardly an exception to the rule

That Norman, Ken and Sidney signalled Prod,
And Seamus (call me Sean) was sure-fire Pape.
Oh, land of password, handgrip, wink and nod,
Of open minds as open as a trap,

Where tongues lie coiled, as under flames lie wicks,
Where half of us, as in a wooden horse
Were cabin'd and confined like wily Greeks,
Besieged within the siege, whispering morse.

IV

This morning from a dewy motorway
I saw the new camp for the internees:
A bomb had left a crater of fresh clay
In the roadside, and over in the trees

Machine-gun posts defined a real stockade.
There was that white mist you get on a low ground
And it was déjà-vu, some film made
Of Stalag 17, a bad dream with no sound.

Is there a life before death? That's chalked up
In Ballymurphy. Competence with pain,
Coherent miseries, a bite and sup:
We hug our little destiny again.

Freedman

> *Indeed, slavery comes nearest to its justification in the early Roman Empire: for a man from a 'backward' race might be brought within the pale of civilization, educated and trained in a craft or a profession, and turned into a useful member of society.*
> R. H. BARROW, *The Romans*

Subjugated yearly under arches,
Manumitted by parchments and degrees,
My murex was the purple dye of lents
On calendars all fast and abstinence.

'*Memento homo quia pulvis es.*' 5
I would kneel to be impressed by ashes,
A silk friction, a light stipple of dust –
I was under the thumb too like all my caste.

One of the earth-starred denizens, indelibly,
I sought to mark in vain the groomed optimi: 10
Their estimating, census-taking eyes
Fastened on my mouldy brow like lampreys.

Then poetry arrived in that city –
I would abjure all cant and self-pity –
And poetry wiped my brow and sped me. 15
Now they will say I bite the hand that fed me.

Singing School

> *Fair seedtime had my soul, and I grew up*
> *Fostered alike by beauty and by fear;*
> *Much favoured in my birthplace, and no less*
> *In that beloved Vale to which, erelong,*
> *I was transplanted . . .*
> WILLIAM WORDSWORTH, *The Prelude*

> *He [the stable-boy] had a book of Orange rhymes, and the days when we read them together in the hay-loft gave me the pleasure of rhyme for the first time. Later on I can remember being told, when there was a rumour of a Fenian rising, that rifles were being handed out to the Orangemen: and presently, when I began to dream of my future life, I thought I would like to die fighting the Fenians.*
> W. B. YEATS, *Autobiographies*

1 *The Ministry of Fear*

for Seamus Deane

Well, as Kavanagh said, we have lived
In important places. The lonely scarp
Of St Columb's College, where I billeted
For six years, overlooked your Bogside.
I gazed into new worlds: the inflamed throat
Of Brandywell, its floodlit dogtrack,
The throttle of the hare. In the first week
I was so homesick I couldn't even eat
The biscuits left to sweeten my exile.
I threw them over the fence one night
In September 1951
When the lights of houses in the Lecky Road
Were amber in the fog. It was an act
Of stealth.
         Then Belfast, and then Berkeley.
Here's two on's are sophisticated,
Dabbling in verses till they have become
A life: from bulky envelopes arriving
In vacation time to slim volumes
Despatched 'with the author's compliments'.
Those poems in longhand, ripped from the wire spine
Of your exercise-book, bewildered me –
Vowels and ideas bandied free
As the seed-pods blowing off our sycamores.
I tried to write about the sycamores
And innovated a South Derry rhyme
With *hushed* and *lulled* full chimes for *pushed* and *pulled*.
Those hobnailed boots from beyond the mountain
Were walking, by God, all over the fine
Lawns of elocution.
                  Have our accents
Changed? 'Catholics, in general, don't speak
As well as students from the Protestant schools.'
Remember that stuff? Inferiority
Complexes, stuff that dreams were made on.

'What's your name, Heaney?'
                    'Heaney, Father.'
                                        'Fair
Enough.'
            On my first day, the leather strap
Went epileptic in the Big Study,
Its echoes plashing over our bowed heads,
But I still wrote home that a boarder's life
Was not so bad, shying as usual.

On long vacations, then, I came to life
In the kissing seat of an Austin Sixteen
Parked at a gable, the engine running,
My fingers tight as ivy on her shoulders,
A light left burning for her in the kitchen.
And heading back for home, the summer's
Freedom dwindling night by night, the air
All moonlight and a scent of hay, policemen
Swung their crimson flashlamps, crowding round
The car like black cattle, snuffing and pointing
The muzzle of a sten-gun in my eye:
'What's your name, driver?'
                    'Seamus . . .'
                                Seamus?

They once read my letters at a roadblock
And shone their torches on your hieroglyphics,
'Svelte dictions' in a very florid hand.

Ulster was British, but with no rights on
The English lyric: all around us, though
We hadn't named it, the ministry of fear.

2 *A Constable Calls*

His bicycle stood at the window-sill,
The rubber cowl of a mud-splasher
Skirting the front mudguard,
Its fat black handlegrips

Heating in sunlight, the 'spud'
Of the dynamo gleaming and cocked back,
The pedal treads hanging relieved
Of the boot of the law.

         His cap was upside down
10   On the floor, next his chair.
         The line of its pressure ran like a bevel
         In his slightly sweating hair.

         He had unstrapped
         The heavy ledger, and my father
15   Was making tillage returns
         In acres, roods, and perches.

         Arithmetic and fear.
         I sat staring at the polished holster
         With its buttoned flap, the braid cord
20   Looped into the revolver butt.

         'Any other root crops?
         Mangolds? Marrowstems? Anything like that?'
         'No.' But was there not a line
         Of turnips where the seed ran out

25   In the potato field? I assumed
         Small guilts and sat
         Imagining the black hole in the barracks.
         He stood up, shifted the baton-case

         Further round on his belt,
30   Closed the domesday book,
         Fitted his cap back with two hands,
         And looked at me as he said goodbye.

         A shadow bobbed in the window.
         He was snapping the carrier spring
35   Over the ledger. His boot pushed off
         And the bicycle ticked, ticked, ticked.

3 *Orange Drums, Tyrone, 1966*

   The lambeg balloons at his belly, weighs
   Him back on his haunches, lodging thunder
   Grossly there between his chin and his knees.
   He is raised up by what he buckles under.

5 Each arm extended by a seasoned rod,
   He parades behind it. And though the drummers
   Are granted passage through the nodding crowd,
   It is the drums preside, like giant tumours.

To every cocked ear, expert in its greed,
His battered signature subscribes 'No Pope'.   10
The goatskin's sometimes plastered with his blood.
The air is pounding like a stethoscope.

4 *Summer 1969*

While the Constabulary covered the mob
Firing into the Falls, I was suffering
Only the bullying sun of Madrid.
Each afternoon, in the casserole heat
Of the flat, as I sweated my way through   5
The life of Joyce, stinks from the fishmarket
Rose like the reek off a flax-dam.
At night on the balcony, gules of wine,
A sense of children in their dark corners,
Old women in black shawls near open windows,   10
The air a canyon rivering in Spanish.
We talked our way home over starlit plains
Where patent leather of the Guardia Civil
Gleamed like fish-bellies in the flax-poisoned waters.

'Go back,' one said, 'try to touch the people.'   15
Another conjured Lorca from his hill.
We sat through death-counts and bullfight reports
On the television, celebrities
Arrived from where the real thing still happened.

I retreated to the cool of the Prado.   20
Goya's 'Shootings of the Third of May'
Covered a wall – the thrown-up arms
And spasm of the rebel, the helmeted
And knapsacked military, the efficient
Rake of the fusillade. In the next room,   25
His nightmares, grafted to the palace wall –
Dark cyclones, hosting, breaking; Saturn
Jewelled in the blood of his own children;
Gigantic Chaos turning his brute hips
Over the world. Also, that holmgang   30
Where two berserks club each other to death
For honour's sake, greaved in a bog, and sinking.

He painted with his fists and elbows, flourished
The stained cape of his heart as history charged.

5 Fosterage

for Michael McLaverty

'Description is revelation!' Royal
Avenue, Belfast, 1962,
A Saturday afternoon, glad to meet
Me, newly cubbed in language, he gripped
My elbow. 'Listen. Go your own way.
Do your own work. Remember
Katherine Mansfield – *I will tell
How the laundry basket squeaked . . .* that note of exile.'
But to hell with overstating it:
'Don't have the veins bulging in your biro.'
And then, 'Poor Hopkins!' I have the *Journals*
He gave me, underlined, his buckled self
Obeisant to their pain. He discerned
The lineaments of patience everywhere
And fostered me and sent me out, with words
Imposing on my tongue like obols.

6 Exposure

It is December in Wicklow:
Alders dripping, birches
Inheriting the last light,
The ash tree cold to look at.

A comet that was lost
Should be visible at sunset,
Those million tons of light
Like a glimmer of haws and rose-hips,

And I sometimes see a falling star.
If I could come on meteorite!
Instead I walk through damp leaves,
Husks, the spent flukes of autumn,

Imagining a hero
On some muddy compound,
His gift like a slingstone
Whirled for the desperate.

How did I end up like this?

I often think of my friends'
Beautiful prismatic counselling
And the anvil brains of some who hate me

As I sit weighing and weighing
My responsible *tristia*.
For what? For the ear? For the people?
For what is said behind-backs?

Rain comes down through the alders,
Its low conducive voices
Mutter about let-downs and erosions
And yet each drop recalls

The diamond absolutes.
I am neither internee nor informer;
An inner émigré, grown long-haired
And thoughtful; a wood-kerne

Escaped from the massacre,
Taking protective colouring
From bole and bark, feeling
Every wind that blows;

Who, blowing up these sparks
For their meagre heat, have missed
The once-in-a-lifetime portent,
The comet's pulsing rose.

UNCOLLECTED POEMS (1975–1979)

A Strange House

Racoons, soft-footed scavengers,
Hustled at the trash-can:
From the blond household timbers,
A whiff of indolent resin.

I sensed hubris of the body
Off steel and sanded grain,
The deliberate nudity
Of a beautiful hard woman.

We whose rooms were hide
And seek, valences and screens –
We were on the wrong side
Of those high, uncurtained panes.

A bare moon stared in
When we put out the light.
Listen.
Trees breathed upon that night

Were clandestine
As our first wedded work,
My eager scavenging,
Your cold nose in the dark.

The Pleasures of the Day

A red and gold roof-boss
jumps in binoculars,
daylight through a lifting window
opens wide the rose of York.

We came through white walls
over a green slope,
we went down to a well
where legionaries threw their coins

and the pleasures of the day
go on, you walking
the drawbridge into the keep,
the children at their hide and seek

in cloisters. It is all
illumination, my chatelaine
15   wears a green duffle-coat and hood,
I parley with her from a stair-head

and the pleasures of the day
go on into the night:
an owl's cry in my forehead
20   and an owl's flight

like the arrow whispering
Sowerby and *Hastings*,
yeoman, *barbican*, and the pigeon
cooing *mole*, and *spinney*.

A Toy for Catherine

'Aren't poems like your toys, Daddy?'
Catherine said,
'And didn't you and mammy make me
And God made the thread?'

FIELD WORK (1979)

for Karl and Jane Miller

Oysters

Our shells clacked on the plates.
My tongue was a filling estuary,
My palate hung with starlight:
As I tasted the salty Pleiades
Orion dipped his foot into the water.

Alive and violated
They lay on their beds of ice:
Bivalves: the split bulb
And philandering sigh of ocean.
Millions of them ripped and shucked and scattered.

We had driven to that coast
Through flowers and limestone
And there we were, toasting friendship,
Laying down a perfect memory
In the cool of thatch and crockery.

Over the Alps, packed deep in hay and snow,
The Romans hauled their oysters south to Rome:
I saw damp panniers disgorge
The frond-lipped, brine-stung
Glut of privilege

And was angry that my trust could not repose
In the clear light, like poetry or freedom
Leaning in from sea. I ate the day
Deliberately, that its tang
Might quicken me all into verb, pure verb.

Triptych

1 *After a Killing*

There they were, as if our memory hatched them,
As if the unquiet founders walked again:
Two young men with rifles on the hill,
Profane and bracing as their instruments.

Who's sorry for our trouble?
Who dreamt that we might dwell among ourselves

In rain and scoured light and wind-dried stones?
Basalt, blood, water, headstones, leeches.

In that neuter original loneliness
From Brandon to Dunseverick
I think of small-eyed survivor flowers,
The pined-for, unmolested orchid.

I see a stone house by a pier.
Elbow room. Broad window light.
The heart lifts. You walk twenty yards
To the boats and buy mackerel.

And today a girl walks in home to us
Carrying a basket full of new potatoes,
Three tight green cabbages, and carrots
With the tops and mould still fresh on them.

II *Sibyl*

My tongue moved, a swung relaxing hinge.
I said to her, 'What will become of us?'
And as forgotten water in a well might shake
At an explosion under morning

Or a crack run up a gable,
She began to speak.
'I think our very form is bound to change.
Dogs in a siege. Saurian relapses. Pismires.

Unless forgiveness finds its nerve and voice,
Unless the helmeted and bleeding tree
Can green and open buds like infants' fists
And the fouled magma incubate

Bright nymphs . . . My people think money
And talk weather. Oil-rigs lull their future
On single acquisitive stems. Silence
Has shoaled into the trawlers' echo-sounders.

The ground we kept our ear to for so long
Is flayed or calloused, and its entrails
Tented by an impious augury.
Our island is full of comfortless noises.'

III *At the Water's Edge*

On Devenish I heard a snipe
And the keeper's recital of elegies
Under the tower. Carved monastic heads
Were crumbling like bread on water.

On Boa the god-eyed, sex-mouthed stone
Socketed between graves, two-faced, trepanned,
Answered my silence with silence.
A stoup for rain water. Anathema.

From a cold hearthstone on Horse Island
I watched the sky beyond the open chimney
And listened to the thick rotations
Of an army helicopter patrolling.

A hammer and a cracked jug full of cobwebs
Lay on the windowsill. Everything in me
Wanted to bow down, to offer up,
To go barefoot, foetal and penitential,

And pray at the water's edge.
How we crept before we walked! I remembered
The helicopter shadowing our march at Newry,
The scared, irrevocable steps.

The Toome Road

One morning early I met armoured cars
In convoy, warbling along on powerful tyres,
All camouflaged with broken alder branches,
And headphoned soldiers standing up in turrets.
How long were they approaching down my roads
As if they owned them? The whole country was sleeping.
I had rights-of-way, fields, cattle in my keeping,
Tractors hitched to buckrakes in open sheds,
Silos, chill gates, wet slates, the greens and reds
Of outhouse roofs. Whom should I run to tell
Among all of those with their back doors on the latch
For the bringer of bad news, that small-hours visitant
Who, by being expected, might be kept distant?
Sowers of seed, erectors of headstones . . .

15 O charioteers, above your dormant guns,
    It stands here still, stands vibrant as you pass,
    The invisible, untoppled omphalos.

A Drink of Water

   She came every morning to draw water
   Like an old bat staggering up the field:
   The pump's whooping cough, the bucket's clatter
   And slow diminuendo as it filled,
5 Announced her. I recall
   Her grey apron, the pocked white enamel
   Of the brimming bucket, and the treble
   Creak of her voice like the pump's handle.
   Nights when a full moon lifted past her gable
10 It fell back through her window and would lie
   Into the water set out on the table.
   Where I have dipped to drink again, to be
   Faithful to the admonishment on her cup,
   Remember the Giver fading off the lip.

The Strand at Lough Beg

In memory of Colum McCartney

*All round this little island, on the strand
Far down below there, where the breakers strive,
Grow the tall rushes from the oozy sand.*
        DANTE, *Purgatorio*, I, 100–103

   Leaving the white glow of filling stations
   And a few lonely streetlamps among fields
   You climbed the hills towards Newtownhamilton
   Past the Fews Forest, out beneath the stars –
5 Along that road, a high, bare pilgrim's track
   Where Sweeney fled before the bloodied heads,
   Goat-beards and dogs' eyes in a demon pack
   Blazing out of the ground, snapping and squealing.
   What blazed ahead of you? A faked road block?
10 The red lamp swung, the sudden brakes and stalling
   Engine, voices, heads hooded and the cold-nosed gun?

Or in your driving mirror, tailing headlights
That pulled out suddenly and flagged you down
Where you weren't known and far from what you knew:
The lowland clays and waters of Lough Beg, 15
Church Island's spire, its soft treeline of yew.

There you used hear guns fired behind the house
Long before rising time, when duck shooters
Haunted the marigolds and bulrushes,
But still were scared to find spent cartridges, 20
Acrid, brassy, genital, ejected,
On your way across the strand to fetch the cows.
For you and yours and yours and mine fought shy,
Spoke an old language of conspirators
And could not crack the whip or seize the day: 25
Big-voiced scullions, herders, feelers round
Haycocks and hindquarters, talkers in byres,
Slow arbitrators of the burial ground.
Across that strand of yours the cattle graze
Up to their bellies in an early mist 30
And now they turn their unbewildered gaze
To where we work our way through squeaking sedge
Drowning in dew. Like a dull blade with its edge
Honed bright, Lough Beg half shines under the haze.
I turn because the sweeping of your feet 35
Has stopped behind me, to find you on your knees
With blood and roadside muck in your hair and eyes,
Then kneel in front of you in brimming grass
And gather up cold handfuls of the dew
To wash you, cousin. I dab you clean with moss 40
Fine as the drizzle out of a low cloud.
I lift you under the arms and lay you flat.
With rushes that shoot green again, I plait
Green scapulars to wear over your shroud.

A Postcard from North Antrim

In memory of Sean Armstrong

A lone figure is waving
From the thin line of a bridge
Of ropes and slats, slung

             Dangerously out between
5   The cliff-top and the pillar rock.
             A nineteenth-century wind.
             Dulse-pickers. Sea campions.

             A postcard for you, Sean,
             And that's you, swinging alone,
10   Antic, half-afraid,
             In your gallowglass's beard
             And swallow-tail of serge:
             The Carrick-a-Rede Rope Bridge
             Ghost-written on sepia.

15   Or should it be your houseboat
             Ethnically furnished,
             Redolent of grass?
             Should we discover you
             Beside those warm-planked, democratic wharves
20   Among the twilights and guitars
             Of Sausalito?

             Drop-out on a come-back,
             Prince of no-man's land
             With your head in clouds or sand,
25   You were the clown
             Social worker of the town
             Until your candid forehead stopped
             A pointblank teatime bullet.

             Get up from your blood on the floor.
30   Here's another boat
             In grass by the lough shore,
             Turf smoke, a wired hen-run –
             Your local, hoped for, unfound commune.
             Now recite me *William Bloat*,
35   Sing of *the Calabar*

             Or of Henry Joy McCracken
             Who kissed his Mary Ann
             On the gallows at Cornmarket.
             Or Ballycastle Fair.
40   'Give us the raw bar!'
             'Sing it by brute force
             If you forget the air.'

Yet something in your voice
Stayed nearly shut.
Your voice was a harassed pulpit 45
Leading the melody
It kept at bay,
It was independent, rattling, non-transcendent
Ulster – old decency

And Old Bushmills, 50
Soda farls, strong tea,
New rope, rock salt, kale plants,
Potato-bread and Woodbine.
Wind through the concrete vents
Of a border check-point. 55
Cold zinc nailed for a peace line.

Fifteen years ago, come this October,
Crowded on your floor,
I got my arm round Marie's shoulder
For the first time. 60
'Oh, Sir Jasper, do not touch me!'
You roared across at me,
Chorus-leading, splashing out the wine.

Casualty

I

He would drink by himself
And raise a weathered thumb
Towards the high shelf,
Calling another rum
And blackcurrant, without 5
Having to raise his voice,
Or order a quick stout
By a lifting of the eyes
And a discreet dumb-show
Of pulling off the top; 10
At closing time would go
In waders and peaked cap
Into the showery dark,
A dole-kept breadwinner
But a natural for work. 15

       I loved his whole manner,
       Sure-footed but too sly,
       His deadpan sidling tact,
       His fisherman's quick eye
20   And turned observant back.

       Incomprehensible
       To him, my other life.
       Sometimes, on his high stool,
       Too busy with his knife
25   At a tobacco plug
       And not meeting my eye,
       In the pause after a slug
       He mentioned poetry.
       We would be on our own
30   And, always politic
       And shy of condescension,
       I would manage by some trick
       To switch the talk to eels
       Or lore of the horse and cart
35   Or the Provisionals.

       But my tentative art
       His turned back watches too:
       He was blown to bits
       Out drinking in a curfew
40   Others obeyed, three nights
       After they shot dead
       The thirteen men in Derry.
       PARAS THIRTEEN, the walls said,
       BOGSIDE NIL. That Wednesday
45   Everybody held
       His breath and trembled.

       II

       It was a day of cold
       Raw silence, wind-blown
       Surplice and soutane:
       Rained-on, flower-laden
5   Coffin after coffin
       Seemed to float from the door
       Of the packed cathedral
       Like blossoms on slow water.

The common funeral
Unrolled its swaddling band,
Lapping, tightening
Till we were braced and bound
Like brothers in a ring.

But he would not be held
At home by his own crowd
Whatever threats were phoned,
Whatever black flags waved.
I see him as he turned
In that bombed offending place,
Remorse fused with terror
In his still knowable face,
His cornered outfaced stare
Blinding in the flash.

He had gone miles away
For he drank like a fish
Nightly, naturally
Swimming towards the lure
Of warm lit-up places,
The blurred mesh and murmur
Drifting among glasses
In the gregarious smoke.
How culpable was he
That last night when he broke
Our tribe's complicity?
'Now you're supposed to be
An educated man,'
I hear him say. 'Puzzle me
The right answer to that one.'

III

I missed his funeral,
Those quiet walkers
And sideways talkers
Shoaling out of his lane
To the respectable
Purring of the hearse . . .
They move in equal pace
With the habitual
Slow consolation

10   Of a dawdling engine,
     The line lifted, hand
     Over fist, cold sunshine
     On the water, the land
     Banked under fog: that morning
15   I was taken in his boat,
     The screw purling, turning
     Indolent fathoms white,
     I tasted freedom with him.
     To get out early, haul
20   Steadily off the bottom,
     Dispraise the catch, and smile
     As you find a rhythm
     Working you, slow mile by mile,
     Into your proper haunt
25   Somewhere, well out, beyond . . .

     Dawn-sniffing revenant,
     Plodder through midnight rain,
     Question me again.

The Badgers

When the badger glimmered away
into another garden
you stood, half-lit with whiskey,
sensing you had disturbed
5   some soft returning.

The murdered dead,
you thought.
But could it not have been
some violent shattered boy
10   nosing out what got mislaid
between the cradle and the explosion,
evenings when windows stood open
and the compost smoked down the backs?

Visitations are taken for signs.
15   At a second house I listened
for duntings under the laurels
and heard intimations whispered
about being vaguely honoured.

And to read even by carcasses
the badgers have come back.   20
One that grew notorious
lay untouched in the roadside.
Last night one had me braking
but more in fear than in honour.

Cool from the sett and redolent   25
of his runs under the night,
the bogey of fern country
broke cover in me
for what he is:
pig family   30
and not at all what he's painted.
How perilous is it to choose
not to love the life we're shown?
His sturdy dirty body
and interloping grovel.   35
The intelligence in his bone.
The unquestionable houseboy's shoulders
that could have been my own.

The Singer's House

When they said *Carrickfergus* I could hear
the frosty echo of saltminers' picks.
I imagined it, chambered and glinting,
a township built of light.

What do we say any more   5
to conjure the salt of our earth?
So much comes and is gone
that should be crystal and kept

and amicable weathers
that bring up the grain of things,   10
their tang of season and store,
are all the packing we'll get.

So I say to myself *Gweebarra*
and its music hits off the place
like water hitting off granite.   15
I see the glittering sound

       framed in your window,
       knives and forks set on oilcloth,
       and the seals' heads, suddenly outlined,
20   scanning everything.

       People here used to believe
       that drowned souls lived in the seals.
       At spring tides they might change shape.
       They loved music and swam in for a singer
25   who might stand at the end of summer
       in the mouth of a whitewashed turf-shed,
       his shoulder to the jamb, his song
       a rowboat far out in evening.

       When I came here first you were always singing,
30   a hint of the clip of the pick
       in your winnowing climb and attack.
       Raise it again, man. We still believe what we hear.

The Guttural Muse

       Late summer, and at midnight
       I smelt the heat of the day:
       At my window over the hotel car park
       I breathed the muddied night airs off the lake
5   And watched a young crowd leave the discotheque.

       Their voices rose up thick and comforting
       As oily bubbles the feeding tench sent up
       That evening at dusk – the slimy tench
       Once called the 'doctor fish' because his slime
10   Was said to heal the wounds of fish that touched it.

       A girl in a white dress
       Was being courted out among the cars:
       As her voice swarmed and puddled into laughs
       I felt like some old pike all badged with sores
15   Wanting to swim in touch with soft-mouthed life.

In Memoriam Seán Ó Riada

He conducted the Ulster Orchestra
like a drover with an ashplant
herding them south.
I watched him from behind,

springy, formally suited,
a black stiletto trembling in its mark,
a quill flourishing itself,
a quickened, whitened head.

'How do you work?
Sometimes I just lie out
like ballast in the bottom of the boat
listening to the cuckoo.'

The gunwale's lifting ear –
trusting the gift,
risking gifts undertow –
is unmanned now

but one whole afternoon
it was deep in both our weights.
We sat awkward on the thwarts
taking turns to cast or row

until mackerel shoaled from under
like a conjured retinue
fawning upon our lures.
He had the *sprezzatura*,

more falconer than fisherman, I'd say,
unhooding a sceptic eye
to greet the mackerel's barred cold,
to pry whatever the cuckoo called.

As he stepped and stooped to the keyboard
he was our jacobite,
he was our young pretender
who marched along the deep

plumed in slow airs and grace notes.
O gannet smacking through scales!

35   Minnow of light.
     Wader of assonance.

Elegy

The way we are living,
timorous or bold,
will have been our life.
Robert Lowell,

5   the sill geranium is lit
     by the lamp I write by,
     a wind from the Irish Sea
     is shaking it –

     here where we all sat
10   ten days ago, with you,
     the master elegist
     and welder of English.

     As you swayed the talk
     and rode on the swaying tiller
15   of yourself, ribbing me
     about my fear of water,

     what was not within your empery?
     You drank America
     like the heart's
20   iron vodka,

     promulgating art's
     deliberate, peremptory
     love and arrogance.
     Your eyes saw what your hand did

25   as you Englished Russian,
     as you bullied out
     heart-hammering blank sonnets
     of love for Harriet

     and Lizzie, and the briny
30   water-breaking dolphin –
     your dorsal nib
     gifted at last

to inveigle and to plash,
helmsman, netsman, *retiarius*.
That hand. Warding and grooming
and amphibious.

Two a.m., seaboard weather.
Not the proud sail of your great verse . . .
No. You were our night ferry
thudding in a big sea,

the whole craft ringing
with an armourer's music
the course set wilfully across
the ungovernable and dangerous.

And now a teem of rain
and the geranium *tremens*.
*A father's no shield
for his child –*

you found the child in me
when you took farewells
under the full bay tree
by the gate in Glanmore,

opulent and restorative
as that lingering summertime,
the fish-dart of your eyes
risking, 'I'll pray for you.'

Glanmore Sonnets

*for Ann Saddlemyer
our heartiest welcomer*

I

Vowels ploughed into other: opened ground.
The mildest February for twenty years
Is mist bands over furrows, a deep no sound
Vulnerable to distant gargling tractors.
Our road is steaming, the turned-up acres breathe.
Now the good life could be to cross a field
And art a paradigm of earth new from the lathe
Of ploughs. My lea is deeply tilled.

       Old ploughsocks gorge the subsoil of each sense
10   And I am quickened with redolence
       Of the fundamental dark unblown rose.
       Wait then . . . Breasting the mist, in sowers' aprons,
       My ghosts come striding into their spring stations.
       The dream grain whirls like freakish Easter snows.

       II

       Sensings, mountings from the hiding places,
       Words entering almost the sense of touch
       Ferreting themselves out of their dark hutch –
       'These things are not secrets but mysteries,'
5   Oisin Kelly told me years ago
       In Belfast, hankering after stone
       That connived with the chisel, as if the grain
       Remembered what the mallet tapped to know.
       Then I landed in the hedge-school of Glanmore
10   And from the backs of ditches hoped to raise
       A voice caught back off slug-horn and slow chanter
       That might continue, hold, dispel, appease:
       Vowels ploughed into other, opened ground,
       Each verse returning like the plough turned round.

       III

       This evening the cuckoo and the corncrake
       (So much, too much) consorted at twilight.
       It was all crepuscular and iambic.
       Out on the field a baby rabbit
5   Took his bearings, and I knew the deer
       (I've seen them too from the window of the house,
       Like connoisseurs, inquisitive of air)
       Were careful under larch and May-green spruce.
       I had said earlier, 'I won't relapse
10   From this strange loneliness I've brought us to.
       Dorothy and William –' She interrupts:
       'You're not going to compare us two . . .?'
       Outside a rustling and twig-combing breeze
       Refreshes and relents. Is cadences.

IV

I used to lie with an ear to the line
For that way, they said, there should come a sound
Escaping ahead, an iron tune
Of flange and piston pitched along the ground,
But I never heard that. Always, instead,   5
Struck couplings and shuntings two miles away
Lifted over the woods. The head
Of a horse swirled back from a gate, a grey
Turnover of haunch and mane, and I'd look
Up to the cutting where she'd soon appear.   10
Two fields back, in the house, small ripples shook
Silently across our drinking water
(As they are shaking now across my heart)
And vanished into where they seemed to start.

V

Soft corrugations in the boortree's trunk,
Its green young shoots, its rods like freckled solder:
It was our bower as children, a greenish, dank
And snapping memory as I get older.
And elderberry I have learned to call it.   5
I love its blooms like saucers brimmed with meal,
Its berries a swart caviar of shot,
A buoyant spawn, a light bruised out of purple.
Elderberry? It is shires dreaming wine.
Boortree is bower tree, where I played 'touching tongues'   10
And felt another's texture quick on mine.
So, etymologist of roots and graftings,
I fall back to my tree-house and would crouch
Where small buds shoot and flourish in the hush.

VI

He lived there in the unsayable lights.
He saw the fuchsia in a drizzling noon,
The elderflower at dusk like a risen moon
And green fields greying on the windswept heights.
'I will break through,' he said, 'what I glazed over   5
With perfect mist and peaceful absences . . .'

Sudden and sure as the man who dared the ice
And raced his bike across the Moyola River.
A man we never saw. But in that winter
Of nineteen forty-seven, when the snow
Kept the country bright as a studio,
In a cold where things might crystallize or founder,
His story quickened us, a wild white goose
Heard after dark above the drifted house.

VII

Dogger, Rockall, Malin, Irish Sea:
Green, swift upsurges, North Atlantic flux
Conjured by that strong gale-warning voice
Collapse into a sibilant penumbra.
Midnight and closedown. Sirens of the tundra,
Of eel-road, seal-road, keel-road, whale-road, raise
Their wind-compounded keen behind the baize
And drive the trawlers to the lee of Wicklow.
L'Etoile, Le Guillemot, Le Belle Hélène
Nursed their bright names this morning in the bay
That toiled like mortar. It was marvellous
And actual, I said out loud, 'A haven,'
The word deepening, clearing, like the sky
Elsewhere on Minches, Cromarty, The Faroes.

VIII

Thunderlight on the split logs: big raindrops
At body heat and lush with omen
Spattering dark on the hatchet iron.
This morning when a magpie with jerky steps
Inspected a horse asleep beside the wood
I thought of dew on armour and carrion.
What would I meet, blood-boltered, on the road?
How deep into the woodpile sat the toad?
What welters through this dark hush on the crops?
Do you remember that pension in *Les Landes*
Where the old one rocked and rocked and rocked
A mongol in her lap, to little songs?
Come to me quickly, I am upstairs shaking.
My all of you birchwood in lightning.

IX

Outside the kitchen window a black rat
Sways on the briar like infected fruit:
'It looked me through, it stared me out, I'm not
Imagining things. Go you out to it.'
Did we come to the wilderness for this?   5
We have our burnished bay tree at the gate,
Classical, hung with the reek of silage
From the next farm, tart-leafed as inwit.
Blood on a pitch-fork, blood on chaff and hay,
Rats speared in the sweat and dust of threshing –   10
What is my apology for poetry?
The empty briar is swishing
When I come down, and beyond, your face
Haunts like a new moon glimpsed through tangled glass.

X

I dreamt we slept in a moss in Donegal
On turf banks under blankets, with our faces
Exposed all night in a wetting drizzle,
Pallid as the dripping sapling birches.
Lorenzo and Jessica in a cold climate.   5
Diarmuid and Grainne waiting to be found.
Darkly aspersed and censed, we were laid out
Like breathing effigies on a raised ground.
And in that dream I dreamt – how like you this? –
Our first night years ago in that hotel   10
When you came with your deliberate kiss
To raise us towards the lovely and painful
Covenants of flesh; our separateness;
The respite in our dewy dreaming faces.

September Song

In the middle of the way
under the wet of late September
the ash tree flails,
our dog is tearing earth beside the house.

In rising ditches the fern subsides.
Rain-logged berries and stones
are rained upon, acorns
shine from grassy verges every morning.

And it's nearly over,
our four years in the hedge-school.
If nobody is going to resin a bow
and test the grieving registers for joy

we might as well put on our old record
of John Field's *Nocturnes* –
his gifts, waste, solitude, reputation, laughter,
all 'Dead in Moscow',

all those gallons of wash for the pure drop,
notes 'like raindrops, pearls on velvet.'
Remember our American wake?
When we first got footloose

they lifted the roof for us in Belfast,
Hammond, Gunn and McAloon
in full cry till the dawn chorus,
insouciant and purposeful.

Gusts, barking, power-lines shaken
and the music wavering. Inside and out,
babes-in-the-wood weather. We toe the line
between the tree in leaf and the bare tree.

An Afterwards

She would plunge all poets in the ninth circle
And fix them, tooth in skull, tonguing for brain;
For backbiting in life she'd make their hell
A rabid egotistical daisy-chain.

Unyielding, spurred, ambitious, unblunted,
Lockjawed, mantrapped, each a fastened badger
Jockeying for position, hasped and mounted
Like Ugolino on Archbishop Roger.

And when she'd make her circuit of the ice,
Aided and abetted by Virgil's wife,

I would cry out, 'My sweet, who wears the bays
In our green land above, whose is the life

Most dedicated and exemplary?'
And she: 'I have closed my widowed ears
To the sulphurous news of poets and poetry.   15
Why could you not have, oftener, in our years

Unclenched, and come down laughing from your room
And walked the twilight with me and your children –
Like that one evening of elder bloom
And hay, when the wild roses were fading?'   20

And (as some maker gaffs me in the neck)
'You weren't the worst. You aspired to a kind,
Indifferent, faults-on-both-sides tact.
You left us first, and then those books, behind.'

High Summer

The child cried inconsolably at night.
Because his curls were long and fair
the neighbours called him *la petite*
and listened to him harrowing the air
that damped their roof-tiles and their vines.   5
At five o'clock, when the landlord's tractor,
familiar, ignorant and hard,
battled and gargled in the yard,
we relished daylight in the shutter
and fell asleep.   10
        Slubbed with eddies,
the laden silent river
ran mud and olive into summer.
Swallows mazed from nests caked up on roof-tiles
in the barn: the double doors stood open,   15
the carter passed ahead of his bowed oxen.

I bought the maggots in paper bags, like sweets,
and fished at evening in the earthy heat
and green reek of the maize.
From that screened bank, as from a plaited frieze,   20
bamboo rods stuck leniently out,

    nodding and waiting, feelers into quiet.
    Snails in the grass, bat-squeak, the darkening trees . . .

    'Christopher is teething and cries at night.
25 But this barn is an ideal place to write:
    bare stone, old harness, ledges, shelves, the smell
    of hay and silage. Just now, all's hot and still.
    I've scattered twenty francs on fishing tackle.'

    On the last day, when I was clearing up,
30 on a warm ledge I found a bag of maggots
    and opened it. A black
    and throbbing swarm came riddling out
    like newsreel of a police force run amok,
    sunspotting flies in gauzy meaty flight,
35 the barristers and black berets of light.

    We left by the high bare roads of the *pays basque*
    where calvaries sentry the crossroads like masts
    and slept that night near goatbells in the mists.

The Otter

    When you plunged
    The light of Tuscany wavered
    And swung through the pool
    From top to bottom.

5   I loved your wet head and smashing crawl,
    Your fine swimmer's back and shoulders
    Surfacing and surfacing again
    This year and every year since.

    I sat dry-throated on the warm stones.
10 You were beyond me.
    The mellowed clarities, the grape-deep air
    Thinned and disappointed.

    Thank God for the slow loadening,
    When I hold you now
15 We are close and deep
    As the atmosphere on water.

    My two hands are plumbed water.
    You are my palpable, lithe

Otter of memory
In the pool of the moment,

Turning to swim on your back,
Each silent, thigh-shaking kick
Re-tilting the light,
Heaving the cool at your neck.

And suddenly you're out,
Back again, intent as ever,
Heavy and frisky in your freshened pelt,
Printing the stones.

The Skunk

Up, black, striped and damasked like the chasuble
At a funeral mass, the skunk's tail
Paraded the skunk. Night after night
I expected her like a visitor.

The refrigerator whinnied into silence.
My desk light softened beyond the verandah.
Small oranges loomed in the orange tree.
I began to be tense as a voyeur.

After eleven years I was composing
Love-letters again, broaching the word 'wife'
Like a stored cask, as if its slender vowel
Had mutated into the night earth and air

Of California. The beautiful, useless
Tang of eucalyptus spelt your absence.
The aftermath of a mouthful of wine
Was like inhaling you off a cold pillow.

And there she was, the intent and glamorous,
Ordinary, mysterious skunk,
Mythologized, demythologized,
Snuffing the boards five feet beyond me.

It all came back to me last night, stirred
By the sootfall of your things at bedtime,
Your head-down, tail-up hunt in a bottom drawer
For the black plunge-line nightdress.

Homecomings

I

Fetch me the sandmartin
skimming and veering
breast to breast with himself
in the clouds in the river.

II

At the worn mouth of the hole
flight after flight after flight
the swoop of his wings
gloved and kissed home.

III

A glottal stillness. An eardrum.
Far in, featherbrains tucked in silence,
a silence of water
lipping the bank.

IV

Mould my shoulders inward to you.
Occlude me.
Be damp clay pouting.
Let me listen under your eaves.

A Dream of Jealousy

Walking with you and another lady
In wooded parkland, the whispering grass
Ran its fingers through our guessing silence
And the trees opened into a shady
Unexpected clearing where we sat down.
I think the candour of the light dismayed us.
We talked about desire and being jealous,
Our conversation a loose single gown
Or a white picnic tablecloth spread out
Like a book of manners in the wilderness.
'Show me,' I said to our companion, 'what
I have much coveted, your breast's mauve star.'

And she consented. O neither these verses
Nor my prudence, love, can heal your wounded stare.

Polder

After the sudden outburst and the squalls
I hooped you with my arms

and remembered that what could be contained
inside this caliper embrace

the Dutch called *bosom*; and *fathom*
what the extended arms took in.

I have reclaimed my polder,
all its salty grass and mud-slick banks;

under fathoms of air, like an old willow
I stir a little on my creel of roots.

Field Work

I

Where the sally tree went pale in every breeze,
where the perfect eye of the nesting blackbird watched,
where one fern was always green

I was standing watching you
take the pad from the gatehouse at the crossing
and reach to lift a white wash off the whins.

I could see the vaccination mark
stretched on your upper arm, and smell the coal smell
of the train that comes between us, a slow goods,

waggon after waggon full of big-eyed cattle.

II

But your vaccination mark is on your thigh,
an O that's healed into the bark.

Except a dryad's not a woman
you are my wounded dryad

in a mothering smell of wet
and ring-wormed chestnuts.

Our moon was small and far,
was a coin long gazed at

brilliant on the *Pequod*'s mast
across Atlantic and Pacific waters.

III

Not the mud slick,
not the black weedy water
full of alder cones and pock-marked leaves.

Not the cow parsley in winter
with its old whitened shins and wrists,
its sibilance, its shaking.

Not even the tart green shade of summer
thick with butterflies
and fungus plump as a leather saddle.

No. But in a still corner,
braced to its pebble-dashed wall,
heavy, earth-drawn, all mouth and eye,

the sunflower, dreaming umber.

IV

Catspiss smell,
the pink bloom open:
I press a leaf
of the flowering currant
on the back of your hand
for the tight slow burn
of its sticky juice
to prime your skin,
and your veins to be crossed
criss-cross with leaf-veins.
I lick my thumb
and dip it in mould,

I anoint the anointed
leaf-shape. Mould
blooms and pigments
the back of your hand
like a birthmark –
my umber one,
you are stained, stained
to perfection.

Song

A rowan like a lipsticked girl.
Between the by-road and the main road
Alder trees at a wet and dripping distance
Stand off among the rushes.

There are the mud-flowers of dialect
And the immortelles of perfect pitch
And that moment when the bird sings very close
To the music of what happens.

Leavings

A soft whoosh, the sunset blaze
of straw on blackened stubble,
a thatch-deep, freshening
barbarous crimson burn –

I rode down England
as they fired the crop
that was the leavings of a crop,
the smashed tow-coloured barley,

down from Ely's Lady Chapel,
the sweet tenor latin
forever banished,
the sumptuous windows

threshed clear by Thomas Cromwell.
Which circle does he tread,
scalding on cobbles,
each one a broken statue's head?

After midnight, after summer,
to walk on a sparking field,
to smell dew and ashes
and start Will Brangwen's ghost

from the hot soot –
a breaking sheaf of light,
abroad in the hiss
and clash of stooking.

The Harvest Bow

As you plaited the harvest bow
You implicated the mellowed silence in you
In wheat that does not rust
But brightens as it tightens twist by twist
Into a knowable corona,
A throwaway love-knot of straw.

Hands that aged round ashplants and cane sticks
And lapped the spurs on a lifetime of game cocks
Harked to their gift and worked with fine intent
Until your fingers moved somnambulant:
I tell and finger it like braille,
Gleaning the unsaid off the palpable,

And if I spy into its golden loops
I see us walk between the railway slopes
Into an evening of long grass and midges,
Blue smoke straight up, old beds and ploughs in hedges,
An auction notice on an outhouse wall –
You with a harvest bow in your lapel,

Me with the fishing rod, already homesick
For the big lift of these evenings, as your stick
Whacking the tips off weeds and bushes
Beats out of time, and beats, but flushes
Nothing: that original townland
Still tongue-tied in the straw tied by your hand.

The end of art is peace
Could be the motto of this frail device
That I have pinned up on our deal dresser –

Like a drawn snare
Slipped lately by the spirit of the corn
Yet burnished by its passage, and still warm.   30

In Memoriam Francis Ledwidge

Killed in France 31 July 1917

The bronze soldier hitches a bronze cape
That crumples stiffly in imagined wind
No matter how the real winds buff and sweep
His sudden hunkering run, forever craned

    Over Flanders. Helmet and haversack,   5
    The gun's firm slope from butt to bayonet,
    The loyal, fallen names on the embossed plaque –
    It all meant little to the worried pet

I was in nineteen forty-six or seven,
Gripping my Aunt Mary by the hand   10
Along the Portstewart prom, then round the crescent
To thread the Castle Walk out to the strand.

The pilot from Coleraine sailed to the coal-boat.
Courting couples rose out of the scooped dunes.
A farmer stripped to his studs and shiny waistcoat   15
Rolled the trousers down on his timid shins.

At night when coloured bulbs strung out the sea-front
Country voices rose from a cliff-top shelter
With news of a great litter – 'We'll pet the runt!' –
And barbed wire that had torn a friesian's elder.   20

Francis Ledwidge, you courted at the seaside
Beyond Drogheda one Sunday afternoon.
Literary, sweet-talking, countrified,
You pedalled out the leafy road from Slane.

Where you belonged, among the dolorous   25
And lovely: the May altar of wild flowers,
Easter water sprinkled in outhouses,
Mass-rocks and hill-top raths and raftered byres.

I think of you in your Tommy's uniform,
A haunted Catholic face, pallid and brave,   30

Ghosting the trenches with a bloom of hawthorn
Or silence cored from a Boyne passage-grave.

It's summer, nineteen-fifteen. I see the girl
My aunt was then, herding on the long acre.
Behind a low bush in the Dardanelles
You suck stones to make your dry mouth water.

It's nineteen-seventeen. She still herds cows
But a big strafe puts the candles out in Ypres:
'My soul is by the Boyne, cutting new meadows . . .
My country wears her confirmation dress.'

'To be called a British soldier while my country
Has no place among nations . . .' You were rent
By shrapnel six weeks later. 'I am sorry
That party politics should divide our tents.'

In you, our dead enigma, all the strains
Criss-cross in useless equilibrium
And as the wind tunes through this vigilant bronze
I hear again the sure confusing drum

You followed from Boyne water to the Balkans
But miss the twilit note your flute should sound.
You were not keyed or pitched like these true-blue ones
Though all of you consort now underground.

Ugolino

(from Dante, Inferno, *xxxii, xxxiii)*

We had already left him. I walked the ice
And saw two soldered in a frozen hole
On top of other, one's skull capping the other's,
Gnawing at him where the neck and head
Are grafted to the sweet fruit of the brain,
Like a famine victim at a loaf of bread.
So the berserk Tydeus gnashed and fed
Upon the severed head of Menalippus
As if it were some spattered carnal melon.
'You,' I shouted, 'you on top, what hate
Makes you so ravenous and insatiable?
What keeps you so monstrously at rut?

Is there any story I can tell
For you, in the world above, against him?
If my tongue by then's not withered in my throat   15
I will report the truth and clear your name.'

That sinner eased his mouth up off his meal
To answer me, and wiped it with the hair
Left growing on his victim's ravaged skull,
Then said, 'Even before I speak   20
The thought of having to relive all that
Desperate time makes my heart sick;
Yet while I weep to say them, I would sow
My words like curses – that they might increase
And multiply upon this head I gnaw.   25
I know you come from Florence by your accent
But I have no idea who you are
Nor how you ever managed your descent.
Still, you should know my name, for I was Count
Ugolino, this was Archbishop Roger,   30
And why I act the jockey to his mount
Is surely common knowledge; how my good faith
Was easy prey to his malignancy.
How I was taken, held, and put to death.
But you must hear something you cannot know   35
If you're to judge him – the cruelty
Of my death at his hands. So listen now.

Others will pine as I pined in that jail
Which is called Hunger after me, and watch
As I watched through a narrow hole   40
Moon after moon, bright and somnambulant,
Pass overhead, until that night I dreamt
The bad dream and my future's veil was rent.
I saw a wolf-hunt: this man rode the hill
Between Pisa and Lucca, hounding down   45
The wolf and wolf-cubs. He was lordly and masterful,
His pack in keen condition, his company
Deployed ahead of him, Gualandi
And Sismundi as well, and Lanfranchi,
Who soon wore down wolf-father and wolf-sons   50
And my hallucination
Was all sharp teeth and bleeding flanks ripped open.
When I awoke before the dawn, my head

    Swam with cries of my sons who slept in tears
55 Beside me there, crying out for bread.
    (If your sympathy has not already started
    At all that my heart was foresuffering
    And if you are not crying, you are hardhearted.)

    They were awake now, it was near the time
60 For food to be brought in as usual,
    Each one of them disturbed after his dream,
    When I heard the door being nailed and hammered
    Shut, far down in the nightmare tower.
    I stared in my sons' faces and spoke no word.
65 My eyes were dry and my heart was stony.
    They cried and my little Anselm said,
    'What's wrong? Why are you staring, daddy?'
    But I shed no tears, I made no reply
    All through that day, all through the night that followed
70 Until another sun blushed in the sky
    And sent a small beam probing the distress
    Inside those prison walls. Then when I saw
    The image of my face in their four faces
    I bit on my two hands in desperation
75 And they, since they thought hunger drove me to it,
    Rose up suddenly in agitation
    Saying, 'Father, it will greatly ease our pain
    If you eat us instead, and you who dressed us
    In this sad flesh undress us here again.'
80 So then I calmed myself to keep them calm.
    We hushed. That day and the next stole past us
    And earth seemed hardened against me and them.
    For four days we let the silence gather.
    Then, throwing himself flat in front of me,
85 Gaddo said, 'Why don't you help me, father?'
    He died like that, and surely as you see
    Me here, one by one I saw my three
    Drop dead during the fifth and the sixth day
    Until I saw no more. Searching, blinded,
90 For two days I groped over them and called them.
    Then hunger killed where grief had only wounded.'
    When he had said all this, his eyes rolled
    And his teeth, like a dog's teeth clamping round a bone,
    Bit into the skull and again took hold.

Pisa! Pisa, your sounds are like a hiss   95
Sizzling in our country's grassy language.
And since the neighbour states have been remiss
In your extermination, let a huge
Dyke of islands bar the Arno's mouth, let
Capraia and Gorgona dam and deluge   100
You and your population. For the sins
Of Ugolino, who betrayed your forts,
Should never have been visited on his sons.
Your atrocity was Theban. They were young
And innocent: Hugh and Brigata   105
And the other two whose names are in my song.

UNCOLLECTED POEMS (1979–1984)

A Cart for Edward Gallagher

The nineteen-twenties
in west Donegal:
between dry stone ditches,
past whitewashed gables
and dank fuchsia bushes
the grocery cart
of *Gallagher and Son,*
Merchant, Publican,
Retail and Import,
rattles back and forward
and so returns me, Edward
to a whitewashed yard,
a grocery cart, a horse
loosed out and watered,
nose-deep in his nose-bag,
the legend on the cart
already legendary:
Teady MacErlean,
The Oldest Firm
in the Bann Valley.
It is a covered waggon,
four-wheeled, wooden-spoked,
and painted green; each wheel
fat-hubbed and still.
It is nineteen-forty-seven.
I am taking it all in.

And why do I tell you?
It is a paradigm
of dream and watchfulness,
the exact gaze of silence.
Like that morning years ago
I came upon you, stilled
and oblivious,
staring into a field
of blossoming potatoes,
your trouser-bottoms wet
and flecked with grass-seed.
On a farm street somewhere
or at the end of a lane

40 your early-rising son
had parked his mobile shop.
Back in your silent bar
last night's glasses soured
in a pure sea-light.
45 If I could have rode up
like Oisin on a horse
and made the morning ring
with heroic Irish,
hoof-beats, bird-song,
50 the dazzle and wet blaze
of sand and ocean,
you would not have been drawn
from the covert of your gaze.

A Hank of Wool

i.m. Elizabeth Bishop

I

'Hank?' I hear you say,
all tact and masquerade.
'Sounds like a name for a cowboy.'

But didn't you hold the wool –
5 shop wool, ticketed bought wool –
until your shoulders ached?

I used to sit like a hermit
with my two arms held out
to stretch the hank between them.

II

To unwind it, Elizabeth,
come back in a cardigan
knitted grey or brown

so that we can imagine
5 the click and flash of needles,
see them like fireflies

in our tranquil recollection

of those supple mysteries,
knit one, drop one, slip one . . .

III

Then say goodbye to Maine,
to shade-card map-colours
of blue and green,

to the doll's afghan
in different coloured squares
your grandmother who 'knitted things for soldiers'

taught you to do, with little sermons.
'But I resented this.
So then I would unravel lots of rows –

And I've never knitted since.'

A Villanelle for Marie

'Love is knowledge: what has been pried and tried,
The worn grain, the song maintained by singing.'
'But love is longing too,' my love replied,

'And hankering for what has been denied.
Who says that that visionary stinging,
Love, is knowledge? What has been pried and tried

Is conjugal, domestic, tamely plied,
The spancelled discipline of two belonging.
But love is longing.' To my love replied

My patient heart, and like a dreamer sighed,
'No, I do not maintain that such a clinging
Love is knowledge. What has been pried and tried

Has gone through fire. Nothing has been shied.
It is hawk and pelican. Its scars are tingling.'
'But love is longing too,' my love replied,

'And to renegue on this is to have lied.'
Still heart kept to its pitch like an old bell ringing:
'Love is knowledge. What has been pried and tried
But love – '
        'Is longing to,' my love replied.

The Well at New Place

I sit on the stone coping wall.

Nothing moved in the courtyard,
in the rose-fed, brick-kept heat.

He had buried his book
yet in the second it took to fall

a yearning fell through him
with the stone he tossed in the well.

The hit water moved of a piece
like an audience rising

and sleepwalking past him, coming to
in his own face, singled and pale.

I toss my stone in the well.

A Lighting Plot

for Brian Friel

Things I saw best when light was rectangular:
A dresser the sun reached framed in door-jambs,
Through a Dutch barn, snowed-in New England farms,
An aerodrome seen through an open hangar.

So not the apron stage: the picture frame.
Under the kilowatts, the croquet lawn,
The lord mayor's parlour, the pub yard at dawn.
Act One, the present time. Act Two, the same.

A window pane lies flattening the grass
And the grass bares itself for inspection.
The real is true hallucination.
Spotlight on Christy Mahon's looking glass.

Conquistadores galloping towards straw
Huts of a pueblo have found El Dorado.

An Open Letter

What is the source of our first suffering?
It lies in the fact that we hesitated to speak ...
It was born in the moment when we accumulated
silent things within us.
    GASTON BACHELARD

1

To Blake and Andrew, Editors,
Contemporary British Verse,
Penguin Books, Middlesex. Dear Sirs,
    My anxious muse,
Roused on her bed among the furze,
    Has to refuse

2

The adjective. It makes her blush.
It brings her out in a hot flush.
Before this she was called 'British'
    And acquiesced
But this time it's like the third wish,
    The crucial test.

3

Caesar's Britain, its *partes tres*,
United England, Scotland, Wales,
Britannia in the old tales,
    Is common ground.
Hibernia is where the Gaels
    Made a last stand

4

And long ago were stood upon –
End of simple history lesson.
As empire rings its curtain down
    This 'British' word
Sticks deep in native and *colon*
    Like Arthur's sword.

5

For weeks and months I've messed about,
Unclear, embarrassed and in doubt,
Footered, havered, spraughled, wrought
    Like Shauneen Keogh,
Wondering should I write it out
    Or let it go.

6

Anything for a quiet life.
Play possum and pretend you're deaf.
When awkward facts nag like the wife
    Look blank, go dumb.
To greet the smiler with the knife
    Smile back at him.

7

And what price then, self-preservation?
Your silence is an abdication.
Your Prince of Denmark hesitation
    You'll expiate
In Act Five, in desperation –
    Too much, too late.

8

And therefore it is time to break
Old inclinations not to speak
Which you defined already, Blake,
    Good advocate,
But if I clammed now for your sake
    I'd always rue it.

9

To think the title *Opened Ground*
Was the first title in your mind!
To think of where the phrase was found
    Makes it far worse!
To be supplanted in the end
    By *British* verse.

10

'Under a common flag,' said Larkin.
'Different history,' said Haughton.
Our own fastidious John Jordan
    Raised an eyebrow:
How British were the Ulstermen?
    He'd like to know.

11

Answer: as far as we are part
Of a new commonwealth of art,
Salute with independent heart
    And equally
Doff and flourish in your court
    Of poesie.

12

(I'll stick to *I*. Forget the *we*.
As Livy said, *pro se quisque*.
And Horace was exemplary
    At Philippi:
He threw away his shield to be
    A naked *I*.)

13

Yet doubts, admittedly, arise
When somebody who publishes
In *LRB* and *TLS*,
    The Listener –
In other words, whose audience is,
    Via Faber,

14

A British one, is characterized
As British. But don't be surprised
If I demur, for, be advised
    My passport's green.
No glass of ours was ever raised
    To toast *The Queen*.

15

No harm to her nor you who deign
To *God Bless* her as sovereign,
Except that from the start her reign
    Of crown and rose
Defied, displaced, would not combine
    What I'd espouse.

16

You'll understand I draw the line
At being robbed of what is mine,
My *patria*, my deep design
    To be at home
In my own place and dwell within
    Its proper name –

17

Traumatic Ireland! Checkpoints, cairns,
Slated roofs, stone ditches, ferns,
Dublin squares where sunset burns
    The Georgian brick –
The whole imagined country mourns
    Its lost, erotic

18

Aisling life. But I digress.
'The pang of ravishment.' Now guess
The author of that sweet hurt phrase.
    Lawrence? Wilde?
No way, my friends. In fact it was
    That self-exiled,

19

Vigilant, anti-cavalier,
Anti-pornographic, fear-
some scourge of diction that's impure,
    That Royal Navy
Poet of water-nymph and shire:
    Donald Davie.

20

The pattern of the patriot
Is Davie's theme: all polyglot
Newspeak conference flies he'd swot
    Who *lhude sing*
Foucault, Foucault. But that is not,   5
    Just now, my thing.

21

It is the way his words imply
That *patria* is maidenly
(Is 'pang of ravishment' not O. K.?)
    That touched me most
Who long felt my identity   5
    So rudely forc'd.

22

Tereu. Tereu. And tooraloo.
A shudder in the loins. And so
The twins for Leda. And twins too
    For the hurt North,
One island-green, one royal blue.   5
    An induced birth.

23

One a Provo, one a Para,
One Law and Order, one Terror –
It's time to break the cracked mirror
    Of this conceit.
It leads nowhere so why bother   5
    To work it out?

24

The hidden Ulster lies beneath.
A sudden blow, she collapsed with
The other island; and the South
    's been made a cuckold.
She has had family by them both,   5
    She's growing old

25

And scared that both have turned against her.
The cuckold's impotent in Leinster
House. The party in Westminster,
    All passion spent,
More down-and-out than sinister,
    Just pays the rent.

26

Exhaustion underlies the scene.
In Kensington, on Stephen's Green,
The slogans have all ceased to mean
    Or almost ceased –
Ulster is British is a tune
    Not quite deceased

27

In Ulster, though on 'the mainland' –
Cf., above, 'the other island' –
Ulster is part of Paddyland,
    And Londonderry
As far away as New England
    Or County Kerry.

28

So let's not raise a big hubbub.
Steer between Scylla and Charyb
A middle way that's neither glib
    Nor apocalyptic,
Suggested by the poet Holub
    In his Aesopic

29

Fable of proper naming, set
In a cinema: a man yells out
When a beaver's called a muskrat
    By the narrator,
Some Actors' Union hack, no doubt,
    Dubbed in later

30

On footage of the beaver dam –
Your usual, B-feature flim-flam.
Anyhow, as the creature swam
    And built and gnawed,
This man breaks out into a spasm
    Of constant, loud

31

And unembarrassed protestation.
Names were not for negotiation.
Right names were the first foundation
    For telling truth.
The audience, all irritation,
    Cries 'Shut your mouth!

32

'Does he have to spoil our evening out?
Who is this self-promoting lout?
Is it an epileptic bout?
    Muskrat? Who cares?
Get the manager. Get him out.
    To hell with beavers!'

33

Need I go on? I hate to bite
Hands that led me to the limelight
In the Penguin book, I regret
    The awkwardness.
But British, no, the name's not right.
    Yours truly, Seamus.

A Summer Night

When we left the bar at one in the morning
the air was balmy. We walked
past the Long Island State Bank
up Gnarled Hollow Road.

'It's eight in the evening at home,' she said
and as we went under the trees

I saw my first fireflies
sparking on the amorous silence.

They were the nearest thing
to what I had forgotten,
the phosphorescence off rat poison
being spread at eight on dark evenings.

They were neuter as the nineteen fifties
I had lived and missed,
standing disappointed at a dance
later on, at one in the morning

under a ball that sparked
and turned above the darkened floor.
I was teetotal, couldn't jive
and duty-danced the plain ones

and that was right
or what I was told was right.
They made do, I made do: we hovered,
clustered, flickered out.

Among the Whins

(from Chekhov's 'Donegal Notebook')

Wasps among sunlit whins. The confidence
Of the three men's punched and well-shod brogues
Faltered on the brae. The hot ditches
Shadowed them, the steep incline took them
From one another into what the whins,
That smelt of confidences, smelt of
To each of them, with the lark
Utterly itself in the afternoon.
They stopped of one accord but did not speak.
They turned away without seeming to turn
From one another into a story.
Which is going to speak? The vet remembers
A reeking horse-box at a point-to-point
Where he guides his partner's wife for shelter
As the crowd starts a rush for the cars
At the end of the meet. Suddenly

He hauls on the taut oiled wires and the door
Half-rises and hangs there, darkening them.
He turns, rubbing his hands clean under his arms
To take hold of the cleft small of her back
And smell deliberately at her perfumed neck
Tender to his half-shaved underlip.
They are excited in seconds but stop
Without speaking once and manage out
Into the crowd hurrying through the mud
To separate naturally and arrive
Hot and bothered with their soaked, half-gathered
Families, asking, 'Where's so and so?' And each
Gets settled, rubbing the windscreen, peering.
This is the vet's story he must tell
So the other two can begin on theirs.
Errigal stands over the horizon
And everything is going on as usual.
For example: as the bookie is telling
Of the local grocer's dud racehorse,
How he insured it first and then one night
Hunted it over the edge of a quarry-hole,
The grocer's son comes rattling on the scene
In an old pick-up and slows down and shouts,
'Some people I know have the great times of it!'

Anniversary Verse

Master Kieley, Guests and friends,
Tutors, tutees, alumni, students,
    You stair-case dwellers
Whose amplified hard rock and reggae
Resound from every dormitory,
You fiftieth anniversary
    Revellers,

Ye maids and swains of Adams House,
Ye actors, athletes, sexy muses,
    Ye gilded youth –
I rise to rise to the occasion
And not disgrace my art or nation
With verse that singe the old equation
    Of beauty and truth.

15 I rise as one who comes and goes
    Beneath your storied walls and windows
        A visitor,
    Part tourist and part faculty,
    An ethnic curiosity
20 Dubbed by grace of poetry
        Guest lecturer,

    Inspire me then, occasional muse,
    With verse to cure the exam blues
        And banished care,
25 To greet the old academic ghosts
    Who once caroused on the gold coast
    Whose love of learning vied with lusts
        For flesh and beer.

    And which we name imagination,
30 A word I cite with much elation
        And some unease
    Because it can sound slight and airy
    An entry in the dictionary,
    A bubble word. Yet while I'm wary
35   I realise

    All need its salutary power
    All men and women must beware
        Who would deny it
    And go against their childhoods grain
40 And dry up like earth parched for rain.
    They'll grow mechanical and then
        No drug or diet,

    No health farm, clinic, yoga course,
    No mantra *om*, no Star Wars force
45   Will compensate
    For what is lost when the mind divides.
    Even science now concedes
    The brain has two conjugal sides,
        The left and right,

50 To have to marry intuition
    To the analytic reason
        For psychic balance.
    Head sleeps with heart, begets a creature

Free yet cornered in its nature.
To be your whole self you must mate to your 55
    Brains and glands

Which is why I blessed the atmosphere
Of Adams House, and toast your master
    And his wife.
I toast good nature in the staff, 60
The way that nothing is done by half –
Those who work hard and still can laugh
    Are the spice of life.

Verses for a Fordham Commencement

Alumnae, alumni, graduates,
Laymen, laywomen, Jesuits
    And other orders,
Doctors, bachelors and masters,
Parents and guests, bishops, sisters, 5
And whoever else old Fordham musters
    Within her borders:

I rise to rise to the occasion
And not disgrace my art or nation
    Because, although 10
The honour of this high degree
Is done to my name and to me,
It's done to poetry equally
    And Ireland also.

By now you've gathered from the rhymes 15
And the tune being played upon the lines
    That these are stanzas;
Yet so far you have felt no pain,
Confusion has not dimmed your brain,
In fact the meaning's made more plain 20
    As sight by lenses.

For clarity's what verse is good for.
It is a kind of *aide-memoire*,
    A metronome
That ticks beneath the pace of talk 25
As feet convey you when you walk,

Shuttling on and shuttling back
    On speech's loom.

And though it's often rhetoric,
It can be casual and domestic,
    It can be quaint.
Its rules are strict, yet curiously
You keep its rules and find you're free
To say all that you need to say
    Without constraint.

Verse comes from *versus*, meaning turns
At the ends of lines, and Robert Burns
    Was master o' it:
Whether in dialogue with a mouse
Or in the Sabbath meeting house
Discoursing with the common louse
    On a lady's bonnet –

And when my speaker's mind was blank
Burns was the man I had to thank
    For inspiration.
Like dancers on a barn-dance floor
His jaunty stanzas called for more.
He said the poet was to the fore
    In every nation.

In ancient Ireland, poems of praise,
In Languedoc, ballades and lays,
    In Greece, the epic;
In Rome, the epistle and the ode;
In Japan, *haiku*; in Wales, *cynghanedd*;
Even the Britons, smeared with woad,
    Spoke verse in public.

And so, to mark commencement day,
I thought, why not the USA?
    Why not recite
A formal ode for graduates
On learning and how it relates
To life, how it disseminates
    Sweetness and light.

Inspire me, then, didactic muse,
Beyond clichés and pompous views

Of art and science,
To be *dulce et utile*,
To speak sweetly and usefully
About the world and th'academy
    And their alliance.

Or is it not a misalliance,
Ivory towers in a world of violence
    And corporate money.
Are college walls perhaps a door
Shut on the workers and the poor
While the privileged and the few ignore
    The unwashed many?

Do we not mystify the facts
And milk the taxpayer of his tax
    By the illusion
That our minds serve much higher ends
Than bending backs and blistered hands?
How much of common good depends
    On education?

In other words, dear graduates,
How do we justify our fates
    As an upper crust
With handfuls of credit cards and dollars
In hands as pale as our white collars?
The question makes me want to holler
    All flesh is dust.

It makes me say such status symbols
Are trivial as sewers' thimbles
    And just as hard
For they can form a callous shell
Against the little pricking needle
Of other people's need, and kill
    The feeling heart

But here, perhaps, I should explain
I was the eldest child of nine
    And I have brothers
Who barkeep, schoolteach – and don't write.
One labours on a building site.
One milks a herd morning and night
    And in all weathers.

My father bargained on fair days.
My mother's father worked the railways
       And linen mills.
One uncle drove a rural breadvan.
One aunt was more farmhand than woman.
One who became an enclosed nun
       Worked in hotels.

So part of me half stands apart
Beyond the pale of books and art
       And is not moved
Until they justify their place
And win their rights and can keep face,
Until their value for the race
       Is really proved.

Poetry even, that I love best,
Was put severely to the test
       In recent years
By guns in streets, bombs on the tracks
Human flesh in plastic sacks,
Excremental prison blocks
       And astonished tears

On the streets of Derry and Belfast
At bombers burst in their own blast,
       At restaurants
Exploding with their clientèle,
At berserk police like hounds of hell,
Shots fired at the funeral,
       The country rampant.

In face of which who can believe
What will survive of us is love,
       As the poet says?
And this is far from the whole story.
There is the nuclear armoury
To blight the earth to a dead berry
       Hung in space.

So the manuscript, the drawing board,
The microscope, the Bronze Age hoard,
       The library,
That studious concentrated hush
When the bird of mind flits from its bush

And sings its truths like a wise thrush
      Inspired and merry –

Long college years cloistered with books
And microfilms and cards and stacks
      Of dictionaries,
Warm afternoons in lecture halls,
Nostalgic walks past ivied walls,
And extra-mural bacchanals
      Seem luxuries,

Seem at times escapes, evasions
Of evil times, the fates of nations,
      But only seem
Because, that evil be withstood,
These acts of mind are kindling wood
To fire the beacons of that good
      Eternal dream

The dream that mind's enlightenment
Will restore man as he was meant
      To be before
His mind was darkened by the Fall.
Or, if that is too pat and doctrinal,
Say instead that man's survival
      In his brute nature

Is not the goal of history
But rather man's self-mastery
      And then, transcendence.
Say understanding civilizes,
Wakens responsibilities,
Promotes ideas of peace and justice
      And demotes vengeance.

Which is why, before the first college
Was built on earth, the men of knowledge
      Were sacrosanct:
Magi, druids, seers and augurs,
Brehons, temple priests, witch doctors
And a thousand other characters
      Long since defunct.

They all had place and influence,
They were, as 'twere, both shrinks and gurus,

185	They all had tenure.
	Then so had the philosopher.
	Aristotle taught Alexander
	So the king of kings learnt to revere
	That learned senior.
190	Yet between the intellectuals and
	The powers that be on sea and land
	Conflict's assumed.
	In any educated forum
	The index of banned *liberorum*
195	And the church's power to censor 'em
	Will be condemned.
	As will the case of Galileo.
	But even popes with names like Leo –
	I love the rhymes –
200	Men orthodox and autocratic
	Who would keep the sum of knowledge static,
	Men stern and anti-democratic
	And behind the times,
	They too praised liberal pursuits,
205	Employed artists and Jesuits
	And blessed the hermits.
	Home decoration was their game.
	Their employees soon made their name.
	Raphael's and Michelangelo's fame
210	Was great as Kermit's.
	So even though some torturers
	And SS men were connoisseurs,
	In general
	History implies equation
215	Between the good and education.
	An unselfish self-cultivation
	Is the ideal.
	And here 'unselfish' must be stressed.
	No good emerging with the best
220	Qualifications
	If that is going to make you proud
	And cut you off from the usual crowd,
	Your neighbours, say, vulgar and loud,
	Your poor relations.

The diapers that you first dressed in
And now your cap and gown of ermine,
    Which, would you say,
Will mean the more at the very end?
Those powdered folds pinned tight around
Your little backside, or this grand
    Scholar's regalia?

All of us are amphibious
Between our universities
    And where we come from.
No one gets born in a campus bed.
Even the trendiest School of Ed.
Has never weaned or bathed or breastfed
    Or cleaned a bum.

No co-ed dorm supplies the joys
Of an attic full of dusty toys
    And old dolls' houses.
No faculty of engineering
Repeats the thrill of tinkering
With model planes, that hankering
    To fly with aces.

It seems illiterate solitude
Is the first place where the true and good
    Awakens in us.
The later freedom we call *leisure*
Cannot supply that buried treasure
Which is the basis and the measure
    Of personalities

And which we name *imagination*,
A word I cite with much elation
    And some unease
Because it can sound slight and airy,
An entry in the dictionary,
A bubble word. Yet while I'm wary
    I realize

I still want to declare its great
Sustaining force, early and late,
    From youth to age.
It does not mean just fancy thoughts.
Accountants, lawyers, graduates

265 　　In medicine, as well as poets
　　　　　Using language –

　　All need its salutary power.
　　All men and women must beware
　　　　Who would deny it
270 　And go against their childhood's grain
　　And dry up like earth parched for rain.
　　　　They'll grow mechanical and then
　　No drug or diet

　　No health-farm, clinic, yoga course,
275 　No mantra *om*, no *Star Wars* force
　　　　Will compensate
　　For what is lost when the mind divides.
　　Even science now concedes
　　The brain has two conjugal sides,
280 　　　The left and right.

　　That have to marry intuition
　　To the analytic reason
　　　　For psychic balance.
　　Head sleeps with heart, begets a creature
285 　Free yet cornered in its nature.
　　To be your whole self, you must mate your
　　　　Brains and glands.

　　So scholarship and art must be
　　Fragrant with personality
290 　　　And moral feeling.
　　Distinction's not an ego-trip.
　　Good luck helps many to the top
　　Yet once up there you still can slip
　　　　And keep on falling.

295 　Everything flows, an old Greek said.
　　Nothing's secure. Gold's only lead
　　　　When you stop to think.
　　On your way up, show consideration
　　To the ones you meet on their way down.
300 　The Latin root of *condescension*
　　　　Means we all sink.

　　Let self-will be anathema.
　　Let the hierarchy and Mafia

    Join hand in glove
To doom and excommunicate   305
Whoever's not compassionate,
Whoever will not contemplate
    The world through love.

So now, together, *gaudeamus*,
Because, as sure as my name's Seamus   310
    To-day's the day
For *homo ludens'* revelry
Ad majorem gloriam dei.
Rejoice then, and as jazzmen say,
    Take it away   315

Onwards towards the sasparilla,
Jack Daniels, Bushmills, Schlitz and Miller,
    The dry martini –
And if the drier types demur
Or if your dates object, declare   320
You were prescribed *whiskey galore*
    By *Doctor* Heaney.

Ulster Quatrains

1 Sectarian Water

I loved soft water, rain water,
Water from the barrel, from the spouts.
It sudded like the vowels in *liturgy*.
It was a soft church-latin *c*.

But ours was a hard water country.   5
Sprung from untainted limestone, cold as glass,
It made the soap scum and ringed the basin.
It was a stiff-necked *k* in the meeting house.

2 Sectarian Latin

Weni, widi, wiki – the black gown
And wide mouth were pure Holbein.
He was pale fingers in a paved text
And spoke black-letter exegesis.

5   We watched him, cute as foxes, and construed
    With the best of them. But when we read
    Our *veni, vidi, vici* was outlandish
    And hedge-schooled as a hunted brush.

   3 *Sectarian Alphabet*

    Here is a sectarian alphabet.
    R is *or* in Dublin, *ar* in Belfast.
    If you *haitch* for *H*, you're Catholic.
    Protestant surnames with an O prefix
5   Descend from soup and turncoat Catholics.
    Enough? Enough. But while we're on to names:
    Seamus – which I got instead of James –
    Our Registrar of Births entered as *Shames*.

Pastoral

White bones that roving dogs had gnawed,
Lying scattered on the grazing
Like prehistoric flint tools, showed
The rock-bottom of living.

5   From soup-pots and brown roasting-pans
    The sawed-up skeletons were cast
    For scavengers to suck and cleanse
    And drop there in the bleaching grass.

    Cows with eyes as round as bowls
10 Chewed their rumbling cuds and stared
    Into nowhere past the gulls
    That keened above the cows' green boneyard.

Expectant

From Cork to Malin the rummaging tide
Sluices, spends itself round promontory,
Lighthouse, harbour and swallowing haven,
A bag of waters at whose centre I
5   Lie staring like an early-wakened bride.

Late May, with its birds, buds and brightening air
Leaves so long from dawn to rising!
I lie still under my mound and the drift
Of white linen, fingering my gold ring,
Knowing this fellow in me will not tire   10

For he works away beyond the heat and cold,
Prospecting light, making me his tunnel.
I finger at the ring: a helm, a landmark.
Like wet grain that will heave apart the hold
My baby moves inside the cargoed dark.   15

Station Island III

I got back into the driver's seat. Sunlight
moved apple-green over the hill farms,
a lough came clear, bog-cotton bowed its wet

grey head, dried white and raced the wind
that shook the car with its soft buffetings.   5
The airiness of being on high ground

lifted me, I let the brake off, ran
rumbling downhill without the engine,
got into gear and started and began

relaxing to the road and the car's rhythms.   10
It was twenty years since I had done the station.
Busloads of students after the exams –

we were a credit, they could be proud of us,
those parents who sacrificed, those other
dour and threadbare founders in birettas   15

whose faces swam and faded: a road-block
swung into view as I took a corner
fluently at speed, so that I had to brake

and creep past soldiers flattened in the hedge
with guns cradled on tripods covering me,   20
up to three halted 'pigs' under camouflage.

The tightness and the stillness round that space
when the car stops in the road, the troops take in
its make and number, and, as one bends his face

25 towards your window, you catch sight of more
in a field beyond, hunkering with intent
behind black pupils with a perfect bore –

it has all the pure calm of nightmare,
like standing throat-deep in a pool, your head
30 a severed head on a pane of water.

'Name, sir? Driving license? Destination?'
The light flotsam of his intonation
skimmed past me, like a bit part in Shakespeare,

Cockney as Keats or O *What A Lovely War*.
35 How different were the words *home, Christ, ale, master*,
on his lips and on mine! 'Just step out, sir.

Open your boot. And sign this document.'
Yet why should I fear him less than my own neighbour
in the khaki of his Ulster regiment,

40 his guttural 'Where are you coming from?'
feral, staccato and familiar
as the muffled drumbeats of a July drum?

'This island, sir. We've had a lot to-day
heading across there. What's it all about?'
45 'They're pilgrims. It's a kind of purgatory,'

I answered. He was handing back the license
but shouted to his mates up in the turret
of a 'pig': 'It's the bible-thumpers

we're getting through this area. O.K.,
50 you can drive on now, sir.' Two riflemen
waved their rifles to motion me away,

a little emptier, as always, drained
bodiless almost, as if their armament
and insolence, natural or trained,

55 had flushed out of me everything I was
so all that was left was bone I had betrayed
and the steering wheel in my obedient paws.

But soon it felt like a fictional event,
the temper of the voice irrelevant
60 to blowing heather, cloud shadow, bent

thorn trees in the roadside, lanes to farms
I never entered but without entering knew
their dog-barks, chain-clinks, puddles and mildew.

To be at one with things. A piled-up cairn,
a ploughed field in Ulster white with gulls.   65
I began to roar, 'I hate where I was born,

I hate my neighbour, hate everything that made me
biddable and unforthcoming.' And so
I drove for the border, a goaded shadow.

Shelf Life

I *Old Perfume Bottle*

When he said *musk* big generative
waterwheels in me plashed and lavished
and all the weirs ran slick and I thought of
the stunted keepsake perfume bottle
I picked out of heavy clay years ago.   5
As I washed and polished at it, welted glass
showed lucent and replete, and puckered too
with trade-mark lettering around the base
that felt like the berried edge of scar tissue.

Not quite an *objet*, and though it does not   10
smell, not absolutely a glass flower.
Breathe on the glass, for example, and it
mists, as if you said *balsam* to it, or *rosewater*.

II *Pussy Willow*

All greying sideburns, a spray of scuts,
diminished antlers and cast antler velvets,
pussy willow neither flowers nor withers
but conjures up the pearled, mid-forties weathers –
a girt Penelope spell-bound in a besom   5
and yearning to unwizen into blossom.

III *Pewters*

Not the age of silver, more a slither
of illiteracy under rafters.
Amoeba-glows in an old pewter plate
full of nebulae, molten and temperate.

Odi et amo, glimmers I am composed of.
Numinous sludge, far conscience-glitters
and the hang-dog, half-truth earnests of true love.
And a whole blizzard-melt of ancestors.

Old pewter, my masters! A soft option
when it comes to metals – next to solder
that beals at the touch of a hot iron.
Doleful and placid as the gloss-barked alder

reflected in the glaucous lid of a pool
where they thought I had drowned one winter day
in nineteen forty-two or three, when the whole
country was mist and I hid deliberately.

Station Island IV

Everything still. The thump as the car door shut
reported like a distant quarry blast
soundproofed across miles of standing heat;

and now the heat was muttering with a boat
I searched for where it bobbed against the glare
in and out of focus like a mote.

Behind it, the black line of the island
with its dome and hostel, and all around
low hills, baled hay, whin bushes blossoming.

Sunshine. *Mea culpa.* I foresaw
penitents in shirtsleeves and blouses
coming barefoot from the basilica

out to an iron cross to renounce the world
that shimmered up at them
toiling among stone beds, intent and sunburned.

Ave and *Gloria*. I had sleepwalked
to the fold, among bead-clicks and murmurs,
back into that dolorous book of hours,

the fug of confessionals, altars
where candles died insinuating slight
intimate smells of wax at body heat.

I heard the boat
clunk to and next thing was being handed down
into it where it rocked on its reflection.

As other pilgrims boarded, a wobbly
tilt and lift rose through me, crouching
on the thwarts, estranged in my own body,

my eyes shut, my arms tight round my knees.
Then the load had filled, the movement steadied,
I relaxed to casual voices,

an outboard motor sputtering, a slow
heave and slicing forward as we cast off
and spray came spitting in over the prow.

Another jetty loomed. Shadows rose
like trees burning in the sun above us,
then through a stirred-up desultory buzz

of voices a voice I recognized
shouted and swore and then apologized
for swearing, all in one breath, as I was hoisted

up off the dipping gunwale. 'Get them off.'
He pointed at my shoes. 'The primrose path
ends here, my boy. On behalf of

your barefoot generations, welcome, welcome!'
As ever, he was stern and humorous
and I was not even surprised to meet him

for he had always seemed a familiar
of famished, stony places, anywhere
heartfelt and desolate – wallsteads, Gaeltacht roads.

He stood there smiling as I bent down
to unlace my shoes, as if I had pleased him
at last, oblivious of the obstruction

                he caused the people who were disembarking
                all around us. Then he started to sing,
                his head to one side, the old turned-in look

55   in his eyes, and the torqued sorrowing gracenotes
                made a well of twilight in the afternoon
                where others gathered quietly in a ring.

                Everything still. They were all listening
                beyond themselves. They had gone round and round
60   the stone circles of beds and round the island

                so many times now everything was wound
                in one fixed gaze ahead. But suddenly
                a shout: 'Is this St Patrick's Purgatory

                or is it not?' A bad-tempered, scuffed soutane
65   and flat biretta came hurrying down
                the jetty, barking, 'Come on, come on,

                what do you think this is? A Dublin disco?
                Back to your pilgrimage, the lot of you.'
                And the place was cleared, as if a warning shot

70   had scared the birds off fields of new-sown corn.

A Night Piece for Tom Flanagan

                The dark has blotted out Howth Head,
                The family have gone to bed,
                The traffic eases on Strand Road,
                    The cork is drawn –
5   The kind of night, Tom, when we could
                    Talk until dawn.

                But since you cannot share the glass
                Familiars will take your place,
                Those famous shades you've raised for us
10   From our own dream;
                They're gathering around the house
                    Like moths round flame.

                I sense the nimble step of Tone,
                Our subtlest, mocking Jacobin.
15   He asks about this Flanagan

Who seems to know
The roll-call of United Men
  From Down to Mayo.

Maria Edgeworth rustles in,
Ripe blackberries piled in her tin,
(She sucks one as she sips the wine)
  She curtsies
To thank you, that you could condone
  Her class neurosis.

Next John Mitchel downs a mouthful,
Struts a bit, salutes your style
As different but still equal
  To bear the brunt.
You smile, he stares: the ironical
  Embalms the violent.

And here's an ironist you like.
A Mr Moore. But which? No pike-
man he, though he can wound and strike
  From his divan.
It is the author of *The Lake*,
  'More mob than man.'

What next? The accents of Tyrone!
The robust stagger of Carleton
(We recognize him, thanks to Ben)
  Has cleared the room
And will demand the poitin soon
  By the look of him.

So I get up, walk to the door,
Hear seabirds on the darkened shore
And think of one out walking there
  With his ash-plant,
Headed from Night-town to the Tower,
  By Sandymount.

Our *genius loci*, fount of inwit,
Our conscience-forger lifts his hat
And tips you an old world salute
  As if to say
'Yes, yes,' to you and all you write,
  Your mastery.

55 And now a bat flits from the trees
    To grow a form I recognize,
    The silent flap of W.B.'s
        Great soul in flight
    He circles thrice to greet you, flies
60   Into the night.

    Seven sages! They speak for me
    Who, this side idolatry,
    (A quote speaks volumes for the shy)
        Year after year
65 Take delight in your artistry,
        Arch-raconteur.

    I know you too recall with pleasure
    At P. J. Clarke's, the steak tartare;
    The night you read, in Terenure
70   Road East,
    The first draft of the first chapter;
        Many a feast

    On Bret Harte Road; Sonny Dalton
    In the rain; and in the sun,
75 Corned beef hash on Highway One.
        And Baggot Street –
    Doheny's snug! Ochone, ochone!
        When can we meet

    Again in that half-lit, musty lair,
80 That confessional atmosphere
    Where red herrings are *plat du jour*
        And reticences
    Are brewed up in the smoky air
        To confidences?

85 The tide is on the turn, though dawn
    Still wears black velvet gloves upon
    Her rosy fingers. But here's the moon
        As clouds unblock it.
    In your time zone, it will rise soon
90   On East Setauket.

    So love to Jean. To Ellen. Kate.
    To Drew. To Hope. And though it's late
    I'm going in to wet my throat

And drink a toast
To you, my friend, the out and out 95
   Gold medallist.

The Hag

She never moved from her corner.
She kept her hands to the blaze,
her elbows apart on her knees,
and savoured the heat off her clothes.

Yet the terrier kicking and kicking 5
wild fantails of mould
at the mouth of the burrow
was no more excited than she

once she found the scent of dissent.
She would pull the shawl to her cheek 10
not to hide but the better to gaze
as she drew you in to bad words

and her smile, that was clear of intent
to win or deceive, an unveiling
under the cowl, like a bride's 15
going drugged to her function.

This was no outburst at random
but a perfecting – as when the arrow's
free flight and absolute fall
prove the acme of rule. 20

A Paved Text

for Norman Nicholson

Dialect landlocked
in a maritime district,
stone walls in earshot
of rowlocks and the seawrack –

those Cumbrian phonetics 5
cracked like a plaited whip

    until the slack, nostalgic
    ambler in me trotted

    on the paved margin
10 of my own black pool –
    Dublin, black pool, *dubh linn*
    in words beyond the Pale,

    beyond Windscale, and Moyle
    that sank in the North Channel.
15 Now nuclear poisons
    re-anglicize a sea

    that is yours and mine as well,
    our saint-crossed, whitecapped, scouse-cursed
    swan-road and path of exile
20 become a dump for waste.

    Windscale: it was pristine,
    imagined and self-cleansing
    as the young, spray-blown Setanta
    at his feats with a *caman* –

25 say bat, or better, hurley –
    striking a silver ball,
    skimming ahead on the waves
    to intercept its fall.

    Setanta, doomed name also,
30 not yet the *Hound* of *Ulster*,
    Cuchulain, guardian, hero,
    dangerous wave-beheader.

The Easter House

    Unseal the undisturbed.
    Go through rock-silence, lime-sharp air,

    the acoustic galleries of *sepulchre*,
    brush past the shaking draperies

5 in the name *Joseph of Arimathea*;
    go back to your easter house behind the nettles.

The sticks are burning in the open,
the eggs boiling with whin blossom

in a corner full of quiet smoke
and the intent breath of children

playing with broken delph and lids
in the middle of the day.

They are in sanctuary,
in the dream that *easter house* has raised

in a marked-off trodden area
canopied with cow-parsley.

And was this all it meant?
They are disappointed with its appointments,

cups with no handles, an old kettle,
the tin blackening on flames that can't be seen

because of the unclouded sun.
No flute is going to sound for them,

no angel out of smoke
like a dusty forkful settling on a ruck

is going to seat himself, for them
or you, on the makeshift hearthstone.

Tremor

'When he jumps down out of a tree
Tarzan shakes the world.'
So Vinny Hunter would tell me
On the road to the school.

I had forgotten for years
Words so seismic and plain
That come back like rocked waters,
Possible again.

(1972)

STATION ISLAND (1984)

for Brian Friel

PART ONE

The Underground

There we were in the vaulted tunnel running,
You in your going-away coat speeding ahead
And me, me then like a fleet god gaining
Upon you before you turned to a reed

Or some new white flower japped with crimson   5
As the coat flapped wild and button after button
Sprang off and fell in a trail
Between the Underground and the Albert Hall.

Honeymooning, moonlighting, late for the Proms,
Our echoes die in that corridor and now   10
I come as Hansel came on the moonlit stones
Retracing the path back, lifting the buttons

To end up in a draughty lamplit station
After the trains have gone, the wet track
Bared and tensed as I am, all attention   15
For your step following and damned if I look back.

La Toilette

The white towelling bathrobe
ungirdled, the hair still wet,
first coldness of the underbreast
like a ciborium in the palm.

Our bodies are the temples   5
of the Holy Ghost. Remember?
And the little, fitted, deep-slit drapes
on and off the holy vessels

regularly? And the chasuble
so deftly hoisted? But vest yourself   10
in the word you taught me
and the stuff I love: slub silk.

Sloe Gin

The clear weather of juniper
darkened into winter.
She fed gin to sloes
and sealed the glass container.

When I unscrewed it
I smelled the disturbed
tart stillness of a bush
rising through the pantry.

When I poured it
it had a cutting edge
and flamed
like Betelgeuse.

I drink to you
in smoke-mirled, blue-black,
polished sloes, bitter
and dependable.

Away from it All

A cold steel fork
pried the tank water
and forked up a lobster:
articulated twigs, a rainy stone
the colour of sunk munitions.

In full view of the strand,
the sea wind spitting on the big window,
we plunged and reddened it,
then sat for hours in conclave
over the last of the claws.

It was twilight, twilight, twilight
as the questions hopped and rooted.
It was oarsmen's backs and oars
hauled against and lifting.
And more power to us, my friend,

hard at it over the dregs,

laying in in earnest
as the sea darkens
and whitens and darkens
and quotations start to rise

like rehearsed alibis:
I was stretched between contemplation
of a motionless point
and the command to participate
actively in history.

'*Actively?* What do you mean?'
The light at the rim of the sea
is rendered down to a fine
graduation, somewhere between
balance and inanition.

And I still cannot clear my head
of lives in their element
on the cobbled floor of that tank
and the hampered one, out of water,
fortified and bewildered.

Chekhov on Sakhalin

for Derek Mahon

So, he would pay his 'debt to medicine'.
But first he drank cognac by the ocean
With his back to all he travelled north to face.
His head was swimming free as the troikas

Of Tyumin, he looked down from the rail
Of his thirty years and saw a mile
Into himself as if he were clear water:
Lake Baikhal from the deckrail of the steamer.

That far north, Siberia was south.
Should it have been an ulcer in the mouth,
The cognac that the Moscow literati
Packed off with him to a penal colony –

Him, born, you may say, under the counter?
At least that meant he knew its worth. No cantor

15   In full throat by the iconostasis
     Got holier joy than he got from that glass

     That shone and warmed like diamonds warming
     On some pert young cleavage in a salon,
     Inviolable and affronting.
20   He felt the glass go cold in the midnight sun.

     When he staggered up and smashed it on the stones
     It rang as clearly as the convicts' chains
     That haunted him. In the months to come
     It rang on like the burden of his freedom

25   To try for the right tone – not tract, not thesis –
     And walk away from floggings. He who thought to squeeze
     His slave's blood out and waken the free man
     Shadowed a convict guide through Sakhalin.

Sandstone Keepsake

It is a kind of chalky russet
solidified gourd, sedimentary
and so reliably dense and bricky
I often clasp it and throw it from hand to hand.

5   It was ruddier, with an underwater
hint of contusion, when I lifted it,
wading a shingle beach on Inishowen.
Across the estuary light after light

came on silently round the perimeter
10 of the camp. A stone from Phlegethon,
bloodied on the bed of hell's hot river?
Evening frost and the salt water

made my hand smoke, as if I'd plucked the heart
that damned Guy de Montfort to the boiling flood –
15 but not really, though I remembered
his victim's heart in its casket, long venerated.

Anyhow, there I was with the wet red stone
in my hand, staring across at the watch-towers
from my free state of image and allusion,
20 swooped on, then dropped by trained binoculars:

a silhouette not worth bothering about,
out for the evening in scarf and waders
and not about to set times wrong or right,
stooping along, one of the venerators.

Shelf Life

1 *Granite Chip*

Houndstooth stone. Aberdeen of the mind.

Saying *An union in the cup I'll throw*
I have hurt my hand, pressing it hard around
this bit hammered off Joyce's Martello
Tower, this flecked insoluble brilliant 5

I keep but feel little in common with –
a kind of stone age circumcising knife,
a Calvin edge in my complaisant pith.
Granite is jaggy, salty, punitive

and exacting. *Come to me,* it says 10
*all you who labour and are burdened, I
will not refresh you.* And it adds, *Seize
the day.* And, *You can take me or leave me.*

2 *Old Smoothing Iron*

Often I watched her lift it
from where its compact wedge
rode the back of the stove
like a tug at anchor.

To test its heat by ear 5
she spat in its iron face
or held it up next her cheek
to divine the stored danger.

Soft thumps on the ironing board.
Her dimpled angled elbow 10
and intent stoop
as she aimed the smoothing iron

            like a plane into linen,
            like the resentment of women.
15   To work, her dumb lunge says,
            is to move a certain mass

            through a certain distance,
            is to pull your weight and feel
            exact and equal to it.
20   Feel dragged upon. And buoyant.

3 Old Pewter

Not the age of silver, more a slither
of illiteracy under rafters:
a dented hand-me-down old smoky plate
full of blizzards, sullied and temperate.

5   I love unshowy pewter, my soft option
    when it comes to the metals – next to solder
    that weeps at the touch of a hot iron;
    doleful and placid as a gloss-barked alder

    reflected in the nebulous lid of a pool
10 where they thought I had drowned one winter day
    a stone's throw from the house, when the whole
    country was mist and I hid deliberately.

    Glimmerings are what the soul's composed of.
    Fogged-up challenges, far conscience-glitters
15 and hang-dog, half-truth earnests of true love.
    And a whole late-flooding thaw of ancestors.

4 Iron Spike

So like a harrow pin
I hear harness creaks and the click
of stones in a ploughed-up field.
But it was the age of steam

5   at Eagle Pond, New Hampshire,
    when this rusted spike I found there
    was aimed and driven in
    to fix a cog on the line.

What guarantees things keeping
if a railway can be lifted
like a long briar out of ditch growth?
I felt I had come on myself

in the grassy silent path
where I drew the iron like a thorn
or a word I had thought my own
out of a stranger's mouth.

And the sledge-head that sank it
with a last opaque report
deep into the creosoted
sleeper, where is that?

And the sweat-cured haft?
Ask the ones on the buggy,
inaudible and upright
and sped along without shadows.

5 Stone from Delphi

To be carried back to the shrine some dawn
when the sea spreads its far sun-crops to the south
and I make a morning offering again:
*that I may escape the miasma of spilled blood,
govern the tongue, fear hybris, fear the god
until he speaks in my untrammelled mouth.*

6 A Snowshoe

The loop of a snowshoe hangs on a wall
in my head, in a room that is drift-still:
it is like a brushed longhand character,
a hieroglyph for all the realms of whisper.

It was to follow the snow goose of a word
I left the room after an amorous blizzard
and climbed up attic stairs like a somnambulist,
furred and warm-blooded, scuffling the snow-crust.

Then I sat there writing, imagining in silence
sounds like love sounds after long abstinence,
eager and absorbed and capable
under the sign of a snowshoe on a wall.

　　　　The loop of the snowshoe, like an old-time kite,
　　　　lifts away in a wind and is lost to sight.
15　　　Now I sit blank as gradual morning brightens
　　　　its distancing, inviolate expanse.

A Migration

　　　　About a mile above
　　　　and beyond our place,
　　　　in a house with a leaking roof
　　　　and cracked dormer windows
5　　　　Brigid came to live
　　　　with her mother and sisters.

　　　　So for months after that
　　　　she slept in a crowded bed
　　　　under the branch-whipped slates,
10　　　bewildered night after night
　　　　by starts of womanhood,
　　　　and a dream troubled her head

　　　　of a ship's passenger lounge
　　　　where empty bottles rolled
15　　　at every slow plunge
　　　　and lift, a weeping child
　　　　kept weeping, and a strange
　　　　flowing black taxi pulled

　　　　into a bombed station.
20　　　She would waken to the smell
　　　　of baby clothes and children
　　　　who snuggled tight, and the small
　　　　dormer with no curtain
　　　　beginning to go pale.

25　　　Windfalls lay at my feet
　　　　those days, clandestine winds
　　　　stirred in our lyric wood:
　　　　restive, quick and silent
　　　　the deer of poetry stood
30　　　in pools of lucent sound

　　　　ready to scare,
　　　　as morning and afternoon

Brigid and her sisters
came jangling along, down
the steep hill for water,   35
and laboured up again.

Familiars! A trail
of spillings in the dust,
unsteady white enamel
buckets looming. Their ghosts,   40
like their names, called from the hill
to 'Hurry', hurry past,

a spill of syllables.
I knew the story then.
Ferry Glasgow–Belfast,   45
then to the Dublin train
with their cases and boxes,
pram and cassette machine,

and then they miss the bus,
their last Wicklow connection –   50
the young ones scared and cross
in the lit bus station,
the mother at a loss.
And so in desperation

they start out for the suburbs   55
and into the small hours.
How it sweetens and disturbs
as they make their homesick tour,
a moonlight flit, street arabs,
the mother and her daughters   60

walking south through the land
past neon garages,
night lights haloed on blinds,
padlocked entries, bridges
swelling over a kind   65
mutter of streams, then trees

start filling the sky
and the estates thin out,
lamps are spaced more widely
until a cold moonlight   70
shows Wicklow's mountainy

　　　　black skyline, and they sit.

　　　　They change the cassette
　　　　but now the battery's gone.
75　　　They cannot raise a note.
　　　　When the first drops of rain
　　　　spit in the dark, Brigid
　　　　gets up and says, 'Come on.'

Last Look

in memoriam E.G.

　　　　We came upon him, stilled
　　　　and oblivious,
　　　　gazing into a field
　　　　of blossoming potatoes,
5　　　　his trouser bottoms wet
　　　　and flecked with grass seed.
　　　　Crowned blunt-headed weeds
　　　　that flourished in the verge
　　　　flailed against our car
10　　　but he seemed not to hear
　　　　in his long watchfulness
　　　　by the clifftop fuchsias.

　　　　He paid no heed that day,
　　　　no more than if he were
15　　　sheep's wool on barbed wire
　　　　or an old lock of hay
　　　　combed from a passing load
　　　　by a bush in the roadside.

　　　　He was back in his twenties,
20　　　travelling Donegal
　　　　in the grocery cart
　　　　of *Gallagher and Son,*
　　　　Merchant, Publican,
　　　　Retail and Import.
25　　　Flourbags, nosebags, buckets
　　　　of water for the horse
　　　　in every whitewashed yard.
　　　　Drama between hedges

if he met a Model Ford.

If Niamh had ridden up 30
to make the wide strand sweet
with inviting Irish,
weaving among hoofbeats
and hoofmarks on the wet
dazzle and blaze, 35
I think not even she
could have drawn him out
from the covert of his gaze.

Remembering Malibu

for Brian Moore

The Pacific at your door was wilder and colder
than my notion of the Pacific

and that was perfect, for I would have rotted
beside the luke-warm ocean I imagined.

Yet no way was its cold ascetic 5
as our monk-fished, snowed-into Atlantic;

no beehive hut for you
on the abstract sands of Malibu –

it was early Mondrian and his dunes
misting towards the ideal forms 10

though the wind and sea neighed loud
as wind and sea noise amplified.

I was there in the flesh
where I'd imagined I might be

and underwent the bluster of the day: 15
but why would it not come home to me?

Atlantic storms have flensed the cells
on the Great Skellig, the steps cut in the rock

I never climbed
between the graveyard and the boatslip 20

are welted solid to my instep.

But to rear and kick and cast that shoe –

beside that other western sea
far from the Skelligs, and far, far
from the suck of puddled, wintry ground,
our footsteps filled with blowing sand.

Making Strange

I stood between them,
the one with his travelled intelligence
and tawny containment,
his speech like the twang of a bowstring,

and another, unshorn and bewildered
in the tubs of his wellingtons,
smiling at me for help,
faced with this stranger I'd brought him.

Then a cunning middle voice
came out of the field across the road
saying, 'Be adept and be dialect,
tell of this wind coming past the zinc hut,

call me sweetbriar after the rain
or snowberries cooled in the fog.
But love the cut of this travelled one
and call me also the cornfield of Boaz.

Go beyond what's reliable
in all that keeps pleading and pleading,
these eyes and puddles and stones,
and recollect how bold you were

when I visited you first
with departures you cannot go back on.'
A chaffinch flicked from an ash and next thing
I found myself driving the stranger

through my own country, adept
at dialect, reciting my pride
in all that I knew, that began to make strange
at that same recitation.

The Birthplace

I

The deal table where he wrote, so small and plain,
the single bed a dream of discipline.
And a flagged kitchen downstairs, its mote-slants

of thick light: the unperturbed, reliable
ghost life he carried, with no need to invent.　　　　　5
And high trees round the house, breathed upon

day and night by winds as slow as a cart
coming late from market, or the stir
a fiddle could make in his reluctant heart.

II

That day, we were like one
of his troubled pairs, speechless
until he spoke for them,

haunters of silence at noon
in a deep lane that was sexual　　　　　5
with ferns and butterflies,

scared at our hurt,
throat-sick, heat-struck, driven
into the damp-floored wood

where we made an episode　　　　　10
of ourselves, unforgettable,
unmentionable,

and broke out again like cattle
through bushes, wet and raised,
only yards from the house.　　　　　15

III

Everywhere being nowhere,
who can prove
one place more than another?

We come back emptied,
to nourish and resist　　　　　5
the words of coming to rest:

*birthplace, roofbeam, whitewash,
flagstone, hearth,*
like unstacked iron weights

afloat among galaxies.
Still, was it thirty years ago
I read until first light

for the first time, to finish
The Return of the Native?
The corncrake in the aftergrass

verified himself, and I heard
roosters and dogs, the very same
as if he had written them.

Changes

As you came with me in silence
to the pump in the long grass

I heard much that you could not hear:
the bite of the spade that sank it,

the slithering and grumble
as the mason mixed his mortar,

and women coming with white buckets
like flashes on their ruffled wings.

The cast-iron rims of the lid
clinked as I uncovered it,

something stirred in its mouth.
I had a bird's eye view of a bird,

finch-green, speckly white,
nesting on dry leaves, flattened, still,

suffering the light.
So I roofed the citadel

as gently as I could, and told you
and you gently unroofed it

but where was the bird now?
There was a single egg, pebbly white,

and in the rusted bend of the spout
tail feathers splayed and sat tight.

So tender, I said, 'Remember this.
It will be good for you to retrace this path

when you have grown away and stand at last 25
at the very centre of the empty city.'

An Ulster Twilight

The bare bulb, a scatter of nails,
Shelved timber, glinting chisels:
In a shed of corrugated iron
Eric Dawson stoops to his plane

At five o'clock on a Christmas Eve. 5
Carpenter's pencil next, the spoke-shave,
Fretsaw, auger, rasp and awl,
A rub with a rag of linseed oil.

A mile away it was taking shape,
The hulk of a toy battleship, 10
As waterbuckets iced and frost
Hardened the quiet on roof and post.

Where is he now?
There were fifteen years between us two
That night I strained to hear the bells 15
Of a sleigh of the mind and heard him pedal

Into our lane, get off at the gable,
Steady his Raleigh bicycle
Against the whitewash, stand to make sure
The house was quiet, knock at the door 20

And hand his parcel to a peering woman:
'I suppose you thought I was never coming.'
Eric, tonight I saw it all
Like shadows on your workshop wall,

Smelled wood shavings under the bench, 25
Weighed the cold steel monkey-wrench
In my soft hand, then stood at the road
To watch your wavering tail-light fade

And knew that if we met again
In an Ulster twilight we would begin
And end whatever we might say
In a speech all toys and carpentry,

A doorstep courtesy to shun
Your father's uniform and gun,
But – now that I have said it out –
Maybe none the worse for that.

A Bat on the Road

*A batlike soul waking to consciousness of itself in
darkness and secrecy and loneliness.*

You would hoist an old hat on the tines of a fork
and trawl the mouth of the bridge for the slight
bat-thump and flutter. Skinny downy webs,

babynails clawing the sweatband . . . But don't
bring it down, don't break its flight again,
don't deny it; this time let it go free.

Follow its bat-flap under the stone bridge,
under the Midland and Scottish Railway
and lose it there in the dark.

Next thing it shadows moonslicked laurels
or skims the lapped net on a tennis court.
Next thing it's ahead of you in the road.

What are you after? You keep swerving off,
flying blind over ashpits and netting wire;
invited by the brush of a word like *peignoir*,

rustles and glimpses, shot silk, the stealth of floods
So close to me I could hear her breathing
and there by the lighted window behind trees

it hangs in creepers matting the brickwork
and now it's a wet leaf blowing in the drive,
now soft-deckled, shadow-convolvulus

by the White Gates. Who would have thought it? At the White Gates
She let them do whatever they liked. Cling there
as long as you want. There is nothing to hide.

A Hazel Stick for Catherine Ann

The living mother-of-pearl of a salmon
just out of the water

is gone just like that, but your stick
is kept salmon-silver.

Seasoned and bendy, 5
it convinces the hand

that what you have you hold
to play with and pose with

and lay about with.
But then too it points back to cattle 10

and spatter and beating
the bars of a gate –

the very stick we might cut
from your family tree.

The living cobalt of an afternoon 15
dragonfly drew my eye to it first

and the evening I trimmed it for you
you saw your first glow-worm –

all of us stood round in silence, even you
gigantic enough to darken the sky 20

for a glow-worm.
And when I poked open the grass

a tiny brightening den lit the eye
in the blunt cut end of your stick.

A Kite for Michael and Christopher

All through that Sunday afternoon
a kite flew above Sunday,
a tightened drumhead, an armful of blown chaff.

I'd seen it grey and slippy in the making,
I'd tapped it when it dried out white and stiff,
I'd tied the bows of newspaper
along its six-foot tail.

But now it was far up like a small black lark
and now it dragged as if the bellied string
were a wet rope hauled upon
to lift a shoal.

My friend says that the human soul
is about the weight of a snipe
yet the soul at anchor there,
the string that sags and ascends,
weigh like a furrow assumed into the heavens.

Before the kite plunges down into the wood
and this line goes useless
take in your two hands, boys, and feel
the strumming, rooted, long-tailed pull of grief.
You were born fit for it.
Stand in here in front of me
and take the strain.

The Railway Children

When we climbed the slopes of the cutting
We were eye-level with the white cups
Of the telegraph poles and the sizzling wires.

Like lovely freehand they curved for miles
East and miles west beyond us, sagging
Under their burden of swallows.

We were small and thought we knew nothing
Worth knowing. We thought words travelled the wires
In the shiny pouches of raindrops,

Each one seeded full with the light 10
Of the sky, the gleam of the lines, and ourselves
So infinitesimally scaled

We could stream through the eye of a needle.

Sweetpea

'What did Thought do?'
                       'Stuck
a feather in the ground and thought
it would grow a hen.'
                     Rod 5
by rod we pegged the drill for sweetpea
with light brittle sticks,
twiggy and unlikely in fresh mould,
and stalk by stalk we snipped
the coming blooms. 10

        And so when pain
had haircracked her old constant vestal stare
I reached for straws and thought:
seeing the sky through a mat of creepers,
like water in the webs of a green net, 15
opened a clearing where her heart sang
without caution or embarrassment, once or twice.

An Aisling in the Burren

A time was to come when we yearned
for the eel-drugged flats and dunes
of a northern shore, its dulse and its seabirds,
its divisions of brine-maddened grass
pouring over dykes to secure 5
the aftermath of the reign of the meek.
That was as much of hope that the purest
and saddest were prepared to allow for.

Out of those scenes she arrived, not from a shell
but licked with the wet cold fires of St Elmo, 10
angel of the last chance, teaching us

the fish in the rock, the fern's
bewildered tenderness deep in the fissure.

That day the clatter of stones
as we climbed was a sermon
on conscience and healing,
her tears a startling deer
on the site of catastrophe.

Widgeon

for Paul Muldoon

It had been badly shot.
While he was plucking it
he found, he says, the voice box —

like a flute stop
in the broken windpipe —

and blew upon it
unexpectedly
his own small widgeon cries.

Sheelagh na Gig

at Kilpeck

I

We look up at her
hunkered into her angle
under the eaves.

She bears the whole stone burden
on the small of her back and shoulders
and pinioned elbows,

the astute mouth, the gripping fingers
saying push, push hard,
push harder.

As the hips go high
her big tadpole forehead
is rounded out in sunlight.

And here beside her are two birds,
a rabbit's head, a ram's,
a mouth devouring heads.   15

   II

Her hands holding herself
are like hands in an old barn
holding a bag open.

I was outside looking in
at its lapped and supple mouth   5
running grain.

I looked up under the thatch
at the dark mouth and eye
of a bird's nest or a rat hole,

smelling the rose on the wall,   10
mildew, an earthen floor,
the warm depth of the eaves.

And then one night in the yard
I stood still under heavy rain
wearing the bag like a caul.   15

   III

We look up to her,
her ring-fort eyes,
her little slippy shoulders,

her nose incised and flat,
and feel light-headed looking up.   5
She is twig-boned, saddle-sexed,

grown-up, grown ordinary,
seeming to say,
'Yes, look at me to your heart's content

but look at every other thing.'   10
And here is a leaper in a kilt,
two figures kissing,

a mouth with sprigs,
a running hart, two fishes,
a damaged beast with an instrument.   15

The Loaning

I

As I went down the loaning
the wind shifting in the hedge was like
an old one's whistling speech. And I knew
I was in the limbo of lost words.

They had flown there from raftered sheds and crossroads,
from the shelter of gable ends and turned-up carts.
I saw them streaming out of birch-white throats
and fluttering above iron bedsteads
until the soul would leave the body.
Then on a day close as a stranger's breath
they rose in smoky clouds on the summer sky
and settled in the uvulae of stones
and the soft lungs of the hawthorn.

Then I knew why from the beginning
the loaning breathed on me, breathed even now
in a shiver of beaded gossamers
and the spit blood of a last few haws and rose-hips.

II

Big voices in the womanless kitchen.
They never lit a lamp in the summertime
but took the twilight as it came
like solemn trees. They sat on in the dark
with their pipes red in their mouths, the talk come down
to *Aye* and *Aye* again and, when the dog shifted,
a curt *There boy!* I closed my eyes
to make the light motes stream behind them
and my head went airy, my chair rode
high and low among branches and the wind
stirred up a rookery in the next long *Aye*.

III

Stand still. You can hear
everything going on. High-tension cables
singing above cattle, tractors, barking dogs,
juggernauts changing gear a mile away.
And always the surface noise of the earth

you didn't know you'd heard till a twig snapped
and a blackbird's startled volubility
stopped short.

   When you are tired or terrified
your voice slips back into its old first place   10
and makes the sound your shades make there . . .
When Dante snapped a twig in the bleeding wood
a voice sighed out of blood that bubbled up
like sap at the end of green sticks on a fire.

At the click of a cell lock somewhere now   15
the interrogator steels his *introibo*,
the light motes blaze, a blood-red cigarette
startles the shades, screeching and beseeching.

The Sandpit

1 *1946*

The first hole neat as a trapdoor
cut into grazing and
cut again as the heft and lift
begin, the plate scrabs field-stones
and a tremor blunts in the shaft   5
at small come-uppances meeting
the driven edge.
     Worms and starlight,
mould-balm on the passing cyclist's face.
The rat's nose in the plastered verge   10
where they walked to clean their boots.

2 *The Demobbed Bricklayer*

A fence post trimmed and packed
into place, but out of place:
       the soldier
not a soldier any more and never
quite a soldier, what has he   5
walked into? This is not the desert
night among cold ambulances,
not the absolute sand

of the world, the sun's whip
and grid –
                this sand,
this lustre in their heavy land
is greedy coppers hammered
in the wishing tree of their talk,
the damp ore of money.
                        Freckled
and demobbed, worked on like the soil
he is inhaling, he stands
remembering his trade, the song
of his trowel dressing a brickbat,
the tock and tap of its butt, the plumb-
line's certitude, the merriment
in the spirit level's eye.

3 The Sand Boom

A fortune in sand then. Sandpits and sandbeds.
River gravel drying in the brickyards.
Clay-scabbed flints, skimming stones of slate,
sandstone pebbles, birds' eggs of flecked granite
all rattled in the caked iron mouth
of the concrete mixer.
                        The first spadeful I saw
pitched up, the handful of gravel
I flung over the cribs,
until they burn in the fireball
or crumble at the edge of the blast
or drink the rain again on their flattened site,
are bonded and set to register
whatever beams and throbs into the wall.
Like undead grains in a stranded cockle shell.
Boulders listening behind the waterfall.

And this as well:
                foxgloves and saplings
on the worked-out pit floor, grass on the cracked
earth face, anglers nested in an overgrown
loading bay above the deepened stream.

4 *What the Brick Keeps*

His touch, his daydream of the tanks,
his point of vantage on the scaffolding
over chimneys and close hills at noontime,
the constant sound of hidden river water
the new estate rose up through –   5
with one chop of the trowel he sent it all
into the brick for ever.
It has not stopped travelling in
in the van of all that followed:
floors hammered down, the pipes' first   10
gulping flow, phone wires and flags
alive on the gable, a bedhead
thumping quickly, banged doors shaking
the joists, rippling the very roof tank.
And my own hands, the size of a grandchild's,   15
go in there, cold and wet, and my big gaze
at the sandpit opening by the minute.

The King of the Ditchbacks

for John Montague

I

As if a trespasser
unbolted a forgotten gate
and ripped the growth
tangling its lower bars –

just beyond the hedge   5
he has opened a dark morse
along the bank,
a crooked wounding

of silent, cobwebbed
grass. If I stop   10
he stops
like the moon.

He lives in his feet
and ears, weather-eyed,

15 all pad and listening,
    a denless mover.

    Under the bridge
    his reflection shifts
    sideways to the current,
20 mothy, alluring.

    I am haunted
    by his stealthy rustling,
    the unexpected spoor,
    the pollen settling.

II

I was sure I knew him. The time I'd spent obsessively in that upstairs room bringing myself close to him: each entranced hiatus as I chainsmoked and stared out the dormer into the grassy hillside I was laying myself open. He was depending on me as I hung out on the limb of a translated phrase like a youngster dared out on to an alder branch over the whirlpool. Small dreamself in the branches. Dream fears I inclined towards, interrogating:

— Are you the one I ran upstairs to find drowned under running water in the bath?
— The one the mowing machine severed like a hare in the stiff frieze of harvest?
— Whose little bloody clothes we buried in the garden?
— The one who lay awake in darkness a wall's breadth from the troubled hoofs?

After I had dared these invocations, I went back towards the gate to follow him. And my stealth was second nature to me, as if I were coming into my own. I remembered I had been vested for this calling.

III

When I was taken aside that day
I had the sense of election:

they dressed my head in a fishnet
and plaited leafy twigs through meshes

5   so my vision was a bird's
    at the heart of a thicket

and I spoke as I moved
like a voice from a shaking bush.

King of the ditchbacks,
I went with them obediently   10

to the edge of a pigeon wood –
deciduous canopy, screened wain of evening

we lay beneath in silence.
No birds came, but I waited

among briars and stones, or whispered   15
or broke the watery gossamers

if I moved a muscle.
'Come back to us,' they said, 'in harvest,

when we hide in the stooked corn,
when the gundogs can hardly retrieve   20

what's brought down.' And I saw myself
rising to move in that dissimulation,

top-knotted, masked in sheaves, noting
the fall of birds: a rich young man

leaving everything he had   25
for a migrant solitude.

PART TWO: STATION ISLAND

Station Island

I

A hurry of bell-notes
flew over morning hush
and water-blistered cornfields,
an escaped ringing
that stopped as quickly   5

as it started. *Sunday*,
the silence breathed

and could not settle back
for a man had appeared
at the side of the field

with a bow-saw, held
stiffly up like a lyre.
He moved and stopped to gaze
up into hazel bushes,
angled his saw in,

pulled back to gaze again
and move on to the next.
'I know you, Simon Sweeney,
for an old Sabbath-breaker
who has been dead for years.'

'Damn all you know,' he said,
his eye still on the hedge
and not turning his head.
'I was your mystery man
and am again this morning.

Through gaps in the bushes,
your First Communion face
would watch me cutting timber.
When cut or broken limbs
of trees went yellow, when

woodsmoke sharpened air
or ditches rustled
you sensed my trail there
as if it had been sprayed.
It left you half afraid.

When they bade you listen
in the bedroom dark
to wind and rain in the trees
and think of tinkers camped
under a heeled-up cart

you shut your eyes and saw
a wet axle and spokes
in moonlight, and me
streaming from the shower,
headed for your door.'

Sunlight broke in the hazels,
the quick bell-notes began
a second time. I turned
at another sound:
a crowd of shawled women   50

were wading the young corn,
their skirts brushing softly.
Their motion saddened morning.
It whispered to the silence,
'Pray for us, pray for us,'   55

it conjured through the air
until the field was full
of half-remembered faces,
a loosed congregation
that straggled past and on.   60

As I drew behind them
I was a fasted pilgrim,
light-headed, leaving home
to face into my station.
'Stay clear of all processions!'   65

Sweeney shouted at me
but the murmur of the crowd
and their feet slushing through
the tender, bladed growth
opened a drugged path   70

I was set upon.
I trailed those early-risers
who had fallen into step
before the smokes were up.
The quick bell rang again.   75

II

I was parked on a high road, listening
to peewits and wind blowing round the car
when something came to life in the driving mirror,

someone walking fast in an overcoat
and boots, bareheaded, big, determined   5
in his sure haste along the crown of the road

so that I felt myself the challenged one.
The car door slammed. I was suddenly out
face to face with an aggravated man

raving on about nights spent listening for
gun butts to come cracking on the door,
yeomen on the rampage, and his neighbour

among them, hammering home the shape of things.
'Round about here you overtook the women,'
I said, as the thing came clear. 'Your *Lough Derg Pilgrim*

haunts me every time I cross this mountain –
as if I am being followed, or following.
I'm on my road there now to do the station.'

'Oh holy Jesus Christ, does nothing change?'
His head jerked sharply side to side and up
like a diver surfacing,

then with a look that said, *who is this cub
anyhow*, he took cognizance again
of where he was: the road, the mountain top,

and the air, softened by a shower of rain,
worked on his anger visibly until:
'It is a road you travel on your own.

I who learned to read in the reek of flax
and smelled hanged bodies rotting on their gibbets
and saw their looped slime gleaming from the sacks –

hard-mouthed Ribbonmen and Orange bigots
made me into the old fork-tongued turncoat
who mucked the byre of their politics.

If times were hard, I could be hard too.
I made the traitor in me sink the knife.
And maybe there's a lesson there for you,

whoever you are, wherever you come out of,
for though there's something natural in your smile
there's something in it strikes me as defensive.'

'I have no mettle for the angry role,'
I said. 'I come from County Derry,
born in earshot of an Hibernian hall

where a band of Ribbonmen played hymns to Mary.
By then the brotherhood was a frail procession
staggering home drunk on Patrick's Day   45

in collarettes and sashes fringed with green.
Obedient strains like theirs tuned me first
and not that harp of unforgiving iron

the Fenians strung. A lot of what you wrote
I heard and did: this Lough Derg station,   50
flax-pullings, dances, summer crossroads chat

and the shaky local voice of education.
All that. And always, Orange drums.
And neighbours on the roads at night with guns.'

'I know, I know, I know, I know,' he said,   55
'but you have to try to make sense of what comes.
Remember everything and keep your head.'

'The alders in the hedge,' I said, 'mushrooms,
dark-clumped grass where cows or horses dunged,
the cluck when pith-lined chestnut shells split open   60

in your hand, the melt of shells corrupting,
old jampots in a drain clogged up with mud – '
But now Carleton was interrupting:

'All this is like a trout kept in a spring
or maggots sown in wounds –   65
another life that cleans our element.

We are earthworms of the earth, and all that
has gone through us is what will be our trace.'
He turned on his heel when he was saying this

and headed up the road at the same hard pace.   70

III

I knelt. Hiatus. Habit's afterlife . . .
I was back among bead clicks and the murmurs
from inside confessionals, side altars
where candles died insinuating slight

intimate smells of wax at body heat.   5
There was an active, wind-stilled hush, as if

in a shell the listened-for ocean stopped
and a tide rested and sustained the roof.

A seaside trinket floated then and idled
in a vision, like phosphorescent weed,
a toy grotto with seedling mussel shells
and cockles glued in patterns over it,

pearls condensed from a child invalid's breath
into a shimmering ark, my house of gold
that housed the snowdrop weather of her death
long ago. I would stow away in the hold

of our big oak sideboard and forage for it
laid past in its tissue paper for good.
It was like touching birds' eggs, robbing the nest
of the word *wreath*, as kept and dry and secret

as her name which they hardly ever spoke
but was a white bird trapped inside me
beating scared wings when *Health of the Sick*
fluttered its *pray for us* in the litany.

A cold draught blew under the kneeling boards.
I thought of walking round
and round a space utterly empty,
utterly a source, like the idea of sound;

like an absence stationed in the swamp-fed air
above a ring of walked-down grass and rushes
where we once found the bad carcass and scrags of hair
of our dog that had disappeared weeks before.

IV

Blurred swimmings as I faced the sun, my back
to the stone pillar and the iron cross,
ready to say the dream words *I renounce* . . .

Blurred oval prints of newly ordained faces,
'Father' pronounced with a fawning relish,
the sunlit tears of parents being blessed.

I met a young priest, glossy as a blackbird,
as if he had stepped from his anointing
a moment ago: his purple stole and cord

or cincture tied loosely, his polished shoes
unexpectedly secular beneath
a pleated, lace-hemmed alb of linen cloth.

His name had lain undisturbed for years
like an old bicycle wheel in a ditch
ripped at last from under jungling briars,

wet and perished. My arms were open wide
but I could not say the words. 'The rain forest,' he said,
'you've never seen the like of it. I lasted

only a couple of years. Bare-breasted
women and rat-ribbed men. Everything wasted.
I rotted like a pear. I sweated masses . . .'

His breath came short and shorter. 'In long houses
I raised the chalice above headdresses.
In hoc signo . . . On that abandoned

mission compound, my vocation
is a steam off drenched creepers.'
I had broken off from the renunciation

while he was speaking, to clear the way
for other pilgrims queueing to get started.
'I'm older now than you when you went away,'

I ventured, feeling a strange reversal.
'I never could see you on the foreign missions.
I could only see you on a bicycle,

a clerical student home for the summer
doomed to the decent thing. Visiting neighbours.
Drinking tea and praising home-made bread.

Something in them would be ratified
when they saw you at the door in your black suit,
arriving like some sort of holy mascot.

You gave too much relief, you raised a siege
the world had laid against their kitchen grottoes
hung with holy pictures and crucifixes.'

'And you,' he faltered, 'what are you doing here
but the same thing? What possessed you?
I at least was young and unaware

that what I thought was chosen was convention.
But all this you were clear of you walked into
over again. And the god has, as they say, withdrawn.

What are you doing, going through these motions?
Unless . . . Unless . . .' Again he was short of breath
and his whole fevered body yellowed and shook.

'Unless you are here taking the last look.'
Suddenly where he stood was bare as the roads
we both had grown up beside, where a sick man

had taken his last look one drizzly evening
when steam rose like the first breath of spring,
a knee-deep mist I waded silently

behind him, on his circuits, visiting.

V

An old man's hands, like soft paws rowing forward,
groped for and warded off the air ahead.
Barney Murphy shuffled on the concrete.
Master Murphy. I heard the weakened voice
bulling in sudden rage all over again
and fell in behind, my eyes fixed on his heels
like a man lifting swathes at a mower's heels.
His sockless feet were like the dried broad bean
that split its stitches in the display jar
high on a window in the old classroom,
white as shy faces in the classroom door.
'Master,' those elders whispered, 'I wonder, master . . .',
rustling envelopes, proffering them, withdrawing,
and 'Master' I repeated to myself
so that he stopped but did not turn or move,
his shoulders gone quiet and small, his head
vigilant in the cold gusts off the lough.
I moved ahead and faced him, shook his hand.

Above the winged collar, his mottled face
went distant in a smile as the voice
readied itself and husked and scraped, 'Good man,
good man yourself,' before it lapsed again
in the limbo and dry urn of the larynx.

The adam's apple in its weathered sac
worked like the plunger of a pump in drought
but yielded nothing to help the helpless smile.
Morning field smells came past on the wind,
the sex-cut of sweetbriar after rain,
new-mown meadow hay, bird's nests filled with leaves.
'You'd have thought that Anahorish School
was purgatory enough for any man,'
I said. 'You've done your station.'
Then a little trembling happened and his breath
rushed the air softly as scythes in his lost meadows.
'Birch trees have overgrown Leitrim Moss,
dairy herds are grazing where the school was
and the school garden's loose black mould is grass.'
He was gone with that and I was faced wrong way
into more pilgrims absorbed in this exercise.
As I stood among their whispers and bare feet
the mists of all the mornings I set out
for Latin classes with him, face to face,
refreshed me. *Mensa, mensa, mensam*
sang in the air like a busy whetstone.

'We'll go some day to my uncle's farm at Toome – '
Another master spoke. '*For what is the great
moving power and spring of verse? Feeling, and
in particular, love.* When I went last year
I drank three cups of water from the well.
It was very cold. It stung me in the ears.
You should have met him – ' Coming in as usual
with the rubbed quotation and his cocked bird's eye
dabbing for detail. *When you're on the road
give lifts to people, you'll always learn something.*
There he went, in his belted gaberdine,
and after him, a third fosterer,
slack-shouldered and clear-eyed: 'Sure I might have known
once I had made the pad, you'd be after me
sooner or later. Forty-two years on
and you've got no farther! But after that again,
where else would you go? Iceland, maybe? Maybe the Dordogne?'

And then the parting shot. 'In my own day
the odd one came here on the hunt for women.'

VI

Freckle-face, fox-head, pod of the broom,
Catkin-pixie, little fern-swish:
Where did she arrive from?
Like a wish wished
And gone, her I chose at 'secrets'
And whispered to. When we were playing houses.
I was sunstruck at the basilica door –
A stillness far away, a space, a dish,
A blackened tin and knocked over stool –
Like a tramped neolithic floor
Uncovered among dunes where the bent grass
Whispers on like reeds about Midas's
Secrets, secrets. I shut my ears to the bell.
Head hugged. Eyes shut. Leaf ears. *Don't tell. Don't tell.*

A stream of pilgrims answering the bell
Trailed up the steps as I went down them
Towards the bottle-green, still
Shade of an oak. Shades of the Sabine farm
On the beds of Saint Patrick's Purgatory.
Late summer, country distance, not an air:
Loosen the toga for wine and poetry
Till Phoebus returning routs the morning star.
As a somnolent hymn to Mary rose
I felt an old pang that bags of grain
And the sloped shafts of forks and hoes
Once mocked me with, at my own long virgin
Fasts and thirsts, my nightly shadow feasts,
Haunting the granaries of words like *breasts*.

As if I knelt for years at a keyhole
Mad for it, and all that ever opened
Was the breathed-on grille of a confessional
Until that night I saw her honey-skinned
Shoulder-blades and the wheatlands of her back
Through the wide keyhole of her keyhole dress
And a window facing the deep south of luck
Opened and I inhaled the land of kindness.
*As little flowers that were all bowed and shut
By the night chills rise on their stems and open
As soon as they have felt the touch of sunlight,*

So I revived in my own wilting powers 40
And my heart flushed, like somebody set free.
Translated, given, under the oak tree.

VII

I had come to the edge of the water,
soothed by just looking, idling over it
as if it were a clear barometer

or a mirror, when his reflection
did not appear but I sensed a presence 5
entering into my concentration

on not being concentrated as he spoke
my name. And though I was reluctant
I turned to meet his face and the shock

is still in me at what I saw. His brow 10
was blown open above the eye and blood
had dried on his neck and cheek. 'Easy now,'

he said, 'it's only me. You've seen men as raw
after a football match . . . What time it was
when I was wakened up I still don't know 15

but I heard this knocking, knocking, and it
scared me, like the phone in the small hours,
so I had the sense not to put on the light

but looked out from behind the curtain.
I saw two customers on the doorstep 20
and an old landrover with the doors open

parked on the street so I let the curtain drop;
but they must have been waiting for it to move
for they shouted to come down into the shop.

She started to cry then and roll round the bed, 25
lamenting and lamenting to herself,
not even asking who it was. 'Is your head

astray, or what's come over you?' I roared, more
to bring myself to my senses
than out of any real anger at her 30

for the knocking shook me, the way they kept it up,
and her whingeing and half-screeching made it worse.
All the time they were shouting 'Shop!

Shop!' so I pulled on my shoes and a sportscoat
and went back to the window and called out,
'What do you want? Could you quieten the racket

or I'll not come down at all.' 'There's a child not well.
Open up and see what you have got – pills
or a powder or something in a bottle,'

one of them said. He stepped back off the footpath
so I could see his face in the street lamp
and when the other moved I knew them both.

But bad and all as the knocking was, the quiet
hit me worse. She was quiet herself now,
lying dead still, whispering to watch out.

At the bedroom door I switched on the light.
'It's odd they didn't look for a chemist.
Who are they anyway at this time of the night?'

she asked me, with the eyes standing in her head.
'I know them to see,' I said, but something
made me reach and squeeze her hand across the bed

before I went downstairs into the aisle
of the shop. I stood there, going weak
in the legs. I remember the stale smell

of cooked meat or something coming through
as I went to open up. From then on
you know as much about it as I do.'

'Did they say nothing?' 'Nothing. What would they say?'
'Were they in uniform? Not masked in any way?'
'They were barefaced as they would be in the day,

shites thinking they were the be-all and the end-all.'
'Not that it is any consolation,
but they were caught,' I told him, 'and got jail.'

Big-limbed, decent, open-faced, he stood
forgetful of everything now except
whatever was welling up in his spoiled head,

beginning to smile. 'You've put on weight
since you did your courting in that big Austin
you got the loan of on a Sunday night.'

Through life and death he had hardly aged. 70
There always was an athlete's cleanliness
shining off him and except for the ravaged

forehead and the blood, he was still that same
rangy midfielder in a blue jersey
and starched pants, the one stylist on the team, 75

the perfect, clean, unthinkable victim.
'Forgive the way I have lived indifferent –
forgive my timid circumspect involvement,'

I surprised myself by saying. 'Forgive
my eye,' he said, 'all that's above my head.' 80
And then a stun of pain seemed to go through him

and he trembled like a heatwave and faded.

VIII

Black water. White waves. Furrows snowcapped.
A magpie flew from the basilica
and staggered in the granite airy space
I was staring into, on my knees
at the hard mouth of St Brigid's Bed. 5
I came to and there at the bed's stone hub
was my archaeologist, very like himself,
with his scribe's face smiling its straight-lipped smile,
starting at the sight of me with the same old
pretence of amazement, so that the wing 10
of woodkerne's hair fanned down over his brow.
And then as if a shower were blackening
already blackened stubble, the dark weather
of his unspoken pain came over him.
A pilgrim bent and whispering on his rounds 15
inside the bed passed between us slowly.

'Those dreamy stars that pulsed across the screen
beside you in the ward – your heartbeats, Tom, I mean –
scared me the way they stripped things naked.
My banter failed too early in that visit. 20

     I could not take my eyes off the machine.
     I had to head back straight away to Dublin,
     guilty and empty, feeling I had said nothing
     and that, as usual, I had somehow broken
25   covenants, and failed an obligation.
     I half-knew we would never meet again . . .
     Did our long gaze and last handshake contain
     nothing to appease that recognition?'

     'Nothing at all. But familiar stone
30   had me half-numbed to face the thing alone.
     I loved my still-faced archaeology.
     The small crab-apple physiognomies
     on high crosses, carved heads in abbeys . . .
     Why else dig in for years in that hard place
35   in a muck of bigotry under the walls
     picking through shards and Williamite cannon balls?
     But all that we just turned to banter too.
     I felt that I should have seen far more of you
     and maybe would have – but dead at thirty-two!
40   Ah poet, lucky poet, tell me why
     what seemed deserved and promised passed me by?'

     I could not speak. I saw a hoard of black
     basalt axe heads, smooth as a beetle's back,
     a cairn of stone force that might detonate,
45   the eggs of danger. And then I saw a face
     he had once given me, a plaster cast
     of an abbess, done by the Gowran master,
     mild-mouthed and cowled, a character of grace.
     'Your gift will be a candle in our house.'
50   But he had gone when I looked to meet his eyes
     and hunkering instead there in his place
     was a bleeding, pale-faced boy, plastered in mud.
     'The red-hot pokers blazed a lovely red
     in Jerpoint the Sunday I was murdered,'
55   he said quietly. 'Now do you remember?
     You were there with poets when you got the word
     and stayed there with them, while your own flesh and blood
     was carted to Bellaghy from the Fews.
     They showed more agitation at the news
60   than you did.'
                    'But they were getting crisis

first-hand, Colum, they had happened in on
live sectarian assassination.
I was dumb, encountering what was destined.'
And so I pleaded with my second cousin. 65
'I kept seeing a grey stretch of Lough Beg
and the strand empty at daybreak.
I felt like the bottom of a dried-up lake.'

'You saw that, and you wrote that – not the fact.
You confused evasion and artistic tact. 70
The Protestant who shot me through the head
I accuse directly, but indirectly, you
who now atone perhaps upon this bed
for the way you whitewashed ugliness and drew
the lovely blinds of the *Purgatorio* 75
and saccharined my death with morning dew.'

Then I seemed to waken out of sleep
among more pilgrims whom I did not know
drifting to the hostel for the night.

IX

'My brain dried like spread turf, my stomach
Shrank to a cinder and tightened and cracked.
Often I was dogs on my own track
Of blood on wet grass that I could have licked.
Under the prison blanket, an ambush 5
Stillness I felt safe in settled round me.
Street lights came on in small towns, the bomb flash
Came before the sound, I saw country
I knew from Glenshane down to Toome
And heard a car I could make out years away 10
With me in the back of it like a white-faced groom,
A hit-man on the brink, emptied and deadly.
When the police yielded my coffin, I was light
As my head when I took aim.'
                              'This voice from blight 15
And hunger died through the black dorm:
There he was, laid out with a drift of mass cards
At his shrouded feet. Then the firing party's
Volley in the yard. I saw woodworm
In gate posts and door jambs, smelt mildew 20

From the byre loft where he watched and hid
From fields his draped coffin would raft through.
Unquiet soul, they should have buried you
In the bog where you threw your first grenade,
Where only helicopters and curlews
Make their maimed music, and sphagnum moss
Could teach you its medicinal repose
Until, when the weasel whistles on its tail,
No other weasel will obey its call.

I dreamt and drifted. All seemed to run to waste
As down a swirl of mucky, glittering flood
Strange polyp floated like a huge corrupt
Magnolia bloom, surreal as a shed breast,
My softly awash and blanching self-disgust.
And I cried among night waters, 'I repent
My unweaned life that kept me competent
To sleepwalk with connivance and mistrust.'
Then, like a pistil growing from the polyp,
A lighted candle rose and steadied up
Until the whole bright-masted thing retrieved
A course and the currents it had gone with
Were what it rode and showed. No more adrift,
My feet touched bottom and my heart revived.

Then something round and clear
And mildly turbulent, like a bubbleskin
Or a moon in smoothly rippled lough water
Rose in a cobwebbed space: the molten
Inside-sheen of an instrument
Revolved its polished convexes full
Upon me, so close and brilliant
I pitched backwards in a headlong fall.
And then it was the clarity of waking
To sunlight and a bell and gushing taps
In the next cubicle. Still there for the taking!
The old brass trumpet with its valves and stops
I found once in loft thatch, a mystery
I shied from then for I thought such trove beyond me.

'I hate how quick I was to know my place.
I hate where I was born, hate everything
That made me biddable and unforthcoming,'

I mouthed at my half-composed face
In the shaving mirror, like somebody
Drunk in the bathroom during a party,
Lulled and repelled by his own reflection.
As if the cairnstone could defy the cairn.
As if the eddy could reform the pool.
As if a stone swirled under a cascade,
Eroded and eroding in its bed,
Could grind itself down to a different core.
Then I thought of the tribe whose dances never fail
For they keep dancing till they sight the deer.

X

Morning stir in the hostel. A pot
hooked on forged links. Soot flakes. Plumping water.
The open door letting in sunlight.
Hearthsmoke rambling and a thud of earthenware

drumming me back until I saw the mug
beyond my reach on its high shelf, the one
patterned with cornflowers, blue sprig after sprig
repeating round it, as quiet as a milestone,

old and glazed and haircracked. It had stood for years
in its patient sheen and turbulent atoms,
unchallenging, unremembered *lars*
I seemed to waken to and waken from.

When had it not been there? There was one night
when the fit-up actors used it for a prop
and I sat in a dark hall estranged from it
as a couple vowed and called it their loving cup

and held it in our gaze until the curtain
jerked shut with an ordinary noise.
Dipped and glamoured from this translation,
it was restored with all its cornflower haze

still dozing, its parchment glazes fast –
as the otter surfaced once with Ronan's psalter
miraculously unharmed, that had been lost
a day and a night under lough water.

And so the saint praised God on the lough shore.

The dazzle of the impossible suddenly
blazed across the threshold, a sun-glare
to put out the small hearths of constancy.

XI

As if the prisms of the kaleidoscope
I plunged once in a butt of muddied water
surfaced like a marvellous lightship

and out of its silted crystals a monk's face
that had spoken years ago from behind a grille
spoke again about the need and chance

to salvage everything, to re-envisage
the zenith and glimpsed jewels of any gift
mistakenly abased . . .

What came to nothing could always be replenished.
'Read poems as prayers,' he said, 'and for your penance
translate me something by Juan de la Cruz.'

Returned from Spain to our chapped wilderness,
his consonants aspirate, his forehead shining,
he had made me feel there was nothing to confess.

Now his sandalled passage stirred me on to this:
How well I knew that fountain, filling, running,
    although it is the night.

That eternal fountain, hidden away,
I know its haven and its secrecy
    although it is the night.

But not its source because it does not have one,
which is all sources' source and origin
    although it is the night.

No other thing can be so beautiful.
Here the earth and heaven drink their fill
    although it is the night.

So pellucid it never can be muddied,
and I know that all light radiates from it
    although it is the night.

I know no sounding-line can find its bottom,
nobody ford or plumb its deepest fathom
    although it is the night.

And its current so in flood it overspills
to water hell and heaven and all peoples
    although it is the night.

And the current that is generated there,
as far as it wills to, it can flow that far
    although it is the night.

And from these two a third current proceeds
which neither of these two, I know, precedes
    although it is the night.

This eternal fountain hides and splashes
within this living bread that is life to us
    although it is the night.

Hear it calling out to every creature.
And they drink these waters, although it is dark here
    because it is the night.

I am repining for this living fountain.
Within this bread of life I see it plain
    although it is the night.

XII

Like a convalescent, I took the hand
stretched down from the jetty, sensed again
an alien comfort as I stepped on ground

to find the helping hand still gripping mine,
fish-cold and bony, but whether to guide
or to be guided I could not be certain

for the tall man in step at my side
seemed blind, though he walked straight as a rush
upon his ash plant, his eyes fixed straight ahead.

Then I knew him in the flesh
out there on the tarmac among the cars,
wintered hard and sharp as a blackthorn bush.

His voice eddying with the vowels of all rivers
came back to me, though he did not speak yet,
a voice like a prosecutor's or a singer's,

cunning, narcotic, mimic, definite
as a steel nib's downstroke, quick and clean,
and suddenly he hit a litter basket

with his stick, saying, 'Your obligation
is not discharged by any common rite.
What you must do must be done on your own

so get back in harness. The main thing is to write
for the joy of it. Cultivate a work-lust
that imagines its haven like your hands at night

dreaming the sun in the sunspot of a breast.
You are fasted now, light-headed, dangerous.
Take off from here. And don't be so earnest,

let others wear the sackcloth and the ashes.
Let go, let fly, forget.
You've listened long enough. Now strike your note.'

It was as if I had stepped free into space
alone with nothing that I had not known
already. Raindrops blew in my face

as I came to. 'Old father, mother's son,
there is a moment in Stephen's diary
for April the thirteenth, a revelation

set among my stars – that one entry
has been a sort of password in my ears,
the collect of a new epiphany,

the Feast of the Holy Tundish.' 'Who cares,'
he jeered, 'any more? The English language
belongs to us. You are raking at dead fires,

a waste of time for somebody your age.
That subject people stuff is a cod's game,
infantile, like your peasant pilgrimage.

You lose more of yourself than you redeem
doing the decent thing. Keep at a tangent.
When they make the circle wide, it's time to swim

out on your own and fill the element
with signatures on your own frequency,   50
echo soundings, searches, probes, allurements,

elver-gleams in the dark of the whole sea.'
The shower broke in a cloudburst, the tarmac
fumed and sizzled. As he moved off quickly

the downpour loosed its screens round his straight walk.   55

PART THREE: SWEENEY REDIVIVUS

The First Gloss

Take hold of the shaft of the pen.
Subscribe to the first step taken
from a justified line
into the margin.

Sweeney Redivivus

I stirred wet sand and gathered myself
to climb the steep-flanked mound,
my head like a ball of wet twine
dense with soakage, but beginning
to unwind.   5
          Another smell
was blowing off the river, bitter
as night airs in a scutch mill.
The old trees were nowhere,
the hedges thin as penwork   10
and the whole enclosure lost
under hard paths and sharp-ridged houses.

And there I was, incredible to myself,
among people far too eager to believe me
and my story, even if it happened to be true.   15

Unwinding

If the twine unravels to the very end
the stuff gathering under my fingernails
is being picked off whitewash at the bedside.

And the stuff gathering in my ear
is their sex-pruned and unfurtherable
moss-talk, incubated under lamplight,

which will have to be unlearned
even though from there on everything
is going to be learning.

So the twine unwinds and loosely widens
backward through areas that forwarded
understandings of all I would undertake.

In the Beech

I was a lookout posted and forgotten.

On one side under me, the concrete road.
On the other, the bullocks' covert,
the breath and plaster of a drinking place
where the school-leaver discovered peace
to touch himself in the reek of churned-up mud.

And the tree itself a strangeness and a comfort,
as much a column as a bole. The very ivy
puzzled its milk-tooth frills and tapers
over the grain: was it bark or masonry?

I watched the red-brick chimney rear
its stamen course by course,
and the steeplejacks up there at their antics
like flies against the mountain.

I felt the tanks' advance beginning
at the cynosure of the growth rings,
then winced at their imperium refreshed
in each powdered bolt mark on the concrete.
And the pilot with his goggles back came in
so low I could see the cockpit rivets.

My hidebound boundary tree. My tree of knowledge.
My thick-tapped, soft-fledged, airy listening post.

The First Kingdom

The royal roads were cow paths.
The queen mother hunkered on a stool
and played the harpstrings of milk
into a wooden pail.
With seasoned sticks the nobles
lorded it over the hindquarters of cattle.

Units of measurement were pondered
by the cartful, barrowful and bucketful.
Time was a backward rote of names and mishaps,
bad harvests, fires, unfair settlements,
deaths in floods, murders and miscarriages.

And if my rights to it all came only
by their acclamation, what was it worth?
I blew hot and blew cold.
They were two-faced and accommodating.
And seed, breed and generation still
they are holding on, every bit
as pious and exacting and demeaned.

The First Flight

It was more sleepwalk than spasm
yet that was a time when the times
were also in spasm –

the ties and the knots running through us
split open
down the lines of the grain.

As I drew close to pebbles and berries,
the smell of wild garlic, relearning
the acoustic of frost

and the meaning of woodnote,
my shadow over the field
was only a spin-off,

my empty place an excuse
for shifts in the camp, old rehearsals
of debts and betrayal.

Singly they came to the tree
with a stone in each pocket
to whistle and bill me back in

and I would collide and cascade
through leaves when they left,
my point of repose knocked askew.

I was mired in attachment
until they began to pronounce me
a feeder off battlefields

so I mastered new rungs of the air
to survey out of reach
their bonfires on hills, their hosting

and fasting, the levies from Scotland
as always, and the people of art
diverting their rhythmical chants

to fend off the onslaught of winds
I would welcome and climb
at the top of my bent.

Drifting Off

The guttersnipe and the albatross
gliding for days without a single wingbeat
were equally beyond me.

I yearned for the gannet's strike,
the unbegrudging concentration
of the heron.

In the camaraderie of rookeries,
in the spiteful vigilance of colonies
I was at home.

I learned to distrust
the allure of the cuckoo
and the gossip of starlings,

kept faith with doughty bullfinches,
levelled my wit too often
to the small-minded wren   15

and too often caved in
to the pathos of waterhens
and panicky corncrakes.

I gave much credence to stragglers,
overrated the composure of blackbirds   20
and the folklore of magpies.

But when goldfinch or kingfisher rent
the veil of the usual,
pinions whispered and braced

as I stooped, unwieldy   25
and brimming,
my spurs at the ready.

Alerted

From the start I was lucky
and challenged, always whacked down
to make sure I would not grow up
too hopeful and trusting –

I was asking myself could I ever   5
and if ever I should
outstrip obedience, when I heard
the bark of the vixen in heat.

She carded the webs of desire,
she disinterred gutlines and lightning,   10
she broke the ice of demure
and exemplary stars –

and rooted me to the spot,
alerted, disappointed
under my old clandestine   15
pre-Copernican night.

The Cleric

I heard new words prayed at cows
in the byre, found his sign
on the crock and the hidden still,

smelled fumes from his censer
in the first smokes of morning.
Next thing he was making a progress

through gaps, stepping out sites,
sinking his crozier deep
in the fort-hearth.

If he had stuck to his own
cramp-jawed abbesses and intoners
dibbling round the enclosure,

his Latin and blather of love,
his parchments and scheming
in letters shipped over water –

but no, he overbore
with his unctions and orders,
he had to get in on the ground.

History that planted its standards
on his gables and spires
ousted me to the marches

of skulking and whingeing.
Or did I desert?
Give him his due, in the end

he opened my path to a kingdom
of such scope and neuter allegiance
my emptiness reigns at its whim.

The Hermit

As he prowled the rim of his clearing
where the blade of choice had not spared
one stump of affection

he was like a ploughshare

interred to sustain the whole field
of force, from the bitted

and high-drawn sideways curve
of the horse's neck to the aim
held fast in the wrists and elbows –

the more brutal the pull
and the drive, the deeper
and quieter the work of refreshment.

The Master

He dwelt in himself
like a rook in an unroofed tower.

To get close I had to maintain
a climb up deserted ramparts
and not flinch, not raise an eye
to search for an eye on the watch
from his coign of seclusion.

Deliberately he would unclasp
his book of withholding
a page at a time and it was nothing
arcane, just the old rules
we all had inscribed on our slates.
Each character blocked on the parchment secure
in its volume and measure.
Each maxim given its space.

Like quarrymen's hammers and wedges proofed
by intransigent service.
Like coping stones where you rest
in the balm of the wellspring.

How flimsy I felt climbing down
the unrailed stairs on the wall,
hearing the purpose and venture
in a wingflap above me.

The Scribes

   I never warmed to them.
   If they were excellent they were petulant
   and jaggy as the holly tree
   they rendered down for ink.
5 And if I never belonged among them,
   they could never deny me my place.

   In the hush of the scriptorium
   a black pearl kept gathering in them
   like the old dry glut inside their quills.
10 In the margin of texts of praise
   they scratched and clawed.
   They snarled if the day was dark
   or too much chalk had made the vellum bland
   or too little left it oily.

15 Under the rumps of lettering
   they herded myopic angers.
   Resentment seeded in the uncurling
   fernheads of their capitals.

   Now and again I started up
20 miles away and saw in my absence
   the sloped cursive of each back and felt them
   perfect themselves against me page by page.

   Let them remember this not inconsiderable
   contribution to their jealous art.

A Waking Dream

   When I made the rush to throw salt
   on her tail the long treadles of the air
   took me in my stride so I was lofted
   beyond exerted breath, the cheep and blur
5 of trespass and occurrence.
   As if one who had dropped off came to
   suspecting the very stillness of the sunlight.

In the Chestnut Tree

Body heat under the leaves, matronly
slippage and hoistings

as she spreads in the pool of the day,
a queen in her fifties, dropping

purses and earrings. What does she care
for the lean-shanked and thorny,

old firm-fleshed Susannah, stepped in
over her belly,

parts of her soapy and white,
parts of her blunting?

And the little bird of death
piping and piping somewhere

in her gorgeous tackling? Surely not.
She breathes deep and stirs up the algae.

Sweeney's Returns

The clouds would tatter a moment
over green peninsulas, cattle
far below, the dormant roadways –
and I imagined her clothes half-slipped
off the chair, the dawn-fending blind, her eyelids'
glister and burgeon.

Then when I perched on the sill
to gaze at my coffers of absence
I was like a scout at risk behind lines
who raises his head in a wheatfield
to take a first look, the throb of his breakthrough
going on inside him unstoppably:

the blind was up, a bangle
lay in the sun, the fleshed hyacinth
had begun to divulge.
Where had she gone? Beyond

the tucked and level bed, I floundered
in my wild reflection in the mirror.

Holly

It rained when it should have snowed.
When we went to gather holly

the ditches were swimming, we were wet
to the knees, our hands were all jags

and water ran up our sleeves.
There should have been berries

but the sprigs we brought into the house
gleamed like smashed bottle-glass.

Now here I am, in a room that is decked
with the red-berried, waxy-leafed stuff,

and I almost forget what it's like
to be wet to the skin or longing for snow.

I reach for a book like a doubter
and want it to flare round my hand,

a black-letter bush, a glittering shield-wall
cutting as holly and ice.

An Artist

I love the thought of his anger.
His obstinacy against the rock, his coercion
of the substance from green apples.

The way he was a dog barking
at the image of himself barking.
And his hatred of his own embrace
of working as the only thing that worked –
the vulgarity of expecting ever
gratitude or admiration, which
would mean a stealing from him.

The way his fortitude held and hardened
because he did what he knew.
His forehead like a hurled *boule*
travelling unpainted space
behind the apple and behind the mountain.

The Old Icons

Why, when it was all over, did I hold on to them?

A patriot with folded arms in a shaft of light:
the barred cell window and his sentenced face
are the only bright spots in the little etching.

An oleograph of snowy hills, the outlawed priest's
red vestments, with the redcoats toiling closer
and the lookout coming like a fox across the gaps.

And the old committee of the sedition-mongers,
so well turned out in their clasped brogues and waistcoats,
the legend of their names an informer's list

prepared by neat-cuffs, third from left, at rear,
more compelling than the rest of them,
pivoting an action that was his rack

and others' ruin, the very rhythm of his name
a register of dear-bought treacheries
grown transparent now, and inestimable.

In Illo Tempore

The big missal splayed
and dangled silky ribbons
of emerald and purple and watery white.

Intransitively we would assist,
confess, receive. The verbs
assumed us. We adored.

And we lifted our eyes to the nouns.
Altar stone was dawn and monstrance noon,
the word rubric itself a bloodshot sunset.

10 Now I live by a famous strand
where seabirds cry in the small hours
like incredible souls

and even the range wall of the promenade
that I press down on for conviction
15 hardly tempts me to credit it.

On the Road

The road ahead
kept reeling in
at a steady speed,
the verges dripped.

5 In my hands
like a wrested trophy,
the empty round
of the steering wheel.

The trance of driving
10 made all roads one:
the seraph-haunted, Tuscan
footpath, the green

oak-alleys of Dordogne
or that track through corn
15 where the rich young man
asked his question –

*Master, what must I
do to be saved?*
Or the road where the bird
20 with an earth-red back

and a white and black
tail, like parquet
of flint and jet,
wheeled over me

25 in visitation.
*Sell all you have
and give to the poor.*
I was up and away

like a human soul
that plumes from the mouth
in undulant, tenor
black-letter latin.

I was one for sorrow,
Noah's dove,
a panicked shadow
crossing the deerpath.

If I came to earth
it would be by way of
a small east window
I once squeezed through,

scaling heaven
by superstition,
drunk and happy
on a chapel gable.

I would roost a night
on the slab of exile,
then hide in the cleft
of that churchyard wall

where hand after hand
keeps wearing away
at the cold, hard-breasted
votive granite.

And follow me.
I would migrate
through a high cave mouth
into an oaten, sun-warmed cliff,

on down the soft-nubbed,
clay-floored passage,
face-brush, wing-flap,
to the deepest chamber.

There a drinking deer
is cut into rock,
its haunch and neck
rise with the contours,

the incised outline
curves to a strained

            expectant muzzle
            and a nostril flared

            at a dried-up source.
70   For my book of changes
            I would meditate
            that stone-faced vigil

            until the long dumbfounded
            spirit broke cover
75   to raise a dust
            in the font of exhaustion.

UNCOLLECTED POEMS (1985–1987)

The Late Paul Cézanne

When Cézanne died watching the empty door
For his son Paul, those late
Unfinishable, half-bare
Canvases had him readied for it.
He could not manhandle
Effulgence of the tree, skull, mountain, apple.
Outrage and silence teemed in him like light.
Space kept standing open and opposite.

It was like when the stroke had quelled her
Yet everyone assumed she could still hear
And petted her and dabbed the lips with water.
Until an hour before that, all morning
When I had been a nagging absent ringing,
She could have seen me in the bedroom door.

Lenten Stuff

Now I can only find myself in one place:
Low-backed island on an inland lough.
A cold chapel takes up half the island.

Three times a day a broad-beamed ferry comes
Sunk to the gunwale, loaded with threescore souls
Who land barefoot to join us barefoot, pacing
Rock, gravel, concrete. Three days and three nights . . .

            I am dispersed
Coherently in these hard exercises,
On the flagged floor, the sharp-edged kneeling board.

Memory is a frozen block, bunging the skull.
Affections walk ahead, behind, shadows
I was that I cannot overtake.
Now is a level the volume of the past
Does not sustain: now fills and drains.

Villanelle for an Anniversary

A spirit moved, John Harvard walked the yard,
The atom lay unsplit, the west unwon,
The books stood open and the gates unbarred.

The maps dreamt on like moondust. Nothing stirred.
The future was a verb in hibernation.
A spirit moved, John Harvard walked the yard.

Before the classic style, before the clapboard,
All through the small hours of an origin,
The books stood open and the gates unbarred.

Night passage of a migratory bird.
Wingflap. Gownflap. Like a homing pigeon
A spirit moved, John Harvard walked the yard.

Was that his soul (look) sped to its reward
By grace or works? A shooting star? An omen?
The books stood open and the gates unbarred.

Begin again where frosts and tests were hard.
Find yourself or founder. Here, imagine
A spirit moves, John Harvard walks the yard,
The books stand open and the gates unbarred.

(1986)

Birthday Tribute to Marie Bullock

Higgledy-piggledy
Mrs Hugh Bullock thought
Poets' Academy:
Oyez! Yes! Yes!

So in a second she
Only begetted the
East Eighty Seven Street
Name and address.

*for Marie Bullock,
with great affection and respect*

THE HAW LANTERN (1987)

for Bernard and Jane McCabe

The riverbed, dried-up, half-full of leaves.
Us, listening to a river in the trees.

Alphabets

I

A shadow his father makes with joined hands
And thumbs and fingers nibbles on the wall
Like a rabbit's head. He understands
He will understand more when he goes to school.

There he draws smoke with chalk the whole first week,
Then draws the forked stick that they call a Y.
This is writing. A swan's neck and swan's back
Make the 2 he can see now as well as say.

Two rafters and a cross-tie on the slate
Are the letter some call *ah*, some call *ay*.
There are charts, there are headlines, there is a right
Way to hold the pen and a wrong way.

First it is 'copying out', and then 'English'
Marked correct with a little leaning hoe.
Smells of inkwells rise in the classroom hush.
A globe in the window tilts like a coloured O.

II

Declensions sang on air like a *hosanna*
As, column after stratified column,
Book One of *Elementa Latina*,
Marbled and minatory, rose up in him.

For he was fostered next in a stricter school
Named for the patron saint of the oak wood
Where classes switched to the pealing of a bell
And he left the Latin forum for the shade

Of new calligraphy that felt like home.
The letters of this alphabet were trees.
The capitals were orchards in full bloom,
The lines of script like briars coiled in ditches.

Here in her snooded garment and bare feet,
All ringleted in assonance and woodnotes,
The poet's dream stole over him like sunlight
And passed into the tenebrous thickets.

He learns this other writing. He is the scribe
Who drove a team of quills on his white field.
Round his cell door the blackbirds dart and dab.
Then self-denial, fasting, the pure cold.

By rules that hardened the farther they reached north
He bends to his desk and begins again.
Christ's sickle has been in the undergrowth.
The script grows bare and Merovingian.

III

The globe has spun. He stands in a wooden O.
He alludes to Shakespeare. He alludes to Graves.
Time has bulldozed the school and school window.
Balers drop bales like printouts where stooked sheaves
Made lambdas on the stubble once at harvest
And the delta face of each potato pit
Was patted straight and moulded against frost.
All gone, with the omega that kept

Watch above each door, the good luck horse-shoe.
Yet shape-note language, absolute on air
As Constantine's sky-lettered IN HOC SIGNO
Can still command him; or the necromancer

Who would hang from the domed ceiling of his house
A figure of the world with colours in it
So that the figure of the universe
And 'not just single things' would meet his sight

When he walked abroad. As from his small window
The astronaut sees all he has sprung from,
The risen, aqueous, singular, lucent O
Like a magnified and buoyant ovum –

Or like my own wide pre-reflective stare
All agog at the plasterer on his ladder
Skimming our gable and writing our name there
With his trowel point, letter by strange letter.

Terminus

I

When I hoked there, I would find
An acorn and a rusted bolt.

If I lifted my eyes, a factory chimney
And a dormant mountain.

If I listened, an engine shunting
And a trotting horse.

Is it any wonder when I thought
I would have second thoughts?

II

When they spoke of the prudent squirrel's hoard
It shone like gifts at a nativity.

When they spoke of the mammon of iniquity
The coins in my pockets reddened like stove-lids.

I was the march drain and the march drain's banks
Suffering the limit of each claim.

III

Two buckets were easier carried than one.
I grew up in between.

My left hand placed the standard iron weight.
My right tilted a last grain in the balance.

Baronies, parishes met where I was born.
When I stood on the central stepping stone

I was the last earl on horseback in midstream
Still parleying, in earshot of his peers.

From the Frontier of Writing

The tightness and the nilness round that space
when the car stops in the road, the troops inspect
its make and number and, as one bends his face

    towards your window, you catch sight of more
on a hill beyond, eyeing with intent
down cradled guns that hold you under cover

and everything is pure interrogation
until a rifle motions and you move
with guarded unconcerned acceleration –

a little emptier, a little spent
as always by that quiver in the self,
subjugated, yes, and obedient.

So you drive on to the frontier of writing
where it happens again. The guns on tripods;
the sergeant with his on-off mike repeating

data about you, waiting for the squawk
of clearance; the marksman training down
out of the sun upon you like a hawk.

And suddenly you're through, arraigned yet freed,
as if you'd passed from behind a waterfall
on the black current of a tarmac road

past armour-plated vehicles, out between
the posted soldiers flowing and receding
like tree shadows into the polished windscreen.

The Haw Lantern

The wintry haw is burning out of season,
crab of the thorn, a small light for small people,
wanting no more from them but that they keep
the wick of self-respect from dying out,
not having to blind them with illumination.

But sometimes when your breath plumes in the frost
it takes the roaming shape of Diogenes
with his lantern, seeking one just man;
so you end up scrutinized from behind the haw
he holds up at eye-level on its twig,
and you flinch before its bonded pith and stone,
its blood-prick that you wish would test and clear you,
its pecked-at ripeness that scans you, then moves on.

The Stone Grinder

Penelope worked with some guarantee of a plot.
Whatever she unweaved at night
might advance it all by a day.

Me, I ground the same stones for fifty years
and what I undid was never the thing I had done.
I was unrewarded as darkness at a mirror.

I prepared my surface to survive what came over it –
cartographers, printmakers, all that lining and inking.
I ordained opacities and they haruspicated.

For them it was a new start and a clean slate
every time. For me, it was coming full circle
like the ripple perfected in stillness.

So. To commemorate me. Imagine the faces
stripped off the face of a quarry. Practise
coitus interruptus on a pile of old lithographs.

A Daylight Art

for Norman MacCaig

On the day he was to take the poison
Socrates told his friends he had been writing:
putting Aesop's fables into verse.

And this was not because Socrates loved wisdom
and advocated the examined life.
The reason was that he had had a dream.

Caesar, now, or Herod or Constantine
or any number of Shakespearean kings
bursting at the end like dams

where original panoramas lie submerged
which have to rise again before the death scenes –
you can believe in their believing dreams.

But hardly Socrates. Until, that is,
he tells his friends the dream had kept recurring

all his life, repeating one instruction:

Practise the art, which art until that moment
he always took to mean philosophy.
Happy the man, therefore, with a natural gift

for practising the right one from the start –
poetry, say, or fishing; whose nights are dreamless;
whose deep-sunk panoramas rise and pass

like daylight through the rod's eye or the nib's eye.

Parable Island

I

Although they are an occupied nation
and their only border is an inland one
they yield to nobody in their belief
that the country is an island.

Somewhere in the far north, in a region
every native thinks of as 'the coast',
there lies the mountain of the shifting names.

The occupiers call it Cape Basalt.
The Sun's Headstone, say farmers in the east.
Drunken westerners call it The Orphan's Tit.

To find out where he stands the traveller
has to keep listening – since there is no map
which draws the line he knows he must have crossed.

Meanwhile, the forked-tongued natives keep repeating
prophecies they pretend not to believe
about a point where all the names converge
underneath the mountain and where (some day)
they are going to start to mine the ore of truth.

II

In the beginning there was one bell-tower
which struck its single note each day at noon
in honour of the one-eyed all-creator.

At least, this was the original idea
missionary scribes record they found

in autochthonous tradition. But even there

you can't be sure that parable is not
at work already retrospectively,
since all their early manuscripts are full

of stylized eye-shapes and recurrent glosses
in which those old revisionists derive
the word *island* from roots in *eye* and *land*.

III

Now archaeologists begin to gloss the glosses.
To one school, the stone circles are pure symbol;
to another, assembly spots or hut foundations.

One school thinks a post-hole in an ancient floor
stands first of all for a pupil in an iris.
The other thinks a post-hole is a post-hole. And so on –

like the subversives and collaborators
always vying with a fierce possessiveness
for the right to set 'the island story' straight.

IV

The elders dream of boat-journeys and havens
and have their stories too, like the one about the man
who took to his bed, it seems, and died convinced

that the cutting of the Panama Canal
would mean the ocean would all drain away
and the island disappear by aggrandizement.

From the Republic of Conscience

I

When I landed in the republic of conscience
it was so noiseless when the engines stopped
I could hear a curlew high above the runway.

At immigration, the clerk was an old man
who produced a wallet from his homespun coat
and showed me a photograph of my grandfather.

The woman in customs asked me to declare
the words of our traditional cures and charms
to heal dumbness and avert the evil eye.

No porters. No interpreter. No taxi.
You carried your own burden and very soon
your symptoms of creeping privilege disappeared.

II

Fog is a dreaded omen there but lightning
spells universal good and parents hang
swaddled infants in trees during thunderstorms.

Salt is their precious mineral. And seashells
are held to the ear during births and funerals.
The base of all inks and pigments is seawater.

Their sacred symbol is a stylized boat.
The sail is an ear, the mast a sloping pen,
The hull a mouth-shape, the keel an open eye.

At their inauguration, public leaders
must swear to uphold unwritten law and weep
to atone for their presumption to hold office –

and to affirm their faith that all life sprang
from salt in tears which the sky-god wept
after he dreamt his solitude was endless.

III

I came back from that frugal republic
with my two arms the one length, the customs woman
having insisted my allowance was myself.

The old man rose and gazed into my face
and said that was official recognition
that I was now a dual citizen.

He therefore desired me when I got home
to consider myself a representative
and to speak on their behalf in my own tongue.

Their embassies, he said, were everywhere
but operated independently
and no ambassador would ever be relieved.

Hailstones

I

My cheek was hit and hit:
sudden hailstones
pelted and bounced on the road.

When it cleared again
something whipped and knowledgeable
had withdrawn

and left me there with my chances.
I made a small hard ball
of burning water running from my hand

just as I make this now
out of the melt of the real thing
smarting into its absence.

II

To be reckoned with, all the same,
those brats of showers.
The way they refused permission,

rattling the classroom window
like a ruler across the knuckles,
the way they were perfect first

and then in no time dirty slush.
Thomas Traherne had his orient wheat
for proof and wonder

but for us, it was the sting of hailstones
and the unstingable hands of Eddie Diamond
foraging in the nettles.

III

Nipple and hive, bite-lumps,
small acorns of the almost pleasurable
intimated and disallowed

when the shower ended
and everything said *wait*.
For what? For forty years

to say there, there you had
the truest foretaste of your aftermath –
in that dilation
10 when the light opened in silence
and a car with wipers going still
laid perfect tracks in the slush.

Two Quick Notes

I

My old hard friend, how you sought
Occasions of justified anger!
Who could buff me like you

Who wanted the soul to ring true
5 And plain as a galvanized bucket
And would kick it to test it?

Or whack it clean like a carpet.
So of course when you turned on yourself
You were ferocious.

II

Abrupt and thornproofed and lonely.
A raider from the old country
Of night prayer and principled challenge,

Crashing at barriers
5 You thought ought still to be there,
Overshooting into thin air.

O upright self-wounding prie-dieu
In shattered free fall:
Hail and farewell.

The Stone Verdict

When he stands in the judgment place
With his stick in his hand and the broad hat
Still on his head, maimed by self-doubt
And an old disdain of sweet talk and excuses,

It will be no justice if the sentence is blabbed out.   5
He will expect more than words in the ultimate court
He relied on through a lifetime's speechlessness.

Let it be like the judgment of Hermes,
God of the stone heap, where the stones were verdicts
Cast solidly at his feet, piling up around him   10
Until he stood waist deep in the cairn
Of his apotheosis: maybe a gate-pillar
Or a tumbled wallstead where hogweed earths the silence
Somebody will break at last to say, 'Here
His spirit lingers,' and will have said too much.

From the Land of the Unspoken

I have heard of a bar of platinum
kept by a logical and talkative nation
as their standard of measurement,
the throne room and the burial chamber
of every calculation and prediction.   5
I could feel at home inside that metal core
slumbering at the very hub of systems.

We are a dispersed people whose history
is a sensation of opaque fidelity.
When or why our exile began   10
among the speech-ridden, we cannot tell
but solidarity comes flooding up in us
when we hear their legends of infants discovered
floating in coracles towards destiny
or of kings' biers heaved and borne away   15
on the river's shoulders or out into the sea roads.

When we recognize our own, we fall in step
but do not altogether come up level.
My deepest contact was underground
strap-hanging back to back on a rush-hour train   20
and in a museum once, I inhaled
vernal assent from a neck and shoulder
pretending to be absorbed in a display
of absolutely silent quernstones.

Our unspoken assumptions have the force
of revelation. How else could we know
that whoever is the first of us to seek
assent and votes in a rich democracy
will be the last of us and have killed our language?
Meanwhile, if we miss the sight of a fish
we heard jumping and then see its ripples,
that means one more of us is dying somewhere.

A Ship of Death

Scyld was still a strong man when his time came
and he crossed over into Our Lord's keeping.
His warrior band did what he bade them
when he laid down the law among the Danes:
they shouldered him out to the sea's flood,
the chief they revered who had long ruled them.
A ring-necked prow rode in the harbour,
clad with ice, its cables tightening.
They stretched their beloved lord in the boat,
laid out amidships by the mast
the great ring-giver. Far-fetched treasures
were piled upon him, and precious gear.
I never heard before of a ship so well furbished
with battle-tackle, bladed weapons
and coats of mail. The treasure was massed
on top of him: it would travel far
on out into the sway of ocean.
They decked his body no less bountifully
with offerings than those first ones did
who cast him away when he was a child
and launched him out alone over the waves.
And they set a gold standard up
high above his head and let him drift
to wind and tide, bewailing him
and mourning their loss. No man can tell,
no wise man in the hall or weathered veteran
knows for certain who salvaged that load.

Beowulf, ll. 26–52

The Spoonbait

So a new similitude is given us
And we say: The soul may be compared

Unto a spoonbait that a child discovers
Beneath the sliding lid of a pencil case,

Glimpsed once and imagined for a lifetime — 5
Risen and free and spooling out of nowhere –

A shooting star going back up the darkness.
It flees him and it burns him all at once

Like the single drop that Dives implored
Falling and falling into a great gulf. 10

Then exit, the polished helmet of a hero
Laid out amidships above scudding water.

Exit, alternatively, a toy of light
Reeled through him upstream, snagging on nothing.

In Memoriam: Robert Fitzgerald

The socket of each axehead like the squared
Doorway to a megalithic tomb
With its slabbed passage that keeps opening forward
To face another corbelled stone-faced door
That opens on a third. There is no last door, 5
Just threshold stone, stone jambs, stone crossbeam
Repeating *enter, enter, enter, enter*.
Lintel and upright fly past in the dark.

After the bowstring sang a swallow's note,
The arrow whose migration is its mark 10
Leaves a whispered breath in every socket.
The great test over, while the gut's still humming,
This time it travels out of all knowing
Perfectly aimed towards the vacant centre.

The Old Team

Dusk. Scope of air. A railed pavilion
Formal and blurring in the sepia
Of (always) summery Edwardian
Ulster. Which could be India
Or England. Or any old parade ground
Where a moustachioed tenantry togged out
To pose with folded arms, all musclebound
And staunch and forever up against it.

Moyola Park FC! Sons of Castledawson!
Stokers and scutchers! Grandfather McCann!
Team spirit, walled parkland, the linen mill
Have, in your absence, grown historical
As those lightly clapped, dull-thumping games of football.
The steady coffins sail past at eye-level.

Clearances

in memoriam M.K.H., 1911–1984

She taught me what her uncle once taught her:
How easily the biggest coal block split
If you got the grain and hammer angled right.

The sound of that relaxed alluring blow,
Its co-opted and obliterated echo,
Taught me to hit, taught me to loosen,

Taught me between the hammer and the block
To face the music. Teach me now to listen,
To strike it rich behind the linear black.

I

A cobble thrown a hundred years ago
Keeps coming at me, the first stone
Aimed at a great-grandmother's turncoat brow.
The pony jerks and the riot's on.
She's crouched low in the trap
Running the gauntlet that first Sunday

Down the brae to Mass at a panicked gallop.
He whips on through the town to cries of 'Lundy!'

Call her 'The Convert'. 'The Exogamous Bride'.
Anyhow, it is a genre piece   10
Inherited on my mother's side
And mine to dispose with now she's gone.
Instead of silver and Victorian lace,
The exonerating, exonerated stone.

2

Polished linoleum shone there. Brass taps shone.
The china cups were very white and big –
An unchipped set with sugar bowl and jug.
The kettle whistled. Sandwich and teascone
Were present and correct. In case it run,   5
The butter must be kept out of the sun.
And don't be dropping crumbs. Don't tilt your chair.
Don't reach. Don't point. Don't make noise when you stir.

It is Number 5, New Row, Land of the Dead,
Where grandfather is rising from his place   10
With spectacles pushed back on a clean bald head
To welcome a bewildered homing daughter
Before she even knocks. 'What's this? What's this?'
And they sit down in the shining room together.

3

When all the others were away at Mass
I was all hers as we peeled potatoes.
They broke the silence, let fall one by one
Like solder weeping off the soldering iron:
Cold comforts set between us, things to share   5
Gleaming in a bucket of clean water.
And again let fall. Little pleasant splashes
From each other's work would bring us to our senses.

So while the parish priest at her bedside
Went hammer and tongs at the prayers for the dying   10
And some were responding and some crying
I remembered her head bent towards my head,

Her breath in mine, our fluent dipping knives –
Never closer the whole rest of our lives.

4

Fear of affectation made her affect
Inadequacy whenever it came to
Pronouncing words 'beyond her'. *Bertold Brek.*
She'd manage something hampered and askew
Every time, as if she might betray
The hampered and inadequate by too
Well-adjusted a vocabulary.
With more challenge than pride, she'd tell me, 'You
Know all them things.' So I governed my tongue
In front of her, a genuinely well-
adjusted adequate betrayal
Of what I knew better. I'd *naw* and *aye*
And decently relapse into the wrong
Grammar which kept us allied and at bay.

5

The cool that came off sheets just off the line
Made me think the damp must still be in them
But when I took my corners of the linen
And pulled against her, first straight down the hem
And then diagonally, then flapped and shook
The fabric like a sail in a cross-wind,
They made a dried-out undulating thwack.
So we'd stretch and fold and end up hand to hand
For a split second as if nothing had happened
For nothing had that had not always happened
Beforehand, day by day, just touch and go,
Coming close again by holding back
In moves where I was x and she was o
Inscribed in sheets she'd sewn from ripped-out flour sacks.

6

In the first flush of the Easter holidays
The ceremonies during Holy Week
Were highpoints of our *Sons and Lovers* phase.

The midnight fire. The paschal candlestick.
Elbow to elbow, glad to be kneeling next
To each other up there near the front
Of the packed church, we would follow the text
And rubrics for the blessing of the font.
As the hind longs for the streams, so my soul . . .
Dippings. Towellings. The water breathed on.
The water mixed with chrism and with oil.
Cruet tinkle. Formal incensation
And the psalmist's outcry taken up with pride:
Day and night my tears have been my bread.

7

In the last minutes he said more to her
Almost than in all their life together.
'You'll be in New Row on Monday night
And I'll come up for you and you'll be glad
When I walk in the door . . . Isn't that right?'
His head was bent down to her propped-up head.
She could not hear but we were overjoyed.
He called her good and girl. Then she was dead,
The searching for a pulsebeat was abandoned
And we all knew one thing by being there.
The space we stood around had been emptied
Into us to keep, it penetrated
Clearances that suddenly stood open.
High cries were felled and a pure change happened.

8

I thought of walking round and round a space
Utterly empty, utterly a source
Where the decked chestnut tree had lost its place
In our front hedge above the wallflowers.
The white chips jumped and jumped and skited high
I heard the hatchet's differentiated
Accurate cut, the crack, the sigh
And collapse of what luxuriated
Through the shocked tips and wreckage of it all.
Deep planted and long gone, my coeval
Chestnut from a jam jar in a hole,

Its heft and hush become a bright nowhere,
A soul ramifying and forever
Silent, beyond silence listened for.

The Milk Factory

Scuts of froth swirled from the discharge pipe.
We halted on the other bank and watched
A milky water run from the pierced side
Of milk itself, the crock of its substance spilt
5   Across white limbo floors where shift-workers
Waded round the clock, and the factory
Kept its distance like a bright-decked star-ship.

There we go, soft-eyed calves of the dew,
Astonished and assumed into fluorescence.

The Summer of Lost Rachel

Potato crops are flowering,
      Hard green plums appear
On damson trees at your back door
      And every berried briar

5   Is glittering and dripping
      Whenever showers plout down
On flooded hay and flooding drills.
      There's a ring around the moon.

The whole summer was waterlogged
10   Yet everyone is loath
To trust the rain's soft-soaping ways
      And sentiments of growth

Because all confidence in summer's
      Unstinting largesse
15 Broke down last May when we laid you out
      In white, your whited face

Gashed from the accident, but still,
      So absolutely still,
And the setting sun set merciless
20   And every merciful

Register inside us yearned
    To run the film back,
For you to step into the road
    Wheeling your bright-rimmed bike,

Safe and sound as usual,   25
    Across, then down the lane,
The twisted spokes all straightened out,
    The awful skid-marks gone.

But no. So let the downpours flood
    Our memory's riverbed   30
Until, in thick-webbed currents,
    The life you might have led

Wavers and tugs dreamily
    As soft-plumed waterweed
Which tempts our gaze and quietens it   35
    And recollects our need.

The Wishing Tree

I thought of her as the wishing tree that died
And saw it lifted, root and branch, to heaven,
Trailing a shower of all that had been driven

Need by need by need into its hale
Sap-wood and bark: coin and pin and nail   5
Came streaming from it like a comet-tail

New-minted and dissolved. I had a vision
Of an airy branch-head rising through damp cloud,
Of turned-up faces where the tree had stood.

A Postcard from Iceland

As I dipped to test the stream some yards away
From a hot spring, I could hear nothing
But the whole mud-slick muttering and boiling.

And then my guide behind me saying,
'Lukewarm. And I think you'd want to know   5
That *luk* was an old Icelandic word for hand.'

And you would want to know (but you know already)
How usual that waft and pressure felt
When the inner palm of water found my palm.

A Peacock's Feather

for Daisy Garnett

Six days ago the water fell
To christen you, to work its spell
And wipe your slate, we hope, for good.
But now your life is sleep and food
Which, with the touch of love, suffice
You, Daisy, Daisy, English niece.

Gloucestershire: its prospects lie
Wooded and misty to my eye
Whose landscape, as your mother's was,
Is other than this mellowness
Of topiary, lawn and brick,
Possessed, untrespassed, walled, nostalgic.

I come from scraggy farm and moss,
Old patchworks that the pitch and toss
Of history have left dishevelled.
But here, for your sake, I have levelled
My cart-track voice to garden tones,
Cobbled the bog with Cotswold stones.

Ravelling strands of families mesh
In love-knots of two minds, one flesh.
The future's not our own. We'll weave
An in-law maze, we'll nod and wave
With trust but little intimacy –
So this is a billet-doux to say

That in a warm July you lay
Christened and smiling in Bradley
While I, a guest in your green court,
At a west window sat and wrote
Self-consciously in gathering dark.
I might as well be in Coole Park.

So before I leave your ordered home,
Let us pray. May tilth and loam,
Darkened with Celts' and Saxons' blood,
Breastfeed your love of house and wood –
Where I drop this for you, as I pass,   35
Like the peacock's feather on the grass.

1972

Grotus and Coventina

Far from home Grotus dedicated an altar to Coventina
Who holds in her right hand a waterweed
And in her left a pitcher spilling out a river.
Anywhere Grotus looked at running water he felt at home
And when he remembered the stone where he cut his name   5
Some dried-up course beneath his breastbone started
Pouring and darkening – more or less the way
The thought of his stunted altar works on me.

Remember when our electric pump gave out,
Priming it with bucketfuls, our idiotic rage   10
And hangdog phone-calls to the farm next door
For somebody please to come and fix it?
And when it began to hammer on again,
Jubilation at the tap's full force, the sheer
Given fact of water, how you felt you'd never   15
Waste one drop but know its worth better always.
Do you think we could run through all that one more time?
I'll be Grotus, you be Coventina.

Holding Course

Propellers underwater, cabins drumming, lights –
Unthought-of but constant out there every night,
The big ferries pondered on their courses.
I envy you your sight of them this morning,
Docked and massive with their sloped-back funnels.   5

The outlook is high and airy where you stand
By our attic window. Far Toledo blues.
And from a shelf behind you

                The alpine thistle we brought from Covadonga
10   Inclines its jaggy crest.

                Last autumn we were smouldering and parched
                As those spikes that keep vigil overhead
                Like Grendel's steely talon nailed
                To the mead-hall roof. And then we broke through
15   Or we came through. It was its own reward.

                We are voluptuaries of the morning after.
                As gulls cry out above the deep channels
                And you stand on and on, twiddling your hair,
                Think of me as your MacWhirr of the boudoir,
20   Head on, one track, ignorant of manoeuvre.

        ## The Song of the Bullets

                I watched a long time in the yard
                        The usual stars, the still
                And seemly planets, lantern-bright
                        Above our darkened hill.

5   And then a star that moved, I thought,
                        For something moved indeed
                Up from behind the massed skyline
                        At ardent silent speed

                And when it reached the zenith, cut
10   Across the curving path
                Of a second light that swung up like
                        A scythe-point through its swathe.

                'The sky at night is full of us',
                        Now one began to sing,
15   'Our slugs of lead lie cold and dead,
                        Our trace is on the wing.

                Our casings and our blunted parts
                        Are gathered up below
                As justice stands aghast and stares
20   Like the sun on arctic snow.

                Our guilt was accidental. Blame,
                        Blame because you must.

Then blame young men for semen or
    Blame the moon for moondust.'

As ricochets that warble close,   25
    Then die away on wind,
That hard contralto sailed across
    And stellar quiet reigned

Until the other fireball spoke:
    'We are the iron will.   30
We hoop and cooper worlds beyond
    The killer and the kill.

Mount Olivet's beatitudes,
    The soul's cadenced desires
Cannot prevail against us who   35
    Dwell in the marbled fires

Of every steady eye that ever
    Narrowed, sighted, paused:
We fire and glaze the shape of things
    Until the shape's imposed.'   40

Now wind was blowing through the yard.
    Clouds blanked the stars. The still
And seemly planets disappeared
    Above our darkened hill.

Wolfe Tone

Light as a skiff, manoeuvrable
yet outmanoueuvred,

I affected epaulettes and a cockade,
wrote a style well-bred and impervious

to the solidarity I angled for,   5
and played the ancient Roman with a razor.

I was the shouldered oar that ended up
far from the brine and whiff of venture,

like a scratching-post or a crossroads flagpole,
out of my element among small farmers –   10

I who once wakened to the shouts of men
rising from the bottom of the sea,

men in their shirts mounting through deep water
when the Atlantic stove our cabin's dead lights in

and the big fleet split and Ireland dwindled
as we ran before the gale under bare poles.

A Shooting Script

They are riding away from whatever might have been
Towards what will never be, in a held shot:
Teachers on bicycles, saluting native speakers,
Treading the nineteen-twenties like the future.

Still pedalling out at the end of the lens,
Not getting anywhere and not getting away.
Mix to fuchsia that 'follows the language'.
A long soundless sequence. Pan and fade.

Then voices over, in different Irishes,
Discussing translation jobs and rates per line;
Like nineteenth-century milestones in grass verges,
Occurrence of names like R. M. Ballantyne.

A close-up on the cat's eye of a button
Pulling back wide to the cape of a soutane,
Biretta, Roman collar, Adam's apple.
Freeze his blank face. Let the credits run

And just when it looks as if it is all over –
Tracking shots of a long wave up a strand
That breaks towards the point of a stick writing and writing
Words in the old script in the running sand.

From the Canton of Expectation

I

We lived deep in a land of optative moods,
under high, banked clouds of resignation.
A rustle of loss in the phrase *Not in our lifetime*,

the broken nerve when we prayed *Vouchsafe* or *Deign*,
were creditable, sufficient to the day.

Once a year we gathered in a field
of dance platforms and tents where children sang
songs they had learned by rote in the old language.
An auctioneer who had fought in the brotherhood
enumerated the humiliations
we always took for granted, but not even he
considered this, I think, a call to action.
Iron-mouthed loudspeakers shook the air
yet nobody felt blamed. He had confirmed us.
When our rebel anthem played the meeting shut
we turned for home and the usual harassment
by militiamen on overtime at roadblocks.

II

And next thing, suddenly, this change of mood.
Books open in the newly-wired kitchens.
Young heads that might have dozed a life away
against the flanks of milking cows were busy
paving and pencilling their first causeways
across the prescribed texts. The paving stones
of quadrangles came next and a grammar
of imperatives, the new age of demands.
They would banish the conditional for ever,
this generation born impervious to
the triumph in our cries of *de profundis*.
Our faith in winning by enduring most
they made anathema, intelligences
brightened and unmannerly as crowbars.

III

What looks the strongest has outlived its term.
The future lies with what's affirmed from under.
These things that corroborated us when we dwelt
under the aegis of our stealthy patron,
the guardian angel of passivity,
now sink a fang of menace in my shoulder.
I repeat the word 'stricken' to myself
and stand bareheaded under the banked clouds
edged more and more with brassy thunderlight.

10   I yearn for hammerblows on clinkered planks,
the uncompromised report of driven thole-pins,
to know there is one among us who never swerved
from all his instincts told him was right action,
who stood his ground in the indicative,
whose boat will lift when the cloudburst happens.

The Mud Vision

Statues with exposed hearts and barbed-wire crowns
Still stood in alcoves, hares flitted beneath
The dozing bellies of jets, our menu-writers
And punks with aerosol sprays held their own
5   With the best of them. Satellite link-ups
Wafted over us the blessings of popes, heliports
Maintained a charmed circle for idols on tour
And casualties on their stretchers. We sleepwalked
The line between panic and formulae, screentested
10   Our first native models and the last of the mummers,
Watching ourselves at a distance, advantaged
And airy as a man on a springboard
Who keeps limbering up because the man cannot dive.

And then in the foggy midlands it appeared,
15   Our mud vision, as if a rose window of mud
Had invented itself out of the glittery damp,
A gossamer wheel, concentric with its own hub
Of nebulous dirt, sullied yet lucent.
We had heard of the sun standing still and the sun
20   That changed colour, but we were vouchsafed
Original clay, transfigured and spinning.
And then the sunsets ran murky, the wiper
Could never entirely clean off the windscreen,
Reservoirs tasted of silt, a light fuzz
25   Accrued in the hair and the eyebrows, and some
Took to wearing a smudge on their foreheads
To be prepared for whatever. Vigils
Began to be kept around puddled gaps,
On altars bulrushes ousted the lilies
30   And a rota of invalids came and went
On beds they could lease placed in range of the shower.

A generation who had seen a sign!
Those nights when we stood in an umber dew and smelled
Mould in the verbena, or woke to a light
Furrow-breath on the pillow, when the talk 35
Was all about who had seen it and our fear
Was touched with a secret pride, only ourselves
Could be adequate then to our lives. When the rainbow
Curved flood-brown and ran like a water-rat's back
So that drivers on the hard shoulder switched off to watch, 40
We wished it away, and yet we presumed it a test
That would prove us beyond expectation.

We lived, of course, to learn the folly of that.
One day it was gone and the east gable
Where its trembling corolla had balanced 45
Was starkly a ruin again, with dandelions
Blowing high up on the ledges, and moss
That slumbered on through its increase. As cameras raked
The site from every angle, experts
Began their *post factum* jabber and all of us 50
Crowded in tight for the big explanations.
Just like that, we forgot that the vision was ours,
Our one chance to know the incomparable
And dive to a future. What might have been origin
We dissipated in news. The clarified place 55
Had retrieved neither us nor itself – except
You could say we survived. So say that, and watch us
Who had our chance to be mud-men, convinced and estranged,
Figure in our own eyes for the eyes of the world.

The Disappearing Island

Once we presumed to found ourselves for good
Between its blue hills and those sandless shores
Where we spent our desperate night in prayer and vigil,

Once we had gathered driftwood, made a hearth
And hung our cauldron like a firmament, 5
The island broke beneath us like a wave.

The land sustaining us seemed to hold firm
Only when we embraced it *in extremis*.
All I believe that happened there was vision.

The Riddle

You never saw it used but still can hear
The sift and fall of stuff hopped on the mesh,

Clods and buds in a little dust-up,
The dribbled pile accruing under it.

Which would be better, what sticks or what falls through?
Or does the choice itself create the value?

Legs apart, deft-handed, start a mime
To sift the sense of things from what's imagined

And work out what was happening in that story
Of the man who carried water in a riddle.

Was it culpable ignorance, or was it rather
A *via negativa* through drops and let-downs?

UNCOLLECTED POEMS (1988–1989)

Valedictory Verses

Composed for the Carysfort Graduation Exercises, 1988

A tuning fork. An era quavers, passes.
Coloured wall-maps fade. And myths of Greece.
Gone with the solfa and the singing classes.

Roll-books. Ink-wells. Motes in sunlight. Stasis.
Aesop. Andersen. The Golden Fleece.　　　　　　　　　5
A tuning fork. An era quavers, passes.

Transcription's gone. And Solemn Latin Masses.
The lace of albs, the wimple's perfect crease –
Gone with the solfa and the singing classes.

Nature study. Names of soils and grasses.　　　　　　　10
Names of county towns. Their singsongs cease.
And tuning forks. That era quavers, passes.

O Ireland of crossroads and comely lasses!
Visionary, historical decease!
Gone with the solfa and the singing classes.　　　　　　15

On a high shelf, catkins moult in vases.
The school clock's stopped all summer. In that peace,
A tuning fork! Another era passes
Beyond the solfa and the singing classes.

Dublin 4

Lit carriages ran through our fields at night
Like promises being speedily withdrawn.
Awakened by train-noise, well-placed, suburban,
I ask myself is this where they were going.

New Worlds

In the country poetry has deserted
Things fall in place like the plate-glass doors in banks.

There is a great calm.
The preserved churches are cool at noon

5   The good life hums and clinks in sidewalk cafés
Along the quays of sun-fed old canals.

Satiety in that air
Is so consistent and unostentatious

The sated traveller returns for more,
10 Grateful that his privilege is condoned.

In the country poetry has deserted,
In a language tonic as their swimming pools,

There are many poets, all insisting
Their poetry brings new worlds into being.

The Strand Hotel

Seagull at first light above the chimney.
Its one skirl has transfixed

Spinster's dulse with its birthmark iodines.
Knickers on sills. More gulls. The morning dogfish.

Resin

Pine cones beyond
The scale of pine cones I knew,
There for the taking, big

As pineapples, dried out,
5   Splayed open, tangy,
Light as a basket.

At sunset, the plink of an engine
Let cool for the first time that day,
Our children with their arms full,

10 And, for a moment, fear
At such an abundance. But then
It was usual, the car all refreshed

With head-clearing resins,
The road on both sides
Littered with them for miles   15

And the weathered piles at each crossroads
Like cone-cairns to Hermes
Lightfooting it north with good news.

from Holdings

Cotyledon, flap your Greek-filmed wings!
Then come to earth, a greener home-grown thing.
I sing the word. She patted sweet-pea mould

In compact, shallow, dead-weight sprouting-boxes
And ranged them in the dark under the bed.   5
Earth to earth, a porous, laden air.

The bedroom was like some dank brooding country
On the verge of a peasant rising,
The forges still, the forged pikes in the thatch.

But then frail seedlings climb the rods in peace, 10
The canopy is borne between stone walls,
Old sills bloom sweetly and the whitewash shines.

§

A molten reddishness scudding with steam.
Shield-walls of stove-heat mustered in the kitchen,
Burnt-brown sweetness wafted off the stove-top

And something summery came wending back
Out of all that sputtering berry-life   5
In the big enamel pot. Fragrance

And promise, subtle inhalations
And dispersals. Rub old jampots now
For the fume that always swayed and disappeared.

Or take a wooden spoon and conduct with it   10
Until each little outburst in the jam
Counts like a missed beat in the dried-up handle.

§

Staccato and reflexive. A barrel rolled
For devilment along the cobbled lane
With one of us inside it, vulnerable

And assailed and exhilarated
5   As a drummer's ear. The storied echo
Of hammering deep under the mountain

Came true a moment, lamplit galleries
Flared and blinded. Everything went wild.
We primed ourselves with hubbub – small scale perhaps
10 But a measure of what was or might be what.
Pitched utterly, like a runner on his mark,
I was hooped and foetal there, the perfect circle.

Five Derry Glosses

> *Derry derives from the Irish word* doire, *meaning an oak grove. The city is associated with Saint Colmcille, 'the dove of the church', who subsequently exiled himself to the island of Iona. The local place-name, Dirraghs, in the fifth poem, is probably another anglicisation of* doire. *The imagery of the third poem is taken from Frances Yates's* The Art of Memory.

Derry was *oak grove*. We believed in that
Like a mystery: the inked-in, thick-bunched,
Green and deckled light, the acorns and dead leaves

Had all been transubstantiated
5   Into a hill-town airiness, Derry's lilt
And pure *éclat* and quick unleavened song.

English or Irish? Transmuted place or name?
A mystery. But Derry Colmcille
Were the clear words of a beginning,

10 The dove, the thing itself and its white sign,
The scribe's illumination, the small boat,
The poem of exile and blindfolded love.

The River Foyle, the Roe, the quick Moyola.
The tense of water is continuous
Past or present. Something in you always

Re-entering its swim, riding or quelling
The very currents that it is comprised of,
Everything you accumulated ever

In river vigils at high college windows,
On gravel beds, or waist-deep in cow parsley
On the banks of self at evening . . .

Lick of fear: the dead leaf borne in silence
Swifter (it seemed) than the water's passage.
Remembered flow the sky-dipped willows trailed in.

Memory as a building or a city,
Well lighted, well laid out, appointed with
Tableaux vivants and costumed effigies:

Statues in purple cloaks, or painted red,
Ones wearing crowns, ones smeared with mud or blood.
Ancient memory primers approved such

Loci et imagines, images
Impressed on sites, like seals impressed on wax,
So that the mind's eye retained the heightened meaning.

And who is this in our haunted townscape staring
But the student of mnemonics and fresh murders,
Incredulous, abstracted, totting, sealing?

Seven years. The usual spellbound term.
The world dreamt through one long suspended gaze
At the shiny glamour and projections

Of a schoolroom wallmap. Shelvings, selvedges
Of blue on blue deepened out from strands,
Colour charts of contours and of soundings

Foretold the heavenly pigments, Atlantic turquoise
Swam immensely north. But green went deep
As the unconscious in *Bann Valley*,

Acre and *holding*, *right-of-way* and *roof*,
Where (landlocked, time-lagged, pent up in gutturals)
We glossed ourselves with earth tones and with leave shades.

The Dirraghs were the fields of the nearly blessed.
Here the oak groves had been retranslated
Into a townland of bog oak and turf stacks

Where gaunt ones in their shirt sleeves dug and barrowed
Or stood alone at dusk out on a spread-field –
Apparitions now, yet active still,

Still territorial, sure of their ground
And interested, not knowing how far
The country of the souls has been pushed back,

How long the lark has stopped outside the Dirraghs
And only seems unstoppable to them
Caught like a far hill in a freak of sunshine.

THE CURE AT TROY (1990)

from Voices from Lemnos: IV

Human beings suffer.
They torture one another.
They get hurt and get hard.
No poem or play or song
Can fully right a wrong
Inflicted and endured.

History says, Don't hope
On this side of the grave,
But then, once in a lifetime
The longed-for tidal wave
Of justice can rise up
And hope and history rhyme.

So hope for a great sea-change
On the far side of revenge.
Believe that a farther shore
Is reachable from here.
Believe in miracles
And cures and healing wells.

Call miracle self-healing,
The utter self-revealing
Double-take of feeling.
If there's fire on the mountain
And lightning and storm
And a god speaks from the sky

That means someone is hearing
The outcry and the birth-cry
Of new life at its term.
It means once in a lifetime
That justice can rise up
And hope and history rhyme.

UNCOLLECTED POEMS (1990–1991)

Grove Hill

Bluebells under trees up on Grove Hill –
I waded them, they waterkissed my shins
And flowed with the light and dark of running tides.

But the light under the trees was driest land-light.
Winnowed. Unscreened. Far-ranging. Stationary.　　　　5
Stand still yourself and everything stood open.

It was four decades before it did again,
After an all-night session of given poems
When I waded in tide-brightness on Long Island.

High water mark dawned straight across my breast,　　　10
A line of bluebells trembling. If I opened my arms
They lay on the level, distanced and sustained.

The Stirling Stanzas

At times in Dublin life is tame
So when a certain letter came
And said in June if I was game
　　　And came to Stirling
They'd put new letters to my name –　　　　5
　　　My heart went birling.

For Stirling was a place I'd been:
I'd read poems there and seen
The ancient castle and the green
　　　And famous campus　　　　10
That had transformed grey academe
　　　Into a pampas.

But how could any place be grey
That had been lucky in its day
To rank a prince of poetry　　　　15
　　　Among its members:
MacCaig (or Norman, as we say,
　　　who lisp his numbers)?

And other friends and potentates –
Like that biographer of Yeats,　　　　20

The Norman who abbreviates
        His name to Derry,
Who edits poems and annotates
        Things literary –

I mean, of course, A Norman Jeffares,
Though there's a score of his successors,
Scholars, critics and professors
        I could praise too;
But just one more name – Alasdair's –
        Will have to do.

I'm being personal, of course,
But I could speak until I'm hoarse
Impersonally and perforce
        On your behalf
To name and flatter and endorse
        The entire staff.

Instead, I hasten to conclude,
To thank you for my gown and hood,
To say what pride and gratitude
        I feel to be
A graduate of this great and good
        Academy.

We 1990 graduates,
We bless our lucky stars and fates,
Our alma mater, parents, mates:
        We're on our knees
To offer thanks and celebrate
        Our new degrees.

SEEING THINGS (1991)

for Derek Mahon

The Golden Bough

(Aeneid, *Book VI, lines 98–148*)

So from the back of her shrine the Sibyl of Cumae
Chanted fearful equivocal words and made the cave echo
With sayings where clear truths and mysteries
Were inextricably twined. Apollo turned and twisted
His spurs at her breast, gave her her head, then reined in her spasms.   5

As soon as her fit passed away and the mad mouthings stopped
Heroic Aeneas began: 'No ordeal, O Priestess,
That you can imagine would ever surprise me
For already I have foreseen and foresuffered all.
But one thing I pray for especially: since they say it is here   10
That the King of the Underworld's gateway is to be found,
Among these shadowy marshes where Acheron comes flooding
    through,
I pray for one look, one face-to-face meeting with my dear father.
Teach me the way and open the holy doors wide.
I carried him on these shoulders through flames   15
And thousands of enemy spears. In the thick of battle I saved him
And he was at my side then through all my sea-journeys,
A man in old age, worn out yet holding out always.
And he too it was who half-prayed and half-ordered me
To make this approach, to find and petition you.   20
So therefore, Vestal, I beseech you take pity
On a son and a father, for nothing is out of your power
Whom Hecate appointed the keeper of wooded Avernus.
If Orpheus could call back the shade of a wife through his faith
In the loudly plucked strings of his Thracian lyre,   25
If Pollux could redeem a brother by going in turns
Backwards and forwards so often to the land of the dead,
And if Theseus too, and great Hercules . . . But why speak of them?
I myself am of highest birth, a descendant of Jove.'

He was praying like that and holding on to the altar   30
When the prophetess started to speak: 'Blood relation of gods,
Trojan, son of Anchises, the way down to Avernus is easy.
Day and night black Pluto's door stands open.
But to retrace your steps and get back to upper air,
This is the real task and the real undertaking.   35

A few have been able to do it, sons of gods
Favoured by Jupiter the Just, or exalted to heaven
In a blaze of heroic glory. Forests spread midway down,
And Cocytus winds through the dark, licking its banks.
Still, if love torments you so much and you so much need
To sail the Stygian lake twice and twice to inspect
The murk of Tartarus, if you will go beyond the limit,
Understand what you must do beforehand.
Hidden in the thick of a tree is a bough made of gold
And its leaves and pliable twigs are made of it too.
It is sacred to underworld Juno, who is its patron,
And it is roofed in by a grove, where deep shadows mass
Along far wooded valleys. No one is ever permitted
To go down to earth's hidden places unless he has first
Plucked this golden-fledged growth out of its tree
And handed it over to fair Prosperina, to whom it belongs
By decree, her own special gift. And when it is plucked,
A second one always grows in its place, golden again,
And the foliage growing on it has the same metal sheen.
Therefore look up and search deep and when you have found it
Take hold of it boldly and duly. If fate has called you,
The bough will come away easily, of its own accord.
Otherwise, no matter how much strength you muster, you never will
Manage to quell it or cut it down with the toughest of blades.'

PART I

The Journey Back

Larkin's shade surprised me. He quoted Dante:

'Daylight was going and the umber air
Soothing every creature on the earth,
Freeing them from their labours everywhere.

I alone was girding myself to face
The ordeal of my journey and my duty

And not a thing had changed, as rush-hour buses

Bore the drained and laden through the city.
I might have been a wise king setting out
Under the Christmas lights – except that 10

It felt more like the forewarned journey back
Into the heartland of the ordinary.
Still my old self. Ready to knock one back.

A nine-to-five man who had seen poetry.'

Markings

I

We marked the pitch: four jackets for four goalposts,
That was all. The corners and the squares
Were there like longitude and latitude
Under the bumpy thistly ground, to be
Agreed about or disagreed about 5
When the time came. And then we picked the teams
And crossed the line our called names drew between us.

Youngsters shouting their heads off in a field
As the light died and they kept on playing
Because by then they were playing in their heads 10
And the actual kicked ball came to them
Like a dream heaviness, and their own hard
Breathing in the dark and skids on grass
Sounded like effort in another world . . .
It was quick and constant, a game that never need 15
Be played out. Some limit had been passed,
There was fleetness, furtherance, untiredness
In time that was extra, unforeseen and free.

II

You also loved lines pegged out in the garden,
The spade nicking the first straight edge along
The tight white string. Or string stretched perfectly
To mark the outline of a house foundation,
Pale timber battens set at right angles 5
For every corner, each freshly sawn new board
Spick and span in the oddly passive grass.
Or the imaginary line straight down

　　　　A field of grazing, to be ploughed open
10　　From the rod stuck in one headrig to the rod
　　　　Stuck in the other.

　　　III
　　　　　　　　All these things entered you
　　　　As if they were both the door and what came through it.
　　　　They marked the spot, marked time and held it open.
　　　　A mower parted the bronze sea of corn.
5　　　A windlass hauled the centre out of water.
　　　　Two men with a cross-cut kept it swimming
　　　　Into a felled beech backwards and forwards
　　　　So that they seemed to row the steady earth.

Three Drawings

1 *The Point*

　　　Those were the days –
　　　booting a leather football
　　　truer and farther
　　　than you ever expected!

5　　It went rattling
　　　hard and fast
　　　over daisies and benweeds,
　　　it thumped

　　　but it sang too,
10　　a kind of dry, ringing
　　　foreclosure of sound.
　　　Or else, a great catch

　　　and a cry from the touch-line
　　　to *Point her!* That spring
15　　and unhampered smash-through!
　　　Was it you

　　　or the ball that kept going
　　　beyond you, amazingly
　　　higher and higher
20　　and ruefully free?

2 *The Pulse*

The effortlessness
of a spinning reel. One quick
flick of the wrist
and your minnow sped away

whispering and silky
and nimbly laden.
It seemed to be all rise
and shine, the very opposite

of uphill going – it was pure
duration, and when it ended,
the pulse of the cast line
entering water

was smaller in your hand
than the remembered heartbeat
of a bird. Then, after all of that
runaway give, you were glad

when you reeled in and found
yourself strung, heel-tip
to rod-tip, into the river's
steady purchase and thrum.

3 *A Haul*

The one that got away
from Thor and the giant Hymer
was the world-serpent itself.
The god had baited his line

with an ox-head, spun it high
and plunged it into the depths.
But the big haul came to an end
when Thor's foot went through the boards

and Hymer panicked and cut
the line with a bait-knife. Then
roll-over, turmoil, whiplash!
A Milky Way in the water.

The hole he smashed in the boat
opened, the way Thor's head

15 opened out there on the sea.
He felt at one with space,

unroofed and obvious –
surprised in his empty arms
like some fabulous high-catcher
20 coming down without the ball.

Casting and Gathering

for Ted Hughes

Years and years ago, these sounds took sides:

On the left bank, a green silk tapered cast
Went whispering through the air, saying *hush*
And *lush*, entirely free, no matter whether
5 It swished above the hayfield or the river.

On the right bank, like a speeded-up corncrake,
A sharp ratcheting went on and on
Cutting across the stillness as another
Fisherman gathered line-lengths off his reel.

10 I am still standing there, awake and dreamy,
I have grown older and can see them both
Moving their arms and rods, working away,
Each one absorbed, proofed by the sounds he's making.

One sound is saying, 'You are not worth tuppence,
15 But neither is anybody. Watch it! Be severe.'
The other says, 'Go with it! Give and swerve.
You are everything you feel beside the river.'

I love hushed air. I trust contrariness.
Years and years go past and I do not move
20 For I see that when one man casts, the other gathers
And then *vice versa*, without changing sides.

Man and Boy

I

'Catch the old one first,'
(My father's joke was also old, and heavy
And predictable.) 'Then the young ones
Will all follow, and Bob's your uncle.'

On slow bright river evenings, the sweet time   5
Made him afraid we'd take too much for granted
And so our spirits must be lightly checked.

Blessed be down-to-earth! Blessed be highs!
Blessed be the detachment of dumb love
In that broad-backed, low-set man   10
Who feared debt all his life, but now and then
Could make a splash like the salmon he said was
'As big as a wee pork pig by the sound of it'.

II

In earshot of the pool where the salmon jumped
Back through its own unheard concentric soundwaves
A mower leans forever on his scythe.

He has mown himself to the centre of the field
And stands in a final perfect ring   5
Of sunlit stubble.

'Go and tell your father,' the mower says
(He said it to my father who told me)
'I have it mowed as clean as a new sixpence.'

My father is a barefoot boy with news,   10
Running at eye-level with weeds and stooks
On the afternoon of his own father's death.

The open, black half of the half-door waits.
I feel much heat and hurry in the air.
I feel his legs and quick heels far away   15

And strange as my own – when he will piggyback me
At a great height, light-headed and thin-boned,
Like a witless elder rescued from the fire.

Seeing Things

I

Inishbofin on a Sunday morning.
Sunlight, turfsmoke, seagulls, boatslip, diesel.
One by one we were being handed down
Into a boat that dipped and shilly-shallied
Scaresomely every time. We sat tight
On short cross-benches, in nervous twos and threes,
Obedient, newly close, nobody speaking
Except the boatmen, as the gunwales sank
And seemed they might ship water any minute.
The sea was very calm but even so,
When the engine kicked and our ferryman
Swayed for balance, reaching for the tiller,
I panicked at the shiftiness and heft
Of the craft itself. What guaranteed us –
That quick response and buoyancy and swim –
Kept me in agony. All the time
As we went sailing evenly across
The deep, still, seeable-down-into water,
It was as if I looked from another boat
Sailing through air, far up, and could see
How riskily we fared into the morning,
And loved in vain our bare, bowed, numbered heads.

II

Claritas. The dry-eyed Latin word
Is perfect for the carved stone of the water
Where Jesus stands up to his unwet knees
And John the Baptist pours out more water
Over his head: all this in bright sunlight
On the façade of a cathedral. Lines
Hard and thin and sinuous represent
The flowing river. Down between the lines
Little antic fish are all go. Nothing else.
And yet in that utter visibility
The stone's alive with what's invisible:
Waterweed, stirred sand-grains hurrying off,
The shadowy, unshadowed stream itself.
All afternoon, heat wavered on the steps

And the air we stood up to our eyes in wavered 15
Like the zig-zag hieroglyph for life itself.

III

Once upon a time my undrowned father
Walked into our yard. He had gone to spray
Potatoes in a field on the riverbank
And wouldn't bring me with him. The horse-sprayer
Was too big and new-fangled, bluestone might 5
Burn me in the eyes, the horse was fresh, I
Might scare the horse, and so on. I threw stones
At a bird on the shed roof, as much for
The clatter of the stones as anything,
But when he came back, I was inside the house 10
And saw him out the window, scatter-eyed
And daunted, strange without his hat,
His step unguided, his ghosthood immanent.
When he was turning on the riverbank,
The horse had rusted and reared up and pitched 15
Cart and sprayer and everything off balance
So the whole rig went over into a deep
Whirlpool, hoofs, chains, shafts, cartwheels, barrel
And tackle, all tumbling off the world,
And the hat already merrily swept along 20
The quieter reaches. That afternoon
I saw him face to face, he came to me
With his damp footprints out of the river,
And there was nothing between us there
That might not still be happily ever after. 25

The Ash Plant

He'll never rise again but he is ready.
Entered like a mirror by the morning,
He stares out the big window, wondering,
Not caring if the day is bright or cloudy.

An upstairs outlook on the whole country. 5
First milk-lorries, first smoke, cattle, trees
In damp opulence above damp hedges –
He has it to himself, he is like a sentry

          Forgotten and unable to remember
10   The whys and wherefores of his lofty station,
          Wakening relieved yet in position,
          Disencumbered as a breaking comber.

          As his head goes light with light, his wasting hand
          Gropes desperately and finds the phantom limb
15   Of an ash plant in his grasp, which steadies him.
          Now he has found his touch he can stand his ground

          Or wield the stick like a silver bough and come
          Walking again among us: the quoted judge.
          I could have cut a better man out of the hedge!
20   God might have said the same, remembering Adam.

1.1.87

Dangerous pavements.
But I face the ice this year
With my father's stick.

An August Night

His hands were warm and small and knowledgeable.
When I saw them again last night, they were two ferrets,
Playing all by themselves in a moonlit field.

Field of Vision

I remember this woman who sat for years
In a wheelchair, looking straight ahead
Out the window at sycamore trees unleafing
And leafing at the far end of the lane.

5   Straight out past the TV in the corner,
     The stunted, agitated hawthorn bush,
     The same small calves with their backs to wind and rain,
     The same acre of ragwort, the same mountain.

She was steadfast as the big window itself.
Her brow was clear as the chrome bits of the chair.   10
She never lamented once and she never
Carried a spare ounce of emotional weight.

Face to face with her was an education
Of the sort you got across a well-braced gate –
One of those lean, clean, iron, roadside ones   15
Between two whitewashed pillars, where you could see

Deeper into the country than you expected
And discovered that the field behind the hedge
Grew more distinctly strange as you kept standing
Focused and drawn in by what barred the way.   20

The Pitchfork

Of all implements, the pitchfork was the one
That came near to an imagined perfection:
When he tightened his raised hand and aimed with it,
It felt like a javelin, accurate and light.

So whether he played the warrior or the athlete   5
Or worked in earnest in the chaff and sweat,
He loved its grain of tapering, dark-flecked ash
Grown satiny from its own natural polish.

Riveted steel, turned timber, burnish, grain,
Smoothness, straightness, roundness, length and sheen.   10
Sweat-cured, sharpened, balanced, tested, fitted.
The springiness, the clip and dart of it.

And then when he thought of probes that reached the farthest,
He would see the shaft of a pitchfork sailing past
Evenly, imperturbably through space,   15
Its prongs starlit and absolutely soundless –

But has learned at last to follow that simple lead
Past its own aim, out to an other side
Where perfection – or nearness to it – is imagined
Not in the aiming but the opening hand.   20

A Basket of Chestnuts

There's a shadow-boost, a giddy strange assistance
That happens when you swing a loaded basket.
The lightness of the thing seems to diminish
The actual weight of what's being hoisted in it.

5   For a split second your hands feel unburdened,
Outstripped, dismayed, passed through.
Then just as unexpectedly comes rebound –
Downthrust and comeback ratifying you.

I recollect this basket full of chestnuts,
10 A really solid gather-up, all drag
And lustre, opulent and gravid
And golden-bowelled as a moneybag.

And I wish they could be painted, known for what
Pigment might see beyond them, what the reach
15 Of sense despairs of as it fails to reach it,
Especially the thwarted sense of touch.

Since Edward Maguire visited our house
In the autumn of 1973,
A basketful of chestnuts shines between us,
20 One that he did not paint when he painted me –

Although it was what he thought he'd maybe use
As a decoy or a coffer for the light
He captured in the toecaps of my shoes.
But it wasn't in the picture and is not.

25 What's there is comeback, especially for him.
In oils and brushwork we are ratified.
And the basket shines and foxfire chestnuts gleam
Where he passed through, unburdened and dismayed.

The Biretta

Like Gaul, the biretta was divided
Into three parts: triple-finned black serge,
A shipshape pillbox, its every slope and edge
Trimly articulated and decided.

Its insides were crimped satin; it was heavy too
But sported a light flossy tassel
That the backs of my fingers remember well,
And it left a dark red line on the priest's brow.

I received it into my hand from the hand
Of whoever was celebrant, one thin
Fastidious movement up and out and in
In the name of the Father and of the Son AND

Of the Holy Ghost . . . I placed it on the steps
Where it seemed to batten down, even half-resist
All of the brisk proceedings of the Mass –
The chalice drunk off and the patted lips.

The first time I saw one, I heard a shout
As an El Greco ascetic rose before me
Preaching hellfire, Saurian and stormy,
Adze-head on the rampage in the pulpit.

Sanctuaries. Marble. Kneeling boards. Vocation.
Some it made look squashed, some clean and tall.
It was antique as armour in a hall
And put the wind up me and my generation.

Now I turn it upside down and it is a boat –
A paper boat, or the one that wafts into
The first lines of the *Purgatorio*
As poetry lifts its eyes and clears its throat.

Or maybe that small boat out of the bronze age
Where the oars are needles and the worked gold frail
As the intact half of a hatched-out shell,
Refined beyond the dross into sheer image.

But in the end it's as likely to be the one
In Matthew Lawless's painting, *The Sick Call*,
Where the scene is out on a river and it's all
Solid, pathetic and Irish Victorian.

In which case, however, his reverence wears a hat.
Undaunting, half domestic, loved in crises,
He sits listening as each long oar dips and rises,
Sad for his worthy life and fit for it.

The Settle Bed

Willed down, waited for, in place at last and for good.
Trunk-hasped, cart-heavy, painted an ignorant brown.
And pew-strait, bin-deep, standing four-square as an ark.

If I lie in it, I am cribbed in seasoned deal
Dry as the unkindled boards of a funeral ship.
My measure has been taken, my ear shuttered up.

Yet I hear an old sombre tide awash in the headboard:
Unpathetic *och ochs* and *och hohs*, the long bedtime
Anthems of Ulster, unwilling, unbeaten,

Protestant, Catholic, the Bible, the beads,
Long talks at gables by moonlight, boots on the hearth,
The small hours chimed sweetly away so next thing it was

The cock on the ridge-tiles.
                      And now this is 'an inheritance' –
Upright, rudimentary, unshiftably planked
In the long ago, yet willable forward

Again and again and again, cargoed with
Its own dumb, tongue-and-groove worthiness
And un-get-roundable weight. But to conquer that weight,

Imagine a dower of settle beds tumbled from heaven
Like some nonsensical vengeance come on the people,
Then learn from that harmless barrage that whatever is given

Can always be reimagined, however four-square,
Plank-thick, hull-stupid and out of its time
It happens to be. You are free as the lookout,

That far-seeing joker posted high over the fog,
Who declared by the time that he had got himself down
The actual ship had been stolen away from beneath him.

The Schoolbag

in memoriam John Hewitt

My handsewn leather schoolbag. Forty years.
Poet, you were *nel mezzo del cammin*
When I shouldered it, half-full of blue-lined jotters,
And saw the classroom charts, the displayed bean,

The wallmap with its spray of shipping lanes
Describing arcs across the blue North Channel . . .
And in the middle of the road to school,
Ox-eye daisies and wild dandelions.

Learning's easy carried! The bag is light,
Scuffed and supple and unemptiable
As an itinerant school conjuror's hat.
So take it, for a word-hoard and a handsel,

As you step out trig and look back all at once
Like a child on his first morning leaving parents.

Glanmore Revisited

1 *Scrabble*

in memoriam Tom Delaney, archaeologist

Bare flags. Pump water. Winter-evening cold.
Our backs might never warm up but our faces
Burned from the hearth-blaze and the hot whiskeys.
It felt remembered even then, an old
Rightness half-imagined or foretold,
As green sticks hissed and spat into the ashes
And whatever rampaged out there couldn't reach us,
Firelit, shuttered, slated and stone-walled.

Year after year, our game of Scrabble: love
Taken for granted like any other word
That was chanced on and allowed within the rules.
So 'scrabble' let it be. Intransitive.
Meaning to scratch or rake at something hard.
Which is what he hears. Our scraping, clinking tools.

2 *The Cot*

Scythe and axe and hedge-clippers, the shriek
Of the gate the children used to swing on,
Poker, scuttle, tongs, a gravel rake –
The old activity starts up again
But starts up differently. We're on our own
Years later in the same *locus amoenus*,
Tenants no longer, but in full possession
Of an emptied house and whatever keeps between us.

Which must be more than keepsakes, even though
The child's cot's back in the place where Catherine
Woke in the dawn and answered *doodle doo*
To the rooster in the farm across the road –
And is the same cot I myself slept in
When the whole world was a farm that eked and crowed.

3 *Scene Shifts*

Only days after a friend had cut his name
Into the ash, our kids stripped off the bark –
The first time I was really angry at them.
I was flailing around the house like a man berserk
And maybe overdoing it, although
The business had moved me at the time;
It brought back those blood-brother scenes where two
Braves nick wrists and cross them for a sign.

Where it shone like bone exposed is healed up now.
The bark's thick-eared and welted with a scar –
Like the hero's in a recognition scene
In which old nurse sees old wound, then clasps brow
(Astonished at what all this starts to mean)
And tears surprise the veteran of the war.

4 *1973*

The corrugated iron growled like thunder
When March came in; then as the year turned warmer
And invalids and bulbs came up from under,
I hibernated on behind the dormer,
Staring through shaken branches at the hill,

Dissociated, like an ailing farmer
Chloroformed against things seasonal
In a reek of cigarette smoke and dropped ash.

Lent came in next, also like a lion
Sinewy and wild for discipline,
A fasted will marauding through the body;
And I taunted it with scents of nicotine
As I lit one off another, and felt rash,
And stirred in the deep litter of the study.

5 Lustral Sonnet

Breaking and entering: from early on,
Words that thrilled me far more than they scared me –
And still did, when I came into my own
Masquerade as a man of property.
Even then, my first impulse was never
To double-bar a door or lock a gate;
And fitted blinds and curtains drawn over
Seemed far too self-protective and uptight.

But I scared myself when I re-entered here,
My own first breaker-in, with an instruction
To saw up the old bed-frame, since the stair
Was much too narrow for it. A bad action,
So Greek with consequence, so dangerous,
Only pure words and deeds secure the house.

6 Bedside Reading

The whole place airier. Big summer trees
Stirring at eye level when we waken
And little shoots of ivy creeping in
Unless they've been trained out – like memories
You've trained so long now they can show their face
And keep their distance. White-mouthed depression
Swims out from its shadow like a dolphin
With wet, unreadable, unfurtive eyes.

I swim in Homer. In Book Twenty-three.
At last Odysseus and Penelope
Waken together. One bedpost of the bed

Is the living trunk of an old olive tree
And is their secret. As ours could have been ivy,
Evergreen, atremble and unsaid.

7 *The Skylight*

You were the one for skylights. I opposed
Cutting into the seasoned tongue-and-groove
Of pitch pine. I liked it low and closed,
Its claustrophobic, nest-up-in-the-roof
Effect. I liked the snuff-dry feeling,
The perfect, trunk-lid fit of the old ceiling.
Under there, it was all hutch and hatch.
The blue slates kept the heat like midnight thatch.

But when the slates came off, extravagant
Sky entered and held surprise wide open.
For days I felt like an inhabitant
Of that house where the man sick of the palsy
Was lowered through the roof, had his sins forgiven,
Was healed, took up his bed and walked away.

A Pillowed Head

Matutinal. Mother-of-pearl
Summer come early. Slashed carmines
And washed milky blues.

To be first on the road,
Up with the ground-mists and pheasants.
To be older and grateful

That this time you too were half-grateful
The pangs had begun – prepared
And clear-headed, foreknowing

The trauma, entering on it
With full consent of the will.
(The first time, dismayed and arrayed

In your cut-off white cotton gown,
You were more bride than earth-mother
Up on the stirrup-rigged bed,

Who were self-possessed now
To the point of a walk on the pier
Before you checked in.)

And then later on I half-fainted
When the little slapped palpable girl
Was handed to me; but as usual

Came to in two wide-open eyes
That had been dawned into farther
Than ever, and had outseen the last

Of all those mornings of waiting
When your domed brow was one long held silence
And the dawn chorus anything but.

A Royal Prospect

On the day of their excursion up the Thames
To Hampton Court, they were nearly sunstruck,
She with her neck bared in a page-boy cut,
He all dreamy anyhow, wild for her
But pretending to be a thousand miles away,
Studying the boat's wake in the water.
And here are the photographs. Head to one side,
In her sleeveless blouse, one bare shoulder high
And one arm loose, a bird with a dropped wing
Surprised in cover. He looks at you straight,
Assailable, enamoured, full of vows,
Young dauphin in the once-upon-a-time.
And next the lowish red-brick Tudor frontage.
No more photographs, however, now
We are present there as the smell of grass
And suntan oil, standing like their sixth sense
Behind them at the entrance to the maze,
Heartbroken for no reason, willing them
To dare it to the centre they are lost for . . .
Instead, like reflections staggered through warped glass,
They reappear as in a black and white
Old grainy newsreel, where their pleasure-boat
Goes back spotlit across sunken bridges
And they alone are borne downstream unscathed,

25 Between mud banks where the wounded rave all night
At flameless blasts and echoless gunfire –
In all of which is ominously figured
Their free passage through historic times,
Like a silk train being brushed across a leper
30 Or the safe conduct of two royal favourites,
Unhindered and resented and bright-eyed.
So let them keep a tally of themselves
And be accountable when called upon
For although by every golden mean their lot
35 Is fair and due, pleas will be allowed
Against every right and title vested in them
(And in a court where mere innocuousness
Has never gained approval or acquittal.)

A Retrospect

I

The whole county apparently afloat:
Every road bridging or skirting water,
The land islanded, the field drains still as moats.

A bulrush sentried the lough shore: I had to
5 Wade barefoot over spongy, ice-cold marsh
(Soft bottom with bog water seeping through

The netted weeds) to get near where it stood
Perennially anomalous and dry,
Like chalk or velvet rooting in the mud.

10 Everything ran into water-colour.
The skyline was full up to the lip
As if the earth were going to brim over,

As if we moved in the first stealth of flood
For remember, at one place, the swim and flow
15 From hidden springs made a river in the road.

II

Another trip they seemed to keep repeating
Was up to Glenshane Pass – his 'Trail of Tears',
As he'd say every time, and point out streams

He first saw on the road to boarding school.
And then he'd quote Sir John Davies' dispatch
About his progress through there from Dungannon
With Chichester in 1608:
'The wild inhabitants wondered as much
To see the King's deputy, as Virgil's ghosts
Wondered to see Aeneas alive in Hell.'

They liked the feel of the valley out behind,
As if a ladder leaned against the world
And they were climbing it but might fall back
Into the total air and emptiness
They carried on their shoulders.

                The old road
Went up and up, it was lover country,
Their drive-in in the sky, where each parked car
Played possum in the twilight and clouds moved
Smokily in the deep of polished roofs
And dormant windscreens.

                   And here they were,
Astray in the hill-fort of all pleasures
Where air was other breath and grass a whisper,
Feeling empowered but still somehow constrained:
Young marrieds, used now to the licit within doors,
They fell short of the sweetness that had lured them.
No nest in rushes, the heather bells unbruised,
The love-drink of the mountain streams untasted.

So when they turned, they turned with the fasted eyes
Of wild inhabitants, and parked in silence
A bit down from the summit, where the brae
Swept off like a balcony, then seemed to drop
Sheer towards the baronies and cantreds.
Evening was dam water they saw down through.
The scene stood open, the visit lasted,
They gazed beyond themselves until he eased
The brake off and they freewheeled quickly
Before going into gear, with all their usual old
High-pitched strain and gradual declension.

The Rescue

In drifts of sleep I came upon you
Buried to your waist in snow.
You reached your arms out: I came to
Like water in a dream of thaw.

Wheels within Wheels

I

The first real grip I ever got on things
Was when I learned the art of pedalling
(By hand) a bike turned upside down, and drove
Its back wheel preternaturally fast.
I loved the disappearance of the spokes,
The way the space between the hub and rim
Hummed with transparency. If you threw
A potato into it, the hooped air
Spun mush and drizzle back into your face;
If you touched it with a straw, the straw frittered.
Something about the way those pedal treads
Worked very palpably at first against you
And then began to sweep your hand ahead
Into a new momentum – that all entered me
Like an access of free power, as if belief
Caught up and spun the objects of belief
In an orbit coterminous with longing.

II

But enough was not enough. Who ever saw
The limit in the given anyhow?
In fields beyond our house there was a well
('The well' we called it. It was more a hole
With water in it, with small hawthorn trees
On one side, and a muddy, dungy ooze
On the other, all tramped through by cattle).
I loved that too. I loved the turbid smell,
The sump-life of the place like old chain oil.
And there, next thing, I brought my bicycle.
I stood its saddle and its handlebars

Into the soft bottom, I touched the tyres
To the water's surface, then turned the pedals
Until like a mill-wheel pouring at the treadles
(But here reversed and lashing a mare's tail)
The world-refreshing and immersed back wheel
Spun lace and dirt-suds there before my eyes
And showered me in my own regenerate clays.
For weeks I made a nimbus of old glit.
Then the hub jammed, rims rusted, the chain snapped.

III

Nothing rose to the occasion after that
Until, in a circus ring, drumrolled and spotlit,
Cowgirls wheeled in, each one immaculate
At the still centre of a lariat.
Perpetuum mobile. Sheer pirouette.
Tumblers. Jongleurs. Ring-a-rosies. *Stet!*

The Sounds of Rain

in memoriam Richard Ellmann

I

An all-night drubbing overflow on boards
On the veranda. I dwelt without thinking
In the long moil of it, and then came to
To dripping eaves and light, saying into myself
Proven, weightless sayings of the dead.
Things like *He'll be missed* and *You'll have to thole.*

II

It could have been the drenched weedy gardens
Of Peredelkino: a reverie
Of looking out from late-winter gloom
Lit by tangerines and the clear of vodka,
Where Pasternak, lenient yet austere,
Answered for himself without insistence.

'I had the feeling of an immense debt,'
He said (it is recorded). 'So many years
Just writing lyric poetry and translating.

10 I felt there was some duty . . . Time was passing.
    And with all its faults, it has more value
    Than those early . . . It is richer, more humane.'

    Or it could have been the thaw and puddles
    Of Athens Street where William Alfred stood
15 On the wet doorstep, remembering the friend
    Who died at sixty. 'After "Summer Tides"
    There would have been a deepening, you know,
    Something ampler . . . Ah well. Good-night again.'

III

The eaves a water-fringe and steady lash
Of summer downpour: *You are steeped in luck*,
I hear them say, *Steeped, steeped, steeped in luck.*
And hear the flood too, gathering from under,
10 Biding and boding like a masterwork
Or a named name that overbrims itself.

Fosterling

'That heavy greenness fostered by water'

At school I loved one picture's heavy greenness –
Horizons rigged with windmills' arms and sails.
The millhouses' still outlines. Their in-placeness
Still more in place when mirrored in canals.
5   I can't remember never having known
The immanent hydraulics of a land
Of *glar* and *glit* and floods at *dailigone*.
My silting hope. My lowlands of the mind.

Heaviness of being. And poetry
10 Sluggish in the doldrums of what happens.
Me waiting until I was nearly fifty
To credit marvels. Like the tree-clock of tin cans
The tinkers made. So long for air to brighten,
Time to be dazzled and the heart to lighten.

PART II: SQUARINGS

1 Lightenings

i

Shifting brilliancies. Then winter light
In a doorway, and on the stone doorstep
A beggar shivering in silhouette.

So the particular judgement might be set:
Bare wallstead and a cold hearth rained into –   5
Bright puddle where the soul-free cloud-life roams.

And after the commanded journey, what?
Nothing magnificent, nothing unknown.
A gazing out from far away, alone.

And it is not particular at all,   10
Just old truth dawning: there is no next-time-round.
Unroofed scope. Knowledge-freshening wind.

ii

Roof it again. Batten down. Dig in.
Drink out of a tin. Know the scullery cold,
A latch, a door-bar, forged tongs and a grate.

Touch the cross-beam, drive iron in a wall,
Hang a line to verify the plumb   5
From lintel, coping-stone and chimney-breast.

Relocate the bedrock in the threshold.
Take squarings from the recessed gable pane.
Make your study the unregarded floor.

Sink every impulse like a bolt. Secure   10
The bastion of sensation. Do not waver
Into language. Do not waver in it.

iii

Squarings? In the game of marbles, squarings
Were all those anglings, aimings, feints and squints
You were allowed before you'd shoot, all those

Hunkerings, tensings, pressures of the thumb,
Test-outs and pull-backs, re-envisagings,
All the ways your arms kept hoping towards

Blind certainties that were going to prevail
Beyond the one-off moment of the pitch.
A million million accuracies passed

Between your muscles' outreach and that space
Marked with three round holes and a drawn line.
You squinted out from a skylight of the world.

iv

Beneath the ocean of itself, the crowd
In Roman theatres could hear another
Stronger groundswell coming through.

It was like the steady message in a shell
Held to the ear in earshot of the sea:
Words being spoken on the scene arrived

Resonating up through the walls of urns.
The cordoned air rolled back, wave upon wave
Of classic mouthfuls amplified and faded.

How airy and how earthed it felt up there,
Bare to the world, light-headed, volatile
And carried like the rests in tides or music.

v

Three marble holes thumbed in the concrete road
Before the concrete hardened still remained
Three decades after the marble-player vanished

Into Australia. Three stops to play
The music of the arbitrary on.
Blow on them now and hear an undersong

Your levelled breath made once going over
The empty bottle. Improvise. Make free
Like old hay in its flimsy afterlife

High on a windblown hedge. Ocarina earth.
Three listening posts up on some hard-baked tier
Above the resonating amphorae.

vi

Once, as a child, out in a field of sheep,
Thomas Hardy pretended to be dead
And lay down flat among their dainty shins.

In that sniffed-at, bleated-into, grassy space
He experimented with infinity.
His small cool brow was like an anvil waiting

For sky to make it sing the perfect pitch
Of his dumb being, and that stir he caused
In the fleece-hustle was the original

Of a ripple that would travel eighty years
Outward from there, to be the same ripple
Inside him at its last circumference.

vii

(I misremembered. He went down on all fours,
Florence Emily says, crossing a ewe-leaze.
Hardy sought the creatures face to face,

Their witless eyes and liability
To panic made him feel less alone,
Made proleptic sorrow stand a moment

Over him, perfectly known and sure.
And then the flock's dismay went swimming on
Into the blinks and murmurs and deflections

10   He'd know at parties in renowned old age
     When sometimes he imagined himself a ghost
     And circulated with that new perspective.)

viii

The annals say: when the monks of Clonmacnoise
Were all at prayers inside the oratory
A ship appeared above them in the air.

The anchor dragged along behind so deep
5   It hooked itself into the altar rails
And then, as the big hull rocked to a standstill,

A crewman shinned and grappled down the rope
And struggled to release it. But in vain.
'This man can't bear our life here and will drown,'

10   The abbot said, 'unless we help him.' So
They did, the freed ship sailed, and the man climbed back
Out of the marvellous as he had known it.

ix

A boat that did not rock or wobble once
Sat in long grass one Sunday afternoon
In nineteen forty-one or two. The heat

Out on Lough Neagh and in where cattle stood
5   Jostling and skittering near the hedge
Grew redolent of the tweed skirt and tweed sleeve

I nursed on. I remember little treble
Timber-notes their smart heels struck from planks,
Me cradled in an elbow like a secret

10   Open now as the eye of heaven was then
Above three sisters talking, talking steady
In a boat the ground still falls and falls from under.

x

Overhang of grass and seedling birch
On the quarry face. Rock-hob where you watched
All that cargoed brightness travelling

Above and beyond and sumptuously across
The water in its clear deep dangerous holes
On the quarry floor. Ultimate

Fathomableness, ultimate
Stony up-againstness: could you reconcile
What was diaphanous there with what was massive?

Were you equal to or were you opposite
To build-ups so promiscuous and weightless?
Shield your eyes, look up and face the music.

xi

To put a glass roof on the handball alley
Where a hopped ball cut merciless angles
In and out of play, or levelled true

For the unanswerable dead-root . . .
He alone, our walking weathercock,
Our peeled eye at the easel, had the right

To make a studio of that free maze,
To turn light outside in and curb the space
Where accident got tricked to accuracy

And rain was rainier for being blown
Across the grid and texture of the concrete.
He scales the world at arm's length, gives thumbs up.

xii

And lightening? One meaning of that
Beyond the usual sense of alleviation,
Illumination, and so on, is this:

A phenomenal instant when the spirit flares
With pure exhilaration before death –
The good thief in us harking to the promise!

So paint him on Christ's right hand, on a promontory
Scanning empty space, so body-racked he seems
Untranslatable into the bliss

Ached for at the moon-rim of his forehead,
By nail-craters on the dark side of his brain:
This day thou shalt be with Me in Paradise.

2 Settings

xiii

Hazel stealth. A trickle in the culvert.
Athletic sealight on the doorstep slab,
On the sea itself, on silent roofs and gables.

Whitewashed suntraps. Hedges hot as chimneys.
Chairs on all fours. A plate-rack braced and laden.
The fossil poetry of hob and slate.

Desire within its moat, dozing at ease –
Like a gorged cormorant on the rock at noon,
Exiled and in tune with the big glitter.

Re-enter this as the adult of solitude,
The silence-forder and the definite
Presence you sensed withdrawing first time round.

xiv

One afternoon I was seraph on gold leaf.
I stood on the railway sleepers hearing larks,
Grasshoppers, cuckoos, dogbarks, trainer planes

Cutting and modulating and drawing off.
Heat wavered on the immaculate line
And shine of the cogged rails. On either side,

Dog daisies stood like vestals, the hot stones
Were clover-meshed and streaked with engine oil.
Air spanned, passage waited, the balance rode,

Nothing prevailed, whatever was in store
Witnessed itself already taking place
In a time marked by assent and by hiatus.

xv

And strike this scene in gold too, in relief,
So that a greedy eye cannot exhaust it:
Stable straw, Rembrandt-gleam and burnish

Where my father bends to a tea-chest packed with salt,
The hurricane lamp held up at eye-level
In his bunched left fist, his right hand foraging

For the unbleeding, vivid-fleshed bacon,
Home-cured hocks pulled up into the light
For pondering a while and putting back.

That night I owned the piled grain of Egypt.
I watched the sentry's torchlight on the hoard.
I stood in the door, unseen and blazed upon.

xvi

Rat-poison the colour of blood pudding
Went phosphorescent when it was being spread:
Its sparky rancid shine under the blade

Brought everything to life – like news of murder
Or the sight of a parked car occupied by lovers
On a side road, or stories of bull victims.

If a muse had sung the anger of Achilles
It would not have heightened the world-danger more.
It was all there in the fresh rat-poison

Corposant on mouldy, dried-up crusts.
On winter evenings I loved its reek and risk.
And windfalls freezing on the outhouse roof.

xvii

What were the virtues of an eelskin? What
Was the eel itself? A rib of water drawn
Out of the water, an ell yielded up

From glooms and whorls and slatings,
Rediscovered once it had been skinned.
When a wrist was bound with eelskin, energy

Redounded in that arm, a waterwheel
Turned in the shoulder, mill-races poured
And made your elbow giddy.

Your hand felt unconstrained and spirited
As heads and tails that wriggled in the mud
Aristotle supposed all eels were sprung from.

xviii

Like a foul-mouthed god of hemp come down to rut,
The rope-man stumped about and praised new rope
With talk of how thick it was, or how long and strong,

And how you could take it into your own hand
And feel it. His perfect, tight-bound wares
Made a circle round him: the makings of reins

And belly-bands and halters. And of slippage –
For even then, knee-high among the farmers,
I knew the rope-man menaced them with freedoms

They were going to turn their backs on; and knew too
His powerlessness once the fair-hill emptied
And he had to break the circle and start loading.

xix

Memory as a building or a city,
Well lighted, well laid out, appointed with
Tableaux vivants and costumed effigies –

Statues in purple cloaks, or painted red,
Ones wearing crowns, ones smeared with mud or blood: 5
So that the mind's eye could haunt itself

With fixed associations and learn to read
Its own contents in meaningful order,
Ancient textbooks recommended that

Familiar places be linked deliberately 10
With a code of images. You knew the portent
In each setting, you blinked and concentrated.

xx

On Red Square, the brick wall of the Kremlin
Looked unthreatening, in scale, just right for people
To behave well under, inside or outside.

The big cleared space in front was dizzying.
I looked across a heave and sweep of cobbles 5
Like the ones that beamed up in my dream of flying

Above the old cart road, with all the air
Fanning off beneath my neck and breastbone.
(The cloud-roamer, was it, Stalin called Pasternak?)

Terrible history and protected joys! 10
Plosive horse-dung on 1940s' roads.
The newsreel bomb-hits, as harmless as dust-puffs.

xxi

Once and only once I fired a gun –
A .22. At a square of handkerchief
Pinned on a tree about sixty yards away.

It exhilarated me – the bullet's song
So effortlessly at my fingertip, 5
The target's single shocking little jerk,

A whole new quickened sense of what *rifle* meant.
And then again as it was in the beginning
I saw the soul like a white cloth snatched away

10   Across dark galaxies and felt that shot
For the sin it was against eternal life –
Another phrase dilating in new light.

xxii

Where does spirit live? Inside or outside
Things remembered, made things, things unmade?
What came first, the seabird's cry or the soul

Imagined in the dawn cold when it cried?
5   Where does it roost at last? On dungy sticks
In a jackdaw's nest up in the old stone tower

Or a marble bust commanding the parterre?
How habitable is perfected form?
And how inhabited the windy light?

10   What's the use of a held note or held line
That cannot be assailed for reassurance?
(Set questions for the ghost of W.B.)

xxiii

On the bus-trip into saga country
Ivan Malinowski wrote a poem
About the nuclear submarines offshore

From an abandoned whaling station.
5   I remember it as a frisson, but cannot
Remember any words. What I wanted then

Was a poem of utter evening:
The thirteenth century, weird midnight sun
Setting at eye-level with Snorri Sturluson

10   Who has come out to bathe in a hot spring
And sit through the stillness after milking time,
Laved and ensconced in the throne-room of his mind.

xxiv

Deserted harbour stillness. Every stone
Clarified and dormant under water,
The harbour wall a masonry of silence.

Fullness. Shimmer. Laden high Atlantic
The moorings barely stirred in, very slight
Clucking of the swell against boat boards.

Perfected vision: cockle minarets
Consigned down there with green-slicked bottle glass,
Shell-debris and a reddened bud of sandstone.

Air and ocean known as antecedents
Of each other. In apposition with
Omnipresence, equilibrium, brim.

3 Crossings

xxv

Travelling south at dawn, going full out
Through high-up stone-wall country, the rocks still cold,
Rainwater gleaming here and there ahead,

I took a turn and met the fox stock-still,
Face-to-face in the middle of the road.
Wildness tore through me as he dipped and wheeled

In a level-running tawny breakaway.
O neat head, fabled brush and astonished eye
My blue Volkswagen flared into with morning!

Let rebirth come through water, through desire,
Through crawling backwards across clinic floors:
I have to cross back through that startled iris.

xxvi

Only to come up, year after year, behind
Those open-ended, canvas-covered trucks
Full of soldiers sitting cramped and staunch,

Their hands round gun-barrels, their gaze abroad
In dreams out of the body-heated metal.
Silent, time-proofed, keeping an even distance

Beyond the windscreen glass, carried ahead
On the phantasmal flow-back of the road,
They still mean business in the here and now.

So draw no attention, steer and concentrate
On the space that flees between like a speeded-up
Meltdown of souls from the straw-flecked ice of hell.

xxvii

Everything flows. Even a solid man,
A pillar to himself and to his trade,
All yellow boots and stick and soft felt hat,

Can sprout wings at the ankle and grow fleet
As the god of fair days, stone posts, roads and cross-roads,
Guardian of travellers and psychopomp.

'Look for a man with an ashplant on the boat,'
My father told his sister setting out
For London, 'and stay near him all night

And you'll be safe.' Flow on, flow on
The journey of the soul with its soul guide
And the mysteries of dealing-men with sticks!

xxviii

The ice was like a bottle. We lined up
Eager to re-enter the long slide
We were bringing to perfection, time after time

Running and readying and letting go
Into a sheerness that was its own reward: 5
A farewell to surefootedness, a pitch

Beyond our usual hold upon ourselves.
And what went on kept going, from grip to give,
The narrow milky way in the black ice,

The race-up, the free passage and return –   10
It followed on itself like a ring of light
We knew we'd come through and kept sailing towards.

xxix

Scissor-and-slap abruptness of a latch.
Its coldness to the thumb. Its see-saw lift
And drop and innocent harshness.

Which is a music of binding and of loosing
Unheard in this generation, but there to be   5
Called up or called down at a touch renewed.

Once the latch pronounces, roof
Is original again, threshold fatal,
The sanction powerful as the foreboding.

Your footstep is already known, so bow   10
Just a little, raise your right hand,
Make impulse one with wilfulness, and enter.

xxx

On St Brigid's Day the new life could be entered
By going through her girdle of straw rope:
The proper way for men was right leg first,

Then right arm and right shoulder, head, then left
Shoulder, arm and leg. Women drew it down   5
Over the body and stepped out of it.

The open they came into by these moves
Stood opener, hoops came off the world,
They could feel the February air

10   Still soft above their heads and imagine
The limp rope fray and flare like wind-borne gleanings
Or an unhindered goldfinch over ploughland.

xxxi

Not an avenue and not a bower.
For a quarter-mile or so, where the county road
Is running straight across North Antrim bog,

Tall old fir trees line it on both sides.
5   Scotch firs, that is. Calligraphic shocks
Bushed and tufted in prevailing winds.

You drive into a meaning made of trees.
Or not exactly trees. It is a sense
Of running through and under without let,

10   Of glimpse and dapple. A life all trace and skim
The car has vanished out of. A fanned nape
Sensitive to the millionth of a flicker.

xxxii

Running water never disappointed.
Crossing water always furthered something.
Stepping stones were stations of the soul.

A kesh could mean the track some called a *causey*
5   Raised above the wetness of the bog,
Or the causey where it bridged old drains and streams.

It steadies me to tell these things. Also
I cannot mention keshes or the ford
Without my father's shade appearing to me

10   On a path towards sunset, eyeing spades and clothes
That turf cutters stowed perhaps or souls cast off
Before they crossed the log that spans the burn.

xxxiii

Be literal a moment. Recollect
Walking out on what had been emptied out
After he died, turning your back and leaving.

That morning tiles were harder, windows colder,
The raindrops on the pane more scourged, the grass   5
Barer to the sky, more wind-harrowed,

Or so it seemed. The house that he had planned
'Plain, big, straight, ordinary, you know,'
A paradigm of rigour and correction,

Rebuke to fanciness and shrine to limit,   10
Stood firmer than ever for its own idea
Like a printed X-ray for the X-rayed body.

xxxiv

Yeats said, *To those who see spirits, human skin
For a long time afterwards appears most coarse.*
The face I see that all falls short of since

Passes down an aisle: I share the bus
From San Francisco Airport into Berkeley   5
With one other passenger, who's dropped

At the Treasure Island military base
Half-way across Bay Bridge. Vietnam-bound,
He could have been one of the newly dead come back,

Unsurprisable but still disappointed,   10
Having to bear his farmboy self again,
His shaving cuts, his otherworldly brow.

xxxv

Shaving cuts. The pallor of bad habits.
Sunday afternoons, when summer idled
And couples walked the road along the Foyle,

We brought a shaving mirror to our window
In the top storey of the boarders' dorms:
Lovers in the happy valley, cars

Eager-backed and silent, the absolute river
Between us and it all. We tilted the glass up
Into the sun and found the range and shone

A flitting light on what we could not have.
Brightness played over them in chancy sweeps
Like flashes from a god's shield or a dance-floor.

xxxvi

And yes, my friend, we too walked through a valley.
Once. In darkness. With all the streetlamps off.
As danger gathered and the march dispersed.

Scene from Dante, made more memorable
By one of his head-clearing similes –
Fireflies, say, since the policemen's torches

Clustered and flicked and tempted us to trust
Their unpredictable, attractive light.
We were like herded shades who had to cross

And did cross, in a panic, to the car
Parked as we'd left it, that gave when we got in
Like Charon's boat under the faring poets.

4 Squarings

xxxvii

In famous poems by the sage Han Shan,
Cold Mountain is a place that can also mean
A state of mind. Or different states of mind

At different times, for the poems seem
One-off, impulsive, the kind of thing that starts
I have sat here facing the Cold Mountain

For twenty-nine years, or *There is no path*
That goes all the way – enviable stuff,
Unfussy and believable.

Talking about it isn't good enough
But quoting from it at least demonstrates
The virtue of an art that knows its mind.

xxxviii

We climbed the Capitol by moonlight, felt
The transports of temptation on the heights:
We were privileged and belated and we knew it.

Then something in me moved to prophesy
Against the beloved stand-offishness of marble
And all emulation of stone-cut verses.

'Down with form triumphant, long live,' (said I)
'Form mendicant and convalescent. We attend
The come-back of pure water and the prayer-wheel.'

To which a voice replied, 'Of course we do.
But the others are in the Forum Café waiting,
Wondering where we are. What'll you have?'

xxxix

When you sat, far-eyed and cold, in the basalt throne
Of 'the wishing chair' at Giant's Causeway,
The small of your back made very solid sense.

Like a papoose at sap-time strapped to a maple tree,
You gathered force out of the world-tree's hardness.
If you stretched your hand forth, things might turn to stone.

But you were only goose-fleshed skin and bone,
The rocks and wonder of the world were only
Lava crystallized, salts of the earth

The wishing chair gave a savour to, its kelp
And ozone freshening your outlook
Beyond the range you thought you'd settled for.

xl

I was four but I turned four hundred maybe
Encountering the ancient dampish feel
Of a clay floor. Maybe four thousand even.

Anyhow, there it was. Milk poured for cats
In a rank puddle-place, splash-darkened mould
Around the terracotta water-crock.

Ground of being. Body's deep obedience
To all its shifting tenses. A half-door
Opening directly into starlight.

Out of that earth house I inherited
A stack of singular, cold memory-weights
To load me, hand and foot, in the scale of things.

xli

Sand-bed, they said. And gravel-bed. Before
I knew river shallows or river pleasures
I knew the ore of longing in those words.

The places I go back to have not failed
But will not last. Waist-deep in cow-parsley,
I re-enter the swim, riding or quelling

The very currents memory is composed of,
Everything accumulated ever
As I took squarings from the tops of bridges

Or the banks of self at evening.
Lick of fear. Sweet transience. Flirt and splash.
Crumpled flow the sky-dipped willows trailed in.

xlii

Heather and kesh and turf stacks reappear
Summer by summer still, grasshoppers and all,
The same yet rarer: fields of the nearly blessed

Where gaunt ones in their shirtsleeves stooped and dug
Or stood alone at dusk surveying bog-banks –   5
Apparitions now, yet active still

And territorial, still sure of their ground,
Still interested, not knowing how far
The country of the shades has been pushed back,

How long the lark has stopped outside these fields   10
And only seems unstoppable to them
Caught like a far hill in a freak of sunshine.

   xliii

Choose one set of tracks and track a hare
Until the prints stop, just like that, in snow.
End of the line. Smooth drifts. Where did she go?

Back on her tracks, of course, then took a spring
Yards off to the side; clean break; no scent or sign.   5
She landed in her form and ate the snow.

Consider too the ancient hieroglyph
Of 'hare and zig-zag', which meant 'to exist',
To be on the *qui vive*, weaving and dodging

Like our friend who sprang (goodbye) beyond our ken   10
And missed a round at last (but of course he'd stood it):
The shake-the-heart, the dew-hammer, the far-eyed.

   xliv

All gone into the world of light? Perhaps
As we read the line sheer forms do crowd
The starry vestibule. Otherwise

They do not. What lucency survives
Is blanched as worms on nightlines I would lift,   5
Ungratified if always well prepared

For the nothing there – which was only what had been there.
Although in fact it is more like a caught line snapping,
That moment of admission of *All gone*,

10   When the rod butt loses touch and the tip drools
And eddies swirl a dead leaf past in silence
Swifter (it seems) than the water's passage.

xlv

For certain ones what was written may come true:
They shall live on in the distance
At the mouths of rivers.

For our ones, no. They will re-enter
5   Dryness that was heaven on earth to them,
Happy to eat the scones baked out of clay.

For some, perhaps, the delta's reed-beds
And cold bright-footed seabirds always wheeling.
For our ones, snuff
10   And hob-soot and the heat off ashes.
And a judge who comes between them and the sun
In a pillar of radiant house-dust.

xlvi

Mountain air from the mountain up behind;
Out front, the end-of-summer, stone-walled fields;
And in a slated house the fiddle going

Like a flat stone skimmed at sunset
5   Or the irrevocable slipstream of flat earth
Still fleeing behind space.

Was music once a proof of God's existence?
As long as it admits things beyond measure,
That supposition stands.

10   So let the ear attend like a farmhouse window
In placid light, where the extravagant
Passed once under full sail into the longed-for.

xlvii

The visible sea at a distance from the shore
Or beyond the anchoring grounds
Was called the offing.

The emptier it stood, the more compelled
The eye that scanned it.
But once you turned your back on it, your back

Was suddenly all eyes like Argus's.
Then, when you'd look again, the offing felt
Untrespassed still, and yet somehow vacated

As if a lambent troop that exercised
On the borders of your vision had withdrawn
Behind the skyline to manoeuvre and regroup.

xlviii

Strange how things in the offing, once they're sensed,
Convert to things foreknown;
And how what's come upon is manifest

Only in light of what has been gone through.
Seventh heaven may be
The whole truth of a sixth sense come to pass.

At any rate, when light breaks over me
The way it did on the road beyond Coleraine
Where wind got saltier, the sky more hurried

And silver lame shivered on the Bann
Out in mid-channel between the painted poles,
That day I'll be in step with what escaped me.

The Crossing

(Inferno, *Canto III*, lines 82–129)

And there in a boat that came heading towards us
Was an old man, his hair snow-white with age,
Raging and bawling, 'Woe to you, wicked spirits!

O never hope to see the heavenly skies!
I come to bring you to the other shore,
To eternal darkness, to the fire and ice.

And you there, you, the living soul, separate
Yourself from these others who are dead.'
But when he saw that I did not stand aside

He said, 'By another way, by other harbours
You shall reach a different shore and pass over.
A lighter boat must be your carrier.'

And my guide said, 'Quiet your anger, Charon.
There where all can be done that has been willed
This has been willed; so there can be no question.'

Then straightaway he shut his grizzled jaws,
The ferryman of that livid marsh,
Who had wheels of fire flaming round his eyes.

But as soon as they had heard the cruel words,
Those lost souls, all naked and exhausted,
Changed their colour and their teeth chattered;

They blasphemed God and their parents on the earth,
The human race, the place and date and seedbed
Of their own begetting and of their birth,

Then all together, bitterly weeping, made
Their way towards the accursed shore that waits
For every man who does not fear his God.

The demon Charon's eyes are like hot coals fanned.
He beckons them and herds all of them in
And beats with his oar whoever drops behind.

As one by one the leaves fall off in autumn
Until at last the branch is bare and sees
All that was looted from it on the ground,

So the bad seed of Adam, at a signal
Pitch themselves off that shore one by one,   35
Each like a falcon answering its call.

They go away like this over the brown waters
And before they have landed on the other side
Upon this side once more a new crowd gathers.

'My son,' the courteous master said to me,   40
'All those who die under the wrath of God
Come together here from every country

And they are eager to go across the river
Because Divine Justice goads them with its spur
So that their fear is turned into desire.   45

No good spirits ever pass this way
And therefore, if Charon objects to you,
You should understand well what his words imply.'

UNCOLLECTED POEMS (1992–1996)

To Sorley MacLean

Dear Sorley, English may be wrong,
Not quite the setting for your song –
Like having just a single tong
    To build the fire
or being served short drinks when long
       's what you require.

Yet this Burns' stanza was the first
Art speech I heard. His lines conversed
In local accents and rehearsed
    A local rhythm.
The whole of Ulster was well versed
    In Burns' wisdom.

His shrewd art pleased them in that land
Where life was fought for hand-to-hand
And elders had you understand
    Each inch was won:
The soul lay wee as riddled sand
    When they had done.

The sunsets of the psyche's west,
The sense that doomed ways might be best,
That heartbreak has the right to crest
    And amplify,
That what has been may be suppressed
    But will not die –

These truths that dawn in widening rings,
This fledging of the mental wings,
The unsealed head that soars and sings,
    This had to wait
Until, Sorley, I read your things.
    But better late

Than never. Lowland worlds expanded,
My ear and being were commanded,
It was as if the Prince had landed
    And won the day.
I did and did not understand it:
    Poetry!

Poetry by its pitch and tone,
Its crises suffered in the bone,
Its tragic magma and ozone
      Survived translation.
The spirit's cover had been blown
      By inspiration.

Which is how poems help us live.
They stretch the meshes in the sieve
We put ourselves through and so give
      Potential speech.
In order to be transitive,
      Poems need not preach.

Sorley, all I say is this:
Your work and you have grown priceless.
There Gaelic finds its fort, its *lios*,
      Its empowered will.
Hallaig survives the clearances.
      The wheel turns still.

The Cuilinn's visionary blue,
Conscience, world and self askew,
Love hurt and justice overdue –
      Your transformed days
Will live forever, big and true
      As the men of Braes.

The Villanelle of Northwest Orient Flight 4

Haikus in English hardly ever scan.
Te-tum, te-tum's no match for brush and ink.
The bard should know. The bard was in Japan.

The bard returned, a shaken, jet-lagged man,
Aghast, displaced, lamenting in his drink,
'Haikus in English hardly ever scan.'

He bought his wife an ornamental fan,
Exclaiming that exchange rates made you think.
The bard should know. The bard was in Japan.

Among geishas he was also-ran.
No matter what, he'd only blush and think,
'Haikus in English hardly ever scan.'

He told us, 'See a Noh play if you can,
But wear your silk kimono, not your mink.'
The bard should know. The bard was in Japan.

Their word for *Mister* is the suffix *-san*.
Their cherry blossom is a perfect pink.
Haikus in English hardly ever scan.
The bard should know. The bard was in Japan.

Skims and Glances

1

Finding the right stone, just weighted so
As not to lose momentum against air,
Just big enough to get the finger hooked
And triggered round it, just plump enough
To skip before it skimmed: the excitement of it
Got me like fiddle music every time.
And not just me. We were all the same,
Casual at first, then warming to the search,
Picking, testing, stockpiling, face to face
With the whole extent of water, refusing
To give up.
           But, in the end, just having
To give up, reluctant and far out,
At arm's length from the throw we never made,
The one that would skim on and on and keep
Momentum, lambency, direction, drag.

2

Another airy nothing? But in your bones
You felt the good of fluency and give,
The lovely danger of it – as years ago
The skid and waltz of a Volkswagen began
Across black ice and the road swam out from under
The whole carload of us, ballasted and braced

And helpless as we'd been an hour before
Careering off the dance-floor at full tilt.

So loosen up, cast off, and go with it.

   3

If thou be'st too hard, thou wilt be broken.
But what of the little reed that was not shaken,
The one who let fly and would not be gone
As he smashed the byre windows at Mossbawn?
That pure refuser, stander of his ground,
Out in the yard, a picked stone in each hand
And a pile of them beside him – but it's me
Pitching in like mad, methodically
Taking out the quarter-panes of two
Fresh-puttied frames the yardsman dared me to.
What of it? Here's my father at the door,
Too late, uncomprehending and unsure,
Looking hurt-eyed, the wind out of his sails.
How answer to the name he calls and calls?
How but own up to it, walk up to him
And start the trek to the land of skip and skim
By way of the old scenes and escapades –
The whirled slingstone, the dangerous crossroads –
Then farther out, compelled and distance-faced,
Until the throwing arm is exorcised?
Until each one comes round, changed through and through,
Yet sheer and steadfast as a broken window,
All-heeding, strange, wide open, equal to.

More River Rhymes

   1

By the harbour down at Smerwick
I couldn't help but think of Derek,
How on the head he hits the nail:
Those Spanish ships around Kinsale!

II

On the banks of River Lagan
He read some 'Fragments of an Agon',
This strange child with a taste for verse,
Coal sheds and Dutch interiors.

III

Far from Ulster fries and farls,
He bided next beside The Charles.
Marked absent from The Crown, The Group,
He graced The Grolier and The Coop.

IV

By Kellswater, by Main and Braid,
We went in poets' cavalcade
To Slemish on a Patrick's Day.
Great times *in illo tempore*.

V

Then east of Strangford Lough he found
MacNeice's shade on that high ground
Who recognized him and cried, 'Hell!
You be Dante, I'll be Virgil.'

VI

Riverrhyme past Adam and Eve's.
Revisions. Revenants. Swirled leaves.
In Trinity Front Square. Gaunt bars.
On Raglan Road . . . What is the stars?

A Landfall

i.m. George Mackay Brown

Far north, in sunlight,
the stone ship ran aground. Larks
sing at the masthead.

Cheers

Proud to be ranked among his gallowglasses
(*Macbeth*, Act One, Scene Two, for note on same)
I join the cheer that's echoing round *Parnassus*
To celebrate Herb's birthday and his name.

In Bellaghy Graveyard

He looked both self-possessed and overcome.
The crowd had gone, the grave had not been filled.
'It's hardly worth my while now going home,'

He murmured as he stood there on its rim
5   Like a man lost to the world in his own field.
He looked both self -possessed and overcome

By something equal to that lostness in him,
A knowledge he was fit for when he felt
It was hardly worth his while now going home.

10   Trees were dark orders, earthy seraphim
Tiding and lavish with the notes they held.
He looked both self-possessed and overcome.

It seemed he stood his ground in running foam,
Having to watch while a boat he'd boarded sailed.
15   It was hardly worth his while now going home.

As he swayed there in the crow's nest of his dream
Above old headstones and the fresh clay piled
He looked both self-possessed and overcome.
It was hardly worth his while now going home.

A Transgression

The teacher let some big boys out at two
    To gather sticks
  (In scanty nineteen forty-six)
And even though I never was supposed to

    I wanted out as well. One afternoon
        I raised my hand
      With those free livers off the land
And found myself at large an hour too soon

Under a raggedy, hurrying sky
        On the road home.
      If ever I felt 'heaven's dome'
Was what I lived beneath, it was that day

I lied myself into my own desire,
        Displaced, afraid
      At what I'd dared to be ahead
Of time. The black spot where the gypsies' fire

Had charred the roadside grass, the rags that blew
        On the stripped hedge,
      The cold – it put me all on edge.
Escape-joy died, one magpie rose and flew

And left an emptiness I walked on through
        To come down to earth
      In my parents' gaze, the whole question of worth,
And their knowledge that loved on without ado.

                (1994)

THE SPIRIT LEVEL (1996)

for Helen Vendler

The Rain Stick

for Beth and Rand

Upend the rain stick and what happens next
Is a music that you never would have known
To listen for. In a cactus stalk

Downpour, sluice-rush, spillage and backwash
Come flowing through. You stand there like a pipe   5
Being played by water, you shake it again lightly

And diminuendo runs through all its scales
Like a gutter stopping trickling. And now here comes
A sprinkle of drops out of the freshened leaves,

Then subtle little wets off grass and daisies;   10
Then glitter-drizzle, almost-breaths of air.
Upend the stick again. What happens next

Is undiminished for having happened once,
Twice, ten, a thousand times before.
Who cares if all the music that transpires   15

Is the fall of grit or dry seeds through a cactus?
You are like a rich man entering heaven
Through the ear of a raindrop. Listen now again.

To a Dutch Potter in Ireland

for Sonja Landweer

Then I entered a strongroom of vocabulary
Where words like urns that had come through the fire
Stood in their bone-dry alcoves next a kiln

And came away changed, like the guard who'd seen
The stone move in a diamond-blaze of air   5
Or the gates of horn behind the gates of clay.

I

The soils I knew ran dirty. River sand
Was the one clean thing that stayed itself
In that slabbery, clabbery, wintry, puddled ground.

Until I found Bann clay. Like wet daylight
Or viscous satin under the felt and frieze
Of humus layers. The true diatomite

Discovered in a little sucky hole,
Grey-blue, dull-shining, scentless, touchable –
Like the earth's old ointment box, sticky and cool.

At that stage you were swimming in the sea
Or running from it, luminous with plankton,
A nymph of phosphor by the Norder Zee,

A vestal of the goddess Silica,
She who is under grass and glass and ash
In the fiery heartlands of Ceramica.

We might have known each other then, in that
Cold gleam-life under ground and off the water.
Weird twins of puddle, paddle, pit-a-pat,

And might have done the small forbidden things –
Worked at mud-pies or gone too high on swings,
Played 'secrets' in the hedge or 'touching tongues' –

But did not, in the terrible event.
Night after night instead, in the Netherlands,
You watched the bombers kill; then, heaven-sent,

Came backlit from the fire through war and wartime
And ever after, every blessed time,
Through glazes of fired quartz and iron and lime.

And if glazes, as you say, bring down the sun,
Your potter's wheel is bringing up the earth.
Hosannah ex infernis. Burning wells.

Hosannah in clean sand and kaolin
And, 'now that the rye crop waves beside the ruins',
In ash-pits, oxides, shards and chlorophylls.

2 *After Liberation*

I

Sheer, bright-shining spring, spring as it used to be,
Cold in the morning, but as broad daylight
Swings open, the everlasting sky
Is a marvel to survivors.

In a pearly clarity that bathes the fields 5
Things as they were come back; slow horses
Plough the fallow, war rumbles away
In the near distance.

To have lived it through and now be free to give
Utterance, body and soul – to wake and know 10
Every time that it's gone and gone for good, the thing
That nearly broke you –

Is worth it all, the five years on the rack,
The fighting back, the being resigned, and not
One of the unborn will appreciate 15
Freedom like this ever.

II

Turning tides, their regularities!
What is the heart, that it ever was afraid,
Knowing as it must know spring's release,
Shining heart, heart constant as a tide?
Omnipresent, imperturbable 5
Is the life that death springs from.
And complaint is wrong, the slightest complaint at all,
Now that the rye crop waves beside the ruins.

from the Dutch of J. C. Bloem (1887–1966)

A Brigid's Girdle

for Adele

Last time I wrote I wrote from a rustic table
Under magnolias in South Carolina
As blossoms fell on me, and a white gable
As clean-lined as the prow of a white liner

Bisected sunlight in the sunlit yard.
I was glad of the early heat and the first quiet
I'd had for weeks. I heard the mocking bird
And a delicious, articulate

Flight of small plinkings from a dulcimer
Like feminine rhymes migrating to the north
Where you faced the music and the ache of summer
And earth's foreknowledge gathered in the earth.

Now it's St Brigid's Day and the first snowdrop
In County Wicklow, and this a Brigid's Girdle
I'm plaiting for you, an airy fairy hoop
(Like one of those old crinolines they'd trindle),

Twisted straw that's lifted in a circle
To handsel and to heal, a rite of spring
As strange and lightsome and traditional
As the motions you go through going through the thing.

Mint

It looked like a clump of small dusty nettles
Growing wild at the gable of the house
Beyond where we dumped our refuse and old bottles:
Unverdant ever, almost beneath notice.

But, to be fair, it also spelled promise
And newness in the back yard of our life
As if something callow yet tenacious
Sauntered in green alleys and grew rife.

The snip of scissor blades, the light of Sunday
Mornings when the mint was cut and loved:
My last things will be first things slipping from me.
Yet let all things go free that have survived.

Let the smells of mint go heady and defenceless
Like inmates liberated in that yard.
Like the disregarded ones we turned against
Because we'd failed them by our disregard.

A Sofa in the Forties

All of us on the sofa in a line, kneeling
Behind each other, eldest down to youngest,
Elbows going like pistons, for this was a train

And between the jamb-wall and the bedroom door
Our speed and distance were inestimable.
First we shunted, then we whistled, then

Somebody collected the invisible
For tickets and very gravely punched it
As carriage after carriage under us

Moved faster, *chooka-chook*, the sofa legs
Went giddy and the unreachable ones
Far out on the kitchen floor began to wave.

*

Ghost-train? Death-gondola? The carved, curved ends,
Black leatherette and ornate gauntness of it
Made it seem the sofa had achieved

Flotation. Its castors on tip-toe,
Its braid and fluent backboard gave it airs
Of superannuated pageantry:

When visitors endured it, straight-backed,
When it stood off in its own remoteness,
When the insufficient toys appeared on it

On Christmas mornings, it held out as itself,
Potentially heavenbound, earthbound for sure,
Among things that might add up or let you down.

*

We entered history and ignorance
Under the wireless shelf. *Yippee-i-ay*,
Sang 'The Riders of the Range'. HERE IS THE NEWS,

Said the absolute speaker. Between him and us
A great gulf was fixed where pronunciation
Reigned tyrannically. The aerial wire

Swept from a treetop down in through a hole

Bored in the windowframe. When it moved in wind,
The sway of language and its furtherings

Swept and swayed in us like nets in water
Or the abstract, lonely curve of distant trains
As we entered history and ignorance.

    *

We occupied our seats with all our might,
Fit for the uncomfortableness.
Constancy was its own reward already.

Out in front, on the big upholstered arm,
Somebody craned to the side, driver or
Fireman, wiping his dry brow with the air

Of one who had run the gauntlet. We were
The last thing on his mind, it seemed; we sensed
A tunnel coming up where we'd pour through

Like unlit carriages through fields at night,
Our only job to sit, eyes straight ahead,
And be transported and make engine noise.

Keeping Going

for Hugh

The piper coming from far away is you
With a whitewash brush for a sporran
Wobbling round you, a kitchen chair
Upside down on your shoulder, your right arm
Pretending to tuck the bag beneath your elbow,
Your pop-eyes and big cheeks nearly bursting
With laughter, but keeping the drone going on
Interminably, between catches of breath.

    *

The whitewash brush. An old blanched skirted thing
On the back of the byre door, biding its time
Until spring airs spelled lime in a work-bucket
And a potstick to mix it in with water.
Those smells brought tears to the eyes, we inhaled

A kind of greeny burning and thought of brimstone.
But the slop of the actual job
Of brushing walls, the watery grey
Being lashed on in broad swatches, then drying out
Whiter and whiter, all that worked like magic.
Where had we come from, what was this kingdom
We knew we'd been restored to? Our shadows
Moved on the wall and a tar border glittered
The full length of the house, a black divide
Like a freshly-opened, pungent, reeking trench.

*

Piss at the gable, the dead will congregate.
But separately. The women after dark,
Hunkering there a moment before bedtime,
The only time the soul was let alone,
The only time that face and body calmed
In the eye of heaven.
                      Buttermilk and urine,
The pantry, the housed beasts, the listening bedroom.
We were all together there in a foretime,
In a knowledge that might not translate beyond
Those wind-heaved midnights we still cannot be sure
Happened or not. It smelled of hill-fort clay
And cattle dung. When the thorn tree was cut down
You broke your arm. I shared the dread
When a strange bird perched for days on the byre roof.

*

That scene, with Macbeth helpless and desperate
In his nightmare – when he meets the hags again
And sees the apparitions in the pot –
I felt at home with that one all right. Hearth,
Steam and ululation, the smoky hair
Curtaining a cheek. 'Don't go near bad boys
In that college you're bound for. Do you hear me?
Do you hear me speaking to you? Don't forget!'
And then the potstick quickening the gruel,
The steam crown swirled, everything intimate
And fear-swathed brightening for a moment,
Then going dull and fatal and away.

    *

Grey matter like gruel flecked with blood
In spatters on the whitewash. A clean spot
Where his head had been, other stains subsumed
In the parched wall he leant his back against
That morning like any other morning,
Part-time reservist, toting his lunch-box.
A car came slow down Castle Street, made the halt,
Crossed the Diamond, slowed again and stopped
Level with him, although it was not his lift.
And then he saw an ordinary face
For what it was and a gun in his own face.
His right leg was hooked back, his sole and heel
Against the wall, his right knee propped up steady,
So he never moved, just pushed with all his might
Against himself, then fell past the tarred strip,
Feeding the gutter with his copious blood.

    *

My dear brother, you have good stamina.
You stay on where it happens. Your big tractor
Pulls up at the Diamond, you wave at people,
You shout and laugh above the revs, you keep
Old roads open by driving on the new ones.
You called the piper's sporrans whitewash brushes
And then dressed up and marched us through the kitchen,
But you cannot make the dead walk or right wrong.
I see you at the end of your tether sometimes,
In the milking parlour, holding yourself up
Between two cows until your turn goes past,
Then coming to in the smell of dung again
And wondering, is this all? As it was
In the beginning, is now and shall be?
Then rubbing your eyes and seeing our old brush
Up on the byre door, and keeping going.

Two Lorries

It's raining on black coal and warm wet ashes.
There are tyre-marks in the yard, Agnew's old lorry

Has all its cribs down and Agnew the coalman
With his Belfast accent's sweet-talking my mother.
Would she ever go to a film in Magherafelt?
But it's raining and he still has half the load

To deliver farther on. This time the lode
Our coal came from was silk-black, so the ashes
Will be the silkiest white. The Magherafelt
(Via Toomebridge) bus goes by. The half-stripped lorry
With its emptied, folded coal-bags moves my mother:
The tasty ways of a leather-aproned coalman!

And films no less! The conceit of a coalman . . .
She goes back in and gets out the black lead
And emery paper, this nineteen-forties mother,
All business round her stove, half-wiping ashes
With a backhand from her cheek as the bolted lorry
Gets revved and turned and heads for Magherafelt

And the last delivery. Oh, Magherafelt!
Oh, dream of red plush and a city coalman
As time fastforwards and a different lorry
Groans into shot, up Broad Street, with a payload
That will blow the bus station to dust and ashes . . .
After that happened, I'd a vision of my mother,

A revenant on the bench where I would meet her
In that cold-floored waiting-room in Magherafelt,
Her shopping bags full up with shovelled ashes.
Death walked out past her like a dust-faced coalman
Refolding body-bags, plying his load
Empty upon empty, in a flurry

Of motes and engine-revs, but which lorry
Was it now? Young Agnew's or that other,
Heavier, deadlier one, set to explode
In a time beyond her time in Magherafelt . . .
So tally bags and sweet-talk darkness, coalman.
Listen to the rain spit in new ashes

As you heft a load of dust that was Magherafelt,
Then reappear from your lorry as my mother's
Dreamboat coalman filmed in silk-white ashes.

Damson

Gules and cement dust. A matte tacky blood
On the bricklayer's knuckles, like the damson stain
That seeped through his packed lunch.
                              A full hod stood
Against the mortared wall, his big bright trowel
In his left hand (for once) was pointing down
As he marvelled at his right, held high and raw:
King of the castle, scaffold-stepper, shown
Bleeding to the world.
                              Wound that I saw
In glutinous colour fifty years ago –
Damson as omen, weird, a dream to read –
Is weeping with the held-at-arm's-length dead
From everywhere and nowhere, here and now.

*

Over and over, the slur, the scrape and mix
As he trowelled and retrowelled and laid down
Courses of glum mortar. Then the bricks
Jiggled and settled, tocked and tapped in line.
I loved especially the trowel's shine,
Its edge and apex always coming clean
And brightening itself by mucking in.
It looked light but felt heavy as a weapon,
Yet when he lifted it there was no strain.
It was all point and skim and float and glisten
Until he washed and lapped it tight in sacking
Like a cult blade that had to be kept hidden.

*

Ghosts with their tongues out for a lick of blood
Are crowding up the ladder, all unhealed,
And some of them still rigged in bloody gear.
Drive them back to the doorstep or the road
Where they lay in their own blood once, in the hot
Nausea and last gasp of dear life.
Trowel-wielder, woundie, drive them off
Like Odysseus in Hades lashing out
With his sword that dug the trench and cut the throat
Of the sacrificial lamb.

                    But not like him –
Builder, not sacker, your shield to the mortar board –
Drive them back to the wine-dark taste of home,
The smell of damsons simmering in a pot,
Jam ladled thick and steaming down the sunlight.

Weighing In

The 56 lb. weight. A solid iron
Unit of negation. Stamped and cast
With an inset, rung-thick, moulded, short crossbar

For a handle. Squared-off and harmless-looking
Until you tried to lift it, then a socket-ripping,
Life-belittling force –

Gravity's black box, the immovable
Stamp and squat and square-root of dead weight.
Yet balance it

Against another one placed on a weighbridge –
On a well-adjusted, freshly greased weighbridge –
And everything trembled, flowed with give and take.

          *

And this is all the good tidings amount to:
The principle of bearing, bearing up
And bearing out, just having to

Balance the intolerable in others
Against our own, having to abide
Whatever we settled for and settled into

Against our better judgement. Passive
Suffering makes the world go round.
Peace on earth, men of good will, all that

Holds good only as long as the balance holds,
The scales ride steady and the angels' strain
Prolongs itself at an unearthly pitch.

          *

To refuse the other cheek. To cast the stone.
Not to do so some time, not to break with

The obedient one you hurt yourself into

Is to fail the hurt, the self, the ingrown rule.
Prophesy who struck thee! When soldiers mocked
Blindfolded Jesus and he didn't strike back

They were neither shamed nor edified, although
Something was made manifest – the power
Of power not exercised, of hope inferred

By the powerless forever. Still, for Jesus' sake,
Do me a favour, would you, just this once?
Prophesy, give scandal, cast the stone.

    *

Two sides to every question, yes, yes, yes . . .
But every now and then, just weighing in
Is what it must come down to, and without

Any self-exculpation or self-pity.
Alas, one night when follow-through was called for
And a quick hit would have fairly rankled,

You countered that it was my narrowness
That kept me keen, so got a first submission.
I held back when I should have drawn blood

And that way (*mea culpa*) lost an edge.
A deep mistaken chivalry, old friend.
At this stage only foul play cleans the slate.

St Kevin and the Blackbird

And then there was St Kevin and the blackbird.
The saint is kneeling, arms stretched out, inside
His cell, but the cell is narrow, so

One turned-up palm is out the window, stiff
As a crossbeam, when a blackbird lands
And lays in it and settles down to nest.

Kevin feels the warm eggs, the small breast, the tucked
Neat head and claws and, finding himself linked
Into the network of eternal life,

Is moved to pity: now he must hold his hand
Like a branch out in the sun and rain for weeks
Until the young are hatched and fledged and flown.

    *

And since the whole thing's imagined anyhow,
Imagine being Kevin. Which is he?
Self-forgetful or in agony all the time
From the neck on out down through his hurting forearms?
Are his fingers sleeping? Does he still feel his knees?
Or has the shut-eyed blank of underearth

Crept up through him? Is there distance in his head?
Alone and mirrored clear in love's deep river,
'To labour and not to seek reward,' he prays,

A prayer his body makes entirely
For he has forgotten self, forgotten bird
And on the riverbank forgotten the river's name.

The Flight Path

1

The first fold first, then more foldovers drawn
Tighter and neater every time until
The whole of the paper got itself reduced
To a pleated square he'd take up by two corners,
Then hold like a promise he had the power to break
But never did.
        A dove rose in my breast
Every time my father's hands came clean
With a paper boat between them, ark in air,
The lines of it as taut as a pegged tent:
High-sterned, splay-bottomed, the little pyramid
At the centre every bit as hollow
As a part of me that sank because it knew
The whole thing would go soggy once you launched it.

2

Equal and opposite, the part that lifts
Into those *full-starred heavens that winter sees*

When I stand in Wicklow under the flight path
Of a late jet out of Dublin, its risen light
Winking ahead of what it hauls away:
Heavy engine noise and its abatement
Widening far back down, a wake through starlight.

The sycamore speaks in sycamore from darkness,
The light behind my shoulder's cottage lamplight.
I'm in the doorway early in the night,
Standing-in in myself for all of those
The stance perpetuates: the stay-at-homes
Who leant against the jamb and watched and waited,
The ones we learned to love by waving back at
Or coming towards again in different clothes
They were slightly shy of.
                      Who never once forgot
A name or a face, nor looked down suddenly
As the plane was reaching cruising altitude
To realize that the house they'd just passed over –
Too far back now to see – was the same house
They'd left an hour before, still kissing, kissing,
As the taxi driver loaded up the cases.

   3

Up and away. The buzz from duty free.
Black velvet. Bourbon. Love letters on high.
The spacewalk of Manhattan. The re-entry.

Then California. Laid-back Tiburon.
Burgers at Sam's, deck-tables and champagne,
Plus a wall-eyed, hard-baked seagull looking on.

Again re-entry. Vows revowed. And off –
Reculer pour sauter, within one year of
Coming back, less long goodbye than stand-off.

So to Glanmore. Glanmore. Glanmore. Glanmore.
At bay, at one, at work, at risk and sure.
Covert and pad. Oak, bay and sycamore.

Jet-sitting next. Across and across and across.
Westering, eastering, the jumbo a school bus,
'The Yard' a cross between the farm and campus.

A holding pattern and a tautening purchase –
Sweeney astray in home truths out of Horace:
Skies change, not cares, for those who cross the seas.

   4

The following for the record, in the light
Of everything before and since:
One bright May morning, nineteen-seventy-nine,
Just off the red-eye special from New York,
I'm on the train for Belfast. Plain, simple 5
Exhilaration at being back: the sea
At Skerries, the nuptial hawthorn bloom,
The trip north taking sweet hold like a chain
On every bodily sprocket.
                      Enter then – 10
As if he were some *film noir* border guard –
Enter this one I'd last met in a dream.
More grimfaced now than in the dream itself
When he'd flagged me down at the side of a mountain road,
Come up and leant his elbow on the roof 15
And explained through the open window of the car
That all I'd have to do was drive a van
Carefully in to the next customs post
At Pettigo, switch off, get out as if
I were on my way with dockets to the office – 20
But then instead I'd walk ten yards more down
Towards the main street and get in with – here
Another schoolfriend's name, a wink and smile,
I'd know him all right, he'd be in a Ford
And I'd be home in three hours' time, as safe 25
As houses . . .
            So he enters and sits down
Opposite and goes for me head on.
'When, for fuck's sake, are you going to write
Something for us?' 'If I do write something, 30
Whatever it is, I'll be writing for myself.'
And that was that. Or words to that effect.

The gaol walls all those months were smeared with shite.
Out of Long Kesh after his dirty protest
The red eyes were the eyes of Ciaran Nugent 35
Like something out of Dante's scurfy hell,

Drilling their way through the rhymes and images
Where I too walked behind the righteous Virgil,
As safe as houses and translating freely:
When he had said all this, his eyes rolled
And his teeth, like a dog's teeth clamping round a bone,
Bit into the skull and again took hold.

5

When I answered that I came from 'far away',
The policeman at the roadblock snapped, 'Where's that?'
He'd only half heard what I said and thought
It was the name of some place up the country.

And now it is – both where I have been living
And where I left – a distance still to go
Like starlight that is light years on the go
From far away and takes light years arriving.

6

Out of the blue then, the sheer exaltation
Of remembering climbing zig-zag up warm steps
To the hermit's eyrie above Rocamadour.
Crows sailing high and close, a lizard pulsing
On gravel at my feet, its front legs set
Like the jointed front struts of a moon vehicle.
And bigly, softly as the breath of life
In a breath of air, a lime-green butterfly
Crossing the pilgrims' sunstruck *via crucis*.

Eleven in the morning. I made a note:
'Rock-lover, loner, sky-sentry, all hail!'
And somewhere the dove rose. And kept on rising.

An Invocation

Incline to me, MacDiarmid, out of Shetland,
Stone-eyed from stone-gazing, sobered up
And thrawn. Not the old vigilante

Of the chimney corner, having us on,
Setting us off, the drinkers' drinker; no,
Incline as the sage of winds that flout the rock face,

As gull stalled in the sea breeze, gatekeeper
Of the open gates behind the brows of birds –
Not to hear me take back smart remarks

About your MacGonagallish propensities –
For I do not – but I add in middle age:
I underprized your far-out, blathering genius.

  *

Those years in the shore-view house, especially.
More intellectual billygoat than scapegoat,
Beyond the stony limits, writing-mad.

That pride of being tested. Of solitude.
Your big pale forehead in the window glass
Like the earth's curve on the sea's curve to the north.

At your wits' end then, always on the go
To the beach and back, taking heady bearings
Between the horizon and the dictionary,

Hard-liner on the rock face of the old
Questions and answers, to which I add my own:
'Who is my neighbour? My neighbour is all mankind.'

  *

And if you won't incline, endure
At an embraced distance. Be the wee
Contrary stormcock that you always were,

The weather-eye of a poetry like the weather,
A shifting force, a factor factored in
Whether it prevails or not, constantly

A function of its time and place
And sometimes of our own. Never, at any rate,
Beyond us, even when outlandish,

In the accent, in the idiom, in
The idea like a thistle in the wind,
A catechism worth repeating always.

  Hugh MacDiarmid 1892–1978

Mycenae Lookout

The ox is on my tongue
   AESCHYLUS, *Agamemnon*

1 *The Watchman's War*

Some people wept, and not for sorrow – joy
That the king had armed and upped and sailed for Troy,
But inside me like struck sound in a gong
That killing-fest, the life-warp and world-wrong
It brought to pass, still augured and endured.
I'd dream of blood in bright webs in a ford,
Of bodies raining down like tattered meat
On top of me asleep – and me the lookout
The queen's command had posted and forgotten,
The blind spot her farsightedness relied on.
And then the ox would lurch against the gong
And deaden it and I would feel my tongue
Like the dropped gangplank of a cattle truck,
Trampled and rattled, running piss and muck,
All swimmy-trembly as the lick of fire,
A victory beacon in an abattoir . . .
Next thing then I would waken at a loss,
For all the world a sheepdog stretched in grass,
Exposed to what I knew, still honour-bound
To concentrate attention out beyond
The city and the border, on that line
Where the blaze would leap the hills when Troy had fallen.

My sentry work was fate, a home to go to,
An in-between-times that I had to row through
Year after year: when the mist would start
To lift off fields and inlets, when morning light
Would open like the grain of light being split,
Day in, day out, I'd come alive again,
Silent and sunned as an esker on a plain,
Up on my elbows, gazing, biding time
In my outpost on the roof . . . What was to come
Out of that ten years' wait that was the war
Flawed the black mirror of my frozen stare.
If a god of justice had reached down from heaven

For a strong beam to hang his scale-pans on
He would have found me tensed and ready-made.
I balanced between destiny and dread
And saw it coming, clouds bloodshot with the red
Of victory fires, the raw wound of that dawn
Igniting and erupting, bearing down
Like lava on a fleeing population . . .
Up on my elbows, head back, shutting out
The agony of Clytemnestra's love-shout
That rose through the palace like the yell of troops
Hurled by King Agamemnon from the ships.

2 *Cassandra*

No such thing
as innocent
bystanding.

Her soiled vest,
her little breasts,
her clipped, devast-

ated, scabbed
punk head,
the char-eyed

famine gawk –
she looked
camp-fucked

and simple.
People
could feel

a missed
trueness in them
focus,

a homecoming
in her dropped-wing,
half-calculating

bewilderment.
No such thing
as innocent.

25 Old King Cock-
of-the-Walk
was back,

King Kill-
the-Child-
30 and-Take-

What-Comes,
King Agamem-
non's drum-

balled, old buck's
35 stride was back.
And then her Greek

words came,
a lamb
at lambing time,

40 bleat of clair-
voyant dread,
the gene-hammer

and tread
of the roused god.
45 And a result-

ant shock desire
in bystanders
to do it to her

there and then.
50 Little rent
cunt of their guilt:

in she went
to the knife,
to the killer wife,

55 to the net over
her and her slaver,
the Troy reaver,

saying, 'A wipe
of the sponge,
60 that's it.

The shadow-hinge
swings unpredict-
ably and the light's

blanked out.'

3 His Dawn Vision

Cities of grass. Fort walls. The dumbstruck palace.
I'd come to with the night wind on my face,
Agog, alert again, but far, far less

Focused on victory than I should have been –
Still isolated in my old disdain   5
Of claques who always needed to be seen

And heard as the true Argives. Mouth athletes,
Quoting the oracle and quoting dates,
Petitioning, accusing, taking votes.

No element that should have carried weight   10
Out of the grievous distance would translate.
Our war stalled in the pre-articulate.

The little violets' heads bowed on their stems,
The pre-dawn gossamers, all dew and scrim
And star-lace, it was more through them   15

I felt the beating of the huge time-wound
We lived inside. My soul wept in my hand
When I would touch them, my whole being rained

Down on myself, I saw cities of grass,
Valleys of longing, tombs, a wind-swept brightness,   20
And far-off, in a hilly, ominous place,

Small crowds of people watching as a man
Jumped a fresh earth-wall and another ran
Amorously, it seemed, to strike him down.

4 The Nights

They both needed to talk,
pretending what they needed
was my advice. Behind backs
each one of them confided

5 it was sexual overload
every time they did it –
and indeed from the beginning
(a child could hardly have missed it)
their real life was the bed.

10 The king should have been told,
but who was there to tell him
if not myself? I willed them
to cease and break the hold
of my cross-purposed silence
15 but still kept on, all smiles
to Aegisthus every morning,
much favoured and self-loathing.
The roof was like an eardrum.

The ox's tons of dumb
20 inertia stood, head-down
and motionless as a herm.
Atlas, watchmen's patron,
would come into my mind,
the only other one
25 up at all hours, ox-bowed
under his yoke of cloud
out there at the world's end.

The loft-floor where the gods
and goddesses took lovers
30 and made out endlessly
successfully, those thuds
and moans through the cloud cover
were wholly on his shoulders.
Sometimes I thought of us
35 apotheosized to boulders
called Aphrodite's Pillars.

High and low in those days
hit their stride together.
When the captains in the horse
40 felt Helen's hand caress
its wooden boards and belly
they nearly rode each other.
But in the end Troy's mothers
bore their brunt in alley,

bloodied cot and bed. 45
The war put all men mad,
horned, horsed or roof-posted,
the boasting and the bested.

My own mind was a bull-pen
where horned King Agamemnon 50
had stamped his weight in gold.
But when hills broke into flame
and the queen wailed on and came,
it was the king I sold.
I moved beyond bad faith: 55
for his bullion bars, his bonus
was a rope-net and a blood-bath.
And the peace had come upon us.

5 *His Reverie of Water*

At Troy, at Athens, what I most clearly
see and nearly smell
is the fresh water.

A filled bath, still unentered
and unstained, waiting behind housewalls 5
that the far cries of the butchered on the plain

keep dying into, until the hero comes
surging in incomprehensibly
to be attended to and be alone,

stripped to the skin, blood-plastered, moaning 10
and rocking, splashing, dozing off,
accommodated as if he were a stranger.

And the well at Athens too.
Or rather that old lifeline leading up
and down from the Acropolis 15

to the well itself, a set of timber steps
slatted in between the sheer cliff face
and a free-standing, covering spur of rock,

secret staircase the defenders knew
and the invaders found, where what was to be 20
Greek met Greek,

    the ladder of the future
    and the past, besieger and besieged,
    the treadmill of assault
25 turned waterwheel, the rungs of stealth
    and habit all the one
    bare foot extended, searching.

    And then this ladder of our own that ran
    deep into a well-shaft being sunk
30 in broad daylight, men puddling at the source

    through tawny mud, then coming back up
    deeper in themselves for having been there,
    like discharged soldiers testing the safe ground,

    finders, keepers, seers of fresh water
35 in the bountiful round mouths of iron pumps
    and gushing taps.

            for Cynthia and Dmitri Hadzi

The First Words

    The first words got polluted
    Like river water in the morning
    Flowing with the dirt
    Of blurbs and the front pages.
5 My only drink is meaning from the deep brain,
    What the birds and the grass and the stones drink.
    Let everything flow
    Up to the four elements,
    Up to water and earth and fire and air.

   from the Romanian of Marin Sorescu

The Gravel Walks

    River gravel. In the beginning, that.
    High summer, and the angler's motorbike
    Deep in roadside flowers, like a fallen knight
    Whose ghost we'd lately questioned: 'Any luck?'

5 As the engines of the world prepared, green nuts

Dangled and clustered closer to the whirlpool.
The trees dipped down. The flints and sandstone-bits
Worked themselves smooth and smaller in a sparkle

Of shallow, hurrying barley-sugar water
Where minnows schooled that we scared when we played –   10
An eternity that ended once a tractor
Dropped its link-box in the gravel bed

And cement mixers began to come to life
And men in dungarees, like captive shades,
Mixed concrete, loaded, wheeled, turned, wheeled, as if   15
The Pharaoh's brickyards burned inside their heads.

　　　　　*

Hoard and praise the verity of gravel.
Gems for the undeluded. Milt of earth.
Its plain, champing song against the shovel
Soundtests and sandblasts words like 'honest worth'.   20

Beautiful in or out of the river,
The kingdom of gravel was inside you too –
Deep down, far back, clear water running over
Pebbles of caramel, hailstone, mackerel-blue.

But the actual washed stuff kept you slow and steady   25
As you went stooping with your barrow full
Into an absolution of the body,
The shriven life tired bones and marrow feel.

So walk on air against your better judgement
Establishing yourself somewhere in between   30
Those solid batches mixed with grey cement
And a tune called 'The Gravel Walks' that conjures green.

Whitby-sur-Moyola

Caedmon too I was lucky to have known,
Back *in situ* there with his full bucket
And armfuls of clean straw, the perfect yardman,
Unabsorbed in what he had to do
But doing it perfectly, and watching you.   5
He had worked his angel stint. He was hard as nails

And all that time he'd been poeting with the harp
His real gift was the big ignorant roar
He could still let out of him, just bogging in
As if the sacred subjects were a herd
That had broken out and needed rounding up.
I never saw him once with his hands joined
Unless it was a case of eyes to heaven
And the quick sniff and test of fingertips
After he'd passed them through a sick beast's water.
Oh, Caedmon was the real thing all right.

The Thimble

1

In the House of Carnal Murals
The painter used it to hold a special red
He touched the lips and freshest bite-marks with.

2

Until the Reformation, it was revered
As a relic of St Adaman.
The workers in a certain foundry cast
A bell, so heavy, it was said,
No apparatus could lift it to the belltower –
And afterwards were stricken one by one
With a kind of sleeping sickness.
In the middle of the fiery delirium
Of metal pouring, they would all fall quiet
And see green waterweed and stepping stones
Across the molten bronze.
So Adaman arrived and blessed their hands
And eyes and cured them, but at that hour
The bell too shrank miraculously
And henceforth was known to the faithful
And registered in the canons' inventory
As Adaman's Thimble.

3

Was this the measure of the sweetest promise,
The dipped thirst-brush, the dew of paradise
That would flee my tongue when they said 'A thimbleful'?

4
         Now a teenager
With shaved head
And translucent shoulders
Wears it for a nipple-cap.

   5
And so on.

The Butter-Print

Who carved on the butter-print's round open face
A cross-hatched head of rye, all jags and bristles?
Why should soft butter bear that sharp device
As if its breast were scored with slivered glass?

When I was small I swallowed an awn of rye.   5
My throat was like standing crop probed by a scythe.
I felt the edge slide and the point stick deep
Until, when I coughed and coughed and coughed it up,

My breathing came dawn-cold, so clear and sudden
I might have been inhaling airs from heaven   10
Where healed and martyred Agatha stares down
At the relic knife as I stared at the awn.

Remembered Columns

The solid letters of the world grew airy.
The marble serifs, the clearly blocked uprights
Built upon rocks and set upon the heights
Rose like remembered columns in a story

About the Virgin's house that rose and flew   5
And landed on the hilltop at Loreto.
I lift my eyes in a light-headed credo,
Discovering what survives translation true.

'Poet's Chair'

for Carolyn Mulholland

Leonardo said: the sun has never
Seen a shadow. Now watch the sculptor move
Full circle round her next work, like a lover
In the sphere of shifting angles and fixed love.

1

Angling shadows of itself are what
Your 'Poet's Chair' stands to and rises out of
In its sun-stalked inner-city courtyard.
On the *qui vive* all the time, its four legs land
On their feet – catsfoot, goatfoot, big soft splay-foot too;
Its straight back sprouts two bronze and leafy saplings.
Every flibbertigibbet in the town,
Old birds and boozers, late-night pissers, kissers,
All have a go at sitting on it some time.
It's the way the air behind them's winged and full,
The way a graft has seized their shoulder-blades
That makes them happy. Once out of nature,
They're going to come back in leaf and bloom
And angel step. Or something like that. *Leaves*
On a bloody chair! Would you believe it?

2

Next thing I see the chair in a white prison
With Socrates sitting on it, bald as a coot,
Discoursing in bright sunlight with his friends.
His time is short. The day his trial began
A verdant boat sailed from Apollo's shrine
In Delos, for the annual rite
Of commemoration. Until its wreathed
And creepered rigging re-enters Athens
Harbour, the city's life is holy.
No executions. No hemlock bowl. No tears
And none now as the poison does its work
And the expert jailer talks the company through
The stages of the numbness. Socrates
At the centre of the city and the day

Has proved the soul immortal. The bronze leaves
Cannot believe their ears, it is so silent.
Soon Crito will have to close his eyes and mouth,
But for the moment everything's an ache
Deferred, foreknown, imagined and most real.

3

My father's ploughing one, two, three, four sides
Of the lea ground where I sit all-seeing
At centre field, my back to the thorn tree
They never cut. The horses are all hoof
And burnished flank, I am all foreknowledge.
Of the poem as a ploughshare that turns time
Up and over. Of the chair in leaf
The fairy thorn is entering for the future.
Of being here for good in every sense.

The Swing

Fingertips just tipping you would send you
Every bit as far – once you got going –
As a big push in the back.
                              Sooner or later,
We all learned one by one to go sky high,
Backward and forward in the open shed,
Toeing and rowing and jackknifing through air.

*

Not Fragonard. Nor Brueghel. It was more
Hans Memling's light of heaven off green grass,
Light over fields and hedges, the shed-mouth
Sunstruck and expectant, the bedding-straw
Piled to one side, like a nativity
Foreground and background waiting for the figures.
And then, in the middle ground, the swing itself
With an old lopsided sack in the loop of it,
Perfectly still, hanging like pulley-slack,
A lure let down to tempt the soul to rise.

*

Even so, we favoured the earthbound. She
Sat there as majestic as an empress

20   Steeping her swollen feet one at a time
In the enamel basin, feeding it
Every now and again with an opulent
Steaming arc from a kettle on the floor
Beside her. The plout of that was music
25   To our ears, her smile a mitigation.
Whatever light the goddess had once shone
Around her favourite coming from the bath
Was what was needed then: there should have been
Fresh linen, ministrations by attendants,
30   Procession and amazement. Instead, she took
Each rolled elastic stocking and drew it on
Like the life she would not fail and was not
Meant for. And once, when she'd scoured the basin,
She came and sat to please us on the swing,
35   Neither out of place nor in her element,
Just tempted by it for a moment only,
Half-retrieving something half-confounded.
Instinctively we knew to let her be.

*

To start up by yourself, you hitched the rope
40   Against your backside and backed on into it
Until it tautened, then tiptoed and drove off
As hard as possible. You hurled a gathered thing
From the small of your own back into the air.
Your head swept low, you heard the whole shed creak.

*

45   We all learned one by one to go sky high.
Then townlands vanished into aerodromes,
Hiroshima made light of human bones,
Concorde's neb migrated towards the future.
So who were we to want to hang back there
50   In spite of all?
                In spite of all, we sailed
Beyond ourselves and over and above
The rafters aching in our shoulderblades,
The give and take of branches in our arms.

The Poplar

Wind shakes the big poplar, quicksilvering
The whole tree in a single sweep.
What bright scale fell and left this needle quivering?
What loaded balances have come to grief?

Two Stick Drawings

1

Claire O'Reilly used her granny's stick –
A crook-necked one – to snare the highest briars
That always grew the ripest blackberries.
When it came to gathering, Persephone
Was in the halfpenny place compared to Claire. 5
She'd trespass and climb gates and walk the railway
Where sootflakes blew into convolvulus
And the train tore past with the stoker yelling
Like a balked king from his iron chariot.

2

With its drover's canes and blackthorns and ash plants,
The ledge of the back seat of my father's car
Had turned into a kind of stick-shop window,
But the only one who ever window-shopped
Was Jim of the hanging jaw, for Jim was simple 5
And rain or shine he'd make his desperate rounds
From windscreen to back window, hands held up
To both sides of his face, peering and groaning.
So every now and then the sticks would be
Brought out for him and stood up one by one 10
Against the front mudguard; and one by one
Jim would take the measure of them, sight
And wield and slice and poke and parry
The unhindering air; until he found
The true extension of himself in one 15
That made him jubilant. He'd run and crow,
Stooped forward, with his right elbow stuck out
And the stick held horizontal to the ground,
Angled across in front of him, as if

20 He were leashed to it and it drew him on
    Like a harness rod of the inexorable.

A Call

'Hold on,' she said, 'I'll just run out and get him.
The weather here's so good, he took the chance
To do a bit of weeding.'
                         So I saw him
5   Down on his hands and knees beside the leek rig,
    Touching, inspecting, separating one
    Stalk from the other, gently pulling up
    Everything not tapered, frail and leafless,
    Pleased to feel each little weed-root break,
10 But rueful also . . .
                         Then found myself listening to
    The amplified grave ticking of hall clocks
    Where the phone lay unattended in a calm
    Of mirror glass and sunstruck pendulums . . .

15 And found myself then thinking: if it were nowadays,
    This is how Death would summon Everyman.

    Next thing he spoke and I nearly said I loved him.

The Errand

'On you go now! Run, son, like the devil
And tell your mother to try
To find me a bubble for the spirit level
And a new knot for this tie.'

5   But still he was glad, I know, when I stood my ground,
    Putting it up to him
    With a smile that trumped his smile and his fool's errand,
    Waiting for the next move in the game.

A Dog Was Crying Tonight in Wicklow Also

in memory of Donatus Nwoga

When human beings found out about death
They sent the dog to Chukwu with a message:
They wanted to be let back to the house of life.
They didn't want to end up lost forever
Like burnt wood disappearing into smoke
Or ashes that get blown away to nothing.
Instead, they saw their souls in a flock at twilight
Cawing and headed back for the same old roosts
And the same bright airs and wing-stretchings each morning.
Death would be like a night spent in the wood:
At first light they'd be back in the house of life.
(The dog was meant to tell all this to Chukwu).

But death and human beings took second place
When he trotted off the path and started barking
At another dog in broad daylight just barking
Back at him from the far bank of a river.

And that is how the toad reached Chukwu first,
The toad who'd overheard in the beginning
What the dog was meant to tell. 'Human beings,' he said
(And here the toad was trusted absolutely),
'Human beings want death to last forever.'

Then Chukwu saw the people's souls in birds
Coming towards him like black spots off the sunset
To a place where there would be neither roosts nor trees
Nor any way back to the house of life.
And his mind reddened and darkened all at once
And nothing that the dog would tell him later
Could change that vision. Great chiefs and great loves
In obliterated light, the toad in mud,
The dog crying out all night behind the corpse house.

M.

When the deaf phonetician spread his hand
Over the dome of a speaker's skull

He could tell which diphthong and which vowel
By the bone vibrating to the sound.

5   A globe stops spinning. I set my palm
On a contour cold as permafrost
And imagine axle-hum and the steadfast
Russian of Osip Mandelstam.

An Architect

He fasted on the doorstep of his gift,
Exacting more, minding the boulder
And the raked zen gravel. But no slouch either

Whenever it came to whiskey, whether to
5   Lash into it or just to lash it out.
Courtly always, and rapt, and astonishing,

Like the day on the beach when he stepped out of his clothes
And waded along beside us in his pelt
Speculating, intelligent and lanky,

10 Taking things in his Elysian stride,
Talking his way back into sites and truths
The art required and his life came down to:

Blue slate and whitewash, shadow-lines, projections,
Things at once apparent and transparent,
15 Clean-edged, fine-drawn, drawn-out, redrawn, remembered . . .

Exit now, in his tweeds, down an aisle between
Drawing boards as far as the eye can see
To where it can't until he sketches where.

The Sharping Stone

In an apothecary's chest of drawers,
Sweet cedar that we'd purchased second hand,
In one of its weighty deep-sliding recesses
I found the sharping stone that was to be
5   Our gift to him. Still in its wrapping paper.
Like a baton of black light I'd failed to pass.

*

Airless cinder-depths. But all the same,
The way it lay there, it wakened something too . . .
I thought of us that evening on the logs,
Flat on our backs, the pair of us, parallel,
Supported head to heel, arms straight, eyes front,
Listening to the rain drip off the trees
And saying nothing, braced to the damp bark.
What possessed us? The bare, lopped loveliness
Of those two winter trunks, the way they seemed
Prepared for launching, at right angles across
A causeway of short fence-posts set like rollers.
Neither of us spoke. The puddles waited.
The workers had gone home, saws fallen silent.
And next thing down we lay, babes in the wood,
Gazing up at the flood-face of the sky
Until it seemed a flood was carrying us
Out of the forest park, feet first, eyes front,
Out of November, out of middle age,
Together, out, across the Sea of Moyle.

*

Sarcophage des époux. In terra cotta.
Etruscan couple shown side by side,
Recumbent on left elbows, husband pointing
With his right arm and watching where he points,
Wife in front, her earrings in, her braids
Down to her waist, taking her sexual ease.
He is all eyes, she is all brow and dream,
Her right forearm and hand held out as if
Some bird she sees in her deep inward gaze
Might be about to roost there. Domestic
Love, the artist thought, warm tones and property,
The frangibility of terra cotta . . .
Which is how they figured on the colour postcard
(*Louvre, Département des Antiquités*)
That we'd sent him once, then found among his things.

*

He loved inspired mistakes: his Spanish grandson's
English transliteration, thanking him

                    For a boat trip: 'That was a marvellous
                    Walk on the water, granddad.' And indeed
45   He walked on air himself, never more so
                    Than when he had been widowed and the youth
                    In him, the athlete who had wooed her –
                    Breasting tapes and clearing the high bars –
                    Grew lightsome once again. Going at eighty
50   On the bendiest roads, going for broke
                    At every point-to-point and poker-school,
                    'He commenced his wild career' a second time
                    And not a bother on him. Smoked like a train
                    And took the power mower in his stride.
55   Flirted and vaunted. Set fire to his bed.
                    Fell from a ladder. Learned to microwave.

                            *

                    So set the drawer on freshets of thaw water
                    And place the unused sharping stone inside it:
                    To be found next summer on a riverbank
60   Where scythes once hung all night in alder trees
                    And mowers played dawn scherzos on the blades,
                    Their arms like harpists' arms, one drawing towards,
                    One sweeping the bright rim of the extreme.

The Strand

The dotted line my father's ashplant made
On Sandymount Strand
Is something else the tide won't wash away.

The Walk

                    Glamoured the road, the day, and him and her
                    And everywhere they took me. When we stepped out
                    Cobbles were riverbed, the Sunday air
                    A high stream-roof that moved in silence over
5   Rhododendrons in full bloom, foxgloves
                    And hemlock, robin-run-the-hedge, the hedge
                    With its deckled ivy and thick shadows –
                    Until the riverbed itself appeared,

Gravelly, shallowy, summery with pools,
And made a world rim that was not for crossing.
Love brought me that far by the hand, without
The slightest doubt or irony, dry-eyed
And knowledgeable, contrary as be damned;
Then just kept standing there, not letting go.

*

So here is another longshot. Black and white.
A negative this time, in dazzle-dark,
Smudge and pallor where we make out you and me,
The selves we struggled with and struggled out of,
Two shades who have consumed each other's fire,
Two flames in sunlight that can sear and singe,
But seem like wisps of enervated air,
After-wavers, feathery ether-shifts . . .
Yet apt still to rekindle suddenly
If we find along the way charred grass and sticks
And an old fire-fragrance lingering on,
Erotic woodsmoke, witchery, intrigue,
Leaving us none the wiser, just better primed
To speed the plough again and feed the flame.

At the Wellhead

Your songs, when you sing them with your two eyes closed
As you always do, are like a local road
We've known every turn of in the past –
That midge-veiled, high-hedged side-road where you stood
Looking and listening until a car
Would come and go and leave you lonelier
Than you had been to begin with. So, sing on,
Dear shut-eyed one, dear far-voiced veteran,

Sing yourself to where the singing comes from,
Ardent and cut off like our blind neighbour
Who played the piano all day in her bedroom.
Her notes came out to us like hoisted water
Ravelling off a bucket at the wellhead
Where next thing we'd be listening, hushed and awkward.

    *

15   That blind-from-birth, sweet-voiced, withdrawn musician
Was like a silver vein in heavy clay.
Night water glittering in the light of day.
But also just our neighbour, Rosie Keenan.
She touched our cheeks. She let us touch her braille
20   In books like books wallpaper patterns came in.
Her hands were active and her eyes were full
Of open darkness and a watery shine.

She knew us by our voices. She'd say she 'saw'
Whoever or whatever. Being with her
25   Was intimate and helpful, like a cure
You didn't notice happening. When I read
A poem with Keenan's well in it, she said,
'I can see the sky at the bottom of it now.'

At Banagher

Then all of a sudden there appears to me
The journeyman tailor who was my antecedent:
Up on a table, cross-legged, ripping out

A garment he must recut or resew,
5   His lips tight back, a thread between his teeth,
Keeping his counsel always, giving none,

His eyelids steady as wrinkled horn or iron.
Self-absenting, both migrant and ensconced;
Admitted into kitchens, into clothes

10   His touch has the power to turn to cloth again –
All of a sudden he appears to me,
Unopen, unmendacious, unillumined.

    *

So more power to him on the job there, ill at ease
Under my scrutiny in spite of years
15   Of being inscrutable as he threaded needles

Or matched the facings, linings, hems and seams.
He holds the needle just off centre, squinting,
And licks the thread and licks and sweeps it through,

Then takes his time to draw both ends out even,
Plucking them sharply twice. Then back to stitching.   20
Does he ever question what it all amounts to

Or ever will? Or care where he lays his head?
My Lord Buddha of Banagher, the way
Is opener for your being in it.

Tollund

That Sunday morning we had travelled far.
We stood a long time out in Tollund Moss:
The low ground, the swart water, the thick grass
Hallucinatory and familiar.

A path through Jutland fields. Light traffic sound.   5
Willow bushes; rushes; bog-fir grags
In a swept and gated farmyard; dormant quags.
And silage under wraps in its silent mound.

It could have been a still out of the bright
'Townland of Peace', that poem of dream farms   10
Outside all contention. The scarecrow's arms
Stood open opposite the satellite

Dish in the paddock, where a standing stone
Had been resituated and landscaped,
With tourist signs in *futhark* runic script   15
In Danish and in English. Things had moved on.

It could have been Mulhollandstown or Scribe.
The byroads had their names on them in black
And white; it was user-friendly outback
Where we stood footloose, at home beyond the tribe,   20

More scouts than strangers, ghosts who'd walked abroad
Unfazed by light, to make a new beginning
And make a go of it, alive and sinning,
Ourselves again, free-willed again, not bad.

September 1994

Postscript

And some time make the time to drive out west
Into County Clare, along the Flaggy Shore,
In September or October, when the wind
And the light are working off each other
So that the ocean on one side is wild
With foam and glitter, and inland among stones
The surface of a slate-grey lake is lit
By the earthed lightning of a flock of swans,
Their feathers roughed and ruffling, white on white,
Their fully grown headstrong-looking heads
Tucked or cresting or busy underwater.
Useless to think you'll park and capture it
More thoroughly. You are neither here nor there,
A hurry through which known and strange things pass
As big soft buffetings come at the car sideways
And catch the heart off guard and blow it open.

UNCOLLECTED POEMS (1996–2001)

A Grace Note for Michael

What stays with me is the rich braid of his voice
As deeply laid as the North Atlantic cable.
When he said 'Seamus' I could hear a wash
Of ocean over me and his person-to-person call
Coming in on the life-line like *sean-nós*.   5

The Road to Derry

On a Wednesday morning early I took the road to Derry
Along Glenshane and Foreglen and the cold woods of Hillhead,
A wet wind in the hedges and a dark cloud on the mountain
And flags like black frost mourning that the thirteen men were dead.

The Roe wept at Dungiven and the Foyle cried out to heaven.   5
Burntollet's old wound opened and again the Bogside bled;
By Shipquay Gate I shivered and by Lone Moor I enquired
Where I might find the coffins where the thirteen men lay dead.

My heart besieged by anger, my mind a gap of danger,
I walked among their old haunts, the home ground where they bled.   10
And in the dirt lay justice like an acorn in the winter
Till its oak would sprout in Derry where the thirteen men lay dead.

Three-Piece

1 *A Suit*

'I'll make you one,' he said, 'and balance it
Perfectly on you.' And I could almost feel
The plumb line of the creased tweed hit my heel,

My shoulders like a spar or a riding scale
Under the jacket, my whole shape realigned   5
In ways that suited me down to the ground.

So although a suit was the last thing that I needed
I wore his words and told him that I'd take it
And told myself it was going for a song.

2 A Tie

    She made
    me one
    of hard
    silk thread,
5   string-thin,
    tight skein
    crocheted
    by hand,
    close-knit
10 and strict
    as *cyng-*
    hanedd,
    all a-
    glitter
15 like rain
    on fern
    or em-
    erald ems
    or fine
20 ground jade,
    my thin
    green line
    for which
    I *grat-*
25 *ias*
    ago
    in Lat-
    in quotes
    (with gen-
30 der change
    in sub-
    ject and
    tense change
    in verb):
35 *nihil*
    tegit
    quod non
    ornat,
    and trans-
40 late thus

(to tie
the knot),
'She puts
a shine
on all   45
she puts
her hand
to.' Love
and thanks
again   50
to her.

3 A Coat

'We're not a mile off it,' I heard him say, with an *ought*
Dragging and lengthening out the sound of that 'not' –
For Mr Simpson, though he worked in Magherafelt,
Was from Antrim and glottal and more of a Pict than a Celt.

But an Ulsterman. An Ulsterman for sure,   5
Calling a spade a spade and the door the *dure*
And any child he was fitting with clothes *the wean*.
My father poked his cattle-dealer's cane

Into the coats on the coatrack for the only one
That took his fancy and when I had put it on,   10
'We're not a mile off it,' Mr Simpson said again,
Uneager and sure of the sale; and confidentially then,

'Ulster, you know, is the name for an overcoat.
The Oxford English Dictionary even gives it.
Ulster.' He paused and he mused. 'All over the world   15
Good cloth and good wear and the whole of your money's worth.'

I hear him still when I reach deep into the long
Cold draught of the sleeve of some ulster I'm fitting on
And wish my hand would come through and beyond all that
Deep glottal purchase and worth, like the virtual flight   20

Of The Red Hand of Ulster beyond the beyond of its myth,
Back to its unbloodied cuff at its unsevered wrist,
Flexing its fingers again and combing the air
And a wild, post-Shakespearean streel of gallowglass hair.

Carlo

for Christopher Reid

I'm afraid the millennium
means nothing to Carlo.
My heart aches for him

with one eye gone blind
and his whole body slowed.
His bark is still loud

but not as aggressive,
not that rampant 'Fuck off'
of a dog in his prime,

hurling and barrelling
round the back yard.
I undervalued

all that at the time,
his just being there
like a bolt from the garden,

woofing and panting
or worrying plastic
bottles or bags,

our mad perforator
and show-off performer.
He once bit a writer

or better say nipped –
regrettably 'nipped'
has to be the *mot juste*.

He went wild at jet trails.
You'd be conscious of nothing
but sunbeat and lawn-heat

when he'd work up a snarl
like a slow Cape Canaveral
burn-up and lift-off,

then launch himself barking
into the blue.
Then quit and come running

like a form of forgiveness.
Now I'd like to relive
those years of aloofness,

am sorry I didn't
give and take more
notice and pleasure

each hour of each day.
I'd stroke him, of course,
at night and at times

when he didn't expect it,
my sudden meltdowns
of hapless affection,

but mostly the case
was live and let live.
Which is hardly enough.

The film on his eye,
his blindsided trot
reminds me of that.

Even his tail
tum-tumming the floor
when I come through the door

reminds me of that.
Ever more slowly
tum-tumming the floor.

Two Paintings by Le Douanier Rousseau

1 *La muse inspirant le poète*

There I was all right, the groom in the suit

With a big white fronded quill
In my right hand, pointing down

And you with your schoolteacher mother's mother's
Fingers pointing up

(Call it 'The School of Us Ones')
When behold I beheld in the quill

That lily of the valley Saint Joseph points
Athwart his brown-robed loins in holy pictures

10 (The meek shall inherit the wroth)
And in the bride a Solomon in drag –

But nowhere near as gloriously arrayed
As you – imitating you

Laying down the law for all you were worth.

2 *'L'enfant aux rochers'*

In the beginning were the words *'Sois Sage'*
So in the end he could be nothing else:

Unyoung, *infans*, outlined in isolation,
Taken up to the mountain and shown all

5 To no avail, then left there unscandalised,
High and dry but never above himself

In his matelot stripes and dainty dumpty shoes,
He's king of the castle again, alert to the first

Faint chant of the namecallers' chorus
10 Ganging up in the playground.

Sonnets from the Peloponnese

Bassae

Up with the cock. The light. The early language
Of goat-bells, barking dogs and answering cocks.
Everyone up. And downstairs with the luggage,
Mad to get going through the mayflowers and warm rocks
5 Of a May morning in the Peloponnese.
Mountain roads, fresh tarmac surfaces,
Car windows down, the car seats buffed like saddles,
Then a last bend to where Bassae's white marble
Columns are conserved now under canvas.
10 We missed their classic ordering and aura,
But had our presence clinched by gravel crunching
Inside the tent acoustic, and by a cuckoo

Calling the whole time as I sat there watching
Butterflies in the pre-Linnaean flora.

Mycenae

That second, unplanned visit: call it fate
Or the unconscious, anything you like,
But with time to spare, we discovered ourselves back
At the Lion Gate, the rath of Atreus,
The founded quiet of Agamemnon's palace   5
Where we climbed the stone path to the *megaron*
And I read the dawn speech of the rooftop watchman
And saw the Aegean from his bastion.
Then later, downhill, at the beehive tomb
Flocks of swallows, like bats out of hell or Hades,   10
Crisscrossed the chamber mouth, and we felt at home
By cairn and *tholos*, cyclopic wall and dolmen.
It was omen and return, an illumined limen
We'd crossed ahead of time, foreshadowed bodies.

The Stick

Whitethorn, not blackthorn,
More a staff than a switch,
So not like the one

The District Inspector
Tucked under the arm   5
Of his dress uniform

When he fronted processions,
As black as his boot
And neater than ninepence.

Mine came from Conor –   10
Illustrissimus donor –
Conor Cruise O'Brien

To whom it had come
Honoris causa
From W. R. Rodgers   15

And Bertie had got it

From Brinsley Mac
Namara, who'd got it

From a man in Avoca,
One Victor Byrne,
Collector, pub owner

And friend of the blacksmith
Who'd shod it with iron,
A hoof-angled ferrule

Put on by instruction
Of the one who had cut it
In Avondale Woods

(Rhyme him with 'carnal'
Yourself if you want to)
Charles Stewart Parnell.

I'm amazed Conor parted
With it at all:
It was intellectual

Property nearly,
His who had written
Parnell and his Party.

The head of it's like
The head of a snake
Being banished by Patrick,

But poised for its comeback,
Rising to strike
As the knot and the curl

And the shine of the grain
Come clean in your palm
Like a *non serviam*.

Now it's mine to pass on
I don't want this baton
Getting into the hands

Of what Mandelstam called
'The symphonic police'.
I'd prefer it to go

To some finder or keeper,

Some rapt son or daughter
Astray like Aeneas

Conducting himself
By the light of the leaves.
I'd see it released

Back into the thickets
And thick of the language,
Into that *selva*

Selvaggia e forte
We cull and come through
As poets, if we're lucky.

Non-U

In memory of Darcy O'Brien

Darcy, child of the stars, of the Hollywood hills,
Of freeways and limos, lemon trees and dude ranches,
To whom the world was an oyster that manners alone

Forbade you to touch, seersuckered Darcy
Of Princeton, of Berkeley, of Claremont, of Dublin and Tulsa,
Why is it deep in the Breughel reek of a crowd

In the sweat-pit of Gallagher's pub in west Donegal
You appear to me now? Me at home in that den
And you like a Daniel who had entered among us protected

By the ironies of correctness, style
As the man, the immaculate black
Of your boot, your timing and smile.

Full as the Baltic, we slept that night in a bothy
Where you rose the next morning unrumpled
And lotioned, like some kind of god.

'I am glad,' your last fax came back
As ever a pure exercise
In the arm's length of diction

'I am glad my piece seems to have had
An emetic effect. I did like the poem.'
In Gallagher's pub,

    In the after-hours blather and surge
    Of that place, in their slug-down and thick-speak,
    An emetic's to help you 'lash off' –

25 A boot-flecking tumult, a locution new-littered
    And fauve as their word for late-night close dancing,
    The word 'belly rub' that you loved,

    So un-lace-curtain, un-Princeton, so us and non-U.

Our Lady of Guadalupe

Our Lady of Guadalupe. Nothing remains
Except daylight across the light of the screen,
The ratchety projector no match for the afternoon,
Disappointment blanching the sense of occasion.

5   An Indian face in close-up. Tropical rainfalls
    Blasting too loudly out of the lousy speakers,
    But none of the miracle cures or the characters.
    Nothing at all. Except for the tightening shawls

    Of those *l*'s in the title, hoisting their burdensome vowels.

Willow, Ophelia, Moyola

    There is a willow grows aslant a brook
    But in the beginning it was sally tree.
    Sallies in hedges and sallies on the bank
    Of the Moyola River and black sallies
5   Like a line of daunted stragglers bogging down
    In the sedge and glarry wetness of our meadow.
    The one in the yard was tetter-barked and hollow,
    Two-timing earth and air: corona top
    Of flick-and-shimmer, sprout-and-tremble growth.
10 Land and sky assembled themselves round it.
    In the protocol of soul, soul might have moved
    Backwards away from it, as from a monarch,
    Then turned to those princess-saplings by the river.
    But they in their turn had stepped a word away
15 And willowed like Ophelias in Moyola.

A Dream of Solstice

Qual è colüi che sognando vede,
che dopo 'l sogno la passione impressa
rimane, e l'altro a la mente non riede,

cotal son io . . .
    DANTE, *Paradiso*, Canto xxxiii

Like somebody who sees things when he's dreaming
And after the dream lives with the aftermath
Of what he felt, no other trace remaining,

So I live now, for what I saw departs
And is almost lost, although a distilled sweetness
Still drops from it into my inner heart.

It is the same with snow the sun releases,
The same as when in wind, the hurried leaves
Swirl round your ankles and the shaking hedges

That had flopped their catkin cuff-lace and green sleeves
Are sleet-whipped bare. Dawn light began stealing
Through the cold universe to County Meath,

Over weirs where the Boyne water, fulgent, darkling,
Turns its thick axle, over rick-sized stones
Millennia deep in their own unmoving

And unmoved alignment. And now the planet turns
Earth brow and templed earth, the corbelled rock
And unsunned tonsure of the burial mounds,

I stand with pilgrims, tourists, media folk
And all admitted to the wired-off hill.
Headlights of juggernauts heading for Dundalk,

Flight 104 from New York audible
As it descends on schedule into Dublin,
Boyne Valley Centre Car Park already full,

Waiting for seedling light on roof and windscreen.
And as *in illo tempore* people marked
The king's gold dagger when he plunged it in

       To the hilt in unsown ground, to start the work
       Of the world again, to speed the plough
30   And plant the riddled grain, we watch through murk

       And overboiling cloud for the milted glow
       Of sunrise, for an eastern dazzle
       To send first light like share-shine in a furrow

       Steadily deeper, farther available,
35   Creeping along the floor of the passage grave
       To backstone and capstone, to hold its candle

       Inside the cosmic hill. Who dares say 'love'
       At this cold coming? Who would not dare say it?
       Is this the moved wheel that the poet spoke of,

40   That star pivot? Life's perseid in the ashpit
       Of the dead? Like his, my speech cannot
       Tell what the mind needs told: *an infant tongue*

Milky with breast milk would be more articulate.

Screenplay

       Scene: a door, a doorstep, a housefront
       And a yard in front of that. The usual, gaunt
       Plonked-down four-squareness of a modern farmhouse.
       Beyond the scene, a sense of light and space.

5   Stillness for a while. Next thing inside
       A door bangs, footsteps start, stop, hesitate,
       And the front door we are watching – panelled glass
       Inside a little porch or roofed recess –

       Screens the moves of someone in the hall,
10   The shadow of a man, broad, not too tall,
       Putting on his overcoat and hat.
       (Much vigorous business here, in silhouette).

       Another pause. He stands, then reaches for
       The Yale-lock snib on the inside of the door
15   But doesn't turn it. Outside, the round bulls-eye
       Of polished brass is pierced by a brass key

       Though we don't, as yet, pay any heed to that
       For now the man has started to come out

Yet still does not, or does not altogether:
He appears to be in two minds as to whether

To cross across the threshold, he turns his back
To take another long, abstracted look
Into the hall. Where there is nobody,
And this no-ness and his thereness in his body

Are like home ground that has suddenly fallen through,
A shock and drop and blow out of the blue.
He turns again, looking a little dazed,
But steadies up between the jambs, arms braced

And feet apart, his whole demeanour stalwart,
As if to say: 'It's not the end of the world,
There are worse fates than to end up on your own.
If God Almighty had left Adam alone

The world would have been a great deal better off.
Earthman to earth, a single perfect life
That hadn't interfered and hadn't done
Injury to a single thing or person.'

Hold, while he hangs there, dead-eyed, in the doorframe,
Then comes to life, cries out, faces the jamb
And beats his brow against it, and one closed fist
Until he disengages and at last

Swings the door shut behind him. Its report
Is solid and dumbfounding. Finally
He reaches up, tugs, twists, withdraws the key
And goes like a man who has betrayed the fort,

Bearing the key in his hand, half-elevated,
As if it were brass flame, a taper lit
And carried as due ceremony dictated
When a threshold was to be deconsecrated

And a locking up occur where heretofore
Day in, day out, a key shone in the door.

An Empty Surfboard on a Flat Sea

You can hardly call him a flat-earther since the roundness of it
wasn't yet in question. This was back in the wonder days when a

map was a new invention and a man with his mind on stars could
end up in a well. The earth, he said, floated on the air as a leaf
floats on the water.

The next time you begin your descent towards Shannon and see
the island steady as she goes, the next time you look from your
balcony across an olive plain or drive on some estuary bridge
beneath the air-socks, spare a thought for Aneximenes and his
floating world.

Úrlár

for Liam O'Flynn

Hull and hawser. Fathom thrum. The rope
And anchor holding, mast-top
And boxed compass move with the gyroscope
Of the big music. Úrlár, meaning floor,
Steadies its foundation in the air.

The Dearest Freshness

Clearable water. There from the start. The sight
And run of it, unpolluting itself
From the muck of dragwork so quickly
I remember eating snow.

          And one night at a party
In Fayetteville, Arkansas, a woman leaving,
Driving home, then driving herself straight back
With the book she meant to read from. Her accent
Was southern, perfect for each voice
In the little scene she chose, from a story set
In a field beside a river.
                  Children playing
Stop and line up and cannot take their eyes off
Something deep in the flow; and then one says
'That's us down there,' and it goes clean through me.

That's us down there. I see us every time.

Postscript to St Lucia

March, the lion, paws the sand
Of Sandymount. The famous strand
Ineluctably rejoices
As scudding gusts and tidal noises

Rise up to where I sit and write   5
At home behind my attic skylight,
Far from Castries and Gros Islet,
Vieux Fort, Soufrière and Rodney Bay,

Far from *en bas gorge* and steel
And catamarans on double-keel,   10
The morning swim, the sunblocked doze,
The urge to throw off *all* the clothes,

Far from our beach-head barbecues,
(Those little deep-fried *balahoos*)
And vinous, long verandah lunches   15
And ruddy sunsets with rum punches.

Dear host and hostess of St Lucia,
Re-work the spell, return us to you!
It's as if in distance set between us
Your fabulous, far *locus amoenus*,   20

Your Prospero-rough-magicked dream
Of cloud-capped *piton*, cove and stream
Grew insubstantial, hazy, weak
As our sometime glimpse of Martinique.

Turquoise, green and blue, the sea   25
Was water-water-coloury:
My first paint-brush and box of paints,
My childhood's puddly wash and tints –

That primal reach for the more of art –
It reawakened in my heart.   30
Under the palms and *Bois-canot*,
Like a punch-drunk Douanier Rousseau

I lounged, luxuriated, drifted.
Tectonic plates inside me shifted.

35 Ice-caps melted. Global warming
    (O most benign and unalarming)

    Entered the body and the soul.
    My tropics stretched from pole to pole.
    Earth and Eden mingled there
40 As in a mural by St Omer.

    Yet earth it was, and no mistake.
    I loved the life, the give and take,
    The stalls of fruit, the roadside rumshops,
    And cows in swamps, and crowds at bus-stops,

45 The breadfruit, the banana plant,
    Helonica and *flamboyante* –
    Not to mention booze at *Buzz*,
    The ice-cold vodka's frigid fuzz,

    Marie's whiskey sours, and lyric
50 Beverages prepared for Derek,
    All recorded by S. Nama –
    'Hold it! Hold it! Where's the camera?'

    So from the wind-whipped Dublin shore
    I walk back towards the open door
55 Of the studio, its siesta calm
    And breathing-space, the light's *I am*

    In which once more I settle, sit
    For one last touch-up to the portrait,
    Sit, drift, hold the pose and stare,
60 Not sure if I am here or there.

Sally Rod

You sharpened the end of a sally rod, a foot to eighteen inches long, and stuck it into a seed potato just heavy enough to bend it at the tip. The art was in gauging how far to stick the rod in so that it had purchase while you swung, but gave when you decided to unleash.

5   Spud-riddance. Whip-slurp. Backlash and wheek of your sally rod through air. Then an equal need to lash your leg with it. Your own bare leg. With a sudden sharper lash. The art was in the hurt you couldn't gauge.

Trea

Nothing definite. Maybe she had the cure, maybe she didn't have the cure, but whether she had or not, time and again I heard them tell the story.

Her house backed on a millrace. With a gooseberry thorn she'd point and pick the sign of the cross, then leave you alone and go in to the bedroom. Time and again I heard and half did not what should happen next.

I sit on a stool at the hearth, feeling the heat of the turf fire on my face, the damp off the busy water all around me, as sycamore keys and big sycamore leaves keep smooching at the window. In imagination, that is, and imagination only. And I wake next morning with the ringworm gone.

Trea, as your moonface bends in towards me and the hooked thorn blurs, with the nib of my pen I point and pick and tick off these three things:

> Your selchie slump and goitre.
> Your bombazine.
> The way they birled the *r* in Trea because of the way you birled it.

A Present from Mr Pause

'*But the structuring, the quality of the feeling . . .?*' At eleven o'clock on a Wednesday we would meet, in hope and strangeness. In *Michaelmas Term*. He made tea from an electric kettle on the floor and allowed us a biscuit each.

Exile from Oxbridge, Conradian, flannel-wearer, he called me *Mr* to my face and made the best he could of my 'contributions'. 'But the *quality* of the feeling, Mr . . .?' Mr Pause. And many, many of them.

Still, he was kind, and so I set between us, in the uselessness of that time and much time since, a structure nothing but structure, yet very dear. Done by the light of an oil-lamp at Hallowe'en, on that first weekend home from boarding school, in what he would have called *an Irish cabin*. Ribbed and sanded according to instructions, nicked and nocked, the balsa wood beginnings of a Spitfire. Dry as a biscuit, right as rain, light as the tissue blueprint it was pinned to. Left unfinished. And unfindable by Christmas.

No Harm

Once I discovered the art of sound effects – galloping coconuts, thunderstorms in corrugated iron – a big noise in me started to come to life. I kept Tom Cushley on edge for a whole summer. Just as he hoisted the loaded mortar board, I'd wobble a sheet of galvanize beneath the scaffolding and 'Swear,' I'd shout, 'Swear, Tom, swear,' to his soft, incensed, ascending 'Jesus, Mary and Joseph, I'll murder you!'

Nobody yields advantage in an art. Nobody should. Let there be mayhem. Sound and fury galore. No harm in that.

Natura Naturans

It was John D. Stewart's ambition to produce a square onion. In the era of the processed cheese-square, a pre-squared onion would be a godsend. He would engineer it somehow. He knocked the bottoms out of his Bushmills empties and lined them up in the rig around each shoot, like globes round horned green flames. Vegetable loves that were the talk of the country and went on display one summer at the show in Ardara.

I thought of the not quite right-angled results the other day as I drove the tree-lined roads into West Cork. Boreens, I nearly said, except you don't expect your boreen to be as juggernaut-friendly as these roads had become. Oak and ash and sycamore still met above them, but the passage of big container lorries had made a squared-off tunnel under the greenwood. I almost expected to meet John D. at the next corner, in his nifty sombrero and high-heeled Spanish boots, drawing a bead on me from behind his theodolite.

Brother Stalk

Cabbage stalks, of kale, of marrowstem, of Brussels sprouts. Left at the end of fields in winter rain, like tramps plastered in wet. Familiar, famine-wobbly, more undead than alive.

Coming up to Christmas, he couldn't help himself. 'If you don't behave,' he'd say, 'you'll be getting a cabbage stalk this year from Santy.' Its old hard toe and shin so imaginable in the stocking, I would stand corrected.

Instruction more than stricture I got from him. Yard catechist, yard-mannerly and most lay. More Brother Stalk to me than Father Christmas.

The Boiling House

Four doors: calves' house, the middle house, the boiling house, the home house. In census terms, three outbuildings, one dwelling. All under the one run of thatched roof, behind one whitewashed, single-storeyed wall.

The boiling house was dug-out dark, peat-dry and oddly sound-proofed, a storage place for bags of meal and grain. Once upon a time it too had been dwelt in, before it knew the scullion life that still seethed in its name.

Heating of gruel, boiling of brock, slop-renderings, washes, fowl-feeds, pig swill, hot water for pig-killings, for scouring of churns and pails, for extra pots on the crane on threshing days.

At the moment of a death (Romans believed) the soul resolved into three. The *manes* went to Elysian Fields or deeper, to Tartarus. The *anima* returned itself to the gods; and the *umbra* hovered, unwilling to quit the body.

I am content with that. Now I know what haunted and hovered there. In an old reluctant breath from behind the bags. In a pelt of soot that trembled in the chimney. In the clay floor that stayed obstinate and simple.

ELECTRIC LIGHT (2001)

for Matthew and Caroline

I

At Toomebridge

      Where the flat water
Came pouring over the weir out of Lough Neagh
As if it had reached an edge of the flat earth
And fallen shining to the continuous
Present of the Bann.
      Where the checkpoint used to be.
Where the rebel boy was hanged in '98.
Where negative ions in the open air
Are poetry to me. As once before
The slime and silver of the fattened eel.

Perch

Perch on their water-perch hung in the clear Bann River
Near the clay bank in alder-dapple and waver,

Perch we called 'grunts', little flood-slubs, runty and ready,
I saw and I see in the river's glorified body

That is passable through, but they're bluntly holding the pass,
Under the water-roof, over the bottom, adoze,

Guzzling the current, against it, all muscle and slur
In the finland of perch, the fenland of alder, on air

That is water, on carpets of Bann stream, on hold
In the everything flows and steady go of the world.

Lupins

They stood. And stood for something. Just by standing.
In waiting. Unavailable. But there
For sure. Sure and unbending.
Rose-fingered dawn's and navy midnight's flower.

            Seed packets to begin with, pink and azure,
            Sifting lightness and small jittery promise:
            Lupin spires, erotics of the future,
            Lip-brush of the blue and earth's deep purchase.

            O pastel turrets, pods and tapering stalks
            That stood their ground for all our summer wending
            And even when they blanched would never balk.
            And none of this surpassed our understanding.

Out of the Bag

I

All of us came in Doctor Kerlin's bag.
He'd arrive with it, disappear to the room
And by the time he'd reappear to wash

Those nosy, rosy, big, soft hands of his
In the scullery basin, its lined insides
(The colour of a spaniel's inside lug)

Were empty for all to see, the trap-sprung mouth
Unsnibbed and gaping wide. Then like a hypnotist
Unwinding us, he'd wind the instruments

Back into their lining, tie the cloth
Like an apron round itself,
Darken the door and leave

With the bag in his hand, a plump ark by the keel . . .
Until the next time came and in he'd come
In his fur-lined collar that was also spaniel-coloured

And go stooping up to the room again, a whiff
Of disinfectant, a Dutch interior gleam
Of waistcoat satin and highlights on the forceps.

Getting the water ready, that was next –
Not plumping hot, and not lukewarm, but soft,
Sud-luscious, saved for him from the rain-butt

And savoured by him afterwards, all thanks
Denied as he towelled hard and fast,
Then held his arms out suddenly behind him

To be squired and silk-lined into the camel coat.
At which point he once turned his eyes upon me,
Hyperborean, beyond-the-north-wind blue,

Two peepholes to the locked room I saw into
Every time his name was mentioned, skimmed
Milk and ice, swabbed porcelain, the white

And chill of tiles, steel hooks, chrome surgery tools
And blood dreeps in the sawdust where it thickened
At the foot of each cold wall. And overhead

The little, pendent, teat-hued infant parts
Strung neatly from a line up near the ceiling –
A toe, a foot and shin, an arm, a cock

A bit like the rosebud in his button-hole.

2

Poeta doctus Peter Levi says
Sanctuaries of Asclepius (called *asclepions*)
Were the equivalent of hospitals

In ancient Greece. Or of shrines like Lourdes,
Says *poeta doctus* Graves. Or of the cure
By poetry that cannot be coerced,

Say I, who realized at Epidaurus
That the whole place was a sanatorium
With theatre and gymnasium and baths,

A site of incubation, where 'incubation'
Was technical and ritual, meaning sleep
When epiphany occurred and you met the god . . .

Hatless, groggy, shadowing myself
As the thurifer I was in an open-air procession
In Lourdes in '56

When I nearly fainted from the heat and fumes,
Again I nearly fainted as I bent
To pull a bunch of grass and hallucinated

Doctor Kerlin at the steamed-up glass
Of the scullery window, starting in to draw
With his large pink index finger dot-faced men

With button-spots in a straight line down their fronts
And women with dot breasts, giving them all
A set of droopy sausage-arms and legs

25 That soon began to run. And then as he dipped and laved
In the generous suds again, *miraculum*:
The baby bits all came together swimming

Into his soapy big hygienic hands
And I myself came to, blinded with sweat,
30 Blinking and shaky in the windless light.

3

Bits of the grass I pulled I posted off
To one going in to chemotherapy
And one who had come through. I didn't want

To leave the place or link up with the others.
5 It was midday, mid-May, pre-tourist sunlight
In the precincts of the god,

The very site of the temple of Asclepius.
I wanted nothing more than to lie down
Under hogweed, under seeded grass

10 And to be visited in the very eye of the day
By Hygeia, his daughter, her name still clarifying
The haven of light she was, the undarkening door.

4

The room I came from and the rest of us all came from
Stays pure reality where I stand alone,
Standing the passage of time, and she's asleep

In sheets put on for the doctor, wedding presents
5 That showed up again and again, bridal
And usual and useful at births and deaths.

Me at the bedside, incubating for real,
Peering, appearing to her as she closes
And opens her eyes, then lapses back

10 Into a faraway smile whose precinct of vision
I would enter every time, to assist and be asked
In that hoarsened whisper of triumph,

'And what do you think
Of the new wee baby the doctor brought for us all
When I was asleep?'   15

Bann Valley Eclogue

Sicelides Musae, paulo maiora canamus. Virgil, *Eclogue IV*

POET

Bann Valley Muses, give us a song worth singing,
Something that rises like the curtain in
Those words *And it came to pass* or *In the beginning.*
Help me to please my hedge-schoolmaster Virgil
And the child that's due. Maybe, heavens, sings   5
Better times for her and her generation.

VIRGIL

Here are my words you'll have to find a place for:
Carmen, ordo, nascitur, saeculum, gens.
Their gist in your tongue and province should be clear
Even at this stage. Poetry, order, the times,   10
The nation, wrong and renewal, then an infant birth
And a flooding away of all the old miasma.

Whatever stains you, you rubbed it into yourselves,
Earth mark, birth mark, mould like the bloodied mould
On Romulus's ditch-back. But when the waters break   15
Bann's stream will overflow, the old markings
Will avail no more to keep east bank from west.
The valley will be washed like the new baby.

POET

Pacatum orbem: your words are too much nearly.
Even 'orb' by itself. What on earth could match it?   20
And then, last month, at noon-eclipse, wind dropped.
A millennial chill, birdless and dark, prepared.
A firstness steadied, a lastness, a born awareness
As name dawned into knowledge: I saw the orb.

VIRGIL

Eclipses won't be for this child. The cool she'll know   25
Will be the pram hood over her vestal head.

Big dog daisies will get fanked up in the spokes.
She'll lie on summer evenings listening to
A chug and slug going on in the milking parlour.
Let her never hear close gunfire or explosions.

POET

Why do I remember St Patrick's mornings,
Being sent by my mother to the railway line
For the little trefoil, untouchable almost, the shamrock
With its twining, binding, creepery, tough, thin roots
All over the place, in the stones between the sleepers.
Dew-scales shook off the leaves. Tear-ducts asperging.

Child on the way, it won't be long until
You land among us. Your mother's showing signs,
Out for her sunset walk among big round bales.
Planet earth like a teething ring suspended
Hangs by its world-chain. Your pram waits in the corner.
Cows are let out. They're sluicing the milk-house floor.

Montana

The stable door was open, the upper half,
When I looked back. I was five years old
And Dologhan stood watching me go off,
John Dologhan, the best milker ever
To come about the place. He sang
'The Rose of Mooncoin' with his head to the cow's side.
He would spin his table knife and when the blade
Stopped with its point towards me, a bright path

Opened between us like a recognition
That made no sense, like my memory of him standing
Behind the half door, holding up the winkers.
Even then he was like an apparition,

A rambler from the Free State and a gambler,
All eyes as the pennies rose and slowed
On Sunday mornings under Butler's Bridge
And downed themselves into that tight-bunched crowd

Of the pitch-and-toss school. Sunlight on far lines,

On the creosoted sleepers and hot stones.
And Dologhan, who'd worked in Montana once,
With the whole day off, in the cool shade of the arch. 20

The Loose Box

Back at the dark end, slats angled tautly down
From a breast-high beam to the foot of the stable wall –
Silked and seasoned timber of the hayrack.

Marsupial brackets . . . And a deep-littered silence
Off odourless, untainting, fibrous horse-dung. 5

*

On an old recording Patrick Kavanagh states
That there's health and worth in any talk about
The properties of land. Sandy, glarry,
Mossy, heavy, cold, the actual soil
Almost doesn't matter; the main thing is 10
An inner restitution, a purchase come by
By pacing it in words that make you feel
You've found your feet in what 'surefooted' means
And in the ground of your own understanding –
Like Heracles stepping in and standing under 15
Atlas's sky-lintel, as earthed and heady
As I am when I talk about the loose box.

*

And they found the infant wrapped in swaddling clothes
And laid in a manger.
                     But the plaster child in nappies, 20
Bare baby-breasted little *rigor vitae*,
Crook-armed, seed-nailed, nothing but gloss and chill –
He wasn't right at all.
                  And no hayrack
To be seen. 25
         The solid stooping shepherds,
The stiff-lugged donkey, Joseph, Mary, each
Figure in the winter crib was well
And truly placed. There was even real straw
On the side-altar. And an out-of-scale, 30

Too crockery, kneeling cow. And fairy lights.
But no, no fodder-billowed armfuls spilling over . . .

At the altar rail I knelt and learnt almost
Not to admit the let-down to myself.

    *

Stable child, grown stabler when I read
In adolescence Thomas *dolens* Hardy –
Not, oddly enough, his Christmas Eve night-piece
About the oxen in their bedded stall,
But the threshing scene in *Tess of the D'Urbevilles* –
That magnified my soul. Raving machinery,
The thresher bucking sky, rut-shuddery,
A headless Trojan horse expelling straw
From where the head should be, the underjaws
Like staircases set champing – it hummed and slugged
While the big sag and slew of the canvas belt
That would cut your head off if you didn't watch
Flowed from the flywheel. And comes flowing back,
The whole mote-sweaty havoc and mania
Of threshing day, the feeders up on top
Like pyre-high Aztec priests gutting forked sheaves
And paying them ungirded to the drum.
Slack of gulped straw, the belly-taut of seedbags.
And in the stilly night, chaff piled in ridges,
Earth raw where the four wheels rocked and battled.

    *

Michael Collins, ambushed at Beal na Blath,
At the Pass of Flowers, the Blossom Gap, his own
Bloom-drifted, soft Avernus-mouth,
Has nothing to hold on to and falls again
Willingly, lastly, foreknowledgeably deep
Into the hay-floor that gave once in his childhood
Down through the bedded mouth of the loft trapdoor,
The loosening fodder-chute, the aftermath . . .

This has been told of Collins and retold
By his biographer:
                  One of his boy-deeds
Was to enter the hidden jaws of that hay crevasse
And get to his feet again and come unscathed

Through a dazzle of pollen scarves to breathe the air.
True or not true, the fall within his fall,
That drop through the flower-floor lets him find his feet 70
In an underworld of understanding
Better than any newsreel lying-in-state
Or footage of the laden gun-carriage
And grim cortège could ever manage to.

                Or so it can be stated 75
In the must and drift of talk about the loose box.

Turpin Song

The horse pistol, we called it:
Brass inlay smooth in the stock,
Two hammers cocked like lugs,
Two mottled metal barrels,
Sooty nostrilled, levelled. 5

Bracketed over the door
Of the lower bedroom, a ghost
Heft that we longed to feel,
Two fingers on two triggers,
The full of your hand of haft. 10

Where was the Great North Road?
Who rode in a tricorn hat?
Bob Cushley with his jennet?
Ned Kane in his pony and trap?
The thing was out of place. 15

When I lift up my eyes at the start
Of Stanley Kubrick's film
A horse pistol comes tumbling
From over the door of the world
And it's nineteen forty-eight 20

Or nine, we have transgressed,
We've got our hands on it
And it lies there, broken in bits.
Wind blows through the open hayshed.
I lift up my eyes with the apes. 25

The Border Campaign

for Nadine Gordimer

Soot-streaks down the courthouse wall, a hole
Smashed in the roof, the rafters in the rain
Still smouldering:
                when I heard the word 'attack'
In St Columb's College in nineteen fifty-six
It left me winded, left nothing between me
And the sky that moved beyond my boarder's dormer
The way it would have moved the morning after
Savagery in Heorot, its reflection placid
In those waterlogged huge pawmarks Grendel left
On the boreen to the marsh.
                        All that was written
And to come I was a part of then,
At one with clan chiefs galloping down paths
To gaze at the talon Beowulf had nailed
High on the gable, the sky still moving grandly.

Every nail and claw-spike, every spur
And hackle and hand-barb on that heathen brute
Was like a steel prong in the morning dew.

Known World

'*Nema problema!*' The Macedonian
Taxi-driver screeched and the taxi screeched
At every unfenced corner on the pass,
Then accelerated.
                '*Beria! Beria! Beria!*'
Screeched Vladimir Chupeski, every time
He smashed a vodka glass and filled another
During those days and nights of '78
When we hardly ever sobered at the Struga
Poetry Festival.
              Rafael Alberti
Was 'honouree' and Caj Westerburg,
A Finnish Hamlet in black corduroy,

Sweated 'on principle' (or was that my projection
Of a northern tweed-wearer's contrariness?). 15

Also there: 'Hans Magnus Enzensberger.
Unexpected. Sharp in panama hat,
Pressed-to-a-T cream linen suit. He gets
Away with it.'
               And a soothsaying Dane 20
Of the avant-garde, squinting up at a squinch,
His eye as clear as the water and coral floor
Of Lake Ohrid. His first words to me were:
'Is this not you, these mosaics and madonnas?
You are a south. Your bogs were summer bogs.' 25

  *

In Belgrade I had found my west-in-east.

'Belmullet melancholy of huckster shops
And small shop windows. Unfresh bread, tinned peas.
Also Belmullet elders in the streets.
Black shawls, straight walk, the weather eye, the beads.' 30

Then I saw men in fezes, left the known world
On the short and sweetening mud-slide of a coffee.

  *

At the still centre of the cardinal points
The flypaper hung from our kitchen ceiling,
Honey-strip and death-trap, a barley-sugar twist 35
Of glut and loathing . . .
               In a nineteen-fifties
Of iron stoves and kin groups still in place,
Congregations blackening the length
And breadth of summer roads. 40
               And now the refugees
Come loaded on tractor mudguards and farm carts,
On trailers, ruck-shifters, box-barrows, prams,
On sticks, on crutches, on each other's shoulders,
I see its coil again like a syrup of Styx, 45
An old gold world-chain the world keeps falling from
Into the cloud-boil of a camera lens.
Were we not made for summer, shade and coolness

And gazing through an open door at sunlight?
50 For paradise lost? Is that what I was taught?

                    *

That old sense of a tragedy going on
Uncomprehended, at the very edge
Of the usual, it never left me once . . .
A pity I didn't know then (for Caj's sake)
55 Hygo Simberg's allegory of Finland,
The one where the wounded angel's being carried
By two farm youngsters across an open field:
Marshland, estuary light, a farther shore
With factory chimneys. Is it the socialist thirties
60 Or the shale and slag and sloblands of great hurt?
A first communion angel with big white wings,
White bandage round her brow, white flowers in hand,
Holds herself in place on a makeshift stretcher
Between manchild number one in round soft hat
65 And manchild number two in a bumfreezer
And what could be his father's wellingtons.
Allegory, I say, but who's to know
How to read sorrow rightly, or at all?

                    *

The open door, the jambs, the worn saddle
70 And actual granite of the doorstep slab.
Now enter another angel, fit as ever,
Past each house with a doorstep daubed 'Serb house'.

                    *

How does the real get into the made-up?
Ask me an easier one.
75   But this much I do know:
Our taxi-man, for all his speed, was late
For the poetry reading we were meant to give
At a cement factory in the mountains.
So a liquid lunch with comrade managers
80 Ended in siesta and woozy wake-ups
Just before sunset. Then, the notebook says,
'People on the move, field full of folk,
Packhorses with panniers, uphill push
Of families, unending pilgrim stream.

Today is workers' day in memory　　　　　　　　　　85
Of General Strike. Also Greek Orthodox
Madonna's Day.'
　　　　　　We followed a dry watercourse,
Rattling stones, subdued by the murmuring crowd
As darkness fell. We passed a water-blesser　　　　90
On his rock apart, El Greco-gaunt and cinctured
('Magician,' said Vladimir), waving his cross
Above the tins and jampotfuls held up.

Then on the mountain top, outside a church,
Icons being carried, candles lit, flowers　　　　　　95
And sweet basil in abundance, some kind of mass
Being celebrated behind the iconostasis,
A censer swung and carried through the crowd.
I had been there, I knew this, but was still
Haunted by it as by an unread dream.　　　　　　100
The sale of holy objects. The little groups
Who'd walked all day now gathering in rings,
Allowing themselves a taste of their bread and olives.

　　　*

As the Boeing's innards trembled and we climbed
Into the pure serene and protocols　　　　　　　　105
Of Air Traffic Control, courtesy of Lufthansa,
I kept my seat belt fastened as instructed,
Smoked the minute the *No Smoking* went off
And took it as my due when wine was poured
By a slight *de haut en bas* of my headphoned head.　110
Nema problema. Ja. All systems go.

　　　　　　　　May 1998

The Little Canticles of Asturias

　I

And then at midnight as we started to descend
Into the burning valley of Gijon,
Into its blacks and crimsons, *in medias res*,
It was as if my own face burned again
In front of the fanned-up lip and crimson maw　　　5
Of a pile of newspapers lit long ago

One windy evening, breaking off and away
In flame-posies, small airborne fire-ships
Endangering the house-thatch and the stacks –
For we almost panicked there in the epic blaze
Of those furnaces and hot refineries
Where the night-shift worked on in their element
And we lost all hope of reading the map right
And gathered speed and cursed the hellish roads.

2

Next morning on the way to Piedras Blancas
I felt like a soul being prayed for.
I saw men cutting aftergrass with scythes,
Beehives in clover, a windlass and a shrine,
The maize like golden cargo in its hampers.
I was a pilgrim new upon the scene
Yet entering it as if it were home ground,
The Gaeltacht, say, in the nineteen-fifties,
Where I was welcome, but of small concern
To families at work in the roadside fields
Who'd watch and wave at me from their other world
As was the custom still near Piedras Blancas.

3

At San Juan de las Harenas
It was a bright day of the body.
Two rivers flowed together under sunlight.
Watercourses scored the level sand.
The sea hushed and glittered outside the bar.
And in the afternoon, gulls *in excelsis*
Bobbed and flashed on air like altar boys
With their quick turns and tapers and responses
In the great re-echoing cathedral gloom
Of distant Compostela, *stela, stela*.

Ballynahinch Lake

Godi, fanciullo mio; stato soave,
Stagion lieta è cotesta.
    LEOPARDI, 'Il Sabato del Villaggio'

for Eamon Grennan

So we stopped and parked in the spring-cleaning light
Of Connemara on a Sunday morning
As a captivating brightness held and opened
And the utter mountain mirrored in the lake
Entered us like a wedge knocked sweetly home   5
Into core timber.
              Not too far away
But far enough for their rumpus not to carry,
A pair of waterbirds splashed up and down
And on and on. Next thing their strong white flex   10
That could have been excitement or the death-throes
Turned into lift-off, big sure sweeps and dips
Above the water – no rafter-skimming souls
Translating in and out of the house of life
But air-heavers, far heavier than the air.   15

Yet something in us had unhoused itself
At the sight of them, so that when she bent
To turn the key she only half-turned it
And spoke, as it were, directly to the windscreen,
In profile and in thought, the wheel at arm's length,   20
Averring that this time, yes, it had indeed
Been useful to stop; then inclined her driver's brow
Which shook a little as the ignition fired.

The Clothes Shrine

It was a whole new sweetness
In the early days to find
Light white muslin blouses
On a see-through nylon line
Drip-drying in the bathroom   5
Or a nylon slip in the shine

Of its own electricity –
As if St Brigid once more
Had rigged up a ray of sun
Like the one she'd strung on air
To dry her own cloak on
(Hard-pressed Brigid, so
Unstoppably on the go) –
The damp and slump and unfair
Drag of the workaday
Made light of and got through
As usual, brilliantly.

Red, White and Blue

1 *Red*

What I loved about that much-snapped scarlet coat
Was the hunting-jacket look of fitted waist
And tailored shoulder, the nifty, tricksy bounce
Of hemline hitting off your knee behind
And your knee in front.
                                  'She's like a wee pony!'
Butter wouldn't melt in that smiler's mouth
So I smiled straight back, as who should say, 'Good God,
You know you're absolutely right.
I love the go and gladsomeness in her,
Something unbroken, her gift for pure dismay
At shits like you.'
                          And had the good fortune
To smile again into his peeky face
Later that night, as you jived with me hell for leather
In the Students Union, the cleared floor like a paddock
Where we gave each other rope and scope and snaffle.

'Redingote!' you'd cry.
                                  And me, back, 'Giddy up!'

2 *White*

The screaming from the pool was bad enough,
Busloads of schoolkids coming in on rota

To the baths next door, the banshee acoustic
Of the glass-and-iron dome upping the wildness.
But in your state you thought the screaming came
From the labour ward.
                 At last-kiss, time-to-go time,
You were dry on the lips, hot-cheeked, already gone,
Drifting away on the high berg of the bed.
They had given you a cut-off top of sorts,
Plain as a flour-bag, orphanage-issue stuff,
White calico demure at the neckline
But unmistakably made for access
Elsewhere.
          Through its laundered weave
I tried to call you back but your quarantine
Was making you touch-proof and my hand
That thought it knew its way got lost and shied.
Oh where was the thick of thickets, the hug and birl
Of pleasures wrought to anger and beyond?
Ahead of us, my love, the small-hours tournaments,
But that afternoon I left the lists and rode
From the sun-daunting keep of Castle Childbirth
And even though you knew as you lay contracting
Behind its bastions that the lilied moat
Was uncrossable, the drawbridge drawn up,
The battlements secure and audience
With the chatelaine denied, behind your eyes
Eye-tooth-tightened shut against the pangs,
What you still could not help making yourself see
Was the Knight of the White Feather turning tail.

3 *Blue*

'Yes, pretty, *veh* pretty.' How many times
Have you mimicked the entirely unaffected
And *veh* genuine touch of class she showed
In her praise of the gate-lodge and the avenue
At Castlebellingham. She was deigning
To bestow that much attention, and in the whim
Of her bestowals we felt ourselves included –
Hitchhikers who must have taken her fancy
Or her husband's, whom I then took to be
Officer class in civvies on weekend leave

             In southern Ireland, as he called it.
                                       'Tell me,
             I mean, you know, in southern Ireland,
             Houses like that, are there many of them left?
15   Your crowd burnt the lot down, did they not,
             In the nineteen-twenties?'
                                       It then being
             1963, we simply dived for cover
             ('We're from the north'), or might surprise attack
20   With a quick torrent of the names of towns
             Burnt in reprisal. But her 'pretty, *veh* pretty',
             Said with the half-interest she might display
             Later that night, letting her warm silks fall
             In the lamplight of some coaching inn in Wicklow,
25   Was like a reminder a goddess might vouchsafe
             To recall a hero to his ardent purpose.

             Doves or no doves, it was a Venus car
             We had thumbed down after more than half an hour
             On the bridge outside Dundalk. You rose before them
30   In a Fair Isle tank-top and blue denim skirt
             And denim jacket. And much blue eye make-up.
             A Botticelli dressed down for the sixties.
             So their big waxed Rolls flows softly to a halt,
             The running board comes level with the footpath
35   And we are borne – sweet diction – south and south.

Virgil: Eclogue IX

             LYCIDAS

             Where are you headed, Moeris? Into town?

             MOERIS

             The things we have lived to see . . . The last thing
             You could've imagined happening has happened.
             An outsider lands and says he has the rights
5   To our bit of ground. 'Out, old hands,' he says,
             'This place is mine.' And these kid-goats in the creel –
             Bad cess to him – these kids are his. All's changed.

LYCIDAS

The story I heard was about Menalcas,
How your song-man's singing saved the place,
Starting from where the hills go doubling back   10
And the ridge keeps sloping gently to the water,
Right down to those old scraggy-headed beech trees.

MOERIS

That's what you would have heard. But songs and tunes
Can no more hold out against brute force than doves
When eagles swoop. The truth is, Lycidas,   15
If I hadn't heard the crow caw on my left
In our hollow oak, I'd have kept on arguing
And that would've been the end of the road, for me
That's talking to you, and for Menalcas even.

LYCIDAS

Shocking times. Our very music, our one consolation,   20
Confiscated, all but. And Menalcas himself
Nearly one of the missing. Who would there be to sing
Praise songs to the nymphs? Who hymn the earth
To grow wild flowers and grass, and shade the wells
With overhanging green? Who sing the song   25
I listened to in silence the other day
And learned by heart as you went warbling it,
Off to the Amaryllis we all love?
The one that goes, 'O heard my goats for me,
Tityrus, till I come back. I won't be long.   30
Graze them and then water them, and watch
The boyo with the horns doesn't go for you.'

MOERIS

And then there was that one he never finished,
Addressed to Varus, about a choir of swans
Chanting his name to the stars, 'should Mantua   35
Survive, Mantua too close to sad Cremona.'

LYCIDAS

If you've any song to sing, then sing it now
So that your bees may swerve off past the yew trees,
Your cows in clover thrive with canted teats
And tightening udders. The Pierian muses   40

Made me a poet too, I too have songs,
And people in the country call me bard,
But I'm not sure: I have done nothing yet
That Varius or Cinna would take note of.
I'm a squawking goose among sweet-throated swans.

MORRIS

MOERIS

I'm quiet because I'm trying to piece together
As best I can a song I think you'd know:
'Galatea,' it goes, 'come here to me.
What's in the sea and the waves that keeps you spellbound?
Here earth breaks out in wildflowers, she rills and rolls
The streams in waterweed, here poplars bend
Where the bank is undermined and vines in thickets
Are meshing shade with light. Come here to me.
Let the mad white horses paw and pound the shore.'

LYCIDAS

There was something I heard you singing by yourself
One night when the sky was clear. I have the air
So maybe I'll get the words. 'Daphnis, Daphnis, why
Do you concentrate your gaze on the old stars?
Look for the star of Caesar, rising now,
Star of corn in the fields and hay in haggards,
Of clustered grapes gone purple in the heat
On hillsides facing south. Daphnis, now is the time
To plant the pear slips for your children's children.'

MOERIS

Age robs us of everything, of our very mind.
Many a time I remember as a boy
Serenading the slow sun down to rest,
But nowadays I'm forgetting song after song
And my voice is going: maybe the wolves have blinked it.
But Menalcas will keep singing and keep the songs.

LYCIDAS

Come on, don't make excuses, I want to hear you
And now's your chance, now this hush has fallen
Everywhere – look – on the plain, and every breeze
Has calmed and quietened. We've come half-way.
Already you can see Bianor's tomb

Just up ahead. Here where they've trimmed and faced   75
The old green hedge, here's where we're going to sing.
Set that creel and those kid-goats on the ground.
We'll make it into town in all good time.
Or if it looks like rain when it's getting dark,
Singing shortens the road, so we'll walk and sing.   80
Walk then, Moeris, and sing. I'll take the kids.

MOERIS

That's enough of that, young fellow. We've a job to do.
When the real singer comes, we'll sing in earnest.

Glanmore Eclogue

MYLES

A house and ground. And your own bay tree as well
And time to yourself. You've landed on your feet.
If you can't write now, when will you ever write?

POET

A woman changed my life. Call her Augusta
Because we arrived in August, and from now on   5
This month's baled hay and blackberries and combines
Will spell Augusta's bounty.

MYLES

      Outsiders own
The country nowadays, but even so
I don't begrudge you. You're Augusta's tenant   10
And that's enough. She has every right,
Maybe more right than most, to her quarter acre.
She knows the big glen inside out, and everything
Meliboeus ever wrote about it,
All the tramps he met tramping the roads   15
And all he picked up, listening in a loft
To servant girls colloguing in the kitchen.
Talk about changed lives! Those were the days –
Land Commissions making tenants owners,
Empire taking note at last too late . . .   20
But now with all this money coming in

And peace being talked up, the boot's on the other foot.
First it was Meliboeus' people
Went to the wall, now it will be us.
25 Small farmers here are priced out of the market.

   POET

Backs to the wall and empty pockets: Meliboeus
Was never happier than when he was on the road
With people on their uppers. Loneliness
Was his passport through the world. Midge-angels
30 On the face of water, the first drop before thunder,
A stranger on a wild night, *out in the rain falling*.
His spirit lives for me in things like that.

   MYLES

Book-learning is the thing. You're a lucky man.
No stock to feed, no milking times, no tillage
35 Nor blisters on your hand nor weather-worries.

   POET

Meliboeus would have called me 'Mr Honey'.

   MYLES

Our old language that Meliboeus learnt
Has lovely songs. What about putting words
On one of them, words that the rest of us
40 Can understand, and singing it here and now?

   POET

I have this summer song for the glen and you:

   Early summer, cuckoo cuckoos,
   Welcome, summer is what he sings.
   Heather breathes on soft bog-pillows.
45   Bog-cotton bows to moorland wind.

   The deer's heart skips a beat; he startles.
   The sea's tide fills, it rests, it runs.
   Season of the drowsy ocean.
   Tufts of yellow-blossoming whins.

50   Bogbanks shine like ravens' wings.
   The cuckoo keeps on calling *Welcome*.

The speckled fish jumps; and the strong
Warrior is up and running.

A little nippy chirpy fellow
Hits the highest note there is;   55
The lark sings out his clear tidings.
Summer, shimmer, perfect days.

Sonnets from Hellas

1 *Into Arcadia*

It was opulence and amen on the mountain road.
Walnuts bought on a high pass from a farmer
Who'd worked in Melbourne once and now trained water
Through a system of pipes and runnels of split reed
Known in Hellas, probably, since Hesiod –   5
That was the least of it. When we crossed the border
From Argos into Arcadia, and farther
Into Arcadia, a lorry load
Of apples had burst open on the road
So that for yards our tyres raunched and scrunched them   10
But we drove on, juiced up and fleshed and spattered,
Revelling in it. And then it was the goatherd
With his goats in the forecourt of the filling station,
Subsisting beyond eclogue and translation.

2 *Conkers*

All along the dank, sunk, rock-floored lane
To the acropolis in Sparta, we couldn't help
Tramping on burst shells and crunching down
The high-gloss horse-chestnuts. I thought of kelp
And foals' hooves, bladderwort, dubbed leather   5
As I bent to gather them, a hint of ordure
Coming and going off their tainted pith.
Cyclopic stone on each side of the path.
Rings of defence. Breached walls. The looted conkers
Gravid in my satchel, swinging nicely.   10
Then a daylight moon appeared behind Dimitri
As he sketched and squared his shoulders like a centaur's

And nodded, nodded, nodded towards the spouses,
Heard but not seen behind much thick acanthus.

3 *Pylos*

Barbounia schooled below the balcony –
Shadows on shelving sand in sandy Pylos.
Wave-clip and flirt, tide-slap and flop and flow:
I woke to the world there like Telemachos,
Young again in the whitewashed light of morning
That flashed on the ceiling like an early warning
From myself to be more myself in the mast-bending
Marine breeze, to key the understanding
To that image of the bow strung as a lyre
Robert Fitzgerald spoke of: Harvard Nestor,
Sponsor and host, translator of all Homer,
His wasted face in profile, ceiling-staring
As he schooled me in the course, not yet past caring,
Scanning the offing. Far-seeing shadower.

4 *The Augean Stables*

My favourite bas-relief: Athene showing
Heracles where to broach the river bank
With a nod of her high helmet, her staff sunk
In the exact spot, the Alpheus flowing
Out of its course into the deep dung strata
Of King Augeas' reeking yard and stables.
Sweet dissolutions from the water tables,
Blocked doors and packed floors deluging like gutters . . .
And it was there in Olympia, down among green willows,
The lustral wash and run of river shallows,
That we heard of Sean Brown's murder in the grounds
Of Bellaghy GAA Club. And imagined
Hose-water smashing hard back off the asphalt
In the car park where his athlete's blood ran cold.

5 *Castalian Spring*

Thunderface. Not Zeus's ire, but hers
Refusing entry, and mine mounting from it.
This one thing I had vowed: to drink the waters

Of the Castalian Spring, to arrogate
That much to myself and be the poet 5
Under the god Apollo's giddy cliff –
But the inner water sanctum was roped off
When we arrived. Well then, to hell with that,
And to hell with all who'd stop me, thunderface!
So up the steps then, into the sandstone grottoes, 10
The seeps and dreeps, the shallow pools, the mosses,
Come from beyond, and come far, with this useless
Anger draining away, on terraces
Where I bowed and mouthed in sweetness and defiance.

6 *Desfina*

Mount Parnassus placid on the skyline:
Slieve na mBard, Knock Filiocht, Ben Duan.
We gaelicized new names for Poetry Hill
As we wolfed down horta, tarama and houmos
At sunset in the farmyard, drinking ouzos, 5
Pretending not to hear the Delphic squeal
Of the streel-haired *cailleach* in the scullery.
Then it was time to head into Desfina
To allow them to sedate her. And so retsina,
Anchovies, squid, dolmades, french fries even. 10
My head was light, I was hyper, boozed, borean
As we bowled back down towards the olive plain,
Siren-tyred and manic on the horn
Round hairpin bends looped like boustrophedon.

The Gaeltacht

I wish, *mon vieux*, that you and Barlo and I
Were back in Rosguill, on the Atlantic Drive,
And that it was again nineteen-sixty
And Barlo was alive

And Paddy Joe and Chips Rafferty and Dicky 5
Were there talking Irish, for I believe
In that case Aoibheann Marren and Margaret Conway
And M. and M. and Deirdre Morton and Niamh

Would be there as well. And it would be great too

10   If we could see ourselves, if the people we are now
     Could hear what we were saying, and if this sonnet

     In imitation of Dante's, where he's set free
     In a boat with Lapo and Guido, with their girlfriends in it,
     Could be the wildtrack of our gabble above the sea.

The Real Names

for Brian Friel

Enter Owen Kelly, loping and gowling,
His underlip and lower jaw ill-set,
A mad turn in his eye, his shot-putter's
Neck and shoulders still a schoolboy's.
5   The hard sticks
He dumped down at the opening of the scene
Raised a stour off the boards, his turnip fists
Swung low out of his ripped tarpaulin smock.
I won't forget his Sperrins Caliban,
10   His bag-aproned, potato-gatherer's Shakespeare:
And I with my long nails will dig thee pig-nuts.

             *

Who played Miranda?
                    Some junior-final day-boy.
Flaxen, credible, incredible
15   In a braided wig and costume, speaking high,
He was a she angelic in the light
We couldn't take our eyes off.
                              House lights down,
Liam McLelland enters, Ferdinand
20   Sleepwalking to the music, spied upon
By Gerry O'Neill cloaked up as Prospero.
'A voice like an organ, so he has, that boy,'
Gallagher (who directed) soliloquized
To the class next day.
25   The previous year
Gerry had been Macbeth, green football socks
Cross-gartered to his Thane of Cawdor knees.
And Anthony Murray, with the hiccups, played
The porter in an ignorant Scotch accent.

*

The smell of the new book. The peep ahead
At words not quite beyond you. At which time
A CARRIER, *with a lantern in his hand*
Entered the small hours, speaking low-life prose,
And a light that sparked when I read that Charles's Wain
Was *over the new chimney* has never stopped
Arriving ever since.
     Pinhead words
In the thick sable of the universe.
Single line to sing along the lifeline.
Sometimes it was as if a chink had opened
Upon a scene foreseen and enterable –
Like the perpetual that shone in the sparks going up
From MacNicholl's chimney:
        I was crossing the yard
When I saw them that one time,
Babe in the world, up to my eyes in it,
Up and about in the winter milker's darkness,
Hand held by one with a lantern in her hand.

*

Shakespeare's father (or so John Aubrey claims)
Was a butcher, and when Shakespeare was a boy
'He exercised his father's trade, but when
He kill'd a Calfe, he would doe it in *high style*
& make a speech.'
     Airiness from the start,
Me on top of the byre, seeing things
In a headier light from that much nearer heaven,
Managing to stand up unsupported
On the deck-tilt of hot zinc: I'm on a roof
That overlooks forever, with a pretend
Gully knife of my own in one raised hand,
Sawing air with the other
      (Call it a stage
That everyone goes through ahead of time).

Cows snuffle at feed buckets in the byre,
The stall-chains clink.
     Call it a home from home.

             *

           There is a willow grows aslant the brook
           But in the beginning it was *sally tree.*
           Sallies in hedges and sallies on the bank
    70   Of the Moyola River and black sallies
           Like a line of daunted stragglers bogging down
           In the sedge and glarry wetness of our meadow.
           The one in the yard was tetter-barked and hollow,
           Two-timing earth and air: corona top
    75   Of flick-and-shimmer, sprout-and-tremble growth.
           Land and sky assembled themselves round it.
           In the protocol of soul, soul might have moved
           Backwards away from it, as from a monarch,
           Then turned to those princess-saplings by the river.
    80   But they in their turn had stepped a word away
           And willowed like Ophelias in Moyola.

             *

           'Frankie McMahon, you're Bassanio.
           Irwin, Launcelot Gobbo. Bredin, Portia.'
           That was the cast, or some of it; the scene,
    85   The right-hand side of Gallagher's low desk,
           A nowhere where the three caskets were placed
           In dumb-show. And off we went again. (And yes,
           Of course, Irwin the fabulous
           Who'd walked out of the gates on the first day
    90   Was typecast as the runaway apprentice.
           And Cassoni the Italian as Lorenzo).
           But who was Jessica?
                              Unforgotten,
           Out of this world, the start of Act Five, Scene One.
    95   '*In such a night* – continue, please, Cassoni!'
           ' – *Stood Dido with a willow in her hand*
           Upon the wild sea banks.'
                                    In summer's language.
           In 1954. In the sun-thwarted
    100   Glass and steel of those new showpiece classrooms.

             *

           Duncan's horses, plastered in wet, surge up
           Wild as the chestnut tree one terrible night

In Mossbawn, the aerial rod like a mast
Whiplashed in tempest, my mother rocking and oching
And blessing herself – 105
                the breach in nature open
As the back of the raiders' lorry hammering on
For the Monaghan border, blood loosed in a scrim
From the tailboard, the volunteer screaming O Jesus!
O merciful Jesus. 110
           Or was it the night
The *Princess Victoria* was lost, when the words *sink*
And *gale-force* and *drowning* broke from their stalls
And whinnied round window and chimney?
                              The newsreader's 115
Voice abreast of the nightmare, striding the airwaves

*

Romantic England live and well. *Twelfth Night*
In open evening air in Regent's Park.
Feste's sad counter-tenor and hugged lute
Erotic as it got. In such a dark 120
McCoo, McAuley, Terrins, me, half tight
In the small-hours fug of an Earls Court student flat . . .
In love with love. And scrumpy. And the bright
Glamour of that phosphorescent mark
They stamped on your hand in *Café des Artistes*. 125

*

Feste, for all the world like an 'ESN'
From Class 1G, those little gutsy suede-heads
I took for PT, Fridays, two to three,
By the cemetery short-cut to Falls Park
And let go early. And then went myself . . . 130

Feste, with his ear to his instrument
And eye on nothing, like the deaf boy in 5A
With his bud-pale hearing aid and clean school tie
And panic when I swooped. 'Sir, no! Please, sir!'

Feste, like catatonic Bobby X 135
With his curled-in shoulders and cabbage-water eyes
Speechlessly rocking, *a little tiny boy*
Shut up inside him. And the doctor shouting,
'Bobby, for Christ's sake, Bobby, catch yourself on.'

140 　　Me in attendance, watching sorrow's elf
　　　Bow his head and hunch and stay beyond us,
　　　Like that moment at the end when '*Exuent*
　　　(*all but* FESTE). FESTE (*sings*.)'
　　　　　　　　　　　　But not Bobby sings.

　　　　　　*

145 　　Then say *chameleon*. And the boy-men reappear
　　　Who's-whoing themselves like changelings.
　　　　　　　　　　　　　　　So will it be
　　　Ariel or the real name, the already
　　　Featly sweetly tuneful Philip Coulter?
150 　　Or his brother Joe as Banquo, dressed in white.
　　　Wise Joe, good Banquo, fairest of the prefects?
　　　Aura and justice, soul in bliss or torment,
　　　Ghost on cue at the banquet, entering
　　　And entering memory like mitigation –
155 　　The table on stage a long, formica-topped
　　　Table for fourteen, on loan from the refectory
　　　Where we, in fourteens, moon-calves, know-nothings,
　　　Stood by our chairs and waited for the grace.

The Bookcase

　　　Ashwood or oakwood? Planed to silkiness,
　　　Mitred, much eyed-along, each vellum-pale
　　　Board in the bookcase held and never sagged.
　　　Virtue went forth from its very shipshapeness.

5 　　　Whoever remembers the rough blue paper bags
　　　Loose sugar was once sold in might remember
　　　The jacket of (was it Oliver & Boyd's?)
　　　Collected Hugh MacDiarmid. And the skimmed milk

　　　Bluey-white of the Chatto Selected
10 　　Elizabeth Bishop. Murex of Macmillan's
　　　Collected Yeats. And their Collected Hardy.
　　　Yeats of 'Memory'. Hardy of 'The Voice'.

　　　Voices too of Frost and Wallace Stevens
　　　Off a Caedmon double album, off different shelves.
15 　　Dylan at full volume, the Bushmills killed.
　　　'Do Not Go Gentle.' 'Don't be going yet.'

   *

Heavy as the gate I hung on once
As it swung its arc though air round to the hedge-back,
The bookcase turns on a druggy hinge, its load
Divulging into a future perfect tense   20

Where we hang loose, ruminating and repeating
The three words, 'books from Ireland', to each other,
Quoting for pleasure the Venerable Bede
Who writes in his *History of the English Church*

That scrapings off the leaves of books from Ireland   25
When steeped in water palliate the effect
Of snake-bite. 'For on this isle,' he states,
'Almost everything confers immunity.'

   *

Chiefly I liked the lines and weight of it.
A measuredness. Its long back to the wall   30
And carpeted right angles I could feel
In my neck and shoulder. And books from everywhere.

Cash in *As I Lay Dying* makes a coffin –
For thirteen stated reasons – 'on the bevel'.
From first, 'There is more surface for the nails   35
To grip,' to last, 'It makes a better job.'

In *Riders to the Sea* Synge specifies
In the opening stage direction 'some new boards
Standing by the wall,' and in Maurya's speech
'White boards' are like storm-gleams on the flood   40

At the very end, or the salt salvaged makings
Of a raft for books, a bier to be borne.
I imagine us bracing ourselves for the first lift,
Then staggering for balance, it has grown so light.

Vitruviana

   for Felim Egan

In the deep pool at Portstewart, I waded in
Up to the chest, then stood there half-suspended

　　　　Like Vitruvian man, both legs wide apart,
　　　　Both arms out buoyant to the fingertips,
5　　　Oxter-cogged on water.
　　　　　　　　　　　　My head was light,
　　　　My backbone plumb, my boy-nipples bisected
　　　　And tickled by the steel-zip cold meniscus.

　　　　　*

　　　　On the hard scrabble of the junior football pitch
10　　　Where Leo Day, the college 'drillie', bounced
　　　　And counted and kept us all in line
　　　　In front of the wooden horse – '*One! Two! In! Out!*' –
　　　　We upped and downed and scissored arms and legs
　　　　And spread ourselves on the wind's cross, felt our palms
15　　　As tautly strung as Francis of Assisi's
　　　　In Giotto's mural, where angelic neon
　　　　Zaps the ping-palmed saint with the stigmata.

　　　　　*

　　　　On Sandymount Strand I can connect
　　　　Some bits and pieces. My seaside whirligig.
20　　　The cardinal points. The grey matter of sand
　　　　And sky. And a light that is down to earth
　　　　Beginning to fan out and open up.

Ten Glosses

1 *The Marching Season*

'What bloody man is that?' 'A drum, a drum!'
Prepossessed by what I know by heart,
I wait for Banquo and Macbeth to come
Unbowed, on cue, and scripted from the start.

2 *The Catechism*

Q. and A. come back. They 'formed my mind'.
'Who is my neighbour?' 'My neighbour is all mankind.'

3 *The Bridge*

Steady under strain and strong through tension,
Its feet on both sides but in neither camp,
It stands its ground, a span of pure attention,
A holding action, the arches and the ramp
Steady under strain and strong through tension. 5

4 *A Suit*

'I'll make you one,' he said, 'and balance it
Perfectly on you.' So I could almost feel
The plumbline of the creased tweed hit my heel,

My shoulders like a spar or arms of a scale
Under the jacket, my whole shape realigned 5
In ways that suited me down to the ground.

So although a suit was the last thing that I needed
I weighed his words and wore them and decided
There and then it was going for a song.

5 *The Party*

Overheard at the party, like wet snow
That slumps down off a roof, the unexpected,
Softly powerful name of Wilfred Owen.
Mud in your eye. Artillery in heaven.

6 *W. H. Auden, 1907–73*

After Oxford and Iceland and Spain and Berlin and Freud,
After Marx and the Thirties, it was New York and Chester and God.
A pause for po-ethics. The moral ascent of Parnassus.
Then retrenchment, libretti, martinis, the slippers, the face.
Conceived in the Danelaw, a language shift and a ruction, 5
He was barker of stanzas, a star turn, a source of instruction,
And the definite growth rings of genius rang in his voice.

7 *The Lesson*

According to Hammond, who heard it out on a spree
From a man who had known the priest who was chaplain on duty

The morning the last man was hanged in Crumlin Road Jail,
What the man said as he shook hands and went to the hangman
5   Was, 'Father, this is going to be a lesson to me.'

8 Moling's Gloss

(from the Irish)

Among my elders, I know better
    And frown on any carry-on;
Among the brat-pack on the batter
    I'm taken for a younger man.

9 Colly

Niamh's horse for Oisin was grand, but saddle me colly,
Giddy on wind and black as the hair on King Billy,

Chimney flakes flecking the air, carbon-dotting the white
Wash on the line, a fly-past, a freak-out of soot.

10 A Norman Simile

To be marvellously yourself like the river water
Gerald of Wales says runs in Arklow harbour
Even at high tide when you'd expect salt water.

The Fragment

            'Light came from the east,' he sang,
'Bright guarantee of God, and the waves went quiet.
I could see headlands and buffeted cliffs.
Often, for marked courage, fate spares the man
5   It has not marked already.'

And when their objection was reported to him –
That he had gone to bits and was leaving them
Nothing to hold on to, his first and last lines
Neither here nor there –
10   'Since when,' he asked,
'Are the first line and last line of any poem
Where the poem begins and ends?'

II

On His Work in the English Tongue

in memory of Ted Hughes

1

Post-this, post-that, post-the-other, yet in the end
Not past a thing. Not understanding or telling
Or forgiveness.
                But often past oneself,
Pounded like a shore by the roller griefs,
In language that can still knock language sideways.

2

I read it quickly, then stood looking back
As if it were a bridge I had passed under –
The single span and bull's eye of the one
Over the railway lines at Anahorish –
So intimate in there, the tremor-drip
And cranial acoustic of the stone
With its arch-ear to the ground, a listening post
Open to the light, to the limen world
Of soul on its lonely path, the rails on either side
Shining in silence, the fretful part of me
So steadied by their cogged and bolted stillness
I felt like one come out of an upper room
To fret no more and walk abroad confirmed.

3

Passive suffering: who said it was disallowed
As a theme for poetry? Already in *Beowulf*
The dumbfounding of woe, the stunt and stress
Of hurt-in-hiding is the best of it –
As when King Hrethel's son accidentally kills
His older brother and snaps the grief-trap shut
On Hrethel himself, wronged father of the son
Struck down, constrained by love and blood
To seek redress from the son who had survived –

10 And the poet draws from his word-hoard a weird tale
Of a life and a love balked, which I reword here
Remembering earth-tremors once on Dartmoor,
The power station wailing in its pit
Under the heath, as if our night walk led
15 Not to the promised tor but underground
To sullen halls where encumbered sleepers groaned.

4

'Imagine this pain: an old man
Lives to see his son's body
Swing on the gallows. He begins to keen
And weep for his boy, while the black raven
5 Gloats where he hangs: he can be of no help.
The wisdom of age is worthless to him.
Morning after morning he wakes to remember
That his child has gone; he has no interest
In living on until another heir
10 Is born in the hall, now that this boy
Has entered the door of death forever.
He gazes sorrowfully at his son's dwelling,
The banquet hall bereft of all delight,
The windswept hearthstone; the horsemen are sleeping,
15 The warriors under earth; what was is no more.
No tune from harp, no cheering in the yard.
Alone with his longing, he lies down on his bed
And sings a lament; everything is too large,
The steadings and the fields.
20   Such were the woes
And griefs endured by that doomed lord
After what happened. The king was helpless
To set to right the wrong committed . . .'

5

Soul has its scruples. Things not to be said.
Things for keeping, that can keep the small-hours gaze
Open and steady. Things for the aye of God
And for poetry. Which is, as Miłosz says,
5 'A dividend from ourselves,' a tribute paid
By what we have been true to. A thing allowed.

Audenesque

in memory of Joseph Brodsky

Joseph, yes, you know the beat.
Wystan Auden's metric feet
Marched to it, unstressed and stressed,
Laying William Yeats to rest.

Therefore, Joseph, on this day,
Yeats's anniversary,
(Double-crossed and death-marched date,
January twenty-eight),

Its measured ways I tread again
Quatrain by constrained quatrain,
Meting grief and reason out
As you said a poem ought.

Trochee, trochee, falling: thus
Grief and metre order us.
Repetition is the rule,
Spins on lines we learnt at school.

Repetition, too, of cold
In the poet and the world,
Dublin Airport locked in frost,
Rigor mortis in your breast.

Ice no axe or book will break,
No Horatian ode unlock,
No poetic foot imprint,
Quatrain shift or couplet dint,

Ice of Archangelic strength,
Ice of this hard two-faced month,
Ice like Dante's in deep hell
Makes your heart a frozen well.

Pepper vodka you produced
Once in Wester Massachussetts
With the reading due to start
Warmed my spirits and my heart

But no vodka, cold or hot,
Aquavit or uisquebaugh
35 Brings the blood back to your cheeks
Or the colour to your jokes,

Politically incorrect
Jokes involving sex and sect,
Everything against the grain,
40 Drinking, smoking like a train.

In a train in Finland we
Talked last summer happily,
Swapping manuscripts and quips,
Both of us like cracking whips

45 Sharpened up and making free,
Heading west for Tampere
(West that meant for you, of course,
Lenin's train-trip in reverse).

Nevermore that wild speed-read,
50 Nevermore your tilted head
Like a deck where mind took off
With a mind-flash and a laugh,

Nevermore that rush to pun
Or to hurry through all yon
55 Jammed enjambements piling up
As you went above the top,

Nose in air, foot to the floor,
Revving English like a car
You hijacked when you robbed its bank
60 (Russian was your reserve tank).

Worshipped language can't undo
Damage time has done to you:
Even your peremptory trust
In words alone here bites the dust.

65 Dust-cakes, still – see *Gilgamesh* –
Feed the dead. So be their guest.
Do again what Auden said
Good poets do: bite, break their bread.

To the Shade of Zbigniew Herbert

You were one of those from the back of the north wind
Whom Apollo favoured and would keep going back to
In the winter season. And among your people you
Remained his herald whenever he'd departed
And the land was silent and summer's promise thwarted.   5
You learnt the lyre from him and kept it tuned.

'Would They Had Stay'd'

1

The colour of meadow hay, with its meadow-sweet
And liver-spotted dock leaves, they were there
Before we noticed them, all eyes and evening,
Up to their necks in the meadow.
                            'Where? I still can't – '   5
'There.'
       'Oh yes. Of course, yes. Lovely.'
                                And they didn't
Move away.
            There, like the air agog.   10
The step of light on grass, halted mid-light.
Heartbeat and pupil. A match for us. And watching.

2

Norman MacCaig, come forth from the deer of Magdalen,
Those startlers standing still in fritillary land,
Heather-sentries far from the heath. Be fawn
To the redcoat, gallowglass in the Globe,
Tidings of trees that walked and were seen to walk.   5

(They did not move and he did not come forth).

3

'Deer on the high hills':
Englished Iain MacGabhainn
Goes into linked verse –
Goes where the spirit listeth –
On its perfectly sure feet.   5

And Shakespeare's 'Into
The air, as breath into the
Wind. Would they had stay'd!'
That too. And Iain's poem
Where sorrow just sits and rocks.

    4

Sorley MacLean. A mirage. A stag on a ridge
In the western desert above the burnt-out tanks.

    5

What George Mackay Brown saw was a drinking deer
That glittered by the water. The human soul
In mosaic. Wet celandine and ivy.
Allegory hard as a figured shield
Smithied in Orkney for Christ's sake and Crusades,
Polished until its undersurface surfaced
Like peat smoke mulling through Byzantium.

Late in the Day

Sir William Wilde, in his *Beauties of the Boyne*,
Tells of a monk of Clonard, working late,
How when his candle burnt out, his quill pen
Feathered itself with a miraculous light

So he could go on working. Shadow-flit,
Ink-gleam and quill-shine, late now in the day
I need their likes, freshets and rivulets
Starting from nowhere, capillaries of joy

Frittered and flittering like the scimitar
Of cowpiss in the wind that David Thomson
Flashed on my inner eye from the murky byre
Where he imagined himself a cow let out in spring

Smelling green weed, up to his hips in grass.
Dark-roomed David, author of the memoir
Nairn in Darkness and Light, whose injured eyes
Saw waves and waterfalls in young girls' hair,

The glee of boyhood still alive and kicking
In the tattered stick-man I would meet and read

A lifetime later – erotic fancy-tickler,
Never more at home than when on the road,   20

Led by amazement as if it were a seal
Walking ahead of him up the Aran shingle
In a clawhammer coat and top hat, dressed to kill,
About to enter a public house or kitchen

The way he would himself, like Arion   25
Arriving in off the waves, off the dolphin's back,
Oblivious-seeming, but taking it all in
And glad of another chance to believe his luck.

Arion

We were all hard at it in the boat,
Some of us up tightening sail,
Some down at the heave and haul
Of the rowing benches, deeply cargoed,
Steady keeled, our passage silent,   5
The helmsman buoyant at the helm;
And I, who took it all for granted,
Sang to the sailors.
                Then turbulent
Sudden wind, a maelstrom: 10
The helmsman and the sailors perished.
Only I, still singing, washed
Ashore by the long sea-swell, sing on,
A mystery to my poet self,
And safe and sound beneath a rock shelf   15
Have spread my wet clothes in the sun.

   from the Russian of Alexander Pushkin

Bodies and Souls

1 *In the Afterlife*

It will be like following Jim Logue, the caretaker,
As he goes to sweep our hair off that classroom floor
Where the school barber set up once a fortnight,
Falling into step as he does his rounds,

Glimmerman of dorms and silent landings,
Of the refectory with its solid, crest-marked delph,
The ground-floor corridor, the laundry pile
And boots tagged for the cobbler. Was that your name
On a label? Were you a body or a soul?

2 Nights of '57

It wasn't asphodel but mown grass
We practised each night after night prayers
When we lapped the college front lawn in bare feet,

Heel-bone and heart-thud, open-mouthed for summer.
The older I get, the quicker and the closer
I hear those labouring breaths and feel the coolth.

3 The Bereaved

Set apart. First out down the aisle
Like brides. Or those boys who were permitted
To leave the study early for music practice –
Privileged and unenvied, left alone
In the four bare walls to face the exercise,
Eyes shut, shoulders straight back, cold hands out
Above the keys. And then the savagery
Of the piano music's music going wrong.

Clonmany to Ahascragh

in memory of Rory Kavanagh

Now that the rest of us have no weeping left
These things will do it for you:
Willows standing out on Leitrim Moss,
Wounds that 'wept' in the talk of those before you,
Rained-on statues from Clonmany to Ahascragh,
Condensation on the big windows
And walls of a school corridor in Derry
Where I drew with warm fingers once upon a time
To make a face that wept itself away
Down cold black glass.

*

Compose yourself again. And listen to me.
You were never up here in my attic study
Beyond the landing, up the second stairwell,
Step-ladder steep, and deep, and leading back
Down to the life going on.   15
                    Even so, appear
Till I tell you my good dream.
                        Be at the door
I opened in the sleepwall when a green
Hurl of flood overwhelmed me and poured out   20
Lithe seaweed and a tumult of immense
Green cabbage roses into the downstairs.
No feeling of drowning panicked me, no let-up
In the attic downpour happened, no
Fullness could ever equal it, so flown   25
And sealed I feared it would be lost
If I put it into words.
                    But with you there at the door
I can tell it and can weep.

*

And if ever tears are to be wiped away,   30
It will be in river country,
In that confluence of unmarked bridge-rumped roads
Beyond the Shannon, between the River Suck
And the Corrib River, where a plentiful
Solitude floods everyone who drives   35
In the unseasonable warmth of a January afternoon
Into places battened down under oyster light,
Under names unknown to most, but available
To you and proclaimable by you
Like a man speaking in tongues, brought to his senses   40
By a sudden plout on the road into Ahascragh.

Sruth

in memory of Mary O Muirithe

The bilingual race
And truth of that water

Spilling down Errigal,

The *sruth* like the rush
Of its downpour translated
Into your accent:

You in your *dishabills*
Washing your face
In the guttural glen.

Mountain and maiden.
The shard of a mirror.
Your head in the air

Or that childhood *breac-Ghaeltacht*,
Those sky-maiden haunts
You would tell me about

Again and again –
Then asked me to visit:
If anything happened

Just to see and be sure
And not to forget.
For your sake to do it.

Splash of clear water.
Things out in the open.
The spoken word, 'cancer'.

And now it has happened
I see what I saw
On the morning you asked me:

Neck-baring snowdrops –
Like you at the *sruth* –
First-footing the springtime,

Fit for what comes.

Seeing the Sick

Anointed and all, my father did remind me
Of Hopkins's Felix Randal.
                          And then he grew
(As he would have said himself) 'wee in his clothes' –

Spectral, a relict –
          And seemed to have grown so
Because of something spectral he'd thrown off,
The unbelonging, moorland part of him
That was Northumbrian, the bounden he
Who had walked the streets of Hexham at eighteen
With his stick and task of bringing home the dead
Body of his uncle by cattle-ferry.

Ghost-drover from the start. Brandisher of keel.

None of your fettled and bright battering sandal.

Cowdung coloured tweed and ox-blood leather.

     *

The assessor's eye, the tally-keeper's head
For what beasts were on what land in what year . . .
But then that went as well. And all precaution.
His smile a summer half-door opening out
And opening in. A reprieving light.
For which the tendered morphine had our thanks.

Electric Light

Candle-grease congealed, dark-streaked with wick-soot . . .
The smashed thumb-nail
Of that ancient mangled thumb was puckered pearl,

Rucked quartz, a littered Cumae.
In the first house where I saw electric light,
She sat with her fur-lined felt slippers unzipped,

Year in, year out, in the same chair, and whispered
In a voice that at its loudest did nothing else
But whisper. We were both desperate

The night I was left to stay, when I wept and wept
Under the clothes, under the waste of light
Left turned on in the bedroom. 'What ails you, child,

What ails you, for God's sake?' Urgent, sibilant
Ails, far off and old. Scaresome cavern waters
Lapping a boatslip. Her helplessness no help.

*

Lisp and relapse. Eddy of sybilline English.
Splashed between a ship and dock, to which,
Animula, I would come alive in time

As ferries churned and turned down Belfast Lough
20   Towards the brow-to-glass transport of a morning train,
The very 'there-you-are-and-where-are-you?'

Of poetry itself. Backs of houses
Like the back of hers, meat-safes and mangles
In the railway-facing yards of fleeting England,

25   An allotment scarecrow among patted rigs,
Then a town-edge soccer pitch, the groin of distance,
Fields of grain like the Field of the Cloth of Gold.

To Southwark too I came,
From tube-mouth into sunlight,
30   Moyola-breath by Thames's 'straunge stronde'.

*

If I stood on the bow-backed chair, I could reach
The light switch. They let me and they watched me.
A touch of the little pip would work the magic.

A turn of their wireless knob and the light came on
35   In the dial. They let me and they watched me
As I roamed at will the stations of the world.

Then they were gone and Big Ben and the news
Were over. The set had been switched off,
All quiet behind the blackout except for

40   Knitting needles ticking, wind in the flue.
She sat with her fur-lined felt slippers unzipped,
Electric light shone over us, I feared

The dirt-tracked flint and fissure of her nail,
So plectrum-hard, glit-glittery, it must still keep
45   Among beads and vertebrae in the Derry ground.

UNCOLLECTED POEMS (2001–2005)

Le Brocquy's *Táin*

Beetle-sparkling blots:
The scribe's dilations, in all
Their opacity.
He has looked into eclipse,
Spilled inkhorns into the light.   5

    *

A taker-outer
Or a putter-in? Decide
For yourself. Until
You see what's not there, look for
What is. And is meant to be.   10

    *

'Deer among dolmens':
Inklings of presence under
The tilted capstone,
Lightfooting it, hightailing
It, now you see them, now you . . .   15

    *

Seeing is saying
'Hurling'. 'The boy Cúchulainn'.
'Magic chariot'.
'Cúchulainn in warp-spasm'.
'Battlefield'. 'Army massing'.   20

    *

And 'Horseman'. A horse
Beneath him as dangerous
As the one that broke
Out of its scroll one midnight
And trampled the paddyfields.   25

    *

Then the tapestries –
Whirlwools, quillpools, text-warps wrought
From a text we took

As read – these loomings, Louis,
30 Meant to be and are believed.

The Snowball

1

It hits the windscreen
Like a full stop and I think –
Feeling the better
For it – 'Somebody out there
5 Wants to give me a white eye.'

2

And am reminded
Of the first years at the wall,
Myself among them,
The broth of bullyboys' breath
5 In that supervised snowfight

3

In January
1952, no place
To go but the wall,
The face at the president's
5 Window the president's face.

4

And reminded too
Of your head-on collision
With the plate glass door,
Your full stop of red lipstick,
5 Ah my dear, lipsticked mid-air.

5

Nothing, all the same,
Like being up against it,
Nothing like being
Faced with what you have to face
5 To make a woman of you.

6

You say contrary,
I say contrary, you say
Contrarier, I
Say contrarier, contrar-
ier and -trarier still.   5

A Present from Old Ardboe

for Paul and Jean

In Royal Avenue once (it was Rag Day at Queen's)
I sat on the kerb and fished in a gullytrap.
Deane sat beside me, and somewhere a photograph
Has me landing a lopsided kipper into his lap.

When I thought of your two birthdays, Jean and Paul,   5
All the old sumps and sinks of association
Rallied and roiled: I was full of life as an eel
In a gurgly grating somewhere in east Manhattan

Silvering, elvering off . . . So here's an eelskin
Like the one Alfie Kirkwood wore on his wrist at school   10
Or the one that lapped together the arms of the flail
James McGuckian used on his 'wee lock of corn',

Salted and cured, but that still might, for all you would know,
Slink off down the Canal Road back to Old Ardboe.

In Memory of Bill Cole

As Dante when he entered Purgatory
Was greeted by Casella, and the song
Casella sang sweetened his memory

Of earthly love and music and their long
Afternoons of wine and poetry,   5
So I, when I heard that William Cole had gone

Among the shades, imagined him and me
Meeting in an earthly paradise
Where we'd never met on earth, in Co Derry,

10 On the banks of the Moyola, and his voice
    Rising to sing in an Irish tenor brogue
    McCormack might have envied, or James Joyce,

    Or Moore in Avoca, by Avonmore and Beg,
    River-rhyming, over-brimming, young
15 At heart again, and younger song by song –

    For always Bill belonged in *Tir na n-Og*.

For Alma Mater

His fresher's face, his fresh-stamped student card,
The glue not set, the course not set: I stare.
Pro tanto quid? Yet what can he afford?

Under the Great Hall's portraits, it's still hard
5 At this stage not to wonder how he'll fare,
This fresher with his fresh-stamped student card.

Then Great Hall turned exam hall where he entered.
First Arts. First Honours. Finals. For each year
Pro tanto quid? For now he can afford.

10 'Re-enter,' said the interviewing board,
    'Take up your notes and be a lecturer
    And cancelled henceforth be your student card.'

He re-enters. He exits. His reward
A Sabine farm and freehold in Glanmore.
15 *Pro tanto quid?* O all he can afford.

Now the course is set and face set by the word.
What then? What's this? *Honoris causa? Doctor?*
Whose was that fresh face on your student card?
Pro tanto quid? O all you can afford.

A Keen for the Coins

O henny penny! O horsed half-crown!
O florin salmon! O farthing wren!
O hare! O hound! O snipe! O bull!
O mint of field and flood, farewell!

Be Ireland's lost ark, gone to ground, 5
And where the rainbow ends, be found.

A Snapshot

Andy, absorbed, sits reading *en plein air*,
The reader over his shoulder the Eiffel Tower.

Sister Clare

'Don't worry, Marie.
I'll be there.'
Thus Clare
Took care
When migrant *pater* 5
Crossed the water
And Strand Road spouse
Rose and shone,
Upped and was gone
To Adams House. 10
Gaudeamus
Igitur.
And likewise
Gratias
Agamus, 15
Say Michael, Chris
And yes, yes,
The Cap of Captains,
Catherine Ann.

Watercolour

for Val

A woman who lives in an old house with stone outbuildings
and an overgrown haggard, at the end of an avenue of
landlordy trees, not a thousand miles from a shining reach
of lough – this woman who seems invented to be a water-
colourist does indeed do watercolours. 5

But I didn't expect her to melt my heart with a vision of
briary hedges and yellowy Nolde skies. Wet clover brushes
her ankles as she disappears down a loaning in search of the
right quiet corner, smelling the glar under a big tree where
cattle have plundered about in the wet weather. She could
keep walking round and round the field for the pure silence
of it. Instead, she sits down and sets up. Now she has
applied the first wash and now she starts to get the picture.
And maybe some day what will catch her eye is the four-
clawed bath-tub just one field farther on, drydocked on
dock-leaves and the lushest grass.

Santiago de Compostela

to Ann and Ignacio

What stays with me from my time in Santiago
Is midnight rain scourging the big Square,
Lashings of water off the fountain lips,
Spouts and gutters plenished and replenished.

          Also stone purgatorial flames –
Unfannable, no matter what wind blew –
Surmounted by stone faces on the carved
Pediment of *Las Animas*.

          And beneath the steps
Of the Hotel of the Catholic Kings, the tongue
Of a panting mongrel, for all the world
As desperate as Dives ever was
For a touch of Lazarus' wetted fingertip.

An Epithalamium

for Rose and Tom

> IRIS: *You nymphs, call'd Naiads, of the wand'ring brooks*
> *With your sedg'd crowns and ever harmless looks,*
> *Leave your crisp channels and on this green land*
> *Answer your summons. Juno does command:*
> *Come, temperate nymphs, and help to celebrate*
> *A contract of true love; be not too late.*
> *Your sunburn't sickle men, of summer weary,*
> *Come hither from the furrow and be merry;*
> *Make holiday; your rye-straw hats put on,*
> *And these fresh nymphs encounter every one*
> *In country footing.*
>   The Tempest

    And now, dear groom, dear Tom,
And dearest Rose, first bride here and first-born,
This Liffey duck must follow Avon's Swan.

Hiberno-English, be now articulate!
Be nuptial, amorous and inebriate.   5
Be 'talking tongues;' be Abbey and be Globe,
Be Cambridge Footlights and the Broadway Strobe.
Be Wooton-Under-Edge. Be Old Ardboe.
Be Tom Brown's Schooldays, Stratford-atte-Bowe.
Rise to the occasion, then descend   10
In couplets on this couple. Help me bend
The boughs of poetry to build their bower,
Their Popean grotto and their Yeatsian tower.

Dear Rose and Tom, on this, your day of days,
I'm no Mark Antony. I come to praise –   15
To praise you whom I love but barely know
Except by instinct, for by instinct I go
And always have done, and will continue to –
So *honi soi qui mal* would *pense de vous*.
Let peacocks' feathers fan, gold torcs adorn you,   20
And a Ro-torc founding father smile upon you.
Increase and multiply. Be Multi-A.
Slieve Gallon's flowers that never will decay.

　　　　And while I'm at it, Orphic with the *vino*,
25　　　I recollect a field in Castellina,
　　　　Another wedding feast in fair Chianti
　　　　When Polly rhymed and coupletted with Andy.
　　　　Across the Tuscan ground in the hot sun
　　　　We walked, or rather wobbled, in procession
30　　　Into a future that's now this present tense,
　　　　This Somerset, this evening, and these friends,
　　　　This stage where we can strut but need not fret,
　　　　This company where all is as you like it,
　　　　Where I make bold, now wedding vows are sealed,
35　　　To misquote Shakespeare: 'All the world's a field',
　　　　A summer's day, a fair field full of folk,
　　　　So here, in summer setting, I invoke
　　　　A Cannwood Avalon, a Garnett Arden
　　　　(Like Monet's poppy field or Marvell's garden)
40　　　A field in the bright side of Dante's wood
　　　　A dream field where the field work is for good,
　　　　Where Polly's syllables name and exhale
　　　　Carnation sedge, sweet grass and tormentil,
　　　　Saxifrage, self-heal, forget-me-not,
45　　　Ribwort plantain, creeping bent and sneezewort.
　　　　– To which, from bonny Marie's bonny brae,
　　　　From Derry moss and the shores of sweet Lough Neagh
　　　　I add the benweeds, seggins, and bog-cotton,
　　　　Fairy thimbles, fairy thorn and docken.
50　　　And, from Brewham's banks, the Daisy and the Bay.

　　　　And finally, for Pookie, on this day
　　　　A wild dog-rose. And that completes my bouquet.
　　　　And as their colours blush and perfumes breathe,
　　　　These blooms and herbs are Tom's and Rose's wreath,
55　　　And in their fragrant names I now repeat
　　　　Come, temperate nymphs, and help to celebrate
　　　　A contract of true love; be not too late.

　　　　　　　　　　　　　With love
　　　　　　　　　　　　　Seamus
　　　　　　　　　　　24 July 1999

The Big Wiper

Finally I had the chance to drive this automatic car. What was new and dangerous was the surge forward the moment you touched the accelerator, an immediate drag of speed through your lower back.

What was more abiding, however, was the action of the big wiper, one blade on a central pivot sweeping the widescreen, to and fro, to and fro, from the passenger's left hand to the driver's right. The surprise was in the strength of the clunk it made with each revolution. The whole car gave a little shudder every time. But the thing you were most conscious of was the steadiness of the action, its lush efficiency.

It used to be I enjoyed turning the three-speed wiper-switch to top gear and watching the blades go frantic. Now I could sit for hours at that other console, in the lumbar hug of good upholstery, eyes straight ahead, the wiper slugging on like oars in rowlocks.

Sophoclean

First he was shivering on the shore in skins,
Or hunkering behind shell-middens in a cave.
Then he took up oars, put tackle on a mast
And steered himself by the stars through gales.

Once upon a time from the womb of earth 5
The gods were born and he bowed down
To worship them. Then he walked tall
From temple to agora, talking against himself.

The wind is no more swift or mysterious
Than his mind and words; he has mastered thinking, 10
Roofed his house against hail and rain
And worked out laws for living together.

Home-maker, thought-taker, measure of all things,
He survives every danger except death
And will yield to nothing else. Nothing 15
Else, good or evil, is beyond him.

When truth is the treadle of his loom
And justice the shuttle, all due honour

Will come his way. But let him once
20 Overbear or overstep

What the city allows, treat law
As something he can decide for himself –
Then let this marvel of the world remember:
When he comes begging we will turn our backs.

Pit Stop Near Castletown

Robert Lowell's incomparable high
What? Pitched voice? Destiny? Mania and style?
Under midnight beeches billowing darkly

We made our pit stop about half a mile
5   From the demesne gates, pissing like men
Together and apart against the wall.

'A large, undangerous drinker,' he called Larkin,
But not undangerous he. His forthright stroan
Went glittering like a foil, Marlovian,

10 As shoulder to shoulder, before we got back in
He intimated he'd probably not be
Returning to Caroline. The headlights shone

Stiffly into a whipped-up swirl and eddy
Of roadside leaves – 'like ghosts from an enchanter
15 Fleeing!' O irremediably

Literary, first-striking Cal, at your
Memorial service later on that autumn
I said the cabbie who'd ferried you to the door

And waited to be paid already had been
20 Paid in the coin of language, that East River was Styx
And so on, rising to the occasion

Perhaps too highly. Mary McCarthy's verdict –
As reported back to me, at any rate –
Took my rhetoric and wrung its neck:

25 'The biggest cover-up since Watergate.'

The Comet at Lullwater

for Bill and JoAn Chace

On top of the world, we'd raised our mint-sprigged bourbon,
Toasted, tasted, drunk and drunk again
Unhurriedly when, like a spoor of pollen
At an astronomic height, the curl and spill
And lucent swish of Hale-Bopp's catkin tail 5
Passed above the roof-deck. We lined the railing,
Silenced, solaced beyond expectation,
And took the measure of the zenith, smiling.

So into my ken swam medieval God
On the top deck of His pageant, overseeing, 10
Summoning Death, His mighty messenger.
And Christy Mahon, the lark of human being
Who felt a pity for God's solitude
All ages sitting in His golden chair.

Beacons at Bealtaine

Phoenix Park, May Day, 2004

Uisce: water. And *fionn*: the water's clear.
But dip and find this Gaelic water Greek:
A phoenix flames upon *fionn uisce* here.

Strangers were barbaroi to the Greek ear.
Now let the heirs of all who could not speak 5
The language, whose ba-babbling was unclear,

Come with their gift of tongues past each frontier
And find the answering voices that they seek
As *fionn* and *uisce* answer phoenix here.

The May Day hills were burning, far and near, 10
When our land's first footers beached boats in the creek
In *uisce*, *fionn*, strange words that soon grew clear;

So on a day when newcomers appear
Let it be a homecoming and let us speak
The unstrange word, as it behoves us here, 15

Move lips, move minds and make new meanings flare
Like ancient beacons signalling, peak to peak,
From middle sea to north sea, shining clear
As phoenix flame upon *fionn uisce* here.

An Iridescence

A chocolate van had crashed. That was the news.
Had skidded off the road at Duggan's Hill.
That night the bedtime cocoa had a smell
Of leaf-mould off it and through Duggan's trees
5   Deep-shining in the polished windowless
Side sheeting of that lumbered vehicle
A moon made headway in the trademark purple,
Made ground light of foil wrappings and smashed glass
And sowed the iris murk with marigold.
10 All that was left next day was a ruined hedge,
Mould and raw verges where a crane had pulled
The van free through an iridescent sludge,
Floatings on it of spoils from the wrecked load
And a trail of silver papers up the road.

Confirmation Day

Examined first in catechism, passed
And ready for a blow upon the cheek
From the bishop's ring, the whole class was released
As if we were at school and this was break.

5   White veils, new suits, new gold-edged daily missals.
Sunlight, stirring branches, dappled grass.
In the cool porch, tea in flask lids, Rich Tea biscuits
And dressed-up parents so unused to us

And them free on a weekday we shall never
10 See ourselves again as we were then
And the camera caught us, in the state of grace
And turned-down ankle socks, with both hands joined.

Monsignors in birettas order us,
Girls on one side, boys on the other, back

Into line. Eyes front, one two, at a left-right lick
We march, God's rank and file, to the front rows.

After Dark

'After dark'
should mean it's morning
but this the language
disallows.

Homunculus
from the age of blackout,
skylight pupil
reflected back

off night-backed glass,
I watch my words
and a starship-placid,
lit up dredger

anchored out
near the Bailey Light.
It pinpoints dark.
It doesn't blink.

A star-wars satellite,
crossing, does,
time and again.
I jot and husband.

Lauds and Gauds for a Laureate

The work you're going to hear to-night
By one who's earned the right to write
    Will have two readers
And is so valued by so many
It hardly needs my praise nor any
    Special pleaders.

Even introducing Joseph
To overcrowding rows on rows of
    Cambridge hotshots

    In mostly just the buzz of showbiz
    For you know who Joseph is
        Since before glasnost.

    The poet Brodsky's held in awe
    For laying down the poetry law
        In these late times.
    He steals the fire and air of words.
    He leaves the clichés for the birds.
        He worships rhymes.

    Uncheckably his poems outrun
    The range and writ and jurisdiction
        Of all Big Brothers.
    He would revive and fortify
    The individual human cry
        Their *newspeak* smothers.

    When I consider Joseph's work
    I recollect, in Stalin's dark,
        How one man wrote,
    Then sealed his manuscript in jars
    And buried them beneath the stars
        Like a deep root.

    The scene is stealthy as a crime.
    The digger working against time,
        A thing being hidden:
    The truth that dare not yet be told,
    The written word like buried gold,
        Rare and forbidden.

    Yet Joseph's tool is not the spade.
    The axe with ice upon its blade
        Is more his thing.
    It splits the frozen sea inside
    And then, You lied! You lied! You lied!
        The echoes ring.

    As if self-launched through hoops of fame –
    The very opposite of tame –
        His poems start
    When whetted sounds get whetted keener
    And spring into the mind's arena
        As uncaged art.

Milosz said it: poems stand
Lashing tails and pawing sand,
   Facing the sun,
For they are visions out of light
Lured down by art from a great height
   Of imagination.

Romantic rhetoric this is not.
This is the poet we have got
   To-night as guest.
For him we'd prime and fire cannon.
In Ireland we would dam the Shannon.
   He is the best.

In Ireland, on a harbour wall,
Among the shipping lanes and all
   Those gulls and gannets,
Joseph, I won't forget the day we spent
last year by Dublin Bay
   Discussing sonnets,

Discussing what it takes and what
Old X might have young Y has not,
   Who's in *pro-tem*.
Praising friends behind their backs
And when it came down to brass tacks,
   Preferring them.

Like you know who, who's here to-night,
The author of 'The Schooner Flight'
   And plays in verse:
Derek Walcott, poet of tides,
The genius of whose music rides
   A winged sea-horse.

His lines are rigging for a mind
Susceptible to each south wind
   And breaking comber
And ere my rhyming fit abates,
For him I quote Joyce quoting Yeats:
   One thinks of Homer.

One thinks of Shakespeare too, for he
Is guardian of the mystery
   Of Wally Shawn.

All actor-playwrights are his friends,
Burning candles at both ends,
    On cue till dawn.

So let your expectations tremble
Now these real presences assemble
    And lights are lowered,
As they unearth the jars and click
The locks wide open on the Slavic
    Poet's word-hoard.

DISTRICT AND CIRCLE (2006)

for Ann Saddlemyer

                            Call her Augusta
Because we arrived in August, and from now on
This month's baled hay and blackberries and combines
Will spell Augusta's bounty.

The Turnip-Snedder

for Hughie O'Donoghue

In an age of bare hands
and cast iron,

the clamp-on meat-mincer,
the double-flywheeled water-pump,

it dug its heels in among wooden tubs
and troughs of slops,

hotter than body heat
in summertime, cold in winter

as winter's body armour,
a barrel-chested breast-plate

standing guard
on four braced greaves.

'This is the way that God sees life,'
it said, 'from seedling-braird to snedder,'

as the handle turned
and turnip-heads were let fall and fed

to the juiced-up inner blades,
'This is the turnip-cycle,'

as it dropped its raw sliced mess,
bucketful by glistering bucketful.

A Shiver

The way you had to stand to swing the sledge,
Your two knees locked, your lower back shock-fast
As shields in a *testudo*, spine and waist
A pivot for the tight-braced, tilting rib-cage;
The way its iron head planted the sledge
Unyieldingly as a club-footed last;
The way you had to heft and then half-rest
Its gathered force like a long-nursed rage
About to be let fly: does it do you good

10   To have known it in your bones, directable,
Withholdable at will,
A first blow that could make air of a wall,
A last one so unanswerably landed
The staked earth quailed and shivered in the handle?

Polish Sleepers

Once they'd been block-built criss-cross and four-squared
We lived with them and breathed pure creosote
Until they were laid and landscaped in a kerb,
A moulded verge, half-skirting, half-stockade,
5   Soon fringed with hardy ground-cover and grass.
But as that bulwark bleached in sun and rain
And the washed gravel pathway showed no stain,
Under its parched riverbed
Flinch and crunch I imagined tarry pus
10   Accruing, bearing forward to the garden
Wafts of what conspired when I'd lie
Listening for the goods train from Castledawson . . .
Each languid, clanking waggon,
And afterwards, *rust, thistles, silence, sky.*

Anahorish 1944

'We were killing pigs when the Americans arrived.
A Tuesday morning, sunlight and gutter-blood
Outside the slaughterhouse. From the main road
They would have heard the squealing,
5   Then heard it stop and had a view of us
In our gloves and aprons coming down the hill.
Two lines of them, guns on their shoulders, marching.
Armoured cars and tanks and open jeeps.
Sunburnt hands and arms. Unknown, unnamed,
10   Hosting for Normandy.
              Not that we knew then
Where they were headed, standing there like youngsters
As they tossed us gum and tubes of coloured sweets.'

To Mick Joyce in Heaven

1

Kit-bag to tool-bag,
Warshirt to workshirt –
Out of your element
Among farmer in-laws,
The way you tied sheaves
The talk of the country,
But out on your own
When skylined on scaffolds –
A demobbed Achilles
Who was never a killer,
The strongest instead
Of the world's stretcher-bearers,
Turning your hand
To the bricklaying trade.

2

Prince of the sandpiles,
Hod-hoplite commander
Watching the wall,
Plumbing and pointing
From pegged-out foundation
To first course to cornice,
Keeping an eye
On the eye in the level
Before the cement set:
Medical orderly,
Bedpanner, bandager
Transferred to the home front,
Rising and shining
In brass-buttoned drab.

3

You spoke of 'the forces'.
Had served in the desert,
Been strafed and been saved
By courses of blankets
Fresh-folded and piled
Like bales on a field.

No sandbags that time.
A softness preserved you.
You spoke of sex also,
10 Talked man to man,
Took me for granted:
The English, you said,
Would do it on Sundays,
Upstairs, in the daytime.

4

The weight of the trowel,
That's what surprised me.
You'd lift its lozenge-shaped
Blade into the air
5   To sever a brick
In a flash, and then twirl it
Fondly and lightly.
But whenever you sent me
To wash it and dry it
10 And you had your smoke,
Its iron was heavy,
Its sloped-angle handle
So thick-spanned and daunting
I needed two hands.

5

'To Mick Joyce in Heaven' –
The title just came to me,
Mick, and I started
If not quite from nowhere,
5   Then somewhere far off:
A bedroom, bright morning,
A man and a woman,
Their backs to the bedhead,
And me at the foot.
10 It was your first leave,
A stranger arrived
In a house with no upstairs,
But heaven enough
To be going on with.

The Aerodrome

First it went back to grass, then after that
To warehouses and brickfields (designated
The Creagh Meadows Industrial Estate),
Its wartime grey control tower rebuilt and glazed

Into a hard-edged CEO-style villa:
Toome Aerodrome had turned to local history.
Hangars, runways, bomb stores, Nissen huts,
The perimeter barbed wire, forgotten and gone.

But not a smell of daisies and hot tar
On a newly-surfaced cart-road, Easter Monday,
1944. And not, two miles away that afternoon,
The annual bright booths of the fair at Toome,

All the brighter for having been denied.
No catchpenny stalls for us, no
Awnings, bonnets, or beribboned gauds:
Wherever the world was, we were somewhere else,

Had been and would be. Sparrows might fall,
B-26 Marauders not return, but the sky above
That land usurped by a compulsory order
Watched and waited – like me and her that day

Watching and waiting by the perimeter.
A fear crossed over then like the fly-by-night
And sun-repellent wing that flies by day
Invisibly above: would she rise and go

With the pilot calling from his Thunderbolt?
But for her part, in response, only the slightest
Back-stiffening and standing of her ground
As her hand reached down and tightened around mine.

If self is a location, so is love:
Bearings taken, markings, cardinal points,
Options, obstinacies, dug heels and distance,
Here and there and now and then, a stance.

Anything Can Happen

after Horace, Odes, *I, 34*

Anything can happen. You know how Jupiter
Will mostly wait for clouds to gather head
Before he hurls the lightning? Well, just now
He galloped his thunder cart and his horses

5   Across a clear blue sky. It shook the earth
And the clogged underearth, the River Styx,
The winding streams, the Atlantic shore itself.
Anything can happen, the tallest towers

Be overturned, those in high places daunted,
10 Those overlooked regarded. Stropped-beak Fortune
Swoops, making the air gasp, tearing the crest off one,
Setting it down bleeding on the next.

Ground gives. The heaven's weight
Lifts up off Atlas like a kettle-lid.
15 Capstones shift, nothing resettles right.
Telluric ash and fire-spores boil away.

Helmet

Bobby Breen's. His Boston fireman's gift
With BREEN in scarlet letters on its spread
Fantailing brim.

Tinctures of sweat and hair oil
5   In the withered sponge and shock-absorbing webs
Beneath the crown –

Or better say the crest, for crest it is –
Leather-trimmed, steel-ridged, hand-tooled, hand-sewn,
Tipped with a little bud of beaten copper . . .

10 Bobby Breen's badged helmet's on my shelf
These twenty years, 'the headgear
Of the tribe', as O'Grady called it

In right heroic mood that afternoon
When the fireman-poet presented it to me
As 'the visiting fireman' –   15

As if I were up to it, as if I had
Served time under it, his fire-thane's shield,
His shoulder-awning, while shattering glass

And rubble-bolts out of a burning roof
Hailed down on every hatchet man and hose man there   20
Till the hard-reared shield-wall broke.

Out of Shot

November morning sunshine on my back
This bell-clear Sunday, elbows lodged strut-firm
On the unseasonably warm
Top bar of a gate, inspecting livestock,
Catching gleams of the distant Viking *vik*   5
Of Wicklow Bay; thinking *scriptorium*,
Norse raids, night-dreads and that 'fierce raiders' poem
About storm on the Irish Sea – so no attack
In the small hours or next morning; thinking shock
Out of the blue or blackout, the staggered walk   10
Of a donkey on the TV news last night –
Loosed from a cart that had loosed five mortar shells
In the bazaar district, wandering out of shot
Lost to its owner, lost for its sunlit hills.

Rilke: After the Fire

Early autumn morning hesitated,
Shying at newness, an emptiness behind
Scorched linden trees still crowding in around
The moorland house, now just one more wallstead

Where youngsters gathered up from god knows where   5
Hunted and yelled and ran wild in a pack.
Yet all of them fell silent when he appeared,
The son of the place, and with a long forked stick

Dragged an out-of-shape old can or kettle
From under hot, half burnt-away house-beams;
And then, like one with a doubtful tale to tell,
Turned to the others present, at great pains

To make them realize what had stood so.
For now that it was gone, it all seemed
Far stranger: more fantastical than Pharaoh.
And he was changed: a foreigner among them.

District and Circle

Tunes from a tin whistle underground
Curled up a corridor I'd be walking down
To where I knew I was always going to find
My watcher on the tiles, cap by his side,
His fingers perked, his two eyes eyeing me
In an unaccusing look I'd not avoid,
Or not just yet, since both were out to see
For ourselves.
              As the music larked and capered
I'd trigger and untrigger a hot coin
Held at the ready, but now my gaze was lowered
For was our traffic not in recognition?
Accorded passage, I would re-pocket and nod,
And he, still eyeing me, would also nod.

~

Posted, eyes front, along the dreamy ramparts
Of escalators ascending and descending
To a monotonous slight rocking in the works,
We were moved along, upstanding.
Elsewhere, underneath, an engine powered,
Rumbled, quickened, evened, quieted.
The white tiles gleamed. In passages that flowed
With draughts from cooler tunnels, I missed the light
Of all-overing, long since mysterious day,
Parks at lunchtime where the sunners lay
On body-heated mown grass regardless,
A resurrection scene minutes before
The resurrection, habitués
Of their garden of delights, of staggered summer.

~

Another level down, the platform thronged.
I re-entered the safety of numbers, 30
A crowd half straggle-ravelled and half strung
Like a human chain, the pushy newcomers
Jostling and purling underneath the vault,
On their marks to be first through the doors,
Street-loud, then succumbing to herd-quiet . . . 35
Had I betrayed or not, myself or him?
Always new to me, always familiar,
This unrepentant, now repentant turn
As I stood waiting, glad of a first tremor,
The caught up in the now-or-never whelm 40
Of one and all the full length of the train.

~

Stepping on to it across the gap,
On to the carriage metal, I reached to grab
The stubby black roof-wort and take my stand
From planted ball of heel to heel of hand 45
As sweet traction and heavy down-slump stayed me.
I was on my way, well girded, yet on edge,
Spot-rooted, buoyed, aloof,
Listening to the dwindling noises off,
My back to the unclosed door, the platform empty; 50
And wished it could have lasted,
That long between-times pause before the budge
And glaze-over, when any forwardness
Was unwelcome and bodies readjusted,
Blindsided to themselves and other bodies. 55

~

So deeper into it, crowd-swept, strap-hanging,
My lofted arm a-swivel like a flail,
My father's glazed face in my own waning
And craning . . .
                Again the growl 60
Of shutting doors, the jolt and one-off treble
Of iron on iron, then a long centrifugal
Haulage of speed through every dragging socket.

And so by night and day to be transported
Through galleried earth with them, the only relict
Of all that I belonged to, hurtled forward,
Reflecting in a window mirror-backed
By blasted weeping rock-walls.
                    Flicker-lit.

To George Seferis in the Underworld

The men began arguing about the spiky bushes that were in brilliant yellow bloom on the slopes: were they caltrop or gorse? ... 'That reminds me of something,' said George. 'I don't know ...'

That greeny stuff about your feet
is asphodel and rightly so,
but why do I think *seggans*?

And of a spring day
in your days of '71: Poseidon
making waves in sea and air
around Cape Sounion, its very name
all ozone-breeze and cavern-boom,
too utterly this-worldly, George, for you
intent upon an otherworldly scene
somewhere just beyond
the summit ridge, the cutting edge
of not remembering.

The bloody light. To hell with it.
Close eyes and concentrate.
Not crown of thorns, not sceptre reed
or Herod's court, but ha!
you had it! A harrowing, yes, in hell:
the hackle-spikes
that Plato told of, the tyrant's fate
in a passage you would quote:
'They bound him hand and foot,
they flung him down and flayed him,
gashing his flesh on thorny *aspalathoi*
and threw him into Tartarus, torn to shreds.'

As was only right
for a tyrant. But still, for you, maybe
too much i' the right, too black and white,
if still your chance to strike
against his ilk,   30
a last word meant to break
your much contested silence.

And for me a chance to test the edge
of *seggans*, dialect blade
hoar and harder and more hand-to-hand   35
than what is common usage nowadays:
sedge – marshmallow, rubber-dagger stuff.

Wordsworth's Skates

Star in the window.
                Slate scrape.
                              Bird or branch?
Or the whet and scud of steel on placid ice?

Not the bootless runners lying toppled   5
In dust in a display case,
Their bindings perished,

But the reel of them on frozen Windermere
As he flashed from the clutch of earth along its curve
And left it scored.   10

The Harrow-Pin

We'd be told, 'If you don't behave
There'll be nothing in your Christmas stocking for you
But an old kale stalk.' And we would believe him.

But if kale meant admonition, a harrow pin
Was correction's veriest unit.   5
Head-banged spike, forged fang, a true dead ringer

Out of a harder time, it was a stake
He'd drive through aspiration and pretence
For our instruction.

10 Let there once be any talk of decoration,
    A shelf for knick-knacks, a picture-hook or -rail,
    And the retort was instant: 'Drive a harrow-pin.'

    Brute-forced, rusted, haphazardly set pins
    From harrows wrecked by horse-power over stones
15 Lodged in the stable wall and on them hung

    Horses' collars lined with sweat-veined ticking,
    Old cobwebbed reins and hames and eye-patched winkers,
    The tackle of the mighty, simple dead.

    Out there, in musts of bedding cut with piss
20 He put all to the test. Inside, in the house,
    Ungulled, irreconcilable

    And horse-sensed as the travelled Gulliver,
    What virtue he approved (and would assay)
    Was in hammered iron.

Poet to Blacksmith

Eoghan Rua Ó Súilleabháin's (1748–84) instructions to Séamus MacGearailt, translated from the Irish

Séamus, make me a side-arm to take on the earth,
A suitable tool for digging and grubbing the ground,
Lightsome and pleasant to lean on or cut with or lift,
Tastily finished and trim and right for the hand.

5   No trace of the hammer to show on the sheen of the blade,
    The thing to have purchase and spring and be fit for the strain,
    The shaft to be socketed in dead true and dead straight,
    And I'll work with the gang till I drop and never complain.

    The plate and the edge of it not to be wrinkly or crooked –
10 I see it well shaped from the anvil and sharp from the file;
    The grain of the wood and the line of the shaft nicely fitted,
    And best thing of all, the ring of it, sweet as a bell.

Midnight Anvil

If I wasn't there
When Barney Devlin hammered
The midnight anvil
I can still hear it: twelve blows
Struck for the millennium.   5

~

His nephew heard it
In Edmonton, Alberta:
The cellular phone
Held high as a horse's ear,
Barney smiling to himself.   10

~

Afterwards I thought
Church bels beyond the starres heard
And then imagined
Barney putting it to me:
'You'll maybe write a poem.'   15

~

What I'll do instead
Is quote those waterburning
Medieval smiths:
'Huf, puf! Lus, bus! Col!' *Such noise
On nights heard no one never.*   20

~

And Eoghan Rua
Asking Séamus MacGearailt
To forge him a spade
Sharp, well shaped from the anvil,
And ringing *sweet as a bell.*   25

Súgán

The fluster of that soft supply and feed –
Hay being coaxed in handfuls from a ruck,

Paid out to be taken in by furl and swivel,
Turned and tightened, rickety-rick, to rope –
Though just as often at the other end
I'd manipulate the hook,
Walking backwards, winding for all I was worth
By snag and by sag the long and the short of it
To make ends mesh –
                    in my left hand
The cored and threaded elderberry haft,
In my right the fashioned wire,
                          breeze on my back,
Sun in my face, a power to bind and loose
Eked out and into each last tug and lap.

Senior Infants

1 *The Sally Rod*

On the main street of Granard I met Duffy
Whom I had known before the age of reason
In short trousers in the Senior Infants' room
Where once upon a winter's day Miss Walls
Lost her head and cut the legs off us
For dirty talk we didn't think she'd hear.
'Well, for Jesus' sake,' cried Duffy, coming at me
With his stick in the air and two wide open arms,
'For Jesus' sake! D'you mind the sally rod?'

2 *A Chow*

I'm staring at the freshly scratched initials
Of Robert Donnelly in the sandstone coping
Of Anahorish Bridge, with Robert Donnelly
Beside me, also staring at them.
                          'Here,' he says,
'Have a chow of this stuff,' stripping a dulse-thin film
Off the unwrapped ounce of Warhorse Plug –
Bog-bank brown, embossed, forbidden man-fruit
He's just been sent to buy for his father, Jock.

The roof of my mouth is thatch set fire to
At the burning-out of a neighbour, I want to lick
Bran from a bucket, grit off the coping stone.
'You have to spit,' says Robert, 'a chow's no good
Unless you spit like hell,' his ginger calf's lick
Like a scorch of flame, his quid-spurt fulgent.

3   One Christmas Day in the Morning

Tommy Evans must be sixty now as well. The last time I saw him was at the height of the Troubles, in Phil McKeever's pub in Castledawson, the first time we'd met since Anahorish School. I felt as free as a bird, a Catholic at large in Tommy's airspace.

Yet something small prevailed. My father balked at a word like 'Catholic' being used in company. Phil asked if we were OK. Tommy's crowd fenced him in with 'What are you having, Tommy?'

I was blabbing on about guns, how they weren't a Catholic thing, how the sight of the one in his house had always scared me, how our very toys at Christmas proved my point – when his eye upon me narrowed.

I remembered his air-gun broken over his forearm, my envy of the polished hardwood stock, him thumbing the pellets into their aperture, The snick of the thing then as he clipped it shut and danced with his eye on the sights through a quick-quick angle of ninety degrees and back, then drilled the pair of us left-right to the back of the house.

The Evans' chicken coop was the shape of a sentry-box, walls and gable of weathered tongue-and-groove, the roofing-felt plied tight and tacked to the eaves. And there above the neat-hinged door, balanced on the very tip of the apex, was Tommy's target: the chrome lid of the bell of his father's bike. Whose little zings fairly brought me to my senses.

The Nod

Saturday evenings we would stand in line
In Loudan's butcher shop. Red beef, white string,
Brown paper ripped straight off for parcelling
Along the counter edge. Rib roast and shin
Plonked down, wrapped up, and bow-tied neat and clean
But seeping blood. Like dead weight in a sling,
Heavier far than I had been expecting
While my father shelled out for it, coin by coin.

Saturday evenings too the local B-Men,
Unbuttoned but on duty, thronged the town,
Neighbours with guns, parading up and down,
Some nodding at my father almost past him
As if deliberately they'd aimed and missed him
Or couldn't seem to place him, not just then.

A Clip

Harry Boyle's one-room, one-chimney house
With its settle bed was our first barber shop.
We'd go not for a haircut but 'a clip':
Cold smooth creeping steel and snicking scissors,
The strong-armed chair, the plain mysteriousness
Of your sheeted self inside that neck-tied cope –
Half sleeveless surplice, half hoodless Ku Klux cape.
Harry Boyle's one-roomed, old bog-road house
Near enough to home but unfamiliar:
What was it happened there?
Weeds shoulder-high up to the open door,
Harry not shaved, close breathing in your ear,
Loose hair in windfalls blown across the floor
Under the collie's nose. The collie's stare.

Edward Thomas on the Lagans Road

He's not in view but I can hear a step
On the grass-crowned road, the whip of daisy heads
On the toes of boots.

                    Behind the hedge
Eamon Murphy and Teresa Brennan –
Fully clothed, strong-arming each other –
Have sensed him and gone quiet. I keep on watching
As they rise and go.
                        And now the road is empty.
Nothing but air and light between their love-nest
And the bracken hillside where I lie alone.

Utter evening, as it was in the beginning,

Until the remembered come and go of lovers
Brings on his long-legged self on the Lagans Road –
Edward Thomas in his khaki tunic
Like one of the Evans brothers out of Leitrim,
Demobbed, 'not much changed', sandy moustached and freckled
From being, they said, with Monty in the desert.

Found Prose

1 *The Lagans Road*

The Lagans Road ran for about three quarters of a mile across an area of wetlands. It was one of those narrow country roads with weeds in the middle, grass verges and high hedges on either side, and all around it marsh and rushes and little shrubs and birch trees. For a minute or two every day, therefore, you were in the wilderness, but on the first morning I went to school it was as if the queen of elfland was leading me away. The McNicholls were neighbours and Philomena McNicholl had been put in charge of me during those first days. Ginger hair, freckled face, green gymfrock – a fey, if ever there was one. I remember my first sight of the school, a couple of low-set Nissen huts raising their corrugated backs above the hedges. From about a quarter of a mile away I could see youngsters running about in the road in front of the buildings and hear shouting in the playground. Years later, when I read an account of how the Indians of the Pacific Northwest foresaw their arrival in the land of the dead – coming along a forest path where other travellers' cast-offs lay scattered on the bushes, hearing voices laughing and calling, knowing there was a life in the clearing up ahead that would be familiar, but feeling at the same time lost and homesick – it struck me I had already experienced that kind of arrival. Next thing in the porch I was faced with rows of coathooks nailed up at different heights along the wall, so that everyone in the different classes could reach them, everyone had a place to hang overcoat or scarf and proceed to the strange room, where our names were new in the rollbook and would soon be called.

2 Tall Dames

Even though we called them 'the gypsies', we knew that gypsies were properly another race. They inhabited the land of eros, glimpsed occasionally when the circus rolled into a field and a fortune-teller, swathed in her silks and beads, inclined to us from the back door of a caravan. The people we called 'the gypsies' we would now call travellers, although at that time in that place 'tinker' was an honourable term, signifying tin-smiths, white-smiths, pony-keepers, regulars on the doorstep, squatters on the long acre. Marvellous upfront women in unerotic woollen shawls, woven in big tartan patterns of tan and mossy green, their baskets full of dyed wooden flowers, their speech cadenced to beg and keep begging with all the stamina of a cantor. Walking the roads in ones and twos, children on their arms or at their heels. Squaws of the ditchback, in step with Yeats's 'tall dames' walking in Avalon.

You encountered them in broad daylight, going about their usual business, yet there was always a feeling that they were coming towards you out of storytime. One of the menfolk on the road with a bit of a halter, you on your way to school, he with a smell of woodsmoke off him, asking if you'd seen an old horse anywhere behind the hedges. The stillness of the low tarpaulin tent as you approached and passed, the green wood in the fire spitting under a pot slung from a tripod. Every time they landed in the district, there was an extra-ness in the air, as if a gate had been left open in the usual life, as if something might get in or get out.

3 Boarders

There's no heat on the bus, but the engine's running and up where a destination should be showing it just says PRIVATE, so it must be ours. We're back in the days of peaked caps and braid piping, drivers mounting steps as ominously as hangmen, conductors with plump bags of coin, the ticket punch a-dangle on its chain. But this is a special bus, so there'll be no tickets, no conductor and no fare collection until the load is full.

The stops are the same as every other time, clusters of us with suitcases assembled in shop doorways or at the appointed crossroads, the old bus getting up speed wherever the going's good, but now she's changing down on the Glenshane Pass. The higher she goes, the heavier she pulls, and yet there's no real hurry. Let the driver keep doing battle with the gear-stick, let his revs and double-clutchings drag the heart, anything to put off that last stop when he slows down at the summit and turns and seems about to take us back. Instead of which he halts, pulls on the handbrake, gives us time to settle, then switches off.

When we start again, the full lock of the steering will be held, the labour of cut and spin leave tyre-marks in the gravel, the known country fall away behind us. But for the moment it's altogether quiet, the whole bus shakes as he bangs the cabin door shut, comes round the side and in to lift the money. Unfamiliar, uninvolved, almost, it seems, angered, he deals with us one by one, as one by one we go farther into ourselves, wishing we were him on the journey back, flailing downhill with the windows all lit up, empty and faster and angrier bend after bend.

The Lift

A first green braird: the hawthorn half in leaf.
Her funeral filled the road
And could have stepped from some old photograph

Of a Breton *pardon*, remote
Familiar women and men in caps
Walking four abreast, soon falling quiet.

Then came the throttle and articulated whops
Of a helicopter crossing, and afterwards
Awareness of the sound of our own footsteps,

Of open air, and the life behind those words
'Open' and 'air'. I remembered her aghast,
Foetal, shaking, sweating, shrunk, wet-haired,

A beaten breath, a misting mask, the flash
Of one wild glance, like ghost surveillance
From behind a gleam of helicopter glass.

A lifetime, then the deathtime: reticence
Keeping us together when together,
All declaration deemed outspokeness.

Favourite aunt, good sister, faithful daughter,
Delicate since childhood, tough alloy
Of disapproval, kindness and *hauteur*,

She took the risk, at last, of certain joys –
Her birdtable and jubilating birds,
The 'fashion' in her wardrobe and her tallboy.

Weather, in the end, would say our say.
Reprise of griefs in summer's clearest mornings,
Children's deaths in snowdrops and the may,

Whole requiems at the sight of plants and gardens . . .
They bore her lightly on the bier. Four women,
Four friends – she would have called them girls – stepped in

And claimed the final lift beneath the hawthorn.

Nonce Words

The road taken
to bypass Cavan
took me west,
(a sign mistaken)
so at Derrylin
I turned east.

Sun on ice,
white floss
on reed and bush,
the bridge-iron cast
in an Advent silence
I drove across,

then pulled in,
parked, and sat
breathing mist
on the windscreen.
Requiescat . . .
I got out

well happed up,
stood at the frozen
shore gazing
at rimed horizon,
my first stop
like this in years.

And blessed myself
in the name of the nonce
and happenstance,
the *Who knows*
and *What nexts*
and *So be its*.

Stern

in memory of Ted Hughes

'And what was it like,' I asked him,
'Meeting Eliot?'
          'When he looked at you,'
He said, 'it was like standing on a quay
Watching the prow of the *Queen Mary*
Come towards you, very slowly.'

          Now it seems
I'm standing on a pierhead watching him
All the while watching me as he rows out
And a wooden end-stopped stern

Labours and shimmers and dips,
Making no real headway.

Out of This World

in memory of Czesław Miłosz

1 *'Like everybody else . . .'*

'Like everybody else, I bowed my head
during the consecration of the bread and wine,
lifted my eyes to the raised host and raised chalice,
believed (whatever it means) that a change occurred.

5   I went to the altar rails and received the mystery
on my tongue, returned to my place, shut my eyes fast, made
an act of thanksgiving, opened my eyes and felt
time starting up again.
                        There was never a scene
10 when I had it out with myself or with another.
The loss occurred off-stage. And yet I cannot
disavow words like 'thanksgiving' or 'host'
or 'communion bread'. They have an undying
tremor and draw, like well water far down.'

2 *Brancardier*

You're off, a pilgrim, in the age of steam:
Derry, Dun Laoghaire, Dover, Rue du Bac
(Prayers for the Blessed M. M. Alacoque,
That she be canonized). Then leisure time

5   That evening in Paris, whence to Lourdes,
Learning to trust your learning on the way:
'*Non, pas de vin, merci. Mais oui, du thé,*'
And the waiter's gone to take you at your word.

Hotel de quoi in *Rue de quoi*? All gone.
10 But not your designation, *brancardier*,
And your coloured bandolier, as you lift and lay
The sick on stretchers in precincts of the shrine

Or on bleak concrete to await their bath.
And always the word 'cure' hangs in the air
Like crutches hung up near the grotto altar.   15
And always prayers out loud or under breath.

Belgian miners in blue dungarees
March in procession, carrying brass lamps.
Sodalities with sashes, poles and pennants
Move up the line. Mantillas, rosaries   20

And the *unam sanctam catholicam* acoustic
Of that underground basilica – maybe
Not gone but not what was meant to be,
The concrete reinforcement of the Mystic-

al Body, the Eleusis of its age.   25
I brought back one plastic canteen litre
On a shoulder-strap (*très chic*) of the Lourdes water.
One small glass dome that englobed an image

Of the Virgin above barefoot Bernadette –
Shake it and the clear liquid would snow   30
Flakes like white angel feathers on the grotto.
And (for stretcher-bearing work) a certificate.

3 Saw Music

Q. *Do you renounce the world?*
A. *I do renounce it.*

Barrie Cooke has begun to paint 'godbeams',
Vents of brightness that make the light of heaven
Look like stretched sheets of fluted silk or rayon
In an old-style draper's window. Airslides, scrims

And scumble. Columnar sift. But his actual palette   5
Is ever sludge and smudge, as if a shower
Made puddles on the spirit's winnowing floor.
What it reminds me of is a wet night

In Belfast, around Christmas, when the man
Who played the saw inside the puddled doorway   10
Of a downtown shop, in light from a display
Of tinselled stuffs and sleigh bells blinking neon,

            Started to draw his bow across the blade.
            The stainless steel was oiled or Vaselined,
15   The saw stood upside down and his left hand
            Pressed light or heavy as the tune required

            Flop-wobble grace note or high banshee whine.
            Rain spat upon his threadbare gaberdine,
            Into his cap where the occasional tossed coin
20   Basked on damp lining, the raindrops glittering

            Like the saw's greased teeth his bow caressed and crossed
            Back across unharmed. 'The art of oil painting –
            Daubs fixed on canvas – is a paltry thing
            Compared with what cries out to be expressed,'

25   The poet said, who lies this god-beamed day
            Coffined in Krakow, as out of this world now
            As the untranscendent music of the saw
            He might have heard in Vilnius or Warsaw

            And would not have renounced, however paltry.

In Iowa

            In Iowa once, among the Mennonites
            In a slathering blizzard, conveyed all afternoon
            Through sleet-glit pelting hard against the windscreen
            And a wiper's strong absolving slumps and flits,

5   I saw, abandoned in the open gap
            Of a field where wilted corn stalks flagged the snow,
            A mowing machine. Snow brimmed its iron seat,
            Heaped each spoked wheel with a thick white brow

            And took the shine off oil in the black-toothed gears.
10   Verily I came forth from that wilderness
            As one unbaptized who had known darkness
            At the third hour and the veil in tatters.

            In Iowa once. In the slush and rush and hiss
            Not of parted but as of rising waters.

Höfn

The three-tongued glacier has begun to melt.
What will we do, they ask, when boulder-milt
Comes wallowing across the delta flats

And the miles-deep shag-ice makes its move?
I saw it, ridged and rock-set, from above,   5
Undead grey-gristed earth-pelt, aeon-scruff,

And feared its coldness that still seemed enough
To iceblock the plane window dimmed with breath,
Deepfreeze the seep of adamantine tilt

And every warm, mouthwatering word of mouth.   10

On the Spot

A cold clutch, a whole nestful, all but hidden
In last year's autumn leaf-mould, and I knew
By the mattness and the stillness of them, rotten,
Making death sweat of a morning dew
That didn't so much shine the shells as damp them.   5
I was down on my hands and knees there in the wet
Grass under the hedge, adoring it,
Early riser busy reaching in
And used to finding warm eggs. But instead
This sudden polar stud   10
And stigma and dawn stone-circle chill
In my mortified right hand, proof positive
Of what conspired on the spot to addle
Matter in its planetary stand-off.

The Tollund Man in Springtime

Into your virtual city I'll have passed
Unregistered by scans, screens, hidden eyes,
Lapping myself in time, an absorbed face
Coming and going, neither god nor ghost,
Not at odds or at one, but simply lost   5
To you and yours, out under seeding grass

And trickles of kesh water, sphagnum moss,
Dead bracken on the spreadfield, red as rust.
I reawoke to revel in the spirit
They strengthened when they chose to put me down
For their own good. And to a sixth-sensed threat:
Panicked snipe offshooting into twilight,
Then going awry, larks quietened in the sun,
Clear alteration in the bog-pooled rain.

~

Scone of peat, composite bog-dough
They trampled like a muddy vintage, then
Slabbed and spread and turned to dry in sun –
Though never kindling-dry the whole way through –
A dead-weight, slow-burn lukewarmth in the flue,
Ashless, flameless, its very smoke a sullen
Waft of swamp-breath . . . And me, so long unrisen,
I knew that same dead weight in joint and sinew
Until a spade-plate slid and soughed and plied
At my buried ear, and the levered sod
Got lifted up; then once I felt the air
I was like turned turf in the breath of God,
Bog-bodied on the sixth day, brown and bare,
And on the last, all told, unatrophied.

~

My heavy head. Bronze-buffed. Ear to the ground.
My eye at turf level. Its snailskin lid.
My cushioned cheek and brow. My phantom hand
And arm and leg and shoulder that felt pillowed
As fleshily as when the bog pith weighed
To mould me to itself and it to me
Between when I was buried and unburied.
Between what happened and was meant to be.
On show for years while all that lay in wait
Still waited. Disembodied. Far renowned.
Faith placed in me, me faithless as a stone
The harrow turned up when the crop was sown.
Out in the Danish night I'd hear soft wind
And remember moony water in a rut.

~

'The soul exceeds its circumstances.' Yes.
History not to be granted the last word
Or the first claim . . . In the end I gathered
From the display-case peat my staying powers,
Told my webbed wrists to be like silver birches,
My old uncallused hands to be young sward,
The spade-cut skin to heal, and got restored
By telling myself this. Late as it was,
The early bird still sang, the meadow hay
Still buttercupped and daisied, sky was new.
I smelled the air, exhaust fumes, silage reek,
Heard from my heather bed the thickened traffic
Swarm at a roundabout five fields away
And transatlantic flights stacked in the blue.

~

Cattle out in rain, their knowledgeable
Solid standing and readiness to wait,
These I learned from. My study was the wet,
My head as washy as a head of kale,
Shedding water like the flanks and tail
Of every dumb beast sunk above the cloot
In trampled gaps, bringing their heavyweight
Silence to bear on nosed-at sludge and puddle.
Of another world, unlearnable, and so
To be lived by, whatever it was I knew
Came back to me. Newfound contrariness.
In check-out lines, at cash-points, in those queues
Of wired, far-faced smilers, I stood off,
Bulrush, head in air, far from its lough.

~

Through every check and scan I carried with me
A bunch of Tollund rushes – roots and all –
Bagged in their own bog-damp. In an old stairwell
Broom cupboard where I had hoped they'd stay
Damp until transplanted, they went musty.
Every green-skinned stalk turned friable,
The drowned-mouse fibres withered and the whole
Limp, soggy cluster lost its frank bouquet

Of weed leaf and turf mould. Dust in my palm
80 And in my nostrils dust, should I shake it off
Or mix it in with spit in pollen's name
And my own? As a man would, cutting turf,
I straightened, spat on my hands, felt benefit
And spirited myself into the street.

Moyulla

In those days she flowed
black-lick and quick
under the sallies,
the coldness off her

5   like the coldness off you –
your cheek and your clothes
and your moves – when you come in
from gardening.

She was in the swim
10 of herself, her gravel shallows
swarmed, pollen sowings
tarnished her pools.

~

And so what, did I hear
somebody cry? Let them
15 cry if it suits them,
but let it be for her,

her stones, her purls, her pebbles
slicked and blurred
with algae, as if her name
20 and addressing water

suffered muddying,
her clear vowels
a great vowel shift,
Moyola to Moyulla.

~

25 Milk-fevered river.
Froth at the mouth

of the discharge pipe,
gidsome flotsam . . .

Barefooted on the bank,
glad-eyed, ankle-grassed, 30
I saw it all
and loved it at the time –

blettings, beestings,
creamery spillage
on her cleanly, comely 35
sally trees and alders.

~

Step into her for me
some fresh-faced afternoon,
but not before
you step into thigh waders 40

to walk up to the bib
upstream, in the give and take
of her deepest, draggiest purchase,
countering, parting,

getting back at her, sourcing 45
her and your plashy self,
neither of you
ready to let up.

Planting the Alder

For the bark, dulled argent, roundly wrapped
And pigeon-collared.

For the splitter-splatter, guttering
Rain-flirt leaves.

For the snub and clot of the first green cones, 5
Smelted emerald, chlorophyll.

For the scut and scat of cones in winter,
So rattle-skinned, so fossil-brittle.

For the alder-wood, flame-red when torn
Branch from branch. 10

But mostly for the swinging locks
Of yellow catkins,

Plant it, plant it,
Streel-head in the rain.

Tate's Avenue

Not the brown and fawn car rug, that first one
Spread on sand by the sea but breathing land-breaths,
Its vestal folds unfolded, its comfort zone
Edged with a fringe of sepia-coloured wool tails.

5 Not the one scraggy with crusts and eggshells
And olive stones and cheese and salami rinds
Laid out by the torrents of the Guadalquivir
Where we got drunk before the corrida.

Instead, again, it's locked-park Sunday Belfast,
10 A walled back yard, the dust-bins high and silent
As a page is turned, a finger twirls warm hair
And nothing gives on the rug or the ground beneath it.

I lay at my length and feel the lumpy earth,
Keen-sensed more than ever through discomfort,
15 But never shifted off the plaid square once.
When we moved I had your measure and you had mine.

A Hagging Match

Axe-thumps outside
like wave-hits through
a night ferry:
            you
5 whom I cleave to, hew to,
splitting firewood.

Fiddleheads

Fiddlehead ferns are a delicacy where? Japan? Estonia?
Ireland long ago?

I say Japan because when I think of those delicious
things I think of my friend Toraiwa, and the surprise I
felt when he asked me about the erotic. He said it
belonged in poetry and he wanted more of it.

So here they are, Toraiwa, frilled, infolded, tenderized,
in a little steaming basket, just for you.

To Pablo Neruda in Tamlaghtduff

Niall FitzDuff brought a jar
of crab-apple jelly
made from crabs off the tree
that grew at Duff's Corner –
still grows at Duff's Corner –
a tree I never once saw
with crab apples on it.

Contrary, unflowery
sky-whisk and bristle, more
twig-fret than fruit-fort,
crabbed
as crabbed could be –
that was the tree
I remembered.

But then –
O my Pablo of earthlife –
when I tasted the stuff
it was freshets and orbs.
My eyes were on stalks,
I was back in an old
rutted cart road, making
the rounds of the district, breasting
its foxgloves, smelling
cow-parsley and nettles, all
of high summer's smoulder
under our own tree ascendant
in Tamlaghtduff,
its crab-hoard and – yes,
in pure hindsight – corona
of gold.

               For now,
      O my home-truth Neruda,
      round-faced as the crowd
      at the crossroads, with your eyes
35   I see it, now taste-bud
      and tear-duct melt down
      and I spread the jelly on thick
      as if there were no tomorrow.

Home Help

1 *Helping Sarah*

And so with tuck and tightening of blouse
And vigorous advance of knee, she was young
Again as the year, out weeding rigs
In the same old skirt and brogues, on top of things
5   Every time she straightened. And a credit.

                    Her oatmeal tweed
With pinpoints of red haw and yellow whin,
Its threadbare workadayness hard and common;
Her quick step; her dry hand; all things well-sped;
10 Her open and closed relations with earth's work;
And everything passed on without a word.

2 *Chairing Mary*

Heavy, helpless, carefully manhandled
Upstairs every night in a wooden chair
She sat in all day as the sun sundialled
Window-splays across the quiet floor . . .

5   Her body heat had entered the braced timber
Two would take hold of, by weighted leg and back,
Tilting and hoisting, the one on the lower step
Bearing the brunt, the one reversing up

Not averting eyes from her hurting bulk,
10 And not embarrassed, but never used to it.
I think of her warm brow we might have once
Bent to and kissed before we kissed it cold.

Rilke: The Apple Orchard

Come just after the sun has gone down, watch
This deepening of green in the evening sward:
It is not as if we'd long since garnered
And stored within ourselves a something which

From feeling and from feeling recollected, 5
From new hope and half-forgotten joys
And from an inner dark infused with these,
Issues in thoughts as ripe as windfalls scattered

Here under trees like trees in a Dürer woodcut –
Pendent, pruned, the husbandry of years 10
Gravid in them until the fruit appears –
Ready to serve, replete with patience, rooted

In the knowledge that no matter how above
Measure or expectation, all must be
Harvested and yielded, when a long life willingly 15
Cleaves to what's willed and grows in mute resolve.

Quitting Time

The hosed-down chamfered concrete pleases him.
He'll wait a while before he kills the light
On the cleaned-up yard, its pails and farrowing crate,
And the cast-iron pump immobile as a herm
Upstanding elsewhere, in another time. 5
More and more this last look at the wet
Shine of the place is what means most to him –
And to repeat the phrase, 'My head is light',
Because it often is as he reaches back
And switches off, a home-based man at home 10
In the end with little. Except this same
Night after nightness, redding up the work,
The song of a tubular steel gate in the dark
As he pulls it to and starts his uphill trek.

Home Fires

1 *A Scuttle for Dorothy Wordsworth*

Dorothy young, jig-jigging her iron shovel,
Barracking a pile of lumpy coals
Carted up by one Thomas Ashburner,
Her toothache so ablaze the carter's name
Goes unremarked as every jolt and jag
Backstabs her through her wrist-bone, neck-bone, jaw-bone.

Dorothy old, doting at the flicker
In a brass companion set, all the companions
Gone or let go, their footfalls on the road
Unlistened for, that sounded once as plump
As the dropping shut of the flap-board scuttle-lid
The minute she'd stacked the grate for their arrival.

2 *A Stove Lid for W. H. Auden*

> *The mass and majesty of this world, all*
>   *That carries weight and always weighs the same ...*
> 'The Shield of Achilles'

The mass and majesty of this world I bring you
In the small compass of a cast-iron stove lid.
I was the youngster in a Fair Isle jersey
Who loved a lifter made of stainless steel,
The way its stub claw found its clink-fast hold,
The fit and weight and danger as it bore
The red hot solidus to one side of the stove
For the fire-fanged maw of the fire-box to be stoked,
Then the gnashing bucket stowed.
                    So one more time,
I tote it, hell-mouth stopper, flat-earth disc,
And replace it safely. Wherefore rake and rattle,
Watch sparks die in the ashpan, poke again,
Think of dark matter in the starlit coalhouse.

The Birch Grove

At the back of a garden, in earshot of river water,
In a corner walled off like the baths or bake-house
Of an unroofed abbey or broken-floored Roman villa,
They have planted their birch grove. Planted it recently only,
But already each morning it puts forth in the sun 5
Like their own long grown-up selves, the white of the bark
As suffused and cool as the white of the satin nightdress
She bends and straightens up in, pouring tea,
Sitting across from where he dandles a sandal
On his big time-keeping foot, as bare as an abbot's. 10
Red brick and slate, plum tree and apple retain
Their credibility, a CD of Bach is making the rounds
Of the common or garden air. Above them a jet trail
Tapers and waves like a willow wand or a taper.
'If art teaches us anything,' he says, trumping life 15
With a quote, 'it's that the human condition is private.'

Cavafy: 'The rest I'll speak of to the ones below in Hades'

'Yes,' said the proconsul, replacing the scroll,
'indeed the line is true. And beautiful.
Sophocles at his most philosophical.
We'll talk about a whole lot more down there
and be happy to be seen for what we are. 5
Here we're like sentries, watching anxiously,
guarding every locked-up hurt and secret,
but all we cover up here, day and night,
down there we'll let out, frankly and completely.'

'That is,' said the sophist, with a slow half-smile, 10
'if down there they ever talk about such things,
if they can be bothered with the like at all.'

In a Loaning

Spoken for in autumn, recovered speech
Having its way again, I gave a cry:
'Not beechen green, but these shin-deep coffers
Of copper-fired leaves, these beech boles grey.'

The Blackbird of Glanmore

On the grass when I arrive,
Filling the stillness with life,
But ready to scare off
At the very first wrong move.
In the ivy when I leave.

It's you, blackbird, I love.

I park, pause, take heed.
Breathe. Just breathe and sit
And lines I once translated
Come back: 'I want away
To the house of death, to my father

Under the low clay roof.'

And I think of one gone to him.
A little stillness dancer –
Haunter-son, lost brother –
Cavorting through the yard,
So glad to see me home,

My homesick first term over.

And think of a neighbour's words
Long after the accident:
'Yon bird on the shed roof,
Up on the ridge for weeks –
I said nothing at the time
But I never liked yon bird.'

The automatic lock
Clunks shut, the blackbird's panic
Is shortlived, for a second

I've a bird's eye view of myself,
A shadow on raked gravel

In front of my house of life.

Hedge-hop, I am absolute
For you, your ready talkback,
Your each stand-offish comeback,
Your picky, nervy goldbeak –
On the grass when I arrive,

In the ivy when I leave.

UNCOLLECTED POEMS (2006–2010)

A Toast for Rand

From Casket-ville he first proceeded.
Now in Hickory he's heeded
As prof. and parent, poetry-guide
Who feeds his poets chicken, fried,
And ribs, well barbecued, and beer 5
Or moonshine, should you so prefer.
At Emory, in his bloom of youth,
I met him when I fared down south.
In Schuchard's yard he baked a hog
And talked of Toome and Toner's Bog. 10
He interviewed for *Salmagundi*.
He annotated words like 'Lundy'.
While Fulbrighting with Beth and Blake
(Who'd crossed the ocean for his sake)
In an attic he was cloistered. 15
In Moran's of the Weir he oystered.
He listed items A, B, C,
Till driven close to lunacy.
He gave us boxes, birdbaths, rainsticks,
Inlaid gourds and compact discs. 20
Wherefore to-day I'm dressed in navy –
My T-shirt from the Blue Trout Café –
And Marie's in her Galway shawl
To raise a brimming glass and call
Good health to Rand, two scored and tenned, 25
Best bibliographer and friend.

Our Mystery

I see him still, a mystery to the islanders, a goad to me in the pub the night before. Why had I caved in? Was I not ready for the inner journey? Now I watched him from the open boat that was taking us back to the mainland, a solitary profile against high sky and a hillside of stone walls. Among the Guinness barrels, under the swagged nets 5 and lobster pots, he'd spoken like a nuncio with news for me, the imperilled one, news he was still imparting when we went our separate ways at the whitewashed gable, I for the family hotel beside the pier, he for the two mile walk to his fisherman's hut, the settle bed and

writing table of planks and tea-chests. As I sat on the thwarts with a
child on either knee, I noticed the man at the tiller would occasionally
turn his head, as if he too were keeping track, so I enquired, 'And what
about our friend? How does he make out?' 'Ach,' the answer came,
'he spends his days just walking round the island, working the head.'

Fragment: 'Nairn in darkness and in light'

One summer night in Nairn, when the Moray Firth
Was a gull-backed, gull-breasted afterglow
We stood out on the pier with other watchers

Sharing their low-voiced, self-contained excitements
As an intermittent silkshine furled and roiled
In the half-light. Then somebody said 'Dolphins!'

Dolphins for certain, though none there could agree
Which shift or gleam contained them
Out at the earth's rim and rondure:

We just kept standing, as if in our twos and threes
We'd gathered providentially
And they'd appeared. I thought of David Thomson's

Unfaulting, damaged eyes that saw waves
And waterfalls in young girls' hair, of sex in Eden,
Sweet-flexed, given, low-voiced, quickening, starry

One summer night in Nairn.

Who Is Billy?

Who is Billy, what is he
The Ireland Funds commend him?
Prince of giving, *saoi, ard-rí*,
His Kerry court around him.

Founder, member, chairman, donor,
Guardsman, oilman, clubman, he:
Veteran, two wounds of honour,
Twice conferred an LL.D.

Cantabrigian, San Franciscan,
Killarney/Kerry patriot

(In verse like this a chap can risk an
Imbecilic rhyme like that –

And better a light touch for Billy
Than po-faced pomp as in *Who's Who*.
But still can you be certain: will he
Smile his smile or barrack you?)

He'll surely smile the smile we love,
His strong man's shyish, shining face
Like sunlight on a Blarney Grove
Or his own ancestral Muckross.

It's nearly, Billy, forty years
Since first we met: the AIF
Awarded me a wad of dollars
To go and write and be myself

And there you were that famous night,
And Marie and Elisabeth,
When supper turned into a wordfight
And the usual right and left

Positions were rehearsed with fury
And friendships thus forever sealed –
As lasting as the walls of Derry,
Perennial as the fourth green field.

And so, old friend and fellow fellow
Of Mary Magdalene's College: all
Hail to you but not farewell-o.
Let's dine when you're next free, in hall.

Cutaways

I

Children's hands in close-up
On a bomb site, picking and displaying
Small shrapnel curds for the cameramen

Who stalk their levelled village. *Ferrum*
And *rigor* and *frigor* of mouse grey iron,
The thumb and finger of my own right hand

Closing around old hard plasticine
Given out by Miss Walls, thumbing it
To nests no bigger than an acorn cup,

10 Eggs no bigger than a grain of wheat,
Pet pigs with sausage bellies, belly-buttoned
Fingerprinted sausage women and men.

II

Or trigger-fingering a six-gun stick,
Cocking a stiff hammer-thumb above
A sawn-off kitchen chair leg; or flying round

A gable, the wingspan of both arms
5 At full stretch and a-tilt, the left hand tip
Dangerously near earth, the air-shearing right

Describing arcs – angelic potential
Fleetly, unforgettably attained:
Now in richochets that hosannah through

10 The backyard canyons of Mossbawn,
Now a head and shoulders dive
And skive as we hightail it up and away

III

To land hard back on heels, like the charioteer
Holding his own at Delphi, his six horses
And chariot gone, his left hand lopped off

A wrist protruding like a waterspout,
5 The reins astream in his right
Ready at any moment to curb and grapple

Bits long fallen away.
The cast of him on a postcard was enough
To set me straight once more between two shafts,

10 Another's hand on mine to guide the plough,
Each slither of the share, each stone it hit
Registered like a pulse in the timbered grips.

A Birl for Burns

From the start, Burns' birl and rhythm,
That tongue the Ulster Scots brought wi' them
And stick to still in County Antrim
    Was in my ear.
From east of Bann it westered in
    On the Derry air.

My neighbours *toved* and *bummed* and *blowed*,
They *happed* themselves until it *thowed*,
By *slaps* and *stiles* they *thrawed* and *tholed*
    And *snedded thrissles*,
And when the rigs were *braked* and hoed
    They'd *wet their whistles*.

Old men and women getting crabbèd
Would hark like dogs who'd seen a rabbit,
Then straighten, stare and have a stab at
    Standard habbie:
Custom never staled their habit
    O' quotin' Rabbie.

Leg-lifting, heartsome, lightsome Burns!
He overflowed the well-wrought urns
Like buttermilk from slurping churns,
    Rich and unruly,
Or dancers flying, doing turns
    At some wild hooley.

For Rabbie's free and Rabbie's big,
His stanza may be tight and trig
But once he sets the sail and rig
    Away he goes
Like Tam-O-Shanter o'er the brig
    Where no one follows.

And though his first tongue's going, gone,
And word lists now get added on
And even words like *stroan* and *thrawn*
    Have to be glossed,
In Burns's rhymes they travel on
    And won't be lost.

Centenary Stanza

Still red brickwork
Remains our bulwark:
Here exercise
Of mind has stood
5   To us, for us
These hundred years,
And will, for good.

The City

   I

Water-slicked hair already wafer-dry
By the start of class, he'd arrive
Wrist-deep in the perpetual soutane,

Still worrying bits of refectory breakfast
5   Between his teeth, the satin lining
Of his tossed-back shoulder-cape

The only thing agleam in the usual
He was inured to: us there in our desks
Observing silence, him readying himself,

10 Then the pause and the unsighed sigh
Before the sighed one, 'Och boys,
I wish it were Book Six.'

   II

But Livy it was instead, in 'selections'
Selected further by our man of sighs,
Resigned to it but sad it couldn't be

Hexameter verse, even that which urged
5   Conquest and imperium on Rome,
Whom to crush, to spare, to pacify.

Yet everywhere in that unremitting prose
Behind the augury and oratory
And carnage, one word shone

Like a Virgilian moon, the feminine-gendered, 10
Argent, birch-barked *urbs*
Risen over chalk-groined *Alba Longa*.

III

Not that Homeric light has not been shed
On 'the city', our Illium now,
Your gate the one where Priam creeps back in

With Hector's body, mine the one
Aeneas slips out from with Anchises, 5
Fathers and sons

The pair of us, grandfathers too,
More pastoral/lyrical than epical,
Inclined to scry the gloom for what might gleam

As when a seal's head rose and streamed and shone 10
For four of us, walking the harbour wall
In the sealight of Ardglass.

With Hindsight

Oisín borne away on the saddled steed
Returns to a different world,
Smaller scaled, in need of help, unhelpful.

Do not, sworn rider, for all your old strength
Stoop. Stay clear and true 5
In the morning world

You left, given fair warning,
Only this morning.
Your good impulse will harm you.

Let them hustle round their boulder. 10
When they call on you, ignore them.
Don't unbend or brace your shoulder.

HUMAN CHAIN (2010)

for
Des and Mary
Peter and Jean

'Had I not been awake'

Had I not been awake I would have missed it,
A wind that rose and whirled until the roof
Pattered with quick leaves off the sycamore

And got me up, the whole of me a-patter,
Alive and ticking like an electric fence:　　　　　　　　　5
Had I not been awake I would have missed it,

It came and went so unexpectedly
And almost it seemed dangerously,
Returning like an animal to the house,

A courier blast that there and then　　　　　　　　　　10
Lapsed ordinary. But not ever
After. And not now.

Album

I

Now the oil-fired heating boiler comes to life
Abruptly, drowsily, like the timed collapse
Of a sawn down tree, I imagine them

In a summer season, as it must have been,
And the place, it dawns on me,　　　　　　　　　　　5
Could have been Grove Hill before the oaks were cut,

Where I'd often stand with them on airy Sundays
Shin-deep in hilltop bluebells, looking out
At Magherafelt's four spires in the distance.

Too late, alas, now for the apt quotation　　　　　　　10
About a love that's proved by steady gazing
Not at each other but in the same direction.

II

Quercus, the oak. And *Quaerite*, Seek ye.
Among green leaves and acorns in mosaic
(Our college arms surmounted by *columba*,

Dove of the church, of Derry's sainted grove)
The footworn motto stayed indelible:
Seek ye first the Kingdom . . . Fair and square

I stood on in the Junior House hallway
A grey eye will look back
Seeing them as a couple, I now see,

For the first time, all the more together
For having had to turn and walk away, as close
In the leaving (or closer) as in the getting.

III

It's winter at the seaside where they've gone
For the wedding meal. And I am at the table,
Uninvited, ineluctable.

A skirl of gulls. A smell of cooking fish.
Plump dormant silver. Stranded silence. Tears.
Their bibbed waitress unlids a clinking dish

And leaves them to it, under chandeliers.
And to all the anniversaries of this
They are not ever going to observe

Or mention even in the years to come.
And now the man who drove them here will drive
Them back, and by evening we'll be home.

IV

Were I to have embraced him anywhere
It would have been on the riverbank
That summer before college, him in his prime,

Me at the time not thinking how he must
Keep coming with me because I'd soon be leaving.
That should have been the first, but it didn't happen.

The second did, at New Ferry one night
When he was very drunk and needed help
To do up trouser buttons. And the third

Was on the landing during his last week,
Helping him to the bathroom, my right arm
Taking the webby weight of his underarm.

V

It took a grandson to do it properly,
To rush him in the armchair
With a snatch raid on his neck,

Proving him thus vulnerable to delight,
Coming as great proofs often come
Of a sudden, one-off, then the steady dawning

Of whatever *erat demonstrandum*.
Just as a moment back a son's three tries
At an embrace in Elysium

Swam up into my very arms, and in and out
Of the Latin stem itself, the phantom
Verus that has slipped from 'very'.

The Conway Stewart

'Medium', 14-carat nib,
Three gold bands in the clip-on screw-top,
In the mottled barrel a spatulate, thin

Pump-action lever
The shopkeeper
Demonstrated,

The nib uncapped,
Treating it to its first deep snorkel
In a newly opened ink-bottle,

Guttery, snottery,
Letting it rest then at an angle
To ingest,

Giving us time
To look together and away
From our parting, due that evening,

To my longhand
'Dear'
To them, next day.

Uncoupled

I

Who is this coming to the ash-pit
Walking tall, as if in a procession,
Bearing in front of her a slender pan

Withdrawn just now from underneath
The firebox, weighty, full to the brim
With whitish dust and flakes still sparking hot

That the wind is blowing into her apron bib,
Into her mouth and eyes while she proceeds
Unwavering, keeping her burden horizontal still,

Hands in a tight, sore grip round the metal knob,
Proceeds until we have lost sight of her
Where the worn path turns behind the henhouse.

II

Who is this, not much higher than the cattle,
Working his way towards me through the pen,
His ashplant in one hand

Lifted and pointing, a stick of keel
In the other, calling to where I'm perched
On top of a shaky gate,

Waving and calling something I cannot hear
With all the lowing and roaring, lorries revving
At the far end of the yard, the dealers

Shouting among themselves, and now to him
So that his eyes leave mine and I know
The pain of loss before I know the term.

The Butts

His suits hung in the wardrobe, broad
And short
And slightly bandy-sleeved,

Flattened back
Against themselves,
A bit stand-offish.

Stale smoke and oxter-sweat
Came at you in a stirred-up brew
When you reached in,

A whole rake of thornproof and blue serge
Swung heavily
Like waterweed disturbed. I sniffed

Tonic unfreshness,
Then delved past flap and lining
For the forbidden handfuls.

But a kind of empty-handedness
Transpired . . . Out of suit-cloth
Pressed against my face,

Out of those layered stuffs
That surged and gave,
Out of the cold smooth pocket-lining

Nothing but chaff cocoons,
A paperiness not known again
Until the last days came

And we must learn to reach well in beneath
Each meagre armpit
To lift and sponge him,

One on either side,
Feeling his lightness,
Having to dab and work

Closer than anybody liked
But having, for all that,
To keep working.

Chanson d'Aventure

Love's mysteries in souls do grow,
But yet the body is his book.

I

Strapped on, wheeled out, forklifted, locked
In position for the drive,
Bone-shaken, bumped at speed,

The nurse a passenger in front, you ensconced
In her vacated corner seat, me flat on my back –
Our postures all the journey still the same,

Everything and nothing spoken,
Our eyebeams threaded laser-fast, no transport
Ever like it until then, in the sunlit cold

Of a Sunday morning ambulance
When we might, O my love, have quoted Donne
On love on hold, body and soul apart.

II

Apart: the very word is like a bell
That the sexton Malachy Boyle outrolled
In illo tempore in Bellaghy

Or the one I tolled in Derry in my turn
As college bellman, the haul of it there still
In the heel of my once capable

Warm hand, hand that I could not feel you lift
And lag in yours throughout that journey
When it lay flop-heavy as a bellpull

And we careered at speed through Dungloe,
Glendoan, our gaze ecstatic and bisected
By a hooked-up drip-feed to the cannula.

III

The charioteer at Delphi holds his own,
His six horses and chariot gone,
His left hand lopped

From a wrist protruding like an open spout,

Bronze reins astream in his right, his gaze ahead 5
Empty as the space where the team should be,

His eyes-front, straight-backed posture like my own
Doing physio in the corridor, holding up
As if once more I'd found myself in step

Between two shafts, another's hand on mine, 10
Each slither of the share, each stone it hit
Registered like a pulse in the timbered grips.

Miracle

Not the one who takes up his bed and walks
But the ones who have known him all along
And carry him in –

Their shoulders numb, the ache and stoop deeplocked
In their backs, the stretcher handles 5
Slippery with sweat. And no let-up

Until he's strapped on tight, made tiltable
And raised to the tiled roof, then lowered for healing.
Be mindful of them as they stand and wait

For the burn of the paid-out ropes to cool, 10
Their slight lightheadedness and incredulity
To pass, those ones who had known him all along.

Human Chain

for Terence Brown

Seeing the bags of meal passed hand to hand
In close-up by the aid workers, and soldiers
Firing over the mob, I was braced again

With a grip on two sack corners,
Two packed wads of grain I'd worked to lugs 5
To give me purchase, ready for the heave –

The eye-to-eye, one-two, one-two upswing
On to the trailer, then the stoop and drag and drain
Of the next lift. Nothing surpassed

That quick unburdening, backbreak's truest payback,
A letting go which will not come again.
Or it will, once. And for all.

A Mite-Box

But still in your cupped palm to feel
The chunk and clink of an alms-collecting mite-box,
Full to its slotted lid with copper coins,

Pennies and halfpennies donated for
'The foreign missions' . . . Made from a cardboard kit,
Wedge-roofed like a little oratory

And yours to tote as you made the rounds,
Indulged on every doorstep, each donation
Accounted for by a pinprick in a card –

A way for all to see a way to heaven,
The same as when a pinholed *Camera
Obscura* unblinds the sun eclipsed.

An Old Refrain

I

Robin-run-the-hedge
We called the vetch –
A fading straggle

Of Lincoln green
English stitchwork
Unravelling

With a hey-nonny-no
Along the Wood Road.
Sticky entangling

Berry and thread
Summering in
On the tousled verge.

II

In *seggins*
Hear the wind
Among the sedge,

In *boortree*
The elderberry's
Dank indulgence,

In *benweed*
Ragwort's
Singular unbending.

In *easing*
Drips of night rain
From the eaves.

The Wood Road

Resurfaced, never widened,
The verges grassy as when
Bill Pickering lay with his gun
Under the summer hedge
Nightwatching, in uniform –

Special militiaman.

Moonlight on rifle barrels,
On the windscreen of a van
Roadblocking the road,
The rest of his staunch patrol
In profile, sentry-loyal,

Harassing Mulhollandstown.

Or me in broad daylight
On top of a cartload
Of turf built trig and tight,
Looked up to, looking down,
Allowed the reins like an adult

As the old cart rocked and rollicked.

Then that August day I walked it
To the hunger striker's wake,

Across a silent yard,
In past a watching crowd
To where the guarded corpse

And a guard of honour stared.

25 Or the stain at the end of the lane
Where the child on her bike was hit
By a speed-merchant from nowhere
Hard-rounding the corner,
A back wheel spinning in sunshine,

30 A headlamp in smithereens.

Film it in sepia,
Drip-paint it in blood,
The Wood Road as is and was,
Resurfaced, never widened,
35 The milk-churn deck and the sign

For the bus-stop overgrown.

The Baler

All day the clunk of a baler
Ongoing, cardiac-dull,
So taken for granted

It was evening before I came to
5 To what I was hearing
And missing: summer's richest hours

As they had been to begin with,
Fork-lifted, sweated-through
And nearly rewarded enough

10 By the giddied-up race of a tractor
At the end of the day
Last-lapping a hayfield.

But what I also remembered
As woodpigeons sued at the edge
15 Of thirty gleaned acres

And I stood inhaling the cool
In a dusk eldorado

Of mighty cylindrical bales

Was Derek Hill's saying,
The last time he sat at our table,   20
He could bear no longer to watch

The sun going down
And asking please to be put
With his back to the window.

Derry Derry Down

I

The lush
Sunset blush
On a big ripe

Gooseberry:
I scratched my hand   5
Reaching in

To gather it
Off the bush,
Unforbidden,

In Annie Devlin's   10
Overgrown
Back garden.

II

In the storybook
Back kitchen
Of The Lodge

The full of a white
Enamel bucket   5
Of little pears:

Still life
On the red tiles
Of that floor.

Sleeping beauty   10
I came on
By the scullion's door.

Eelworks

I

To win the hand of the princess
What tasks the youngest son
Had to perform!

For me, the first to come a-courting
In the fish factor's house,
It was to eat with them

An eel supper.

II

Cut of diesel oil in evening air,
Tractor engines in the clinker-built
Deep-bellied boats,

Landlubbers' craft,
Heavy in water
As a cow down in a drain,

The men straight-backed,
Standing firm
At stern and bow –

Horse-and-cart men, really,
Glad when the adze-dressed keel
Cleaved to the mud.

Rum-and-peppermint men too
At the counter later on
In her father's pub.

III

That skin Alfie Kirkwood wore
At school, sweaty-lustrous, supple

And bisected into tails
For the tying of itself around itself –

For strength, according to Alfie.
Who would ease his lapped wrist

From the flap-mouthed cuff
Of a jerkin rank with eel oil,

The abounding reek of it
Among our summer desks   10

My first encounter with the up close
That had to be put up with.

   IV

Sweaty-lustrous too
The butt of the freckled
Elderberry shoot

I made a rod of,
A-fluster when I felt   5
Not tugging but a trailing

On the line, not the utter
Flip-stream frolic-fish
But a foot-long

Slither of a fellow,   10
A young eel, greasy grey
And rightly wriggle-spined,

Not yet the blueblack
Slick-backed waterwork
I'd live to reckon with,   15

My old familiar
Pearl-purl
Selkie-streaker.

   V

'That tree,' said Walter de la Mare
(Summer in his rare, recorded voice
So I could imagine

A lawn beyond French windows
And downs in the middle distance)   5
'That tree, saw it once

Struck by lightning . . . The bark – '
In his accent the *ba-aak* –
'The bark came off it

10   Like a girl taking off her petticoat.'
White linen *éblouissante*
In a breath of air,

Sylph-flash made flesh,
Eelwork, sea-salt and dish cloth
15   Getting a first hold,

Then purchase for the thumb nail
And the thumb
Under a v-nick in the neck,

The skinpeel drawing down
20   Like silk
At a practised touch.

VI

On the hoarding and the signposts
'Lough Neagh Fishermen's Co-operative',

But ever on our lips and at the weir
'The eelworks'.

Slack

I

Not coal dust, more the weighty grounds of coal
The lorryman would lug in open bags
And vent into a corner,

A sullen pile
5   But soft to the shovel, accommodating
As the clattering coal was not.

In days when life prepared for rainy days
It lay there, slumped and waiting
To dampen down and lengthen out

10   The fire, a check on mammon
And in its own way
Keeper of the flame.

II

The sound it made
More to me
Than any allegory.

Slack schlock.
Scuttle scuffle. 5
Shak-shak.

And those words –
'Bank the fire' –
Every bit as solid as

The cindery skull 10
Formed when its tarry
Coral cooled.

III

Out in the rain,
Sent out for it
Again

Stand in the unlit
Coalhouse door 5
And take in

Its violet blet,
Its wet sand weight,
Remembering it

Tipped and slushed
Catharsis 10
From the bag.

A Herbal

after Guillevic's 'Herbier de Bretagne'

Everywhere plants
Flourish among graves,

Sinking their roots
In all the dynasties
Of the dead. 5

*

Was graveyard grass
In our place
Any different?

Different from ordinary
Field grass?

Remember how you wanted
The sound recordist
To make a loop,

Wildtrack of your feet
Through the wet
At the foot of a field?

*

Yet for all their lush
Compliant dialect
No way have plants here
Arrived at a settlement.

Not the mare's tail,
Not the broom or whins.

It must have to do
With the wind.

*

Not that the grass itself
Ever rests in peace.

It too takes issue,
Now sets its face

To the wind,
Now turns its back.

*

'See me?' it says,
'The wind

Has me well rehearsed
In the ways of the world.

Unstable is good.
Permission granted!

Go then, citizen
Of the wind.
Go with the flow.'

    *

The bracken
Is less boastful.

It closes and curls back
On its secrets,

The best kept
Upon earth.

    *

And, to be fair,
There is sun as well.

Nowhere else
Is there sun like here,

Morning sunshine
All day long.

Which is why the plants,
Even the bracken,

Are sometimes tempted
Into trust.

    *

On sunlit tarmac,
On memories of the hearse

At waking pace
Between overgrown verges,

The dead here are borne
Towards the future.

    *

When the funeral bell tolls
The grass is all a-tremble.

			But only then.
65		Not every time any old bell

			Rings.

				*

			Broom
			Is like the disregarded
			And company for them,

70		Shows them
			They have to keep going,

			That the whole thing's worth
			The effort.

			And sometimes
75		Like those same characters
			When the weather's very good

			Broom sings.

				*

			Never, in later days,
			Would fruit

80		So taste of earth.
			There was slate

			In the blackberries,
			A slatey sap.

				*

			Run your hand into
85		The ditchback growth

			And you'd grope roots,
			Thick and thin.
			But roots of what?

			Once, one that we saw
90		Gave itself away,

			The tail of a rat
			We killed.

We had enemies,
Though why we never knew.

Among them,   95
Nettles,

Malignant things, letting on
To be asleep.

       *

Enemies –
Part of a world   100

Nobody seemed able to explain
But that had to be
Put up with.

There would always be dock leaves
To cure the vicious stings.   105

       *

There were leaves on the trees
And growth on the headrigs

You could confess
Everything to.

Even your fears   110
Of the night,

Of people
Even.

       *

What was better then

Than to crush a leaf or a herb   115
Between your palms,

Then wave it slowly, soothingly
Past your mouth and nose

And breathe?

*

If you know a bit
About the universe

It's because you've taken it in
Like that,

Looked as hard
As you look into yourself,

Into the rat hole,
Through the vetch and dock
That mantled it.

Because you've laid your cheek
Against the rush clump

And known soft stone to break
On the quarry floor.

*

Between heather and marigold,
Between sphagnum and buttercup,
Between dandelion and broom,
Between forget-me-not and honeysuckle,

As between clear blue and cloud,
Between haystack and sunset sky,
Between oak tree and slated roof,

I had my existence. I was there.
Me in place and the place in me.

*

Where can it be found again,
An elsewhere world, beyond

Maps and atlases,
Where all is woven into

And of itself, like a nest
Of crosshatched grass blades?

Canopy

It was the month of May.
Trees in Harvard Yard
Were turning a young green.
There was whispering everywhere.

David Ward had installed
Voice-boxes in the branches,
Speakers wrapped in sacking
Looking like old wasps' nests

Or bat-fruit in the gloaming –
Shadow Adam's apples
That made sibilant ebb and flow,
Speech-gutterings, desultory

Hush and backwash and echo.
It was like a recording
Of antiphonal responses
In the congregation of leaves.

Or a wood that talked in its sleep.
Reeds on a riverbank
Going over and over their secret.
People were cocking their ears,

Gathering, quietening,
Stepping on to the grass,
Stopping and holding hands.
Earth was replaying its tapes,

Words being given new airs:
Dante's whispering wood –
The wood of the suicides –
Had been magicked to lover's lane.

If a twig had been broken off there
It would have curled itself like a finger
Around the fingers that broke it
And then refused to let go

As if it were mistletoe
Taking tightening hold.

35   Or so I thought as the fairy
       Lights in the boughs came on.

1994

The Riverbank Field

Ask me to translate what Loeb gives as
'In a retired vale . . . a sequestered grove'
And I'll confound the Lethe in Moyola

By coming through Back Park down from Grove Hill
5   Across Long Rigs on to the riverbank –
Which way, by happy chance, will take me past

The *domos placidas*, 'those peaceful homes'
Of Upper Broagh. Moths then on evening water
It would have to be, not bees in sunlight,

10   Midge veils instead of lily beds; but *stet*
To all the rest: the willow leaves
Elysian-silvered, the grass so fully fledged

And unimprinted it can't not conjure thoughts
Of passing spirit-troops, *animae, quibus altera fato*
15   *Corpora debentur*, 'spirits,' that is,

'To whom second bodies are owed by fate'.
And now to continue, as enjoined to often,
'In my own words':

'All these presences
20   Once they have rolled time's wheel a thousand years
Are summoned here to drink the river water

So that memories of this underworld are shed
And soul is longing to dwell in flesh and blood
Under the dome of the sky.'

after Aeneid VI, 704–15, 748–51

Route 110

for Anna Rose

I

In a stained front-buttoned shopcoat –
Sere brown piped with crimson –
Out of the Classics bay into an aisle

Smelling of dry rot and disinfectant
She emerges, absorbed in her coin-count,   5
Eyes front, right hand at work

In the slack marsupial vent
Of her change-pocket, thinking what to charge
For a used copy of *Aeneid* VI.

Dustbreath bestirred in the cubicle mouth   10
I inhaled as she slid my purchase
Into a deckle-edged brown paper bag.

II

Smithfield Market Saturdays. The pet shop
Fetid with droppings in the rabbit cages,
Melodious with canaries, green and gold,

But silent now as birdless Lake Avernus.
I hurried on, shortcutting to the buses,   5
Parrying the crush with my bagged Virgil,

Past booths and the jambs of booths with their displays
Of canvas schoolbags, maps, prints, plaster plaques,
Feather dusters, artificial flowers,

Then racks of suits and overcoats that swayed   10
When one was tugged from its overcrowded frame
Like their owners' shades close-packed on Charon's barge.

III

Once the driver wound a little handle
The destination names began to roll
Fast-forward in their panel, and everything

      Came to life. Passengers
5   Flocked to the kerb like agitated rooks
      Around a rookery, all go

      But undecided. At which point the inspector
      Who ruled the roost in bus station and bus
      Separated and directed everybody

10   By calling not the names but the route numbers,
      And so we scattered as instructed, me
      For Route 110, Cookstown via Toome and Magherafelt.

          IV

      Tarpaulin-stiff, coal-black, sharp-cuffed as slate,
      The standard-issue railway guard's long coat
      I bought once second-hand: suffering its scourge

      At the neck and wrists was worth it even so
5   For the dismay I caused by doorstep night arrivals,
      A creature of cold blasts and flap-winged rain.

      And then, come finer weather, up and away
      To Italy, in a wedding guest's bargain suit
      Of finest weave, loose-fitting, summery, grey

10   As Venus' doves, hotfooting it with the tanned expats
      Up their Etruscan slopes to a small brick chapel
      To find myself the one there most at home.

          V

      Venus' doves? Why not McNicholls' pigeons
      Out of their pigeon holes but homing still?
      They lead unerringly to McNicholls' kitchen

      And a votive jampot on the dresser shelf.
5   So reach me not a gentian but stalks
      From the bunch that stood in it, each head of oats

      A silvered smattering, each individual grain
      Wrapped in a second husk of glittering foil
      They'd saved from chocolate bars, then pinched and cinched

10   'To give the wee altar a bit of shine.'
      The night old Mrs Nick, as she was to us,
      Handed me one it as good as lit me home.

VI

It was the age of ghosts. Of hand-held flashlamps.
Lights moving at a distance scried for who
And why: whose wake, say, in which house on the road

In that direction – Michael Mulholland's the first
I attended as a full participant,   5
Sitting up until the family rose

Like strangers to themselves and us. A wake
Without the corpse of their own dear ill-advised
Sonbrother swimmer, lost in the Bristol Channel.

For three nights we kept conversation going   10
Around the waiting trestles. By the fourth
His coffin, with the lid on, was in place.

VII

The corpse house then a house of hospitalities
Right through the small hours, the ongoing card game
Interrupted constantly by rounds

Of cigarettes on plates, biscuits, cups of tea,
The antiphonal recital of known events   5
And others rare, clandestine, undertoned.

Apt pupil in their night school, I walked home
On the last morning, my clothes as smoke-imbued
As if I'd fed a pyre, accompanied to the gable

By the mother, to point out a right of way   10
Across their fields, into our own back lane,
And absolve me thus formally of trespass.

VIII

As one when the month is young sees a new moon
Fading into daytime, again it is her face
At the dormer window, her hurt still new,

My look behind me hurried as I unlock,
Switch on, rev up, pull out and drive away   5
In the car she'll not have taken her eyes off,

The brakelights flicker-flushing at the corner
Like red lamps swung by RUC patrols
In the small hours on pre-Troubles roads

10   After dances, after our holdings on
And holdings back, the necking
And nay-saying age of impurity.

IX

And what in the end was there left to bury
Of Mr Lavery, blown up in his own pub
As he bore the primed device and bears it still

Mid-morning towards the sun-admitting door
5   Of Ashley House? Or of Louis O'Neill
In the wrong place the Wednesday they buried

Thirteen who'd been shot in Derry? Or of bodies
Unglorified, accounted for and bagged
Behind the grief cordons: not to be laid

10   In war graves with full honours, nor in a separate plot
Fired over on anniversaries
By units drilled and spruce and unreconciled.

X

Virgil's happy shades in pure blanched raiment
Contend on their green meadows, while Orpheus
Weaves among them, sweeping strings, aswerve

To the pulse of his own playing and to avoid
5   The wrestlers, dancers, runners on the grass.
Not unlike a sports day in Bellaghy,

Slim Whitman's wavering tenor amplified
Above sparking dodgems, flying chair-o-planes,
A mile of road with parked cars in the twilight

10   And teams of grown men stripped for action
Going hell for leather until the final whistle,
Leaving stud-scrapes on the pitch and on each other.

XI

Those evenings when we'd just wait and watch
And fish. Then the evening the otter's head
Appeared in the flow, or was it only

A surface-ruck and gleam we took for
5   An otter's head? No doubting, all the same,
The gleam, a turnover warp in the black

Quick water. Or doubting the solid ground
Of the riverbank field, twilit and a-hover
With midge-drifts, as if we had commingled

Among shades and shadows stirring on the brink   10
And stood their waiting, watching,
Needy and ever needier for translation.

XII

And now the age of births. As when once
At dawn from the foot of our back garden
The last to leave came with fresh-plucked flowers

To quell whatever smells of drink and smoke
Would linger on where mother and child were due   5
Later that morning from the nursing home,

So now, as a thank-offering for one
Whose long wait on the shaded bank has ended,
I arrive with my bunch of stalks and silvered heads

Like tapers that won't dim   10
As her earthlight breaks and we gather round
Talking baby talk.

Death of a Painter

i.m. Nancy Wynne Jones

Not a tent of blue but a peek of gold
From her coign of vantage in the studio,
A Wicklow cornfield in the gable window.

Long gazing at the hill – but not Cézanne,
More Thomas Hardy working to the end   5
In his crocheted old heirloom of a shawl.

And now not Hardy but a butterfly,
One of the multitude he imagined airborne
Through Casterbridge, down the summer thoroughfare.

And now not a butterfly but Jonah entering   10
The whale's mouth, as the Old English says,
Like a mote through a minster door.

Loughanure

i. m. Colin Middleton

I

Smoke might have been already in his eyes
The way he'd narrow them to size you up
As if you were a canvas, all the while

Licking and sealing a hand-rolled cigarette,
Each small ash increment flicked off
As white as flecks on the horizon line

Of his painting of Loughanure, thirty guineas
Forty-odd years ago. Whitewashed gables
Like petals stripped from hawthorn, heather ground

A pother of Gaeltacht turf smoke. Every time
He came to the house, he would go and stand
Gazing at it, grunting a bit and nodding.

II

So this is what an afterlife can come to?
A cloud-boil of grey weather on the wall
Like murky crystal, a remembered stare –

This for an answer to Alighieri
And Plato's Er? Who watched immortal souls
Choose lives to come according as they were

Fulfilled or repelled by existences they'd known
Or suffered first time round. Saw great far-seeing
Odysseus in the end choose for himself

The destiny of a private man. Saw Orpheus
Because he'd perished at the women's hands
Choose rebirth as a swan.

III

And did I seek the Kingdom? Will the Kingdom
Come? The idea of it there,
Behind its scrim since font and fontanel,

Breaks like light or water,
Like giddiness I felt at the old story
Of how he'd turn away from the motif,

Spread his legs, bend low, then look between them
For the mystery of the hard and fast
To be unveiled, his inverted face contorting

Like an arse-kisser's in some vision of the damned
Until he'd straighten, turn back, cock an eye
And stand with the brush at arm's length, readying.

IV

Had I sufficient Irish in Rannafast
In 1953 to understand
The *seanchas* and *dinnsheanchas*,

Had not been too young and too shy,
Had even heard the story about Caoilte
Hunting the fawn from Tory to a door

In a fairy hill where he wasn't turned away
But led to a crystal chair on the hill floor
While a girl with golden ringlets harped and sang,

Language and longing might have made a leap
Up through that cloud-swabbed air, the horizon lightened
And the far 'Lake of the Yew Tree' gleamed.

V

Not all that far, as it turns out,
Now that I can cover those few miles
In almost as few minutes, Mount Errigal

On the skyline the one constant thing
As I drive unhomesick, unbelieving, through
A grant-aided, renovated scene, trying

To remember the Greek word signifying
A world restored completely: that would include
Hannah Mhór's turkey-chortle of Irish,

The swan at evening over *Loch an Iubhair*,
Clarnico Murray's hard iced caramels
A penny an ounce over Sharkey's counter.

Wraiths

for Ciaran Carson

I *Sidhe*

She took me into the ground, the spade-marked
Clean-cut inside of a dugout
Meant for calves.

Dung on the floor, a damp gleam
And seam of sand like white gold
In the earth wall, nicked fibres in the roof.

We stood under the hill, out of the day
But faced towards the daylight, holding hands,
Inhaling the excavated bank.

Zoom in over our shoulders,
A tunnelling shot that accelerates and flares.
Discover us against weird brightness. Cut.

II *Parking Lot*

We were wraiths in the afternoon.
The bus had stopped. There was neither waiting room
Nor booth nor bench, only a parking lot

Above the town, open as a hillfort,
A panned sky and a light wind blowing.
We were on our way to the Gaeltacht,

Between languages, half in thrall to desire,
Half shy of it, when a flit of the foreknown
Blinked off a sunlit lake near the horizon

And passed into us, climbing and clunking up
Those fretted metal steps, as we reboarded
And were reincarnated seat by seat.

III *White Nights*

Furrow-plodders in spats and bright clasped brogues
Are cradling bags and hoisting beribboned drones
As their skilled neck-pullers' fingers force the chanters

And the whole band starts rehearsing
Its stupendous, swaggering march 5
Inside the hall. Meanwhile

One twilit field and summer hedge away
We wait for the learner who will stay behind
Piping by stops and starts,

Making an injured music for us alone, 10
Early-to-beds, white-night absentees
Open-eared to this day.

Sweeney Out-Takes

for Gregory of Corkus

I *Otterboy*

'Eorann writes with news of our two otters
Courting yesterday morning by the turnhole.
I can see them at their shiny romps

And imagine myself an otterboy
Kneeling where Ronan stands in cleric's vestment, 5
His hand outstretched to turn the bordered page

Of a massbook I hold high for his perusal,
My brow inclined to those big thong-tied feet
Protruding from the alb. Then shake myself

Like a waterdog that bounds out on the bank 10
To drop whatever he's retrieved and gambol
In pelt-sluice and unruly riverbreath.'

II *He Remembers Lynchechaun*

'That three-leggèd, round-bellied, cast-iron pot
Deep in the nettle clump, cobweb-mouthed
And black-frost cold

After its cauldron life of plump and boil,
Reminds me of the cool consideration
Behind the busy warmth

Of Lynchechaun; and its heaviness
When I'd lift it off the crane,
Its lightening once I'd tilt and drain it

I now see as premonitions
Of my seeing through him, the dizziness
As scales fell from my eyes.'

III *The Pattern*

'Full face, foursquare, eyelevel, carved in stone,
An ecclesiastic on the low-set lintel
Vested and unavoidable as the one

I approached head-on the full length of an aisle –
Unready as I was if much rehearsed
In the art of first confession.

What transpired next was meltwater,
A little trickle on the patterned tiles,
Truthfunk and walkaway, but then

In the nick of time, heelturn, comeback
And a clean breast made
Manfully if late. The pattern set.'

Colum Cille Cecinit

I *Is scíth mo chrob ón scríbainn*

My hand is cramped from penwork.
My quill has a tapered point.
Its bird-mouth issues a blue-dark
Beetle-sparkle of ink.

Wisdom keeps welling in streams
From my fine-drawn sallow hand:
Riverrun on the vellum
Of ink from green-skinned holly.

My small runny pen keeps going
Through books, through thick and thin,
To enrich the scholars' holdings –
Penwork that cramps my hand.

    II *Is aire charaim Doire*

Derry I cherish ever.
It is calm, it is clear.
Crowds of white angels on their rounds
At every corner.

    III *Fil súil nglais*

Towards Ireland a grey eye
Will look back but not see
Ever again
The men of Ireland or her women.

        11th–12th century

Hermit Songs

    for Helen Vendler

    Above the ruled quires of my book
    I hear the wild birds jubilant.

    I

With cut-offs of black calico,
Remnants of old blackout blinds
Ironed, tacked with criss-cross threads,
We jacketed the issued books.

Less durable if more desired,
The mealy textured wallpaper:
Its brede of bosomed roses pressed
And flattened under smoothing irons.

Brown parcel paper, if need be.
Newsprint, even. Anything
To make a covert for the newness,
Learn you were a keeper only.

II

Open, settle, smell, begin.
A spelling out, a finger trace:
One with Fursa, Colmcille,
The riddle-solving anchorites –

Macóige of Lismore, for instance,
Who, when asked which attribute
Of character was best, replied
'Steadiness, for it is best

When a man has set his hand to tasks
To persevere. I have never heard
Fault found with that.' Tongue-tried words
Finger-traced, retraced, lip-read.

III

Bread and pencils. Musty satchel.
The age of lessons to be learnt.
Reader, ours were 'reading books'
And we were 'scholars', our good luck

To get such schooling in the first place
For all its second and third handings.
The herdsman by the roadside told you.
The sibyls of the chimney corner.

The age of wonders too, such as:
Rubbings out with balls of bread-pith,
Birds and butterflies in 'transfers'
Like stamps from Eden on a flyleaf.

IV

The master's store an otherwhere:
Penshafts sheathed in black tin – was it? –
A metal wrap, at any rate,
A tight nib-holding cuticle –

And nibs in packets by the gross,
Powdered ink, bunched cedar pencils,

Jotters, exercise books, rulers
Stacked like grave goods on the shelves.

The privilege of being sent
To fetch a box of pristine chalk 10
Or perfect copperplate examples
Of headline script for copying out.

    V

'There are three right ways to spell *tu*.
Can you tell me how you write that down?'
The herdsman asks. And when we can't,
'Ask the master if *he* can.'

Neque, Caesar says, *fas esse* 5
existimant ea litteris
mandare. 'Nor do they think it right
To commit the things they know to writing.'

Not, that is, until there comes
The psalm book called in Irish *cathach*, 10
Meaning 'battler', meaning victory
When borne three times round an army.

    VI

Sparks the Ulster warriors struck
Off wielded swords made Bricriu's hall
Blaze like the sun, according to
The Dun Cow scribe; and then Cuchulain

Entertained the embroidery women 5
By flinging needles in the air
So as they fell the point of one
Partnered with the eye of the next

To form a glittering reeling chain –
As in my dream a gross of nibs 10
Spills off the shelf, airlifts and links
Into a giddy gilt corona.

    VII

A vision of the school the school
Won't understand, nor I, not quite:
My hand in the cold of a running stream
Suspended, a glass beaker dipped

　　　　And filling in the flow. I'm sent,
　　　　The privileged one, for water
　　　　To turn ink powder into ink –
　　　　Out in the open, the land and sky

　　　　And playground silent, a singing class
　　　　I've been excused from going on,
　　　　Coming out through opened windows,
　　　　Yet still and all a world away.

　　　　VIII

　　　　'Inkwell' now as robbed of sense
　　　　As 'inkhorn': a dun cow's, perhaps,
　　　　Stuck upside down at dipping distance
　　　　In the floor of the cell. Hence Colmcille's

　　　　Extempore when a loudmouth lands
　　　　Breaking Iona silence:
　　　　This harbour shouter, it roughly goes,
　　　　Staff in hand, he will come along

　　　　Inclined to kiss the kiss of peace,
　　　　He will blunder in,
　　　　His toe will catch and overturn
　　　　My little inkhorn, spill my ink.

　　　　IX

　　　　A great one has put faith in 'meaning'
　　　　That runs through space like a word
　　　　Screaming and protesting, another in
　　　　'Poet's imaginings

　　　　And memories of love':
　　　　Mine for now I put
　　　　In steady-handedness maintained
　　　　In books against its vanishing.

　　　　Books of Lismore. Kells. Armagh.
　　　　Of Lecan, its great Yellow Book.
　　　　'The battler', berry-browned, enshrined.
　　　　The cured hides. The much tried pens.

'Lick the Pencil'

I

'Lick the pencil' we might have called him
So quick he was to wet the lead, so deft
His hand-to-mouth and tongue-flirt round the stub.

Or 'Drench the cow', so fierce his nostril-grab
And peel-back of her lip, so accurately forced
The bottle-neck between her big bare teeth.

Or 'Catch the horse', for in spite of the low-set
Cut of him, he could always slip an arm
Around the neck and fit winkers on

In a single move. But as much for the surprise
As for the truth of it, 'Lick the pencil'
Is what it's going to be.

II

A 'copying pencil', so called who knows why,
That inked itself and purpled when you licked,
About as short

As the cigarette butts in his pocket
And every bit as tangy, in constant need
Of sharpening, then of testing

On the back of his left hand, the line as bright
As bloodlines holly leaves might score
On the back of a bird-nester's,

Indelible as the glum grey pocks
White dandelion milk
Would mark your skin with as it dried.

III

In memory of him, behold those pigmentations
Moisten and magnify to resemble marks
On Colmcille's monk's habit

The day he died, the day he didn't need
To catch the horse since the horse had come to him
Where he sat beside a path

Because, as the *Vita* says, 'he was weary'.
And the horse 'wept on his breast
So the saint's clothes were made wet.'

10 Then 'Let him, Diarmait, be,' said Colmcille
To his attendant, 'till he has sorrowed for me
And cried his fill.'

'The door was open and the house was dark'

in memory of David Hammond

The door was open and the house was dark
Wherefore I called his name, although I knew
The answer this time would be silence

That kept me standing listening while it grew
5 Backwards and down and out into the street
Where as I'd entered (I remember now)

The streetlamps too were out.
I felt, for the first time there and then, a stranger,
Intruder almost, wanting to take flight

10 Yet well aware that here there was no danger,
Only withdrawal, a not unwelcoming
Emptiness, as in a midnight hangar

On an overgrown airfield in late summer.

In the Attic

I

Like Jim Hawkins aloft in the cross-trees
Of *Hispaniola*, nothing underneath him
But still green water and clean bottom sand,

The ship aground, the canted mast far out
5 Above a sea-floor where striped fish pass in shoals –
And when they've passed, the face of Israel Hands

That rose in the shrouds before Jim shot him dead
Appears to rise again . . . 'But he was dead enough,'
The story says, 'being both shot and drowned.'

II

A birch tree planted twenty years ago
Comes between the Irish Sea and me
At the attic skylight, a man marooned

In his own loft, a boy
Shipshaped in the crow's nest of a life,
Airbrushed to and fro, wind-drunk, braced

By all that's thrumming up from keel to masthead,
Rubbing his eyes to believe them and this most
Buoyant, billowy, topgallant birch.

III

Ghost-footing what was then the *terra firma*
Of hallway linoleum, grandfather now appears,
His voice a-waver like the draught-prone screen

They'd set up in the Club Rooms earlier
For the matinee I've just come back from.
'And Isaac Hands,' he asks, 'Was Isaac in it?'

His memory of the name a-waver too,
His mistake perpetual, once and for all,
Like the single splash when Israel's body fell.

IV

As I age and blank on names,
As my uncertainty on stairs
Is more and more the lightheadedness

Of a cabin boy's first time on the rigging,
As the memorable bottoms out
Into the irretrievable,

It's not that I can't imagine still
That slight untoward rupture and world-tilt
As a wind freshened and the anchor weighed.

A Kite for Aibhín

after 'L'Aquilone' by Giovanni Pascoli (1855–1912)

Air from another life and time and place,
Pale blue heavenly air is supporting
A white wing beating high against the breeze,

And yes, it is a kite! As when one afternoon
All of us there trooped out
Among the briar hedges and stripped thorn,

I take my stand again, halt opposite
Anahorish Hill to scan the blue,
Back in that field to launch our long-tailed comet.

And now it hovers, tugs, veers, dives askew,
Lifts itself, goes with the wind until
It rises to loud cheers from us below.

Rises, and my hand is like a spindle
Unspooling, the kite a thin-stemmed flower
Climbing and carrying, carrying farther, higher

The longing in the breast and planted feet
And gazing face and heart of the kite flier
Until string breaks and – separate, elate –

The kite takes off, itself alone, a windfall.

UNCOLLECTED POEMS (2010–2014)

'Of all those starting out'

Of all those starting out
High-horsed and spirited,
Instepped in their stirrups,

Who will stay young in the end?
Who'll be the merrymen old,   5
Weird sisters, the mockers of mockers?

Be poet enough to survive
Those delusions the king of the world
Presented once to Buddha?

'After the first of desire   10
And the second, terror of death,
That of social obligation.'

Actaeon

High burdened brow, the antlers that astound,
Arms that end now in two hardened feet,
His nifty haunches, pointed ears and fleet
Four-legged run . . . In the pool he saw a crowned
Stag's head and heard something that groaned   5
When he tried to speak. And it was no human sweat
That steamed off him: he was like a beast in heat,
As if he'd prowled and stalked until he found

The grove, the grotto and the bathing place
Of the goddess and her nymphs, as if he'd sought   10
That virgin nook deliberately, as if
His desires were hounds that had quickened pace
On Diana's scent before his own pack wrought
Her vengeance on him, at bay beneath the leaf-

lit woodland. There his branchy antlers caught   15
When he faced the hounds
That couldn't know him as they bayed and fought
And tore out mouthfuls of hide and flesh and blood
From what he was, while his companions stood
Impatient for the kill, assessing wounds.   20

On the Gift of a Fountain Pen

Now that your pen is in my hand
And I have fears
That poems may cease,

What of the years
5   Of every other obligation
Imposed and undertaken?

All that 'Do unto others
As you would have done unto you'?
Mistaken? Virtue?

10 Yes and no. I dip and fill
And start again: doubts
Or no doubts, let flow.

Lauds for Loretta

How can we laud her? Let me count the ways.
Her ready smile, serene attentive gaze,
Her hostess role on both sides of the ocean,
Her work for peace when the land was in commotion.

5   Philanthropy, unstinted, open-handed,
Requests for help from every quarter granted,
Benefactor, with her mighty spouse,
Of galleries, colleges and Ireland House.

The edifice off 1 Fifth Avenue –
10 Fit monument to herself and Lew –
Is like a small translated Clonmacnoise,
An amplifier for the native voice

Of Irish writing, culture, scholarship,
An answer given to the famine ship,
15 A feis, a court of poetry, a seisiún,
Academy and legacy, a boon.

Twenty years ago, a kilted piper,
The Taoiseach, Albert Reynolds, at his heel,
Led a starry crowd across the Square:
20 Jay Oliva, James Galway, Brian Friel,

Loretta, Lew himself, the whole aosdána,
With supporting cast, O'Shea, Cusack, O'Hara.
That April day, a mark was made in time
As we processed in step like words in rhyme,

As dúchas met diaspora and combined   25
Indomitable Irishry of mind
With the Big Apple of Knowledge: thus we set a
Crown upon the labours of Loretta

And great Lew, while Cathleen ni Houlihan
Looked down upon this lass of Allentown   30
And recognized her as an aisling geal,
A presence, guardian spirit, and a pal.

'She is foremost of those that I would hear praised'
Said Yeats of Maud, but for us LBG
Is she to whom all glasses must be raised,   35
So rise up now and toast our honouree.

February 26, 2013

In a Field

And there I was in the middle of a field,
The furrows once called 'scores' still with their gloss,
The tractor with its hoisted plough just gone

Snarling at an unexpected speed
Out on the road. Last of the jobs,   5
The windings had been ploughed, furrows turned

Three ply or four round each of the four sides
Of the breathing land, to mark it off
And out. Within that boundary now

Step the fleshy earth and follow   10
The long healed footprints of one who arrived
From nowhere, unfamiliar and de-mobbed,

In buttoned khaki and buffed army boots,
Bruising the turned-up acres of our back field
To stumble from the windings' magic ring   15

And take me by a hand to lead me back
Through the same old gate into the yard
Where everyone has suddenly appeared,

All standing waiting.

In Time

for Síofra

Energy, balance, outbreak:
Listening to Bach
I saw you years from now
(More years than I'll be allowed)
Your toddler wobbles gone,
A sure and grown woman.

Your bare foot on the floor
Keeps me in step; the power
I first felt come up through
Our cement floor long ago
Palps your sole and heel
And earths you here for real.

An oratorio
Would be just the thing for you:
Energy, balance, outbreak
At play for their own sake
But for now we foot it lightly
In time, and silently.

18 August 2013

The Latecomers

He saw them come, then halt behind the crowd
That wailed and plucked and ringed him, and was glad
They kept their distance. Hedged on every side,

Harried and responsive to their need,
Each hand that stretched, each brief hysteric squeal –
However he assisted and paid heed,

A sudden blank letdown was what he'd feel
Unmanning him when he met the pain of loss
In the eyes of those his reach had failed to bless.

And so he was relieved the newcomers 10
Had now discovered they'd arrived too late
And gone away. Until he hears them, climbers

On the roof, a sound of tiles being shifted,
The treble scrape of terra cotta lifted
And a paralytic on his pallet 15

Lowered like a corpse into a grave.
Exhaustion and the imperatives of love
Vied in him. To judge, instruct, reprove,

And ease them body and soul.
Not to abandon but to lay on hands. 20
Make time. Make whole. Forgive.

Banks of a Canal

Gustave Caillebotte, c.1872

Say 'canal' and there's that final vowel
Towing silence with it, slowing time
To a walking pace, a path, a whitewashed gleam
Of dwellings at the skyline. World stands still.
The stunted concrete mocks the classical. 5
Water says, 'My place here is in dream,
In quiet good standing. Like a sleeping stream,
Come rain or sullen shine I'm peaceable.'
Stretched to the horizon, placid ploughland,
The sky not truly bright or overcast: 10
I know that clay, the damp and dirt of it,
The coolth along the bank, the grassy zest
Of verges, the path not narrow but still straight
Where soul could mind itself or stray beyond.

COMMENTARY

UNCOLLECTED POEMS (1959–1966)

Before *Death of a Naturalist* (1966) and its predecessor publication *Eleven Poems* (1965), SH had brought into print more than fifty poems in journals and newspapers. The publications extended from two magazines published at Queen's University in 1959–60, *Q* and *Gorgon* (to which he submitted poems under the self-questioning pen-name 'Incertus'), to printings in the *Belfast Telegraph*, the *Irish Times* and the *Times Literary Supplement* (1962–5). In the earliest poems the influence of his predecessors is noticeable: Gerard Manley Hopkins, as SH observed himself, in 'October Thought' and 'Nostalgia in the Afternoon'; Dylan Thomas in 'Song of my Man-Alive'; R. S. Thomas and Patrick Kavanagh in the MacKenna poems. But also evident is a more distinctive voice on rural subjects, with features that anticipate what came to be seen as his own manner: poems like 'Tractors', 'Fisher' and 'Lint Water'. The descriptive and evocative clarity admired in *Death of a Naturalist* is only occasionally evident here, while the inconsistent use of personal experience can risk banality ('Taking Stock') or simplistic reminiscence ('Going In'). There is some variety in prosodic assurance too, between the skill of 'On Hogarth's Engraving' and the lexical instability of 'Poor Man's Death'. The group has the marks of apprentice work, with some signs of the clear-eyed confidence that will emerge consistently in *Death of a Naturalist*. The process of working through Advancements of Learning, the typescript SH submitted to Liam Miller at the Dolmen Press in 1964 (Appendix II), to the more sustained focus in *Death of a Naturalist* and *Door into the Dark* (1969) can be partially traced through these probationer years.

Reaping in Heat

Published in *Q* (Michaelmas 1959): 27, under the pseudonym 'Incertus'.

8 The mower] the mower *Q* (error)
16 And deeper] and deeper *Q* (error)
17 sycamore's] sycamores *Q* (error)

1–5 See 'a South Derry rhyme / With *hushed* and *lulled* full chimes for *pushed* and *pulled*' (*North*, 67; *PSH*, 204).

October Thought

First published in *Q* (Michaelmas 1959): 27, under the pseudonym 'Incertus'; subsequently in Jon Stallworthy (ed.), *First Lines: Poems Written in Youth, from Herbert to Heaney* (Manchester: Carcanet, 1987).

[text: *Q*]

2 shoots] breaks *First Lines*
3 cobwebs, like] cobwebs like *First Lines*
6 Haystalks straw-broken] Haystalks, straw-broken *First Lines*
8 The iron-bound] the iron-bound *Q* (error)
8^9] [stanza break] *First Lines*
10 heaven-hue plum-blue] heaven-hue, plum-blue *First Lines*   gorse pricked] gorse-pricked *First Lines*
11 through] under *First Lines*
12 bells, well] bells well *First Lines*

SH mentions Hopkins among the 'masters' who influenced his earliest poems, and that poetic influence is marked here, in compounds, alliteration and assonance. The influence of Keats (of whom SH tells Dennis O'Driscoll he had learned 'a whole lot of' by heart: *SS*, 404) is strong also. In a late letter, SH says the earliest poem he would like to see in Marco Sonzogni's anthology of Italian translations, *Poesie Scelte*, is '"October Thought" . . . Then perhaps "McKenna's [*sic*] Saturday Night"' (*LSH*, 799).

6 *Haystalks straw-broken*: a curious linking since hay and straw are different things (as SH would certainly have known). The Hopkins-derived compounds are particularly marked in this poem, as SH acknowledged in a later Note prepared for *First Lines*:

> Laurence Lerner, who was a lecturer at Queens University, Belfast, during my time there as an undergraduate, commended the phrase 'gorse-pricked with gold' when 'October Thought' appeared in a student magazine in, I think, 1959. It was published under the pseudonym 'Incertus' and while this first brush with a critical audience did not altogether confer certitude upon me, it did suggest that words I wrote might be capable of transmitting a live signal. Yet the words were more Hopkins' than mine; and yet again, while they were overdone and pastiche, they opened a seam of phonetic ore that kept tempting me to come back and try again. This was among the first four or five attempts I made at writing verse and is, I suppose, the 'best' of them. (NLI 49,493/79)

Nostalgia in the Afternoon

Published in *Gorgon*, 3 (Nov. 1959): 17 with erratic indentation, under the pseudonym 'Incertus'.

20 scoop] scoope *Gorgon* (error)

Like 'October Thought', the influence of Hopkins is very marked, especially from 'Hurrahing in Harvest'.

Aran

Published in *Gorgon*, 4 (Feb. 1960): 7, under the name Seamus J. Heaney.

The Heaneys visited the Aran Islands off the west coast of Ireland in the early 1960s. There are two Aran-based poems in *Death of a Naturalist*, 'Lovers on Aran' (*DN*, 47; *PSH*, 42) and 'Synge on Aran' (*DN*, 52; *PSH*, 45). In this poem the description of the hardships of Aran life recalls J. M. Synge's *Riders to the Sea* (1904).

Lines to Myself

Published in *Gorgon*, 5 (Dec. 1960): n.p., under the misspelt name Sheamus Heaney; reprinted in *Washington Post* (2 Jan. 1996): C10.

[text: *Gorgon*]

6 violence,] violence. *Washington Post* (error)

Song of My Man-Alive

Published in *Gorgon*, 6 (Hilary Term 1961): 19 with erratic indentation and capitalisation, under the pseudonym 'Incertus'.

The influential master here is Dylan Thomas rather than Hopkins. Thomas is the subject of 'Dylan the Durable? On Dylan Thomas', a lecture SH delivered on 21 November 1991 during his term as Oxford Professor of Poetry, later collected in *RP* (124–45).

Her Home

Published in *Gorgon* (Michaelmas Term 1961): 18, under the pseudonym 'Incertus'.

6 Sunday] Sunday, *Gorgon* (error)
8 notice] notice. *Gorgon* (error)

Tractors

First published in the *Belfast Telegraph* (24 Nov. 1962): 5, under the name Seamus J. Heaney.

Scotch Fir in City Cemetery

Published in *Interest*, 3. 4 (Jan. 1963): 13.

Going In

Published in *Interest*, 3. 4 (Jan. 1963): 13.

Essences

Published in *Interest*, 3. 6 (May 1963): 16.

Welfare State

Published in *Interest*, 3. 6 (May 1963): 16.

Poor Man's Death

Published in the *Dubliner*, 2. 2 (Summer 1963): 54.

MacKenna's Saturday Night

Published in the *Kilkenny Magazine*, 10 (Autumn/Winter 1963): 17.

Fair

Published in Tom Lowenstein (ed.), *Universities' Poetry Five* (London: Managing Committee of Universities' Poetry, 1963), 7.

The 'ancestral photographs' of the third stanza anticipate 'Ancestral Photograph' in *DN* (*DN*, 26; *PSH*, 31).

Fisher

First published in the *Irish Times* (8 Feb. 1964): 11, under the name James Heaney; subsequently in *Interest*, 4. 3 (May 1964): 10 and *PM*.

[text: *Irish Times*]

6 He watched happily] Each day he gloated *Interest*
7 of the river-bed;] of riverbed *Interest* | of river-bed *PM*
12 hold it cold in his thrilled hand] hold it in his thrilled hand *PM*
15 angling is more] fishing was more *PM*
16] Than good luck, and skill more than fun: *Interest* | Than good luck and skill more than fun *PM*
19–20] I think of him much now, who am / Snatching once more at life that has lain *Interest* | I think of him much now who am / Angling for life that has lain *PM*
22 I cast a line baited with metre] I cast a line, baited with metre, *Interest*
23 scatter.] scatter – *Interest*
24 verse, dead] verse dead *PM*

The first poem in which SH makes a thematic link between writing poetry (*l.* 22) and other activities. Cf. 'A Daylight Art' (*HL*, 10; *PSH*, 361): 'practising the right one from the start – / poetry, say, or fishing' (*ll.* 19–20).

The Indomitable Irishry

Published in *Poetry Ireland*, 3 (Spring 1964): 104.

Title Yeats, 'Under Ben Bulben': 'That we in coming days may be / Still the indomitable Irishry' (section v, *ll.* 14–5; Albright 1990, 375). But Yeats is thinking of the Irish upper orders, not the London-based stage-Irish students here.
   5 *The Proclamation*: of 'The Provisional Government of the Irish Republic' in 1916.

Easter Son

Published in *English* (Spring 1964): 15.

Such Men Are Dangerous

Published in *Interest*, 4. 3 (May 1964): 9.

Title Said of Cassius in Shakespeare's *Julius Caesar*: 'Yond Cassius has a lean and hungry look, / He thinks too much; such men are dangerous' (1.2.194–5).
   13–14 *inscaped*: a term devised by Hopkins, not exactly 'a school of thought'.

Writer and Teacher

First published in *Interest* (Nov. 1964): 16; subsequently in the *Irish Times* (20 Feb. 1965): 8.

[text: *Interest*]

3 market-place] market place *Irish Times*
8–9 bone- / heads] bone- / Heads *Irish Times*
13 tale] story *Irish Times*
14–15 drive towards the gale / Of living – once his] imperceptibly / Grow into men. The *Irish Times*
17 review:] review. *Irish Times*

Based on SH's job as teacher in St Thomas's Secondary Intermediate School in Ballymurphy, Belfast, in 1962. The first of a number of works which show the influence of his work as a teacher, which he sustained in various forms until his resignation from Harvard in 1996.

Young Bachelor

Published in *Interest* (Nov. 1964): 16.

Soliloquy for an Old Resident

First published in *Interest* (Nov. 1964): 17; subsequently in P. L. Brent (ed.), *Young Commonwealth Poets '65* (London: Heinemann, 1965), 136–8.

[text: *Interest*]

Taking Stock

Published in the *Kilkenny Magazine*, 12–13 (Spring 1965): 42–3.

Dated 5 April 1964 in MS (NLI 49,493/1).
   9–10 Cf. Yeats, *Responsibilities* (1914), 'Although I have come close on forty-nine, / I have no child, I have nothing but a book' in an introductory poem beginning 'Pardon, old fathers' (Albright 1990, 148).

On Hogarth's Engraving 'Pit Ticket for the Royal Sport'

Published in the *Irish Times* (10 April 1965): 8.

Title The original engraving by the satirist William Hogarth (1697–1764) is called *Pit Ticket: The Cockpit* and dated 1822. It features several of the figures and details apparent in SH's poem: drunkards betting on the cock fight or taking snuff, while the blind noble arbitrates. The term 'Royal Sport' was introduced with colour-tinted copies of Hogarth's engraving from the eighteenth century onwards. This is the first of many poems by SH which responds to a work of visual art.

Saint Patrick's Stone

First published in *Outposts*, 65 (Summer 1965): 3; subsequently in Wolfgang Görtschacher, James Hogg and Ronald John (eds), *Salute to 'Outposts' on Its Fiftieth Anniversary* (Salzburg: University of Salzburg, 1994), 123.

[text: *Outposts*]

Peter Street at Bankside

First published in the programme for the laying of the Foundation Stone of the Lyric Players Theatre, Belfast (12 June 1965), and reprinted in *EP* and in Mary O'Malley and John Boyd (eds), *A Needle's Eye* (Belfast: Lyric Players Theatre, 1979), 45.

[text: Lyric Players Theatre]

epigraph December, 1598,] December 1598, *EP*   Theatre, and] Theatre and *EP*
   Theatre.] theatre. *EP*   woods] wood *Lyric Players Theatre* (error)
3 water:] water. *EP* | water; *Needle's Eye*
10 crew,] crew *EP*
18 players] player *EP*

Lint Water

Published in the *Times Literary Supplement* (5 Aug. 1965): 681.

12 graip] grape *TLS* (error)

Gate

Published in the *Dublin Magazine*, 5. 1 (Spring 1966): 38.

Dated 1 February 1966 in MS (NLI 49,493/5).

For a Young Nun

Published in *Tomorrow* (March 1966): 7.

DEATH OF A NATURALIST (1966)

Death of a Naturalist was published in hardback in London by Faber & Faber on 19 May 1966, and in New York by Oxford University Press on 3 June 1966; it took its title from a poem that had first appeared as 'End of a Naturalist' in *Poetry Ireland* in the spring of 1965. While the publisher's archives do not record the initial print run, the sale of 1,000 bound copies to Oxford University Press, late in the production process in April 1966, forced Faber into a pre-publication reprint to accommodate the American order (a 'confounded nuisance', according to production archives), to which the London office added 500 copies reserved for itself as 'a reasonable gamble'.* Oxford University Press would be the publisher of SH's American volumes up to *North*. By May 1968, the edition had, according to a Belfast journal at the time, 'already sold well over 2,000 copies locally' (*Square Times*, May 1968: 15). The volume first appeared in Faber's Paper Covered Editions in 1969, and sold sufficiently in that format to generate reprints of 6,000 copies in paperback in both 1972 and 1976, which were followed by seven further reprints before the book was reset with the author's amendments in 1991, the only time that SH would retrospectively amend a collection as a whole. The 1991 amended edition became the standard for subsequent printings, and was the basis for the hardback's fiftieth anniversary edition, published by Faber in 2016, from which this edition draws its text.

When Charles Monteith, the poetry editor at Faber, read three poems by SH published in the *New Statesman* by the magazine's literary editor Karl Miller in December 1964, he asked the poet to submit a manuscript (a request which SH said was 'like getting a letter from God the Father'; Corcoran 1986, 23). SH shared with Monteith a version of a manuscript that he had in circulation, aware that it might underwhelm Faber in its present form. 'I sent them what I had and they didn't think there was a book there but they would like first refusal if ever I thought I had a book,' he later reported. 'So in about four months I wrote a hell of a lot, and I think I sent them another thing in about May or June' (Corcoran 1986, 23–4). The volume had a substantial prehistory: a pamphlet called *Eleven Poems* had been published as one of a series by Belfast Festival Publications on 2 November 1965, along

---

* Oxford University Press, New York, were offered the book in February 1966, after it had been turned down for publication by Alfred Knopf and by SH's long-standing future publisher Farrar, Straus and Giroux, who wrote, 'Though we all like them, we doubt in the end we can put them over successfully right now' (FF P/Rdlm/547/4). The OUP order arrived at the same moment as Faber's bound copies, meaning that new sheets had to be both printed and bound.

with editions of twelve and ten poems by Derek Mahon and Michael Longley respectively. Ten of the eleven poems that fulfilled SH's edition would be published in *Death of a Naturalist*. Moreover, SH had already, late in 1964, submitted to Liam Miller at Dolmen Press a manuscript entitled Advancements of Learning which was returned by Dolmen at the author's request with the approach from Faber.* The Dolmen manuscript is in three sections: 'Home Territory', 'MacKenna Country' and 'Portraits and Landscapes', and it lacks several of the most celebrated poems of *Death of a Naturalist*, such as 'Follower', 'Blackberry-Picking', 'The Diviner' and 'Personal Helicon'.

With its composition in August 1964, 'Digging' would become the first poem in all the collections in which it featured. 'Where else could it be placed? It decided its position for itself,' SH said to O'Driscoll (*SS*, 82). Despite SH's insistence that he wrote 'a hell of a lot' in the four months between his submitting to Faber and their offer of publication, the contents of the volume nevertheless cover quite a range in time. 'Turkeys Observed', published in the *Belfast Telegraph* on 15 December 1962, was the earliest written of the collection's poems; the last was 'The Diviner', first published by the Poetry Book Society at Christmas 1965. Even so, the 'hell of a lot' include many of the most celebrated poems in the book, which served to replace the central section of the Advancements of Learning poems with its comparatively derivative 'MacKenna' poems.

That SH's conception of *Death of a Naturalist*, as well as its size and contents, changed in the brief time between its acceptance by Faber in June 1965 and its publication in May 1966 can be seen from the opening group of Uncollected Poems included here, 1959–66. Rand Brandes tells us that 'Fisher', later published in *Poems and a Memoir* (1982), was the last poem in Advancements of Learning (Brandes 2009, 21). None of the seven poems of 'MacKenna Country', the middle section of Advancements of Learning, are printed in *Death of a Naturalist* or anywhere else, until their collection in this edition. They are, SH tells O'Driscoll, derivative from R. S. Thomas's Iago Prytherch and Patrick Kavanagh's Paddy Maguire in *The Great Hunger* (*SS*, 81).

---

* In a later reflection on the episode, SH commented that 'Liam Miller sent the manuscript back to me and said they weren't quite sure' (Corcoran 1986, 23). Later still, he clarified that he had worried at the 'protocol' of having poems under consideration of two presses simultaneously, and that the 'two and a half, or three' months that the collection had been with Miller constituted a reasonable period for decision-making: SH wrote to Dolmen accordingly, that 'if they had not decided to accept the book, then I'd like to have it back' (*SS*, 80–1). The subsequent emergence of Liam Miller's accompanying letter of 5 February 1965 indicated the hope on his part of resubmission: 'I return your manuscript herewith and will be very glad to hear from you at a later date. If you are in Dublin some time perhaps you would like to telephone me and we might meet' (*Irish Times*, 18 May 2017). Instead, the collection was accepted by Faber in the early summer of 1965.

Death of a Naturalist was received from the first, both in England and Ireland, with great acclaim. Christopher Ricks praised it highly in the *New Statesman*, while Michael Longley said the book's 'childhood landscape has acquired the validity of myth' (*Irish Times*, 24 May 1966), an observation that was prophetic of the themes and concerns of SH's subsequent books. John Carey, who had already admired *Eleven Poems*, lavished praise on the new book too. It had extraordinarily widespread public recognition, winning the Geoffrey Faber Prize, the Somerset Maugham Award, a Cholmondeley Award and the Eric Gregory Award for Young Writers. Mostly the book was praised for the fidelity with which it evoked the life and setting of SH's rural background in Co. Derry.

Despite its critical and publishing success, *Death of a Naturalist* was relatively lightly drawn on in SH's own selections from his work, and we are left wondering on what grounds he dropped seven pieces from the collection for *Poems 1965–1975* (FSG, 1979), a volume published as an introduction to SH for American readers. Some of those omitted poems, such as 'Storm on the Island' and 'Synge on Aran', seem impressive in the SH manner. His declaration in *Stepping Stones* that he 'would never interfere with the contents of the volume per se – the volume, I mean, reprinted under its own title' (*SS*, 86), is not of course contradicted by this change. We know from *Stepping Stones* that the omission of these seven poems was SH's own initiative: 'I dropped seven of the poems' (*SS*, 86). He does not give the grounds for that judgement but says that 'the *Naturalist* had been out for fourteen years at that stage and I felt free to exercise my judgement'.

Many of the poems in *Death of a Naturalist* achieved their fame straight away and maintained it through the growing admiration for SH's work. But it might be borne in mind that he selected fewer poems from the volume than from the other volumes, from *Door into the Dark* onwards. This means that, as with all the volumes, there are impressive poems to be recuperated in this collected volume. Examples are two powerfully evocative poems, 'Ancestral Photograph' and 'Trout'; 'An Advancement of Learning' is an example of a later disprized poem that *PSH* brings back into view. (Later, SH tells O'Driscoll that the only changes he could remember making in proof to *Death of a Naturalist* – which went to the typesetter for production on 18 August 1965 (FF P/Rdlm/547/4) – were to 'the last three or four stanzas of "An Advancement of Learning"' (*SS*, 83).) The description of an encounter with a rat at which the narrator's 'throat sickened' fits well into the concerns of the whole volume: with the much-anthologised title poem for example. It might be felt that its reinforcement of the volume's theme makes it an important recovery now. In his introduction to *Poems and a Memoir*, Thomas Flanagan says that SH's work from *Death of a Naturalist* on 'has balanced a twinned fascination, with the natural world and with the man-created world of language' (*PM*, x), linking the two fascinations to Antaeus and Hercules respectively; the poem 'Hercules and Antaeus' was published in *North* in 1975, as was the poem 'Antaeus' which is back-dated to 1966 in the text here. One might add to these twin interests a recurrent imagery of violence, particularly in the context of guns, establishing from the start a theme in the book which has death in its final title. It is there from the second line of 'Digging', to 'Dawn Shoot', to the first line of 'Trout' as 'a fat gun-barrel', and on to the 'grenade' of 'In Small Townlands'.

By contrast with parts of the Dolmen manuscript, Advancements of Learning, *Death of a Naturalist* is already an achieved indicator of what SH's distinctive subjects and strengths are. Other characteristics of the early work can be seen in 'Digging', for example the contrast between hard and soft materials – the 'clean rasping sound' of the spade digging through gravel, and the spade's 'bright edge', as against the milk-bottle 'corked sloppily with paper' and 'the squelch and slap / of soggy peat'. The preference for the potatoes' 'cool hardness' anticipates later aesthetic preferences, as does the verb 'love' to describe that preference. Already local usage is drawn on with the word 'tops', as is the specialist farming terminology with words like the 'lug' and 'shaft' of the spade. There is local topographical reference too, to 'Toner's bog' and the colloquialism 'the old man'. The significance of memory is already established by the way the present view of the poet's ageing father, Patrick Heaney, digging in the garden recalls his digging the larger-scale potato drills twenty years before, and his father's father cutting turf a generation before (SH tells us later that this archetypal turf-cutter was in fact his father's uncle). There is even a suggestion of the underground theme which will become central in the poetry from *North* to *District and Circle* in 'going down and down / For the good turf'. What Longley meant by 'the validity of myth' in 'the childhood landscape' is evident.

These local and mythic themes in 'Digging' feature prominently in other poems in *Death of a Naturalist* as the first commentators all noted: the frogs and flax-dams of the title poem, the 'two-lugged sacks' of 'The Barn', and the poems of obsolescent agricultural activity like 'Churning Day' and 'At a Potato Digging'. The drowning of unwanted kittens in 'The Early Purges' was deplored by the Conservative politician Eldon Griffiths, according to an anonymous letter in the *Daily Telegraph*, bringing SH to early public notice. But there is also a marked movement towards familial and personal matters, which remain a prominent poetic subject throughout his career. 'Follower' returns to the poet's father, the subject of 'Digging' and of the uncollected poem 'Boy Driving His Father to Confession'; 'Ancestral Photograph' again takes his father back to an earlier generation. 'Mid-Term Break', describing the death of the poet's four-year-old brother Christopher, attracted wide notice and sympathy. The poems draw on such personal subjects, especially on his early marital experience, in a way that retains central importance throughout his writing life, culminating in the great parental and marital poems of *Human Chain*. And Irish history, which will have a marked presence in *Wintering Out* and *North*, is anticipated in 'At a Potato Digging' and 'For the Commander of the Eliza' with their recall of the Famine. Already in *Death of a Naturalist*, SH has made what Coleridge called 'a bid to influence the climate of taste in which his poems will be read'.

[text: DN2016]

Digging

First published in the *New Statesman* (4 Dec. 1964): 880. Collected with revisions in *DN*. Subsequently published in Andrew Carpenter (ed.), *Eight Irish Writers* (Paris: Adrien Maeght, 1981); also in *Gravities*, *SP*, *PM*, *NSP1990*, *OG*, *100P*.

3 Under] Beneath *New Statesman*
3 clean] rich *New Statesman*
4 sinks into] sinks clean into *New Statesman*
11 inside knee] inside-knee *New Statesman*
13 picked,] picked *New Statesman*, *DN1966*, *NSP1990*, *100P*
15 spade.] spade; *New Statesman*
17 turf] peat *New Statesman*

Written in August 1964, SH says that from the first he recognised 'Digging' as 'a strength-giver' (*SS*, 82). It was not SH's first significant poetry publication; but of its opening place in all the volumes it occurs in – that is, in *DN* and all the selected volumes throughout his career (it was omitted only from *Eleven Poems*) – he says to Dennis O'Driscoll 'where else could it be placed'? (*SS*, 82) The poem launches several recurrent SH themes: relations with his father (as in 'Follower', 'Making Strange', and 'Boy Driving His Father to Confession'); comparison between agricultural work and writing, still prominent in the first of the 'Glanmore Sonnets' in *Field Work* which provided the title for his major selected volume in 1998: 'Vowels ploughed into other: opened ground' (*FW*, 28; *PSH*, 231); exploration of what is underground: here 'going down and down / For the good turf (*ll.* 23–4), later associated with violence in the bog poems. As often in SH, there is an unexpressed subtext: 'the pen is mightier than the sword' which lies behind the poem's concluding declaration of vocation: 'I'll dig with it' (the sense of which requires a stress on 'it' that occurs in some Northern Irish accents).

2 *snug as a gun*: the first occurrence of martial imagery.

6 *rump*: belongs to a local, or reductive register, like 'old man' for father in *ll*. 15 and 16.

12 *tops*: the top green parts of the potato plant.

18 *Toner's bog*: the place name is particularised in the same way as country customs, like the bottle of milk corked sloppily with twisted paper. Toner's Bog (where turf is cut for fuel) was, Eugene Kielt has confirmed in correspondence with the editors, a bank in the larger Moneystaghan Bog, where SH's father's family had cutting (or turbary) rights. It lies north-west of The Wood, the farm bequeathed to SH's father by his uncle Hugh Scullion, to which the Heaney family moved in 1954. So the 'grandfather' here was in fact SH's great-uncle (*SS*, 25). Cf. the 'big-voiced Scullions' in *Beowulf* (Faber, xxvi; Norton, xxxvi).

Death of a Naturalist

First published under the title 'End of a Naturalist' in *Poetry Ireland* (Spring 1965): 8–9. Collected with revisions as 'Death of a Naturalist' in *EP* and *DN*, and subsequently published in *FP*, *SP*, *PM*, *Seamus Heaney: Readings in Contemporary Poetry* (New York: Dia Art Foundation, 1988), *NSP1990*, *OG* and *100P*. Much recorded in audio by SH.

2 heavy headed] heavy-headed *Poetry Ireland, OG*
3 weighted down by] weighted down *Poetry Ireland*
7 dragon-flies] dragonflies *OG*
10 spring,] spring *DN1966, SP NSP1990, OG*
16 bullfrog,] bullfrog *Poetry Ireland, EP, DN1966, SP, NSP1990, OG*
17 croaked,] croaked *Poetry Ireland, EP, DN1966, SP, NSP1990, OG*
23 grass,] grass *EP, DN1966, SP, NSP1990*
27 dam,] dam *EP, DN1966, SP, NSP1990, OG*
30 Poised like] Poised-like *Poetry Ireland*
31 and ran. The] and ran – the *Poetry Ireland*
32 vengeance,] vengeance *Poetry Ireland, EP, DN1966, SP, NSP1990, OG*

The poem is a classic instance of what was praised by the reviewers as SH's 'power and precision' (Christopher Ricks in the *New Statesman*) and 'accuracy and freshness' (Richard Kell in the *Guardian*). The terminology of the linen industry – the rotted flax, 'weighted down by huge sods' – occurs in other early poems, such as the uncollected 'Lint Water'. The child's dark view of the natural world is indicated by the change of title from the 'end' to the 'death' of the naturalist, culminating with the horror of the 'gross-bellied frogs . . . the great slime kings' of the poem.

2 *townland*: standard, though somewhat inexact, unit of division in the Irish countryside since the Middle Ages (*baile fearann* in Irish). Given prominence in poetry by Yeats's early poem 'The Happy Townland'. See 'In Small Townlands' below.

15 *Miss Walls*: the first use of a real name for which SH has a penchant, recognised in the poem 'The Real Names' in *Electric Light* (2001) and in *SS*, 242. The detail of the child's learning process parallels the learning of literacy in 'Alphabets' in *The Haw Lantern* (1987).

The Barn

First published in *Vogue* (1 Sept. 1965): 134. Collected with revisions in *DN*, and subsequently published in *FP*, *SP* and *OG*.

1 Threshed] Clean *Vogue*
2 sacks.] sacks; *Vogue*
10 clean] bright *Vogue*
13 yard –] yard. *DN1966*, *SP*
17 gulfed] yawned *Vogue*
18 shot] swept *Vogue*

3 *armoury*: a martial term.

11–12 The major theme of the early parts of this anti-pastoral volume is the invasion of an idyllic world of bright objects by darker, more sinister things – *cobwebs clogging up your lungs*. The poem ends comparing the sacks of corn to *great blind rats*, a figure of horror like the frogs at the end of the previous poem.

14–15 *when bats were on the wing /Over the rafters of sleep*: echo of Yeats's 'Song of Wandering Aengus' 'when white moths were on the wing', and of the influence of Dylan Thomas in poems like 'Fern Hill' which SH identified in his own early poetry.

An Advancement of Learning

First published in the *Irish Times* (9 March 1963): 8. Collected with considerable revisions in *DN*, but not in any Faber selected.

3 past,] past *Irish Times*
9 curtly] dirtily *Irish Times*
12 quickly] thickly *Irish Times*
16 Arcs on the stones.] Orbit. *Irish Times*
20 hitherto snubbed] ever-disgusting *Irish Times*
25–36] I reflected: 'Why turn sick?
    He is a perfect creature –
    Theologically preferable
    To you, stuck with your fallen nature.

>   Plague-bearer, who cold-clawed my thought
>   Across dark childhood ceiling-boards,
>   Henceforth skip on grace-full legs
>   Amid grey apocalyptic hordes.' *Irish Times*

Title The poem's title was the last to arrive of all those for *DN*, and too late for the first proof, where it appeared on the contents page as '? ? ? ? ?' and as '(TITLE UNKNOWN)' on the poem page itself; a publisher's memo of 10 August 1965 records: 'He said he also wanted to make some alterations to "An Advancement of Learning" and – as I can't find this poem anywhere – I think he must have taken it away with him!' (FF E/18/45/1).

It is striking that the attempt in the *Irish Times* version to overcome philosophically the revulsion aroused by the rat is discarded in the final version, in keeping with the theme of the volume, enabling the poem to end unconsoled with 'terror' as the rat 'cold, wet-furred, small-clawed, / Retreated up a pipe for sewage'.

Blackberry-Picking

First published in the *New Statesman* (30 July 1965): 156, subsequently in *Critical Quarterly Poetry Supplement*, 7 (1966): 8. Collected with revisions in *DN*, and subsequently published in *SP*, *PM*, *NSP1990*, *OG* and *100P*.

8 inked up,] inked up *New Statesman*, *Critical Quarterly*, *DN1966*, *SP*, *NSP1990*, *OG*, *100P*
9 milk-cans, pea-tins, jam-pots] milk cans, pea tins, jam pots *OG*, *100P*   jam-pots] jampots *New Statesman*
10 our] out (error) *New Statesman*
11 potato-drills,] potato drills *OG*, *100P*
14 green ones,] green ones *New Statesman*
16 thorn pricks] thorn-pricks *New Statesman*
17 byre.] byre *OG*
20 bush,] bush *New Statesman*, *Critical Quarterly*, *DN1966*, *SP*, *NSP1990*, *OG*, *100P*

Although it ends less wholly traumatically than the preceding poems with their threatening frogs and rats, its 'rat-grey fungus' keeps it in the world of childhood horror, with the extraordinary comparison of the blackberries to 'a plate of eyes', evoking Bluebeard's castle.

Churning Day

First published in *Critical Quarterly Poetry Supplement*, 7 (1966): 8–9: *New Poems 1966*. Collected in *DN*, and subsequently published in *SP*, *PM* and *OG*.

4 udder,] udder *Critical Quarterly*, *DN1966*, *SP*

12 whisky muddler] whiskey-muddler *OG*
16^17] [stanza break] *DN1991* (error)
17^18 [stanza break]] [omitted] *DN1991* (error)
23 churned up] churned-up *OG*

Although it ends with the stink of 'sour-breathed milk', making the house 'acrid as a sulphur mine', 'Churning Day' is the first of the farm poems that describes activity and implements in a neutral way, in the course of a collaborative family enterprise. There is even a magical suggestion of alchemy in *ll.* 18–19 when 'gold flecks / began to dance'. As well as the accuracy and precision of observation, some features of SH's style are beginning to be identifiable.

1 *coarse-grained*: SH famously called 'Digging' a 'big, coarse-grained navvy of a poem' ('Feeling into Words', *Preoccupations*, 43).
3 *pottery bombs*: sustains the theme of armaments.
9 *flagged*: standard Irish term for stone floor.
24 *coagulated sunlight*: recalls the 'thickened wine' of 'Blackberry-Picking' (*l.* 6).

The Early Purges

First published in the *Kilkenny Magazine* (Spring 1965): 42, subsequently in the *Northern Review*, 1. 2 (1965): 7–8, and collected in *DN*.

17 drown,] drown *Kilkenny Magazine, Northern Review, DN1966*
18 shrug,] shrug. *Kilkenny Magazine*

The poem, which continues the anti-pastoral childhood theme, attained some notoriety when the Conservative politician Eldon Griffiths called it 'sick' in the House of Commons, according to an anonymous *Daily Telegraph* letter of 20 July 1976, which ascribes it to 'Sean Heany'.

2 *Dan Taggart*: real name Jimmy Taggart. SH was less ready to use 'real names' in his early poems than he was later. No doubt the local usage 'scraggy wee shits' was a factor in prompting Griffiths's outrage.

Follower

First published in *EP*, and then the *New Statesman* (3 Dec. 1965): 888; also published in *Threshold*, 21 (Summer 1967): [31]. Collected with minor revisions in *DN, Gravities, SP, PM, NSP1990* and *OG*.

8 headrig] head-rig *EP*
10 hob-nailed] hobnailed *100P*
15 back,] back *EP, New Statesman, DN1966, SP, NSP1990, OG, 100P*
18 arm.] arm: *EP*
24 me,] me *EP*

'Follower' is one of SH's best-known poems, on one of his dominant themes: his relationship with his father, dwelt on in many other poems throughout his career such as 'Boy Driving His Father to Confession' (*PSH*, 54), 'Making Strange' (*SI*, 32; *PSH*, 302), 'The Stone Verdict' (*HL*, 19; *PSH*, 366), 'Album' (*PSH*, 643) and 'Lick the Pencil' (*PSH*, 679). The culmination of the theme is the translation *Aeneid Book VI*, published posthumously in 2016, acknowledging the idea of a posthumous encounter with a dead father, like that of Aeneas with Anchises, which SH said was a major motivation towards the translation.

1 *worked*: SH says the verb was originally the local term 'wrought' (as used by his father-in-law) and that the substitution of the standard term 'worked' deprived the poem of its 'one touch of individuality' (see 'John Clare's Prog', *RP*, 63; *FK*, 275; first delivered as a lecture during SH's term as Oxford Professor of Poetry, 20 October 1992). But of course outside the locality the term 'wrought' would have inappropriate overtones of poetic diction.

1, 3 etc. The rhyming of monosyllables with the unstressed part of a disyllable ('plough', 'furrow'; 'wing', 'breaking'; 'plough', 'follow') is a favoured practice among Irish poets writing in English, including Austin Clarke and Paul Muldoon. The poem's rhyming system is notable for the half-rhymes that are widely used by SH: 'sock', 'pluck', 'wake', 'back'.

23–4 The metaphorical idea that the father cannot be banished from the poet's mind – 'and will not go away' – is a strong statement of the theme of the father–son relationship.

Ancestral Photograph

First published in *Vogue* (1 Sept. 1965): 134. Collected with revisions in *DN*.

10 faded] whitened *Vogue*
16–7 cattlemen / Who] cattlemen. / They *Vogue*
17 handled rumps, groped teats,] handled teats, felt rumps *Vogue*
20 Heckled] Hackled *Vogue*
26–7 shopped / Like housewives] shopped, / Like housewives, *Vogue*
29–30 Closing this chapter of our chronicle, / I take your uncle's portrait to the attic.] A long chase ends here and I sense a kill / Taking your uncle's portrait to the attic *Vogue*

The subject of the poem is SH's father's maternal uncle, Hugh Scullion, who left Patrick Heaney his farm in The Wood near Bellaghy. 'To me he was always the ur-ancestor on the Heaney side of the family,' SH tells O'Driscoll (*SS*, 25).

29 *Closing this chapter of our chronicle*: declaring the autobiographical nature of the farming poems in *Death of a Naturalist*.

Mid-Term Break

First published in *Kilkenny Magazine* (Spring 1963): 25, and subsequently in the *Listener* (29 July 1965): 158. Collected with minor revisions in *EP*, *DN*, *SP*, *NSP1990*, *OG* and *100P*.

1 sick bay] sick-bay *Kilkenny Magazine*
1 bay,] bay *Listener*, *EP*, *DN1966*, *SP*, *NSP1990*, *OG*, *100P*
10 'sorry for my trouble'] sorry for my trouble *Kilkenny Magazine*
10 trouble'.] trouble', *DN1966*, *SP*
12 held] clamped *Kilkenny Magazine*
13 angry tearless] tearless angry *Kilkenny Magazine*
14 the] an *Kilkenny Magazine; Listener*
18 now,] now. *EP*
20, 22 four foot] four-foot *Listener*; *OG*, *100P*
21 scars, the] scars – the *Kilkenny Magazine*

Possibly SH's best-loved poem, the subject is the death of the poet's four-year-old brother Christopher, struck by a car outside their farmhouse Mossbawn (an event which SH says was part of the motivation for their moving to the farm at The Wood in the following year, 1954).

16 *the room:* a term for the parlour or sitting-room, only used for special occasions, as distinct from the kitchen, which was the general family room.

Dawn Shoot

First published in the *New Statesman* (1 April 1966): 473.

3 sleepers,] sleepers *DN1966*
30 barrel. This] barrel. // This *DN1991*
30 his.] his, *DN1991* (error?)
31 more.'] more' *DN1966*
33 more,'] more', *DN1966*
35 And got him.] And got him. I finished him off. *DN1966*

Military metaphors run throughout the poem.

41 *cut out the tongue*: as evidence for payment of the bounty given for the killing of animals that threatened farming crops.

At a Potato Digging

First published in *New Ireland* (1966): 37–8. Collected with revisions in *DN*, and subsequently published in *SP* and *PM*.

I–IV] *New Ireland* employs initial capitals for each line.
I 8 stand] stand. *New Ireland*

II 4 clotted,] clotted *New Ireland; DN1966*
II 10–11 insides / promise] inside / promises *New Ireland; DN1966*
III 14 the earth,] the bitch earth, *New Ireland; DN1966*
III 19 are,] are *New Ireland; DN1966*
IV 1 gay] white *New Ireland*

The poem makes a complicated and chthonic series of connections between the everyday agricultural activity of potato harvesting and the historical significance of the potato in nineteenth-century Ireland and the period of Famine in the 1840s.

    I 1 *A mechanical digger*: although the machine is modernised, the beginning recalls Patrick Kavanagh's *The Great Hunger*, as well as SH's 'Digging' in this volume.

    I 8–9 the workers straightening and then stumbling back echoes the 'grandfather'/great-uncle cutting turf in 'Digging'.

    I 12 *Mother*: term for the 'mother tuber' in growing potatoes, which rots and turns black in the course of generating the new potatoes. The potato-gatherers form a procession like a religious group, here paying tribute to the 'famine god'. But this black tuber anticipates the poisonous, blight-rotted potatoes of part III of the poem.

    II 13 *live skulls, blind-eyed*: this deathly image at the end of part II is immediately repeated at the start of part III to link with the historical skulls.

    III 3 *'forty-five*: 1845 was the first year of the Great Famine in Ireland (generally dated 1845–52). The worst year of the Famine was called 'Black Forty-seven'.

    IV 6 *timeless fasts*: the poem's observances return to the present and the respite from farming tasks, as in 'The Wife's Tale' in *DD*, and 'The Seed Cutters' in *North*.

For the Commander of the 'Eliza'

First published in *EP*, and subsequently in the *Cambridge Review* (7 May 1966): 389. Collected with revisions in *DN*.

Title the 'Eliza'] 'The Eliza' *EP, Cambridge Review*
Epigraph] officer reported to Sir James Dombrain . . . and Sir James,] officer in charge reported the incident to Sir James Dombrain, the Inspector General . . . and Sir James *EP, Cambridge Review*
12 Bia'. In] Bia,' in *EP, Cambridge Review*
14 shortage,] shortage *EP, Cambridge Review, DN1966*
16 men's,] men's. *Cambridge Review*
17 distress] distress. *EP, Cambridge Review*
18–19] There was relief available in Westport / Though these poor brutes would clearly never make it. *EP, Cambridge Review*
20 food:] food; *Cambridge Review*
21 privates.] privates *Cambridge Review*

27 bunks] bunk EP, *Cambridge Review*
28 ship,] ship EP, *Cambridge Review*, DN1966

'For the Commander of the "Eliza"' shares with 'At a Potato Digging' historical reflections on the Irish Famine, drawing on Cecil Woodham-Smith's highly influential *The Great Hunger* (1962). The poem's narrative dramatises Woodham-Smith's account of a report by an 'officer' mentioned in the epigraph, to Captain James Dombrain, the inspector general of the Coast Guard who became a relief commissioner during the Famine. He exceeded his authority by having relief brought by sea to the worst-affected areas by the west coast. He reported to Sir Randolph Isham Routh who from 1845 to 1848 was responsible for the distribution of famine relief in the West of Ireland. According to *ll.* 30–2 of the poem, Dombrain urged free relief for famine victims in the Westport Sector and was reprimanded by Routh for exceeding his brief.

11–12 *'Bia, bia / Bia'*: *bia* means 'food' in Irish. The divided lineation is like this in all versions.

31 *the Westport Sector*: a sector was one of the subdivisions of a coastal frontier. Westport is a town in west Co. Mayo.

32 *Whitehall*: the centre of UK government in London. The 'good' is ironic.

The Diviner

First published in EP, subsequently in the Poetry Book Society's *Poetry Supplement* (Christmas 1965): [5]. Collected with revisions in DN, and then published in SP, OG and *100P*. Early version and two final drafts of the poem also included in the exhibition catalogue for Poetry in Manuscript, Queen's University Belfast exhibition of poets' worksheets, Feb. 1970. Quoted in full in SH's important early essay 'Feeling Into Words' (*Preoccupations*, 48) in 1974.

6 jerked] jerked down EP, DN1966, SP
8 hazel] aerial EP, DN1966, SP
11 till, nonchalantly,] till nonchalantly EP, DN1966, SP

This was the last poem added to DN in August 1965 (SS, 83).

7–8 *broadcasting . . . secret stations*: the earliest of several radio images and references in SH's work, of which the most familiar is 'the absolute speaker' in 'A Sofa in the Forties' (*SL*, 8; *PSH*, 467).

Turkeys Observed

First published in the *Belfast Telegraph* under the name Seamus J. Heaney (15 Dec. 1962): 5. Subsequently published in *Universities' Poetry Five* (May 1963): 6, and collected with revisions in DN.

1] One observes them; one expects them; *Belfast Telegraph*
7–8 hook maintains / That] hook / Maintains that *Belfast Telegraph*
12] An ink-blotchy slump of putty. *Belfast Telegraph*
13 extravagantly] loudly *Belfast Telegraph*
17–20] Now, in my winter woollens and turned-up collar, / I pass the butcher's bleak December dazzle, / And casually note the importance / Of plumage and perpendicularity. *Belfast Telegraph*

SH tells O'Driscoll 'Turkeys Observed' is 'the earliest poem in *DN*. Written in November or December 1962, partly as a result of reading Ted Hughes's "View of a Pig", and partly as a result of butchers' window displays coming up to Christmas' (*SS*, 79).

11 *poor forked thing*: cf. Lear to Edgar in *King Lear*, 3.4.106–8: 'Thou art the thing itself: unaccommodated man is no more but such a poor, bare fork'd animal as thou art.'

Cow in Calf

First published in *DN*, but not in any Faber selecteds.

2 haunches,] haunches *DN1969*

Trout

First published in the *Listener* (4 Feb. 1965): 193. Collected with revisions in *DN*.

1 Hangs] hangs *Listener* | gun-barrel] gun barrel *Listener*
6 bull's eye] bull's-eye *Listener*
15 is] in *DN1966* (error)

The gun theme is strikingly sustained in the first line of this unlikely context, before turning to a more evocatively descriptive mode. This is the first of a number of fish poems, about salmon and eels for example. The later poem closest to this is 'Perch' (*EL*, 4; *PSH*, 527).

Waterfall

First published in *Vogue* (1 Sept. 1965): 134, and subsequently in *EP*, then collected in *DN*. Not in *P1980*.

5 braking;] braking. *Vogue, EP*
8 reverse:] reverse; *Vogue, EP*
10–11 falls with / Hurtling] falls / With hurtling *Vogue, EP*
12 thus] thus, *Vogue, EP*

'Waterfall' is one of the seven poems omitted by SH from the American selection, *P1980*, which otherwise included all the poems published in the first four Faber volumes.

1 *burn:* the term may be suggested by the opening of 'Inversnaid' – 'This darksome burn, horseback brown' – by Hopkins, who was a major influence on SH's early poems; *drowns . . . in its own downpour:* Christopher Ricks discusses this self-referential motif in Andrew Marvell and other English poets in *The Force of Poetry* (Ricks 1987, 51).

Docker

First published in the *Dublin Magazine* (Spring 1965): 69, with 'Poor Women in a City Church', under the title 'Belfast Snapshots'. Subsequently collected in *EP*, *DN* and *PM*. Later published in Padraic Fiacc (ed.), *The Wearing of the Black* (Belfast: Blackstaff, 1974) and the *Washington Post* (3 May 1985): C4.

1 There,] There *Dublin Magazine*
3 Cowling plated] Cowling-plated *Dublin Magazine* | sledgehead] sledge-head *Dublin Magazine*
6 again.] again; *Dublin Magazine*, *EP*
15 Tonight] To-night *EP*

The poem is unusually stereotyping in its sectarian identification, added to which the journalist Jenny McCartney said that SH ruefully told her later that the dockers tended to be Catholics; the shipbuilders were the Protestants (*Spectator*, 7 Sept. 2013). But, apart from the title, the references and imagery in the poem ('cowling', 'rivets', 'clamped') belong to shipbuilding.

Poor Women in a City Church

First published in the *Dublin Magazine* (Spring 1965): 69, with 'Docker', under the title 'Belfast Snapshots'. Collected in *DN*. One of the seven poems omitted by SH from the FSG *P1980* and not included in any of the selected editions.

4 right,] right *Dublin Magazine*, *DN1966*
12 Golden] Gold *Dublin Magazine*
15 beeswax] waxen *Dublin Magazine*

4 The Virgin's altar is usually on the right as seen from the main altar, on the Gospel side: on the left as seen from the body of the church.
6 'Old dough-faced women with black shawls' was admired by Ciaran Carson.

Gravities

First published in *DN*, and subsequently in *Gravities*.

1 freely,] freely *DN1966*

11 Colmcille was banned from walking on Irish soil in Ireland, so on Iona he had Irish mould in his sandals. Another version of the legend is that he abided by the command that he must never walk on Irish soil by returning to Ireland with Scottish soil in his sandals. Such homesickness narratives are also told of Yeats and Joyce, as well as by SH in 'The Tollund Man in Springtime' (*DC*, 57; *PSH*, 617).

Twice Shy

First published in the *Listener* (28 Jan. 1965): 156, and collected with revisions in *DN*. Subsequently published in *ND*, *P1980* and *100P*.

2 suede] suède *Listener*
10 swam,] swam; *Listener*
16 apart,] apart; *Listener*
17 decorum,] decorum *Listener*
18 Deployed our talk] Deploying talk *Listener*
26 hawk,] hawk *Listener*

One of the many love poems to the poet's wife in *DN*. It is one of only two poems (the other is 'Scaffolding') which is included in the family's anthology *100 Poems* without having been included in any earlier Faber selected edition.

Title The expression 'once bitten, twice shy' is ageless. The wisdom of holding back after the first encounter with love is perhaps questioned here.

Valediction

First published in *Poetry Ireland* (Spring 1965): 9, and subsequently collected in *DN*.

3 you left] you have left *Poetry Ireland*
10 calendar,] calendar *DN1966*
15 command,] command *Poetry Ireland*

Taken to be dismay at the poet's temporary separation from his young wife.

Lovers on Aran

First published in *Vogue* (1 Sept. 1965): 134, and subsequently collected in *EP*, *DN* and *SP*. Also included in *ND*.

1 bright,] bright *Vogue*, *EP*, *DN1966*, *SP*

Poem

First published in *Northern Review*, 1. 2 (1965): 8, and subsequently published in *SP*, *PM*, *NSP1990* and *OG*.

7 exclude] keep out *NSP1990*, *OG*
10 drain,] drain *Northern Review*, *DN1966*, *SP*, *NSP1990*, *OG*
16] And square the circle: four walls and a ring. *NSP1990*, *OG*

This poem, dedicated expressly to SH's wife, had an immediate popularity on the publication of *DN*. The established images of digging and agriculture are given metaphorical application to family circumstances, as are the ideas of flowing water and the construction of protective walls to pregnancy. The failed protection of the child's garden will become perfect in a new future.

Honeymoon Flight

First published in the *Kilkenny Magazine* (Spring/Summer 1966): 19, and collected in *DN*. Also published in *ND*.

5 world] earth *Kilkenny Magazine*
8 wing-tip] wingtip *Kilkenny Magazine*
9 fire,] fire *Kilkenny Magazine*; *DN1966*
10 hang, miraculous, above] hang miraculous above *Kilkenny Magazine*

In a memo to Charles Monteith, 10 August 1965, Faber's Rosemary Goad records SH's presence at the firm's Russell Square offices while on honeymoon in London with Marie:

> Seamus Heaney called here 10th August. He has written 2 new poems (one called 'Honeymoon Flight'!) which Carol Gower is typing out now, together with the one ['Lint Water'] that appeared in the *TLS* of August 5th. She is also typing 'Turkeys Observed', as he has made some alterations to it. She will get in touch with S.H. when she has finished them, and will either take them round to him or he will call here. He and Marie are staying at Polly Devlin's flat: Flat 24, Great Russell Mansions, W.C.1. (Museum 0202) until next Wednesday.
>
> He said he also wanted to make some alterations to An Advancement of Learning and – as I can't find this poem anywhere – I think he must have taken it away with him!
>
> He is planning to have the complete ms. in its final form to give you at lunch on Monday [16 August 1965]. (FF E/18/45/1)

Scaffolding

First published in the *New Statesman* (4 Dec. 1964): 880, and then in P. L. Brent (ed.), *Young Commonwealth Poets '65*. Collected in *EP* and *DN*, published in *Threshold* (Summer 1967): 32, and then included in *ND*, *PM* and *100P*.

5 done,] done *New Statesman, Young Commonwealth Poets, DN1966*
8 me,] me *New Statesman, Young Commonwealth Poets, EP, DN1966*
9 fall,] fall *New Statesman, Young Commonwealth Poets, EP, DN1966*

One of the three poems published in the *New Statesman* by Karl Miller which caught the attention of Charles Monteith at Faber. It shares with 'Poem' *(for Marie)* and 'Honeymoon Flight' imagery of building as a sustaining force against fragility and anxiety. Although it was included in the FSG *P1980*, it was not included in any of the selected editions, even *OG*, until 2018 when *100P*, edited by the poet's family, was published, perhaps in response to the poem's popularity at Irish weddings noted by SH himself. Shortly after its first publication it was included (along with the uncollected 'Soliloquy for an Old Resident') in an anthology of *Young Commonwealth Poets*: a context which was recalled after SH published *An Open Letter* in 1983, objecting to his inclusion in *The Penguin Book of Contemporary British Poetry*, edited by Blake Morrison and Andrew Motion in 1982 (*PSH*, 257).

Storm on the Island

First published in the *New Statesman* (4 Dec. 1964): 880, subsequently collected in *DN*.

13 cliffs,] cliffs *DN1966*

This poem sustains very effectively the building image and is one of the most surprising of the omissions from *P1980*.
    5 *stooks*: a structure of sheaves, propped together in a cornfield before being brought into the farmyard for threshing.

Synge on Aran

First published in *New Statesman* (30 July 1965): 156; subsequently collected in *DN*.

Arguably another surprising omission from the FSG *P1980*. These sea poems are reminiscent of poems by SH's contemporary and friend Richard Murphy, also prominently published by Faber in the 1960s.

Saint Francis and the Birds

First published in the *Irish Times* (9 Jan. 1965): 8, and subsequently collected in *DN*, although omitted from the FSG *P1980*, and from all selected editions.

1 birds,] birds *Irish Times, DN1966*

9 *the best poem Francis made*: Possibly an echo of Ben Jonson's line on his dead son 'Ben Jonson his best piece of poetry'.

In Small Townlands

First published in *Interest* (March 1965): 48, then in the *New Statesman* (16 April 1965): 611, and *Northern Review*, 1. 2 (1965): 7. Collected with revisions in *DN*.

12 Pares] Bares *Northern Review* (error?)
14 thick, greedy] thick greedy *Interest; New Statesman*
15 This] The *Interest*

This poem was dedicated to SH's friend, the Belfast painter Colin Middleton (1910–83). His work is semi-surrealist, though his expressionist use of colour is also influenced by Van Gogh. SH wrote the elegy 'Loughanure' for him (*HC*, 61; *PSH*, 670), which celebrates a painting of Donegal which the Heaneys bought for 'thirty guineas / forty-odd years ago': about the time of this poem.

    1 *townlands*: see note to 'Death of a Naturalist' above.

    7–8 *bright grenade . . . safety catch*: the recurrent gun imagery of the volume is in a surprising context here.

The Folk Singers

First published in *Envoi*, 24 (1964): 10, then collected with revisions in *DN*. Not included in the FSG *P1980*, or in any of the Faber selected volumes.

3 harmony,] harmony *Envoi*
11 tale] take *DN1966*
14 all broken hearts. Death's edge] the broken heart *Envoi*
14–15] Solders the broken heart. / Death's edge blunts on the narcotic strumming. *Envoi*

The Play Way

First published in *Outposts*, 62 (Autumn 1964): 14, then collected with revisions in *DN*. Not included in the FSG *P1980*, or in any of the Faber selected volumes.

1 glass,] glass; *Outposts*

2 drinking straws and old dry crusts] sour drinking straws, old crusts *Outposts*
3 it,] it *Outposts*
5–8 [italics]] [no italics] *Outposts, DN1966*
9 record,] record *Outposts*
11 firmer,] firmer *Outposts*
12 tyre,] tyre *Outposts; DN1966*
14 wide. They] wide: they *Outposts*
15 The pens are busy, the tongues mime] Pencils are chewed, tongues mime *Outposts*

This poem about school-teaching draws on SH's experience as an English teacher at St Thomas's school in Belfast between 1961 and 1963.

    4 T. S. Eliot's *The Waste Land*, ll. 2–4: 'mixing / Memory and desire, stirring / Dull roots with spring rain.'

    6 *Beethoven's Concerto Number Five*: the 'Emperor' Concerto for Piano and Orchestra, opus 73.

Personal Helicon

First published in the *New Statesman* (9 July 1965): 446, then collected in *EP, DN, Gravities, SP, PM, NSP1990, OG* and *100P*.

1 mulch,] mulch *New Statesman, DN1966, SP, NSP1990, OG, 100P*
15 scaresome] scaresome, *OG*

DN, like all subsequent SH volumes, ends with a major poem of statement. 'Personal Helicon', addressed to his fellow poet and friend Michael Longley, summarises the way that the experiences of his early life in the countryside inspire him to an exploratory view of the world which results in his vocation: to 'rhyme / To see myself, to set the darkness echoing'.

    Title *Helicon*: Mount Helicon in Greek mythology is a mountain in the Boeotian region of Greece, the location of Hesiod's farm, from which originated the Hippocrene spring, regarded as the source of poetic inspiration.

    18 *big-eyed Narcissus*: it was on Mount Helicon that Narcissus fell in love with his own reflection. The well into which the child-poet peers reflects 'a white face', but it also 'gave back your own call / With a clean new music in it'. This reflexive view of inspiration recurs throughout SH's career, like the burn which has already drowned 'steadily in its own downpour' in 'Waterfall'.

UNCOLLECTED POEMS (1966–1969)

After the acclaim with which *Death of a Naturalist* was received, poems by SH were easy to place in the most prestigious poetry outlets in Ireland and England, and two were published in the US. The thirty-four uncollected poems between *Death of a Naturalist* and *Door into the Dark* (including two substantial sequences) amount to an uncollected gathering of as much weight as any in the poet's career: indeed SH himself said to Dennis O'Driscoll: 'A few of the poems that were published in magazines – and which I still like – didn't appear in *Door into the Dark*' (*SS*, 89). It is tempting to speculate what those poems were, but there are many strong candidates, several on major SH themes. Various kinds of violence feature in the poems of this group (the impressive 'Idyll' for example) which connects with themes such as gun imagery in *Death of a Naturalist*. There are also a number of significant unpublished poems from this period. Although it is generally true that SH rarely published 'the same poem twice in the same country' (Brandes 2008, xiv), there are several instances of multiple publication in Britain and Ireland in this group: maybe further evidence of SH's high regard for poems like 'Rookery' and 'Corncrake'. It is a group that certainly does not diminish the standing of the early poems.

Thaw

First published in the *Irish Times* (28 May 1966): 8; subsequently in *PM*.

[text: *Irish Times*]

1] Last snow piebalding the ditches *PM*
2 into all the] into the *PM*
4 flopping] rising *PM*
5–10] *PM* omits the second stanza
11 Remember that walk] Remember walking *PM*
12 god,] god *PM*
13 Dived] And dived *PM*
15 forward, stiff] forward stiff *PM*

Aries

Published in *Encounter* (June 1966): 40.

Title Aries is the celestial sign of the Ram, 21 March to 19 April. SH's birthday on 13 April fell within this sign.

9–12 The felloe (12) is the circular wooden rim of a wheel into which the spokes (9) are fixed.

Rookery

First published in the *Listener* (29 Sept. 1966): 475; subsequently in *three* (1969), *PM* and *Midsummer Feast* (Oldham: Incline Press, 2002).

[text: *Listener*]

Dedication [no dedication]] for Helen *Midsummer Feast*
2 sailers (error)
5 twigs] branches *PM, Midsummer Feast*
6 With each foot-loose, sure-footed landing, *Midsummer Feast*
7 rest. There] rest – there *three*
10] Like muttered thunder through radio *three*

Dedication In *Midsummer Feast*, the poem bears the dedication 'for Helen', Marie Heaney's sister. The notable rookery was at Ardboe, Helen and Marie's home place.

Aubade

Published in the *New Statesman* (14 Oct. 1966): 556.

Dated 20 May 1966 in MS; an unrelated poem of the same title appeared in the *New Yorker* (Nov. 1971), and was later incorporated into 'Summer Home' (*WO*, 47; *PSH*, 140).

1 *From Cork to Malin*: the scenic west coast of Ireland, from Co. Cork in the south-west to Malin Head in the north-west.

Triptych for the Easter Battlers

Published in the *New Statesman* (23 Dec. 1966): 942.

1 7 *Five counties*: the illegal practice of cockfighting (*l.* 12) was prevalent in Ulster from the late nineteenth century, though it was banned from the beginning of the twentieth century.

The third part incorporates language and imagery from 'On Hogarth's Engraving "Pit Ticket for the Royal Sport"', published in the *Irish Times*, 10 April 1965 (*PSH*, 18), in which distaste for the cruelty of cockfighting, implicit in the first two sections, is overt. Also striking is the Easter religious imagery throughout, from the chapel at the start to the Crucifixion of the conclusion.

Boy Driving His Father to Confession

First published in *Phoenix*, 1 (March 1967): 35; subsequently with revisions as a separate edition by the Sceptre Press, Surrey, in 1970 under the title *A Boy Driving His Father to Confession* (although the poem retains its original title within this edition); then collected with revisions in *PM*, then in the *Honest Ulsterman*, 97 (Spring 1994): 19, which reprinted the *Phoenix* text without variant.

[text: *Phoenix*]

5–6] [omitted] *A Boy, PM*
9 Again, last year, I] Again last year I *PM*
10 off: in] off. In *A Boy, PM*
12 long-threatened, two-week holiday.] long-talked-of, two-week holiday: *A Boy, PM*
17 toilet; we] toilet. We *A Boy, PM*
19 Today] To-day *A Boy, PM*
20 You asked me to drive up to church] You asked to be driven to the church *PM*
22 at pot-holes] for potholes *A Boy* | at potholes *PM*
24 Beneath that thick grey hair?] Under that thick grey skull? *A Boy, PM*
25 preparing?] preparing. *A Boy*
28 ground.] ground; *PM*
29 You grunt and] You grunt, and *A Boy*
A Boy includes the date – '1965' – after the poem
29–30 I watch another / Who gropes as awkwardly to know his father.] And when the curtain's drawn / It will be 'Bless me, father', and 'Yes, my son'. *PM*

7–8 The event described in 'Mid-Term Break'.

28 *the fourth time*: SH returns to the subject of failed physical contact with his father in 'Album iv' (*HC*, 7; *PSH*, 644) when three such failed encounters across a lifetime are recalled.

South Derry Evening

Published in *Hibernia*, 31. 7 (July 1967): 21.

6 *a tractor gargled*: the verb used for tractors a number of times by SH.

Corncrake

First published in the *Listener*, 78. 214 (2 Nov. 1967): 573. Subsequently published in *three* (1969), and collected with revisions in *PM*.

[text: *Listener*]

1 [initial caps]] [sentence case] *PM* | catacombs] cloisters *PM*
4 these dark acres] these acres *three, PM*
5–6 his own responses: / Solace and reproach,] his own responses. Solace / And reproach, *three* | his own responses, / his litany of solace and reproach *PM*

9] All night a prayer wheel ratchets in his throat. *three*

3 *tenebrae*: darkness, the term for the three pre-Easter days at the end of Lent.

Chestnut Time

Published in *Words* (Dec. 1967): n.p.

Last Look

First published in *Outposts*, 76 (Spring 1968): 7; subsequently in *Broadsheet*, 4 (May 1968); and in *Room to Rhyme: An Anthology of Poems by Seamus Heaney and Michael Longley and of ballads collected by David Hammond* (Belfast: Arts Council of Northern Ireland, 1968): [23].

[text: *Outposts*]

4 shoots] clumps *Broadsheet*

Child Lost

Published in *Square Times* (May 1968): 15.

3 giant] gaint *Square Times* (error)

The subject of the child hiding in the fields is one SH returns to more than once (e.g. 'Cauled' (*Stations*, 4; *PSH*, 161)). The child lost amid the pea drills recalls the poetry of Theodore Roethke whom SH mentions as 'one of the invoked spirits' between 1964 and 1968 (*SS*, 85).

The Survivor

Published in *Square Times* (May 1968): 15.

The violence of dynamite is here confined to an agricultural rather than a political context.

The Evening Land – Ceili on the Deck – Inisheer – The Oarsmen's Song – The Basket-Maker – The Basket-Maker's Song – Michael – Neddy – The Dealing Man – The Dealer – The Cargo – Lullaby

Published as a BBC pamphlet, *The Island People*, with the description 'An Irish sequence of music and poetry by Seamus Heaney. Music by Gerard

Victory.' It accompanied the BBC Radio for Schools Music Workshop (Stage 1) series, which was first broadcast on BBC Radio 4 from 1 May to 27 June 1968. The poems appear under the title *The Island People: An Irish Sequence of Music and Poetry by Seamus Heaney*. All but two of the poems ('Inisheer' and 'The Dealing Man') were set to music by Gerard Victory and appear as lyrics within the text. The pamphlet was illustrated by Doreen Roberts. 'The Evening Land', 'Inisheer' and 'The Oarsmen's Song' were subsequently published in *The Aran Islands: A World of Stone* (Dublin: O'Brien Educational, 1977).

[text: *The Island People*]

THE EVENING LAND

Title Approaching the Aran Islands, 'the three stepping-stones out of Europe' (*l*. 3), by boat in the evening: Inis Oírr, Inis Meáin, Inis Mór.
    10 Aranmore, the largest of the three islands: usually termed Inis Mór (Inishmore) 'big island'.

CEILI ON THE DECK

15 *The Sailor on the Rock*: reel from Doolin in West Clare from where a ferry to the Aran Islands sails; famously played by the accordionist Joe Cooley who was much admired by SH.
    16 *The Girl I Left Behind Me*: popular song, dating back to the seventeenth century in Ireland and England. Well known in the US, especially the Carolinas.

INISHEER

9–12] And down where the waves break in white lace.
         The bobbing boats all plunge and race
         And row right under the steamer's bows –
         Then back they ride with homely cargoes. *Aran Islands*

Title The smallest and most easterly of the three islands, Inis Oírr ('eastern island').
    7 *currachs*: small boats, with wooden frames covered with animal hides or canvas.

THE OARSMEN'S SONG

11 comes –] comes *Aran Islands*
21 And black] As black   hollow,] hollow *Aran Islands*

Bachelor Deceased

Published in the *Honest Ulsterman*, 2 (June 1968): 5.

Frogman

First published in the *Listener*, 80. 2049 (4 July 1968): 11; subsequently in Penny Blackie (ed.), *Things Working* (Harmondsworth: Penguin, 1970) (series title Penguin English Project Stage One).

[text: *Listener*]

I 6 in contact –] in contact, *Things Working*
III 8 bridges –] bridges. *Things Working*

Driving in the Small Hours

Published in *Poetry Review*, 59. 3 (Autumn 1968): 166–7.

Birdwatcher

Published in *Everyman*, 1 (1968): 126, and subsequently in *three* (1969), grouped in a selection under the title 'Five Short Poems'.

[text: *Everyman*]

1 died] died, *three*
3] The dormers, the gables, the ridge-tiles *three*
6 screened by] screened in by *three*

In an Airport Coach

Published in the *Honest Ulsterman*, 13 (May 1969): 16.

5 New Jersey.] New Jersey *Honest Ulsterman* (error)

The first poem to be located in the US. The Bowery (*l.* 29) is a neighbourhood in Lower Manhattan.

DOOR INTO THE DARK (1969)

Door into the Dark was published in London by Faber & Faber on 16 June 1969 in a hardback printing of 3,000 copies, and in New York by Oxford University Press in 1,000 copies printed and bound by Faber, despite a reluctance in London to renew the US partnership.* It became a Choice of the Poetry Book Society – the first of the six books by SH across his career that would be granted the accolade – and was reprinted by Faber in hardback in 1969, and first produced as a Faber Paper Covered Edition in 1972. It was reprinted in paperback in 5,000 copies in 1974, and reprinted again in 1976, reset in 1991 and reset once more in a corrected edition of 2002, our copy-text here.

The volume, which was delivered in manuscript to Faber by SH on 18 July and 3 October 1968 (FF P/Rdlm/604/6), takes its title from the first line of the sixth poem, 'The Forge':

All I know is a door into the dark.

This poem became the first to be reprinted by SH from the collection in most selected editions, meaning that the titling line would take on increasing significance over time. Apart from its remarkable aptness for the underground theme that becomes increasingly prominent in the poetry – what SH described as 'an emblem for the instinctive, blurred stirring and shaping of some kinds of art' (*PBS Bulletin*, 61, Summer 1969) – Barney Devlin's local forge is an important archetypal location (*SS*, 91), confirmed by its function in two poems in *District and Circle* (2006), 'Poet to Blacksmith' and 'Midnight Anvil'. In alighting on the line for a book title, SH said that it was only after its selection as a title for the new book that he realised that it followed directly from the last line in the previous book; it was a happy connection, he said, between books that he described very differently, in which the 'recollected emotion' of the debut collection was now to be 'contained rather than confessed' in the second book (*PBS Bulletin*, 61). Even so, common themes opened the new collection, leading to a series of domestic poems that he described as 'the heart of the book', before the working life cycles of fishermen and eels gave backdrop to 'A Lough Neagh Sequence', to be concluded with the final 'meditative landscape poems' with their allusions towards history and nationality (*PBS Bulletin*, 61).

---

* Matthew Evans–Charles Monteith, 27 July 1968: 'I think we all agree that OUP, New York, did a pretty poor job with *Death of a Naturalist* and that we should try and get Heaney published properly in the States with this new book' (FF E/18/45/1).

There are only seven of the twenty-eight poems of *Door into the Dark* (thirty-four if the component parts of 'A Lough Neagh Sequence' are seen as distinct poems) in the 1980 *Selected Poems*, and fifteen in *Opened Ground*. Between 1966 and 1969, there were twenty-three uncollected poems, some of which (as noted) SH told O'Driscoll he still liked in 2008 (*SS*, 89). As late as 2013, SH makes clear that the volume's dominant item that signalled a change of direction was the concluding poem, 'Bogland', which confirmed him as 'a ground person . . . sedimentary': relocating his poetic homeland, and confirming, too, the prominence of a chthonic underground theme: 'going down and down and finding origin there' (*Irish Times*, 3 Sept. 2013).

Door into the Dark was mostly well received and regarded as manifesting the same virtues as *Death of a Naturalist* and a continuity of the rural skills, for example, in 'Thatcher'. However, there are features of the collection that distinguish it from its predecessor, based partly on developments in SH's personal life. One such element is a tendency towards a more visionary or religious language in the later work. Henry Hart saw the book as an adventurous depiction of a kind of secular mysticism, drawing on the classical ideas of Christian mysticism and deploying them in the description of the verities of the home place which had been celebrated in *Death of a Naturalist* (Hart 1992). In 'The Forge' (effectively the title poem), the hieratic associations of the blacksmith, Hephaestus, and his anvil, 'horned as a unicorn' are displaced, as 'profane denotations undercut their sacred connotations'. The anvil 'resembles a mysterious omphalos at the center of space and time' (Hart 1992, 4). The dark in this poem, and in the book generally, becomes the positive element of the creative imagination, rather than the locus of physical and sexual threat that it was in *Death of a Naturalist*. There is also a dominant set of images, centring on water (waves breaking on the shore in three poems, for example) as a kind of Heraclitean flux, associated with pregnancy, motherhood, and abundance. There is a movement from evocative description to reflection on wider significances. SH tells O'Driscoll that the notebook he used during his wife's first pregnancy shows that 'pregnancy is the theme or the preoccupation' (*SS*, 97). There were poems on the theme 'that were published, like "Aubade" and "Cana Revisited" and "Elegy for a Stillborn Child" (lost by another couple who got married the same time as us), other ones that weren't worth publishing' (*SS*, 97). O'Driscoll observes that, though SH gave virtually equal space to work from the first two books in the 1990 *New Selected Poems*, he gave a good deal more space to poems from *Door into the Dark* in *Opened Ground* in 1998.

O'Driscoll notes the prescience of SH's placing of 'Bogland' at the end of the book because it points forward to the many places where SH uses bog as a metaphor. 'A Lough Neagh Sequence', which was first published in January 1969 in the series of Phoenix Pamphlet Poets, also marks a move from the agricultural farming of *Death of a Naturalist* to the underground of the bogland and the fishing world of the eelworks (associated with his wife's family). And, though there isn't a direct link between the final poem of *Door into the Dark* and the opening poem of *Wintering Out*, as often happens with subsequent volumes in what Patrick Crotty (1994, 193) calls 'this poet's delight in Janus-faced volume-endings', there is a thematic link between the deliquescent imagery of many poems in the former volume and the emerging bog poems in both the latter volume and the limited-edition *Bog Poems* of May 1975 that contains eight poems subsequently collected in *North*. In the same way that SH says he recognised 'Digging' from the first as 'a strength-giver', he says to O'Driscoll: 'From 'the moment I wrote it, I felt promise in "Bogland" . . . It seemed the right poem to close with since it didn't seem to stop after the last line' (*SS*, 90–1). The last line, 'The wet centre is bottomless', did indeed open up what was to be a major and productive thematic vein.

Door into the Dark marked the growing involvement by SH in the way his editions were both produced and sold. He took close interest in the aesthetic appearance of the printing, reordering the prelims of the publisher's proof 'so that there's a clean page opposite the first poem' (9 January 1969; FF P/Rdlm/604/6). It also witnessed his sense of disappointment at the manner in which Oxford University Press had published the edition in the US, as he told Faber on 26 September 1970: 'I never even knew when they released *Door into the Dark* and I had to buy the American editions of each book myself, in bookshops' (FF E/16/41/20; *LSH*, 53).

[*text*: DD2002]

Night-Piece

Published in *DD*.

As in the volume's second poem, 'Gone', the close focus on the horse recalls SH's observation to O'Driscoll that when he was a child 'the comfort sound in the bedroom was the horse beyond the wall. You'd hear these occasional big body rolls and foot stamps in the stable. Big flubby snorts of contentment' (*SS*, 15). Later he tells O'Driscoll how as a child his night fears were associated with the horse in the stable 'on the other side of the bedroom wall. The home horse turned night mare' (*SS*, 96). The moment is recalled once more in the Nobel speech 'Crediting Poetry' (1995).

Gone

Published in *DD*.

Another horse poem of accurate, technical observation.
    13 *shods*: iron tips on shoes.

Dream

Published in *DD*.

A surreal nightmare, of the kind associated with the filmmaker Luis Buñuel.

The Outlaw

First published in the programme for the Cheltenham Festival of Literature (3–8 Oct. 1966): 43, subsequently in *Phoenix*, 1 (March 1967): 37, and collected with revisions in *DD*. It was also included in *OG*.

2 road:] road; *Cheltenham Festival of Literature, DD1969* | you risked] one risked *Cheltenham Festival of Literature*
8 Go by.] Go by *DD1969*
10 business-like] businesslike *Cheltenham Festival of Literature, OG*
16 and,] and *Cheltenham Festival of Literature, DD1969, OG*
20 ash-plant] ashplant *Phoenix*
22 slack,] slack *Cheltenham Festival of Literature, DD1969, OG*

Title 'Oh Brave New Bull' in TS (HFC).
    2 Bulls on farms had to be licensed, in a period when insemination of cattle was normally done by an artificial process.

The Salmon Fisher to the Salmon

First published in *Outposts*, 68 (Spring 1966): 1, and collected with revisions in *DD*.

6 river cramming under me] river, cramming under me, *Outposts*
7 net] net, *Outposts*
11 best, but] best. But *Outposts*
12 through] by *Outposts*
14 water] rhythms *Outposts*   leg,] leg: *Outposts*
16 I go, like you, by] I go like you by *Outposts*
18 on] with *Outposts*

9 *Walton*: Izaak Walton, *The Compleat Angler. Or The Contemplative Man's Recreation. Being a Discourse of Fish and Fishing, Not Unworthy the Perusal of most Anglers* (1653).

The Forge

First published in the *Times Literary Supplement* (19 May 1966): 426, subsequently in *St Stephen's* (Hilary Term 1967): 21, and *Critical Quarterly Poetry Supplement*, 10 (1969): 3, then collected with revisions in *DD*, and included in *PM*, *SP*, *OG* and *100P*. It was also published as a special limited edition, *The Forge*, with an etching by Breon O'Casey, in 1994.

2 rusting;] rusting. *TLS*
8 immovable] immoveable *TLS*, *Critical Quarterly*, *DD1969*, *SP*, *PM*, *The Forge*, *OG*, *100P* | immovable: an altar] immoveable like an altar *TLS*] immoveable – an altar *St Stephen's*
12 hoofs] hooves *TLS* rows;] rows. *TLS*

The sixth poem in the volume, but the preceding five (with the exception of 'The Outlaw' in *OG*) are not reprinted by SH in his selected editions so this poem effectively becomes the first poem in practice – appropriately, since its first line provides the volume's title.

Thatcher

First published as 'The Thatcher' in *Honest Ulsterman*, 6 (Oct. 1968): 3, and later in *New Republic* (27 March 1976): 24. Collected with revisions in *DD* and subsequently included in *SP*, *PM*, *NSP1990* and *OG*. One of the poems included in 'Singing Schools', the linen scroll produced by Queen's University Belfast in 1996.

9 well-honed] well honed *Honest Ulsterman*, *DD1969*, *SP*, *PM*
13 rafters,] rafters *Honest Ulsterman*, *DD1969*, *SP*, *PM*

13 *Couchant*: the heraldic term suits the artistic subject, as well as describing accurately the thatcher's posture, lying on the thatch with his head raised.
   16 King Midas turned all he touched into gold.

The Peninsula

First published in the *Dublin Magazine* (Spring 1966): 38, then in the *Cambridge Review* (7 May 1966): 389. It was included in James Gibson (ed.), *Let the Poet Choose* (London: Harrap, 1973). Collected with revisions in *DD* and included in *SP*, *PM*, *NSP1990*, *OG* and *100P*.

4 marks] marks, *OG*, *100P*
12 fog] fog, *OG*, *100P*
15 upon] on *Dublin Magazine*, *PM*, *SP*, *NSP1990*, *OG*, *100P*

Dated 23 January 1966 in MS (NLI 49,493/10). This is the first of many poems by SH about driving. The setting is the Ards peninsula in Co. Down.

In Gallarus Oratory

Published in *DD*.

4 alone,] alone *DD1969*
5 creature,] creature *DD1969*
8 barrow,] barrow *DD1969*
12 censer] censer, *DD1969*

Gallarus Oratory is a small stone structure, dating perhaps from the eleventh or twelfth century CE, in the Irish-speaking Dingle peninsula in Co. Kerry. It is one of the most distinctive and best-known archaeological monuments in Ireland, shaped like an upside-down boat. It is not certain whether the building was a small church or served some other sheltering function. The Heaneys spent several holidays in Corca Dhuibhne, the Dingle area, in the 1960s.

    8 *barrow*: in archaeology a burial-mound.

Girls Bathing, Galway, 1965

First published in the *Dublin Magazine* (Summer 1966): 48–9, then collected with revisions in *DD* and *ND*. This poem is also reproduced in a plaque on the promenade in Salthill, Galway, as part of the Galway Poetry Trail, organised by Kennys Bookshop and unveiled by SH in 2006.

Title Galway,] Galway *Dublin Magazine*, *DD1969*, *ND*
2 catherine-wheel] catherine wheel *DD1969*, *ND*   hand;] hand. *Dublin Magazine*
6 shore.] shore; *Dublin Magazine*
7 pirate queen] pirate-queen *Dublin Magazine*
18] Brown-legged, smooth-shouldered and bare-backed *Dublin Magazine*   long-backed,] long-backed *DD1969*

7–8 The 'pirate queen in battle clothes' is Granuaile, Grace O'Malley, a historical queen of Umhaill in west Co. Mayo in the Elizabethan era. There are many legends associated with her.

Requiem for the Croppies

First published in the *Dublin Magazine* (Summer 1966): 48, then in *Room to Rhyme*, the Arts Council anthology which accompanied the tour of Northern Ireland by SH, Michael Longley, and David Hammond in 1968. It was collected with revisions in *DD*, and included in *SP*, *PM*, *NSP1990*, *OG* and *100P*. It was recorded for inclusion on *The Northern Muse: Seamus Heaney and John Montague Reading Their Poetry* (Dublin: Claddagh, 1968).

5 people, hardly] people hardly *Dublin Magazine*
6 day:] day. *Room to Rhyme*
7–9] Horseman and horse fell to the twelve foot pike, / We'd stampede cattle into infantry, / Retreat through hedges where cavalry must be thrown *Dublin Magazine*
14 August the barley] August barley *Dublin Magazine*

The poem is set in Wexford in the 1798 Rebellion, when at Vinegar Hill the ill-armed Irish rebels died in great numbers, 'shaking scythes at cannon' (*l.* 11). Croppy was a term applied to the rebels who wore their hair cropped as an expression of sympathy for the French revolutionaries; the term was positive, if tragic, for the rebels (there are two celebrated songs called 'The Croppy Boy'), and negative for the unionists (as in the anti-republican song 'Croppies Lie Down'). SH says that the poem became too sensitive to read in the course of the early 1970s as political divisions became more fraught (*SS*, 118–19). He did, however, include the poem in his first public reading at Harvard in 1975 (see Lavan 2020, 99).

The poem was read as part of Poets' Offering at the Abbey Theatre on 25 August 1968, a reading in aid of the victims of the Biafra conflict in Nigeria. It is the first of a group of poems in *DD* assigned to a particular speaker – in this case a representative of the Croppies.

14 the idea is that the grain the local soldiers had in their pockets as food sprouted in the autumn where they lay dead.

Rite of Spring

First published as 'Persephone' in the *Cambridge Review* (4 June 1966): 464 and under the same title in *Broadsheet*, 2 (1968), then collected with revisions as 'Rite of Spring' in *DD* and selected for inclusion in *FP* (Belfast: Crannog Press, 1975).

Title Rite of Spring] Persephone *Cambridge Review, Broadsheet*
3 lump] lump. *Cambridge Review*
4–5 ice founding itself / Upon iron. The handle] ice / Founding itself upon iron. The handle *Broadsheet*
7 twisting] twin string *Cambridge Review*
11 latch,] latch. *Cambridge Review*

12 and] but *Cambridge Review*

SH tells O'Driscoll that this is one of the poems he would 'like to revise, or better still lose, as much for artistic as ideological reasons'. Educated as he was by 'living with a woman of independent spirit', it is no doubt the sexist imagery of the conclusion that leads him to call it 'a crude bit of work' (*SS*, 312).

Undine

First published in *Icarus* (Nov. 1966): n.p. Subsequently published in the *Listener* (11 April 1968): 474 and then in *Broadsheet*, 3 (1969) and *Critical Quarterly Poetry Supplement*, 10 (1969): 3. Collected with revisions in *DD* and then included in *ND*, and in *SP* and *OG*. SH also includes and discusses it in 'Feeling into Words' (1974), collected in *Preoccupations* (53–4).

2 right of way] right-of-way *Icarus, Listener, Broadsheet, OG*
4 disrobed,] disrobed *Icarus*
5 unconcern.] unconcern *Broadsheet*
11 grain –] grain. *Icarus, Listener, Broadsheet*
13 reflection.] reflection: *Icarus*
15 freedom. Human] freedom; human *Icarus, Listener, Broadsheet*

Dated 21 April 1966 in MS (NLI 49,493/5).

This poem was first published in the Trinity College Dublin magazine *Icarus*. When the copies of this fiftieth issue went on sale they were confiscated and destroyed when the poet Brendan Kennelly, then a junior lecturer in English at Trinity and chair of the *Icarus* board, objected to a story in the magazine by its editor, Tony Lowes, on the grounds of literary quality and explicit content deemed to be harmful. However, some copies survived, having already been sent to subscribers. The incident was covered in the student press and the *Irish Times*, and cited in 1967 as being one of the prompts for the formation of the Union of Student Journalists in Ireland. A new fiftieth issue was later produced and published, but 'Undine' was not included.

By contrast with 'Rite of Spring', SH says he would 'still stand by "Undine", farm drainage and burgeoning sexuality yoked by violence – literary violence, that is together' (*SS*, 312). He chose it for the *Critical Quarterly Poetry Supplement*, 10 (1969).

The Wife's Tale

First published in *Phoenix*, 2 (Summer 1967): 10–11, then in *Critical Quarterly Poetry Supplement*, 10 (1969): 2. Collected with revisions in *DD*, then included in *ND*, *SP*, *PM*, *NSP1990* and *OG*. A recording appears on *The Northern Muse*.

7 twenty] thirty *Phoenix*
8 theirs.] theirs, *Phoenix, NSP1990, OG* | theirs. *Critical Quarterly, DD1969, ND, SP, PM*
10–11 'That looks well.' / (He nodded at my white cloth on the grass.)] 'That looks well,' – / He nodded at my white cloth on the grass – *Phoenix*
17 good] right *Phoenix*
24 stuck] struck *Phoenix*
26 them back] them, back *Phoenix*
27 dregs] dregs, *Phoenix*

Written in the wife's voice, SH later said that he felt this poem 'gets something right about man/woman companionship and contesting', despite being 'picturesque' (*SS*, 312–13). It anticipates in some ways the harder-edged 'Seed Cutters' poem at the start of *North*. SH wrote of it on publication:

> 'The Wife's Tale' began as an irrational desire to write about a woman bringing tea to a harvest field. Earlier I might have set down the picture and trusted that it was redolent of the emotion which it evoked for me. But this time the initial memory began to coordinate with questions about the balance between man and woman in marriage and the poem turned into a dramatic monologue that ended with a reference to Brueghel's painting of the cornfield. (*PBS Bulletin*, 61)

Mother

Published in *DD*, included in *ND*. It was also recorded for *The Northern Muse*.

12 ready-made] readymade *DD1969, ND*

The first of three motherhood and pregnancy poems, again assigned to the voice of the mother. The poems were written while Marie Heaney was pregnant with their first child.

Cana Revisited

First published in the *Irish Times* (8 and 9 April 1966): 8; collected with revisions in *DD*.

3 taps] tap *Irish Times*

Dated 16 January 1966 in MS (NLI 49,493/5).
    The imagery of pregnancy is prominent in *l.* 5, 'the bone-hooped womb'. The west face of the high cross of Ardboe, the birthplace of Marie Heaney, portrays the Miracle of Cana.

Elegy for a Still-born Child

First published in *Phoenix*, 1 (March 1967): 36, and then in *Room to Rhyme*. Collected with one revision in *DD*, and included in *ND*. It was also recorded for *The Northern Muse*.

III 4 reaching] groping *Phoenix*

Dated 10 April 1966 in MS (NLI 49,493/5); entitled 'Elegy for an Unborn Child' in TS.

    SH tells O'Driscoll that this poem was written about a child lost by a couple who got married at the same time as he did (*SS*, 97).

Victorian Guitar

First published in the *Listener* (18 Jan. 1968): 85, and collected with one revision in *DD*. It was also included in the programme for Poets Loused with Song, an event at the City Hotel in Derry on 12 December 1969, in aid of the Derry Itinerant Settlement Committee, and in *ND*.

10 is obviously] is so obviously *Listener*

Written for SH's close friend, the singer and broadcaster David Hammond. Together with Michael Longley, they went on the Arts Council Room to Rhyme tour across Northern Ireland in May 1968, aiming to cross the sectarian divide (Hammond and Longley were Protestants). The poem was performed on 12 December 1969, as part of Poets Loused with Song: 'an entertainment for the cultural edification of the Citizens and the financial edification of the Derry Itinerant Settlement Committee', at the City Hotel, Derry at which the participants were SH, Hammond, Longley and Derek Mahon. (The redress of inequality and improvement of conditions in housing were central to civil rights activity in Derry in the 1960s.) SH continued to perform and consort with Hammond until his friend's death in 2008. Hammond is the subject of SH's late memorial poem, 'The door was open and the house was dark' (*HC*, 82; *PSH*, 680).

Night Drive

Published in *DD* and then in the special edition *ND*. Subsequently included in *SP*, *NSP1990*, *OG* and *100P*.

6 Abbéville] Abbeville *OG*, *100P*
10 its] *DD1969* (error)

Title poem of a pamphlet produced by Richard Gilbertson, Bow, Crediton, Devon, containing twelve poems, all previously published in *DN* or *DD*, published in July 1970.

At Ardboe Point

First published in *Phoenix*, 5 (Summer 1969): 6, and later in *Ardboe* (1970): 38. Collected in *DD* and selected for inclusion in *SP* and *PM*.

> 6 whisper] whisper. *Ardboe*
> 12–13 closes. // Tonight] closes. / To-night *Ardboe*
> 13 Tonight] To-night *Phoenix*; *Ardboe*, *SP*
> 15 moonlight] moonlinght *Ardboe* (error)
> 15 go] go. *Ardboe*
> 17 pollen.] pollen *Ardboe*
> 18 further,] further *Phoenix*, *SP*, *PM*
> 21 wings] wings. *Ardboe*
> 26 Pharaoh's.] Pharaoh's – *Phoenix*, *Ardboe*, *SP*
> 27 mosquitoes] mosquitoes. *Ardboe*
> 30 innocent, shuttling] innocent shuttling *Ardboe*
> 32 only] only, *Ardboe*

Ardboe, Co. Tyrone, on the western shore of Lough Neagh, was the birthplace of SH's wife, Marie Devlin, on 14 September 1940.

    26 *Pharaoh's*: the plague of locusts, sent by God to punish Pharaoh.

Relic of Memory

First published in the *New Statesman* (14 Oct. 1966): 556, and collected with revisions in *DD*. Subsequently included in *NSP1990* and *OG*.

> 2 wood:] wood. *New Statesman*
> 4 Over the years] In seven years *New Statesman*
> 9 take:] take. *New Statesman* | take – *DD1969*
> 11 love] love, *New Statesman*
> 21 stored –] stored: *New Statesman* | stored. *DD1969*
> 24 Oatmeal coloured] Oatmeal-coloured *New Statesman*

One of the 'pre-bog poems', dated July 1966 in MS, where the formative draft is a quatrain of what became the final lines:

> A Local Legend
> On a shelf at school,
> A piece of stone
> Oat-meal coloured. (NLI 49,493/5)

A Lough Neagh Sequence

First published in the *University Review*, 4. 3 (Winter 1967): 286–90, and then in a separate edition from the Phoenix Pamphlet Poets' Press in January 1969. Collected with revisions in *DD* and included in *SP*, *PM* and *OG*. *SP* includes only the first part of section 4, 'Setting' (*ll*. 1–9); that section also published separately, with 'At Ardboe Point', in *Ardboe* (1970): 38.

1 UP THE SHORE

ll 4 stones] stone *University Review*, *DD1969*, *SP*, *PM*, *OG*
III 4 out] out, *DD1969*, *SP*, *PM*, *OG*
IV 1 down,'] down', *DD1969*, *SP*, *PM*   say.] say – *University Review*, *DD1969*, *PM*

I 1 *The lough will claim a victim every year* (repeated in speech marks at the end): this piece of folk wisdom (like the phrase 'Once the season's in' at the end of 5 'Lifting') seems to anticipate the ageless determinism of the bog poems. In the same way that the first volume became beset by threatened horror with rats and the nightmarish frogs in the title poem, in the last lines of this powerful sequence the eels are figures of repugnance:

> Phosphorescent, sinewed slime
> Continued at his feet. Time
> Confirmed the horrid cable.

III 4 In many coastal parts of Ireland, sailors don't learn to swim so they won't suffer too long before drowning.

2 BEYOND SARGASSO

13 rapids,] rapids *University Review*, *DD1969*, *SP*, *PM*
20 day,] day *University Review*, *DD1969*, *SP*, *PM*, *OG*

Title The Sargasso Sea, an area of the Atlantic to the north-east of the Caribbean, where the eels go to hatch before returning to Europe to spawn.

3 BAIT

11 dew-lapped] dewlapped *University Review*, *DD1969*, *SP*, *PM*, *OG*
11 blades,] blades *University Review*, *DD1969*, *SP*, *PM* *OG*
12 night] might *DD1969* (error), *PM*
13 ground,] ground *University Review*, *DD1969*, *SP*, *PM*, *OG*

4 SETTING

ll 1 and] an *University Review*, *DD1969*, *PM*

5 LIFTING

14 furling, slippy] furling, fat, slippy *University Review*

6 THE RETURN

Part number] [unnumbered] (error) *University Review*
1 canals,] canals *University Review, DD1969, SP, PM, OG*
6 turn] stop *OG*
8 lough] loch *University Review*
14 direction?] direction; *University Review, DD1969, SP, PM*
15 She's] she's *University Review, DD1969, SP, PM*

7 VISION

1 fine-combed,] fine-combed *University Review, DD1969, SP, PM, OG*
4 doomed,] doomed *University Review, DD1969, SP, PM*
7 trunk,] trunk] *University Review, DD1969, SP, PM*

The poem marks a move from the farming agricultural setting of *Death of a Naturalist* to the underground of the bogland and the fishing world of the eelworks, associated with his wife's family. SH wrote of it:

> I envisaged this sequence as a kind of Celtic pattern: the basic structural image is the circle – the circle of the eel's journey, the fishermen's year, the boats' wakes, the coiled lines, the coiled catch, and much else; and in places the connotations of the language are meant to relate the compulsions and confrontation of fish and fishermen to sexual compulsions and confrontations that occur beyond Lough Neagh. (*PBS Bulletin*, 61)

Of the seven poems of the sequence, the fourth, 'Setting' was published with 'At Ardboe Point' in *Ardboe* (1970), of which SH explains to O'Driscoll: 'When I started to visit Ardboe in the sixties, I got introduced to the whole eel business and couldn't help being fascinated by the life cycle, the mysterious drift of elvers from the Sargasso and the programmed drive of the mature eel back to the original spawning ground' (*SS*, 93). The volume's fixation with pregnancy (noted by the author, *SS*, 97) is remarkably transferred to the female eel in the sixth poem in the sequence, 'The Return'.

The Given Note

Published in *DD* and subsequently included in *SP*, *OG* and *100P*. Recording included on *The Poet and the Piper* (Dublin: Claddagh Records, 2003) a collaboration between SH and his friend Liam O'Flynn, who used 'The

Given Note' in other projects, including as the title for his 1995 Tara Records album for which SH wrote the sleeve note.

9 easy,] easy *DD1969*, *SP*, *OG*, *100P*

This poem draws on a familiar west of Ireland legend, about a slow air called 'Port na bPúcaí' ('The Fairies' Tune'). Three islanders, rowing back to Inishvickillane Island, one of the Blasket islands off Dingle in West Kerry, hear unearthly sounds coming from the hull of their curragh, and one of them plays along on his fiddle. It has been suggested that it may have been the song of the hump-backed whale. The tune was a great favourite with SH's friend the piper Liam O'Flynn, who plays it as the first track on the album *The Poet and the Piper* (2003). It was the only poem by SH read (by the publisher Peter Fallon) at his funeral in Donnybrook.

Whinlands

First published in the *Listener* (24 April 1969): 571, along with 'Bann Clay', and collected in *DD*. Subsequently included in *OG*, and published as a separate limited edition by the English Department of Meredith College, Raleigh, North Carolina, to celebrate a reading given there by SH on 4 October 1998.

9 oxidize] oxidise *Listener*
18 thorn –] thorn. *Listener*, *DD1969*, *OG*
21 frilled,] frilled *Listener*, *DD1969*, *OG*

Whin is one of the Irish terms for gorse, also known there as furze.

The Plantation

First published in *Phoenix*, 3 (Spring 1968): 16–17, and collected with revisions in *DD*. Subsequently included in *SP*, *PM* and *OG*.

1 point] point, *PM*
6 line,] line *Phoenix*, *DD1969*, *PM*, *OG*
12 fire,] fire *Phoenix*, *DD1969*, *PM*
18 Campers, gipsies] Campers gipsies *Phoenix* | Campers gypsies *OG*
21 so,] so *Phoenix*, *DD1969*, *PM*, *OG*

11 *bleyberries*: like 'blaeberries', a dialectal variant for 'bilberry' or 'whortleberry' (known as whorts in other parts of Ireland; the late Middle English form *hurte* also survives in an Irish usage, 'hurts'). This poem, like 'Whinlands', uses local nomenclature for botanical items, in the same way that *WO* will use local pronunciation.

36 Hansel and Gretel, as figures of the return-to-self by retracing items encountered along the way, recur in 'The Underground' (*SI*, 13; *PSH*, 291) at the start of *SI*.

Shoreline

First published in *Phoenix*, 4 (Summer/Autumn 1968): 13, and later in *New Republic* (27 March 1976): 35. Collected in *DD* and included in *FP*, and also in *SP* and *PM*.

5 foreshore] bottom *Phoenix*, *DD1969*, *New Republic*, *SP*, *PM*
6 Dead-eyed as fish.] Saying 'Back in ten minutes.' *Phoenix*
7–8 craters march / The] craters / March the *Phoenix*

'The book ends with a number of meditative landscape poems, some of which are meant to encompass notions about history and nationality – "Shoreline" and "Bogland", for example,' wrote SH on publication (*PBS Bulletin*, 61). The end of the poem itemises Irish distinctiveness in place names, corresponding to the dialectal botanical terms of the two preceding poems, the 'languagey' poems of *WO*, and the Irish language tradition of place-name poetry, *dinnseanchas*, which SH explains himself more than once, notably in 'The Sense of Place' in 1977 (*Preoccupations*, 131).

Bann Clay

Published with 'Whinlands' in the *Listener* (24 April 1969): 571, and collected in *DD*, selected for inclusion in *OG*.

9 grass,] grass *Listener*, *DD1969*
18 drain,] drain *Listener*, *DD1969*, *OG*

The fixation with the substructure of terrain, whether on land or water, underlies this poem too.

17 *Mesolithic*: the middle period of the Stone Age; in Ireland its start date is usually said to be the eighth millennium BCE.

Bogland

First published in the *Listener* (2 Nov. 1967): 573, collected in *DD*, and selected for inclusion in *SP*, *PM*, *NSP1990*, *OG* and *100P*. Also included in Gibson (ed.), *Let the Poet Choose* (1973), and *Seamus Heaney: Readings in Contemporary Poetry* (New York: DIA Art Foundation, 1988). Recorded for *The Northern Muse*, *Seamus Heaney at Harvard* (Poetry Room, Harvard College Library, 1990), *Stepping Stones* (London: Penguin Audiobooks, 1995) and *The Poet and the Piper*.

Dedication For T. P. Flanagan] [no dedication] *Listener OG, NSP1990, 100P*

Dedication T. P. Flanagan (1929–11) was an Irish landscape painter and teacher, born in Enniskillen. Colleague of SH in St Joseph's College of Education, Andersonstown, Belfast, the teacher training college where SH took his teaching diploma in 1962, and returned to lecture in English from 1963 until 1966. SH was introduced to Flanagan by Michael McLaverty (*SS*, 54). His paintings often represent the Yeats country around Sligo, and the lake areas around Fermanagh.

10 *the Great Irish Elk*: Megaloceros, a giant extinct deer (not an elk), the largest deer species ever. It ranged throughout Europe, North Africa and Northern Asia; though fossils of the deer are found preserved in lakes and bogs in Ireland, no complete specimen has been found there, so no whole skeleton has been taken 'from the peat', strictly speaking. The last one in Ireland probably died about 11,000 years ago.

28 *The wet centre is bottomless*: when SH said of the poem that it 'didn't seem to stop after the last line' (*SS*, 90–1), he was acknowledging the opening up of what was to be a major and productive thematic vein. But it was also rounding off a theme that has been prominent in several of the poems in the volume: the underlying layer of land and water as a figure of history and its presence in the current situation. In the early essay 'Belfast', SH says that the bog 'was a wide low apron of swamp on the west bank of the River Bann [. . .] the bog was rushy and treacherous, no place for children. They said you shouldn't go near the moss-holes because "there was no bottom in them"' (*Preoccupations*, 35). 'Moss', as in 'Mossbawn' or 'moss-holes', is the local term for bog or swamp.

UNCOLLECTED POEMS (1969–1972)

Few periods of SH's writing life involved such wide-ranging development as the period between *Door into the Dark* in 1969 and *Wintering Out* in 1972, partly because of major changes in his life circumstances. He and his family spent the academic year 1970–1 in Berkeley, California, where he was a visiting lecturer. In 1972 they moved south to Co. Wicklow. Major changes in the corpus over the period are evident from a comparison of the contents of the unpublished volume Winter Seeds (Appendix II), semi-completed in Berkeley, with the poems of *Wintering Out* as proposed to Faber and as published in the event in 1972. In addition, some poems from Winter Seeds are adapted in *Wintering Out*: for example section II of the poem 'Last Camp' is adapted as 'Tinder', section 5 of 'A Northern Hoard'. The uncollected poem rather mysteriously entitled 'Retort' about a child seeing dead relatives is again published along with 'The Last Mummer' and 'Icon' here. 'Scullion', the poem about SH's 'Big-voiced' ancestors, contains phrases drawn on for 'The Strand at Lough Beg' in *Field Work*. The outspoken, unusually explicit 'Craig's Dragoons', a bitterly satirical song written for the composer Seán Ó Riada to be broadcast on radio, is included in this group.

Medallion

Published in the *Listener*, 82. 2110 (4 Sept. 1969): 311.

Epigraph *Reverend George Walker:* (c.1645–1690), joint governor of Derry during the siege in 1689, killed at the Battle of the Boyne, 1 July 1690, reputedly when going to the aid of the wounded Duke of Schomberg, a leader of William of Orange's army in the battle.

Icon

First published in the *Listener*, 82. 2110 (4 Sept. 1969): 311; subsequently in *Michigan Quarterly Review*, 9. 3 (Summer 1970): 167.

[text: *Listener*]

The myth of St Patrick ridding Ireland of snakes, with an ironic negative conclusion with the 'worm-clot' wrapped round the crozier.

Idyll

Published in the *Listener*, 82. 2110 (4 Sept. 1969): 311.

5 The line about hunted animals 'That die barking on the slopes' is strikingly evocative of the hunting scenes in *Sir Gawain and the Green Knight*: 'What, thay brayen and bleden, bi bonkkes thay deyen' ('They scream and they bleed, they die on the hillsides', 1163).
   Cf. 'Land' (*WO*, 11).

Offerings

Published in the *Honest Ulsterman*, 19 (Nov. 1969): 4. 'High Street, 1786' was collected with revisions as 'Linen Town' in *WO* and subtitled there as 'High Street, Belfast, 1786', the title under which it was previously published in *Critical Quarterly*, 11. 4 (Winter 1969): 293, but it is retained here, among the uncollected poems, in order to note its significant place in this sequence dedicated to Patrick Rooney. 'September Song' here differs from the later poem of that title published in the *Honest Ulsterman*, 54 (Jan./Feb. 1977) and collected in *FW*.

Dated 24 May 1971 in MS (NLI 49,493/16).
   Dedication Patrick Rooney, aged nine, was the first child killed in the Northern Ireland Troubles; he was struck by an RUC tracer bullet which entered his home in the Divis Flats, Belfast, on 14 August 1969, during rioting outside. (See McKittrick 1999, 34.)

1 TURNIP MAN

At Hallowe'en turnips are hollowed out to make a lighted head as pumpkins are in England and the US.
   1–4 A popular Belfast street song, made famous by its recording by David Hammond, SH's friend and fellow performer; see 'The Singer's House' (*FW*, 27; *PSH*, 227).
   4 *Fornenst*: in front of (Ulster-Scots)

2 HIGH STREET, 1786

17] Forever arrested, pre-revolution. *Critical Quarterly*

Title From the etching *High Street, Belfast, 1786*, by J. Nixon. A watercolour based on it was done by Joseph William Carey in 1917: cf. 'this civic print unfrozen' (12) and 'water tint' (18).
   10–11 *the Linen Hall / or Cornmarket*: centres of civic operation in Belfast.

14 Henry Joy McCracken (1767–98), one of the leaders of the United Irishmen in Belfast in 1798, executed in July of that year: a heroic figure in Republican lore, the subject of the song 'Henry Joy', recorded by the Dubliners and others.

24–7 *reasonable . . . a last turn with citizens / In the tang of possibility*: terms of the Enlightenment associated with the revolutionary 1790s.

3 FROM CAVE HILL

Title The basalt outcrop that overhangs Belfast.

4 SEPTEMBER SONG

Title Also the title of the 1938 song by Kurt Weill and Maxwell Anderson, and of a much admired 1968 poem by Geoffrey Hill; later the title of a very different poem by SH (*FW*, 38; *PSH*, 235).

3 *Tele*: the *Belfast Telegraph*.

5 Patrick Rooney's name will be expunged from the school register, and he will be absent from the Hallowe'en games, associated with apples. Hallowe'en is sometimes called 'snap-apple night' in Ireland.

An Evening at Killard

Published in the *Irish Press* (29 Nov. 1969): 9.

Title Killard, in the Lecale area of Co. Down on Strangford Lough was where Michael McLaverty lived at the end of his life. SH spoke at an event commemorating his centenary in Downpatrick in September 2004.

Dedication Michael McLaverty (1904–92), born in Carrickmacross, Co. Monaghan, was headmaster of St Thomas's secondary school when SH taught there. Admired writer of short stories and novels.

6 *neb*: northern Irish or Scottish term for a bird's beak.

7 *St Patrick's Rock*: pair of black basalt columns near Downpatrick.

14 The same advice McLaverty is credited with in 'Fosterage', section 5 of 'Singing School' (*North*, 74; *PSH*, 203).

Their Brother

Published in the *Listener* (18 Dec. 1969): 864.

This poem and the next one may be about the same boy.

Crowing Man

Published in the *Listener* (18 Dec. 1969): 864.

Lictor

Published in the *Listener* (18 Dec. 1969): 864.

Title Like 'Freedman' in *North* (61; *PSH*, 203) 'Lictor' was derived from a prose poem called 'Romanist' which draws on official functions in Imperial Rome. A lictor was a magistrate's attending officer whose role is here compared to the priesthood of the Catholic Church. The politically divided sense of the poem is paralleled by the epigraph from R. H. Barrow's *The Romans*, added in 'Freedman' from the prose poem: 'slavery comes nearest to its justification in the early Roman Empire'.

1–2 A gully-knife was a sharp kitchen knife, here being used to cut marrowstem kale, which left big stalks when the cabbage-head was cut off. The sheathing of the knife suggests the completion of a violent action against 'casualties'.

A Twilight

Published in *three* (1969).

4. *lien*: used here to mean 'weed', as with 'Maighdean Mara' (I, 7; *WO*, 56; *PSH*, 144).

Yank

Published in *Everyman* (1969): 14–15.

Elegy for a Postman

First published in the *Listener* (5 Feb. 1970): 182, and subsequently included in Peter Porter (ed.), *New Poems 1971–1972: A PEN Anthology of Contemporary Poetry* (London: Hutchinson, 1972), 86.

[text: *Listener*]

William Rooney, a fifty-four-year-old postman who was frozen to death in his boat on Lough Erne on 29–30 December 1961.

Rags

Published in *The Tablet*, 224. 6773 (21 March 1970): 276.

Third Degree

Published in the *New Statesman* (10 April 1970): 515.

Retort

Published in *Michigan Quarterly Review*, 9. 3 (Summer 1970): 165, with 'The Last Mummer' and 'Icon', in an issue entitled *New Poetry from England* guest edited by Donald Hall.

11 *scapular*: a long band around the neck, worn as a symbol of religious devotion and of the wish for the grace of a happy death.

Last Camp

Published in the *New Statesman* (12 June 1970): 840.

Cf. 'Tinder', Part V of 'A Northern Hoard' in WO, in which some of these images are developed.

Intimidation

Published in *Malahat Review*, 17 (Jan. 1971): 34; subsequently as 'A Midsummer' in the *Irish Times* (13 Feb. 1971): 5.

15–16] Drifts in the street and soot / Off his blackened holding *Irish Times*
\>16]   Falls like a conjurer's scarf.
         He has a premonition
         Of winnowing, quicklime
         In the whitewashed dust. *Irish Times*

Rubric

Published in *Malahat Review*, 17 (Jan. 1971): 36.

Cf. 'The Blinker' below. The idea of transmitting ill-fortune through votive objects or activities was widespread in rural communities: called *piseoga* in Irish. Here it is linked to more overt anti-neighbour activities like setting things on fire, and to the July bonfire season in Ulster in the poems 'Intimidation' and 'A Midsummer' in this series. It suggests wider contexts for the notoriously powerful phrase 'neighbourly murder' ('Funeral Rites', *North*, 18).

Museum Pieces

Published in the Irish Times (13 Feb. 1971): 5.

This is the first poem in Winter Seeds.

   Dedication Michael S. Harper (1938–2016) was a New York-born poet who wrote to heal the various divisions of the times, notably between black and white experience, often using the history of jazz as a common element. The crucial term for him was 'kinship', and in his Yeats-derived collection Nightmare Begins Responsibility: Poems in 1974 he wrote about his own family antecedents as well as public artistic figures such as John Coltrane and the novelist Richard Wright. Images of Kin in 1977 was nominated for a National Book Award. Both in terminology and subject his writing parallels SH's in the 1970s.

Craig's Dragoons

Published in Review (Autumn/Winter 1971–2): 47; the poem is published in an essay by Karl Miller titled 'Opinion'.

Title William Craig (1924–2011), Northern Irish politician and founder of the unionist Ulster Vanguard party after an early career in the Ulster Unionist Party. As Minister of Home Affairs in Terence O'Neill's government, he banned a march planned by the Derry Housing Action Committee and the Northern Irish Civil Rights Association march in Derry on 5 October 1968. The march went ahead and its violent suppression by the RUC, who baton-charged the peaceful protestors, was captured by television cameras to the shock of international audiences; it is routinely cited as one of the key starting points of the Troubles. When O'Neill dismissed Craig, he became head of the Ulster Loyalist Association and, after he lost the UUP whip, he founded Vanguard in 1972. They were influential in the Ulster Unionist Council which opposed and defeated the Sunningdale Agreement between the British and Irish governments in 1974.
   2 Craig's Dragoons is derived from the Irish Jacobite song 'Clare's Dragoons'.
   9 Eddie McAteer leader of the Catholic Nationalist Party; Austin Currie and Gerry Fitt of the Social Democratic and Labour Party.

Letter to an Editor

Published in the Honest Ulsterman, 31 (Nov./Dec. 1971): 7.

The addressee is Michael Foley, editor of the *Honest Ulsterman*, who had written disparagingly about SH in the summer issue of 1971, and to whom SH now responds. Foley would later write an article in the *Irish Times*, 'How I Learned to Love Seamus Heaney's Poetry' (1 June 2020), regretting and rejecting his early view that SH's work was 'everything that poetry should not be, a rejection of the urban world for pastoral nostalgia, and of adult life for childhood nostalgia, a cautious upholding of all the Irish pieties (especially the Holy Trinity of nation, church and family), and an avoidance of anything emotionally disturbing or intellectually challenging'.

9 *H.U.*: the *Honest Ulsterman* poetry journal.

16–17 *The Great Hunger, Collected Pruse*: works by Patrick Kavanagh.

Slieve Gallon's Brae

Published in *Broadsheet*, 13 (Dec. 1971): [verso].

Title A familiar and admired Ulster song, named from the local mountain.

Epigraph The first two lines of the song's chorus.

1ff. Marie Heaney singing with her eyes closed occurs again in 'At the Wellhead' (*SL*, 65; *PSH*, 499).

Woodcut

Published in *Workshop*, 11 (1971): 4.

Father of the Bride

Published in *Aquarius* (1971): 44, along with 'Mother of the Groom' (*PSH*, 139).

Baptism

Dated 17 December 1971 and dedicated to Ellen and Kate Flanagan, and posthumously published in the *Atlantic* (Jan. 2025): 39.

12 those] thsoe *Atlantic* (reproduction of author TS)

The poem, written for the daughters of his Berkeley friend Tom Flanagan, was read by SH at the Flanagan children's baptism in Dublin, December 1971. It was gifted in typescript to the children on a 'piece of onionskin he typed that poem on, so thin that it's almost translucent', as described by co-dedicatee Caitlin Flanagan, who recounted the import of receiving the poem as 'my certificate of belonging, in this world and the next'. The poem is collected here in the chronological moment of its gifting, rather than in its occasion of posthumous publication.

The Blinker

Published in *Fortnight*, 43 (July 1972): 20.

Cf. 'Rubric' above. This poem is an extensive list of the elements of Irish rural black magic: good and diseased eyes, coffin nails, rancid butter and sour milk, action on the border between farms.

Scullions

Published in the *Irish Times* (7 Oct. 1972): 9.

Note how SH returns to this poem and lifts phrases for 'The Strand at Lough Beg'.
    7, 14 *Ballyscullion*: a parish connected to Bellaghy, the Catholic church attended by SH's Scullion granduncles.
    22 *mongol*: the now unacceptable term for people with Down syndrome. Possibly the person mentioned in 'Their Brother' and 'Crowing Man' above.

January God

Published with an illustration by T. P. Flanagan as a broadside by the Arts Council of Northern Ireland in 1972. Subsequently included in Helen Hickey's *Images of Stone* (Belfast: Blackstaff, 1976), 12.

Sile na Gig

Published in Seamus Heaney (ed.), *Soundings: An Annual Anthology of New Irish Poetry* (Belfast: Blackstaff, 1972), 24.

An independent poem from the like-titled 'Sheelagh na Gig' in *SI*. For a consideration of this controversial poem, and SH's collaborations with Barrie Cooke on it, see Heather Clark, '"Diving for Crucibles": Seamus Heaney, Barrie Cooke, and Bog Poems' (*Éire-Ireland*, Spring/Summer 2023, 14–49).

WINTERING OUT (1972)

Wintering Out was published as a paperback original on 20 November 1972 in 2,500 copies by Faber & Faber in London, and in New York by Oxford University Press on 26 April 1973 in 500 cased copies produced by Faber from original sheets. A hardback edition for UK and Ireland was initially cancelled but later released in the autumn of 1973, marking the first time that SH had been originated in Britain and Ireland in paper covers. The paperback edition was reprinted in 1975 and reprinted again in 1978 in 3,000 paper copies and again in 1980; by the time it was reset in 1993 it had been reprinted nine times.

The book was launched at the Abbey Theatre in Dublin on 6 November 1972, with advance copies supplied a fortnight before publication. It had not received the smoothest of starts: Faber had learned in July 1972 that the book was to be, like its predecessor, the Choice of the Poetry Book Society that autumn, only to learn in August that a mistake had been made and the book had been awarded neither the Choice nor a Recommendation. Nevertheless, the publication quickly found its critical place. Even allowing for the general enthusiasm with which the first two books had been received, several commentators greeted *Wintering Out* as a major development. Peter Porter in the *Guardian* wrote that SH's fastidious use of language had never been so well employed as in this volume. Eavan Boland in the *Irish Times* believed that the collection went further and with more maturity onto new grounds of 'desolation and isolation'. Harold Bloom told readers of the *TLS* that SH was now simply 'unlike any other significant poet at work in the language anywhere'. Clive James, reviewing the book in the *Observer*, suggested that, with *Wintering Out*, SH now stood above all his contemporaries, and that comparisons to Yeats were imminent. Neil Corcoran would later confer upon the book an assessment that it had been 'the seminal single volume of the post-1970 period of English poetry' (Corcoran 1993, 182).

SH had spent the academic year 1970–1 at Berkeley in California, giving his emerging collection a rather different starting point to its predecessors. He had given the working collection the title Winter Seeds after the grains imagined in the stomach of the Tollund Man (*SS*, 121), and less directly perhaps also recalling the seeds from which the barley grew in 'Requiem for the Croppies'. Winter Seeds resides in various iterations in the NLI (49,493/18–23), but there exists a preliminary version of the typescript in the Thomas Flanagan Archive at Amherst, Massachusetts, headed in SH's hand 'Winter Seeds (most of them)', gifted to Thomas and Jean Flanagan, prominent hosts of the Heaneys in California ('our best friends about the place', *LSH*, 137), in the winter of 1970–1.* A comparison between the Amherst and NLI typescripts testifies to the considerable degree of revision that the poems of <u>Winter Seeds</u> underwent at that time, well before SH made the radical changes to the assembly that were about to come.

SH tells O'Driscoll that the title for the volume came 'from memories of cattle in winter fields. Beasts standing under a hedge, plastered in wet, looking at you with big patient eyes, just taking what came until something else came along. Times were bleak, the political climate was deteriorating. The year the book was published was the year of Bloody Sunday and Bloody Friday' (*SS*, 121). (Bloody Sunday, 30 January 1972, is one of the defining events of the Troubles: members of the Parachute Regiment opened fire on unarmed protestors during a civil rights demonstration in Derry, killing thirteen people and injuring at least fifteen others, one fatally. Bloody Friday, 21 July 1972, was an especially brutal day of paramilitary violence, when the Provisional IRA planted twenty-two bombs across Belfast which killed nine people and seriously injured more than 130.) But finding a governing title for the book was not straightforward. *No Man's Land* and *A Dreamer at the Ford* had also been prospective titles before the volume narrowed its focus to become *Wintering* around April 1971, *en route* to its final formation. SH can be seen ascribing the spirit of a book to the public conditions of its time, saying in an interview in 1972 something that has been very widely quoted, particularly during the Covid-19 pandemic (though the phrase is not expressly used in the poetry): 'If we winter this one out, we can summer anywhere,' an expression that draws on a line from the poem 'Sarah Ann' by the Tyrone Presbyterian minister-poet, W. F. Marshall, spoken in the voice of an exploited farm-labourer:

> I wunthered in wee Robert's, I can summer anywhere.†

Many of the poems that would give the collection its distinctiveness were written after SH's return from California to Belfast, in the autumn and winter of 1971. *Wintering Out* was recorded by that name as 'Accepted' in the Faber Book Register for 14 October 1971, and although the title for the collection would now remain fixed, the content was nevertheless still to undergo considerable transformation

---

* The Amherst TS: 'WINTER SEEDS / (most of them) / Tom's and Jean's / 8th January 1970 / Seamus'; the date, which cannot be correct as SH was first introduced to the Flanagans in September 1970, may conceivably be a new-year 'slip' for 8 January 1971.

† This source was suggested to us by Marie Heaney.

after that date, despite its interim delivery to the publisher. Several of the volume's most admired and iconic poems – including those that SH referred to as 'the languagey poems' (*SS*, 124): 'Anahorish', 'Broagh' and 'Fodder' – were written over a few days between 11 and 15 January 1972. The latter, with its vernacular correction of pronunciation in its opening lines ('Or, as we said, / *fother*'), was just one of a number of local phonetic details that marked new ground for the volume.

The introduction by SH of a subsequent suite of five pieces sent to Charles Monteith on 9 April 1972, two months after the typescript had been passed to the compositors Latimer Trent on 16 February 1972 for typesetting, would introduce another defining character of the collection. Those poems – 'Oracle', 'Backward Look', 'Traditions', 'A New Song' and 'The Other Side' – were to appear together in a first part of a book that SH wanted to perceive as 'a single breath' (*SS*, 122) that could be felt 'moving in and out of the theme of language and Ulster and identity' (*LSH*, 81). In that same submission to Monteith, SH had asked about 'dividing the book' in a bipartite format. The request, together with the additional poems, triggered an increase in the extent from seventy-two to eighty pages: it pushed the text of the book in an ungainly way up against the inside covers, but it emphasised the division that would so characteristically mark not only *Wintering Out* but *North* and some later volumes.

At the same time – and for the first time – an early poem in one volume ('Bog Oak' is the second poem) extends the material that concludes a previous volume ('Bogland' is the last in *Door into the Dark*), and so begins to make links that can be seen as both reflecting upon and anticipating each other: an instance of the Janus-faced volume-endings noted by Patrick Crotty (Crotty 1994, 193).

Of equal moment is the first emergence of the bog as subject in 'The Tollund Man', written in West Kerry in Easter 1970. SH had read P. V. Glob's *The Bog People*, published in Denmark in 1965 and translated into English in 1969, and been captivated by the haunting black-and-white photographs of what Glob believed to be victims of ritual killing. In 1973, SH met Glob on a visit to Denmark and saw the Tollund Man in the Silkeborg Museum, fulfilling the declaration of the poem's opening, 'Some day I will go to Aarhus / To see his peat-brown head.'

The volume is more substantially represented in SH's selected editions than either of its predecessors, and it is at the same time more discerning. When O'Driscoll asked him why certain early poems were held back ('Orange Drums, Tyrone 1966' from Winter Seeds is printed as section 3 of 'The Ministry of Fear', the concluding sequence in *North*, for example), SH says that he felt they did not suit 'the more inward, broody style' of the final *Wintering Out* (*SS*, 123–4). The 'inward, broody style' might describe Part Two of *Wintering Out*, but there is some suggestion here of the more marked political–personal division between the two parts that will characterise *North*.

Some of the early Winter Seeds poems took on a later life in this way. Others had more restrictive outings in the form of sole printing in journals. On 19 May 1969, SH told Charles Monteith that, in a remarkable burst of activity, he had composed twenty-three poems in the past week, 'nearly all of which I believe I'll be keeping' (*LSH*, 41); later, in an apparent escalation of remembrance, SH tells O'Driscoll that the tally had been 'about forty poems' (*SS*, 147). While several of the poems of that extraordinary week appeared in *Wintering Out*, 'a lot more saw the light of day just once, in spreads in *The Listener*', in September 1969, then edited by Karl Miller, including 'Idyll', 'Medallion', 'Their Brother', 'Crowing Man' and 'Lictor', collected here for the first time (*PSH*, 95–100). Other poems from Winter Seeds ('Hawthorns' (*PSH*, 1179) and 'Museum Pieces' (*PSH*, 106)) were gutted for new poems in *Wintering Out*, or stripped down to provide material in SH's next three collections. Several more poems were included in *Wintering Out* after substantial adaptation: 'High Street, Belfast, 1786' in Winter Seeds appears here as 'Linen Town'; 'Dream of the Trenches' (Winter Seeds) as 'Veteran's Dream' (*WO*).

Tellingly, Michael Parker (2007, 133) makes the interesting observation that 'several of the poems that SH originally chose to start Winter Seeds were never published.' Of forty poems published in journals and magazines between 1969 and 1972, only fourteen found their way into *Wintering Out*, which, in the words of Michael R. Molino, represented 'an unprecedented selectivity' (Molino 1993, 57). Molino argues that it was the darkening of the Troubles that imposed this selectivity, and one issue with this change of tack from Winter Seeds is indeed whether it represents a move in a more political direction. Patrick Crotty writes, 'Nothing in *North* mines the ore of terror half so hair-raisingly' as 'the visionary gore of "The Tollund Man"' in *Wintering Out*, with its 'Tell-tale skin and teeth' (Crotty 1994, 196). 'A generation after their first appearance,' he goes on, 'the best poems in *Wintering Out* still have something disturbed and disturbing about them.' So, when SH says to John Haffenden, 'Up to *North*, that was one book' (Haffenden 1981, 64), there are important distinctions between the component volumes of that 'one book'. SH makes it clear that the turn towards the political was partly suggested by his time in California (it could hardly fail to be), and that his encounters with Tom Flanagan with his emphasis on the 'historical and political and biographical' aspects of criticism assuaged the bias towards the circumscribed textuality of the Eliotic New Criticism in which SH had been schooled.

Furthermore, SH had, he told Charles Monteith in the delivery of the April 1972 suite of poems, come to believe that poetry had become an 'urgency' in response to the political situation, and that he hoped that *Wintering Out* might 're-define' the climate for at least a few people on both sides (*LSH*, 81). Such a goal inevitably must place weight upon the poems that can be difficult to balance, as he told the poet Brendan Hamill in January 1973:

> Even as the violence proceeded, I still sought ways of keeping within the style and landscape of my earlier poetry; still waited for poems to accrue round seminal images; refused to allow the will to direct the motion of the imagination; tried to be non-partisan and to comprehend all that was happening within the terms of history and myth. (*LSH*, 99)

For all that right and artful need for balance, *Wintering Out* nevertheless remains, as SH himself has observed, 'the collection where language and its historical/political charge come into focus' (*LSH*, 776).

In the end, *Wintering Out* is, as Neil Corcoran writes, a more aspirational, ambitious book than the two previous volumes, and it is more challenging to read: similarly, some of the uncollected poems of 1969–72, such as 'Last Camp', are difficult to interpret precisely. A sequence like 'A Northern Hoard', although its harsh themes are forceful enough, seems to evade detailed scrutiny, both in vocabulary and narrative: a complexity carried over from its interim, unresolved predecessor-forms in Winter Seeds. The book is allusive in a way that the earlier books were not, and among the most 'languagey'. Last of all to be added to the collection, Michael Parker tells us, was 'The Backward Look' which, though it comes in the middle of the book, serves well as a summation of the ideas about those 'languagey' poems with a snipe 'fleeing . . . into dialect, / into variants'. The political context is tested at the end when the snipe 'corkscrews away . . . / through the sniper's eyrie, / over twilit earthworks / and wallsteads', and where the snipe–sniper echo is suggested all the more threateningly for its inexplicitness. The closing poem 'Westering' glances towards the orientation of John Donne's 'Good Friday. Riding Westward', and acts as a kind of valedictory to the US as the Janus face turns east and north again.

[text: WO2002]

For David Hammond and Michael Longley

Published in *WO*.

In 1968 SH went on an Arts Council poetry and song tour in Ulster called Room to Rhyme with Hammond and Longley. In July 2003, he called his Greatest Minds Lecture at the University of Dundee 'Room to Rhyme'; it was published by the university in 2004. The three quatrains of this epigraph make up an apparently independent poem in the archive; the dedication to his collaborators on Room to Rhyme is a recognition of the cross-cultural aim of the tour in the difficult circumstances of 1968. The same quatrains are reprinted as section IV of 'Whatever You Say Say Nothing' in *North* (60; *PSH*, 200).

2 *the internees*: on 9 August 1971 the British Army's Operation Demetrius began, introducing internment without trial to Northern Ireland. The measure had been proposed to the British government by the Unionist government at Stormont, and involved mass arrests of people from Catholic and nationalist backgrounds suspected of involvement with the IRA. It is regarded as a major exacerbating factor in inter-community tensions as well as in tensions between the British Army and the nationalist community.

8 *Stalag 17*: a German prisoner-of-war camp near Krems in Austria, familiar from a 1953 film directed by Billy Wilder, based on a play written by two survivors about their experiences there.

10 *on a wall downtown*: when this epigraph is reprinted in 'Whatever You Say Say Nothing' this phrase is replaced by the more territorially definitive 'In Ballymurphy', which evokes the Ballymurphy Massacre of 9–11 August 1971 in which the Parachute Regiment killed eleven civilians in the course of Operation Demetrius.

PART ONE

Fodder

First published in the *TLS* (17 March 1972): 314, and subsequently collected in *WO* and *OG*.

8 itself] itself, *TLS*

Dated 15 January 1972 in MS (NLI 49,493/5), the first of the series of language-themed poems SH said he wrote at that time, as additions and changes to the prototype version of the book, Winter Seeds, which had mostly been assembled in the course of his year at Berkeley. This poem is called 'Museum Pieces' in <u>Winter Seeds</u>, and is unrelated to the uncollected poem of that title in this edition (*PSH*, 106). SH calls the series 'languagey poems' (*SS*, 124) which centre on the components of the linguistic amalgam of Northern Ireland.

Title '"Fodder", pronounced "fother" where I grew up, rhyming with mother, half-rhyming with father' (*LSH*, 776).

2 The substitution of the voiced dental ð for the alveolar d in some Irish accents is accurately observed.

6 *vise*: the US spelling for 'vice', pronounced 'vize' by SH on his audio recordings.

Bog Oak

First published in the *Listener* (23 March 1972): 372, and later in the *New Republic* (27 March 1976): 24. Collected in *WO*, and subsequently included in *SP*, *PM*, *NSP1990* and *OG*.

6 I] We *Listener*

11–12 Cf. 'The Dirraghs', *ll*. 14–16: 'as blow-downs of smoke / struggling over half-doors . . . / into the drizzle' (*PSH*, 1181).

26–8 From *A View of the Present State of Ireland, Discoursed by way of a Dialogue between Eudoxus and Ireneus* (1596) by Edmund Spenser. Spenser (*c*.1552–99), the poet of *The Faerie Queene*, became private secretary to Arthur Grey, the Lord Deputy of Ireland, in July 1580. He spent most of his last twenty years unhappily in Ireland and he was sheriff-designate for Co. Cork at the end of his life. Kilcolman Castle near Buttevant, Co. Cork was his principal residence from 1583 until the year before his death in London. *A View of the Present State of Ireland* is his only prose work. In this passage, Ireneus explains to Eudoxus that in the desperate conditions the Irish are reduced to, 'there perished not many by the sword, but all by the extremitie of famine, which they themselves had wrought' (Hadfield 1997, 101). SH quotes part of this passage in 'The Trade of an Irish Poet' (*Guardian*, 25 May 1972: 17); the evocative term 'geniuses' (*l*. 25) in this Irish vernacular sense is supplied by him.

Anahorish

First published along with 'Broagh' and 'Toome', under the collective title 'Watermarks' in *Stand* (July 1972): 4. Later published alongside facsimile manuscript version, dated 11 January 1972, in 'Poet's Worksheets' in *Phoenix*, 13 (Spring 1975). Collected in WO and included in the limited-edition *Toome*, illustrated by Jane Proctor and published by the National College of Art and Design, Dublin, in 1980, and *Seamus Heaney: Readings in Contemporary Poetry* (New York: Dia Art Foundation, 1988). Recordings were included on *Seamus Heaney and Tom Paulin* (Faber Poetry Cassette, London, 1983) and *Seamus Heaney at Harvard*. It was used as the title poem for the programme for Seamus Heaney–Derek Walcott, a joint poetry reading at the DIA Center for the Arts, New York (12 April 1996). It was also included in SP, PM, NSP*1990*, OG and *100P*.

6 lane.] lane: *Stand*

Dated 11 January 1972 in MS (NLI 49,493/5), although SH's work on the poem continued deep into the production of the proofs of WO, writing to Faber about *l.* 10 on 7 June 1972 long after author revisions would be viable: 'If it's still in time, I want to make a niggling alteration in stanza 3 of Anahorish. Can you alter "swung in its yards" to "swung through the yards"? Is my ear too pernickety, or is there more dark and swing in the second? I think it's worth changing. I take a vow of silence until the next book' (ALS SH–Lorna Simmonds, 7 June 1972: FF P/Rdlm/667/3).

1 Anahorish, a townland near Magherafelt, close to SH's birthplace and the location of his primary school. The name is usually glossed as a translation of the Irish *áit an fuar uisce*, 'place of the cold water', or *anach fhior uisce*, meaning roughly 'swamp of pure water'. As in 'Broagh', the first line is a calque translation of the place name.

Servant Boy

First published as a broadside by the Red Hanrahan Press, Detroit (20 June 1971), in *Responses*, a limited-edition book from the National Book League and the National Poetry Society (1971): 24, and in the *Honest Ulsterman*, 31 (Nov./Dec. 1971): 5. Collected in WO and subsequently included in SP, PM and OG. It was also included in Desmond Egan and Michael Hartnett's *Choice: An Anthology of Irish Poetry Selected by the Poets Themselves* (Castleknock: Goldsmith Press, 1973), 38–9.

10^11] [stanza break] (error) *Honest Ulsterman*

Title 'Hired-Boy' in TS (NLI 49,493/13).
    1 *wintering out*: effectively the title poem of the volume, in the same way as 'The Forge' was in DD. 'Wintering Out' has been interpreted as meaning 'living through a bad time' without relief; in

Irish agricultural terms, it means leaving cattle out in the fields for the winter rather than in barns and stalls.

6 *Old work-whore*: in Irish vernacular usage the term 'servant boy' was used for men of all ages (like 'postboy' for 'postman').

7 *fair-hills*: the fairs at which agricultural workers called 'spalpeens' (*spailpíní* in Irish) stood waiting to be hired belong to an earlier period. It is said to have been the employment of Eoghan Rua Ó Súilleabháin (1748–84), the eighteenth-century poet celebrated in SH's poem 'Poet to Blacksmith' (*DC*, 25; *PSH*, 604). The poem's terminology ('jobber' (5), 'bidder' (8)) comes from the cattle-dealing which was SH's father's employment.

13 *haggard*: Irish vernacular for farmyard (via 'hay-yard').

16 *first-footing*: a practice mostly in evidence in Scotland and Northern England, applied to the first person to come into the house at New Year. The term 'first-footer' occurs at the end of 'Belfast's Black Christmas', SH's *Listener* piece which became 'Christmas 1971', Part 2 of 'Belfast' (*Preoccupations*, 33). The term 'first footers' is used in the previously uncollected poem 'Beacons at Bealtaine' (*PSH*, 585), delivered at an EU Enlargement Ceremony in the Phoenix Park on 1 May 2004, to refer to the mythological invasion of Ireland.

The Last Mummer

Privately printed as a Christmas card in 1969. Part I published in the *Honest Ulsterman*, 22 (March/April 1970): 15, where the poem is misnamed 'Last Summer' in the contents list, in *Michigan Quarterly Review*, 9. 3 (Summer 1970): 166 and in the *Guardian* (9 July 1970): 11, and then, revised and extended to three parts, again in the *Honest Ulsterman*, 31 (Nov./Dec. 1971): 5–6. Collected thereafter in *WO* and included in *SP*.

I–III] [initial caps] *HU1970*, *Michigan Quarterly*, *Guardian*
I 3–4 out of the fog / on the lawn, pads] out of the fog on the lawn, / Pads *HU1970*

The poem has an involved textual history. Like 'Linen Town' (*WO*, 28; *PSH*, 131), it is derived from 'High Street Belfast, 1786' in Winter Seeds. Only section I appears initially under the poem's title in its earlier sonnet-publications in the first 1970 *Honest Ulsterman* printing, before a full-length version appears in the same journal in 1971.

I 8 *St George, Beelzebub and Jack Straw*: characters from the traditional mummers' play which provided the title of the Arts Council tour undertaken by SH with Michael Longley and David Hammond in 1968, Room to Rhyme. The Christmas mummers' play was enacted in Co. Derry (and throughout Ulster) in SH's childhood, as he explains in his lecture at the University of Dundee in 2003, published as *'Room to Rhyme'* (Dundee, 2004).

III 11 *monstrance*: an ornate vessel used in Catholic ritual to display the Eucharistic host for veneration.

III 13–14 Cf. 'In a Yard', stanza 3 (*c*.1967–71; *PSH*, 1180).

Land

First published as a broadside by Poem-of-the-Month Club (Greenfield: John Roberts Press, 1971), and then in *Hibernia* (17 Nov. 1972): 15. Collected in *WO* and subsequently included in *OG*. A reading of the poem was also included on the Faber Poetry Cassette *Seamus Heaney and Tom Paulin*.

I 7 hedges] hedges, *OG*
II 1 leave] leave, *OG*
II 2 branchy] branchy, *OG*
II 6 open-work] open work *Hibernia*

Gifts of Rain

First published in *Poetry*, 119. 5 (Feb. 1972): 280–2, and then in the *Irish Press* (18 Nov. 1972): 7. Subsequently collected in *WO* and included in *SP*, *PM*, *NSP1990* and *OG*.

I 8 stepping stones] stepping-stones *Poetry, Irish Press*
III 7 slabbering] unfurling *Poetry, Irish Press*
III 16 calling] voices *Poetry, Irish Press*

Dated 11 January 1971 in MS (NLI 49,493/14).

I 1ff. The theme and medium of the poem are the senses of touch and hearing in response to water, from the sensing of weather by skin (*l.* 6) to the 'soundings' that measure depth and register sounds.

I 12 *Soundings* was the name of a poetry publication, the first two of which were edited by SH.

III 8, IV 2 *Moyola*: the local river near Broagh and Mossbawn which flows from the Sperrin Mountains to Lough Neagh, much mentioned by SH.

IV This final section is an example of the 'gutting' by SH of one poem for another that is common in *WO*: in this case, a compression of sections IV and V of an unpublished poem, 'A Dreamer at the Ford', which was temporarily adopted as the title poem for *WO*.

Toome

First published, with 'Anahorish' and 'Broagh', under the title 'Watermarks' in *Stand* (July 1972): 5. Subsequently collected in *WO* and included in *OG*. Also published in the special limited edition, *Toome* (Dublin: National College of Art and Design, 1980)

2 blastings,] blastings: *Stand*
7 what] what's *Stand*

Title Toome (also called Toomebridge) a village at the northwest corner of Lough Neagh in Co. Antrim, the location of the execution of a young United Irishman, Roddy McCorley, in 1800, commemorated in a popular republican ballad. SH returns to it in the poem at the start of *EL*, 'At Toomebridge' (*EL*, 3; *PSH*, 527).

  6 *souterrain*: Iron Age underground chamber or passage, widely found in Ireland.

  10 *ware*: archaeological term for pottery; also an Irish country term for crockery, chinaware.

  11 *torcs*: Celtic neck-rings of the Bronze Age. Prized golden torcs are on display in the National Museum in Dublin.

Broagh

First published, with 'Anahorish' and 'Toome' under the collective title 'Watermarks' in *Stand* (July 1972): 5. Subsequently collected in *WO* and included in *SP*, *NSP1990*, *OG* and *100P*. Also published in the special limited-edition *Toome* (Dublin: National College of Art and Design, 1980).

1 Riverbank] Riverback (error) *WO1993*

Dated 12 January 1972 in MS (NLI 49,493/28).

  Title The place name Broagh comes from the Irish *bruach*, 'riverbank', as translated in *l*. 1.

  1 *rigs*: Ulster-Scots term for 'ridges'.

  2 *docken*: dock plants. This word is Ulster-Scots from Old English *doccan*, signalling the poem's etymological complex of source languages.

  11 *boortrees*: Ulster-Scots term for elder.

Oracle

First published in the *Listener* (23 March 1972): 372, collected in *WO* and subsequently included in *Gravities*, *SP*, *PM*, *NSP1990* and *OG*.

The Backward Look

First published in the *Guardian* (25 May 1972): 17, collected with revisions in *WO* and subsequently included in *OG*.

1 A stagger in air] italicised in *Guardian*
6 nesting ground] nesting-ground *OG*
10 reserves –] reserves: *Guardian*
14–28] It disappears
    with the yellow bittern
    into the vaults

    that we live off, its flight
    through the sniper's eyrie,
    over twilit earthworks
    and wall-steads,

    its bleak dabbing among
    gleanings and leavings
    in the combs
    of an archive. *Guardian*
24 wall-steads] wallsteads *OG*

Title 'Snipe' in TS (NLI 49,493/12).

11–13 Variations on the Irish for snipe, *gabhairín reo*, 'little goat of the frost'. Cf. 'bleat' (*l.* 5). See Lysaght 1997, 443.

14–28 The second part of the poem was heavily revised by SH at proof stage from the initial *Guardian* printing: 'Here is the proof – corrected, and a little altered. Nothing drastic, I hope. Just a revision of the Acknowledgements, one stanza of "Bog Oak" and the last half of "Backward Look" . . . I feel the revisions are absolutely necessary in the two poems' (2 June 1972, FF P/Rdlm/667/3).

Traditions

First published in the *Listener* (23 March 1972): 372, and subsequently collected in *WO* and *SP*.

Dedication] [no dedication] *Listener*
II 4 us;] us: *Listener*
III 1 MacMorris] Macmorris *Listener*
III 11 replied,] replied. *Listener*

Dedication Tom Flanagan (1923–2002) was Professor of English at UC Berkeley when SH was guest lecturer (1970–1): author of *The Year of the French* (1979), a major novel about the Rebellion of 1798; with his wife Jean, initially dedicatee of Winter Seeds; acknowledged as major hosts of the Heaneys at Berkeley. SH wrote his obituary in the *New York Review of Books*.

I 3 *the alliterative tradition*: the formal poetic tradition in Old English poems such as *Beowulf*, as distinct from the rhyming and syllable-counting European tradition. Here, and elsewhere, SH represents Ireland as female, aggressed by England, and the English language as male.

I 9–10: *Othello* 1.3.226–9: 'That most sovereign mistress of effects . . . The tyrant custom.'

II 3ff. The dialectal survival of words or senses from earlier English (such as 'varsity', 'deem', 'allow') in Ireland is a recurrent theme of *WO*. Some of the senses here – the verb 'allow' meaning admit or say – are shared with Southern US usage.

III 1 MacMorris in Shakespeare's *Henry V* (3.2.1253) is often named as the first stage Irishman in English literature. He asks 'What ish my nation?' (III 8), a question which is answered here by Leopold Bloom of Joyce's *Ulysses* (III 11–12).

A New Song

First published in *WO*, and subsequently included in *SP*, *NSP1990* and *OG*.

9 just,] just: *NSP1990*, *OG*
10 water,] water – *NSP1990*, *OG*

Dated 6 April 1972 in MS under the working title 'The Girl from Derrygarve'.

1 *Derrygarve*: a townland near Castledawson (*l.* 17) in Co. Derry.

16 *Demesnes staked out in consonants*: associated in *WO* with English, by contrast with the 'vowelling embrace' linked to Irish.

18 *bawn*: fortified dwelling built by English settlers in Ireland (in the introduction to *Beowulf* (xxx), SH derives the word from Irish *bó dhún*, 'a fort for cattle'): hence 'planted', in contrast to the Irish terms *rath* and *bullaun* (20), meaning 'fort' and 'circular depression in a stone'. The invader's consonants and smooth greens are replaced by vowels and geological features.

The Other Side

First published in *Fortnight*, 43 (July 1972): 21, collected in *WO*, and subsequently included in Padraic Fiacc (ed.), *The Wearing of the Black* (Belfast: Blackstaff, 1974), *SP*, *NSP1990*, *OG* and *100P*.

1 marigolds] marigolds, *OG*, *100P*
4 It's poor as] It's as poor as *OG*, *100P*
6 leafage:] leafage. *NSP1990*, *OG*
8 fallow,] fallow *Fortnight*

11 dismissal,] dismissal *Fortnight*
27 big] bid (error) *Fortnight*
30 book] Book *Fortnight*, OG, *100P*

Title 'The Other Side' is another of WO's compound poems that emerged from other beginnings: *ll*. 1–6 of part I being reworked from part I of 'A Dreamer at the Ford' (see note on 'Gifts of Rain', *PSH*, 760), and part III being drawn from a discrete TS called 'The Other Sort', that clearly suggested the eventual title for the WO poem (NLI).

I 2 *a neighbour*: the Heaneys' Protestant farming neighbour Johnny Junkin, after the family moved to the farm at The Wood in 1954, as SH tells O'Driscoll (*SS*, 126). In an early draft of the poem in NLI, 'Community Relations', he arrives by bicycle.

I 4 The biblical Lazarus, like the names in II 3–4, associated with Protestant fidelity to the Bible, by contrast with Catholic liturgical practices which 'hardly rule by the book (the Bible) at all' (II 9).

The Wool Trade

First published in WO.

Title Applies particularly to the trade between England and the Low Countries in the late Middle Ages. Bruges (*l*. 8) in Belgium is a celebrated centre of fine clothing industries, especially lace. A working title for the poem in TS had been 'Tweed' (NLI 49,493/17).

Epigraph From James Joyce, *A Portrait of the Artist as a Young Man*, chapter 5. Stephen Dedalus reflects on how much more the English language belongs to the English Dean of Studies, 'a countryman of Ben Jonson', than to him. (Joyce 1992, 205).

Linen Town

First published in WO.

'Linen Town' is closely related to the poem 'High Street, 1786', published in the 'Offerings' sequence in the *Honest Ulsterman*, 19 (Nov. 1969): 5.

A Northern Hoard

First published in *Hibernia* (17 Dec. 1971): 21 and collected in WO. 'Roots' first published as 'Nocturne' in *Malahat Review*, 17 (Jan. 1971): 35. The full sequence was included in *PM*, 'Roots', 'Stump' and 'Tinder' were included in *SP*, 'Tinder' was included in *OG*.

1 ROOTS

2 streetlamp's] street lamp's *Hibernia*
4^5] [no stanza break] *Malahat Review*
5–11] Sleeping beauty, the touch of love
      Operative as faith to move
      Your small mountains
      And shift your gradual plains
      Is stilled.
              Above each slated terrace
      Gunshot and siren dwindle towards us
      Like well-timed noises off.
      The fault is opening at last – my love,
      How should we love our old Gomorrah? *Malahat Review*
16^17] [no stanza break] *Malahat Review*
19 loam] loam.

2 NO MAN'S LAND

2 awning] yawning (error) *PM*

5 *spirochete*: disease-causing bacteria, including syphilis and Lyme disease.

3 STUMP

1 I am riding] Riding *Hibernia*
2–5] Sometimes from the top of a bus / I see children on waste ground / Stoning the helpless unremembering / Air. Sometimes under a sooty wash *Hibernia*

5 TINDER

6 fingered,] fingered *Hibernia*

Titled 'The Tinder Box' and dated February 1970 in TS (NLI 49,493/28).

Midnight

First published in the *Listener* (4 Sept. 1969): 311, and collected with revisions in *WO*.

5–16] In Ireland. Forests
      Cut down for timber
      That casked each wine of France
      Dwindled. The packs

      Scoured bogland and moor
      Till a Quakerbuck and his dogs

>   Killed the last one
>   In some scraggy waste of Kildare.
>
>   The wolf-hound was crossed
>   With inferior strains.
>   Her ladyship, crinolined,
>   Could flower in the woodland.
>
>   I am thinking tonight
>   The rain sogs turf-banks
>   And heather, sets glinting
>   Outcrops of basalt and granite *Listener*

22–4] Nothing is coursing, / Snuffling, panting and lolling. /The howl sticks in my throat. *Listener*

1 *the professional wars*: the demise of wolves in Ireland is sometimes linked to the loss of habitat caused by the Cromwellian wars of the seventeenth century.

8 The last wolf in Ireland is said to have been killed near Mount Leinster in Co. Carlow in 1786, by a sheep-farmer called John Watson. There are many stories about the end of the wolf in Ireland, here a kind of figure for imperial spoliation.

The Tollund Man

First published in *Threshold* (Summer 1970): 5–6, and then in *Poetry Supplement* (1971) [2–3], before collection in *WO*. Subsequently included in Padraic Fiacc (ed.), *The Wearing of the Black* (Belfast: Blackstaff, 1974), *SP*, *PM*, *Seamus Heaney: Readings in Contemporary Poetry* (New York: Dia Art Foundation, 1988), *NSP1990*, *OG* and *100P*. It was also published in Bryony Coles, J. M. Coles and Mogens Schou Jørgensen (eds), *Bog Bodies, Sacred Sites, and Wetland Archaeology* (Exeter: WARP, 1999).

I 3 eye-lids] eyelids *Threshold*; *OG*, *100P*
I 5 nearby] near by *NSP*
I 6 out,] out – *Threshold*
I 9–10 Naked except for / The cap, noose and girdle,] Naked except for the cap, / Noose and girdle – *Threshold*
II 6 labourers,] labourers; *Threshold*
II 7 Stockinged corpses] The stockinged corpses *Threshold*
II 8 in the farmyards,] in farmyards; *Threshold*
II 11 brothers,] brothers *Threshold*
II 12 along] between *Threshold*
III 3–4 to me, driving, / Saying] to me / Driving, saying *Threshold*
III 5] Grauballe] Grabaulle (error) *WO1972*

Title The Tollund Man is the preserved body of a strangled man, found in 1950 in the Bjaeldskovdal bog in Jutland near the village of Tollund. It is a particularly graphic figure, dated to the fourth century BCE. SH makes his fate a figure for the violence of Northern Ireland, saying he will feel 'unhappy and at home' in the old man-killing parishes there.

I 1 *Aarhus*: the largest city in Jutland and the second largest in Denmark, dating back to the eighth century. SH's attention was drawn to it by reading P. V. Glob's *The Bog People*, which describes with vivid black-and-white photographic illustrations a group of bodies preserved by bog-water. Two decades after his visit to Denmark in 1973, SH made a memorable return to the Silkeborg Museum, an event noted in the poem 'Tollund' at the end of *SL*, dated September 1994 (*SL*, 69; *PSH*, 501).

I 12 *the goddess*: Celtic goddess of fertility. See next poem.

I 13 *torc* (or torque): circular metal necklace found in several Celtic archaeological hoards. The Tollund Man has a leather thong tied round his neck which is thought to be how he was killed.

III 5 Place names in Jutland, here liturgically intoned in the way Irish lists of place names are itemised in the medieval *dinnseanchas* (*Preoccupations*, 131). 'Grauballe' is misspelled in the early editions of *WO*: it is correct in 'The Grauballe Man' in *North*.

Nerthus

First published in the *Listener* (23 March 1972): 372, collected in *WO*, and subsequently included in *SP* and *OG*. Also included in *Toome*.

3 weather,] weather *OG*

Dated 24 March 1970 in MS (NLI 49,493/5), where *ll*. 1–2 appear as a draft of six lines; revised on 12 January 1972 on the same MS page, when *ll*. 3–4 are brought in to replace *ll*. 3–6 of the 1970 version.

Title Nerthus in Germanic culture was a goddess associated with fertility, referred to by Tacitus. SH represents her as the deity to whom the bog bodies may have been sacrificed. The terminology of the poem verges on violence throughout: 'staked', 'gouged', etc.

4 *loaning*: local term for pathway, occurring as 'loaney' in Northern Irish songs.

Cairn-maker

First published in the *Listener* (23 March 1972): 372, collected in *WO*.

Dedication] [no dedication] *Listener*
6 in the Burren] on the mountain *Listener*
15 heather-bells] heather bells *Listener*

Dedication Barrie Cooke (1931–2014) was a painter from Knutsford in Cheshire who lived for much of his life in Kilkenny with his partner, the Dutch ceramic artist Sonja Landweer. Both of them were close friends of the Heaneys, and of Ted Hughes. At the time when SH was preparing *WO* he was working with Cooke, who illustrated some of his poems. Even further collaboration was planned between them, and they remained close friends. They fished together (*SS*, 95 and 335) and painted and wrote about shared experiences. Cooke was an abstract expressionist, much of whose work was set in Ireland. A significant occasion when the Heaneys stayed with Cooke and Landweer is commemorated in a MS archive poem, 'The Island', dated 13 November 1971 (BC 1280725).

Navvy

First published in the *Listener* (4 Sept. 1969): 311, and then in *Capella*, 4 (April 1970): 26. Collected with extensive revisions in *WO*.

1–20]   The moleskins stiff as bark,
        The pick grafting his wrists
        To the shale:
        This old photograph

        Belonged to the railway.
        Two miles from here
        Sleepers and lines without gradients
        Sunk in a bog

        Going far under
        With lake-dwellings and dug-outs.
        But they pile-drove a bed
        That sagged and bobbed

        Just a few inches
        Under buggies, goods and expresses.
        Now all is trucking and cars.
        Where the surface is weavy

        And the camber tilts
        In the slow lane, he still
        Flags you down. The morass
        The macadam snakes over

        Swallowed his yellow bulldozer
        Only four years ago. His drill
        Has him plugged to the hard-core.
        He has not relented.   *Listener, Capella*

Title Slang term for Irish labourers in England, derived from 'navigation workers' from their work on building railways from the early nineteenth century and on motorways in the twentieth.

Veteran's Dream

Published in WO.

Title 'Dream of the Trenches' in TS (NLI 49,493/12).
  1 The figure on whom the veteran was based was a much-liked next-door neighbour of the young married Heaneys in Belfast.
  6 *indifferently*: the war-damaged soldier is indifferent to his harsh surroundings as the navvy was to his ('Navvy', *l*. 13).
  8 *gangrene*: flesh-eating bacterial condition, commonly incurred in the trenches of World War I. Maggots (*l*. 15) were bred to kill its bacteria and stimulate healing.

Augury

First published under the title 'As We Roved Out' in *Malahat Review*, 17 (Jan. 1971): 33. Subsequently in *Criterion* (Galway, 1971): 35–6, collected with revisions in WO. Also included in *Toome*.

5–10]   Sure enough, a neat crusted sore
        Made a white eyepatch
        From one gill to the working jaw
        As it supported itself

        Against the rush of the race.
        Behind us, great wheels and belts
        In the powerhouse hummed and quivered
        The catwalk where we were standing.

        The fish flashed, wound away –
        A slurring
        And running, a creep
        And clearance of murk.

        At the trembling rail
        We hang charmed: *Malahat Review*

Title John Montague has pencilled disapproval of the original title on SH's typescript which may have influenced the change.

PART TWO

Wedding Day

First published in ND, then in *Phoenix*, 6–7 (Summer 1970): 5, and subsequently collected in WO and included in SP, PM, NSP*1990*, OG and *100P*. Also published in the programme for An Evening of Poetry and Music presented by Claddagh Records at the Peacock Theatre, Dublin, 5 July 1970.

2 Sound] The sound *ND, Phoenix*
7–8] Of mourning has gorged / Our friends on the steps. *ND* | Of mourning has gorged / Our friends on the step. *Phoenix*
13 gents] Gents *NSP1990, 100P*
13–14 love. Let me / sleep on your breast to the airport.] love. / Let me sleep on your breast to the airport. *ND; Phoenix*
14 Sleep] sleep (error) *WO1993*

Dated 28 December 1970 in TS (NLI 49,493/26).

Title The first of a series of wedding poems named for the various roles of those involved, of which only the first two are in WO.

Mother of the Groom

First published in *Aquarius*, 4 (1971): 44–5, and then collected in WO. Also published in *New Republic* (27 March 1976): 24. Collected in OG.

5 lap,] lap *Aquarius*
12 her] his *Aquarius* (error?)

Summer Home

Published as 'Summer Home' in WO and subsequently included in SP, PM, NSP1990 and OG. Part I was published as 'The Smell' in *Occident* (Fall 1971): 49. Part II was published as 'Home' in the *New Yorker* (1 May 1971): 48. Parts III and IV appeared as parts I and III of *Chaplet*, a broadside limited to fifty copies (Tara Telephone Publications, Dec. 1971). Part V first published as 'Aubade', *New Yorker* (27 Nov. 1971): 47.

I] [initial caps] *Occident*
I 8 whip off the mat] Whip the mat off *Occident*
I 9 moving] creeping *Occident*
II] [initial caps] *New Yorker* (May 1971)
II 4 hall,] hall *New Yorker* (May 1971)
V 3 you] you, *New Yorker* (Nov. 1971)
V 4 pillow,] pillow – *New Yorker* (Nov. 1971)
V 7 dark –] dark. *New Yorker* (Nov. 1971)

Serenades

First published in the *Listener* (4 Sept. 1969): 311, collected in WO, and subsequently included in SP, PM and OG.

6 the] a *Listener*
15 no man's land] no-man's-land *Listener*; OG
17 love,] love. *Listener*
19–20 us, well, /So] us – / Well, so *Listener*

Somnambulist

Published in *WO*.

Title Dated 12 Jan. 1972 in MS (NLI 49,493/5), and titled 'Virgo' in MS and TS (NLI 49,493/14).

A Winter's Tale

First published in the *Listener* (30 Oct. 1969): 592, collected with significant revisions in *WO*.

8 babble] gabble *Listener*
11 whimper] whimper, *Listener*
12 brandy –] brandy *Listener*
16^17] // So she became a byword.
    By the shocked button-lipped
    Her bare act was embroidered.
    And she began to be met
    By the drunk, the vicious
    Who told of lewd invitings
    And tumbles in cold ditches
    And hot, secret whisperings –
    Even though during this time
    She sat bandaged by the fire,
    Moved from there to the bedroom
    Obedient, behind her stare. // *Listener*
17 Still] Till *Listener*
18 Some nights] At night *Listener*

The first of a series of poems 'about women in distress' (*SS*, 124).

Shore Woman

First published in the *Irish Press* (1 March 1969): 7, then in the *Listener* (7 May 1970): 611, and selected for inclusion in Jeremy Robson's anthology *The Young British Poets* (Chatto & Windus, 1971) and Robson's *Corgi Modern Poets in Focus*: 2 (1971). Collected with revisions in *WO* and included in *SP*, *PM* and *OG*.

6–7 At the far rocks / A pale sud comes and goes.] A pale sud at the far rocks / Comes and goes. *Irish Press*; *Listener*
7^8] [inset] Out there he put me through it.
8 Under boards] Under the boards *Irish Press*; *Listener*
9 Yet still we] Yet we still *Irish Press*; *Listener*; *PM*, *OG*
14 called] called: *Irish Press*] called, *Listener*
25–6 more / Than] me / More than *Irish Press*; *Listener*
31 him] John *Irish Press*; *Listener*
35 sloped oily] thick slimy *Irish Press*; *Listener*

37 open rocking] open, rocking *Listener*
46 gasping] grasping (error) *PM*
47 to-night] tonight *OG*
47–8] But to-night such moving, sinewed life patrols / The blacker fathoms out beyond the head. *Irish Press* | But to-night such moving sinewed life patrols / The blacker fathoms out beyond the head. *Listener*
49 a debris of scrubbed shells] a detritus of shells, *Irish Press*
50 wave,] wave *Irish Press*; *Listener*
51 have rights] claim rights *Irish Press*; *Listener*

1 *I*: the first-person 'I' is unusual in SH's corpus in being partly in a woman's narrative voice.

9 *we*: the companion on the trip the poem is based on was Seán Ó Riada, composer and Professor of Music at University College, Cork. (*SS*, 124).

31 *him*: the original printing of 'John' (*Irish Press*, *Listener*) might be a reminiscence of the name of Ó Riada who, in his earlier life, was known as John Reidy; but by this point it seems in both versions that the narrative voice in the poem is a woman's, in keeping with the poem's title.

Maighdean Mara

First published in the *Irish Press* (29 Nov. 1969): 9, then *Poetry Supplement* (Christmas 1971): [3]–[4], under the title 'Sea-Wife' in *Workshop*, 11 (1971): 3–4, and in *Criterion* (Galway, 1971). Collected in *WO*, and subsequently included in *SP*.

Title] Sea-Wife *Workshop*, *Criterion*
Dedication For Seán Oh-Eocha] (For Sean O h-Eocha) *Irish Press* | [no dedication] *Poetry Supplement*, *Workshop*
I 7 Liens] Weeds *SP*
I 11 dishevelled.] dishevelled: *Irish Press*
II 1 garments] garment *Irish Press*; *Poetry Supplement*; *WO1972*; *SP*
II 5 there,] there: *Irish Press*
II 10 Patterns of home] A home pattern *Irish Press*
II 11 tidesong] tide-song *Irish Press*
III 3 smoke-reeks] smoke reeks *Irish Press*
III 4 Straw-musts] straw musts *Irish Press*
III 7 fisher wives] fisher-wives *Irish Press* | fisherwives *Poetry Supplement*

Title *Maighdean mhara* is the Irish for 'mermaid'.

Dedication Seán Ó hEochaidh (1913–2002) was a leading Irish folklorist (his name is misspelt in *WO*). His *Síscéalta Ó Thír Chonaill* (*Fairy Legends from Donegal*) is one of the anthologies containing the folk story on which the poem draws. The tale of the man who marries a mermaid is widely attested in the west of Ireland; cf. Eamon Kelly, 'The Shea Man and the Mermaid'. SH updates it movingly to apply to a young woman drowned in reality, among the series here that he described to O'Driscoll as 'poems about women in distress' (*SS*, 124). The Heaneys' friend David Thomson (1914–88) wrote *The People of the Sea: Celtic Tales of the Sea-Folk* about such stories (Edinburgh: Canongate Classics, 1954); SH wrote an introduction to a reprint in 2000.

Limbo

First published in the *Listener* (5 Feb. 1970): 182, then in *Criterion* (Galway, 1971): 34–6. Collected in *WO*, and subsequently included in *SP*, *NSP1990* and *OG*.

1 at] in *Listener*

Title Limbo was traditionally the area of the afterlife to which unbaptised infants were sent.

Bye-Child

First published in Jeni Couzyn (ed.), *Twelve to Twelve* (London: Poets Trust for Poetry D-Day, 1970). Subsequently published in the *Irish Press* (7 Aug. 1970): 9, collected in *WO*, and then included in *SP*, *NSP1990* and *OG*.

Epigraph *anything*] any words *Irish Press*
17 Under the roosts] Mouldy under the roosts *Irish Press*
28 gaping] squawked-out *Irish Press*

Good-night

First published in the *Listener* (22 May 1969): 729, and in *three* (1969), collected in *WO*, and subsequently included in *SP* and *OG*. Also as a broadside for *Poetry in Motion* (1996).

Title] Good-Night *Listener* | Good Night *three*
1 den] cave *Listener*   light] light, *three*
3 corridor,] corridor *three*
6 steady] neatly *three*   brightness.] brightness *Listener*

First Calf

First published in the *Listener* (4 Sept. 1969): 311, and *Capella*, 4 (April 1970): 26–7, then collected in *WO*, and included in *Toome* (1980)

2 hedge] hedge, *Listener*
5–7] Somewhere about / The cow stands with her head / Almost outweighing her tense, sloped neck, *Listener*
11 plaque] plinth *Listener*

14 nothing.] nothing: *Listener*
15 The] Those *Listener*

May

First published in the *Irish Press* (7 Aug. 1971): 9, and then in *Poetry*, 119. 5 (Feb. 1972): 282–3. Collected in WO.

7 juice] juice! *Irish Press*
19 ladysmock] lady's-smock *Poetry*

9 *fontanel*: space between the plates of a baby's skull.

Fireside

Published in WO, and then in the *New Yorker* (26 May 1973): 48. Also included in OG.

Title The subject of the poem is various folk stories that might be told around Irish firesides. The first few references are to tales of diabolical apparitions: such as lights in bushes, goats and chains.

Dawn

First published in *Critical Quarterly*, 11. 4 (Winter 1969): 294–5, and included in WO.

8 cobbles,] cobbles *Critical Quarterly*
15 window / Displays] window- / Displays *Critical Quarterly*

Travel

Published in WO.

Westering

Published in WO, included in *Gravities* and subsequently in SP, *NSP1990*, OG and *100P*.

Title 'Easy Rider' working title in TS (NLI 49,493/13), suggesting the 1969 film by Dennis Hopper.
   1 *Rand McNally*: an American publishing company specialising in mapping.
   6 *'Pitiscus'*: a series of craters on the surface of the Moon, named after Bartholomeo Pitiscus (1561–1613) who is credited with the first use of the term 'trigonometry'.

16 Along with the poem's title, perhaps a reference to John Donne's poem 'Good Friday Riding Westward' with a similar implication of travelling in the wrong direction.

33 The distance from California to Ireland is roughly five thousand miles.

UNCOLLECTED POEMS (1973–1975)

'A New Life', the four-sonnet sequence with which this short uncollected group begins, develops the somewhat controversial sexualised metaphor of some poems in *Door into the Dark* and the second part of *Wintering Out*; versions of two of the sonnets here are published in the notes to 'Act of Union' in *North* (*PSH*, 197), to the second part of which they correspond closely. But this group's five poems do not have a clear overall affinity with either *Wintering Out* or *North*. Two of the poems feature major figures in Irish musical history; the Belfast Harp Festival was a significant moment in the development of Irish nationalist culture.

A New Life

First published in the *Listener* (22 Feb. 1973): 239, and subsequently in *Lynx* 1. 2 (Spring 1973): 21. The first and last of the sonnets were revised and collected as 'Act of Union' in *North*: sonnet 4 much revised.

[text: *Listener*]

Four unnumbered sonnets, the second and fourth being inset in their first printing in *Listener*.
    See also McGuinness 1979: 62–91.

A Flourish for the Prince of Denmark

Published in Graham Fawcett (ed.), *Poems for Shakespeare 2* (London: Globe Playhouse/Trust Publications, 1973), 37.

Commissioned by the Globe Theatre in a celebration of Shakespeare's birthday, 1973.
    9 'For he was likely, had he been put on, / To have prov'd most royally.' (*Hamlet*, 5.2.397–8.)

The Belfast Harp Festival 1792

Published in the *Cambridge Review* (18 May 1973): 145.

The Belfast Harpers Assembly, 11–14 July 1792, celebrated radical events such as the French Declaration of the Rights of Man, American liberties and the Polish constitution of 1791, as well as the national music of Ireland. The 1792 event is most remembered for the activity of Edward Bunting (*l.* 1), who collected tunes from the ten harpers present. This formed the major part of his *General Collection of the Ancient Irish Music* (1796) upon which Thomas Moore drew for the tunes of his *Irish Melodies* (1808–34).

1 Edward Bunting (1773–1843), born in Armagh, was a trained classical musician who was a pianist (*l.* 4) as well as an inheritor of the native Irish harping tradition, noted since the Middle Ages.

9 *planxty*: a tune associated with the harper and prolific composer Turlough O'Carolan (1670–1738), whose works Bunting collected and published. The etymology in Irish is obscure, though one rather fanciful suggestion is that it might be a transliteration of the word *sláinte*, 'health'. Many of O'Carolan's most admired tunes are titled by linking the word with the name of a presumed patron of his: for example 'Planxty George Brabazon', 'Planxty Lady Wrixon' and 'Planxty Irwin'. The word was adopted as the name of a leading Irish folk group of the 1970s, including in its number Liam O'Flynn with whom SH performed in their album, *The Poet and the Piper*.

11, 13 Theobald Wolfe Tone (1763–98), one of the leaders of the 1798 Rebellion who cut his throat in prison.

John Field

Published in the *Cambridge Review* (18 May 1973): 145. Subsequently published under the same title in a heavily revised form, and accompanied by a French translation, in *Digraphe* (June 1982): 45:

> Technique is vehicular: the slow pains
> Of making each hand pry what was there
> And not unbalance the coin laid on it
> Cast him in silence when he faced the keyboard.
> His wrists 'seemed cast in bronze' but his touch
> Exfoliated, 'raindrops . . . pearls on velvet'.
> Morose and stylish, slothful, drunken Field,
> Artist in residence, stuttering out
> Your legend, paying court to the court
> Till cancer of the rectum wrecked your puns:
> Knowing technique expendable and still
> Dissipating melody, sinking
> Your reputation like champagne in Moscow
> Under those somnolent nocturnes of snow. *Digraphe*

Title John Field (1782–1837), Irish pianist-composer, credited with the invention of the nocturne pre-Chopin; he died in Moscow (*l.* 13) where he spent the last part of his life as a piano impresario.

1 It is said that some early nineteenth-century pianists, including Chopin, had coins placed on the back of their wrists as students.

Field, born in Dublin in 1782, as a child prodigy might have been disciplined in such ways by his father and by his tutor, Tommaso Giordani. Field was greatly admired in his own time. He travelled from Ireland to England and thereafter to St Petersburg and to Moscow where he died in 1837 at the end of a colourful life there.

3, 5 Muzio Clementi (1752–1832), born in Rome but mostly based in London and the west of England – virtuoso musician and piano maker. Field was one of his many students.

The Poet Crowned

Published in the *New York Review of Books* (15 May 1975): 41.

13 lonely.] lonely (error) *NYRB*

STATIONS (1975)

Stations, a pamphlet of twenty-one prose poems, was published in Belfast by Ulsterman Publications with an introduction by SH dated 'Glanmore, March, 1975'. Eight of the poems were subsequently reprinted in the *Irish Times* under the heading 'Autobiographical Borings' (8 July 1975), with a further eleven pieces republished in *Exile*, later in 1975.

SH tells us that the prose poems of *Stations* were begun in California in 1970/1 as what he experimentally regarded as 'stolen marches in a new form' (*Stations*, 3), but discontinued when his foray into verse form was 'headed off by a work of complete authority': the publication of Geoffrey Hill's *Mercian Hymns* in 1971. Nevertheless, SH returned to the task in the early summer of 1974, telling us that the 'greater part of them came rapidly to a head in May and June' of that year, and that their resumption took place in what he called 'the "hedge-school" of Glanmore in Wicklow', where SH had moved with his family from Belfast in August 1972. Wicklow was seen, as California had been, as a setting at some remove from the poems' subjects, at a distance where 'the sectarian dimension of that pre-reflective experience presented itself as something asking to be uttered also' (*Stations*, 3). An interim title for the collection in TS had been Seed-Time.

Since *Stations* and *North* were published in the same year, commentators have often taken them together for comparison and contrast, sometimes arguing that the prose poems (SH suggested that the term 'writings', as used by David Jones, might be more appropriate; *SS*, 180) were a more democratic form to represent personal experience. It is striking that the drilling image he famously used for the poetic method of *North* was also applied by him to the prose method of *Stations*: 'autobiographical borings, narrow shafts let down into one stratum of a northern consciousness' (*Irish Times*, 8 July 1975), despite the great formal difference between the clear and open prose of *Stations* and the narrow lines of the quatrain poems in *North*. It has been suggested that the direct narration of *Stations* has more in common with 'Whatever You Say Say Nothing' (*North*, 60–3; *PSH*, 200) and with 'Singing School' (*North*, 65–76; *PSH*, 203) – which is headed with Wordsworth's 'Fair seedtime had my soul' – than it has with the narrow-shaft poems of the first part of *North*.

The series begins with some of the child's earliest memories with what SH calls 'pre-reflective experience' (*Stations*, 3) before moving on to personal recollections of the social and political conditions of the contested Northern Ireland for which he finds the straightforward prose form more fitting and maybe less contentious. The first five poems, before he moves to more public comment, are reports in the child's third person singular 'he'. As with many poems in *Death of a Naturalist* what promises to be an evocation of an Edenic world is quickly undermined by fear and revulsion. References in the commentary here are to the text and page numbers of the 1975 Ulsterman edition, the only place that *Stations* has been published in full, and as a single book.

SH envisaged a text of fluid lineation, common in prose, variable in page width, meaning that each of the first three printings carried a differing typographic complexion. The *Irish Times* printed the poems ragged right, while *Exile* set them justified. Our text follows *Stations*, and reproduces the original ragged-right lineation of the Ulsterman edition; it follows *New Selected Poems 1966–1987* in replacing the bold type of that edition with small caps.

[text: *Stations 1975*]

Cauled

Published in *Stations* and subsequently in *Exile*, 2. 3–4 (1975): 108.

1 *They thought he was lost*: Henry Hart (Hart 1992, 110) notes the closeness of this childhood story of the child lost in the pea drills to childhood memories in Theodore Roethke's *The Lost Son*, including a description of the child's memory of being lost behind his father's greenhouses; SH had reviewed Roethke's *Collected Poems* in the *Listener* in 1968 (reprinted as 'Canticles to the Earth', *Preoccupations*, 190–4). The same childhood reminiscence is described in the 'Omphalos' section of the early essay 'Mossbawn' (*Preoccupations*, 17) and in *SS* (16).

3 in his Roethke review, SH quotes from 'The Meadow Mouse' (Hart 1992, 110).

6ff. Hart compares the prepubescent imagery to Roethke too.

Branded

Published in *Stations*.

The event here is described in *SS* (9).

2 *haggard*: etymology: 'hay-yard'.

13 *pastern*: part of the horse's leg, above the hoof. SH says more than once that the sound of the horse shifting on the other side of the bedroom wall was reassuring and comforting in his early childhood (*SS*, 15) so this memory is a stark contrast.

Hedge-School

Published in *Stations* and subsequently in *New Blackfriars* (June 1975): 7, and *Exile*, 2. 3–4 (1975): 109.

Title Hedge-school was the term for the informal countryside places where Catholic children were taught before the establishment of National Schools in Ireland by the British government in 1831.

3 *ditchback*: the base of a roadside fence (called 'ditch' in Ireland, made of earth and stones). Familiar from SH's poems 'The King of the Ditchbacks', dedicated to John Montague (*SI*, 56) among a series of poems of which this prose poem is reminiscent.

12 *Pull them*: the Hiberno-English verb for picking flowers, rather than 'pluck' or 'pick'; *the May altar*: flowers were arranged in small private altars made by Irish Catholic children in honour of the Blessed Virgin to whom the month of May was dedicated.

13 *Legs of nestlings*: the child cries at the thought of birds' legs lurking in the 'cool and wet' of the hedge, anticipating the revulsion of the next poem.

Nesting Ground

Published in *Stations* and subsequently in *Exile*, 2. 3–4 (1975): 110; collected in *NSP1990* and *OG*.

Title Nesting-ground] Nesting-Ground *NSP1990*, *OG*
3 he once] he had once *OG*

4 *a dead robin's claw*: a major intrusion into the child's Eden, like the rat's nest in the corn stack (*l.* 8) and the rat in 'The Advancement of Learning' in *DN*.

12 'the silence under the ground' anticipates the subterranean themes of the bog poems and elsewhere.

Sinking the Shaft

Published in *Stations* and subsequently in *Exile*, 2. 3–4 (1975): 111.

Title Drilling a shaft for an electric pump, which was a major project in the modern development of farming from the 1950s onwards, fits SH's developing symbol of the underground, as in the last line of the previous poem.

15 The upright helmeted pump, set on its pediment, acts as the kind of world-centring omphalos that SH uses as a symbol in the opening section of 'Mossbawn' (*Preoccupations*, 17) and elsewhere (*SS*, 8).

17 *inscribed by the points of their trowels*: like the plasterer 'Skimming our gable and writing our name there / With his trowel point' in 'Alphabets' (*HL*, 3; *PSH*, 357).

Waterbabies

Published in *Stations* and subsequently in *Exile*, 2. 3–4 (1975): 112.

This sixth poem shifts from the third person to the first person plural to represent memory.

1 *Botany Bay*: Kamay, where James Cook landed in Australia. Notable in Irish history as a penal colony where transported convicts were imprisoned.

2 It is unclear who the child being played with and addressed is: probably one of the Heaney siblings, perhaps Sheena.

6 The ripples quivering across the children's delta recalls the quiver the train caused in the bucket of household drinking water.

7ff. the destruction of this Edenic scene by the fouling of the toy, 'a marvellous lightship', (*l*. 10) parallels the 'death' of the naturalist's ideal in *DN*. Cf. John Donne, 'Twickenham Garden':

> And that this place may thoroughly be thought
>   True Paradise, I have the serpent brought. (Robbins 2008, 1255)

Patrick and Oisin

Published in *Stations* and subsequently in *New Blackfriars* (July 1975): 328, and *Exile*, 2. 3–4 (1975): 113.

3 solemnizations] solemnisations *New Blackfriars*

The narrative changes to reporting in the first person singular; there is also a move towards a more educated language in a shift which parallels the development in 'Alphabets' (*HL*, 1–3; *PSH*, 357).

Here it is the stern and opaque polysyllabic language of Catholic education, derived from the school catechism with an emphasis on sin. The implication of the largely symbolic title is the imposition of church authority represented by St Patrick on the secular narrative personified by the legendary Fenian hero Oisín, a confrontation whose most famous poetic treatment is Yeats's *The Wanderings of Oisin*. The technical catechetical terms 'calumny and detraction' (*l*. 6) describe the gossipy criticism and 'back-biting' (*l*. 5) of neighbours in kitchen conversation. The decorated script of the medieval texts is suggested by the uncurling of the names and the child's hand reaching upward like the botanical figures in the manuscripts with their 'creeping greenery' (*l*. 13).

Sweet William

Published in *Stations* and subsequently in *Irish Times* (8 July 1975): 2.

3 the clumped growth] the clump *Irish Times*

Prompted by the 'creeping greenery' at the end of the previous poem, this poem remembers a clump of sweet william surviving in a vegetable garden which had gone to seed, startlingly described as looking as if it had been shot apart by a cluster of ammunition: another unexpected intrusion of violent imagery.

    5 Banners of William of Orange usually show him with long, curly dark hair: heraldry the Catholic child-narrator could not assent to.

    8–9 *the many men / so beautiful*: Coleridge, 'The Ancient Mariner', Part IV. The appropriateness here is not obvious, except perhaps by raising a contrast with the putrefying things in Coleridge's context:

> The many men, so beautiful!
> And they all dead did lie;
> And a thousand thousand slimy things
> Lived on; and so did I. (Coleridge 1912, 196–7)

    But SH may have been led to the source in Coleridge by David Jones, whose *In Parenthesis* (1937) he admired greatly; the title of Part 1 of that work is 'The many men so beautiful'.

The Discharged Soldier

Published in *Stations* and subsequently in the *Irish Times* (8 July 1975): 2, under the title 'An Ulster Twilight'.

8 Drunk] Full *Irish Times*

10–11 Aye they all went down, they all went down but Danny.] Aye they all went down, they all went down and none came back but Danny. *Irish Times*
12 old rip] ould rip *Irish Times*
13 old bastard] ould bastard *Irish Times*   Flanders.'] Flanders. They've little to do, bejasus, with their army pensions, when they're handing them out to a boy like that.' *Irish Times*
16 there for sure.'] there, all right.' *Irish Times*
16^17] [no paragraph break] *Irish Times*

1 *Flanders*: shorthand for the main arena of conflict in World War I, incorporating Ypres, the Somme and Passchendaele, much recalled by Northern Irish unionists, among others.

6 After the killing of a pig on a farm, children were given the bladder to inflate as a football.

8 *the Boyne*: the river, sacred in Ulster Protestant iconography.

10 *they all went down*: referring to the vast numbers of fatalities in World War I.

12 *rip*: outdated Irish term of abuse, of obscure origin.

17 *Pew*: Blind Pew in the first scene of R. L. Stevenson's *Treasure Island* turns up at the Admiral Benbow inn, trying to get the map of the island from Billy Bones, but he is trampled to death without getting it. But he gives Billy the 'black spot' which means imminent death among pirates. Sure enough, Billy collapses and dies of 'thundering apoplexy'.

18 *built-up hoof*: Danny's club foot. Maybe suggesting too Pew's tapping of his stick as he approached, a celebrated shock-horror motif in the book.

The Sabbath-Breakers

Published in *Stations* and subsequently in *Irish Times* (8 July 1975): 2.

7 honeysuckles. To-morrow] honeysuckles. // Tomorrow *Irish Times*
9 children] the children *Irish Times*
12 air. So] air. // So] *Irish Times*
13–14 when a dog barked from an outlying farm] when a dog barked at the back of a house *Irish Times*
19 liberty. Undaunted] liberty? // Undaunted *Irish Times*
13 IN SPITE OF DUNGEON, FIRE AND SWORD.] In spite of dungeon, fire and sword. *Irish Times*

Title The Gaelic Athletic Association's games, hurling and Gaelic football, were traditionally played on Sunday which is a breach of the Sabbath in Protestant thinking. The term 'an old Sabbath-breaker' is applied to the local Traveller figure called Simon Sweeney (real name Charlie Griffin: *SS*, 240) in *SI* (61; *PSH*, 318).

1 *pattern*: term used to refer to celebratory parish events such as dancing competitions in Catholic Ireland, derived from 'patron' meaning a saint's commemorative day.

4–5 *the summer grass / marked out with sawdust*: the touchline the field's edges; the square the area around the goal corresponding to the penalty area; the twenty-one and the fifty (yards) line were where frees were taken from; there was also a fourteen for football; the twenty-one was for hurling.

7 *To-morrow night*: Saturday night, before the Sunday game. The poem has some affinity with Leopardi's 'Il sabato del villaggio', in the way the keen excitement of anticipation is thwarted.

10–11 *'The Soldier's Song'*: the Irish national anthem, 'Amhrán na bhFiann'.

14 Setanta, the original name of Cú Chulainn, the leading hero of the Ulster Cycle of Irish legends. The boy Setanta was returning from a game of hurling on the way to a feast at the house of Culann. When he reaches the house he is attacked by Culann's guard dog which he kills by flinging his sliotar (hurling ball) down its throat. To repair the loss of the dog, Setanta takes on its role as the hound of Culann, Cú Chulainn, which thereafter is his name.

16 *pattern*: at its second mention the term means 'the usual practice'. Pogrom is too strong a term to describe this destruction of the prepared playing-field by the puritanical 'roundhead elders' (l. 17–18).

19–20 *the gap of danger*: Irish *bearna baoil* (usually untranslated when the song is sung in English): the phrase in 'The Soldier's Song' for what the singers have to 'man'. The tricolour is the Irish flag.

24 *In spite of dungeon, fire and sword*: l. 2 from 'Faith of Our Fathers', the Catholic anthem which was sung before 'The Soldier's Song' before the start of GAA matches up to the 1950s.

Kernes

Published in *Stations* and subsequently in *Irish Times* (8 July 1975): 2.

4 saddled declamatory] saddled, declamatory *Irish Times*

Title Kern is an English borrowing from the Old Irish term *ceithearn*, a band of foot-soldiers; in English it can be collective or singular. The first syllable in Irish links to *caith*, battle. In 'Exposure' at the end of *North* the speaker calls himself 'a wood-kerne / Escaped from the massacre'.

1 The English flagpole in response to the Irish tricolour near the end of the previous poem.

2 *a fairy thorn*: in Northern Ireland a tree standing alone with various vatic and magical influences, often negative.

4 *king of the castle*: a claim of superiority in a children's rhyme.

5 *papish*: derogatory vernacular term for papist – Catholic.

9 Raleigh bicycle, popular in Ireland. Raleigh 'in his inflated knickers' corresponds to William of Orange 'with crinkling feminine black / curls' in 'Sweet William' (*Stations*, 11; *PSH*, 164, *ll*. 6–7).

16 *glib*: thick fringe of hair over the forehead, perhaps loosely evoking the croppies.

July

First published in Padraic Fiacc (ed.), *The Wearing of the Black* (Belfast: Blackstaff, 1974), and subsequently in *Stations* and OG.

16 skeins] a skein OG
18] [omitted] OG

The subject is the Orange demonstrations in Northern Ireland, on and around the Twelfth of July, also evoked more trenchantly in 'Intimidation' (*PSH*, 105).

10–11 The terms 'red sea' and 'chosen people' draw on Old Testament narratives associated with Northern Irish Protestant discourse.

14, 15 The violent references (butcher's apron; skeins of blood) are again in keeping with the raising of tensions in SH's poetry of the period.

England's Difficulty

Published in *Stations* and subsequently in *Irish Times* (8 July 1975): 2, and *Exile*, 2. 3–4 (1975): 114, and collected in *NSP1990* and OG.

3 machine. It was a] machine, a mechanical *Irish Times*
5 bitter] bitterest *NSP1990*, OG
10 tired-out] tired out *NSP1990*, OG
15 an artist] a playboy *Irish Times*
15–16 He can fairly leave it into them.] By God, he's the boy can leave it into them! *Irish Times*
17–21 Ulster', the scullions outside the walls. Squires of the cockpit, barkers of auction notices, arbitrators of the burial grounds. An adept at banter, I crossed the lines with carefully enunciated passwords,] Ulster' – squires of the cockpit, barkers of auction notices, arbitrators of the burying grounds. Adept at banter and disguise, I crossed lines with elocuted passwords, *Irish Times*

The first of three poems about Northern Ireland's relations with England in the two world wars.

Title 'England's difficulty is Ireland's opportunity', a political catchphrase associated with several Irish leaders from Daniel O'Connell up to 1914. SH's take on it in this poem is complicated, recalling the child's experience as a double agent who overhears the rhetoric of confrontation among concepts – like 'enemy' – which are too big for him.

5–6 The Belfast Blitz occurred in spring 1941. Clearly a voice which is unsympathetic to the 'bitter Orange parts' of Belfast even as it is being bombed, the same voice as in *ll.* 15–16.

15 *Haw Haw*: William Joyce (1906–46), a New York-born commentator who broadcast pro-German bulletins from Germany throughout World War II, dubbed Lord Haw Haw because of his affected upper-class English voice. He grew up in Ireland from the age of three to fifteen with Anglophile Irish Protestant parents. He claimed to be American, then (fraudulently) British, then German before he was hanged for treason in Wandsworth Prison.

17 *the enemies of Ulster*: Northern Irish Catholics who were thought to be unsympathetic to the Allied cause: the child learns to cross the lines with passwords, reporting back to nobody and manning 'every speech with checkpoints' (*l.* 21), which is a characterisation that SH returns to much later in the parable poems in *HL* such as 'From the Republic of Conscience' (*HL*, 12–13; *PSH*, 363); *scullions*: among the lower orders listed in the last six lines are those responsible for menial tasks outside the walls of privilege. SH is punning on the names of his father's forebears, the 'big-voiced Scullions'.

Visitant

Published in *Stations* and subsequently as 'A Visitant' in *Exile*, 2. 3–4 (1975): 115; collected in *NSP1990* and *OG*.

7 with toothbrush] with bits of toothbrush *NSP1990*

The figure that emerges from the tremor of the heat-haze is a German prisoner-of-war on parole from his prison camp at the local aerodrome (*SS*, 180), a 'real visitant' rather than the ghostly figure of the opening. The middle section lists the things that the skilled Germans make, admired by the local 'harbourer's' appraising comment on 'these Germans'. Then the visitant goes back through his medial spectral condition into the reality of his prison fatigues.

Trial Runs

First published in Padraic Fiacc (ed.), *The Wearing of the Black* (Belfast: Blackstaff, 1974) and subsequently in *Stations*; collected in *NSP1990* and *OG*.

10 papish] Papish OG
11 O] Oh OG
12 pope's] Pope's OG
16 over] across OG

Title 'Timeo danaos' in TS (NLI 49,493/31).

1 The message painted along the demesne wall addressed to soldiers returning from World War II joins the traditional Northern Irish unionist inscriptions; all three are textually emphasised in the poem which describes a trial run at light-hearted exchanges between Catholic and Protestant neighbours, with the khaki of the returned soldier (one of the demobbed Evans brothers: *SS*, 180) and his jokey gift of heavy rosary beads. The repressed unease is all 'above my head' from the child's perspective.

The Wanderer

Published in *Stations* and subsequently in *Exile*, 2. 3–4 (1975): 116; collected in *OG*.

1 semi-circle] semicircle OG
3 jamjar] jam jar OG
6 him winning] him, for winning OG

The subject is the schoolmaster Barney Murphy at Anahorish school giving SH money as a reward for winning a scholarship to St Columb's College in Derry. The master's dispensing money is compared to the ring-giving of the Germanic chieftain in *Beowulf* and elsewhere, which determines the detail of the poem in the second paragraph: halls in flames, filled and emptied hall-benches as in *Beowulf*. The title is taken from the great Exeter Book elegy, 'The Wanderer' (also translated by Auden and many others) who is an *anhaga* (solitary dweller) in the Old English: the source of the 'migrant solitude' (*l.* 9 here). The 'rich young man' of the closing lines is a figure from the Synoptic Gospels who is told by Jesus to seek perfection by selling his possessions and giving to the poor.

Cloistered

Published in *Stations* and subsequently in *Exile*, 2. 3–4 (1975): 117; later in John Quinn (ed.), *Must Try Harder: Tales Out of School* (Dublin: Mount Salus Press, 1985). Collected in *NSP1990* and *OG*.

2 terrazzo] terrazo *Stations* (error)
20–1] [omitted] *NSP1990*, *OG*

Recalling the setting of the college chapel at St Columb's, the poet notes in paragraph 2 the resemblances there to the detailed illustrations in medieval Books of Hours (such as the *Très Riches Heures du Duc de Berry*). Paragraph 3 recalls the detailed school subjects, such as geometry and Latin. At the end he recalls his academic prowess, contrasting it with the undeclared lust which scalded him in this very cloistered world.

Ballad

Published in *Stations* and subsequently in *Irish Times* (8 July 1975): 2, and *Exile*, 2. 3–4 (1975): 119.

3 them] them, *Irish Times*
7–8 question and doubting] question or doubting *Irish Times*
11 and the anthem] and anthem *Irish Times*

The subject is one of the IRA border raids in the mid-1950s in which one of the volunteers, an 'ascetic boy' (*l*. 2), bleeds to death after the attack. He is probably Fergal O'Hanlon who is named in Dominic Behan's song 'The Patriot Game', very popular at ceilis and Irish dances in the 1970s: 'My name is O'Hanlon, I'm just gone sixteen.' O'Hanlon and Seán South (also the subject of a nationalist ballad) were killed in an attack on Brookeborough RUC Barracks on 1 January 1957. The opening section of the poem is unique in *Stations* in describing at a remove events that the poet could not have known at first hand or from local report. The second and third sections recount the impact on the narrator's personal experience of the violent event in section 1. At the end, he tells of the love of Irish traditional music – the piper's chanter and the fiddle-bows – that grew from such occasions, once the public event was replaced by 'quiet' (*l*. 13) and the 'exhaustion' from violence 'had been nominated peace' (*l*. 5).

The Stations of the West

Published in *Stations*. Subsequently as 'Mo Thuras go Rann na Feirste', *Irish Times* (8 July 1975): 2, and as 'Turas' in *Exile*, 2. 3–4 (1975): 118; collected in *NSP1990* and *OG*.

6 EPHETE] *Ephete NSP1990, OG*

Title The Irish 'turas' means journey in general, but it has particular application to pilgrimage and religious journeys or circuits, like the Stations of the Cross or the *Camino di Santiago* to Compostela.

1 *the Gaeltacht*: the Irish-speaking areas in the west of Ireland, visited by schoolchildren and Higher Education students of Irish to improve their grasp of the language. The one visited by SH was Rannafast, Co. Donegal, officially known by its Irish name Rann na Feirste (roughly 'The area of the sandbar').

2 Often the visits to the Gaeltacht during the school holidays were the first absence from their parents for young children and a cause of homesickness. Here the child is homesick for English, the language he was in the Gaeltacht to extirpate.

7–8 *the fasting spittle of / our creed*: fasting was a major distinguishing practice in Catholic culture. The spittle is a reference to Christ's restoration of sight to a blind man by rubbing his spittle to his eyes and pronouncing the Greek version of an Aramaic word *ephphatha*, meaning 'be opened': *Ephete* (*l.* 8) here.

10 *gift of tongues*: the form in which the linguistic enlightenment of the Holy Ghost was transmitted to the Apostles at Pentecost.

12ff. The Gaeltacht areas down the west coast are all places of great natural beauty, which is what the child carries back from the west rather than an enhanced grasp of the language.

Inquisition

Published in *Stations* and subsequently as 'The Gents' in *Irish Times* (8 July 1975): 2.

This scary encounter with 'Loyalists in the Gents of a Belfast hotel' (*SS*, 180), beginning with a crudely misogynist line, comes from a later period of the young narrator's development.

2 Cf. Yeats's 'Porter-drinkers' randy laughter' ('Under Ben Bulben' V, 10, in a section beginning 'Irish poets, learn your trade'; Albright 1990, 375).

5 *combination*: introducing the running theme of systems of communication.

9 *christened in Boyne water*: i.e. on the Protestant side.
12 'live and let live' with its sinister air evokes 'Whatever You Say Say Nothing': '"Religion's never mentioned here", of course . . . "One side's as bad as the other, never worse"' (*North*, 62; *PSH*, 201–2).
15–16 Even the expression to describe escape is indirect and evasive.

Incertus

Published in *Stations* and subsequently as 'Alias' in *Exile*, 2. 3–4 (1975): 120; collected in *NSP1990* and *OG*.

2 latin] Latin *NSP1990*, *OG*

Title Familiar as the pseudonym (*l.* 5) under which SH submitted and published his first student poems in Belfast.
2 *church-latin c*: as initially in 'si:zer' rather than with a 'hard' initial 'k'.
3 In *A Portrait of the Artist as a Young Man*, Stephen feels 'obeisance' before the linguistic authority of the English dean of studies: 'My soul frets in the shadow of his language.' (Joyce 1992, 205). The uncertainty of the young poet is the same for SH.

NORTH (1975)

North was published in London by Faber & Faber on 9 June 1975 simultaneously in 2,000 hardback and 6,750 paperback copies, and in 1976 by Oxford University Press in New York in 1,250 copies bound from Faber's sheets. It was the Choice of the Poetry Book Society, and was, far and away, the most widely distributed of SH's books to date. By March 1977, less than two years into publication, it had sold in excess of 60,000 copies – 'Pretty good I'd say!' Faber's Rosemary Goad wrote to the family at the time (FF E/18/45/1). Nine reprints followed before the book was reset in 1992; it was reset again in 1996 for the Faber Library Edition in hardback, from which the 2001 paperback takes its text, and reset once more in a corrected edition in 2025, from which this edition takes its text.

Following on from Neil Corcoran's accolade for *Wintering Out* as the 'seminal single volume of post-1970 English poetry', great claims were made for this successor volume. Helen Vendler describes her first encounter with *North* at the Yeats Summer School at Sligo in 1975: a book 'which I thought then – and still think now – one of the crucial poetic interventions of the twentieth century, along with *Prufrock* and *Harmonium* and *North of Boston*' (Vendler 1998, 3). It is crucially important, Vendler goes on to say, as 'an *oeuvre* of strong social engagement, looking steadily and with stunning poetic force at what it means to be a contemporary citizen of Northern Ireland – at the intolerable stresses put on the population by conflict, fear, betrayals, murders'. Conor Cruise O'Brien said something similar in his more troubled tribute: he had 'the uncanny feeling, reading these poems, of listening to the thing itself, the actual substance of historical agony and dissolution, the tragedy of a people in a place: the Catholics of Northern Ireland' (O'Brien 1975, 204).

The most quoted positive response to *North* alongside Vendler's was Robert Lowell's judgement in the *Observer* that SH was 'the most important Irish poet since W. B. Yeats'. Less frequently quoted is Lowell's significant characterisation of *North* in the same sentence – that it was 'a new kind of political poetry'. Because of its 'strong social engagement', the volume was controversial from the first, regarded as a further increase in the political momentum that many commentators had seen between *Door into the Dark* and *Wintering Out*: indeed, in the smaller window of time between Winter Seeds and *Wintering Out* after SH's return from California in 1971. We have noted already SH's telling O'Driscoll that the political poem 'Orange Drums, Tyrone' in

<u>Winter Seeds</u> was held back from the 'more inward, broody style of *Wintering Out*' to find its home eventually in the more political context of 'Singing School' in *North*. Similarly, the poem 'Antaeus', which had been published in the Irish journal *Hibernia* in 1966, appears as the first poem of Part I of the collection, exceptionally dated '1966' on the page, making it evident that it is a resurrection of a poem that has been omitted from earlier collections. However, the address to political subjects in the volume is deferred by starting with 'Mossbawn: Two Poems in Dedication', a diptych (though originally the poems were published separately) of two personal, domestic poems in celebration of the calm and continuity of home life which serves as a kind of prologue to the book. The first, 'Sunlight', is one of SH's best-loved poems, a tribute to his father's sister Mary Heaney, who lived with the family and to whom the two poems are dedicated, ending with a much-quoted quatrain which could not be more remote from public tensions:

> And here is love
> like a tinsmith's scoop
> sunk past its gleam
> in the meal-bin.

The second dedicatory poem, 'The Seed Cutters', mentions Breughel in the first line, matching the Dutch-interior, Vermeer-like feeling of 'Sunlight'. In the prominent positioning of this title, SH shows the continued and defining importance he attributes in this period to the symbolism of the granular 'seed', which had been a word in the working titles of the two previous gatherings, *Wintering Out* (once <u>Winter Seeds</u>) and *Stations* (<u>Seed-Time</u>).

North, SH said in interview, 'is the first book of mine that is to some extent designed' (Kinahan 1982, 410). Like *Wintering Out*, it is again divided into two parts, and this time even more decisively than before. For the first time, the partition was a feature of the typescript's design, rather than the printer's setting, bearing two part titles that boldly carried epigraphs by Eliot and by SH himself, before SH came to consider them 'heavy-handed' and removed them as 'interferences with the reader's response' (FF P/Rdlm/716/10).

Nevertheless, the division and the twin part-title pages would remain. Part I begins with 'Antaeus' and ends in 'Hercules and Antaeus', a sequence in which invincibility is lost when contact with the earth is broken. The poems of this first part continue from 'The Tollund Man' of *Wintering Out* to draw upon the sagas and historic excavations of Northern Europe; they centre once again on P. V. Glob's characterisation of the Bog People, albeit with direct application to the worsening socio-political circumstances of Northern Ireland. The word 'bog', SH reminds us, is a rare borrowing in English from the Irish, meaning 'soft'; whereas in Northern Ireland the peat bog was called the 'moss', a word of Norse origin carried in with Scots planters. 'So in the bog/moss syndrome,' he tells readers at the time, 'one can diagnose a past of invasion, colonization and language shift' (*PBS Bulletin*, 85, (Summer 1975)). Part II, SH wrote on publication, 'is the result of a need to be explicit about pressures and prejudices watermarked into the psyche of anyone born and bred in Northern Ireland' (*PBS Bulletin*, 85). It is a volume of apparently clear division, for which the compass had been aligned, with the book's title a gesture towards the twin norths of Ireland and of Europe.

When O'Driscoll asked about what was sometimes seen as the stark difference between the unqualified politics of Part I, centring on the bog poems, and what O'Driscoll called 'the more conversational and personal poems' of Part II (*SS*, 179), SH said the division was not so clear cut. The sequence 'Whatever You Say Say Nothing' in the second, 'personal' part pre-dated the bog poems of the first part, and it is decidedly political in social terms. And that sequence ends in revisiting the poem for Longley and Hammond which gave *Wintering Out* its epigraph, but to very different effect. In *North*, where the poem is reprinted as the culmination of the influential sequence, it carries one significant difference in text: the piece of graffiti 'Is there a life before death?', which in the dedicatory poem of the 'more inward, broody' *Wintering Out* is 'chalked up / on a wall downtown', is in *North* instead 'chalked up / in Ballymurphy', a name by then inseparable in public association from the killing of eleven people by the Parachute Regiment in the course of Operation Demetrius, which was the beginning of internment without trial in Northern Ireland. Whatever it is saying, it is not saying nothing.

The controversy over the bog poems and their political context in *North* has been more intense than about anything else SH has written. Edna Longley expressly contrasted *North* and its central symbolism with the preceding volume: 'in contrast with the fecund variety of *Wintering Out*, there is system, homogenisation' (Longley 1982, 161). Ciaran Carson in a trenchant review in *The Honest Ulsterman* refers to SH as 'the laureate of violence – a mythmaker, an anthropologist of ritual killing' (*Honest Ulsterman*, 50 (Winter 1975): 183–6). The poem which has provoked this controversy and conflict most pointedly is 'Punishment', which draws on the image of the figure Glob called the 'Windeby girl'. Later examiners of the body have suggested that it is probably that of a young man, and prefer to refer to the Windeby Child, which clearly radically affects what some commentators have seen as the disturbingly gendered nature of the sexualised language of the early part of the poem. It is evident from the number and variety of drafts in SH's archive that the poet sensed the delicacy of the subject and that his view of it was by no means monolithic: in working drafts, the poem is entitled 'Shame' among other titles (NLI 49,493/67/ 187).

Importantly, this poem and others of the era became focal points for feminist engagement with SH's work. Notable interventions by Patricia Coughlan and Elizabeth Butler Cullingford in the early 1990s identified the restricting gendered perspective SH took on some female subjects. Their readings were endorsed by SH's expansion of these ideas into his prose poetics of the early 1970s, in such pieces as 'Feeling into Words', where he mapped them onto the 'sectarian division' in Northern Ireland, presenting his gendered vision as an extension of the nationalist conceit of Ireland as woman, or as he put it – in terms apparently borrowed from his reading of David Jones – 'an indigenous territorial numen, a tutelar of the whole island, call her Mother Ireland, Kathleen Ni Houlihan, the poor old woman, the Shan Van Vocht, whatever' (*Preoccupations*, 57). SH addressed feminist critiques of his work obliquely in 'Orpheus in Ireland', his Oxford lecture on the eighteenth-century poet Brian Merriman delivered on 21 October 1993, which revealed a somewhat defensive intolerance of literary analysis of this kind (*RP*, 38–62). Fran Brearton surveyed this complicated area in her essay 'Heaney and the Feminine', in which she concluded that 'perhaps, ironically enough, Heaney's gender politics prove less "dismaying", even for the feminist reader, with the recognition that his voice is rather more uncertain than it sometimes purports to be' (Brearton 2009, 89).

It is important to note that SH himself never lost faith in *North*. Patrick Crotty observes that 'the biggest difference between the treatment of the opening decade of the career in the 1980 and 1990 compilations is in the weighting given to *North*', which is far greater in the later *New Selected Poems 1966–1987* than in the earlier books. 'It looks as if, having entertained the doubts of his critics in 1980, the poet has finally had the courage of his initial convictions and come down decisively in favour of *North*' (Crotty 1994, 194). The dominant representation of *North* among the earlier books is maintained in *Opened Ground*.

Although the debates over the bog poems have been the main talking points about *North*, the high claims made for the volume as one of the 'crucial poetic interventions of the twentieth century', in Vendler's words, are not just founded on the force and directness with which it addresses public matters and the predicament of Northern Ireland. Just as *Wintering Out* established its linguistic note with 'the languagey poems', *North* has a new striking poetic form, which was anticipated in 'Tollund Man' in *Wintering Out*. These forms have been described as 'skinny quatrains' composed of short lines which suggest a kind of augur or drill, penetrating down and therefore metaphorically suited to the underground, archaeological theme. And the claim for precision and accuracy is spelled out towards the end of the title poem:

> Keep your eye clear
> as the bleb of the icicle.

Some of SH's most effective and admired locutions come in this book: the devastating summary of the northern civil war as 'neighbourly murder'; the self-location in 'Kinship':

> I grew out of all this
> like a weeping willow
> inclined to
> the appetites of gravity.

There is a literary force of personal experience that SH himself was insistent on and desired to see preserved against and beyond the politics of the moment:

> During the last few years there has been considerable expectation
> that poets from Northern Ireland should 'say' something about 'the
> situation', but in the end they will only be worth listening to if they are
> saying something about and to themselves. The truest poetry may be
> the most feigning but there are contexts, and Northern Ireland is one of
> them, where to feign a passion is as reprehensible as to feign its absence.
> (*PBS Bulletin*, 85)

There is in abundance continuity from *Wintering Out* that lies not only in the bog poems of *North*, but in the further maturing of SH's poetics. The volume ends notably with 'Exposure', section 6 of 'Singing School', a significant statement of SH's situation that serves as a kind of political *ars poetica*. Has he missed what that poem's final lines call the 'once-in-a-lifetime portent', by escaping 'from the massacre' to this wood-kerne's retreat? Is the troubled North of Ireland the place where the momentous present is marked by an impending comet? *Field Work*, the next book, which follows the four that were 'one book', will answer these questions in the negative.

[text: *North*2025]

Mossbawn: Two Poems in Dedication

Charting the publication history of these two poems is complicated by the fact that, while they are gathered under the one title in *North*, they had been published separately before. The notes here draw upon the three related entries in Brandes 2008: for 'Mossbawn: Two Poems in Dedication', 'Mossbawn Sunlight', and 'The Seed Cutters'. The poems are first published together under the title 'Mossbawn: Two Poems in Dedication' in *North*, and subsequently included thus in *SP*, *PM*, *Seamus Heaney: Readings in Contemporary Poetry* (New York: Dia Art Foundation, 1988), *NSP1990*, *OG* and *100P*. 'Mossbawn Sunlight' was first published in Seamus Heaney (ed.), *Soundings '72: An Annual Anthology of New Irish Poetry* (Belfast: Blackstaff, 1972), 23, in *Antaeus* (Winter 1973): 59, and in John Montague (ed.), *The Faber Book of Irish Verse* (London: Faber, 1974), 361–2. 'The Seed Cutters' was first published in the *Irish Times* (5 May 1973): 10 (as 'The Seed-Cutters'), and then in the *Times Literary Supplement* (28 March 1975): 336 (as 'Seed Cutters').

Dedication Mary Heaney was SH's aunt, his father's sister, who lived with the family throughout the poet's childhood, first in Mossbawn and later at The Wood. He was deeply attached to her. Her later life and death are commemorated in 'Chairing Mary', Part 2 of 'Home Help' (*DC*, 67, *PSH*, 624); she is the dedicatee of 'In a Yard' (*PSH*, 1180).

1 SUNLIGHT

Title] Mossbawn Sunlight *Soundings, Antaeus, FBO Irish Verse*

Title 'A Guardian' in TS (NLI 49,493/36).
   7 *griddle*: a flat cooking plate, used for baking bread.
   10 'her' identifies Mary Heaney, from here to the end of the poem.
   23 *scone*: loaf of home-made soda bread.
   24 *two clocks*: perhaps with some coded significance: there are also two clocks audible in 'A Call' (*SL*, 53; *PSH*, 494).

2 THE SEED CUTTERS

Title] The Seed-Cutters *Irish Times* | Seed Cutters, *TLS*
3 hedge] hedge, *Irish Times* half-circle] half-circle, *Irish Times* | half circle *TLS*
4 windbreak] wind-break *Irish Times*
4^5, 8^9, 12^13] [stanza breaks] *Irish Times*
5 seed cutters] seed-cutters *Irish Times*
7 kill,] kill *TLS*, *SP*, *PM*
12 O,] Oh *Irish Times*, *TLS*, *SP*, *PM*, *NSP1990* the] that *Irish Times*
13 Yellowing over] That yellows over *Irish Times*

1 *Breughel*: Pieter Brueghel the Elder (*c.*1525–69), Flemish Renaissance painter, famous for his depiction of country scenes and landscapes.

PART I

North, like its predecessor volume *Wintering Out*, is explicitly divided into two parts (as well as the prefatory 'Mossbawn: Two Poems in Dedication'). Although one of the most powerful of the bog poems, 'The Tollund Man', comes in Part One of *Wintering Out*, there is not such a thematic divide between the two parts as has been found in *North*; here, Part I has been seen as driven by what Seamus Deane called the 'enabling myth' of the bog poems, which other commentators saw as a fatalistic view of violence in Northern Ireland, while Part II returns to a more personal response to current circumstances.

Epigraph Page 11 of SH's personal uncorrected proof copy of *North* prints and deletes (with diagonal lines inside a rectangle) *ll*. 156–65 of T. S. Eliot's *Little Gidding*, beginning 'This is the use of Memory' (see Cuda 2005, 172 n. 12).

Antaeus

First published in *Hibernia* (Oct. 1966): 17. Collected with revisions in *North*, and also included in *PM* and *OG*. Interestingly, in *OG*, the poem is not placed with the others from *North* which are included, but set alone as a kind of inter-text between the selections from *DN* and *DD*.

2 as] like *Hibernia*
7 the earth's long contour] her breasts' firm contour *Hibernia*
8 cave] cave, *Hibernia*, *PM*, *OG*
9 Girdered] Girded *Hibernia*, *PM*, *OG*
11–12 *Hibernia* reading:

> And recharge from each worming artery.
> My limbs bulge like a wheat sack. *Hibernia*

14 Atlas.] Atlas: *OG*
17 royal:] royal. *Hibernia*, *OG*
18 birth] birth. *Hibernia*

Title Antaeus is the giant son of Poseidon and Ge (Sea and Earth): in SH the earth-bound antitype, with whom he first identifies, of the 'sky-born' Hercules. Cf. 'Hercules and Antaeus' (*North*, 55; *PSH*, 198). He lost his strength when he lost contact with the earth. Because the poem was published in October 1966 in *Hibernia* and is collected with revisions here, '1966' is written at the foot of the text in *North* in 1975.

Belderg

First published in *Encounter* (Dec. 1974): 63, and then in the Rainbow Press limited edition, *BP*. After collection in *North* it was included in *PM*, and later in Richard Murphy (ed.), *The Mayo Anthology* (Ballina: Mayo County Council, 1990).

Dated 26 July 1974 in MS (NLI 49,493/39).
Title Village in north Co. Mayo, also called Belderrig (from Irish *béal dearg*, 'red mouth or inlet'). The quernstones were discovered in the nearby bog in an area now known as the Céide Fields by a farmer Patrick Caulfield whose archaeologist son, Séamus Caulfield, excavated the site, finding Neolithic fields under the bog there (though some archaeologists claim it dates to later in the Bronze Age). Entitled 'A Visit to Belderg' in TS (NLI 49,493/35), and 'Ode on an Ancient Site' (NLI 49,493/39).
1 The speaker is presumably Séamus Caulfield whom SH knew and who showed him around the excavations.
5 *quernstones*: circular stones used for grinding grain.
11 *glib*: Irish term for pendulous tufts of hair.
27 *moss* and **34** *bawn*: SH had dwelt in 1972 on the etymology of both elements of the name in his early essay 'Belfast' (*Preoccupations*, 35); he returns to the derivation of *bawn* in the introduction to his translation of *Beowulf* (1999, xxx).
43 *world-tree*: in many mythologies, a tree that supports the heavens. Here SH is probably thinking of the Norse version, Yggdrasil (as in *l.* 39).

Funeral Rites

First published in the *Irish Times* (9 Nov. 1974): 10, and in *Exile*, 2. 1 (1974): 5–7. After collection in *North* it was also published in *New Republic* (27 March 1976): 26, and Maurice Harmon (ed.), *Image and Illusion: Anglo-Irish Literature and its Contexts, A Festschrift for Roger McHugh* (Dublin: Wolfhound, 1979), and in *SP, PM, Seamus Heaney: Readings in Contemporary Poetry* (New York: Dia Art Foundation, 1988), *NSP1990*, *OG* and *100P*.

I 2 to lift] the lift (error) *North1975*
I 15 courteously] courteously, *Irish Times*
I 16 all] all, *Irish Times*
II 6 cortège] cortege *Irish Times*
II 11 cupmarked] cup-marked *Irish Times*
II 12 bye-roads] by-roads *Irish Times*
III 7 placated] suspended *Irish Times*

I: The first section describes the traditional procedures at Catholic funerals, pre-Troubles.

I 2 *to lift the coffins:* first edn (1975) erroneously has 'the lift', corrected in 1992 reset edition.

I 13 *dulse:* also called dillisk or sea lettuce, an edible seaweed, very popular in the North of Ireland (*duilleog uisce:* 'water leaf' in Irish).

I 26 *soapstone:* material from which Inuit sculptures are traditionally carved (hence 'igloo', l. 27).

II 7 *blinded home:* reference to practice of drawing curtains shut as funeral processions pass.

II 9 *great chambers of Boyne:* Neolithic monuments in Co. Meath, collectively called Brú na Bóinne, near the reputed location of the Battle of the Boyne and of Tara: Newgrange, Knowth and Dowth. The grandest of them, Newgrange, is a huge passage-tomb, dated to about 3200 BCE. Knowth is a complex of mounds (l. 22).

II 26 *the Gap of the North:* the Moyry Pass that runs past Slieve Gullion mountain, the classic route from the South of Ireland to the North (through which SH's own funeral cortège from Dublin to Bellaghy passed in 2013).

III 4 Strangford and Carlingford are two great sea loughs in the east of Northern Ireland, which are named from the Norse term *fjord*.

III 9 *Gunnar:* one of the heroes of the medieval Norse *Njáls saga*. SH interprets the verses 'about honour' he was chanting in his burial-chamber as hopeful so he looks with a joyful face at the moon because his 'feud [is] placated' (7). But cf. O'Donoghue 2009, 197–8.

North

First published in the *Irish University Review*, 4. 2 (Autumn 1974): 200–1, collected in *North* and then in Eric White (ed.), *Poetry Book Society: The First Twenty-Five Years* (London: Poetry Book Society, 1979). Subsequently included in *SP*, *PM*, *NSP1990* and *OG*.

2 shod] curve *NSP1990*, *OG*
24 thick-witted] thick witted *Irish University Review*
25 behindbacks] behind-backs *OG*
35–6 *Irish University Review* reading: in the long foray of your art / but no cascade of light
38 of] or *Irish University Review*
39 treasure] treasures *Irish University Review*

Title 'Northerners' in TS (NLI 49,493/35).

10 *Orkney and Dublin:* both Viking settlements. The location of the first Viking raids on Ireland is usually identified as Lambay Island off north Co. Dublin in 795.

22 *Thor:* the Norse warrior god.

26 *the althing:* the medieval Icelandic political meeting-house, and the name of the modern Icelandic parliament.

30 *word-hoard:* term for poetic vocabulary. Beowulf's first speech is introduced by the formula 'the leader of the troop unlocked his word-hoard' (*l.* 258).

33 *compose in darkness*: the Irish bards were said to have been locked up in darkness while they composed.

34 *aurora borealis:* the Northern Lights.

Viking Dublin: Trial Pieces

First published in the *New Review* (June 1974), the *Irish University Review*, 4. 2 (Autumn 1974): 201–3, and in the *Irish Press* (7 June 1975): 6. Collected in *North* with revisions, and then included in *SP, PM, NSP1990* and *OG*, and in Pat Boran and Gerard Smyth (eds), *If Ever You Go: A Map of Dublin in Poetry and Song* (Dublin: Dedalus, 2014), 223.

I 1 jaw-bone] jaw bone *Irish University Review*
I 12 itself] itself, *Irish University Review, Irish Press, SP, PM, NSP1990, OG*
I 13 eluding] outrunning *Irish University Review*
II 1 trial pieces] 'trial pieces' *Irish University Review*
II 16] coins and scale-pans. *Irish University Review*
III] *Irish University Review* reading:

> Its clean line
> ran aground, hardening
> the spine of *Dublin*:
> the name of the town
>
> clinker-built.
> The shallows continued
> their assonance, conspiring
> under the hurdles,
>
> curraghs ghosted the run
> of the dark pool
> but the longship's keel
> struck fast in the uvular
>
> slip of the bank,
> like a long sword
> sheathed in its moisting
> burial clays.

III 16 migrant line.] migrant line *Irish Press* [presumed typo]
IV, V] [omitted] *Irish University Review*
VI 9 and] And *Irish University Review*

Title Dublin was founded by Norwegian Vikings in 841. A celebrated series of Viking excavations led by Breandán Ó Ríordáin (1927–2017) started in 1974, so SH is interested early in the process. In 1978–9 there were forceful and sustained protests at the plans of Dublin Corporation to build its headquarters on Wood Quay on a site next to Christ Church Cathedral in the heart of the old city, destroying a major part of its foundations. On 23 September 1978 there was a protest by 20,000 people at the destruction of the astonishingly well preserved underground remains of the medieval city. Trial pieces are carvings done to test an artist's skill and 'the craft's mystery' (II 2).

II 11 The 'migrant prow' of the invading Vikings.

III 6 *clinker-built*: a method of boat building with overlapping planks, originating in Scandinavia.

IV 3 *zoomorphic*: the tracing of capital letters in animal shapes, in Celtic and insular Germanic texts.

IV 6 *Hamlet the Dane*: 'Danes' was the term traditionally used to refer to the Norwegian Vikings who came to Ireland, linking the conditions of Troubles-era Northern Ireland to the poison and 'jumping in graves' of the last act of Shakespeare's play.

V 9ff. *butcher's aplomb*: describes the – probably fictitious – torture called 'blood-eagling' in which the victim's lungs were spread across their shoulders.

V 13 *Old fathers*: probably recalling Yeats's appeal to his forebears in the 'Introductory Verses to *Responsibilities*' (Albright 1990, 148).

VI 10 *pan*: probably brainpan, i.e. a skull; *'an old Dane'*: one of the Danes that first founded Dublin.

VI 15 *pampooties*: rawhide shoes, made and worn on the Aran Islands.

The Digging Skeleton

First published as 'The Digging Skeleton (After Baudelaire)' in *Fuse*, a magazine of St John's College, Oxford in (Nov. 1973): 34, and then in the *TLS* (16 Aug. 1974): 880, before collection in *North*.

Title] The Digging Skeleton (After Baudelaire) *Fuse*

From Baudelaire's 'Le Squelette laboureur' (*Les Fleurs du mal*).

After the fairly close translation of the beginning, SH's hallmark themes – 'boneyard' (II 8); 'spade' (II 20) – become prominent. In I 12, the term 'navvies', applied in England to Irish labourers, confirms this shift of association.

Bone Dreams

First published in *Arts in Ireland* (Autumn 1972): 52–3 and *Phoenix*, 10 (July 1973): 6–7. Before collection in *North* it also appeared in Stewart Conn (ed.), *New Poems 1973–1974: A PEN Anthology of Contemporary Poetry* (London: Hutchinson, 1974), and in *BP*, in which it was dedicated to Barrie Cooke. After collection in *North* it was included in *PM*, *NSP1990* and *OG*. Part VI was previously published under the title 'In Devon', in *Aquarius*, 4 (1971): 45.

III 4 ban-hus] ban bus (error) *PM* | bān-hūs *NSP1990*, *OG*

Dated 'Written at Wotton-under-Edge / Gloucestershire, 15–16 July 1972 / Seamus Heaney' (BC 1280758), the house of Polly Devlin, Marie Heaney's sister (*SS*, 157).

    II 1 *Bone-house*: translation of Old English compound *ban-hus* (III 4), a kenning for body.

    II 6 The 'dictions' of English work backwards progressively from Elizabethan, to the Middle Ages of the Normans and Provençal, to the Old English of the *scop* (poet) where he finds the original of 'bone-house' *ban-hus* (above).

    III 15 The trochaic compounds 'love-den, blood-holt', were 'ring-hoard, bone-box' in a version sent to Barrie Cooke; 'bone-box' is the term invented by Cooke for an image with which he illustrated these Heaney poems.

    IV 7 my *lady*: the English scheme of reference, linguistic and geographical, is personalised and sexualised throughout the rest of the poem.

    IV 12 A chalk giant such as the Cerne Abbas Giant on a hillside in Dorset, which is fifty-five metres high, carrying a club and featuring a prominent erection.

    V 14 *Hadrian's Wall*: defensive Roman fortification wall, seventy-three miles long, from coast to coast across the north of England from Bowness in the west to Wallsend in the east, begun in the reign of the Emperor Hadrian in CE 122.

    V 16 *Maiden Castle*: Iron Age fort near Dorchester in Dorset, visited by the Heaneys in 1972 (*SS*, 157): one of the biggest hillforts in Britain, excavated in the 1930s by Mortimer Wheeler who discovered several skeletons there bearing evidence of wounds.

    VI In a version of the poem sent to Barrie Cooke, the poem 'Come to the Bower' was included as section VI.

    VI 5 *coulter*: the digging blade at the front of a plough.

    VI 14 *Pennines*: range of hills in the north of England.

Come to the Bower

First published, under the title 'Bog Bower', in Douglas Dunn (ed.), *New Poems, 1972–1973: A PEN Anthology of Contemporary Poetry* (London: Hutchinson, 1973), and the first poem in *BP*, with illustrations by Barrie Cooke. After collection in *North* it was included in *Toome*.

Title 'Will You Come to the Bower' is the name of a well-known Irish nationalist song, recorded by the Dubliners and very popular in the 1960s.

 1 *My hands*: the narrative voice explores in the bog the body of 'the dark-bowered queen' (l. 5) dug up on the Moira Estate in Co. Down, twenty miles south of Belfast. This is the first of the six bog poems in *North*.

Bog Queen

First published in the *Listener* (23 Nov. 1972): 712, subsequently in the *James Joyce Quarterly*, 11. 3 (Spring 1974): 221–3, and in *Antaeus* (Spring 1975): 43–4. Before collection in *North* it also appeared in Stewart Conn (ed.), *New Poems 1973–1974*, and in *BP*. After collection in *North* it was included in *SP*, *PM*, *NSP1990* and *OG*.

6–7 influences: / dawn] influences. / Dawn *James Joyce Quarterly*
25–6 carious, / gemstones] carious. / Gemstones *James Joyce Quarterly*
30 wrinkling, dyed weaves] wrinkling. Dyed weaves *James Joyce Quarterly*
31 phoenician] Phoenician *OG*
36–8] at my thighs. // The soaked fledge, / the weight of the hides. *James Joyce Quarterly*
42–3 I was barbered / and stripped] I was barbered and stripped / and stripped (error?) *James Joyce Quarterly*
46 coomb] mould

Title 'The Viking Queen of Ulster' in TS (NLI 49,493/34).

 1ff. The narrative voice is assigned to a female body dug up on the Moira Estate near Lisburn, Co. Antrim, in 1780, preserved by the bog water like the Jutland bodies in Glob's book, so this poem joins the poems about them in SH's pamphlet *BP*. Unlike the Jutland bodies, there is no suggestion of ritual killing, though the process of digging her up is represented as a kind of violation. Links to the terrain of Jutland ('moraines' as a material pushed ahead by glaciers, for example) are made throughout the poem.

 21 *Baltic amber*: the Baltic Sea washes the east coast of Jutland. Amber is a fossilised tree resin, prized as the material of decorative jewellery.

 46 *coomb*: Ulster term for soft vegetative material.

The Grauballe Man

First published in the *Listener* (15 Nov. 1973): 663, and then in the *James Joyce Quarterly*, 11. 3 (Spring 1974): 225–6. Later also published in *New Republic* (27 March 1976). Before collection in *North*, it was included in *BP*, and subsequently in *SP, PM, NSP1990, OG* and *100P*.

Title A body found in the bog by turf-cutters near Grauballe in South Denmark, now on display in the Moesgaard Museum near Aarhus, illustrated and discussed in P. V. Glob's *The Bog People*. Glob assumed the body was the victim of violent ritual killing.

43 *the Dying Gaul*: ancient Roman marble semi-recumbent figure now in the Capitoline Museums in Rome. It is a copy of a bronze Hellenistic original so, strictly speaking, probably not a Gaul or Celt.

Punishment

First published in *Broadsheet*, 17 (March 1973): [1], then in the *James Joyce Quarterly*, 11. 3 (Spring 1974): 224–5, and in the *Listener* (23 May 1974): 663. Worksheets for the poem were included in *Quarto* (Coleraine, Nov. 1974). The poem also appeared in *BP*, and later in Maurice Harmon (ed.), *Image and Illusion: Anglo-Irish Literature and Its Contexts* (Dublin: Wolfhound Press, 1979). After collection in *North*, it was included in *SP, PM, NSP1990, OG* and *100P*.

3–4 frail rigging / of] frail / rigging of *Broadsheet*
10 bog] pool *Broadsheet*
14–15 barked sapling / that] barked / sapling, that *Broadsheet*
16 brain-firkin:] brain-firkin. *Broadsheet*
17–44] They have breached
    her shaved head, her stubble
    of black corn, spied
    on her glutted furrows

    and numbered all her bones.
    Beneath the stone
    her unshorn loins
    had been atoning,

    gradually her red
    and yellow headband,
    tied for a blindfold,
    was a soiled halo

    and the birch scourge
    they had thrown across her
    settled, at the angle
    of a palm.

    Sated with bog juice

          the oxhide collar
          was a ring that stored
          the memories of love.

          Little adultress, we hear
          that you were flaxen haired,
          undernourished, and your
          tar-black face was beautiful

          into your meek gaze
          I commit the stone-casters
          and your punished sisters
          weeping under the lamp-post. *Broadsheet*
33–4] of your brain's / historic ridges *James Joyce Quarterly*
36 bones:] bones. *James Joyce Quarterly*: this is the end of the poem in this version.

Dated 18 November 1972 in TS (NLI 49,493/34).

Notably, the development of this poem altered during its publication life: the *Broadsheet* outing of 1974 presenting a dramatically different text after *l*. 17, while the version published in the *James Joyce Quarterly* had yet to include the poem's final two stanzas, which would appear from the *Listener* printing onward.

38ff. The linking of the girl in the poem, assumed to be the victim of a ritual killing, with the barbaric punishment of some young Catholic women in Northern Ireland who consorted with British soldiers was the point of greatest controversy in the poem, especially because of the understanding of the 'tribal, intimate revenge' at the end.

Strange Fruit

First published, as 'Strange Fruits', in the *Times Literary Supplement* (4 April 1975): 352. After collection in *North*, it was included in *Toome*, and subsequently *SP*, *NSP1990* and *OG*.

Title] Strange Fruits, *TLS*

Title 'Strange Fruit' was written by Abel Meeropol and famously sung by Billie Holiday, who recorded it in 1939. It describes the brutal practice of the lynching of African Americans in the United States. Originally a poem titled 'Bitter Fruit', Meeropol was moved to write it after seeing a photograph by Lawrence Beitler of the lynching of Thomas Shipp and Abram Smith in Indiana on 7 August 1930. Previously titled in TSS 'Severed Head' (NLI 49,493/37), 'Head' in TS (NLI 49,493/34), 'Tete Coupee' (NLI 49,493/35) and 'Reliquary' (NLI 49,493/39).

9 *Diodorus Siculus*: Diodorus of Sicily, a Greek historian who wrote in the first century BCE, whose *Bibliotheca Historica*, a monumental universal history in forty books of which fifteen survive, begins with the culture and history of Ancient Egypt. It is primarily concerned with the Mediterranean area, so Diodorus's ease with Northern Europe might be called gradual (*l.* 10). There is a passage in the *Bibliotheca* which may refer to Stonehenge.

Kinship

First published in *James Joyce Quarterly*, 11. 3 (Spring 1974): 227–32, then in *Phoenix*, 13 (Spring 1975): 11–12, and later in *New Republic* (27 March 1976): 26. After collection in *North* it was included in *SP*, *PM* and *OG*.

I 1–2 hieroglyphic / peat on] hieroglyphic peat / on *James Joyce Quarterly*
I 2 spreadfield] spread-field *James Joyce Quarterly*
I 3 strangled] sundered *James Joyce Quarterly*
I 14–15] the black spade-marks, / the layered secrets *James Joyce Quarterly*
II 6–8] meaning soft, borrowing / windless falls of rain, / the pupil of amber. *James Joyce Quarterly*
II 12 pollen-bin] pollen bin *James Joyce Quarterly*
II 14–16] embalmer of sacrifice / and staked murders, / tanner of sunlight. *James Joyce Quarterly*
III 16 that obelisk:] my obelisk: *James Joyce Quarterly*
III 20–2] catkin and bog-cotton // tremble as they set up / the cloven oak branch. *James Joyce Quarterly*
V 2–8] of the cart-wheels, buried
    in the turf mould,
    the curve of the tail-board,

    the socketed cribs –
    all come together
    and I have retrieved
    a ritual chariot. *James Joyce Quarterly*
VI 5] in a desolate peace *James Joyce Quarterly*
VI 17] of the sacrificed, *James Joyce Quarterly*

II 5 *bog*: soft (Irish).

II 17 *Insatiable bride*: see 'Nerthus' (*WO*, 38; *PSH*, 136); a Germanic goddess, described by Tacitus in *Germania* as a figure of Mother Earth, like Ge.

IV 1 *This centre holds*: by contrast with the centre that cannot hold in the anarchy of Yeats's 'The Second Coming' (Albright 1990, 235).

V 5 The cupid's bow design was common on the tailboard of carts.

V 11 *God of the waggon*: Hermes, often associated with SH's father, with whom the poet as child is linked as 'his privileged attendant' (*ll.* 13–14)

VI 1 Publius Cornelius Tacitus, Roman historian, born *c.*56 CE whose *Germania* (*c.*98 CE) was a major Latin work about the Germanic peoples, whom he admired.

VI 5 *a desolate peace*: 'ubi solitudinem faciunt pacem appellant' ('where they make a desert they call it peace'), according to Tacitus, said of the Romans under Agricola by Calgacus, the leader of the Caledonian conspiracy at the Battle of Mons Graupius in 83/4. But the idea is a commonplace in Greek and Roman history.

VI 19–20 In this northern territory, in contrast to Tacitus's more positive view of the Germanic peoples, they 'slaughter / for the common good' while the occupying 'legions stare / from the ramparts' (VI 11–12).

Ocean's Love to Ireland

First published in the *Irish University Review*, 4. 2 (Autumn 1974): 199–200. After collection in *North* the poem was also included in the *New Republic* (27 March 1976).

I 2 Ralegh] Raleigh *Irish University Review*

Title Derived from Walter Raleigh's long poem of appeal to Elizabeth I, 'Ocean's Love to Cynthia'. See Moloney 1991.

I 6 this verbal account of the rape of the maid, with 'Sweet Sir Walter' syncopated, is taken from the description of the episode in John Aubrey's late seventeenth-century *Brief Lives*, though the victim is not Irish there.

II 1 Cynthia, the moon, the term used in poetic celebration of Queen Elizabeth.

II 3 *Lee and Blackwater*: the two principal rivers in Co. Cork. Raleigh's house was in Youghal, where the Blackwater reaches the sea.

II 4–5 The story that Raleigh spread his coat on the ground in a 'plashy' place for the queen to walk on is first told in Thomas Fuller's *Worthies of England* (1662).

II 7–9 Smerwick Harbour (Cuan Árd na Caithne) on the Dingle peninsula in West Kerry where 600 Spanish and Italian seamen were butchered after surrendering on the orders of Raleigh. The characterisation of the victims as 'gallant and good' is attributed by Aubrey to Lord Grey, Lord Deputy of Ireland.

III 1ff. The Spanish attempts, including the Armada, to help Irish resistance to English rule 'failed her'.

III 6 Onan in Genesis 38 was slain by God because he failed to perform his levirate duty by sleeping with his brother's wife to perpetuate his tribe.

Aisling

Published in *North*.

Title The aisling is an Irish poetic form, chiefly associated with eighteenth-century political poetry, in which the poet reports a vision of a woman representing Ireland. This poem probably links with the preceding one; here the male lover employs 'sweet art' rather than the violence of Raleigh. But he is still linked to Actaeon who was torn to pieces by his hunting dogs for the voyeuristic crime of seeing the chaste Diana naked. See also the late uncollected poem 'Actaeon' (*PSH*, 685).

Act of Union

'Act of Union' emerges from a poem called 'A New Life', comprising four sonnets, published in the *Listener* (22 Feb. 1973): 239; two of these sonnets are collected with revisions under the title 'Act of Union'. 'A New Life' was also published in *Lynx* 1. 2 (Spring 1973): 21. 'Act of Union' was then published in *Broadsheet*, 21 ([June] 1974):7, and *Aquarius* (1974): 108–9, as well as in Stewart Conn (ed.), *New Poems 1973–1974: A PEN Anthology of Contemporary Poetry* (London: Hutchinson, 1974) and later Maurice Harmon (ed.), *Image and Illusion: Anglo-Irish Literature and its Contexts* (1979). After collection in *North*, it was included in *SP*, *NSP1990* and *OG*.

I 1 To-night] Tonight *NSP1990, OG*

Title Historically the Act of Union was the legal union of Britain and Ireland in 1800, forcing the closure of the Parliament of Ireland (Grattan's Parliament) in Dublin, which had been led by Henry Grattan from 1782.

I 9ff. The tall kingdom is the island of Great Britain, represented as male, and the addressed 'you' is Ireland, with its 'half-independent' shore, represented, as in several poems here, as female and violated by conquest, as in the 'stretchmarked body' in II 13.

The Betrothal of Cavehill

Published in *North*.

Title Cavehill is a rocky basalt hill overlooking Belfast.

2 *profiled*: an outcrop on the rock is called 'Napoleon's Nose' because it is said to resemble Napoleon's profile. Here, though, it represents the 'proud, protestant' north, looking towards the Catholic south in Ireland.

Hercules and Antaeus

First published in the *Irish Times* (31 May 1975): 10, and later in *Strawberry Fare* (London: St Mary's College, Strawberry Hill, 1980). After collection in *North*, it was included in *SP*, *PM*, *NSP1990* and *OG*.

28 shaken,] shaken *Irish Times*, *SP*, *PM*, *NSP*

Title Cf. 'Antaeus' (*North*, 15; *PSH*, 174). That poem was first published in 1966, so this poem is a kind of sequel. But while the resistant earth-giant Antaeus is the centre of the earlier poem, here Hercules 'has the measure' of 'Antaeus, the mould-hugger'.

23–4 All native opponents of the dominant political order: Balor was in Irish mythology the leader of the Fomorians, a malevolent supernatural giant with a single destructive eye. Byrhtnoth was a leader of Anglo-Saxon warriors in East Anglia, defeated by the invading Norwegians at the Battle of Maldon in 991. Sitting Bull (1831–90) was chief of the Hunkpapa Lakota people, who led their resistance against the United States government, victorious over Custer's 7th Cavalry at the Battle of Little Bighorn (1876). But their causes have all died or will die.

32 'Pap for the dispossessed' was taken as the title of a 1985 article about SH by David Lloyd, questioning what he saw as the acquiescent view of the inevitability of Northern Irish violence and its role in nationalist mythology.

PART II

The Unacknowledged Legislator's Dream

First published in *North*.

Title Shelley's *A Defence of Poetry* (written 1821 and published posthumously in 1841) ends by claiming that 'poets are the unacknowledged legislators of the world'. A working title in TS had been 'The Unacknowledged Legislator' (NLI 49,493/35).

1 Archimedes' principle of the lever states that unequal weights on a lever can produce balance at the fulcrum in inverse proportion to the distance of each from the fulcrum. So an agent of lesser strength can equal the strength of a greater by being placed proportionately further from the fulcrum. The metaphorical sense here might be applied to the opponents in 'Hercules and Antaeus', the last poem in Part One of *North*.

3 Tarzan, from the novels of Edgar Rice Burroughs, was probably familiar to SH and his school-age friends like Billy Hunter from a series of films which began in the 1930s. The inequality here between the mass of Tarzan and of the world is reduced by the length of the creeper on which he jumps from the treetop.

4–6 The principle of inequality is applied in the political realm in which the narrator of the poem undermines the masonry of state and statute by swinging on a creeper into the Bastille prison and sinking his crowbar into a point of weakness.

9 *strappado*: a brutal form of torture in which the victim is suspended by their arms and dropped on a long rope, another kind of suspending mechanism. The 'wronged people cheer', but the power remains with the commandant who mockingly claims to be honoured to add a poet to the victims (*l.* 12) while claiming he will be safer in prison.

13–15 The imprisoned narrator jumps on the concrete flagstones of the cell to test the principle of equivalence. But every act in prison is under surveillance.

Whatever You Say Say Nothing

First published in the *Listener* under the headline 'Whatever You Say, Say Nothing: Seamus Heaney Gives His View on the Irish Thing' (14 Oct. 1971): 496–7, and then in the *Irish Press* (11 Dec. 1971): 9. It was included in Padraic Fiacc (ed.), *The Wearing of the Black* (Belfast: Blackstaff, 1974), then collected in *North*, and subsequently in *PM*. Parts I, III and IV of the poem were included in *NSP1990*, *OG* and *100P*.

Title] Whatever You Say, Say Nothing *Listener* | Whatever you say, say nothing *Wearing of the Black*
Passim] [sentence case] *Listener, Wearing of the Black*
I 1 I'm writing this just] I'm writing just *Irish Press, Wearing of the Black, PM*
I 5 media-men] media men *Wearing of the Black*
I 6 recorders] and Uhers *Listener, Irish Press* | uhers *Wearing of the Black*
I 10] Of leader writers or those marvellous men *Listener, Irish Press* | of leader-writers or newspapermen *Wearing of the Black*
I 12 And protest to gelignite and sten,] to gelignite, whose day begins at ten, *Listener* sten] Sten *OG*
I 14] provisional] Provisional *Listener, Wearing of the Black*
I 15 hate'.] hate', *Wearing of the Black*
I 16 sing,] sing *Wearing of the Black*
I 17 civil-tongued] civil tongued *PM, NSP*
I 19 fake] false *Wearing of the Black*

I 21 agree.] agree, *Listener, Wearing of the Black*
I 22 worse.] worse, *Listener, Wearing of the Black*
I 21 murderers.] murderers, *Listener, Wearing of the Black*   understandably . . .]
  understandably, *Wearing of the Black*
II 2 gelignite's] gelignite, *Wearing of the Black*   effect:] effect; *Wearing of the Black*
II 3 The Pope] the Pope, *Listener, Wearing of the Black*
II 9 tit,] tit *Listener, Irish Press, Wearing of the Black*
II 10 swallow,] swallow *Listener, Irish Press, Wearing of the Black, PM*
II 11] leaves us fork-tongued on the partition bit: *Listener, Irish Press*
II 14 all] our *Listener, Irish Press*
II 15 It's tempting here to rhyme] It's hard here not to rhyme *Listener, Irish Press*
II 23 I sit here with a] I suffer this *Listener, Irish Press*
II 27 sham,] sham *Listener, PM, Wearing of the Black*
II 27] could cut a line through enmity and sham *Listener, Irish Press*
II 28 Given the right line] give me the right line] *Irish Press*
III 3 never] never *Listener, Irish Press*
III 5–6] in the great dykes that always barricade / the dutchmen from the jacobites
  among us. *Listener, Irish Press*
III 8–10] I am about as capable as fungus // of breaking my soft grip on the sick place /
  or its on me. Of the 'wee six' I sing *Listener, Irish Press*
III 10 'wee six'] wee six, *Wearing of the Black*
III 13–24]
  And I belong to that strange generation
  who got the message on the road to school
  that 'party tunes' made up for segregation:
  'Fenian' and 'Prod' and 'fanny', 'ball' and 'tool'

  dirtied our cleanish tongues at dinner-time.
  But we learnt the rules of company, sang dumb
  for to be found out was the only crime.
  We learnt to be too sweet and not wholesome.

  Enter, in our twenties, the great O'Neill.
  The Great O'Neill! Those 'two cultures' again!
  He might as well have never turned a wheel.
  The tone was raised and things went down the drain.

  And at the age of thirty-two I hear
  the old mythologies explode with death
  and lie with my fellow brutes, with my ear
  to the ground, lie, sick of my bad breath. *Listener, Irish Press*
III 17 Prod,] Prod *Wearing of the Black, PM, NSP1990, 100P*
III 19 Oh,] O *Wearing of the Black, PM, NSP1990, OG, 100P*
IV 2 internees:] internees, *Listener, Irish Press*
IV 4 roadside,] roadside *Listener, Irish Press*
IV 7 déjà-vu,] déjà-vu – *Listener, Irish Press*
IV 10 In Ballymurphy.] on a wall down town. *Listener, Irish Press*
IV 11 sup:] sup, *Irish Press, Wearing of the Black, OG*

One of SH's most familiar titles and sequences, expressing in its title an attitude of wariness ascribed to Irish political attitudes of SH's time. It also links to the reserve that SH associated with his father in poems like 'The Stone Verdict' (*HL*, 17; *PSH*, 366): here 'the famous / Northern reticence' (III 8–9). Entitled 'Views' in TS (NLI 49,493/39).

I 5 *stringers*: freelance journalists or photographers.

I 7 *The times are out of joint*: 'The time is out of joint: O cursed spite / That ever I was born to set it right'. *Hamlet*, 1.5.188–9.

I 16 *'I live here too'*: perhaps again recalling Leopold Bloom in *Ulysses* 35–6, the passage quoted in 'Traditions' (*WO*, 21; *PSH*, 128) answering the question 'What ish my nation?' '"Ireland," said Bloom, / "I was born here. Ireland."' Also echoes the closing lines of American poet and political activist (1901–67) Langston Hughes's poem 'Freedom': 'I live here, too. / I want freedom / Just as you.'

I 17 'expertly civil-tongued', recalling 'connive / in civilized outrage' in 'Punishment' (*North*, 40; *PSH*, 191).

II 3 Celtic is Glasgow Celtic FC, the Catholic-supporting Glasgow club. The claim that the Pope rejoices in their victories, especially over their Protestant-supporting rivals Rangers, is a familiar Northern Irish joke.

II 9 *the hind tit*: the idea that the sow's last teat is smaller and less nutritious so it is left for the runt of a litter. Cf. 'pap for the dispossessed' in 'Hercules and Antaeus' (*North*, 55; *PSH*, 199).

II 20 *Pearse*: Patrick Pearse (1879–1916), leader of the Easter Rising in Dublin in 1916.

II 21 *'little platoons'*: in his *Reflections on the Revolution in France*, Edmund Burke (II 23) argues against revolutionary action, claiming that attachment to 'the subdivision, to love the little platoon we belong to in society, is the first principle (the germ as it were) of public affections. It is the first link in the series by which we proceed towards a love to our country and to mankind.'

II 22 Conor Cruise O'Brien (1917–2008), Irish and international politician and writer, latterly mostly associated with opposition to the traditions of activist Irish Republicanism. Author of *The Great Melody*, a biography of Edmund Burke (see II 23). Like his hero Burke, he became more conservative despite his originally liberal politics; Burke is now often seen as the founding father of modern, 'big society' Conservatism.

II 23 Edmund Burke (1729–97), Irish political philosopher, author of *Reflections on the Revolution in France* (1790). He disapproved of the French Revolution, despite his originally liberal, Whig politics.

II 28 *aere perennius*: *exegi monumentum aere perennius* (I have built a monument more lasting than brass), Horace *Odes*, 3.30.1 (23 BCE). There is also an echo here of Shakespeare's 'Sonnet 55', 'Not marble nor the gilded monuments / Of princes shall outlive this powerful rhyme.' 'The right line', as always in SH, means a written line as well as a moral-political one.

III 5 *The Dutchman*: William of Orange, 'King Billy', the hero of Northern Irish Orange politics.

III 6 *Seamus*: James II, defeated by William of Orange at the Battle of the Boyne in 1691.

III 7 *sedentary trade*: Yeats, 'The Tower', l. 60 (Albright 1990, 245): 'This sedentary trade' – the writer's trade rather than that of the men of action.

III 10 *the 'wee six'*: the Six Counties in Northern Ireland that remained part of the United Kingdom after Partition in 1922: Antrim, Derry, Armagh, Down, Fermanagh and Tyrone.

III 17–18 Prod is Protestant, Pape is Catholic (the derogatory 'papist').

III 19 *Oh, land of password . . .*: Cf. Louis MacNeice, *Autumn Journal*, xvi (which is a major influence on this section of the poem): 'The Land of scholars and saints: / Scholars and saints my eye, the land of ambush, / Purblind manifestoes, never-ending complaints, / The born martyr and the gallant ninny . . .'

III 23 'cabin'd, cribb'd, confined, bound in / to saucy doubts and fears' (*Macbeth*, 3.4.24–5).

III 24 *Besieged within the siege*: the breaking of the Siege of Derry by Protestant forces was seen as a major triumph.

IV These lines had been included as an epigraph to WO, with one significant variation: the first half of *l.* 10 of WO 'on a wall downtown' (WO, v; PSH, 117) is replaced in *North* by the more explicit and inflammatory 'In Ballymurphy', evoking the Ballymurphy Massacre of August 1971 in which eleven civilians were killed by the Parachute Regiment.

Freedman

First published as a prose poem 'Romanist' in Padraic Fiacc (ed.), *The Wearing of the Black* (Belfast: Blackstaff, 1974) and subsequently heavily revised as 'Freedman' in *New Blackfriars*, 56. 660 (May 1975): 213. After collection in *North*, it was included in *Gravities*.

ROMANIST

I was subjugated under arches, manumitted at a graduation ceremony, for years a humble client at the lattice of confessionals. My murex was the purple of lent on a calendar patterned with fish-days.

I knelt to take the impress of the celebrant's ashy thumb, a silk friction, the spread palps of his fingers cold as mushrooms at my temples. An infinitesimal fall of dust itched down over my nose. Stipple of the first spadeful. *Memento homo quia pulvis es et in pulverem reverteris.*

>   Caste-marked annually, I went among the freemen of the city for their
>   inspection. In forum and theatre I felt their gaze bend to my mouldy brow and
>   fasten like a lamprey on the mark. In vain I sought it myself on the groomed
>   *optimi*, on the hammerheads of lictor and praetorian. I was estimated and
>   enumerated with my own, indelibly one with the earth-starred denizens of
>   catacomb and campagna.

5 [speech marks]] [no speech marks] *New Blackfriars*

Title Entitled 'Romanist' in its earlier, prose-poem iteration, the poem's theme is the freeing of the poet-narrator from the various forms of subservience under which he grew up: political (*l.* 1) and ecclesiastical (*ll.* 3–8), as slaves were sometimes granted freedom under the Roman Empire.

Epigraph R. H. Barrow, *The Romans* (1949; Penguin 1954). A book often thought to be unduly forgiving of the Romans, as in this epigraph.

3 *murex*: a dye made from snail shells, here used on parchment.

5 *Memento homo quia pulvis es*: 'Remember, man, thou art but dust.' Latin formula, pronounced on Ash Wednesday as ash was put on the forehead to remind the recipient of their mortality.

8 *all my caste*: Catholics.

9ff. Tied to the earth (like Antaeus); the Catholic is indelibly marked by the stipple of dust, of which he sees no trace in the 'groomed optimi' (*l.* 10), the higher social orders like the socially dominant unionists in Ulster.

13ff. Poetry comes to the rescue in his life, to wipe his brow and promote him. But when he pays this tribute, he will be accused of not recognising his promoters or liberators.

Singing School

The sequence is published in full in *PM* and *OG*, and extracts have been included in the other three selected editions, as detailed below; in *NSP1990*, as in *PM* and *OG*, these are accompanied by the epigraphs from Wordsworth and Yeats which head the entire sequence in *North*.

Title 'Nor is there singing school but studying / Monuments of its own magnificence' (Yeats, 'Sailing to Byzantium' in Albright 1990, 239).

I THE MINISTRY OF FEAR

First published as 'From Singing School' in Padraic Fiacc *The Wearing of the Black* (Belfast: Blackstaff, 1974). After publication in *North*, the poem was included in *SP*, *PM*, *OG* and *100P*. In May 1999 an extract was published in the *Irish Times* to accompany feature on St Columb's College (Anne Byrne, 'Columb's Men', *Irish Times*, 11 May 1999).

23 seed-pods] seed-pots *North*1996 (error)
33^4] [stanza break] *North*1996
41 Sixteen] 16 *OG*, *100P*

Title *The Ministry of Fear* (1943) was a novel by Graham Greene, made into a film by Fritz Lang, starring Ray Milland, in 1944.

Dedication Seamus Deane (1940–2021) was SH's student contemporary at St Columb's College, Derry and Queen's University Belfast, and his lifelong friend. With David Hammond and Tom Paulin, Deane and SH served as directors of the Field Day Theatre Company from 1981, after its founding by the playwright Brian Friel and the actor Stephen Rea in 1980; in 1988, the playwright Tom Kilroy also joined the board. Field Day published a series of major books and pamphlets, including SH's 'An Open Letter' (*PSH*, 257) and the three-volume *Field Day Anthology of Irish Writing* (1991).

1 *we have lived*: an allusion to Patrick Kavanagh's 'Epic': 'I have lived in important places, times / When great events were decided.'

4 *your Bogside*: at St Columb's, SH was a boarder and Deane a dayboy from the Bogside. The Bogside is a predominantly Catholic, working-class area of Derry City, infamous as the location of Bloody Sunday in 1972.

6 *Brandywell*: sportsground in Derry, with a dogtrack. Now the home of Derry City FC.

13–14: *an act / Of stealth*: Quoting the 'boat-stealing' episode in Wordsworth, *The Prelude* I, 361/388.

16 'Ha! here's three on's are sophisticated!' (*King Lear*, 3.4.105–6.)

17–18 'A man innocently dabbles in words and rhymes, and finds that it is his life' (Patrick Kavanagh, Author's Note to *Collected Poems*, 1964, xiii).

26ff. see 'Reaping in Heat' (*PSH*, 5): 'Hushed / And lulled / Lay the field, under a high-sky sun. / Pushed / And pulled / Came the rasp of steel on stone.'

35 'We are such stuff / As dreams are made on'. (*The Tempest*, 4.1.156–7)

60 *your hieroglyphics*: Deane's florid handwriting.

2 A CONSTABLE CALLS

First published as a prose poem in Padraic Fiacc (ed.), *The Wearing of the Black* (Belfast: Blackstaff, 1974) and was also published in *Aquarius* (1974) before collection in *North*. It was then included in *SP*, *PM*, *NSP*1990, *OG* and *100P*.

A CONSTABLE CALLS

His bicycle stood at the windowsill, its fat black handlegrips heating in sunlight, the 'spud' of the dynamo gleaming and cocked back, the pedal treads hanging relieved of the boot of the law.

His cap was upside down on the floor next his chair: the line of its pressure tan like bevel in his slightly sweating hair. He had unstrapped the heavy ledge and my father was making tillage returns in acres, roods and perches.

Arithmetic and fear. I sat staring at the polished holster with its buttoned flap, the braid cord lopped into the revolver butt.

'Any other root crops? Mangolds, marrowstems, anything like that?'

'No.'

But there was – that drill of turnips where the seed ran out in the potato field. I assumed small guilts and sat imagining the black hole in the barracks.

'Well, I'll have to be beating on.'

He stood up, shifted the baton case more accurately to his haunch, scabbarded and pocketed the fountain pen, fitted his cap back with two hands and looked at me for the first time when he'd said goodbye.

A shadow bobbed in the window as he clipped his trousers and snapped the carrier-spring over the leger. His boot pushed off and the bicycle ticked, ticked, ticked.

The original prose-poem form of this piece (above) suggests that SH may have originally prepared it for *Stations*, before its redevelopment in verse form for *North*.

5 *spud*: common Irish term for the dynamo hub powering a bicycle light.

6 *cocked back*: the first of several gun images in the poem, culminating in the suggestion of a bomb in the last line.

30 The Domesday Book was the general record of land and possessions in England and Wales conducted by William the Conqueror in 1086. Here with a more threatening overtone of the word 'Doomsday'.

3 ORANGE DRUMS, TYRONE, 1966

First published in the *Listener* (29 Sept. 1966), and then in *Fortnight* (July 1972). After collection in *North*, it appeared in *PM* and *OG*.

3 knees.] knees: *Listener* | knees *Fortnight*
7 crowd,] crowd *Listener*; *PM*
8 preside,] preside *Listener*; *Fortnight*
9 To every cocked ear, expert in its greed,] Training the note of hate on the ear's greed, *Listener* | Each cocked ear gloating, expert in its greed, *Fortnight*
11 The goatskin's sometimes plastered with his blood.] The pigskin's scourged until his knuckles bleed. *Listener*; *Fortnight*   goatskin's] goatskins (error) *PM*

1 *lambeg*: the huge 'Lambeg drum', beaten on Orange marches in Northern Ireland.

4 SUMMER 1969

After publication in *North*, the poem appeared in *PM, NSP1990, OG* and *100P*.

17 death-counts] death counts *PM, NSP1990*
28 children;] children, *PM, NSP1990, OG, 100P*

2 The Falls Road, the main road through Catholic West Belfast, the location of particular tension between soldiers and populace as the Troubles worsened in 1969.
   3 *Madrid*: the Heaney family went in the summer of 1969 to France and Spain in fulfilment of the terms of the Somerset Maugham Award for *Death of a Naturalist*.
   6 SH was reading Richard Ellmann's *James Joyce* (1959).
   7ff. the opening section of the poem develops similarities between the environment in mid-Spain and Co. Derry.
   16 Federico García Lorca (1898–1936), Spanish poet and playwright, assassinated by the Franco authorities in the early weeks of the Spanish Civil War.
   20 The Prado, the principal art gallery in Madrid, containing major paintings by Francisco Goya (1746–1828) including the nightmarish *Third of May, 1808* (l. 21), Saturn consuming his son (ll. 27–8), and *The Colossus*: all themes responding to the violence of the simultaneous world of Northern Ireland.

5 FOSTERAGE

After publication in *North*, the poem appeared in *SP, PM, NSP1990* and *OG*.

10 biro] Biro *OG*

SH tells O'Driscoll (*SS*, 215) that this sixteen-line poem – which he calls a 'section' of 'Singing School' – is 'an unrhymed sonnet, modelled on those unrhymed sonnet-portraits of writers in *Notebook and History*' by Lowell.
   Dedication '"Fosterage" could equally well have been called Michael McLaverty' (*SS*, 215). McLaverty (1904–92) was a novelist and short-story writer, born in Carrickmacross, Co. Monaghan, and headmaster of St Thomas's in the Ballymurphy area of Belfast where SH taught 1962–3. He encouraged SH's writing and is one of the 'masters' in 'Station Island' V where he quotes Hopkins, whose *Journals* he gave SH (l. 11). His advice to SH to 'Go your own way' (l. 5) anticipates SH's Joyce's advice in 'Station Island' XII.

1 *'Description is revelation'*: Wallace Stevens, 'Description Without Place', in *Collected Poems* (Faber & Faber, 1955) 344: presumably quoted by McLaverty to SH, like the other quoted pieces in the poem.

1–2 *Royal Avenue*: the principal shopping thoroughfare in Belfast.

7 Katherine Mansfield (1888–1923) New Zealand-born short-story writer.

16 *obols*: Greek coins; 'Charon's obol' is the coin placed in the mouth of a dead person before burial and crossing to the afterlife.

6 EXPOSURE

After publication in *North*, the poem appeared in *Gravities* (1979), *SP*, *PM*, *NSP1990*, *OG* and *100P*.

Dated 28 November 1973 in TS (NLI 49,493/36).

Title Recognised as a signalling point, indicating a change of direction and exposure to negative judgement (*SS*, 162), and perhaps also alluding to Wilfred Owen's poem of the same name.

1 December in Wicklow, presumably 1973, dated by the comet.

5 Comet Kohoutek, visible from March to December 1973. It attained perihelion, the point nearest the sun and its brightest display, on 28 December.

10 *meteorite*: longed for because of its sense of occasion, in contrast with the depressed 'flukes of autumn'. Throughout the poem, as often in early SH, hard substances are positive, and soft negative. Cf. 'diamond absolutes' (*l.* 29).

22 *tristia*: written by Ovid from exile in Tomus on the Black Sea after his expulsion from Rome.

30 *internee nor informer*: the two negative figures in Northern Irish nationalist demonology: the victim of internment without trial, and the informer who reports suspected terrorist activity to the authorities.

31 'inner émigré' takes the French phrase *émigré de l'intérieur*, an internally displaced person, which SH applies to his move from Northern Ireland to the South. Mostly the term was applied to samizdat writers in the Soviet Union such as Osip Mandelstam (*SS*, 174ff.).

UNCOLLECTED POEMS (1975–1979)

The small number of uncollected poems between *Wintering Out* and *North* had close affinities with those volumes, acting almost as a kind of glue between them. But the even smaller number of uncollected poems between *North* and *Field Work* are much less related to their place in the development of the corpus; they are either entirely personal – private, seemingly – or non-political in a way fitting for SH's declared move towards a more 'open' poetry, stepping into the light, away from the dark pressure of the poems of *North*.

A Strange House

First published in *Thames Poetry* (Nov. 1977): 13 and then collected with revisions in Peter Fallon and Seán Golden (eds), *Soft Day: A Miscellany of Contemporary Irish Writing* (Notre Dame: University of Notre Dame Press, 1980).

The Pleasures of the Day

Published in *Broadsheet*, 26–30 (June 1978): 3, by Hayden Murphy in Edinburgh.

In a letter of 17 March 1978 accompanying delivery of the poem to Hayden Murphy for *Broadsheet*, Edinburgh, SH writes: 'I apologise for the boorish silence – it's just that I never seem to get time to settle to do the things I should be doing: thinking about poems and poets and editors. I enclose a little versing which I hope you can use some time, some where' (NLS 8845/75, 217).

A Toy for Catherine

Published in *FA*, an edition of fifty hand-numbered copies printed by Peter Woolfenden at the Byron Press 1979, having previously appeared as 'Catherine's Poem' in a private printing for the family as a Christmas card in 1975. Subsequently published as 'Catherine's Poem' in Angela Huth (ed.), *Island of the Children: An Anthology of New Poems* (London: Orchard Books, 1987).

[text: *FA*]

Title] Catherine's Poem *Island of the Children*

FIELD WORK (1979)

Field Work was published simultaneously in London in 3,500 hardback and 12,000 paperback copies on 15 October 1979 by Faber & Faber, and, for the first time, by Farrar, Straus and Giroux in New York, in a hardback edition of the same month. A paperback reprint from Faber followed swiftly in the new year of 1980, while an inaugural American paperback was published 1 April 1981. The text was reset in London in 2001 providing the copy-text for a Faber Modern Classics edition of 2017 and for *PSH*. As *North* and *Door into the Dark* had been, the volume was again the Choice of the Poetry Book Society, for Autumn 1979.

Field Work showed SH giving ever closer scrutiny to the production of his editions. He had been invested in the partitions of *North*, but he hadn't cared for the way the section-opening poems had appeared on title versos, and with *Field Work* he wished to see this changed, and the first poem granted its own recto. He wished, also, to see two-page poems occupying a spread, and had endeavoured to organise the running order of the book to effect such a balance, which didn't prove possible in the event. 'So here it goes to you and the printer,' SH wrote to Faber of the proofs on 13 May 1979. 'I believe it may well be my first error-free publication. Let's hope it is anyhow.' But the edition would be beset with problems at the firm's new printer, Ebenezer Baylis in Worcester, who, despite a meticulously elegant setting in Ehrhardt type – a marked redesign from Whitstable's iconic Caslon setting of the first four books – had to acknowledge that their advance copies in the summer of 1979 were 'atrocious' after they misfed the machine with waste sheets that became erroneously folded into the production; a rushed reprint in the new year of 1980 was crippled by what was modestly called 'a discrepancy' in the evenness of the inking. (FF P/Rdlm/759/34).

It was a shorter volume in extent than either *Wintering Out* or *North*, and had departed from those books' entrenched partitions to return to the single sequence of the first two collections. In a series of interviews SH said that in this new book he wanted to move away from the various constrictions of *North* – the narrow lines, the inescapable imagery of the bodies buried under the ground, all the senses of moral and political answerability – towards a freer expression, more like the 'devil-may-careness' of the place-name poems of *Wintering Out*. It was, he said, an attempt 'to do something deliberately: to change the note and to lengthen the line', and to bring into play 'elements of my social self, elements of my usual nature' (Kinahan 1982, 411). In a letter to Brian Friel he said that he no longer wanted a door into the dark, but 'a door into the light' (*LSH*, 135); he wanted, he said in an interview with O'Driscoll in 1979, to be able to use the first person to refer to himself and his own experience again, rather than to be a spokesman for a community. It is a wish to escape the 'responsible *tristia*' of 'Exposure' at the end of *North*, and a desire to find a mode that captures the domestic to 'fortify the quotidian into a work' (Kinahan 1982, 411).

This wish for personal freedom of action as well as expression is put forcefully in the first poem 'Oysters' with its resentment at the guilt that attends the eating of the 'alive and violated' oysters, 'ripped and shucked and scattered'. But, like so many of SH's poems, it answers its own challenge; the poem sets up wonderfully the ambivalence of this versatile book, as its artful title does too. 'Field work' does not in fact mean work in the fields; it means the preparatory research work for some kind of declaration. SH himself said of the title: 'I gave *Field Work* that title partly because there's an element of samplings in it. But I think there's an opener note in it as well. What holds *Field Work* together – this is only my view of it – is a certain ease of the voice' (Kinahan 1982, 411). Rand Brandes reports the earlier titles SH had considered for this conciliatory book: 'Polder' (*FW*, 48; *PSH*, 241), a Dutch-derived word for a patch of land surrounded by water, rejected at least in part because of uncertainty about its pronunciation expressed by Charles Monteith, but also perhaps for its narrowness of application; and 'Easter Water', rejected because of its undue benignity (Brandes 2009, 19).

The jagged assertiveness of 'Oysters' is a surprising start to this book's aspiration to be 'a door into the light', just as the luminously personal 'Mossbawn: Two Poems in Dedication' was a misleading preparation for the urgency of the 'new kind of political poetry' of *North*. Ambivalence and the avoidance of the doctrinaire are always the hallmarks of SH's expressed positions. And the book ends echoing where it began, with a translation of the Ugolino section of Dante's *Inferno* in which Ugolino gnaws the head of his enemy Archbishop Ruggiero 'like a dog's teeth clamping round a bone'. So the book is far from single-minded in its pursuit of personal freedoms and indulgence; 'Oysters' is followed by a series of powerful poems about the painful intrusion of the public world into this avowed personal attempt to use the first person to express private experience, extending from 'After a Killing' about the killing of Christopher Ewart-Biggs, the British Ambassador to Ireland, not far from the Heaneys' new home in Dublin (a variation on the terrible theme of 'neighbourly murder' in *North*) to the series of elegies culminating in 'Casualty' about the poet's acquaintance, the fisherman Louis O'Neill who was blown up when he refused to depart from the personal practice of his normal life. These poems make up the first third of the book, ending with a stark warning in 'The Badgers': 'How perilous is it to choose / not to love the life we're shown?'

After a pair of elegies, the book takes a turn for the lyrical, more in keeping with SH's declared ambition for it, in the series of ten 'Glanmore Sonnets', dedicated to Ann Saddlemyer, the Canadian scholar on the work of J. M. Synge who let to the Heaneys at a modest rent the cottage at the edge of the Synge estate and who is celebrated as a major benefactor in *Electric Light*. SH celebrated the pastoral delights of the family's circumstances in 'the hedge-school of Glanmore', often placing them within memories of the poet's rural childhood and in the context of his happy marriage. There follow a series of admired love poems to his wife, including the erotic 'The Skunk'. This personal, even idyllic tone is sustained until it is interrupted by the last two poems in the book: 'Ugolino' following 'In Memoriam Francis Ledwidge,' about the painful dilemma of the young Irish nationalist soldier who was killed at Passchendaele. The poem quotes Ledwidge's observation, 'I am sorry / That party politics should divide our tents.' It is the same conflict as for the poet who has left the North of Ireland and its violence for the pastoral peace of Wicklow 'among the dolorous / And lovely: the May altar of wild flowers'. And the book ends with the savagery of the revenge of Dante's Ugolino, with his teeth biting into his enemy's skull. The journey into the light is not an unclouded one. 'Up to *North*, that was one book', SH said. But the new departure that followed that book in *Field Work* was by no means in a single direction. It is far from his longest book; but it is arguably the book which is powerful in the greatest variety of forms, subjects and emotions.

Like its predecessor volumes, *Field Work* was much admired on its appearance and it has maintained its standing as one of SH's best loved books (a judgement shared by the poet himself and by his family). Denis Donoghue in *The New York Times* called it 'a superb book, the most eloquent and far-reaching book he has written', but suggested too that 'readers who want Heaney to go on writing political poems, as in *North*, may be disappointed with *Field Work*' (2 Dec. 1979). Later, in a 1997 interview with Henri Cole in *The Paris Review*, SH himself called it 'one of my favorites', saying that it moved him 'from the intensity of *North* to something more measured, in both formal and emotional terms'. In a review in *The New York Review of Books*,

Al Alvarez spoke for those who wanted SH to go on writing political poems, rather than reverting to what Alvarez in his anthology of *The New Poetry* in 1962 had disapprovingly called 'the gentility principle': reinforcing 'the British audience in their comfortable prejudice that poetry, give or take a few quirks of style, has not changed essentially in the last hundred years' (6 March 1980). SH vigorously rejects this criticism of *Field Work* in *Stepping Stones* (*SS*, 64), remarking that Alvarez had already done 'a hatchet job' on *Door into the Dark* in the *Observer*. Even David Lloyd, who would famously express reservations about *North* in his 1985 essay 'Pap for the Dispossessed', said *Field Work* was 'a startling advance for Heaney because the poet takes up the themes of the second half of *North* . . . but does so while returning to the richer language and imagery of his earlier work', concluding that *Field Work* is 'his best work to date and a major contribution to modern poetry' (Lloyd 1981, 87, 92).

In 1979, the book had been originally published in covers that featured a local map of the area around Glanmore Castle, where, in a gate lodge marked in the map's bottom left-hand corner, the Heaney family had lived until November 1976. Almost forty years later, in 2017, it was reissued as a Faber Modern Classic with a cover photograph of the author with his daughter at the kitchen table of the property they had moved to from Glanmore, the house in Dublin that would become the family home of SH for the rest of his life.

[text: *FW2001*]

Dedication Karl Miller (1931–2014) was the editor of the *London Review of Books*, which he had founded along with Mary-Kay Wilmers and Susannah Clapp. During his tenure as literary editor of the *New Statesman* he published three poems by SH on 4 December 1964, bringing them to the attention of Charles Monteith, the poetry editor of Faber. As editor of the *Listener* from 1967 to 1973 he continued to publish poems by SH, and to commission articles, which often addressed the situation in Northern Ireland. The Millers remained close friends of the Heaneys throughout their lives. In a letter to Karl Miller of 20 October 1978, SH says that the book will be 'published in a year's time under the title *UMBER*', adding that he has 'had a lot of bother settling on' the title (*LSH*, 166). The inclusion of Jane Miller, also a writer, in the dedication was, said SH, 'the most crucial addition' he made to the book's proofs during their production (FF P/Rdlm/759/34). Decades later, Jane and SH were still reading each other's work and exchanging ideas with enthusiasm (*LSH*, 674).

Oysters

First published in *Thames Poetry* (Nov. 1977): 12, and after collection in *FW* in *PM*, *NSP1990*, *OG* and *100P*.

5 foot] brilliant foot *Thames Poetry*
7 ice:] ice, *Thames Poetry*
10 them] them, *Thames Poetry*
16–20] [omitted] *Thames Poetry*
21 And] I *Thames Poetry*
22 light,] light *Thames Poetry*
23 Leaning] Lifting *Thames Poetry*

The setting of the poem is a meal with friends in Moran's Bar in Clarinbridge, Co. Donegal, expressing resentment that it could not be savoured fully because of feelings of guilt at 'the glut of privilege' (*l.* 20) like the Romans returning south with their booty across the Alps.

11 *that coast*: somewhere on the Irish west coast (flowers and limestone might suggest the Burren in West Clare). In the 1970s the Heaneys also stayed frequently near Dingle in West Kerry.

16ff. The Romans carried oysters back to Rome across the Alps from Northern European coasts, notably Brittany, packed in baskets of ice, snow and hay. Their passion for oysters is widely attested, by Pliny, Lucilius and others.

Triptych

First published in the *Irish Press* (12 March 1977): 9, then in the *Listener* (23 June 1977): 832; where the poems are numbered I, II and II, and their subtitles are not included. Subsequently published in *Antaeus* (Spring 1979), and *DAM Poetry International Documents* (Summer 1980): 24–6. In the latter two, 'At the Water's Edge' bears the title 'Song of Erne'. After collection in *FW*, 'Triptych' was included in *PM*, *NSP1990* and *OG*.

I AFTER A KILLING

8 headstones] headstone *DAM*   leeches.] leeches *PM* (error)
16 And today] Today *Irish Press* | And to-day *DAM*

Title Christopher Ewart-Biggs, the UK Ambassador to Ireland, was killed together with Judith Cook, Private Secretary to the Permanent Under-Secretary of the Northern Ireland Office, on 21 July 1976 when his car was blown up by an IRA landmine near his official residence in Sandyford, Dublin (see McKittrick 1999, 663–4). Jane Ewart-Biggs, his widow, established a literary prize in his memory in

1977, which is awarded to works which promote understanding and reconciliation between Britain and Ireland. SH had not met him, but in 1984 he presented the Ewart-Biggs Prize to the Irish historian and broadcaster John Bowman, for his book *De Valera and the Ulster Question* (1983). Entitled 'What Will Become of Us' in TS (NLI 49,493/48).

2 *unquiet founders*: the rebels who fought against British rule in Ireland, such as the 'Old IRA men of the West Cork Flying Column', as SH glosses it (*SS*, 211).

10 Brandon in West Kerry in the south-west of Ireland; Dunseverick in the north-east near the Giant's Causeway. Thus, the longest diagonal across the island.

II SIBYL

3–4] And as water in the shaft of a forgotten well / Might shake at an explosion under morning *Listener*
4 morning] morning. *DAM* (error)
6] She trembled into speech. *Irish Press*
12 And the fouled magma] And the creeping fundament *DAM*

Title The speaker approaches the sibyl for a prophecy, as Virgil approached the Cumaean sibyl in *Aeneid*, 6.

8 *Saurian*: lizard-like; *Pismires*: ants. Humanity regresses, like evolution in reverse: perhaps prompted by the dehumanising killing in Part I. The term 'pismires' had been used in an uncollected poem 'Intimidation', published in the *Malahat Review*, 17 (1970) in a bitter characterisation of Loyalist bonfires around the twelfth of July as 'midsummer madness . . . a nest of pismires / At his drystone walls' (*PSH*, 105).

10 *bleeding tree*: in *Inferno*, 13, Virgil and Dante encounter Pier delle Vigne, transformed into a tree, in the wood of the suicides (based on *Aeneid*, 3.22–68).

12 *magma*: subterranean material from which igneous rocks are formed.

20 Cf. Caliban's words, 'Be not afeard. The isle is full of noises' (*The Tempest*, 3.2.130). The noises for Caliban are 'Sounds, and sweet airs, that give delight, and hurt not.' On SH's island, Ireland, they are comfortless.

III AT THE WATER'S EDGE

5 stone] stone, *Listener*
14 windowsill] window-sill *NSP1990*, *OG*

Title 'Song of Erne in TS (NLI 49,493/49).

1 *Devenish*: an island in Lower Lough Erne, Co. Fermanagh, a monastic foundation dating from the sixth century.

3 *tower*: a monastic round tower.

5 *Boa*: another island in Lough Erne, where two stone statues can be found; they are thought to date from either the pre-Christian Iron Age or from early Christian times. The most famous statue is called a Janus figure because it has two faces, looking different ways. The name Boa comes from the Celtic goddess of war, Badhbh.

6 *trepanned*: having a hole bored through the skull.

8 *Anathema*: a formal curse by the Catholic Church.

9 *Horse Island*: there are two islands of this name in Lough Erne. It is a common island name throughout Ireland, from West Cork to Strangford Lough.

19 *our march at Newry*: a civil rights march on Sunday 6 February 1972 in Newry, called as a response to the Bloody Sunday massacre of the week before, attended by SH and Michael Longley.

The Toome Road

First published in *Threshold* (Spring 1979): 35, in an issue for which SH served as poetry editor, and subsequently in the *New York Review of Books* (27 Sept. 1979): 8. After collection in *FW*, the poem was also included in *NSP1990* and *OG*.

4 turrets.] turrets *Threshold*
7 rights-of-way] right-of-way *Threshold*
9 Silos] Siloes *Threshold, NYRB*
11 back doors] backdoors *Threshold*
13^14] Those crossers of themselves, averters of eyes,
    Assessors of flattened crops and opening skies,
    That long procession rustling through the windows
    In mown graveyards and in hard-won meadows,

Title Toome (also called Toomebridge) is a village at the north-west corner of Lough Neagh, the subject of the poem 'Toome' (*WO*, 16; *PSH*, 124) and 'At Toomebridge' (*EL*, 3; *PSH*, 527).

1 *One morning early*: common start to popular ballads, such as 'The Boys of Mullaghbawn'.

17 *omphalos*: the opening term in SH's early essay 'Mossbawn' (1974): 'the Greek word, *omphalos*, meaning the navel, and hence the stone that marked the centre of the world' (*Preoccupations*, 17).

A Drink of Water

First published as 'A Visitant' in the *American Irish Foundation Report* (Spring 1974). Revised as 'A Drink of Water' and published in *St Stephen's* (Autumn 1974): 17, later in *Poetry Wales*, 2. 1 (1975): 25, and *New Republic* (27 March 1976): 24, in which it was the only previously unpublished poem in a selection that included poems from *DD*, *WO* and *North*, and was accompanied by an appreciation by Robert Fitzgerald. After collection in *FW* it was also included in *NSP1990*, *OG* and *100P*. It was also published as a separate edition, the second in the Anna Livia Books Broadsheet series, by the American Ireland Fund for the San Francisco Dinner (March 1998).

1 water] water, *St Stephen's*
2 Like an old bat staggering up the field:] An old bat struggling up the field. *St Stephen's*
2 field:] field. *Poetry Wales*
4 filled,] filled *St Stephen's*, *Poetry Wales*, *New Republic*
6 pocked white enamel] pocked enamel *St Stephen's*, *New Republic*
7 bucket, and] bucket and *St Stephen's*
11 water set out on] water on *St Stephen's*
12–14] Where I would dip and drink again if only / I could lay hands on her old drinking cup – / Remember the Giver fading round its lip. *St Stephen's*
14 Giver] Giver, *NSP1990*, *OG*, *100P*
14 the lip] its lip *New Republic*

Title 'A Visitant' in TS (NLI 49,493/47).
1 'The old lady in the poem was a neighbour [near Mossbawn], a crone, as she might have been described. Who lived on her own, down the fields from us . . . In the poem she becomes more like a muse offering the cup of poetry to the child Incertus' (David Cohen Prize speech, 2009). Identified as Annie Devlin (*SS*, 173).

14 *Remember the Giver*: injunction to remember God as the source of his benefits, Isaiah 23:9.

The Strand at Lough Beg

First published in *Antaeus* (Spring 1979), then in *Threshold* (Spring 1979): 34–5 (the issue for which SH was poetry editor), the *London Magazine* (June 1979): 3–4, which also includes John Haffenden's interview 'Meeting Seamus Heaney', and later in *Envoy*, 47 (1985): 3, 47. After collection in *FW*, it was also included in *PM*, *NSP1990*, *OG* and *100P*.

Epigraph strive,] strive *Threshold*, *London Magazine*   100–103] 100–102 *London Magazine*
2 And a few] And few *London Magazine*
6] [omitted] *Threshold*

9 block?] block *Threshold*
10–11] The red lamp swung, the sudden brakes and stalling / Engine, voices, heads hooded and the cold-nosed gun? *Threshold*
17 used hear] once heard *NSP1990*, *OG*, *100P*
26 herders, feelers] herders feelers *Threshold*
28–9 ground. / Across] ground. // Across *Envoy*, *NSP1990*, *OG*, *100P*
34 half shines] half-shines *OG*, *100P*

Title Lough Beg is a small freshwater lake north of Lough Neagh, near Bellaghy, on the border of Co. Antrim and Co. Derry. See 'Mossbawn' (1974) (*Preoccupations*, 19).

Dedication Colum McCartney was SH's second cousin, related to him through the Scullions on his father's maternal side. His family lived on the shore of Lough Beg; he was a carpenter in Armagh. He was murdered alongside John P. Farmer on 24 August 1975 on their way back from the All-Ireland semi-final in Dublin. It is believed they were killed by loyalist paramilitaries, masquerading as members of the security forces who had erected a fake checkpoint (see McKittrick 1999, 565–6).

Epigraph In 'Station Island VIII' SH represents McCartney as rebuking him for the way he 'whitewashed ugliness and drew / the lovely blinds of the *Purgatorio* / and saccharined my death with morning dew' (*SI*, 83; *PSH*, 331).

3–4 *Newtownhamilton*: a small town in south Co. Armagh, near the Fews Forest, the large wooded area which is the location of some of Sweeney's flight in *SA* (6).

26 *Big-voiced scullions*: punning on the surname of SH's paternal forebears. SH recalls this family epithet in his introduction to *Beowulf* (xxvi).

39 *cold handfuls of the dew*: *Purgatorio* 1.121–2, 124–5: 'la rugiada / pugna col sole . . . ambo le mani in su l'erbetta sparte / soavemente 'l mio maestro pose' (Kirkpatrick 2007, 8). 'The dew fought against the sun . . . my master placed both his hands spread gently on the grass.'

43 *rushes that shoot green again*: *Purgatorio* 1.134–6: 'oh maraviglia! ché qual elli scelse / l'umile pianta, cotal si rinacque / subitamente là onde l'avelse' (Kirkpatrick 2007, 8). 'Oh wonder! That when he chose that modest plant, one like it rose up immediately where he had plucked it.'

44 *scapular*: a symbolic necklace-type appendage made of cloth, hung round the neck as a sign of Christian fidelity.

A Postcard from North Antrim

First published in the *Irish Press* (29 April 1978): 14, and then in *Poetry Review*, 67. 4 (1978): 11–12, and *Literary Review* (Madison, NJ; Winter 1979): 213–14. It was also included in Maurice Harmon's *Irish Poetry after Yeats: Seven Poets* (Dublin: Wolfhound, 1979), 221–2.

6 nineteenth-century] nineteenth century *Irish Press, Poetry Review, Literary Review, Irish Poetry After Yeats*
8 A postcard] An old postcard *Irish Press*
15 your houseboat] your far-out houseboat *Irish Press*
16 furnished] furbished *Poetry Review*
45 harassed] harnessed *Irish Press* | harrassed *Literary Review*

Dedication Sean Armstrong was a friend of SH's from his university days at Queen's (*SS*, 222). SH told James Randall that Armstrong went to 'Sausalito where he became part of the commune-pot-smoking generation – he came back to Belfast in the early seventies to get involved in social work and worked at children's playgrounds. And he was shot by some unknown youth' (*Ploughshares*, 5. 3, 1979). Armstrong was killed on 30 June 1973 by Ulster Defence Association/Ulster Freedom Fighters paramilitaries at his flat in south Belfast. His work included cross-community initiatives for children. (See McKittrick 1999, 138.)

13 The Carrick-a-Rede Rope Bridge is a spectacularly vertiginous suspension bridge near Ballintoy, Co. Antrim, stretching from the mainland to the small island of Carrick-a-Rede.

34 *William Bloat*: a ghoulish popular comic poem and song, extolling the strength of Belfast linen.

35 'The Cruise of the *Calabar*' is a parodic sea-shanty by Cyril Tawney from Lisburn, sung by, among others, SH's friend David Hammond.

36 *Henry Joy McCracken*: a leader of the United Irishmen in the 1798 Rebellion in Ulster: subject of a popular Republican song 'Henry Joy', beginning 'An Ulsterman I am proud to be. From the Antrim glens I come.' He was hanged in Cornmarket, Belfast, on 17 July 1798.

37–9 The song 'The Auld Lammas Fair' (held in Ballycastle) says 'you can treat your Mary Ann to Dulse and Yalla Man'. Yalla Man was a popular variety of sweets in Northern Ireland.

50 *Bushmills*: Ulster whiskey, sometimes referred to as 'Protestant whiskey'. The details in these stanzas evoke a non-sectarian, celebratory Ulster in gatherings where Armstrong is a kind of Lord of Misrule.

59 Marie Heaney, whom SH first met in 1962. A couple of days after their first meeting they went to a party at Armstrong's flat together, 'and the thing took off from there' (*SS*, 222).

Casualty

First published in the *New Yorker* (2 April 1979): 38, the *Dutch Quarterly Review of Anglo-American Letters*, 9. 1 (1979): 2–3, and Maurice Harmon (ed.), *Irish Poetry after Yeats*: 218–21. This latter version is not broken into numbered sections. After collection in *FW*, it was included in *PM*, *NSP1990*, *OG* and *100P*.

I 5 blackcurrant] black currant *New Yorker*
I 9 dumb-show] dumb show *New Yorker*
I 13] Out into the dark *Irish Poetry*
I 27 slug] slug, *New Yorker*
I 36 my tentative art] my kept wilting art *Irish Poetry*
I 37 watches too:] watches, too: *New Yorker*
I 38 blown to bits] blown to wet bits *Irish Poetry*
I 40–6] That wiser citizens
      Observed behind closed doors
      When we mourned the thirteen killed
      By British paratroopers. *Irish Poetry*
I 46 His] Their *Dutch Quarterly Review*, *OG*, *100P*
II 2 wind-blown] windblown *New Yorker*, *OG*, *100P*
II 4 flower-laden] flower laden *Dutch Quarterly Review*
II 19 bombed] bombed, *New Yorker*
II 22 cornered] cornered, *New Yorker*
III 12–12 sunshine / On] sunshine // On *Dutch Quarterly Review*
III 14] When he took me in his boat *NSP1990*, *OG*, *100P*
III 17^18] [stanza break] *New Yorker*, *Dutch Quarterly Review*

Dated 1/2 August 1977 in TS (NLI 49,493/51).
    I 1 The subject of this celebrated elegy is Louis O'Neill, an eel fisherman from Ardboe, who was a regular customer in Marie Heaney's father's public house (*SS*, 214ff.). He was killed in the Imperial Bar in Stewartstown, Co. Tyrone on 3 February 1972, when a bomb exploded without warning. Officially the pub was closed, like others, as a mark of respect for the funerals of those killed on Bloody Sunday, and this led to speculation that the IRA was behind the attack, but it was subsequently assumed that loyalist paramilitaries were responsible (see McKittrick 1999, 150).
    I 43 *PARAS*: the 1st Battalion of the Parachute Regiment of the British Army who shot dead thirteen civil rights protestors in the Bogside, Derry, on Bloody Sunday, 30 January 1972.
    III 14–15 *that morning / I was taken in his boat*: SH says his friendship 'with Louis was special because of that unforgettable

summer morning when I went out on Lough Neagh with him and another companion to lift the eel lines' (*SS*, 214).

The Badgers

First published in the *Sewanee Review* (Winter 1976): 121–2, in the Arts Council of Northern Ireland pamphlet *In Their Element: A Selection of Poems by Seamus Heaney and Derek Mahon* (1977): n.p., and in *Outposts*, 120 (Spring 1979): 4–5. Later included in *NSP1990* and *OG*, under the title 'Badgers'.

Title] Badgers *NSP1990*, *OG*
9 boy] boy? *Sewanee Review*, *In Their Element*
10–13] [omitted] *Sewanee Review*, *In Their Element*
29–31] for what he is: pig family / and not at all what he's painted. *Sewanee Review*, *In Their Element*
31^2] [stanza break] *NSP1990*, *OG*

'The Badgers' had been one of the longer poems that SH had specifically identified in typescript with Faber as requiring typesetting on a single spread; nonetheless, when the proof broke the poem across a turning page, SH accepted the setting on the grounds that narrative sequence should take priority: 'I think we should let the sequence stand as printed from Casualty, to Badgers, to Singer's House: although visually I prefer to see Badgers on a double-page spread, I think this order is systematically preferable' (FF P/Rdlm 759/34).

Title The title occurs without the definite article in some versions which changes the sense from the particular animals to a more metaphorical sense.

16 *duntings*: thumping sounds.

The Singer's House

First published in *Thames Poetry* (Nov. 1977): 11. After collection in *FW*, it was included in *PM*, *Seamus Heaney: Readings in Contemporary Poetry* (New York: Dia Art Foundation, 1988), 27–8. It was also selected for *OG* and *100P*.

1 Carrickfergus] Carrickfergus *Thames Poetry*
8 kept] kept, *OG*, *100P*
13–14] Now I grope for what I'm after / Gweebarra breaks on my tongue *Thames Poetry*
19–20 and the seals' heads, suddenly outlined, / scanning everything.] And the seals' heads / Suddenly outlined, dark and intelligent. *Thames Poetry*
21–4] [omitted] *Thames Poetry*
25] When you came here first, you were always singing, *Thames Poetry*

Title The singer is SH's friend David Hammond, whose best-known album, *The Singer's House*, was named after this poem and had a sleeve note by SH; a working title for the poem had been 'The Seals'. SH explained the origins of the poem in 'The Interesting Case of Nero, Chekhov's Cognac and a Knocker', the prefatory essay to *GT*: one night in 1972 he and Hammond had arranged to meet at the BBC in Belfast to record a tape of poetry and music for a friend, but as they made their way to the studio a series of explosions occurred across the city. Distressed by the news of casualties and the general atmosphere, they did not have the heart to continue. The experience prompts a serious meditation on the tension between what SH calls 'Song and Suffering' ('melodramatically' refining the juxtaposition of 'Art and Life'): 'What David Hammond and I were experiencing, at a most immediate and obvious level, was a feeling that song constituted a betrayal of suffering' (*GT*, xii). But ultimately SH found himself compelled to voice a renewed faith in artistic expression, and the result was 'The Singer's House', which he wrote for Hammond.

 1 'Carrickfergus' is a well-known song, which refers to the town in Co. Antrim.

 2 *saltminers*: the only salt mine in Ireland is at Kilroot, three miles north-east of Carrickfergus on the northern shore of Lough Neagh.

 13 *Gweebarra*: a bay in North Donegal, where the river Gweebarra reaches the sea.

 22 The idea that the souls of drowned people were transfigured into seals is commonly found in Celtic mythology. See Martin Puhvel, 'The Seal in the Folklore of Northern Europe', *Folklore*, 74. 1 (Spring 1963). The term 'selkies' was used of shape-changing seal-people who could shed their skins to become human.

 24 The seals swimming in for the music recalls the music that comes out of the night on the 'most westerly Blasket' in 'The Given Note' (*DD*, 36; *PSH*, 87).

 27 A black-and-white photograph on the LP sleeve shows Hammond leaning against the door-jamb of a whitewashed shed.

The Guttural Muse

First published in the *New Yorker* (25 June 1979): 28, and after collection in *FW* included in *PM*, *NSP1990* and *OG*.

5 discotheque] discothèque *New Yorker*, *NSP1990*
9 the 'doctor fish'] the doctor fish *New Yorker*

The TS was sent to Barrie Cooke with an appended handwritten message, 19 September 1978: 'Two evenings swam together here –

our memorable elderberry-blooming Sunday and another night when I stayed in the Nuremore hotel in Monaghan and heard the muddy healing dialect of the north.'

Title SH describes the occasion of this poem a number of times. A working title for the poem had been 'The Fishing Trip' in manuscript, where it then carried a dedication for Derek Mahon that was withdrawn before publication (NLI 49,493/49).

In Memoriam Sean Ó Riada

First published in *Cyphers* (Summer 1976): 33, subsequently in the *Sewanee Review* (Winter 1976): 120–1, *Encounter* (July 1977): 14, and *Poetry Review* (June 1978): 4–5. It was also included in the programme for Ó Riada Retrospective, three concerts in Ó Riada's memory held at the National Concert Hall, Dublin, April 1987.

Title] In Memoriam: Sean O'Riada *Cyphers, Sewanee Review, Encounter, Poetry Review*
>1] Ó Riada's white head was Easter snow, / the silver knob on a swordstick. *Cyphers, Encounter,* and *Poetry Review*
2^3 [stanza break] *Sewanee Review, Encounter, Poetry Review*
4–8]   I watched him from behind,
         springy, formally suited,
         a black stiletto trembling in its mark,

         a quill flourishing itself.
         He had a cornered energy.
         He was in the fallow hell,
         a snowball that would neither

         thaw nor flow. *Cyphers, Sewanee Review, Encounter, Poetry Review*
11^12] [stanza break] *Cyphers, Sewanee Review, Encounter, Poetry Review*
15 gifts] gift's *Cyphers, Encounter, Poetry Review*
15^16] [stanza break] *Cyphers, Sewanee Review, Encounter, Poetry Review*
19 thwarts] thwarts, *Cyphers, Sewanee Review*
19^20] [stanza break] *Cyphers, Sewanee Review, Encounter, Poetry Review*
22 retinue] retinue. *Cyphers, Sewanee Review, Encounter, Poetry Review*
23] [omitted] *Cyphers, Sewanee Review, Encounter, Poetry Review*
27 mackerel's] mackerels' *Cyphers* | mackerel *Poetry Review*
27–8 cold, / to] cold. / To *Cyphers, Sewanee Review*
29–36] [omitted] *Cyphers, Sewanee Review*
33 grace notes] grace-notes *Encounter, Poetry Review*

Title Seán Ó Riada (1931–71), born in Cork, was the foremost Irish composer and musicologist of his time and a lecturer in Irish traditional music at University College Cork where he studied Music and Classics as a student. Most famous for developing and recreating a sophisticated body of Irish traditional music with a group of musicians called Ceoltóirí Chualann, several of whom later formed the celebrated band the Chieftains.

17ff. the afternoon when SH and Ó Riada fished together is also drawn on in 'Shore Woman' (*WO*, 54; *PSH*, 143)

24 *sprezzatura*: Renaissance term for studied carelessness or innate style, coined by Baldassarre Castiglione in *The Book of the Courtier* (1528).

30 *jacobite*: follower of the movement to restore the Stuart dynasty to the English throne: in Ireland associated with the nationalist tradition. Ó Riada moved from a general interest in European classical music to concentrate on the Irish tradition.

31 'The Young Pretender' was Charles Edward Stuart, Bonnie Prince Charlie, defeated at the Battle of Culloden in 1746. There was an active Irish cult associated with him.

32 From 'My Dark Rosaleen' (1846) by James Clarence Mangan: 'The priests are on the ocean green, / They march along the deep.'

33 *slow airs and grace notes*: classic elements of Irish traditional music, as Ó Riada established.

Elegy

First published privately by Faber & Faber in *Robert Lowell: A Memorial Address and an Elegy* (1978): 5–13, in an edition of 250 copies, which included SH's address from Lowell's memorial service, held in London on 5 October 1977. Subsequently published in *After Summer* (Deerfield/Gallery, 1978), 8–9, in an edition of 250 copies, with illustrations by Timothy Engelland, in an edition limited to 250 copies. Also published in *Encounter* (Feb. 1979): 93, the *Cork Review* (Nov./Dec. 1979): 25 and, accompanied by the memorial address, in *Agenda* (Autumn 1980): 21–2. Collected with revisions in *FW*, and then included in *PM* and *100P*.

42 music] music, *Encounter*
46 tremens] tremens *100P*

4 Robert Lowell (1917–77), American poet and friend of SH, born into a patrician Boston family. His book *Life Studies* (1959), centring on his family and his own psychological problems, was seen as a founding text in confessional poetry. At Boston University he taught Sylvia Plath and Anne Sexton. SH first met him at a party given by Sonia Orwell in 1972 to celebrate Lowell's wedding to his third wife, Caroline Blackwood (1931–96). SH invited him to the Kilkenny Arts Week in 1975 and they met a number of times in Lowell's last years when he and Caroline lived in Castletown House near Dublin. He was imprisoned as a conscientious objector to military service

in 1943, and in 1965 he refused an invitation to Lyndon Johnson's White House as a protest against the Vietnam War. After reading *North*, he famously described SH as the best Irish poet since Yeats, saluting *North* as 'a new kind of political poetry'.

27–9 Lowell's book of sonnets, *For Lizzie and Harriet* (1973). Elizabeth Hardwick (1916–2007) was Lowell's second wife, and Harriet was their daughter (born 1957).

30 *dolphin*: Lowell's 1973 volume, *The Dolphin*.

34 *retiarius*: the net-bearer in gladiatorial combat (sustaining the link with fishing here).

47–8 *A father's no shield / for his child*: from Lowell's poem 'Fall 1961' (*For the Union Dead*, 1964), which is shadowed by anxiety over nuclear war.

Glanmore Sonnets

I

First published as 'Opened Ground' in *Poetry Wales*, 2. 1 (1975): 24, then in *Prospice*, 5 (1976): 64–5, gathered under the title 'Glanmore' with II, and as 'Vowels ploughed into the other: opened ground', accompanied by illustrations by Cecil King in the limited-edition *GS*. It was also published in *DAM: Poetry International Documents* (Summer 1980): 27. Collected with revisions in *FW*, and subsequently included in *PM*, *NSP1990* and *OG*.

Title] Opened Ground *Poetry Wales* | Glanmore *Prospice* | 'Vowels ploughed into
   the other: opened ground' *GS*
2 twenty] sixty *Poetry Wales*
3 mist bands] mist-bands *Poetry Wales*
8–11] Of ploughs. Appeasements, plenary and old,
      Surrenders to this quickening redolence
      Of the fundamental dark unblown rose
      Subside below the subsoil of each sense. *Poetry Wales*
10 redolence] a redolence *DAM, PM, NSP1990, OG*
11] Of farmland as a dark unblown rose. *PM, NSP1990, OG*
12 Wait then . . .] Wait then.] *Poetry Wales*   sowers'] sower's *Poetry Wales*
13 My ghosts] Ghosts *Poetry Wales*

II

First published under the title 'Glanmore' with I in *Prospice*, 5 (1976): 64–5. It was also published in *DAM: Poetry International Documents* (Summer 1980): 27. Collected with revisions in *FW*, and subsequently included in *PM*, *NSP1990*, *OG* and *100P*.

Title] Glanmore *Prospice*
2 touch] touch, *NSP1990, OG, 100P*

III

First published under the title 'This evening the cuckoo and the corncrake' with illustrations by Cecil King in the limited-edition GS. It was also published in *DAM: Poetry International Documents* (Summer 1980): 28. Collected with revisions in *FW*, and subsequently included in *PM*, *NSP1990* and *OG*.

Title] 'This evening the cuckoo and the corncrake' *GS*

IV

First published under the title 'The Train' in *Poetry Wales*, 2. 1 (1975): 24. It was also published in *DAM: Poetry International Documents* (Summer 1980): 24–30. Collected with revisions in *FW*, and subsequently included in *PM*, *NSP1990* and *OG*.

Title] The Train *Poetry Wales*
1 used] use *NSP*
4 piston] pistol *PM*   ground,] ground. *Poetry Wales*
11 Two fields] One field *Poetry Wales*
12–13 water / (As they are shaking now across my heart)] water – / As they are shaking now across my heart – *Poetry Wales*

V

Published in *FW*, and subsequently included in *PM*, *NSP1990* and *OG*.

VI

First published in *Aquarius*, 11 (1979): 85, as 'Glanmore Sonnets V'. Collected with revisions in *FW*, and subsequently included in *PM*, *NSP1990* and *OG*.

Title] Glanmore Sonnets V *Aquarius*
12 founder,] founder *NSP*

VII

First published in the *Listener* (5 June 1975): 745, under the title 'Remembering Forecasts', and as 'Dogger, Rockall, Malin, Irish Sea' in *GS*. It was also published in *DAM: Poetry International Documents* (Summer 1980): 29. Collected with revisions in *FW*, and subsequently included in *PM*, *NSP1990*, *OG* and *100P*.

Title] Remembering Forecasts *Listener* | 'Dogger, Rockall, Malin, Irish Sea' *GS*
2 Green, swift] Green swift *Listener*
3 gale-warning] peremptory *Listener*   voice] voice, *OG*, *100P*
8–14] Lundy, Fastnet, Minches, Cromarty –
    Unforgettable annunciation
    The boy attended to and rode like a spar

> Cast up inevitably from commotion
> On to bewildered shores. And now his house
> Is built around it, as round the pole star
> Those demarcations, fixed and tempestuous. *Listener*

9 Le Belle Hélène] La Belle Hélène *PM, NSP1990, OG, 100P*
11 marvellous] marvelous] *DAM*
13 deepening] deepending *DAM* (error)

VIII

First published in the *Listener* (5 June 1975): 745, under the title 'Thunderlight', then in *Little Word Machine* (1975): 38, under the title 'Hiatus', then 'as 'Thunderlight on the split logs' in *GS*. It was also published in *DAM: Poetry International Documents* (Summer 1980): 29. Collected with revisions in *FW*, and subsequently included in *PM, NSP1990* and *OG*.

Title] Thunderlight *Listener* | Hiatus *Little Word Machine* | 'Thunderlight on the split logs' in *GS*
1 logs: big] logs. Big *Listener*
2] At body heat, and gorged with omen *Listener* | Pentecostal and gorged with omen *Little Word Machine*
4 morning] morning, *Little Word Machine*
7 What] Who *Little Word Machine*
10 pension] pension *Listener, Little Word Machine, NSP1990, OG* Les Landes] Les Landes *Listener, Little Word Machine, DAM, OG*
12 old one rocked] old rocked *DAM*
13 quickly] quick *Listener, DAM, PM, NSP1990* | quick. *Little Word Machine*

IX

First published in *Aquarius*, 11 (1979): 85, as 'Glanmore Sonnets VIII'. Collected in *FW* and subsequently included in *PM, NSP1990* and *OG*.

Title] Glanmore Sonnets VIII *Aquarius*
9 pitch-fork] pitchfork *OG*
13 beyond, your] beyond, inside, your *NSP1990, OG*

X

First published in *Prospice*, 5 (1976): 64–5, under the title 'A Night in the Cold'. It was also published in *DAM: Poetry International Documents* (Summer 1980): 30. Collected with revisions in *FW*, and subsequently included in *PM, NSP1990* and *OG*.

Title] A Night in the Cold *Prospice*

In a typescript dated Dublin 1978, SH writes:

> In August 1972 we moved from Belfast in the North of Ireland to live in Co. Wicklow, some thirty miles South of Dublin. During the previous ten years I had been teaching in Belfast but now, thanks to

Ann Saddlemyer who gave us the run of Glanmore Cottage, I was casting adrift into a life where my commitments as a writer would take precedence over my commitments as an employee. The sonnets sprang out of the four intense and enhancing years that we spent in 'the hedge-school of Glanmore'. (NLI 49, 493/49)

Title Parts I–III initially collected in typescript under the working title 'Preludes in Glanmore' (NLI 49,493/51).

Dedication Ann Saddlemyer, a Canadian scholar of Anglo-Irish literature, rented the Heaneys their cottage at Glanmore at a modest rate. She is celebrated in 'Glanmore Eclogue' (*EL*, 35; *PSH*, 547): 'A woman changed my life. Call her Augusta / Because we arrived in August' – but also because that was the name of Lady Gregory, Yeats's benefactor who stands in the same relation to him as Saddlemyer stands to SH.

I 2 The weather was very mild in February 1972.

I 4 *gargling tractors*: same adjective in uncollected 'Tractors', where they 'gargle / Sadly, astraddle unfolding furrows' (*PSH*, 9).

II 5 Oisín Kelly (1915–81), celebrated Irish sculptor.

II 9 *hedge-school*: methods of illicit rural education in Ireland before the National School system began in 1831.

III 11 Dorothy and William Wordsworth. The demurring voice is the poet's wife, rejecting equivalence with the Wordsworth siblings.

IV 12 SH mentions the ripple on the surface of the bucket of drinking water in the first paragraph of his Nobel lecture: 'Every time a passing train made the earth shake, the surface of that water used to ripple delicately, concentrically, and in utter silence' (*OG*, 447).

V 1 *boortree*: Northern Irish term for the elder (cf. *l*. 5).

VI 10 The late winter and spring of 1946–7 were notoriously cold and snow-ridden.

VII 1 The sea-areas around Britain and Ireland lend themselves to these trochaic lines which SH is fond of (as in *l*. 6 here). The other sea-area names (*l*. 14) end the poem with a contrasting rhythm. The *Shipping Forecast*, broadcast two to three times daily on BBC Radio since 1925, is sometimes referred to as 'the most famous poem on the radio'.

VII 9 Presumably real trawler names.

VIII 7 *blood-boltered*: Macbeth's term for Banquo when he meets him after his murder (*Macbeth*, 4.1.123). 'Boltered' is obscure: perhaps a past participle of a rare Middle English verb *balter*, to tangle/mat (of hair).

VIII 10 *Les Landes*: a department in the south-west of France. The Heaneys stayed in the nearby Bas Pyrénées in July 1969 (*SS*, 100)

IX 5 Recalling the self-questioning of 'Exposure' at the end of *North*.

IX 8 *inwit*: conscience or inner awareness, linked by Stephen Dedalus with guilt in the first chapter of Joyce's *Ulysses*.

X 1 *moss*: Ulster term for turf-bog (as in 'Mossbawn').

X 5 Lorenzo and Jessica: romantic lovers in Shakespeare's *The Merchant of Venice*.

X 9 *how like you this?*: 'They Flee from Me' (Thomas Wyatt): *ll.* 13–14: She 'therewithal sweetly did me kiss / And softly said, "Dear heart, how like you this?"'

September Song

First published in the *Honest Ulsterman*, 54 (Jan./Feb. 1977): 61, and collected with revisions in *FW*.

10–11 school. / If] school: / if *Honest Ulsterman*
11 resin] rosin *Honest Ulsterman*
14 *Nocturnes*] Nocturnes *Honest Ulsterman*
14–17 of John Field's Nocturnes – his gifts, waste,
　　　solitude, reputation, laughter, all
　　　'Dead in Moscow', all those gallons of wash

　　　　for the pure drop, *Honest Ulsterman*
21 Belfast,] Belfast – *Honest Ulsterman*

In 1976, SH had been given leave from Carysfort College of Education to return to Berkeley as Beckman Professor. Our Lady of Mercy College, Carysfort, was a training college for female primary teachers in Blackrock, Dublin, from its foundation in 1877 and was recognised as a constituent college of the National University of Ireland in 1975. SH became a lecturer in English in 1975, and then served as head of English. The autumnal feel of the poem and the end of the four years in the 'hedge school' suggest SH is anticipating the end of his first sojourn in Wicklow and even his final resignation from Carysfort in 1981. The Heaney family will all soon spend much of 1979 at Harvard so there is a sense of the kind of change in educational settings associated with September.

Title A different poem of the same title was published as the final part of 'Offerings' (*PSH*, 98).

1 From the opening line of Dante's *Divine Comedy*, 'Nel mezzo del cammin . . .'

10 *hedge-school*: as in 'Glanmore Sonnets II' above, the term for unofficial, secret schools in Ireland, notably in the eighteenth century.

Here, four years since the Heaneys came to Glanmore in 1972 (the poem was first published in 1977).

11 *resin*: variant for verb 'rosin'

14 John Field (1782–1837), Irish composer, credited with the invention of the nocturne. SH chose his *Nocturne no. 1 in E Flat Major* on *Desert Island Discs*, 19 Nov. 1989; see 'John Field' (*PSH*, 157).

16 *'Dead in Moscow'*: Field died in Moscow and is buried there.

18 'His fingers [. . .] glided like raindrops, like pearls on velvet' (Russian composer Mikhail Glinka (1804–57) on Field, who taught him).

19 *American wake*: the party held by Irish people before a family member emigrated to America.

22 David Hammond (1928–2008), Belfast singer and broadcaster, close friend of SH; Tommy Gunn (1912–2001), fiddler, singer, from Co. Fermanagh; Sean McAloon (1923–98), also from Fermanagh, uilleann piper and pipe-maker.

An Afterwards

First published in *VIA* (Jan. 1977): 1; then in the *New Review* (Feb. 1978): 24; the *New Republic* (25 Aug. 1979): 30; and in Peter Fallon and Dennis O'Driscoll (eds), *The First Ten Years: Dublin Arts Festival Poetry* (Dublin: Dublin Arts Festival, 1979), 20. Collected with revisions in *FW*, and subsequently included in *NSP1990* and *OG*. It was also published in *Readings in Contemporary Poetry* (1988): 29–30.

4 daisy-chain] daisychain *New Review*, *The First Ten Years*

1 *she*: SH's wife, humorously presented; *ninth circle*: the place of punishment for the treacherous in Dante's *Inferno*.

2 tooth in skull, as Ugolino in the ninth circle gnaws on the skull of Archbishop Ruggiero who had left him and his sons and grandsons to starve to death locked in a tower (l. 8). See 'Ugolino' (*FW*, 60–3; *PSH*, 246).

9 the sufferers in the ninth circle are imprisoned in ice.

21 *some maker gaffs me in the neck*: the poets' backbiting in action (as *ll*. 1–2, 3–4, 5–6).

High Summer

First published in the *Honest Ulsterman*, 60 (July/Oct. 1978): 8–9, then in the *Harvard Advocate* (May 1979): 9, and collected with revisions in *FW*.

10 asleep. / Slubbed] asleep. // Slubbed. *Honest Ulsterman, Harvard Advocate*
12 the laden silent river] the glaucous laden silent river *Honest Ulsterman, Harvard Advocate*
34 sunspotting] suns potting] *Honest Ulsterman* (error)

1 *The child*: revealed in *l*. 24 as the Heaneys' second son Christopher (born 1968). The poem is once again set in the family's visit to the South of France and Spain in 1969 in fulfilment of the conditions of the Somerset Maugham Award (cf. 'Summer Home', *WO*, 49; *PSH*, 141: 'My children weep out the hot foreign night').

3 *la petite*: because of his long curls, the French locals think Christopher is a girl.

8 'gargled' is a familiar SH term for the sound of a tractor. Cf. 'Tractors' (*PSH*, 9) and 'Glanmore Sonnets' I, *l*. 4, 'distant gargling tractors' (*FW*, 28; *PSH*, 231).

11 *Slubbed*: the dialect term is glossed as 'Twisted; irregular' (Johnston 2020, 49).

24–8 The quotation marks round these lines suggest that they are an extract from a journal written at the time. Cf. use of notebooks in 'Known World' (*EL*, 19–20; *PSH*, 536).

30ff. The loathsomeness of the swarm of maggots is reminiscent of earlier poems, and in particular of section 1 of 'Summer Home: 'the mat // that was larval, moving – / and scald, scald, scald' (*WO*, 47; *PSH*, 140). The image of the 'police force run amok' (*l*. 33) is part of the guilt at escape from responsibility, both of the father escaping into the barn to write, avoiding the crying child, and of the Northern Irishman escaping the troubles of 1969.

36 The *pays basque* was the end of the French part of the trip before crossing into Spain where the family stayed in Madrid.

The Otter

First published as 'Otter' in *Aquarius*, 9 (1977): 32, then as 'The Otter' in Geoffrey Elborn (ed.), *Hand and Eye: An Anthology for Sacheverell Sitwell* (Edinburgh: Tragara Press, 1977): n.p. [19–20], and in *Antaeus* (Spring 1979): 20–31. Collected with revisions in *FW* and subsequently included in *PM*, *NSP1990*, *OG* and *100P*.

Title] Otter *Aquarius*
23 Re-tilting] Retilting *OG*, *100P*

2 *The light of Tuscany*: the representation of the poet's wife in the poem is suffused with light: either literally in Tuscany (where the Heaneys had been), or in Tuscan painting. The poem is an enamoured

recall of the figure in her absence, often assumed to be while the poet was in California in 1976 and his wife at home in Ireland.

In *Éire-Ireland* (2023), an additional four lines are given, taken from a BBC audio recording *In Their Element* and printed by the 'best guess' of the article author, Alex Alonso (2023, 243):

> Riverbank marigolds,
> Seepage through alder root.
> Back there, on the patterning mud-slick,
>   I would pounce, otter, and revel.

The Skunk

First published in *Cyphers* (Winter 1977–8): 36–7, and then in the *New Review* (Feb. 1978): 25. After collection in *FW* it was also included in Dannie Abse (ed.), *Best of the Poetry Year 6* (London: Robson Books, 1979), 149, and then in *PM*, *NSP1990*, *OG* and *100P*. It was also published in *Readings in Contemporary Poetry* (1988): 31.

2 mass] Mass *OG*, *100P*
6 verandah] veranda *NSP1990*

1–2 The priest's vestments, notably the chasuble, the most visible covering vestment, are black and white, matching the skunk's coloration, in masses for the dead, which suits the elegiac mood of the poet in his wife's absence.

   10 *wife*: confirming the identification of the image with SH's wife, as 'California' in *l.* 13 with the poet's love-lorn marital separation in 1976.

   21 *It all came back to me*: both the erotic memory and its source when the poet is back in the physical reality of his wife's presence.

Homecomings

First published in *mars*, 1 (1976): 35, collected with revisions in *FW*, and included in Peter Fallon and Dennis O'Driscoll (eds), *The First Ten Years: Dublin Arts Festival Poetry* (Dublin: Dublin Arts Festival, 1979), 62.

Title Resolving the theme of love in absence of the two preceding poems.

   I 1 *Fetch me*: bring me the bird as an image of return to self and home.

   II 4 *gloved*: perfectly fitted in greeting.

A Dream of Jealousy

First published in *Quarto* (Coleraine, Nov. 1975): 2, and in *Little Word Machine*, 7 (1975): 38, and *Blue Moon News*, 1. 2 (1976): 24, and 'Y' (1977): 9. Collected with revisions in *FW* and subsequently included in *NSP1990* and *OG*.

4–5 a shady / Unexpected] an unexpected, shady *Quarto*
13 O] Oh *OG*   these verses] epiphanies *Little Word Machine*

A sonnet on the model of the poems in Dante's *Vita Nuova*, which is concerned with debates about love and poetry.

1 Many of the poems of Dante and his poetry colleagues involve the presence of a beloved and a mysterious third lady, such as the relationship between Beatrice, the major love of the *Vita Nuova*, and the figure called the *donna gentile*. The *Vita Nuova* also celebrates a new kind of art-writing.

After the death of Beatrice Dante's new love was a figure of Philosophy which should not have displaced her in Dante's affections. Another influence on this poem in the same genre was Yeats's 'Adam's Curse' which similarly features 'you and I' and 'a beautiful mild woman', where they sat together 'and talked of poetry' (Albright 1990, 106).

Polder

First published in the *Honest Ulsterman*, 60 (July/Oct. 1978): 9, and in the *Paris Review* (Spring 1979): 233. Also published in the *Harvard Advocate* (May 1979): 6. Collected with revisions in *FW*.

1 sudden outburst and the squalls] dyke-burst and receding floods *Honest Ulsterman*
6] what the arms took in extended *Honest Ulsterman*

Title To the English words – etymologically related to Dutch – 'bosom' and 'fathom', linked to physical embrace, SH adds 'polder', a reclaimed waterland, to describe the reclamation of a beloved after a marital conflict.

Field Work

Part I published under the title 'Field Work' in the *New England Review* (Autumn 1978): 31; the complete poem (I–IV) was then published in *Stone Ferry Review* (Winter 1978): 66–69, and in *Antaeus* (Spring 1979): 22–3. Collected with revisions in *FW*, and included in *PM* and *OG*. Parts I, III and IV were included in *NSP*.

I 1] Where the yellowhammer flared out of the bushes *New England Review*
I 4] I watched you through the mossed shins of the hedge *New England Review*
I 5 gatehouse] gate-house *New England Review*
I 6 and reach to lift] And lean to pick *New England Review*
I 8 arm,] arm *New England Review*
II 5 wet] leaves *Stone Ferry Review*

The volume's title sequence describes the physical restoration of eroticism after separation and interruption. All the poems evoke the physical basis of the amorous.

  II 3 *dryad*: in Greek mythology a tree-nymph, originally linked to the oak.

  II 9 *Pequod* is the name of the ship in *Moby-Dick*. In origin the word is Algonquian, perhaps meaning 'people of the swamp'. But here the sense is far-travelled in the course of marriage.

  IV 1–4 The word 'catspiss' is often used to describe the tart smell of flowering currant leaves when pressed between the fingers.

  IV 13 *anoint*: religious terminology applied to erotic subjects is characteristic of the love-poetry of Dante and his friends.

  18 *my umber one*: in a letter to Charles Monteith, 19 October 1978, SH seems to have decided on 'Umber' as a title for the book published as *FW* (*LSH*, 165). 'Umber' was a working title for this section of the poem while it was an independent piece, before its incorporation into 'Field Work', as was 'Catherine's Fancy', 'Folk Art' and 'Jen'.

Song

First published in *Antaeus* (Spring 1979): 24, and in *Recorder*, 40 (1979): 40–3. Collected in *FW* and included in *NSP1990*, *OG* and *100P*.

  1 The association of colours in nature with the human is continued, like 'umber' in the previous poem.

  6 *immortelle*: grave decorations or wreaths, of hard materials and usually flower-shaped: symbols of immortality.

  8 *the music of what happens*: in one of the medieval Irish Fenian legends, Fionn mac Cumhaill and his followers debate what was the finest music in the world. The cuckoo is suggested and the ring of a spear on a shield; 'the belling of a stag across water, the baying of a tuneful pack heard in the distance; the song of a lark, the laughter of a gleeful girl, or the whisper of a moved one.' But finally, good as all those sounds are, '"The music of what happens," said great Fionn, "that is the finest music in the world"' (James Stephens, *Irish Fairy Stories*, quoted in Montague 1974, 79–80). Unusually, SH time-stamped the addition of this single line in his typescripts, marking it

as '13/4/78 3 a.m.' in a formative draft that explored the working titles 'King's Island', 'The Straying Kerne's Song', 'A Woodkerne's Song' and, seemingly, 'Polders' (NLI 49,493/49/189).

Seamus Heaney: The Music of what Happens (2019), a film about SH released after his death, was made by Adam Low and Martin Rosenbaum for the BBC arts programme *Arena*, in the course of which this poem was read twice.

Leavings

First published in *After Summer* (Old Deerfield, MA, and Dublin: Deerfield and Gallery, 1978), then in *Cyphers* (Winter 1977–8): 36–7; *Poetry Australia* (March 1978): 18; *Listener* (18 Jan. 1979): 121; the *Paris Review* (Spring 1979): 234; and *Straight Lines*, 2 (1979): 27. Collected in FW and later published in OG.

10 latin] Latin OG
18 on] in *Poetry Australia*, *Listener*, Straight Lines, OG
18 sparking] sparkling *Poetry Australia*

9 The Lady Chapel attached to Ely Cathedral in Cambridgeshire was one of the most extravagant monuments of English Decorated style of the fourteenth century, but was almost entirely denuded of its distinctive qualities in the course of the iconoclastic Dissolution of the Monasteries in the sixteenth century.

13 *Thomas Cromwell* (*c.*1485–1540): chief minister to Henry VIII, who had him beheaded. A major force in the establishment of the Reformation in England and in the Dissolution of the Monasteries.

14 *Which circle*: in Dante's *Inferno*, Canto 14 has a plain of burning sand, but the scalding cobbles made up of broken statues' heads seem to be SH's invention.

20 *Will Brangwen*: the central male character in D. H. Lawrence's *The Rainbow* (1915); also a character in the sequel *Women in Love* (1920), in which his daughters Ursula and Gudrun are central. He represents a kind of mysticism which has largely been thought less sympathetic than the modernism of his Polish wife, Anna. Here his mysticism seems to suggest a way of countering the various instances of English iconoclasm through the ages.

The Harvest Bow

First published in the *Times Literary Supplement* (28 May 1976): 634, as a poem of only three stanzas (the first, second and last stanza of the collected version); then in *Poetry Australia* (March 1978): 19; and the *Literary Review*

(Winter 1979) 212–13. Collected with revisions in *FW* and subsequently included in *NSP1990*, *OG* and *100P*.

7] Your hands that aged round the cattle-dealer's sticks *TLS*
8 gamecocks] game-cocks *TLS*] game cocks *Poetry Australia, Literary Review*
12 palpable,] palpable. *TLS*
17 An] And *Literary Review* [error]
24–5 hand. // The] hand. / The *Literary Review* (error)
27 dresser –] dresser *Poetry Australia, Literary Review*
28 Like a drawn snare] Like faith, or like a drawn snare *TLS*

1 'you' is the poet's father. Various qualities associated with him occur through the poem: silence (*l.* 2), and his agriculturally adept hands, especially associated with ashplants (*l.* 7), for example.

12 This line has often been said to encapsulate the essence of SH's poetic aesthetic.

14 The homesick recollection of an evening with his father anticipates the wish to encounter him after his death.

25 *The end of art is peace*: a notion from the Victorian poet-critic Coventry Patmore, paraphrased with admiration by W. B. Yeats in *Samhain* (1905; collected in *Explorations*). The Yeats passage is used as the epigraph to SH's *Preoccupations*.

27 *deal dresser*: pinewood kitchen storage unit.

In Memoriam Francis Ledwidge

First published in the *Irish Times* (19 Nov. 1977): 11, then in *Stand*, 19. 2 (1978): 21, and in *New Republic* (7 July 1979): 32. After collection in *FW* it was included in *NSP1990*, *OG* and *100P*. It was also published in Dermot Bolger's volumes *Francis Ledwidge: Selected Poems* (Dublin: New Island, 1992), 79–80, and *The Ledwidge Treasury: Selected Poems* (Dublin: New Island, 2007), 15–16, and John Quinn (ed.), *A Little Book of Ledwidge: A Selection of the Poems and Letters of Francis Ledwidge* (Dublin: Veritas, 2017), 117–19.

6 gun's] guns's *Irish Times* (error)
8 worried pet] papish get *Irish Times, Stand*
8 pet] pet. *Ledwidge Treasury* (error)
17–20 [omitted] *NSP1990*, *OG*, *Ledwidge Treasury*, *A Little Book of Ledwidge*, *100P*
24 Slane.] Slane *Irish Times, Stand, New Republic, NSP1990, OG, Ledwidge Treasury, A Little Book of Ledwidge, 100P*
31 with] like *Irish Times, NSP1990, OG, Ledwidge Treasury, 100P*
32 cored] coned *Irish Times*

Title Francis Ledwidge (1887–1917), Irish poet born near Slane in Co. Meath, the eighth of nine children of a poor family. He died fighting in the British Army at Passchendaele in the Third Battle of Ypres. He was a friend of a local landowner, Lord Dunsany, who encouraged his writing and introduced him to major poetic contemporaries such as Yeats, Oliver St John Gogarty, AE and Katherine Tynan. He was a trade union activist who read the political writings of James Connolly, and a keen Irish nationalist who sided with the Irish Volunteers, which opposed participation in the war. Nevertheless, encouraged by Dunsany, he enlisted in the Royal Irish Inniskilling Fusiliers in 1914. He continued to write poems, some of them pinned to posts in the battlefield, and sent them back to Dunsany who published three volumes of his poems and a collected edition of 122 poems in 1919 after the poet's death. The irony of his position is most poignantly evident in his most celebrated poem 'Lament for Thomas MacDonagh', an elegy for the poet-academic who was executed as one of the leaders of the 1916 Easter Rising in Dublin. Ledwidge's poems continued to appear throughout the twentieth century; updated collected editions were published by Alice Curtayne in 1974 and by Peter Fallon in 2022.

11 *Portstewart*: a seaside destination, near Portrush in Co. Derry. The bronze soldier of the poem's opening features in the Portstewart World War I memorial.

22 *Drogheda*: port town in Co. Louth, roughly halfway between Dublin and the border.

32 *Boyne passage-grave*: one of the Megalithic passage tombs in Co. Meath near Ledwidge's birthplace.

34 *the long acre*: roadside grass on which cattle were sometimes led to graze.

35 *the Dardanelles*: the strait in north-western Turkey where a disastrous campaign was conducted against the Ottomans in February–March 1915.

37–8 Two years later, SH's Aunt Mary as a young girl is herding cows in the same place when Ledwidge is killed in Ypres.

41ff. Ledwidge's dilemma: to be called a British soldier while Ireland has no place among nations (recalling the death speech of Robert Emmet in 1803: 'When my country takes her place among the nations of the earth, then and not till then, let my epitaph be written').

Ugolino

First published in *Antaeus* (Spring 1979): 29–31, and in *lower stumpf lake review* (Spring 1979): 6–7. Also published as *Ugolino*, a special edition with two lithographs by Louis le Brocquy, by Andrew Carpenter in Dublin in September 1979 and printed by Liam Miller at the Dolmen Press. After collection in *FW* it was also included in *OG*.

21–2 relive all that / Desperate time makes] live all that / Desperate time again *lower stumpf lake review*

33 malignancy.] malignancy, *lower stumpf lake review*, OG
34 held,] held *lower stumpf lake review*
49 Lanfranchi] Lanafranchi *lower stumpf lake review*
55 bread.] bread . . . *lower stumpf lake review*
56–8 These lines are omitted in *lower stumpf lake review*
67 daddy] Daddy *lower stumpf lake review*
74–5 desperation / And] desperation. // And *lower stumpf lake review*
84 throwing] stretching *lower stumpf lake review*
100 Capraia] Caprara *lower stumpf lake review*

Title Ugolino della Gherardesca, Count of Donoratico (d.1289), belonged to an emperor-supporting Ghibelline family of Pisa. In 1271 his daughter was married to Giovanni Visconti of a family that led the papal-supporting Guelphs in Pisa. Ugolino and Giovanni were imprisoned as enemies of Pisa; Giovanni died and Ugolino was freed. He made common cause with the Guelphs of Florence and Lucca and attacked Pisa, which had to make peace on humiliating terms. After warfare between Pisa and the Guelph cities, Ugolino became joint leader of Pisa with his grandson Nino Visconti, Giovanni's son. But they quarrelled and Ugolino negotiated with Archbishop Ruggiero degli Ubaldini of Pisa, drove Nino and other Guelph families out of Pisa and had himself proclaimed Podestà on his own. After the resulting conflict, the Archbishop had Ugolino, along with his two sons and two grandsons, locked in the Muda, a tower belonging to the Gualandi family, and ordered the keys to be thrown into the Arno leaving Ugolino and his family to starve. In *Inferno*, 32 and 33, among those guilty of treachery in the depths of Hell, Dante and Virgil meet Ugolino and Ruggiero together in a frozen hole with Ugolino mounted on the Archbishop's back and chewing his skull. In Canto 33, Ugolino tells the story of their capture and incarceration. SH's poem is a relatively close translation of Dante, whose version of the story was one of the recurrent narratives of the Middle Ages: for example in Chaucer's Monk's Tale in the *Canterbury Tales* (*TSH*, 6; 535–6).

Given its date of first publication, this starvation narrative has inevitably been seen in the context of the Republican protests in the H-Blocks of HM Prison Maze, near Lisburn, Co. Antrim, though the prominent hunger strikes of 1980 and 1981 post-date the poem. The protests were staged by Republican prisoners to demand the reinstatement of Special Category Status (recognising them as political, as opposed to criminal, prisoners). They began in September 1976 with the Blanket protest, during which prisoners refused to wear prison uniform. The Dirty/No Wash protest, during which prisoners refused to leave their cells to wash or use lavatory facilities, and covered the cell walls in excrement, began in 1978. The first hunger strike involving seven prisoners began in October 1980, but was called off in December that year. The second, led by Bobby Sands, began in March 1981 and ended that August, after the deaths of ten men.

SH himself tells Dennis O'Driscoll that he 'translated "Ugolino" in order for it to be read in the context of the "dirty protests" in the Maze prison' (*SS*, 425). In a 24 May 1978 letter to Michael Longley about this translation, SH says 'no prizes for guessing who figures there. In a way, it merges with the elegies for Sean Armstrong and Louis O'Neill – and matches what's happening in H Block' (*LSH*, 159). He also tells Dennis O'Driscoll that he 'had toyed with the idea of dedicating the Ugolino translation to the prisoners. But our friend's [Danny Morrison's, as recounted in 'The Flight Path' (*SL*, 24–5; *PSH*, 475)] intervention put paid to any such gesture. After that, I wouldn't give and wasn't so much free to refuse as unfree to accept' (*SS*, 258). 'Free to refuse' is a reference to Yeats's line in 'The Tower': 'The people of Burke and of Grattan / That gave, though free to refuse' (Albright 1990, 244).

UNCOLLECTED POEMS (1979–1984)

After the 'more political context of *North*' and a declared aspiration to return to the 'devil-may-careness' of the language poems in *Wintering Out*, and before a return to the more public subjects of the 'Sweeney Complex' in *Station Island* and *Sweeney Astray*, SH published twenty-two uncollected poems, including two sequences, nineteen of which are collected here for the first time. Some of these poems were notable statements of his current poetics: the controversial but witty 'An Open Letter' (1983) published by Field Day, objecting to his featuring under the heading 'British' in Motion–Morrison's *Penguin Book of Contemporary British Poetry*, and the 322-line-long 'Lines for a Fordham Commencement'. A poem of similar substance is the highly inventive translation 'The Names of the Hare' (*see TSH*, 11 and 546–8). The absence of all three items from *Station Island* (1984), SH's next full-length volume, may largely be explained by their length; 'An Open Letter' and the Fordham poem are absent from *Opened Ground* as well. There are some uncollected poems with connections to poems in the main collections: in this version of the 'Shelf Life' sequence, 'iii, Pewters' corresponds to 'Old Pewter' in *Station Island*; 'Station Island III' and 'IV' were not included in that book's title sequence. 'Tremor' is published by the Gallery Press in a 1984 pamphlet, *Hailstones*. The most striking unpublished item is 'A Night-Piece for Tom Flanagan', with its roll-call of seven significant Irish figures from Wolfe Tone to W. B. Yeats. The 'Villanelle for Marie' occurs in *A Family Album* in 1979. Overall, although these poems emerge at a transitional time in SH's working life and from a painful period of Northern Irish history, there is no consistent concern to them that would place them decisively between *Field Work* and *Station Island*. The most significant development in the uncollected pieces of this period is the new frequency of publication in the US after SH takes up his new his role at Harvard in 1982.

The publication on 20 October 1980 in London of *Selected Poems 1965–1975* in 3,000 hardback and 12,000 paperback by Faber would provide a popular and accessible introduction to SH's work to date. A compendium edition by Farrar, Straus and Giroux in New York, entitled *Poems 1965–1975*, was published that year in hardback and on 1 October 1981 in paperback, and featured the first four books in their entirety with the exception of seven poems for *Death of a Naturalist*, which were omitted. These sibling editions would serve as key surveys of SH's work until their replacement in 1990 by a unified UK–US volume, *New Selected Poems 1966–1987*.

A Cart for Edward Gallagher

This poem undergoes significant revision to become 'Last Look' in *SI*, but the differences between this and its earlier incarnations warrant its inclusion here among the uncollected poems. It was first published in the *Recorder*, 40 (1979): 40–3, and in the *Times Literary Supplement* (8 Feb. 1980): 136, and then in Kevin M. Cahill (ed.), *The American Irish Revival: A Decade of 'The Recorder', 1974–1983* (Port Washington, NY, and London: Associated Faculty Press, 1984), 39–1.

[text: *TLS*]

>1] // I *American Irish Revival*
4 whitewashed] turf stacks at *American Irish Revival*
10 forward] forward. *American Irish Revival*
10^11] But the son's mind's far away.
      Grain-ships locked in ice
      on the far St Lawrence,
      dark skies, flurried snow –
      each pent-up cargo
      of Canadian wheat
      falls golden and slow
      through a daydream of chutes
      along Derry Quay
      into bags of flour, bins
      of yellow meal and bran . . .
      I gaze into a bucket,
      smell a near horses's sweat
      and hear him mashing corn
      on my uncle's street.
      It is nineteen forty-seven. *American Irish Revival*
11–12] // 11 / Edward, you return me / to that archaic yard, *American Irish Revival*
23 and painted] painted *American Irish Revival*
25] [omitted] *American Irish Revival*
26^27] // III *American Irish Revival*
28 is a] is all a *American Irish Revival*
29^30] the music of what happens, *American Irish Revival*
36 trouser-bottoms] trouser bottoms *American Irish Revival*

The figure is identified on the 2009 RTÉ audio recording and in 'Last Look' (*SI*, 28; *PSH*, 56) as Edward Gallagher, who travelled Donegal selling various provisions.

    18–20 Teady (or Teddy) McErlean's of Clady near Ballymena, Co. Antrim, 'the oldest firm in the Lagan Valley' dealt with agricultural materials. Seamus McErlean, Chair of the Bellaghy Historical Society, cherished the reference in this poem.

    29^30 A revised printing of this poem in the *American Irish Revival* carries a refrain from SH's famous line of Fionn mac

Cumhaill's published in 'Song' (*FW*, 53; *PSH*, 243): 'the music of what happens'.

A Hank of Wool

Published in the *Times Literary Supplement*, 7 March 1980.

Dedication SH only met Elizabeth Bishop (1911–79) in the last year of her life, in the course of his first year at Harvard, but he was 'often in [her] company' in that time (*LSH*, 168, 663). Bishop taught poetry at Harvard from 1970 until her retirement in 1977 (*SS*, 268–9). She won the Pulitzer Prize for Poetry in 1956 and the National Book Award in 1970. SH's Oxford lecture 'Counting to a Hundred: On Elizabeth Bishop' was delivered on 2 December 1992 and included in *RP* (164–85).

A Villanelle for Marie

Published in *FA*, and subsequently in *Quarto* (Coleraine, Summer 1980): 34.

The Well at New Place

Published in *New Departures*, 12 (1980), an anthology issued in celebration of the first Poetry Olympics, launched at Poet's Corner in Westminster Abbey on 26 September 1980.

A Lighting Plot

First published in Andrew Carpenter and Peter Fallon (eds), *The Writers: A Sense of Ireland* (Dublin: O'Brien, 1980), and later in the Dublin *Sunday Independent* (8 Jan. 1989), which included a feature marking Brian Friel's sixtieth birthday.

[text: *The Writers*]

7 dawn.] dawn *The Writers*, *Sunday Independent* (error)

Dated 21 August 1979 in TS (NLI 49,493/50).
    12 In Act II of Synge's *The Playboy of the Western World*, Christy Mahon, the ingénu hero, is captivated by his clean face in a looking-glass.

An Open Letter

First published in Derry by Field Day Theatre Company in 1983, the second of the three inaugural Field Day Pamphlets. Subsequently collected in Seamus Deane (ed.), *Ireland's Field Day* (London: Hutchinson, 1985), and published again in *Harper's Magazine* (March 1987).

[text: *An Open Letter*]

In its Field Day publications, the poem was accompanied by SH's own Notes, which read as follows:

- Stanza 1   This open letter is prompted by the writer's inclusion in *The Penguin Book of Contemporary British Poetry*, edited by Blake Morrison and Andrew Motion, Harmondsworth, 1982. I have to apologize for changing the *Poetry* of the title to *verse* – a result of the constrictions of rhyme.

- Stanza 8   'Good advocate'. Blake Morrison is the author of a critical study, *Seamus Heaney*, in Methuen's Contemporary Writers series, London, 1982.

- Stanza 9   *Opened Ground* is a quotation from 'Glanmore Sonnets, 1' in the writer's *Field Work*, London, 1979.

- Stanza 10   References to reviews of the Penguin anthology by Philip Larkin, Hugh Haughton and John Jordan in *The Observer*, *Times Literary Supplement*, and *Irish Press* respectively.

- Stanza 20   See Donald Davie, 'Poet: Patriot: Interpreter', *Critical Quarterly*, Volume 9, Number 1, Chicago, 1982.

- Stanza 28   See Miroslav Holub's 'On the Necessity of Truth', in *Sagittal Section*, translated by Stuart Frieberg and Dana Habova, Ohio, 1980.

Epigraph Gaston Bachelard (1884–1962), French philosopher of poetics and science, author of *The Poetics of Space*. The quotation is a translation of *L'eau et les rêves: Essai sur l'imagination de la matière* (Paris: José Corti, 1942), 262 by Colette Gaudin in her Introduction to *On Poetic Imagination and Reverie: Selections from the Works of Gaston Bachelard* (Indianapolis: Bobbs-Merrill, 1971), xxxvii.

Stanza 1 Blake Morrison and Andrew Motion, editors of *The Penguin Book of Contemporary British Poetry* (1982).

Stanza 3 Caesar's *De Bello Gallico* begins, 'Gaul as a whole is divided into three parts.'

Stanza 5 In Synge's *The Playboy of the Western World* (1907), Shauneen Keogh is the feeble comic suitor of the heroine Pegeen Mike.

Stanza 12 *pro se quisque* (each for himself): a recurrent phrase in Livy's *Ab Urbe Condita*. Horace fought in Brutus's army at Philippi in 42 BCE. He said he fled from the battle, leaving his shield behind, thus ending his military career.

Stanza 19 *Donald Davie*: conservative poet, author of *Purity of Diction in English Verse* (1952), and dedicatee of the first published version of 'The Flight Path' in *PN Review* (Nov.–Dec. 1992): 31–2, which is collected in *SL* (22ff.; *PSH*, 475).

Stanza 20 'Lhude sing cuccu' is from the Middle English 'Sumer is icumen in'. Here the cuckoo's call is improbably replaced by the name of the French historical literary theorist Michel Foucault (1926–84), a hero of the new theoretical criticism.

Stanza 21–2 *So rudely forc'd*: the rape of Philomela in T. S. Eliot's *The Waste Land* (1922), whose song as nightingale is represented as 'jug jug . . . tereu' by John Lyly.

A shudder in the loins: Yeats's 'Leda and the Swan' (Albright 1990, 260); 'a sudden blow' in stanza 24.

Stanzas 23–4 The opposing parties in literary criticism are compared to the opposing forces in Northern Ireland: the Provisional IRA versus the Parachute Regiment. 'The hidden Ulster' derives from Daniel Corkery's decidedly Irish literary history *The Hidden Ireland* (1924).

Stanza 25 The Middle English cuckoo song (st. 20) has been interpreted as echoing the word cuckold. Leinster House is the seat of government in Dublin.

Stanza 27 A common complaint by unionists in Northern Ireland is that their unionist state is not recognised in London as something distinct from nationalist Ireland.

Stanza 28ff. the concluding fable from Holub weighs the merits of factual correction (like SH's here) against 'letting it go' (st. 5) for a quiet life.

A Summer Night

Published in *Bananas*, 26 (April 1981): 26.

Among the Whins

First published in the *New Statesman* (29 Jan. 1982), and subsequently collected in the Linen Hall Library limited edition, *TC*. The latter version does not include the subtitle, and has been significantly revised. It is transcribed here in full.

[text: *New Statesman*]

AMONG THE WHINS

Wasps in foxgloves. And the three walkers
Faltered on the brae. The hot ditches
Shadowed them, the steep incline took them
From one another into themselves
And on into the mood of confidences –
Accountant, vet and bookie, among the whins.
They stopped of one accord but did not speak
(The lark unstoppable over their heads).
Who is going to tell? The vet remembers
A reeking horse-box at a point-to-point,
Guiding his partner's wife in there for shelter
As the crowd starts a big rush for the cars
At the end of the meet. Ancient rain
Drums on the roof above them. Suddenly
He hauls on the taut oiled wires and a door
Half-rises and hangs there, darkening them.
He turns, rubbing his hands under his arms,
To take hold of the small cleft of her back
And smell deliberately at her perfumed neck,
So tender to his half-shaved underlip.
They are roused inside a second but then stop
Without speaking and manage out
Into the crowd still hurrying through the mud,
To separate naturally and arrive
Hot and bothered with their soaked, half-gathered
Families, asking, 'Where's so and so?' And each
Gets settled, rubbing the windscreen, peering.
This is the vet's story he must tell
So the other two can begin on theirs.
Errigal stands guard on the horizon
And everything is going on as usual.
For example, when the bookie's compliments
Have been expressed – 'Aren't you the right cute whore!' –
He starts on the tale of his own dud racehorse,
How he insured it first and then one night
Hunted it over the edge of a quarryhole.
And now it's the vet's partner, rattling into shot
In an old pick-up, slowing down and shouting,
'Haven't some bastards the greatest times of all!'
And now it's the accountant: 'That reminds me . . .'

Anniversary Verse

Read at Harvard University on 19 May 1982, subsequently published to mark the dedication of the Heaney Suite, Adams House, Harvard University, 28 March 2015.

Verses for a Fordham Commencement

First published in a four-page leaflet for the Commencements (usually termed graduation in Britain and Ireland) ceremony at Fordham University, New York, on 23 May 1982. Also published in the university magazine *Fordham* (Summer 1982): 8–9, and in the *Irish Literary Supplement* (Fall 1982): 22–3. It was subsequently published, by Nadja in 1984, in a limited run of twenty-six cased and 200 paper covers.

[text: leaflet, *Fordham*]

5] Parents, guests and bishops, sisters *Nadja*
7 borders:] borders – *Irish Literary Supplement*
8–14] [omitted] *Irish Literary Supplement, Nadja*
16 And the tune] And tunes *Nadja*
20 In fact] In fact, *Nadja*
54] Japan, haiku; and Wales, cynghannedd; *Nadja*   cynghanedd] cynghannedd (error) *leaflet, Irish Literary Supplement*
63 light.] light? *Nadja*
64–77 [omitted] *Nadja*
78] Yet do we not elide the facts *Nadja*
98 heart] heart. *Irish Literary Supplement, Nadja*
130 clientèle] clientele *Irish Literary Supplement*
141–75] [omitted] *Nadja*
148–54 [omitted] *Irish Literary Supplement*
154] All seem at times escapes, evasions *Irish Literary Supplement*
161 dream] dream, *Irish Literary Supplement*
176–7] And yet, before the first college / Was built, the men of art of knowledge *Nadja*
179 seers] seers, *Irish Literary Supplement*
182 defunct.] defunct, *Irish Literary Supplement* | defunct – *Nadja*
183 influence,] influence *Irish Literary Supplement*
186 Then so had] And so had *Nadja*
212 And SS men] and SS men *leaflet, Fordham* (error) | And commandants *Irish Literary Supplement, Nadja*
225–31, 232–8] [stanza order reversed] *Nadja*
227 Which] which *leaflet, Fordham, Nadja* (error)
238 cleaned] wiped *Irish Literary Supplement*
239–45] [omitted] *Nadja*
260–6] [omitted] *Nadja*
271 rain.] rain – *Nadja*
280 right.] right, *Nadja*
286 whole self] wholeself *Irish Literary Supplement*
289 Fragrant with] Integral with *Irish Literary Supplement* | The fume off *Nadja*
290 moral feeling] your own feeling *Irish Literary Supplement*

295–301] [omitted] *Nadja*

Title Fordham University is a private Catholic University in New York City, established in 1841 by the Jesuits, originally located in the Bronx.

33 SH's idea that formal rules are liberating rather than constraining in poetry is often associated with Robert Frost.

37ff. SH's poem, like 'An Open Letter' is written in the Burns or Habbie Stanza. Two of Burns's most familiar poems are noted in these lines, 'To a Mouse, on Turning Her Up in Her Nest With the Plough, November, 1785', and 'To a Louse, On Seeing one on a Lady's Bonnet at Church', 1786.

50–6 Listing the poetic forms native to various cultures and languages, from Homer to Japan to the medieval courtly poets of Languedoc to the poetry of Ireland, England and Wales.

54 *cynghanedd*: intricate Welsh poetic form, admired by Hopkins, who replicated its consonantal structure in English, influencing SH.

135–6 *What will survive of us is love*: the last line of Philip Larkin's 'An Arundel Tomb'.

295 See, for example, the Heraclitean poem 'Crossings' xxvii (*ST*, 85; *PSH*, 438).

Ulster Quatrains

First published in the *Recorder* (1982), and subsequently collected in Kevin M. Cahill (ed.), *The American Irish Revival: A Decade of 'The Recorder', 1974–1983* (Port Washington, NY, and London: Associated Faculty Press, 1984).

1 SECTARIAN WATER

4 *church-latin c*: by contrast with 'stiff-necked *k*' (*l*. 8) – in words like *caelum* Catholics in church liturgy pronounced the initial consonant 'ch' (as in 'child') but when they studied school Latin learned to pronounce it 'k' (as in 'kind'). SH extends this opposition into public political usage. Similarly (*ll.* 9 and 15) students of Latin were told to pronounce initial v as w: Wirgil rather than Virgil.

2 SECTARIAN LATIN

2 Holbein's portraits of Erasmus and Thomas More, for example, do have black gowns and thin spread lips. But the extension of this into phonetics is fanciful if evocative.

3 SECTARIAN ALPHABET

1ff. The identifying shibboleths here have sinister associations in Troubles Northern Ireland, culminating in the ambivalent term *Shames*.

Pastoral

Published in *PM*, in the section titled 'Early Uncollected Poems'.

Expectant

Published in *PM*, in the section titled 'Early Uncollected Poems'.

Station Island III

Published in the *Hudson Review* (Summer 1983): 262–4, where it appeared with the first published versions of the first and second poems from the sequence.

While this poem bears some relation to the published 'Station Island IX' (notably correspondence of *ll*. 66–8 here with 'IX' *ll*. 57–9 (*SI*, 85; *PSH*, 332)), it is uncollected.

Shelf Life

Published in *Outposts: Poetry Quarterly*, 138 (Autumn 1983). Part iii, 'Pewters', was significantly revised and collected as 'Old Pewter', Part 3 of the sequence also titled 'Shelf Life' in *SI* (22; *PSH*, 296).

iii 7 love.] love *Outposts* (error)

Station Island IV

Published in the *Yale Review* (Autumn 1983): 136–8, with three other sections numbered VII [i.e. V], VIII [i.e. VI] and IX [i.e. VII], which were collected in *SI*.

Working title in TS 'The Purgatory Ferry' (NLI 49,493/81).

A Night Piece for Tom Flanagan

First published in the *Recorder* (1983), and subsequently collected in Kevin M. Cahill (ed.), *The American Irish Revival: A Decade of 'The Recorder'*, *1974–1983* (Port Washington, NY, and London: Associated Faculty Press, 1984).

The Hag

Published in *Critical Quarterly* (Spring and Summer 1984).

Initially envisaged as part of the SWEENEY REDIVIVUS sequence in *SI* under the working title 'Sweeney's Awe of the Hag'.

A Paved Text

Published in William Scammell (ed.), *Between Comets: for Norman Nicholson at 70* (n.p.: Taxus, 1984), 22–3.

The Easter House

Published in *Pequod* (1984).

5 Arimathea] Arimithea *Pequod* (error)

Dated 'April' [1980] in MS, between drafts of 'Station Island' (NLI 49,493/57).

Tremor

Published in *Hailstones*, in a limited edition of 750 copies.

This is one of the relatively rare instances of SH dating a poem in print, which here is given as 1972. After *Hailstones*, the poem was considered for *HL* as its opening piece, but later cancelled in TS. In its draft iterations, the poem carried the working titles 'Earthshaker', 'Poetic Diction' and 'Waves', as well as family-framed 'for Ann and Hugh and Jeananne' (HFC, NLI 49,493/84).

STATION ISLAND (1984)

Station Island was published simultaneously in 3,000 hardback copies and 10,000 paperback copies on 15 October 1984 by Faber & Faber in London and was Recommendation of the Poetry Book Society for the Winter of 1984. It was subsequently published in New York in 6,000 copies by Farrar, Straus and Giroux in New York on 1 January 1985 in dual hardback and paperback bindings. The book can be profitably read in conjunction with *Sweeney Astray*, SH's translated version of the medieval Irish *Buile Suibhne*, which was published by Faber in London in a printing of 500 hardback and 5,500 paperback copies on the same day as *Station Island*; it had been previously published in Ireland by Field Day, Derry in 1,000 hardback and 4,000 paperback copies in November 1983, and in New York by Farrar, Straus and Giroux in 5,500 hardback copies in May 1984, and subsequently there in paperback in April 1985. The publication history and subjects of the two books are intricately linked, especially because they are connected by Part Three of *Station Island*, which is headed SWEENEY REDIVIVUS, and to which SH appends the following note:

> The poems in this section are voiced for Sweeney, the seventh-century Ulster king who was transformed into a bird-man and exiled to the trees by the curse of St Ronan. A version of the Irish tale is available in my *Sweeney Astray*, but I trust these glosses can survive without the support system of the original story.*

Station Island is a small island in Lough Derg in Co. Donegal, also known as St Patrick's Purgatory, a place of Europe-wide pilgrimage since the Middle Ages. SH made the Lough Derg pilgrimage three times while he was a student; he had thought of writing a poem based on it a few years after those occasions. He tells O'Driscoll that 'as early as 1966 I'd written a short piece called "Lenten Stuff" that began "Now I can only find myself in one place, / Lowbacked island on an

---

* There is a formidable literary predecessor here (acknowledged by SH in the opening paragraph of his introduction to *Sweeney Astray*) which probably tempted him to undertake his translation. The story of Sweeney is one of the interlocking subjects of Flann O'Brien's masterpiece *At Swim-Two-Birds* (1939). The story is introduced by one of the book's characters as 'about this fellow Sweeney that argued the toss with the clergy and came off second-best at the wind-up. There was a curse – a malediction – put down in the book against him. The upshot is that your man becomes a bloody bird.' Flann O'Brien, *At Swim-Two-Birds* (London: MacGibbon and Kee, 1960: 85). Almost thirty years after its first publication, *At Swim-Two-Birds* gained enormous popularity when it was published by Penguin in 1967. The attraction for SH was no doubt partly O'Brien's fine poetic translations of the nature lyrics in the medieval text.

inland lough. / A cold chapel takes up half the island"' (*PSH*, 353). He knew from its place in his notebooks that it was written in May 1966; the title 'Lenten Stuff' is taken from Thomas Nashe's 1599 pamphlet in praise of herring. But it was when SH read Dante in the early 1970s that he really thought of working on this purgatorial poetic enterprise: the 'three-part Dantean journey scaled down into the three-day station, no hell, no paradise, just "Patrick's Purgatory", which is how the place is known to this day' (*SS*, 235). The term 'stations', as in 'Stations of the Cross', describes a sequence of stopping points in a series of penitential meditations.*

For the first time, a book of SH's is expressly divided into three parts, rather than the twofold division of several of his earlier volumes. Part One, SH summarised at the time, 'brings together shorter poems written over the last five years where some of the concerns of the book's later sections are implicit – art and conscience, place and displacement, the transfigurations possible in the erotic and the remembered life' (*PBS Bulletin*, 123, Winter 1984). It has no distinct title, and consists of thirty lyric poems, starting with two resonant personal poems, the first of which, 'The Underground', is a mythological take on a journey out of the London Underground, lightly sustaining the chthonic theme of the preceding volume. The lyric poems of Part One mostly develop the metaphorical potential of memories of people and objects.

Part Two, STATION ISLAND, shares the book's title and describes imaginary post-mortem encounters (what SH calls 'voices and visitations', *PBS Bulletin*, 123) with twelve figures, several of whom are personal acquaintances, but also including William Carleton and James Joyce, who advises the poet to give priority to his artistic work rather than the 'peasant pilgrimage' of Lough Derg. Its purpose, writes SH, is 'the pilgrim's journey, its pattern of withdrawal and return, its encounters with people and memories, its moods of self-examination and re-dedication', intent on offering 'a way of dramatizing contradictory awareness' (*PBS Bulletin*, 123). O'Driscoll quotes to SH Paul Breslin's observation that '"Station Island" is one of those crisis poems that poets sometimes have to write in order to break an impasse' (Breslin 1996, 341), and SH concurs, saying he 'needed to butt my way through a blockage, a pile-up of hampering stuff, everything that had gathered up inside me because of the way I was both in and out of the Northern

---

* In the series in Lough Derg, there are seven stopping points, called 'beds', dedicated to seven Irish saints. For an attractive account of the representations of Lough Derg in modern Irish literature, see Peggy O'Brien, *Writing Lough Derg: From William Carleton to Seamus Heaney* (New York: Syracuse University Press, 2006).

Ireland situation' (*SS*, 235–6). In an interview with Melvyn Bragg in 1991, he says: '"Station Island" is a poem of self-accusation' in which 'the sweetness of lyric is refused . . . It tries to put the boot into lyric. It is a big container, full of subject matter which has no lyric charm' (*South Bank Show*, 27 Oct. 1991).

Part Three is titled SWEENEY REDIVIVUS, twenty short poems, many related to medieval Irish monastic prototypes. The section takes its title from the central figure in *Buile Suibhne*, the medieval Irish epic in prose and verse of which SH was making his own translation at the same time, and is 'spoken by the freed voice of the legendary Sweeney' (*PBS Bulletin*, 123), a figure, SH says in the introduction to *SA*, 'of the artist, displaced, guilty, assuaging himself by his utterance' (*SA*, [vi]). The note on the poems of SWEENEY REDIVIVUS quoted above ends: 'Many of them, of course, are imagined in contexts far removed from early medieval Ireland' (*SI*, 123).* There are other poems, 'voiced for Sweeney', which are not in SWEENEY REDIVIVUS: one is included in the Appendix of unpublished poems in this volume.

The crisis and 'hampering stuff' that the 'Station Island' sequence was resolving were not simply making a settlement with the Northern Ireland situation. Partly in response to his reading of Dante, SH was examining his whole relationship with the Catholic Christendom in which he was raised. When O'Driscoll asked him if it was a confessional book, using the term as it applied to American poets such as Robert Lowell, he replied that it was more like an examination of conscience. His ambition now was to 'get as free as Sweeney': hence the need to take the book in conjunction with *Sweeney Astray*; and, although he says the poems of Part Three were 'voiced' for Sweeney, it is not always clear whether the first person in which most of the poems are written is the poet or the bird-narrator of the medieval poem. A composite persona, 'Sweeney–Heaney' has often been suggested; original reviewers called the book 'Heaney's Sweeney' (echoing the somewhat invidious rhyme 'famous Seamus', first coined by Clive James as Seamus Famous).

SH describes the order of composition of the volume to O'Driscoll in some detail (*SS*, 234ff.). The first section was written in September 1979, becoming section VIII of the central sequence, about Tom Delaney, the Heaneys' archaeologist friend who died aged thirty-two in 1979. The original idea of writing the sequence was to 'get as free as Sweeney' because Sweeney's flight from Ulster had 'a similar purgatorial element', and to end the sequence in the last section of the

---

* For a brief account of the medieval history of St Patrick's Purgatory, see O'Donoghue 2016, 414–26.

poem, but the part written for Sweeney 'ended up in a cycle he got to himself, the "Sweeney Redivivus" poems that conclude the book' (SS, 236). In the event, the concluding twelfth encounter in the 'Station Island' sequence is with James Joyce, who returns to the theme established by SH in the bid for artistic freedom claimed in the movement from the politics of North to the artistic freedom of Field Work. In some ways the subject of the volume is history: the book is balanced between the dedication to Brian Friel, whose powerful, historically set play Translations appeared in Derry 1980 (and went on to pip Station Island to the post for the Ewart-Biggs Memorial Prize in 1985), and the absolution from Joyce in the final section of the central sequence in which he says, 'That subject people stuff is a cod's game'. The fact that this section comes at the end of the poem doesn't alter the fact that the sequence is set in real periods of time and politics. This quality was well summarised by Helen Vendler in her review of the book in the New Yorker (23 September 1985, 116) when she described it as 'poetry so conscious of cultural and social facts which nonetheless remains chiefly a poetry of awareness, observation and sorrow'. The conflict between artistic freedom and public responsibility – 'doing the decent thing' – has not been resolved in any simple terms.

Critical reactions to Station Island varied, partly in response to the relatively unenthusiastic things the poet himself said about it. Many critics admired Part Three, SWEENEY REDIVIVUS, the most; but Paul Muldoon in his review of the book in the London Review of Books thought that was the weakest section and Part One the strongest, before concluding in summary that the collection was SH's 'best since Wintering Out'. Some of the poems in Part Three adapt material originally included as part of the Sweeney Astray project in application to figures from SH's life and art: notably the poem originally published as 'Sweeney as Novice' is reworked as 'The Master' (SA, 110) with reference to Czesław Miłosz (some very informed readers, including Dennis O'Driscoll, had taken it to be a tribute to Yeats).

After the printing difficulties that beset Field Work, Faber had returned with Station Island to working with Whitstable Litho in Kent, adamant that a repeat of poor results must be avoided with their old print partner, as the publisher explained: 'Seamus is one of our very coveted poets and a lovely man and I am particularly anxious that the machining of Station Island does him justice' (Michael Wright, 2 Aug. 1984). Whitstable had imposed such stylish design upon the first four books, but in a transitional age of production, their role was no longer to be that of typesetter. Wilmaset, in Birkenhead, would employ a Linotron 202 for that task, a pioneering machine that dispensed with sort-by-sort setting in order to code computer tape into a photoset of line, column and even entire pages at once. Wilmaset were asked to follow what they were instructed by Faber as 'the now established style' for the poetry list in which they had recently and carefully produced Paul Muldoon's *Quoof* (1983). But the results for *Station Island* were nothing like so subtle, with the clunky Palatino setting poorly spaced and positioned; it would be the most ungainly of the productions that SH would endure in the six decades through which he would work with Faber.

Nevertheless, SH's work on the proofs in the early summer of 1984, had seen little by the way of major amendment, with the exception of the author's addition of 'On the Road', which, the publisher explained apologetically to the setter on 2 July 1984, 'has been slipped in not very surreptitiously at the end of the book'. The three new pages that were hurried into production would break clumsily, mid-stanza, across the page, before camera-ready copy was supplied to Whitstable for printing on 2 August 1984 (FF P/Rdlm/778/6).

Station Island was not the sole publication of SH's in production at that moment, as Faber was simultaneously issuing *Sweeney Astray*. For the first time, the origination of a SH volume was led by the US partner, Farrar, Straus and Giroux, whose 1983 production from which Faber would offset was not pleasing London. 'The running-heads are horrendous and should be deleted from every page,' Faber instructed the off-setting printer on 15 May 1984. But the finish was at least upmarket: 'sewn and not perfect bound,' Faber had decided for their production, 'which makes a nice change' (FF P/Rdlm/778/6).

SH's own notes on *SI*, partly incorporated below, are published at the end of the volume, and dated February 1984.

[text: *SI1984*]

Title Station Island is the name of an island in Lough Derg in Co. Donegal, known since the Middle Ages as St Patrick's Purgatory. It is an ancient and modern place of Catholic penitential pilgrimage, 'a laboratory of the spirit' (*PBS Bulletin*, 123) that has inspired writers for generations.

Dedication Brian Friel (1929–2015), leading Irish playwright and short-story writer, was a close friend of SH; he was a founder with Stephen Rea of the Field Day Theatre Company on the board of which he and SH served together. The first play staged by Field Day was Friel's *Translations* in the Guildhall in Derry in 1980; SH's review of Friel's play *Volunteers* in the *TLS* was headed 'Digging Deeper'. Both plays share SH's interests in archaeological and linguistic themes.

PART ONE

The Underground

First published in *Thames Poetry*, 2. 9 (Feb. 1981): 5, and then in *Sequoia*, 27. 3 (Autumn 1983): 1, and *Poetry Ireland Review*, 9 (Winter 1983–4): 23. Collected with revisions in *SI* and subsequently included in *NSP1990*, *OG* and *100P*. Also published as a limited-edition broadside on 7 April 1991 by the Folger Shakespeare Library for the inaugural reading in the Folger Poetry Board Reading series.

1 running,] running: *Thames Poetry*
3 me, me then] me – me, then, *Thames Poetry*
5 japped] slashed *Thames Poetry*, *Sequoia*
6 wild] wide *Poetry Ireland Review*
7 fell] feel *Poetry Ireland Review* [obvious error]
8 Underground] underground *Thames Poetry*, *Sequoia*, *Poetry Ireland Review*   moonlighting] mooning around *NSP1990*, *OG*, *100P*   for] from *Poetry Ireland Review* [again, an obvious error?]
10 that] the *Thames Poetry*

The occasion was the Heaneys' honeymoon in London when they went by Underground to the Royal Albert Hall. There is a vaulted tunnel from South Kensington Station towards the Albert Hall.

11ff. The story of Hansel and Gretel morphs ominously into the myth of Orpheus (*l.* 16), after the poem's opening with the myth of Syrinx, who was pursued by Pan ('a fleet god', humorously identified with the poet) and turned into a reed (*l.* 4).

La Toilette

First published in *Horizon* (June 1984): 27, and collected with revisions in *SI*.

2 wet,] wet *Horizon*
3 first coldness] magnolia coolness *Horizon*
12 slub] slubbed *Horizon*

Title Working titles in TS 'Receiving' and 'Le Bain'.
5–6 'Do you not know that your body is a temple of the Holy Spirit?' (1 Corinthians 6:19).
7–8 The lidded chalice was covered with small, divided cloth drapes.
9 *chasuble*: the topmost garment worn by the Mass celebrant.
12 *slub silk*: medium-weight silk fabric, here associated with female undergarments.

Sloe Gin

First published in the *Listener* (23 and 30 Dec. 1982): 38, and in *Poetry Ireland Review*, 9 (Winter 1983–4): 24. Collected with revisions in *SI* and subsequently included in *NSP1990* and *OG*.

2, 4, 6, 8, 10, 12, 14, 16] [indented] *Listener*
5 unscrewed it] screwed the lid off *Listener*
13–16] in smoky, polished / blue-black sloes, / bitter and reliable. *Listener*
14–15 blue-black, / polished sloes,] blue- / black slows, *OG*
15–16 bitter / and dependable.] savage / and reliable. *Poetry Ireland Review*

Dated 18 January 1981 in MS.

12 *Betelgeuse*: the second brightest star in the constellation Orion. It is not particularly 'flaming', as this synaesthetic reference suggests.

Away from it All

Published in *SI*.

SH provided the following note on this poem, at the end of *SI* (122):

> '*I was stretched* . . .' from Czeslaw Milosz's *Native Realm* (University of California Press, 1981), p. 125.

Title Implication of being away from the challenges of Northern Irish Troubles perhaps, with an air of guilt at the life of self-indulgence (as in 'Oysters', *FW*, 3; *PSH*, 217), reinforced by the cold steel of the cruel forking of the lobster (*l*. 3). SH tells O'Driscoll that the poem is concerned with the dilemma of deciding between declaring active political interest or the artist's 'contemplation / of a motionless point' as in the quotation from Czesław Miłosz's *Native Realm* (*ll*. 22–5). Working titles for the poem in TS were 'Home from Home' and, somewhat confusingly, 'An Ulster Twilight', under which title a separate poem had already been published in 1977 that SH had also gathered in *SI* (38–9; *PSH*, 305).

8 *we*: the poet and his interlocutor, Brian Friel (information from Marie Heaney).

13ff. The to-and-fro of the conversational 'conclave' echoes the book's cover image from a medieval edition of Giraldus Cambrensis (*c*.1146–*c*.1223) showing two oarsmen, working, it seems, against each other.

16 *hard at it*: not working but drinking, requiring the 'rehearsed alibis' from Miłosz's participation 'actively in history' (*l*. 25).

30 *inanition*: a striking word in the context of the IRA hunger strikes of 1980–1. Cf. the graphic and surreal imagining of the experience of two hunger strikers in 'Station Island' IX (*PSH*, 331).

35 *fortified*: a term from food and drink, ironic given the fate of the tortured lobster.

Chekhov on Sakhalin

First published in the Field Day Theatre Company programme for Brian Friel's *Three Sisters* (1981): [8], then in the *New Statesman* (29 Jan. 1982): 21, and the *Cumberland Poetry Review* (Spring 1982): 28–9. It was also published as a leaflet to mark SH's receipt of the Bennett Award 1982 from the *Hudson Review*, at a ceremony in New York City on 16 November 1982. Collected with revisions in *SI* and subsequently included in *NSP1990* and *OG*.

Dedication] [no dedication] *Three Sisters*, *New Statesman*, *Cumberland Poetry Review*
3 north] there] *NSP*
5 Tyumin] Tyumen *OG*
9 north,] north *Three Sisters*, *New Statesman*, *Cumberland Poetry Review*
9–11] So far away, Moscow was like lost youth. / And who was he, to savour in his mouth / Fine spirits that the puzzled literati *NSP1990*, *OG*
10 an ulcer in the mouth] 'an ulcer in the mouth' *New Statesman*, *Cumberland Poetry Review*
13 counter?] counter. *New Statesman*
14 At least that meant he knew its worth.] That meant he knew its worth, at least. *Three Sisters*
16 glass] glass. *Three Sisters*
17–20 This stanza does not appear in the *Three Sisters* version
18 pert young] old bitch's *Cumberland Poetry Review*
19 Inviolable and affronting.] It was too much, it affronted suffering. *New Statesman*, *Cumberland Poetry Review*
23 In the months to come] All through the months to come *NSP1990*, *OG*
Postscript] In the programme for Friel's *Three Sisters* the following note by SH appears beneath the poem:

> CHEKHOV ON SAKHALIN was inspired by talks with Brian Friel about Chekhov and is dedicated to everybody involved with this production of THREE SISTERS. In 1890, Chekhov surprised his literary friends by going to live on the convict island of Sakhalin. He worked hard at gathering and marshalling facts about conditions there and, when he had published his findings in a book, wrote that he was glad that this 'rough convict's smock will hang in my literary wardrobe.' On his way to the island Chekhov had been much impressed by the cursing of Siberian coachmen and ferrymen. 'May you get an ulcer in the mouth!' was the only curse he felt he could print.

Postscript] In the *Cumberland Poetry Review*, the following 'Editor's Note' appears after the poem:

It was in 1890 that Chekhov, as a physician, visited the settlement on the Pacific island of Sakhalin. This was before he wrote most of the stories and plays for which he is remembered.

SH provided the following note on this poem, at the end of *SI* (122):

> Chekhov's friends presented him with a bottle of cognac on the eve of his departure for the prison island of Sakhalin, where he spent the summer of 1890 interviewing all the criminals and political prisoners. His book on conditions in the penal colony was published in 1895.

Title Sakhalin is a Russian island, north of Japan. The writer Anton Chekhov (1860–1904) went there in the summer and autumn of 1890 to conduct a medical research project in the penal colony though he was already suffering from tuberculosis himself. There is a Chekhov Museum there. His travel notes, called 'Sakhalin Island', describe his experiences and research there, as well as his revulsion from the savagery of its punishments (*l.* 26). Before setting off for Sakhalin he drank the bottle of cognac he had been given: an indulgence like the lobster in the previous poem here. SH tells O'Driscoll that if he had followed the logic of this poem, he would have gone to the Maze Prison where the Republican prisoners were on hunger strike, as Chekhov went to Sakhalin (*SS*, 259).

Dedication Derek Mahon (1941–2020) was poetry editor of the *New Statesman* when this poem appeared, which may explain the absence of the poem's dedication in that publication.

Sandstone Keepsake

First published in the *New Yorker* (9 July 1984): 36. Collected with revisions in *SI* and subsequently included in *NSP1990* and *OG*.

1 chalky russet] chalky-russet *New Yorker*

SH provided the following note on this poem, at the end of *SI*:

> Guy de Montfort. See *Inferno*, 12.118–20, and also Dorothy Sayers's note in her translation (Penguin Classics).

10 *the camp*: Magilligan Prison at Limavady, Co. Derry. Visible across Lough Foyle from Inishowen (*ll.* 7, 18). *Phlegethon*: the river of fire and boiling blood, one of the five rivers in Hades (Dante, *Inferno*, 12.117ff.) in the seventh circle of Hell which punishes people guilty of crimes of violence, such as murder and tyranny.

14 *Guy de Montfort*: son of Simon de Montfort who led the English barons against Henry III. Simon was killed by Henry's son Edward at the Battle of Evesham in 1265. In 1271 Guy avenged his

father by killing the king's nephew Henry of Almayne in a church at Viterbo, an act of both violence and sacrilege. The heart of the peacemaker Henry of Almayne was put in a casket and placed on a pillar over London Bridge, or in the hand of his statue in Westminster Abbey (*l.* 16).

19 *free state*: punning on the cross-border vantage point and the Irish Free State of 1922, though, as often in SH, metaphorically the 'free state of image and allusion' is language.

24 *the venerators*: usually of the practice of art and language in SH: in contrast perhaps to Shelley's poets as 'legislators' of the world who do 'set things wrong or right' (*l.* 23).

Shelf Life

Title Shelf Life is a very Heaneyesque title (like 'field work' or 'wintering out') in the way it develops a theme subtly different from what it suggests. It means 'the durability of things', which is one of the major themes of this book (as in 'Iron Spike').

1 GRANITE CHIP

Published in *SI* and later included in *NSP1990* and *OG*.

1 Aberdeen, north Scotland, known as 'the granite city'.

2 *Hamlet*, 5.2.271–2: 'The king shall drink to Hamlet's better breath / And in the cup an union shall he throw.' A union is a precious pearl; but what the king Claudius has put in the cup is poison intended for Hamlet, which in the event kills his mother.

11 'Come to me, all of you who are weary and burdened, and I will give you rest' (Matthew 11:28).

12–13 *Seize / the day*: *carpe diem*, Horace, *Odes*, 1.

2 OLD SMOOTHING IRON

Published in *SI* and in *In Touch* 2 (1985): 30. Subsequently included in *NSP1990* and *OG*.

5–6 by ear / she spat] she'd stare / and spit] *NSP1990*, *OG*
8 divine the] imagine the *In Touch* 2
10 dimpled] dimpled, *In Touch* 2
17 distance,] distance *In Touch* 2
18–20] distance – / so you'll salvage words for the iron / exact and equal to it, / and make them pull their weight, // each one like a single, built-up / orthopaedic boot, / or a diver's soled with lead / and dragging what was buoyant. *In Touch* 2

3 OLD PEWTER

First published as 'Pewters', the third in a three-part sequence called 'Shelf Life' in *Outposts: Poetry Quarterly*, 138 (Autumn 1983): 72–3 (the other two poems, 'Old Perfume Bottle' and 'Pussy Willow', are uncollected). Collected with revisions in *SI*.

3–4] Amoeba-glows in an old pewter plate / full of nebulae, molten and temperate. *Outposts*
5–16 In *Outposts*, the remaining four stanzas read as follows:

> *Odi et amo*, glimmers I am composed of.
> Numinous sludge, far conscience-glitters
> and the hang-dog, half-truth earnests of true love
> And [*sic*] a whole blizzard-melt of ancestors.
>
> Old pewter, my masters! A soft option
> when it comes to metals – next to solder
> that beals at the touch of a hot iron.
> Doleful and placid as the gloss-barked alder
>
> reflected in the glaucous lid of a pool
> where they thought I had drowned one winter day
> in nineteen forty-two or three, when the whole
> country was mist and I hid deliberately.

4 IRON SPIKE

First published as 'An Iron Spike' in *American Poetry Review* (July/Aug. 1983): 48. Collected in *SI*, and later published as a limited-edition broadside by William B. Ewert, Concord, New Hampshire, in June 1992.

8^9] In *American Poetry Review* there is an additional stanza:

> It flakes like dead maple leaves
> in the track of the old railway,
> eaten at and weathered
> like birch stumps dressed by beavers.

11 ditch growth] ditch-growth *American Poetry Review*
13] in its still, grassed-over path *American Poetry Review*
15–16] or a dialect word of my own / warm from a stranger's mouth. *American Poetry Review*
17 sank] drove *American Poetry Review*
21] And its sweat-cured, polished haft? *American Poetry Review*
22 the ones] those ones *American Poetry Review*

5 *Eagle Pond, New Hampshire*: the home of the poets Donald Hall and Jane Kenyon, where Hall grew up. The couple were friendly with the Heaneys.

5 STONE FROM DELPHI

First published in the limited-edition *Mandeville's Travellers* (Hitchin, Herts: Mandeville Press, 1984). Collected with revisions in *SI* and subsequently included in *NSP1990* and *OG*.

Title By 1984, SH had not yet been to Delphi so the source of the stone is not known.

4ff. Oliver Taplin (2019, 15), like Helen Vendler, reads these italicised lines as a hymn to Apollo.

5 *govern the tongue*: a favourite idea for SH, as in the title of his next collection of critical prose, *GT*.

6 A SNOWSHOE

First published as 'Alba' in *Hibernia* (27 April 1978): 22, and collected with revisions in *SI*. In TS (NLI 49,493/49) the title had likewise been 'Alba'.

3 longhand] cursive *Hibernia*
5 snow goose] snow-goose *Hibernia*
6 I left the room after an] I got up after our *Hibernia*
7 and climbed up attic stairs like a somnambulist,] And climbed the attic stair: somnambulist *Hibernia*
8 scuffling the] scuffling over the *Hibernia*
9–10 Then I sat there writing, imagining in silence / sounds like] And so I hear myself on the white expanse / Make sounds like *Hibernia*
10 abstinence,] abstinence: *Hibernia*
12 a snowshoe] the snowshoe *Hibernia*
13–16] Now the loop of the snowshoe, like an old-time kite,
     Lifts in a swish of wind, is lost to sight.
     Now buoyant over drifts, at a dream's pace
     I face back into your white distances. *Hibernia*

Title 'Mercury Snowbound' in TS.

A Migration

First published as 'A Deer in Glanmore' in the *London Review of Books* (25 Oct. 1979): 20, and then collected with revisions in *SI*.

dedication [no dedication]] *for B.C. LRB*
41 names,] names *LRB*
42 'Hurry', hurry past,] hurry, hurry past *LRB*
43 a spill of] a stone's-throw of *LRB*
45–8] With their margarine boxes, / pram wheels and biscuit tins, / they had missed their last bus on that first night in Dublin *LRB*
49–54 [omitted] *LRB*
55–6] and walked miles of suburbs / all through the small hours. *LRB*
59 street arabs] street-arabs *LRB*
63 night lights] night-lights *LRB*

64 entries] churchyards *LRB*
65 swelling] sturdy *LRB*
73–8] Brigid, now I am Davin / walking a dark road, / you are the young woman / who crept into his head / out of a roadside cabin / still following, and followed. *LRB*

Dated 5 February 1979 in MS (NLI 49,493/61); working title 'A Deer for Brigid Coyle' (NLI 49,493/50).

Marie Heaney identifies the event and the family as people called Coyle from Lincolnshire who arrived to live in a cottage near Glanmore Castle, not far from the Heaneys in Wicklow. Brigid's mother, Minnie, came from Donegal, and her father from Galway. Much of the detail in the poem suggests negative associations with the Troubles: black taxi (*l*. 18), bombed station (*l*. 19). In the *LRB* version, Brigid is linked at the end to the young woman encountered by Davin in Joyce's *A Portrait of the Artist as a Young Man*. Cf. italicised epigraph to 'A Bat on the Road' (*SI*, 40–1; *PSH*, 306).

Last Look

First published as 'A Cart for Edward Gallagher' in the *Recorder*, 40 (1979): 40–3, and in the *Times Literary Supplement* (8 Feb. 1980): 136. The poem also appeared under this title in Kevin M. Cahill (ed.), *The American Irish Revival: A Decade of 'The Recorder', 1974–1983* (Port Washington, NY, and London: Associated Faculty Press, 1984), 39–41. These printings and variants are recorded in the notes on the Uncollected Poems 1975–1979 (*PSH*, 856). It was first published as 'Last Look' in *Illuminations* (Autumn 1982): 1, then collected in *SI*.

Dated 2 and 5 February 1979 in MS (NLI 49,493/61).

Dedication: *in memoriam E.G*: he is named in full on the RTÉ recording where SH says 'in memoriam Edward Gallagher'. Gallagher sold groceries from a horse-drawn cart. Presumably he is the older man watching a field over a gate at the beginning, absorbed in reflections on his past.

30 *Niamh*: legendary Irish queen of great beauty. She carried her lover Oisín away with her to Tír na nÓg, the Land of Youth. Oisín appears towards the end of 'A Cart for Edward Gallagher' (*PSH*, 254).

Remembering Malibu

Published as a limited edition by Scripps College Press, Claremont, California, 1982, with an accompanying linocut by Carol Wehrmann; a second edition was published in 1983. Also published in *Fiction Magazine*

(Autumn 1982): 29, and the *Recorder*, 43 (1982): 61–2, *Sequoia* (Autumn 1983): 3, and Kevin M. Cahill (ed.), *The American Irish Revival: A Decade of 'The Recorder', 1974–1983* (Port Washington, NY, and London: Associated Faculty Press, 1984), 44–5. Collected with revisions in *SI* and later published in the *Sunday Tribune* (17 Jan. 1999): 2, to mark the death of Brian Moore, with the following note by SH:

> This poem is about the windblown day on the beach at Malibu when we visited Brian Moore in 1971. It was a truly Pacific experience. Obviously we were talking about Belfast and the whole Northern Irish Catholic culture that we shared – asceticism and repression and self-denial and all that. About how we were more prepared by our background to go barefoot on a pilgrim's path on, say, the Skelligs, than to go barefoot on a pleasure beach in California. But Brian had made the journey, nevertheless.

2 notion] notions *Fiction, Recorder, American Irish Revival*
6 our] your *Recorder, American Irish Revival*
12 sea noise] sea-noise *Fiction, Recorder, Sequoia, American Irish Revival*
14 I'd] I *Fiction*] I had *Recorder, American Irish Revival*
18 the Great Skellig] Skellig Michael *Fiction, Recorder*
21 my instep.] our insteps. *Fiction, Recorder, American Irish Revival*
22 shoe – // beside] shoe! // Beside *Fiction, Recorder, Sequoia, American Irish Revival*

Dedication Brian Moore was a celebrated Irish novelist (1921–99), born in Belfast, who emigrated to Canada and later lived in Malibu, California where he and his wife Jean were visited by the Heaneys in 1971 and visited them in turn on return trips to Ireland.

9 Piet Mondrian (1872–1944), Dutch painter, most associated with geometrical blocks of primary colours.

17–18 *Atlantic storms . . . the Great Skellig*: Moore's first major success was the novel *Catholics* (1972), set on an offshore Irish monastic island.

20 *the graveyard and the boatslip*: from the top to the foot of the Great Skellig, a vertiginous path.

22 *cast that shoe*: a liberation from physical duty (equine).

26 *footsteps filled with blowing sand*: recalling stories of St Columba whose shoes were filled with Irish soil after his departure to Iona.

Making Strange

First published in *Ploughshares*, 5. 3 (1979): 24, under the title 'Near Anahorish'; and then as 'Near Anahorish: A Visitation', in the *London Review of Books* (25 Oct. 1979): 20. Collected with revisions in *SI*, the poem subsequently appeared in *Envoy*, 47 (1985): 2, *NSP1990* and *OG*.

No dedication] For Louis Simpson *LRB*
Form] In *Ploughshares* and the *LRB*, the poem is arranged in two sections numbered I. and II.; the first comprises two four-line stanzas; the second is a single fourteen-line verse paragraph.
2 travelled] tawny *Ploughshares* | scanning] *LRB*
3–4] and fencer's containment, / his speech like a bowstring, *Ploughshares*
9–10 a cunning middle voice / came out of the field] the cunning voice of poetry / came out of the wood *Ploughshares*
9 a cunning middle voice] the cunning voice of poetry *LRB*
22 departures] betrayals *Ploughshares*
22 go back] renege *Ploughshares*
23–8 These lines do not appear in the *Ploughshares* or *LRB* versions.

Dated Cambridge, Massachusetts, 2 February 1979 in TS.

Title Irish phrase to describe the shyness of a child. Typescripts carry a working title, 'The Stranger'.

2ff. 'the one' is the American poet Louis Simpson; 'another' (*l.* 5) is SH's father.

16 *Boaz*: in the biblical Book of Ruth, Naomi is a foreigner who finds favour in the cornfields of Boaz.

The Birthplace

First published in the *London Review of Books* (7–20 Oct. 1982): 20, and in the *New England Review and Bread Loaf Quarterly*, 5. 4 (Summer 1983): 567–8, where it is accompanied by the following reflection on the theme of this issue, 'Writers in the Nuclear Age':

> The poem I have always cherished in this context is Edwin Muir's 'The Horses' which conveys gravely and tenderly a sense of the world emptied and then the world stirring to replenish itself. Yet by now Muir's vision can feel almost too consoling, though its consolations are a true effect of its wisdoms. Muir could trust the memories of his archaic Orcadian culture and weave a minimal shelter out of that remote ghost-life. It struck me that 'The Birthplace', which had no intention of being a 'nuclear' poem, nevertheless touches upon our inability to trust too far a language of continuity: words, especially hallowed words, can now turn into weightless chimaeras. Yet they remain our truest means of sifting the chances of earth and pledging ourselves to a possible life in a threatened future. The best art continues to find occasions where it is possible to contemplate, without being overwhelmed, man pitted against dread.

After collection in *SI*, the poem appeared again in the *New England Review*, 15. 1 (Winter 1993), the fifteenth anniversary issue, and later in *OG*.

I 3^4] [no stanza break] *LRB, NER1983, NER1993*
I 5 ghost life] ghost-life *LRB, NER1983, NER1993*

I 6 round] around *NER1983*, *NER1993*
I 6^7] [no stanza break] *LRB*, *NER1983*, *NER1993*
I 8 market,] market *LRB*, *NER1983*, *NER1993*
II 1 pairs] couples *OG*
II 8 heat-struck] heart-struck *NER1993*
III 4 We come back] So we go back *LRB*
III 9–10 weights // afloat] weights / afloat *LRB*
III 15–16 aftergrass // verified] aftergrass / verified *LRB*

Dated 3–7 August [1982?] in MS.

Title The birthplace of Thomas Hardy is at Upper Bockhampton near Stinsford in Dorset. His heart is buried in the graveyard at Stinsford. SH tells Dennis O'Driscoll that he read Hardy's 'The Darkling Thrush' in the graveyard there on 31 December 2000, to mark a hundred years since Hardy wrote and dated the poem (*SS*, 252).

III 1 'To be everywhere is to be nowhere,' Seneca (4 BCE–65 CE), *Letters from a Stoic*.

III 14 *The Return of the Native* by Thomas Hardy (1878).

Changes

First published in the *London Review of Books* (18 Sept.–1 Oct. 1980): 10, and then in Michael Mason (ed.), *London Review of Books: Anthology One* (London: Junction Books, 1981), 13. Also published in *Antaeus* (Autumn 1984): 90–1, and in *Pequod*, 16–17 (1984): 36. Collected with revisions in *SI*, and later included in *OG*.

13 speckly white] speckled and white *LRB*
14 on] in *LRB*
21 in the rusted bend of the spout] from the rusted bend of the snout *LRB*
22 tail feathers] tail-feathers *LRB*, *Pequod*
25–6] when you fear you have grown up at last / and come forever to the empty city.' *LRB*

Dated 31 July 1980 in TS (NLI 49,493/58).

Title SH tells Dennis O'Driscoll that the title comes from the Chinese *I Ching* (*The Book of Changes*) (*SS*, 255).

24 *you*: taken by Dennis O'Driscoll to be one of SH's children (*SS*, 235).

An Ulster Twilight

First published as 'The Workshop' in the *RTÉ Guide* (23 Dec. 1977): 3, and then on a limited-edition Christmas card printed by Peter Fallon in 1978. Published as 'An Ulster Twilight' in *Outposts*, 129 (Summer 1981): 3, and in the *New Statesman* (17/24 Dec. 1982): 43, and collected with revisions in *SI*.

13] Eric Dawson, where are you now? *New Statesman*
16 him] you *New Statesman*
18 his] your *New Statesman*
20 was] is *New Statesman*
21 his] your *New Statesman*
26 monkey-wrench] monkey wrench *New Statesman*
34 uniform] black tunic *New Statesman*

Title Derived from Daniel Corkery's *A Munster Twilight* (1917), a collection of short stories mostly set in the countryside of West Cork, in the same way as the 'hidden Ulster' derived from Corkery's *The Hidden Ireland*.

4 *Eric Dawson*: a member of a family of Protestant neighbours with whom the Heaneys were on very good terms (*SS*, 18).

A Bat on the Road

First published under the title 'Davin on the Broagh Road' in *Broadsheet*, unnumbered edition [Feb. 1983]: 2, and in *Pequod* 16–17 (1984): 38. Collected with revisions in *SI*, and included in *OG*.

Epigraph] Portrait of the Artist as a Young Man [attribution] *Pequod*
8 Railway] railway *Pequod*
11 tennis court] tennis-court *Pequod*
14 netting wire] netting-wire *Pequod*
21 deckled,] deckled *Pequod*
23 liked.] liked! *Pequod*

Originally 'Davin on the Broagh Road'. See Jonathan Allison, 'The Erotics of Heaney's Joyce' (*Colby Quarterly* 30. 1 (March 1994)).

Epigraph In *A Portrait of the Artist as a Young Man*, Stephen's friend Davin tells him about a young woman who invited him into her house in the countryside late at night where she is alone; he refused the offer and watched her standing in the doorway as he walked away. Stephen sees reflected in her 'other figures of the peasant women he had seen standing in the doorways at Clane as the college cars drove by, as a type of her race and his own, a batlike soul waking to the consciousness of itself in darkness and secrecy and loneliness and, through the eyes and voice and gesture of a woman without guile, calling the stranger to her bed' (Joyce 1992, 198). Stephen uses the image of bats several times in relation to Ireland. SH had used it in 'A Drink of Water' (*FW*, 8; *PSH*, 220), also in relation to a woman.

In this poem, the Joycean allusion unravels along the Broagh Road of Heaney's childhood, as the original title suggests. In private correspondence with the editors, Eugene Kielt identified the 'stone bridge' (l. 7) as a railway bridge over the river Moyola close to a redbrick and black stone house called The Bungalow. The house was built in 1906 by the Clark family who owned the linen factory in Castledawson where several members of Heaney's mother's family, the McCanns, worked. The Bungalow, which had both a tennis court and white gates, was a short distance from Heaney's father's birthplace in one direction, and from Mossbawn in the other. The Clarks were related to James Chichester-Clark – prime minister of Northern Ireland between 1969 and 1971, and later Baron Moyola, whose family seat was Moyola Park, at Castledawson – and to the novelist Joyce Cary (1888–1957).

11 *tennis court*: suggesting that on the grounds of The Bungalow.

17 Davin tells Stephen that 'she stood so close to me I could hear her breathing' (Joyce 1992, 198).

22 *the White Gates*: again, suggesting those of The Bungalow.

23 The italicised sentence is the culmination of the theme of male fantasy through the poem.

A Hazel Stick for Catherine Ann

First published on a limited-edition Christmas card printed by Peter Fallon in 1983, then in *SI*, and included in *NSP1990*, *OG* and *100P*.

24 cut] pared *OG*, *100P*

The events of this poem, dedicated to SH's daughter, are localised by Marie Heaney to the south-east of France in 1981.

A Kite for Michael and Christopher

First published in *Ploughshares*, 5. 3 (1979): 23, then in *FA*, 3–7, and in *Aquarius* (Dec. 1980): 34–5. After collection in *SI*, the poem was also included in *NSP1990*, *OG* and *100P*.

2 above Sunday] above the Sunday *Ploughshares*
16 weigh] weighs *Ploughshares*, *NSP1990*, *OG*, *100P*

A companion poem to the preceding one, dedicated to SH's two sons. It is echoed in the last poem in *HC*: 'A Kite for Aibhín', for the daughter of his son Michael (*HC*, 85; *PSH*, 682). SH tells Dennis O'Driscoll that the poem is based on a memory of his father launching such a home-made kite in his own childhood (*SS*, 254).

12 The friend has been identified as Michael Longley.

21 Perhaps an echo of the penultimate line of Hopkins's 'Spring and Fall': 'It is the blight man was born for.'

The Railway Children

First published in Andrew Motion (ed.), *Poetry Book Supplement 1981* (Christmas 1981): 16, then in *Antaeus* (Autumn 1984): 92. Collected in *SI* and subsequently included in *NSP1990*, *OG* and *100P*. The poem appeared on a poster in the Poems on the Underground series in January 1986.

5–6 us, sagging / Under] us, / Sagging under *Poetry Book Supplement*
8 though words] thought that words *Poetry Book Supplement*

Title A children's book written by E. Nesbit in 1905, frequently adapted for the screen, though without much bearing on the poem. SH tells Dennis O'Driscoll that the poem was written quickly one afternoon in Carysfort (*SS*, 254). The remarkably literal description of the view from the railway cutting in Broagh is perpetuated by a photograph by Larry Herman of the young Heaney family there, reproduced in the schools' anthology *Worlds* by Geoffrey Summerfield (Harmondsworth: Penguin, 1974).

Sweetpea

Published in *SI*.

12 'her' refers to Mary Heaney, SH's aunt with whom he tended the garden.

An Aisling in the Burren

Published in *SI*.

Title Originally envisioned for the SWEENEY REDIVIVUS sequence in *SI* under the title 'His Vision in the Burren'. The aisling is an Irish poetic form, most prominently associated with eighteenth-century political poetry, in which a female figure representing Ireland appears in a vision to the poet, lamenting her woes, already familiar in the SH corpus from the poem 'Aisling' (*North*, 51; *PSH*, 197). (See SH's note on 'The Glamoured' in *TSH*, 576–7.) In this poem she is lamenting the condition of modern Troubles-era Ireland, and the poet seeks consolation from the seashore of the Burren in the north of Co. Clare (though the 'northern shore' and the 'dulse' of l. 3 primarily evoke the landscape of SH's native Northern Ireland from which he is exiled).

9 'she', the visionary figure, may also evoke Sonja Landweer, the Dutch potter who was the partner of the painter Barrie Cooke. SH

collaborated with both of them at many stages of his career. She is the subject of the poem 'To a Dutch Potter in Ireland' (*SL*, 2–4; *PSH*, 463).

10 *St Elmo*: St Elmo's fire is a light phenomenon caused by plasma in the atmosphere, sometimes found by rocky shores. In 'To a Dutch Potter in Ireland', Landseer as a child is imagined as 'luminous with plankton, / A nymph of phosphor by the Norder Zee' (*SL*, 2) and later working with 'glazes' which 'as you say, bring down the sun' (*SL*, 3).

Widgeon

First published in *Aquarius* (Dec. 1980): 35, and after collection in *SI* also included in *OG*.

TS titles include 'Decoy', and also 'Widgeon Cries', which carried a second and third part, cancelled in typescript (NLI 49,493/58):

> ii
> Widgeon was you[r] pet-name
>
> but, widgeon,
>
> if I call you alder
> the last drops of a shower
> blow across my face,
>
> silk enters the wind
> and a starry grass
> brushes your ankles.
>
> iii
> A great bell-mouth of air,
> the tongue pliant
> among caesurae:
>
> et bendictus
> fructus ventris tuae . . .
>
> Windfall, plumlines,
> my little
> apple-bellied Eve.

Dedication Paul Muldoon (b.1951), Irish poet, was a student of SH's at Queen's University Belfast.

Sheelagh na Gig

First published as 'Síle na Gig' in Glenn Storhaug (ed.), *The Kilpeck Anthology* (Hereford: Five Seasons Press, 1981), 18–19. Collected as 'Sheelagh na Gig' in *SI* and later included in *OG*.

II 2 barn] outhouse *Kilpeck Anthology*
II 9 rat hole] rathole *Kilpeck Anthology*
II 14 under heavy] under the heavy *Kilpeck Anthology*
III 4 flat,] flat – *Kilpeck Anthology*
III 7 grown-up] grown up *Kilpeck Anthology*
III 9 'Yes, look] 'Look *Kilpeck Anthology*

TSS under the working titles 'At Kilpeck' dated Bradley Court, 30 July 1980, and 'The Figures at Kilpeck' (NLI 49,493/60). An entirely different SH poem of the same title was published in *Soundings* (1972) (*PSH*, 112).

Title Also 'sheela-na-gig' and 'Síle na gig': architectural figures of naked women displaying and drawing attention to their exaggerated vulva. Found across western Europe from about 1000 BCE, and commonly in Ireland, mostly within Romanesque religious sculpture. The etymology of the term is obscure; in Irish, *Síle* may be a standard female name, and *na gig* might be derived from *na gCíoch*, 'of the breasts' – though breasts are not the most prominent bodily feature.

Epigraph *at Kilpeck*: there is a particularly expressive sheela-na-gig at the church of St Mary and St David at Kilpeck in Herefordshire, a small twelfth-century Norman church, visited by SH with Barrie Cooke.

The Loaning

Part I first published as 'The Loaning' in the *London Review of Books* (5–18 Feb. 1981): 11, and Parts I–III published under the same title in the *Sunday Tribune Magazine* (27 Dec. 1981): 4, and in *Cumberland Poetry Review* (Spring 1982): 30–1, and *Antaeus* (Autumn 1984): 93–4. Collected with revisions in *SI*. Part III published under the title '"Aye"' in *OG*.

Title] in *OG* the title 'Aye' is followed by the incorrect attribution (*from* 'The Loaning') | in the *Cumberland Poetry Review*, the title is accompanied by the following: '*Editors' Note*: See *Shorter Oxford English Dictionary*: "Loaning: an open uncultivated piece of ground near a farm house or village, on which the cows are milked."'
I 1–2 loaning / the wind shifting] loaning to the fields / the wind shifting *LRB* | loaning to the fields / the wind whispering *Sunday Tribune Magazine*
I 2–3 hedge was like / an old] hedge / was like an old *LRB*
I 3 whistling speech. And] whispering speech. Then *Sunday Tribune Magazine*

I 3–4 speech. And I knew / I was in the limbo of lost words.] speech. / I knew then I was in the limbo of lost words. *LRB* | speech. Then I knew / I was *Cumberland Poetry Review*

I 5 raftered sheds] outhouses *LRB, Sunday Tribune Magazine, Cumberland Poetry Review*

I 6 the shelter of gable ends and turned-up carts.] under rotten carts and churchyard walls. *LRB* | under churchyard walls and turned-up carts *Sunday Tribune Magazine, Cumberland Poetry Review* | the shelter of church gables and turned-up carts. *Antaeus*

I 8–9] to nest a while in those old places, then *LRB* | and fluttering over bedsteads / until the soul would leave the body. *Cumberland Poetry Review*

I 10 Then on] on *LRB*

I 11–12] rising in smoky clouds on the summer sky / to settle in the uvulae of mossed stones *LRB*

I 14 Then I knew why] I knew then why *LRB*

I 15–17] the loaning breathed upon me / though now each hole in the hedge was blowing cold / as I went stooped and shivering beneath / the spit blood of a few last haws and rose-hips. *LRB*

II 1 Big] Bit *Sunday Tribune Magazine* (error)

II 6 again and, when] again, and when *Cumberland Poetry Review*

II 7 boy! I] boy! / I *OG* [the line becomes two half-lines]

III 2 High-tension] High tension *Sunday Tribune Magazine, Cumberland Poetry Review, Antaeus*

III 3 singing] sizzling *Sunday Tribune Magazine, Cumberland Poetry Review, Antaeus*

III 4 [omitted] *Antaeus*

III 5 always] always, *Sunday Tribune Magazine, Cumberland Poetry Review*

III 9 When] In the *Sunday Tribune Magazine* (left aligned)

III 10 old first] first old *Sunday Tribune Magazine*

III 11 make there . . .] would make . . . *Sunday Tribune Magazine, Cumberland Poetry Review, Antaeus*

III 15 cell lock] cell-lock *Antaeus*

III 16] [omitted] *Sunday Tribune Magazine, Cumberland Poetry Review*

Dated 2 January 1981 in MS (NLI 49,493/58). Dedicated 'for Derek and Doreen Mahon' in TS.

Title Loaning is a Northern Irish term for a narrow grassy lane in the countryside by the side of a house. See note on Title above.

I 3 *an old one*: an old woman.

I 12–13 Uvulae and lungs are voice-producing organs, in a poem that is largely focused on sound.

II 1 *Big voices*: the voices of the 'big-voiced Scullions', SH's forebears.

III 12ff. Dante, *Inferno*, 13.40–2; the voice is that of Pier delle Vigne (d.1249).

III 16 *introibo*: the first word of the Latin Mass, 'I shall go (to the altar of God)'.

III 17 *blood-red cigarette*: implication of torture.

The Sandpit

Published in *SI*.

1 1946

The four sections of this poem trace the stages of the child's sightings of a building project, from his first observation in Part 1 in 1946 (when SH was seven) of how the spade cuts the first sod, hitting a stone in the ground which sends a tremor up through the handle. The child's gardening at Bellaghy School with Master Murphy encounters 'the little clinks of spades and rakes and hoes on the occasional pebble' (*SS*, 244).

4 *scrabs*: Ulster dialect term for scratch or scrape.

2 THE DEMOBBED BRICKLAYER

The ex-soldier of the early part is Mick Joyce, a Corkman who was the brother-in-law of SH's father. SH remembers him arriving in Mossbawn in his khaki outfit (*SS*, 256); he was a medical orderly in the North African desert in World War II. He reappears in the poem 'To Mick Joyce in Heaven' (*DC*, 8; *PSH*, 595) and unnamed in the posthumous poem 'In a Field'. Here, demobbed, he returns from the sands of the desert to working with sand as a builder.

3 THE SAND BOOM

The gravel dug out from the pit used in the building process, an active industry that led to the boom in sand in the 1950s and after.

9 *cribs*: the sideboards of the wagon carrying sand or gravel. The fireball is caused by the ammunition that is used to 'blast' the gravel out of the rock, widening the stream at the bottom of the pit.

4 WHAT THE BRICK KEEPS

1 'His' refers to Mick Joyce's observations again, as he works on the building of the new estate. 'My own hands' at the end returns to the child's observation of the new buildings taking shape. 'What the brick keeps' is the history of its construction of the buildings.

The King of the Ditchbacks

An early version of part I of the poem was published under the title 'Shadowed' in *Fortnight*, 43 (July 1972): 20, and part III was published under the title 'The Pigeon Shoot' in the *New Yorker* (31 Jan. 1977): 34. The full poem was published under the title 'Sweeney Astray' in Andrew Carpenter and Peter Fallon (eds), *The Writers: A Sense of Ireland* (Dublin: O'Brien Press, 1980), 52–4. After collection with revisions in *SI* it was included in *NSP1990*, *Sweeney's Flight* and *OG*. In his note on this poem at the end of *SI*, SH referred readers to his note on Part Three [SWEENEY REDIVIVUS], reproduced below (*PSH*, 889).

I 3 the growth] the soft growth *Fortnight, The Writers*
I 10 grass] grasses *Fortnight, The Writers*
I 10–12 I stop / he stops / like the moon.] I stop, / he stops, like the moon / used to. *Fortnight*
I 14 weather-eyed] a haunter *Fortnight*] I stop / he stops, like the moon / used to. *The Writers*
I 17–20 This stanza does not appear in the *Fortnight* version.
I 18 his reflection] his pale reflection *The Writers*
I 21 haunted] shadowed *Fortnight*
I 22 rustling] melodies *Fortnight*
II ¶1 out the dormer] out of the dormer *The Writers*   on to an alder] on an alder *The Writers*   Small dreamself] Dream face *The Writers*
III Title] The Pigeon Shoot *New Yorker*
III 4 meshes] the branches *New Yorker*
III 11 wood –] wood, *New Yorker*] wood's *The Writers*
III 13 in silence.] like effigies. *New Yorker, The Writers*
III 14] None came, but I waited silent *New Yorker* | No birds came, but I waited silent *The Writers*
III 15–16 or whispered / or broke the watery gossamers] or whispered, / Or infringed waterlogged cobwebs *New Yorker*
III 20 gundogs] gun-dogs *The Writers*

Dated 18 March 1972 in MS under the title 'Initiate'.

Title 'Ditchback' probably dialect for 'ditchbank', the term for the clay-based fence called 'ditch' in Ireland or 'bank' in the poem (*l.* 7). The trespasser of the opening is significant for the effect of his action rather than in his own right, though his anonymity as a creature of the wild invites comparison with Sweeney in *SA*. As a figure for the impermanence of things, the ripping of the tangled grass here recalls the railway which can be lifted like a 'long briar' in 'Shelf Life' (*SI*, 23; *PSH*, 297), and the 'old bicycle wheel in a ditch / ripped at last from under jungling briars' in section IV of 'Station Island' (*SI*, 69; *PSH*, 323).

In typescript, part I had carried working title 'Trespasser', then 'Haunted', with 'Midas's Barber' briefly considered and discarded; part III carried 'Change of Life', then 'Initiate', before retitling as 'The Pigeon Shoot' and carrying a dedication 'for Robert Parker and Barrie Cooke'.

Dedication John Montague (1929–2016), Irish poet, was an older contemporary and friend of SH. His poem 'The Water Carrier' provides the epigraph to SH's 'Fosterling' (*ST*, 50; *PSH*, 426): 'That heavy greenness fostered by water.'

II ¶1 *I was sure I knew him*: the trespasser of part I, even more plausibly linked to Sweeney of *SA*.

II ¶2 This series of questions is reminiscent of the syntactic patterns in poems by T. S. Eliot such as 'Marina' (to which the answer is 'Death').

III This section establishes the link between the narrative first person with the poem's title and with the bird-figure Sweeney. The section corresponds closely to the MS archive poem 'The Island' (BC 1280725), both referring to the day when the Heaneys arrived in Co. Kilkenny to visit Cooke and Landweer in 1972 and sharing ritualistic-sounding references to the narrator's head 'dressed . . . in a fishnet' and a journey to 'a pigeon wood'.

PART TWO: STATION ISLAND

Station Island

SH provided the following note on the sequence that would comprise PART TWO: STATION ISLAND, at the end of *SI* (122):

> *Station Island* is a series of dream encounters with familiar ghosts, set on Station Island on Lough Derg in Co. Donegal. The island is also known as St Patrick's Purgatory because of a tradition that Patrick was the first to establish the penitential vigil of fasting and praying which still constitutes the basis of the three-day pilgrimage. Each unit of the contemporary pilgrim's exercises is called a 'station', and a large part of each station involves walking barefoot and praying round the 'beds', stone circles which are said to be the remains of early medieval monastic cells.

A formative moment is captured in a journal diary for the poem that SH kept between September 1979 and the summer of June 1983:

> September 4 1979
> On Saturday in Barry Cooke's I began what I hope will be a large undertaking, the poem I have been thinking about set on Lough Derg – a big open form that will turn like a wheel – one of those wheels laden with water scoops that go down empty and come up full. Here I hope to keep notes for the thing, images and drafts.
>   This morning the sea was bright with sunlight, the tide was in to the strand, Catherine was off to school again for the first time since

America – Marie off with her, the boys away to Conleth's. I posted cards and sat in the clear glittering weather, looking out at Howth Head, the smoke drifting a sulphurous dissolving brush from the Pigeon House, the red and white chimneys of the power station hallucinatory. I felt the lift I used to sense at the seaside in Portstewart, or on the coast at Dingle or Donegal. I felt that the seven years since leaving Belfast had paid off, that perhaps steady inward effort would be possible. I felt I could trust. I have been lucky but also I think I have worked to earn this. I pray to God or whatever means the good to keep us all safe here and to sustain this effort. I am now in the study upstairs. The trains rattle through the sunlit suburban morning, the birds chatter in the garden bushes, the red leaves of the creeper on the gable flutter. (NLI 49,493/57)

Progress was initially encouraging. Composition began on 4–5 September 1979 with manuscript passages that would become the concluding lines of section VIII. By mid-October, section V was under way; section II was started on 27 October; by November, section IX was also begun, and would incorporate an earlier poem, 'Contrition', that itself dated back to a MS draft of 30 July 1977 (NLI 49,493/58). But SH struggled to advance from a promising start and was unable to add to the poem for three months. He began a draft of section I in February 1980, and, in March that year, sketched materials that would be adapted for section XII, after which progress stalled altogether. SH admitted to becoming 'exhausted and despondent' at his inability to settle at the poem in the face of external commitments. He said the poem was akin to 'broken bare' ground: 'It is like a building site, abandoned in November. Cold. Mucky. Puddled. Promising. Hopeless. Tempting. Promising nothing but work. But hope still there, even as you shiver at the barefaced, broken nothingness of it all' (16 Nov. 1980, NLI 49,493/57).

Work on the poem didn't resume again until January 1981 with the beginnings of section VII. In a note at the time, SH recorded the pressing need to realise 'some developing scheme' within the poem: 'Now that I feel some grip on the way to do individual pieces, the next thing is to conceive the emerging shape, which should involve, I suppose, changes in the self, as well as definite developments in the kind of character encountered at different stages.' The poem was to trace a metamorphosis of spirit released from the fetlocks of tribal allegiance towards 'an emergence into a kind of independent life': one in which the imagination was freed, so that the writer might discover 'the necessary autonomy of the "artist" within the "domestic man"', and 'to help one into middle age' (16 Jan. 1981; NLI 49,493/57).

Drafts for section III began in April 1981, but once again progress quickly stalled, and it was not until a train ride from Birmingham to London on 8 November 1981 that SH jolted his efforts back into life, when he began to annotate an existing draft of section XII that by now he had put into TS. Through November and December, the sequence regained its momentum in MS. The poem was now two years into drafting, and SH pressed upon himself a need to clarify the actions and the motivations of the work. 'As I meet people on the island, what am I doing?' he asked himself. 'Re-entering the whirlpool,' came the answer. 'Finding out what I embraced, what embraced me, so that I can divest it and be divested of it.' The challenge in the mind of the author now feels distinctly Dantesque. He writes that the overall action is one of 'descending into the belly' of the affliction, back to the 'womb life' of church and community.

> The freedom sort is not just psychological or political – not just the honesty of one's newfound adulthood, if that can be penetrated to, or the truth of one's political grounding, if that can be stripped [. . .] The freedom is spiritual; it has surrendered to a larger whole or *gestalt* than the community, national papistical force of experience that has been so far dominant in my system. (14 Dec. 1981, NLI 49,493/57)

Section IV took shape at this time.

It would be a further six months before SH returned to manuscript work, and then it was not to 'Station Island' but, revealingly, to a translation of Dante's *Inferno*, 3 (*TSH*, 38–42; 563–5n.), which occupied him in June and July of 1982. It was not until the end of October 1982 that SH progressed his next instalment for 'Station Island', with the beginning of section VI, and a return to section IX, begun three years previously. The first MS workings of section XI are traceable to just after Christmas 1982 and are the last part of the sequence to have been begun. By then, section X, which had lived an autonomous life as 'Going Back', had been published for a Field Day Theatre Company production in the autumn of 1982.

I

First published in the *Hudson Review* (Summer 1983): 257–9, and collected with revisions in *SI*.

In the *Hudson Review*, the following note appears at the beginning of the sequence:

> Station Island is on Lough Derg in Co. Donegal in the northwest of Ireland. It is also known as St Patrick's Purgatory because there is a tradition that

the pilgrimage which thousands of people still do there every summer was established by the saint. It lasts for three days and involves fasting, praying barefoot around stone 'beds' and various other penitential exercises which make up the 'station.' The nineteenth-century Irish novelist William Carleton wrote about it in his story 'The Lough Derg Pilgrim.' These are the opening sections of a longer poem.

1–5]   It was a close grey morning,
            a reek of early summer
            pith-life, rotted things,
            reed-beds, thick young corn
            hushed and water-blistered.

            Something beat on iron:
            a hurry of bell-notes
            flew over sedge and iris,
            an escaped ringing
            that stopped as quickly *Hudson Review*

8 back] quite *Hudson Review*
9 man had appeared] man appeared *Hudson Review*
10 side of the field] back of the hedge *Hudson Review*
14–15 up into hazel bushes, / angled his] at the shins of hazel trees, / then angled the *Hudson Review*
17 move] moved *Hudson Review*
20] that has been dead for years!' *Hudson Review*
35 half afraid] half-afraid *Hudson Review*
36 bade] made *Hudson Review*
41 and saw] to see *Hudson Review*
65] 'Stay clear of that procession –' *Hudson Review*
66]   he was shouting angrily,
            'Don't turn your back again.
            Sooner or later, son,
            you will have to face me
            with both eyes open.' *Hudson Review*
66 me] me, *OG*
69–70] the tender bladed growth / was another scent picked up, / a drugged and open path *Hudson Review*
70 opened] had opened *NSP1990*, *OG*
73 who had fallen into step] fallen into step *NSP1990*, *OG*

The first of the twelve encounters making up the book's central sequence is with a different Sweeney, an Irish Traveller called Simon Sweeney, 'an old Sabbath-breaker', who is amalgamated with a neighbour called Charlie Griffin who went around with a bow-saw cutting branches for firewood (*SS*, 250). In the fiction of SH's pilgrimage, Sweeney calls out to him, 'Keep clear of all processions,' a resonant and possibly salutary injunction in Northern Irish culture.

36ff. Some earlier poems, such as 'Hawthorns' (*PSH*, 1179), contain this instruction to children to think of the hardships of the Travellers (there referred to as 'gypsies') in bad weather and to appreciate their beds, in some versions ascribed to SH's father.

II

First published in the *Hudson Review* (Summer 1983): 259–62, and collected with revisions in *SI*.

7 so that I felt] and I somehow felt *Hudson Review*
17 followed,] followed *Hudson Review*
21 diver] diver's surfacing after a plunge *Hudson Review*, OG | diver's *NSP*
22 who] Who *OG*
23 anyhow,] anyhow? *Hudson Review*
25 softened by] rinsed clear after *Hudson Review*
33 their] those *Hudson Review*
34 hard, I] hard, then I *Hudson Review*
36 there's] there is *Hudson Review*
40 'I have no mettle for the angry role,'] 'The angry role was never my vocation,' *NSP*
41 said.] said, *Hudson Review*
42–6] where the last marching bands of Ribbonmen // on Patrick's Day still played their Hymn to Mary. *NSP1990*, *OG*
50–2 station, / flax-pullings, dances, summer crossroads chat // and] station. / Flax-pullings. Dances. Summer crossroads chat. // And *Hudson Review*
51 summer crossroads chat] fair-days, crossroads chat *NSP1990*, *OG*
65 in wounds –] in wounds for desperate ointment *Hudson Review*, *OG*

Working titles in TS include 'The Road to Lough Derg' and 'The Lough Derg Pilgrim' (a working title shared with section XII).

SH provided the following note on this poem, at the end of *SI* (122):

> William Carleton (1794–1869), a Catholic by birth, had done the pilgrimage in his youth, and when he converted to the Established Church he published his critical account of it in 'The Lough Derg Pilgrim' and launched himself upon his most famous work, *Traits and Stories of the Irish Peasantry* (1830–3).

The overcoated figure seen in the driving mirror of the car (not yet on the island) is the nineteenth-century Ulster fiction writer William Carleton (1794–1869), named in *l*. 63, whose 'The Lough Derg Pilgrim' (*l*. 15) features among his *Traits and Stories of the Irish Peasantry*. Born a Catholic in Clogher, Co. Tyrone, he became a Protestant with a virulently hostile attitude to the Catholic Church in Ireland, who describes himself here as an 'old fork-tongued turncoat' (*l*. 32). Both conflicting traditions are presented negatively by the Carleton figure here, as in MacNeice's *Autumn Journal*, xvi: the 'hard-mouthed Ribbonmen and Orange bigots' (*l*. 31), nationalist and unionist stereotypes respectively.

41ff. Bipartisan description of SH's place of origin, between the band of Ribbonmen 'staggering home drunk on St Patrick's Day' (*l*. 45) and 'the neighbours on the roads at night with guns' (*l*. 54).

III

First published as 'In a Basilica', *Observer* (6 Feb. 1983): 33. After collection with revisions in *SI* the poem also appeared in *Envoy*, 47 (1985): 4.

1–5]   I knelt inside *basilica*. I knelt
       In its mother-of-pearl sounds of *s* and *l*,
       Its pointed tesserae of *ic* and *ba*,
       And faced the cut marble of *tabernacle*

       Inlaid in the gules of *sanctuary*. *Observer*

7 in a shell the listened-for ocean stopped] The listened-for ocean stopped in a shell *Observer*
9 floated then and] floated and *Observer*
10 in a vision, like] In vision like *Observer*
11 mussel shells] mussel-shells *Observer*
12 it,] it. *Observer*
13–14] Little shimmering ark, pale morning star, / Tower of Ivory and House of Gold *Observer*
15 her] a *Observer*
17 it] it, *Observer*
21 name which they] name they *Observer*
22 but was] But which was *Observer*
28 sound;] sound *NSP*
29 like an absence stationed in the] or like the absence sensed in *NSP1990*, *OG*
30 a ring of walked-down grass and rushes] a circle of trodden rushes *Observer*

Working title in TS of 'Turas'. A notebook entry dated '4.00. a.m. 5th January 1982' reads:

> Have just got up in a kind of ferment. Recollected little shell grotto that belonged to Aunt Agnes. A whole world glowing in the mother-of-pearl. The dead Heaneys, the fever bout, the decline, all of them ghostly in the rainbow sperm-freeze, the pink shimmer of the baby-nail shells[.]
> (5 Jan. 1982, NLI 49,493/57)

1–5 The first five lines replace the corresponding lines of 'In a Basilica' published in the *Observer*, 6 February 1983, given in the variant text above. The change may have been prompted by the appearance of the lines 'In a Basilica' in 'Pseuds Corner' in the London satirical magazine *Private Eye*.

2 *back*: on the island for the first time in the sequence, in the church amid the items of Catholic piety associated with SH's childhood, 'Habit's afterlife' (*l*. 1).

7 The seaside trinket is a memorial of SH's aunt Agnes who died in her teens of tuberculosis (the fate of three of SH's father's siblings). SH tells Dennis O'Driscoll that the trinket 'had the status of relic in the house' adding that it 'is one of my first and last things' (*SS*, 247).

14 'House of gold' is one of the terms in the Litany of the Virgin Mary (l. 24), as is 'Ark of the Covenant', the 'ark' in the same line, and 'Health of the Sick' (l. 23).

27–8 The 'space utterly empty / utterly a source' associated with death, returns in relation to SH's mother's death in 'Clearances' 8: 'I thought of walking round a space / Utterly empty, utterly a source' (*HL*, 34; *PSH*, 373). The idea is associated with the Romanian pessimist philosopher Emil Cioran (1911–95).

29–32 Author's notebook: 'the Kerns: the dead dog, Nora, decomposing in the rushes, the rusted water, the wet rank smell of dead bushes, old black leaves, the child's full sense of the cycle there and then, foreknowledge of the essential now long forgotten and ready to be retrieved' (5 Jan. 1982, NLI 49,493/57).

IV

First published in *SI*.

10 tied loosely] loosely tied *OG*
21 masses] Masses *OG*
26 off drenched] off the drenched *OG*
53 bare] empty *OG*
54 we both had grown up] we both grew up *NSP1990*, *OG*   a] the *NSP1990*, *OG*
56 when steam rose like the] when the tarmac steamed with the *NSP1990*, *OG*

3 *I renounce* . . . : the opening words of the vow in the Sacrament of Confirmation (and originally in the Sacrament of Baptism), 'I renounce Satan and all his works and pomps.' The pilgrimage of Station Island is a renewal of those vows.

7 The young priest is Terry Keenan, a childhood friend of SH and the brother of Rosie Keenan, the blind pianist in 'At the Wellhead' (*SL*, 65; *PSH*, 499). He became a missionary priest in the tropical rainforests. In the earlier part of the poem, the clerical student who becomes a priest is a local celebrity, though 'doomed to the decent thing' that SH's James Joyce figure will represent as a loss of self in XII. By the end of this poem, the exchange between the pilgrim and the priest represents the priest's choice which has left him fatally ill as a failure to escape into real personal life because he was young and unaware. The mystery for the young priest is why the poet-pilgrim, having escaped into secular life, is now going through these penitential motions again: unless he is 'here taking the last look' (l. 54): as near as SH ever comes to declaring his loss of faith (see also 'Out of this World', *DC*, 47; *PSH*, 614). In a notebook entry from mid-December 1981, SH writes:

T. Keenan represents idealism and renunciation strictly within terms of the tribe. There is a beauty and inadequacy about it: beauty because of the surrender and ideal of abnegation and service, the emptying of the self; inadequacy because of its ultimately sectarian nature, the egotism of the whole venture. His life a symbol for what might have happened if I had gone with the 'call' of Fr O'Connor, sweating and wheezing at the gable, asking me to consider before I went into 'the world'. (n.d. [14–26 Dec. 1981], NLI 49,493/57).

24 *In hoc signo vinces* . . . ('in this sign you will triumph'). The pagan Emperor Constantine before the Battle of Milvian Bridge across the Tiber on 28 October 312 saw a sign in the sky with these words in Greek, inspiring him to become a Christian. The sign is the chi-rho (XP), the first two letters of Christ's name; cf. the Chi-Ro Page in the Book of Kells.

28ff. 'to clear the way / for other pilgrims queuing to get started': one of many passages in *SI* modelled on the journey of Dante and Virgil through Purgatory.

39ff. *holy mascot*: like the grotto of the previous section and the iconography of the kitchen grottoes in the following lines (*ll.* 41–2).

48 *withdrawn*: the idea of the *deus absconditus* (Isaiah 45:15), 'the withdrawn god'. The biblical phrase has been used in modern sceptical discussion to indicate that God has disappeared from view, as the young priest suggests here.

V

First published under the title 'A Vision of Master Murphy on Station Island' in R. L. Cook (ed.), *A Garland of Poems for Leonard Clark* (Kinnesswood and London: Lomond and Enitharmon, 1980), 17–18, and then in the *Yale Review* (Autumn 1983): 138–9, where it is identified as 'Station Island' VII. Collected with revisions in *SI*.

headnote]: Station Island – or St Patrick's Purgatory – is on Lough Derg in County Donegal and has been a place for penance and retreat since Celtic times. Pilgrims still go there by the busload every summer to complete the three day 'station', fasting, praying and carrying out prescribed exercises in their bare feet. *Garland*
1 like soft paws rowing forward,] like the paws of a soft toy *Garland*
2 groped for and warded off] Warded and rowed into *Garland*
8 broad bean] broad-bean *Garland*
10 window] window-ledge *Garland*
11–13] Whitish, calloused, the poor toes curling buds . . . // Bud-white elders loomed in the classroom door. / 'Master,' they whispered humbly, 'I wonder, master – ' / Rustling letters, proffering, *Garland*
13–14] rustling envelopes, proffering them, withdrawing, / waiting for him to sign beside their mark, / and 'Master' I repeated to myself *NSP1990, OG*
16 going] gone *Garland* gone quiet in the shoulders, his small head *NSP1990, OG*

17 the cold gusts off the lough.] the wind that gusted round us. *Garland*
18 I moved ahead and] Then I moved on and *Garland*
18–19 hand. // Above] hand: / 'Seamus Heaney, master, from Mossbawn.' / Above *Garland*
20 smile] smile, *Garland*
21 and husked and scraped,] and scraped and husked *Garland*
22 before it] then *OG*
23 in] into *OG*
24 adam's] Adam's *OG*
25 weathered] withered *Garland*
27 but] And *Garland*
27–44] 'You would have thought that Anahorish School
    Was purgatory enough for any man,'
    I said, seeing a swarm of scholars
    Darken the tall-hedged road for fifty years,
    As morning field-smells came past on the wind,
    The sex-cut of sweet briar after rain,
    Littered chestnut pith, birds' nests filled with leaves.
    Then a soft rush like scythes in meadow grass:
    'Birch trees have overgrown Leitrim moss,
    Dairy herds are grazing where the school was
    And the school garden's loose black mould is grass.
    But you keep it in mind. And keep the florin
    I gave you for a prize. To give to Charon.'
    But he was gone and I was faced wrong way
    Into pilgrims absorbed in this station.
    As I turned to join their whispers and bare feet
    The mists of those lost mornings I set out
    For Latin classes with him, face to face,
    Refreshed me. *Mensa, mensa, mensam*
    Rang through the air like busy sharping-stones.
    I was lifting swathes for him. The scythe
    Swept and swept like a pendulum. *Garland*
29 new-mown] new *OG*
29 bird's] birds' *OG*
29–30 leaves. / 'You'd] leaves. // 'You'd *OG*
32 You've] You have *NSP1990*, *OG*
41 I] I'd *OG*
44 in the air like a busy whetstone] on the air like a busy sharping-stone *NSP1990*, *OG*
55 a third] another *OG*
61–2 Dordogne?' // And] Dordogne?' / And *NSP*

SH provided the following note on this poem, at the end of *SI* (122):

> 'Forty two years on . . .' Patrick Kavanagh wrote his posthumously published poem, 'Lough Derg', in 1942.
>
> 3 Barney Murphy, SH's teacher at Anahorish Primary School who prepared SH for the scholarship examination for St Columb's, including introductory Latin. Hence the first declension Latin noun mensa at the end of his exchange (*l.* 43).

12 *'Master', those elders whispered*: 'Master' was the term used to address the headmaster in Irish primary schools: also the term used to translate the word used to address Christ in biblical translation.

35 *Leitrim Moss*: an area of bogland near Anahorish.

46 *another master*: Michael McLaverty (1904–92), headmaster of St Thomas's Secondary Intermediate School in Belfast where SH taught 1962–3. SH wrote the introduction to his *Collected Short Stories* and his obituary in the *Irish Times*. SH dedicated two poems to him: section 5 'Fosterage' in 'Singing School' (*North*, 74; *PSH*, 208) and the uncollected 'An Evening at Killard' (*PSH*, 99).

46ff. *'For what is the great . . .'*: Gerard Manley Hopkins, 'Feeling, love in particular, is the great moving power and spring of verse.'

51 *'met him'*: i.e. McLaverty's uncle. McLaverty advises 'When you're on the road . . .' before giving way to a third fosterer of SH's writing (*l*. 56), Patrick Kavanagh.

59 *Forty-two years on*: since the publication of Kavanagh's poem 'Lough Derg' (1942). Like Carleton in section II, Kavanagh deplores the lack of progress in pilgrimage travels or in Irish Catholicism and its rituals.

VI

First published in the *Yale Review* (Autumn 1983): 140–1, where it is identified as 'Station Island' VIII. The third stanza was published as 'From Station Island' in *Poetry Ireland Review* (Winter 1983–4): 23. Collected with revisions in *SI*.

24 that bags] that packed bags OG
33 Shoulder-blades] Shoulderblades OG
39 sunlight,] sunlight – *Poetry Ireland Review*

SH provided the following notes on this poem, at the end of *SI*:

> 'Till Phoebus . . .', Horace, *Odes*, Book III, xxi, *l*. 24. 'As little flowers . . .', Dante, *Inferno*, Canto II, lines 127–32.

1 The child recalled in the memory of the opening lines of this three-sonnet section (freckle-faced, red-haired) seems to be identifiable as the neighbouring child who took SH to school, Philomena McNicholl, 'a fey, if ever there was one' (*SS*, 242). The memory seems to have been prompted by Kavanagh's remark about the motivation of the pilgrimage at the end of the previous section, 'on the hunt for women', a link supported by the reference to 'the Sabine farm' (*l*. 18) from which the women were abducted, which was also an idealised retreat in Horace.

37ff. A translation of Dante *Inferno*, 2.127–32, describing the revival of the pilgrim's spirit as flowers open out at sunrise, here continuing the theme of sexual development: quoted in SH's translation with minor variations (see *TSH*, 36).

VII

First published in the *Yale Review* (Autumn 1983): 141–4, where it is identified as 'Station Island' IX, and in the *Irish Times* (13 Sept. 1984): 13. An excerpt from this section was also included in *Inside Tribune* (30 Sept. 1984): 1–3. Collected with revisions in *SI* and later included under the title 'From Station Island' in *Seamus Heaney: Readings in Contemporary Poetry* (New York: Dia Art Foundation, 1988), 32–5, and in *100P*.

22 street] street, *OG*, *100P*
32 whingeing] whinging *Irish Times*
41 street lamp] streetlamp *OG*, *100P*
48 time] hour *OG*, *100P*
67 on weight] on a bit of weight *OG*, *100P*
72 him] him, *OG*, *100P*

A working title for this section in TS was 'A Ghost'.

4 The figure encountered here is William Strathearn, with whom SH had played Gaelic football. Eugene Kielt has pointed out, in private correspondence with the editors, that in the *Derry Journal* of Friday, 8 April 1955, the minor Gaelic Football panel for South Derry includes both W. Strathearn (Bellaghy) and S. Heaney (Castledawson). Strathearn was the proprietor of a chemist's shop in Ahoghill, Co. Derry, victim of a random sectarian murder on 19 April 1977 for which two members of the UVF, John Weir and Billy McCaughey, were convicted (*l.* 63). (See also McKittrick 1999, 716–8.) The poem is an imaginative fictional representation of the killing, and the Strathearn family were pleased with it as an elegy in tribute.

82 This is formally the most Dante-like of all SH's purgatorial poems, reading like a canto made up of triads with a concluding single line.

VIII

First published as 'Encounter on Station Island' in the programme for the Tom Delaney Memorial Concert at the Ulster Museum in Belfast (7 Dec. 1979). Subsequently published under the title 'From Station Island' in *Agenda* (Summer 1984): 3–5, where the following note was given before the poem:

> *Note*: Station Island, on Lough Derg in Co. Donegal, is the site of a penitential pilgrimage where the exercises include praying while making the rounds of various stone circles called 'beds'.

An excerpt from this section was also included in *Inside Tribune* (30 Sept. 1984): 1–3, and after collection with revisions in *SI* an excerpt (ll. 1–28) appeared in *Envoy*, 47 (1985): 5.

5 Bed] bed *Agenda*
11 over] across *Agenda*
22 straightaway] straight away OG
43 axe heads] axeheads *Agenda*, OG
49 house.'] house – ' OG

Working title in TS 'Visions on Station Island'.

7 'my archaeologist' is SH's friend Tom Delaney (1947–79), a Dubliner who worked in the Ulster Museum and who at his early death from a heart complaint was head of the Department of Medieval Archaeology at Queen's University Belfast. This section was the first written of the sections of 'Station Island' (*SS*, 235, 240). Delaney reappears in 'Scrabble', the first sonnet in 'Glanmore Revisited' (*ST*, 31).

2 *the magpie is seen as a bird of ill omen here*: SH says his starting point was the story that a rook flew into the church at Delaney's funeral (*SS*, 235).

17ff. SH describes the pain of his failure to provide consolation at Delaney's deathbed when he visited him in hospital.

40 *Lucky Poet* (1943) was a book by Hugh MacDiarmid: though here SH's luck relative to Delaney seems to be his still living.

47 *the Gowran master*: the creator of a series of carved faces at St Mary's Collegiate Church at Gowran near Jerpoint in Co. Kilkenny, which SH visited with Barrie Cooke.

50ff. *But he had gone . . .* : Delaney is replaced by SH's murdered cousin Colum McCartney, the 'pale-faced boy' who was the subject of SH's 'The Strand at Lough Beg' (*FW*, 9–10; *PSH*, 220). Now he accuses the poet of staying with poets in Jerpoint during his funeral in Bellaghy.

58 The Fews Forest in Co. Armagh where McCartney was killed, which is a prominent location in *SA*.

74 *the lovely blinds of the Purgatorio*: in 'The Strand at Lough Beg', SH imagines weaving a scapular of 'rushes that shoot green again' for his dead cousin, drawing on Dante's *Purgatorio*, 1.124–7.

IX

First published in *Inside Tribune* (30 Sept. 1984): 1–3, 6, and collected with revisions in *SI*.

16 mass] Mass OG

Working title in TS 'Nightpiece'.

1ff. The opening voice 'from blight and hunger' (15–16) in the first of the five sonnets of this sequence has been thought to be an amalgam of two the IRA hunger strikers who died in 1981, SH's neighbour Francis Hughes and his cousin Thomas McElwee. Hughes, once described by the security forces as 'the most wanted man in Northern Ireland', died on 12 May 1981 after fifty-nine days on hunger strike; his death prompted 'heavy rioting' (see McKittrick 1999, 806). SH was in Oxford at the time; as a guest of Charles Monteith at All Souls College that evening he attended the Anglican evensong service in the College chapel, and he was allocated rooms belonging to the Conservative minister Keith Joseph in which to spend the night. He was keenly aware of the clash of cultures and experiences which this coincidence of events represented, and wrestled with it privately in drafting his first Oxford lecture as Professor of Poetry eight years later, in 1989. He did eventually describe that evening in the final Oxford lecture, 'Frontiers of Writing', delivered on 23 November 1993 (*RP*, 186–203), and returned to the subject in a lecture given in April 2004 for the American Philosophical Society, 'Title Deeds: Translating a Classic' (pp. 860–1).

17–18 SH did attend the wake of his neighbour Thomas McElwee; he was known not to be sympathetic to IRA observances, but as he later explained in 'Title Deeds' (2004), he respected the traditions of his community in marking a death. McElwee, from Tamlaghtduff, was the ninth man to die on the hunger strike and also the youngest, aged twenty-three. He died on 8 August 1981 after sixty-two days without food (McKittrick 1999, 875).

29 '*I dreamt*': in the course of the one night's sleep allowed on the pilgrimage after the first sleepless night. The nightmare atmosphere and imagery, especially in the third sonnet of the sequence, are strikingly consistent with the medieval accounts of Lough Derg which describe the descent of a knight, Owein, and others into a purgatorial pit in a cave on the island, where, according to the chronicler Froissart, they encounter terrible dreams in the course of their night in the pit. Dante seems to have been aware of the nightmarish horrors in the accounts.

43ff. The nightmare visions of the previous section settle into a memory of a brass trumpet, hidden in the loft in his childhood, which gives way to the waking sounds of a bell and a gushing tap in a neighbouring cubicle on the island.

57ff. The poet, apparently in his own voice, returns to the theme of his failure to overcome the limitations of his own biddable heritage, as in the appeal to William Strathearn or Colum McCartney for forgiveness for it, an appeal which Strathearn in section VII said was 'above his head'.

X

First published under the title 'Going Back' in the programme for the Field Day Theatre Company production of Brian Friel's *The Communication Cord* (Sept. 1982), and collected with revisions in *SI*.

1] The tackle of the fireplace: a pot *Communication Cord*
2 links. Soot flakes. Plumping] links, black iron, plumping *Communication Cord*
3 The] An *Communication Cord*   letting in] brilliant with *NSP1990, OG*
3–4 sunlight. / Hearthsmoke rambling and a] sunlight, / hearthsmoke rambling, a *Communication Cord*
5] on the common table. Then I saw the mug *Communication Cord*
6 its] a *Communication Cord*
7 with cornflowers, blue sprig] with blue cornflowers, sprig *NSP1990, OG*
7–8 patterned with cornflowers, blue sprig after sprig / repeating] with a pattern of cornflowers, a blue sprig / repeated round *Communication Cord*
8 quiet] still *Communication Cord*   milestone,] milestone . . . *NSP*
9–12] [omitted] *NSP1990, OG*
11 unchallenging,] unchallenging *Communication Cord*
14 when the fit-up] when fit-up *NSP1990, OG*   when the fit-up actors used it] when actors borrowed it *Communication Cord*
15 in a dark hall] in the hall *Communication Cord*
16 couple vowed] pair kissed *Communication Cord*
18 an ordinary] a slight ordinary *Communication Cord*
19 from this] then by this *NSP1990, OG*
20 it was restored with all its cornflower haze] it reappeared ringed in its blue-eyed haze *Communication Cord*
20–1 with all its cornflower haze // still dozing,] to its old haircracked doze // on the mantelpiece *NSP1990, OG*
21 still dozing] back in place *Communication Cord*   fast,] fast – *Communication Cord*
22] like the psalter restored once by an otter *Communication Cord*
25] The saint praised God aloud on the lough shore. *Communication Cord*
25–8] And so the saint praised God on the lough shore
  for that dazzle of impossibility
  I credited again in the sun-filled door,
  so absolutely a light it could put out fire. *NSP1990, OG*

Continuing with the morning after the nightmares of section X, the resumed normality reminds the poet-pilgrim of a mug decorated with cornflowers, which in his childhood was borrowed as a prop for a local play performance.

11 *lars*: Latin term for a household votive object (more commonly *lares*, and linked with *penates*). Associated with spirits of the dead, the lares guarded homes, crossroads and the city.

22 *Ronan's psalter*: in *SA*, Sweeney's throwing of the bishop Ronan's psalter into the lake started the hostility between them that led to Sweeney's wandering 'astray' through Ireland. An otter miraculously brought the psalter back to Ronan.

XI

First published under the title 'Song of the soul that delights in knowing God by faith (from the Spanish of St John of the Cross)' in Martin Booth's limited-edition *Tenfold: Poems for Frances Horovitz* (Wellingborough: Skelton's Press, 1983): [9–10] (this version comprises the translation (*ll*. 17–51) alone). Collected with revisions in *SI* and subsequently included in *Envoy*, 47 (1985): 6.

1–16] [omitted] *Tenfold*
22 one,] one *Tenfold*
38 wills to,] wills, *Tenfold*
47 drink these waters, although] lap at these waters, though *Tenfold*

SH provided the following note on this poem, at the end of *SI* (122):

> The St John on [*sic*] the Cross poem translated here is 'Cantar del alma que se huelga de conoscer a Dios por fe'.

The last votive object in the sequence is the child's kaleidoscope (given to SH as a child by his Aunt Sally) which was ruined by being plunged into muddy water; restored now, the pilgrim sees in it the face of a Franciscan priest, based on a monk who taught in the Philosophy Department at Queen's (with 'his sandalled passage', *l*. 16) to whom the pilgrim is confessing, a conclusive stage of the pilgrimage. As penance, the priest enjoins the poet to translate a poem by San Juan de la Cruz (the Spanish mystical poet, St John of the Cross, 1542–91) and the translation follows. It is a translation of one of St John's most famous poems, written while he was in prison, 'Cantar de la alma que se huelga de conocer a Dios por fe' ('Song of the soul that rejoices to know God by faith'). The idea most famously associated with St John is 'the dark night of the soul', the emptying of the mind and consciousness that makes them ready for divine inspiration: here 'although it is the night'. 'The living fountain' (*l*. 49) at the end of the poem represents the culmination of the poet's pilgrimage.

XII

First published as 'A Familiar Ghost' in the *Irish Times* (2 Feb. 1982), in its special centenary supplement 'James Joyce 1892–1982': A1, where it is preceded by the note: 'The following is envisaged as part of a sequence of poems centred on the Lough Derg pilgrimage.' Later that year it appeared with revisions under the title 'Leaving the Island', in W. J. McCormack and Alistair Stead (eds), *James Joyce and Modern Literature* (London: Routledge & Kegan Paul, 1982), 74–6, where it is preceded by the note: '"Leaving the Island" is envisaged as part of a sequence of poems set on Station Island in Lough Derg in County Donegal. A Pilgrimage [*sic*] to the island, supposedly initiated by Saint Patrick, has been part of the penitential sub-culture of Irish Catholicism for generations.' Also published as 'From Station Island', and described as section XIV of the sequence, in *Studies in Medievalism* (Summer 1983): 15–17. Collected with revisions in *SI* and later included in *100P*.

>1] In the *Irish Times* and *James Joyce and Modern Literature*, the poem begins with these four stanzas (perhaps modelled on Dante's *Purgatorio* where the spirits sing the psalm *In exitu Israel de Aegypto* as they sail towards Purgatory, II, 46–8); variants in the latter publication are indicated here in square brackets:

> Hail Glorious Saint Patrick! The pilgrims in the boat
> were singing when the throttle opened
> and spray came gusting and each lazing note
>
> warped as it lifted off in gusts of wind.
> Close-packed [Close packed], loaded deep, we sang our way
> across the choppy water, like a band
>
> of starved [starving] monks out of the western sea.
> But we had done with peregrinatio.
> Lough Derg flowed up, flowed under, back, away
>
> astern and Station Island was a mirage now
> already as we readied for the land
> nearing the widening up beyond the bow.

9 ash plant] ashplant *James Joyce*] ash-plant *Studies in Medievalism*
10 in the flesh] in a flash *Irish Times, James Joyce, Studies in Medievalism*
13 eddying] fluent *Irish Times, James Joyce*
17 downstroke] cursives *Irish Times, James Joyce, Studies in Medievalism*
18 litter] little *Irish Times*
19–22] with his stick, saying, 'What I did on my own
　　　was done for others but not done with them – and this
　　　you have failed to learn. Your obligation

　　　is not discharged by pious exercise.
　　　When I refused to take the sacrament /
　　　I made my life an instrument of grace

　　　so all of you had more abundant
　　　life. I was at nobody's service
　　　the way you are at theirs – ' and the ash-plant

　　　went jerking backwards towards the landing place

where the last pilgrims were still hanging about.
'This was a backsliding enterprise.

Get back in harness. The main thing is to write
for your own joy in it. Cultivate a work-lust *Irish Times, James Joyce*
21 What you must do must be done] What you do you must do *NSP1990, OG, 100P*
22-3 own // so get back in harness. The main thing is to write] own. // The main thing is to write *NSP1990, OG, 100P*
25 a] her *Irish Times*
28 let others wear the] so ready for the *OG, 100P*
34 as I came to. 'Old father, mother's son,] as I came to and heard the harangue and jeers / going on and on. *NSP1990, OG*
34-41 'Old father [. . .] 'any more?'] [omitted] *NSP1990, OG,* or *100P.*
37-8 stars – that one entry / has been a sort of password in my ears,] stars. That day's my birthday / and those words are vagitus in my ears *Irish Times, James Joyce*
39 of] for *Irish Times, James Joyce*
40 Tundish.'] Tundish!' *Irish Times, James Joyce*
41 jeered] said *Irish Times, James Joyce*
43] rehearsing the old whinges at your age. *NSP1990, OG, 100P*
45 infantile,] infantile – *Irish Times, James Joyce*   your] this *NSP1990, OG, 100P*
47-8] doing the decent thing. The way of the blunt] sleek dolphin has to be your way: swim *Irish Times*] The way to cement] community is the dolphin's way: swim *James Joyce, Studies in Medievalism*
53 shower broke in] shower in *Irish Times*

Dated 8 November 1981 in TS as 'The Lough Derg Pilgrim' (a working title shared with section II).

SH provided the following note on this poem, at the end of *SI* (122):

'Stephen's diary'. See the end of James Joyce's *A Portrait of the Artist as a Young Man*.

4 'the helping hand . . . fish-cold and bony' is that of James Joyce.

8 Joyce suffered from a number of serious eye conditions throughout his life.

9 The 'ashplant' links Stephen Dedalus, who carries one in *Ulysses*, with SH's cattle-dealing father, who urges his sister travelling to London to 'Look for a man with an ashplant on the boat' (*ST*, 85).

15 'eddying with the vowels of all rivers', referring to Anna Livia, the Liffey, in *Finnegans Wake*.

28 Sackcloth and ashes, the penitential garb of those guilty of sin in the Sacrament of Penance.

35-6 Stephen's diary in *A Portrait of the Artist as a Young Man*. 'April the thirteenth' is SH's birthday. Cf. Joyce 1992, 270-6.

40 *The Feast of the Holy Tundish*: Stephen's Dean of Studies at university is English, and he thinks Stephen's use of the term 'tundish' for 'funnel' is Irish dialect. But this entry in Stephen's diary in the last pages of the book says 'That tundish has been on my

mind for a long time. I looked it up and find it English and good old blunt English too' (Joyce 1992, 274). So in the context of *SI* it is another declaration of freedom from ethical constraints, like the abandonment of the 'peasant pilgrimage' (*l.* 45) the Joyce figure advises.

41–2 *The English language / Belongs to us*: Stephen's diary entry for 13 April ends, 'Damn the Dean of Studies and his funnel! What did he come here for to teach us his own language or to learn it from us? Damn him one way or the other' (Joyce 1992, 274).

PART THREE: SWEENEY REDIVIVUS

Throughout his career, SH wrote poems in the first person, often in his own voice, from 'I'll dig with it' in 'Digging' onwards. But, like all poets who write in a personal voice, there is not a single fixed identification of that voice with the author's. SH uses familiar grammatical and rhetorical stand-ins for the poet. The most obvious and familiar is the narrative 'you'; 'In Gallarus Oratory' (*DD*, 12; *PSH*, 75) begins 'You can still feel the community pack / This place'; these pronouns shift further to the third person in the personal narrative of 'Alphabets': 'He understands / He will understand more when he goes to school' (*HL*, 1; *PSH*, 357).

Such narrative strategies are familiar enough. But a new, strikingly significant avatar is made use of when SH works on his translation of *Sweeney Astray*. SH uses the figure of Sweeney in several ways. It can be taken directly from the medieval poem, as when Sweeney narrates his own experience of the weather: 'I have gone north and south. / One night I was in the Mournes' (*SA*, 28; *TSH*, 152). But, as well as translating Sweeney's narratives like this, SH makes a quite different use of the figure of Sweeney as a kind of figure for his own experience. In doing this SH is drawing on a powerful lyric predecessor. In his early poetry, and especially in the 1899 volume *The Wind Among the Reeds*, W. B. Yeats represented his personal experience or views through a number of such stand-in figures: first as 'The Lover', in 'The Lover mourns for the Loss of Love' (1898), whose title is implicit in the four poems that follow it as 'He', and in a further twelve poems in the volume (including the title of the celebrated 'He wishes for the cloths of Heaven') in which the lover shares the title with the poet. Moreover, and closer to SH's case, Yeats draws on figures from medieval Irish legend to serve as the poetic first person: Aengus, Red Hanrahan and briefly Mongan, the son of the god of the sea, Manannán mac Lir, in poems like 'Mongan Thinks of his Past Greatness' and 'Mongan laments the change that has come upon him and his Beloved'.

The reason for raising this parallel here is to bring back into consideration a number of SH's Sweeney poems beyond those that appear in the SWEENEY REDIVIVUS section of *Station Island*. The poems in that section are included here as poems published within the twelve canonical volumes, but there are a number of Sweeney poems, uncollected and unpublished, that were candidates for inclusion here too. A series of uncollected Sweeney poems were published in 1984 and republished in *NSP1990*, all closely derived from the text of *SA*. But there are a number of what might be called the Heaney–Sweeney poems (SH himself noted the rhyme) where the persona has the name of Sweeney but the experience of Heaney: unpublished poems like 'Sweeney Truant' and 'Sweeney's Artistic Conscience' which, like the Yeats avatar poems, express the experience or opinion of the poet. Also derived from this practice in Yeats is a series of poems in the NLI archive where an unnamed female third person has various dreams: 'She dreams Sile na Gig', 'She dreams Bogside', 'She Dreams an Ulster Bestiary', as well as 'Her Nightmare Bestiary'. Obviously this is a different case from the persona to stand in for the poet's voice, but the use of an identified personal pronoun as subject is similarly derived from Yeats.

SH provided the following note on this section, at the end of *SI* (123):

> The poems in this section are voiced for Sweeney, the seventh-century Ulster king who was transformed into a bird-man and exiled to the trees by the curse of St Ronan. A version of the Irish tale is available in my *Sweeney Astray*, but I trust these glosses can survive without the support system of the original story. Many of them, of course, are imagined in contexts far removed from early medieval Ireland.

The First Gloss

First published in *SI*, and later in *OG*.

Sweeney Redivivus

First published in *The Times* (11 Oct. 1984): 8, and after collection in *SI* also included in *OG*.

8 *scutch mill*: a common sight in Ulster in the 200-year heyday of the linen industry, offering the same service to flax growers as corn mills

to corn growers: i.e. a central mill to which the growers brought their flax to be 'scutched' – beaten into a form ready for spinning.

Unwinding

First published in the *London Review of Books* (20 Oct.–2 Nov. 1983): 14, and collected in *SI*.

In the Beech

First published in the *London Review of Books* (20 Oct.–2 Nov. 1983): 14, and after collection in *SI* included in *NSP1990* and *OG*.

5–6 discovered peace / to touch himself in the reek of churned-up mud.] found peace to weigh / his chances with the pale thug in his fork. *LRB*
7 a strangeness and a comfort,] an old one and a new one, *LRB*
11 red-brick] red brick *LRB*
12 stamen] stamen, *OG*

SH told O'Driscoll: 'I *did* sit hidden in the fork of the beech tree at the head of our lane as the tanks and armoured cars and marching soldiers passed below' (*SS*, 264).

The First Kingdom

First published in *SI*, then included in *NSP1990* and *OG*.

Working titles in TS are 'Sweeney Remembers' and 'Sweeney's First Life'.

The First Flight

First published in *SI*, then included in *NSP1990* and *OG*.

Dated 11 September 1983 in MS as 'Sweeney's First Flight', also as 'Sweeney Recalls his First Flight' in TS.
   24 *a feeder off battlefields*: accusations that SH exploited Troubles violence for poetic profit, in *North*, for example.

Drifting Off

First published as 'Sweeney Reminisces' in *Aquarius* (1983/4): 55, and then as 'Sweeney Drifts Off' in *Runway* (Feb./March 1984): 25. Collected with revisions in *SI* and later included in *NSP1990* and *OG*.

2 gliding] cruising *Runway*
4 gannet's strike] gannet's perfect strike *Runway*

12 starlings,] starlings. *Runway*
13 kept faith] I kept faith *Runway*
19–21] [omitted] *Runway*
25 stooped] rose *Runway*
26–7 brimming, / my spurs at] brimming, my spurs / at *Runway*

Dated 7 September 1983 in MS (NLI 49,493/70); in TS as 'Sweeney Rates Himself'.

Alerted

Published in *SI*.

Dated 15 September 1983 as 'Sweeney Infans' in MS (NLI 49,493/70).

The Cleric

First published as 'Sweeney and the Cleric' in *Thames Poetry* (March 1984): 28, and under the same title, after collection with revisions as 'The Cleric' in *SI*, in *Graham House Review* (Winter 1985): 7. Also included in *NSP1990* and *OG*.

13 Latin] latin *Graham House Review*
22 whingeing] whinging *Graham House Review*

In TS as 'Sweeney's Verdict on Ronan' (NLI 49,493/70).

The Hermit

First published in *Critical Quarterly* (Spring and Summer 1984): 20, with the following note: 'These poems are from a sequence in which the imagined speaker is Sweeney, the legendary King of Ulster who was cursed and outcast among the trees.' After collection in *SI* it was also published in *Graham House Review* (Winter 1985): 8, under the title 'Sweeney Remembers the Hermit'. Later included in *OG*.

7 high-drawn] high-drawn, *Critical Quarterly, Graham House Review*
9 in the wrists and elbows –] in elbows and wrists – *Critical Quarterly*
10 time] time, *OG*

In TS as 'Sweeney Recalls the Hermit Briton' and 'Sweeney recalls the Briton in the Wood'.

The Master

First published in *Critical Quarterly* (Spring and Summer 1984): 19, and after collection with revisions in *SI* also in *Graham House Review* (Winter 1985): 9. Later included in *NSP1990* and *OG*.

13–15] Each maxim given its space. / Each character blocked on the parchment secure / in its volume and measure. *Critical Quarterly, Graham House Review*
15–16] Each maxim given its space. // *Tell the truth. Do not be afraid.* / Durable, obstinate notions, / like quarrymen's hammers and wedges proofed *NSP1990, OG*
16–17 wedges proofed / by] wedges / proofed by *OG*

Dated 16 September 1983 in MS as 'Sweeney as Novice' (NLI 49,493/69).

A much-discussed poem because authoritative readers originally assumed the title referred to Yeats, particularly in the light of the 'unroofed tower' (*l.* 2), before SH said the primary reference was to Miłosz (*SS*, 262).

The Scribes

First published as 'Sweeney and the Scribes' in *Thames Poetry* (March 1984): 29, and after collection in *SI* also included in *Seamus Heaney: Readings in Contemporary Poetry* (New York: Dia Art Foundation, 1988), 36, *NSP1990* and *OG*.

Dated 29 August 1983 in TS (NLI 49,493/70).

A Waking Dream

Published in *SI*.

Dated 7 September 1983 in TS (NLI 49,493/70).

In the Chestnut Tree

First published as 'Sweeney in the Chestnut Tree' in *Aquarius* (1983/4): 55–6, and collected with revisions in *SI*.

Sweeney's Returns

Published in *SI*.

Holly

Printed privately for the author as a Christmas card by Peter Fallon in 1981, then published in *Quarryman* (Aug. 1982): 2, and *Sequoia* (Autumn 1983): 2. Collected with revisions in *SI* and included in *NSP1990* and *OG*.

3–5] the ditches were swimming, / we were wet to the knees, // our hands were all jags and water ran up our sleeves *Quarryman*

9 Now here I am, in a room that is decked] Thirty years on, the living room's decked *Sequoia*
9–12] Thirty years on, I have nearly forgotten
    what it's like to be wet to the skin

    or to long for a snowfall – and the living room's decked
    with the red-berried waxy-leafed stuff. *Quarryman*
14 want] would like *Sequoia*

An Artist

First published in *SI*, and later included in *NSP1990* and *OG*.

Dated 31 August 1983 in MS as 'Sweeney redresses the artist'; also, 'Sweeney Praises an Artist' (NLI 49,493/69). SH confirms Dennis O'Driscoll's suggestion that the artist is Cézanne (*SS*, 262ff.), quoting the first line of the poem: 'I love the thought of his anger.'

The Old Icons

First published in the *London Review of Books* (20 Oct.–2 Nov. 1983): 14, and after collection in *SI* also included in *OG*.

Dated 20 August 1983 in TS; working titles in TS 'Sweeney's Gallery' and 'Sweeney Considers His Icons' (NLI 49,493/70).

In Illo Tempore

First published in the *Observer* (5 Feb. 1984): 52, and after collection in *SI* also included in *NSP1990* and *OG*.

8 Altar stone] Altar-stone *Observer*, *NSP1990*, *OG*
9 rubric] 'rubric' *OG*
13 range wall] range-wall *Observer*

On the Road

First published in *SI*, and later included in *NSP1990* and *OG*.

32 latin] Latin *NSP1990*, *OG*
36 deerpath] deer path *OG*
59 wing-flap] wingflap *OG*

Dated June 1983 in MS (NLI 49,493/57).
    'On the Road' was the last poem to be supplied for *SI*, and was 'slipped in' to the author's returning proofs for the volume on 2 July 1984 (FF P/Rdlm/778/6).

17-18 *Master, what must I / do to be saved?* The exchange between Jesus and a rich young man is woven through the poem: Acts 16:30, as well as in all the Synoptic Gospels, e.g. Matthew 19:16ff.

UNCOLLECTED POEMS (1985–1987)

There is no particularly distinctive emphasis in the small number of poems uncollected between *Station Island* and *The Haw Lantern*. Perhaps the thematic dominance of personal poems such as 'Clearances' in *The Haw Lantern* after the death of SH's mother reduced the appeal of external subjects.

The Late Paul Cézanne

First published in *Word & Image* (Jan./March 1986), and then in *Clearances*, a special limited edition from the Cornamona Press, December 1986.

Dated 18–19 June 1985 in MS under the title 'Latecomer' (NLI 49,493/83); unrelated to the uncollected poem 'The Latecomers', *PSH*, 688.
  The painter Paul Cézanne (1839–1906) was a great favourite of SH: he tells Dennis O'Driscoll, 'the first art book I bought for myself was about Cézanne' (*SS*, 262–3) and confirms that he is the subject of 'An Artist' in the SWEENEY REDIVIVUS series (*SI*, 116; *PSH*, 346). When he went to the Picasso Museum in Paris he 'tended to note the Picassos but to linger with the Cézannes' (*SS*, 333).
  Title The prefix 'the late' usually means deceased; the phrase for the late works of an artist usually omits the first name and the definite article ('late Cézanne') as in *l.* 2 here. But there is some kind of wordplay here since the title could apply to the son as well as the father.
  2 *his son*: Paul (1872–1947), son of Cézanne and his mistress Hortense Fiquet. A close friend of filmmaker Jean Renoir, whose parents treated him as their son. He was a painter's model and was involved in the production of some of Jean Renoir's films.

Lenten Stuff

Published in *Erato*, 1 (Summer 1986): [1].

Dated April 1966 in MS (NLI 49,493/5).

Villanelle for an Anniversary

First published as a card by Harvard University, as part of its 350th anniversary celebrations. The poem was read by SH at the Second Convocation event at the university, on 5 September 1986. Subsequently published in *Erato* (Fall/Winter 1986), and in the *Harvard Magazine* (Nov./Dec. 1986). It was collected with revisions in OG.

[text: OG]

1 moved,] moved. *Erato*, *Harvard Magazine*
2 unwon,] unwon. *Erato*, *Harvard Magazine*
4] New Town bore its new name. Still nothing stirred. *Harvard Magazine*
9 books] Books *Harvard Magazine*
11 Wingflap.] Wingbeat. *Erato*, *Harvard Magazine*
11 pigeon] pigeon, *Erato*
13 (look)] (look!) *Erato*, *Harvard Magazine*
17 Here,] Here. *Erato*, *Harvard Magazine*
18–19 yard, / The] yard. // The *Harvard Magazine*

Title Harvard University was founded as Harvard College in 1636; its 350th anniversary was marked in 1986 with great display including the featuring of John Harvard's face on a 56c US stamp.

1 John Harvard (1607–38), an English Puritan born in Southwark in 1607 who emigrated to New England in 1637, donated in his will his library of 400 volumes and half of his estate 'to the schoale or colledge'. In gratitude for his bequest the college (at Newtowne, renamed Cambridge in recognition of the university which Harvard attended at Emmanuel College) named the college after him. Harvard Yard is the oldest part of the campus.

2 The atom was split in 1932.

3 The books acknowledge John Harvard's donation of books to the university's origins.

Birthday Tribute to Marie Bullock

Published in *Poetry Pilot* (Feb. 1987): 7.

Marie Bullock (c.1912–86) was founder in 1934 (with her husband Hugh) and president of the Academy of American Poets at East 87th Street, New York. SH's poem is in an issue of *Poetry Pilot* devoted to tributes to her on her birthday, where it appears untitled; the title given here follows Brandes 2008.

THE HAW LANTERN (1987)

The Haw Lantern was published in London by Faber & Faber in June 1987 in 30,000 simultaneous hardback and paperback copies, and in New York by Farrar, Straus and Giroux on 1 October 1987 in 7,250 hardback copies and in paperback on 1 February 1989. It was reprinted in London in 1990 and reset in 2006.

The volume had numerous earlier working titles, among them 'Alphabets', after the book's first poem, and 'The Globe in the Window', from a line in the same. When the typescript was delivered by SH to Faber in the summer of 1986, it was done so under the title 'The Shape of Things', which was taken from a line in 'The Song of the Bullets'. SH tells O'Driscoll that *'The Stone Verdict* was a definite favourite for a while' (*SS*, 290). A possible disqualification was the actual death of SH's father in 1986: when the poem was published in *Hailstones* he was still alive and the poem was a pre-elegy, inviting the verdict, rather than a post-mortem judgement. The poem, casting the father as Hermes, offered itself as a suitable title with its foregrounding of the theme of grieving for lost relatives. In the years between the publication of the 'Sweeney Complex', *Station Island* and *Sweeney Astray*, and *The Haw Lantern*, both of the poet's parents died, his mother in 1984 and his father in 1986, and his niece Rachel was killed in 1985 in a road accident terribly reminiscent of the death of the poet's brother Christopher memorialised in 'Mid-Term Break'. Rachel is commemorated in the beautiful poem 'The Summer of Lost Rachel' in *The Haw Lantern*. Of the commemorative poems in the book, the most loved is the series of elegiac sonnets for SH's mother called 'Clearances' of which SH says 'for all the loss' in them, 'they were actually a pleasure to write'. Number 3 in the series, beginning 'When all the others were away at Mass', was voted the Irish nation's favourite poem in 2015 in the RTÉ poll 'A Poem for Ireland'.

In the end, the title was chosen for the book because – with its scrutinising figure of Diogenes with his lamp 'seeking one just man' – *The Haw Lantern* was 'requiring strict self-examination from everybody' (*SS*, 290): something which might be read as the opposite of the artistically permissive advice from James Joyce at the end of the 'Station Island' sequence 'to write / for the joy of it' and to 'Let go, let fly, forget' (*SI*, 93; *PSH*, 336). Despite its subjects for mourning and the claim for 'strict self-examination', SH tells O'Driscoll that he sees *The Haw Lantern* as after all 'a recovery book – recovery of writing "for the joy of it"', as enjoined by Joyce at the end of 'Station Island' and as he had claimed himself for *Field Work*. Of the thirty-nine poems in *The Haw Lantern* (taking 'Clearances' as nine poems, including its italicised heading poem), twenty-six are included in *Opened Ground*, including all the poems of 'Clearances'. By that measure, the book is highly valued by SH despite his description of it as 'a light craft' in *Stepping Stones* (291) and its relative slighting by commentators including Michael Allen in an influential review. Praise was not as fulsome as before (the *New York Times* spoke of a poet 'enlarging his powers of invention' and the London *Independent* of poems that 'irradiate . . . with a humanity'), but 'light craft' or not, *The Haw Lantern* is one of the most learned and allusive of all SH's books.

Because of the centrality and power of the parental elegies, *The Haw Lantern* does not lend itself as readily as its predecessors to the binary contrasting of artistic freedom versus public responsibility as those bear on the politics of Northern Ireland. But there is another, less local politics here. The book turns to a different, more abstract kind of political perspective, and it can even be seen as the last of SH's books in which politics in any form is a primary concern. 'The Stone Verdict', as well as its personal elegiac subject, links to the series of poems in what SH calls 'the parable mode': poems set in a series of abstract states such as 'Parable Island', 'From the Republic of Conscience', 'The Frontier of Writing', 'The Land of the Unspoken' and 'The Canton of Expectation'. Even poems whose titles do not follow this naming pattern invent such polities – 'The Mud Vision' and 'The Disappearing Island'. When Dennis O'Driscoll suggested an influence here from East European poets or the fables of Borges, SH says that the American poet Richard Wilbur's poem 'Shame' (which opens, 'It is a cramped little state', and whose capital is 'Scusi') was the immediate influence in the development of the political-allegorical strain (*SS*, 291). There is also a move beyond the politics of Ireland altogether, as in 'From the Republic of Conscience', written in 1985 at the request of Heaney's local branch of Amnesty International in Sandymount, to mark United Nations Day. From this point onwards SH is more disposed to declare in public liberal political positions, free of any contamination with violence, as his earlier exclusive concentration on Irish politics widens.

It has also been said that what gives the volume a consistency is the theme of education, from 'Alphabets' onwards.[*] Indeed if 'Alphabets' had survived as the book's title, it would have established autobiographical learning as an abiding theme of the whole book, especially

---

[*] Florence Impens notes that SH's 'eclectic readings of that period [at Harvard in the mid-1980s] would certainly be reflected in the multiplication and variety of classical allusions in *The Haw Lantern*' (Higgins 2021, 223; see also Dillon 1995).

the learning of writing and symbolic representation. (Learning, as SH explains to O'Driscoll, is the prescribed concern of the Harvard Phi Beta Kappa poem for which 'Alphabets' was written; *SS*, 291.) But education is not an unmodified progress in imaginative terms: the astronaut's vision of the risen earth at the end of 'Alphabets' is as 'pre-reflective' and new as the child watching the plasterer, tracing the family name on the gable. It might even be said that the volume's dominant subject is the emergence of language and learning from the 'pre-articulate', and that the process begun in 'Alphabets' reaches its logical conclusion in 'Hermit Songs' in *Human Chain*, which revisits 'The age of lessons to be learnt' (*HC*, 75; *PSH*, 676). *The Haw Lantern*'s second poem 'Terminus' is concerned with the child's learning of local borders and limits rather than the representation of them, derived from the preliterate objects and perceptions of childhood.

A learning-related idea in *The Haw Lantern* which becomes increasingly prominent in the poetry from here on relates to SH's declaration of feeling what he called 'shy of condescension' in 'Casualty' in *Field Work* (*FW*, 14–17; *PSH*, 224); in 'Clearances' 4 it is the poet's mother's 'fear of affectation' which prompts her to affect linguistic inadequacy 'as if she might betray / The hampered and inadequate by too / Well-adjusted a vocabulary' (*HL*, 28; *PSH*, 372). This will link to the concern for the unregarded that is voiced in 'Mint' (*SL*, 6; *PSH*, 466) and other poems in *The Spirit Level*, and in the minatory Horace translation 'Anything Can Happen' (*DC*, 13; *PSH*, 598).

The poem 'Fosterling' in *Seeing Things* famously expresses surprise that the poet waited until 'nearly fifty / To credit marvels'; but that moment of belief is anticipated in the poem 'Hailstones' here. Things that were 'intimated and disallowed' said '*wait*', prompting a rejoinder from the voice of the poem saying 'wait for what?' Has he waited for forty years to recognise the moment of learning what was 'the truest foretaste of your aftermath'? And any expectation that the borderlines between the individual volumes are impermeable must be modified in the light of the fact that the poem 'From the Frontier of Writing' occurs in the course of an earlier version of section III of the 'Station Island' sequence where there is no suggestion that it is a single poem.*

The Haw Lantern is a book of self-dedication; one word for the attitude of these poems is 'votive'. The voice in each of the poems, from the child in 'Alphabets' onwards, is devoted to some belief system or set of values. In some of the poems, it could be called a cult (in 'The Mud Vision' and 'Parable Island' for example). Indeed it might be

---

* Version of *ST* in *Hudson Review*, 36. 2 (1983) where 'Station Island III' has a closing section beginning 'I got back into the driver's seat'.

argued that the parable poems do after all fit in with the binary of poetry and politics by proposing a series of abstract cults which do not demand fealty in the way that the two sides of the Northern Irish religious divide do. Before the two relatively low-key short poems which end the volume, the strange parable poem 'The Mud Vision' acts as a kind of summary conclusion to the volume's themes. It begins with clear application to Irish devotional iconography with the images of the Sacred Heart and the Crown of Thorns in the first line, joined by more modern developments: 'the blessings of popes' and 'idols on tour', and Richard Long's hand circles from Avon, 1984. This is a move away from the personal politics of *Station Island* and the alter ego figure of Sweeney to a more collective view of observance.

The new themes of *The Haw Lantern* were matched by a new look typographically. Faber had directed the book's photosetting to Goodfellow and Egan, in Cambridge, who produced the book in Lapidary 333, a digitisation of Eric Gill's Perpetua, in a comparatively delicate cast for the poems well suited to their content; the book was the first of SH's to be printed by Clays in Bungay, Suffolk, which would carry the share of Faber's poetry printing for many decades to come. And even if the critical response had been somewhat muted, the volume was swiftly embraced by its readership, as an enthusiastic memo of 10 July 1987 from Matthew Evans, who would become a trusted voice for SH at Faber:

> We printed 30,000 and have sold nearly 18,000 since publication 10 days ago, and this Sunday it will be No. 3 in the best-seller lists in *The Sunday Times*. There may be some hope for British culture yet, even though the author is Irish! (FF ME140)

[text: *HL2006*]

[For Bernard and Jane McCabe]

First published as the dedicatory poem in *HL*, and subsequently included in *NSP1990* and *OG*.

1 half-full] half full *NSP1990*

Working titles in MS/TS 'Anticipation' and 'Vigil' (NLI 49,493/84).

Epigraph and dedication SH tells O'Driscoll that he gave the completed manuscript of the book (which was published in June 1987) to the McCabes on a visit to Lincolnshire in the summer of 1986. The moment recalled in the epigraph was one shared by the Heaneys and McCabes when they stopped at the small Saxon church of St Gregory's in Kirkdale near Pickering in North Yorkshire some time earlier (*SS*, 286). The phrase 'the river in the tree' occurs in Emily Dickinson's 'letter to Mrs J. G. Holland' (May 1866), but SH tells O'Driscoll that he didn't know of it (*SS*, 289). In both *NSP1990* and *OG*, the dedication is given the same weight and position typographically as a poem title and appears on the contents pages in that form also.

Alphabets

First published in *Harvard Magazine* (July/Aug. 1984): 31, then in the Gallery Press limited-edition *Hailstones*: 10–12, *Harper's* (Dec. 1984): 31, and *Paris/Atlantic* (Summer 1985): 50–2. Collected with revisions in *HL* and subsequently included in *NSP1990*, *OG* and *100P*.

I 5] Once there he draws smoke with chalk for a week, *Harvard Magazine, Hailstones, Harper's*
I 6 stick that they] stick they *Harvard Magazine, Hailstones, Harper's*
I 12 pen] pen, *Harvard Magazine*
I 13 out',] out' *Harvard Magazine, Hailstones, Harper's*
II 1 hosanna] hosannah *Hailstones*
II 1–24] II

    SANCTUS, SANCTUS, SANCTUS, in gold appliqué
    A foot high on the altar's baize:
    Silence came beating through the sanctuary.
    Then a faint peal of etymologies

    Got lost in the side altar's HOSANNA
    For years, until, column after column,
    Book One of Elementa Latina,
    Marbled and minatory, rose up in him.

    So he learned U could be written like a V,
    That V could be sounded V or W,
    And began to think the soft Church Latin c
    And the New Learning's hard c stood for two

    Ways with the world, the eroticism
    of [sic] yielding versus puritan fury.
    He dwelt in phonetics. His first volume
    Was published in MCMLXVI.

        III
    Meanwhile, in that enclosure on a hill
    Called after the saint of the oak wood
    He changed classrooms to the sound of a bell,
    Leaving paved Latin for the branchy shade

    Of an alphabet with letters named for trees.
    Scrolled capitals stood like thorns in bloom,
    The lines were briary as summer ditches –
    Calligraphy which made him feel at home.

> With leaves stuck to her shawl-frills and bare feet,
> All ringleted in assonance and woodnotes,
> The poets' dream stole over him like sunlight
> And passed into the tenebrous thickets.
>
> He learns this other writing. He is the scribe
> Who drove a team of quills on his white field.
> Round his cell door the blackbirds dart and dab.
> Then self-denial, fasting, the pure cold.
>
> By rules that hardened the farther they reached north
> He bends to his desk and begins again.
> Christ's sickle has been in the undergrowth.
> The script grows bare and Merovingian. *Harvard Magazine*

II 5–12 Named after the saint of the oak wood
    Where he changed classrooms to the sound of a bell,
    Leaving paved Latin for the branchy shade

    Of an alphabet with letters named for trees.
    Here capitals lifted heads in blossom
    From lines scrolled thick as briars on the ditches –
    Calligraphy which made him feel at home. *Hailstones, Harper's*
II 14 ringleted] ringletted *Hailstones, Harper's*
II 15 poet's] poets' *Hailstones, Harper's*
III 1–24] [IV 1–24] *Harvard Magazine*
III 4 printouts] print-outs *Harvard Magazine, Hailstones, Harper's*
III 6–7] And the long delta of the potato pit / Hardened its outline against early frost. *Harvard Magazine*
III 9 good luck horse-shoe] good-luck horseshoe *OG, 100P*
III 18 all he] all that he *OG*
III 21 wide] wide, *Harvard Magazine*
III 23 our name] my name *Harvard Magazine*

'Alphabets' was the Phi Beta Kappa poem at Harvard University in 1984, the year SH's temporary contract at Harvard was altered to a tenured position as Boylston Professor of Rhetoric and Oratory, in succession to the classical scholar Robert Fitzgerald, the subject of an SH elegy (*HL*, 24; *PSH*, 369). The elegy was also published in the *Irish Press* and in the *New York Review of Books* in 1987.

    I 16 The turning of the globe as an image for the developing understanding of writing is the crucial image in the poem. Herbert McCabe, Bernard's brother, said that SH considered *The Globe in the Window* as a possible title for the volume (private conversation with BO'D).

    II 3 *Elementa Latina*, or *Latin Lessons for Beginners*, W. H. Morris (London: Longman, 1914).

    II 6 *the patron saint of the oak wood*: sixth-century St Columba (Colmcille), after whom SH's secondary school, St Columb's in

Derry, was named. The Irish name of the city is Doire Cholm Cille, 'the oakwood of Colmcille'.

II 10 Some letters of the Gaelic Ogham alphabet (like some letters of the Old English alphabet) are named after trees, e.g. *Beith* (birch).

II 12 *briars coiled in ditches*: descriptive of the ornate margins of Old Irish manuscripts. The following lines list some of the typical subjects of Irish monastic poetry, like the blackbird at the cell door (II 19), recalled in the blackbird of the final poem in *DC* and the much-translated poem about the blackbird of Belfast Lough.

II 24 *Merovingian*: the Gallo-Roman script from which the traditional script for Irish was drawn until it was replaced by the *cló Rómhánach* (Roman form) in the 1950s. Historically the Merovingian script was replaced in the ninth century by the Carolingian script which thereafter became the standard in Western Europe.

III 6ff. The 'shape-note language' (III 10) in these lines begins with the shapes of the Greek letters λ, δ and ω applied to farming items, such as the horseshoe commonly attached to outhouse walls on Irish farms. 'IN HOC SIGNO' refers to the sign of the vision of the cross by the Emperor Constantine in 312, a vision of the initial Greek letters of the name of Christ chi-rho (XP) which led to 'The Donation of Constantine' giving jurisdiction of the Western Empire to the Papacy. The Chi-Rho Page in the Book of Kells is admired as one of the great works of medieval illustration. See notes on *SI* (*PSH*, 896).

III 13ff. The third spin of the globe in the poem's running conceit returns the poet to the now bulldozed old school where the modern symmetrical printout-like bales of corn-straw have replaced the sheaves and stooks of corn of the poet's childhood.

III 23–4 It was a common practice when building houses in the Irish countryside to write the family name or initials in the wet plaster.

Terminus

First published in the *LRB* (1–14 Nov. 1984): 8, then in *Hailstones*: 14–15. Collected with revisions in *HL* and subsequently included in *NSP1990* and *OG*.

13–14 This stanza does not appear in the *LRB*.
20 stepping stone] stepping-stone *LRB*
22 peers] kernes *LRB*

Title The poem and its title are discussed in 'Something to Write Home About' (1998) in *FK*, 48ff.

I 1 *hoked*: Ulster-Scots from Scots dialect 'howk', to dig, root round, rummage.

II 3 'make friends of the mammon of iniquity' (The Parable of the Unjust Steward, Luke 16:1–9).

III 2 SH's birthplace was in fact on the border between what he describes as 'the predominantly Protestant and loyalist village of Castledawson' and the 'generally Catholic and nationalist district of Bellaghy' (FK, 50).

III 7 *the earl on horseback in midstream*: Hugh O'Neill, an Ulsterman of the noble Uí Néill clan, who was brought up in the Elizabethan English Court but who led the Irish rebellion against the Crown in the Nine Years War at the turn of the seventeenth century, which ended with the defeat of the Irish at the Battle of Kinsale in 1601 and 'the Flight of the Earls' to the Continent. O'Neill's deliberations are the subject of the play *Making History* by SH's friend Brian Friel (first performed by Field Day in Derry in 1988).

From the Frontier of Writing

First published in the *TLS* (1 Nov. 1985): 1224. After collection with minor revisions in *HL* it was included in *Readings in Contemporary Poetry*, *NSP1990* and *OG*.

3 number] number, *TLS*
12 obedient.] obedient . . . *TLS*
23 flowing and receding] fluently receding *TLS*

Title in TS 'From the Place of Writing'. The first of the state-parable poems in the book, which are widely recognised to have been influenced by Eastern European writers. The poem is written in a modified terza rima. It is a particularly successful metaphorical reworking of a real situation (the challenge by soldiers at a checkpoint) into a conceit for the writer's self-scrutiny.

The Haw Lantern

First published in Lynda Moran (ed.), *Poets for Africa* (n.p.: Leinster Leader, 1986): 83–4. All proceeds from this book were donated to Band Aid. Also published in *Verse*, 6 (1986): 23–4, and in the *Irish Press* (20 June 1987): 9. After collection in *HL* it was also included in *NSP1990*, *OG* and *100P*.

Title SH discusses the choice of the title as 'requiring strict self-examination from everybody, be they poets, pundits, priests, party political jabberwocks', which fits with the challenging frontiers of the previous poem.

7 Diogenes of Sinope (*c*.412–323 BCE), one of the founders of Greek Cynic philosophy. He held a lamp up to the faces of the

Athenians, looking for an honest man: a popular subject with Renaissance artists.

    12 The idea of being scrutinised by the modest haw is original with SH – 'its pecked-at ripeness that scans you, then moves on', like the soldiers and metaphorical interpreters of the previous poem.

The Stone Grinder

First published in *Verse*, 6 (1986): 23–4.

    1 Penelope, the wife of Odysseus in Homer's *Odyssey*. In the absence of her husband, she promises to respond to the suitors' overtures when she has completed the shroud she is weaving for her father-in-law Laertes; but every night she unpicks her day's work so that the task will never be completed. The implication of SH's employment of the conceit seems to be that the artist never works back to a clean slate, even if it seems so to the new practitioner.

A Daylight Art

First published in the *Scotsman* (15 Nov. 1985): 11, and in Lynda Moran (ed.), *Poets for Africa* (n.p.: Leinster Leader, 1986): 83–4, *Cumberland Poetry Review* (Spring 1986): 43–4, and *Gown* (1986): 10. Collected with revisions in *HL*.

4–6]   And this was not for the reasons you'd expect,
          that Socrates was a lover of wisdom
          and an advocate of the examined life.

          No. The extremist of reason
          was scanning lines in those last precious hours
          because he'd had a dream. *Scotsman, Cumberland Poetry Review*

10 original panoramas] the far panoramas *Scotsman, Cumberland Poetry Review*
13 Socrates. Until,] Socrates – until, *Scotsman, Cumberland Poetry Review*
14 the] this *Scotsman, Cumberland Poetry Review*   had] has *Scotsman, Cumberland Poetry Review*
16–17] *Practice the art,* which he had always taken / until that momnent [*sic*] to mean philosophy. *Scotsman | Practice the art,* which until that moment / he always took to mean philosophy. *Cumberland Poetry Review*
19 one from the start –] art from the start, *Scotsman, Cumberland Poetry Review*

Dedication Norman MacCaig (1910–96) was one of a group of Scottish poets greatly admired by SH. Like several of SH's friends, notably Ted Hughes, MacCaig was a fisherman-poet. The title of this poem is a tribute to the luminous clarity for which MacCaig's poetry is admired.

2 *Socrates*: the Greek philosopher was condemned to death by self-administering poison in 399 BCE. In Plato's *Phaedo*, the dialogue which tells of the death of Socrates, he says that he has occupied his last days before taking the poison in versifying Aesop's fables, describing a fable about pain and pleasure. Aesop is said to have suffered an unjust death, like Socrates. Linking the translation of Aesop to fishing is SH's initiative.

22 The comparison of the nib to the fishing rod recalls SH's substituting the pen for the spade in 'Digging'.

Parable Island

First published in John Carey (ed.), *William Golding: The Man and His Books* (London: Faber & Faber, 1986), 169–70, to mark Golding's seventy-fifth birthday.

SH tells O'Driscoll that, though most of the parable poems in *The Haw Lantern* were written in the Heaneys' house in Strand Road, 'a good bit' of this one was done in Iceland in 1985 (*SS*, 286). This poem can in some ways be seen as a mirror image of 'Alphabets' because here the glossators and archaeologists are working their way back to origins which were the starting point for the child in 'Alphabets'.

I Clearly the imaginary island of the opening section bears a strong resemblance to Ireland, whose 'only border is an inland one'. In *l.* 8, 'Cape Basalt' refers to the Giant's Causeway, the most prominent natural landmark in 'the far north'. The running conceit in the poem is of a 'traveller' visiting this strange island and encountering for the first time the various conflicting historical claims – traditional or revisionist – that are made on it, from the monastic to the archaeological to the theological.

II 6 *autochthonous*: sprung from the soil, rocks and trees. Of population, indigenous, rather than immigrant or colonising: etymologically 'of the land itself' (Greek): a recurrent idea in SH as in 'Tollund' in *SL*.

II 11 *revisionists*: one of the themes of the poem is the conflict between the traditional narrative of Irish history, versus the various 'revisionist' questionings of that narrative. Here the 'old revisionists' are seekers out of deconstructive etymologies, which undermines the simple opposition.

III Develops the paradoxical Irish 'Island Story' of section II. Section IV ends the poem with an interpretation that is unquestionably wrong (the draining away of the Atlantic). The story can't be got 'straight' (III 9); the elders' stories of 'boat-journeys and havens' recall the legendary arrival of the mythical settlers, the Milesians from north-west Spain, as the first colonisers of the autochthonous territory of Ireland.

From the Republic of Conscience

First published as a pamphlet on 10 December 1985, for Amnesty International, Irish section, with an illustration by John Behan. Parts I and II of the poem were included in a pamphlet published by University College Galway Amnesty Group in 1987, and the original Amnesty pamphlet was reissued as a broadside and card in 1989. Also published in *Reflections: Journal of the Society of Writers, United Nations Staff Recreation Council* (Sept. 1986): 4–5, and *American Poetry Review* (July/Aug. 1987): 6, before collection in *HL*, and later inclusion in *NSP1990*, *OG* and *100P*.

The second of the parable poems in *HL*, the poem was written in 1985 to celebrate the twenty-fifth anniversary of the founding of Amnesty International. SH tells O'Driscoll that Richard Wilbur's 'Shame' helped him 'to get started' on the project (*SS*, 291–2).

I Section I begins with a literal arrival on Orkney, where the immigration officers have allegorical associations, side by side with the real curlew's call compared by SH to Yeats's 'Paudeen' with its 'sweet crystalline cry' (*SS*, 292). The arriving passenger bears the poet's responsibilities: to his family heritage (given a picture of his grandfather) and beyond it. In the absence of porters and taxis, he has to carry his 'own burden', and the 'symptoms of creeping privilege' have gone: an established SH theme – in 'Oysters' (*FW*) for example.

I^II In a TS dated 14 August 1985, the poem carries an additional section, numbered II, and sequenced between the published text's final parts I and II:

> Their creation stories tell how earth arose
> from salt in tears that the sky-god wept
> after he dreamt his solitude was endless.
>
> Salt is their precious mineral. Seashells
> are held to the ear at births and funerals.
> The base of their inks and pigments is seawater.
>
> They have no word for foreigner or jury
> and the same monosyllable signifies
> 'poem', 'conspiracy', 'government' and 'orgasm'.
>
> Their sacred symbol is a stylized boat.
> The sail is an ear, the mast a sloping pen,
> the hull a mouth shape, the keel an open eye. (NLI 49,493/84)

II Section II is an Audenesque extension of the practices and values of this conscience-ruled republic. Salt, in itself or in seawater or in tears, is the stock in trade. The solitary sky god weeps this republic into existence, and its leaders 'weep / to atone for their presumption to hold office': the poet's self-privileged responsibility again.

III Section III describes the poet passing back through customs, now as a dual citizen of the republic of conscience as well as the republic of letters (SH's familiar dilemma of answerability to the public world of conscience or to artistic licence). Because of his dual citizenship the poet must now speak on behalf of conscience in his native tongue; Conscience's embassies are everywhere and the ambassador's appointment is for life. They can never be relieved of its responsibilities.

Hailstones

First published in the *London Review of Books* (1–14 Nov. 1984): 8, then in the Gallery Press limited-edition *Hailstones*: 16–7, and in *Dánta idir ghaeilge agus bhéarla*, a limited-edition publication from Wake Forest University Press for distribution at the annual meeting of the American Committee for Irish Studies (1984), 10–1. Also published in the *Seneca Review*, 16. 2 (1986): 40–1. Collected in *HL* and included in *NSP1990* and *OG*.

I 1 hit:] hit *Seneca Review*
I 12 absence.] absence *Seneca Review*
II 8 had his orient] had orient *LRB*, *Hailstones*
II 12 nettles.] nettles *Seneca Review*
III 5 wait.] wait *Seneca Review*
III 7–9] to say there, there's where / to taste and test it: / disappointment *LRB* | to say there, there's where / to taste and test it: / disappointment *Hailstones*
III 10 when the light opened] as the light opens *LRB*, *Hailstones*   in silence] in the silence *Seneca Review*
III 12 laid] lays *LRB*, *Hailstones*

Dated Ardour House, 4–6 February 1984 in TS (NLI 49,493/80).

See 'Two Poems', *LRB* (1 Nov. 1984), and *Hailstones*, the short collection of which it is the title poem (Gallery Press, 1984). The physical hail in section I is a figure for 'this' poem now, made of 'the real thing' and 'smarting into its absence'. Section II calls the hail that provided the 'real' material from which the poem was composed as 'brats of showers' that refused permission for use as poetic material and rapidly deteriorated into 'dirty slush', a symbol which returns in 'The Mud Vision' (*HL*, 50).

II 8–9 The religious Metaphysical poet Thomas Traherne (1637–74): 'The Corn was Orient and Immortal Wheat which never should be reaped, nor was ever sown. I thought it had stood from everlasting to everlasting. The Dust and the Stones of the Street were as precious as Gold' (*Centuries of Meditations*, no. 3).

II 11 *Eddie Diamond*: the son of a farmer near the Heaneys, between Castledawson and Bellaghy.

III The forty-year wait for the aftermath anticipates the fifty years of waiting to 'credit marvels' of 'Fosterling' in *ST*. The perfect lines made by the car wipers in the slush on the windscreen is a clarification of the slush waiting for form in section I.

Two Quick Notes

First published in *Verse*, 6 (1986): 23–4.

Working title in TS 'A Quick Note' (NLI 49,493/81, /83). Possibly an address to Conscience, as in 'The Republic of Conscience'.

The Stone Verdict

First published in *Hailstones*: 19, then in *Poetry Australia*, 102 (1985): 32, *University of Toronto Review* (Summer 1987): 31. Collected with revisions in *HL*, and then included in *NSP1990*, *OG* and *100P*.

1, 8 judgment] judgement *Hailstones*, *Poetry Australia*, *University of Toronto Review*, *OG*, *100P*
4 excuses,] excuses *University of Toronto Review*
12 apotheosis] absolution *OG*, *100P*
13 wallstead] wall *University of Toronto Review*

SH tells O'Driscoll this was a strong candidate for title poem of the volume. The figure of the opening with his stick in his hand and a broad hat is Hermes (named in *l*. 8) but identified by his speechlessness (*l*. 7) and his 'disdain of sweet talk and excuses' (*l*. 4) with SH's father, who died in 1986. It is important to remember, though, that the poem in identical form was published in *Hailstones* in 1984, two years before his death, so the poem is a kind of preliminary elegy, considering what will be appropriate when death comes. Even the brief recognition of the pile of stones round the figure of Hermes as the place where 'his spirit lingers' will already be saying 'too much' for this very taciturn man. SH's interest in Aeneas's search for his father Anchises in the underworld links to a wish to debrief in the afterlife his own much-loved, reserved father (as he says to Karl Miller and Andrew O'Hagan, *Guardian*, 2 Sept. 2013).

From the Land of the Unspoken

First published in the *TLS* (1 Nov. 1985): 1224, and collected in *HL*.

13 hear their legends] hear legends *TLS*
16 sea roads] sea-roads *TLS*
20–1 train / and] train. And *TLS*
23–4] pretending to be absorbed in a display / of absolutely silent quernstones.] that seemed all concentration on a quernstone. *TLS*
26 revelation. How] revelation: how *TLS*
27–8 first of us to seek / assent and votes] first to speak the word] that sues for votes *TLS*

Following on from the speechlessness of 'The Stone Verdict', this report from the land of the unspoken – not the unspeaking, but something like the unsayable – connects with the guilt and responsibility which are the book's wider themes.

1ff. The 'bar of platinum' of the poem's opening sounds like the Bank of England with its 'standard of measurement' as guarantor of value. This 'logical and talkative nation' seems as remote from the taciturn subject in 'The Stone Verdict' as they are from 'the dispersed people' of the second stanza, who are in exile among 'the speech-ridden' – a term which still implies that speech is an aberration. The legends of the 'speech-ridden' here are multiple: the 'infants discovered / floating in a coracle towards destiny' include the biblical Moses but also link to Scyld at the start of *Beowulf* who appears *umborwesende* ('being an infant') and whose funeral ship disappears on 'the sea roads', a burden which no one knows who receives. Thirdly the reference is to the burial of the legendary Irish king Cormac mac Airt who was buried against his wishes at Brú no Bóinne (Newgrange) but is borne by the flooded waters of the Boyne to be anonymously interred at his chosen burial place of Rosnaree ('the Headland of the Kings'). In a strange personal twist, what are recognised in the third stanza as 'our own' are equally 'unspoken' and not admitted to: the passing erotic brushes in a rush-hour train or a museum, things which are not connected with value or destiny at all. The poem's last stanza declares that our real revelations are assumptions which we leave unspoken, like the ripples that survive the jump of the fish which we haven't seen.

A Ship of Death

First published in *Numbers* (Autumn 1986): 96.

A translation of *Beowulf*, ll. 26–52, it is the first translation of any part of *Beowulf* published by SH. The text varies in several details from the translation of these lines in SH's 1999 translation of the complete poem.

1 Scyld is the eponymous legendary founder of the Scyldings, the Danes, in *Beowulf*. The disposal of his body by casting it out on to the sea ends with a declaration of ultimate doubt which fits the indeterminacy of this book: the failure to know for certain 'who salvaged that load'.

The Spoonbait

First published in *Hailstones*: 13, then in *Poetry Australia*, 102 (1985): 32. After collection in *HL* it was included in *NSP1990* and *OG*.

1–2] Since this text does not exist, let us / Invent it: The soul of man may be likened *Poetry Australia*
4 case,] case. *Poetry Australia*

This poem is a variation on the parabling that the book employs, beginning with the New Testament formula of similitude. A spoonbait in fishing is a lure in the form of a shining metal plate with a hook attached to it. SH tells O'Driscoll that the image is concerned with loss of faith (*SS*, 287), and the idea seems to be a kind of delusive visionary gleam, 'a toy of light / . . . snagging on nothing'. The fact that it occurs as a glimpse once in a child's pencil case suggests that it is a memory of a real event from childhood. In a file in National Library of Ireland (l.vi.1, Image 11), the 'bill' element is linked to Old English *bil* (sword) (NLI 49,493/32).

In Memoriam: Robert Fitzgerald

First published in the *Irish Press* (20 June 1987): 9, and then in the *NYRB* (17 Dec. 1987): 9.

1 axehead] axhead *NYRB*
6 Just threshold] Just a threshold *NYRB*
12 test over] test is over *NYRB*

Robert Fitzgerald (1910–85), poet most celebrated as translator of Homer and of Virgil's *Aeneid*, and as a collaborating translator of Euripides and Sophocles. He was SH's predecessor as Boylston Professor of Rhetoric and Oratory at Harvard (1965–81), and a friend of the Heaneys there. The poem is an extreme statement of the book's elegiac theme, of beginnings that open on to absence and empty centres.

The Old Team

First published in the *Honest Ulsterman*, 80 (Spring 1986): 5.

9 FC!] F.C. *Honest Ulsterman*
13 dull-thumping] long-shadowed *Honest Ulsterman*

Dated 1 May [1985] in MS. In TS, this poem was the first of two numbered sonnets under the working title 'Perspectives'; the second, 'A cobble thrown a hundred years ago', became the opening to 'Clearances'.

The poem's colonial setting evokes a picture of an association soccer team, as distinct from the Castledawson Gaelic football team for which SH played (his maternal uncle, Matt Sonny McCann, the son of 'Grandfather McCann' in *l*. 10, was a major player at the club and also played for Derry and Ulster). But the elegiac figures here have gone 'in your absence': while the poet was somewhere else. The 'dull-thumping games of football' in the penultimate line evoke playing Gaelic football, also grown historical in the time of the poem.

Clearances

The sequence is reproduced in full in *NSP1990* and *OG*. The limited-edition *Clearances* (Amsterdam: Cornamona Press, 1986) included versions of poems 'Clearances' 1, 2, 3, 4, 6, 7, and 8, and the uncollected 'The Late Paul Cézanne' (*PSH*, 353).

This series of elegies for his mother, Margaret Kathleen McCann, who died in 1984, are among SH's best-loved poems. In the 2009 RTÉ recording of the collected poems, SH reads the dedication (*HL*, 26) as 'in memoriam Margaret Kathleen Heaney', without her dates. After the nine-line introductory poem there are eight sonnets. 'Things to Share' was a working title for the sequence (Brandes 2008, 132): see publication history of sonnet VII below.

['SHE TAUGHT ME WHAT HER UNCLE ONCE TAUGHT HER']

First published as one of the two poems in 'Diptych', *LRB* (3 July 1986): 10.

Dated 2 June 1986 in MS (NLI 49,493/85); working title in TS 'Things to Share' (NLI 49,493/80).

SH's mother, Margaret Kathleen Heaney (*née* McCann), died in 1984. This introductory poem takes the physical action of going with the grain in splitting coal as a figure for the writer's aim for precision. In some later poems, such as 'Weighing In', SH returns to this image of balance and force. The 'linear black' of the conclusion has perhaps an ageless air of 'Linear B', the originary linguistic writing system, to it.

1

First published in the *Honest Ulsterman*, 80 (Spring 1986): 3, the limited-edition *Clearances*, and in Jonathan Barker (ed.), *Poetry Book Society Anthology 1986/87* (London: Poetry Book Society, 1986), 49–50.

The first of the 'Clearances' sonnets tells the story of SH's Protestant maternal great-grandmother who married a Catholic husband and 'ran the gauntlet' of her disapproving community.

    8 'He' is the husband, driving her to Mass in the pony-and-trap.

    'Lundy!': Robert Lundy, a Scottish Army Officer, born in Dumbarton, who became Governor of the city during the early stages of the Siege of Derry in 1690. He failed to defend the city against the attacking Jacobite forces and has become a byword for a traitor in Orange iconography. Hence the cries of 'Lundy!' at the wife here, who has married outside her cultural tradition, an 'Exogamous Bride' (9).

2

First published in the *Honest Ulsterman*, 80 (Spring 1986): 3, then in *Field* (Spring 1986): 44, the limited-edition *Clearances*, and in Jonathan Barker (ed.), *Poetry Book Society Anthology 1986/87* (London: Poetry Book Society, 1986), 49–50.

4 teascone] tea scone OG

The second poem describes the orderliness of SH's mother's home at 5, New Row, Castledawson where we know from poem 7 (*ll.* 3–5) her husband came to court her.

    5 What are 'present and correct' are the household rules of mannerly behaviour as imposed on children. O'Driscoll reminds SH (*SS*, 310) that he has said in his *Paris Review* interview that the McCanns 'were strict adherents of dress codes and table manners'.

    9 *Land of the Dead*: both figures here, the grandfather and the married daughter visiting her premarital home, are now dead.

    11 The 'clean bald head' of Grandfather McCann is described to O'Driscoll (*SS*, 27).

3

First published in the *Honest Ulsterman*, 80 (Spring 1986): 4, then in *Field* (Spring 1986): 44, the limited-edition *Clearances*, and in Jonathan Barker (ed.),

Poetry Book Society Anthology 1986/87 (London: Poetry Book Society, 1986), 49–50. Also included in *100P*.

3 all the others were] the other woman was *Honest Ulsterman*, *Field*
8 each] the *Honest Ulsterman*, Field

The opening line originally read 'When the other woman was away at Mass', referring to the poet's paternal aunt Mary, the other candidate for his feminine domestic affections and the dedicatee of the poem 'Sunlight' at the start of *North*. SH writes in 'Clearances' 6 of his '*Sons and Lovers* phase', going to religious devotions with his mother.

SH's most well-known sonnet did not begin in that form, but as a poem of sextets in five parts initially called '"Dear Mam and Aunt Mary . . ."', preserved in an annotated TS in the National Library of Ireland (49,493/80), that SH subsequently revised, in a fair-copy TS titled 'A Chaplet', dedicated 'for my mother'.

A CHAPLET
for my mother

I

When all the others were away at Mass
I was all yours, peeling the potatoes:
They broke the silence, let fall one by one
Like solder weeping off the soldering iron.
Cold comforts set between us, things to share
Gloaming in a bucket of clean water.

II

Earlier you let fall memorial cards
Out of your missal, between the kneeling boards,
Black-rimmed, black-lettered, each with its photograph
Of the deceased . . . *Pray for the soul of* . . .
Our Lady of the Seven Dolours
Pined on the obverse in her sepia colours.

III

Your breath in my breath those Sunday mornings
Intimated the natural cold of things
And how you stood them just by understanding.
What age was I then when I came weeping
With news along the road from Castledawson
That your father had died? 'There now. Don't worry, son.'

iv

Once when you were carrying one of us
I watched you at the pump, bottling potatoes,

And I was old enough, though young and growing,
To see your youth and freedom then were going.
Wind and rain, the grey blown overall –
I'm grey at the temples now, grey Paul Morel.

   v

Let the wind blow high, let the wind blow low,
At the set times now I come and go.
And now the tears of things, now your resentments
At others' whimpering, or incontinence,
O mother, mother, in each departing kiss,
The lents, the christenings, the rosaries.

4

First published in *Field* (Spring 1986): 45, and in the limited-edition *Clearances*; in both publications it appears as the fifth poem in the sequence. Also in Jonathan Barker (ed.), *Poetry Book Society Anthology 1986/87* (London: Poetry Book Society, 1986), 49–50.

The poet is 'shy of condescension' ('Casualty' in *FW*, 14–17; *PSH*, 224). SH's book-reading mother, fearing affectation, affects wrong grammar ('all them things') and pronunciation ('Brek' for Brecht) so as not to betray 'the hampered and inadequate', like the disregarded in 'Mint' in *SL*, 6 (*PSH*, 466), and in 'Anything Can Happen' in *DC*, 13 (*PSH*, 598).

  9 *I governed my tongue*: SH's collection of essays *The Government of the Tongue* was published in 1988, the year following *The Haw Lantern*.

5

First published as 'Sonnet' in *Poetry Ireland Review* (Autumn 1986): 6. After collection in *HL* also included in *Seamus Heaney: Readings in Contemporary Poetry* (New York: Dia Art Foundation, 1988), 39.

6 cross wind] cross-wind *Poetry Ireland Review*
13 x] X *OG* o] O *OG*

The activity of folding sheets with his mother replicates the advancing and retiring of the 'allied and at bay' at the end of the previous poem. The theme is again partly competition without hostility: 'just touch and go'; 'I was x and she was o'.

  14 Making sheets out of flour bags was an extreme case of household economy.

6

First published in the *Honest Ulsterman*, 80 (Spring 1986): 4, the limited-edition *Clearances*, and in Jonathan Barker (ed.), *Poetry Book Society Anthology 1986/87* (London: Poetry Book Society, 1986), 49–50: in all three publications it appears as the fourth poem in the sequence.

The continuation of the theme of activities undertaken with his mother.

3 The dominant relationship in D. H. Lawrence's *Sons and Lovers* is between the self-referential central character Paul Morel and his mother.

9 Cf. Psalm 42:1.

11 *chrism*: a mixture of oil and balsam, used in anointing rituals of the Catholic Church, notably Baptism but also – significantly here – in anointing the sick.

7

First published in *Field* (Spring 1986): 45, then as the broadside 'In the last minutes he said more to her . . .', *from Things to Share: in memoriam M.K.H., 1911–1984*, by the Friends of Irish Studies, Boston College (9 Dec. 1986), and in the limited-edition *Clearances*. After collection in *HL*, also included in *Seamus Heaney: Readings in Contemporary Poetry* (New York: Dia Art Foundation, 1988), 39–40, and also included in *100P*.

2 in all their] in their whole *Field*
5 door . . .] door. *Field*
12 it penetrated] we tasted it *Field*
13–14 In a pure change that suddenly triumphed. / High cries were felled in us and brightenings happened. *Field*

Dated 17 June 1985 in MS. The death bed of the poet's mother.

1 The poet's taciturn father finally speaks in terms of affection.

3 *New Row*: Margaret Heaney's childhood home (no. 5) in Castledawson.

11 *The space we stood around had been emptied*: the semi-mystical theme of the substance of emptiness becomes prominent from this point onwards.

8

First published in the *Honest Ulsterman*, 80 (Spring 1986): 5, then in *Field* (Spring 1986): 46, the limited-edition *Clearances* (1986), and as a broadside ('I thought of walking round and round a space') with illustrations by Robert Perkins (Cambridge, Mass.: Char Press, 1987). After collection in *HL*, also included in *Seamus Heaney: Readings in Contemporary Poetry* (New York: Dia Art Foundation, 1988), 40.

5 high] high. *Honest Ulsterman*, *Field*, *NSP1990*, *OG*, Readings

6–7 differentiated / Accurate cut,] undifferentiated / Accurate cuts *Honest Ulsterman*
7 cut] cuts *Field*
11 jam jar] jamjar *Honest Ulsterman, Field*
12 become] became *Honest Ulsterman*

Dated in TS 13 April 1985 (NLI 49,493/84), under the queried title 'The Soul-Tree? (As a title?)', and with a pencilled author note at the foot: 'for Peter & Lynn with love from the ramifying Aries. Seamus' and a subsequent note 'And thank you for the welcome – and the stamina – of your hospitality. S.'

1–2 The 'space / Utterly empty, utterly a source' continues from the end of the previous poem.

3 *chestnut tree*: SH's 'coeval chestnut' (*ll.* 10–11) was planted in the year of his birth, as he tells us in the essay 'The Placeless Heaven: Another Look at Kavanagh' (*GT*, 3ff.). The felling of the tree and the sigh of its collapse link to the death of the mother in the 'Clearances' series, in creating 'a bright nowhere', and also perhaps to the sound of 'the river in the trees' in the book's epigraph.

The Milk Factory

First published in *Hailstones*, and after collection in *HL* included in *NSP1990* and *OG*.

1 *discharge pipe*: from the Nestlé factory in Castledawson (*l.* 6).

3 the phrase 'pierced side' comes in Gospel narratives of the Crucifixion. 'But when they came to Jesus and saw that he was already dead, they did not break his legs. Instead, one of the soldiers pierced his side with a spear, and at once blood and water came flowing out' (John, 19:33–4).

The Summer of Lost Rachel

First published in *Poetry Kanto*, 4 (Summer 1987): 16–17.

7 drills.] drills, *Poetry Kanto*
9 waterlogged] waterlogged. *Poetry Kanto*
10 loath] loth *Poetry Kanto*
17 accident,] accident *Poetry Kanto*
24 bike,] bike *Poetry Kanto*
25 usual,] usual *Poetry Kanto*

Rachel Heaney, the nine-year-old daughter of SH's brother Hugh, was killed when she was knocked off her bicycle outside their house at The Wood in May 1985. Sadly the tragedy was reminiscent of the death of SH's brother Christopher, the subject of 'Mid-Term Break'.

The poem is written in the ballad stanza, suggestive of clarity and innocence here.

8 'a ring around the moon' in folklore predicted precipitation of rain and snow.

The Wishing Tree

First published as the second of the two poems in 'Diptych', *LRB* (3 July 1986): 10, and then in *Poetry Kanto*, 4 (Summer 1987): 17. After collection in *HL* also included in *NSP1990*, *OG*, *Midsummer Feast*, where it appears with the dedication '*In memoriam* E. D.', and *100P*.

Dated 3 June 1986 in MS. The title refers to the practice of hammering coins into a particular tree, with each coin representing a wish or a prayer. The tree was located in Ardboe, Co. Tyrone, and the poem was written after the death of Eileen Devlin, SH's mother-in-law. In SH's elegiac poem the coins are 'needs'; the image links to the assumption of the Virgin Mary, body and soul, into Heaven, imagining that as the fitting fate for Rachel of the previous poem. The concluding vision of the branch-head rising up over the 'turned-up faces where the tree had stood' evokes the expressive space left by the removal of SH's 'coeval' chestnut in the last of the 'Clearances' poems (*HL*, 35; *PSH*, 373).

A Postcard from Iceland

Published in *HL*.

Dated 'for Marie, with much love, / September 14 1985' in MS, under the working title 'A letter from Iceland'.

1ff. The Icelandic geyser is well evoked in the opening lines.

6 The uncommon Old Icelandic word *lukr* means the hollow of the hand, held like a cup, so 'lukewarm' means at hand-temperature. 'The inner palm of water' recalls 'the pierced side / Of milk itself' in 'The Milk Factory' (*HL*, 50; *PSH*, 374).

A Peacock's Feather

First published in Andrew Carpenter and Peter Fallon (eds), *The Writers: A Sense of Ireland* (Dublin: O'Brien, 1980), 51–2, then in *Numbers*, 1 (Autumn 1986): 94–5. After collection in *HL* it was also included in *Midsummer Feast*. Dated in typescript Bradley Court, 1972.

2–3] To name and bless your fontanel / That seasons towards womanhood. *The Writers* | To name and bless your fontanel / That seasons towards womanhood – *Numbers*

9 as] like *The Writers, Numbers*
15 have] has *The Writers*
17 cart-track] cart-rut *The Writers*
21 own. We'll] own, we'll *The Writers*
22 wave] live *The Writers*
23 With] In *The Writers*
24 billet-doux] billet doux *Numbers*
26 Bradley] Bradley. *The Writers*
30 Park.] Park! *The Writers*
32 pray. May] pray: may *The Writers*
34 wood –] wood. *The Writers*
35 Where] And *The Writers*
36 on] in *The Writers*
Date 1972] Bradley Court, 1972 *The Writers, Numbers* | [no date] *Midsummer Feast*

Working titles in TS 'A Daisy Chain' and 'Bradley Court'.

Dedication Daisy Garnett is the 'English niece' of Marie Heaney, the middle daughter of her sister Polly Devlin and her husband the industrial engineer and entrepreneur Andy Garnett; taken with the Rachel elegy, the poem forms a diverse diptych of child-niece poems. Like her mother, Daisy went on to write for *Vogue* magazine. The child, with her Tyrone mother and her Etonian father, is born in a 'loam / Darkened with Celts' and Saxons' blood' (*ll*. 32–3).

26 Bradley is their Elizabethan manor house Bradley Court (the 'green court' of *l*. 27) near Wotton-under-Edge in Gloucestershire which is where SH found the peacock feather and rapidly wrote the poem.

28ff. SH, 'at a west window' in 'the green court' performs a role like that of Yeats in the Gregory house at Coole Park (*l*. 30). The 'ordered home' of Daisy contrasts with the rain-soaked Northern Irish summer of Rachel.

Grotus and Coventina

First published in *Verse*, 1 (Oct. 1984): 3, and then in *Hailstones*. After collection in *HL* it was also included in *OG*.

5 the stone where he cut his name] anywhere he had left his mark *Verse, Hailstones*
10 rage] angers *Verse*
11 phone-calls] phonecalls *Verse*
11–13 door / For somebody please to come and fix it? / And] door? / And *Verse, Hailstones*
17 through all that one] through that just one *Verse, Hailstones*
18] You be Coventina, I'll be Grotus. *Verse, Hailstones*

Title Coventina was a Romano-British goddess of wells and springs, recorded in inscriptions near the Roman fort and Temple of Mithras at Carrawburgh on Hadrian's Wall in Northumberland, at a point called 'Coventina's Well'. The well has a great number of votive objects in it, including two dedication slabs to the goddess Coventina and ten small altars to her, as well as a great number of Roman coins. Grotus only occurs as a name cut crudely into the stone so his identification as a Roman soldier 'Far from home', and his attraction to running water, are SH's inventions.

9ff. The application of the homely appreciation of running water to the relief at the restoration of domestic water recalls an event in Glanmore (*SS*, 295): a love poem in which the deity is the female and the votive the male.

Holding Course

First published in *Numbers*, 1 (Autumn 1986): 91.

7 Toledo] toledo *Numbers*

Working titles in TS: 'A Distance', 'Strand Road, 'The Strand Road', 'The Mid-Passage' and 'The Middle Passage' (NLI 49,493/78, /84).

1ff. The Heaneys' house in Sandymount looks eastward to the sea where the ferries pass, visible from the attic window.

7 'Toledo Blues' is a song by the jazz pianist Art Tatum recorded in the early 1940s.

9ff. The poem is recalling a shared visit to Spain: Covadonga is in Asturias, where the Heaneys visited Marie Heaney's sister Anne, who lives there.

13 The thorny items they brought back are compared to Grendel's steel-like claw, which is nailed to the roof as a symbol of victory over him in *Beowulf*.

19 MacWhirr in Conrad's *Typhoon* is single-minded in the pursuit of what he wants.

The narrative voice's envy of the morning sight of the ferries (*l.* 4) might suggest that the voice of the poem speaks a kind of 'home thoughts from abroad'.

The Song of the Bullets

First published as 'The Ballad of the Bullets' in *Ploughshares*, 11. 4 (1985): 38–40, then as 'The Song of the Bullets' in *An Múinteoir* (Autumn 1986): 12, and the *Irish Press* (20 June 1987): 9, before collection in *HL*.

>1]   Late summer breathed from earth and stones,
        Tall lupins probed the air,
    The Milky Way was combed-out light,
        The sheen off midnight's hair. *Ploughshares*
6 For something] And then it *Ploughshares*

8 speed] speed. *An Múinteoir*
10 curving] high swung *Ploughshares*
11 second light that swung up] twinned star moving *Ploughshares*
12 through] in *Ploughshares*
12^13] Two glow-worms that described pure arcs,
        And as these sink, there rise
      From complementary compass-points
        Two brilliant fireflies –

      Or better say mosquitoes, since
        I heard a panicked note,
      So laser-thin it flayed the round
        Huge silence of the night.

      And then like speeded tapes that slow
        And ease their chalk-screech noise,
      This modulated gradually
        To a far choral voice: *Ploughshares*
14 one began to] the first stars *Ploughshares*
15 lie] like *Ploughshares* [typo?]
19] Where justice whets its dream on us *Ploughshares*
28 reigned] reigned. *An Múinteoir*
29 fireball] fireballs *Ploughshares*
33 Mount Olivet's] The Olive Mount's *Ploughshares*
36 marbled] blue-rimmed *Ploughshares*
37–8]   Of carbon hurts and diamond laws
      Haughtily self-empowered.
     We fire and glaze the shape of things
      Until the shape cools hard.' *Ploughshares*
41 Now wind] Now the wind *Irish Press*

Working title in TS 'The Ballad of the Bullets'. In a book containing many poems that are untypical of SH's writing, this poem is perhaps the most untypical. It is written in the ballad stanza: quatrains rhyming *abcb*, with alternating lines of eight and six syllables, and of four and three stresses.

    1ff. The first-person narrative voice is a standard ballad opening. The quiet of the starry evening is broken by a moving star that rises from the skyline. At its zenith it cuts across another, similar line of light which now establishes these 'stars' as tracer bullets. The tracers 'sing' in the sky about their ugly material origins: the 'slugs of lead' and casings and 'blunted parts' which remain on the ground.

    21ff. No blame attaches to the bullets themselves whose action is seen as natural to them. The question of blame and guilt seems to belong to the book's theme rather than to the imagery of the poem.

    25ff. The musical image of the title is sustained through terms like 'warble', 'contralto' and 'cadenced', as if the aesthetic action of the tracers has no connection with the destruction it enables. The abstract generalisation 'Justice stands aghast' recalls the justice that lay 'like an acorn in the winter' in 'The Road to Derry', the uncollected poem, written as a song, about Bloody Sunday (*PSH*, 505).

33ff. The defeat of the 'cadenced desires' of the soul according to the beatitudes shows the action of the bullets to be against the spirit of the Sermon on the Mount. The return of the perspective of the opening at the end shows the real stars blanked out.

41ff. The poem has been interpreted as a gloomy prognostic of the times to come in Northern Ireland, the 'yard' and 'darkened hill' of the poem.

Wolfe Tone

First published in *Verse*, 6 (Autumn 1986): 24 and then, after collection in *HL*, in the *New York Times Book Review* (27 Dec. 1987): 27. Also included in *NSP1990* and *OG*.

Title Theobald Wolfe Tone (1763–98) was one of the founding members of the United Irishmen who led a French military force to Ireland during the rebellion of 1798. He was a London-trained Protestant lawyer from Dublin. After the failure of the rebellion, he died in prison after cutting his own throat. He is one of the major heroes of Irish republicanism. Working title in MS 'The Hero Yearns [to Outsing] His Moment'.

6 'played the ancient Roman with a razor' by cutting his own throat.

7 The oar recalls the ending of seafaring by Odysseus. In an archive file of writings before *HL*, there are varying handwritten versions of this couplet: 'I who had thought of myself as an oar / ended up like a parched winnowing fan' (NLI 49,493/77).

10 Tone went to America in 1795 with the intention of farming there. But, like Tennyson's Ulysses, he was reawakened to the call of seafaring adventure.

15–16 The French fleet led by Tone failed in its attempt to aid the Irish revolutionaries: it 'split and Ireland dwindled'.

A Shooting Script

First published in the *Sunday Tribune Magazine* (27 Dec. 1981): 4, then in *American Poetry Review* (July/Aug. 1987): 6, and collected in *HL*.

2 in a held shot;] in longshot; *Sunday Tribune Magazine*
3 bicycles, saluting native speakers,] bicycles on Gaeltacht roads *Sunday Tribune Magazine*

4 like the future] like water *Sunday Tribune Magazine*
6 anywhere and not getting away.] anywhere, not going away. *Sunday Tribune Magazine*
8 Pan] Hold *Sunday Tribune Magazine*
9] Voices over, in differently weathered Irish, *Sunday Tribune Magazine*
11 nineteenth-century] nineteenth century *Sunday Tribune Magazine, American Poetry Review*
11 verges,] verges *Sunday Tribune Magazine*
12] names like Quentin Durward and R. M. Ballantyne. *Sunday Tribune Magazine*
13 A close-up] Close-up *Sunday Tribune Magazine*
15] a roman collar, an adam's apple, a biretta. *Sunday Tribune Magazine*
16 his] the *Sunday Tribune Magazine*
16–17 run // And] run. // and *Sunday Tribune Magazine*
17 it is] it's *Sunday Tribune Magazine*
18] a tracking shot of a long wave on a strand *Sunday Tribune Magazine*
20 Words] names *Sunday Tribune Magazine*

SH tells O'Driscoll (*SS*, 315) that the poem 'belongs in a cluster of poems towards the end of *HL*, all of them about the doubleness of Irish experience', between the 'dwindling' at the end of 'Wolfe Tone' and the 'constant possibility of renewal' at the end of 'The Disappearing Island'.

Title Suggests playfully a possible script for a film about the Gaelic world of the 1920s, particularly in relation to the revival of the Irish language. Though at the beginning the figures in the poem are 'riding . . . Towards what will never be' and 'Not getting anywhere', SH points out to O'Driscoll that 'the writing in the sand' to which the revival movement is compared 'will go on, "just when it looks as if it is all over"' (*SS*, 315).

9 *in different Irishes*: different dialects of the language were spoken and studied by the visitors in the major Gaeltachts (Irish-speaking areas): Connemara, West Kerry and Donegal.

12 R. M. Ballantyne (1825–94), Scottish author of *The Coral Island* (1858) and other adventure stories for children, especially boys. Likening it to a 'milestone in grass verges' suggests the durability of the landmarks of writing in English even in Ireland in the nineteenth century.

20 *the old script*: the insular script used for Gaelic manuscripts before the general introduction of Roman script in the twentieth century.

From the Canton of Expectation

First published in the *TLS* (24 Jan. 1986): 95, and after collection in *HL* also included in *NSP1990* and *OG*.

I 4 when we prayed *Vouchsafe* or *Deign*,] in prayers with *vouchsafe* or *deign*, *TLS*
I 10 the] our *TLS*
I 11–2 we always took for granted, but not even he / considered this, I think, a call to action.] the whole backlog of outrage and exaction / we always took for granted. But not even he / considered this, I think, a call to action. *TLS*
I 15 shut] shut, *TLS*
I 16 harassment] harassments *TLS*
II 2 newly-wired] newly wired *TLS*, *NSP1990*, *OG*
II 9 for ever] forever *TLS*
II 13 anathema,] anathema: *TLS*
III 1–2] 'What looks the strongest has outlived its term.' / 'The Future lies with what's affirmed from under.' *TLS*
III 13 action,] action; *TLS*
III 14 indicative,] indicative; *TLS*

Title A canton (as in Switzerland) is an administrative unit, responsible for its own cultural affairs. It is applied here to the expectant but resigned 'state within a state' that the Catholics of Northern Ireland constitute. Working titles 'Folk' (MS) and 'From the Canton of Exhaustion' (TS, NLI 49,493/80 /81, /84).

I 1 *We*: the Catholic nationalists of Ulster (and other parts of Ireland); *optative moods*: the grammatical mood that expresses a wish rather than a reality.

I 3 *Not in our lifetime*: a phrase of resignation, often used to concede the unlikelihood of political progress.

I 4 *Vouchsafe or Deign*: typical terms of the anachronistic Latinate language of Catholic prayer.

I 6ff. The scenes of the Gaelic *Feis* – a festival of Irish cultural observance, involving dancing and songs 'in the old language'.

I 9 *the brotherhood*: the Irish Republican Brotherhood, a secret movement devoted to Irish Independence, lasting from 1858 to 1924, known in the USA as the Fenian Brotherhood. W. B. Yeats was briefly a member, inspired by John O'Leary who was President of the IRB 1891–1907. It is significant that the auctioneer doesn't regard the 'humiliation . . . a call to action'.

I 15 *our rebel anthem*: the Irish national anthem, 'Amhrán na bhFiann' ('The Soldier's Song', though it could be called 'The Fenians' Song').

II Part II of the poem describes the radical 'change of mood' that overcame Irish nationalist culture in SH's lifetime as a primarily agricultural economy turned partly towards textual activity (as the poet himself did). President Mary McAleese, when she received an honorary doctorate from the National University of Ireland in 1998, quoted the poem's theme of advances in Irish education.

ll 7ff. The resigned, optative mood of the opening is replaced in the new order by a more confident grammar of 'imperatives' and 'demands'. The 'conditional' mood of the unfulfilled is banished.

ll 11 *de profundis*: the opening of Psalm 129 and a major text in Catholic Liturgy, 'Out of the depths I have cried to thee, O Lord.'

ll 12ff. 'It is not those who can inflict the most, but those who can suffer the most who will prevail.' Terence MacSwiney, the playwright-politician Mayor of Cork who died on hunger strike in Brixton Prison in 1920.

lll 1 Part III of the poem longs for decisive action in the indicative rather than the resignation and passivity that characterised this canton of the optative. The missing 'mood' is the subjunctive with its air of unfulfillment and perhaps subjugation.

The Mud Vision

First published in *Hailstones*, then in *Threepenny Review* (Fall 1985): 8, *Poetry Australia*, 102 (1985): 33–4, and *Numbers*, 1 (Autumn 1986): 92–3. After collection in HL also included in *Seamus Heaney: Readings in Contemporary Poetry* (New York: Dia Art Foundation, 1988), 41–3, *NSP1990* and *OG*.

6 heliports] helipads *Hailstones, Threepenny Review, Poetry Australia*
15 rose window] rose-window *Hailstones, Poetry Australia*
20 colour,] colour *Hailstones, Threepenny Review, Poetry Australia*
31 placed in range of] under the skirts of *Hailstones, Threepenny Review, Poetry Australia*
34 verbena,] verbena *Hailstones, Threepenny Review, Poetry Australia*
40 hard shoulder] hard-shoulder *Hailstones, Threepenny Review, Poetry Australia, Numbers*
52 in tight] around *Hailstones, Threepenny Review, Poetry Australia*
55 origin] founded *Hailstones, Threepenny Review, Poetry Australia*

Working title in MS 'The Mud Window' (NLI 49,493/79).

SH explains to O'Driscoll that the poem is 'set in the Irish midlands, but the actual memory behind it was of thronged roads and gardens around a housing estate in County Tyrone in the late 1950s, when the Virgin Mary was supposed to have appeared to a woman in Ardboe' (*SS*, 286). There was a series of reported moving statues of the Blessed Virgin in the summer of 1985, most notably in Ballinspittle, Co. Cork. The idea of a mud vision was suggested by a 1984 installation by the artist Richard Long, 'a huge circle of muddy handprints that he'd made on the high wall of the [Guinness] Hop Store' in Dublin (*SS*, 287). SH wrote an extensive gloss on the poem's meaning (*Irish Times*, 28 Sept. 2013), published the month after his death.

1ff. The poem opens with a miscellaneous list of Irish images – the religious iconography of statues and barbed-wire crowns is mixed with a new kind of secular visionary event in Ireland.

19ff. A connection of the sun with visions of the Virgin Mary in Fatima and elsewhere was often claimed.

22 The murky windscreen recalls the closing lines of 'Hailstones' (*PSH*, 366).

25–6 The 'smudge on their foreheads' recalls the ash mark made on the forehead on Ash Wednesday.

53 'our one chance to know the incomparable' recalls the missed 'comet's pulsing rose' at the end of 'Exposure' (*North*, 76; *PSH*, 209), as well as MacNeice's fear that he would be 'missing history' if he stayed in the USA. The poem's conclusion seems to see that Ireland is returning to a traditional world of myth. Although it was written in the economically straitened 1980s, SH was later inclined to reread the poem in the wake of the extraordinary affluence of the Celtic Tiger era of the 1990s and early 2000s, and the financial crash which followed (*SS*, 287–8).

The Disappearing Island

First published as 'A Last Word on the Island' in the *Irish Times* (26 Oct. 1985): 13, and then as 'The Disappearing Island' in *American Poetry Review* (July/Aug. 1985): 6. After collection in *HL* it was also included in *NSP1990* and *OG*.

Title SH tells O'Driscoll that the poem is 'a form of *aisling*, a vision poem about Ireland, even though it is an *aisling* inflected with irony' (*SS*, 289).

9 The irony SH notes seems to refer to this line: 'All I believe that happened there was vision', as if the visionary here is the imaginary, founded on willed belief and the land (Ireland) seems only to support its occupants *in extremis*.

The Riddle

First published in *Hailstones*: 18, and after collection in *HL* included in *OG*.

7 start a mime] you begin *Hailstones*
9 And work out what was happening in that story] Puzzling over, say, the old story *Hailstones*

The poem starts with the double sense of riddle, as enigma or – when it is resolved – a winnowing sieve.

5 'Which would be better' lends itself to the metaphor of poetry's appropriate material, 'to lift the sense of things from what's imagined' and determine whether the literal or the imaginative sense is primary. It is the question SH returns to ('Known World' in *EL*, 21; *PSH*, 538): 'How does the real get into the made up?'

UNCOLLECTED POEMS (1988–1989)

Between the abstracting allegorical poems of *The Haw Lantern* and the visionary poems of *Seeing Things*, there are fifteen uncollected poems, including the atmospheric sequence of twelve-liners 'Five Derry Glosses'. As well as that sequence, SH publishes five translations of Romanian poems by Marin Sorescu (see *TSH*, 15–20).

In March 1990, Faber & Faber in London had published *New Selected Poems: 1966–1987* in simultaneous hardback and paperback, to replace the 1980 *Selected Poems*. Farrar, Straus and Giroux issued the same text in New York on 22 August 1990 in hardback, and on 4 December 1991 in paperback, in place of their *Poems 1965–1975*. The edition would become a perennial seller.

Valedictory Verses

First edition printed as a card, dated 13 May 1988, for the Carysfort College of Education Graduation Exercises, 1988, to mark the closure of the college. Published in *Education Today* (Spring 1993).

[text: Carysfort College]

Title Our Lady of Mercy College, Carysfort, in Blackrock, South Dublin, was founded in 1877 as a women's training college for National School (primary) teachers. From 1975 until its closure in 1988 it was a recognised college of the National University of Ireland, open to both sexes and conferring a BEd degree. SH accepted the invitation to become a lecturer in English there in 1975, and he became Head of English the following year. In 1976 he was also given leave of absence to return to UC Berkeley as Beckman Professor. He taught in Carysfort for six years until he was invited to take up a more permanent but less demanding role at Harvard where he had been an occasional teacher in the spring of 1981. His poem 'Corncrake' (*PSH*, 56) was dedicated to an admired English teacher there, Mother Assisium Skelly, for her hundredth birthday.

1ff. The villanelle begins with the skills inculcated into the trainee primary teachers, among which singing (sight-reading by sol-fa) was prominent, and with the tools of their profession, mostly now associated with a recent bygone era.

7–8 The closure of the college is linked to the weakening of Catholic clerical authority in Ireland, along with the decline of vocations to the priesthood and convents.

13 Reference to an ideal Ireland expressed by Éamon de Valera in a much-misquoted radio speech on St Patrick's Day 1943, 'On Language and the Irish Nation': 'with the romping of sturdy children, the contest of athletic youths and the laughter of happy maidens'. The crossroads were a persistent addition to the representation of the speech.

Dublin 4

Published by Poems on the DART in 1988; subsequently in Jonathan Williams (ed.), *Between the Lines: Poems on the DART* (Dublin: Lilliput Press, 1994), 11.

Jonathan Williams recalls that 'Dublin 4' was the second of two poems for the DART written 'especially for the venture'; the first, supplied about a week before, was 'Waiting for the Gates', a quatrain that was unused in the project, set at the Merrion Gates level crossing near the author's home (*Irish Independent*, 9 May 2025).

New Worlds

Published in W. J. McCormack (ed.), *In the Prison of His Days* (Dublin: Lilliput, 1988), 62, which was reissued as a special limited edition in 1990 to celebrate Nelson Mandela's visit to Ireland on 1 July 1990.

The Strand Hotel

Published in *Orbis* (Summer/Autumn 1988).

Resin

Published in *Oxford Poetry*, 5. 1 (Winter 1989/90): 15.

from Holdings

Published in *Poetry Review* (Winter 1989/90).

Dated 20 March and 17 May 1989 as 'A molten reddishness scudding with steam' in TS (NLI 49,493/91).
 Title 'Holdings' had been a working title for the second sequence in what would become Part II of *ST*, SQUARINGS. Of the four 'twelve-liners' published in *Poetry*, the three here were uncollected, while a fourth ('What were the virtues of an eelskin?') was re-published in *ST* as 'Squarings' xvii (*ST*, 73; *PSH*, 434).

1 *Cotyledon*: the embryonic leaf in seed-bearing plants like the sweet peas here being grown by SH's Aunt Mary, the 'she' of *l*. 3. A characteristic SH image for the growth of an idea.

9 *the forged pikes*: weapons, hidden in house thatches, associated with the 'peasant rising' of 1798.

Five Derry Glosses

Published in Donovan Wylie, *32 Counties* (London: Secker & Warburg, 1989). The first poem was also published separately as 'A Gloss on Derry' in *Drumragh Parish Magazine* (1989); the second, third and fifth are collected with significant revisions in *ST* as 'xli', 'xix' and 'xlii' respectively, but the original sequence is preserved here.

[text: *32 Counties*]

The fifth in the sequence has its origins in a MS 'The Dirrahs' dated 19 January 1972 (NLI 49,493/5), a poem that in a revised form is included in Appendix I (*PSH*, 1180).

1 'Doire' in Irish means oak. The city name in Irish is Doire Cholm Cille, 'the oak-grove of Colmcille'. But the form 'Derry Colmcille' (*l*. 8), a kind of linguistic hybrid, does not normally occur in English.

THE CURE AT TROY (1990)

The Cure at Troy, SH's version of Sophocles' *Philoctetes*, his first of two dramatic productions, was published in Northern Ireland by Field Day in hardback, and in London by Faber & Faber in paperback, in October 1990. It was published in New York in a revised text by Farrar, Straus and Giroux simultaneously in hardback and paperback on 4 December 1991. It is reprinted in *TSH*, 193–253; 552–7n.

from Voices from Lemnos: IV

First published in CT and subsequently as 'Excerpt from *The Cure at Troy*. A Version of Sophocles' *Philoctetes*', in Oscar Gilligan (ed.), *The Birmingham Six: An Appalling Vista* (Dublin: Literéire, 1990), 66–9. Reprinted with revisions as 'A Chorus', *New York Times* (1 Jan. 1991), A29, and as 'Chorus from The Cure at Troy', *Arion: A Journal of Humanities and the Classics* (Spring 1991): 131–8. Subsequently as 'Chorus', a programme for *The Cure at Troy*, directed by Derek Walcott, Poetry Center of the 92nd Street YMCA, New York City, 15 March 1993; and as 'Chorus from The Cure at Troy', Atlantic Foundation Irish Odyssey, private circulation 1997. Collected as 'Voices from Lemnos': IV Chorus in OG, and as '*from* The Cure at Troy' in *100P*, with the introduction of *ll*. 28–30.

[text: OG]

2 another.] another, *CTa*
6^7   The innocent in gaols
      Beat on their bars together.
      A hunger-striker's father
      Stands in the graveyard dumb.
      The police widow in veils
      Faints at the funeral home. *CTa*
7–8 History says, *Don't hope / On this side of the grave.*] *CTa*
11 up] up, *100P*
19 self-healing,] self-healing: *CTa*
20 utter] utter, *CTa*
28–30] [omitted] *CTa*

Of the five extracts from *The Cure at Troy* included in *Opened Ground*, the fourth, delivered by the chorus commenting on Philoctetes, has attained great familiarity because of its pronouncement in 1991 of hope for an end to political violence in a period when there was some movement towards disarmament in Northern Ireland. Their message that for once it is possible that 'hope and history rhyme' (l. 12) was quoted by President Clinton and several others, including Nadine Gordimer and Gerry Adams (see *SS*, 421). This declaration of a political ideal is unusual in SH's work. Elsewhere in the same extracts, 'Voices from Lemnos', Philoctetes declares his determination to go 'Away to the house of death. / To my father, sitting waiting / Under the clay roof' (*OG*, 329–30; *TSH*, 241), in lines that SH will recall in 'The Blackbird of Glanmore' at the end of *DC* (75; *PSH*, 628).

UNCOLLECTED POEMS (1990–1991)

In the eight months between the publication of the verse drama *The Cure at Troy* (1990) and the collection *Seeing Things* (1991), SH published just two poems, which take their settings from Northern Ireland and Scotland.

Grove Hill

Published in *Thames Poetry* (1990).

8 all-night] all night *Thames Poetry* (error)

Title An area just to the east of Castledawson, thought to be the remnants of an ancient ring fort, renowned locally for its bluebells.

The Stirling Stanzas

Published in the *Airthrey Journal* (Spring 1991), where it is accompanied by the following note:

> Seamus Heaney included *The Stirling Stanzas* in the eloquent reply he made on behalf of graduates at the conclusion of graduation ceremonies on 29 June 1990 – when the University conferred the honorary degree of Doctor of the University on him.
> The presence at that graduation of the distinguished poets Norman MacCaig, Sorley MacLean and Iain Crichton Smith underlined the special nature of the University's award to Professor Heaney.

25 A. N. Jeffares (1920–2005), scholar of Anglo-Irish literature, especially Yeats, and Professor of English at the University of Stirling.
   29 The addressee is SH's friend, the poet and scholar Alasdair Macrae.

SEEING THINGS (1991)

Seeing Things was published in London by Faber & Faber on 3 June 1991 in 5,000 hardback, 25,000 paperback and 250 limited-edition copies; it was published in New York by Farrar, Straus and Giroux on 1 December 1991 in 6,500 hardback copies, and in paperback on 1 April 1993 (FF L8). It was Waterstones' Book of the Month for June 1991, and was dedicated to SH's contemporary Belfast friend and poet, Derek Mahon. In its first decade in print, it sold all of its 5,000 hardback printing and 61,000 paperback copies in its Faber & Faber editions (FF L7).

The book is divided into two parts, and framed by two translations which serve as a kind of prologue and coda. The prologue is 'The Golden Bough', a translation of the episode early in *Aeneid*, 6 (SH's translation of the whole book was published posthumously by Faber in 2016 (*TSH*, 491–522)), in which Aeneas finds the golden bough that will serve as a passport through the afterlife in search of his father Anchises; the coda, 'The Crossing', is part of Canto 3 of Dante's *Inferno* in which Dante and his guide Virgil are challenged by the ferryman Charon as they attempt to cross the Acheron into the underworld. Expanding on these framing passages, Faber's press release for the book said, 'Journeys to underworlds and otherworlds correspond to the journeys made by poetic language itself elsewhere in the book.' Both passages can also be seen as SH's response to the death of his father in 1986, making a link to 'The Stone Verdict' and 'Clearances' in *The Haw Lantern*. SH described in positive terms the spirit in which he turned to the new book, saying that around 1988–9, he experienced a kind of visitation, a surge of poetic energy, that resulted in the forty-eight twelve-line poems he called SQUARINGS.

Between the two framing translations, Part I of the book is forty-four pages of lyric poems, and Part II of forty-eight poems each composed of four triplets, later referred to by SH as 'twelve-liners'. As a formal feature, this series was noted from the first as an eye-catching departure. The full series is headed SQUARINGS, and is subdivided into four groups of twelve, each with its own subheading verbal noun: '1 Lightenings' – '2 Settings' – '3 Crossings' – '4 Squarings', the last being a co-adoption of the series title. Archive papers show that arrangements for the four divisions had been in flux ('1 Squarings' – '2 Holdings' – '3 Farings' – '4 Offings' is an earlier order), but when SQUARINGS later became the governing name for the series as a whole, the subsection titles were reshuffled accordingly. Even so, the final order retains traces of its earlier archaeology: when 'Lightenings' became the new title of the first subsection, it retained as its third poem the piece that explains that the term 'Squarings' comes from the game of marbles where 'those anglings, aimings, feints and squints' (*ST*, 57; *PSH*, 428) were a prelude to the actual shot: a figure therefore for the artistic preparedness brought about by practice – or field work – which SH had called 'technique' in an early essay, 'Feeling into Words' (1974: *Preoccupations*, 47). Similarly, the volume's epilogue from Dante is entitled 'The Crossing', so it is perhaps surprising that 'Crossings' is not the concluding, rather than the third, subsection, since the notion of crossing to the afterlife is one of the crucial themes of the whole series. Clearly SH had been uncertain about the order and application of the various verbal nouns as section titles.*

However, there was no such uncertainty about the title of the book as a whole. SH told Rand Brandes, 'When I wrote the "Seeing Things" poem – I think in the summer of 1990, after I came home from Harvard, early summer – I suddenly knew that I had the name of the volume' (Brandes 2009, 29). Even then, other titles remained under consideration, and a manuscript held in the National Library of Ireland shows SH crossing out *Seeing Things* for 'The World of Light' and 'The Journey Back' and 'The Light of Morning', before writing once again above them all 'Seeing Things' (NLI 49,493/94). This decision about the title had enormous impact on the effect of the book and on its reception. *Seeing Things* was regarded from the first as a change of tack, from the public and political concerns of *Station Island* particularly, to a more internalised, visionary emphasis, as indicated in 'Fosterling' at the end of Part I: 'Me waiting until I was nearly fifty / To credit marvels' (*ST*, 50; *PSH*, 426). This poem can also be linked to 'Hailstones' in *The Haw Lantern* (and in the 1984 Gallery book *Hailstones*) where the end of the hail shower is said to wait 'For forty years / to say there, there you had / the truest foretaste of your aftermath – / in that dilation / when the light opened in silence'. 'Fosterling' though can be most enlighteningly read, as SH said to O'Driscoll (*SS*, 317ff.), as a kind of general prologue to SQUARINGS, the forty-eight twelve-line poems of Part II with their liberated personal reflections on the poet's experiences: a more explicit response to the injunction of SH's Joyce at the end of 'Station Island' to 'strike his own note' rather than examine his conscience and obligations. Nevertheless, when O'Driscoll asked SH about his view of Yeats's *A Vision*, he quoted

---

* SH edited two anthologies of new Irish poetry called *Soundings* (Belfast: Blackstaff Press, 1972 and 1974) – his first use of such a verbal noun, though there with a more Frostian-phonetic and aquatic overtone.

in response Yeats's description of the work as 'a fardel of old stories', and when O'Driscoll asked him if there was a connection between the forty-eight Squarings and his '"fardel" of Catholic beliefs', he decisively replied, 'Undoubtedly.' The marvels credited beyond 'the doldrums of what happens' are an opening to the visionary in all its forms, new and old.

Any enduring doubt about a visionary, rather than an elegiac or responsible emphasis, as well as exhilaration at it, was dispelled by the book's title. As with other SH titles such as *The Government of the Tongue* or *The Spirit Level*, the associations of 'seeing things' are richly and ambiguously suggestive. As in 'Fosterling', it means 'crediting marvels', an idea which is most memorably expressed in the last line of the most popular item of the series, poem viii beginning 'The annals say: when the monks of Clonmacnoise'. A late medieval Irish story translated in Kenneth Hurlstone Jackson's *A Celtic Miscellany* (1971, 165) tells how the monks saw 'a ship sailing over them in the air, going as if it were on the sea'. The ship's crew drop anchor on to the floor of the church and the monks seize hold of it. One of them comes down to retrieve the anchor and begs the monks to release him: '"For God's sake let me go!" said he, "for you are drowning me."' So they let him go and he swims back up to the ship, holding the anchor. SH's most significant – and thematically characteristic – addition to the story is the last line which describes the crewman's return 'Out of the marvellous as he had known it'. The marvellous, like the mythology of 'Punishment', is not single-stranded.

Of course, the idiom 'seeing things' also means imagining things which are not real or verifiable by literal observation. SH tells O'Driscoll that his memory of the details of the Wicklow folk story about 'the tree-clock of tin cans / The tinkers made', the example of a 'marvel' in 'Fosterling', is imprecise, but 'the tree clock pointed an orphic hand up towards the light' (*SS*, 317). He goes on to describe the 'strange and unexpected' process by which the twelve-line structure first came about as *'les vers donnés'* rather than *'les vers calculés'*, in the elegant reading room in the National Library in Dublin the day he finished his annotations for a selection of Yeats's poetry for the *Field Day Anthology of Irish Writing* (1990). 'Suddenly I wrote a few lines and it became a twelve-line, four three-lines, thing. It felt given, strange and unexpected; I didn't quite know where it came from, but I knew immediately it was there to stay . . . The form operated for me as a generator of poetry' (*SS*, 320–1). When O'Driscoll asks 'How long did the inspiration last?', he accepts this characterisation of the process, answering 'About sixteen to eighteen months, from September 1988 until the end of the next year' (SS, 320). There were about 'six or eight' further poems in the series which were not included in *Seeing Things*.

Seeing Things was published two years after the first of SH's Oxford lectures 'The Redress of Poetry' was given on 24 October 1989, which starts with a consideration of whether poetry must be 'of present use', as well as providing an imaginative counterweight to redress what Simone Weil in *Gravity and Grace* (1947) called 'the force of gravity' in harsh reality (*RP*, 3). One of SH's most imaginative readers, Michael Hofmann, said *Seeing Things* was 'Heaney's most plainspoken and autobiographical work to date . . . a departure in style, tone and purpose' (*LRB*, 13. 15, 15 Aug. 1991). Hofmann says of the book, 'Heaney has understood the need to move on, to remake himself from book to book.'

The forty-eight twelve-line poems end with a secular visionary moment of a Wordsworthian kind that SH favours as a volume-ending from here on (in the closing poems of *The Spirit Level*, 'Tollund' and 'Postscript', for example): 'when light breaks over me / The way it did on the road beyond Coleraine . . . I'll be in step with what escaped me'. The 'seventh heaven' may be 'a sixth sense come to pass'. But after this moment of revelation, there is a further confirmatory moment of epilogue with 'The Crossing' in which the pilgrim Dante is reassured by Virgil of his status as a good spirit when Charon's identification of him as one of the damned on his way to punishment is corrected. It is a conclusion that will be reaffirmed in the penultimate poem in the next book, *The Spirit Level* in 1996, 'Tollund', which concludes 'alive and sinning, / Ourselves again, free-willed again, not bad' (*SL*, 69).

[text: *ST1991*]

The Golden Bough

SH's translation of *Aeneid*, 6.98–148. First published, as a longer translation, in the Irish Issue of *Translation* (Fall 1989): 197–201, guest edited by Seán Ó Tuama, where it carries the dedication 'In Memory of Jack and Máire Sweeney'. In *Translation*, the poem continues as follows:

> But there is other news, alas, that you did not yet know.
> The body of one of your friends lies emptied of life
> And his death is polluting your fleet while you bide your time
> On my doorstep, consulting and suing.
> Carry this man to his right resting place. Put him into the tomb.
> Offer up herds of black sheep as your first reparation.
> Then and then only will you see the forests of Styx,
> Realms that are barred to the living.' She said these things,
> Pressed her lips shut and went silent.

Aeneas's face was saddened and his eyes downcast
As he walked away from the cave, musing to himself
About the blind outcome. Trusty Achates
Walked at his side, matching his friend's step and mood.
Between them, they talked many different things through,
Such as who their dead comrade might be, the one the prophetess said
Would have to be buried. And then they saw him, Misenus,
On the high, dry part of the shore – they arrived there and saw
Misenus, the son of Aeolus, unfairly called to his death,
A man unsurpassed at inflaming the spirits of fighters
With his bronze trumpet, and rousing up Mars when he played.
Once this Misenus had been great Hector's lieutenant,
At his side in all battles, well known by his trumpet and spear.
Then after Achilles had savaged the life out of Hector,
The staunchest of heroes joined with Dardan Aeneas,
Refusing to follow any inferior cause.
But a mad moment came, when impulse drove him to blow
Resonant notes from a conch shell over the waves
And to challenge the gods themselves to a musical contest.
Triton was shaken with envy – hard as this is to believe –
And seized him and drowned him in a foaming surge among rocks.
So the Trojans all gathered round and lamented, especially
Aeneas the Good. Then, still in tears, they hurried along
Eager to perform the tasks that the Sibyl commanded,
Piling up logs in an altar-pyre that rose to the heavens.
They head into virgin forest, up among the wild beasts,
Making the holm-oaks echo the crack of their axes,
Pitching down spruce trees, splitting up beams of ash wood
And grained oak, with their wedges, rolling immense rowan trees
To the foot of the slopes.
                   In the midst of all this activity
Aeneas was to the fore, encouraging comrades
And geared out with tools like the rest. But he kept gazing up
At that huge belt of forest, sadly preoccupied,
Pondering things in his heart, until he happened to pray
In words that came out like this: 'If only that golden bough
Would reveal itself to us out of such deep forest dens.
For all that the prophetess spoke about you, Misenus,
Was true, altogether too true!' And immediately then
A pair of doves happened to fly down out of the sky
Under the man's very eyes, and settled on the green grass;
And in them the great hero knew his own mother's birds
And prayed and rejoiced: 'O, if a way can be found.
Be you my guides! Take your course through the air. Lead on into groves
Where that blessed bough casts its shade on the rich forest floor.
And you, O my mother divine, do not abandon me
In this time of confusion.' He said this, then halted his steps
To watch for what signs they might give or where they might make for
But the doves kept on going, now feeding, now flying ahead,
Always staying in view of the eyes that pursued them.
Then when they came to the gorge of thickly fuming Avernus,
They flew quickly up and swept back down through clear air

> To the perch they had chosen, a tree that grew like two trees
> For a glow came from it, and a gold aura tarnished its branches.
> Like mistletoe shining with cold in the mid-winter woods,
> Gripping its tree but not grafted to it, always in leaf,
> Its yellowy berries in sprays all curled round the bole –
> The leaf-sprouting gold looked like that in the gloom of the oak
> While its bright foil chimed in the breeze. There and then,
> Aeneas took hold of it and although it resisted
> He greedily tore it away and carried it back
> To the Sibyl's retreat.

Also published in *Poetry Review* (Spring 1991): 73–4. Collected with revisions in *ST*, and an extract was included in *OG* and *NSP2014*. An extended translation from 6.98–211 formed the text of a limited edition featuring screenprints by Jan Hendrix (Mexico D.F. and Banholt: Imprenta de los Tropicos and Bonnefant Press, 1992), accompanied by a note on the translation by SH.

1–29] [omitted] *OG*, *NSP2014*
2 fearful] scaresome *Translation*
9 foresuffered all] foresuffered them all *Translation*
21 Vestal] kind lady *Translation*] vestal *Poetry Review*
22 for nothing is out of your power] you who have power to do everything, *Translation*
28 speak of] harp on *Translation*
30] Aeneas was praying and holding on the altar *OG* | Aeneas was praying and holding on to the altar *NSP2014*
31 relation] relations *Poetry Review*
36 sons of gods] sons of the gods *OG*, *NSP2014*
37 Jupiter the Just] Jupiter Justus *OG*, *NSP2014*
38 Forests spread midway down] Halfway down is all forests *Translation*
38 midway] half-way *OG*, *NSP2014*
40 need] desire *OG*, *NSP2014*
42] The underworld dark, if you must go beyond what's permitted, *OG*, *NSP2014*
46 underworld] Underworld *Translation*
47 it is roofed in by a grove,] is all roofed in by a grove, *Translation*] overtopped by a grove *OG*, *NSP2014*
50 growth] tree-branch *OG*, *NSP2014*
51 handed it over to] bestowed it on *OG*, *NSP2014*
52 plucked,] plucked *Translation*, *OG*, *NSP2014*
53 one always grows] one grows *OG*, *NSP2014*
53 again,] once more, *OG*, *NSP2014*
54 on it has the same metal sheen.] upon it glimmers the same. *OG*, *NSP2014*
56 you,] you *OG*, *NSP2014*
57 come away easily, of] come easily, and of *Translation*
57 own accord.] own sweet accord. *OG*, *NSP2014*
58–9 never will / Manage to quell it or cut it down] won't / Ever manage to quell it or fell it *OG*, *NSP2014*

Line references to the Latin original are not directly equivalent to the line numbers in SH's full *Aeneid Book VI* because the Latin hexameters are longer than the loose pentameter form of SH's translation. Thus, for example, the original Latin corresponding to *ll.* 98–148 here are, in SH's version, *ll.* 140–203 (*ABVIa*, 8–10). In *OG* and *NSP2024*, the shorter passage translated as 'The Golden Bough' is the Latin *ll.* 124–48 (*OG*, 333–4, and *NSP2014*, 1–2). For SH's treatment of the episode in detail, see Falconer 2022, 21ff.

1 *the Sibyl of Cumae*: Cumae was a Greek colony near Naples; Sibyl in Greek is normally translated as 'prophetess'. She is the most celebrated of the many Sibyls in Roman art and writing, perhaps because of the proximity of Cumae to Rome; she is the most massive figure of the four Sibyls in Michelangelo's Sistine Chapel ceiling. Virgil names her 'Deiphobe', the daughter of Glaucus, and priestess of Phoebus and Trivia. Her primary association is with Apollo, god of artistic beauty (*l.* 4).

11 *King of the Underworld*: not named but capitalised by SH, called 'Dis' by Virgil in *l.* 127 (in the genitive, *ianua Ditis*, gateway of Dis, where SH calls him 'Pluto').

12 *Acheron*: river in Greek mythology; in Virgil the river across which Charon had to ferry the dead into the underworld.

13 Aeneas's wish to see his father Anchises, his motivation in travelling to the underworld realm of the dead, is applied by SH to his wish to encounter his father, who had died in 1986.

15ff. Aeneas's carrying of his father from the ruins of Troy is described in *Aeneid*, 2 in Aeneas's account to Dido.

23 *Hecate*: given authority over the underworld by Zeus. *Avernus* is the lake near Cumae, seen here as the fateful entrance to the underworld.

24–5 Orpheus was permitted to visit the afterlife underworld in pursuit of his wife, Eurydice, who was killed by a snakebite. She was allowed to leave with him because of his skill in playing his lyre but was lost again when he broke the agreement not to look back at her as she followed him to the upper air. He is the first of the examples here of figures who moved between the lands of the living and the dead.

26 *Pollux*: of the mythological twins, Castor was mortal and Pollux was a demigod. When Castor died, Pollux asked Zeus if he could join him in death. Zeus, moved by his loyalty, agreed they could stay together for eternity, half the time in the underworld and half in the physical world so they passed from one realm to the other.

28 Theseus went with Pirithous to the underworld to rescue Persephone who had been raped by Hades (Dis). But they were confined there until Heracles (Hercules) came to release Theseus.

29 Aeneas is himself the son of a goddess; his mother, Venus, was the daughter of Jupiter.

37 *Jupiter the Just*: 'Jupiter Justus' in *OG* and *NSP2014* (though neither in Virgil nor other SH versions).

39 *Cocytus*: one of the five rivers encircling Hades. 'The river of wailing', it flows into Acheron.

41 *Stygian*: the Styx is another of the five rivers around Hades, which has to be crossed to enter Hades, though the same is said of Acheron.

42 *Tartarus*: the deepest level of the infernal underworld.

44ff. The golden bough seems to be Virgil's invention.

46 *underworld Juno*: is Proserpina (*l.* 51), wife of Dis, as Juno in the upper realms is the wife of Jupiter.

PART I

The Journey Back

First published as 'MCMLXXXV, December 22nd', in George Hartley (ed.), *Philip Larkin: A Tribute* (London: Marvell Press, 1988), 39, and then as 'The Journey Back' in *New Nation* (Nov. 1988): 21, where it bears the dedication 'i.m. Philip Larkin', and *stet* (Autumn 1990): 7. Included in *TC*, 15, and then collected with revisions in *ST*. It was the subject of an exchange between Michael O'Toole and SH in the *Evening Press* in autumn 1992.

1 This line is not present in *Philip Larkin* or *New Nation*
4 everywhere.] everywhere: *Philip Larkin, New Nation, TC*
11 forewarned] forwarned *Philip Larkin*

The first poem here is the sixth in *TC*.

1 The Dante improbably quoted by Philip Larkin is *Inferno*, 2.1–3.

Markings

First published in *Field*, 44 (Spring 1991): 52–3, and then in *Oxford Today* (Trinity Issue, 1991): 21. Collected with revisions in *ST* and included in *OG*, *NSP2014* and *100P*. In *Oxford Today*, the poem was prefaced by the note:

> At the opening of 'Talking Shop: the Playthings in the Playhouse' (a lecture given in Michaelmas 1990), Professor of Poetry Seamus Heaney reminisced about the football pitch he had known as a child, where the Castledawson Magpies played. He explained that he liked the evocative emptiness of the vacated pitch, with its markings of whitewash or sawdust, adding, somewhat tantalizingly, 'You'll guess from the personal nature of these remarks that I have just written a poem about a football pitch. But about a different one!' *Oxford Today* is delighted to be able to give the poem its first appearance in print.

I 4 bumpy thistly ground] bumpy ground *Field, Oxford Today, OG, NSP2014, 100P*

I 9–10 playing / Because] playing – / Because *Field, Oxford Today*
I 14 world . . .] world. *Field, Oxford Today*
I 16 out. Some] out: some *Field, Oxford Today*
I 18 time that was extra, unforeseen and free.] playtime that was ordinary and extra. *Field, Oxford Today*
II 2 nicking the] nicking a *Field, Oxford Today*
III 1 All these] These *Oxford Today*
III 3 time] time, *Field, Oxford Today*

Dated Glanmore, 7 September 1990 in MS, 11 September and 12 October 1990 in TS, under working titles 'Learning Lines' and 'Headlines'.

Title 'Markings' is the first occurrence of the -ings verbal-noun formulas used as headings in Part II of the book.

I 2 *squares*: the areas in Gaelic football, corresponding to the penalty area in soccer.

II 14–16 *another world*: some limit had been passed: in keeping with the otherworld theme of 'The Golden Bough'.

II 1 *You*: the impersonal for the poet's childhood memory.

II 10 *headrig*: the first ridge at the edge of a ploughed field.

III 2 *the door and what came through it*: reminiscent of moments of passage in 'Clearances' 7 and 8 (*HL*).

Three Drawings

1 THE POINT

First published in *Oxford Poetry* (Winter 1989/90): 15–16, and in *Alpha* (21 Dec. 1989): 2A [insert]. Included in *TC*, 9, and collected in *ST*.

4–6] than you ever expected // with a spot-on drop kick. / It went rattling *Oxford Poetry*
8–14] it thumped / but it sang too, / a kind of dry, ringing / foreclosure of sound. // 'Point her!' / they shouted. / That spring *Oxford Poetry*

Title A point is the lesser score in Gaelic football; the greater is a goal which is worth three points.

7 *benweed*: term sometimes used in Northern Ireland for ragwort, a much decried plant, poisonous to cattle.

2 THE PULSE

First published in *stet* (Autumn 1990): 7, and collected in *ST*.

13–16] of a distant purchase and thrum
    out in the river, as you reeled
    and strung yourself tighter again
    from heel-tip to rod-tip. *stet*

4 The minnow here is a fake one, used as a lure in trout fishing.

3 A HAUL

Published in *ST*.

2 Thor is the Norse god who went fishing with the giant Hymir and caught the world serpent. The story is told by Snorri Sturluson in the *Prose Edda*, but also alluded to elsewhere in Icelandic literature. It may be that Hymir's cutting of the fishing line saves the world by enabling the world serpent to survive. In the 2009 RTÉ recording, SH calls Hymir 'god' rather than 'giant'. The Norse word is *jötunn*, usually translated 'giant', cognate with the Old English *eoten*.

14 *the way*: 'the way that' is an Irish idiom, meaning 'so that', 'with the result that'.

Casting and Gathering

First published in the *LRB* (27 September 1990): 6, and in *Field*, 44 (Spring 1991): 55, and collected with revisions in *ST*.

2 bank,] bank *LRB*
7 went] kept *LRB*
10 dreamy,] dreamy. *LRB*, *Field*
14 are not] aren't *LRB*
15 Watch it! Be severe.'] So watch Number One!' *LRB*
19 do not] cannot *LRB*, *Field*

Dedication *for Ted Hughes*. Among the many interests shared between SH and Hughes was a common enthusiasm for fishing, also shared with Barrie Cooke. The terms casting and gathering are also used in ploughing, for ploughing next to unploughed and ploughed ground respectively.

Man and Boy

First published in *Poetry Review* (Spring 1991): 72, and then in *Tikkun* (July/Aug. 1991): 67. Collected with revisions in *ST* and later included in *OG* and *NSP2014*.

I 4 uncle] Uncle *Tikkun*
II 1 the salmon] that salmon *Poetry Review*, *Tikkun*
II 3–4 scythe. // He] scythe. / He *Tikkun*
II 4 He] he *Poetry Review* [error]
II 8 me)] me), *OG*, *NSP2014*

The first poem in *ST* about SH's relationship with his father, as well as in this case the father's tragic experience of his own father's early death. The theme is continued in the following poems 'Seeing Things' III and 'The Ash Plant'.

Seeing Things

First published in *Salmagundi* (Fall 1990–Winter 1991): 78–81, and then in the *Irish Times* (2 Feb. 1991): A9. Collected in *ST* and later included in *OG*, *NSP2014* and *100P*.

I 12 reaching] grabbing *Salmagundi*
I 13 the shiftiness] the quick response *Salmagundi*
I 15 quick response] fluency *Salmagundi*
I 20 could see] was being shown *Irish Times*
I 21 riskily we fared into the morning,] openly we fared in the light of morning, *Salmagundi*
II 6 façade] facade *Salmagundi, Irish Times*
III 13 immanent] imminent *Irish Times*

Dated 9 July 1990 in MS (NLI 49,493/95).
Title Decided by the time of SH's return from Harvard to Dublin in the summer of 1990.
  I 1 *Inishbofin*: island off Connemara, reached by boat from Cleggan.
  I 8 *the boatmen*: performing the role of Charon in *Aeneid*, 6 and *Inferno*, 3 (*ST*, 111–3), referred to in the last line of the final poem in the 'Crossings' sequence here, xxxvi (*ST*, 94).
  I 13 *panicked*: SH comments in other places on his nervousness on the water. Here it suits the underworld setting.
  I 19–20 The boat 'sailing through air, far up' famously appears in 'Lightenings' viii (*ST*, 62; *PSH*, 430).
  II 1 *claritas:* this 'dry-eyed Latin word' is taken from Stephen Dedalus's use of it in Joyce's *A Portrait of the Artist as a Young Man*, drawing on the scholastic philosophy of St Thomas Aquinas (Joyce 1992, 230–1). Stephen translates it as 'radiance', going on to define it as 'the artistic discovery and representation of the divine purpose in anything or a force of generalisation which would make the esthetic image a universal one'.
  II 3ff. The Baptism of Jesus, a mosaic on the façade of Orvieto cathedral which SH tells Shane Murphy he and Marie saw in 1986.
  II 10 The 'utter visibility' corresponds to the 'deep, still, seeable-down-into water' of I 18, introducing a theme of lucidity and perspicuity which will be central to part II of the book, SQUARINGS (51ff.).
  II 16 The 'hieroglyph for life itself' is usually represented, not as a zig-zag, but by a symbol called the 'ankh', which is a T-shape with a liquid droplet on top. In 'Squarings' xliii, it says 'Consider too the

ancient hieroglyph / Of "hare and zig-zag", which meant "to exist", / To be on the *qui vive*' (*ST*, 103; *PSH*, 445).

III This childhood memory of a traumatic episode in SH's father's life is one of the major father-and-son poems in SH's corpus.

III 1 *Once upon a time*: as at the start of a fairytale narrative; *undrowned*: suggestion of the 'undead'.

III 13 *his ghosthood immanent*: the religious idea of immanence, as applied to God, is something actual but unsensed. The 'unguided' recalls Anchises's dependence on Aeneas in *Aeneid*, 2.

III 15 *rusted*: dialect term for 'shied', grew restive.

III 22 *face to face*: continuing the theme of immanence and the line between life and death. Cf. Tennyson's 'Crossing the Bar': 'I hope to see my pilot face to face / When I have crossed the bar'.

III 25 *happily ever after*: the fairytale conclusion to the story begun at *l.* 1.

The Ash Plant

First published in *Antaeus* (Spring 1988): 184, and in the commemorative programme *An Upstairs Outlook: An Evening of Poetry by Seamus Heaney and Michael Longley*, held at Elmwood Hall in Belfast on 4 May 1989 in aid of the Linen Hall Library Development Campaign: 4. Collected in *ST*.

6 milk-lorries] milk lorries *Antaeus*   cattle] Friesians *Antaeus*
7 damp hedges] the hedges *Antaeus*

Dated 15–16 September 1986 in MS.

The association of SH's father with the ash plant of the cattle drover is memorably recalled in poem xxvii in the 'Crossings' series: 'Look for a man with an ashplant on the boat' (*ST*, 85; *PSH*, 438) where the 'broad-backed, low-set man' of 'Man and Boy' reappears as 'a solid man' in the first line.

1 the old man after his death is ready to cross back to the land of the living, like Anchises in *Aeneid*, 6.

17–18 The ash plant is the cattle-dealer's bough, golden or silver, as he walks 'again among us', immanent after his death.

1.1.87

Privately published under the title 'Dangerous Pavements', as a Christmas card printed for Heaney family by Gallery (1987). After collection in *ST*, included in *100P*.

Title This haiku is named for the first New Year after the death of SH's father. The title is read on the RTÉ recording as, 'The first of the first, eighty-seven.'

An August Night

Published in *ST*, and later included in *OG* and *NSP2014*.

A dream in which SH's father's hands appear to him in a dream (different in 'Squarings' xi; *ST*, 65; *PSH*, 431).

Field of Vision

First published privately by the Gallery Press as a Christmas card in 1990, with an illustration by Catherine Heaney, then in the *Irish Times* (2 Feb. 1991): A9, *Field*, 44 (Spring 1991): 54, and in the *Spectator* (13 April 1991): 36. After collection in *ST* it was included in *OG*, *NSP2014* and *100P*.

9 steadfast] upfront *Irish Times*

1 *this woman*: SH's Aunt Mary, a major presence in his life and poetry, most centrally in 'Sunlight' (*North*, 9–10; *PSH*, 173), 'In a Yard' (*PSH*, 1180), and 'Chairing Mary' (*DC*, 67; *PSH*, 624). Her setting here recalls the preferences of her brother, SH's father: 'one of those lean, clean, iron, roadside [gates] / Between two whitewashed pillars' parallels Patrick Heaney's ideal for a newly built house in 'Squarings' xxxiii: 'plain, big, straight, ordinary, you know' (*ST*, 91; *PSH*, 441).

The Pitchfork

First published in *Antaeus* (Spring 1988): 183, then in *Orbis* (Summer/Autumn 1988): 23, and in the *Irish Times* (5 Aug. 1989): A7. It appeared in *An Upstairs Outlook*: 5, and in *TC*, 12. Collected in *ST* and later included in *OG* and *NSP2014*.

7 grain] shaft *Antaeus*
8 its own natural] its natural *Orbis*
9 Riveted] Rivetted *Antaeus*, *Orbis*, *Irish Times*, *TC*
11 tested,] rounded, *Orbis*
13 And then when] And when *Antaeus*, *Orbis*
15 imperturbably] imperturbably, *Antaeus*

Dated 15 September 1986 in MS (NLI 49,493/85).
 An extreme example of the dematerialisation of a wholly material object, one of the book's salient themes.

A Basket of Chestnuts

First published as 'A Basket of Chestnuts' in the *New Yorker* (27 May 1991): 36, and in Brian Fallon (ed.), *Edward McGuire* (Dublin: Irish Academic Press, 1991), 94. Collected in *ST*. In *ST* McGuire's surname appears as 'Maguire'.

6] Dismayed, passed out, gone through. *Edward McGuire*
17] Since the portrait painter walked out of our house *New Yorker*
18 1973,] nineteen seventy-three, *Edward McGuire*
19 A] That *Edward McGuire*
20 me –] me *Edward McGuire*
23 toecaps] toe caps *New Yorker*
27 foxfire] fox-fire *New Yorker*

17 Edward McGuire (1932–86): Irish painter of the portrait of SH that appears on the back cover of *North*, held in the Ulster Museum. The occasion of McGuire's 1973 visit to the Heaney house is described in *Stepping Stones* (328). In a MS note to accompany the Brian Fallon edition, entitled 'Edward Maguire Exhibition', SH describes McGuire as 'one of the indispensable Irish painters of the century', not only for his 'mastery' of portraiture but as 'a painter of still lives' (NLI 49,493/106).

The Biretta

Commissioned by Brian P. Kennedy, this poem is a response to Matthew James Lawless's painting *The Sick Call*, for Kennedy (ed.), *Art Is My Life: A Tribute to James White* (Dublin: National Gallery of Ireland, 1991), 83. Also published in the *TLS* (25 Jan. 1991): 3, and collected with revisions in *ST*.

6 flossy] glossy *Art Is My Life*, *TLS*
15 Mass –] Mass *Art Is My Life*
17–20] [omitted] *Art Is My Life*, *TLS*
34] In Matthew J. Lawless's *The Sick Call*, *Art Is My Life*, *TLS*
37 which] this *Art Is My Life*, *TLS*
38 Undaunting, half domestic,] Clerical yet domestic, *Art Is My Life*, *TLS*
39 each long] the long *TLS*

Dated 8 December 1990 in MS (NLI 49,493/88).
   Title The biretta is a small three-cornered hat, worn by Catholic clergy on various ceremonial occasions.
   1 At the start of his *De Bello Gallico*, Julius Caesar says 'The whole of Gaul is divided into three parts', occupied by the Belgae in the north and east, the Aquitani in the south, and the Gauls or Celts in the west.

12 The capitalisation of 'AND' reflects a familiar priestly stress in the articulation of the formula for a blessing.

18 *an El Greco ascetic*: a puritanical figure, thin as in the paintings of El Greco (1541–1614).

19 *Saurian*: lizard-like. SH also uses this uncommon word in a list of repulsive creatures in 'Sibyl', part II of 'Triptych' (*FW*, 5; *PSH*, 218), where the Sibyl says 'I think our very form is bound to change. / Dogs in a siege. Saurian relapses. Pismires'. The context there is an unusually forceful denunciation of circumstances in Ireland, contemporary and historical.

27 The boat that wafts into the first lines of the *Purgatorio* is a metaphorical one, *la navicella del mio ingegno* – 'the little boat of my wit' (2).

29 The bronze age boat is an eighteen-centimetre-long gold boat in the Broighter Hoard from the first century BCE, found in 1896 on a farm near Limavady, Co. Derry, now in the National Museum of Ireland.

34 *The Sick Call* in the National Gallery of Ireland is the only known painting by Matthew James Lawless (1837–64), dated 1863 and much reproduced.

37 Here 'his reverence' wears a large-brimmed hat, not a biretta. But SH tells O'Driscoll that that hat was the starting point of the poem (*SS*, 326).

For a strongly positive and enlightening reading of the poem, see O'Driscoll, 1999, 74–9.

The Settle Bed

Printed privately by the Gallery Press as a Christmas card in 1989, with an illustration by Catherine Heaney. Published in *Parnassus* ([July] 1990): 103, and in the limited-edition *Robert Greacen: A Tribute at the Age of Seventy* (Dublin: Poetry Ireland, 1991): 8. After collection in *ST* it was also included in *OG* and *NSP2014*.

9 Anthems] Sigh-life *OG*, *NSP2014*
15 the long ago] the long long ago *OG*, *NSP2014*

Title A precious family heirloom, left to SH in her will by Biddy Carmichael, a distant cousin of his father's from Co. Derry. There was no room for it in the house in Strand Road, but suited the style of the Glanmore cottage perfectly (*SS*, 326).

1 *willed down*: i.e. passed down in a will; cf. *ll*. 15–6 'willable forward / Again and again and again.'

21–2 The settle bed is the most striking of the solid objects that are conceptually reimagined.

25 *posted high over the fog*: like Jim Hawkins in 'In the Attic' (*HC*, 83).

The Schoolbag

First published in October 1987 in the catalogue for *A Poet's Pictures: A Selection of Works of Art Collected by John Hewitt (1907–1997)*, an exhibition held at the Shambles Art Gallery, Hillsborough, Co. Down, 4. Subsequently published in the *Irish Times* (30 July 1988): A7, and in *An Upstairs Outlook*: 3 and *TC*, 16. Collected with revisions in *ST*.

4–5 bean, // The] bean, / The *Irish Times*, *TC*
5 wallmap] wall-map *Irish Times*, *TC*
11 school conjuror's] school-conjuror's *Irish Times*, *TC*
12 a word-hoard and a handsel,] your word-hoard and your handsel, *Irish Times*
12–13 handsel, // As] handsel, / As *Irish Times*, *TC*
13–14] As you step out, trig as ever, behind weavers, / Journeymen, spalpeens and cattle-drovers. *Irish Times*

Title SH and Ted Hughes called their second Faber anthology of poems *The School Bag* (1997), a successor to their 1984 *The Rattle Bag*.

Dedication John Hewitt (1907–87) a Belfast poet of the generation before SH, was appointed first poet-in-residence at Queen's University Belfast in 1976. He was an art historian and left-wing political activist who was a founding member of the Belfast Peace League. In 1930 he was appointed art assistant at the Belfast Museum and Art Gallery and remained in that secondary role until 1957 when he moved to Coventry as Director of the Herbert Art Gallery and Museum, before retiring back to Belfast in 1972. His study of Ulster poets was published in 1974 as *Rhymers, Weavers and Other Country Poets of Antrim and Down*. SH's review of his *Collected Poems 1932–67* (London: MacGibbon and Kee, 1968) was republished in *Preoccupations*, 207–10.

2 Addressing Hewitt, who was thirty-two years senior to SH; *nel mezzo del cammin*: opening of Dante's *Divine Comedy*, set in 1300 when Dante was thirty-five.

4 *displayed bean*: nature-illustrating poster.

12 *word-hoard and handsel*: word-hoard as the Old English term for a poet's vocabulary, and handsel as an archaic term for a gift: both decidedly English rather than Hiberno-English.

13 *trig*: meaning neat or trim, from Old Norse *trygr*.

14 *leaving parents*: moving from the domestic to the learned.

Glanmore Revisited

The title indicates that these seven sonnets are a return to the form of the ten 'Glanmore Sonnets' (*FW*, 28–37; *PSH*, 231–5).

1 SCRABBLE

First published in Gearóid Mac Niocaill and Patrick F. Wallace (eds), *Keimelia: Studies in Medieval Archaeology and History in Memory of Tom Delaney* (Galway: Galway University Press, 1988), [vii], and then in *Owl* (Nov. 1989): 10; in *Antaeus* (Spring/Autumn 1990): 48, with the fourth, third and fifth poems; and under the title 'Glanmore Sonnets' with all but 'Scene Shifts' in the *English Review* (Nov. 1990): 21. It was also one of four poems from the sequence included in *TC*, 17. Collected with revisions in *ST* and subsequently included in *OG* and *NSP2014*.

1 Winter-evening] Winter evening *Owl, Antaeus, English Review, TC*
3 hearth-blaze] hearth blaze *Owl*
9 Scrabble] scrabble *Owl, Antaeus, English Review, TC*
10–11] granted, another low-score word / In that game of breaks and moves cut off and rules. *Owl*
14] It's us you hear, that scrape and clink of tools. *Owl, Antaeus* | Which is what he hears. A scrape and clink of tools. *English Review, TC*

Dated 1 August 1988 in MS (NLI 49,493/86).

Dedication Tom Delaney, an archaeologist (1947–79), was born in Dublin and educated at University College Dublin. His major archaeological project was at Carrickfergus. At the time of his death he was head of the Department of Medieval Archaeology at Queen's University Belfast; he specialised in the study of bog bodies, as did his wife, Máire Delaney, who was a granddaughter of Éamon de Valera. He had also appeared in 'Station Island VIII' (*SI*, 81), as 'my archaeologist, very like himself'.

2 *Our backs*: the couple happily settled back into Glanmore Cottage – not with Delaney at this point.

2 THE COT

First published with all but 'Scene Shifts' as part of the sequence in the *English Review* (Nov. 1990): 21, collected in *ST*, and later included in *OG* and *NSP2014*.

3 Poker, scuttle, tongs,] Poker and coal-scuttle, *English Review*

6 *locus amoenus*: beautiful place, fit for love (like the garden of love in medieval courtly love writings). The word *amoenus* may be linked to *amare*, to love.

7 *Tenants no longer*: the Heaneys have now bought the cottage from Ann Saddlemyer, rather than renting it.

9 *keepsakes*: things kept for their sentimental associations. The implication here though is that the verb 'keeps' in the previous line has more permanency to it.

10 *Catherine*: SH's daughter, who had occupied the cot in Glanmore: the same cot that SH had occupied in Mossbawn.

3 SCENE SHIFTS

First published in *Owl* (Nov. 1989): 11, with the fifth, first and fourth poems from the final sequence, and under the sequence title 'Glanmore Revisited' with the first, fourth and fifth poems in *Antaeus* (Spring/Autumn 1990): 50. Collected in *ST*.

1] The weekend after each had cut his name *Owl*] The weekend after a good friend cut his name *Antaeus*
2 ash] tree *Owl, Antaeus*
4 around] round *Owl, Antaeus*
9 now.] now *Antaeus*
10–11] But, even so, there is another scene / Preparing in the ash-tree's welted scar *Owl* | But, even so, there is another scene / Secluded in the ash tree's welted scar *Antaeus*
11–12 scene / In] scar // In *Owl*
14 veteran] verteran *Antaeus* (error)

Dated 27 July 1988 in MS (NLI 49,493/86).

1 *a friend*: Originally David Hammond and Brian Friel on the occasion of Michael Heaney's First Communion ('each' in *Owl*), but reduced to one in *ST*.

12 *old nurse*: Eurycleia recognises Odysseus from the scar on his leg in the *Odyssey*.

4 1973

First published in *New Nation* (Nov. 1988): 21, and in *Owl* (Nov. 1989): 12, with the fifth, first and third poems from the final sequence. Also published under the sequence title 'Glanmore Revisited' with the first, third and fifth poems in *Antaeus* (Spring/Autumn 1990): 49, and in the *English Review* (Nov. 1990): 21. It was also one of four poems from the sequence included in *TC*, 18. Collected with revisions in *ST*.

1 The] Our *Owl, Antaeus, English Review*
1–2 The corrugated iron growled like thunder / When March came in; then as] Our March-buffed zinc made natural stage-thunder – / Proverbial. And as *New Nation*

2-4 warmer / And invalids and bulbs came up from under, / I hibernated] warmer, / Invalids and bulbs came up from under. / I hibernated *New Nation*
4 dormer,] dormer *New Nation*
6 an ailing] a sick *New Nation*
8 ash.] ash . . . *TC*
8-9 ash. // Lent came in next,] ash . . . / Then Lent came in, *New Nation*
10 for] with *New Nation*
11 through the] as a *New Nation*
12 it] him *New Nation, Owl, Antaeus*

Dated 27 July 1988 in MS.

1973 was the year of Catherine Heaney's birth, and was a significant point of change for the Heaneys following their move to Wicklow the year before. In a note with this poem to O'Driscoll, SH refers to it as 'Glanmore Rewardless'.

12 *taunted it*: smoking was commonly given up for Lent by Catholics.

5 LUSTRAL SONNET

First published in *Orbis* (Summer/Autumn 1988): 22; in *Owl* (Nov. 1989): 9, with the fifth, first and fourth poems from the final sequence; under the sequence title 'Glanmore Revisited' with the first, fourth and third poems in *Antaeus* (Spring/Autumn 1990): 51; and in the *English Review* (Nov. 1990): 21. It was also one of the four poems from the sequence included in *TC*, 20. Collected in *ST* and later included in *OG* and *NSP2014*.

3 did,] did *Owl, TC*
3-11] And for long after I came into my own
       Masquerade as man [*sic*] of property.
       Even then my first impulse was never
       To double-lock a door on the inside;
       And people always pulling curtains over
       Seemed too stand-offish, self-preoccupied.

       Then I broke to enter here. And now it scares us
       To recollect my practical instruction
       To saw up the old bedstead, since the staircase *Orbis*

3-12] Even when I'd 'come into my own'
       And owned a house, a man of property
       Who lacked the proper outlook. I would never
       Double-bar the door or lock the gate
       Or draw the blinds or pull the curtains over
       Or give 'security' a second thought.

       But all changed when I took possession here
       And had the old bed sawn on my instruction
       Since the only way to move it down the stair
       Was to cut the frame in two. A bad action, *OG, NSP2014*
4 as a man] as man *Owl, Antaeus*
5 then,] then *Owl, Antaeus*

6 double-bar a door or lock a gate;] double-lock a door on the inside; *Owl, Antaeus*
8] Seemed to boast that there were things to hide. *Owl, Antaeus* | Half-countermanded their own command: *Keep Out. English Review, TC*
9–10] Then I broke re-entering here. And now I scare, / Remembering my commonsense instruction *Owl, Antaeus*
10 bed-frame] bed frame *Owl, Antaeus*
12 action,] action *Orbis, Owl, Antaeus*
13 dangerous,] dangerous *Orbis*

Dated 2 August 1988 in MS (NLI 49,493/86). *Lustrum* was a five-year period of purification in Ancient Rome. This sonnet and 'Scene Shifts' (no. 3), date from the start of a long period of sabbatical from June 1988 to January 1990 so might be seen as 'lustral', purificatory.

13 The most famous phrase in the poem, 'So Greek with consequence', occurs in all versions. See Oliver Taplin, *Greek With Consequence* (London: Classical Association, 1999).

6 BEDSIDE READING

First published, with 'The Skylight', under the title 'from "Glanmore Sonnets"' in *Poetry Ireland Review* (Summer 1990): 4, and in the *English Review* (Nov. 1990): 21. Collected in *ST*.

9 Twenty-three] Twenty Three *Poetry Ireland Review, English Review*
13–14 As ours could have been ivy, / Evergreen, atremble and unsaid.] As ours will be ivy, / Stringent, evergreen, dark-berried, fretted. *Poetry Ireland Review, English Review*

13 A twelve-syllable line results from the expansion of the journal printings' 'will be ivy' to *ST*'s 'could have been ivy'.

7 THE SKYLIGHT

First published, with 'Bedside Reading', under the title 'from "Glanmore Sonnets"' in *Poetry Ireland Review* (Summer 1990): 3, and then in the *English Review* (Nov. 1990): 21. It was also one of the four poems from the sequence included in *TC*, 19. After collection in *ST* it was included in *OG*, *NSP2014* and *100P*.

1 skylights.] skylights, *Poetry Ireland Review*
3 closed,] closed. *English Review*
5 Effect.] Effect, *Poetry Ireland Review*
7 hatch.] hatch, *Poetry Ireland Review*
10 open.] open, *Poetry Ireland Review*

1 *You*: Marie Heaney, who first argued for a skylight in the cottage. The opposing 'I' is SH.
8 Thatch was the roof material of SH's childhood.

12ff. SH returns to another biblical narrative of an ailing figure being carried in 'Miracle' (*HC*, 17) with reference to his helpers after his stroke of August 2006.

A Pillowed Head

First published in the *Observer* (10 September 1989): 50, and then in *Parnassus* ([July] 1990): 102. Collected with revisions in *ST* and included in *OG*, *NSP2014* and *100P*.

8–11] begun. To be prepared
       And clued in to a different sense

       Of 'grave matter, full knowledge
       And full consent of the will.' *Observer*
15 bed,] bed.) *Observer*
16–18 [omitted] *Observer*.
21 as usual] as usual, *Observer*
22–7 Even after a small death like that,
       Came to in eyes
       That had been farther dawned into that ever,

       Slower and wider and duller
       Than all the mornings of waiting, your brow
       A held silence, the dawn chorus anything but. *Observer*
22 in two wide-open] in wide-open *Parnassus*
23–7] That had been farther dawned into
       Than ever, and slower and duller

       Than all those mornings of waiting
       When your brow was a cairn of held silence
       And the dawn chorus anything but. *Parnassus*

Celebrating the day when the Heaneys' daughter Catherine was born (25 April 1973).

    1 The formal Latinate term for the morning period suggests the significance of the moment.

    7 *this time*: Marie Heaney had given birth twice before to the couple's two sons, Michael and Christopher.

    27 'dawn chorus is anything but' silence; the poem might have been called 'aubade', dawn-song.

A Royal Prospect

First published in the *LRB* (2 March 1989): 9, and then in *Threepenny Review* (Summer 1991): 5. It was also included in *TC*, 25. Collected with revisions in *ST*, and included in *OG* and *NSP2014*.

2 Hampton] Hampden *LRB*
9 dropped] drooped *LRB*

21–2] They rematerialize as in a black / And white old grainy newsreel, where their boat *LRB, Threepenny Review, TC*
36–8] That test the grounds even of blamelessness. *LRB*
37–8 [omitted] *TC*

SH explains to Dennis O'Driscoll that the occasion of the poem was coming across photographs of a visit to Hampton Court during the Heaneys' London honeymoon in 1965 (*SS*, 325). The poem is entirely a third-person narrative description of the elements in the photograph, including the couple, apart from the brief identification of them as 'We' in *l*. 15, shifting back to 'them' two lines later.

2 *Hampton Court*: palace on the north bank of the Thames, about ten miles south-west of central London, a celebrated tourist attraction, with a famous maze in its gardens.

12 *dauphin*: son and heir apparent of the French king. The mock-heroic presentation of the male figure recalls the poem 'The Underground', remembering the same occasion – 'me then like a fleet god' (*SI*, 3; *PSH*, 291).

A Retrospect

Part I first published as 'May Day' in the *New Statesman* (14 Oct. 1966): 556, and subsequently in *PM*. Published in full as 'A Retrospect' in the *LRB* (7 Feb. 1991): 8, where part I is dated 1966, and collected in *ST*.

I 3–4 the field drains still as moats. // A bulrush sentried the lough shore:] lough and burn turned moat. // That bulrush at attention. *New Statesman*
I 6 Soft bottom with bog water] No bottom, just water *New Statesman*
I 7 weeds] weed *New Statesman*
I 10 water-colour] water colour *LRB*
I 8–15] Perennially dry among May blossoming,
    Chalky, velvety, rooted in liquid.

    The elements running to watercolour,
    The skyline filled up to the very brim.
    The globe was flooded inwardly, fuller

    Than a melon, the rind not even solid
    For remember, in a ditch, the unstanched spring
    Flushing itself all over the road. *New Statesman*
II 4 boarding school] boarding-school *LRB*
II 5 dispatch] despatch *LRB*
II 26 used] apt *LRB*

'May-Day in Fermanagh' dated 1966 in MS (NLI 49,493/5); 'A Retrospect' dated 21 August 1990 in MS (NLI 49,493/93).

II 1 *they*: the Heaneys, principally SH and Marie.

II 2 *Glenshane Pass*: the road pass through the Sperrin Mountains by Lough Neagh, between Derry and Belfast. *'Trail of Tears'*: term applied to the routes by which Native Americans were forcibly moved westward from the south-east of the USA between the 1830s and 1850s. Applied here to 'his' (the poet's in his schoolgoing days) unhappy return to boarding school at the end of the weekend at home. The 'sword of sorrow' and 'unblaming, unavailing grief' at being left at St Columb's by his parents is described to Dennis O'Driscoll (*SS*, 32–3).

II 5 Sir John Davies (1569–1626), poet, lawyer and politician, Attorney General for Ireland. He was vehemently anti-Catholic and active in the Plantation of Ulster after the Flight of the Earls in 1608–9. The lines quoted here were written after his visit to the escheated lands of O'Neill and O'Donnell; they are apt in this book beginning with Aeneas in the underworld.

II 9 *the King's deputy*: Davies himself.

II 11 *They*: SH and Marie.

II 26 *Young marrieds*: returning by car to the location of their premarital courting.

The Rescue

Published in *ST*, and later selected for the London Underground's Poems on the Underground poster series, 1997.

Wheels within Wheels

Published in *ST*, and later included in *OG* and *NSP2014*.

II 15 *mare's tail*: vernacular term for an invasive weed which grows through soil in early summer.

III 6 *Stet!*: proof instruction to 'let it stand' – i.e. to leave an amended word or apparent error uncorrected. Here for the aptness of the image.

The Sounds of Rain

First published in a limited edition by Emory University on 11 April 1988, to inaugurate the Richard Ellmann Lectures at Emory, then in the *Georgia Review* (Fall 1988): 481–2, *Agenda* (Spring 1989): 5–6, and the *Oxford Magazine* (Eighth Week, Trinity Term 1989): 12. It was included in *TC*, 26–7, before collection in *ST*.

I 2 veranda] verandah *Georgia Review, Agenda, Oxford Magazine, TC*
I 5 dead.] dead, *Georgia Review, Agenda*
I 9 late-winter] late winter *Georgia Review, Agenda, Oxford Magazine, TC*

I 21 the wet] a wet *Oxford Magazine*   the friend] his friend *Georgia Review*
II 16–18] Only sixty when Charon stopped the clock. / 'There would have been a deepening, you know, / Something ampler . . . like in Day by Day.' *Georgia Review*
III 4–5] As a flood gathers according to its laws / Like work going forward silently beyond me *Georgia Review*

Dedication Richard Ellmann (1918–87) was a friend of SH and celebrated literary critic, notably of twentieth-century Irish literature, and biographer of Joyce, Yeats and Wilde. SH gave the first Richard Ellmann Lecture in Modern Literature at Emory in April 1988.

I 3 *moil*: dialect term for 'drudgery'.

I 6 *thole*: to suffer or endure (Ulster-Scots, from Old English *þolian*). In this case, endure the death of Ellmann.

II 2 *Peredelkino*: the house-museum of Boris Pasternak, south-west of Moscow. Pasternak is buried in the cemetery there.

II 5 Pasternak (1890–1960): Russian poet and novelist. When he was awarded the Nobel Prize in 1958, the Russian authorities, who had banned his novel *Doctor Zhivago*, forced him to decline it by preventing him from travelling to receive it.

II 14 William Alfred (1922–99), US playwright and colleague of SH at Harvard. Athens Street is a select address in Cambridge, Massachusetts, near Harvard Square. SH's translation of *Beowulf*, ll. 88–98, was dedicated to Alfred and appeared as 'A Skilled Poet', published by Kathleen McCanless at the Bow and Arrow Press, Adams House, Harvard.

III 2–3 *steeped in luck*: in the exchange with Tom Delaney in 'Station Island VIII', the Delaney figure lamented his own early death, addressing the poet by contrast as 'poet, lucky poet' (*SI*, 82), something which SH frequently concedes. It corresponds to Pasternak's sense of duty in section II (9–10), beyond 'just writing lyric poetry'.

Fosterling

First published in Thomas Dillon Redshaw, *Hill Field: Poems and Memoirs for John Montague on his Sixtieth Birthday, 28 February 1989* (Minneapolis and Oldcastle: Coffee House Press and Gallery, 1989), 16, then in *Poetry Ireland Review* (Spring 1989): 1, and included in the programme for *50/60*, an event which marked Montague's sixtieth birthday and SH's fiftieth, at the Gate Theatre, Dublin, 11 June 1989. It was included in *TC*, 28, before collection in *ST*, and in *OG*, *NSP2014* and *100P*.

Epigraph] [attribution] John Montague *OG, NSP2014, 100P*
1–2 heavy greenness – / Horizons rigged with windmills' arms and sails.] gloominess: / Stalled windmills on the skyline. Arms and sails. *Hill Field*
5 never] not ever *OG, NSP2014, 100P*

13 marvels. Like] marvels: like *Hill Field*

This important poem acts as a kind of hinge between the poems up to this point and the turn 'to credit marvels' which pervades Part II of the book, SQUARINGS.

Epigraph *l.* 18 of the poem 'The Water Carrier' by John Montague (1929–2016), published in *Six Irish Poets* (1962), edited by Robin Skelton; John Montague, *Collected Poems* (Gallery Books, 1995), 189.

6 *hydraulics*: water is the dominant element in the early part of *ST*, as earth was in *DN*, and as air will be dominant in *ST* from this point on.

7 *glar*: mud; *glit*: ooze, scum; *dailigone*: dusk (i.e. 'daylight gone'), all Ulster-Scots. See Johnston 2020, and Richard Wall, 'A Dialect Glossary for Seamus Heaney's Works' (1998).

10 *the doldrums of what happens*: by contrast with 'the music of what happens' in 'Song' (*FW*, 53; *PSH*, 243). The original is the translation by James Stephens of a debate from the Fenian Cycle about what is the finest music, where Fionn mac Cumhaill is asked for his opinion by one of his followers: '"The music of what happens," said great Fionn, "that is the finest music in the world."' (Quoted in Montague 1974, 80. If Montague's book is SH's source, the cross-reference is apt in this poem.)

12 SH explains this as a Wicklow folk tale about a group of Travellers who escape a contract with the devil by making a clock which deceives him about the time (*SS*, 317).

13–4 The air brightening and the heart lightening, overcoming the depressed 'doldrums' of *l.* 10.

PART II SQUARINGS

All forty-eight poems were published in a special edition, *Squarings48*, with drawings by Sol LeWitt and an introduction by Helen Vendler.

1 Lightenings

Title SH says he found a dictionary entry that defined the term as 'a flaring of the spirit at the moment before death' (*SS*, 321). See the notes on poem xii of the series below. For the various terms used to describe the four groups of the twelve-line poems, see Brandes, 2009. The term 'Lightenings' picks up from the closing lines of 'Fosterling' and it was briefly considered as a title for the whole series. SH tells

Dennis O'Driscoll about the moment in the National Library in Dublin when the twelve-liners first came to him, saying he wrote the first three poems then 'in the order in which they eventually appeared in the book' (*SS*, 320–1).

i

First published in the sequence 'From Lightenings' in *Agenda* (Spring 1989): 9, and, before inclusion in OG and *NSP2014*, in the limited-edition collaboration with Felim Egan, *Squarings12*. SH's Author's Note stated:

> In 1986, when Felim Egan and I worked together on a small exhibition entitled 'Towards a Collaboration', we had no exact sense of how the collaboration would be fulfilled. Yet the paintings on the walls and the writing in the catalogue had this much in common: they were about natural landmarks that had become marked absences. Two years later, therefore, when I got going on these twelve-line poems (the whole sequence was published in *Seeing Things*), I realized it was time for our next move. What I was doing seemed to have real connection with Felim's approach, since the writing was usually an attempt to catch at something fleet and promising, and the lines I liked best had a quality which recalled my earlier characterization of certain Egan paintings as 'brightness air-brushed on the air.' This book is intended to provide a setting for some of those commonly intuited 'lightenings'.

11 old truth dawning] the old dawning *Agenda*

4 *the particular judgement*: the judgement of each soul on their individual death (as distinct from the general judgement when all souls are judged at the end of time).

7 *the commanded journey*: the point of death.

11 *no next-time-round*: interpreted as a declaration of disbelief in the Catholic doctrine of life after death, though elsewhere SH expresses a more indefinite position, saying that any loss of faith occurred 'offstage'. The poem that this may be thought to be in intertextual conversation with is Yeats's great point-of-death poem 'The Cold Heaven', a connection with which is most marked in the final and culminating poem of 'Lightenings', xii (*ST*, 66).

12 *Unroofed scope*: SH says to Dennis O'Driscoll 'My father's death in October 1986 was the final "unroofing" of the world' (*SS*, 322).

ii

First published in the sequence 'From Lightenings' in *Agenda* (Spring 1989): 10, and included in OG and *NSP2014*.

2 cold,] cold. *Agenda*
4 wall,] wall. *Agenda*
6 coping-stone] coping stone *Agenda*
6 chimney-breast] chimney breast *Agenda*

9 Make your study the unregarded floor.] Study the ultimate homelessness of floors. *Agenda*

1 *Roof it again*: the 'unroofed scope' at the end of the previous poem. The details in the opening lines are a wish to restore the conditions of a simple rural childhood.

8 *squarings*: the first occurrence of the overall term for the forty-eight twelve-line poems.

9 *unregarded floor*: SH's first use of the term 'unregarded' which becomes a major theme from 'Mint' in *SL* onwards; in response to the 'gravity-free cabin' he experienced while reading John Ashbery at Harvard in the mid-1980s, SH described his need 'to keep my poetic feet in the equivalent of divers' boots' and recover a metrical floor to his writing: 'in the nick of time, a poem came to the rescue. It was the second of what would turn out to be a sequence of 48 twelve-liners' ('Threshold and Floor', *Metre* (Spring/Summer 2000): 267). See also 'Úrlár' (*PSH*, 518).

iii
First published in the sequence 'From Lightenings' in *Agenda* (Spring 1989): 11, and included in *OG* and *NSP2014*.

12 squinted out from] pulled back to *Agenda*

1 Starting with the word 'Squarings?', which SH explains is derived from games of marbles 'in the school playground. How the preparation involved "anglings, aimings, feints and squints", "test-outs and pull-backs, re-envisagings" – all of which suggested ways of proceedings with more poems' (*SS*, 321).

7 All the preparations are hoping for the prevailing of 'certainties' which are 'blind' but the product of the exercise of muscles, physical or artistic.

iv
First published in the sequence 'From Lightenings' in *Agenda* (Spring 1989): 12.

2 theatres] amphitheatres *Agenda*
2–3 hear another / Stronger] hear / Another stronger *Agenda*
12 carried] brimming *Agenda*

2 A roofless Roman theatre like the Colosseum in Rome.
10 *How airy and how earthed*: SH said to Dennis O'Driscoll 'You could think of every poem in "Squarings" as the peg at the end of a tent-rope reaching up into the airy structure, but still with purchase

on something earthier and more obscure' (*SS*, 320). Here this dual attachment is applied to sound as it 'amplified and faded' (*l*. 9).

v

First published in *ST*, and later included in *OG* and *NSP2014*.

1 *marble holes*, cf. *iii*, *ll*. 3–4: the marble-player who went to Australia was the twin brother of SH's father. See 'Twins' (*PSH*, 1181).
  5 *the music of the arbitrary*: see note on 'Fosterling' 10 above.
  6 *an undersong*: like the groundswell resonating through the Roman urns in the previous poem, recalled in the last line's 'amphorae'.
  10 *Ocarina*: a bulbous wind instrument, held in the hands and with several finger-holes (between four and twelve).

vi

First published, with *vii*, as one of two poems under the title 'Diptych' in the *Irish Times* (7 Jan. 1989): A8, and with the selection 'From Lightenings' in *Agenda* (Spring 1989): 14. Also included in *Squarings12*, *OG*, and *NSP2014*.

4 sniffed-at] snuffed-at *Agenda*

As the next poem reveals, this story about Thomas Hardy (1840–1928) is based on SH's false memory of an episode in *The Early Life and Later Years of Thomas Hardy* (the book was attributed to Florence Emily Dugdale, Hardy's second wife, though largely written by Hardy himself).

vii

First published as the second poem in 'Diptych', *Irish Times* (7 Jan. 1989): A8, and with the selection 'From Lightenings' in *Agenda* (Spring 1989): 15. Later included in *OG* and *NSP2014*.

2 *Florence Emily*: Hardy's second wife; *ewe-leaze*: a meadow, used for sheep-grazing; cf. Hardy's poem 'In a Eweleaze near Weatherbury' (Hardy 1976, 70–1).

viii

First published in the sequence 'From Lightenings' in *Agenda* (Spring 1989): 16, and then with a selection of other poems under the title 'Lightenings', and described as 'a sequence of poems in progress', in the *Irish Times* (8 April 1989): A1. Also published under the title 'The Ship in the Air, *from* Lightenings' in the Japanese periodical *Edge* (July 1990): 1, and included in *Squarings12*, *OG*, *NSP2014* and *100P*.

One of SH's best-loved and most admired poems.

1 *the annals*: SH has taken the basis of the story from Jackson 1971, 165, where it is called 'The Air Ship'. In that version, the anchor is dropped on to the floor of the church and the priests seize hold of it. The man who comes down to retrieve it 'was swimming as if he were in the water', but the priests were dragging him down. '"For God's sake let me go!" said he, "for you are drowning me." Then he left them, swimming in the air as before, taking his anchor with him.' Jackson's source is Kuno Meyer's transcription in *Anecdota from Irish Manuscripts*, vol. 3, 8–9. This source is fourteenth or fifteenth century, and the story is repeated in various annals. The earliest written version of this form of the story (likely from an oral source) is the Norse *Konungs Skuggsjá* (c.1250). This also locates the event in the church of St Ciarán in Clonmacnoise. The monastery was founded in the sixth century, one of the great European centres of learning in its time.

ix

First published in the *Irish Times* (8 April 1989): A1, and in Christopher Reid (ed.), *The Poetry Book Society Anthology 1989–1990* (London: Hutchinson, 1989), 47. Later included in *OG* and *NSP2014*.

Another boat poem, like viii and the first part of the volume's title poem. Again, air and water as the volume's elements. This boat on dry land does not wobble, unlike the Inishbofin boat with 'its shiftiness and heft' that kept SH in agony.

11 The well-dressed sisters are probably SH's mother and her two sisters.

x

First published in the *Irish Times* (8 April 1989): A1, and in Christopher Reid (ed.), *The Poetry Book Society Anthology 1989–1990* (London: Hutchinson, 1989), 47. A special limited edition was published by the Friends of the Cheltenham Festival of Literature, *The Air Station* (Whittington Press, 1992), and it was later included in *OG* and *NSP2014*.

8–12] Stony up-againstnesss: it was both
an inglenook of homelessness and open

Chimney to the knowable, testing place
Where you would place yourself to face the music –
Those big-hulled questions looming in the air-slips. *Irish Times*

5 The quarry was one of the dangerous places of water, recurrent in SH from 'Bogland' (*DD*, 43; *PSH*, 91) to 'Seeing Things' (*ST*, 16, 18).

xi
Published in *ST*.

1 Only SH's friend Barrie Cooke (1931–2014), an abstract expressionist painter, the 'walking weathercock' (5), would turn a glass-roofed handball alley into a painter's studio. SH worked with him on various projects from the early 1970s.

2 Angles in the rectangular handball alley are the link to the squaring, geometrical theme of the series; cf. ii (*ST*, 56).

6 The eye 'peeled at the easel' confirms that the figure in the poem is the painter Barrie Cooke.

xii
First published in the *Irish Times* (8 April 1989): A1, and in Christopher Reid (ed.), *The Poetry Book Society Anthology 1989–1990* (London: Hutchinson, 1989), 47. Also included in *OG* and *NSP2014*.

6 promise] words *Irish Times*
8 empty] terrible *Irish Times*
9 bliss] promise *Irish Times*
10 Ached for at] That blazes on *Irish Times*
11 By] In *Irish Times*

The final poem of the 'Lightenings' group begins with the particular sense of the term that applies here when 'the spirit flares / With pure exhilaration before death': a moment of exhilaration that is even closer to Yeats's 'The Cold Heaven' than the first poem in the series.

12 *This day*: Christ's address to the good thief at the crucifixion (Luke 23:43).

2 Settings

The title of the second of the four groups of twelve poems, 'Settings', suggests the contexts in which the events of the poems are set, most of them memories of childhood.

xiii
First published under the title 'Bothar Bui' in *Thames Poetry*, 3. 7 (1990): 43, and later included in *OG* and *NSP2014*.

10 *the adult of solitude*: the grown-up perspective on a hot day in the childhood home place.

12 *first time round*: echoing 'no next-time round' (*l.* 11) in the corresponding first poem in 'Lightenings'.

xiv
First published with 'Squarings' xv and xvi as 'Three Rich Hours' with the dedication 'For Benedict Kiely' in Gordon Brown (ed.), *High on the Walls: An Anthology Celebrating Twenty-Five Years of Poetry Readings at Morden Tower* (Newcastle: Morden Tower and Bloodaxe, 1990), 66, then in *Squarings12*, and included in *OG* and *NSP2014*.

Title Published as 'Three Rich Hours', identifying the gold leaf of this poem and the following one as a reference to the *Très Riches Heures du Duc de Berry*, a richly decorated Book of Hours from the early fifteenth century. In a partial TS, a working title had been 'A Triptych of Rich Hours' dedicated 'for Benedict Kiely', with this part as section I, and xv (below) as section II; the third section (unknown) has become detached.

 1 The Seraphim is the highest rank in the hierarchy of angels.

xv
Printed privately for the author as 'A Rich Hour', a Christmas card, by the Gallery Press, December 1988. First published as the second poem in 'Three Rich Hours' in Gordon Brown (ed.), *High on the Walls: An Anthology Celebrating Twenty-Five Years of Poetry Readings at Morden Tower* (Newcastle: Morden Tower and Bloodaxe, 1990), 66, then in *Squarings12*, and later in *OG* and *NSP2014*.

1 And strike] Strike *A Rich Hour* relief] crude relief *A Rich Hour*
2 it:] it; *A Rich Hour*
4 my father] he *A Rich Hour*
5 The] A *A Rich Hour*
9] To be weighed by feel, guessed, coveted, put back. *A Rich Hour*

One of the sequence's most admired poems.

 1 Another preeminent scene, 'in gold' like that in the previous poem.

 3 Many of Rembrandt's paintings have a burnished centre of light, as with the hurricane lamp (*l.* 5).

 4 After the killing of a pig on a farm, the meat was preserved in coarse salt in a tea-chest or large wooden tub.

 10 Reference to a Rembrandt etching in Vienna, depicting Joseph distributing grain in Egypt, against forthcoming famine.

 12 *blazed upon*: reference to Yeats's 'Vacillation', section IV: 'My body of a sudden blazed' (Albright 1990, 301).

xvi
First published as the third poem in 'Three Rich Hours' in Gordon Brown (ed.), *High on the Walls: An Anthology Celebrating Twenty-Five Years*

of Poetry Readings at Morden Tower (Newcastle: Morden Tower and Bloodaxe, 1990), 67.

5 sight] charge *Three Rich Hours*
8 would] could *Three Rich Hours*
9 rat-poison] rat poison, *Three Rich Hours*

2f. Continuing the theme of shine and burnishing with its 'phosphorescent' and 'rancid shine', but repulsive here.

7 *the anger of Achilles*: l. 1 of the *Iliad*. An encounter in childhood with the destructive power of rat poison was a preparation for all the negative things witnessed in later life, public and personal.

10 *Corposant*: archaic term for the phenomenon called St Elmo's fire, an apparent phosphorescence on the surface of objects. Here the miasma of the poison hovers above the repulsive crusts. There may also be an ironic play on the Portuguese etymology of the word as 'holy body': far from rat-poison material.

xvii

First published, with three uncollected poems, under the title 'From Holdings' in *Poetry Review* (Winter 1989/1990): 4–5.

12 supposed] thought *Poetry Review*

1 *virtues of an eelskin*: the restorative powers that it confers (cf. 'Eelworks', III (*HC*, 29; *PSH*, 654), for SH's schoolfriend Archie Kirkwood's tying the eelskin round him 'for strength'). SH's interest in eels was founded on the eel business operated by his wife's family at Ardboe on Lough Neagh (*SS*, 93). This poem draws on two myths about the eel: that it took shape out of water, and Aristotle's view that it was generated out of mud, lacking sexual organs.

xviii

First published under the title 'The Fair Hill' in the *New Yorker* (29 April 1991): 36.

1 foul-mouther] foulmouthed *New Yorker*
2 rope-man] rope man *New Yorker*
7 belly-bands] bellybands *New Yorker*
9 rope-man] rope man *New Yorker*

1 *god of hemp*: the only known deities of hemp are female in eastern religions like Taoism so it is an imaginative extension here.

2 *the rope-man*: salesman of rope at country fairs and markets.

8 A childhood memory again, given his height.

9 The freedom he menaces the farmers with is the freedom to buy.

11 He loses his power once his customers have left the fair-hill.

xix

First published in Donovan Wylie, *32 Counties* (London: Secker & Warburg, 1989), 70, as part of the sequence 'Five Derry Glosses' (the full text of this version is given with 'Five Derry Glosses' in Uncollected Poems 1988–1989 (*PSH*, 391)), and then as the first of 'Two Settings' in Barry Humphries (ed.), *A Garland for Stephen* (Edinburgh: Tragara, 1991), 24. Also included in *OG* and *NSP2014*.

6–7] In order that the mind's eye be impressed // And so retain and then learn to read *Garland for Stephen*
11 a code of] haunting *Garland for Stephen*
12 In each] By your *Garland for Stephen*

The early parts of this poem are the same as the start of the third of 'Five Derry Glosses' (*PSH*, 391).

1 *Memory as a building*: as in the classical art of memory, which worked by associating places with 'With a code of images' (11). SH is drawing on Frances Yates's celebrated book *The Art of Memory* (London: Routledge & Kegan Paul, 1966) which had a great vogue in SH's period as a student. The images here in *ll.* 3–5 are taken from Yates's book, and it has been suggested that the violent images are an application to Northern Ireland of her images, especially in the Derry Glosses version.

xx

First published as the second of 'Two Settings' in Humphries (ed.), *A Garland for Stephen*: 24.

11 1940s'] nineteen-forties *Garland for Stephen*

1ff. The Heaneys visited Moscow as part of the 'festival of Youth and students' in 1985, when they visited Yevgeny Yevtushenko (1932–2017) in his *dacha* in Peredelkino (*SS*, 308–9).

xxi

First published under the title 'A Rent' in the *TLS* (19–25 Jan. 1990): 53.

10 shot] rent *TLS*
12 phrase] term *TLS*

1 Cf. 'One Christmas Day in the Morning': 'I was blabbing on about guns, how they weren't a Catholic thing' (*DC*, 31).

8 *as it was in the beginning*: the liturgical phrase introduces the child's image of the soul – as in Yeats's 'Coole and Ballylee, 1931' where the soul is said to be 'So arrogantly pure, a child might think / It can be murdered with a spot of ink' (Albright 1990, 294).

xxii

First published as 'Small Fantasia for W.B.' in the *TLS* (27 Jan. 1989): 76, and later reprinted in John Gross (ed.), *A 'TLS' Companion: The Modern Movement* (London: Harvill, 1992), 304. Also published in Christopher Reid (ed.), *The Poetry Book Society Anthology 1989–1990* (London: Hutchinson, 1989), 47, then in *Squarings12*, and later in *OG* and *NSP2014*.

6 the] some *TLS*, *'TLS' Companion*
10–12] What was learned from the midwife and the hangman? / What's the use of a held note or held line / That cannot be assailed for reassurance? *TLS*, *'TLS' Companion*

12 W.B.: Yeats. As in xxi, the poem raises the very Yeatsian question: where does the soul live?

xxiii

Published in *ST*.

1 *saga country*: Iceland.
 2 Ivan Malinowski (1926–89), Danish modernist poet and actor.
 3–4 Both the American naval base at Keflavik and the ethics of whale-hunting were major issues in Icelandic politics in the later twentieth century.
 9 Snorri Sturluson (1179–1241), famed Icelandic historian and poet, author of the *Prose Edda*, a crucial handbook of poetics.
 10 Snorralaug ('Snorri's pool'), a hot spring, can still be visited in Iceland today.

xxiv

First published in the *Irish Times* (8 April 1989): A1, then in Christopher Reid (ed.), *The Poetry Book Society Anthology 1989–1990* (London: Hutchinson, 1989), 47, and later included in *OG* and *NSP2014*.

Perhaps the 'utter evening' wanted by the speaker in the preceding poem (*l.* 7). The themes and atmospheres of the settings of this group are brought together in this quiet conclusion, dominated by air and water.

3 Crossings

The title of the third group of twelve poems, 'Crossings', seems the most applicable to the theme of its poems, particularly given the volume's framing by two highly significant literary crossings, by Virgil and Dante into the afterlife, and the death of the poet's father in the years leading up to it. Change and movement, especially of water, is a recurrent theme in the series. The first four of these twelve-line poems, along with 'Squarings', xliii (*ST*, 103), were published together as a single poem called 'Crossings' in the *LRB* in April 1989 which shows that the poems in the four groups of these twelve-line poems are to some degree interchangeable and their borders permeable. But generally the poems in 'Crossings' are more thematically connected than in any of the other groups.

xxv

First published with five other poems under the title 'Crossings' in the *LRB* (20 April 1989): 12.

4 stock-still] stock still *LRB*
5 Face-to-face] Face to face *LRB*

1 The first word established the theme of crossing and travelling from one state or place to another.
  10 *Let rebirth come*: meaning whether it comes through water or desire: two forms of Baptism.
  11 *backwards*: backways. The fox's eye is the imagination's route to a new world.

xxvi

First published in the *LRB* (20 April 1989): 12, and later in *Squarings12*.

11 that flees] fleeing *LRB*
12 Meltdown of souls from the straw-flecked ice of hell.] Melt-down of souls from hell's deep, straw-flecked ice. *LRB*

3ff. The encounter with soldiers here recalls 'From the Frontier of Writing' (*HL*, 6; *PSH*, 359).
  12 The straw-flecked ice of hell is reminiscent of the environment of the last canto of Dante's *Inferno*.

xxvii

First published in the *LRB* (20 April 1989): 12, and later in *OG*, *NSP2014* and *100P*.

12 dealing-man] dealing men *LRB*

Another of the most admired and popular poems in the sequence of forty-eight.
  1 'Everything flows' translates the Greek phrase attributed to Heraclitus, *panta rhei*, the doctrine that everything is constantly in flux and changing.
  3 *yellow boots*: Johnston glosses this: 'Light brown/yellowish laced boots traditionally worn by cattle dealers' (Johnston 2020, 57).

4 The association of SH's recently dead father with Hermes, the messenger between the gods and the world, is a major theme in the 'Crossings' poems.

5–6 Hermes is established as god of all these things, especially travel which is the subject of 'Crossings'.

7 One of SH's most quoted lines: a figure both of Hermes and the cattle-dealer, as well as recalling Stephen Dedalus in the 'Circe' section of *Ulysses*.

xxviii
Published in *ST*.

The slide on the ice in childhood is another irresistible movement, like Heraclitus's flux.

xxix
First published as 'A Latch' in the *TLS* (27 Oct.–2 Nov. 1989): 1172, and later in *OG* and *NSP2014*.

1 A latch evocative of the entrance to a church, leading to the religious terms of the poem.

4 *binding and loosing*: Christ's words to St Peter: 'Truly I tell you, whatever you bind on earth will be bound in heaven, and whatever you loose on earth will be loosed in heaven' (Matthew 18:18).

6 *at a touch renewed*: the cold tactility of the steel latch revives the memory.

8 *threshold*: the classic crossing point.

xxx
First published with seven other poems under the title 'Crossings' in the *New Yorker* (17 April 1989): 35, and later included in *OG* and *NSP2014*.

2 rope:] rope. *New Yorker*
5 arm] arm, *New Yorker*
11 wind-borne] windborne *New Yorker*
12 ploughland] plowland *New Yorker*

A traditional seasonal practice, reminiscent of 'The Harvest Bow' (*FW*, 55; *PSH*, 244).The next seven poems, beginning with this, printed as 'Crossings' in *New Yorker* (17 April 1989), are referred to by Rachel Falconer as a 'smaller clutch of threshold-related poems' (Falconer 2022, 42).

1 *St Brigid's Day*: First of February, coinciding with Imbolc, the first day of spring in the Celtic calendar, associated with renewal.

11 *flare*: St Brigid's Celtic prototype is a goddess of fire as well as renewal.

xxxi
First published as 'The Road at Frosses' in Simon Rae (ed.), *The Orange Dove of Fiji: Poems for the World Wide Fund for Nature* (London: Hutchinson, 1989), 53, and in the *New Yorker* (17 April 1989): 35. Also included in *Squarings*12.

2 quarter-mile] quarter mile *New Yorker*

    4 The line of Scotch fir trees at Frosses near Ballymena.
    10 *Of glimpse and dapple. A life all trace and skim*: the diction and atmosphere of the poem is reminiscent of Hopkins, especially of 'That Nature is a Hericlitean Fire and of the comfort of the Resurrection', perhaps suggested by Heraclitus in *xxvii*.

xxxii
First published in the *New Yorker* (17 April 1989): 35, and later included in *OG* and *NSP2014*.

10 eyeing] eying *New Yorker*
11 turf cutters] turf-cutters *New Yorker*

    2 *Crossing water*: making this poem crucial to the sequence.
    3 The *Stepping Stones* interviews may not require a particular source. But this line identifying them as 'stations of the soul' fits O'Driscoll's book well.
    4–6 The local terms 'kesh' and 'causey' recall the method of learning and remembering in poems like 'Alphabets'.
    11 The clothes the turf cutters cast off before they crossed the burn link to the souls waiting to cross the Acheron in *Aeneid*, 6.

xxxiii
First published in the *New Yorker* (17 April 1989): 35, and later included in *OG* and *NSP2014*.

7–8 planned / 'Plain, big, straight, ordinary, you know,'] planned – / 'Plain, big, straight, ordinary, you know?' – *New Yorker*
9 rigour] rigor *New Yorker*
11 idea] idea, *New Yorker*

    1 *literal*: address to self, to represent real events and people, rather than symbols for them like the Virgilian figures at the end of the previous poem.
    3 *he died*: SH's father.

10 The paradigm in the father's ideal, a 'shrine to limit', recalls the idea of squaring in poems like *ii* (*ST*, 56; *PSH*, 427).

xxxiv

First published in the *New Yorker* (17 April 1989): 35, and later in OG and *NSP2014*.

1 Yeats said, To those who see spirits, human skin] To those who have seen spirits, human skin *New Yorker*
2 afterwards] afterward *New Yorker*
7 base] base, *New Yorker*
8 Half-way] Halfway *New Yorker*
9 one of the newly dead] one newly dead *New Yorker*
11 farmboy] farm-boy *New Yorker*, OG, *NSP2014*

1–2 These lines do not exactly occur in the works of Yeats, though the idea seems appropriate. The opening phrase 'Yeats said' does not occur in earlier draft versions of the poem. This revenant is like someone crossed back from the land of the dead with his otherworldly brow (*l.* 12).

xxxv

First published in the *New Yorker* (17 April 1989): 35.

5 storey] story *New Yorker*
12 a dance-floor.] the gene pool. *New Yorker*

1 The shaving cuts of the young GI at the end of the previous poem suggests this memory of misbehaviour in the dorms at St Columb's.

xxxvi

First published in the *New Yorker* (17 April 1989): 35, later in *Squarings12*, OG and *NSP2014*.

1 we too] we, too, *New Yorker*
2 streetlamps] street lamps *New Yorker*
3 As danger gathered and the march dispersed.] When scaresome night made *valley* of that town. *New Yorker*

Dated 15 September 1988 in MS (NLI 49,493/86).
1 The friend is Michael Longley (1939–2025). Longley and SH attended a Northern Ireland Civil Rights Association march in Newry on 6 February 1972, to protest against the Bloody Sunday shootings which had taken place the previous week. An estimated 100,000 people joined this march. Longley recalled the experience in Adam Low's film *Seamus Heaney and the Music of What Happens* (2019).

1–2 'Even though I walk through the valley of the shadow of death, I will fear no evil, for you are with me' (Psalm 23:4).

6 The fireflies image from Dante is *Inferno*, 26.25ff.

12 Cf. 'The Crossing', *ST*, 111–2; *PSH*, 448. 'the faring poets': Virgil and Dante in *Inferno*, 3.

4 Squarings

The final group of twelve poems shares the title of the whole forty-eight-poem section that comprises *Seeing Things* Part II.

xxxvii

First published under the title 'Quoting' in the *TLS* (19–25 Jan. 1990): 53, and then with a selection of other poems 'From Squarings' in *Force 10* (Winter 1990): 31. Later included in *OG* and *NSP2014*.

1 Han Shan is the name associated with a collection of Buddhist poems from the Chinese Tang Dynasty in the ninth century. The name means 'Cold Mountain' (*l.* 2), so it can refer to a place, a state of mind, or the poet himself – if he ever existed. Beginning the group with this poem signals a move towards a more internal focus in the poems.

12 'an art that knows its mind' has been suggested as a description of SH's poems as a whole.

xxxviii

First published in *Force 10* (Winter 1990): 31, and later in *OG* and *NSP2014*.

1 the Capitoline Hill in Rome.

2 *temptation on the heights*: suggesting the biblical Transfiguration which occurs in all three of the Synoptic Gospels, in which Jesus is taken up to a mountaintop with three of his followers and transfigured in radiant glory.

11 The grandiloquent exclamations are undercut by the return to the everyday of the others, waiting at the Forum Café.

xxxix

First published as one of 'Six Poems' in the *LRB* (26 Oct. 1989): 20; then as 'The Wishing Chair' in John F. Deane (ed.), *Thistledown: Poems for UNICEF* (Dublin: Dedalus, 1990), 21; in *Force 10* (Winter 1990): 31, and in *Agni*, 29. 30 (1990): 168. Later included in *OG* and *NSP2014*.

3 very solid sense.] sense of the firmament. *LRB, Agni*
10 gave a savour] gave savour *LRB, Agni*
11 freshening] sharpening *LRB, Agni*
12 what you thought you'd settled for.] of possibility. *LRB, Agni*

1–2 The 'wishing chair' is a natural space between the base columns of basalt in the Giant's Causeway in North Antrim. The 'you' in the first line has been taken to be Marie Heaney, though the 'your/you' in the last two lines reads like the impersonal 'you' SH mostly uses for childhood memories, as in note to 'Markings' II 1.

xl

First published in the *LRB* (26 Oct. 1989): 20; then in *Force 10* (Winter 1990): 31; and in *Agni*, 29. 30 (1990): 169. Also included in *Squarings12*, *OG* and *NSP2014*.

6 terracotta] terra cotta *LRB, Agni*

4–5 The crude drinking holes in the earth for the cats are paralleled in the Sweeney story.

xli

First published in the *LRB* (26 Oct. 1989): 20; then in *Force 10* (Winter 1990): 31; and in *Agni*, 29. 30 (1990): 170. Also included in *Squarings12*, *OG* and *NSP2014*.

2 river shallows] river-shallows *LRB*

9–10 The squarings which are both literal measurements and indexes of the inner condition of 'self'.

xlii

First published in 32 *Counties* as the fifth of the 'Five Derry Glosses': 71 (the full text is given with the sequence in Uncollected Poems 1988–1989 (*PSH*, 392), then in Force *10* (Winter 1990): 31; and in *Agni*, 29. 30 (1990): 171. Later included in *OG* and *NSP2014*.

4 shirtsleeves] shirt-sleeves *Agni*
9 back,] back. *Agni*

1 *kesh*: from Irish *ceis*, a causeway made of wickerwork across a small river. Cf. Irish *ciseán*, basket.
   3 Cf. 'Fields of the Blessed', the Elysian Fields, the territory of heroes in the Greek afterlife where the blessed continued whatever gave them happiness in life.

xliii

Published as 'The Spring' in the *Sunday Tribune* (26 Feb. 1989), accompanied by an essay by SH marking the first anniversary of the death of David Thomson, to whom the poem is dedicated; subsequently published in *Force 10* (Winter 1990): 31, and later in OG and NSP2014.

Dated 5 February 1989 in TS, where it is titled 'The Spring', 'i.m. David Thomson' (NLI 49,493/93); Thomson (1914–88), was a writer and BBC presenter, and with George Ewart Evans joint author of *The Leaping Hare* (London: Faber & Faber, 1972). *Woodbrook*, his memoir of ten years as a tutor with the Anglo-Irish Kirkwood family near Sligo, was a major publishing success in 1974.

11 *missed a round*: of buying drinks; *stood it*: the hare's dodging its pursuer is like the drinker not paying for his round.

12 Cf. SH's 'The Names of the Hare' (*OG*, 210; *TSH*, 11–12; 546–8): two of the phrases for the hare 'the dew-hammer' and 'the shake-the-heart' occur verbatim in the poem; 'the far-eyed' echoes 'the bleary-eyed, the wall-eyed' in the poem. The Middle English original is in the Bodleian Library, Oxford, Ms Digby 86 from the last quarter of the thirteenth century. For notes on the original, see Margaret Laing, in *Medium Aevum*, 67. 2 (1998): 201–11. The poem is named in French in the manuscript, 'Les Nouns de un levre en englais', edited by A. S. C. Ross, 'The Middle English Poem on the Names of a Hare', *Proceedings of the Leeds Philosophical and Literary Society*, 3 (1932–5), 347–77.

xliv

First published in the *LRB* (26 Oct. 1989): 20; then in *Force 10* (Winter 1990): 31; and in *Agni*, 29. 30 (1990): 172. Later included in OG and NSP2014.

1 'They are all gone into the world of light' is the first line of one of the best-known poems by the Welsh Metaphysical poet Henry Vaughan (1621–95), on the perspective of the bereaved on the dead; his religious poems were published as *Silex Scintillans* in 1650.

3 Vaughan's religious poems are suffused with imagery of light.

7 The fisherman, 'well prepared for the nothing there', here corresponds to the admission in the '*All gone*' of the absolute absence of the dead. The positive view of death in Vaughan's poem is rejected.

xlv

First published in the *LRB* (26 Oct. 1989): 20; then in *Force 10* (Winter 1990): 31; and in *Agni*, 29. 30 (1990): 173. Later included in OG and NSP2014.

7 reed-beds] reed beds *LRB*, *Agni*

1ff. Like the 'Otherwise / They do not' of the previous poem, a stark distinction is made between the 'certain ones' for whom 'what was written may come true' and 'our ones' for whom it won't.

3 The dead living on at the mouths of rivers alludes to the afterlife in *Aeneid*, 6.

xlvi

First published as 'A Window' in the *TLS* (27 Oct.–2 Nov. 1989): 1172, and then in *Force 10* (Winter 1990): 31. Later included in *OG* and *NSP2014*.

7 'La musique de Bach est la seule preuve tangible de l'existence de Dieu' (Emil Cioran, *Syllogismes* 19–20). Cf. 'Clearances' 8 for application of Cioran's nihilist philosophy, 'a space / Utterly empty' (*HL*, 34; *PSH*, 373), and *SS*, 409 for influence of Cioran on SH.

xlvii

First published in the *LRB* (26 Oct. 1989): 20, and then in *Force 10* (Winter 1990): 31. Later included in *OG* and *NSP2014*.

7 Argus in Greek mythology was also known as Panoptes because he had a hundred eyes in his head and all over his body.

xlviii

First published in the sequence 'From Lightenings' in *Agenda* (Spring 1989): 13, and then in *Force 10* (Winter 1990): 31. Included in *Squarings12*, and later in *OG* and *NSP2014*.

9 Where wind] Where the wind *Agenda*
10 lame] lamé *Agenda*, *OG*, *NSP2014*

1 *in the offing*: not in the literal sense of the previous poem, but in the metaphorical sense of 'about to happen'.

7 *light breaks over me*: like the lambency of the previous poem. The images for transcendence recall moments in earlier poems in the series, such as the end of xv (*ST*, 71; *PSH*, 433) 'unseen and blazed upon'.

The Crossing

First published in the 'Seamus Heaney Fiftieth Birthday Issue' of *Agenda* (Spring 1989): 7–8, and included in *TC*, 23–4.

10 By another] But another *Agenda*
13 Quiet your anger] Do not anger yourself *Agenda*, *TC*

22 on the earth] on earth *Agenda, TC*
35 off that] from *TC*

 1 *us*: Dante and his guide Virgil, waiting to cross the Styx into the underworld.

 2 *an old man*: Charon, the ferryman across the Styx.

 7 *the living soul*: Dante who is uniquely crossing to the underworld with his living soul.

 12 *a lighter boat*: after death his soul must travel to the afterlife by a different route than this infernal one.

 21 *their teeth chattered*: the 'lost souls' are terrified by the appearance among them of a living spirit, and by their own terrible eternal fate.

 39 *a new crowd*: as the first group cross to the realm of the damned, another group gathers on the shore to follow them.

 47–8 Charon objects to the appearance of Dante there because he is not one of 'the bad seed of Adam' (*l.* 34) and should not travel in his boat. 'What his words imply' is that Dante is one of the 'good spirits' (*l.* 46) who does not belong there.

UNCOLLECTED POEMS (1992–1996)

The considerable number (twenty-three) of uncollected poems between the crediting of marvels in *Seeing Things* and the continued self-scrutiny in *The Spirit Level* is largely attributable to two factors: first, the number of translations, all included in *TSH* (from Irish, from SH's forthcoming *Beowulf*, and from the Romanian of Ana Blandiana, whose poems had featured prominently in John Fairleigh's anthology of Romanian translation *Where the Tunnels Meet*, published by Bloodaxe in 1996); and second, the number of tribute poems from this time: for Derek Mahon, George Mackay Brown, Herb Leibowitz (the editor of the New York poetry journal *Parnassus*). SH did not include any of the poems in these categories in the later canonical volumes. The Blandiana translations hit a particular note of self-representation not otherwise found in SH; her prominence as an environmentalist and her activity with PEN might also have held appeal for SH at a stage of his career when he was actively interested in Index on Censorship (cf. *TSH*, 43–52). This group has an interesting place between the decisive crediting of marvels and the full-scale epic translation of *Beowulf*. One much-admired elegiac poem 'In Bellaghy Graveyard' was written for the opening of Bellaghy Bawn in 1996.

To Sorley MacLean

Published in Angus Peter Campbell (ed.), *Somhairle, Dàin is Deilbh: A Celebration on the 80th Birthday of Sorley MacLean* (Stornaway: Acair, 1991).

7, 12 Burns'] Burn's *Somhairle* (error)
21 That] Tha *Somhairle* (error)
27 unsealed] unseeled *Somhairle* (error)

Sorley MacLean (1911–96), Scottish Gaelic poet born in Raasay. SH first met him in Kilkenny in 1976 and often declared his admiration for him, describing him in the *LRB* (6 Nov. 1986) as one of 'those poets who later become vital to us'.

33 *the Prince*: Bonnie Prince Charlie.
51 *lios*: Scottish Gaelic and Irish for fort.
53 *Hallaig*: MacLean's most celebrated poem, translated by SH (*TSH*, 85–6). SH visited Hallaig in Raasay in 2004, fifty years after the publication of 'Hallaig' in 1954 and 150 years since the clearance of Raasay.

55 *The Cuillin*: spectacular mountain range in the Isle of Skye, prominently visible from Raasay.

The Villanelle of Northwest Orient Flight 4

Published in a limited edition of 500 copies to mark the inaugural Emerald Ball in Tokyo, 12 March 1993.

Skims and Glances

Published in Colm Tóibín (ed.), *Soho Square Six: New Writing from Ireland* (London: Bloomsbury, 1993), 30–1.

More River Rhymes

Published in the *Irish University Review* (Spring–Summer 1994): 60, a special issue on Derek Mahon.

I 2–4 Derek Mahon described himself as a strange child with a taste for verse ('Courtyards in Delft', *New Selected Poems*, Faber & Faber and Gallery, 2016, 43). He lived for much of his later life in Kinsale, Co. Cork; in this clerihew SH in Smerwick on the Dingle peninsula rhymes on Mahon's first name.
 II 2 *'Fragments of an Agon'*: dramatic fragment by T. S. Eliot (1927).
 II 4 *Dutch interiors*: as in 'Courtyards in Delft', based on the painting by Pieter de Hooch.
 III 1 *farls*: small scones of soda bread or potato-cake in Ulster cuisine: an element in the celebrated Ulster fry.
 III 2 The Charles River in Eastern Massachusetts.
 III 3 *The Crown*: one of Mahon's places of resort in Belfast; *The Group*: Philip Hobsbaum's writers' group.
 III 4 Comparable places of poetic resort at Harvard near the Charles River, the Grolier Bookshop and The Coop university shop.
 IV 1 Three rivers in Northern Ireland.
 IV 3 *Slemish*: Slieve Mish (Irish *Sliabh Mis*), a hill near Ballymena in the Glens of Antrim where St Patrick is said to have herded sheep after his enslavement in youth.
 V 1 *east of Strangford Lough*: Carrowdore Churchyard where Louis MacNeice is buried, here imagined as the tutelary guide to Mahon as Virgil was to Dante in *The Divine Comedy*. The three poets in cavalcade (Mahon, Longley and SH) made a pilgrimage together there in 1963.

VI 1 A riff on the opening of Joyce's *Finnegans Wake*: 'riverrun, past Eve and Adam's'.

VI 3 The Front Square of Trinity College Dublin, where Mahon was a student.

VI 4 Two of the most familiar of Irish twentieth-century texts: 'Raglan Road' by Patrick Kavanagh, and the 'darlin' question' posed by Captain Boyle in Seán O'Casey's *Juno and the Paycock* (1924).

A Landfall

Published in *Oar*, 8 (Nov. 1995), and then collected in *Dove-Marks on Stone: Poems for George Mackay Brown* (Schondorf: Babel, 1996).

[text: *Oar*]

George Mackay Brown (1921–96), Scottish writer from Stromness in Orkney where SH visited him in 1982; he had visited SH in Belfast in 1968. SH admired him greatly as a poet deeply rooted in his locality.

Cheers

Published in the influential journal *Parnassus* (1995), in the supplement honouring Herb Leibowitz (1923–2011), its co-founder and editor, on the occasion of his sixtieth birthday. SH poems featured in *Parnassus: Poetry in Review*, 25. 1 and 2 (2001).

1–2] 'from the Western Isles / Of kerns and gallowglasses is supplied' (*Macbeth* 1.2.12–3).

In Bellaghy Graveyard

Published as a broadside of 500 copies by Robin Wade, London, in 1996 by the Northern Ireland Department of the Environment to mark the opening of Bellaghy Bawn.

Title The graveyard where SH's parents are buried and where he was to be buried in 2013. The speaker in this villanelle is probably SH's father at the funeral of his wife who died in 1984, only two years before him.

Bellaghy Bawn, a museum and arts centre on Castle Street in Bellaghy, is an early seventeenth-century fortified house, originally called 'The Castle'. It was opened by SH in 1996.

A Transgression

Privately printed for the family by the Gallery Press as a Christmas card limited to 125 copies (1991), and later included in a revised form in OG, after a selection from ST, with the date 1994.

[text: OG]

4 I was never supposed] our family didn't need *Gallery*
5 I wanted out as well. One afternoon] I felt the lure of it: one afternoon *Gallery*
15 At] Of *Gallery*   dared to] dared just to *Gallery*

THE SPIRIT LEVEL (1996)

The Spirit Level was published in London by Faber & Faber in 5,000 hardback and 30,000 simultaneous paperback copies on 6 May 1996 (a further 1,750 hardback copies were prepared for the Book Club Associates); it was published in New York by Farrar, Straus and Giroux in hardback on 30 June 1996 and in paperback on 10 April 1997. Two significant events had intervened since the publication of *Seeing Things*, with its emphasis on marvels and the transcendental. In Northern Ireland, the first IRA ceasefire was declared on 31 August 1994; the Combined Loyalist Military Council announced their ceasefire on 13 October. In December 1995 SH had been awarded the Nobel Prize in Literature. If these events were too close to the publication date of *The Spirit Level* to be reflected in great detail in the volume's contents (except for the dating of the penultimate poem 'Tollund' as 'September 1994' and the declared readiness in that poem 'to make a new beginning / And make a go of it'), they affected significantly the way in which SH was read. (A discussion of this appears in *SS*, 350.) The Nobel Prize also impacted upon the circulation of the book. Faber had tripled its print order for the paperback in the wake of the award, and even that turned out to be insufficient for demand. A reprint of 1,800 hardbacks was required for the Book Club Associates and for the trade after only six weeks of publication, while a paperback reprint of some 15,000 copies was in circulation on 24 January 1997. In the first four years of publication, Faber sold 15,000 hardbacks and 67,000 paperbacks of the edition (FF L7).

As had become a pattern over the years, it would take delivery of the TS in the summer of 1995 to help focus SH's final perception of how it should be organised and produced. Design work was undertaken by Faber's eminent typographer, Ron Costley, whose textual specification went into production at the end of August 1995.* The resulting proof was not exactly as SH had hoped, however, and featured crowded subheadings, ineffectual partitions and poor page breaks, and saw him responding in his most diplomatic mode in encouraging Faber to 'seize opportunities' to give the poems 'some breathing-space' on the page. Author revisions were to make production still more challenging, as

---

* Ron Costley had taken over as head of design at Faber from Shirley Tucker, who worked for the firm 1959–87, and had famously produced Sylvia Plath's iconic cover for *The Bell Jar* in 1966. Tucker, in turn, had taken over the position from the legendary Berthold Wolpe, who had joined Faber in 1941 and retired in 1975. Costley retired in 2005, but maintained close relations with Faber's poetry team until his death in 2015.

SH had returned his proof in November 1995 with the middle third of the book reordered, 'Tollund' moved second to last, and with substantive reworkings of 'The Flight Path', 'A Sofa in the Forties' and 'Weighing In'. He also removed all but one of the translations.

Those changes landed with good effect. Michael Hofmann in *The Times* described the book as 'irresistibly coherent'; Nicholas Jenkins in the *TLS* praised an internal balance that was both 'buoyant and sombre, cryptic and forthright', in an effect that was 'dazzling'. The book, described by Mick Imlah in his review in the London *Independent* as 'magnificent and mould-breaking' with its 'redemptive effect', begins in the positive, marvelling spirit of *Seeing Things*. The opening poem, 'The Rain Stick', recalls the last of the forty-eight twelve-line poems of *Seeing Things* with its 'glitter-drizzle' reflecting the 'silver lame shivered on the Bann'; the last words of the poem, 'Listen now again', were used as the title of the celebrated National Library of Ireland exhibition in the Bank of Ireland Cultural and Heritage Centre in Dublin, curated by Geraldine Higgins, which opened in 2018. Another of its poems, 'The Gravel Walks', provides the inscription that was selected for the poet's headstone in the graveyard at Bellaghy, a line that is entirely in the transcendental spirit of *Seeing Things*: 'walk on air against your better judgement'. And the final poem, 'Postscript', has become one of the great favourites among the poet's work, again celebrating light and apperception of the marvellous. By the shore in Co. Clare, the ocean 'is wild / With foam and glitter', and the resulting feelings of exaltation 'catch the heart off guard and blow it open'.

But, if the book begins and ends with light and exaltation, no book of SH's hits darker notes than this one: for example, a very different employment of the idiom 'Against our better judgement' appears in the pugnacious 'Weighing In' (*SL*, 17; *PSH*, 473). In 'Keeping Going', the tribute to the poet's beloved and grounded brother Hugh, the apparent childhood idyll of its opening with Hugh humorously playing the piper gives way to 'Macbeth helpless and desperate / In his nightmare' and Hugh's witnessing of the 'Part-time reservist' shot against a wall, 'Feeding the gutter with his copious blood'. The mood of the book is mixed: not a simple conflict between the marvellous and the violent but a series of poems in which both sentiments occur within the same setting. Hugh Heaney is in the location where the reservist was murdered but can 'shout and laugh above the revs' of the tractor. The ultimate tribute is the haunting line

> But you cannot make the dead walk or right wrong,

where, in keeping with the ambivalence of the book, 'right' functions equally as transitive verb and adjectival noun (*SL*, 12; *PSH*, 470). The familiar similarly encounters the violent in the sestina 'Two Lorries' where the lorry of the flirtatious coalman gives way to 'a different lorry . . . with a payload / That will blow the bus station to dust and ashes' (*SL*, 13; *PSH*, 471). This in turn prompts 'a vision of my mother / A revenant on the bench' in that bus station. The ambivalence is sustained in 'Damson', where the bricklayer's implement might be seen as providing the volume's undeclared title poem and which is another unnerving combination of the normal-domestic with the injurious in the 'matte tacky blood' on his knuckles, preparing the way for Odysseus in Hades 'lashing out / With his sword that dug the trench and cut the throat / Of the sacrificial lamb' (*SL*, 16; *PSH*, 472). The ambivalence is succinctly expressed in the address to the bricklayer as 'Trowel-wielder, woundie.' It may be the phrases 'coming clean' and 'mucking in' that suggest the combative 'Weighing In' in the poem placed next in the book in which four twelve-line Squarings-type poems are used to balance the 'unearthly pitch' of 'the angels' strain' against the obligation to 'follow-through' with 'a quick hit'. Shockingly in the context of 'Damson' the poem concludes

> I held back when I should have drawn blood . . .
> At this stage only foul play cleans the slate. (*SL*, 18–19)

The stage is set for the volume's two most controversial poems, which are in various ways as extreme as SH ever gets: 'The Flight Path' and 'Mycenae Lookout'. 'The Flight Path' follows the same contour as 'Keeping Going', from the domestic playful to the conflicted: in this case from the poet's father making paper boats at which 'a dove rose in my breast' to a disturbing encounter with a republican ideologue and another with a hostile policeman, to a conclusion in which – this time – peace has the last word: 'the dove rose. And kept on rising.'

The Spirit Level was dedicated to Helen Vendler, who said she found 'Mycenae Lookout' 'shocking' when she first read it (*SS*, 349). Like other poems in the book such as 'The Thimble' it is at the violent end of the continuum of this ambivalent book. SH says he always had 'confidence in the sequence', including the second section, 'Cassandra', with its uncompromising language, which was the most controversial publication by him since 'Punishment' in *North*. He tells O'Driscoll that the extremity of the mood of the poem was prompted by 'a rage at what had gone on in the previous twenty-five years, "That killing-fest", as the poem calls it' (*SS*, 350), though in an exchange of letters with O'Driscoll he expresses some anxiety about such language as 'camp-fucked' (EU 1420). And we recall the bitter conclusion of 'Weighing In': 'At this stage only foul play cleans the slate.'

Overall, it is clear that by this time there is no simple subject or sentiment (in the way that *Death of a Naturalist* might be called home-based, or *North* politically charged, or *Seeing Things* marvel-centred). This post-ceasefire and post-Nobel book, poem by poem, is unstably placed between the extremes of violence and virtue. This is perhaps the way in which Imlah found the book 'mould-breaking'. Among the closing poems, 'Tollund' may attempt to warrant the evocation of 'The Townland of Peace' and aspire at the end to be 'alive and sinning, / Ourselves again, free-willed again, not bad'; 'Postscript' pleads the virtue of finding the freedom 'to make the time' to drive west and wait for the wind's 'big soft buffetings' to 'catch the heart off guard and blow it open'. But the terminology of even this seemingly idyllic scene still contains an element of threat.

[text: *SL1996*]

The Rain Stick

First published in the *Observer Review* (10 September 1995): 17; and included in the programme for a reading presented by the Academy of American Poets and the Pierpoint Morgan Library, New York (13 Nov. 1996): 3. Included in *OG*, *NSP2014* and *100P*.

1 Upend] Up-end *OG*, *NSP2014*, *100P*
12 Upend] Up-end *OG*, *NSP2014*, *100P*

Dated 27 July 1992 in TS (NLI 49,493/106).

The rain stick is in origin a Chilean musical instrument made from a dried-out cactus, containing dry seeds or pebbles which flow up and down inside it, producing a sound like rain falling. The particular one here was given to SH by Rand and Beth Brandes; he says the poem is about keeping 'the lyric faith' and as much 'about middle age as about a rain-stick' (*SS*, 345). The musical terminology of the poem shows SH's descriptive power at its most evocative. The 'diminuendo' sound is 'undiminished' by the fact that it has happened many times before, so the rain stick is an image of the imaginatively new and the familiar.

To a Dutch Potter in Ireland

First published as a poem of three parts in the limited-edition *KG*, 10–12, and in the *Threepenny Review* (Spring 1993): 15, where part 2 is an early version of 'The Gravel Walks' (variants are recorded below with the notes on that poem) and part 3 is 'After Liberation'. Published as a two-part poem in *Poetry Ireland Review* (Autumn/Winter 1995): 62–4; and included in the programme for *Poetry International, Poetry on the Road*, Rotterdam (19/20 June 1993): 2. 'After Liberation' appeared in Peter Van De Kamp (ed.), *Turning Tides: Modern Dutch and Flemish Verse in English Versions by Irish Poets* (Irving: Taylor Publishing Company, 1994), 133.

I 3 bone-dry] bone dry *Poetry Ireland Review*
I 3–4 kiln // And] kiln – / And *Threepenny Review*
I 9 that] the *Threepenny Review*
I 14 scentless / sticky *Poetry Ireland Review*
I 15 sticky] lustrous *Threepenny Review* | scentless *Poetry Ireland Review*
I 22 might] could *Threepenny Review*
I 23 Cold gleam-life] Gleam-life *Threepenny Review*
I 23 water.] water, *Threepenny Review*, *Poetry Ireland Review*
I 25–7 This stanza is not present in the *Threepenny Review* version.
I 29 night instead, in the Netherlands,] night in the burning Netherlands *Threepenny Review*
I 30 kill; then,] kill, but, *Threepenny Review*
I 31] Came backlit from the fire a second time *Poetry Ireland Review*
I 31–2] You came through fire safe a second time / And now this third and ever-after time, *Threepenny Review*
I 38 And, 'now that the rye crop waves beside the ruins',] And *now that the rye crop waves beside the ruins Threepenny Review*

A poem of intertextual genesis, which in early drafts included formative versions of 'An Education' (*PSH*, 1184), 'The Gravel Walks' (*SL*, 39–40; *PSH*, 486) and 'The Clay Pipes' (*TSH*, 25) under working titles 'An Education' and 'The Freedom of Ceramica' (NLI 49,493/f. 102, 106, 108, 109; HFC).

The Dutch potter is Sonja Landweer (1933–2019), a celebrated artist born in Amsterdam who lived in Ireland from the 1960s and was the partner of the painter Barrie Cooke. The Heaneys visited them in Co. Kilkenny in the early 1970s on their return from California and considered moving to that area to be near them, as commemorated in the MS archive poem 'The Island' (BC 1280725). Both Landweer and Cooke remained close friends of SH until the end of his life. See also the commentary note to 'An Education' (*PSH*, 1200).

I 1–6 The italicised preamble to the poem describes Landweer's working studio in Co. Kilkenny, drawing on the end of 'An Education' (*PSH*, 1184).

Part I of the poem compares the childhoods of SH in Co. Derry and Landweer in Holland by the Norder Zee, contrasting her experience in World War II (her father was shot by the Nazis as they withdrew from the Netherlands: *SS*, 357) with his quiet country upbringing. Part II, 'After Liberation', is SH's translation of the poem

'Na de Bevrijding' by J. C. Bloem (1887–1966) which is 'an iconic celebration of Dutch liberation' (*TSH*, 27, 563) though Bloem was sometimes accused of Nazi sympathies or anti-Semitism. Published several times between 1993 and 1996, SH's translation is usually taken to be making an implicit comparison with the improving situation in Northern Ireland.

A Brigid's Girdle

First published in *Parnassus* 20: 1 and 2 (1995): 284.

5 sunlit] shadowed *Parnassus*
8 delicious,] delicious *Parnassus*
15 hoop] hoop, *Parnassus*
18 To handsel and to heal,] Immemorially *Parnassus*
19 lightsome] healing *Parnassus*

Dedication Adele Dalsimer (1939–2000) was a friend of SH in Boston who established the Irish Studies Program at Boston College and who died of cancer at the age of sixty. She was one of the group of Massachusetts friends that SH lists as first acquaintances of the Heaneys on their arrival in 1979 (*SS*, 269). The poem, written in early spring in Wicklow, recalls his previously writing to her from South Carolina at the same time of year, presumably before she was ill.

9 *Dulcimer*: perhaps an echo of Dalsimer's surname.

10 *feminine rhymes*: rhymes on more than one syllable (as opposed to masculine rhymes on stressed monosyllables), in which this poem is very rich: 'table'/'gable' etc. The whole spirit of the poem is feminine, including the dominant saint and clothing ('crinoline').

13 St Brigid's Day, 1 February, regarded in Ireland as the first day of spring, as it was in the ancient Celtic and Anglo-Saxon calendars. The 'Brigid's Girdle' was a circle (Irish *crios*) made of plaited straw rope through which people passed as a spring ritual. Cf. 'Squarings', xxx (*ST*, 88): 'On St Brigid's Day the new life could be entered / By going through her girdle of straw rope'.

16 *trindle*: to force into a circular shape (from Old English *trindel*, a circle).

18 *handsel*: a New Year's gift to bring good luck, associated with healing here. The poem's elegiac subtext contrasts the remembered period of happiness of the opening with the time when Adele 'faced the music and the ache of summer' with the ambiguous 'going through the thing' – at once enduring a period of suffering and physically passing through the circular straw device.

Mint

First published in May 1991 as a limited-edition broadside *Mint* by William B. Ewert, dedicated to the Corbett family of Boston; and then in *Soho Square Four* (London: Bloomsbury, 1991), 102; subsequently in *KG*: 14; *New Republic* (21 June 1993): 45; and *Fortnight* (Nov. 1995): 27. Also included in *OG* and *NSP2014*.

3 our refuse and old bottles:] our tins and bottles. *Soho Square Four*
4] Usual and unverdant, a bit like us. *Soho Square Four*
6 newness in the back yard] newfangledness in the yard *Soho Square Four*, *New Republic*
7 callow] vivid *Soho Square Four*

15–16 Concern for the rights of the disregarded is a recurrent SH theme from this point onwards, as in 'Anything Can Happen' (*DC*, 13; *PSH*, 598) where 'those overlooked regarded' (*l*. 10) is a reversal of the normal order.

A Sofa in the Forties

First published as the shorter poem 'A Wave from the Distance' in *Forward into the Past: For May Sarton on Her Eightieth Birthday* (Concord, NH: William B. Ewert, 1992), 28, where it reads:

> A WAVE FROM THE DISTANCE
>
> All of us on the sofa, all lined up
> Behind each other, eldest down to youngest,
> All going *chooka-chook*, for this was a train
>
> And between the jamb-wall and the bedroom door
> Our speed and distance were inestimable.
> First we shunted, then we whistled, then
>
> Somebody collected the invisible
> For tickets and very gravely punched it
> As carriage after carriage under us
>
> Moved faster, *chooka-chook*, the sofa legs
> Went giddy and the unreachable ones
> Far out on the kitchen floor began to wave.
>
>   For May Sarton, on her 80th birthday.
>
>   Seamus Heaney
>   Cambridge, Massachusetts
>   3 March 1992

Subsequently published in *Verse* (Winter 1992): 6–7; the limited-edition *Poems for Alan Hancox* (Herefordshire: Whittington Press, 1993): n.p.; then in *KG*: 22–3; and the programme for *Poetry International, Poetry on the Road*. Also in Hans-Christian Oesr (ed.), *Transverse II: Seamus Heaney in*

Translation ([Dublin]: Irish Translators' Association, 1994), 129–30, and later included in *OG*, *NSP2014* and *100P*.

14 ornate] bier-like *Verse, Poems for Alan Hancox*
16 castors on tip-toe,] ballerina castors, *Verse, Poems for Alan Hancox*
16 tip-toe] tiptoe *OG, NSP2014, 100P*
19–20 straight-backed, / When it] straight backed, when / It *Verse, Poems for Alan Hancox*
20–1 remoteness, / When the] remoteness, when / The *Verse, Poems for Alan Hancox*
22 mornings,] morning *Verse, Poems for Alan Hancox*
25–36] [as *ll*. 37–48] *Verse*
26 Yippee-i-ay] Yippee-yi-yay *Verse, Poems for Alan Hancox*
31–2 hole / Bored in] hole bored / In *Verse, Poems for Alan Hancox*
37–48] [as *ll*. 25–36] *Verse*
44 seemed;] seemed, *Verse, Poems for Alan Hancox*
46 unlit] lit-up *Verse, Poems for Alan Hancox*

A group of four twelve-line poems on the model of the SQUARINGS section of *ST*, recalling the childhood home of SH and his siblings. The twelve-line form is often used for personal and family contexts, culminating in *HC*.

13 The idea of the 'Death-gondola', suggested by the circular carvings of the sofa's arms (comparable perhaps to the crinoline's 'trindle') may derive from Nicholas Roeg's film *Don't Look Now* (1993) which features a memorable funeral gondola.

26–7 In fact 'yippee-i-ay' is the refrain of Stan Jones's 'Ghost Riders in the Sky' (most familiar as sung by Johnny Cash). *The Riders of the Range* was a popular western as BBC radio serial and comic strip in the British boys' magazine *Eagle*, both launched in 1949, and in Lesley Selander's 1950 film.

27–8 HERE IS THE NEWS / *Said the absolute speaker*: the voice of authority of the BBC with its 'gulf' between the newsreader's pronunciation and the country accent of Co. Derry.

44 'The Last Thing on My Mind', a song by Tom Paxton, very popular in Irish 1960s dance halls. All the cultural references in the poem are to things with marked popularity in SH's childhood and teenage years.

Keeping Going

First published, without dedication, in the *New Yorker* (12 Oct. 1992): 76–7; and in *KG*: 26–8; then in Patrick Crotty (ed.), *Modern Irish Poetry: An Anthology* (Belfast: Blackstaff, 1995), 217–19, where it carries the dedication *For H. H.*; *Fortnight* (Nov. 1995): 26, with the same dedication; and the programme for *Poetry International, Poetry on the Road*. Also included in *OG*, *NSP2014* and *100P*.

3 Wobbling] Bobbling *New Yorker*
6 pop-eyes] pop eyes *New Yorker*
7–8 keeping the drone going on / Interminably,] keeping up the drone / Inside your nose, *New Yorker, Modern Irish Poetry*] keeping up the drone / Interminably *Fortnight*
11 work-bucket] work bucket *New Yorker*
23 freshly-opened] freshly opened *New Yorker, OG, NSP2014, 100P*
27 alone,] alone. *New Yorker, Modern Irish Poetry*
29 heaven.] Heaven *New Yorker*
40 nightmare – when] nightmare, when *New Yorker*
46 forget!'] forget.' *New Yorker*
48 crown] clown *Fortnight*
55 morning like] morning just like *New Yorker, Modern Irish Poetry*
62 and heel] and his heel *Fortnight*
72 piper's] pipers' *New Yorker, Modern Irish Poetry*
78 to in] to to *New Yorker, Modern Irish Poetry*
79 is] Is *New Yorker*

1 *The piper coming from far away is you*: addressed to SH's brother Hugh, to whom the poem is dedicated. The poem is a sustained work of praise to the brother who stayed on in the family farm, despite its various hardships, ending by saluting his 'good stamina' in staying on 'where it happens': a tribute reminiscent of Derek Mahon's in 'Afterlives': 'if I'd stayed behind / and lived it bomb by bomb'. Most of the poem's six sections are centred on Hugh, admiring his resolve in 'keeping going' on the same ground in good humour throughout his life. The final section shows him waiting 'until your turn goes past' (Hugh was epileptic); his experiencing of the death of Christopher, his child-brother (in 'Mid-Term Break') and of his own daughter Rachel (in 'The Summer of Lost Rachel') is not mentioned here; but section five describes graphically the killing of David McQuillan, an Ulster Defence Regiment reservist from Bellaghy, who was shot by the IRA on 15 March 1977 in Hugh's area (see McKittrick 1999, 709).

Patrick Crotty points out that the opening line is taken from the end of Hugh MacDiarmid's poem 'With the Herring Fishers': 'Look! Is that only the setting sun again? Or a piper coming from far away?' The play-acting piper with the whitewash brush continues the theme of family childplay in 'A Sofa in the Forties'. The nexus of images throughout the poem is remarkably sustained: whitewash, tar-borders, bloodstains, dung and putrefaction.

19–20 The pristine whitewashed world of childhood memory.
57–8 Castle Street and the Diamond – near the centre of Bellaghy.

Two Lorries

First published as 'The Modern Mistress' in *Verse* (Winter 1993): 87; and as 'Two Lorries' in *Oxford Poetry* (Summer 1994): 6–7; and *Fortnight* (Nov. 1995): 27. Later included in *OG*, *NSP2014* and *100P*.

5] Does she ever go to the films in Magherafelt? *Verse*
11 mother:] mother. *Verse*
13 And films no less!] And films, no less. *Verse*] And a film, no less! *Oxford Poetry*
13 coalman . . .] coalman! *Verse*
15 this nineteen-forties mother,] 'The Modern Mistress' mother, *Verse*] mother,] mother. *Oxford Poetry*
16 her] that *Verse*
17 her] one *Verse*
18 for] towards *Verse*
19 Oh,] O, *Oxford Poetry*, *Fortnight*
19–39] In *Verse*, these stanzas read as follows:

> Where the bus has gone already. Magherafelt.
> O dream of dark plush near a city coalman!
> O plasm and blinding flash! For a different lorry
> Is nosing into Broad Street with its load
> To blow the bus station to dust and ashes
> And when the dust settles, I meet my mother
>
> In the empty waiting room, now less a mother
> Than a pilgrim revenant in Magherafelt
> On an Ash Wednesday, her silky brow all ashes.
> Death walks out past her like a dust-faced coalman
> Refolding body-bags, plying his load
> Empty upon empty. Again a lorry
>
> Is getting revved and turned, again a lorry
> Is moving into Broad Street, the usual mother-
> Loded heavy hijacked one that will explode
> Its payload soon in a nowhere Magherafelt.
> So sweet-talk darkness and tally dust, coalman.
> Exhume old shit from the ashpit and the ashes.
>
> There was a load that blew up Magherafelt.
> There was a lorry and a stove-proud mother.
> There was a coal-man, there are warm-wet ashes.

20 Oh,] O, *Oxford Poetry*, *Fortnight*
21 a different] another *Oxford Poetry*
22 shot, up Broad Street, with] shot up Broad Street with *Oxford Poetry*, *Fortnight*
23 That will blow the bus station] To blow the bus-station *Oxford Poetry*] bus station] bus-station *Fortnight*
20 that] what *Fortnight*
25 on the bench] on bare forms *Oxford Poetry*
26 Magherafelt.] Magherafelt, *Oxford Poetry*
27 bags full up with] bags were full of *Oxford Poetry*
31 motes] notes *Oxford Poetry*

32 Was it now? Young Agnew's or that other,] Is it now? Agnew's own or that other *Oxford Poetry*
33 In a time beyond her time in Magherafelt . . .] In 1992 in Magherafelt . . . *Oxford Poetry*
37 a load] the load *Oxford Poetry*
37 Magherafelt] Magherafalt [typo] *Oxford Poetry*
39 Dreamboat] Glorified *Oxford Poetry*

Working title in TS: 'The Modern Mistress' (NLI 49,493/108, /112).

'Two Lorries' is SH's only sestina, notable among other things for the virtuoso requirement of 'Magherafelt' as one of the six recurrent words. The initial story of the flirtatious coalman 'sweet-talking' the poet's mother changes to a dark event when the bus station in Magherafelt, where SH used to meet his mother, is blown up by an IRA bomb on 23 May 1993, the same dramatic shifting of tone as in 'Keeping Going' and other poems in *SL*.

Damson

First published in *Antaeus* (Autumn 1994): 278–9, and later in *OG* and *NSP2014*.

5 wall,] wall; *Antaeus*
5 big] big, *Antaeus*
6 (for once)] for once *Antaeus*
8 King of the castle,] The profiled one, *Antaeus*
13 Is weeping with the held-at-arm's-length dead] Streams with the desperate, held-at-arm's-length dead *Antaeus*
17 bricks] bricks, *Antaeus*
24 point and skim] dint and trim *Antaeus*
26 kept hidden.] rehidden. *Antaeus*
29 rigged in bloody gear.] rigged out in killing gear. *Antaeus*
38 mortar board] mortarboard *Antaeus*

The poem begins with the blood and cement dust that the preceding poem's explosion ends with and concludes with sunlight and the jam-making that the poem's title might have led us to expect, maintaining the ambivalent atmosphere of the book. The bricklayer of the opening section is probably SH's uncle-in-law, Mick Joyce from Cork, who appears as an exotic figure on his return from the Army and who is the subject of 'To Mick Joyce in Heaven' (*DC*, 8; *PSH*, 595). The blood-seeking ghosts appear like the congregating dead by the farmhouse in 'Keeping Going', before the pastoral ending.

33 *woundie*: rare word, someone who treats wounds, as the bricklayer is a builder, not a sacker (of cities).

Weighing In

First published in the *TLS* (17 Jan. 1992): 28. The third section appeared as 'To refuse the other cheek. To cast the stone' in *Mica* (Winter 1992): 31–2. Later included in *OG* and *NSP2014*.
Note: see 'Resolutions' (NLI 49,493/106), which is partly collected in this poem.

In the *TLS*, the poem appears as three numbered sections (the first, second and fourth sections of the final version), and with significant variants.

1–12 Enter the brute fact of a 'fifty-six':
Half a hundredweight of solid iron
With an inset, thick-set, integral crossbar

For a handle. Squared-off and ordinary
Until you lifted it, then a life-belitting,
Socket-ripping force. The gates of heaven

Could not prevail against it, flesh-proof,
Dormant, inoppugnable,
A tabernacle of dead weight. Yet balance it

Against a second one on a weighbridge
That had been well greased and adjusted
And everything grew lambent, touch had force. *TLS*

13–24 In other words, this principle of bearing –
Bearing one another, bearing up
Or down – changes everything. Which is

The extent of the good tidings in the end,
This having to balance the intolerable
In others against our own, the sealed vault

In everyone where an undead thing just keeps
And keeps because it's not let walk.
Peace on earth, men of good will, all that

Is workable when the fulcrum's trembling,
When truth weighs in, scales rest, the angels' song
Prolongs its strain and overload defers. *TLS*

37] Two sides to every question, obviously . . . *TLS*
38 just weighing in] putting the boot in *TLS*

Another poem made up of four twelve-liners, starting with a literal contrast between the weighed down and the smoothly flowing. The second section applies this principle of balance to personality types, developing this in the third and fourth sections to a disconcerting argument for retribution rather than forbearance, against the ideal of turning the other cheek.

1 *56 lb. weight*: half a hundredweight: a common measure of sacks of domestic fuel or animal feed.

29ff. Matthew 26:68. The precise wording 'Prophesy who struck thee' seems to be SH's own: not the terms of the RSV or Douay–Rheims version.

37 *yes, yes, yes . . .*: recalling 'connive / in civilized outrage' in 'Punishment' (*North*, 41; *PSH*, 191).

47 *old friend*: probably a notional opponent in debate.

St Kevin and the Blackbird

First published as parts I and III of 'Triptych' in *From Erudition to Inspiration: A Booklet for Michael* (Belfast: Belfast Byzantine Enterprises, Department of Greek and Latin, Queen's University, 1992), 1–2. The book marked the occasion of the retirement of Professor Michael McGann from Queen's. Published as 'Diptych' in the programme for *Poetry International, Poetry on the Road*; Carmen Horst and Wanda Kraybill (eds), *A Whistle Over the Water: A Broadside Sampler* (Goshen, Indiana: Pinchpenny Press, 1994); *CutBank*, 42 (Summer 1993): 47–8; and *Tracks*, 11 (1996): 23–3. Published as 'Saint Kevin and the Blackbird' in Brendan Flynn (ed.), *The Clifden Anthology* (Clifden: Clifden Community Arts Week, 1995), 46; *Fortnight* (Nov. 1995): 27; *Link-Up* (Dec. 1995): 25; here the two sections of the poem are not separated by the asterisk. Also included in Maurice Riordan and John Burnside (eds), *Wild Reckoning* (London: Picador, 2004), 193, and in Robert Perkins, *The Written Image* (London: Benjamin Spademan Rare Books, 2017), 52, where stanza breaks are not observed and the text is accompanied by an illustrated facsimile manuscript of the poem. Later included in *OG*, *NSP2014* and *100P*.

14 he?] he: *CutBank*
18 shut-eyed] shut-eye *Link-Up*

The first of the two twelve-line sections tells an Irish legend of the sixth-century St Kevin of Glendalough; in the second SH constructs an imaginative account of the physical and mental condition of Kevin during his unmoving vigil and the loss of self-awareness it produces.

The Flight Path

First published in *PN Review* (Nov./Dec. 1992): 31–2, and then in *Threepenny Review* (Winter 1993): 5; in both it is dedicated to Donald Davie. Section 5 of the poem was published under the title 'Far Away' in the *New Yorker* (26 Dec. 1994–2 Jan. 1995): 88; and part of the poem was published as 'Up and Away' in Maurice Hayes (ed.), *The Flight Path: Writings by the Winners of the American Ireland Fund Literary Award, 1972–1996* (Oldcastle: Gallery, 1996), 18. Sections 4 and 5 were included in *OG* and *NSP2014*.

1 4–5 corners, / Then] corners / And *PN Review, Threepenny Review*
1 7] Whenever my father's hands came clean apart *PN Review, Threepenny Review*
1 10 High-sterned, splay-bottomed,] High-sided, splayed *PN Review, Threepenny Review*
1 11 centre every] centre of it every *PN Review*
2 8 The sycamore speaks in sycamore from darkness,] The sycamore now's all surge and reassurance *PN Review*
2 9–10 lamplight. // I'm] lamplight. / I'm *PN Review, Threepenny Review*
2 11] Standing in in my own shoes for all those *PN Review*
2 12–13 stay-at-homes / Who leant against the jamb and watched and waited, / The ones] stay-at-homes, / The ones *PN Review, Threepenny Review*
2 18 nor] or *PN Review, Threepenny Review*
2 19–22] As their plane reached cruising altitude, / Too late to get an angle on the house / They'd left hours earlier, kissing, kissing *PN Review, Threepenny Review*
3 1–18] The final section 3 does not appear in *PN Review* or *Threepenny Review*. Instead after *l.* 35 this third section is included:

> Horace was right: there is no alibi.
> Sunk in the home truths is the way to fly.

PN Review and *Threepenny Review* then include this section 4:

> The following for the record, in the light
> Of everything before and since.
>
> Not long after the Birmingham bombings
> A couple of us flew from Belfast, drunk
> As lords, miming into sick bags, doing
> Photo-cartoons on the in-flight magazines –
> Rent-a-Paddy Inc., in full production!
> In which state, IN BLOCK CAPITALS, one filled out
> (As instructed) an Embarcation Card.
> Previous Address. Address in Britain.
> Duration of Visit. Purpose of . . . We were
> Headed for a seminar (what else)
> On art and politics. At any rate,
> Under Purpose of Visit, this bard wrote
> TO EDUCATE (IF POSS.) SOME ENGLISH PEOPLE
> And thought no more about it.
>   The plainclothes man
> Who checked us through Arrivals took his time.
> 'What's this then, sir.?' [*sic*: *PN Review*]
>   'What's what?'
>   'This here, sir.'
>   'That?
> Oh, that's what I'm across here for. You see
> The address? It's the university.'
> 'All the same, it's a bit sarcastic, sir.'
> 'It's what we call in Ireland an English joke.'
> And all jokes stopped. Anti-terrorism,
> Special powers and acts, arrests, detentions –
> At least our story held when they phoned out.
> We sobered up and a second form was brought.

4 1–3] Also the following. May, seventy-nine, *PN Review, Threepenny Review* [NB this is the opening of section 5 in this version]
4 6 Exhilaration] Exultation *PN Review, Threepenny Review*
4 7 the nuptial hawthorn bloom,] the nuptials of the hawthorn, *PN Review, Threepenny Review*
4 8 The trip north] The familiar *PN Review, Threepenny Review*
4 9 This line is not broken in *PN Review* or *Threepenny Review*.
4 11 some] your *PN Review, Threepenny Review*   guard –] guard *PN Review, Threepenny Review*
4 12]   A presence out of my recurring dream,
   More grimfaced than his phantom self who'd smiled
   And dallied at the mountain crossroads, leaning
   An elbow on the car roof to explain *PN Review, Threepenny Review*
4 17 a van] the van *PN Review*
4 20] I were going to bring forms to the office *PN Review, Threepenny Review*
4 21 ten yards more down] on ten yards farther *PN Review, Threepenny Review*
4 27 So he enters and] Naturally *PN Review, Threepenny Review*
4 28–9 on. / 'When, for] on. 'When, / For *PN Review, Threepenny Review*
4 30 something,] something,' *PN Review, Threepenny Review*
4 31–5] (This is one line I remember clearly) / 'It'll be for me, not you or anybody / About to tell me what I should be writing.' / Those were the months of jail walls smeared with shite, / The red eyes then were eyes on dirty protest *PN Review, Threepenny Review*
5 1–8] These lines do not appear in *PN Review* or *Threepenny Review*. Instead this section (headed '6') follows; square brackets indicate a variant in the latter publication:

Your 'Ireland of the Bombers'. Your yes and no
And praises and dispraises and poems to me.
Your Royal Navy days. Your TCD.
England your England. Low Church. High ground. Heigh-ho. [Heigho!]
We're in holding pattern; a near miss over Heathrow.

5 8 light years] light-years *New Yorker*
6 1–12] These lines do not appear in *PN Review* or *Threepenny Review*; instead the following seventh and eighth sections of the poem follow. The section headed '8' is clearly an early version of the published section 6.

7.
Milosz launches his home-made boats of bark
Into inviolable rivers. 'I feel,'
He always says, 'just like a boy,'
But he writes like a papal Merlin.
Not civic. Grievous. And unfoolable
And giving. When he names the haywagons
And orchards and processions on feastdays,
I'm on a bridge of air that spans the deep
Clear flooded valley of the heart; beyond
Infliction, as if it were Glenshane Pass,
My head light from the outlook and dissolve
Of memory into what's in front of me,
As if a foreseen and a suffered love
Passed through each other like the north and south

>   In a tremor of the compass.
>   The great ones
>   Prevent us always. And sometimes literally,
>   As Czeslaw did at the shrine of Rocamadour.
>   Pilgrim, poet, praiser of what is,
>   He wrote about the small miraculous virgin
>   In distance and homecoming and known loss
>   And robbed me of the chance (till now) of printing
>   Lines I jotted down extempore
>   In nineteen eighty-one, on the same old path.
>   Lines out of the blue that we leave alone.
>
>   8.
>   All hail, St Amadour of Rocamadour!
>   Rock-lover, enduring loner, sky-sentry.
>
>   My bones feel like articulated air,
>   Remembering the lime green butterfly
>   Going softly past on the Way of the Cross:
>   It was all zig-zags up a scraggy hillside
>   To this last station, *Jesus Laid in His Tomb*,
>   In an open cave. Crows sailing high and close.
>   On the gravel at my feet, a lizard
>   With shoulders pulsing, its front legs set
>   Like the struts of a moon vehicle.
>   Eleven in the morning. The climb done.
>   The coach parties below still out of earshot.

SH says to O'Driscoll: 'this poem has always been problematical for me': a difficulty largely due to the application of the ambivalence of *SL* to the positives and negatives of travel. The difficulty is evident from the various versions here; the *SL* version is in six sections of different lengths. The first one describes the poet's father making a paper boat; the second describes watching from Wicklow a late jet flying out of Dublin Airport (a subject returned to poignantly in the late unpublished poem 'Those Winter Evenings', *PSH*, 1192). The third section is about 're-entry' after travelling – to America or with exhilaration back to Glanmore. The orientation of the journeys is a central theme: 'At bay, at one, at work, at risk' from the section that ends with Horace's reminder that '*Skies change, not cares, for those who cross the seas*' (*Epistles*, 1.2.27).

   2 2 'Watching the full-starred heavens that winter sees' in Thomas Hardy, 'Afterwards' (Hardy 1976, 553).

   3 8 *Reculer pour sauter*: to draw back in order to jump (as for the long jump in athletics) makes sense; but the usual phrase is *Reculer pour mieux sauter*: to draw back in order to jump better. This is probably a typo; but the adapted phrase might mean that the return to the USA was a necessary withdrawal to enable return to Glanmore at all in the complex allusiveness of the poem's travels.

4 Section 4 is the most discussed part of the poem and perhaps the core of what made the poem problematical, describing encounters with republicans, actual or dreaming. Having flown back from New York (with red eyes after a sleepless night), the poet is exhilarated at his re-entry to Ireland and on the way to Belfast when someone he'd 'last met in a dream' sits across from him on the train and asks him 'head on' when he is 'going to write something for us' (the republican movement: SH later identified the figure as Danny Morrison, who was director of publicity for Sinn Féin – *SS*, 257). This was in 1979, the period of the dirty protest by republican prisoners, so the section ends after the poet's refusal to write for the cause with a painful imagining of what life for the protesting prisoners was like. Here the red eyes belong to Kieran Nugent (1958–2000, not usually known as Ciaran), the first IRA 'blanket man' in the Maze Prison (one of the group who refused to wear prison uniform and were draped only in a blanket), not now to the transatlantic traveller, the poet walking 'behind the righteous Virgil' and translating Dante, 'free as houses'. The section ends with lines from SH's 'Ugolino', translated from *Inferno*, 33 (as at the end of *Field Work*; *FW*, 60–3; *PSH*, 246).

5 Section 5 is a brief threatening encounter with a policeman who mishears the poet's description of his address 'far away' as the name of some unfamiliar place 'up the country' – which the hostile questioner is made suspicious by. 'Far Away' was a working title for this section in a TS, which has its origins in a MS dated *c*.19 June 1992.

6 The final section recalls another remote journey to the 'hermit's eyrie' above Rocamadour, a clifftop village in the Dordogne, dominated by its medieval religious buildings, one of the most visited places of pilgrimage in France. The exaltation here is at the spiritual climb upwards, recalling the dove of peace and security in the breast of the opening section of the child's trust in his father.

An Invocation

First published in the *LRB* (6 Aug. 1992): 16; and the *Harvard Review* (Fall 1992): 25–6. In September 1992 it was published as a broadside by the Turret Book Shop, London. It also appeared as 'An Invocation: In Memoriam Hugh MacDiarmid' in *Hermathena* (1992): 113–14; and in *KG*: 46–7. These printings employed numbered section heads replaced in *SL* by asterisks.

6 winds that flout] wind that flouts *LRB, Harvard Review, Hermathena*
6 rock face] rockface *LRB, Harvard Review*
7 sea breeze] seabreeze *Harvard Review*
8 Of the open] Of open *LRB, Hermathena*
10–11 MacGonagallish propensities – / For I do not – but] McGonaglish propensities, / For I do not, but *LRB, Harvard Review, Hermathena*
12 blathering] blethering *LRB, Harvard Review, Hermathena*
13 especially.] especially – *LRB, Harvard Review, Hermathena*
15 writing-mad] writing mad *LRB, Harvard Review, Hermathena*
20 heady bearings] cognizance *LRB, Harvard Review, Hermathena*
22–3] Hardliner on the rockface of the old / Questions and answers, to which I also add: *LRB, Harvard Review, Hermathena*
29 factored in] entering *LRB, Harvard Review, Hermathena*
31–2 A function of its time and place / And sometimes of our own.] Tuned in, of its time and place – and ours / If we're lucky. *LRB, Hermathena*] A variable, of its time and place, / Sometimes of our own. *Harvard Review*
33 outlandish,] outlandish. *LRB, Harvard Review, Hermathena*

Dated 3 January 1992 in MS, entitled 'MacDiarmid upon Scotland'.

Hugh MacDiarmid, the pen name of Christopher Murray Grieve (1892–1978), the leading Scottish modernist poet in Scots and English and the dominant figure in the Scottish Literary Renaissance, was born in Langholm, Dumfries. He taught briefly in Edinburgh and was a journalist in Wales before joining the Royal Army Medical Corps at the outbreak of World War I. He stood for Parliament for both the Scottish National Party (1945, 1950) and the Communist Party (1964). He moved in 1933 to the Shetland Island Whalsay and lived at the end of his life in Biggar near Edinburgh where SH visited him in 1977. SH gave the first Hugh MacDiarmid Lecture in 2002 in Langholm where MacDiarmid is buried.

'An Invocation' is another triptych of twelve-liners.

2 *stone-gazing*: one of MacDiarmid's major poems is 'Stony Limits' in 1934, written after he moved to Shetland. Cf. *l.* 15.

3 *thrawn*: Scottish term meaning perverse, from Northern Middle English 'thrawen', to twist.

4 *the chimney corner*: where MacDiarmid sat in his house in Biggar.

10 *MacGonagallish*: William MacGonagall (1825–1902), Scottish poet born and died in Edinburgh, but who spent most of his life in Dundee. Famous for the banal tragedy of his subjects and the crudeness of his poetic forms among which only rhyme was sustained without regard to stress or line length. At this stage SH does not withdraw his ascribing such propensities to some of MacDiarmid's verse, though later he would.

13 The shore-view house on Whalsay.

21 *the dictionary*: MacDiarmid drew on John Jamieson's *Etymological Dictionary of the Scottish Language* (1808) and other dictionaries in writing his much-loved Scots poems in a language which has been called 'synthetic Scots'.

27 MacDiarmid, 'My song today is the storm-cock's song / When the cold winds blow and the driving snow / Hides the tree-tops' ('The Storm-Cock's Song'). The storm cock is the mistle thrush.

Mycenae Lookout

Full sequence first published in the *Harvard Review* (Spring 1996): 15–21. Later included in *OG* and *NSP2014*.

1 THE WATCHMAN'S WAR

Published under the title 'The Watchman at Mycenae' in the *Notre Dame Review* (Spring 1995): 1–2; and as 'The Watchman Remembers, from Mycenae Wavelengths', in *College Green* (Autumn 1995): n.p. [46–9].

Epigraph] The rest is silence. The ox is on my tongue.
                    Aeschylus, AGAMEMNON. *Notre Dame Review*
5 pass,] pass *Notre Dame Review, College Green*
17 I would] I'd *Notre Dame Review, College Green*
45 from the ships] from ships *Notre Dame Review*

2 CASSANDRA

Published in the *Threepenny Review* (Winter 1996): 9.

44–5 god. / And] god – / and *Threepenny Review*
45 a] the *OG, NSP2014*

3 HIS DAWN VISION

First published under the title 'Mycenae Lookout' in the *TLS* (16 Dec. 1994): 15.

20 wind-swept] windswept *OG, NSP2014*

4 THE NIGHTS

Published under the title 'Mycenae Nightwatch' in *Poetry* (Oct./Nov. 1995): 2–4, where the epigraph for the final published sequence is given.

34–5 alley, / bloodied] alley, // bloodied *Harvard Review*
57 blood-bath] bloodbath *OG, NSP2014*

5 HIS REVERIE OF WATER

Published as 'A Water Seer' in the *TLS* (7 July 1995): 8.

6 that the far] the far *TLS*
34–6] finders, keepers, seers of fresh water. *TLS*

One of SH's most controversial poems; even Helen Vendler found it shocking on first reading it. The setting is Mycenae at the end of the Siege of Troy in *Agamemnon* by Aeschylus, the first play in the *Oresteia*. Agamemnon has sailed for Troy, leaving his queen Clytemnestra behind to have a love affair with Aegisthus. The narrator is Clytemnestra's Watchman; in the first section he recalls the point when the Greek army set sail for Troy and the start of the 'killing-fest, the life-warp and world-wrong' that ensued.

Title Working title in TS 'Mycenae Wavelengths'.

Epigraph A Greek epigrammatic phrase *bous epi glottes*, 'ox on tongue', meaning unable to speak freely: the condition of the watchman in the poem. His role is to tell the queen when her husband Agamemnon is returning. SH has supported the interpretation of the violence and bitterness of the ten-year siege of Troy as a figure for the waste and destruction of the war in Northern Ireland for the past twenty-five years.

Section 2, 'Cassandra', is the most controversial part of the poem. Cassandra was a Trojan princess brought back by Agamemnon as a trophy of war. Apollo had granted her the gift of prophecy, but after she rejected him he added the curse that her prophecies would not be believed. Though this section says there is no such thing as innocent bystanding, she is decidedly a victim in this section and Agamemnon, 'King Kill-the-child', as guilty as Clytemnestra and Aegisthus.

Section 3, 'His Dawn Vision', turns to a quieter interlude in two twelve-liners. In the first of the two the war is 'stalled in the pre-articulate' and the reporter weeps for the time-wound they have lived inside. The circumstances translate readily into the conditions of Northern Ireland in the period of its civil war with 'Mouth athletes . . . quoting dates' to justify the 'grievous distance' between the warring sides. The second begins with a lyrical Dantesque image, reminiscent of the epigraph to 'The Strand at Lough Beg' from *Purgatorio*. The section ends with an image of civil war: a man jumping over a fresh earth-wall and another running 'amorously, it seemed, to strike him down'.

Section 4 is concerned with Clytemnestra and Aegisthus, whose 'real life was the bed' and the complex of loyalties and betrayals of the watchman's situation. Section 5 'His Reverie of Water' begins with the bath in which Agamemnon was killed by Clytemnestra who wrapped him in a net, like the lined well-shaft 'puddling through tawny mud'. He ends more positively by considering the purgative effects of water.

Section 5 'finders, keepers' (*l.* 34) would be used as the title of SH's last collected essays in 2002.

for Cynthia and Dmitri Hadzi: SH reads the dedication at the beginning of the poem on the 2009 RTÉ recording.

The First Words

First published in *The Biggest Egg in the World* (Newcastle: Bloodaxe, 1987), 71; then in *TC*, 21. Collected in *TSH*, 19.

4 Of blurbs] Of the blurbs *Biggest Egg in the World*
6 and the grass and the stones] and grasses and stones *Biggest Egg in the World, TC*
9] Up to fire and air and water and earth *Biggest Egg in the World*

The theme of polluted or clean water continues naturally from the preceding poem.

The Gravel Walks

First published in a limited edition, *The Gravel Walks*, by Lenoir-Rhyne College, North Carolina (14 March 1992): 8–9, on the occasion of the annual meeting of the American Conference for Irish Studies Southern Region; in William Scammell (ed.), *The Poetry Book Society Anthology 3* (London: Hutchinson, 1992), 27–8; *Thinker Review* (Summer 1992): 307–8; and the *Observer Review* (8 Oct. 1995): C16. Later included in *OG, NSP2014* and *100P*. An early version of the poem can be found in the *Threepenny Review* version of 'To a Dutch Potter in Ireland', which reads as follows:

> When sandbeds opened and mixers came to life
> And men in dungarees, like sunstruck shades,
> Loaded concrete, wheeled, turned, wheeled, as if
> The Pharaoh's brickyards burned inside their heads,
>
> I began to know the verity of gravel.
> Gems for the undeluded. Milt of earth.
> Its plain, champing song against the shovel
> Tested and sandblasted the scales of worth.
>
> Beautiful [*sic*] in or out of the river,
> The kingdom of gravel is inside us too –
> Deep down, far back, clear water running over
> Pebbles of caramel, hailstone, mackerel blue.
>
> But the actual washed stuff kept all slow and steady
> As men went stooping with their barrows full
> Into an absolution of the body,
> The shriven life tired bones and marrow feel.

> So we walk on air against our better judgement,
> Imagining a place or state between
> Those solid batches mixed with grey cement
> And a tune called 'The Gravel Walks' that conjures green.

6 Dangled and clustered] Kept hanging their cheeks *PBS Anthology 3*, *Thinker Review*
9 hurrying] hurrying, *PBS Anthology 3*, *Thinker Review*
10 that we scared when we played –] and bare-assed children bathed – *PBS Anthology 3*, *Thinker Review*
12 link-box] link box *Observer*
12 gravel bed] riverbed *PBS Anthology 3*, *Thinker Review*
13 life] life, *PBS Anthology 3*, *Thinker Review*
14 captive] sunstruck *PBS Anthology 3*, *Thinker Review*
22 too –] too *Thinker Review*
24 caramel] carmel *PBS Anthology 3*, *Thinker Review*
26 full] full – *Thinker Review*
28 tired] your *PBS Anthology 3*, *Thinker Review*
29 judgement] judgement, *PBS Anthology 3*, *Thinker Review*
30 yourself somewhere] real presence *PBS Anthology 3*, *Thinker Review*
31 Those] The *PBS Anthology 3*, *Thinker Review*

Title 'The Gravel Walks' is a popular Irish reel (*l*. 24). The first line of the last stanza was inscribed on SH's headstone in Bellaghy graveyard. Another diptych of two twelve-liners, the poem germinated from the confluent drafting of 'To a Dutch Potter in Ireland' (*PSH*, 463) and 'An Education' (*PSH*, 1184).

13–16 SH repeatedly takes gravel as a figure for work and 'honest worth'; elsewhere he says that this poem is about heavy work.

19 Clear water, in response to the polluting water of the previous two poems.

Whitby-sur-Moyola

First published in the *Honest Ulsterman*, 100 (Autumn 1995): 40. Later included in *OG* and *NSP2014*.

1–2 too I was lucky to have known, / Back] too, when the gift deserted him, / was back *Honest Ulsterman*
3 yardman] yard man *Honest Ulsterman*
13–15] unless it was a case of sniff and test] after he'd passed them through a sick beast's water. *Honest Ulsterman*

Title, 1 Cædmon was a monk of Whitby in North Yorkshire whose story is told in Latin in Bede's *History of the English Church and People* (*c*.730). The nine-line 'Cædmon's Hymn' about God's creation of the world is the earliest surviving poem in English, written in Old English alliterative verse. Bede's Latin narrative tells how Cædmon withdrew from the assembled monks when they broke into song at beer-drinking because he couldn't sing so he went out to the cattle stall. An angel appeared to him in a dream and asked him to sing about Creation. Cædmon sang his hymn and when he woke up he sang it for the town reeve and the Abbess of Whitby. SH transfers the story to the area of his local river, the Moyola, and his native farming environment where a 'yardman' (*l*. 3) would be a familiar figure.

The Thimble

Published in *SL*.

The poem's five short sections play with various manifestations of a thimble.

    1 1 *the House of Carnal Murals*: an unclear location; Helen Vendler says the formula suggests Pompeii. SH says the idea for the poem came by chance.

    2 2 *St Adaman*: presumably the saint normally called Adamnán or Adomnán (628–704), abbot of Iona who wrote a life of St Columba shortly after his lifetime.

    2 4ff. There are legends connected to bells named after Adomnán in a number of places in Scotland, including one at Glenlyon Church believed to date back to his time.

The Butter-Print

First published in Lawrence Sail (ed.), *First and Always: Poems for The Great Ormond Street Children's Hospital* (London: Faber & Faber, 1988), 30; in *The Times* (7 Oct. 1988): G20, in a series called 'Poems for Great Ormond Street' featuring contributions to Sail's book; and in *TC*, 13.

    6–7] I felt like a standing crop probed by a scythe. / I took its cut and scare far in and deep *First and Always*, *Times* | I was like a standing crop felt by a scythe. / I took its cut and scare far in and deep *TC*
    12 relic] blessed *TC*

For an admiring reading of this poem, see James Fenton, 'The Orpheus of Ulster' in the *New York Review of Books* (11 July 1996), reprinted in Fenton's Oxford lectures, *The Strength of Poetry* (Oxford, 2001). Fenton succeeded SH as Oxford Professor of Poetry.

Remembered Columns

First published in *Poetry* (Oct./Nov. 1995): 2.

5 An early Marian legend says the house of Mary was transported from Palestine to Loreto on the Adriatic coast where it became a place of pilgrimage. The event fits the balance of weight and lightness which is the central theme of *SL*. An order of nuns named Loreto was founded by the Englishwoman Mary Ward in France in 1609; transplanted to Ireland in 1821, it became influential in girls' education.

'Poet's Chair'

First published under the title 'Shifting Angles' in the exhibition catalogue for Carolyn Mulholland and Breon O'Casey, Narrow Water Gallery, Warrenpoint, Co. Down (24 Sept.–21 Oct. 1992): 3; then under the title 'Here for Good' in the *TLS* (22 Jan. 1993): 10. Published as 'Poet's Chair' in *Agni*, 38 (1993): 1–2; also in *KG*: 38–9, and published as a separate limited-edition broadside by William B. Ewert/Bow and Arrow Press on 15 May 1993 to mark the twenty years' service of Robert and Jana Kiely, Master and Associate Master of Adams House at Harvard. An early version of the poem, from a paper SH delivered in 1993, was included in Patrick Primeaux (ed.), *Humanizing the City: Politics, Religion, the Arts in Critical Conversation* (San Francisco: Catholic Scholars Press, 1997): 104–5. Collected in *OG* and *NSP*2014.

The *TLS* version is significantly different and transcribed below. Section 1, and aspects of section 2, of the final published poem appear as sections 4 and 5 in this version.

    1
Romulus and Remus and the wolf, all
Pointy canty teats, the twins suck-mad –
In the beginning, the perennial bronze
Was cast and carnal equally. *Uber*
(Third declension, neuter, *breast* or *bosom*)
Rang true and short-pitched as knuckles hitting at
A burnished flank, that test by clang and contour
Itself the echo of an echo:
                   a cub
With a stick once hammered a tar barrel.

    2
He also once stood open-mouthed beneath
The horse's belly, when it was being clipped:
Cub's eye view of vein systems and cock.
Trojan's eye view, come to that. Chinese
Emperor's ceramicist's eye view.
                   The fizz
Of the driven clippers kept going on
And on, I could see through to the railway
(The horse stood on a flat earth, in clear air),
Could see green grass in sunlight on Slieve Gallon.

Hoofier than their own idea in
Eternity, the four hoofs stood their ground
Imitating nothing but themselves.
Only the fawnish shorn skin, all angry
Little bites and scrab-marks, lived as body.

In equestrian statuary, bronze
Or marble, in the lustrous belly-sweep –
Like gazing up from under at the globe's
Taut ocean-sheen, starlit from inside – in that
Close encounter with mass and girth triumphant,
Sculpture begins its gravitational
Withdrawal. *Noli me tangere* says
The absolutely tangible. *Ergo*,
Hoof, black-rimmed and minatory. Stirrup,
Mailed. Spur, cruel but not extraneous.
All rearing to go.
              (But here for good as well.)

3
Leonardo said: the sun has never
Seen a shadow. Now watch the sculptor move
Full circle round a figure, ptolemaic
In the sphere of shifting angles and no give.

4
Angling shadows of itself are what
Your 'Chair in Leaf' stands to and rises out of.
Nothing hoofy there. Its four legs land
On their feet, catsfoot, goatfoot, maybe splay-foot too;
Its straight back sprouts two bronze and twiggy saplings.
Every flibbertigibbet in the town,
Old birds and boozers, late night pissers, kissers,
All have a go at sitting in it some time.
It's the way the air behind them's winged and full,
The way a graft has seized their shoulder-blades,
That makes them happy. Once out of nature,
They're going to come back in leaf and bloom
And angel step. Or something like that. *Leaves*
On a bloody chair? Would you believe it?

5
Athenian space, let's call it, less known
Than foreknown, most real when most imagined.
I see your lanky chair in a white prison
With Socrates sitting on it, bald as a coot,
Clearing his friends' minds, warming their hearts,
Tormenting them in sunlight with the truth.
His time is short. The day his trial began
A garlanded ship sailed to Apollo's shrine
In Delos, for the annual rite
Of commemoration. Until its wreathed
And creepered rigging re-enters Athens'
Harbour, the city's life is holy.

No executions. No hemlock bowl. No tears
As the poison works its way up from the feet
And the expert jailer talks everybody through
The stages of the numbness. Socrates
At the centre of the city and the day
Has proved the soul immortal. The bronze leaves
Cannot believe their ears, it is so silent.
It is for all the world like the moment when
The master's face will be uncovered and
Crito will have to close the eyes and mouth.

[0] 3–4 her next work, like a lover / In the sphere of shifting angles and fixed love.] a figure, ptolemaic / In the sphere of shifting angles and no give – / As if a wall of air stood there to prove / The ne plus ultra of a whole technique. *Agni*
1 3 sun-stalked inner-city] sun-stalked, inner city *Agni*
1 4 On the *qui vive* all the time, its] Plenty of give there. Its *Agni*
1 5] On their feet, catsfoot, goatfoot, maybe splay-foot too; *Agni*   catsfoot, goatfoot,] cat's-foot, goat-foot, *OG, NSP2014*
1 5 leafy] twiggy *Agni*
1 9 on] in *Agni*
1 11 shoulder-blades] shoulder-blades, *Agni*
2 3 bright] broad *Agni*
2 4 began] began, *Agni*
2 5 boat sailed from] boat had sailed to *Agni*   from] for *OG, NSP2014*
2 8 re-enters Athens] re-entered Athens' *Agni*
2 9 is] was *Agni*
2 17 mouth,] mouth *Agni*

This poem and 'M.' (*SL*, 57; *PSH*, 495) share common ancestry in a TS poem 'Clang and Contour', whose first two sections formed the basis of those in the *TLS* printing of 'Poet's Chair', and whose third section was first published as 'In Touch' (*Listener*, 1979) before adoption in 'M.' A fourth part of 'Clang and Contour', not reused in any other poem, read:

> In the tin horse's belly's where I learnt it,
> Inside the tar barrel, tumbled for a dare
> For fifty yards or more down Connor's Brae,
> Rattling and banging over the cobblestones.   (Private collection)

Title The poem's title invariably appears in quotation marks.
Dedication Carolyn Mulholland (b.1944), is a sculptor born in Lurgan, Co. Armagh, and a friend of the Heaneys when she was an art student in Belfast. She made a bust of SH in 1967–8 which remained in the Heaney house in Strand Road. Her 'Poet's Chair' was a public commission in 1988 to mark the Dublin Millennium. It was positioned in a courtyard at the end of George's Street, Dublin, from which it was removed because its bronze leaves were too easy to steal (*SS*, 356).

Preliminary stanza: SH says that an entry in Leonardo's Notebooks was part of the inspiration for the poem (*SS*, 356).

2 15 The bronze leaves seem to be the connection with Socrates because Mulholland's Chair is in bronze.

2 17 Crito in the late Platonic dialogue named for him is Socrates' wealthy friend who comes to Socrates' prison to tell him of his impending death. Crito tries to persuade Socrates to escape but he refuses on the grounds that his death is the choice of the Athenians.

3 3-4 The thorn tree they never cut out of regard for tradition.

3 9 The good in every sense is derived from Socrates' clinching argument with Crito: only the good life is worth living.

The Swing

First published in the *Southern Review* (July 1995): 676–8. Later included in *OG* and *NSP2014*.

5 learned] learnt *Southern Review*
7 jackknifing] jack-knifing *OG*, *NSP2014*
12 nativity] Nativity *OG*, *NSP2014*
22-3 an opulent / steaming arc] opulent steaming arcs *Southern Review*
41 backed on into it] backed into it *Southern Review*
45] One by one we learned to go sky-high. *Southern Review*

Working title in TS 'Sweet Chariot'.

1ff. Learning the balance of weight and momentum on the swing is again a central theme in *SL*.

8 Jean-Honoré Fragonard's *The Swing* (1767) in the Wallace Collection in London is a major Rococo oil painting, controversial for its flouncing titillation with the shoe of the young woman on the swing flying off as she is watched by a pensive putto and an elegant young man who looks on lasciviously.

8 Pieter Breughel the Elder, here as the painter of *Children's Games* (1560).

9 Hans Memling (1430–94), a more solemn religious painter, nearer to the grounded setting of the Heaneys' rural swing.

18 'She' is SH's mother whose ablutions are described with careful attention, as her family role was described in 'The First Kingdom' where 'the royal roads were cow paths' (*SI*, 101). Here she sits on the swing, 'half-retrieving' a childhood activity.

The Poplar

First published in the *Sunday Times* Books supplement (8 Oct. 1995): 9.

4 come to grief?] run aground? *Sunday Times*

1 Quicksilver is mercury, the agent of change, as the evanescent wind changes the whole big tree.

3–4 The swing of the compass from the bright scale to grief – again, the theme of the book.

Two Stick Drawings

First published in *Parnassus*, 20. 1–2 (1995): 281–2. Later included in OG and *NSP2014*.

1 1, 5 Claire] Clare *Parnassus*
1 8 tore] roared *Parnassus*
2 1–3] Another one. The ledge behind the back seat
  Of my father's car was a kind of stick museum,
  All blackthorns and ashplants and drovers' canes.
  It looked like a sales display, my mother said, *Parnassus*

1 4 Persephone was detained in the underworld for six months of each year because she ate six pomegranate seeds while she was held there.

1 9 The engine stoker is a balked king, like Persephone's captor Dis in the underworld.

2 5 The boy Jim is familiar as the 'Crowing Man' (*PSH*, 100) and 'Their Brother' (*PSH*, 99).

A Call

First published in the *Spectator* (23 September 1995): 39; and then in *Parnassus*, 20. 1–2 (1995): 283. Also included in the *Programme for 25*, a poetry reading presented by the Gallery Press, to celebrate its twenty-fifth anniversary, in association with the National Theatre Society at the Abbey Theatre (2 July 1995): 16. Later included in OG, *NSP2014* and *100P*.

9 also . . .] also – *Parnassus*

Title A call is the general term for a telephone call.
1 'she' is Anne Friel, and 'him' is Brian Friel (reported verbally by SH).
12 Hall clocks (plural), like the two clocks in 'Sunlight' (*North*, 9).
16 In the medieval play *Everyman*, Death summoned Everyman in person; nowadays he would do it by phone.

The Errand

First published in the *Atlanta Review*, 2. 2 (1996): 25. Later included in *OG* and *NSP2014*.

A Dog Was Crying Tonight in Wicklow Also

First published in the *Independent on Sunday* (16 Aug. 1992): 22; and then, accompanied by a photograph by Rachel Brown, as a broadside and poster by White Fields Press, Louisville, Kentucky (1994); and in *Poetry* (Oct./Nov. 1995): 1–2. Later included in *OG*, *NSP2014* and *100P*. In the *Independent on Sunday* it is accompanied by a short biographical note which concludes: 'This new poem is based on an Igbo story and is dedicated to the memory of the Nigerian scholar and critic Donatus Nwoga, who was a student with Heaney at Queen's University, Belfast, in the 1950s.'

9–11 [omitted] *Independent*
17 is] was *Independent*
24–6] To where there were no roosts or nests or trees / And his mind reddened and darkened all at once *Independent*
29 In obliterated light] Obliterating light *Independent*

Dedication Donatus Nwoga (1933–91) was a professor of African literature at the University of Nigeria, Nsukka, with a focus on traditional Igbo poetry; he was a fellow student of SH at Queen's University Belfast.
    2 *Chukwu*: etymologically 'great god', the supreme deity in Igbo cosmology, responsible for all things on the earth and beyond it.

M.

First published in part under the title 'In Touch' in the *Listener* (20 and 27 Dec. 1979): 871. Published in a revised form as 'The Articulation of Siberia' in *Soho Square Four* (London: Bloomsbury, 1991), 103.

1 spread his hand] laid his hands *Listener*
2 Over the dome of a speaker's] On the warm bowl of another's *Listener*
4 to the sound.] under his hands. *Listener*
5–8] Think of his fingertips stored with dark and clear sound. / Then think too of your script written into mine / And all that went to making a fair hand / Of your cursives and your firm runes. *Listener*

Title 'M.' is Osip Mandelstam (1891–1938), Polish-born Russian poet from a wealthy Jewish family who moved to St Petersburg soon after his birth. He was a leading member of the Acmeists. He was arrested in the 1930s and sent into internal exile along with his wife Nadezhda. They moved to Voronezh, where Mandelstam was arrested again in 1938; he died in a transit camp near Vladivostok on the way to a labour camp in the Soviet Far East. Greatly admired by SH as poet and critic, especially for his 'Conversation about Dante'.

The forerunner to this poem, the 1979 'In Touch', bore no reference to the 'M.' of the later piece, Mandelstam, whose emergence as a subject for the piece can be traced to SH's work towards *HL*, 1985–6, and a typescript called 'Soundings', which reused the first stanza of the published poem but replaced the second. The new poem was temporarily subsumed as part III of a typescript 'Clang and Contour', before regaining independent status as 'The Articulation of Siberia', in which the deaf phonetician can hear inaudible sounds through the skull by touch. The idea is that the silencing of censorship can be overcome. The title 'M.' is first adopted in *SL*.

An Architect

First published in Anne Stevenson (ed.), *The Poetry Book Society Anthology* 2 (London: Hutchinson, 1991), 67.

Dated 3 March 1991 in TS (NLI 49,493/103).

Title The architect is Robin Walker (1924–91) who, along with his wife, Dorothy Walker (1929–2002), hosted the Heaneys in the elaborate house-complex called Bóthar Buí, which he designed, near Ardgroom in West Cork. See 'A Tie' (1997) (*PSH*, 506).

1 *fasted on the doorstep*: like the poet Seanchan in Yeats's *The King's Threshold* (1903), who after his banishment from the court starves himself on the doorstep of King Guaire's palace in protest against the failure to recognise the value of art.

The Sharping Stone

First published in the *New Yorker* (23 Oct. 1995): 62–3. An extract [*ll.* 41–56] was also included in *Midsummer Feast*: 15, with the dedication '*In memoriam* T.F.D.'

8 something] something, *New Yorker*
17 fence-posts] fence posts *New Yorker*
20 thing] thing, *New Yorker*
25 out,] out *New Yorker*
40 That we'd] We'd *New Yorker*
40 once, then] once and *New Yorker*
44 granddad] Granddad *New Yorker*

5 *Our gift to him*: to Marie Heaney's father.

25 *the Sea of Moyle*: the sea to the north-east of Northern Ireland, between Ireland and Scotland.

26 *Sarcophage des époux*: a sixth-century BCE terracotta Etruscan funerary monument in the Louvre. It depicts a man and a woman lying on a dining couch. The Heaneys had sent a postcard of it to Marie's father, which now they find among his possessions (*l*. 40).

52 '*He commenced his wild career*': from the ballad 'Brennan on the Moor.'

The Strand

First published in the *Sunday Times* Books supplement (8 Oct. 1995): 8; and as a card, with a watercolour by Felim Egan, by Gallery in November 1995, without the title. Later included in Irene de Angelis and Joseph Woods (eds), *Our Shared Japan: An Anthology of Contemporary Irish Poetry* (Dublin: Dedalus, 2007), 74, and Pat Boran and Gerard Smyth (eds), *If Ever You Go: A Map of Dublin in Poetry and Song* (Dublin: Dedalus, 2014), 299. Also included in OG and NSP2014.

The Walk

First published in *Agenda* (Autumn/Winter 1996): 5; and included in OG and *NSP2014*.

14^15 [section break]] [stanza break] *Agenda*

Dated 2 January 1995 in TS (NLI 49,493/108).

This double sonnet anticipates some of the early poems in HC, the first about the poet as child on a day out with his parents. The second is the 'erotic woodsmoke' of the relations of the poet and his wife.

At the Wellhead

First published in the *New Yorker* (28 March 1994): 74; and in *Transverse II*: 135. Later included in OG, *NSP2014* and *100P*.

Another double sonnet, under the working title 'Country Roads' in TS.

1 'you' is Marie Heaney, singing with her eyes closed, compared to Rosie Keenan (*l*. 10), the blind piano teacher who lived next door to SH's grandparents in Castledawson.

19 SH also uses braille as a case of 'gleaning the unsaid off the palpable' in 'The Harvest Bow', (FW, 55; PSH, 244).

At Banagher

First published in the *New Welsh Review* (Summer 1992): 11; and in *Verso*; *Oxford Poetry* (Hiver 1992): 47–51; *KG*: 50; *Transverse II*: 133; and *Fortnight* (Nov. 1995): 26–7. Also included in *OG*, *NSP2014* and *100P*.

2] My greatgrandfather, the journeyman tailor, *New Welsh Review*] antecedent:] antecedent. *Fortnight*
4 or] and *New Welsh Review*
6 always, giving none,] like Odysseus *New Welsh Review*
7] Eyelids steady as wrinkled horn or iron, *New Welsh Review*
8 ensconced;] ensconced, *New Welsh Review*
10 again –] again. *New Welsh Review*
13 So more power to him] And I love him, *New Welsh Review*] And I love him *Fortnight*
16 the] up *New Welsh Review*
23 Buddha] Bhudda *New Welsh Review*

Dated 3 January 1992 in MS (NLI 49,493/106); working title in TS 'An Apparition'.

After the group of sonnets, a return to the twelve-liners, as earlier in the book.

2 *my antecedent*: a travelling artist, like the poet.

23 *Buddha*: by his posture 'up on a table, cross-legged' (l. 3).

Tollund

Printed privately for the family as a card by Gallery (September 1994); then in the *New Yorker* (3 Oct. 1994): 92. Also included in *OG* and *NSP2014*.

7 farmyard; dormant] farmyard. Dormant *New Yorker*
9–16 [omitted] *New Yorker*
18–20] The byeroads had their names on them, the map / Of the country and the country added up. / We were truant and at home outside the tribe, *New Yorker*
21 More scouts than strangers,] Like scouts in old haunts, *New Yorker*

1–2 *travelled far*: to Tollund Moss. This is the first visit to 'the actual bog in Tollund' (*SS*, 350), twenty-one years after SH went to Jutland and saw the Tollund Man. On Wednesday 31 August 1994, the IRA declared a ceasefire, so the Sunday in the poem must have been 4 September, since he says it was in the days immediately after the ceasefire.

10 '*Townland of Peace*': poem by John Hewitt (1907–87), beginning 'Once walking in the county of my kindred'.

15 *futhark*: any of several runic Germanic alphabets, including the one used for writing early Old English; the name is derived from its first six letters.

17 *Mulhollandstown or Scribe*: as Eugene Kielt has confirmed in private correspondence with the editors, Mulhollandstown is a small area in the townland of Ballymacombs Beg; the Heaney family farm The Wood is about a mile to the south-east. Scribe, or the Scribe, is another small area in the locality, immediately west of Mulhollandstown and north of Tamlaghtduff, just inside the boundary of the townland of Ballymacpeake Upper.

20 *at home beyond the tribe*: by contrast with the end of 'Tollund Man': 'lost, unhappy and at home' (WO, 36).

24 *ourselves again*: suggestion of *sinn féin*: ourselves.

Postscript

First published in the *Irish Times* Weekend Books supplement (10 Oct. 1992): 9; and in the Admission Catalogue for Burren College of Art (1993): 15; *Tandem* (Summer 1995): 2; and later as a limited-edition broadside by Anna Livia Books, to mark a reading by SH at 'A Night of Irish Poetry', Fox Theatre, Redwood, California (9 Oct. 2002). Also included in OG, NSP2014 and 100P.

1 And some time] Some time *Irish Times*
2 Into County Clare,] Into Clare, *Irish Times*
8–9 lit / By the earthed lightning] hit / By the bolt lightning *Irish Times*
12–13] Useless to park and think you'll capture it /More thoroughly or indelibly. You are / At one with what is here and there and gone, *Irish Times*
16 catch the heart off guard] find the heart unlatched *Tandem*

2 *the Flaggy Shore*: the North Clare shoreline on the south of Galway Bay, visited by the Heaneys with Brian and Anne Friel, and perhaps on other occasions too. Later, SH wondered if that wouldn't have made for the better book title. 'It's windier and stranger – nobody quite liked it, but I always felt it had a contrary rightness about it. A lesson there – go with your own contrariness' (*LSH*, 615).

UNCOLLECTED POEMS (1996–2001)

Like the uncollected poems between *Seeing Things* and *The Spirit Level*, the even more considerable number of uncollected poems between the latter and *Electric Light* (some forty-six poems) is explained for the most part by the great number of translations, from Irish, Romanian and Russian, as well as a short section of Dante's *Paradiso* 33 at the start of 'A Dream of Solstice' and, most particularly, from the remarkable rendering of *Beowulf* that was published in London in October 1999 by Faber & Faber, and New York by Farrar, Straus and Giroux on 15 February 2000. The title would become a bestseller in the UK – selling 93,000 hardbacks in its first nine months, while subsequent paperback editions would surpass 100,000 copies in its author's lifetime (FF L7); it would be awarded the Whitbread Book of the Year 1999, as *The Spirit Level* was before it.* There are variations from the full and final text of *Beowulf* in all the extracts, which are therefore self-contained episodes rather than extracts proper, including many of the tale's most celebrated passages under new titles: 'Paths to Power' (a translation of *ll.* 1–25); 'Grendel Attacks Hrothgar's Hall' (*ll.* 86–163); 'A Sea Crossing' (*ll.* 193–228); 'The Haunted Mere' (*ll.* 1310–79); 'The Last Survivor' (*ll.* 2241–70); 'Beowulf Fights With the Dragon' (*ll.* 2542–91); 'Funeral of Beowulf' (*ll.* 3137–82). In keeping with our general practice, we have included extracts from *Beowulf* and other translations only when they were included in the twelve volumes; for a full text and editorial notes see *TSH*, 285–366; 582–90. In *Electric Light* there are translations of other memorable episodes: 'The Fragment' (*ll.* 569ff.; *EL*, 57; *PSH*, 560) and 'The Father's Lament' in 'On His Work in the English Tongue' (*ll.* 2444–65; *EL*, 62–3; *PSH*, 562). There are also a number of tribute poems in this group between *Beowulf* and *Electric Light*: to Harvard, W. H. Auden, Liam O'Flynn, Derek Walcott and his partner Sigrid Nama, and Paul Muldoon and Jean Hanff Korelitz, and an elegy for the Heaneys' friend Darcy O'Brien. The proportion of traditional lyric poems is relatively small, in both verse and prose.

The period also marks the first publication in which SH had the time to respond to the award of the Nobel Prize in Literature. *Opened Ground: Poems 1966–1996* was a generous selection of SH's poetry to date, some 496 pages in binding, that concluded with the Nobel

---

* The Whitbread (and later Costa) Book Awards ran from 1971 to 2021; in that time, it conferred thirty-seven overall Books of the Year, of which eight were poetry titles; of these, only SH (1996, 1999) and Ted Hughes (1997, 1998) were awarded it twice.

Lecture he delivered in Stockholm on 7 December 1995, 'Crediting Poetry' (also published separately by the Gallery Press). It was published in simultaneous hardback and paperback in London by Faber & Faber in October 1998, and in New York by Farrar, Straus and Giroux in hardback on 9 November 1998 and in paperback on 25 October 1999. By the summer of 2000, the Faber edition had tallied 5,400 hardback and 24,000 paperback sales in little more than its first eighteen months in print (FF L7).

A Grace Note for Michael

First published in *Michael J. Durkan* (Swarthmore, PA: Swarthmore College, 1996), 2, in a letterpress printing of 550 copies for a celebration of the life of Michael J. Durkan, held at Swarthmore College, 15 November 1996, and subsequently in Rand Brandes and Michael J. Durkan, *Seamus Heaney: A Bibliography 1959–2003* (London: Faber & Faber, 2008): ix.

A draft TS for this poem is entitled 'Slow Air' (NLI 49,493/115).

Michael J. Durkan (1930–96) was Head Librarian at Swarthmore College, Pennsylvania, and co-author of *Sean O'Casey: A Bibliography*, and, with Rand Brandes, *Seamus Heaney: A Bibliography 1959–2003*. The poem 'Raftery's Killeadan', a translation of Antoine Ó Raifteirí, is also dedicated to his memory (*TSH*, 57–8).

The Road to Derry

First published in the *Derry Journal* (31 Jan. 1997): 3, and then in the *Guardian* (1 Feb. 1997): 2.

[text: *Derry Journal*]

The ballad form here follows the measure of a popular nationalist song 'The Boys of Mullaghbawn'.

Title The event that the poem recalls is Bloody Sunday, a massacre on 30 January 1972 when British soldiers of the Parachute Regiment, the 'Paras', shot twenty-six unarmed civilians during a protest march in the Bogside area of Derry. Thirteen men were killed and another died later of gunshot wounds from the incident. Luke Kelly, lead singer with the Dubliners, had asked SH to write something commemorating Bloody Sunday for him to perform. In conversation with O'Driscoll SH recalled that 'it didn't seem to work for Luke, he didn't sing it, and the moment passed', and he explained why he refrained from including the poem in any of his collections afterwards: 'It belonged to the moment that produced it. It was what Wordsworth called 'a timely utterance' that gave relief. Like any song, it was made for the communal voice. If it had been sung by Luke Kelly, it would have functioned immediately and rightly as an expression of shared grief and outrage. If, on the other hand, I had reprinted it later in a book, I'd have felt I was currying favour with a certain constituency, writing propaganda and basically letting myself down' (*SS*, 213, 214).

9 *The gap of danger*: *bearna baoil* in Irish, a phrase from the Irish national anthem.

11 *acorn*: Derry (Doire in Irish) means oak tree.

Three-Piece

Published in *Poetry*, 171: 1 (Oct./Nov. 1997): 30–2. 'A Suit' is subsequently the first of 'Three Glosses', *London Magazine*, 41. 1–2 (April/May 2001): 33, collected with revisions as the fourth of 'Ten Glosses' in *EL*.

[text: *Poetry*]

1 A SUIT

9 'And told myself', will be revised to 'There and then' in 'Three Glosses' (*London Magazine*) and 'Ten Glosses' (*EL*, 54–5; *PSH*, 558).

2 A TIE

1 'She' is Dorothy Walker, the prominent Irish art critic. SH stayed with her family in their house Bóthar Buí (see *PSH*, 1032) near Ardgroom in West Cork, and she made a tie for him. Her husband, Robin, who died in 1991, was the subject of 'An Architect' (*SL*, 58, *PSH*, 496).

11–12 *cynghanedd*, Welsh poetic form, drawn on by Hopkins.

24–6 *gratias ago*: 'I give thanks', a Latin formula increasingly used by SH from this point onwards.

35–8 *nihil tegit quod non ornat*: 'she touches nothing that she does not adorn'. A frequently applied Latin compliment, not attributable to any particular source.

3 A COAT

4 *more of a Pict than a Celt*: Celt is a very uncertain, all-embracing term. But the distinction made here is that the Picts (a term meaning 'painted people' assigned by the Romans) describes the people of the more easterly parts of Ulster, east of the Bann, while the Gaels (called

Celts here) occupied the area west of the Bann. Magherafelt in SH's native area is on a dividing line. But the crucial point is that both Mr Simpson and SH's father were Ulstermen.

13 An ulster in the *OED* is 'a long loose overcoat of frieze or other rough cloth' made since the Victorian period.

21–2 SH makes the coat a symbol of pre-violent but traditional Ulster values.

Carlo

First published in the *Princeton Library Chronicle* 59. 3 (Spring 1998): 441–3, then in *Thumbscrew*, 11 (Autumn 1998): 2–4, and the *Times* Metro section (27 March – 2 April 1999): 17.

[text: *Princeton Library Chronicle*]

dedication] [no dedication] *Times*
7 aggressive, / not] aggressive. / not *Times*
8 off'] off!' *Times*
48 enough.] enough *Times*
51 reminds] remind *Times*

Title Carlo was the Heaneys' much-loved dog (named, according to Patrick Crotty on SH's authority, after the Irish county Carlow, though spelt without the w).

Dedication Christopher Reid (b.1949) was SH's editor at Faber and friend; he is the editor of *LSH*.

29 Cape Canaveral in Florida, the launch point for space satellites and unmanned space vehicles.

Two Paintings by Le Douanier Rousseau

First published in *Graph*, 3. 2 (Autumn/Winter 1998): xv, and then in the *Irish Times* Weekend supplement (12 Dec. 1998): 11, where it is accompanied by the note: '*This poem appears in a special memorial supplement for Lar Cassidy in the current issue of the cultural review,* Graph'.

[text: *Graph*]

Title SH tells Dennis O'Driscoll that Le Douanier Rousseau was one of the painters he would like to have been (*SS*, 335). Henri Rousseau (1844–1910), French Primitivist painter. His popular name, Le Douanier ('the Customs Officer'), derives from his initial employment as an inspector at a toll station on the outskirts of Paris.

1 LA MUSE INSPIRANT LE POÈTE

1 *The Muse Inspiring the Poet*, 1909 painting now in the Kunstmuseum in Basel, depicting the French poet Guillaume Apollinaire (1880–1918) and the French Post-Impressionist painter Marie Laurencin (1883–1956). SH describes it as 'that painting of the poet and his muse as a shabby old couple standing in their ordinary old doorway' (*SS*, 335).

1–4 SH identifies the couple with himself and his wife (whose mother was a schoolteacher) as 'a worn-out image of themselves as bride and groom' (*SS*, 335).

6 (Call] Call *Graph* (error)

9 Sentimental pictures of the Holy Family, often displayed in Irish Catholic houses in the twentieth century, show St Joseph carrying a spray of lilies which symbolise his purity: held in the way the poet in Rousseau's painting holds a quill.

10 *wroth*: in place of 'earth' as in the Beatitudes.

12ff. The lilies bring to mind Solomon, who 'in all his glory' was not 'adorned like one of these'. The narrator sees in this bride a poor imitation of his bride which she competes with.

2 'L'ENFANT AUX ROCHERS'

Title *The Boy of the Rocks*, the second Rousseau painting dating from 1895–7, now in the National Gallery of Art in Washington.

1 '*Sois Sage*': 'be sensible', as a command to a child. This child in his set posture and with his 'unyoung' mature person's face can't be anything else. To the end of the poem, the references are to children's dress or games, responding to the strange child and his location in the picture, sitting on top of a range of pointed miniature mountains.

4 'Taken up to the mountain' as Christ was, to be transfigured (in all the Synoptic Gospels: e.g. Luke 9:8–36). This sensible child 'high and dry' will not be transfigured.

9 *namecallers' chorus*: maybe in response to the painting's naivete.

Sonnets from the Peloponnese

'Bassae' and 'Mycenae' published, with 'Into Arcadia', in *Cara*, 31. 5 (Sept./Oct. 1998): 14–17, the Aer Lingus in-flight magazine, with this headnote:

> These sonnets are from a sequence written to commemorate holidays spent in Greece in 1995 and 1997, when my wife and I travelled with two friends who were in effect guides to the ancient sites. Everywhere we went we had a tremendous sense of the literary and the legendary past: just saying the names of the places we visited was like speaking lines from Homer.

In a single day in October 1995, for example, we drove from Mycenae, across the plains of Argos, into the mountains of Arcadia and ended up in Sparta. Everywhere was backlit with associations, so that no matter how many tourists crowded the ramparts of Agamemnon's palace or how many drab tavernas lined the main street of Sparta, it was impossible not to feel connected to the classical world. The ruins, the rocks, the earth, the very air consolidated that heritage within us: it was our first time there and yet it was as if we had known the place ahead of time.

The sonnets arose out of this sense of being two-timed, of experiencing the actual Greece in the light of one we had already imagined.

'Into Arcadia' was collected in *EL*, the first of the 'Sonnets from Hellas' (*EL*, 38; *PSH*, 549).

BASSAE

An archaeological site in the north-eastern part of Messenia in Greece. Celebrated for its Temple of Apollo Epicurius in which the three Greek architectural orders – Doric, Ionic and Corinthian – are found together. Its marble frieze consists of twenty-three panels depicting the battle between the Greeks and Amazons against the Lapiths and Centaurs.

MYCENAE

An archaeological site in the north-eastern Peloponnese, built on a hill rising 240 metres above the sea, one of the major centres of Greek civilisation in the second millennium BCE, the period of Greek history called the Mycenean. It is strongly connected to the Homeric epics.

4–5 Lion Gate at the ancient cemetery. SH applies the Gaelic term *rath* ('fort') to the cemetery as he used the term *bawn* in translating Beowulf and as he applies the Celtic terms 'cairn' and 'dolmen' to the *tholos* ('tomb') in *l.* 12 here. Atreus was king of Mycenae, the father of Agamemnon and Menelaus.

6 *megara*: the great hall at the centre of Mycenean palaces.

7 *the rooftop watchman*: familiar from SH's 'Mycenae Lookout' (*SL*, 29; *PSH*, 480).

The Stick

Privately published on 18 August 1998 as a broadside limited to a hundred copies by the Gallery Press, 'to mark the presentation of the Parnell Stick by Seamus Heaney to Nuala Ní Dhomhnaill in the presence of Conor Cruise O'Brien, Guest of Honour'; published in Richard English and Joseph

Morrison Skelly (eds), *Ideas Matter: Essays in Honour of Conor Cruise O'Brien* (Dublin: Poolbeg, 1998), 51–3, and then in *LL*.

[text: Gallery]

6 uniform] uniform, *LL*
7] A rod of correction *LL*
15 W. R.] WR *Ideas Matter*
16–37] And to him by succession
   From the one who had cut it
   In Avondale Woods:

   Charles Stewart Parnell.
   (I'm amazed Conor parted
   With it at all.) *LL*
45 serviam.] serviam *Ideas Matter* (error)

In *Ideas Matter*, the poem is preceded by the following note by SH:

> This poem was read at a gathering in Dublin on 18 August 1998, where Conor Cruise O'Brien was guest of honour. The lines were specially written for the occasion and celebrate the passing on to the poet Nuala Ní Dhomhnaill of the walking stick that had once belonged to Charles Stewart Parnell. The provenance of this stick is rehearsed in the poem: Conor had received it in 1962 from the poet WR Rodgers, with the proviso that he pass it on at an appropriate time to another Irish writer younger than himself. This Conor did, more than 20 years ago, honouring me mightily and, at the same time, putting me *faoi gheasa* to hand it on in turn. Now it is Nuala Ní Dhomhnaill's, and she too will eventually have to 'see it released / Back into the thickets / And thick of language'.

Faoi gheasa: under a semi-magical obligation. The current holder of the stick is the Tralee-born Irish-language poet, Ailbhe Ní Ghearbhuigh to whom Ní Dhomhnaill passed it in 2017.

   11 *Illustrissimus donor*: 'most illustrious donor'.

   12 Conor Cruise O'Brien (1917–2008). Irish writer, diplomat, controversialist and politician, writer of an influential review of *North*. Major representative of the United Nations in the Congo in 1961; Labour Party minister in the Irish coalition government 1973–7, editor-in-chief of the London *Observer* 1978–81.

   15–16 W. R. Rodgers (1909–69), Belfast-born poet, essayist and broadcaster, and Presbyterian minister, always called Bertie.

   17–18 Brinsley Macnamara (1890–1963), Irish writer.

   36 *Parnell and His Party, 1880–90* (1957) by Conor Cruise O'Brien.

   52 *finder or keeper*: cf. 'Mycenae Lookout: 5. His Reverie of Water', l. 34 (*SL*, 37; *PSH*, 486).

60–1 *selva* / *Selvaggia e forte*: Dante, *Inferno*, 1.5: 'a wood savage and grim'. The language to which SH committed the stick was the Irish of Nuala Ní Dhomhnaill (b.1952).

Non-U

Published in Christopher Cahill et al., *In Memoriam Darcy O'Brien*, a supplement to *the Recorder* (Fall 1998): 22–3.

[text: *In Memoriam Darcy O'Brien*]

Dedication Darcy O'Brien (1939–98) was born in Los Angeles to Hollywood-movie star parents, George O'Brien and Marguerite Churchill, as the poem says. In 2001 SH wrote the introduction to the reprint of his first novel, a comic fictionalised autobiography, *A Way of Life, Like Any Other* (1977), the title of which was ascribed to SH. A friend of the Heaneys in both California and Dublin, he wrote first in a comic vein but more sombrely in his later work. The tone of the poem is dandyish ('seersuckered' as the title suggests).

Our Lady of Guadalupe

Published in *LL* under the title 'Our Lady of Guadeloupe'.

Title Guadalupe] Guadeloupe *LL*
1 Guadalupe] Guadeloupe *LL*

Our Lady (or the Virgin) of Guadalupe appeared four times to a Mexican farm-labourer called Juan Diego and once to his uncle, said to have occurred in December 1531. The basilica there is the most visited Marian shrine in the world and the third most visited religious site anywhere. The cult began in Guadalupe in Spain, the home-place of some Spanish conquistadores.

Willow, Ophelia, Moyola

Published in *LL*.

A Dream of Solstice

First published on the front page of the *Irish Times* (21 Dec. 1999): 1, and then with revisions in the *Kenyon Review* 23: 1 (Winter 2001): 1–3. The *Kenyon Review* version was selected for inclusion in Philip Zaleski and Natalie Goldberg (eds), *The Best Spiritual Writing 2002* (San Francisco: HarperCollins, 2002), 85–6.

[text: *Irish Times*]
Before the epigraph from *Paradiso*, the *Kenyon Review* and *Best Spiritual Writing* versions include the following explanatory epigraph:

> The sun's rays enter Newgrange – 5,000-year-old passage grave north of Dublin – on December 21 every year. A slot in the stone entrance, 70 feet away from the burial chamber at the core of the tumulus, admits the light.

Epigraph 3 non] no *Kenyon Review*, *Best Spiritual Writing* (error)
17–18 the corbelled rock / And unsunned tonsure of the burial mounds,] the crowd grows still / In the wired-off precinct of the burial mounds, *Kenyon Review*, *Best Spiritual Writing*
19–21 [omitted] *Kenyon Review*, *Best Spiritual Writing*
36 to hold its candle] holding its candle *Kenyon Review*, *Best Spiritual Writing*
37–43] To the world inside the astronomic cave. *Kenyon Review*, *Best Spiritual Writing*
[line notes]

Epigraph Dante, *Paradiso*, 33.58–61, midway through the final canto of *The Divine Comedy*. After the epigraph, SH begins the poem by continuing to translate *Paradiso*, 33.62–5, before composing the new text of his poem. (For preceding lines 49–57 of Canto 33, see 'The Light of Heaven', *TSH*, 89.)

1–8 SH continues from the lines in the epigraph to translate *Paradiso*, 33.58–65.

39 The moved wheel recalls the '*rota*' that moves equally ('*egualmente*') as a figure of universal love in the penultimate line of *Paradiso*.

Screenplay

Published in the *Cork Review* (1999): 6.

The poem seems to dramatically imagine SH's father leaving the house empty after the death of his wife. An earlier TS draft, entitled 'The Locking Up' (HFC), bears a more comforting ending than carried in 'Screenplay' *ll.* 45–50:

> Saying over and over, 'It's not the end
> Of the world,' bearing the key in his hand
> As if it were a relic being translated
> And his words the words due ceremony dictated
>
> For the locking up of a house where heretofore
> All day and night the key stayed in the door
> In case (as she put it) there should come a moment when
> 'Somebody might be needing to get in.'

An Empty Surfboard on a Flat Sea

Published in the *Paris Review* (Spring 2000): 97–8, this was SH's contribution to a feature called 'Pomework: An Exercise in Occasional Poetry', in which poets were invited to write in response to a selection of titles.

[text: *Paris Review*]

Aneximines of Miletus (*c*.586–525 BCE) was a pre-Socratic Greek philosopher who believed that air was the foundational element underlying everything.

Úrlár

Published in *Metre*, 7–8 (Spring/Summer 2000): 268, where the poem is accompanied by the following note:

Author's Note: 'úrlár' is a term used in relation to the 'floor' of sound in Scottish piping.

Dedication Liam O'Flynn (1945–2018) was an Irish uilleann piper and whistle player, soloist and founding member of Planxty, friend and collaborator with SH in live performance and notably on the recording *The Poet and the Piper*.

The Dearest Freshness

Published in the *Threepenny Review*, 80 (Winter 2000): 7.

Title 'There lives the dearest freshness deep down things' (Gerard Manley Hopkins, 'God's Grandeur', *l.* 10).

A Postscript to St Lucia

Published in *Poetry Review*, 91. 1 (Spring 2001): 41–3. Subsequently published in *The Formalist*, 14. 2 (2003): 15–17.

[text: *Poetry Review*]

25 Turquoise] Torquoise *Poetry Review* (error)

Title St Lucia, Caribbean island nation, the home of SH's friend, the poet Derek Walcott (1930–2017) and his German-born partner Sigrid Nama, visited by the Heaneys in 2005 and later years. SH's impressions of Castries and Gros Islet in St Lucia are evoked with great enthusiasm for O'Driscoll (*SS*, 343–4). SH first met Walcott in New York in 1980, and afterwards in Boston and Dún Laoghaire.

40 Sir Dunstan St Omer was the foremost painter of St Lucia and the designer of the national flag. He was a close friend of Walcott.

Sally Rod

Published in the *Dublin Review*, 2 (Spring 2001): 40, together with the following five poems under the title '*from* Private Excursions'.

An independent poem from 'The Sally Rod' (*DC*, 29; *PSH*, 606).

Trea

Published in the *Dublin Review*, 2 (Spring 2001): 41

Title Trea is probably a short version of Theresa.
   15 *selchie*: perhaps a variant on selkie, a seal-woman.
   16 *bombazine*: thick black material, traditionally used for mourning clothes.
   17 *birled*: to spin or turn: here apparently to emphasise the rhotic 'r' consonant.

A Present from Mr Pause

Published in the *Dublin Review*, 2 (Spring 2001): 42.

No Harm

Published in the *Dublin Review*, 2 (Spring 2001): 43.

3 There are several Cushleys on the committee of Castledawson GAC.
   5 '*Swear, Tom, swear*': as in *Hamlet* 1.5: the Ghost's urging, 'Swear! Swear!'

Natura Naturans

Published in the *Dublin Review*, 2 (Spring 2001): 44.

1 John. D. Stewart (1917–88) was a Belfast-born playwright, a leading figure in the Belfast Humanist Group.

Brother Stalk

Published in the *Dublin Review*, 2 (Spring 2001): 45.

4–6 The kind of humorous warning associated by SH in childhood with his father.

The Boiling House

First published in *The SHOp*, 5 (Spring 2001): 10, and then in *To Stanley Kunitz, With Love from Poet Friends, for his 96th Birthday* (Riverdale-on-Hudson: Sheep Meadow Press, 2002), 29.

[text: *The SHOp*]

5–8] The boiling house too had been a dwelling once. Now it was dug-out dark, peat-dry and oddly sound-proofed, a storage place for bags of meal and grain. But in the meantime it had lived the scullion life that seethed still in its name. *To Stanley Kunitz*
11 for extra pots on the crane on threshing days.] for extra pots on the crane at harvest homes. *To Stanley Kunitz*
13 Elysian Fields] Elysian fields *To Stanley Kunitz*
16–19] I am content with that, and opt for a hover-home where others hovered. An old reluctant breath comes off the bags. A pelt of soot is trembling in the chimney. The clay floor has stayed obstinate and simple. *To Stanley Kunitz*

1ff. The component rooms of a long, single-storey house like Mossbawn.

ELECTRIC LIGHT (2001)

Electric Light, dedicated to Matthew Evans and Caroline Michel, was published in London on 19 March 2001 by Faber & Faber in simultaneous hardback and paperback, and in New York by Farrar, Straus and Giroux in hardback on 8 April 2001 and in paperback on 3 April 2002. It was the Choice of the Poetry Book Society in Summer 2001. In its structure, it returns to the binary divisions of *Wintering Out* and *North*: the twenty-eight poems of part I a series of travel poems, classical eclogues and personal memories; part II, eleven elegies for poets, friends and family that establish a commemorative note that is pervasive in SH's late work.

Electric Light would be among the more hard-won of the titles that would come to SH. 'For a long time I couldn't decide what to call the collection,' he told readers on publication; but, 'Once "Electric Light" got written, I had no doubt about it as the title poem' (*PBS Bulletin*, 189, Summer 2001). Working papers in the National Library of Ireland, however, reveal a more complex picture, in which even once it had been discovered, further titles would remain under consideration. SH ran experimental print-outs of four title pages ('Real Names', 'Known World', 'Electric Light', with 'Between the Sleepers' seemingly the last among them), and annotated no fewer than thirty alternatives in manuscript leading up to and beyond those pages, indicating that, at minimum, he had entertained thirty-four titles for the collection, and seemingly a further seven after the arrival of 'Electric Light'.* Rand Brandes says that three in particular were uppermost in SH's mind, all with tragedy lying behind them to various degrees: 'The Real Names', 'Known World' and 'Duncan's Horses' (Brandes 2009, 32); the latter being the author's preference until his friend, Derek Walcott, published the proximate *Tiepolo's Hound* in April 2000 (*LSH*, 615). Brandes sees a tragic view of the world behind much of SH's work, between Anglo-Saxon gloom and the catastrophe implicit in actions that are

---

* From undated papers in the NLI archive, it is possible to construct a speculative sequence in which SH tested out titles for *EL*, with the following representing the earliest first: 'Milker's Darkness', 'Lupins', 'Real Characters', 'Duncan's Horses', 'Gallowglass Hair', Educations' (49,493/115); 'Playground Wind' (49,493/115); 'Itty-Bitties' (49,493/115); 'Now and Again', 'Red, White and Blue' (49,493/115); 'The Flow', 'Real Names' (49,493/116); 'Known World', 'Known World, Real Names' (49,493/117); 'Time and Again', 'On the Cusp', 'Feste's Lute', 'Open Air', 'Feste (Sings)', 'Ears and Awns' (49,493/117); 'Pignuts', 'Footer', 'Steady Go', 'Mull', 'A Venus Car', 'Moyola', 'Electric Light' (49,493/117); 'The Playthings in the Playhouse', 'Over the Door', 'The Coolth', 'Between the Sleepers', 'Into Arcadia', 'Acanthus', 'Arion' (49,493/117).

'Greek with consequence' ('Lustral Sonnet', *ST*, 35; *PSH*, 419). The immediate predecessors here are the decidedly violence-threatened political world of *Beowulf* in 1999, and the temperamentally unstable world of *The Spirit Level*. Furthermore, a book being completed in 2000 had an unavoidable millenarian context, reinforced by the world of SH's most recent complete work, the translation of *Beowulf* with its tragic ending. So, even before the elegiacs of part II here, the book begins with 'At Toomebridge' where Roddy McCorley 'the rebel boy was hanged in '98'. Earlier versions of the poem begin by striking a stark note on the millennial bell.

The book was not as enthusiastically received as other SH volumes, maybe to some extent because the two immediately preceding publications, *The Spirit Level* and *Beowulf*, had each been Whitbread Books of the Year, with the former considered as an exceptionally powerful collection. The developing reception of *Electric Light* was complicated, too, by the 9/11 attacks, a few months after its appearance, which changed the subject of public discourse, as SH reflected later: 'the whole condition of the world was altered henceforth, the spirit of the age had darkened' (*SS*, 424). Patrick McGuinness's review in the *LRB* was more insightful than most, describing the book as 'freighted with memory and allusion', but even he concedes 'This is not [SH's] best book, but some of the poems it contains are among the best he has written'. The poems he particularly admires are 'Perch', 'The Bookcase' and the title poem.

Of the poems in the first part of the book, 'Out of the Bag', about the doctor who presided over the birth of each of the Heaney children, sets the tone by the way it links childhood perception of events (the poem was originally entitled 'Miraculum', and the word still survives in the text to describe the doctor's miraculous action in assembling the baby bits 'into his soapy big hygienic hands') with various medical history, as a classic instance of the linking of memory with allusion that McGuinness believes characterises the volume. The more substantial Part I of the book moves from domestic origins to three Virgilian eclogues, one relocated to the Bann Valley, another to Wicklow, and a third a relatively close translation of the ominous *Eclogue 9*. The two dominant locales of this first part – Hellas, in a six-sonnet sequence, and the Northern Ireland of SH's schooldays – are both highly ambiguous in atmosphere: from the Theocritan idyll of the apples on the road in the first of the 'Sonnets from Hellas', to the horror of the brutal killing of Sean Brown in the fourth of the sonnets, 'The Augean Stables'. The poem 'Known World' contains both sentiments: between the irresponsible hilarity of *Nema problema!* at the start and the end, the narrator admits that that 'old sense of a tragedy going on / Uncomprehended, at the very edge / Of the usual, it never left me once'. The fluctuation between the tragic and the nostalgic extends even to the influence of *Beowulf* in this book: from the anxiety of 'The Border Campaign', with its memory of the IRA campaigns on the border of Northern Ireland in the 1950s (earlier versions of the poem are entitled 'Attack'), to 'The Fragment', the hypnotic hymn of creation from early in *Beowulf*.

Painful emotions pervade the whole of the shorter second part, mostly comprising elegies for Ted Hughes, Joseph Brodsky, Zbigniew Herbert, various Scottish makars, and family friends Mary Ó Muirithe and Rory Kavanagh, and ending with poems about SH's maternal grandfather and his grandmother, buried in the Derry ground at the end of the title poem. 'It is full of *mortalia*,' SH told readers, 'by people and things we must pass away from or that have had to pass away from us' (*PBS Bulletin*, 189); it might even have a carried an epigraph from the *Aeneid*, he confided, in which Aeneas encounters a memorial wall to his fallen friends of the Trojan War – *Sunt lacrimae rerum et mentem mortalia tangunt* – in SH's much-treasured translation by Robert Fitzgerald: 'they weep here / For how the world goes, and our life that passes / Touches their hearts' (*Aeneid*, 1.462; Fitzgerald 1983, 20: 1.628–30).[*] By its conclusion, *Electric Light* is yet another SH book in which the pastoral world is evoked only to be undermined.

[text: *EL2001*]

Dedication Matthew Evans (1941–2016) joined Faber in 1963, and was chairman 1980–2000; the literary agent Caroline Michel (b.1959) was his wife.

I

At Toomebridge

First published in *Thumbscrew* (Autumn 1998): 4, then in *College Green* (September 2000): 6. Collected with revisions in *EL*.

≤1] The year two thousand. *Thumbscrew*
5–10] Present of the Bann, the sky above
   Was hurdle and hurdler all at once,
   The furl of inner light in the overspill
   Axle and portal and crystal as the warp

---

[*] In his personal copy of Fitzgerald's translation, SH has ruled off the section in pencil with what looks like the shape of an arrowhead.

> Those words make in the mind:
> > 'The year two thousand.'
> At Toomebridge.
> > Where the checkpoint used to be.
> Where the Civil Righters bulldozed the RUC's
> Tenders into the river. Where the rebel boy
> Was hanged on the bridge in 1798.
> Where poetry can take it and leave it. *Thumbscrew*

Toome is a village at the north-east edge of Lough Neagh. An earlier draft of the poem begins 'The year two thousand' (Emory H, 1613).

5 *the Bann*: the Lower River Bann which flows north from Lough Neagh to the sea.

6 *the checkpoint*: army checkpoints were common on the Irish border, but were considerably reduced after the paramilitary ceasefires of 1994 and are now no longer used.

7 *the rebel boy*: Roddy McCorley, Irish nationalist from Co. Antrim who was hanged 'near the Bridge of Toome' on 28 February 1800 for alleged participation in the 1798 rebellion: the subject of a popular nationalist song named after him, with words written by Ethna Carbery a century later.

Perch

First published as 'The Perch' in the *New Yorker* (18 Jan. 1999): 30. After collection in *EL* it was included in *NSP2014*.

1 water-perch] water perch *New Yorker*
3 we] they *New Yorker*
6 adoze,] adoze *New Yorker*
7 Guzzling] On *New Yorker*

Dated 'Boston–LA', 22 April 1998 in MS (NLI 49,493/117).

4 *glorified body*: theological term for the resurrected body after death.

Lupins

First published as 'The Lupins' in the *Sunday Times* Books section (17 Aug. 1997): 9. After collection with revisions in *EL* it was included in *NSP2014*.

4 *Rose-fingered dawn*: the Homeric epithet for the goddess Eos, the Dawn, *rododaktylos*.

Out of the Bag

First published in *Threepenny Review* (Fall 2000): 8. Later included in Martin Dyar (ed.), *Vital Signs: Poems of Illness and Healing* (Dublin: Poetry Ireland, 2022), 40–5. After collection in *EL*, parts 1 and 4 were included in *NSP2014* and *100P*.

3 4 midday] mid-day *Threepenny Review*

Dated Tuesday 13 April [1999] in TS as 'Hygiea' (NLI 49,493/118), then as 'Miraculum' (NLI 49,493/113, 49,493/117–18), corrected first to 'Tender' (NLI 49,493/114) then to 'Out of the Bag' (NLI 49,493/118).

 1 1 *Doctor Kerlin*: Joseph Philip Kerlin, local doctor based in Magherafelt.

 1 17 *a Dutch interior gleam*: the light effects of painters like Vermeer, also suggested in the first of the opening pair of dedicatory poems to *North*, 'Sunlight' (*North*, 9; *PSH*, 173).

 1 27 *Hyperborean*: realm of eternal spring, beyond the home of the North Wind, and so 'hyper-north'. Also, the penetrating blue of skimmed milk (l. 29–30).

 1 34ff. *infant parts*: Oliver Taplin (2019, 24–5) suggests these components of infants might have been suggested to SH by a room leading to the museum of Asclepius at Epidaurus (l. 44), visited by SH in 1995, and recalled by him in conversation with O'Driscoll (*SS*, 294). The room contains many clay models of such infant parts. Cf. *asclepions* (l. 39).

 2 1 *poeta doctus*: 'learned poet'. Peter Levi (1931–2000) was SH's immediate predecessor as Oxford Professor of Poetry.

 2 4 *Lourdes*: a modern Catholic equivalent of the curative properties of Asclepius at Epidaurus.

 2 5 Robert Graves (1895–1985) was also a predecessor of SH's as Oxford Professor of Poetry.

 2 10 *'incubation'*: as well as the definition given here, and more obviously, 'incubation' means the preparation of young creatures (birds or human beings) for birth. The word returns in the last section of the poem when the child, 'incubating for real' is about to see the baby delivered by his mother and the doctor.

 2 14 *thurifer*: the altar boy who swung the thurible, the metal censer that dispersed incense.

 2 26 *miraculum* is perhaps a vestige of the poem's earlier title.

 3 2 Possibly Adele Dalsimer (d.21 March 2000) or Mary Ó Muirithe (d.1998); see 'Sruth' (*EL*, 77; *PSH*, 569).

3 11 *Hygeia*: daughter of Asclepius and associate of Aphrodite, goddess of love and procreation, and initial working title for the poem.

Bann Valley Eclogue

First published in the *TLS* (8 Oct. 1999): 32, then in the *Sunday Business Post* (26 Dec. 1999): l 1. Extract published as a limited-edition broadside under the title 'The Child That's Due' by Bank of Ireland Group Treasury (Dec. 1999), with some proceeds going to the Irish Peatland Council's 'Save the Bog Campaign'. The poem also featured on BBC Radio Four's *Today* programme in the 'Thought for the Day' slot on 7 October 1999, and was read on RTÉ radio on the eve of the millennium. Collected with revisions in *EL*.

epigraph] [no epigraph] *TLS*   canamus.] canamus! *Sunday Business Post*
8 gens.] gens, *TLS*, *Sunday Business Post*
8^9] Ferrea, aurea, aetas, scelus, Lucina. *TLS*, *Sunday Business Post*
11] then an infant birth] iron and gold. *TLS*, *Sunday Business Post*
12] [omitted] *TLS*, *Sunday Business Post*
12^13] POET

    *Lucina. Rhyming with Sheena. Vocative. First
    Declension. Feminine gender. The Roman
    St Anne. Who is casta Lucina, chaste
    Star of the birth-bed. And secular star,
    Meaning star of the *saeculum*, brightness gathering
    Head great month by month now, waiting to fall.

    You were raised on the land they drove your father off.
    You had his country accent and little to learn
    Of the facts of life when you read your first poems out
    To Octavian, feeling the length of the line
    As if you were dressing husks off a hank of tow
    Or measuring wheat for thatch. Holding your own

    In your own way. *Pietas* and stealth. If ex-servicemen
    Were cocks of the walk at home, hexameters
    Would rule the roost in Rome. You would understand us
    Latter-day scholarship boys and girls, on the cusp
    Between elocution and *duchas*. Faces that were japped
    With cowdung once now barefaced to camera, live. *TLS*

*Lucina. Rhyming with Sheena. The Roman
    St Anne. Who is *casta Lucina*, chaste
    Star of the birth-bed. And secular star,
    Meaning star of the *saeculum*, luminous
    Ominous sign, a brightness gathering
    Head great month by month now, waiting to fall. *Sunday Business Post*

>42] [stanza break]
    We know, little one, you have to start with a cry
    But smile soon too, a big one for your mother.

> Unsmiling life has had it in for people
> For far too long. But now you have it in you
> Not to be wrong-footed but to first-foot us
> And, muse of the valley, give us a song worth singing. *TLS, Sunday Business Post*

Dated 23 August 1999 in MS with the title 'Eclogue for a Godchild'.

Epigraph Opening line of Virgil *Eclogue* 4: 'Sicilian Muses, let us sing slightly greater things.'

3 *And it came to pass*: a common formula in biblical translations. The exchange between 'Poet' and Virgil is a departure; the original Virgilian eclogue is not a dialogue. *In the beginning*: most familiar as the opening phrase of St John's Gospel.

4 *hedge-schoolmaster*: teacher when formal Catholic schooling was prohibited in the Irish countryside from 1695 until the introduction of the National School system in 1831.

5 *the child that's due*: SH's grandniece, whose birth is imminent. The focus on this event continues the childbirth theme of the preceding poem. This Virgilian predecessor was chosen because in the Middle Ages the appeal to Juno as here to smile on the birth of an expected child was sometimes interpreted as a prophecy of the coming of Christ.

8 SH's Virgil sets the poet a kind of sestina-type exercise in which he will have to find a place for five words found at various points in Virgil's Latin.

19 *Pacatum orbem*: l. 17 in Virgil: 'the world made peaceful' by a father's strength.

22 *birdless and dark*: recalling the term *aornos* 'birdless' at the entrance to Avernus in *Aeneid*, 6.242. The seeing of the 'orb' (l. 24) has a 'millennial chill', though the poem returns to post-violence rural peace with the expectant young mother at the end and the 'child on the way' (l. 37).

Montana

Published in *EL*.

Dated 20 April 2000 in TS, under the title 'Dologhan' (NLI 49,493/117).

3–4 John Dologhan as a milker, suggested by 'the milk-house floor' at the end of the previous poem.

6 'The Rose of Mooncoin', one of the most popular Irish songs of locality, about a small town in Co. Kilkenny: the anthem of the Kilkenny hurling team.

11 *the winkers*: Irish term for horse blinkers, familiar from Patrick Kavanagh's poem 'Kerr's Ass'.

13 The internal rhyme 'rambler', 'gambler' may derive from another popular song, 'The Moonshiner', the chorus of which begins, 'I'm a rambler, I'm a gambler, I'm a long ways from home'; *the Free State*: the twenty-six counties of Ireland which became the Irish Republic in 1949: commonly used in the North of Ireland to differentiate it from Northern Ireland.

14–17 The game 'pitch and toss' was commonly played out of doors, often in the hidden space under bridges. Butler's Bridge is near Castledawson, just east of the village. Betting on it was illegal, so Dologhan should not have been 'a gambler' (*l.* 13).

The Loose Box

Third section first published privately under the title 'The Manger' as a Christmas card by the Gallery Press (Christmas 1998); another section published under the title 'Threshing Day' on the cover of *Open Door: Linen Hall Library Millennium Festival* (16–24 September 2000): cover, and reprinted in *Images & Reflections: Photographers and Writers Seeing Our Century* (Belfast: Linen Hall Library, 2000), 26. Full poem first published in M. E. J. Hughes, John Mole and Nick Seddon (eds), *Figures of Speech: An Anthology of Magdalene Writers* (Cambridge: Magdalene College, 2000), 212–14, then in *Parnassus*, 25 (Feb. 2001): 275–7. Also published as a limited-edition broadsheet of 101 numbered copies by *Parnassus: Poetry in Review* (2001), to mark the journal's twenty-fifth anniversary.

22 Crook-armed] Crook-kneed *The Manger*
24 hayrack] manger *The Manger*
32] But no, no arm-filled, fodder-billowy manger-mouth. *The Manger*
41 rut-shuddery] rut-shedder-fast *Parnassus*
51^2] [stanza break] *Parnassus*
74^5] [no stanza break] *Parnassus*

3 'hayrack' is a synonym for 'manger', as a trough from which animals feed.

8 *glarry*: Ulster term for 'muddy'. Cf. 'glar' as one of the dialect terms in 'Fosterling' (*ST*, 50; *PSH*, 426).

15 *Heracles*: in earlier Heaney poems, like 'Hercules and Antaeus', Hercules (Heracles) overcomes Antaeus by lifting him off the ground. 'Stepping in and standing under' are terms for helping to carry the coffin in Irish Catholic funerals, as in 'The Lift' (*DC*, 43; *PSH*, 611).

18–19 Luke 2:12. In the Bible text, it is a directive by the angel, not a report as here.

36 *dolens*: sorrowful (Latin). Appropriate but not common description of the English writer Thomas Hardy (1840–1928).

37 *his Christmas Eve night-piece*: Hardy, 'The Oxen'.

38 *their bedded stall*: for original 'their strawy pen' ('The Oxen').

39 *the threshing scene*: Hardy's *Tess of the d'Urbervilles* (1891), chapter 47.

55 Michael Collins (1890–1922), Irish revolutionary leader and politician, born near Clonakilty, Co. Cork, was killed by gunfire a few miles away at Béal na Bláth in the Irish Civil War after he had signed the Anglo-Irish Treaty, which partitioned Ireland, in 1921.

57 *Avernus-mouth*: entrance to the underworld and the afterlife.

60 *the hay-floor that once gave in his childhood*: a story told by biographers of Collins.

65 *boy-deeds*: a formula derived from the medieval Irish genre 'boyhood deeds' (of Fionn mac Cumhaill or Cú Chulainn, for example).

Turpin Song

First published in the *London Magazine* (April/May 2001): 31.

Title Dick Turpin (1706–39) was a notorious highwayman and cattle-thief from Essex, the subject of a substantial popular literature. The Heaney children associated him with a horse pistol that was attached to the wall in their childhood home.

11 *the Great North Road*: the main south–north axis in England, from London to York. A stagecoach route, liable to highwayman hold-ups in popular stories.

12 *tricorn hat*: in 'Linen Town' (*l.* 9), 'young [Henry Joy] McCracken', an executed republican leader of the 1798 rebellion, was watched on the gallows by a 'low-necked belle and tricorned fop' (*WO*, 38; *PSH*, 131).

16–17 At the start of Kubrick's *2001: A Space Odyssey* (1968) a group of apes discover how discarded bones can be used as weapons, a moment of the loss of innocence; cf. *l.* 25 here.

The Border Campaign

First published under the title 'An Image from Beowulf' in Andries Walter Oliphant (ed.), *A Writing Life: Celebrating Nadine Gordimer* (Penguin [South Africa], 1998), 121, and in *Crab Orchard Review* (Fall/Winter 1998): 102. Collected with revisions in *EL*.

5 fifty-six] fifty *Crab Orchard Review*

6–7] Something or other, it left me winded. / From my boarder's dormer, I watched the big sky move *Crab Orchard Review*
12–19]   I am in awe,
    Back there with clan chiefs giddy in the head
    At the sight of the talon Beowulf tore off
    Nailed to the gable, the sky still moving grandly ... *Crab Orchard Review*

Title The Border Campaign was the term used to describe IRA attacks on the Irish border between 1956 and 1962. A draft version in TS was called 'Attack' (cf. *l*. 4, here).

Dedication Nadine Gordimer (1923–2014), South African novelist and activist, won the Nobel Prize in Literature in 1991.

1 The courthouse in Derry, visible from St Columb's where SH started as a boarder in 1951.

9 *Savagery in Heorot*: the attacks by the monster Grendel on the Danish hall Heorot in *Beowulf*.

15 After the hand-fight with Grendel, Beowulf nails Grendel's claw to the wall in Heorot as a trophy.

17–19 *Beowulf*, *ll.* 983–5. These lines are different from their translation in SH's full *Beowulf* and from their version in 'Attack'.
         Every nail,
    claw-scale and spur, every spike
    and welt on the hand of that heathen brute
    was like barbed steel.   *Beowulf*

Known World

First published in the *TLS* (21 May 1999): 21, and collected with revisions in *EL*.

10^11] [stanza break] *TLS*
45] I see that tarnished, bletted coil again, *TLS*
47^8] [stanza break] *TLS*
55 Hygo] Ilygo *TLS*
71 Now enter] Enter *TLS*
85 Today] To-day *TLS*
91 El Greco-gaunt] Giotto-gaunt *TLS*
99] I had been there before, it seemed, but still *TLS*
100 Haunted] Was haunted *TLS*
108 *No Smoking*] No Smoking *TLS*
>111 May 1988] [no date] *TLS*

Working title in TS 'Kosovo Summer'.

1 '*Nema problema!*': the occasion recalled is the Poetry Festival at Struga of 1978, in the south-west of what is now North Macedonia (9–10). Struga is a popular holiday destination on the shore of Lake

Ohrid. The dramatic sequence published now recalls a return to Struga in May 1998 (dated at the end, *EL*, 23).

1 *Belgrade*: capital of the former Yugoslavia and now of Serbia, 400 miles north of Struga. SH visits it in 1998.

5 *Beria!*: Lavrentiy Pavlovich Beria (1899–1953), a Georgian Bolshevik, was the Soviet head of the secret police under Stalin, removed by Khrushchev in 1953. He was tried for treason and various other indefinite offences and executed in December 1953. Why the unidentified Vladimir Chupeski (who reappears at *l.* 13 on page 22) uses his name as a vodka-drunk imprecation is not clear.

11 Rafael Alberti (1902–99): the Spanish winner of the Struga Golden Wreath in 1978 (won by SH in 2001).

12 Caj Westerburg (b.1946): Finnish poet and translator.

16 Hans Magnus Enzensberger (1929–2022): German poet and translator.

19 The soothsaying Dane is unidentified.

21 *squinch*: in architecture, an interior arch supporting a tower or pinnacle.

27 *Belmullet*: town in west Co. Mayo, at the eastern end of the Erris peninsula. Here used adjectivally to mean deeply rural. Presumably these lines are in quotation marks because SH is drawing on notebooks written at the time (see *l.* 81, 'the notebook says', followed by quotation marks: Karl Miller describes 'Known World' as 'a notebook poem' (Miller 2000, 27)).

33 *the still centre*: cf. 'the still point of the Turning World' (Eliot, *Four Quartets* (1941): 'Burnt Norton', *l.* 64).

34 Hanging strips of flypaper were commonly used, and universally detested, in Irish farm kitchens in the 1950s: a powerful image as 'a syrup of Styx' (*l.* 45) in contrast to the summer 'open door at sunlight' (*l.* 49). SH tells Karl Miller that seeing the displaced refugees with their rural effects in the Balkan Wars brought to his mind the image of 'those old-fashioned sticky fly-papers hanging from the ceiling of a deserted house, a house that the family was driven from' (Miller 2000, 26).

51ff. 'tragedy . . . at the very edge / Of the usual' is the condition of the Balkan and the Northern Irish wars alike, characteristic too of the contrasting atmospheres in this book. The irresponsible lightheartedness of the poets conflicts with the hardships of the refugees, as the 'Sonnets from Hellas' will vary from the 'opulence and amen' of the first poem to the brutal murder of Sean Brown in 'The Augean Stables'.

55 Hugo Simberg (1873–1917), Finnish painter, therefore invoked for the sake of Caj Westerburg, the 'Finnish Hamlet in black

corduroy' of the opening section of the poem. Simberg's painting *The Wounded Angel* was already familiar in Irish poetry as the front-cover illustration of Paul Durcan's book *Daddy, Daddy* (Blackstaff, 1990) which contained the poem 'Seamus Heaney's Fiftieth Birthday'.

71 *another angel*: the angel of death.

72 *'Serb house'*: in the conversation with Karl Miller SH says 'This was a message which was painted on thresholds in order to dissuade those who would otherwise enter the house and kill everyone inside' (Miller 2000, 27). Cf. Exodus 12:13: 'The blood on your doorposts will serve as a sign, marking the houses where you are staying. When I see the blood, I will pass over you.'

83 *field full of folk*: Langland, *Piers Plowman* (B-text, Prologue, 17).

85–6 *workers' day*: 1 May. 'Greek Orthodox Madonna's Day' is perhaps also Mayday, First of May, though Orthodox celebrations of the Virgin Mary are primarily observed on 15 August.

91 *El Greco-gaunt*: Doménikos Theotokópoulos (1541–1614), Greek painter of the Spanish Renaissance. His figures are thin and elongated; it has even been suggested that their gauntness was a product of an eye condition in the painter.

97 *iconostasis*: screen with icons on it in Eastern Orthodox churches, separating the sanctuary from the nave.

110 *de haut en bas*: a gracious gesture of superiority – literally 'from high to low'.

The Little Canticles of Asturias

First published online in *'Slate* the internet magazine' on 24 June 1996, and later in *Slate on Paper* (September 1996): 59. Also published in *LL*, and in *Chapman* (1999): 38. Collected with revisions in *EL* and included in *NSP2014*.

2 2 for.] for, *LL, Chapman*
2 2^3] Giddy and replenished all at once. *LL, Chapman*
3 1–2] San Juan de la Cruz
      Had his dark night of the soul.
      At San Juan de las Harenas
      It was bright day. *Chapman*

Title *Asturias*: an autonomous region in north-west Spain where Marie Heaney's sister Anne lives.

1 The opening sonnet-section has a Dantesque, infernal atmosphere, concluding with the 'hellish' roads.

1 2 *Gijón*: a city on the coast of Asturias.

1 9 'stacks' of corn or straw in the farmyard.

2 1 *Piedras Blancas*: the capital of the municipality of Castrillón in Asturias, thirty-two kilometres west of Gijón.

3 1 *San Juan de las Harenas*: one of the five parishes in the municipality of Soto del Barco in Asturias. An earlier version carried 'San Juan de la Cruz / Had his dark night of the soul' at the head of the text here.

3 6ff. There are two suggestions of a Dantesque heaven to respond to the hell of part I: *in excelsis* (in *l.* 6) and the concluding word *stela*, echoing the last word of Paradiso, '*stelle*'.

Ballynahinch Lake

First published in Marco Sonzogni (ed.), *Or Volge L'Anno: At the Year's Turning: An Anthology of Irish Poets Responding to Leopardi* (Dublin: Dedalus, 1998), 146–7, and then in two private limited editions: an Italian translation by Marco Sonzogni to mark SH's sixtieth birthday (Dec. 1999), and by Ballynahinch Castle Hotel, Co. Galway (Dec. 1999). After collection in *EL* it was also included in *NSP2014*.

2^3] The freshly surfaced tarmacadam road, / The stockpiled peat on the verge, the sunstruck bonnet / Seemed to enter sleeping beauty time *Or Volge L'Anno*
5 Entered] Eked *Or Volge L'Anno*
20 the wheel] her thought *Or Volge L'Anno*
21–2 indeed / Been useful] indeed been / Useful *Or Volge L'Anno*

Title A lake near Clifden in Connemara, the location of a celebrated luxury hotel.

Epigraph Giacomo Leopardi (1798–1837), Italian Romantic poet. '*Il sabato del villaggio*' ('The Village Saturday') is one of his best-known poems, about a young girl's happy anticipation of the day of rest on Saturday night which is dashed by bad weather on the Sunday morning. 'Rejoice, my child; be calm, / This is a happy season.'

Dedication Eamon Grennan (b.1941), Dublin-born poet, was Professor of English at Vassar College before retiring to the west of Ireland.

1 *So we stopped and parked*: some commentators have read this opening as a continuity to 'Postscript' at the end of *The Spirit Level*. There is a correspondence, too, between the strong waterbirds and the 'headstrong-looking' swans there (*SL*, 70; *PSH*, 502), though of course the locations are different: Connemara here and North Clare in 'Postscript'.

2 Cf. the opening of 'Seeing Things': 'Inishbofin on a Sunday morning' (*ST*, 16; *PSH*, 955).

The Clothes Shrine

Private edition limited to a hundred copies produced on 14 September 2000 by the Bonnefant Press, Banholt, to mark Marie Heaney's sixtieth birthday. Published in *The Harp*, 15 (2000): 5, and included in *Midsummer Feast*, with the dedication 'for Marie': 31. After collection in *EL* it was also included in *NSP2014* and *100P*.

dedication [no dedication]] for Marie *Bonnefant, MF*

2 In the early days of the Heaneys' marriage.

8–11 Referring to a medieval legend of the Irish St Brigid drying her cloak on a sunbeam.

Red, White and Blue

'Blue' first published in *Poetry Ireland Review* (Winter 1998): 75–6; and published in full in the *Sunday Times*, Culture section (11 April 1999): 13. Collected with revisions in *EL*.

3 2 mimicked the] mimicked her and the *Poetry Ireland Review*   unaffected] unaffected, *Poetry Ireland Review*
3 3 And *veh*] Veh *Poetry Ireland Review*
3 9 then took] assume *Poetry Ireland Review*
3 3 And *veh*] Veh *Poetry Ireland Review*
3 18 cover] cover, *Poetry Ireland Review*
3 19 north] north, *Poetry Ireland Review*
3 32 A Botticelli] Botticelli *Poetry Ireland Review*

Title The trio of colours associated with Britain: here three episodes from the earlier lives of SH and his wife Marie together.

1 RED

18 *Redingote*: a fitted long coat.

2 WHITE

31 *the Knight of the White Feather*: the husband fleeing from the hospital delivery room (in the poem's imagery, Castle Childbirth).

3 BLUE

1, 3, 21 *veh*: upper-class English pronunciation of 'very', mocked and imitated here.

5 *Castlebellingham*: a village in Co. Louth, most familiar for its seventeenth-century castle, now an exclusive luxury hotel. SH and

Marie (Devlin then, in 1963) are picked up as hitchhikers by this upper-class English couple, 'officer class', who have been staying in the hotel.

11, 13 *southern Ireland*: a term for the Irish Republic, only used in Britain.

15 *Your crowd*: the Irish republicans who burned an estimated 300 Anglo-Irish Big Houses during the revolutionary period in Ireland.

21 *Burnt in reprisal*: several Irish towns and cities – Cork and Mallow for example – were set on fire in reprisal for anti-British activities in the Troubles during the War of Independence.

24 *coaching inn in Wicklow*: moving on to the next exclusive overnight resting place.

26 *recall a hero to his ardent purpose*: by contrast with the fleeing prospective father in 'Blue', *l.* 31.

30 *tank-top*: a sleeveless shirt, originally US. Marie is dressed in blue, in the regulation garb of the liberated 1960s.

33 Rolls-Royce, the foremost British luxury car.

Virgil: Eclogue IX

Published in *EL*.

Virgil's *Eclogue 9* is the second of two of the eclogues (the other is *Eclogue 1*) concerned with grievance about land distribution. It describes the meeting of two shepherds (herdsmen, as in the term Bucolics), Lycidas and Moeris. Moeris has been turned out of his farm and he is taking some kid goats to town, to the market on behalf of the new occupant. Lycidas is surprised because he had heard that Menalcas (Virgil) had saved the district by his poetry. (The identification of Menalcas as Virgil is because of the phrase 'should Mantua / Survive': Mantua was Virgil's birthplace.) SH's version retains the names of the original pastoral. Moeris is probably the displaced landowner, though some commentators used to identify him as a bailiff.

28 *Amaryllis*: the standard female object of the pastoral poet's affections.

29ff. The ostensible extracts from earlier works of Menalcas, in quotation marks here and later, are not specifically identified though similarly marked in the original.

40 *Pierian muses*: the Muses were said to have been born in Pieria at the foot of Mount Olympus so they were called Pierian as well as Olympian.

59 *the star of Caesar*: the *Iulium sidus* (Horace, *Odes*, 1.12.47): the comet which appeared just after the death of Julius Caesar was commonly said to be his deified soul.

74 *Bianor's tomb*: Bianor was a Trojan killed in an Achaian counterattack led by Agamemnon in the *Iliad*. His tomb seems to be used as a well-known landmark; Servius says that Bianor founded Mantua.

Glanmore Eclogue

First published in Nicholas Grene (ed.), *Interpreting Synge: Essays from the Synge Summer School 1991–2000* (Dublin: Lilliput, 2000), 17–19, and collected with revisions in *EL*. Later included in *NSP2014*.

SH's own pastoral, on the model and subjects of the Virgilian eclogue. There are similarities in the setting to *Eclogue 1*, SH's bay tree corresponding to Virgil's beech. Of the two shepherds there, Tityrus is the 'Poet'.

1ff. *Myles*: name taken from Flann O'Brien (Myles na Gopaleen), whose poetic translations from sections of *Buile Suibhne* in his novel *At Swim-Two-Birds* (1939) were an important influence on *Sweeney Astray*. His interlocutor, 'Poet', speaks in the voice of SH himself. This Myles is also a figure of the small farmer, corresponding to Moeris in the previous poem.

4ff. *a woman*: Ann Saddlemyer (b.1932), Canadian scholar and authority on Irish literature, who sold Glanmore Cottage to the Heaneys at a modest price, performing the same function, SH says, as Yeats's patron Augusta Gregory had served for him. Hence Saddlemyer is called Augusta.

14 Meliboeus corresponds to J. M. Synge, whose family earlier owned the Glanmore estate; he is the interlocutor with Tityrus in Virgil's *Eclogue 1*.

16–17 Meliboeus 'listening in a loft / To servant girls colloguing in the kitchen' echoes a famous episode in Synge's *The Aran Islands* (1907).

18 The Land Commission, the body responsible for the redistribution of Irish lands, often by giving tenants the rights of ownership.

20 The British Empire taking note too late of tenant hardship.

23 *Meliboeus' people*: corresponding to the Anglo-Irish, Synge's people.

24 *us*: Myles's people, representing tenant farmers.

26 *empty pockets*: recalling the empty pockets that the poet Antoine Ó Raifteirí complained of performing for; see *TSH*, 59.

31 '*out in the rain falling*': from the opening of Synge's one-act play *In the Shadow of the Glen* (1904).

36 'Mr Honey' was a term of address in Synge's play *The Playboy of the Western World* (1907). So his equivalent Meliboeus would rename Heaney as 'Honey'.

37 Synge studied Irish at Trinity College Dublin and was famously urged by Yeats to go and live on the Irish-speaking Aran Islands.

41ff. The poem this 'Poet' produces is an amalgam of Irish nature poems, including pieces that SH translated or composed himself; see *TSH*, 78–9. The poem at the end of 'Glanmore Eclogue' (*EL*, 37; *PSH*, 548–9) draws largely on Marie Heaney's *The Names Upon the Harp: Irish Myth and Legend* (1999) in which this poem begins with 'throaty blackbirds', a recurrent bird in SH's poetry.

Sonnets from Hellas

Sequence first published in full in the *Guardian Saturday Review* (7 April 2001): 8, and after collection in *EL* included in *NSP2014*.

1 INTO ARCADIA

First published in *Cara*, 31. 5 (Sept./Oct. 1998): 14, with two other uncollected sonnets, under the sequence title 'Sonnets from the Peloponnese', that included an author headnote (*PSH*, 1041). Included in the catalogue *University College Dublin, International Summer School 50th Anniversary* (July 1998): 8, and published, with 'Conkers' and 'Pylos', as 'Sonnets from Hellas' in *Mondogreco* (Fall 2000): 5–7. Later included in *100P*.

5 Hellas] the country *Cara*

Dated 5 October 1995 in MS; working titles for the sequence in TS 'Sonnets from the Peloponnese' and 'Sitings' (NLI 49,493/117).

Title *Arcadia*: ancient Greek province, associated with pastoralism and harmony.

5 *Hellas*: Greece; *Hesiod*: ancient Greek poet, c.750–650 BCE (see Fowler 2019, 38ff.).

7 *Argos*: city in the Peloponnese.

12 *goatherd*: definitive figure of the eclogue (bucolic).

2 CONKERS

First published in *Persephone* (Spring 1999): 36. Also published, with 'Into Arcadia' and 'Pylos', as 'Sonnets from Hellas' in *Mondogreco* (Fall 2000): 5–7. Earlier 'Conquerors' in archive.

11 Dimitri Hadzi (1921–2006), sculptor and photographer, was a friend of SH from Harvard. He and his wife, Cynthia, were with the Heaneys in Greece when SH's Nobel Prize was announced. They are the dedicatees of 'Mycenae Lookout' (*SL*, 37; *PSH*, 480).

3 PYLOS

First published under the title 'Mycenae' in *Persephone* (Spring 1999): 34. Also published, with 'Into Arcadia' and 'Conkers', as 'Sonnets from Hellas' in *Mondogreco* (Fall 2000): 5–7.

1 *Barbounia*: a sand-fish, the red mullet.

4 *Telemachos*: son of Odysseus in the *Odyssey*.

10 Robert Fitzgerald (1910–85), celebrated translator of Homer and Virgil, friend of SH at Harvard and his predecessor as Boylston Professor of Rhetoric there 1965–81; *Nestor*, king of Pylos, figure of venerable wisdom in Homer.

4 THE AUGEAN STABLES

First published in the *New Yorker* (20 March 2000): 66, and in *College Green* (September 2000): 6.

12 GAA] G.A.A. *New Yorker*
13 Horse-water] Horsewater *New Yorker*

Title The fifth of the twelve labours of Hercules was to clean the stables of Augeas, the mythical king of Elis, who had a vast herd of animals. Hercules did this by deflecting the course of the river Alpheus into the yard.

1ff. Athene shows Hercules where to make a breach in the bank, causing the river to flow through Augeas's yard.

10 *lustral*: by ceremonial purification.

11ff. Sean Brown, chairman of Wolfe Tone's GAA club in Bellaghy, was abducted while locking up the grounds at the end of the day on 12 May 1997, and murdered by members of the Loyalist Volunteer Force (see McKittrick 1999, 1407–8). SH was in Greece when he heard of Brown's murder, and on 14 May 1997 he faxed a letter to the Belfast *Irish News*, the leading nationalist paper in the North, to pay tribute to Brown as a friend, neighbour and community figure. The paper carried it on the front page, and it was much cited in other media outlets:

> Sean Brown's murder was shocking and sinister. I have known two generations of the Brown family. They are people of great probity, much respected in the Bellaghy district, so my heart goes out to them

at this moment. I heard the news in Olympia, just after I had visited the stadium where the original Olympic games were held, and given Sean Brown's role as chairman of the Gaelic Athletic Club in Bellaghy, I could not help thinking of his death as a crime against the ancient Olympic spirit.

    The Greeks recognised that there was something sacrosanct about the athletic ideal and regarded any violence during the period of the games as sacrilegious. Athletics and drama, two of the great civilising activities of Greece, were two of the activities which Sean Brown promoted, in his capacity as a lifelong member of the local Wolfe Tone's club. He was a man of integrity and good will, qualities which were manifest when he presided at an event organised in January last year to celebrate the award of the Nobel prize to this particular Bellaghy man. Many things were precious about that evening, including Sean's presentation to me of a painting of Lough Beg and the country around it, where we both grew up.

    But even more important was the fact that the celebration was attended by people from both sides of the Bellaghy community, Protestant and Catholic. He represented something better than we have grown used to, something not quite covered by the word 'reconciliation' because that word has become a policy word – official and public. This was more like a purification, a release from what the Greeks called the miasma, the stain of spilled blood. It is a terrible irony that a man who organised such an event should die at the hands of a sectarian killer.
(*Irish News*, 15 May 1997, 1)

In the poem, SH thinks of the water washing Brown's blood off the walls as the equivalent of the rivers Alpheus and Peneus washing the defilements from the walls of the Augean stables.

5 CASTALIAN SPRING

Published as a limited-edition broadsheet, *Castalian Spring / Loose for a Little While* by Pressed Wafer / Bow & Arrow Press (Boston), to celebrate the inaugural Stratis Haviaras Lecture which SH delivered at Harvard on 6 April 2000. 'Loose for a Little While' is a prose text by Haviaras dedicated to SH. Also published as 'Castilian Spring' [*sic*] in the combined issue of *Kenyon Review* (Spring 2001) and *Stand* (March 2001): 48.

Title The location in Delphi where the oracle was consulted and where the pilgrims washed before the consultation. Another source of poetic inspiration.

    1 *Thunderface*: a name for Zeus or Jupiter, as in 'Anything Can Happen' (*DC*, 13; *PSH*, 598). Here the obstructer is Juno, represented by the modern doorkeeper.

6 DESFINA

First published under the title 'Desfina: An Chailleach' in the combined issue of *Kenyon Review* (Spring 2001) and *Stand* (March 2001): 48–9.

Epigraph [no epigraph]] *Cailleach*: old woman, c. *feasa*: wise woman, fortune-teller *Kenyon Review*
2 Filiocht] Filíocht *Kenyon Review*
4 houmos] hoummos *Kenyon Review*

Title A mountain village near Delphi overlooking the gulf of Corinth. In modern times popular for its culinary prominence.

2 The Celtic places of poetic inspiration, corresponding to Parnassus: in Ireland, Bards' Mountain and Poetry Hill; and in Wales, Poems' Hill.

7 *cailleach*: Irish term often translated by the sexist term 'hag'; here her 'squeal' is a parody of the Delphic priestess.

11 The word 'hyperborean' is broken into its etymological components with an interruption by the term 'boozed', drunk. In linguistics 'tmesis', which means cutting: a device used humorously.

14 *boustrophedon*: written left to right and right to left in alternating lines: also associated by SH with the alternating progress of ploughing with horses.

The Gaeltacht

Published in *EL* and subsequently in the *London Magazine* (April/May 2001): 32, and later in a separate limited-edition broadside accompanied by *Land Link*, a mixed media image by the artist Eileen Ferguson, by the Keough Institute for Irish Studies to mark SH's reading at Dante's Cultures: Le Culture di Dante, University of Notre Dame, September 2003.

Title The term Gaeltacht refers to the parts of Ireland, mostly in the west, where Irish is still spoken as a mother tongue. The theme of the poem is the practice in the Irish Republic and Irish-teaching schools in Northern Ireland of sending schoolchildren – mostly of secondary-school age – to stay in the Gaeltacht for a period during school vacations to speak only Irish. Cf. 'The Stations of the West' (*Stations*, 22; *PSH*, 169). It was famously a context in which children of both sexes could mingle free of the supervision of their parents. However, the occasion recalled in this poem was while SH was a student at Queen's University Belfast in 1960. Working title in TS 'Rosguill'.

1 *mon vieux*: humorous address to 'my old friend', presumably one of the poem's students, now in adulthood.

2 *Rosguill*: in September 2013 the *Derry Journal* published a photograph taken at Ros Guill, West Donegal, which featured 'Seamus Heaney pictured with friends on a trip to the Donegal Gaeltacht at Easter 1960'. Identified in the picture was Peter Gallagher, who said in an article in the *Derry Journal* that he first met SH when they sat the entrance examination for St Columb's together, 'developing a friendship that carried them through school, Queen's University and Teacher Training college together'. Gallagher says: 'In 1960 I organised a trip to Ros Guill . . . We went for a week during the Easter holidays. Seamus came on the trip with his girlfriend at that time, Aoibheann Marren [*l*. 7], while I was accompanied by a girl called Margaret Conway [*l*. 7]' (who became Gallagher's wife). Among the people named in the poem and identified in the photograph in the *Derry Journal* is Vera Rafferty (called Chips after the archetypal Australian actor Chips Rafferty). The real names here anticipate the procedure of the next poem.

10ff. The Dante sonnet is 'Rime', LII to Guido Cavalcanti, beginning '*Guido, I' vorrei che tu e Lapo ed io / fossimo presi per incantamento / e messi in un vasel*' ('Guido, I wish that you and Lapo [Gianni] and I could be taken by magic and put in a boat') (Foster 1967, 30–1). The ladies who might accompany them are also named there: 'Vanna and Lagia' and a cryptic third 'who stands on number thirty'. The last is thought to be an associate for Dante. They are all to speak happily of love, as in all the early sonnets of Dante and his *stilnovisti* associates.

The Real Names

First published in the *Irish University Review* (Spring/Summer 1999), 1–5; then in *Threepenny Review* (Spring 2000), 34–5; *Around the Globe* (Summer 2000): 28–9; the *Times Educational Supplement* (16 June 2000): 21–2; and *Reader*, 8 (2000): 5–10. Collected with revisions in *EL*.

10 Shakespeare:] Shakespeare *Irish University Review* | Shakespeare. *Threepenny Review*
13 day-boy] dayboy *Irish University Review, Threepenny Review*
32] A CARRIER, with a lantern in his hand *Irish University Review* | A CARRIER, with a lantern in his hand *Threepenny Review*
34 Charles's Wain] Charles's Wain *Irish University Review*
52 *high style*] high style *Irish University Review*
61^62] [stanza break] *Irish University Review*
87 In] By *Irish University Review, Threepenny Review*
96 ' – Stood] 'Stood *Irish University Review*
104 oching] oching *Irish University Review*
112 *Princess Victoria*] Princess Victoria *Irish University Review*
116 airwaves [without full stop]] [all texts] (error?)
128 two to three] 2 to 3 *Irish University Review, Threepenny Review*

135 Bobby X] Bobby Sproule *Irish University Review*, *Threepenny Review*
137 *a little tiny boy*] a little tiny boy *Irish University Review*
143 (all but FESTE)] [All but FESTE] *Irish University Review*, *Threepenny Review*
145 *chameleon*] chameleon *Irish University Review*
146 Whos'-whoing] Who's whoing *Irish University Review*, *Threepenny Review*

Title One of the titles considered for *Electric Light*; an early draft appears in TS under the title 'Shakespeare'.

Dedication Brian Friel (1929–2015) was a prominent Northern Irish playwright and close friend of SH: the subject of 'A Call' (*SL*, 53; *PSH*, 494). Dedicatee also of *Station Island*, he dedicated his play *Volunteers* (1975) to SH.

1 *Owen Kelly*: schoolmate of SH in St Columb's, first named of the members of St Columb's Dramatic Society in which SH took an active part (as he had in local dramatics in Bellaghy); *gowling* (Scottish): grimacing.

7 *stour* (Ulster): dust disturbed by feet or wheels on floor or road (pronounced 'stu:r').

9 *Sperrins*: mountain range in Co. Tyrone and Co. Derry.

11 Caliban's speech to Stephano (*The Tempest*, 2.2.175).

12 *Miranda*: heroine of *The Tempest*.

19ff. Real names of schoolboy actors, and of the teacher-director Gallagher.

27 *Thane of Cawdor*: Macbeth, and his predecessor in that capacity.

29 The Porter is a celebrated comic character in Macbeth.

32 Shakespeare, *Henry IV, Part One*, 2.1: opening stage direction.

34 *Charles's Wain*: Charlemagne's waggon (Ursa Major); *over the new chimney*: the Carrier's time calculation for the morning.

43 *MacNicholl's* [sic] *chimney*: the neighbours' house along the road or across the fields from the Heaneys' in Mossbawn; the family spelling is McNicholl.

49 John Aubrey (1626–97): English writer of *Brief Lives*, short biographical pieces, including one of Shakespeare.

67 Gertrude's monologue describing the drowning of Ophelia (*Hamlet*, 4.7.166).

68 *sally tree*: term for willow in Ireland.

70 *Moyola*: the local river in SH's childhood, passing by the Broagh at the eastern end of Castledawson.

72 *glarry*: wet, muddy (Ulster). Cf. *glar* in 'Fosterling' (*ST*, 50; *PSH*, 426). From Donegal Irish, *glár*, silt.

73 *tetter-barked*: a skin disease, marked by white patches of eruption.

82f. Cast listing for *The Merchant of Venice*.

83 *Irwin*: fled St Columb's days after arriving there, like Launcelot Gobbo fleeing Shylock's house; *Bredin*: Hugh Bredin (1939–2024), later lecturer in Scholastic Philosophy at Queen's University Belfast, writer on Aquinas and Dante.

91 *Cassoni*: 'the Italian' suitable as Lorenzo (or indeed any Venetian role in the play).

95 'In such a night . . .': repeated phrase in *The Merchant of Venice*, 5.1.1ff.

96 'Stood Dido . . . banks': *The Merchant of Venice*, 5.1.12–13.

101ff. Duncan's horses, an image of a disordered world, briefly considered by SH as a book title for *EL*; *Macbeth*, 2.4.14ff.: 'And Duncan's horses (a thing most strange and certain), / Beauteous and swift, the minions of their race, / Turn'd wild in nature, broke their stalls, flung out, / Contending gainst obedience, as they would make / War with mankind.'

109 *volunteer*: an IRA member, injured in a raid.

112 *the Princess Victoria*: a car-ferry which operated from Stranraer to Larne and sank off the coast of Co. Down in a storm on 31 January 1953 with the loss of 135 lives.

113 Disasters like the unnatural behaviour of Duncan's horses: hence image 'broke from their stalls / and whinnied'.

117 *Romantic England live and well*: on the syntactic model of 'Romantic Ireland's dead and gone' in Yeats's 'September 1913' (Albright 1990, 159); *Twelfth Night*: Shakespeare comedy of 1601.

119–26 Feste is the witty 'clown' in the play, compared in *l.* 14 to the ESN ('educationally subnormal', in the brutal terminology of the time for children with special educational needs and disabilities) pupils taught by SH in class 1G at St Thomas's Secondary Intermediate School in Ballymurphy, Belfast, 1961–2.

121 More real names, here of Northern Irish friends of SH in London, where he had a holiday job in the Passport Office in the summer of 1962.

123 *scrumpy*: English cider.

125 *Café des Artistes*: probably the café of that name at 266a Fulham Road in South Kensington.

135 Bobby X was Bobby Sproule, taken by SH to the school clinic.

137 Feste's closing song, *Twelfth Night*, 5.1.389.

145 *chameleon*: the changed men remembered as boys, the 'boy-men'.

149 Ariel played by Phil Coulter (b.1942), later a highly successful songwriter, composer of 'The Town I Loved So Well' about the

damaging effects of the Troubles on Derry, the Eurovision-winning 'Puppet on a String' and other celebrated songs.

The Bookcase

First published under the title 'Books from Ireland' in *Honest Ulsterman*, 110 (Summer 2001): 34, and collected with revisions in *EL*.

4 shipshapeness] ship-shapeness *Honest Ulsterman*

A triptych of twelve-liners.
    7–8 *Collected Poems of Hugh MacDiarmid* (Edinburgh and London: Oliver and Boyd, 1962).
    9f. Elizabeth Bishop, *Selected Poems* (London: Chatto and Windus, 1967).
    10 *Murex*: Tyrian purple cover of *Collected Poems of W. B. Yeats* (New York: Macmillan, 1933; or probably 2nd edn, London: Macmillan, 1950).
    11 *Collected Poems of Thomas Hardy* (Macmillan, 1928).
    12 'Memory' in Yeats, *Collected Poems*, 168 (Albright 1990, 199). 'The Voice' in Hardy 1976, 346.
    14ff. *The Caedmon Treasury of Modern Poets Reading Their Own Poetry* (New York, n.d.): two long-playing records, featuring Robert Frost, Wallace Stevens, Dylan Thomas and others.
    16 Dylan Thomas's elegiac villanelle for his father, 'Do Not Go Gentle Into That Good Night', in *Collected Poems* (New York: New Directions, 1957), 128. 'Don't be going yet' is SH's Irish paraphrase of the poem. Thomas was thought to have died of alcoholism, but the post-mortem gave pneumonia as the primary cause of death: Bushmills is the most famous Northern Irish whiskey.
    23–4 Bede (673–735), *History of the English Church and People* (*c.*731).
    33 William Faulkner, *As I Lay Dying* (1930). Cash is the eldest son of Addie Bundren in the central family.
    37 Maurya is the bereaved mother of the family in J. M. Synge's *Riders to the Sea* (1904). She specifies the white boards (*l.* 38) that will make the coffin of her drowned son.

Vitruviana

The third section of the poem was first published in *Felim Egan: S. M. A. Cashiers*, 18, an exhibition catalogue of Egan's work for the Stedelijk Museum, Amsterdam (1999): [7], and later as an edition of 1,000 broadsides by Hieroglyph Editions (May 2003), accompanied by a watercolour by Egan.

The poem was first published in full in *Reader*, 8 (2000): 5–10, collected with revisions in *EL*, and later included in *NSP2014*.

Dated 22 January 1999 in a fax accompanying a revision of the poem (NLI 49,493/121).

Title Vitruvian Man: a drawing by Leonardo da Vinci, dated *c.*1490, inspired by the ancient Roman architect Vitruvius (first century BCE). The drawing superimposes a nude man on the same figure in a different posture, contained in both a circle and a square. One of the postures has 'both legs wide apart' (*l.* 3), the other with legs together. Again, 'both arms buoyant to the fingertips' correspond to the placing of the fingers in the drawing.

Dedication Felim Egan (1952–2020), an Irish abstract painter from Strabane, Co. Tyrone, was 'attracted to the vanishing point, the far-out place where the visible and the invisible meet'. After a year at the British School in Rome, he came back to Dublin where he lived in Sandymount near the Heaneys. SH wrote in 'A Catalogue Note' (NLI 49,493/117):

> When I think of Felim Egan's work, or rather of the intelligence behind it, I think of the lantern room at the top of a lighthouse, a place full of prisms and reflections, precise lines and symmetries, a Euclidean system; but then too I see something different, a seascape, the offing veiled in mist, the withheld commingling with the revealed, the actual scene that I too can contemplate from the top window of my house on Strand Road – a scene where the far-out solitary figure might just be the artist himself.

1 *Portstewart*: a seaside resort in Co. Derry, near Portrush (on the north Antrim coast).

9 The junior football pitch at St Columb's.

15ff. St Francis receiving the stigmata is a panel painting in tempera by Giotto, now in the Louvre but painted *c.*1300 for the Church of St Francis in Assisi.

18 Cf. T. S. Eliot, *The Waste Land* (*ll.* 300–2): 'On Margate Sands. / I can connect / Nothing with nothing.' Sandymount Strand is where SH lived.

Ten Glosses

The tenth gloss, 'A Norman Simile' was first published in the limited-edition *Norman MacCaig: A Celebration: Tributes from Writers in Honour of Norman MacCaig's 85th Birthday* (Chapman Publishing, 1995), 41. The fourth gloss, 'A Suit', was first published in *Poetry*, 171. 1 (Oct./Nov. 1997): 30. The third gloss ('The Bridge') was written as an untitled poem 'Steady under the strain and strong through tension' for the trilingual

Council of Europe publication *Écrire les frontières: le Pont de l'Europe – Grenzüberschreibung: Die Europabrücke* (1999): 65–7, then published as 'The Bridge' in *Forbes* (4 Oct. 1999): 95. The fourth, fifth and seventh glosses ('A Suit', 'The Party', 'The Lesson') were published in the *London Magazine*, 41. 1–2 (April/May 2001): 31–4. The sequence was first published in full in the *Guardian Saturday Review* (24 March 2001): 12.

1 THE MARCHING SEASON

Title The period in Northern Ireland when Orange marches take place, typically from April to October, though the marches in the first twelve days of July are the most prominent.

1 'What bloody man is this?' (*Macbeth*, 1.2.1); 'A drum, a drum' (*Macbeth*, 1.3.30).

2 THE CATECHISM

Title The Catholic method of religious instruction in schools by question and answer.

3 THE BRIDGE

Title Implication of bridging a gap between opposing parties.

4 A SUIT

Title Originally the first part of a trio of apparel poems called 'Three-Piece' (*Poetry*, 1997), where its last line appears in an earlier form (*PSH*, 505).

5 THE PARTY

3 Wilfred Owen (1893–1918). World War I poet, who composed most of his most celebrated poetry between August 1917 and November 1918. 'Mud in your eye' is an imprecation as a glass is raised to drink from.

6 W. H. AUDEN, 1907–73

A sketch of Auden's cosmopolitan life.

3 *po-ethics*: a compound of poetry and ethics as a resolution of the political poetry dilemma. Not Auden's term.

5 *the Danelaw*: the north-eastern area of England; Auden was born in York.

7 THE LESSON

A commonly told Irish joke: here to illustrate another kind of inter-community tension: Crumlin Road Jail was regarded with bitterness by the nationalist population.

1 David Hammond (1928–2008): prominent Northern Irish broadcaster and singer and close friend of SH. On the board of directors of Field Day. SH's elegy for him, 'The door was open and the house was dark' is in *HC*, 82 (*PSH*, 680).

8 MOLING'S GLOSS

There are various stories and legends about St Moling whose origin is in Leinster, and some of whose associations are with Suibhne Geilt (as in *SA*) in the seventh century. The story touched on here is that Moling was an aged hermit who impersonated Jesus descending from the Cross to a young nun who wanted to embrace him before she encountered him as her bridegroom in Paradise. He was later seen as a serious saint, the original of St Mullin in various places in Leinster. See *TSH*, 80.

9 COLLY

1 In the story of Niamh and Oisín, Oisín returns to Ireland from Tír na nÓg, from the Land of Youth, where he has been living for hundreds of years. Niamh lends him her horse and asks him to vow not to get off and touch the ground in Ireland; when he falls off the horse, he ages dramatically. This poem declares a preference for the down-to-earth horse Colly (an occasional horse name) with the imperfections and defilements of the everyday.

10 A NORMAN SIMILE

Dated 1995 in TS as 'A Norman Simile Culled for Norman MacCaig', corrected to 'Arklow Harbour' (NLI 49,493/113), before publication under the present title in celebration of MacCaig's eighty-fifth birthday. SH states that it was the first poem written after the Nobel Prize: 'The muses were instructing me, I thought, to be myself, not to go with public expectations of something oceanic and tidal and super-Nobelish, but to stay fresh and true to the old channels' (*SS*, 373).

2 Another appearance of the Norman historian Giraldus Cambrensis (*c.*1146–*c.*1223) who reports this phenomenon in his *Topografia Hibernica*; see 'Away from it All' (*SI*, 16; *PSH*, 292).

The Fragment

First published in the *Harvard Review*, 10 (Spring 1996): 12; then the *Irish Review*, 19 (Spring/Summer 1996): 108; and *Tabla*, 6 (April 1997): 5. Collected with revisions in *EL*.

1–12 [initial caps]] [sentence case] *Harvard Review, Irish Review, Tabla*
1, 5, 10 [indent]] [no indent] *Irish Review*
7–9]   namely, that his work had turned to fragments,
        that they weren't sure any more where they stood with him,
        that they recognized no first line or last line –
        he answered with a question. *Harvard Review*
8 that they could no longer be sure of where they were, *Irish Review* | that they were no longer be sure how they should take it *Tabla*
11 any] a *Harvard Review*

Translation of *Beowulf, ll.* 569ff., during Beowulf's response to the Danish king's spokesman Unferth (whose name might be translated as Discord). A working title in TS was 'The Old Scop' (NLI 49,493/117).

   2 *Bright guarantee of God*: '*beorht beacen godes*' in the original poem, one of the few occasions in *Beowulf* when the hero, rather than the poet, apparently refers to the Christian God.

   6 The objection of the listeners to Beowulf, which SH applies to the readers of poetry.

II

On His Work in the English Tongue

First published as 'On First Looking into Ted Hughes's "Birthday Letters"' in the *New Yorker* (5 Oct. 1998): 64–5; then as 'On a New Work in the English Tongue' in both the *Sunday Times* Books supplement (11 Oct. 1998): 7 and *LL*. Collected with revisions in *EL*.

dedication] [no dedication] *New Yorker, Sunday Times* | for Ted Hughes *LL*
1 5 griefs,] griefs *New Yorker, Sunday Times, LL*
2 3–4] [omitted] *New Yorker, Sunday Times, LL*
2 8 limen] limen *New Yorker, Sunday Times, LL*
2 9 rails on either side] railway lines *New Yorker, Sunday Times, LL*
2 10 fretful part of] railway child in *New Yorker, Sunday Times, LL*
2 11] Stepped in so deep in unshadowed apprehension *New Yorker, Sunday Times, LL*
3 2 Beowulf] 'Beowulf' *New Yorker* | Beowulf *Sunday Times*
3 4^5] [stanza break] *New Yorker*
3 6^7] [stanza break] *Sunday Times, LL*
3 7–16] And the poet draws from his word-hoard a parallel
         Story of balked love which I reword here,

> Remembering night-tremors once on Dartmoor
> Where three of us walked after dark and heard
> The power-station wailing in its pit
> Under the heath, as if Lear's breaking heart
> And Cordelia's breaking silence called to you
> Chooser of poem light, ploughshare of fields unsunned. *Sunday Times, LL*

3 8–9] Struck down, honor bound to exact / The death price from his own surviving son – *New Yorker*

3 10 word-hoard] word hoard *New Yorker*

4] 'It was like the misery endured by an old man
Who has lived to see the body of his son
Swing on the gallows. He begins to keen
And weep for his boy, watching the black raven
Gloat where he hangs: he can be of no help.
The wisdom of his years is worthless to him.
Morning after morning he wakes to remember
That his child has gone; he has no more interest
In living on until another heir
Is born in the hall, now that his first-born
Has departed through the door of death forever.
He gazes sorrowfully at his son's dwelling,
The banquet hall bereft of all delight,
The windswept hearthstone; the horsemen are sleeping,
The warriors under ground; what was is no more.
No tunes from the harp, no cheering in the yard.
Alone with his longing, he lies down on his bed
And sings a dirge, suddenly without joy
In his steadings and wide fields.
　　　　　　　　　Such were the woes
And pains of loss that the lord of the Geats endured
After Herebeald's* death. The king was helpless
To set to right the wrong that had been committed.'† *New Yorker, Sunday Times, LL*

　　* Herebeard's *Sunday Times* (error)　† committed . . .' *Sunday Times, LL*

5 3 aye] *aye New Yorker, Sunday Times, LL*

Dedication Ted Hughes (1930–98), Poet Laureate from 1984 until his death on 28 October 1998, was a close friend and associate of SH. SH's *Beowulf* and his poem 'Stern' (*DC*, 46; *PSH*, 613) were also dedicated in memory of Hughes.

　1 1 *Post-this* . . .: perhaps a disapproving reference to various theories of literary criticism: post-structuralist, etc.

　1 6 A tribute to the power of the English language, descended from Old English.

　2 1 *I read it quickly*: what was read was Hughes's *Birthday Letters*, about his life with Sylvia Plath, published by Faber in March 1998.

　3 1 'Passive suffering is not a theme for poetry.' W. B. Yeats, introduction to *Oxford Book of English Verse* (1936, xxxiv), on

which grounds he 'rejected' the inclusion of the poets of World War I, including Wilfred Owen, who is quoted by SH at the end of this section (*l. 16*).

3 5 *King Hrethel*: Beowulf's maternal grandfather, ultimately succeeded as king of the Geats by his youngest son Hygelac. Hrethel's second son Haethcyn accidentally kills his eldest brother Herebeald (*l. 6*); Hrethel's tragedy is that he cannot exact vengeance for the death of Herebeald because the killer was also his son (*Beowulf*, *ll.* 2430ff.). As elsewhere in this poem, there seems to be an implicit reference to the tragic death of Sylvia Plath and the part indirectly played in it by her husband Hughes.

3 16 Wilfred Owen, 'Strange Meeting' (*l. 4*): 'Yet also there encumbered sleepers groaned' – another example of a tragic conflict of interests as in the poem's famous closing, 'I am the enemy you killed, my friend' (*l. 40*).

4 *Beowulf, ll.* 2444–65. SH continues with the theme of Hrethel's tragedy with this episode, sometimes called 'The Father's Lament'.

5 4 *as Miłosz says*: Czesław Miłosz (1911–2004), Lithuanian-Polish poet and friend in the US of SH, who greatly revered him and spoke at his funeral in Krakow. He received the Nobel Prize in Literature in 1980.

Audenesque

First published in the *TLS* (9 Feb. 1996): 11; and in *Atlanta Review*, 2. 2 (1996): 22–3. Also published as a limited edition, accompanied by lithographs by Max Neumann, by Maeght in Paris (25 May 1998); in *LL*; and in Michael Horovitz (ed.), *Welcome Aboard the Poetry Olympics Party* (London: New Departures, 2000), 47–9. After collection in *EL* it was also included in *NSP2014*.

34] *Aquavit or uisquebaugh LL* uisquebaugh] uisequebaugh, *TLS*
59] You hijacked] Hijacked *TLS*, *Atlanta Review* | You'd hijacked *LL*

Title Written in the form used by Auden for the closing section of 'In Memory of W. B. Yeats', beginning 'Earth, receive an honoured guest; / William Yeats is laid to rest.'; so SH's poem is 'Audenesque', Auden-like.

Dedication Joseph Brodsky (1940–96), Russian poet and essayist born in Saint Petersburg, was expelled from the Soviet Union in 1972, after which he lived in the USA where he was championed by Auden, among others. He received the Nobel Prize in Literature in 1987. Brodsky was a close friend of SH, who attended his memorial service in New York in 1996.

6 *Yeats's anniversary*: Brodsky, like Yeats, died on 28 January.

11 *On Grief and Reason* (1995) was a collection of essays by Brodsky.

17 *cold*: Auden's Yeats elegy begins 'He disappeared in the dead of winter: / The brooks were frozen, the air-ports almost deserted'.

22 *Horatian ode*: in English, a poem of regular rhyme and metre, in two- or four-line stanzas.

27 *Ice like Dante's*: the lowest part of Dante's Inferno is a region of ice (canti 32, 33).

41 *In a train in Finland*: SH travelled with Brodsky by rail in September 1994 (*SS*, 378).

46 *Tampere*: city in Southern Finland, host of SH's event with Brodsky in September 1994, whose cathedral is famous for its macabre frescoes.

65 *Gilgamesh*: Sumerian epic, claimed to be the oldest epic in existence. Gilgamesh's ancestor Utanapishtim in Mesopotamian mythology anticipates Noah in being the chosen survivor of a universal flood. He tells Gilgamesh that the water turned the dust of people into clay.

To the Shade of Zbigniew Herbert

First published as 'A Hyperborean' in the *New Yorker* (18 Jan. 1999): 56, and as 'Hyperborean' in *LL*, before inclusion in revised form in *EL*, and collected in *NSP2014*.

dedication [no dedication]] *i.m. Zbigniew Herbert LL*
≤1]   Ruined temples. Poetry. Zbigniew Herbert,
       The inside of your head was a littered Delphi
       Where satellites and eagles sailed in orbit
       Above the god's besieged hill sanctuary
       And the oracle was the one thing still uncensored,
       The via sacra a via crucis partly
       And partly actual stone, the untransfigured
       Hill itself. You were a Hyperborean, *New Yorker, LL*
1] One of those at the back of the north wind *New Yorker, LL*
3 In the winter season] Every winter *LL*

Title Zbigniew Herbert (1924–98) was a Polish poet and moral essayist, born in Lviv in western Ukraine (which in 1924 was Lwów in Poland). As an opponent of communism and a supporter of the Solidarity movement he was prohibited from publication in Poland; he lived in several places in Western Europe until 1992 when he returned to Poland where he lived until his death. SH admired his moralistic poetry and explored this in the important essay 'Atlas of

Civilization', a review of works by Herbert and Miłosz, published in *Parnassus* in 1986 and collected in *GT* and *FK* (54–70; 153–67).

1 *those from the back of the north wind*: the legendary Hyperboreans again, explicit in the *New Yorker* and *LL* versions (cf. 'Out of the Bag', *EL*, 7; *PSH*, 528).

2 Apollo as god of the arts.

'Would They Had Stay'd'

Published privately as a Christmas card by the Gallery Press in 1997; then in Noel King (ed.), *Podium IV: An Anthology of Poetry from Samhlaíocht Chiarraí* (n.p.: Kerry Arts, 1999), 20; *Poetry Review* (Winter 1997/98): 7; and in *LL*. Collected with revisions in *EL*.

1 4^5] [stanza break] *LL*
1 5 I still can't –'] I still –' *Gallery*
1 7 Of course] Oh God *Gallery*
1 5] away.] away *Gallery*
1 10 agog] on hold *Gallery, LL*
2 6] [omitted] *Gallery, LL*
3 1–10] [omitted] *Gallery, LL*
5 4 a figured] Earl Rognvald's *Gallery*
5 5] [omitted] *Gallery*

Title *Macbeth*, 1.3.82: Macbeth's wish after the disappearance of the witches. Here an expression of sadness at the proximate deaths of various Scottish poets who were friends of SH and whom he admired.

1 2 Not yet named, but 'they' are either the deer in the deer park of Magdalen College, Oxford, where the Heaneys stayed regularly during SH's incumbency of the Oxford Poetry Chair, or deer seen in Scotland. SH was elected a Fellow of Magdalen in 1989.

2 1 Norman MacCaig (1910–96), Scottish poet and teacher. Friend of SH, to whom 'A Daylight Art' (*HL*, 10; *PSH*, 361) is dedicated.

2 2 *fritillary land*: the Magdalen deer park is noted for its rich crop of snake's head fritillaries in the spring.

3 2 *Iain MacGabhainn*: Iain Crichton-Smith (1928–98), Scottish poet and novelist who wrote in both Gaelic and English. Born in Glasgow, he grew up on the Isle of Lewis from the age of two.

3 4 'where the wind listeth' (John 3:8).

3 6ff. *Macbeth*, 1.3.81–2.

4 1 Sorley MacLean (1911–96), leading Scottish Gaelic poet born in Oskaig. His 'Hallaig' translated by SH (2002), beginning 'Time, the deer, is in Hallaig Wood' (*TSH*, 85–6).

5 1 George Mackay Brown (1921–96), Scottish poet from Stromness, Orkney. He visited SH in Belfast in 1968; SH wrote in the *Listener* 'I have never seen his poetry sufficiently praised'. Along with Ted Hughes and Christopher Fry, featured with SH in *Four Poets for St Magnus* (Orkney: Breckness Press, 1987). SH was one of the patrons of the George Mackay Brown Fellowship, and he wrote 'A Landfall' in his memory (*PSH*, 457).

Late in the Day

Published in *EL*.

This poem emerged from a TS 'Dialogue', where it was intertwined with lines that would become the TS poem 'Clang and Contour', to become its own independent poem (NLI 49,493/58); also in TS under the working title 'On the Pier in Nairn', which is corrected to the present title (NLI 49,493/117).

1 Sir William Wilde (1815–76), Irish ophthalmologist surgeon born in Castlerea, Co. Roscommon, who wrote widely on medicine and on the folklore and archaeology of Ireland. Father of Oscar Wilde and husband of 'Speranza', Jane Elgee (1821–96), who was a prominent Irish nationalist and folklorist. *The Beauties of the Boyne, and Its Tributary, the Blackwater* was published in 1849.

2 Clonard Abbey, early medieval monastery on the river Boyne in Co. Meath, reputedly founded by St Finnian who is perhaps a relocating of St Finnian of Movilla, who founded Movilla Abbey near present-day Newtownards, Co. Down.

10 David Thomson (1914–88), born in India to Scottish parents, BBC radio producer and friend of the Heaneys; author of *The People of the Sea* (1954) about the seals of the coast of Ireland and Scotland (*l.* 21), and of *The Leaping Hare* (1972) in collaboration with George Ewart Evans (father of Matthew Evans, the dedicatee of *EL*). But he is best known for three memoirs: *Woodbrook* (1974), *In Camden Town* (1983) and *Nairn in Darkness and Light* (1987), from which the details mentioned in the poem are taken (*ll.* 12–15).

14 *Dark-roomed*: at the age of eleven, Thomson sustained an eye injury which nearly blinded him and required him to have special schooling after a recuperative period spent with his grandmother in Nairn.

25 *Arion*: see next poem.

Arion

First published in Elaine Feinstein (ed.), *After Pushkin: Versions of the Poems of Alexander Sergeevich Pushkin* (London: Folio Society, 1999), 83; in the *TLS* (15 Oct. 1999): 28; and later in a separate limited edition, with a note on the Russian by Olga Carlisle, by the Arion Press, San Francisco (2002).

10 maelstrom:] maelstrom; *TLS*

Title Arion in Ancient Greece was a Dionysiac poet, attributed with the invention of the wild choral hymn, the dithyramb; in Herodotus' account he was saved from drowning by a dolphin. SH translates the poem by Pushkin (1799–1837) quite closely; the text in *EL* is a slightly revised version of an earlier, closer translation (see *TSH*, 70). Among this group of elegies, SH adopts the persona of Arion, the survivor of shipwreck. Where all others are drowned, the poem's first person is the sole survivor, still singing (*l*. 12).

Bodies and Souls

Parts 1 and 2 first published as separate poems under their respective titles in *Harvard Review*, 18 (Spring 2000): 6; 'Nights of '57' reprinted in the *New Yorker* (20 March 2000): 62. Part 3 'The Bereaved' first published in *EL*, where the three poems are collected under the title 'Bodies and Souls', the form in which it was included in *NSP2014*.

1 IN THE AFTERLIFE

Title The afterlife of doubtful privilege of the senior school students.

1 *Jim Logue*: this 'real name' was that of the caretaker at St Columb's, one of whose tasks was to sweep up the cut hair left behind by the school barber.

4 *Falling into step*: SH as a prefect or trusty who helped the caretaker on his rounds.

5 *Glimmerman*: term for inspectors who were employed to detect illicit use of gas in Ireland during World War II: here applied to the school employee who watched the activities of the school boarders.

2 NIGHTS OF '57.

In 1957, SH was in the sixth form at St Columb's and such senior students had various activities after night prayers, as described here. As he gets older, the memory of those physical activities bears down heavily on him.

6 *coolth*: unusual abstract noun derived from the adjective 'cool', as warmth is from 'warm', first found *c*.1500 but said to be commonest in the mid-twentieth century. Cf. 'Banks of a Canal' (*PSH*, 689): 'The coolth along the bank'.

3 THE BEREAVED

Title Bereft of normal freedoms, the student practising the piano is isolated within the unfriendly context of the four bare walls of the bleak practice room.

Clonmany to Ahascragh

Published in *EL*.

Working title in TS 'Weeping' (NLI 49,493/113, /115).
  Dedication Rory Kavanagh was the son of SH's great friends and supporters Des and Mary Kavanagh; he died at the age of twenty-five. Des Kavanagh is from Clonmany in the north-west of Co. Donegal and was a boarder with SH at St Columb's; Mary is from Ahascragh in east Galway.
  6ff. The falling of tears and rain reminds the poet of tracing a face in the condensation on the school windows at St Columb's in Derry where SH and Des Kavanagh were close friends from their first day together there.
  33 The river Ahascragh flows into the Suck, which is a tributary of the Shannon.

Sruth

First published in the *Sunday Times*, Books section 7 (30 March 1997): 2, and collected with revisions in *EL*.

Dedication] For Mary O Muirithe *Sunday Times*
4–6] [omitted] *Sunday Times*
7 *dishabills*] disabhills *Sunday Times*
12 air] air. *Sunday Times*
13–31] The day is a looking-glass
    Backed by a future,
    The *sruth* like its rush

    Reflected translated
    In a bum in a dream.
    You come to the stream

    That you'll ask me to visit
    Fifty years on –

If anything happens

Just to see and be sure
And not to forget
For your sake to do it.

Splash of clear water.
Things out in the open.
The *sruth* in your accent.

Of course I will do it.
And not forget what I've seen
On this visit to you:

Your neck-baring snowdrops
First-footing the morning,
Fit for what comes. *Sunday Times*

Title *sruth*: Irish for 'stream'.

Dedication Mary Ó Muirithe was the first wife of the Irish scholar Diarmaid Ó Muirithe. She died of cancer in 1998 (*l.* 24).

1 The 'bilingual race' refers to the speakers of Irish and English at Irish school-age summer schools, as attended by SH and by Mary, who was four years older than him.

3 *Errigal*: a 750-metre peak in Co. Donegal near Gweedore: one of the iconic geographical features in the north of Ireland.

7 *dishabills*: a colloquial version of the French word déshabillé (like negligée).

9 *guttural*: here an onomatopoeic term for the noise of the stream.

10 *Mountain and maiden*: perhaps an echo of the alliterative medieval Marian formula 'Mother and Maiden' ('I sing of a maiden / That is makeles').

13 *breac-Ghaeltacht*: the Gaeltacht is the place where Irish is spoken, often the location of summer schools; the Irish word *breac* means 'speckled' (as in Hugo Hamilton's novel *The Speckled People*). So a speckled Gaeltacht is one where Irish is intermingled with English.

Seeing the Sick

First published in the *Guardian Saturday Review* (24 March 2001): 12; and in the *London Magazine* (April/May 2001): 32–3. Later included in Joaquin Kuhn and Joseph J. Feeney, SJ (eds), *Hopkins Variations: Standing round a Waterfall* (Philadelphia and New York: Saint Joseph's University Press and Fordham University Press, 2002), 3–4.

17 year . . .] year *Guardian*

Title From Gerard Manley Hopkins's 'Felix Randal' (cf. *l.* 2): 'This seeing the sick endears them to us.'

   1 *Anointed and all*: Hopkins's poem says that the dead blacksmith was 'mended / Being anointed and all'.

   14 *bright and battering sandal*: 'Felix Randal' ends by recalling the dead blacksmith when he had his strength and 'Didst fettle for the great grey drayhorse his bright and battering sandal!'

   20 *A reprieving light*: *l.* 7 of 'Felix Randal' mentions 'our sweet reprieve and ransom' for the Sacrament of Extreme Unction administered by Hopkins as priest. The 'reprieving light' in SH's poem is the morphine which is tendered to deaden pain.

Electric Light

First published in the *New Yorker* (19 and 26 June 2000): 152–3; and as a limited edition by the Press at Colorado College to commemorate SH's reading of 16 April 2001. Collected with revisions in *EL* with *ll.* 16–30 included in *NSP2014*.

1–45] [sentence case] *New Yorker*
1 wick-soot . . .] wick-soot. *New Yorker*
2] Rucked alps from above. The smashed thumbnail. *New Yorker*
4 Rucked] moonlit *New Yorker*   littered] beached and littered *New Yorker*
10 stay, when I wept and wept] stay with her and wept *New Yorker*
13 sibilant] sorrowing *New Yorker*
14 far off] far-off *New Yorker*
17 Splashed] Splashes *New Yorker*
23 meat-safes] meat safes *New Yorker*
27 Gold.] Gold, *New Yorker*
28–9] tunnel gauntlet and horizon keep. To Southwark, / too, I came, from tube mouth into sunlight, *New Yorker*

SH never placed a title poem first or last in his twelve collections, with the exception of *EL*.

   4 The reference is to the Sibyl of Cumae, a figure of unfamiliar female venerability. Here the subject of the poem, the poet's grandmother, speaks cryptic 'sybilline English' (16).

   6 'She' is SH's maternal 'grandmother McCann' (*SS*, 27) who lived at New Row, Castledawson where SH stayed overnight with her on his first night away from home, identified in the poem as the first house where he saw electric light (*l.* 5). It contrasts with the 'candle-grease' and 'wick-soot' of the opening, a vestige of the previous source of light.

   12 '*What ails you?*': a common historic Irish synonym for 'what is the matter?', asked of children in the generation before SH's.

18 *Animula*: poem among the Ariel Poems (1936) of T. S. Eliot, beginning with 'the simple soul' issuing 'from the hand of God'. Here applied by SH to the start of the child's journey 'to a flat world of changing light and noise' ('Animula', *l.* 2), suited to the poem's topic.

27 The Field of the Cloth of Gold was a meeting between Henry VIII of England and Francis I of France, 5–24 of June 1520.

28 Recalling T. S. Eliot, *The Waste Land*, *l.* 307, 'To Carthage then I came', applied to Southwark as the location of Thomas Becket's last sermon before his murder in Canterbury Cathedral, and as the starting point of Chaucer's *Canterbury Tales*, the source of the 'straunge strondes' (*l.* 30; *Canterbury Tales*, 13). The straunge strondes are 'the foreign shores' sought by the palmeres travelling abroad like the growing speaker in this poem for whom the Thames is 'straunge'. (Strictly the Chaucerian singular should be 'straunge strond'.)

37 *Big Ben*: the clock of the Houses of Parliament in Westminster, rung to mark the hours of 6 p.m. and midnight during World War II.

39 The blackout marked the end of the day's BBC broadcast at the end of the News during World War II. Cf. 'the absolute speaker' in 'A Sofa in the Forties' (*SL*, 8; *PSH*, 467), announcing 'HERE IS THE NEWS'.

UNCOLLECTED POEMS (2001–2005)

After the tragic and elegiac tones of *The Spirit Level*, *Beowulf* and *Electric Light*, the uncollected poems in this group are dominated by the observation of celebratory occasions: the various domestic celebrations in *A Midsummer Feast* (2002), and the expansion of the European Union on 1 May 2004 ('Beacons at Bealtaine'). Even the elegiac pieces – for the demise of Yeats's Irish coinage and the memory of a last car trip with Robert Lowell – are light-hearted in contrast to their surrounding books.

Le Brocquy's *Táin*

Published in an exhibition catalogue for Louis le Brocquy's 'Aubusson Tapestries', 2–29 May 2001: Agnew's, Bond Street, London: [5].

Six tankas in honour of Louis le Brocquy (1916–2012), one of Ireland's foremost painters, who illustrated with brush drawings Thomas Kinsella's influential translation of *An Táin Bó Cuailnge* (Dublin: Dolmen, 1969), the pre-Christian Irish epic recounting the legendary battle of Queen Medb and the men of Connaught against Cú Chulainn.

The Snowball

Published in *Metre* (Autumn 2001): 95–6.

3 4 *the president*: the term for the headmaster at St Columb's.

A Present from Old Ardboe

Published in the *Cork Literary Review* (2001): 1.

14 Ardboe] Arboe *Cork Literary Review* (error)

Dedication For Paul Muldoon and Jean Hanff Korelitz (b.1961), to whom the poem was sent on 7 September 2001 (*LSH*, 558).

   3 *Deane*: Seamus Deane, fellow student of SH at both St Columb's and Queen's University Belfast.

   14 *Ardboe*: the *Cork Literary Review* spelling may conceivably be purposeful, reflecting the local pronunciation, rather than a typo. The homeplace of Marie Heaney.

In Memory of Bill Cole

First published in *The Brooklyn Rail* (Oct./Nov. 2001), and subsequently in Brendan Flynn (ed.), *Clifden 35: The Clifden Anthology* (Clifden: Clifden Community Arts Week, 2012), and subsequently as 'Bill Cole's LPs' in the *Irish Times* (30 Aug. 2014): 10, and in *Irish Pages*, 8. 2 (30 Aug. 2014): 9–10.

[text: *Brooklyn Rail*]

Title] Bill Cole's LPs *Irish Times, Irish Pages*
4 Of earthly love] Of loves they'd known and music and many a long *Irish Times, Irish Pages*
5 Afternoons] Long afternoon *Irish Times, Irish Pages*
7 Among] To meet *Irish Times, Irish Pages*
8 Meeting] Meeting again *Irish Times, Irish Pages*   paradise] paradise – *Irish Times, Irish Pages*
8^9] Not in his old off-Broadway Flat 6b, / His book grotto, his cove of revery, / Of trysts daydreamt while we replayed the LPs – *Irish Times, Irish Pages*
9 Where we'd never met on earth] But where we'd never meet *Irish Times, Irish Pages*
11 Rising to sing] Rising up there *Irish Times, Irish Pages*
13 Beg,] Beg. *Irish Times, Irish Pages*
14 River-rhyming] River rhyming *Irish Times, Irish Pages*
15 At heart again,] At heart, *Irish Times, Irish Pages*   song –] song. *Irish Times, Irish Pages*
16] [omitted] *Irish Times, Irish Pages*

William Rossa Cole (1919–2000) was a New York writer and editor, of whom SH wrote, 'I loved him and had some of my sweetest moments in his company.' He was a grandson of the nationalist leader Jeremiah O'Donovan Rossa. SH sent a draft of this poem to Cole's son, Williams Cole, on 29 September 2000, explaining: 'I woke this morning and had a vision of him by the banks of the River Moyola, and slipped into terza rima as easily as I slipped into a reverie many an afternoon in the armchair under the bookshelves. I send the lines with love from Marie and myself to you and Rossa and Galen and all the rest of the family and friends' (*LSH*, 542).

2 Dante's friend Casella, a musician from Florence or Pistoia, meets him in *Purgatorio*, 2, and sings to him a version of Dante's canzone 'Love that in my mind speaks to me'.

16 *Tir na n-Og*: the land of youth, representing the ease and light-heartedness of Cole.

For Alma Mater

Published first by Queen's University Belfast with the brochure distributed to guests on 8 November 2001, marking the launch of the Campaign for Queen's, and then, on 9 November 2001, in the *Irish News*.

A villanelle, tracing the stages of development in higher education.
  3 *Pro tanto quid retribuamus* (What shall we give back for so much?) is the motto of Belfast city.

A Keen for the Coins

First published as an untitled poem in Hans van de Waarsenburg (ed.), *Hotel Europa: 12 Europese dichters over de euro* ([Maastricht]: Gemeente Maastricht, 2001), 13, then in *Irish Pages*, 1. 1 (Summer 2002): 116, where it appeared with images of Carolyn Mulholland's accompanying bronze reliefs, of the poem in SH's hand, and of the coins the poem laments. The images are accompanied by the following text:

> The bronze collaboration with Seamus Heaney [. . .] marks the demise of Irish coinage, whose design was overseen, after independence, by W. B. Yeats in his capacity as a Senator in the Dáil. (117)

The poem was subsequently published as *A Keen for the Coins*, a limited edition by Lenoir-Rhyne College, Hickory, North Carolina, accompanied by illustrations by Todd Rivers, on 6 October 2002. This publication marked the opening of *Seamus Heaney's Ars Poetica*, an exhibition of Heaney rare books and manuscripts, at the Hickory Museum of Art.

[text: *Hotel Europa*]

2] O farthing wren!] O sixpence hound! *Irish Pages*
3] O woodcock! Piglets! Hare and bull! *Irish Pages*

In 1926 a Coinage Committee of five, chaired by Yeats, was appointed by the Irish Free State government. A competition to design the new coinage without the British monarch as figurehead was won by the English artist and sculptor Percy Metcalfe whose set of animal figures, as listed in the poem, were greatly admired, so their replacement by the new Euro coins on 1 January 2002 with an imaginative set of designs from ancient Irish art was not immediately popular. Hence SH's exuberant lament for the animal coinage.

A Snapshot

Published in *Midsummer Feast* (Oldham: Incline Press, 2002), 11, a limited edition to mark an extended family celebration centred on Cannwood

House, the home of Polly Devlin and her industrialist husband Andy Garnett, and the marriage of their daughter Rose in July 1999. The snapshot is of Andy in Paris on a shared visit there.

Sister Clare

Published in *Midsummer Feast*: 25.

Claire Devlin, the sister of Marie Heaney, declared her willingness to look after the Heaney children in Dublin for two weeks a year so that Marie could join SH in Boston. The thanks of the three children as well as their parents are expressed at the end of the poem.

Watercolour

Published in *Midsummer Feast*: 28.

Santiago de Compostela

Published in *Midsummer Feast*: 33, and in *Irish Pages*, 1. 1 (Summer 2002): 116.

[text: *Midsummer Feast*]

2 Square] square *Irish Pages*
6 Unfannable] unfannable *Irish Pages*

Dedication Anne is Marie Heaney's sister, Ann Devlin, and Ignacio is her Spanish husband. Visited on several occasions by the Heaneys.
    8 Capilla de las Ánimas (of the souls), church in Compostela dating from 1784.
    10 *Hotel of the Catholic Kings*: the Parador de Santiago de Compostela in the Plaza do Obradoiro next to the Cathedral, founded in 1499 as lodgings for pilgrims who had completed the pilgrimage of St James.

An Epithalamium

Published in *Midsummer Feast*: 35–7.

13^14] [stanza break indeterminate due to page break] *Midsummer Feast*

Written for the wedding of Polly Devlin's daughter, Rose Garnett, now a film production executive, to Tom Browne (whose acting name is Tom Fisher), 24 July 1999.
    4 *Hiberno-English*: usually applied to language but here because Rose's mother is Irish and Tom English.

6ff. Both Rose and Tom were involved with the theatre in England (the Cambridge Footlights and the Globe). The interference of Strobe lighting with American productions was a passing issue in the 1990s.

8 *Wooton-under-Edge*: Rose's childhood home in Gloucestershire; Old Ardboe was the home of her mother Polly.

9 *Tom Brown's Schooldays* was a novel by Thomas Hughes (1857), set in the English public school Rugby in the 1830s, no doubt just suggested to SH by Tom's name; *Stratford-atte-Bowe*: the setting-off point in Chaucer's *Canterbury Tales*.

13 *Popean grotto*: the grotto (1720–5) is the last surviving structure from Alexander Pope's villa and gardens in Twickenham, south-west London, after the house was demolished and the grounds overhauled in 1808. Yeats's Tower is at Ballylee, Co. Galway.

15 In *Julius Caesar*, Mark Antony says over Caesar's body that he has 'come to bury Caesar, not to praise him' (3.2.74).

19 *honi soit qui mal y pense*: 'shame on anyone who thinks ill of it': the motto of the Order of the Garter, founded by Edward III in 1348.

20 *peacocks' feathers*: thinking of SH's poem written in 1972 for Rose's sister Daisy (*HL*, 40–1; *PSH*, 376).

23 A reference to the song 'Slieve Gallon's Brae': 'thinking of your flowers all a-going to decay' (see *PSH*, 109).

27 *Polly and Andy*: Rose's parents, who were married in Tuscany.

31 *this Somerset*: where the wedding party is taking place at Cannwood House (*l.* 50).

35–6 'All the world's a field': the Shakespearean 'all the world's a stage' (*As You Like It*, 2.7.139: cf. *l.* 33, and Arden, the pastoral setting of the play in *l.* 37), changed to the West Country setting of Piers Plowman.

51 *Pookie*: Rose's dog.

The Big Wiper

Published in *The Worcester Review* (2002): 47.

Sophoclean

Published in Matthew Hollis and Paul Keegan (eds), *101 Poems Against War* (London: Faber & Faber, 2003), 15, and in the *New Yorker* (3 March 2003): 78.

[text: *101 Poems Against War*]

1 skins,] skins *New Yorker*
3 mast] mast, *New Yorker*

13 'Man is the measure of all things', ascribed to the fifth-century pre-Socratic philosopher Protagoras. The poem is a condensed history of man and his propensity for war.

Pit Stop Near Castletown

Published in *Agni*, 57 (2003): 4–5. Subsequently reprinted in *Irish Pages*, 3. 1 (Spring/Summer 2005): 30–1.

[text: *Agni*]

Title Pit Stop] Pit-Stop *Irish Pages*
13 Stiffly] Level *Irish Pages*
16–17 at your / Memorial service later on that autumn] two months later, / At your memorial arranged by Caroline *Irish Pages*

Describing one of SH's last meetings with Robert Lowell shortly before his death in 1977. Lowell was called Cal (*l.* 16) from his teenage years, perhaps drawing on the name of a tyrannical Emperor Caligula or a Shakespearean monster Caliban.

    12 It seems a strange moment for Lowell to tell SH such a momentous thing – that he is going to leave his wife Caroline Blackwood.

    14–15 P. B. Shelley, 'Ode to the West Wind', *l.* 3.

    22ff. Mary McCarthy (1912–89), American writer, critic and vigorous political commentator.

The Comet at Lullwater

Published as a broadside by Emory University, 23 September 2003, to mark the conclusion of Dr William M. Chace's tenure as president of the university, and the acquisition of the Seamus Heaney papers by Emory's Robert W. Woodruff Library.

The comet Hale–Bopp was watched by SH with William and JoAn Chace at the Emory president's home in 1997.

    12 *Christy Mahon*: hero of Synge's *Playboy of the Western World* (1907), an innocent who finds the world a wonder: often alluded to by SH.

Beacons at Bealtaine

This poem was delivered at the EU Enlargement Ceremony in the Phoenix Park, Dublin, on 1 May 2004, during Ireland's presidency of the European Union, and published in the commemorative programme produced for the occasion, *The Day of Welcomes* (Dublin: European Union, 2004). It was accompanied by the following introduction by SH:

> In the Celtic calendar that once regulated the seasons in many parts of Europe, May Day, known in Irish as *Bealtaine*, was the feast of bright fire, the first of summer, one of the four great quarter days of the year. The early Irish *Leabhar Gabhála* (*The Book of Invasions*), tells us that the first magical inhabitants of the country, the *Tuatha Dé Danaan*, arrived on the feast of Bealtaine, and a ninth century text indicates that on the same day the druids drove flocks out to pasture between two bonfires. So there is something auspicious about the fact that a new flocking together of the old European nations happens on this day of mythic arrival in Ireland; and it is even more auspicious that we celebrate it in a park named after the mythic bird that represents the possibility of ongoing renewal. But there are those who say that the name Phoenix Park is derived from the Irish words, *fionn uisce*, meaning 'clear water' and that coincidence of language gave me the idea for this poem. It's what the poet Horace might have called a *carmen sæculare*, a poem to salute and celebrate an historic turn in the *sæculum*, the age.

It was also published online, on the website of Ireland's EU presidency. The poem was subsequently published in the Dublin *Sunday Independent*, *Sunday Tribune* (both 2 May 2004) and *Irish Times* (3 May 2004): 8, *Irish Pages* (Autumn/Winter 2004): 99, and later in Pat Boran and Gerard Smyth (eds), *If Ever You Go: A Map of Dublin in Poetry and Song* (Dublin: Dedalus, 2014), 94.

An Iridescence

Published in John Burningham (ed.), *When We Were Young: A Compendium of Childhood* (London: Bloomsbury, 2004), 11, with an accompanying note from the author (11):

> I was late on the scene. What I remember are smashed bushes and cut up ground, the bark skinned off the thorn trees and bits of trampled down chocolate everywhere. Rain had fallen, adding melancholy to the mystery. It was only a hole in the hedge but it could have been an entrance to the underworld. When I came to recall it in a sonnet, I wanted to keep the actuality of Cadbury's 'trademark purple', although the scene had the aura of a place where (in the words of Patrick Kavanagh) 'some strange thing had happened'.

2, 4 *Duggan's*: in private correspondence with the editors, Eugene Kielt has located Dougan's Hill in Anahorish, on the Hillhead Road, about a mile from Mossbawn heading towards Toome. The Duggan family moved to Anahorish from the nearby parish of Lavey in the 1920s, and the spelling of their name was changed to Dougan, possibly when the children began attending Anahorish School. Kielt suggests that SH would have been aware of this change in the spelling of the family's name, and some among the older generations of the family continue to pronounce the name as 'Duggan' rather than 'Dougan'. The incident described in the poem is still recalled in the Dougan family.

Confirmation Day

First published as part 2 of 'Out of This World', in *Agni*, 61 (April 2005): 227, but excluded when the poem was collected in *DC* (*DC*, 47–51; *PSH*, 614). Subsequently reprinted in Brian Doyle (ed.), *The Best Catholic Writing* (Chicago: Loyola Press, 2006), 109.

[text: *Agni*]

After Dark

Published in *Irish Pages* (Spring/Summer 2005): 32.

Lauds and Gauds for a Laureate

Published in *Ars Interpres*, 4 and 5 (Oct. 2005). Subsequently in the *London Magazine* (Aug./Sept. 2007): 67–70.

[text: *Ars Interpres*]

Written for a celebration of Joseph Brodsky that took place at the American Repertory Theater, Cambridge, Massachusetts, 15 February 1988. Brodsky was awarded the Nobel Prize in Literature in 1987.

DISTRICT AND CIRCLE (2006)

District and Circle was published in London by Faber & Faber in 10,000 hardback copies on 6 April 2006 and in 10,000 paperback copies on 5 October 2006, and in New York by Farrar, Straus and Giroux in hardback on 30 May 2006 and in paperback on 4 April 2007. It came at a point of extraordinary activity in SH's life and work. Since *Electric Light* in 2001, he had travelled widely – to Prague, Lithuania and Russia, as well as to Greece twice and to Spain, Denmark, Italy and Hong Kong, and to South Africa; and he was awarded the prestigious Golden Wreath at Struga in what is now North Macedonia (a return to the scene of the 1978 festival that was commemorated in 'Known World' in *EL*, 19; *PSH*, 536). He was also very productive in publication. *Finders Keepers: Selected Prose 1971–2001*, the successor to *Preoccupations* (1980), had appeared in London from Faber & Faber in hardback on 8 April 2002 (paperback 7 April 2003), and in New York in hardback on 26 June 2002 (paperback 16 April 2003). *The Burial at Thebes*, the second of SH's dramatic adaptations from Sophocles, *Antigone*, had been published in London by Faber & Faber in hardback on 4 March 2004 (paperback 17 March 2005), and in New York by Farrar, Straus and Giroux in hardback on 3 November 2004 (paperback 13 October 2005) (see *TSH* 376–421; 614–22). In 2007, the Gallery Press published *The Riverbank Field* in an edition limited to 500 hand-numbered copies, signed by the author, which was to be an important part of his final Faber volume, *Human Chain*, in 2010. It is hard not to link the stroke he suffered later in 2006 to this tireless level of activity, especially travel. In any case, physical health made SH limit his public undertakings for the next twelve months.

In July 2005, SH described *District and Circle* to a Faroese journalist in the clear-sighted terms:

> I try to use memories of a childhood spent far from the horrors of World War II as a way into the eerie new conditions of our menaced twenty-first century where most of us live far from the danger yet are still haunted by a feeling that 'anything can happen'. And then there's a movement where the theme is renewal, at a personal and general level. I suppose the volume is about standing one's ground and gaining refreshment in the process, about the resolution and independence that can come from recollection and dash and even from the experience of loss. (FF N50)

Despite such understanding of the content, SH had struggled to identify a title for the collection. 'Works and Days' is a working title page for the collection held in the National Library of Ireland (NLI 49,493/126). Another, 'Midnight Anvil', had been rejected, SH told Rand Brandes, in case it was inadvertently seen to be 'approving of the manifest deadliness' of Western reprisal attacks in Afghanistan and Iraq (Brandes 2009, 33–4). 'Planting the Alder' had been the leading contender until it was discarded as 'a bit too beautiful'; it was replaced with 'District and Circle' on 19 May 2005 ('And I have my own district which I've been circling for a while now,' *LSH*, 635). By 3 July, SH had reverted to a simplified 'Alder', but, later that same month, confided to his publishers of 'an ongoing uncertainty' as to what the volume might be called. '*Alder* is still workable. I also thought of *Breard*, and then, having inserted the word "braiding" in "Súgán", I wondered about *Braid*. And then there's always *Saw Music*' (27 July 2005, FF N50). Sure enough, 'Saw Music' replaces a crossed-out 'Alder' on yet another title page in the National Library of Ireland (NLI 49,493/126), although it would not last for long. By August, SH had alighted on *Braird* ('I had thought of *New Braird* as another possible title – since "braird" is in the *OED* as "the first shoots of grass, corn, or other crops"'), and told his publisher that this was the title that he felt committed to, 'for better or worse' (3 May and 3 Aug. 2005, FF N50).

It was not until 22 August that he returned to the title 'District and Circle'. The wording recalled the summer of 1962 in which SH had commuted daily on the District Line on the London Underground ('taking the Green Line every day from Earls Court to St James's Park', *SS*, 418), and it now 'seemed right for a collection that returned to places and preoccupations to be found in my earlier books' (*PBS Bulletin*, 189). However, the terrorist attacks of 7 July 2005 in London would apply doubts of a moral nature onto those existing of a literary kind. Four devices were detonated across central London on 7/7: three on the Underground, and one on a double-decker bus; fifty-two people were killed. SH confessed that he 'hesitated' in his use of the title in the wake of the bombings (*LSH*, 637), until he came to see his moral uncertainties as something emblematic that had to be embraced.

> By that time, I had already written poems that took cognizance of September 11 2001 and all that it entailed. The subject matter of those poems belonged in a world far removed from Ground Zero, falling bombs and insurgent bombers, yet it was coloured by a darkened understanding. A wielded sledgehammer, a cold bladed turnip cutter, a memory of American troops in battledress on the byroads of Co. Derry

– these things bore for me 'the heavy trappings of inner necessity' (to use a phrase of Susan Sontag's), but they also seemed capable of bearing the brunt of present realities. (*PBS Bulletin*, 189)

It took the arrival of a poem featuring the Tollund Man, 'my old soul-guide' from the Jutland bogs of *Wintering Out*, to restore what SH called 'a renewed trust in the lyric *qua* lyric', and so construct a literary form sturdy enough to withstand those present realities.

District and Circle was immediately well received, and it won the T. S. Eliot Prize and the *Irish Times* Poetry Now Award. It was the Choice of the Poetry Book Society Summer 2006, and sold, in the author's lifetime, 40,000 hardback and 34,000 paperback copies. Many reviewers interpreted the title as suggesting a return to the home district after moving out from it. Brad Leithauser's review in the *New York Times* was representative, saying that the book 'plays rich variations on old themes', turning again to the world of agricultural implements, albeit sometimes in an arcane language.

The book's dedication to Ann Saddlemyer makes a link to *Electric Light* by quoting the lines written for her in 'Glanmore Eclogue' (*EL*, 35; *PSH*, 547). But *District and Circle* quickly establishes its own theme of physical solidity in the snedder (pulper or mangler), sledgehammer and railway sleepers of its opening poems. These are followed by a series of poems about distant conflicts: the passing through Northern Ireland of American soldiers in World War II, and the attacks on the Twin Towers which, like the moment of the millennium, happened too late for any allusion in *Electric Light*. Northern Irish sensitivities are delicately revisited in poems like 'The Nod', and the five-sonnet title poem brings the source district and the outside world together again as the poet sees in his reflection in a Tube train window the face of his father. 'The Birch Grove' near the end of the book ends with a definite declaration by SH's friend Bernard McCabe, which SH has attributed elsewhere to Joseph Brodsky's Nobel acceptance speech, 'If art teaches us anything . . . it's that the human condition is private.'* Translation is felt through Latin, German and Irish, and would also have embraced French, had SH included the version of René Char's 'L'Adolescent Soufflété' that he entitled 'The Playground' in an unpublished draft of 27 February 2005 (NLI 49,493/131–2), and which he briefly proposed as an addition to a TS in August 2005 TS (FF N50). The closing poem, 'The Blackbird of Glanmore', decisively revisits the earlier work, recalling both 'The Blackbird of Belfast Lough', the

---

* Joseph Brodsky, Nobel Lecture, 8 December 1987: 'If art teaches anything (to the artist, in the first place), it is the privateness of the human condition' (translated for the Nobel Prize from the Russian by Barry Rubin).

anonymous ninth-century Irish poem SH had first translated in 1980 (*TSH*, 9, 537–9n), and the poet's dead child-brother of 'Mid-Term Break' in an emotional return prompted by the ominous remark of a neighbour who reveals, 'I never liked yon bird.' Here the poet says it is the blackbird's 'picky, nervy goldbeak' that he loves as it recalls the young brother 'cavorting through the yard'. The crucial reversion is to the lines that SH translated from Sophocles in *The Cure at Troy*:

> 'I want away
> To the house of death, to my father
>
> Under the low clay roof.' (*CT*, 64; *TSH*, 241)

It is a wish that is kept in the poet's mind while he is translating *Aeneid*, 6 throughout these years, centring on Aeneas's journey to the afterlife in search of his father Anchises. The complete translation would be published posthumously in 2016.

[text: *DC2006*]

Dedication Ann Saddlemyer, Canadian scholar and biographer of George Yeats, let her house – a gate lodge of the Synge Glanmore Estate in Co. Wicklow – in 1972 to the Heaneys at a modest rent and finally sold it to them in 1988. The dedication quotes SH's own lines in praise of her from 'Glanmore Eclogue' (*EL*, 35; *PSH*, 547), calling her Augusta because that was the name of Yeats's patron Lady Gregory.

The Turnip-Snedder

First published in the *New Yorker* (20 March 2006). Collected with revisions in *DC*.

4 double-flywheeled water-pump] double flywheeled water pump *New Yorker*
16 turnip-heads] turnip heads *New Yorker*
18 turnip-cycle] turnip cycle *New Yorker*

Originally envisioned as a middle-order poem within the collection, SH promoted 'The Turnip-Snedder' to becoming the opening piece after delivery of his typescript to Faber & Faber (FF N50).

   Title Snedder was a local term for the farmyard implement elsewhere called 'turnip-mangler' or 'pulper'. The more usual term 'mangle' is used in 'Electric Light', *l*. 23 (*EL*, 81).
   Dedication Hughie O'Donoghue (b.1953), a Manchester-born painter, who lives and works in London and Erris, Co. Mayo, was the illustrator of SH's *Testament of Cresseid*.

12 *greaves*: the cast-iron legs of the snedder, by analogy with the pieces of metal armour that protected the legs (from French *grève*).

14 *seedling-braird*: the first shoots of grass or corn. The term 'braird' reappears in the first line of 'The Lift'.

A Shiver

Published in the *New Yorker* (25 Oct. 2004) and subsequently in *A Shiver* (Thame: Clutag Press, 2005), in a limited printing of 200 copies. Collected with revisions in *DC* and later in *NSP2014*.

3 testudo] testudo *New Yorker*
6 club-footed] clubfooted *New Yorker*
9 fly:] fly – *New Yorker*
11 Withholdable] Witholdable *A Shiver* (error)

3 *testudo*: Roman shield-wall in which straight-edged shields were held side by side to form a wall or above the soldiers' heads as a defensive roof. The Latin word means *tortoise*, to indicate its shell-like toughness.

Polish Sleepers

Published in the *New Yorker* (17 Jan. 2005). Collected with revisions in *DC*.

1 criss-cross] crisscross *New Yorker*
4 half-skirting, half-stockade] half skirting, half stockade *New Yorker*
5 ground-cover] ground cover *New Yorker*
7–13] Our gravel darkened and a tarry pus,
   Imagined yet pervasive, reeked and ran
   Like the breathing, bleeding bad in Dante's wood,
   Unsettling, bearing forward to the garden
   What I couldn't hear in the forties when I lay
   Listening for that might come down the line . . .
   Each deadlit, boarded, languid, clanking wagon. *New Yorker*

Title Sleepers are the large rectangular wooden planks on which railway lines were laid, creosoted to delay rotting in the wet.

12 *Castledawson*: the nearest village to SH's home farm Mossbawn, near Magherafelt, Co. Derry. SH's maternal grandparents lived in New Row, Castledawson.

Anahorish 1944

First published under the title 'Testimony' in the *Irish Times* (16 March 2002): 9; the *Guardian Review* (15 Feb. 2003): B36; and *101 Poems Against War* (London: Faber & Faber, 3 March 2003): 113. Also published as 'Testimonies', a limited-edition broadside by Shari DeGraw and Nicole Flores at the University of Iowa Center for the Book, to mark SH's receipt of the Truman Capote Award on 25 September 2003, and in *A Shiver*. After collection with revisions (including the adoption of the present title) in *DC* it was reprinted in the *Irish Times* (16 Jan. 2007) and also included in *NSP2014* and *100P*.

Title] Testimony *Irish Times, Guardian, 101 Poems Against War* | Testimony: Anahorish 1944 *A Shiver*
1–13] [no inverted commas] *Irish Times*
1 Americans] Yanks *Irish Times, Guardian, 101 Poems Against War*
3 slaughterhouse] slaughter house *A Shiver*
4 squealing] screaming *Irish Times, Guardian, 101 Poems Against War, A Shiver*
9 Unknown, unnamed] Unnamed, in step *Irish Times, Guardian, 101 Poems Against War*
10^11] [stanza break] *Irish Times*

Title SH attended Anahorish Primary School from 1944 to 1951, location of the poem 'Anahorish' in *Wintering Out*. In 1944, American forces of the 82nd Airborne Division were stationed at Creagh (pronounced 'crake'), near Mossbawn ('The Aerodrome', *l*. 3, *DC*, 11; *PSH*, 597).

1ff. *We*: the notional speakers are the workers in a local abattoir who, SH tells Dennis O'Driscoll, 'are tuned to an Ulsterese register' (*SS*, 365). 'In the Beech' (*SI*, 100; *PSH*, 338) records the young poet watching the arriving soldiers from a perch in a beech tree (*SS*, 264).

8 *Armoured cars and tanks and open jeeps*: recalls 'Armoured cars and tanks and guns / Came to take away our sons', the opening lines of the rebel song 'The Men Behind the Wire', composed by Paddy McGuigan of the folk group the Barleycorn in the wake of Operation Demetrius. It spent three weeks at number 1 in the Irish charts in early 1972, and was quickly covered by the Wolfe Tones, Liam Clancy, and others.

12 *like youngsters*: it is left open whether this applies to the young airmen or to the aproned workers or both.

To Mick Joyce in Heaven

Published in *DC*.

Dated 6 March 2005 in MS (NLI 49,493/131). The poem consists of five sonnets in a short-lined, driving dactylic rhythm.

Title Mick Joyce is identified in *Stepping Stones* (256) as SH's uncle-in-law (*l*. 4 here) from Cork, the husband of SH's father's sister Susan. He had been in the North African desert campaign as a medical orderly. He has also appeared in 'Damson' (*SL*, 15–16; *PSH*, 472).

The Aerodrome

First published in *Salmagundi* (Fall 2005–Winter 2006): 98–9, and subsequently in *A Shiver*. Collected in *DC*.

4 rebuilt] blanched *Salmagundi, A Shiver*
5 CEO-style] CEO style *Salmagundi, A Shiver*
6^7]   Barn Loaning, name and laneway,
       Disappeared. And the meadows too
       Where no man need appear who couldn't mow
       His acre between dawn and dailigone. *Salmagundi, A Shiver*
7] Hangars, bomb stores, nissen huts, the line *Salmagundi, A Shiver*
8 The perimeter] Of perimeter *Salmagundi, A Shiver*
9 a smell] the smell *Salmagundi, A Shiver*
11 away that afternoon] away, *Salmagundi, A Shiver*
21 perimeter.] perimeter *Salmagundi* | perimeter, *A Shiver*
21^2]   Snapped in black and white, a torn print,
        As if the sky were riven, as if already
        The light itself could no longer be trusted. *Salmagundi, A Shiver*
22 then like] then came like *Salmagundi*
25] With the airman under his nose-up Thunderbolt *Salmagundi, A Shiver*
25^6] Offering her a free seat in his cockpit? *Salmagundi, A Shiver*
28 mine] my hand *Salmagundi, A Shiver*

Title The aerodrome at Creagh, Toomebridge, where the American airmen mentioned in 'Anahorish 1944' (*DC*, 7; *PSH*, 594) were quartered; the poem shares the location with an unpublished archive poem, 'Toome Aerodrome: 1943' (HFC).

4 *control tower*: especially in the context of World War II, the phrase has perhaps a suggestion of the concentration camps. It also carries connotations of the British Army watchtowers installed for surveillance in Northern Ireland, most notably in south Co. Armagh, during the Troubles.

5 *CEO-style villa*: a grandiose modern house such as a chief executive officer might aspire to.

11 *1944*: recalling the subject of 'Anahorish 1944' (*DC*, 7; *PSH*, 594). On Easter Monday 1944, the child recalls going there rather than to the more entertaining fair at Toome (two miles away).

18 *B26 Marauders*: American World War II bombers.

19 Presumably a compulsory order applying to Northern Ireland during the war.

20 *her*: whoever the child had to go to the airfield with rather than to the Toome fair, most likely the poet's mother or one of his aunts.

25 *Thunderbolt*: another US fighter plane in World War II, the P-47, whose pilot calls to the woman: the child wonders if this is a

possible proposition, explicitly in an additional line from the pre-*DC* printings of the poem: 'Offering her a free seat in his cockpit?'

Anything Can Happen

First published under the title 'Horace and the Thunder' in the *Irish Times Weekend* magazine (17 Nov. 2001): 10, 'in the aftermath of the September 11 attacks'; then in the *TLS* (18 Jan. 2002): 40; *Translation Ireland* (Spring 2002): 8–11; *Irish Pages* (Autumn/Winter 2002/2003): 54, and as *Horace and the Thunder*, a broadside limited to twenty-six copies to mark SH's reading at MIT, Cambridge, Mass., 17 October 2002. Subsequently as *Anything Can Happen: A Poem and Essay by Seamus Heaney with Translations in Support of Art for Amnesty* (Dublin: Townhouse, THCH, 2004), 8. Collected with revisions in *DC* and later included in *NSP2014* and *100P*.

4 thunder cart] thunder-cart *Irish Times, Irish Pages*
8 towers] things *Irish Times, TLS, Irish Pages*
10 regarded] esteemed *Irish Times, TLS*   Stropped-beak] Hooked-beak *TLS*
11 the crest off one,] off *Irish Times, TLS*
12] Crests for sport, letting them drop wherever. *Irish Times, TLS*
14 kettle-lid.] kettle lid, *Irish Times, TLS,* | kettle lid. *Irish Pages*
16 boil away] darken day *TLS, Irish Pages*

Dated to Bernard and Jane, 29 September 2001, Bologna, in MS under the title 'Horace, Odes, I, 34' (NLI 49,602/32).

Title Previously published as 'Horace and the Thunder', a manuscript draft has the title 'Out of the Blue' (NLI 49,602/32). For a detailed history of the text of the poem, see *TSH*, 599–601.

Epigraph SH's poem is a fairly free translation of stanzas 2 and 3 (roughly *ll*. 5–12) of Horace's *Odes* 1.34, omitting the first stanza, which questions Horace's earlier Epicurean materialist beliefs and returns to regard for the gods, and adding a new stanza at the end (*DC, ll*. 13–16).

1 *Anything can happen*: representing Horace's *valet deus* (roughly 'God prevails'); *Jupiter*: Diespiter ('Day-father') in Horace (*l*. 5), which is an alternative name for Jupiter.

10 *stropped-beaked*: sharp-beaked, like a razor sharpened by a leather strop; hence wounding. Horace '*cum stridore acuto*' (*l*. 15), 'with sharp screech'.

14 *Atlas*: the Titan required to hold up the heavens (taking the place of Fortuna in Horace, *l*. 15). The Atlantic (*l*. 7; Horace, *l*. 11) is derived from the Sea of Atlas.

Helmet

First published in the *New York Review of Books* (25 Sept. 2003): 52; subsequently in *A Shiver*. Collected with revisions in *DC* and later included in *100P*.

3 brim.] brim, *NYRB*, *A Shiver*
8 Leather-trimmed, steel-ridged] Steel ridge, leather-trimmed *NYRB* | Leather-lapped, steel-ridged, *A Shiver*
9 bud] clasp *NYRB*
10–11] Emblazoned with the number 17, and on my shelf
   Like a trophy, like 'headgear, *NYRB*
15 fireman' –] fireman,' twenty years ago – *NYRB*
20 hose man there] hose man *NYRB*

Dated Glanmore, 31 May 2003 in MS.
   1 Bobby Breen, a Boston firefighter, gave SH his helmet, which gained a new significance with the heroics of New York firefighters on 9/11 when 343 of them lost their lives. After his retirement, Bobby Breen published poems in Brunswick. This poem fits the series of conflict-related poems in *DC*, extending from 'Anahorish 1944' to 'Out of Shot', particularly centring on non-violent figures.
   12 *O'Grady*: Irish poet Desmond O'Grady (1935–2014) whose family were close friends of the Heaneys.
   14 *the fireman-poet*: what Breen became after retirement.
   17 *fire-thane*: modelled on an Old English compound (like the 'shield-wall' in *l.* 21 which does occur in Old English poetry such as SH's *Beowulf*).

Out of Shot

First published in *Salmagundi* (Fall 2005–Winter 2006) and subsequently in *A Shiver* and the *Guardian Review* (15 Oct. 2005): 21. Collected in *DC*.

7 raiders] warriors *A Shiver*, *Guardian*
7^8] [stanza break] *Guardian*

Dated 3 December 2003 in TS (NLI 49,493/126).
   5 *vik*: inlet (Icelandic). The mood of the sonnet has its *volta* with a dramatic deterioration at this point after its 'unseasonably warm' opening.
   7–8 'Norse raids . . .' A celebrated and much translated monastic poem from the eighth–ninth century is found in the margin of a manuscript from St Gall in Switzerland. The poem reflects that the wild weather on the sea means that the Viking raiders will not come this night. SH translated it with an illustration by Tim O'Neill,

published by the Gallery Press in 2007: 'Wind fierce tonight. / Mane of the sea whipped white. / I am not afraid. No ravening Norse / On course through quiet waters.' Reprinted in Maurice Riordan (ed.), *The Finest Music* (London: Faber & Faber, 2014), 11 under its Irish title 'Is aicher in-gáeth in-nocht'. See *TSH*, 94, 643–4.

13 *the bazaar district*: of the war-torn Middle East (perhaps with an overtone of the biblical scapegoat).

Rilke: After the Fire

Published in the *London Review of Books* (5 May 2005): 10. Collected in *DC* and included in *TSH* (98).

5 gathered up] in a pack *LRB*
6] Went rip-roaring wild and yelled and wrecked. *LRB*
9 out-of-shape] out of shape *LRB*
10 half burnt-away] charred, half-consumed *LRB*
16 a foreigner among them.] as from a far-off land. *LRB*

Dated 'Outdoors in Glanmore', 19 March 2005 in MS entitled 'Burnt Out House' (NLI 49,493/131).

A translation of 'Die Brandstätte' (*Neue Gedichte*, 1908). In a letter to Dennis O'Driscoll on 29 March 2005, SH referenced comments he had written earlier that day to a PhD student on the act of translation, which seemed '*à propos*' to the Rilke poems he had just sent to his friend:

> The ideal situation would be to come at the poems without mediation, but that's an ideal that's rarely lived up to. I know Latin and French, for example, well enough to think for myself about what might be equivalents, but I'd still go hunting for other people's translations, not to rip them off, just for some kind of reassurance that I'd got the sense right. And then, of course, once you see that other version, your instinct is to make your own translation more your own, as it were, make it diverge so that it doesn't look like a copy. (Same thing happens with a good crib . . .)
>
>   Come to think of it, that is the problem with cribwork – you're dropping your bucket into the well of meaning all right, but it doesn't go down all the way to the bottom. The haulage work, which is part of the joy of poetry, is lighter than it should be. You may get beneath the surface, but not very far. (*LSH*, 633)

For Rilke translations, see *TSH*, 97–9 and 626–7.

District and Circle

First published in *DC* and later included in *NSP2014* and *100P*.

Fragments dated July 2005, and 11 and 17 August 2005 in MS (NLI 49,493/131); working title 'Testimony: District & Circle, 1962' in TS (NLI 49,493/126).

Title The title poem of the book, made up of five sonnets (though the third, middle 'sonnet' has only thirteen lines and there are several truncated lines throughout the poem). It was expanded from the two sonnets it originally comprised, the first and last of the five: this 'double sonnet' was the form in which the poem called 'District and Circle' existed in May 2005 but, SH said, in the wake of the London 7 July bombings, a poem of that title 'was going to have to bear additional scrutiny' (*SS*, 410). A third part was added in early June, with fourth and fifth parts introduced that summer. Of all the poems in the collection, this was the one that SH struggled most to complete, telling his publishers on 13 June 2005 of having had 'forty-second thoughts' about it (Faber N40). Following the attack of 7/7, SH retitled the poem 'Relict', a word that survives in the final lines of the poem, admitting that 'post-July 7, this poem looms odder and odder' (27 July 2005, FF N50).

> In the summer of 1962, I had a holiday job in London. Every morning I took the District Line or the Circle Line from Earls Court to St James's Park, and came back the same way every evening. The sonnet sequence that gives the new book its name originated in that rush hour experience.
>
> At first there were only two poems, a diptych I liked because the setting was just that bit unexpected. The title moreover seemed right for a collection that returned to places and preoccupations to be found in my earlier books. Then the attacks of July 7 occurred and I realized that a poem named for two lines of the London Underground would be scrutinized for its relation to that atrocity. So, in order to deepen and strengthen the tunnels of suggestion, as it were, I added three more sections.

The first sonnet describes a repeated encounter by a figure identified by SH as the Tollund Man (*SS*, 410) with a tin whistle player busking in the Underground when SH had a holiday job in the Passport Office in London in 1962. The final sonnet describes the same journey forty years later when the older poet is reminded of his father by his own reflection in the train window. Rachel Falconer points out the elements throughout the five sonnets which recall the Virgilian journey to the underworld in *Aeneid Book VI*: the tin-whistle player is probably Irish, given that his traffic with the poet is in recognition (*l.* 12). But he is another figure for Charon who has to be paid an 'obolus', kept by the dead traveller under their tongue; the vision of the father at the end recalls Aeneas's search for his father Anchises, a search SH will return to in his translation of *ABVIa*; and the 'roof-wort' in sonnet four which enables the poet to keep his balance corresponding to the golden bough which leads Aeneas on his way. See Falconer 2022, 136ff.

12 Recognition, as Charon comes to recognise that Aeneas is warranted in crossing the Styx.

35 *Street-loud . . . herd-quiet*: in a later interview, SH said: 'I always like to make a play on two words which sound the same: there's H-E-A-R-D, *heard*, and there's H-E-R-D, *herd*. I think that in writing poetry especially in times of crisis, political crisis, you've got to be aware of H-E-R-D feelings as opposed to individual H-E-A-R-D. The writer is there to be H-E-A-R-D singularly, not to be part of the tribe, although, at moments of crisis, this is a very fine and important distinction' (*NewsHouse*, 14 April 2010).

36 *betrayed*: the question of Irish loyalty, declared or undeclared, is a familiar SH dilemma.

47 *well girded*: the term for chivalric readiness for action.

59 SH plausibly seeing his reflection as his father recalls Aeneas's search for his father in *Aeneid*, 6 with which the poet was so preoccupied, especially in this underworld setting.

65 *relict*: term associated with bereavement, appropriate for the vision of the dead father and for the unstated theme of tragedy on the Underground; the word was temporarily adopted as a title for the poem, and is returned to here after its use in 'Seeing the Sick' (*EL*, 79; *PSH*, 571).

To George Seferis in the Underworld

Published in *Times Literary Supplement* (19 March 2004): 4. Collected in *DC*.

27–8] for a tyrant. But maybe,
    dare I say it, George, for you
    too much i' the right, *TLS*
32 much contested] elected *TLS*
34–6] of a word like *seggans*, smuggle it back in
    like a dialect blade, hoar and harder
    than what it has turned into
    these latter days: *TLS*
37 sedge –] sedge, *TLS*

Dated Glanmore 19 January 2004 in MS under the working title 'To George Seferis in Elysium' (NLI 49,493/126).

Title George Seferis (Georgios Seferiadis, 1900–71), Greek Symbolist poet and diplomat born in Smyrna, was the first Greek winner of the Nobel Prize in Literature in 1963. SH did a presentation on him for the Greek Department at Harvard to mark his anniversary in 2000. His appeal for SH was reinforced by his temperamental disinclination to express political views (cf. *l.* 32: 'your much contested silence'), though at the end of his life he did speak out against the dictatorial military Junta of the Colonels in Greece (1967–74). His funeral was marked by anti-Junta demonstrations and public recitations of his poems (*SS*, 388). Seferis's last poem 'On Aspalathoi' turned to Plato in his consideration of the underworld; several of his own poems feature katabasis, underworld journeys, some inspired by the reflections of Socrates in the closing sections of Plato's *Apology* as he anticipates his death and also in Plato's fable of Er in the *Republic*.

SH often quotes Seferis as saying in troubled times 'poetry is strong enough to help'; in fact Seferis said 'Cavafy, in times of stress, is not strong enough to help' (1974) (see Fowler (2014)). SH himself returns to Cavafy and the underworld in a close translation of a famous Cavafy poem near the end of *DC* (73; *PSH*, 627).

Epigraph Quoted from Roderick Beaton's *George Seferis: Waiting for the Angel* (New Haven and London: Yale University Press, 2003); SH tells O'Driscoll he was fascinated by the account of the Colonels in it (*SS*, 388). *The spiky bushes*: asphodels, which still grow wild in Greece as in Elysium, the abode of the blessed in Greek antiquity. However, the word is botanically vague, perhaps referring to a variety of spiky broom. The debate about what the plant is leads metonymically to the uncertainty that SH shares with Seferis about the public or private duties of art.

3 *seggans*: local term for rough rushes: maybe connected with Irish *seagal*, rye-grass. The uncertainty here is about what plant exactly the local term refers to.

5 *your days of '71*: the year of Seferis's death.

7 *Cape Sounion*: a promontory south of Athens, in English associated with Byron.

19 *hackle-spikes*: hackle is a prickly plant once used in Ulster for carding flax.

22–3 The graphic description of flaying as a punishment suitable for tyrants comes from Seferis's poem 'On Aspalathoi', *ll.* 13–8, in George Seferis, *Collected Poems: Revised Edition*, ed. and trans.

Edmund Keeley and Philip Sherrard (Princeton University Press, 1995), 223. The reprehensibility of tyrants is a running theme in Plato's *Republic*; the particular passage here is marked in Seferis's copy of the *Republic*.

25 *Tartarus*: the area of infernal punishment.

27ff. The poem concludes with uncertainty about the absoluteness of political judgement and punishment, 'for you': that is, given Seferis's innate judiciousness.

Wordsworth's Skates

First published in the *New Yorker* (13 Feb. 2006). Collected in *DC* and later included in *NSP2014*.

Dated 22 June 2004 in MS; a working title in TS was 'Listen' (NLI 49,493/126).

Title In a letter to Coleridge, 24 December 1799, Wordsworth writes that he has obtained a pair of ice skates and will use them the next day (Christmas Day, his sister Dorothy's birthday) to skate on frozen Lake Windermere and 'give [his] body to the wind'. In a celebrated passage in the *Prelude* (Wordsworth 1985, 1.425–46), Wordsworth recalls skating in 'the frosty season' in childhood. The skates are on display in the Wordsworth Museum at Grasmere. SH's poem recaptures the vivid diction of the Wordsworth passage: 'All shod with steel / We hiss'd along the polish'd ice' (433–4).

1 *star in the window*: the window in Dove Cottage when SH visited it. At the end of the Wordsworth passage, 'the stars, / Eastward, were sparkling clear' (444–5).

5 and 8 SH's first use of the 'Not the ... But the' verbless opposition: again in 'Miracle' (*HC*, 17; *PSH*, 649). In a faxed draft of 29 Aug 2005, l. 5 was still in evolution, at that time in the alliterative form, 'Not the toppled strigil shapes seen once' (FF N50).

The Harrow-Pin

Published in *Metre* (Spring 2005): 10–13.

Title] The Harrow Pin *Metre*
1 We'd be told] He would say *Metre*
4 harrow pin] harrow-pin *Metre*

Title Pins are the components of a spike harrow; the individual pins are strong steel prongs, about eight inches long. They were often used to support heavy shelves in farm outhouses, as in the stable-wall here (l. 15).

3 *kale stalk*: agricultural kale is a rough brassica fed to cattle. 'Him' is SH's father, identified in this role elsewhere.

17 The tackle of a working farm-horse: the hames fitted over the collar on the horse's back and the reins passed through it.

22 In Book 4 of Swift's *Gulliver's Travels* (1726), the figures of moral strength are the horses, the Houyhnhnms, which Gulliver admires more than mankind on his return home.

Poet to Blacksmith

First published in 1997 in a limited edition by Pim Witteveen in Hoogevenn, the Netherlands, to mark the first twenty years of Hans van Eijk's private press, In de Bonnefant; and in Louis de Paor (ed.), *Leabhar Sheáin Uí Thuama* (Dublin: Coiscéim, 1997), 1. Later in Patrick Crotty (ed.), *The Penguin Book of Irish Poetry* (London: Penguin, 2010): 317.

In an undated TS draft of the poem, SH records a list of poems in MS in an annotation that he dates 4 August 1997 (NLI 49,493/108).

SH's twelve-line poem is a loose translation of the first eight lines of Eoghan Rua Ó Súilleabháin's long poem in quatrains 'A Chara Mo Chléibh', 'Friend of my Breast'. It is addressed to the blacksmith Séamus MacGearailt, asking him to provide the poet with a spade for his work as a travelling labourer, a 'Spailpín Fánach'. The first two of Ó Súilleabháin's quatrains are reworked into three quite different quatrains by SH. It is only the early section of Ó Súilleabháin's poem that is about the request for the spade; his poem goes on to dwell on the life of drinking shared with MacGearailt, the 'friend of his breast'. Ó Súilleabháin (1748–84) was a kind of *poète maudit*, also famous as a writer of the political visionary form, the aisling. A precedent to SH's poem is 'His Request' by Joan Keefe, published in Montague 1974, 161, which similarly translates the opening quatrains of the original into three stanzas.

Midnight Anvil

The first section was privately printed for the author as a Christmas card, 'At The Hillhead', the Gallery Press, 2000. First published in a lengthened form under the title 'Linked Verses' in the *Irish Times Weekend* magazine (30 Dec. 2000): 8; then in *Agni*, 57 (2003): 8. Collected with revisions in *DC* and later included in *100P*. The first section was independently published as 'At the Hillhead'.

Title] At the Hillhead *Gallery* Linked Verses *Irish Times, Agni*
Passim] [no ornaments between stanzas] *Irish Times*

12 heard] heard. *Irish Times*
15^16] What I'll do instead
    Is quote lines from 'Blacksmith Shop':
    It seems I was called
    For this: to glorify things
    Just because they are. That's it. *Irish Times*
16–18] Also worth hearing:
    Those waterburners shouting
    In Middle English *Irish Times*
21 Eoghan] Owen *Irish Times, Agni*
22 Asking] Requesting Irish *Times*
24] Clear-sheened, tapered and lightsome *Irish Times, Agni*
25 And ringing sweet] And ringing true *Irish Times, Agni*
25^]   Where I mean to be,
    For all that, this New Year's Eve
    Is Hardy country,
    Lychgate and hoarfrost country,
    In search of a darkling thrush. *Irish Times*

Title The midnight is the turning point of the millennium in 1999–2000 when SH's friend, the blacksmith Barney Devlin, whose forge was near Mossbawn, struck twelve blows on his anvil to mark the millennium and was heard on a cellphone by his nephew in Canada. The poem follows naturally from the blacksmith MacGearailt in the preceding poem, returned to in *ll.* 21–2, and ending identically. The title was briefly considered by SH for the book.

    12 *Church bels beyond the starres heard*: George Herbert, 'Prayer 1'.

    17ff. *waterburning / Medieval smiths*: see the anonymous alliterative poem from the fifteenth century (British Museum MS Arundel 292), beginning 'Swarte-smeked smethes' ('Black-smocked smiths'). The last line is 'May no man for brenwateres on night han his rest' ('No one can sleep at night with these waterburners': burning the water by plunging the hot iron horseshoes into it to cool).

    19ff. *l.* 3 of the poem is 'Swich nois on nights ne herd man never'; the smiths cry out for 'Col! Col!' (coal). 'Huf, puf! Lus, bus! Col!': 'Huf, puf' (*l.* 7), and 'Lus, bus, lus, das' (*l.* 20 of the original). See R. T. Davies, *Medieval English Lyrics* (London: Faber & Faber, 1963), 213.

Súgán

Published in *Poetry London*, 52 (Autumn 2005): 3.

'Súgán' was marked as a 'new addition' to the TS of *DC* on 3 June 2005 (FF N50), where it would be intended as the opening poem until demotion in the running order by SH after delivery to Faber. 'Late revisions' can be dated to 8 August 2005 in TS (FF N50).

Title *Súgán* is the Irish word for a rope made by twisting hay.

6 *hook*: used for twisting the hay into a rope, while the other hand fed out the hay from an elder stick.

7 *Walking backwards, winding*: the most famous literary application of the process is Yeats's story 'The Twisting of the Rope' (from the Irish *Casadh an tSúgáin*) in *Stories of Red Hanrahan* (1904) (a figure based partly at least on Eoghan Rua Ó Súilleabháin) in which Hanrahan is tricked into walking backwards out the door while winding the rope.

14 *power to bind and loose*: the power conferred by Christ on St Peter to remit sin or not.

Senior Infants

First published in *Pretext* (Autumn 2005): 1–5, including 'A Nod'.

Title The early years in Irish primary schools were known as low and high (or junior and senior) infants.

1 THE SALLY ROD

Dated 6 December 1998 under the title 'The Bond' in MS (NLI 49,493/117); also in MS as 'Unspoiled' (NLI 49,493/117) and in TS as 'Duffy' (NLI 49,493/116 and 117).

Title 'Sally' is the common Irish term for willow.

1 *Granard*: a town in northern Co. Longford.

4 *Miss Walls*: SH's teacher at Anahorish primary school, familiar from 'Death of a Naturalist' (*DN*, 15; *PSH*, 26).

9 *D'you mind*: local usage for 'Do you remember'.

2 A CHOW

Title Local usage for a 'chew' of tobacco.

6 Dulse is an edible seaweed, popular in Northern Ireland.

15 *quid-spurt*: 'quid' is another term for a chew of tobacco.

3 ONE CHRISTMAS DAY IN THE MORNING

1 *Tommy Evans*: the Evans family were Protestant neighbours of the Heaneys at Mossbawn, featured in 'Edward Thomas on the Lagans Road' (*DC*, 35; *PSH*, 609), as well as earlier appearances in 'Mid-Term Break' (*DN*, 28; *PSH*, 32) and 'Trial Runs' (*Stations*, 18; *PSH*, 167).

The Nod

Published in *The Village* (2–8 Oct. 2004): 23. Subsequently in *Pretext* (Autumn 2005): 1–5 before collection in *DC*.

Dated 3 June 2003 in TS (NLI 49,493/127).

2 Loudan's butcher shop on King's Street, Magherafelt, now closed. Usually spelled 'Louden's'.

9 *B-Men*: the B-Specials, the special constabulary, almost exclusively Protestant. Their mention here is the most explicit point in the subtle sectarian implications of this poem and the preceding one. In a letter of 3 May 2005 to his US publisher, SH explains: 'B-Men: These were also know[n] as the B-Specials, short in its turn for the B-Special Constabulary. They were supplementary to a regular A Force, The Royal Ulster Constabulary tout court. Basically, the B-Specials were loyalist laymen recruited as part-timers in the security forces, notably sectarian and bitterly resented by their nationalist catholic neighbours' (FF N50).

11 *Neighbours with guns*: established as not 'a Catholic thing' in the preceding poem (*DC*, 31).

14 *not just then*: while they were among their own milieu.

A Clip

First published in the *New Yorker* (20 March 2006).

11 shoulder-high] shoulder high *New Yorker*

Dated Glanmore 3 December 2003 in MS (NLI 49,493/126); working title 'Why Not Say What Happened?' (NLI 49,493/127).

Title The standard term for a male haircut (as in *l.* 3). Harry Boyle's real name was Harry Mullan; he cut hair in his spare time in his small house in Castledawson, quite close to Mossbawn. The working title references a favoured line from Robert Lowell's poem 'Epilogue', from *Day by Day* (1977).

7 *surplice*: the white blouse-like garment worn by mass-servers. A very different register from the white Ku Klux Klan cape.

Edward Thomas on the Lagans Road

First published as 'To Edward Thomas on the Lagans Road' in *Remember Fontenoy!*, 1 (Irish Literary Society, 2005), viii–ix, and subsequently in the *TLS* (16 Sept. 2005): 25. Collected in *DC* and subsequently in the *Guardian* (20 Jan. 2007) and in Guy Cuthbertson and Lucy Newlyn (eds), *Branch*

Lines: Edward Thomas and Contemporary Poetry (London: Enitharmon, 2007), 136.

Title Edward] To Edward *Remember Fontenoy*, TLS
1 He's] You're *Remember Fontenoy*, TLS
3^4] [stanza break] [*sic*] *Branch Lines*
5 Murphy] Stinson *Remember Fontenoy*, TLS | Brennan] Keenan *Remember Fontenoy*, TLS
6 Fully] Embowered, *Remember Fontenoy*, TLS
7 him] you *Remember Fontenoy*, TLS
8 As] Until *Remember Fontenoy*, TLS
9–11] Nothing but air and light / Between their love-nest and the whinny hill / Where I lie alone. And now the road is empty, *Remember Fontenoy*
11 bracken] whinny *TLS*
12^13] [no stanza break] *Remember Fontenoy*
14 his] your *Remember Fontenoy*, TLS on the Lagans Road] in khaki trousers *Remember Fontenoy*, TLS
15 in his khaki tunic] on the Lagans Road *Remember Fontenoy*, TLS
18 desert.] desert, *Remember Fontenoy*
>18] Putting the wind up me about mankeepers, / Talking in solemn tones about blitterwheets' eggs. *Remember Fontenoy*

Title The English poet Edward Thomas (1878–1917) was killed in World War I. SH imagines him on leave from the war on the Lagans Road, a small grassy road near Mossbawn and New Row in Castledawson (see next poem, 'The Lagans Road', in 'Found Prose', *DC*, 36; *PSH*, 609).

 1 *not in view*: not even in the imagined scenario of the poem.

 4ff. The imagining of the young lovers is drawn from Thomas's poem 'As the Team's Head Brass' (*l.* 2: 'The lovers disappeared into the wood'), which, SH wrote later, 'is perhaps my favourite poem by Edward Thomas and it was on my mind when I set him walking on the Lagans Road' (*Branch Lines*, 134). He responded to it in a late uncollected poem, 'In a Field', at the invitation of Carol Ann Duffy who was compiling an anthology to mark the centenary of the outbreak of World War I (Duffy 2013, 94; *PSH*, 687). SH particularly admired the 'Homeric plane' in Thomas's poem in which, all but disguised, 'a big wheel of danger is turning above and beyond the poignant and the ordinary': the woodland lovers, the war in Flanders, lives given and taken 'out of shot'.

 15 Khaki tunic of the British Army.

 16 The Evans brothers, Protestant neighbours near Mossbawn.

 17 *not much changed*: a reflection on Thomas's 'Everything / Would have been different' (*ll.* 29–30) and the many possible 'changes' of world that the original poem imagines.

 18 *Monty*: Field Marshal Bernard Law Montgomery (1887–1976), who served in World War I and went on to be a pivotal commander

in World War II, notably in the North African campaign and on D-Day. From an Anglo-Irish family whose seat was at New Park near Moville, Co. Donegal, he also served as a brigade major based in Cork during the War of Independence. In 1943 he was said to have remarked to soldiers of the 9th Londonderry Heavy Anti-Aircraft Regiment, 'I am a Derry man myself.'

Found Prose

First published in *DC* and included in *NSP2014*. 'Tall Dames' is adapted from 'A Gate Left Open', a programme note for the Dublin performance of Janáček's *Diary of One Who Vanished* (Gaiety Theatre, 14–16 Oct., 1999).

1 THE LAGANS ROAD

Title A small country road near Mossbawn. See previous poem, 'Edward Thomas on the Lagans Road' (*DC*, 35; *PSH*, 608).

1–30 The prose 'found' here was taken from an interview transcript produced as part of the *Stepping Stones* process, in which SH was asked by O'Driscoll for 'a more detailed look' at being taken to school for the first time (*SS*, 242).**12** The school is Anahorish primary school.

18 *the Indians of the Pacific Northwest*: their arrival in the land of the dead: another instance of the SH theme of crossing over to the afterlife.

2 TALL DAMES

Title The phrase, as the poem says (*ll.* 16–17) comes from the one-line refrain of Yeats's poem 'A Statesman's Holiday' (1939): *'Tall dames go walking in grass-green Avalon'* (Albright 1990, 372). Like the 'fey' presentation of the child Philomena McNicholl in the previous section, these women are encountered in normal life but also seem outside of 'the usual life'.

3 BOARDERS

Title SH went away from home to board at St Columb's College when he was twelve. In this version of the transition, change-of-life poem, the bus is Charon's barge and the driver Charon who (like the whistle player in the title poem of this volume) does not exact his payment while 'the known country' falls away behind the passengers. A working title in TS had been 'Private Excursion'; *'from* Private

Excursions' was the title of a suite of poems that appeared in the *Dublin Review* in 2001 (*PSH*, 520–3).

The Lift

First published in *Poetry Ireland Review* (Summer 2002): 74–5, in a variant form (below); subsequently as a limited-edition broadside by the University of Kentucky as a keepsake for Helen Vendler's lecture 'W. B. Yeats and Lyric Form' on 13 Feb. 2003 that marked the opening of the university's exhibition 'Irish Literature 1699–1944'; then in *Irish Pages* (Autumn/Winter 2002/2003): 55–6. Later included in *NSP2014* and *100P*.

1–30] Too timely spring: the hawthorn half in leaf.
Her funeral filled the road as it moved off,
The walkers four abreast, soon falling quiet.

Then came the throttle and articulated whops
Of a helicopter crossing and afterwards
Awareness of the rhythm of our footsteps,

Of open air and the life behind those words
'Open' and 'air'. I remembered her aghast,
Shaking, sweating, gathered, shrunk, wet-haired,

A beaten breath, a misting mask, the flash
Of one wild glance, like ghost surveillance
From behind a gleam of helicopter glass.

A lifetime, then the deathtime: reticence
Keeping us together when together,
All declaration deemed outspokenness.

Delicate since childhood, tough alloy
Of kindness, disapproval, and hauteur,
Living by herself, she knew the score

But took the risk at last of certain joys –
Her birdtable and jubilating birds.
The 'fashion' in her wardrobe and her tallboy –

And even pinned poems on her notice board.
In the end, though, it was weather said our say.
Reprise of griefs in summer's clearest mornings,

Child anniversaries that would bloom in May
Out of the simplest depths, the empyrean
There when the curtains opened every day . . .

They bore her lightly on the bier. Four women,
Four friends – she would have called them girls – stepped in
And claimed the final lift beneath the hawthorn. *Poetry Ireland Review*

1 braird: the hawthorn] braird. The hawthorn *Irish Pages*
8 crossing,] crossing *Irish Pages*
12 Foetal, shaking, sweating, shrunk, wet-haired,] Shaking, sweating, gathered, shrunk, wet-haired, *Irish Pages*

20 kindness and *hauteur*] *tendresse* and hauteur *Irish Pages*
21 risk, at last,] risk at last *Irish Pages*
27 Whole requiems] Tears springing *Irish Pages*

Title The lifting of a coffin to take a dead person to their grave.

1 *braird*: like the seedling-braird in 'The Turnip-Snedder', the first shoots of a plant (here in spring).

2 *her*: the funeral of SH's second-eldest sister Ann, who died in 2002, having been 'delicate since childhood' (*l.* 14).

4 *Breton pardon*: ritual funeral procession in rural Brittany.

24 'fashion' is the rural Irish term for someone's best clothes.

30 The four 'girls' were Ann's friends, two of them sisters called McGuiggan.

Nonce Words

First published in a series of cards edited by John F. Deane at the Waxwing Press, Dublin (2003): [2]; in *Irish Pages* (Autumn/Winter 2002/2003): 56–7; and in *Agni*, 57 (2003): 6–7. Collected with revisions in *DC* and later included in *NSP2014*.

10 bridge-iron] bridge *Irish Pages*, *Agni*
11 Advent] advent *Irish Pages*, *Agni*
14 parked,] parked *Irish Pages*, *Agni*

Dated 7 January 2003 in MS, where the first draft is written on the back and front of an envelope; a working title in TS is 'The Road Taken' (NLI 49,493/131).

Title Strictly, nonce words are words that are only attested once.

5 *Derrylin*: a village in Co. Fermanagh on the Cavan border.

11 *Advent*: the penitential period before Christmas.

17 *Requiescat*: here meaning take a rest from driving; but usually a pious wish in the Mass for the Dead.

26 *nonce*: a chance event, so the poem ends with resignation to what happens.

Stern

First published in *Irish Pages* (Spring/Summer 2005): 30. Collected in *DC* and later included in *NSP2014*.

Dedication SH's close friend Hughes died in October 1998.

2 T. S. Eliot had been instrumental in the publication by Faber & Faber of Ted Hughes's debut, *The Hawk in the Rain* (1957).

Out of this World

First published in *Agni*, 61 (April 2005): 226–30.

Dedication Czesław Miłosz (1911–2004), born in Lithuania into a Polish family, died in Poland (in Krakow where SH spoke at his funeral, quoting Sophocles' *Oedipus at Colonus*: 'Wherever that man went, he went gratefully'). Greatly revered by SH, who got to know him in the US. He is the subject of 'The Master' (*SI*, 110; *PSH*, 343).

1 'LIKE EVERYBODY ELSE . . .'

First published as 'A Found Poem', part 1 of 'Out of This World', in *Agni*, 61 (April 2005): 226. Subsequently published in *The God Factor: Inside the Spiritual Lives of Public People*, ed. Cathleen Flasani (New York: Farrar, Straus and Giroux, [7 March] 2006), 165–9. Collected with revisions in *DC*. Later in *Czesław Miłosz Literary Festival* (Krakow, 2009), 28–33 and as 'A Found Poem' in *Irish Pages*, 8. 2 (30 Aug. 2014): 9, where neither the poem nor the title is given in quotes.

Title] A Found Poem *Agni, God Factor, Irish Pages*
4^5 [stanza break]] [no stanza break] *Irish Pages*
8^9] [stanza break] *God Factor*
9 [inset]] [ranged left] *Irish Pages*
11 off-stage] offstage *Agni* | off stage *God Factor, Irish Pages*
12 disavow] disrespect *Agni, God Factor, Irish Pages*
13 bread] wafer *Agni, God Factor, Irish Pages*
14 tremor] pallor *Agni, God Factor, Irish Pages*

1–14 The sonnet is a recension of a prose passage that later appears in *Stepping Stones* in answer to a question, 'Did you have to wrestle with concepts (or words!) like "transubstantiation" and "real presence"?', to which SH replies:

> Not in the beginning. Like everybody else, I bowed my head at Mass during the consecration of the bread and wine, lifted my eyes to the raised host and the raised chalice. I believed (whatever it means) that a change occurred: I went to the altar rails and received the mystery on my tongue, returned to my place, shut my eyes fast, made an act of thanksgiving, opened my eyes and felt time starting up again. It was phenomenally refreshing and, when I began to admit to myself that I was losing faith in it, I was very sorry. Intellectually speaking, the loss of faith occurred offstage, there was never a scene where I had it out with myself or with another. But the potency of those words remains for me, they retain an undying tremor and draw; I cannot disavow them. Nor can I make the act of faith. In 'Station Island', I arranged for John

of the Cross to help my unbelief by translating his 'Song of the Soul that Knows God by Faith'. (*SS*, 234)

4 *A change occurred*: at the Consecration of the Mass when bread and wine are changed into the Body and Blood of Christ, according to the Catholic belief in Transubstantiation with which SH, like Miłosz, was brought up.

9–10 A scene when the speaker (SH or Miłosz) 'has it out' definitively whether or not he 'believed (whatever it means)'.

12–13 Terms associated with the sacrament of Communion.

2 BRANCARDIER

First published in the *Irish Examiner* (10 Feb. 2005): 14, and subsequently as part 3 of 'Out of This World', in *Agni*, 61 (April 2005): 228–9.

3 M. M. Alacoque] Mary Alacoque *Agni*
8^9 [additional stanza in *Agni*]:

> Now Cathleen Conroy's in the corridor
> Where you've been standing. *Vierge. Vivace.* '*Ma fille*',
> As Mr Conroy calls her, who calls you 'ye'
> And 'Son'. 'Son, what's the time?' 'Son, would ye shut that door.'

11 coloured] little *Agni*
19 poles] poles, *Agni*
20 rosaries] rosaries, *Agni*

Title French for stretcher-bearer. See *SS*, 288–9; glossed on first publication as 'Someone who assists infirm pilgrims at a shrine' (*Agni*). Working title in TS 'Testimony: Lourdes 1956' (in error for 1958) (NLI 49,493/132).

1 A student pilgrim to Lourdes in 1958 (*SS*, xxi).

11 *bandolier*: sash over the shoulders worn by the helper-volunteers.

19 *Sodalities*: confraternities, particularly of membership of Catholic guilds.

20 *Mantillas*: traditional Spanish light veils, confined in the twentieth century to liturgical wear, mainly to conform to the Catholic rule that women had to wear a head-covering in the church. Very common in Catholic countries before the rule was relaxed in the 1960s, after Vatican II.

21 *unam sanctam catholicam*: from the Nicene Creed said in the Latin Mass: 'one, holy, catholic and apostolic church'. 'Catholic' means universal but its restrictive application to Roman Catholicism is hard to exclude.

24–5 *Mystic- / al Body, the Eleusis of its age*: the Mystical Body means the union of all Christians with Christ as the head; hence the collective of pilgrims here. Eleusis in Athens was famous for annual festivities in honour of Demeter and Persephone.

27 The Lourdes pilgrims bring home water from the well because of its supposed curative properties.

29 Bernadette Soubirous (1844–79), Saint Bernadette of Lourdes to whom a young lady appeared several times between 11 February and 16 July 1858, finally declaring herself to be the Virgin Mary and asking for a chapel to be built at the grotto at Massabielle.

3 SAW MUSIC

First published in *The Door Stands Open: Czesław Miłosz 1911–2004* (Dublin: Irish Writers' Centre, printed by the Book Art Museum, Łódź, 2005), in an edition limited to 300 copies. Subsequently as part 4 of 'Out of This World', in *Agni*, 61 (April 2005): 230 and as a broadside by Green River Press limited to 250 copies (2006). Collected in *DC*.

epigraph] [no epigraph] *Agni*
4 scrims] scrims, *Agni*
14 Vaselined] vaselined *Agni*
18 gaberdine] gabardine *Agni*

The conclusion of 'Saw Music', like that of 'District and Circle', was one of the very last that SH said was 'still being tampered with' in May 2005, and was marked 'Revised' on 3 June 2005 resubmission of TS (FF N50).

Epigraph A question and answer from vows made at Baptism.

1 *'godbeams'*: a new term for the crepuscular rays of the sun when it has just gone below the horizon at twilight, used by Barrie Cooke to refer to his paintings of the breaking of the rays of the sun through clouds. It is a variant on the term sunbeam.

9ff. 'the man / Who played the saw': William (Willie) Campbell (d. January 1970) was a familiar busker in Belfast city centre for over twenty years (see Jack Loudan, 'Master of Music – with a Saw', *Belfast Telegraph*, 17 April 1964).

22–3 The quoted passage ascribed to Miłosz.

25ff. The poet is Czesław Miłosz, buried in Krakow now he is 'out of this world'.

In Iowa

First published in the *New Yorker* (18 April 2005), and subsequently in the *Boston Irish Reporter*, 17. 10 (Oct. 2006).

6 corn stalks] cornstalks *New Yorker*
8 brow] brow, *New Yorker*

Written on 30 March 2005 with 'Chairing Mary' (under the title 'Carrying Mary') and sent to SH's close reader Dennis O'Driscoll that morning as a handwritten postscript to a letter of the previous day, SH–DOD, 29 March 2005 (EU 1420).

Seen as the first of three poems about climate change, a recurrent theme in *DC*, discussed with O'Driscoll (*SS*, 408ff.); see also 'The Tollund Man in Springtime' and 'Höfn'. In 'Seamus Heaney's Cold Heaven: "The Ecological Lament"' (*Irish Pages*, 10. 1, 2018, 127–45), Brendan Corcoran argues for a different ecological triad: 'In Iowa', 'Höfn' and 'Anything Can Happen' in that order.

1 Mennonites, 'a Christian sect who reject, among other things, infant baptism' (*SS*, 408).

10–11 The biblical term 'Verily' introduces a portentous note, reinforced by 'unbaptised' and 'darkness'.

12 Crucial moments in the narrative of Christ's passion: crucified at the third hour, and 'Behold, the veil of the temple was rent in twain from the top to the bottom' (Matthew 27:51).

14 The waters parted in Exodus 14:21 so the Israelites could pass over the Red Sea, but rising waters are an ominous indication of climate change.

Höfn

First published in *Metre*, 17 (Spring 2005): 10–13, and subsequently in the *Guardian Review* (15 Oct. 2005): 21 and *Irish Times* (31 March 2007): 3. Collected in *A Shiver* (Clutag, 2005) and with revisions in *DC* and later included in *NSP2014* and *100P*.

3 shag-ice] shag ice *Guardian*
10 mouthwatering] mouth-watering *Metre*

Dated 6 June 2004 in MS (NLI 49,493/126), and sent to Liam O'Flynn the following day.

Title Höfn is a small town in the south-east of Iceland under the slopes of the glacier Vatnajökull, the largest ice cap in Iceland. In 2004, SH flew there in a small plane from Reykjavik with Liam O'Flynn for a performance of 'The Poet and the Piper'. After flying over the 'stony great scar of ice' and imagining a freezing death on it, SH reflects that the real threat is the rising temperature (*SS*, 411). In a fax to O'Flynn on 7 June 2004: 'That glacier chilled me to the bone:

I don't know if I've done it justice, but, good or bad, I thought the poem should be sent to you' (NLI 49,493/128).

6 *Undead*: the ghoulish condition of returning dead to dwell among the living, as the frozen glacier melts to take its place in the 'warm, mouthwatering' world of nature.

On the Spot

'On the Spot' was commissioned by Maurice Riordan and John Burnside for their anthology, *Wild Reckoning* (London: Picador, 2004). Subsequently published in *Metre* (Spring 2005): 10–13 and collected in *DC*.

4 death sweat] death-sweat *Wild Reckoning*

Undated TSS acknowledged by John Burnside (27 Jan. 2003) and Paul Muldoon (25 Feb. 2003).

Title *l.* 13, in the colloquial sense 'immediately'; working titles for the poem had been 'Early Riser' (*l.* 8) and 'The Spot'.

1 *A cold clutch*: a batch of eggs left by a hen who was 'laying out', continuing the theme of what should be living and vibrant but is dead or dying.

13 *addle*: of an egg, to become rotten and barren through heat.

14 *planetary stand-off*: as with the glacier in 'Höfn', small pieces of evidence of huge disturbance. Perhaps recalling Donne's 'A Valediction: Forbidding Mourning', 'Moving of th'earth brings harms and fears / Men reckon what it did, and meant; / But trepidation of the spheres, / Though greater far, is innocent.' Donne was a fixture in A-Level English courses of SH's time. His poem 'The Ecstasy' is a crucial component of 'Chanson d'Aventure' (*HC*, 14; *PSH*, 648).

The Tollund Man in Springtime

Sections three ('My heavy head') and five ('Cattle out in rain') published as '*from* The Tollund Man in Springtime' in *TLS* (29 April 2005): 4; sections one ('Into your virtual city'), four ('The soul exceeds') and six ('Through every check') published as 'The Tollund Man in Springtime' in *Metre* (Spring 2005): 10–13. Collected in *A Shiver* and *DC*. Later included in *NSP2014*.

3 myself in time] time in myself *Metre*
15 Scone of peat, composite] *Bakey turf*: composite of *A Shiver*
20 a sullen] sullen *A Shiver*
21 . . . And] . And *A Shiver*
23 plied] sighed *A Shiver*
24 At my] And my *A Shiver*
26 turned turf] a turned leaf *A Shiver*
29 the ground] ground *A Shiver*

53 the air] first smoke *A Shiver*
57–70] [omitted] *A Shiver*
59 My study was] I stood by in *TLS*
63 gaps] mud *TLS*
59 lough] long lough *TLS*
77 withered] dried up *Metre*
78 frank bouquet] bouquet *Metre*

Title The Tollund Man is the preserved body of a strangled man, found in 1950 in the Bjældskovdal bog in Jutland near the village of Tollund. It is a particularly graphic figure, dated to the fourth century BCE. In *WO* the poem 'The Tollund Man' ends by making his fate a figure for the violence of Northern Ireland, saying the poet will feel 'unhappy and at home' in the old man-killing parishes there. In the poem 'Tollund' in *SL*, dated September 1994, the Danish landscape is the backdrop for cautious hopes of renewal implicitly prompted by the IRA ceasefire of 31 August 1994 (*SL*, 69; *PSH*, 501). The voice in the six-sonnet poem in *DC* is assigned to the bog body in the Silkeborg Museum in Jutland; the conceit of the poem is that this figure comes back to earthly life by reviving in a plant-like way in springtime. As Rachel Falconer says, it is a reversal of the descent of the living body into an afterlife in the *Aeneid* or Dante but dealing with the same katabatic narrative of movement between death and life (Falconer 2022, 146ff.). For SH himself, the Jutland figure arrived restoratively out of the peat bog 'as if in defiance of the desolations that threatened', and allowed the author to break through onto new ground: 'It was mostly thanks to him that I then wrote several quick and quickening short poems and could have exclaimed with George Herbert "I once more smell the dew and rain / And relish versing"' (*PBS Bulletin*, 189). In a later letter, SH identifies the Tollund Man as 'a second self of sorts for SH' (*LSH*, 687).

1 'I' is the awakening revenant figure, addressing the 'you' of modern reality, whether the 'virtual' reality evoked by the commuter in *l*. 1 or the 'you and yours' of the physical world of humanity in *l*. 6, though SH said the 'I' was neither a dramatised persona or any reporting voice but 'a transfusion', a 'guardian other, risen out of the Jutland bog' ('One Poet in Search of a Title', *The Times*, 26 March 2006: 7). The figure, which had been buried in the bog, is reviving in spring like a planted organism. Like the shades restored to the world of the living at the end of *Aeneid*, 6, it reawakens 'to revel in the spirit' (*l*. 9) at the volta before the sestet of the first sonnet.

3 *Lapping myself in time*: become invisible after burial with the passage of time, so passing 'undetected' through modern time.

15ff. In the second sonnet, the image changes from the buried body as plant to the bog figured as food and drink: bread-making dough ('scone' is the Northern Irish term for 'loaf'), or wine ('trampled like a muddy vintage'). The peat is kneaded and left out to cook and dry in the sunshine of day (17). This metaphor is sustained: not dry (cooked) 'the whole way through' (18), the slow-burn no more than lukewarm: slow to cook because the peat has been 'so long unrisen' (21).

22ff. The metaphor is resolved with the identification of the bog-dough with the human figure ('me', 21) revealed by the lifting of the bog body out of the wet ground.

25ff. The figure feels the air like turf in the drying breath of God as the bog body 'on the sixth day', the last day of Creation before God rested.

28 *unatrophied*: again, the counter-normal restoration of wholeness when the atrophying normal to the death of the body is reversed.

29ff. The third sonnet begins with an evocative detailed description of how this bog body looks in its museum case.

36 *was meant to be*: the excavation of the bog body was fated like the springtime growth of plants.

37 *On show*: potentially visible though its protection by time kept it undetected and unregistered.

43 'The Soul exceeds its circumstances' (Czesław Miłosz). Used as the title of a collection of essays on SH's later poetry edited by Eugene O'Brien (University of Notre Dame Press, 2016). The soul or spirit cannot be accounted for in purely material terms.

50ff. By an act of faith (in the aesthetic) the reporting voice becomes reconciled to its circumstances in the display case, rather than the environmentally damaged world he is returning to with exhaust fumes, silage reek and traffic.

70 *Bulrush*: in a letter to Dennis O'Driscoll of 29 March 2005 to thank him for draft criticism, SH remarked that his friend's commentary had sparked 'a remembrance' in the sequence, an example of how images can reside untapped in the mind to be accessed later: 'that bulrush has been waiting to get into the right place for decades' (EU 1420).

71ff. The final sonnet shows the revenant becoming reconciled to the world of nature. He in the voice of the poet now carries a bunch of Tollund rushes as Yeats kept a piece of the earth of Sligo in his pocket in London.

Moyulla

First published in *DC* and subsequently in *Scintilla*, 10 (Spring 2007): 31–2.

Dated Glanmore, 26 February 2005 in MS (NLI 49,493/131).

Title The river Moyola or Moyulla flows through Castledawson and by Mossbawn, from its source in the Sperrin Mountains to the northern end of Lough Neagh. SH calls this 'a praise poem', but says it is 'keenly aware of "green issues", so, to a degree its drift is also political' (*SS*, 406). Working title in TS 'In those days she flowed' (NLI 49,493/132).

1 *those days*: before the river became polluted.

13 *so what*: the graceless colloquial response to concern about environmental issues.

19 *algae*: the pollution of the river is a prominent idea in the poem.

23–4 The middle vowel variation between Moyola and Moyulla is not great. The play is on the Great Vowel Shift in English during the fifteenth and sixteenth centuries, in the course of which most prominent vowels were fronted.

25 *milk-fevered*: the pollution of rivers and the water-table was caused by some aspects of farming activity. Cf. 'The Milk Factory' (*HL*, 35; *PSH*, 374) describing the effect of the Nestlé factory in Castledawson in the 1940s.

28 *gidsome*: a nonce-word, derived from 'gid', a disease of herbivores contracted from pollutants in water. 'flotsam' is refuse on water.

33 *blettings*: bletting is a stage of the over-ripening of fruit which is suggestive but unidiomatic here.

33 *beestings*: the first, enriched milk of a cow after calving, not used as milk for general drinking.

40 *thigh waders*: necessary perhaps as a protection against pollution; but the general spirit of this section is positive.

Planting the Alder

First published in the *New Yorker* (19 Dec. 2005). Later included in *NSP2014*.

Dated February 2005 in MS (NLI 49,493/131).

Title Alder trees grow in plenty unplanted along the banks of the Moyola. The poem proposes planting them as an environmental action and for the various beauties of the tree.

1 *argent*: a heraldic colour, dulled silver.

14 *streel-head*: from Irish-English term 'streelish', unkempt.

Tate's Avenue

Published in the *Irish Times: Weekend Review* (11 Feb. 2006): 11. Collected in *DC* and later included in *NSP2014* and *100P*.

Title A street in south Belfast where Marie Heaney had a flat in the early days of the couple's courtship, the domicile of the poem's rug in the third quatrain (9).

3 *vestal*: virginal. The family seaside rug, spread chastely on the sand: SH calls this 'abstinent' (*SS*, 406).

7 *Guadalquivir*: the Heaneys went to Spain in 1969 in fulfilment of the terms of the Somerset Maugham Award, in the course of which they went to a bullfight ('corrida', *l*. 8) before which they had a picnic by the Guadalquivir river further south in Spain (*SS*, xxiii).

A Hagging Match

First published in the *New Yorker* (20 March 2006).

A late introduction to *DC*, with the author marking 'Addition/Alternative?' beside 'Fiddleheads / A Hagging Match' on a TS contents page for Faber of 3 June 2005 (FF N50).

Title 'Hag' means to chop, cut or split logs. Overhearing wood being split by his wife outside, the narrator reflects on their match which is not split: another unlaboured love poem like 'Tate's Avenue'.

Fiddleheads

Published in *DC*. Later included in *NSP2014*.

A late introduction to *DC* as above (FF N50).

Title Fiddlehead ferns are a delicacy in Japan (*l*. 1).

4 Masazumi Toraiwa (1932–2023), Japanese authority on modern Irish literature and friend of SH. See *LSH*, 634.

To Pablo Neruda in Tamlaghtduff

Published in *Poetry London*, 52 (Autumn 2005): 3.

Pablo Neruda (1904–73), aka Ricardo Eliécer Neftalí Reyes Basoalto, was a Chilean poet-diplomat who won the Nobel Prize in Literature in 1971. He was a senator in the Chilean Communist party before it was outlawed, and a friend and advisor to Chile's murdered socialist president Salvador Allende.

Title Tamlaghtduff is a townland next to Bellaghy near the Glenshane Pass mentioned in 'Boarders' (*DC*, 40; *PSH*, 611), the birthplace of the IRA hunger striker Francis Hughes, who is the subject of Christy Moore's song 'Boy from Tamlaghtduff'.

1 Niall Fitzduff, a friend of the Heaneys from Ardboe, was active in community work in Northern Ireland. He cycled long distances for charitable causes throughout Ireland, Europe and the USA, including a cycle ride from Boston to Key West, Florida.

4 Duff's Corner in Ardboe. The crab apple tree near it is a well-known local landmark.

16 *Pablo of earthlife*: SH links the unshowy appeal of the crabapple to the 'home-truth Neruda', taking him as a fitting figure for this series of optimistic poems. Neruda was celebrated for his poems about everyday objects: see Neruda's *Odes to Common Things*, selected and illustrated by Ferris Cook, trans. Ken Krabbenhoft (New York: Bulfinch Press, 1994). But the poem has a fitting edge of tragedy too, captured in the tear-duct (*l*. 35).

Home Help

First collected under this title in *DC*.

1 HELPING SARAH

Published singularly in the *New Yorker* (20 March 2006): 94.

Dated 16 Mar. [2005] in MS (NLI 49,493/131).

Title SH's aunt and godmother, Sarah Heaney, his father's sister, a schoolteacher, was influential on his development of bookish interests (*SS*, 26). Like SH, she was prepared for a scholarship examination by the teacher Barney Murphy (*SS*, 247). Lived in the family house at The Wood until she moved to her own house in Bellaghy where she lived alone and where SH, aged eleven or twelve, used to visit her to help in her garden ('weeding' *l*. 3, and 'earth's work' *l*. 10).

3 *rigs*: local term for ridges, as in 'Broagh' (*WO*, 17; *PSH*, 125) and 'A Call' (*SL*, 53; *PSH*, 494).

2 CHAIRING MARY

Published singularly in the *New Yorker* (27 June 2005): 60.

Written on 30 March 2005 with 'Iowa' (see 'In Iowa' above).

Title SH's aunt Mary Heaney, his father's sister, lived in the family houses throughout SH's childhood; she is the subject of 'Sunlight' (*North*, 9; *PSH*, 173): 'the familiar of the yard', a household baker and a family gardener. Until late in the preparation of the collection, the poem had borne the title 'Carrying Mary' (EU, Faber, NLI).

1 *carefully manhandled*: SH tells Dennis O'Driscoll that Mary developed arthritis in old age and had to be carried up and down stairs in a chair by her nephews (*SS*, 172).

Rilke: The Apple Orchard

First published in *London Review of Books* (5 May 2005): 10, under the title 'Three Poems', but referenced on the front page as 'Three Rilke Translations'. Cf. *TSH*, 626.

9 Here under trees] Under trees here *LRB*
16 mute] quiet *LRB*

Like Rilke's German original, 'Der Apfelgarten', SH's poem is in four quatrains over a single sentence. In the *LRB* printing the poem is headed, like the original, BORGEBY-GARD, the place in Sweden where Rilke saw the apple orchard.

3–4 The Wordsworthian idea of the stored memory is confirmed by the word 'recollected' in *l.* 5.

See Resch 2021, 128–33.

Quitting Time

First published in the *New Yorker* (14 Feb. 2005). Later included in *NSP2014*.

8 phrase, phrase *New Yorker*
13 tubular steel] tubular-steel *New Yorker*

Working title 'Turkeys' in TS.

1 *chamfered*: concrete flooring layered in corrugated lines; *him* is SH's farmer-brother Hugh, also the subject and dedicatee of 'Keeping Going' (*SL*, 10–12; *PSH*, 468).

4 *herm*: Greek architectural statue of a head and torso on a square plinth.

8 '*My head is light*': Hugh suffered from epilepsy. Cf. his 'turn' in 'Keeping Going' (*SL*, 12; *PSH*, 470).

12 *redding up*: tidying up (Northern Irish and USA).

Home Fires

First published in *Irish Pages* (Spring/Summer 2005): 29 and subsequently in *Tatler* (September 2005): 126. 'A Scuttle for Dorothy Wordsworth' published singularly in *Harvard Review*, 28 (2005): 113.

1 A SCUTTLE FOR DOROTHY WORDSWORTH

Published singularly in *Harvard Review*, 28 (2005): 113.

Title Dorothy Wordsworth (1771–1855), sister of and collaborator with William Wordsworth. The coal-scuttle still stands by the fireside in their house, Dove Cottage at Grasmere in the Lake District.

3 *Thomas Ashburner*: a neighbour of the Wordsworths who brought them coal from Keswick (see Dorothy Wordsworth, *Grasmere Journals*, ed. Pamela Woof, Oxford: Oxford University Press, 1991).

7 *doting*: an outdated term used to describe senility.

2 A STOVE LID FOR W. H. AUDEN

Published singularly in a signed edition limited to seventy-five copies by Oxford Poetry Broadsides, printed by Evergreen Press.

Epigraph 'The Shield of Achilles'] [omitted] *Irish Pages*, *Tatler*
10 time,] time *Irish Pages*, *Tatler*
13 ashpan] ashpit *Oxford Poetry Broadsides*, *Irish Pages*, *Tatler*

Dated 8 October 2004 in a TS entitled 'To W. H. Auden by his Fireside' (NLI 49,493/126).

Title W. H. Auden (1907–73): major English poet, much admired by SH.

Epigraph 'The Shield of Achilles', poem by Auden, published in 1952, and title of a volume of poems published in 1955.

3 *Fair Isle jersey*: multi-coloured knitwear of a striped pattern, very common in mid-twentieth century.

7 *solidus*: burnt through coals welded together.

8 *maw*: the yawning mouth on top of the stove when the circular lid has been lifted off.

The Birch Grove

Published in the *TLS* (18 March 2005): 10, and subsequently in the *Guardian* (1 April 2006).

1 back] foot *TLS*
4 only,] only *TLS*

4 'They' are SH's friends, Bernard and Jane McCabe who lived in Ludlow, Shropshire.

15–16 *'If art teaches us anything . . .'*: the theme of the Nobel Prize speech by Joseph Brodsky. In SH's Lecture 'Writer and Righter' for the Irish Human Rights Commission (9 Dec. 2009), he says Brodsky 'once said to me in conversation, "if art teaches us anything, it is that the human condition is private"'.

Cavafy: 'The rest I'll speak of to the ones below in Hades'

Published as the last of six translations under the title 'Poets, Sculptors, Sophists and Other Clients: Six Poems by Constantine Cavafy', in *Hermathena*, 179 (Winter 2005): 12.

Title] 6. 'The rest I'll speak of to the ones below in Hades' *Hermathena*
8 all we cover up] everything we guard *Hermathena*
11 about such] about about *Hermathena*

Title Constantin P. Cavafy (1863–1933), Greek poet who lived in Alexandria. The words are the last words spoken by Ajax in Sophocles' *Ajax* before he dies on his own sword.

1 The civilised proconsul believes that Ajax may be able to atone in Hades for his crimes. Cf. 'Testimony: The Ajax Incident' (*TSH*, 69; 613–14n).

2 *the line*: the quotation in the poem's title.

10 *the sophist*: the sceptic who is doubtful whether they care about worldly 'hurt and secret' in the afterlife at all. SH's poem is a close translation of the Greek original.

In a Loaning

Published in the *New York Times* (31 Dec. 2005) in an opinion piece entitled 'Closing Time; In a Loaning'.

Title Loaning is the Ulster word for a small roadway in the countryside, used on several occasions by SH.

3–4 Declaration of a preference for local usage in poetry over the traditional English diction of 'beechen green'.

The Blackbird of Glanmore

First printed by the King Library Press (2004) and published in *The Yellow Nib*, 1 (2005): 1. Later included in *NSP2014* and *100P*.

Title Set by the Heaneys' house in Co. Wicklow, the poem returns to several themes and events from SH's poetry. This blackbird links to several earlier poems and translations by SH, especially the versions of the poem called (among other titles) 'The Blackbird of Belfast Lough' (*TSH*, 9; 537–8n) and 'The Drowned Blackbird' (*TSH*, 133).

10–12 *CTa*, *ll*. 1368–70: 'Away to the house of death, / To my father, sitting waiting there / Under the clay roof' (*TSH*, 241).

13ff. SH's brother Christopher, killed in a road accident at the age of four, the event commemorated in 'Mid-Term Break' (*DN*, 28; *PSH*, 32); SH told Dennis O'Driscoll: '"The Blackbird of Glanmore", contains a memory of my young brother Christopher. The first time I came home from St Columb's College, when he was just about two or three, he actually frolicked and rolled around the yard for pleasure. That stayed with me forever and came up more than fifty years later in the poem' (*SS*, 408).

20ff. The neighbour's post-factum reported premonition is a familiar Irish – and universal – trope.

UNCOLLECTED POEMS (2006–2010)

The small number of uncollected poems between the publication of *District and Circle* and the profoundly personal last collected volume *Human Chain* doesn't possess a single thematic coherence; nevertheless, in the wake of the exposed subject of the former collection, there follows a marked move towards interior conditions, as SH wrote in a review at the time: 'Poetry is a domestic art, most itself when most at home' (*Guardian*, 24 Nov. 2007). The beginning of that period was marked by SH's stroke in August 2006 which will become the subject of the haunting poem 'Chanson d'Aventure' (*HC*, 14–16; *PSH*, 648). As in other uncollected groups, this short series is dominated by occasional poems written in tribute to friends and institutions, recognising the devotion to classical literature shared with Michael Longley in 'The City', the title of which refers to Livy. SH's work on the translation of *Aeneid Book VI* continues with the publication of a fifth excerpt, 'The Fields of Light' (see *TSH*, 651). The Heaneys' friend David Thomson, author of the highly successful memoir *Woodbrook*, is commemorated in the poem 'Fragment: "Nairn in darkness and in light"'. Most of all, SH can be seen in preparation for the personal poems that were to emerge in *Human Chain*, telling a Dublin audience for a celebration of his seventieth birthday in 2009, 'If poetry and the arts do anything, they can fortify your inner life, your inwardness' (*Irish Times*, 14 April 2009).

A Toast for Rand

Gifted to mark the fiftieth birthday of Rand Brandes on 19 April 2006. Subsequently published in Rand Brandes (ed.), *Seamus Heaney: A Life Well Written. Selections from the Collections of Carolyn and Ward Smith, Alan M. Klein, and Rand Brandes* (New York: Grolier Club, and Hickory, NC: Lenoir-Rhyne University, 2014), 108.

Title Rand Brandes, American scholar of Irish literature and author with Michael Durkan of the authoritative *Seamus Heaney: A Bibliography 1959–2003* (London: Faber & Faber, 2008); second edition, 2026. The poem is collected here in the chronological moment of its gifting, rather than in its occasion of posthumous publication.

Our Mystery

Published in *Archipelago*, 1 (Summer 2007): 1.

Title 'Mystery' in the archaic sense of reserved art.

Fragment: 'Nairn in darkness and in light'

Published in *Archipelago*, 1 (Summer 2007): 62.

Title Nairn is a small fishing port in the Scottish Highlands east of Inverness.

12 David Thomson (1914–88), though he was born in India, came from Nairn. SH, like many other Irish readers, greatly admired *Woodbrook* (1974), his memoir of acting as tutor to Phoebe Kirkwood of an Anglo-Irish family in Co. Roscommon and his falling in love with her. SH characterised his writing as having a 'delicate wildness' to it, a phrase which was used by Julian Vignoles as the title of his biography of Thomson (Dublin: Lilliput Press, 2015). Thomson suffered from poor eyesight as well as mental ill-health.

Who Is Billy?

Maurice Hayes (ed.), *Billy: A Tribute to AWB Vincent*, Dublin: The Ireland Funds (23 June 2007): v, an edition limited to 500 copies to commemorate the Ireland Funds Gala evening honouring A. W. B. Vincent.

William Bourn ('Billy') Vincent (1919–2012), whose family owned Muckross House and Estate in Killarney, Co. Kerry. After service in the Royal Inniskilling Fusiliers in World War II he became a successful businessman in California (his mother came from San Francisco). The family gave the Muckross Estate to the Irish state, and among other philanthropic activities he was a major figure in the work of the American Ireland Fund (now the Ireland Funds). His later life was shared between Killarney, California and Monaco, where he died in 2012.

1–4 Cf. *Two Gentleman of Verona*, IV.2.39–42:

Who is Silvia? What is she,
That all our swains commend her?
Holy, fair and wise is she
The heaven such grace did lend her.

Cutaways

Published in *Irish Pages*, 4. 1 (2007), 24–5. Part I subsequently in *Poems for 2008* (Oxfam, 2008): [1] in a revised form; part III subsequently in 'Chanson d'Aventure' III in a revised form.

[text: *Irish Pages*]

I 12]Fingerprinted woman- and man-bodies *Poems for 2008*
>I 12] [additional single-line stanza]: Laid out side by side in a little row. *Poems for 2008*
III] *see* 'Chanson d'Aventure' (*PSH*, 648).

Title In his accompanying letter to his contribution to Oxfam Books, 27 May 2007, SH explained: 'Incidentally, the third meaning given for "cutaway" in my Collins English Dictionary reads: "*Films, television*, a shot separate from the main action of a scene, to emphasize something or to show simultaneous events". But I think it would be heavy-handed to include that as either a note or epigraph. Nowadays more or less everybody would have a grasp of that sense of the word.' SH offered an extended draft of thirteen lines for the Oxfam calendar, which he described as 'part of a longer sequence and may not hold its own as a thirteen liner' (private collection).

A Birl for Burns

Published in Andrew O'Hagan (ed.), *A Night Out with Robert Burns* (Canongate, [4 Jan.] 2008): viii–ix, and subsequently in the *Daily Telegraph* (25 Jan. 2008): 34, also in Douglas Gifford (ed.), *Addressing the Bard: Twelve Contemporary Poets Respond to Robert Burns* (Edinburgh: Scottish Poetry Library, 2009), 71.

[text: *A Night Out with Robert Burns*]

SH's tribute to the poet Robert Burns (1757–96) was inspired by a tour of Ayrshire in the company of his friends Andrew O'Hagan and Karl Miller, a trip that he later described as 'miraculous' (*A Night Out with Robert Burns*, 48).

Title 'Birl' means twisting or turning in Scots, so here something like a musical turn.

Centenary Stanza

Published in a limited-edition broadside for the Queen's University of Belfast Centenary Luncheon (19 March 2008) [2]. Subsequently in the *Irish Times* (20 March 2008): 9, and BBC News Northern Ireland (3 Dec. 2008).

On 19 March 2008, Elizabeth II (1926–2022) attended ceremonies in the Black and White Hall of the Lanyon Building, Queen's University Belfast, to mark the centenary of the institution's grant of a Royal Charter of independence. A limited broadside published to mark the occasion records, 'During the visit, Her Majesty unveiled the Centenary Stone on which is carved the Centenary Stanza, penned to mark the occasion by one of the University's most distinguished graduates, Nobel Laureate, Dr Seamus Heaney'. The stanza was read by the author at the occasion.

The City

Published in Robin Robertson (ed.), *Love Poet, Carpenter: Michael Longley at Seventy* (London: Enitharmon, 2009), 66–7.

Title From Livy, *Ab Urbe Condita*, a history of Rome from its foundations (identified from *urbs*, II 11).
 I 1–2 The figure arriving at the start of the poem is identifiable as Father Michael McGlinchey, SH's Latin teacher at St Columb's, by his sighing wish in I 10–12 'Och boys, / I wish it were Book Six', the same wish assigned to him on the first page of SH's 'Translator's Note' to *ABVIa* (vii).
 II 5 *Conquest and imperium*: much as SH admired Book Six, he called it the worst of books as well as the best because of its 'imperial certitude' (*ABVIa*, 51).
 II 12 *Alba Longa*: an ancient Latin city in the Alban Hills in Central Italy, defeated in the seventh century BCE by the Romans, who took over its leadership of the Latin League, described in *Ab Urbe Condita*, 1.3 and 29. Livy says Aeneas's son Ascanius founded the city and named it from its location along the Alban Ridge.
 III: SH addresses Michael Longley, the dedicatee of the poem, for his evocation of Troy from the *Iliad* when Priam creeps back in the gate with the body of his son Hector given to him by his triumphant enemy Achilles (the story told in Longley's celebrated poem 'Ceasefire', in *The Ghost Orchid*, 1995), joining it to SH's recalling of Aeneas's escape from Troy with his father Anchises in the *Aeneid*. Both poets are now grandfathers (III 6), linked by their devotion to the Classics and their ageless application to them.

With Hindsight

Published in *Poetry Ireland Review*, 100 (March 2010): 33; subsequently as part I of *Triptych*, a letterpress broadside limited to twenty-six copies (Boston: Back Pages Books, 2013).

[text: *Poetry Ireland Review*]

Title] Triptych: I *Triptych2013*
1–12] [sentence case] *Triptych2013*
12 shoulder.] shoulder (error) *Poetry Ireland Review*

'With Hindsight' was returned in proof for *Poetry Ireland Review* on 10 February 2010, accompanied by 'The Mite-Box' and a short instruction by SH marked 'With Hindsight OK' (private collection). The text of *Triptych* (2013) appears at *PSH*, 1166.

HUMAN CHAIN (2010)

Human Chain was published in London by Faber & Faber on 2 September 2010 in hardback, and in paperback on 3 June 2011; it was published in New York by Farrar, Straus and Giroux in hardback on 14 September 2010 and in paperback on 30 August 2011. It was Book of the Week in the *Guardian*, and Book of the Month in the *Observer*, and was the Autumn Choice of the Poetry Book Society, marking the sixth occasion that a collection by SH had the accolade conferred. It won both the Forward Prize for Best Collection 2010 and the *Irish Times Poetry Now* Award for 2011. In the author's lifetime it sold 48,000 copies in hardback and 10,000 in paperback in the UK and Ireland, and would outsell every one of SH's single volumes in the year after his death.

It was at once recognised critically as a major development. Colm Tóibín described it in the *Guardian* as SH's 'best single volume for many years, and one that contains some of the best poems he has written'. Paul Batchelor in *The Times* agreed that it marked 'the best volume in his later phase'. Fintan O'Toole praised the book's force of 'social connection' (*Observer*) and Sian Hughes wrote that it 'strikes to the heart' in its metaphor for humanity (*Spectator*). Epithets for the book were swift to pour in. 'Masterly' (*Observer*); 'unerring certainty' (*The Times*); 'firing on all cylinders' (*Evening Standard*) with 'no sense of diminishment' (*Daily Telegraph*); it was, wrote John Carey in an influential summary, 'complete, brilliant and assured' (*Sunday Times*). There were demurrals, naturally, and compliments that were backhanded (the *Irish Independent* review said that it was a book of many pleasures, 'though more often in individual lines or images than in complete poems'); but the overwhelming tone was one of appreciation for what Eamon Grennan astutely identified in the *Irish Times* as 'a new departure' in SH's work: namely, that it was his 'first book of old age', and one that saw him moving with the human body's inevitable frailty on a voyage into 'metaphysical ache and observation'. It was in this sense that Adam O'Riordan in the *Daily Telegraph* expressed a hope that these were 'simply late and not last poems'.

The serious stroke that SH suffered in August 2006 inevitably left its mark. In March 2010, he gave an advance reading from *Human Chain* at the StAnza Festival in St Andrews in an effort to return to public readings, but it wasn't entirely a success, as he wrote to his publicist at Faber & Faber:

> It was the first time I'd read some of those new poems in public, 'Album' and 'Chanson d'Aventure', for example – things that I like very much, but which arise from and are explicit about truly intimate experience. Afterwards it struck me that any interviewer is bound to ask again about my stroke and my parents and all that the 'Album' entails/contains, and that these are subjects that I do not want to address other than in the poems themselves. (FF N50; *LSH*, 742)

With that, he decided sagely that he would not be available for press interviews when the book was to be published in six months' time.

'Truly intimate experience' had risen to dominance in a volume that is shadowed throughout by a sense of mortality and physical fragility, and that culminates in a series of powerful elegies for his parents and others. It is a spirit that pervades a sequence of poems modelled on the episodes in *Aeneid Book VI*, 'The Riverbank Field' and 'Route 110', gathered by the Gallery Press in 2007, and evidencing SH's continuing work towards a translation for Book VI of the *Aeneid*. And it is a spirit that fuses all areas of the book, especially the sequences that become a structural form more defining of this collection than previous volumes, both in eulogy (for Colin Middleton) and friendship (for Helen Vendler). The guiding themes and matters of *Human Chain* are family and elegy, often taken together, in what SH dubbed the 'many instances of separations and partings' that possessed the book, as in the affecting tributes to the poet's father 'The Butts' and 'Lick the Pencil'. SH explained to readers at the time:

> The links which hold the book together are various – parallels between different lives and landscapes, literary and cultural patternings, generational and familial connections. My grandfather, for example, appears in the penultimate poem, our first granddaughter at the end of 'Route 110'; our second in the last poem of the collection. [. . .] Yet for all these intimations of connection, there are many instances of separations and partings (as in 'Uncoupled' and the 'in memory' poems), of mortality ('Human Chain', 'The Baler'), of the far-off being glimpsed rather than retrieved ('Derry Derry Down', 'Loughanure').
> (*PBS Bulletin* 226, Autumn 2010)

Human Chain was delivered to Faber for 'a preliminary read' on 14 November 2009. In doing so, SH wrote that he was mindful of T. S. Eliot's litmus test on determining the moment at which a book has enough material to be considered complete (it remains *incomplete*, Eliot had explained to Marianne Moore in 1934, 'when one feels that the poems written require the cooperation of certain poems not yet written, in order to be themselves quite'; *The Letters of T. S. Eliot*, Vol. 7, 54). SH told his publisher, 'I have been waiting for those unwritten necessary ones to arrive. And when I found a way of including the second grandchild – "A Kite for Aibhín" – and "The Conway Stewart" (to link to the parent poems early on and look forward to the Columcille translations, "Lick the Pencil" and "Hermit Songs" in the latter part) I felt the book was near to being itself quite' (FF N50; *LSH*, 738). Throughout his correspondence with his publisher, SH can be seen in confident command of his production, showing meticulous care for which sequences were to be granted separate pages and which were to be run on, for which titles should take upper- or lower-case roman, for which elements should be small or initial caps. In so doing, and with a precision and attention that had characterised a lifetime's production, SH ensured that his final book had, in every way, become 'near to being itself quite'.

> There's an argument that a poem should be as tightly moulded and mum as an oyster, but the poems in *Human Chain* are not like that. The experience of writing them was more like opening a shell than sealing it, the twelve-line form in which most of them are cast providing – like an oyster knife – points of entry, little quick twists, and then, if the job were successful, a gleam of secreted life. (*PBS Bulletin* 226)

[text: *HC2010*]

Dedication The collection was dedicated to Des and Mary Kavanagh, and to Peter Fallon and Jean Barry, while the title poem was dedicated to Terence Brown.

'Had I not been awake'

Published in *Poetry Ireland Review*, 98 (20 July 2009): 5, and subsequently in *Little Star*, Inaugural Issue (2010): 69–71. Collected with revisions in *HC* and reprinted in the *Guardian* (6 Oct. 2011). Later in *NSP2014* and *100P*.

Title] 'Had I not been awake . . .' *Poetry Ireland Review*
5 fence:] fence; *Poetry Ireland Review*
6 it,] it *Poetry Ireland Review*
9 Returning like an animal to] Hurtling like an animal at *Little Star*]
11 After] Afterwards *Poetry Ireland Review*, *Little Star*

In a rare interview in 2010, SH commented in abstraction upon poetry in a way that seems especially relevant to the opening and closing poems that bookend the collection: 'So I think the difference in a poem, or a work of literary art, shall we say – story, novel – is that it isn't for the moment utilitarian communication, it is its own kind of housing of a moment, a snapshot of consciousness that can be looked upon by other persons' (*NewsHouse*, 14 April 2010).

11–12 SH continued to revise these final lines after delivery to his publisher in search of what he called an 'end-of-fairytale echo': temporarily becoming: 'Lapsed. But not / Into the ordinary. Ever' (10 Jan. 2010), then: 'Lapsed. But never after / Into the ordinary' (9 Feb. 2010), before reverting on proof to something closer to the original journal phrasing, which he revised to the version printed here (FF N50).

Album

First published as 'Now the oil-fired heating boiler comes to life' in *Parnassus*, 30: 1–2 (2008): 75. Subsequently, as 'Lapse of Time', *Poetry Ireland Review*, 98 (20 July 2009): 6–8; collected with revisions in *HC* under the title 'Album'; later in *NSP2014*.

Title] Now the oil-fired heating boiler comes to life *Parnassus* | Lapse of Time *Poetry Ireland Review*
I 3 I imagine them] another time and lapse *Poetry Ireland Review*
I 4] That must have fallen around midsummer *Poetry Ireland Review*
I 5 And the place] Come swimming up, and the place *Poetry Ireland Review*
I 6 oaks] trees *Poetry Ireland Review*
I 7 I'd often stand] I often stood *Poetry Ireland Review*
II 1 Seek] seek *Poetry Ireland Review*
II 8 A grey] There is a grey *Poetry Ireland Review*
IV 9 up trouser] up his trouser *Poetry Ireland Review*
V 2 rush him] rush in and surprise him *Poetry Ireland Review*
V 6 one-off] one off *Poetry Ireland Review*

Although published only as a whole from 2008, part III was drafted as an independent sonnet *c.*1985 for *The Haw Lantern* but not included in that volume (NLI 49,493/83).

Title SH abandoned the title 'Lapse of Time' after delivery of his typescript to his publisher to avoid what he described as 'an unintended pointless association/trial' with 'Lapsed' in *l.* 11 of the previous poem, 'Had I not been awake'. He considered 'Rushes' ('as in the film, but with my history it will be read as marsh vegetation') and 'Home Movie' ('not very appealing', 9–10 Jan. 2010); he then tried 'Family Album' but felt that 'clunks and prompts a bit loudly', before proposing 'the bare Album' (9 Feb. 2010). But the 'bare' title may not have provided as much personal cover as SH had desired, as he had acknowledged in a 25 March 2010 letter with his publisher, following a reading in St Andrews (FF N50; *LSH*, 742), for which 'Album' had been one of the poems that he did not wish to address in interview.

I 3 *them*: SH's parents.

I 6 *Grove Hill*: a circular tract of land with trees, possibly remnants of an old ring fort, near Broagh to the east of the village of Castledawson.

I 11–12 This idea is found in *Le Petit Prince* by Antoine de Saint-Exupéry (1943).

II 1 *Quercus*: Latin, corresponding to Irish *doire*, Derry (II 4).

II 3–4 *columba / Dove*: St Columb's is named from St Colmcille or St Columba.

II 1 and 6 *Quaerite autem primum regnum*: 'But seek ye first the kingdom' (Matthew 6:33).

II 8 'An old grey eye, weeping for lost renown': Frank O'Connor's translation of a line in Aodhagán Ó Rathaille's poem 'Valentine Browne' (*Kings, Lords and Commons*, Dublin: Gill & Macmillan, 1959, p. 102).

III 1 'they' are SH's parents. The 'I' of III 2 is the unborn poet who is also present, confirmed by the 'we' of III 12.

IV 1 *him*: the poet's father.

IV 7 New Ferry is a village near Ballymena in Co. Antrim, by the northern shore of Lough Beg.

V 1 A young grandson who is innocent of the inhibitions of the mature Irish male.

V 7 *quod erat demonstrandum*: the positive conclusion of a Euclidean theorem: 'what was to be shown'.

V 8 The most celebrated son's three attempts were Aeneas's failed attempts to embrace the shade of his father Anchises in *Aeneid*, 6.700–2, the *ter conatus* motif.

V 12 'very' from *verus*, true.

The Conway Stewart

First published in *Many Mansions* (Dublin: Stoney Road Press, 2009), in a limited printing of 125 copies, and subsequently in *Honouring the Word: Poetry and Prose Celebrating Maurice Harmon on his 80th Birthday* (Cliffs of Moher, Co. Clare: Salmon Poetry, 2010), 30, a limited printing of 250 copies. Collected in HC and reprinted in the *Poetry Society Bulletin*, 226 (Autumn 2010): 4–7. Later included in *NSP2014* and *100P*.

Title A small, elegant fountain pen, the Series 58 of which is accurately described in the poem, often the first fountain pen given by parents to pupils starting secondary school, and, in SH's case, 'a pen which my parents bought me the day I went to the school as a boarder' at St Columb's College in Derry (*PBS Bulletin*, 226).

17 *Dear*: the first employment of the pen, given by the parents, will be to write home the next day, the first day after parting from them (*l.* 15).

Uncoupled

First published in *HC* and subsequently in the *Guardian* (24 Jan. 2011), before inclusion in *NSP2014*.

Working title 'Diptych' in MS (NLI 49,493/135).
   I 1 *Who*: the poet's mother.
   II 1 *Who*: the poet's father.

The Butts

Published in *Agenda*, 44. 4–45. 1 (Winter 2009): 82. Collected in *HC* and included in *NSP2014*.

21 pocket-lining] pocket lining *Agenda*

Working titles in TS 'A Restitution' and 'As Close as We Got' (NLI 49,493/135).
   Title Cigarette butts; cf. 'Lick the Pencil' (*HC*, 80–1; *PSH*, 679).
   1 *His suits hung*: after the death of the wearer, the poet's father.

Chanson d'Aventure

Published in the *Irish Times* (11 April 2010): 7. Included in *NSP2014* and *100P*.

Epigraph 2] [indent] *Irish Times*
I 8 laser-fast] laser fast *Irish Times*
II 7 Warm] Soft *Irish Times*
II 10 Dungloe] Glendoan *Irish Times*
II 11 Glendoan] Churchill *Irish Times*
III 5 astream] wrapped *Irish Times*
III] see 'Cutaways' (*PSH*, 636).

SH wrote that '"Miracle" and "Chanson d'Aventure" treat the experience of stroke through a story from the New Testament, a poem by John Donne and a sculpture from Delphi respectively' (*PBS Bulletin*, 226).
   Title Medieval lyric form, telling the story of an experience of the speaker, usually in love: literally 'song of a happening'. The happening in this poem is the stroke which SH suffered in 2006 and the ambulance journey with his wife after it.
   Epigraph John Donne, 'The Ecstasy', *ll.* 71–2.

I 2 *the drive*: by ambulance to Letterkenny Hospital from the guesthouse in Co. Donegal where the Heaneys had been celebrating the seventy-fifth birthday of their friend Anne Friel.

I 4 'you' is Marie Heaney. The poem's first section draws repeatedly on the detail of Donne's 'The Ecstasy', quoted in the epigraph: 'everything and nothing spoken' (*l.* 7); 'All day, the same our postures were, / And we said nothing, all the day' ('Ecstasy', *ll.* 19–20). 'Our eyebeams threaded laser-fast' (*l.* 8); 'Our eye-beams twisted, and did thread / Our eyes, upon one double string' ('Ecstasy', *ll.* 7–8).

I 12 *love on hold, body and soul apart*: a concise summary of the theme of 'The Ecstasy'.

II 1 Cf. 'Forlorn! The very word is like a bell / To toll me back from thee to my sole self!' (Keats, *Ode to a Nightingale*, *ll.* 70–1).

II 2 The sexton of the Catholic church at Bellaghy.

II 5 College bellman at St Columb's.

II 7 Cf. 'This living hand, now warm and capable', *l.* 1 (Keats): the hand without feeling after the stroke.

II 10–11 *Dungloe, Glendoan*: towns in Co. Donegal, between Lifford and Letterkenny.

III 1ff. The Charioteer of Delphi is an original bronze statue, excavated in 1896 by French archaeologists near the north-west region of the temple of Apollo at Delphi. The upright figure is only identified as a charioteer (or horseman of some kind) by the reins he holds in his right hand; the left arm is missing from above the elbow. SH makes it a figure for his attempts to recover manual movement by physiotherapy in the hospital in Dublin.

Miracle

Privately produced for SH as a Christmas card by the Gallery Press (2006) and subsequently in a commemorative programme limited to 150 copies by the Keough Naughton Notre Dame Center, Dublin. Published in *Czesław Miłosz Literary Festival* (Krakow: 2009): 28–33, and the *Irish Times* (11 April 2010): 7. Collected in *HC* and later in the *Guardian* (24 Jan. 2011), *NSP2014* and *100P*.

3 in –] in *Irish Times*
11 lightheadedness] light-headedness *Irish Times*

Title After SH's stroke, various friends carried him downstairs; here this is compared to the biblical miracle at Capernaum in which a paralysed man is lowered by his friends through the roof to be healed by Christ (Mark 2:1–12, and Luke 5:17–26).

1 The one who takes up his bed and walks is a different miracle of Christ (John 5:8–16).

Human Chain

First published in Nicholas Allen and Eve Patten (eds), *That Island Never Found: Essays and Poems for Terence Brown* (Dublin: Four Courts Press, 2007), 195, and subsequently in *Irish Times Special Supplement* (13 Feb. 2008): 3. Collected with revisions in *HC* and reprinted in the *Guardian* (24 Jan. 2011).

5 wads of grain I'd] wads I had *That Island Never Found*

For all its importance to this collection, 'Human Chain' had a roundabout route to becoming title poem for the book. An early two-stanza sonnet of that name was revised in TS into tercets of twelve lines under the title 'Seeing the bags of meal', and although the formative title would become fixed from the next draft, the structure of the poem continued to undergo formal development. Following its first printing as 'Human Chain' in 2007, SH expanded the poem into a triptych under that title, of which this poem formed part i, a fifteen-line draft of 'The Mite-Box' comprised part ii, and an unpublished twelve-line poem beginning 'Midnight rain scourging Santiago' made up part iii. In a TS dated 11–12 November 2009, this final section was dropped to produce a diptych, still under the title 'Human Chain', that adopted two part titles: i becoming 'Lent Hands', and ii 'The Mite-Box', before a separation of the two poems by early 2010 (NLI 49,493/135).

Dedication Terence Brown (b.1944), Emeritus Professor of English at Trinity College Dublin, a friend of SH, and a leading scholar of Irish history and poetry in English.

1 The passing of sacks of food among aid workers, as well as the strain of the biblical lifters in the previous poem, reminds SH of lifting heavy bags of grain in farming.

11–12 The letting go of the heavy weight is a release which brings to mind the final release from life connections, in a poem SH described 'of mortality' (*PBS Bulletin*, 226).

A Mite-Box

Published in *Poetry Ireland Review*, 100 (March 2010): 32. Collected in *HC*.

11 Camera] camera *Poetry Ireland Review*

Dated 23–4 October 2009 in MS (NLI 49,493/135), and briefly incorporated in TS into 'Human Chain' in autumn of that year (above).

Title A box for collecting coins for charity, from the biblical story of 'the widow's mite' (Luke 21:1–4). As in the preceding two poems, the power of touch by hand is a pressing theme here.

5 *'The foreign missions'*: a common requirement from Irish Catholic schoolchildren was to collect coins in this way for the conversion of people, mostly in Africa and the Far East.

8 *every doorstep*: the children went from door to door, asking for contributions from the neighbours.

9 *pinprick*: a method of calculating the amount of money accrued was to make a pinprick for every penny in a card (called a 'prickcard') with about sixty spaces.

11–12 *Camera / Obscura*: a device by which a pinprick of light is shone through a black box onto one of its walls on which it casts an inverted image of the figure inside it.

An Old Refrain

Published in *Poetry Review*, 993 (Autumn 2009): 18–20. Collected in *HC* and reprinted in the *Poetry Society Bulletin*, 226 (Autumn 2010): 4–7.

I 1 Robin-run] Robin run *Poetry Review* (proof)
III]   You could say
        When the wordscape changes
        You don't know where

        You are, or who.
        That an unheard world
        Will fail.

        But no. Ken
        Otherwise,
        For you can,

        Trick-o'-the-loop man,
        Conjure
        Every where. *Poetry Review*

In an initial TS, the poem is a single part draft of twelve lines (NLI 49,493/135); by the time SH submitted the poem to *Poetry Review* in the summer of 2009, it was a piece of three parts of twelve lines, the third of which, given above, was abandoned before the poem's inclusion in *HC*.

Throughout his career, SH had all but unconsciously adopted initial capitals at the start of each line of lyric verse as a system he 'hardly thought about', even though, as he put it in correspondence for *HC*, capitals operated 'like stop signs' and 'the hovering, discreet, antenna-feel of the slender versing is made clumpier'. But for *HC* he now considered introducing sentence case in certain places, the first of which in the running order was 'An Old Refrain', as he wrote to his publisher: 'Then as to lower case and all that. Once it raises itself as a problem at all, it becomes too much of a problem. Heretofore I hardly thought about it. But I incline to think that "Eelworks", "Slack" and "A Herbal" could well be without the capitals (except, as I said, the original Guillevic maintains them). "An Old Refrain" and "Derry Derry Down" suggest themselves for demotion too, but in those cases I like the braking factor the caps introduce into the short lines. And then there are those hermit songs. I've got used to them the way they are.' In the event, he retained his characteristic initial caps throughout. (9 Jan. and 2 March 2010, FF N50.)

I Title Introducing various Elizabethan, mostly Shakespearean, terms for plants familiar from SH's childhood.

I 8 The Wood Road is the semi-official road outside the farmhouse at The Wood where the Heaneys lived: the title of the next poem.

II 1 *seggins*: local term for rough grass or rushes.

II 4 *boortree*: local term for elder, used a number of times by SH, notably in 'Broagh' (*WO*, 17; *PSH*, 125).

II 7 *benweed*: ragwort.

II 10 *easing* (of rain): moderating.

The Wood Road

Published in *Magma Poetry* (Winter 2006): 28. Subsequently in a programme guide for Irish Seminar, 26 June–12 July 2007, directed by Seamus Deane, Luke Gibbons and Kevin Whelan, South Bend, Indiana: Keough-Naughton Institute for Irish Studies (2007): 26–42; in Melissa Sihra and Paul Murphy (eds), *The Dreaming Body: Contemporary Irish Theatre* (Buckinghamshire: Colin Smythe, 2009): ix–x; and then the *Irish Times* (11 April 2010): 7.

1 widened,] widened. *Magma*
10 staunch patrol] patrol *Magma*
11] Sentry-still, in profile, *Magma*
12 Harassing] Guarding *Magma*
15 built trig and tight,] hand-built and squat. *Magma* | built neat and tight, *Irish Times*
16–18] As a drystone beehive hut, / Looked up to, looking down, // Allowed the reigns like an adult – *Magma*
18^19] In the picture at last,
    The one on the whitewashed wall

>   Of a horse and cart and turfman
>   Embroidered on calico
>   In what they called 'the long ago',
>
>   Framed in passe-par-tout. *Magma*

19 Then] Or *Magma*
25–30] [omitted] *Magma*
33] This was/is the Wood Road. *Magma, Irish Times*
35 milk-churn] milk-can *Magma* | milk churn *Irish Times*

Dated Glanmore 5–7 August 2006 in TS (NLI 49,493/135).

Title Officially Ballymacombs Road, by the Heaney farmhouse at The Wood.

3 *Bill Pickering*: Special Militiaman – a 'B-Special', a member of the auxiliary group in the RUC, largely Protestant, and disbanded in 1970; see 'The Nod' (*DC*, 33; *PSH*, 608).

12 *Mulhollandstown*: small area to the north-west of the Heaneys' house at The Wood. Mentioned in 'Tollund' (*SL*, 69; *PSH*, 501) as the equivalent of the byroads in Jutland.

20 SH's neighbour from Tamlaghtduff, Thomas McElwee was the eighth of the IRA hunger strikers to die, on 8 August 1981. SH attended his wake as a neighbourly courtesy though he makes it clear that he was not sympathetic to the IRA campaign of violence.

26 SH's niece, Hugh Heaney's daughter Rachel, was knocked off her bike and killed outside the house at The Wood in May 1985, a tragedy which is commemorated in SH's poem 'The Summer of Lost Rachel' (*HL*, 36–7; *PSH*, 374).

33 The Wood Road 'as it is and was' is seen as inescapably a location of conflict and tragedy.

The Baler

Published *HC* and subsequently in the *Guardian* (9 Oct. 2010).

Dated Glanmore 10 August 2006 in MS in a pencil draft entitled 'Another August' (NLI 49,493/135); a poem 'of mortality' (*PBS Bulletin*, 226).

1 *All day*: a day when the ageing poet hears a hay-baler working in a nearby field and is reminded of similar days in his earlier life.

19 Derek Hill (1916–2000) was an English-born landscape and portrait painter who lived much of his life in Donegal. Commissioned by Faber to paint a portrait of SH for his fiftieth birthday in 1989.

Derry Derry Down

Published in *Poetry Review*, 993 (Autumn 2009): 18–20.

An instance of 'the far-off being glimpsed rather than retrieved (*PBS Bulletin*, 226).

Title The refrain of a popular English folk song called 'The Keeper', apparently about a gamekeeper hunting a series of female deer but with sexual insinuations which may carry over into SH's poem, though its primary appeal for him was probably the geographical echo of 'Derry'. John Redmond points out that there are two county names in the title.

I 10 Annie Devlin was a neighbour of the Heaneys near their farmhouse The Wood.

II 3 *The Lodge*: probably an invented 'big house' name.

II 7 *Still life*: a painting, typically of fruit like the gooseberry and pears here.

II 10 *Sleeping beauty*: the inaccessible figure of the fairytale, in contrast to the 'unforbidden' fruit of the opening section. In II 12 the reporting voice enters her world by the scullion's (servants') door, echoing the family name of SH's forebears in that house, the 'Scullions'.

Eelworks

First published in the *TLS* (20 Nov. 2009): 8. Collected with revisions in *HC* and included in *NSP2014*.

I–VI] [sentence case] *TLS*
I 3 perform!] perform *TLS*
II 10 Horse-and-cart] horse and cart *TLS*
II 13 Rum-and-peppermint] rum and peppermint *TLS*
V 20 Like silk] like a silk stocking *TLS*

Title The term for the eel-fishing industry worked in by Marie Heaney's forebears at Ardboe on the western shore of Lough Neagh.

I 1 *the princess*: returning to the fairytale theme of the previous poem, to apply to SH's courting of his wife (the 'me' of *l.* 4). The term 'a-courting' also has a children's cultural source, the nursery song 'Frog Went a-Courtin'.

II 15 Marie Heaney's father did run a public house in Ardboe, Co. Tyrone.

III 1 Alfie Kirkwood, classmate of SH at primary school, wore an eelskin round his wrist 'for strength'. Cf. 'Settings', xvii

(*ST*, 73; *PSH*, 434) 'When a wrist was bound with eelskin, energy / Redounded in that arm'.

IV 18 *Selkie-streaker*: selkies are mermaids or seal-women, invoked here with the eel which seems to operate similarly between the underwater and above ground. A favourite figure for SH since early poems like 'Maighdean Mara' (*WO*, 56; *PSH*, 144).

V 1ff. Walter de la Mare (1873–1956), English poet and short-story writer, familiar among other things for his writing for children. The setting is Southend House, Montpelier Row, in St Margarets, Twickenham, where on 20 September 1955 de la Mare recorded a reminiscence of seeing the 105-foot tree at the bottom of the garden 'reflected in a looking glass struck by lightning' (Walter de la Mare, *Reading and Speaking*, Caedmon Literary Series TC1046, 1956). The image of de la Mare looking through the same window at a 'Vista of Hanoverian trees' had previously been recorded by T. S. Eliot in February 1947 after a visit to Southend House ('Montpelier Row', *Poems of T. S. Eliot*, I, 309). The house overlooks the River Thames, and there are no downs in the middle distance (V 5).

V 9 The link here is with the eel stripping its skin.

V 11 *éblouissante*: dazzling.

Slack

Published as a limited-edition of 1,000 cards and fifty broadsides to commemorate SH's attendance at the opening of the Newcastle Centre for the Literary Arts in October 2009 (Newcastle-upon-Tyne: Newcastle Centre for the Literary Arts, 2009). Subsequently published in *Little Star*, Inaugural Issue (2010): 69–71, and collected in *HC*.

III 11 *Catharsis*] Catharsis *Slack*

Title Coal-dust, kept as a slow-burning means of keeping a fire alight without flaming.

III 7 *blet*: soft, over-ripened fruit.

A Herbal

First published in Jane Conroy (ed.), *Franco-Irish Connections: Essays, Memoirs and Poems in Honour of Pierre Joannon* (Four Courts Press, 2009), 123–8. Collected in *TSH* (110–15; 635–6).

Dated 16 January 2009 in TS as 'A Bellaghy Herbal' (NLI 49,493/138).

'Guillevic's Brittany grows into and out of my own Broagh and Bellaghy', SH told readers of this translation of Breton poet, Eugène Guillevic (1907–97), whose *Herbier de la Bretagne* (1975) is a poem of decay and renewal. Guillevic was hosted by SH at the Kilkenny Arts Festival in 1976 (*SS*, xxiv). SH tells O'Driscoll that Guillevic's *Living in Poetry*, published in Paris in 1980 and in Dublin in 1999, was one of the 'auspicious precedents' he considered when he agreed 'to an interview book' (*TSH*, 636).

2 *graves*: SH brings explicit death-related images while Guillevic is more purely botanical.

11 'you' is Marie Heaney: a personal memory added to the French original. She wanted the sound recordist on a film to record the sound of feet through the wet grass.

15 *Through the wet*: SH's TS had carried 'Slushing through the wet', which he changed at proof stage to avoid acoustic similarities with the previous poem, 'Slack', initially considering 'Through the slushed wet' before alighting on the chosen phrase (9 April 2010, FF N50).

18ff. *dialect*: the anthropomorphising of plants is sustained through the poem, like the grass in *l.* 25.

40ff. The bracken is SH's localising of the poem's botany.

For further annotations see *TSH*, 635–6.

Canopy

First published in the Harvard University Art Museums exhibition catalogue for David Ward, *Canopy: A Work for Voice and Light in Harvard Yard* (Cambridge, Mass.: Harvard University Busch-Reisinger, 1997), 12–13; then in *Metre*, 3 (Autumn 1997): 36–7. Collected with revisions in *HC*.

1–36] [sentence case] *Canopy, Metre*
5 installed] hung *Canopy, Metre*
9 gloaming –] gloaming *Canopy, Metre*
10] or shadow adam's apples. *Canopy, Metre*
11 That] They *Canopy, Metre*
15–16] tree congregations stirring, / giving thanks for the summer. *Canopy, Metre*
18 Reeds] Or reeds *Canopy, Metre*
25 airs:] airs. *Canopy, Metre*
26–8] I met the artist and told him / Dante's whispering wood / of the suicides had its answer: *Canopy, Metre*
30–2] it would have curled like fingers / or a tendril of mistletoe / around the fingers that broke it. *Canopy* | it would have curled like lover's / fingers or mistletoe / around the fingers that broke it. *Metre*
33–5] His work had confounded hell / in elysium. Avalon. / Or so I thought as we parted *Canopy, Metre*

36] and the pinprick lights came on. *Canopy* | like shades, and the lights came on. *Metre*

Dated 1987 and 1994 in TS (NLI 49,493/135).

Canopy was a temporary audiovisual exhibition by the British artist David Ward, installed in Harvard Yard in May 1994 that, for two weeks between dusk and darkness, replayed recorded voices in multiple languages from sound sources hanging in the trees. On publishing the poem in 1997, SH noted the need to allow time to circulate before writing about the immediate: 'it takes a while', he wrote, 'for the familiar to sink deep enough to resurface in an imaginable way' (*Metre*, 3 (Autumn 1997): 14).

14–15 *recording*: picking up the themes of sound recording and anthropomorphic sounds in nature from the previous poem.

26 Dante, *Inferno*, 13: the wood of the suicides, the violent against themselves.

29 *a twig had been broken off*: following *Aeneid*, 3.39–43 where the tree in Thrace damaged by Aeneas reveals itself to be Polydorus, the son of Priam; Dante says he plucks a small branch from a tree which then cries out in pain and reveals itself to be the suicide Pier delle Vigne (*Inferno*, 13.31–6). The spirit of this violent passage is markedly opposed to the celebratory context in SH's poem, represented by the lover's mistletoe.

The Riverbank Field

First published with 'Route 110' in *RF*. Collected with revisions in *HC*, and subsequently in *SD*. Included in *NSP2014*.

1–24] [sentence case] *RF*
9 bees] butterflies *RF*
12 Elysian-silvered] Elysian silvered *RF*
20] once they have done their turn of a thousand years *RF*
22–4] so that memories of life on this side are shed / and soul repines to dwell in flesh and blood /under the dome of heaven'. *RF*

This passage from *Aeneid Book VI* is the second excerpt to be collected by SH among his twelve collections, and the third to be published. SH told members of the *Poetry Book Society*: 'In "The Riverbank Field" the landscape of that same Broagh merges with the landscape of Book VI of *The Aeneid*, and episodes from Book VI continue to be matched in the autobiographical sequence that follows' (*PBS Bulletin*, 226).

Title A field by the river Moyola near Castledawson. 'Riverbank' is also the translation of the first line and title of SH's early poem 'Broagh' (*WO*, 17).

1 *Loeb*: the edition of *Aeneid*, 6 in *Virgil: Eclogues, Georgics, Aeneid 1–6*, edited by G. P. Goold with an English translation by H. Rushton Fairclough (Harvard University Press, 1916).

2 Loeb, 555, *ll.* 703–4.

3 Lethe, the river of forgetfulness in Virgil; Moyola, SH's local river.

4–5 Back Park, Grove Hill, Long Rigs: named fields near Castledawson.

7 *domos placidas*: Loeb, 555 (*l.* 705).

9 *bees in sunlight*: Loeb, 555 (*l.* 707).

10 *stet*: let it stand.

14–15 *animae ... debentur*: the words of Aeneas's father Anchises: 'spirits ... to whom second bodies are owed by fate': i.e. a second life in the world (*Aeneid*, 6.713–14).

18 '*In my own words*': the schoolroom injunction to rephrase a received text.

Route 110

First published with 'The Riverbank Field' in *RF*. Collected with revisions in *HC*, and subsequently in *SD*. Included in *NSP2014* and *100P*. Section X published as 'A Sports Day in Bellaghy' in Irish Seminar, 26 June–12 July 2007, directed by Seamus Deane, Luke Gibbons and Kevin Whelan, South Bend, Indiana: Keough-Naughton Institute for Irish Studies (2007): 26–42.

II 7 with their displays] festooned *RF*
II 8] with canvas schoolbags, heads for brushes, caps, *RF*
II 12 close-packed] close packed *RF*
IV 2 standard-issue] standard issue *RF*
IV 3 second-hand] second hand *RF*
IV 5] For the dismay caused by my late night doorsteppings *RF*
IV 8 bargain suit] light suit *RF*
IV 10] expats] ex-pats *RF*
IV 11–12] To a deconsecrated chapel on their slopes / Only to sense oneself the only one at home. *RF*
VI 9 Sonbrother] Landsman *RF*
VIII 8–9] Like lamps at road blocks manned by the RUC / On those small hours, pre-Troubles roads *RF*
VIII 11 the necking] our necking *RF*
VIII 12 impurity] piety *RF*
IX 6–8]Bomb-blasted after hours the Wednesday

    The thirteen Bloody Sunday dead were buried?
    Or of bodies unglorified, accounted for and bagged *RF*

XI 1–2] The stillness of long evenings when we'd stand / Just watching. *RF*
XI 8–11]Beneath our feet, long since vacated
   Yet returnable to, still twilit and ahover

   As if among shadows stirring on the brink
   We had commingled, and were standing watching, *RF*
XII 3 fresh-plucked] fresh plucked *RF*
XII 5–7] Would linger on, in spite of hoovering / Where mother and child were due to enter later // So now, for a morning offering to one *RF*

The poem's twelve sections correspond in subject to episodes in Virgil's *Aeneid*, 6, which SH had been translating over many years, and was published posthumously in 2016.

Title The bus route by which SH travelled between Magherafelt and Belfast: pronounced 'One-ten'

Dedication *Anna Rose*: SH's first grandchild, the daughter of his son Christopher.

II 4 *Aeneid*, 6.242. The derivation of Avernus from a possible Greek antecedent, Aornos. But the famous line – 'from which the Greeks named the place "Birdless"' – was thought an interpolation by early commentators on Virgil.

II 12 Charon's barge, which carried the shades of the dead in the *Aeneid*.

III 5 The passengers flock to the bus as the shades pushed their way towards Charon's barge; the inspector divides them as Charon divided the shades between those who could cross and those who couldn't.

IV 10 Doves were sacred to Aeneas's mother, Venus, and their appearance before him convinces him that his quest (to find his father in the underworld) will be successful (*Aeneid*, 6.190–2). They lead him to the golden bough.

V 1ff. The McNicholls were a family who lived near the Heaneys in Mossbawn. Mrs McNicholl's silvered foil-wrapped oats-stalk led SH home as the golden bough led Aeneas on his quest. A further echo is that Philomena McNicholl – 'a fey if ever there was one' (*SS*, 242) – led SH to school on his first day.

VI 4 *Michael Mulholland*: a neighbour of the Heaneys, he was drowned in the Bristol Channel and his wake was held without his body, as the lost steersman Palinurus was unburied *(Aeneid*, 6.337ff.).

VIII 1 *Aeneid*, 6.454–5; the moment when Aeneas sees Dido in the underworld, linked to a girlfriend that SH has abandoned as Aeneas abandoned her.

IX 2 *Mr Lavery*: John F. Lavery, Catholic publican, killed on 21 December 1971 as he carried an IRA bomb out of his pub on the corner of the Lisburn Road and Ashley Avenue, where the Heaneys lived (see McKittrick 1999, 134).

IX 5 *Louis O'Neill*: Catholic fisherman from Ardboe, killed when a bomb exploded without warning at the Catholic-owned Imperial Bar in Stewartstown, 3 February 1972. The bar had been closed in mourning for those killed on Bloody Sunday but some customers went in through the back door for a drink. O'Neill is the subject of SH's poem 'Casualty' (*FW*, 14–17; *PSH*, 223) which says O'Neill was kept away from the pub 'by his own crowd', though the bomb was probably placed by loyalist paramilitaries.

IX 7 *Thirteen who'd been shot in Derry?:* on Bloody Sunday, 30 January 1972.

X 1 *Virgil's happy shades*: Aeneid, 6.645ff. (*ABVIa*, 35, 874ff.).

X 7 Slim Whitman (1923–2013) was an American country singer of unrivalled popularity in 1950s Ireland at events such as village carnivals and the sports day described here.

XII 1 *the age of births*: as of SH's granddaughter Anna Rose, the dedicatee of the whole sequence.

XII 9 Like the light-givers in part V.

Death of a Painter

Printed as 'In Memory of Nancy Wynne Jones' as a private funeral card 2006 and published as 'In Memory of Nancy Wynne-Jones' in *Stony Thursday* (Autumn 2008): 1–2, and in *New Republic* (8 July 2010): 38.

Epigraph i.m.] In Memory *New Republic*

Dedication Nancy Wynne-Jones (1922–2006) was a Welsh and Irish painter, born in Dolgellau, North Wales. She studied music at the Royal Academy of Music in London (1940–3). She moved to Cornwall, and then Kinsale, Co. Cork (in 1972) before settling in Rathdrum, Co. Wicklow, where she died. SH said of her painting that it was 'place and palette and spirit, all equal' (*Guardian*, 29 Nov. 2006).

3 One of Wynne-Jones's most admired paintings is *Cornfields with Red Farm* (1980).

4 *Cézanne*: compared here because of his many paintings of Mont Sainte-Victoire in Provence.

Loughanure

First published in *Archipelago*, 2 (Spring 2008): 11–14.

I–V] [unnumbered parts, separated by asterisks] *Archipelago*
I 8 Forty-odd] Forty odd *Archipelago*
II 2 the wall] a wall *Archipelago*
II 5 Plato's Er? Who watched] the man of Er? Who saw *Archipelago*
II 8 far-seeing] farseeing *Archipelago*
III] [omitted] *Archipelago*
IV] [fifth section] *Archipelago*
IV 4–12]Had heard the tale of Caoilte and the fawn
    He hunted from Tory Island to the door
    Of a fairy hill where he wasn't turned away

    But led to a crystal chair on the hill floor
    Where he saw warriors seated with their women
    On one side of the house, while a girl with yellow hair

    Harped and then drank from horns they handed her,
    The horizon might have lightened and the far
    'Lake of the yew tree' gleamed in that cloud-swabbed air. *Archipelago*
V] [sixth section] *Archipelago*
V 1–2 turns out / Now that I] turns out, now / My brazen car *Archipelago*

One of the two poems that SH described as 'of the far-off being glimpsed rather than retrieved' (*PBS Bulletin*, 226).

Title Loughanure is a village halfway between Gweedore and Dungloe in Co. Donegal.

Dedication Colin Middleton (1910–83), friend of the Heaneys, was a Northern Irish modernist/surrealist painter, who was born in Belfast, and died in Dublin. SH's poem 'In Small Townlands' was dedicated to him (*DN*, 54; *PSH*, 46).

I 1, 4 Middleton was a heavy smoker.

I 7 The painting by Middleton bought by the Heaneys 'thirty years ago' was hung in their house in Dublin.

II 4–5 Dante Alighieri and Plato, famous literary accounts of the afterlife, in *The Divine Comedy* and *Republic*.

II 10 Er, on his return from the afterlife, says that he saw souls returning from heaven to choose new lives, including the soul of Orpheus changing into a swan.

III This section added after delivery to the publisher, an addition that SH knew 'ups the ante a bit' with its reference to 'the Kingdom', adding, 'I confess I like the lift of the big word' (9 Feb. 2010; FF N50).

III 1–2 *the Kingdom / Come*: variant on 'Thy Kingdom come' in the 'Our Father'.

III 3 *scrim*: a semi-revealing screen in theatre; *fontanel*: soft spot on a newborn infant's head.

III 6–10 Middleton's strange posture for a new look at his work is likened to a vision of the damned in a mannerist Renaissance painting.

IV 1 *Rannafast*: a village (Rann na Feirste in Irish) in the Rosses area of north-west Co. Donegal, a Gaeltacht area where students went for courses in Irish. SH was fourteen in 1953.

IV 3 *seanchas*: local history; *dinnseanchas*: local history in poetic form, mostly associated with place names.

IV 5 *Caoilte*: Caoilte mac Rónáin, nephew of Fionn mac Cumhaill in Irish legend; he could communicate with animals.

IV 6 *Tory*: island nine miles off the north-west coast of Co. Donegal. Because of his speed of foot, Caoilte was able to capture pairs of animals from all around Ireland.

IV 12 *'Lake of the Yew Tree'*: 'Loch an Iubhair' in Irish, as in V 10 below, is Loughanure.

V 3 *Mount Errigal*: 750-metre mountain near Gweedore in Co. Donegal, a notable local landmark.

V 7 The Greek word may be *apokatastasis*, in theology the restoration of creation to a condition of perfection.

V 9 Hannah Mhór, big Hannah, presumably an Irish speaker known to SH.

V 10 *Loch an Iubhair*: Loughanure in Irish (as in IV, 12 above).

V 11 Clarnico-Murray's hard iced caramels were very popular in Ireland in the 1950s.

V 12 *Sharkey's*: presumably a shop in the Gaeltacht area.

Wraiths

First published in Des Lally with Peter Fallon and John Fanning (eds), *Captivating Brightness: Ballynahinch* (Connemara: Occasional Press [July] 2008): 40; subsequently in *From the Small Back Room: A Festschrift for Ciaran Carson* (Belfast: Netherlea, 2008), 230–1.

Dedication Ciaran Carson (1948–2019), Northern Irish poet, was born in Belfast where he lived all his life; he was a student of SH's at Queen's University. He grew up speaking Irish, a decision for the household made by his parents, and he was a notable singer and flute-player.

I SIDHE

Sidhe (pronounced 'she') is the Irish term for the people of the fairy world, here imagined as dwelling underground.

1 *She*: literally the companion who leads the speaker into an underground cattle shelter, but also a homophone for the poem's title.

10 The situation of the couple is represented in cinematic terms: the first incarnation of the poem's insubstantial wraiths.

II PARKING LOT

Title A stopping point for the bus on its way to deliver the students to their Gaeltacht base for a summer school.

7 *Between languages*: between English and Irish: the condition of Ciaran Carson in some ways.

III WHITE NIGHTS

1 *Furrow-plodders*: the Rannafast Pipers Band in their regalia.

3 *neck-pullers*: the action required to kill chickens, reinforcing the rural image of the opening line; *chanters*: the finger-stopped section of the bagpipes.

8 *We*: the children, early to bed, remote from the band proper, even in the brightness of the summer night.

Sweeney Out-Takes

Published in *Agenda*, 43. 4–44. 1 (Autumn 2008): 75–6.

Title All three of these poems are in fact extracts from SH's recensions of his work towards *SA*.

Dedication For Greg Delanty (b.1958), Cork poet and friend of SH. The spoof name here is on the pattern of Delanty's similarly spoof book, *The Greek Anthology: Book XVII* (Manchester: Carcanet 2012), with mock-attributions to various recognisable renamed Irish poets (there are only sixteen books in *The Greek Anthology*). Gregory of Corkus is what Delanty calls himself. See Greg Delanty, *Collected Poems 1986–2006* (Manchester: Carcanet Oxford Poets, 2006), xiii.

I OTTERBOY

1 Eorann is the wife of mad Sweeney who tried to prevent his flight by seizing hold of his cloak.

3 *I*: the narrative voice is Sweeney's (though SH says that Sweeney is to be identified with him).

5 In the story Sweeney throws St Ronan's breviary (massbook here) into the lake and it is restored by an otter.

9 *alb*: the full-length white garment worn by clerics.

10 *waterdog*: the Irish for otter is *madra uisce*, 'dog of the water'.

II HE REMEMBERS LYNCHECHAUN

Title In the Sweeney story 'some say Lynchechaun was a half-brother of Sweeney's, some say he was a foster-brother, but whichever he was, he was deeply concerned for Sweeney and brought him back three times out of his madness' (cf. *SA* section 26); 'He' and 'I' of *l.* 8, and the quotation marks for the whole, reinforce the Heaney–Sweeney identification in the SWEENEY REDIVIVUS section of *SI* and elsewhere.

8 *crane*: the assembly over the fire in old kitchens from which pots were hung for cooking.

III THE PATTERN

6 The pattern of Catholic observance, set from this child's first confession.

Colum Cille Cecinit

Published in *HC*.

Translations by SH of three famous short bardic poems, headed with their first lines in Irish, in Gerard Murphy's *Early Irish Lyrics*. See *TSH*, 129.

Title *Cecinit* (Latin): sang. Colmcille/Columba was a sixth-century saint whose name means 'dove of the church'. SH wrote in regard to *HC*:

> Saint Colmcille, poet, scribe and patron saint of the St Columb's College I attended once in Derry, is a presence throughout. His quill with·its 'beetle-spark of ink' ghosts 'The Conway Stewart', a pen which my parents bought me the day I went to the school as a boarder; it glitters again in the reeling nibs of 'Hermit Songs'; and is still wet on the lead in 'Lick the Pencil'. (*PBS Bulletin*, 226)

I IS SCÍTH MO CHROB ÓN SCRÍBAINN

Published as *Columcille the Scribe* (Royal Irish Academy, 2004), an edition of 150 signed copies handwritten onto vellum by Tim O'Neill; reprinted in a limited edition of fifty copies by Wild Apple Press, Bethesda, Maryland

2011. Subsequently under the same title in the *Irish Times* (7 June 1997): B9, and the *Gazette of the Grolier Club*, 50 (Spring 1999): 5. Collected with revisions in *HC* and later as a poster in the Poems on the Underground series (2011).

1 from] with *Irish Times*   penwork.] penwork *Royal Irish Academy*
3 bird-mouth] bird mouth *Royal Irish Academy*   issues] spurts *Irish Times*   blue-dark] dark blue *Gazette*
4 Beetle-sparkle] Beetle-spark *Irish Times*
6 fine-drawn] fine-drawn, *Irish Times, Gazette*
8 green-skinned] green skinned *Royal Irish Academy*
10 books,] books *Royal Irish Academy*   thin,] thin *Irish Times, Gazette*
11 holdings –] holdings: *Royal Irish Academy, Irish Times, Gazette*

Title *Is scíth mo chrob ón scríbainn*: 'My hand is cramped from writing.' The three quatrains comprising SH's poem come from a twelfth-century poem in Irish (Poem 33, Murphy 1956, 71; Irish text Oxford Laud MS 615, 55; cf. *TSH*, 63).

II IS AIRE CHARAIM DOIRE

Published as 'Colmcille's Derry', the second in five translations from the Old Irish called 'A Note-Spurt' and dedicated to Anne Stevenson, in John Lucas and Matt Simpson (eds), *The Way You Say the World: A Celebration for Anne Stevenson* (Beeston: Shoestring, 2003), 64. Also published privately as a Christmas card by Gallery (2008) and as the fifth in a sequence in Felix M. Larkin (ed.), *Librarians, Poets, and Scholars: A Festschrift for Dónall Ó Luanaigh* (Dublin: Four Courts in association with National Library of Ireland, 2009), 156.

1–4]   Why I love Derry:
        it is calm, it is clear,
        transparent angels in every
        breath of air. *A Note-Spurt*

1–4]   Why I love Derry:
        It is calm, it is clear.
        Rustle of white-robed angels
        at every corner. *Librarians, Poets, Scholars*

Title *Is aire charaim Doire*: 'Why Derry is dear to me' (Poem 32, Murphy 1956, 68; Irish text from Royal Irish Academy MS Leabhar Breac; cf. *TSH*, 81).

III FIL SÚIL NGLAIS

Published in *HC*.

Title *Fil súil nglais*: 'A blue eye will look back' (Poem 29, Murphy 1956, 64; cf. *TSH*, 129). Said to be Colmcille's farewell to Ireland as he travelled to Iona, one of the most admired and frequently translated of the medieval Irish monastic poems.

Hermit Songs

First published in Stephen Burt and Nick Halpern (eds), *Something Understood: Essays and Poetry for Helen Vendler* (Charlottesville: University of Virginia Press, 2009). Collected with revisions in *HC*.

Dedication Helen Vendler (1933–2024), American critic and literary scholar, was a long-term friend of SH and his colleague at Harvard.

Epigraph Two lines of a celebrated monastic poem. It is most familiar in Frank O'Connor's 1963 version called 'In the Country' in *The Little Monasteries* (Dublin: Dolmen Press, 1976), 11, although the lines here are presumably SH's own.

I The first section of the nine-poem sequence of stages in the learning process recalls the practice of covering new schoolbooks with various protective materials.

I 11 *covert*: presumably an error for 'cover', although the author's TSS have 'covert'.

II 3 *Fursa*: mostly known as Fursey, Irish monk mostly associated with East Anglia and later France where he died *c.*650.

II 4ff. Abbot MacÓige of Lismore is reported to praise steadiness above other virtues, including charity, humility and abstinence in a medieval manuscript (see E. J. Gwynn and W. J. Purton, 'The Monastery of Tallaght', *Proceedings of the Royal Irish Academy: Archaeology, Culture, History, Literature*, 29 (1911–12): 158–9, §76).

III Section 3 returns to the primary school world with the evocative contents of the satchel.

III 4 *scholars*: the usual Irish term for schoolgoing children.

III 6 *second and third handings*: by contrast with the covert 'newness' of section 1.

III 7 *the herdsman*: the bearer of countryside wisdom.

IV 1 *The master*: standard Irish term for headmaster.

IV 3–4 The 'metal wrap' . . . 'cuticle' was known as the 'nib-holder'.

V 1 The answer to the riddle (recalling the 'riddle-solving anchorites' of II 4) is *to, too* and *two*.

V 5–8 Caesar in *De Bello Gallico* 6.14.4 says of the education of the Druids that 'they do not think it right to entrust to writing' the verses that young people learn by heart.

V 10 *cathach*: the Old Irish term for psalm-book: here because of the competitiveness that learning entails: writing versus oral, country lore versus scholarship, etc.

VI Section VI draws on two Irish legends from the twelfth-century miscellany Lebor na hUidre (The Book of the Dun Cow) which contains *Bricriu's Feast*, the *Voyage of Bran* and the *Táin*.

VI 1 The Ulster warriors Cú Chulainn, Conall Cearnach and Lóegaire are invited to a feast by the mischievous Bricriu, where they compete to win the champion's portion. The warriors' clashing swords make the hall blaze like the sun and Cú Chulainn creates a glittering chain by throwing needles into the air where they knit together as the nibs link letters together to form texts.

VII Returning to the literal memory of early school, SH as a privileged student has been sent out to get water to mix with powder to make ink.

VIII 1 The standard schoolroom term 'inkwell' is as historical now as the Renaissance term 'inkhorn'.

VIII 6 Iona in the Hebrides was Colmcille's monastery.

VIII 7ff. Although his name means 'dove', Colmcille's quick temper is described by Adomnán in his late-seventh century *Vita Sancti Columbae* (*Life of Columba*).

IX 1 *A great one*: Czesław Miłosz (1911–2004), with his faith in 'meaning', the public substance of poetry: cf. his poem 'Meaning' (*New and Collected Poems* (2001), 569).

IX 3 *another*: W. B. Yeats. 'Poets' imaginings / And memories of Love' ('The Tower', III, 40–1, Albright 1990, 245).

IX 9–10 The Great Books of the Irish tradition: the Book of Lismore (also called the Book of MacCarthaigh Riabhach), a late fifteenth-century manuscript from Kilbrittain, Co. Cork, connecting Ireland with the European tradition and now in University College Cork; the Book of Kells, a major illuminated manuscript, now in Trinity College Dublin; the Book of Armagh (or the Codex Ardmachanus, or Leabhar Ard Mhacha), a manuscript dating from c.807, also in Trinity College Dublin; the Yellow Book of Lecan, a late-medieval Irish manuscript in Trinity College Dublin, containing much of the Ulster Cycle, centring on Conchobhar mac Nessa and Cú Chulainn. The Ulster Cycle is a modern name given to a body of heroic narratives from medieval Ireland.

'Lick the Pencil'

First published in *Many Mansions* (Dublin: Stoney Road Press), 2009.

I Title A nickname for SH's father, based on a personal practice. The odd idiomatic formula for naming might echo the Dublin figure 'Skin the Goat' in Joyce's *Ulysses*.
  I 4 The process of force-feeding a cow with liquid medicine was called 'drenching'.
  II 1 Also known as 'indelible pencil'; cf. II 10.
  II 4 Cf. 'The Butts' (*HC*, 12; *PSH*, 646).
  III 5 Didn't need to catch the horse, unlike SH's father in section I.
  III 7 *Vita Sancti Columbae* by Adomnán, abbot of Iona.
  III 10 Diarmit, Columba's faithful servant in the *Vita*.

'The door was open and the house was dark'

Published in the *Irish Times* (11 April 2010): 7. Included in *NSP2014* and *100P*.

Dedication] [at footer] *Irish Times*
1] [omitted] *Irish Times*
8] I felt myself, for the first time then, a stranger, *Irish Times*
13 late] high *Irish Times*

In a letter to the poetry editor at the *Irish Times*, Gerard Smyth, 24 March 2009, SH said that the poem was 'written after a dream before David Hammond died, but . . . can now stand as a memorial' (*LSH*, 728).
  Title The enclosing of the title in quotation marks perhaps reflects the dream-origin of the poem.
  Dedication David Hammond (1928–2008), broadcaster and singer, was a close friend of SH from the early 1960s until his death. Originally he was a teacher who was appointed to the schools department of BBC Northern Ireland in 1964 for which he made many important radio series, including *Explorations* (1974–5), a BBC schools service production on literature which SH presented. As a filmmaker his work for BBC television includes *Dusty Bluebells* (1971) about Belfast children's street games, and, much later, *Something to Write Home About: Seamus Heaney* (1998). The text of SH's script for *Something to Write Home About* was included in *FK* (48–58). With SH and Michael Longley, he went on the Room to Rhyme Arts Council of Northern Ireland tour in 1968. He is the subject of SH's poem 'The Singer's House' (*FW*, 20; *PSH*, 227).
  1 After delivery of his typescript to Faber, SH revised the structure of this poem so that the title was repeated as the first line and its then-opening line, 'Wherefore I called his name, although I knew'

became the second, expanding the poem from 12 to 13 lines and setting the finale as a single line out on its own.

2 *Wherefore*: the formal register of the term may also be a reflection of the poem's dream origin.

6 *(I remember now)*: putting together the details of the dream.

13 *late summer*: at proof stage for *HC*, SH revised the final line of this poem from the typescript 'high summer'.

In the Attic

Published in the *New Yorker* (9 and 16 Feb. 2009). Collected with revisions in *HC* and included in *NSP2014*.

I 5 sea-floor] seafloor *New Yorker*
III 2 appears,] appears *New Yorker*
III 3–5] Above me just back from the matinée, / His voice awaver like the draft-prone screen / They'd set up in the Club Rooms earlier. *New Yorker*
III 6 Was Isaac] was Isaac *New Yorker*
III 7 a-waver] awaver, *New Yorker*
IV 3 lightheadedness] light-headedness *New Yorker*

Dated 24–5 April 2008 in TS, entitled '"Like Jim Hawkins aloft"', and titled in an earlier TS 'Wind-Drink' (NLI 49,493/135).

I 1 Jim Hawkins is the young narrator of R. L. Stevenson's *Treasure Island*.

I 2 *Hispaniola*: the ship in *Treasure Island*.

I 6 *Israel Hands*: in *Treasure Island*, the villainous sidekick of Long John Silver; in chapter 26 he throws a knife at Jim as the boy tries to escape him by climbing to the crow's nest of the mast, and Jim shoots him dead.

II 2 SH's attic workroom in Dublin looks out on the Irish Sea, aloft in another kind of crow's nest.

III 2 Grandfather McCann, SH's maternal grandfather in New Row, Castledawson, who also appears in 'The Old Team' (*HL*, 25; *PSH*, 370) and in 'Clearances' 2 (*HL*, 28; *PSH*, 371). The 'hallway linoleum' recalls the 'polished linoleum' of 'Clearances' in this well-kept house.

III 4 The GAA Club Rooms in Castledawson where a makeshift cinema had been set up for the screening of *Treasure Island* where SH watched it as a child.

III 6 In a classic memory-lapse in old age, the grandfather with his voice 'a-waver' calls Israel Hands Isaac.

IV 1 As the poet himself ages in turn and blanks on names, memory becomes irretrievable, though the imagination survives (IV 7).

A Kite for Aibhín

Adapted from 'L'Aquilone', by Giovanni Pascoli, and first published as 'The Kite', dedicated to Mary Kelleher, in Fergus Mulligan (ed.), *Auguri: To Mary Kelleher* (Dublin: Royal Dublin Society, 2009), 4–6. Subsequently with revisions in Andrea Battistini, Marco A. Bazzocchi and Gino Ruozzi (eds), *Rivista pascoliana*, 24–5 (2012–13): 39–40, and in Gabriella Morisco, 'Two Poets and a Kite: Seamus Heaney and Giovanni Pascoli', *Linguæ &*, 12 (2013): 40, 42, 44. Published in an abridged version (*ll.* 31–64) as 'From The Kite' in Geoffrey Brock (ed.), *The FSG Book of Twentieth Century Italian Poetry: An Anthology* (New York: Farrar, Straus and Giroux, 2012), 15 and 17. Collected in *TSH* (116–17; 636–8). A reworking of 'L'Aquilone' *ll.* 10–15 and 25–33, 'A Kite for Aibhín' is first collected in *HC*. Produced in a limited broadside of 200 copies to commemorate the opening of the exhibition, curated by Geraldine Higgins, 'Seamus Heaney: The Music of What Happens', Emory University, February 2014. Included in *NSP2014* and *100P. See* also *TSH* (636–8).

'A Kite for Aibhín' is a relatively close translation of *ll.* 10–30 of Pascoli's sixty-five-line Italian original, which SH translated as a whole for *Auguri: To Mary Kelleher* (RDS, 2009), printed in *TSH*, 116–17.

    Title Aibhín is SH's second granddaughter, the daughter of his son Michael, who is himself the shared dedicatee of SH's poem 'A Kite for Michael and Christopher' (*SI*, 44). So this is another poem in 'the age of births' *(HC,* 59).

    1 *another life and time and place*: different from the 'one afternoon' (*l.* 4) when in his childhood SH and his family – 'all of us there' – trooped out on Anahorish Hill with his father to fly a kite. Now they are 'back in that field' (*l.* 9) to fly a kite again.

    5 *All of us there*: revised by SH from the TS 'All in the house' after delivery to the publisher, as a 'back echo to "The Seed Cutters" in *North* and the title of Polly Devlin's memoir some years ago' (9 Feb. 2010, FF N50). Devlin's book was published in 1983.

    19 The liberation of the kite corresponds to the birth of the child.

UNCOLLECTED POEMS (2010–2014)

'I'm going to afford myself a year off, and wait and see, and live in panic for the next poem,' SH said in September 2010 in interview for the publication of *Human Chain* (BBC, 23 September 2010). He would supervise the production of eight poems, three of which he saw into print: '"Of all those starting out"' (which would be revised for *Triptych*), 'Actaeon' for the National Gallery in London, and an appreciation for the Law Society of Ireland. A further four poems would be prepared by SH for publication: commissions for Glucksman Ireland House, his publisher Faber & Faber, *Poetry Ireland Review* and the National Gallery of Ireland, that would each publish posthumously, as well as his final poem, written for his third granddaughter, in the days immediately before his death.

'Of all those starting out'

Published in *Dàin Do Shomhairle: Poems for Sorley* (Sorley MacLean Trust/ Scottish Poetry Library, 2011), 32, and, to mark the appearance of that pamphlet, in the *Guardian* (17 June 2011). The poem was later incorporated in a revised form as part III of *Triptych* (Boston: Back Pages Books, 2013). Subsequently in John Halliday (ed.), *Don't Bring Me No Rocking Chair: Poems on Ageing* (Newcastle: Bloodaxe, 2013), in a form that reprints the first outing in *Dàin Do Shomhairle*.

[text: *Dàin Do Shomhairle*]

Title] [no inverted commas] *Guardian* | III] *Triptych*2013
1-12] [sentence case] *Triptych*2013
1] All poets are young poets *Triptych*2013
3 stirrups,] stirrups *Triptych*2013
4-9]   until the lapse.
         A wise upstanding one
         has put it thus:

         'Beware the three delusions
         The King of this world presented
         to the pupil as temptations: *Triptych*2013
10 'After] after *Triptych*2013

A working title 'The Third Temptation' in TS.
   A formative unpublished TS draft of this poem in a private collection includes the line 'Edwin at ninety', which may reference the birthday on 27 April 2010 of the poet Edwin Morgan (1920–2010), to whom SH paid tribute for his 'magnificent work as poet

and translator, whose mind and hand went together, who cast a warm eye on life and whose achievement shines fuller and steadier as the decades pass' (Marsack 2010, 30). SH may later have adapted the poem to mark the centenary of the birth of Sorley MacLean (1911–96), in preparing the poem for publication in *Dàin Do Shomhairle*.

1 *Of all those starting out*: for his 2013 letterpress *Triptych*, SH reverts to an earlier TS version of this opening, 'All poets are young poets', seemingly an echo of a sentiment that he had expressed in giving the Robert Lowell Memorial Lecture at the Graduate School of Arts and Sciences, Boston University, 2 October 2008: 'One of the great joys of assembling like this with poets of all ages, is to realise that when you come together we're all young poets: there's no such thing as an old poet once there are two or three gathered together' (with thanks to Marco Sonzogni).

On 22 December 2012, SH shared a typescript with his Italian translator, Marco Sonzogni, that showed he was preparing this poem as the third section of *Triptych* that would appear in 2013 in a limited letterpress broadside of twenty-six copies, hand set by Alex Green of Back Pages Books, an independent bookshop that traded on Moody Street in Waltham, Massachusetts, 2005–15. It was not the first time that SH had unified three discrete poems under such a title: he had used the format in 1977 for a gathering that would appear in *FW* under that name, and more variously for the 1966 poem 'Triptych for the Easter Battlers'.

Triptych (2013) incorporated 'With Hindsight' (*PSH*, 639) as its opening part, together with twelve previously unpublished lines in its middle section, published in broadside by Back Pages in the text:

TRIPTYCH

I
Oisin borne away on the saddled steed
returns to a different world,
smaller scaled, in need of help, unhelpful.

Do not, sworn rider, for all your old strength
stoop. Stay clear and true
in the morning world

you left, given fair warning
only this morning.
Your good impulse will harm you.

Let them hustle round their boulder.
When they call on you, ignore them.
Don't unbend or brace your shoulder.

II
You felt the girth
give way,
fell to earth

and in a minute
aged. It was a deer
that dropped you first

on native ground
where now you're drowned,
undone, your covenant

with the wonder land ir-
reparable. Old and cold you are
and one to lie with.

III
All poets are young poets,
high-horsed and spirited,
instepped in their stirrups

until the lapse.
A wise upstanding one
has put it thus:

'Beware the three delusions
The King of this world presented
to the pupil as temptations:

after the first of desire,
and the second, terror of death,
that of social obligation.'

Actaeon

Published in Kate Bell (ed.), *Metamorphosis: Poems Inspired by Titian* (London: National Gallery, 2012), 41. Also in *Granta*, 120, Online Edition (Summer 2012), and in *SD*, 115. Collected in *TSH*.

[text: *Metamorphosis*]

1 brow] brown *Granta* (error)
6 And it was no] Nor was it *Granta*
12 desires] desire *Granta*
15 lit] Lit *SD*
18 tore out] tore *Granta*
19 From] from *Guardian* (error) | Out of *Granta*

In Book 3 of Ovid's *Metamorphoses* the hunter Actaeon sees Diana bathing naked in a spring and she turns him into a stag which is torn to pieces by his own hunting dogs.

On the Gift of a Fountain Pen

First published as a limited-edition broadside to mark SH's appearance at the Baylor University Beall Poetry Festival, 4 March 2013. Fair copy MS previously presented to the Law Society of Ireland in October 2012 following an address SH delivered to the Society on 2 October 2012, subsequently reproduced posthumously in SH's memory in the Society's magazine, *Gazette* (8 Oct. 2013): 13. It was, with variants, given general publication in Marco Sonzogni's *Poesie* (Mondadori, 2016), 930.

[text: *Poesie*]

3 cease] cease to be *Gazette, Baylor*
11–12] And start again, / After the spade, the hoe. *Gazette* | And start again, doubts /
   Or no doubts. Heigh-ho! *Baylor*
Footer] October 2012 *Gazette*

Following an address at Blackhall Place in Dublin, 2 October 2012, SH wrote to thank the Law Society of Ireland for the presentation of a Mont Blanc fountain pen by gifting them a fair copy of this poem, which he dated to that month, with an accompanying note: 'I just wish my handwriting was better' (*Gazette*, 12).

   In an 'Author's Note' of 31 January 2013 (revised 19 February 2013) for a prospective Italian edition of his work with Mondadori, SH described the poem as 'a backward look' at a life in writing that remained 'convinced of the importance of the art although aware now that it has to earn its place and stand its ground in face of the other demands that a committed life must answer'. In positioning the poem as the last of that volume, SH calculatedly wished to set it against 'Digging', which he had placed first, as a work 'looking forward', just as his new poem was to look back. The edition – and by inference, his life work – would, he wrote, 'begin with a pen and end with a pen' (*Poesie*, cxxxv).

   On 4 March 2013, SH read at a special event for the nineteenth Beall Poetry Festival, at Baylor University's Jones Concert Hall, Waco, Texas, before an audience of nearly a thousand people, an event that was marked by the production of fifty commemorative broadsides for which SH had now revised the ending from the manuscript he gave to the Law Society of Ireland. By 13 June that year, when he read the poem at the Marché de la Poésie festival at the Centre Culturel Irlandais, Paris, SH had further refined the ending.

By 8 August 2013, three weeks before his death, SH had settled upon the Paris ending and had made an additional revision of the third line, with its reference to John Keats's 'When I Have Fears that I May Cease to Be', explaining to the editor for his Mondadori edition, Marco Sonzogni: 'I have indeed changed the fountain pen poem to end as in the attached – and cut out "to be", since whether I write or not, poems will not cease to be' (8 Aug. 2013, Sonzogni).

Lauds for Loretta

Published in the *American Journal of Irish Studies*, 10 (2013): 175–6. Subsequently in Terry Golway (ed.), *Being New York, Being Irish: Reflections on Twenty-Five Years of Irish America and New York University's Gluksman Ireland House* (Irish Academic Press, 2018), 203–4.

[text: *American Journal of Irish Studies*]

Loretta Brennan Glucksman (b.1925) was a philanthropist and Chairman Emerita of the Ireland Funds. In 1993 Glucksman Ireland House, the Centre for Irish Studies at New York University, was founded. She lived partly in Cobh, Co. Cork, where her husband, Lew, died in 2006.

The poem was the first of SH's posthumous printings, recorded by the journal's editors in a stop-press note addendum beneath the poem:

> As we went to press in late August we learned of the passing of Seamus Heaney, a great friend of Glucksman Ireland House, NYU. We send our deepest condolences to his wife, children, grandchildren, extended family, and friends around the world. The loss is both personal and professional to us. Seamus has shared our podium in the past and we anticipated his presence in our classroom for a series of lectures and an oral history in the spring. He was also part of our celebration earlier this year as we looked back on two decades of commitment to Irish and Irish-American scholarship and culture in New York City at GIH. His tribute to Loretta Brennan Glucksman in this volume was part of our planned editorial lineup so his departure not only elevates its power and poignancy but heightens our sense of loss. We will find the words to put our feelings in perspective and continue our tribute to Seamus Heaney in our next issue. Ar dheis Dé go raibh a anam dílis. (*May his soul be at the right hand of God.*) (177)

In a Field

First published in Carol Ann Duffy (ed.), *1914: Poetry Remembers* (London: Faber & Faber, 2013): 94, for which it was commissioned, and in the *Guardian* (26 Oct. 2013). Subsequently in *Irish Pages*, 8. 2 (30 Aug. 2014): 10–11.

[text: *1914*]

Once again, SH is responding to Edward Thomas's poem, 'As the Team's Head Brass', as he did in *District and Circle* (*DC*, 35; *PSH*, 608). Here the commission, from the then Poet Laureate, Carol Ann Duffy, is a commemoration of World War I, for which SH delivered an initial draft on 25/6 April 2013 (Duffy 2013, 94). The poignant ending of the young, hand-held SH being received into the company of his family was introduced late in the proof stage (24 June 2013).

 2 *furrows . . . gloss*: the furrows in Thomas's original poem 'flashed' (*l*. 11).

 6 *furrows turned*: 'horses turned' in Thomas (*l*. 6).

 7–8 *the four sides / Of the breathing land*: Thomas: 'a yellow square / Of charlock' (*ll*. 5–6).

 11–12 *one who arrived / From nowhere*: identified by SH in his initial draft of 25–6 April 2013 for *1914* as 'my demobbed uncle', Cork bricklayer and serviceman, Mick Joyce: 'I always remember him arriving at Mossbawn in his khaki outfit, coming up the field from the railway, either when he was on leave or had been demobbed. Mick was tall and exotic to us because of his accent and his tales of having been in England and in the North African desert as a medical orderly. And he had this big canvas bag full of bricklayer's tools – mortar board and trowel and skimmer and plumb line and what have you. All of them heavier than you'd have expected, Achillean gear of sorts, really. You had to be a hero to wield it' (*SS*, 256).

In Time

First published in the *New Yorker* (23 and 30 Dec. 2013): 87, and subsequently collected in *NSP2014* and *100P*.

[text: *NSP2014*]

 dedication] [no dedication] *New Yorker*

The author's final poem, dated 18 August 2013, twelve days before his death, and dedicated to his youngest granddaughter, Síofra, is a eulogy cast finely between a life beginning and one that is nearing completion. Like the revolving familial hourglass of *HC*, the poem returns in its trace of the granddaughter's infant footsteps to those of the poet's own childhood, in a moment recalled in 'Squarings' (xl, *ll.* 1–3; *ST*, 100; *PSH*, 444), where young feet make first contact with the ground (*SS*, 14–15; see *Poesie*, 1071–2, 1136). The poem culminates enigmatically stepping into time and silence.

The Latecomers

Published in *Poetry Ireland Review*, 112 (April 2014): 122; reprinted in *Irish Pages*, 9. 1 (2014): 131–2. Collected here for the first time.

[text: *Poetry Ireland Review*]

Invited as a contribution to *Poetry Ireland Review* by John F. Deane, for an issue 'seeking new work that might offer a personal answer to the question of what the personal Christ meant to contributors'. Deane records that SH replied to the invitation saying, 'it's quite a commission, a test of truth and art, but one worth risking'; he interpreted SH within this poem as 'Christ himself, surrounded by the needy who press around seeking help and healing. Seamus was then constantly being badgered for signatures, for readings, for statements' (*Irish Pages*, 131).

Banks of a Canal

First published in *Irish Pages*, 8. 2 (30 Aug. 2014): 10, and subsequently in the *Guardian*, 3 Oct. 2014, and Janet McLean (ed.), *Lines of Vision: Irish Writers on Art* (London: Thames & Hudson, 2014), 100; subsequently in *Ploughshares*, 42. 1 (Spring 2016): 66.

[text: *Irish Pages*]

This poem was commissioned by the National Gallery of Ireland to celebrate its 150th anniversary. SH submitted a draft of the poem less than a week after visiting the gallery in February 2013, when he selected Gustave Caillebotte's (1848–94) impressionist oil painting, *Banks of a Canal, Near Naples* (c.1872) as the artwork to which he would respond. SH revised the poem in the summer of 2013, delivering a final draft on 20 August, ten days before he died.

APPENDICES

I: UNPUBLISHED POEMS

The twenty-five poems included in this appendix were chosen by Seamus Heaney's family – Marie, Michael, Christopher and Catherine – in consultation with the three volume editors. The poems are drawn from the large number of unpublished poems in varying states of completeness dating from all stages of the author's life, many housed in the National Library of Ireland, where he deposited his literary papers in 2011, as well as other archives and private collections. They range from works that predate his first collection, *Death of a Naturalist* (like the early love poem 'Mirror'), to poems written not long before his death – such as 'Black Walnuts' and 'Those Winter Evenings' – that echo the late personal works of *Human Chain*. Some fit in with the themes and subjects of the author's most celebrated poems: family, artistic dedication, language and public concern. Others feature familiar and significant family figures, such as Aunt Mary in 'In a Yard' and his mother in 'The Cassette', as well as poems like 'Hawthorns' and 'Twins' which add to an existing body of work about his father. What this selection aims to represent is the wealth of subjects, familiar and unfamiliar, that exist beyond the collected and uncollected poems.

However, their presence here also, inevitably, raises the question of why we decided to include work that the author had chosen not to publish during his lifetime. It was a responsibility that weighed heavily on us, and we considered it together as a family and individually over months. However, ultimately, we were convinced that the delight of encountering these poems for the first time – an experience we wanted to share with Seamus Heaney readers – outweighed our natural sense of caution and trepidation. We chose poems that appeared to be in a finished state – often reworked over several drafts – and a few which we knew were in contention for inclusion in the collections. Overall, we concluded that the pages of this landmark volume were the right place to share these previously unseen glimpses into a long and rich writing life.

Marie, Michael, Christopher and Catherine Heaney

At Yeats's Grave

I came expectant, as one learning the trade,
To find the grave plain, the verge and stone well-made.
But under Ben Bulben in the August rain
One grave is much like others: suddenly there
I feared the trade itself might be all vain.   5

Lighting the Lamp

Was a bright ritual.
In days before the main
Brought power to fingertips,
At evening down our lane
The brute darkness shambled   5
And lay against the pane.

My mother lit a torch
For the oil lamp; pumped up tight
Until the mantle glowed
A grape of solid light   10
Spilling joy and safety,
Driving away the night.

I left that bright kitchen
Where the tall lamp hissed low
And cannot ever return.   15
I shut all doors and go
Forward into the dark:
I have my own house now

Where I grope in the half-light –
No power has been switched on.   20
But when you close the circuit
We'll come into our own
And love will shine bright here,
Stronger than all lamps shone.

Mirror

The room's one eye
that is chill and lashless.

Hard clear rink
where her gentlest move is
calculated, practised:
where she skates towards
her perfect replica.

The clean plate where she
is dressed and served to herself.

Her crystal shield,
her shut porthole.

1965

Omen and Plan

Feathering the village church,
Cresting the cooling ridge-tiles of each house,
The storks had settled.

We bore their clumsy racket
On the roofs, their clacks and scrapings,
Away into the hot night.

Their big bodies stagger in circles
Over those memories now.
They meant good for the village

Where people rigged roosting and coops
And kept luring them back –
And I rely on their haphazard landing,

Their big-footed, matter-of-fact blessing.
We must be deliberate like that,
Feather a love-nest, a decoy, for luck.

Hawthorns

I

Somebody would say
'Think of the gipsies out
Under a hedge on a night like that
And go to your sleep.'
So we lay, alert   5
To rats across the ceiling boards,
The moonlight pining through
A tree-soft rain, our eyelids
Pulled back on the dark, taut
As the sapling sprung down   10
To shape the tent-mouth.
'Good-night, now.'

Somewhere, green boughs sputter and hiss,
Raindrops smutch the ash
And one last flame licks a sheen   15
On the grass; and a sleepless eye
Camped far in the shadows
Sparks, like those drops travelling
Along the thorns.

II

When I imagine civil war
It's always a local ambush
With a scared young son
Tucked in the drenching hedge.
Drops are webbing the tiny crook   5
Between thorn and twig, and maybe
He leaves go the trigger to pick
(Breaking a silent gossamer)
And palp a crimson haw
That bloodies along miles and miles   10
Of road and each winter lights
Its pustules between small farm
And small farm.

In a Yard

for Mary Heaney

Where the strange bird
Arrived, pecking dropped grain,
To bring our first death.

Where I took your hand
On dark mornings and watched
For sparks from Wards chimney.

Your trail, untousling
The dewy growth
Of summer grazing

Or broken
From scullery to byre
On Christmas mornings,

Is fresh as ever.
Those gentle arts
Of watering, foddering,

A straggle of hay
Between puddles,
A mutter of froth

In the pail.
God love you now, warming
The chrome lap
Of a wheelchair.

The Dirraghs

To say 'oak groves'
translates the sour ground
to tonsured hillocks
in a classical sunlight

and every brawny liar
who ever cut turf
along the banks
is unnaturally gilded.

It is worn-out country.
The trees turned up
as bog oak, hagged
and buried in the heart

of the stack;
as blow-downs of smoke
struggling over half-doors
into the drizzle.

Does the rutted kesh
lead back among
green clearings, among
the cutters of mistletoe?

I doubt it.
Here come the moustached
dead, the creel-fillers,
the wives afield.

Twins

You came to print your future after dark
and left three marble-holes in the concrete road
like three black eyes, your wrists messed with the skim
and sticky as the wrists of blood-brothers.

I have known one only through the other
who sits quiet for hours like a bushman
asking the outback. In the back of his head
three holes are black as borings to down-under.

Oral English

'The lips, the teeth, the tip of the tongue.
Repeat it. Again. Again. Again.'

He would cultivate the slobland of the larynx,
Deliver laws to my outlandish breath.
Words, summoned up the aisle of the mouth,
Came forward singly and self-consciously.
I heard then how the melodious Greeks

       Named barbarians by their ugly talk.
       I blushed with Peter in the outer court
       Whose speech betrayed him. And once I hitched a lift
       With an MP who told me that success
10   Depended much on good pronunciation.

       It's a well-spoken world, my masters.
       Last night, beside an armoured car in Derry,
       A Sandhurst officer could not quite catch
       That place I'd just said I was travelling to . . .
15   I find it hard to arbitrate between
       Disdains and intonations, and I sense
       Attentions of more than vowels
       In many an improved accent. Perhaps
       I am too pious in my guttural
20   Fidelities but, set like a tripwire,
       My tongue can hardly be a trampoline.

Grief in North Antrim

          I

       The sunlit basalt spondee of Fair Head
       has her daydreaming of the larks on Tor,

       a bark of rifles, a winded silence, then
       a click of hoes among the stony ridges

5   for now she sees herself as one of two
       long-skirted, faraway, farming sisters

       in a grainy sepia photograph.
       And everything behind her and ahead

       comes to her through a grief as she drives
10   in the light of Ulster, behind the school-bus,

       past the lock-up of an old police-barracks
       and tractors on the equable ploughland.

          II

       All afternoon, as the sun moved
       across their concrete yard

where swallows whiten and blacken and are gone
into the shadow of the tall silo,

the ladder stood without a tremor,
cogged by its stone, up to the high trapdoor

where one mouthful of silage gas
poisoned the husband who drank at its black hole.

All afternoon he slumped on the top rungs,
a weighted comma above the electric wires,

a sentry of the usual, still at his post
millions of years after the lava cooled.

The Discovery of the Eel

A smell of chain-oil, worms raddling in brick-dust,
horse dung intact and plosive on the road –

and the eel drawn like a rib of water
out of the water, an ell yielded up
from glooms and slatings and whorls,

for the smoky ridge to unsheathe with a mute
wet rip as his left boot fastens its head
and his right hand doubles its length outside in

and he straps his wrist up tight with an eelskin
so his arm sings high and mighty and light
as if his whole spirit were rilling in it

and out of it, like the river out of its own
roundy backward contractions, backwards
and smaller to raindrops and horsehairs of dew.

'Chestnut was the whitest wood veneer'

Chestnut was the whitest wood veneer
In the veneer kit. Sycamore for sky
Gone faintly pink, and English walnut burr
For cloud mottle: my teenage marquetry
Was the one art she paid attention to.
My hands cramped from fine work, blistered with glue,

      Must have consoled her, since the devil finds
      (She would repeat it) work for empty hands.
      The smell of them when I lifted eel-lines,
10   Unshelled an acorn from its Latin *glans*
      Or dyed them black with dandelion milk.
      In chests of drawers, the feel of slips and silk
      When I slipped from the bedroom desk to wait
      For whitewashed walls or snowcappped peaks to set.

An Education

    (*Thomastown, 1972*)

      The clamour of arrival. Banging doors.
      Gravel and gundogs. Hugs. But rolled-up sleeves
      And paint-smudged cheeks meant interrupted work.
      'It's pike for supper! And nettle soup. All right?'
5   Then cold stone floors. The river in the night.
      Ourselves displaced, exposed to damps and dark
      And wind in the small hours plenishing the leaves.
      In high-ceilinged spare-rooms, off corridors

      Crammed with primed canvases and bags of clay,
10   We woke to treetops in uncurtained windows
      And the coldest running water in the world.
      Routine for the pair of you, for us a chance
      To space-walk in a vernal ambience:
      Our spirits trampolined and our heads birled
15   At the thought we too might opt for nine beanrows
      And a small cabin down there in Kilkenny.

      Potter and painter. Peacock owners. Growers
      Dug in far from bombs and marching seasons,
      Putting your faith in things like cress and mint:
20   You were, in Ulsterspeak, 'an education'
      To the pair of us who were like two reeds shaken
      But steadying in the calm of your intent –
      Among caked palettes, 'friendly feathered demons',
      That whole quiet congregation of good powers.

25   As branchy light moved over us, I found
      A cotyledon in me green and grow
      Venturesome, heliotropic even:

Something germane had come through germination.
Obedient as big sunflowers in the sun,
We went with it, and into circulation   30
Around the sunwheel of the studio
Where purpose gathered force and went to ground.

And in a strongroom of vocabulary,
Words like urns that had come through the fire
Stood in their bone dry alcoves next a kiln: 35
I remembered a night pantry, the cold dream
Of crocks in moonlight, the hard glaze on each rim,
And left your house like a tomb-guard who had seen
The stone move in a diamond-blaze of air
And the gates of horn behind the gates of clay.   40

Ribbons

In the name of the colours,
Emerald, cornflower blue,
Ruby, primrose and white,

In the name of ringlets and curls,
Polka dots, partings and plaits   5
And double-tied bows . . .

To-day the photographer comes
With his tripod and cowl
And plaited retractable snout,

A five-legged beast   10
Of gesticulation and blather
They'll outface together,

Steady and far off and solemn
As orphans posed at a rail
In the last days of sail,   15

Beyond the pale of the selves
They are due to become,
The one thing immutable still

The roughcast grey of the wall
Of the school, plus   20
The knitted classic Fair Isle

Patterns, plus their names on the roll
As transcribed on the slats of the bench,
In a copperplate hand –

25 All that, and the strictly tied bows,
And one right arm and one left,
Each placed to be seen round the other's

Shoulder, as ordered.

The Whirligig

When I was a child I thought as a grown-up.
Not all the time, but once I had overheard
I was helpless to unhear.

Michael and Brendan Joyce played cars in the sand
5 With little cut-offs of resinous pitch-pine
Their father brought from the building site for kindling.

'Bizzing', they called it. When Hughie Scullion died
The Joyce boys talked that night about him bizzing
In the sand on heaven's floor, but how on earth –

10 How could he not come falling down again
Since heaven's floor was air? That was my grown-up thought
But the grown-ups themselves just kept on quoting,

Hughie bizzing in heaven! so I couldn't know
If heaven itself up there were child's play only
15 Or anything but. And then they would break down

And double up and say the words again – words, it seemed,
As glee-flecked as the Christ child's whirligig
In Hieronymus Bosch, his little busy body

Pelting ahead in its child's play zimmer-frame.

The Race

The race at Clarke's Mill
Its quick surly gleam
Under brick walls and willows

Blackwater trench
Channel of lavish
All in the ear

A hiss then and rip
Of wheels on wet tarmac
Like hot steam let off

Along the Broagh Road
Who's that on his bike
Tears on cold cheeks

A grandfather dead
Little more than an hour
Him first with the news

Most odd to be crying
And pedalling hard
The breath of fresh air

As old as the hills
Full in his face
His eye on the road

Arkansas

Cast-iron waffle-irons,
Horse-shoe nails, mouse-traps, furled down
Bean bags full of beans:
I keep going on about
That hardware store in Conway.

  *

Hunk armadilloes
(That came, they said, from Texas)
Were the roadkill, not
The famous razorback hog
They call soo-ee, soo-ee to.

  *

At Big Jim Whitehead's
Later, Jim praised a poet

       Possessed of 'the same
15   Suicidal urges as
       A full-grown Bengal tigress.'

              *

       And later again
       A woman drove home, came back
       With a book, and read
       This one good line, just to prove
20   One good line could be worth it.

              *

       Two firsts that happened
       In my first hour in the state:
       I was driven through
       A dry county (at high speed,
25   Yes), and then a paddy field.

Sweeney as Lyre

   Because I perched sometimes on the woodwormed joists
   Of condemned buildings and on scaffolding round new ones
   He called me 'forest-steeplejack' and said
   He'd make me his lyre.

5 To lament the one who fell hard through a roof,
   One who missed his footing on ill-placed planks.

   The former (my instructor bids me tell) discovered
   On a midden of slate bits like the smithereens
   Of Bakelite 78s he once let fall –
10 The least applauded of his much recounted boy-deeds.

   And of the latter, what? Small boy at school,
   Next thing small-paunched in housepainter's overalls,
   And if gone, gone having made a mark
   As workaday as his daubs on sawn-off board.

Chair, Pocket Knife, Guitar

The slatted folding chair you sat upon,
The scantlings and ad hoc stuff of that playroom
You screened out as you just rocked on and on
In perfect time before the television,
To-day let all that tick-tock bric-a-brac   5
Come like a drumstick stick-man rolling home.

The one-blade pocket knife you coveted
In a shop window that first evening in France
And I bought then on the spot in thanksgiving
For us just being there: although it's lost   10
I stand like a glad Macbeth faced with its ghost
Handle towards my hand, saying, 'Thank, thank God'.

The guitar you got the day you started school
And were photographed with, up on the picnic table,
Play it again to-day, fierce Andalucian   15
Serenades and country wedding songs,
Then hang it on the wall, your true love's token,
Last thing before she sleeps, first when you waken.

Working the Head

1 *Plasterseed*

The sound of clay being slapped, the shine of it, every now and
again the dampening with water: just looking and listening as she
worked was like regressing. She rolled little mud-pod shapes and
primped and patted them round the armature to model the bulk of
it. Then took my measure with a set of calipers, the sharp steel   5
points just tipping nose and forehead, cheek and temple, ear and
chin, each fleet touch a surprise, a reminder that you weren't all
inwardness, that your head was shape as well as source. Years later
when I carried the heavy cast into one of her exhibitions, it felt cold
and hard-set as the used plasticine we were issued with in Senior   10
Infants, and when I remembered that – our 'plasterseed' – the bronze
nearly slipped my grip.

2 Plaster Cast

That head. She cast it first in plaster and so it remained for thirty
years. Coloured like bronze, weighty as concrete. No ring, all solid,
dud. Slap it with your hand and your hand met sheer refusal. Yet
slap it I often did, for the flat small sound of it, the maidenly
vincibility of the palm, the loutish invincibility of the medium. The
most decided thing about it was the sharp uneven edge of the
modelled neck. There, where she had done with it, a severance
occurred. Staked on a marble plinth, the head was all tilt and
attitude, face-off and jut-jaw down to this point of abandon, this utter
cut-away. Whatever it amounted to stopped there. I hit the thing
again, but to what end? As I slapped and hurt, I was needy far and
away beyond my reach.

The Cassette

Then at Christmas he'd return,
in cahoots with her again –
dependable pinner-up

of the decorations
he found for her in Woolworth's.
They'd flex each garland open,

stretch and hoist and tack it
criss-cross with another
on the tongue-and-groove low ceiling,

then hang a round-earth bauble
of sectioned coloured paper
folded back on itself.

Then themselves stand back
to admire the place festooned:
swags of tissue-fetters

trembling in the convection –
like her voice on a cassette
decades later, unexpected

voice from before the grave
played once
and only once.

In the Loft

When the new house was nearly finished, soon after the stairs and
floors and windows had been fitted, my brothers and I slept in the
place for a night. It still smelled of plaster and timber, there were no
carpets down, no curtains up and no wiring in, so we clattered and
banged from room to room with a couple of old yard lamps, enjoying
the echo of bare boards and our big fitful shadows on the walls.

But what everybody remembered most about that night was
something said the next day by Jim Boorman. Jim lived at the end of
our lane and had a gift for the wrong word or the strange word. He
talked about eating a 'snatch' when he meant a snack, and spoke of
'completely recognizing' people when he meant completely ignoring
them. This time it was the concept of an upstairs that eluded him. 'I
saw you last night,' he said, 'near bedtime, moving about in the loft.'

But for once, Jim was on to something. Before it meant the upper
chamber or attic of a house, 'loft' signified the upper region of the air
or sky, and was related to the first sense of the word 'lift', which
signifies the high fetch of the heavens.

It's early but it's dark and I'm back at the end of the lane, looking up at
the same old shadow play going on in the lamplit rooms, still there, still
familiar, myself and Jim and all the rest.

Swallow

Citadel. Hill town.
Our first time in Pienza.
Flagstoned hot *piazza*.
Stone coping round the well.

Migrate then, little soul,
Swoop to your window seat
In the back room of that café
Or *gelateria*, was it?

Where, from the sheered off hill,
We overlooked the drop,
Table and chairs, it seemed,
Ready-steady for take-off

Phantasmagorical
Fathoms and fathoms above
Autostrada and farms
On the level valley floor.

Well-wall the drystone colour
Of layered and feathered mud.
Nest-juts. Roofspace. Rafters.
Breast the air, little soul.

Black Walnuts

Black walnuts hitting a barn roof
Fairly rapped the morning.
                          Massachusetts,
Autumn. Orioles and pumpkins.
And the crack of those round shells
Like a hardwood mallet hammering a wedge
Into the moment, splitting it ever open

Up ahead, letting it travel with us,
Us into it, articulated
Ongoing: whatever was to happen next
Anticipated as half-consciously
As the smack of the next mailed walnut
On the roof, but at exactly what

Interval none of us could tell.

Those Winter Evenings

Those winter evenings we walked the strand
Watching lights of planes coming in above
Howth Head, sailing down the dark,
Beginning their descent high in the east,
Each on the same flight path
At staggered intervals –

It was like that dream of a kite-flier,
The string taut in his hand and the lift
Palpable but the kite itself
Invisible to him: a heavyweight

Drag upwards through the mist-roof:
Yet in the breast a kind of settlement

As on those winter evenings when we walked
And watched for lights of planes.

COMMENTARY

Composition dates are given below the title, with conjectured dates in square brackets, followed by source material MS (manuscript) and TS (typescript), in an order of probable composition constructed by the editors with the copy-text given last. Archive sources are given in parenthesis: BC (the Barrie Cooke Archive, Pembroke College Cambridge), EU (Emory University, Stuart A. Rose Manuscript, Archives, and Rare Book Library: Dennis O'Driscoll Papers, MS Collection 1420; Ted Hughes Papers, MS Collection 644) and NLI (National Library of Ireland, Dept of Manuscripts, Seamus Heaney Literary Papers, MS 49,493), with box numbers given as 'b.' and folders as 'f.'; HFC denotes papers in the Heaney family collection.

At Yeats's Grave

August 1964, TS1 (HFC)

Recording a visit to the cemetery in Drumcliffe near Sligo in which W. B. Yeats is buried, the poem expresses an early uncertainty about the whole poetic enterprise relatively rare in SH's writing. The TS is dated by the author in blue ink.

Lighting the Lamp

[*c.*1964–5], TS1–2 (NLI 49,493/8)

Familiar through its recitation by Ireland's former President Mary McAleese on RTÉ in 2020, this early poem was originally conceived for inclusion in *DN*, and appears listed on a MS contents for that collection in SH's hand, signalled to appear between 'Lovers on Aran' and 'Poem', tenth-last in the running order, making its latest date of composition spring 1965 (NLI 49,493/8). No earliest date of composition is indicated, but the typewriter on which its two surviving drafts were produced was in active use by the author *c.*1963–6.

Mirror

1965, TS1 (NLI 49,493/47)

Fair copy carbon typescript, dated 1965, produced on a typewriter that was in active use *c.*1959–65. An early love poem overlooked for *DN* and seemingly reconsidered for *FW*, where the draft resides among the poems in a folder marked 'Field Work'.

Omen and Plan

[1]–2 November 1969, MS1–2 (NLI 49,493/11), TS1 (HFC)

Written shortly after SH's first arrival in the United States, and seemingly the first of the author's American poems. Two MS drafts, the first, a sketch of *ll.* 1–3, is given on the verso of MS 'Tweed', which itself is dated '1/11/69'; the second, a fair copy draft in black ink, is author dated '2/11/69', and subsequently transferred to an undated typescript with annotations.

Hawthorns

[*c.* September 1970–June 1971], TS1 (NLI 49,493/29) TS2 (f.21), TS3 (f.18, 20), TS4a (f.29), TS4b (f.27), TS5a (f.28), TS5b (f.12)

Originally considered for *WO*, 'Hawthorns' is listed on MS and TS contents pages for that collection, where it appears as the fourth poem in the running order (NLI 49,493 f.28, 14). A much worked-on poem with considerable variations, composed on manual and electric Berkeley typewriters, initially as a three-part poem beginning 'My father would say', revised to two parts with the less explicit opening 'Somebody would say'. Part I appears in an unpublished sequence called 'No Man's Land', where that figure is once again identified as 'My father' (NLI 49,493/29). 'No Man's Land' is also the heading for a separate poem that appears as section 2 of 'A Northern Hoard' (*WO*, 29; *PSH*, 132).

In a Yard

[*c.* September 1970–June 1971], TS1 (NLI 49,493/14), TS2 (f.12), TS3 (f.14), TS4 (f.12), TS5 (f.14)

Originally considered for *WO*, two undated typescripts of thirteen lines are followed by three subsequent typescripts of twenty-two lines, produced on the same typewriter and watermarked paper stock as the author's initial TSS of 'Hawthorns', placing both poems in Berkeley, 1970–1.

Dedication Mary Heaney, the sister of SH's father, who lived with the family: the subject of several poems, most notably 'Sunlight', the first of the two 'Mossbawn' poems at the beginning of *North*.

1 The strange bird interpreted as an ill omen, as recalled in 'The Blackbird of Glanmore': 'But I never liked yon bird' (*DC*, 76; *PSH*, 628).

3 *our first death*: the death of SH's young brother Christopher, the subject of 'Mid-Term Break' (*DN*, 28; *PSH*, 32).

4 *'your hand'*: Aunt Mary's: the first of several contacts with her through the poem.

22 *wheelchair*: the condition in which we finally encounter Aunt Mary in 'Chairing Mary', section 2 of 'Home Help' (*DC*, 67; *PSH*, 624).

The Dirraghs

[15–]19 January 1972, MS1–2 (NLI 49,493/5), TS1a (f.14), TS1b (f.12), TS2 (f.28), TS3 (f.15)

Written in a very productive week after SH's return from Berkeley when he produced the *WO* 'languagey' poems 'Anahorish', 'Broagh' and 'Fodder', the last dated '15/1/72' in a MS notebook, followed immediately by a first draft of 'The Dirrahs' (*sic*). A second draft in MS turquoise ink dated '19th January 1972' is seemingly transferred to TS at that time. The poem is included in a TS contents page for *WO* (NLI 49,493/28).

In private correspondence with the editors, Eugene Kielt has identified the Dirraghs (also referred to locally as the Dirah) as a hilly piece of scrubland surrounded by bog in the small area known as Mulhollandstown, about a mile from the Scullion–Heaney farm at The Wood. The name – as SH describes in 'The Trade of an Irish Poet', an article contemporary with this poem published in the *Guardian* on 25 May 1972 and later collected as '1972', the third part of 'Belfast' in *Preoccupations* (36) – is drawn from the Irish: 'The Dirraghs from *doire* as in Derry, also usually Englished as "oak grove"' (*Preoccupations*, 36).

'The Dirraghs' may have been a starting point for the fifth of the 'Five Derry Glosses' (*PSH*, 392), which in turn is taken up as 'Squarings', xlii, 'Heather and kesh and turf stacks' (*ST*, 102; *PSH*, 444).

Twins

[*c*.20 January–18 March 1972], MS1 (NLI 49,493/5) TS1a–2 (f.14)

Undated MS notebook, sequenced between entries of '20 Jan. 1972' and '18/3/72', subsequently transferred to undated TS draft of twenty-four lines, before a TS revision of eight lines.

Title The twins are SH's father Patrick Heaney and his brother Charlie, who emigrated to Australia.

5 The 'one' whom SH only knows through the 'other' is the absent twin; the 'other' is SH's reserved father, whose reticence is ironically described in Australian terms: like a bushman in the outback 'down under'. As children the brothers made holes in setting concrete with a marble which remain as evidence.

Oral English

[*c.*1972–4?], TS1a (NLI 49,493/47), TS1b (f.31), TS2 (f.47)

Considered for *Stations* as an undated prose poem TS entitled 'Finding a Voice', produced on an early typewriter, *c.*1972–4, then revised, re-lineated and retitled as a verse poem 'Oral English' in an undated TS, seemingly produced at the same time, but recorded in the NLI among the *FW* papers suggesting that it may have been revised for consideration for that later volume.

Epigraph The first line is an American choral warm-up routine, itemising the significant organs in the production of speech.

1 *He*: a teacher of elocution.

5–6 The term 'barbarian' is believed to have been devised by the Greeks and Romans to apply to the uncivilised speech of the northern peoples who overran the Empire, derived from the sound 'ba, ba' which they attributed to them.

7–8 Peter in the outer court betrayed Christ by denying knowledge of him even though his accent identified him as a fellow countryman of his. (Matthew 26:72).

9 *MP*: a member of the British Parliament who is 'well-spoken'.

13 *Sandhurst*: the Royal Military Academy which trains the officer class of the British Army.

15 SH reports the same confusion in section 5 of 'The Flight Path' (*SL*, 25; *PSH*, 478) when he says he is from 'far away' and 'The policeman at the roadblock snapped, "Where's that?"' ('Far Away', *New Yorker*, December 1994).

Grief in North Antrim

[*c.* February–28 October 1982], TS1 (HFC), TS2 (EU 644, b.9, f.16)

Formative single-part TS entitled 'The Light of Ulster' composed on typewriter and paper stock in use at Harvard University, probably February 1982. Revised and retitled as a two-part TS enclosed in a letter to Ted Hughes, 28 October 1982, in which SH describes the poem as 'a little flutter above a strange accident I heard about in Antrim where one whiff of the silage gas killed a man who went up to inspect it' (*LSH*, 212).

I 1 *Fair Head*: spectacular basalt coast formation in the north of Co. Antrim.

I 2 *Tor*: Torr Head, a headland on the north-east coast of Co. Antrim.

I 10 *the light of Ulster*: the title of the earlier draft.

The Discovery of the Eel

8 September 1983, MS1–2 (NLI 49,493/70), TS1 (NLI 49,493/22)

Two consecutive MS drafts, the second dated '3:00 a.m. / 8/9/83', followed by TS enfolding MSS corrections.

4 *ell*: a measure of a strip of cloth.

'Chestnut was the whitest wood veneer'

[*c*. [June?] 1985], MS1, TS1–2 (NLI 49,493/83)

MS and two subsequent TSS, untitled and undated, although proximate MSS dated 17–19 June 1985 include the first draft of 'Clearances' 7, author dated '17/6/85', which may suggest that this untitled sonnet was composed in a similar moment, most likely for consideration in the 'Clearances' sequence of *HL*.

5 'she' is SH's mother, as in 'Clearances' 4: 'You / Know all them things' (*HL*, 30; *PSH*, 372), gratified by his teenage activity in marquetry (assembling thin pieces of wood veneer to create pictures or designs on furniture: here composing a landscape). Her invocation of proverbial wisdom fits her role in 'Clearances' too.

10 *glans*: Latin for acorn or chestnut.

12 *slips and silk*: (made of) tactile materials like the chestnut and the eel-lines.

14 The setting of the woodwork picture corresponds to the completion of the poem.

An Education

[*c*.1992–8?], MS1 (NLI 49,493/109), TS1–3 (HFC), TS4a (NLI 49,493/108), TS4b–5 (f.106), TS5 (f.106), TS6a (f.102), TS6b (f.108), TS7 (HFC), TS8 (NLI 49,493/115, HFC)

The MS notebook origins for this poem, as well as those for 'The Gravel Walks' (*SL*, 39–40; *PSH*, 486), are formatively intertwined with 'To a Dutch Potter in Ireland' (*SL*, 2; *PSH*, 463), for which 'An Education' provided an opening section of thirty-two lines and a title for its initial drafts, before reduction to a six-line epigraph that SH described to his publishers on 7 September 1995 as 'the last remaining stanza of an earlier section' (EU 1420, b.4). Following the publication of 'To a Dutch Potter in Ireland', SH returned to the unused 'earlier section' to compose a discrete, undated TS of forty lines, entitled 'An Education' that is collected with *EL* papers in the NLI, and formatted in kind, suggesting that it was produced for consideration for that volume at that time. In an essay of 1998, SH quotes *ll*. 17–32, referring to it as a poem written 'a few years ago', which would reasonably date the genesis of the draft ('Total Absorption', in *Barrie Cooke*, Belfast: Gandon Editions, 1998, 6).

The occasion described in the poem is a visit to Barrie Cooke and Sonja Landweer at The Island, Co. Kilkenny, in February 1972 by the Heaneys after they had decided to move to the south of Ireland and were looking for somewhere to live. They gave serious consideration to the area around Kilkenny to be near Cooke and Landweer, whose 'vision and example proved important in those days, when we ourselves had just come back from Berkeley and were feeling a need for a change of direction and rededication of purpose' ('Total Absorption', 6). The poet's somewhat ritualistic experience on the occasion is described in 'The King of the Ditchbacks, III' (*SI*, 57–8; *PSH*, 316–17) and in the MS archive poem 'The Island' (BC 1280725).

Title Colloquial idiom in Ulsterspeak meaning something like a lesson to 'the pair of us' (*l*. 21).

Epigraph *Thomastown, 1972*: town close to The Island, where Cooke and Landweer lived before moving to Jerpoint in December 1972.

3 The host's 'paint-smudged cheeks' identifies him as Cooke.

6 They are displaced because they have moved from their home in Belfast.

14 As at the end of 'Oral English' the trampoline is an image of artistic life and progress.

15–16 The details of the idealised new environment – 'nine beanrows' and 'a small cabin' – are taken from Yeats's 'The Lake Isle of Innisfree'.

18 The marching season in July in Ulster and the bombs in the Netherlands during World War II.

26 *cotyledon*: the first leaves that develop from the embryo of a seed plant (cf. '*from* Holdings' (*PSH*, 389)).

33–40 Close correspondence to the epigraph to 'To a Dutch Potter in Ireland':

> *Then I entered a strongroom of vocabulary*
> *Where words like urns that had come through the fire*
> *Stood in their bone-dry alcoves next a kiln*
>
> *And came away changed, like the guard who'd seen*
> *The stone move in a diamond-blaze of air*
> *Or the gates of horn behind the gates of clay.* (SL, 2; PSH, 463)

Ribbons

[*c*.1998?], MS1, TS1–5a (HFC), TS5b–6 (NLI 49,493/113), TS7 (HFC)

Undated MS notebook draft, followed by annotated TSS of thirty-three lines then subsequent revisions of twenty-eight lines from pre-*EL* period, 1998–2001.

The children in the poem are SH's sisters, Sheena and Ann, who were the oldest of his seven younger siblings. They are having their school photograph taken and a sense of occasion is given by the prayer-like anaphoric opening, 'In the name of'.

The Whirligig

[1998–2001], TS1–5 (HFC)

Five undated TSS *c*.1998–2001 initially entitled 'Bizzing'.

7 *Hughie Scullion*: SH's granduncle, who willed his farm at The Wood to SH's father in 1954.

17ff. Reference to Hieronymus Bosch, *Christ Child with a Walking Frame*, *c*.1480 (Kunsthistorisches Museum, Vienna) in which the naked child is carrying a toy windmill or whirligig. The image was used on the cover of *OG*.

18 *Hieronymus*: silently corrected from TS 'Hieronymous' (error).

The Race

[*c*.1998–2009], TS1–3 (HFC)

An undated TS produced *c*.1996–8 on electric typewriter, revisited in two later word-processed drafts, *c*.2009–10.

Title Mill race; also the child racing on his bicycle to bring his mother the news of her father's death.

1 William Clark & Sons at Maghera, said to be the oldest linen mill in Northern Ireland.

11 *Who's that*: introducing the poet as child; the same questioning formula is used to introduce the poet's parents in the two twelve-line poems of 'Uncoupled' (*HC*, 10–11; *PSH*, 646).

Arkansas

[*c*.2000–1?], TS1 (HFC)

Undated TS. In a letter to the piper Liam O'Flynn, 5 January [2001], SH writes: 'I've been fiddling with this Japanese form called the tanka – two lines longer than the haiku, and a development of it – consisting of five lines of five-seven-five-seven-seven syllables. It's like a wee pastry cutter I nick into the ould dough inside the head, just to give it shape. Verse-nips from Nippon' (*LSH*, 519). 'Arkansas' is one of a series of five tanka sequences drafted (and in some cases published) between later 2000 and May 2001.

5 *Conway*: city location of the University of Central Arkansas; in a letter to Jean Kennedy Smith, 5 March 1996, SH writes: 'I was proud not only to have been quoted in the President's speeches but also to be able to tell him about my long-standing affection for Arkansas – especially a certain hardware store in the town of Conway!' (*LSH*, 450.)

11 *Jim Whitehead*: poet and teacher of Creative Writing in the University of Arkansas, SH's host there.

Sweeney as Lyre

[*c*.2002–10?], TS1–4 (HFC)

Undated TSS, *EL* and *DC* period. As well as in *SA* itself and the Sweeney-connected poems in the 'Sweeney Redivivus' section of *SI*, there are a number of poems in the author's archives that employ the figure of Sweeney or just his name. Several of those are connected to events in the Sweeney epic itself ('Sweeney's Verdict on Ronan', for instance), but others, like the poems using his name in 'Sweeney Redivivus', escape the context of the framework story altogether and are adapted to constitute new lyrics. For example, 'The Master', which SH says is 'a transmogrified account of meeting Czesław Miłosz' (*SS*, 262), was originally called 'Sweeney as Novice'; similarly, the Cézanne poem 'An Artist' had been 'Sweeney Praises an Artist'. Here, 'Sweeney as Lyre' is included as sole representative of the poems in which Sweeney is no more than a name; for more on SA, see *TSH* (539–46).

Title Lyre perhaps as the instrument that accompanies elegy.

1 The 'I' figure in these poems, perched on wooden joists, is aptly balanced between bird and narrator of child's experience.

3 *He*: identified in *l.* 7 as 'my instructor', is a workman that the child accompanies.

5 The one who falls to his death through a slate roof is the first of the stories of warning to the child; the second in *l.* 6 lost his footing on wet planks. The phrase 'the one who' to refer to a death victim is used by SH in 'The King of the Ditchbacks', II (*SI*, 57; *PSH*, 316) in a series reminiscent of T. S. Eliot's 'Marina' (1930).

9 *Bakelite 78s*: the 78 rpm records played on old gramophones.

10 *boy-deeds*: the childhood achievements of Fenian heroes like Fionn and Cú Chulainn, used also in 'The Loose Box', *l.* 65, in description of Michael Collins (*EL*, 16; *PSH*, 534).

14 The child's using scraps of building wood to paint on (as in 'The Whirligig', *PSH*, 1186).

Chair, Pocket Knife, Guitar

[24 July 2004], TS1 (HFC, NLI 49,493/129)

Undated TSS, written for the wedding of SH's son Christopher and his wife Jenny and read by SH at the wedding on 24 July 2004. Christopher is a drummer.

Working the Head

[*c*.2006–9], TS1 (HFC)

Undated TS in two leaves from the *DC* era, taking its title from the Irish colloquialism meaning 'acting cleverly', although here meaning literally the sculpting in the 1960s of SH's head by Carolyn Mulholland, leading Irish sculptor born in Lurgan, Co. Armagh in 1944, dedicatee of 'Poet's Chair' (*SL*, 46–7; *PSH*, 490). SH's daughter Catherine has said it was the likeness of her father that had 'most resonance' for the family.

The Cassette

31 July 2009, TS1–11 (HFC)

Multiple TSS numbered 1–9 from which the first in the sequence is dated '31/7/09', followed by unnumbered TSS that include an apparently final draft, describing a return home for Christmas from college or university and helping his mother to put up the household decorations.

In the Loft

[*c.* [Summer] 2009], TS1 (HFC)

Undated prose poem; proximate archive texts date from July 2009.
    1 The family moved from Mossbawn to the new house at The Wood in 1954.
    12 *upstairs*: the house at Mossbawn was single-storey, so the upstairs at The Wood was a novelty.

Swallow

27 February 2010, TS1 (HFC)

TS author dated by hand '27/2/10 Glanmore'.
    2 *Pienza*: citadel town in Tuscany in the Val d'Orcia, a UNESCO World Heritage Site and first example of Humanist urban planning in Italy. Birthplace of Pope Pius II in 1405, Pienza means 'city of Pius' as he renamed it when he became pope.
    18 Layered and feathered mud of the swallow's nest.

Black Walnuts

[12]–13 July 2013, MS1, TS1–4 (HFC)

Undated MS draft on the back of initial 'Those Winter Evenings' TS in identical brown ink, suggesting a concomitant path for the two poems; first TS dated '13/7/13' revised in brown ink.
    Black walnuts, native to central and eastern North America, are often found by water, as in Massachusetts.

Those Winter Evenings

12–13 July 2013, TS1–3 (HFC)

First TS dated '12/13 July 2013' containing MS additions in brown ink that continue overleaf into first MS draft of 'Black Walnuts'.

SH is reflecting on evening walks with Marie in their later years, on Sandymount Strand just across the road from their house, and looking north together across Dublin Bay towards Howth Head and Dublin Airport.

7 The kite-flier recalls earlier kite-poems, especially 'A Kite for Michael and Christopher' (*SI*, 44; *PSH*, 308), weighed down with its 'long-tailed pull of grief' and 'A Kite for Aibhín' (*HC*, 85; *PSH*, 682) at the end of *Human Chain*.

II: UNPUBLISHED COLLECTIONS IN TYPESCRIPT

Advancements of Learning

Unpublished TS submitted to Dolmen Press, Dublin, Autumn 1965, 41 fos.; HFC.

ADVANCEMENTS OF LEARNING | Poems | by | Seamus Heaney | Seamus Heaney, c/o St Joseph's Training College, Belfast 11.

[i], cover, as above, serves as title-page; [ii], acknowledgements; 1, Contents; 2–39, text.

Contents: *I: Home Territory*: Digging—The Play Way—Mid-Term Break—End of a Naturalist—An Advancement of Learning—The Early Purges—Grand-Uncle—Lighting the Lamp.

II: MacKenna Country: A Pillar of the Community—Progress—MacKenna's Saturday Night—Men's Confessions—MacKenna's Son—Obituary—Fair.

III: Portraits and Landscapes: Taking Stock—Turkeys Observed—On Hogarth's Engraving 'Pit Ticket for the Royal Sport'—At St Enda's Settlement on Aran—In Glenelly Valley—The Folk Singers—Ex-Champ—Easter Son—Poor Women in a City Church—Docker—Storm on the Island—Soliloquy for an Old Resident—Fisher.

Winter Seeds

Unpublished TS gifted to Thomas and Jean Flanagan, Berkeley, January 1970 [1971], 41 fos.; Box 6, Folder 24, Thomas A. Flanagan Collection (AC 1945) Papers MA-00171, Amherst College Archives and Special Collections.

WINTER SEEDS | (most of them) | Tom's and Jean's | 8th January 1970 | Seamus

[i], cover, as above, serves as title-page; [1]–[40], text.

Contents: Home [Summer Home, II]—The Smell [Summer Home, I]—As We Roved Out [Augury]—Wedding Day—Mother of the Groom—Limbo—Bye-Child—A Winter's Tale—Shore Woman—Maighdean Mara—Good-night—Serenades—Nocturne—Dream of the Trenches [Veteran's Dream]—First Calf—The Last Mummer—Intimidation—Tinder—Idyll—Orange Drums, Tyrone 1966—High Street, Belfast, 1786 [Linen Town]—Icon—The Tollund Man—Midnight—Their Brother—Navvy—Frogman—Westering.

Note: cover page in author's hand, likely a misdating of 8 January 1971.

In addition to the Amherst TS, six undated TSS in the National Library of Ireland carry the title page WINTER SEEDS | by | SEAMUS HEANEY in extents ranging from 9–60 folios, four of which carry the dedication, '*For David Hammond and Michael Longley* | Room, room, my gallant boys, | And give us room to rhyme.' (NLI 49,493/18–23, Seamus Heaney Literary Papers, 1963–2010, National Library of Ireland). Poems that appear in addition to the Amherst TS are:

Aubade (Summer Home, V)—Bathing (Summer Home, III)—Dawn—A Dreamer at the Ford [The Other Side, I]—Dulse—Fireside—Fodder—A Gift of Rain—Hawthorns—Impetigo—May—Museum Pieces for Michael S. Harper—Roots—Rubric—Slieve Gallon's Brae—Sometimes—Spell—Spile [Summer Home, IV]—Waves—The Wool Trade.

III: SELECTED EDITIONS AND RECORDINGS

SELECTED EDITIONS

Eleven Poems

Belfast: Festival Publications, Queens University of Belfast, 1965, 20pp.

An edition in three issues, beginning November 1965, featuring poems that will, with the exception of 'Peter Street at Bankside', be collected in *Death of a Naturalist* (1966). The back cover reads 'This pamphlet is one in a series to be published monthly and to include Michael Longley | Seamus Heaney | Derek Mahon | Arthur Terry | Joan Watton | Philip Hobsbaum | Stewart Parker | James Simmons | Seamus Deane'.

Contents: Personal Helicon—Mid-Term Break—Follower—The Diviner—Peter Street at Bankside—Waterfall—Docker—For the Commander of 'The Eliza'—Lovers on Aran—Scaffolding—Death of a Naturalist.

Bog Poems

London: The Rainbow Press, 1975, 44pp.; illustrations by Barrie Cooke.

An edition of 150 copies, May 1975, published between *Stations* and *North*, featuring poems that will be collected in *North*.

Contents: Bone Dreams—Come to the Bower—Bog Queen—Punishment—The Grauballe Man—Tête Coupée—Kinship—Belderg.

Poems and a Memoir

New York: The Limited Editions Club, 1982, 176pp.

An edition of 2000 copies selected by Henry Pearson, introduced by Thomas Flanagan, with a Preface by the author. Founded in 1929, the Limited Editions Club produced fine-press, illustrated signed editions on subscription.

Contents: EARLY UNCOLLECTED POEMS: Fisher—Pastoral—Thaw—Rookery—Corncrake—May Day—Expectant—Boy Driving his Father to Confession.
from DEATH OF A NATURALIST: Digging—Death of a Naturalist—Blackberry-Picking—Churning Day—Follower—Mid-Term Break—At a Potato Digging—The Diviner—Docker—Poem—Scaffolding—Personal Helicon.

from DOOR INTO THE DARK: The Forge—Thatcher—The Peninsula—Requiem for the Croppies—The Wife's Tale—At Ardboe Point—A Lough Neagh Sequence: 1. Up the Shore; 2. Beyond Sargasso; 3. Bait; 4. Setting; 5. Lifting; 6. The Return; 7. Vision—The Plantation—Shoreline—Bogland.

from WINTERING OUT: Bog Oak—Anahorish—Servant Boy—Gifts of Rain—Oracle—A Northern Hoard: 1. Roots; 2. No Man's Land; 3. Stump; 4. No Sanctuary; 5. Tinder—The Tollund Man—Wedding Day—Summer Home—Serenades—Shore Woman.

from NORTH—Mossbawn: Two Poems in Dedication: 1. Sunlight; 2. The Seed Cutters—Antaeus.—Belderg—Funeral Rites—North—Viking Dublin: Trial Pieces—Bone Dreams—Bog Queen—The Grauballe Man—Punishment—Kinship—Hercules and Antaeus—Whatever You Say Say Nothing—Singing School: 1. The Ministry of Fear; 2. A Constable Calls; 3. Orange Drums, Tyrone, 1966; 4. Summer 1969; 5. Fosterage; 6. Exposure.

from FIELD WORK: Oysters—Triptych: 1. After a Killing; 2. Sibyl; 3. At the Water's Edge—The Strand at Lough Beg—Casualty—The Singer's House—The Guttural Muse—Elegy—Glanmore Sonnets—The Otter—The Skunk—Field Work.

Selected Poems 1965–1975

London: Faber & Faber, 1980, 136pp.

The first retrospective, *Selected Poems* drew upon the first four published volumes, *Death of a Naturalist* (1966), *Door into the Dark* (1969), *Wintering Out* (1972) and *North* (1975), in an edition comprising 71 poems. In Britain and Ireland it was the sole trade selection of the author's work until its replacement in 1990 by *New Selected Poems 1966–1987*.

Contents: *from* DEATH OF A NATURALIST: Digging—Death of a Naturalist—The Barn—Blackberry-Picking—Churning Day—Follower—Mid-Term Break—At a Potato Digging—The Diviner—Lovers on Aran—Poem—Personal Helicon.

from DOOR INTO THE DARK: The Forge—Thatcher—The Peninsula—Requiem for the Croppies—Undine—The Wife's Tale—Night Drive—At Ardboe Point—A Lough Neagh Sequence: 1. Up the Shore; 2. Beyond Sargasso; 3. Bait; 4. *from* Setting; 5. Lifting; 6. The Return; 7. Vision—The Given Note—The Plantation—Shoreline—Bogland.

from WINTERING OUT: Bog Oak—Anahorish—Servant Boy—The Last Mummer—Gifts of Rain—Broagh—Oracle—Traditions—A New Song—The Other Side—*from* A Northern Hoard: 1. Roots; 3. Stump; 5. Tinder—The Tollund Man—Nerthus—Wedding Day—Summer Home—Serenades—Shore Woman—Maighdean Mara—Limbo—Bye-Child—Good-Night—Westering.

from NORTH: Mossbawn: Two Poems in Dedication: 1. Sunlight; 2. The Seed Cutters—Funeral Rites—North—Viking Dublin: Trial Pieces—Bog Queen—The Grauballe Man—Punishment—Strange Fruit—Kinship—Act of Union—Hercules and Antaeus—*from* Singing School: 1. The Ministry of Fear; 2. A Constable Calls; 5. Fosterage; 6. Exposure.

Poems 1965–1975

New York: Farrar, Straus and Giroux, 1980, 240pp.

A compendium edition of the author's work published by FSG on becoming SH's US publisher, reprinting the contents of his first four collections that had been originally issued by OUP New York, with the omission of seven poems from *Death of a Naturalist* and one from *Wintering Out*. The selection comprised 136 poems.

Contents: DEATH OF A NATURALIST: Digging—Death of a Naturalist—The Barn—An Advancement of Learning—Blackberry-Picking—Churning Day—The Early Purges—Follower—Ancestral Photograph—Mid-Term Break—Dawn Shoot—At a Potato Digging—For the Commander of the 'Eliza'—The Diviner—Turkeys Observed—Cow in Calf—Trout—Docker—Gravities—Twice Shy—Valediction—Lovers on Aran—Poem—Honeymoon Flight—Scaffolding—In Small Townlands—Personal Helicon.

DOOR INTO THE DARK: Night-Piece—Gone—Dream—The Outlaw—The Salmon Fisher to the Salmon—The Forge—Thatcher—The Peninsula—In Gallarus Oratory—Girls Bathing, Galway, 1965—Requiem for the Croppies—Rite of Spring—Undine—The Wife's Tale—Mother—Cana Revisited—Elegy for a Still-born Child—Victorian Guitar—Night Drive—At Ardboe Point—Relic of Memory—A Lough Neagh Sequence: 1. Up the Shore; 2. Beyond Sargasso; 3. Bait; 4. Setting; 5. Lifting; 6. The Return; 7. Vision—The Given Note—Whinlands—The Plantation—Shoreline—Bann Clay—Bogland.

WINTERING OUT: Part One: Fodder—Bog Oak—Anahorish—Servant Boy—The Last Mummer—Land—Gifts of Rain—Toome—Broagh—Oracle—The Backward Look—Traditions—A New Song—The Other Side—The Wool Trade—Linen Town—A Northern Hoard: 1. Roots; 2. No Man's Land; 3. Stump; 4. No Sanctuary; 5. Tinder—Midnight—The Tollund Man—Nerthus—Cairn-maker—Navvy—Veteran's Dream—Augury. Part Two: Wedding Day—Mother of the Groom—Summer Home—Serenades—Somnambulist—A Winter's Tale—Shore Woman—Maighdean Mara—Limbo—Bye-Child—Good-night—First Calf—May—Fireside—Dawn—Travel—Westering.

NORTH: Mossbawn: Two Poems in Dedication for Mary Heaney; 1. Sunlight; 2. The Seed Cutters. Part One: Antaeus—Belderg—Funeral Rites—North—Viking Dublin: Trial Pieces—The Digging Skeleton—Bone Dreams—Come to the Bower—Bog Queen—The Grauballe Man—Punishment—Strange Fruit—Kinship—Ocean's Love to Ireland—Aisling—Act of Union—The Betrothal of Cavehill—Hercules and Antaeus. Part Two: The Unacknowledged Legislator's Dream—Whatever You Say Say Nothing—Freedman—Singing School: 1. The Ministry of Fear; 2. A Constable Calls; 3. Orange Drums, Tyrone, 1966; 4. Summer 1969; 5. Fosterage; 6. Exposure.

Hailstones

Dublin: Gallery Press, 1984, 28pp.

An edition limited to 750 copies, published on 12 December 1984, featuring poems that will, with the exception of 'Tremor', be collected in *The Haw Lantern* (1987).

Contents: Tremor—Alphabets—The Spoonbait—Terminus—Hailstones—The Riddle—The Stone Verdict—Grotus and Coventina—The Milk Factory—The Mud Vision.

New Selected Poems 1966–1987 | Selected Poems 1966–1987

London: Faber & Faber, 1990, 256pp. | New York: Farrar, Straus and Giroux, 1990, 288pp.

A successor to the 1980 *SP*, revising that selection to include poems from three subsequent volumes, *Field Work* (1979), *Station Island* (1984) and *The Haw Lantern* (1987), as well as a selection from *Stations* and SH's translation of the medieval Irish work *Buile Suibhne*, *Sweeney Astray* (1983). The selection was a co-edition with the US, comprising 118 poems.

Contents: from DEATH OF A NATURALIST: Digging—Death of a Naturalist—Blackberry-Picking—Follower—Mid-Term Break—Poem—Personal Helicon.

from DOOR INTO THE DARK: Thatcher—The Peninsula—Requiem for the Croppies—The Wife's Tale—Night Drive—Relic of Memory—Bogland.

from WINTERING OUT: Bog Oak—Anahorish—Gifts of Rain—Broagh—Oracle—A New Song—The Other Side—The Tollund Man—Wedding Day—Summer Home—Limbo—Bye-Child—Westering.

from STATIONS: Nesting Ground—England's Difficulty—Visitant—Trial Runs—Cloistered—The Stations of the West—Incertus.

from NORTH: Mossbawn: Two Poems in Dedication; 1. Sunlight; 2. The Seed Cutters—Funeral Rites—North—Viking Dublin: Trial Pieces—Bone Dreams—Bog Queen—The Grauballe Man—Punishment—Strange Fruit—Act of Union—Hercules and Antaeus—*from* Whatever You Say Say Nothing—*from* Singing School: 1. The Ministry of Fear; 2. A Constable Calls; 4. Summer 1969; 5. Fosterage; 6. Exposure.

from FIELD WORK: Oysters—Triptych: I. After a Killing; II. Sibyl; III. At the Water's Edge—The Toome Road—A Drink of Water—The Strand at Lough Beg—Casualty—The Badgers—The Singer's House—The Guttural Muse—Glanmore Sonnets—An Afterwards—The Otter—The Skunk—A Dream of Jealousy—*from* Field Work—Song—The Harvest Bow—In Memoriam Francis Ledwidge.

from SWEENEY ASTRAY: Sweeney Praises the Trees—Sweeney Astray—Sweeney's Lament on Ailsa Craig—Sweeney in Connacht—Sweeney's Last Poem.

from STATION ISLAND: The Underground—Sloe Gin—Chekhov on Sakhalin—Sandstone Keepsake—*from* Shelf Life: Granite Chip; Old Smoothing Iron; Stone from Delphi—Making Strange—A Hazel Stick for Catherine Ann—A Kite for Michael and Christopher—The Railway Children—The King of the Ditchbacks—Station Island—*from* SWEENEY REDIVIVUS: In the Beech—The First Kingdom—The First

Flight—Drifting Off—The Cleric—The Master—The Scribes—Holly—An Artist—In Illo Tempore—On the Road.

from THE HAW LANTERN: For Bernard and Jane McCabe—Alphabets—Terminus—From the Frontier of Writing—The Haw Lantern—From the Republic of Conscience—Hailstones—The Stone Verdict—The Spoonbait—Clearances—The Milk Factory—The Wishing Tree—Wolfe Tone—From the Canton of Expectation—The Mud Vision—The Disappearing Island.

The Tree Clock

Belfast: Linen Hall Library, 1990.

An edition limited to 870 copies, September 1990, featuring poems which, with the exception of 'Among the Whins' and 'Proper Names', will be collected in *Seeing Things* (1991), *The Spirit Level* (1996) and *Opened Ground* (1998).

Contents: The Point—Among the Whins—The Pitchfork—The Butter-Print—The Ash Plant—The Journey Back—The Schoolbag—Glanmore Revisited: 1. Scrabble; 2. 1973; 3. The Skylight; 4. Lustral Sonnet—The First Words—Proper Names—The Crossing—A Royal Prospect—The Sounds of Rain—Fosterling.

Opened Ground: Poems 1966–1996 | Opened Ground: Selected Poems 1966–1996

(London: Faber & Faber, 1998, 494pp. | New York: Farrar, Straus and Giroux, 1998, 494pp.)

An expansion edition, *Opened Ground* revised the earlier selections up to 1987, adding poems from the two subsequent single volumes, *Seeing Things* (1991) and *The Spirit Level* (1996), and 'a very few poems not printed in previous volumes' (*OG*, vi), as well as extracting from *The Cure at Troy* (1990) and including his Nobel speech, 'Crediting Poetry' (1995). Approximately 240 poems.

Contents: from DEATH OF A NATURALIST (1966): Digging—Death of a Naturalist—The Barn—Blackberry-Picking—Churning Day—Follower—Mid-Term Break—The Diviner—Poem—Personal Helicon.

Antaeus (1966).

from DOOR INTO THE DARK (1969): The Outlaw—The Forge—Thatcher—The Peninsula—Requiem for the Croppies—Undine—The Wife's Tale—Night Drive—Relic of Memory—A Lough Neagh Sequence—The Given Note—Whinlands—The Plantation—Bann Clay—Bogland.

from WINTERING OUT (1972): Fodder—Bog Oak—Anahorish—Servant Boy—Land—Gifts of Rain—Toome—Broagh—Oracle—The Backward Look—A New Song—The Other Side—Tinder (*from* A Northern Hoard)—The Tollund Man—

Nerthus—Wedding Day—Mother of the Groom—Summer Home—Serenades—Shore Woman—Limbo—Bye-Child—Good-night—Fireside—Westering.

from STATIONS (1975): Nesting Ground—July—England's Difficulty—Visitant—Trial Runs—The Wanderer—Cloistered—The Stations of the West—Incertus.

from NORTH (1975): Mossbawn: Two Poems in Dedication: 1. Sunlight; 2. The Seed Cutters—Funeral Rites—North—Viking Dublin: Trial Pieces—Bone Dreams—Bog Queen—The Grauballe Man—Punishment—Strange Fruit—Kinship—Act of Union—Hercules and Antaeus—*from* Whatever You Say Say Nothing—Singing School: 1. The Ministry of Fear; 2. A Constable Calls; 3. Orange Drums, Tyrone, 1966; 4. Summer 1969; 5. Fosterage; 6. Exposure.

from FIELD WORK (1979): Oysters—Triptych: After a Killing; Sibyl; At the Water's Edge—The Toome Road—A Drink of Water—The Strand at Lough Beg—Casualty—Badgers—The Singer's House—The Guttural Muse—Glanmore Sonnets—An Afterwards—The Otter—The Skunk—A Dream of Jealousy—Field Work—Song—Leavings—The Harvest Bow—In Memoriam Francis Ledwidge—Ugolino.

from SWEENEY ASTRAY (1983): Sweeney in Flight.

The Names of the Hare (1981).

from STATION ISLAND (1984): The Underground—Sloe Gin—Chekhov on Sakhalin—*from* Shelf Life: Granite Chip; Old Smoothing Iron; Stone from Delphi—Making Strange—The Birthplace—Changes—A Bat on the Road—A Hazel Stick for Catherine Ann—A Kite for Michael and Christopher—The Railway Children—Widgeon—Sheelagh na Gig—'Aye' (*from* The Loaning)—The King of the Ditchbacks—Station Island—*from* Sweeney Redivivus: The First Gloss; Sweeney Redivivus; In the Beech; The First Kingdom; The First Flight; Drifting Off; The Cleric; The Hermit; The Master; The Scribes; Holly; An Artist; The Old Icons; In Illo Tempore; On the Road.

Villanelle for an Anniversary (1986).

from THE HAW LANTERN (1987): For Bernard and Jane McCabe—Alphabets—Terminus—From the Frontier of Writing—The Haw Lantern—From the Republic of Conscience—Hailstones—The Stone Verdict—The Spoonbait—Clearances—The Milk Factory—The Wishing Tree—Grotus and Coventina—Wolfe Tone—From the Canton of Expectation—The Mud Vision—The Disappearing Island—The Riddle.

from THE CURE AT TROY (1990): Voices from Lemnos.

from SEEING THINGS (1991): The Golden Bough—Markings—Man and Boy—Seeing Things—An August Night—Field of Vision—The Pitchfork—The Settle Bed—*from* Glanmore Revisited—A Pillowed Head—A Royal Prospect—Wheels within Wheels—Fosterling—*from* Squarings: Lightenings; Settings; Crossings; Squarings.

A Transgression (1994).

from THE SPIRIT LEVEL (1996): The Rain Stick—Mint—A Sofa in the Forties—Keeping Going—Two Lorries—Damson—Weighing In—St Kevin and the Blackbird—*from* The Flight Path—Mycenae Lookout—The Gravel Walks—Whitby-sur-Moyola—'Poet's Chair'—The Swing—Two Stick Drawings—A Call—The Errand—A Dog Was Crying Tonight in Wicklow Also—The Strand—The Walk—At the Wellhead—At Banagher—Tollund—Postscript.

Crediting Poetry (1995).

A Shiver

Thame: Clutag Press, 2005.

An edition limited to 200 copies, that will, with the exception of 'Testimony: The Ajax Incident', be collected in *District and Circle* (2006).

Contents: Höfn—Horace and the Thunder—Helmet—Testimony: The Ajax Incident—Testimony: Anahorish 1944—The Aerodrome—A Shiver—Out of Shot—The Tollund Man in Springtime.

New Selected Poems 1988–2013 | Selected Poems 1988–2013

London: Faber & Faber, 2014, 240pp. | New York: Farrar, Straus and Giroux, 2014, 236pp.

A posthumous selection of SH's later work, discussed by the author with his publisher, and informed by preferences supplied to Marco Sonzogni for an Italian selection of his work. *NSP2014* draws on five volumes from *Seeing Things* (1991) to *Human Chain* (2010), culminating with 'In Time' (2013), and comprises 132 poems.

Contents: from SEEING THINGS (1991): The Golden Bough—Markings—Man and Boy—Seeing Things—An August Night—Field of Vision—The Pitchfork—The Settle Bed—*from* Glanmore Revisited—A Pillowed Head—A Royal Prospect—Wheels within Wheels—Fosterling—*from* Squarings: Lightenings; Settings; Crossings; Squarings.
from THE SPIRIT LEVEL (1996): The Rain Stick—Mint—A Sofa in the Forties—Keeping Going—Two Lorries—Damson—Weighing In—St Kevin and the Blackbird—*from* The Flight Path—Mycenae Lookout—The Gravel Walks—Whitby-sur-Moyola—'Poet's Chair'—The Swing—Two Stick Drawings—A Call—The Errand—A Dog Was Crying Tonight in Wicklow Also—The Strand—The Walk—At the Wellhead—At Banagher—Tollund—Postscript.
from BEOWULF (1999): lines 1–163—lines 3137–3182.
from ELECTRIC LIGHT (2001): Perch—Lupins—*from* Out of the Bag—The Little Canticles of Asturias—Ballynahinch Lake—The Clothes Shrine—Glanmore Eclogue—Sonnets from Hellas—Vitruviana—Audenesque—To the Shade of Zbigniew Herbert—Bodies and Souls—*from* Electric Light.
from DISTRICT AND CIRCLE (2006): A Shiver—Anahorish 1944—Anything Can Happen—District and Circle—Wordsworth's Skates—Found Prose: 1 The Lagans Road, 2 Tall Dames, 3 Boarders—The Lift—Nonce Words—Stern—*from* Out of this World: 1 'Like everybody else...'—In Iowa—Höfn—The Tollund Man in Springtime—Planting the Alder—Tate's Avenue—Fiddleheads—Quitting Time—The Blackbird of Glanmore.
from HUMAN CHAIN (2010): 'Had I not been awake'—Album—The Conway Stewart—Uncoupled—The Butts—Chanson d'Aventure—Miracle—Human Chain—The Baler—Eelworks—The Riverbank Field—Route 110—Wraiths—'The door was open and the house was dark'—In the Attic—A Kite for Aibhín.
In Time (2013).

100 Poems

London: Faber & Faber, 2018; New York: Farrar, Straus and Giroux, 184pp.

A posthumous selection of SH's work made by his family. 'It includes many of his best-loved and most celebrated poems, as well as others that were among his favourites to read and which conjure up that much-missed voice. However, we also made some choices that have special resonance for us individually: evocations of departed friends; remembered moments from a long-ago holiday; familiar objects from our family home.' (*100P*, ix).

Contents: Digging—Death of a Naturalist—Blackberry-Picking—Follower—Mid-Term Break—The Diviner—Twice Shy—Scaffolding—Personal Helicon—The Forge—The Peninsula—Requiem for the Croppies—Night Drive—The Given Note—Bogland—Anahorish—Broagh—The Other Side—The Tollund Man—Wedding Day—Westering—Mossbawn Two Poems in Dedication: 1. Sunlight—2. The Seed Cutters—Funeral Rites—The Grauballe Man—Punishment—*from* Whatever You Say Say Nothing—*from* Singing School: 1. The Ministry of Fear; 2. A Constable Calls; 4. Summer 1969; 6. Exposure—Oysters—A Drink of Water—The Strand at Lough Beg—Casualty—The Singer's House—Elegy—*from* Glanmore Sonnets: II; VII—The Otter—The Skunk—Song—The Harvest Bow—In Memoriam Francis Ledwidge—The Underground—A Hazel Stick for Catherine Ann—A Kite for Michael and Christopher—The Railway Children—*from* Station Island: VII; XII—Alphabets—The Haw Lantern—From the Republic of Conscience—The Stone Verdict—*from* Clearances: 3; 7—The Wishing Tree—*from* The Cure at Troy—Markings—Seeing Things—1.1.87—Field of Vision—*from* Glanmore Revisited: VII. The Skylight—A Pillowed Head—Fosterling—*from* Lightenings: viii—*from* Crossings: xxvii—The Rain Stick—A Sofa in the Forties—Keeping Going—Two Lorries—St Kevin and the Blackbird—The Gravel Walks—A Call—A Dog Was Crying Tonight in Wicklow Also—At the Wellhead—At Banagher—Postscript—Out of the Bag—The Clothes Shrine—*from* Sonnets from Hellas: 1. Into Arcadia—Anahorish 1944—Anything Can Happen—Helmet—District and Circle—Midnight Anvil—The Lift—Höfn—Tate's Avenue—The Blackbird of Glanmore—'Had I not been awake'—The Conway Stewart—Chanson d'Aventure—Miracle—Human Chain—Route 110: i, iii, xii—'The door was open and the house was dark'—In the Attic—A Kite for Aibhín—In Time.

SELECTED RECORDINGS

The Northern Muse

Seamus Heaney and John Montague reading their poetry

Dublin: Claddagh Records, 1968

Twelve-inch vinyl recording on 33 1/3 rpm (side one).

Contents: Personal Helicon—The Diviner—The Barn—Follower—Requiem for the Croppies—The Wife's Tale—Mother—Elegy for a Still-born Child—Bogland—A Lough Neagh Sequence.

Seamus Heaney and Tom Paulin

A Faber Poetry Cassette

London: Faber & Faber, 1983

Single audio cassette (side one).

Contents: Death of a Naturalist—Anahorish—Gifts of Rain—The Tollund Man—Bone Dreams—Funeral Rites—Exposure—The Otter.

Seamus Heaney at Harvard

Heaney reads his own poems and poems of Dunbar, Wyatt, Raleigh, Shakespeare, Marvell, Blake, Wordsworth, Hardy and Yeats

Harvard, Massachusetts: Poetry Room, Harvard College Library, 1990

Twin audio cassette recorded on 18 November 1987.

Contents: Death of a Naturalist—Personal Helicon—Bogland—Tollund Man—Anahorish—Mossbawn: Sunlight—Bone Dreams—Funeral Rites—Exposure—Casualty—The Singer's House—The Otter—The Skunk—Station Island, VII; XII—The Scribes—Alphabets.

Readings

A collection of poems introduced and read by the poets

London: Faber & Faber, 1994

Single audio cassette featuring Philip Larkin, Thom Gunn, Ted Hughes, SH, Douglas Dunn, Tom Paulin and Paul Muldoon (side two).

Contents: Death of a Naturalist—Anahorish—Gifts of Rain—The Tollund Man.

The Poet Speaks

A twentieth-century anthology read by the poets

London: Argo/Polygram Records, 1995

Twin audio cassette featuring a selection of poets (side three).

Contents: Follower—Poor Women in the City Church—Poem for Marie—St Francis and the Birds—Death of a Naturalist.

Stepping Stones

London: Penguin Audiobooks, 1995

Single audio cassette.

Contents: Mossbawn: Sunlight—Personal Helicon—Bogland—The Tollund Man—Punishment—Strange Fruit—Exposure—Oysters—Casualty—Glanmore Sonnets: 2; 3; 7; 10—Station Island: VII—Ugolino—Alphabets—From the Republic of Conscience—Clearances: Prologue; 2; 3; 5; 8—The Wishing Tree—Fosterling—Lightenings: i; ii; vi; vii; viii—Crossings: xxvii; xxxii; xxxiii; xxxiv—Tollund—St Kevin and the Blackbird—Mint—At the Wellhead.

The Poet and the Piper

Dublin: Claddagh Records, 2003

Single CD collaboration with Liam O'Flynn, uilleann pipes.

Contents: The Given Note—Digging—Bogland—At the Wellhead—The Otter—The Yellow Bittern (*An Bonná Buí*)—The Glamoured (*Gile na Gile*)—The Tollund Man—Mid-Term Break—Clearances: III; V—A Call—Seeing Things: iii—St Kevin and the Blackbird—The Annals Say—Postscript.

New Selected Poems

London: Faber & Faber, 2014

Twin CD to mark the publication of *New Selected Poems 1988–2013*, featuring a selection made by Faber and the Heaney family from *NSP1990* (disc one) and *NSP2014* (disc two).

Contents: from NEW SELECTED POEMS 1966–1987:

from DEATH OF A NATURALIST (1966): Digging—Death of a Naturalist—Blackberry-Picking—Follower—Mid-Term Break—Personal Helicon.

from DOOR INTO THE DARK (1969): The Peninsula—Requiem for the Croppies—Night Drive—Bogland.

from WINTERING OUT (1972): Anahorish —Broagh—The Tollund Man—Wedding Day.

from NORTH (1975): Mossbawn: Two Poems in Dedication: 1. Sunlight; 2. The Seed Cutters—Funeral Rites—Punishment—*from* Singing School: 2. A Constable Calls; 6. Exposure.

from FIELD WORK (1979): Oysters—The Toome Road—A Drink of Water—The Strand at Lough Beg—Casualty—The Singer's House—Glanmore Sonnets: VII; X—The Otter—The Skunk—The Harvest Bow—In Memoriam Francis Ledwidge.

from STATION ISLAND (1984): The Underground—A Hazel Stick for Catherine Ann—A Kite for Michael and Christopher—The Railway Children—Station Island: VII; XII.

from THE HAW LANTERN (1987): Alphabets—The Haw Lantern—From the Republic of Conscience —The Stone Verdict—Clearances: 2; 3; 5; 8—The Wishing Tree.

from NEW SELECTED POEMS 1988–2013:

from SEEING THINGS (1991): Markings—Seeing Things—Field of Vision—Glanmore Revisited: I. Scrabble; VII. The Skylight—*from* Squarings: Lightenings: i; viii; Settings: xxii; xxiv; Crossings: xxvii; xxxii; Squarings: xxxix; Squarings: xlviii.

from THE SPIRIT LEVEL (1996): Mint—A Sofa in the Forties—Keeping Going—Two Lorries—St Kevin and the Blackbird—A Call—The Errand—At the Wellhead—Tollund—Postscript.

from BEOWULF (1999): [lines 1–163]; [lines 3137–3182].

from ELECTRIC LIGHT (2001): Perch—Out of the Bag: I; IV—The Clothes Shrine—Sonnets from Hellas: I. Into Arcadia; II. Conkers.

from DISTRICT AND CIRCLE (2006): Anything Can Happen—District and Circle—The Lift—Stern—Höfn—Tate's Avenue—The Blackbird of Glanmore.

from HUMAN CHAIN (2010): 'Had I not been awake'—Chanson d'Aventure—Miracle—Human Chain—A Kite for Aibhín.

Collected Poems

Dublin: RTÉ, 2009; London: Faber & Faber, 2018

Fifteen-CD box set produced for RTÉ by Tim Lehane in 2009 comprising an unabridged recording of SH's eleven collections, *Death of a Naturalist* to *District and Circle*; subsequently rereleased in an expanded format by Faber & Faber in 2018 including a sixteenth disc featuring live recordings of eleven poems from *Human Chain*.

Contents: DEATH OF A NATURALIST —DOOR INTO THE DARK—WINTERING OUT—NORTH—FIELD WORK—STATION ISLAND—THE HAW LANTERN—SEEING THINGS—THE SPIRIT LEVEL—ELECTRIC LIGHT—DISTRICT AND CIRCLE—[*from*] HUMAN CHAIN (Live): 'Had I not been awake'—The Conway Stewart—Uncoupled—The Butts—Chanson d'Aventure—Miracle—Human Chain—The Baler—'The door was open and the house was dark'—In the Attic—A Kite for Aibhín.

Bibliography

The following texts are cited in abbreviated form in the commentary:

Albright 1990	Daniel Albright (ed.), *W. B. Yeats: The Poems*, London, J. M. Dent, 1990
Allen 1997	Michael Allen (ed.), *Seamus Heaney: Contemporary Critical Essays*, Basingstoke and London: Macmillan New Casebooks, 1997
Alonso 2023	Alex Alonso, 'Seamus Heaney's Audio Archive', *Éire-Ireland* (Spring–Summer 2023): 227–48
Brandes 1988	Rand Brandes, 'An Interview with Seamus Heaney', *Salmagundi*, 80 (Fall 1988): 4–21
Brandes 1994	Rand Brandes, 'Secondary Sources: A Gloss on the Critical Reception of Seamus Heaney 1965–1993', *Colby Quarterly*, 30. 1 (March 1994): 63–77
Brandes 2008	Rand Brandes and Michael J. Durkan, *Seamus Heaney: A Bibliography 1959–2003*, London: Faber & Faber, 2008
Brandes 2009	Rand Brandes, 'Seamus Heaney's Working Titles: From "Advancements of Learning" to "Midnight Anvil"', in Bernard O'Donoghue (ed.), *The Cambridge Companion to Seamus Heaney*, Cambridge: Cambridge University Press, 2009, 19–36
Brearton 2009	Fran Brearton, 'Heaney and the Feminine', in Bernard O'Donoghue (ed.), *The Cambridge Companion to Seamus Heaney*, Cambridge: Cambridge University Press, 2009: 73–92
Breslin 1996	Paul Breslin, 'Heaney's Redress', *Poetry*, 168. 6 (September 1996): 337–51
Carson 1975	Ciaran Carson, 'Escaped from the Massacre?', *Honest Ulsterman*, 50 (Winter 1975): 183–6
Coleridge 1912	Samuel Taylor Coleridge, *Poetical Works*, ed. Ernest Hartley Coleridge, Oxford: Clarendon, 1912
Corcoran 1986	Neil Corcoran, *A Student's Guide to Seamus Heaney*, London: Faber & Faber, 1986

Corcoran 1993	Neil Corcoran, *English Poetry since 1940*, London and New York: Longman, 1993
Crotty 1994	Patrick Crotty, 'All I Believe That Happened There Was Revision', in Tony Curtis (ed.), *The Art of Seamus Heaney*, third edn, Bridgend: Seren Books, 1994: 191–224
Cuda 2005	Anthony J. Cuda, 'The Use of Memory', *Journal of Modern Literature*, 28. 4 (Summer 2005), 152–75
Dennison 2015	John Dennison, *Seamus Heaney and the Adequacy of Poetry*, Oxford: Oxford University Press, 2015
Dillon 1995	John Dillon, 'Classical Allusions in Seamus Heaney's *The Haw Lantern*', *Classics Ireland*, 2 (1995): 55–66
Duffy 2013	*1914: Poetry Remembers*, ed. Carol Ann Duffy, London: Faber & Faber, 2013
Falconer 2022	Rachel Falconer, *Seamus Heaney, Virgil and the Good of Poetry*, Edinburgh: Edinburgh University Press, 2022
Fitzgerald 1983	Virgil, *The Aeneid*, trans. Robert Fitzgerald, Harmondsworth: Penguin, 1983
Foster 1967	Kenelm Foster and Patrick Boyde (eds), *Dante's Lyric Poetry*, Oxford: Oxford University Press, 1967
Fowler 2014	Rowena Fowler, 'Plato, Seferis, Heaney: Poetry as Redress', in Dimitris Tziovas (ed.), *Re-imagining the Past: Antiquity and Modern Greek Culture*, Oxford: Oxford University Press, 2014
Fowler 2019	Rowena Fowler, 'Heaney and Hesiod', in Stephen Harrison, Fiona Macintosh and Helen Eastman (eds), *Seamus Heaney and the Classics*, Oxford: Oxford University Press, 2019
Hadfield 1997	Andrew Hadfield and Willy Maley (eds), *Edmund Spenser: A View of the State of Ireland*, Oxford: Blackwell, 1997
Haffenden 1981	John Haffenden, *Viewpoints: Poets in Conversation*, London: Faber & Faber, 1981
Hardy 1976	*The Complete Poems of Thomas Hardy*, ed. James Gibson (London: Macmillan, 1976)
Hart 1992	Henry Hart, *Seamus Heaney: Poet of Contrary Progressions*, New York: Syracuse University Press 1992
Heaney 2000	Marie Heaney, *The Names Upon the Harp: Irish Myth and Legend*, London: Faber & Faber, 2000

Higgins 2021	Geraldine Higgins (ed.), *Seamus Heaney in Context*, Oxford: Oxford University Press 2021
Jack 1985	Ian Jack, 'A Choice of Orders', in Jerome J. McGann (ed.), *Textual Criticism and Literary Interpretation*, Chicago, Illinois: University of Chicago Press, 1985
Jackson 1971	Kenneth Hurlstone Jackson, *A Celtic Miscellany: Translations from the Celtic Literatures* (1951), London: Penguin Books, 1971
Johnston 2020	Maura Johnston, *From Aftergrass to Yellow Boots: A Glossary of Seamus Heaney's Hearth Language*, Derry: Colmcille Press, 2020
Joyce 1992	James Joyce, *A Portrait of the Artist as a Young Man* (1916), ed. Seamus Deane, London: Penguin, 1992
Kinahan 1982	Frank Kinahan, 'An Interview with Seamus Heaney', *Critical Inquiry*, 8. 3 (Spring 1982): 405–14
Kirkpatrick 2007	Dante, *Purgatorio*, trans. Robin Kirkpatrick, London: Penguin Classics, 2007
Lavan 2020	Rosie Lavan, *Seamus Heaney and Society*, Oxford: Oxford University Press, 2020
Lloyd 1981	David Lloyd, 'Seamus Heaney's "Field Work"', *Ariel*, 12. 2 (April 1981): 87–92
Lloyd 1985	'"Pap for the Dispossessed": Seamus Heaney and the Poetics of Identity', *Boundary*, 2 (Winter 1985): 319–42
Longley 1982	Edna Longley, '*North*: "Inner Emigré"' or "Artful Voyeur"?', in Tony Curtis (ed.), *The Art of Seamus Heaney*, third edn, Bridgend: Seren Books, 1994: 63–96
Lysaght 1997	Sean Lysaght, 'Contrasting Natures: the Issue of Names', in J. W. Foster (ed.), *Nature in Ireland: A Scientific and Cultural History*, Dublin: Lilliput Press, 1997
McGuinness 1979	Arthur E. McGuinness, 'The Craft of Diction: Revision in Seamus Heaney's Poems', *Irish University Review* (Spring 1979): 62–91
McKittrick 1999	David McKittrick, Seamus Kelters, Brian Feeley and Chris Thornton (eds), *Lost Lives: The Stories of the Men, Women and Children who Died as a Result of the Northern Ireland Troubles*, Edinburgh and London: Mainstream Publishing, 1999

Marsack 2010	Robyn Marsack and Hamish Whyte (eds), *Eddie at 90*, Edinburgh: Scottish Poetry Library and Mariscat Press, 2010
Miller 2000	*Seamus Heaney in Conversation with Karl Miller*, London: Between the Lines, 2000
Molino 1993	Michael R. Molino, 'Flying by the Nets of Language and Nationality: Seamus Heaney, the "English" Language, and Ulster's Troubles', *Modern Philology*, 91. 2 (1993): 180–201
Moloney 1991	Karen M. Moloney, 'Heaney's Love to Ireland', *Twentieth Century Literature*, 3, in *Wesno*, 3 (Autumn 1991): 273–88
Montague 1974	John Montague (ed.), *The Faber Book of Irish Verse*, London: Faber & Faber, 1974
Murphy 1956	Gerard Murphy (ed.), *Early Irish Lyrics: Eighth to Twelfth Century*, Oxford: Oxford University Press, 1956
O'Brien, 1975	O'Brien, Conor Cruise, 'A Slow North-east Wind', *Listener* (25 September 1975), in Michael Allen (ed.), *Seamus Heaney: Contemporary Critical Essays*, Basingstoke and London: Macmillan New Casebooks, 1997, 25–9
O'Donoghue 2009	Heather O'Donoghue, 'Heaney, Beowulf and the Medieval Literature of the North', in Bernard O'Donoghue (ed.), *The Cambridge Companion to Seamus Heaney*, Cambridge: Cambridge University Press, 2009
O'Donoghue 2016	Bernard O'Donoghue, 'Lough Derg', in David Wallace (ed.), *Europe: A Literary History 1348–1418*, 1, Oxford: Oxford University Press, 2016: 414–26
Parker 2007	Michael Parker, 'From *Winter Seeds* to *Wintering Out*: The Evolution of Heaney's Third Collection', *New Hibernia Review*, 11. 2 (Samhradh/Summer 2007): 130–41
Resch 2021	Stephan Resch 'The Memory of Things', in Marco Sonzogni and Marcella Zanetti (eds), *Raids and Settlements: Seamus Heaney as Translator*, Wellington, NZ: Cuba Press, 2021: 117–34
Ricks 1987	Christopher Ricks, *The Force of Poetry*, Oxford University Press 1987
Robbins 2008	John Donne, *Poems,* 1, ed. Robin Robbins, London: Routledge, 2008

Singleton 1973	Dante Alighieri, *The Divine Comedy: Purgatorio*, trans. Charles S. Singleton, Princeton, NJ: Princeton University Press, 1973
Sonzogni 2021	Marco Sonzogni and Marcella Zanetti (eds), *Raids and Settlements: Seamus Heaney as Translator*, Wellington, NZ: Cuba Press, 2021
Taplin 2019	Oliver Taplin, 'Boustrophedon between Hellas and Home', in Stephen Harrison, Fiona Macintosh, and Helen Eastman (eds), *Seamus Heaney and the Classics*, Oxford: Oxford University Press, 2019
Vendler 1998	Helen Vendler, *Seamus Heaney*, London: HarperCollins, 1998
Wordsworth 1985	William Wordsworth, *The Fourteen-Book Prelude*, ed. W. J. B. Owen, Ithaca: Cornell University Press, 1985

FURTHER READING

In addition to the textual references cited above, the following works have contributed to the reading and research for this edition:

Andrews, Elmer (ed.), *The Poetry of Seamus Heaney*, Cambridge: Icon Books, 1998
Cavanagh, Michael, *Professing Poetry: Seamus Heaney's Poetics*, Washington, DC: Catholic University of America Press, 2009
Corcoran, Neil, *The Poetry of Seamus Heaney: A Critical Study*, London: Faber & Faber, 1998
——, 'Heaney's Shakespeare', *Essays in Criticism*, 70. 1 (January 2020): 64–86
Coughlan, Patricia, 'Bog Queens: The Representation of Women in the Poetry of John Montague and Seamus Heaney', in Toni O'Brien Johnson and David Cairns (eds), *Gender in Irish Writing*, Milton Keynes: Open University Press, 1991: 88–112
Crowder, Ashby Bland, 'Seamus Heaney's Revisions for *Death of a Naturalist*', *New Hibernia Review*, 19. 2 (Summer/Samhradh 2015): 94–112
Cullingford, Elizabeth Butler, 'Thinking of Her . . . as . . . Ireland': Yeats, Pearse and Heaney', *Textual Practice*, 4. 1 (Spring 1990), 1–21
Curtis, Tony (ed.), *The Art of Seamus Heaney*, third edn, Bridgend: Seren Books 1994
Foster, J. W. (ed.), *Nature in Ireland: A Scientific and Cultural History*, Dublin: Lilliput Press, 1997

Foster, Roy, *On Seamus Heaney*, Princeton, NJ: Princeton University Press, 2020

Harrison, Stephen, Fiona Macintosh and Helen Eastman (eds), *Seamus Heaney and the Classics*, Oxford: Oxford University Press, 2019

Laverty, Christopher, *Seamus Heaney and American Poetry*, London: Palgrave Macmillan, 2022

Marshall, W. F., *Livin' in Drumlister: The Collected Ballads and Verses of W. F. Marshall 'The Bard of Tyrone'*, Dundonald: Blackstaff Press, 1983

Morrison, Blake, *Seamus Heaney*, London and New York: Methuen, 1982

O'Brien, Peggy, 'Lough Derg, Europe and Seamus Heaney', *Irish Review*, 13 (Winter 1992–3): 122–30

O'Driscoll, Dennis, '"The Biretta": Heaney's Boater', *Harvard Review*, 17 (Fall 1999): 74–9

Parker, Michael, *Seamus Heaney: The Making of the Poet*, Dublin: Gill & Macmillan, 1993

——, '"His Nibs": Self-Reflexivity and the Significance of Translation in Seamus Heaney's *Human Chain*', *Irish University Review*, 42. 2 (Autumn/Winter 2012), 327–50

Passannanti, Erminia (trans.), *Poesie Scelte di Seamus Heaney*, Oxford: Vortex, 2011

Regan, Stephen, 'Seamus Heaney and the Making of *Sweeney Astray*', *Hungarian Journal of English and American Studies*, 21. 2 (Fall 2015), 317–39

Russell, Richard Rankin, *Seamus Heaney's Regions*, Notre Dame, Indiana: University of Notre Dame Press, 2014

Wall, Richard, 'A Dialect Glossary for Seamus Heaney's Works', *Irish University Review*, 28. 1 (Spring/Summer 1998): 68–86

Woodham-Smith, Cecil, *The Great Hunger: Ireland 1845–1849*, London: Harper and Row and Penguin Books, 1962

Index of First Lines

A boat that did not rock or wobble once 430
A carter's trophy 118
A chocolate van had crashed. That was the news 586
A cobble thrown a hundred years ago 370
A cold clutch, a whole nestful, all but hidden 617
A cold steel fork 292
A fence post trimmed and packed 313
A first green braird: the hawthorn half in leaf 611
A fortune in sand then. Sandpits and sandbeds 314
A gland agitating 83
A house and ground. And your own bay tree as well 547
A humble master of two trades 15
A hurry of bell-notes 317
A latch lifting, an edged den of light 147
A line goes out of sight and out of mind 85
A lone figure is waving 221
A mechanical digger wrecks the drill 34
A pallor in the headlights' 142
A red and gold roof-boss 213
A rowan like a lipsticked girl 243
A salmon sunk on the stiff tines of his fork 103
A shadow his father makes with joined hands 357
A shadow lurches on the sandy ring 18
A smell of chain-oil, worms raddling in brick-dust 1183
A soft whoosh, the sunset blaze 243
A spirit moved, John Harvard walked the yard 354
A stagger in air 126
A thick crust, coarse-grained as limestone rough-cast 29
A time for confidences 66
A time was to come when we yearned 309
A tramp whom parents made crow 100
A tuning fork. An era quavers, passes 387
A wave of Christ's love blood has washed 21
A woman who lives in an old house with stone outbuildings 579
A year has gone, twelve salaries have been spent 17
About a mile above 298
According to Hammond, who heard it out on a spree 559
'After dark' 587
After Oxford and Iceland and Spain and Berlin and Freud 559
After the sudden outburst and the squalls 241
Air from another life and time and place 682
All along the dank, sunk, rock-floored lane 549
All day the clunk of a baler 652
All gone into the world of light? Perhaps 445
All greying sideburns, a spray of scuts 279
All I know is a door into the dark 73

All of us came in Doctor Kerlin's bag 528
All of us on the sofa in a line, kneeling 467
All the times I have heard you sing it 109
All through that Sunday afternoon 308
All year round the whin 88
All year the flax-dam festered in the heart 26
Although they are an occupied nation 362
Alumnae, alumni, graduates 267
Always there would be stories of lights 149
Among my elders, I know better 560
An all-night drubbing overflow on boards 425
An old man's hands, like soft paws rowing forward 324
And lightening? One meaning of that 431
And now, dear groom, dear Tom 581
And so with tuck and tightening of blouse 624
And some time make the time to drive out west 502
And still the youngsters commandeer the trolleys 98
And strike this scene in gold too, in relief 433
And then at midnight as we started to descend 539
And then there was St Kevin and the blackbird 474
And there I was in the middle of a field 687
And there in a boat that came heading towards us 448
'And what was it like,' I asked him 613
And yes, my friend, we too walked through a valley 442
Andy, absorbed, sits reading *en plein air* 579
Angling shadows of itself are what 490
Anointed and all, my father did remind me 570
Any point in that wood 89
Anything can happen. You know how Jupiter 598
Archimedes thought he could move the world if he could 199
'Aren't poems like your toys, Daddy?' 214
As a child, they could not keep me from wells 47
As Dante when he entered Purgatory 577
As he prowled the rim of his clearing 342
As I dipped to test the stream some yards away 375
As I went down the loaning 312
As I work at the pump, the wind heavy 78
As if a trespasser 315
As if he had been poured 189
As if the prisms of the kaleidoscope 334
As you came with me in silence 304
As you plaited the harvest bow 244
Ashwood or oakwood? Planed to silkiness 556
Aside from their tenebrous conversation, I sat learning my catechism 163
Ask me to translate what Loeb gives as 664
At first, in oil-swirls of shadow, in whirlpools of sound 7
At school I loved one picture's heavy greenness 426
At the back of a garden, in earshot of river water 627
At times in Dublin life is tame 399
At Troy, at Athens, what I most clearly 485
Axe-thumps outside 622

Back at the dark end, slats angled tautly down 533
Bann Valley Muses, give us a song worth singing 531
Barbounia schooled below the balcony 550
Bare flags. Pump water. Winter-evening cold 417
Barrie Cooke has begun to paint 'godbeams' 615
Be literal a moment. Recollect 441
Because I perched sometimes on the woodwormed joists 1188
Beetle-sparkling blots 575
Below, the patchwork earth, dark hems of hedge 43
Beneath the ocean of itself, the crowd 428
Bespoke for weeks, he turned up some morning 74
Between my finger and my thumb 25
Big-voiced ancestors 111
Black walnuts hitting a barn roof 1192
Black water. White waves. Furrows snowcapped 329
Blood ran a jewelled delta down the back of the lorry, the 169
Bluebells under trees up on Grove Hill 399
Blurred swimmings as I faced the sun, my back 322
Bobby Breen's. His Boston fireman's gift 598
Body heat under the leaves, matronly 345
Breaking and entering: from early on 419
But still in your cupped palm to feel 650
'*But the structuring, the quality of the feeling . . .?*' At eleven o'clock 521
But your vaccination mark is on your thigh 241
By the harbour down at Smerwick 456

Cabbage stalks, of kale, of marrowstem, of Brussels sprouts. Left at 522
Caedmon too I was lucky to have known 487
Call it a pattern. We called it a tournament. Two pavilions 164
Candle-grease congealed, dark-streaked with wick-soot . . 571
Candystriped red, white and blue, ringed with influence 165
Carries a stone in his pocket 120
Cast-iron waffle-irons 1187
'Catch the old one first,' 409
Catspiss smell 242
Chestnut was the whitest wood veneer 1183
Children's hands in close-up 635
Choose one set of tracks and track a hare 445
Citadel. Hill town 1191
Cities of grass. Fort walls. The dumbstruck palace 483
Claire O'Reilly used her granny's stick 493
Clearable water. There from the start. The sight 518
Cloudburst and steady downpour now 122
Clouds ran their wet mortar, plastered the daybreak 33
Come all ye Ulster loyalists and in full chorus join 107
Come just after the sun has gone down, watch 625
Cotyledon, flap your Greek-filmed wings! 389
Cut from the green hedge a forked hazel stick 37

Dangerous pavements 412
Darcy, child of the stars, of the Hollywood hills 513
Dear Sorley, English may be wrong 453

Derry I cherish ever 675
Derry was *oak grove*. We believed in that 390
'Description is revelation!' Royal 208
Deserted harbour stillness. Every stone 437
Dialect landlocked 285
Discovered rigid as an abandoned plough 64
Dogger, Rockall, Malin, Irish Sea 234
'Don't worry, Marie 579
Dorothy young, jig-jigging her iron shovel 626
Downpours overhead 112
Dusk. Scope of air. A railed pavilion 370

Early autumn morning hesitated 599
Ease him towards the strict arrest of bone 156
Edward Bunting, organist of St Anne's 157
Elbows snugged on the low bridge-wall 13
Energy, balance, outbreak 688
Enter Owen Kelly, loping and gowling 552
'Eorann writes with news of our two otters 673
Even now at twenty-five 14
Even though we called them 'the gypsies', we knew that 610
Everything flows. Even a solid man 438
Everything still. The thump as the car door shut 280
Everywhere plants 657
Examined first in catechism, passed 586

Far from home Grotus dedicated an altar to Coventina 377
Far north, in sunlight 457
Fear of affectation made her affect 372
Feathering the village church 1178
Fetch me the sandmartin 240
Fiddlehead ferns are a delicacy where? Japan? Estonia? 622
Finally I had the chance to drive this automatic car. What was new 583
Finding the right stone, just weighted so 455
Fingertips just tipping you would send you 491
First he was shivering on the shore in skins 583
First it went back to grass, then after that 597
Fishermen at Ballyshannon 146
Flanders. It sounded heavy as an old tarpaulin being dragged 164
For beauty, say an ash-fork staked in peat 136
For certain ones what was written may come true 446
For the bark, dulled argent, roundly wrapped 621
Four doors: calves' house, the middle house, the boiling house, the 523
Four times now I have seen you as another 54
Freckle-face, fox-head, pod of the broom 326
From Casket-ville he first proceeded 633
From Connemara, or the Moher clifftop 58
From Cork to Malin the rummaging tide ('Aubade') 52
From Cork to Malin the rummaging tide ('Expectant') 276
From the mantelpiece my lecture program stares 15
From the start, Burns' birl and rhythm 637
From the start I was lucky 341

'Full face, foursquare, eyelevel, carved in stone 674
Furrow-plodders in spats and bright clasped brogues 673

Glamoured the road, the day, and him and her 498
Go easy, now, go steady 61
Great blue-scooped sky, arching above me 6
Green froth that lathered each end 71
Grey as slugs 9
Gules and cement dust. A matte tacky blood 472
Gunfire barks its questions off Cavehill 198

Had I not been awake I would have missed it 643
Haikus in English hardly ever scan 454
Hangs, a fat gun-barrel 38
'Hank?' I hear you say 254
Harry Boyle's one-room, one-chimney house 608
Hazel stealth. A trickle in the culvert 432
He comes to Aran's scanty grass 62
He conducted the Ulster Orchestra 229
He courted her 197
He draws four of five straws from the stack that stands in 161
He dwelt in himself 343
He fasted on the doorstep of his gift 496
He has given her away 110
He is wintering out 119
He lived there in the unsayable lights 233
He looked both self-possessed and overcome 458
He robbed the stones' nests, uncradled 136
He saw them come, then halt behind the crowd 688
He slashed the briars, shovelled up grey silt 77
He was standing like a milestone 56
He would cultivate the slobland of the larynx 1181
He would drink by himself 223
Heather and kesh and turf stacks reappear 444
Heavy, helpless, carefully manhandled 624
He'll never rise again but he is ready 411
Her scarf *à la* Bardot 41
Here are men in tricorn hats 97
Here is a sectarian alphabet 276
Here is Patrick 95
Here is the girl's head like an exhumed gourd 191
Here they come, freckling the sunset 51
He's a trouble to them 99
He's not in view but I can hear a step 608
He's run away from rocking-horse and toys 57
Hide in the hollow trunk 125
Higgledy-piggledy 354
High burdened brow, the antlers that astound 685
High-riding kites appear to range quite freely 40
His bicycle stood at the window-sill 205
His boots would bruise the crackling detritus 56
His fresher's face, his fresh-stamped student card 578

His hands were warm and small and knowledgeable 412
His suits hung in the wardrobe, broad 646
His touch, his daydream of the tanks 315
'Hold on,' she said, 'I'll just run out and get him 494
Houndstooth stone. Aberdeen of the mind 295
How can we laud her? Let me count the ways 686
Hull and hawser. Fathom thrum. The rope 518
Human beings suffer 395
Hushed 5

I am afraid 139
I am riding to plague again 133
I am the dealer from Tipperary 62
I came expectant, as one learning the trade 1177
I came from water through the hoop of bone 110
I can feel the tug 190
I deserted, shut out 132
I dreamt we slept in a moss in Donegal 235
I expected the lettering to carry 80
I got back into the driver's seat. Sunlight 277
I had come to the edge of the water 327
I have crossed the dunes with their whistling bent 143
I have heard of a bar of platinum 367
I heard new words prayed at cows 342
I knelt. Hiatus. Habit's afterlife . . 321
I lay waiting 187
I love the thought of his anger 346
I loved soft water, rain water 275
I met a girl from Derrygarve 128
(I misremembered. He went down on all fours 429
I moved like a double agent among the big concepts 166
I never warmed to them 344
I remember this woman who sat for years 412
I returned to a long strand 178
I rode south through the petty kingdoms 158
I sat all morning in the college sick bay 32
I see him still, a mystery to the islanders, a goad to me in the pub 633
I shouldered a kind of manhood 176
I sit on the stone coping wall 256
I sit under Rand McNally's 150
I stepped it, perch by perch 121
I stirred wet sand and gathered myself 337
I stood between them 302
I thought of her as the wishing tree that died 375
I thought of walking round and round a space 373
I took the embankment path 27
I used to lie with an ear to the line 233
I was a lookout posted and forgotten 338
I was four but I turned four hundred maybe 444
I was parked on a high road, listening 319
I was six when I first saw kittens drown 30
I watched a long time in the yard 378

I went disguised in it, pronouncing it with a soft 170
I wish, *mon vieux*, that you and Barlo and I 551
If I wasn't there 605
If the twine unravels to the very end 338
'I'll make you one,' he said, 'and balance it ('Three-Piece: A Suit') 505
'I'll make you one,' he said, 'and balance it ('Ten Glosses: A Suit') 559
I'm afraid the millennium 508
I'm staring at the freshly scratched initials 606
I'm writing this just after an encounter 200
In a semi-circle we toed the line chalked round the master's 168
In a stained front-buttoned shopcoat 665
In an age of bare hands 593
In an apothecary's chest of drawers 496
In drifts of sleep I came upon you 424
In famous poems by the sage Han Shan 442
In Iowa once, among the Mennonites 616
In poetry I wish you would 7
In ponds, drains, dead canals 86
In Royal Avenue once (it was Rag Day at Queen's) 577
In small townlands his hogshair wedge 46
In the beginning were the words '*Sois Sage*' 510
In the country poetry has deserted 387
In the deep pool at Portstewart, I waded in 557
In the first flush of the Easter holidays 372
In the gloomy damp of an old garden with its gooseberry bushes 164
In the House of Carnal Murals 488
In the last minutes he said more to her 373
In the middle of the way 235
In the name of the colours 1185
In the wet catacombs of the grass 56
In this cobbled gabled village under 12
In those days she flowed 620
Incline to me, MacDiarmid, out of Shetland 478
Inishbofin on a Sunday morning 410
Inside sleek satin cribs 104
Into your virtual city I'll have passed 617
It could be a jaw-bone 180
It drew them compulsively as a lover 52
It had been badly shot 310
It hits the windscreen 576
It is a kind of chalky russet 294
It is December in Wicklow 208
It kept treading air, as if it were a ghost with claims 167
It looked like a clump of small dusty nettles 466
It rained when it should have snowed 346
It seems she has swallowed a barrel 38
It was a whole new sweetness 541
It was John D. Stewart's ambition to produce a square onion. In the era 522
It was more sleepwalk than spasm 339
It was opulence and amen on the mountain road 549
It was the month of May 663
It wasn't asphodel but mown grass 568

It will be like following Jim Logue, the caretaker 567
It's a long time since I saw 147
It's Hallowe'en. The turnip-man's lopped head 133
It's only twice a week she comes 59
It's raining on black coal and warm wet ashes 470
It's twenty to four 131

Jaws puff round and solid as a turnip 31
Joseph, yes, you know the beat 563

Kelly's kept an unlicensed bull, well away 72
Kennedy thought he'd test him from the start 101
Kinned by hieroglyphic 192
Kit-bag to tool-bag 595

Labourers pedalling at ease 91
Lady with the frilled blouse 42
Lamps dawdle in the field at midnight 84
Larkin's shade surprised me. He quoted Dante 404
Last snow remaindered everywhere on ditches 51
Last time I wrote I wrote from a rustic table 465
Late August, given heavy rain and sun 28
Late summer, and at midnight 228
Leaf membranes lid the window 132
Leave a holed flint on the shelf 106
Leave a holed flint on the shelf 111
Leaving the white glow of filling stations 220
Leonardo said: the sun has never 490
'Lick the pencil' we might have called him 679
Light as a skiff, manoeuvrable 379
'Light came from the east,' he sang 560
Light was calloused in the leaded panes of the college chapel 168
Like a convalescent, I took the hand 335
Like a foul-mouthed god of hemp come down to rut 434
'Like everybody else, I bowed my head 614
Like Gaul, the biretta was divided 414
Like Jim Hawkins aloft in the cross-trees 680
Like somebody who sees things when he's dreaming 515
Lit carriages ran through our fields at night 387
Love, I shall perfect for you the child 42
'Love is knowledge: what has been pried and tried 255

March, the lion, paws the sand 519
Masons, when they start upon a building 44
Master Kieley, Guests and friends 265
Matutinal. Mother-of-pearl 420
'Medium', 14-carat nib 645
Memory as a building or a city ('Five Derry Glosses') 391
Memory as a building or a city ('Settings' xix) 434
Michael, you know I'm expert with the spade 108
Mr Dickson, my neighbour 137
Morning stir in the hostel. A pot 333

Mount Parnassus placid on the skyline 551
Mountain air from the mountain up behind; 446
Mouth loose like an open waistband 12
Must you know it again? 71
My Aunt Jane, she's awful smart 97
'My brain dried like spread turf, my stomach 331
My cheek was hit and hit 365
My father worked with a horse-plough 31
My favourite bas-relief: Athene showing 550
My hand is cramped from penwork 674
My hands come, touched 187
My handsewn leather schoolbag. Forty years 417
My mouth holds round 124
My old hard friend, how you sought 366
My 'place of clear water' 119
My shed is full of long green willow shoots 60
My tongue moved, a swung relaxing hinge 218

Neighbours collected 11
'Nema problema!' The Macedonian 536
Nestrobber's hands 142
Niall FitzDuff brought a jar 623
Niamh's horse for Oisin was grand, but saddle me colly 560
No round-shouldered pitchers here, no stewards 79
No such thing 481
Not a tent of blue but a peek of gold 669
Not an avenue and not a bower 440
Not coal dust, more the weighty grounds of coal 656
Not the age of silver, more a slither ('Shelf Life (1983): Pewters') 280
Not the age of silver, more a slither ('Shelf Life (1984): Old Pewter') 296
Not the brown and fawn car rug, that first one 622
Not the mud slick 242
Not the one who takes up his bed and walks 649
Nothing definite. Maybe she had the cure, maybe she didn't have the 521
November morning sunshine on my back 599
Now, from the basket-maker's door 61
Now, the currachs put out again 63
Now I can only find myself in one place 353
Now that the rest of us have no weeping left 568
Now that your pen is in my hand 686
Now the oil-fired heating boiler comes to life 643

O henny penny! O horsed half-crown! 578
Of all implements, the pitchfork was the one 413
Of all those starting out 685
Often I watched her lift it 295
Oh young boy sad upon the strand 63
Oisín borne away on the saddled steed 639
Old men in distant country summers 11
On a Wednesday morning early I took the road to Derry 505
On Devenish I heard a snipe 219
On my first night in the Gaeltacht the old woman spoke to me 169

INDEX OF FIRST LINES | 1235

On Red Square, the brick wall of the Kremlin 435
On St Brigid's Day the new life could be entered 439
On the bus-trip into saga country 436
On the day he was to take the poison 361
On the day of their excursion up the Thames 421
On the grass when I arrive 628
On the main street of Granard I met Duffy 606
On the most westerly Blasket 87
On top of the world, we'd raised our mint-sprigged bourbon 585
'On you go now! Run, son, like the devil 494
Once, as a child, out in a field of sheep 429
Once and only once I fired a gun 435
Once he woke late, the sun already warm on the linoleum 162
Once I discovered the art of sound effects – galloping coconuts 522
Once they'd been block-built criss-cross and four-squared 594
Once we presumed to found ourselves for good 383
One afternoon I was seraph on gold leaf 432
One morning early I met armoured cars 219
One observes them, one expects them; 37
One summer night in Nairn, when the Moray Firth 634
Only days after a friend had cut his name 418
Only to come up, year after year, behind 438
Or, as we said 117
Our guttural muse 127
Our Lady of Guadalupe. Nothing remains 514
Our Lars always at stud 104
Our shells clacked on the plates 217
Outside the kitchen window a black rat 235
Overhang of grass and seedling birch 431
Overheard at the party, like wet snow 559
Oxen supporting their heads 150

Penelope worked with some guarantee of a plot 361
Perch on their water-perch hung in the clear Bann River 527
Pine cones beyond 388
Polished linoleum shone there. Brass taps shone 371
Post-this, post-that, post-the-other, yet in the end 561
Potato crops are flowering 374
Propellers underwater, cabins drumming, lights 377
Proud to be ranked among his gallowglasses 458

Q. and A. come back. They 'formed my mind' 558

Racoons, soft-footed scavengers 213
Rat-poison the colour of blood pudding 433
Resurfaced, never widened 651
Re-turning time-turned words 46
Right along the lough shore 81
River gravel. In the beginning, that 486
Riverbank, the long rigs 125
Robert Lowell's incomparable high 584
Robin-run-the-hedge 650

Roof it again. Batten down. Dig in   427
Routine patrol off West Mayo; sighting   36
Running water never disappointed   440

Salt off the sea whets   45
Sand-bed, they said. And gravel-bed. Before   444
Saturday evenings we would stand in line   608
Say 'canal' and there's that final vowel   689
Scene: a door, a doorstep, a housefront   516
Scissor-and-slap abruptness of a latch   439
Scuts of froth swirled from the discharge pipe   374
Scyld was still a strong man when his time came   368
Scythe and axe and hedge-clippers, the shriek   418
Seagull at first light above the chimney   388
Séamus, make me a side-arm to take on the earth   604
Seeing the bags of meal passed hand to hand   649
Sensings, mountings from the hiding places   232
Set apart. First out down the aisle   568
Seven years. The usual spellbound term   391
Shaving cuts. The pallor of bad habits   441
She came every morning to draw water   220
She made   506
She never moved from her corner   285
She sleeps now, her cold breasts   144
She taught me what her uncle once taught her   370
She took me into the ground, the spade-marked   672
She would plunge all poets in the ninth circle   236
Sheer, bright-shining spring, spring as it used to be   465
Shifting brilliancies. Then winter light   427
Since the professional wars   134
Sir William Wilde, in his *Beauties of the Boyne*   566
Six days ago the water fell   376
Sky-born and royal   198
Slept (with a boast) on the parquet floor beneath   13
Slowly into his whispering pad   101
Smoke might have been already in his eyes   670
So, he would pay his 'debt to medicine'   293
So a new similitude is given us   369
So from the back of her shrine the Sibyl of Cumae   403
So like a harrow pin   296
So we stopped and parked in the spring-cleaning light   541
So winter closed its fist   76
Soft corrugations in the boortree's trunk   233
Some day I will go to Aarhus   135
Some evenings the city smokes   98
Some people wept, and not for sorrow – joy   480
Somebody lets up a blind   149
Somebody would say   1179
Soot-streaks down the courthouse wall, a hole   536
Speaking broad Devonshire   196
Spoken for in autumn, recovered speech   628
Squarings? In the game of marbles, squarings   428

Star in the window 603
Starling thatch watches, and sudden swallow 5
Statues with exposed hearts and barbed-wire crowns 382
Steady under strain and strong through tension 559
Still red brickwork 638
Strange how things in the offing, once they're sensed 447
Strapped on, wheeled out, forklifted, locked 648
Subjugated yearly under arches 203
Sudden, stunted, crooked-cross 8
Sunlight pillars through glass, probes each desk 47
Sunlight twitches on leaves 10

Take hold of the shaft of the pen 337
Technique is vehicular: the slow pains 157
That dull land was ringed 57
That greeny stuff about your feet 602
That head. She cast it first in plaster and so it remained for thirty 1190
That second, unplanned visit: call it fate 511
That Sunday morning we had travelled far 501
'That three-leggèd, round-bellied, cast-iron pot 674
That's a shooting range 96
'That's what three women could never do – piss in the same po!' 170
The air here, laundered as a nurse's apron 14
The annals say: when the monks of Clonmacnoise 430
The bare bulb, a scatter of nails 305
The big missal splayed 347
The bilingual race 569
The bronze soldier hitches a bronze cape 245
The burn drowns steadily in its own downpour 39
The child cried inconsolably at night 237
The clamour of arrival. Banging doors 1184
The clear weather of juniper 292
The clouds would tatter a moment 345
The colour of meadow hay, with its meadow-sweet 565
The cool that came off sheets just off the line 372
The corrugated iron growled like thunder 418
The dance floor rocks the wind frocks 58
The dark has blotted out Howth Head 282
The dark swooned and flung out a shower 10
The deal table where he wrote, so small and plain 303
The Dirraghs were the fields of the nearly blessed 392
The door was open and the house was dark 680
The dotted line my father's ashplant made 498
The drumming started in the cool of the evening, as if the 166
The effortlessness 407
The 56 lb. weight. A solid iron 473
The first fold first, then more foldovers drawn 475
The first hole neat as a trapdoor 313
The first real grip I ever got on things 424
The first words got polluted 486
The fish faced into the current 138
The flax was pulled by hand once it ripened 20

The fluster of that soft supply and feed 605
The gully flashes 100
The guttersnipe and the albatross 340
The head like a death-mask 95
The horse pistol, we called it 535
The hosed-down chamfered concrete pleases him 625
The ice was like a bottle. We lined up 438
The Irish nightingale 141
The Lagans Road ran for about three quarters of a mile 609
The lambeg balloons at his belly, weighs 206
The legend tells how Patrick 19
The living mother-of-pearl of a salmon 307
The loop of a snowshoe hangs on a wall 297
The lough waters 82
The lough will claim a victim every year 83
The lush 653
The mass and majesty of this world I bring you 626
The moleskins stiff as bark 137
The mouths of tunnels 67
The nineteen-twenties 253
The one that got away 407
The Pacific at your door was wilder and colder 301
The piper coming from far away is you 468
The place has gone down badly. Not like then 16
The pockets of our great coats full of barley 76
The race at Clarke's Mill 1186
The rain smouldered 55
The ram, my sign, wheels into his own now 51
The ridged lip set upstream, you flail 73
The River Foyle, the Roe, the quick Moyola 390
The riverbed, dried-up, half-full of leaves 355
The road ahead 348
The road taken 612
The rock breaks out like bone from a skinned elbow 6
The room's one eye 1178
The royal roads were cow paths 339
The sandmartins' nests were loopholes of darkness in the 162
The screaming from the pool was bad enough 542
The slatted folding chair you sat upon 1189
The small wax candles melt to light 40
The smells of ordinariness 80
The socket of each axehead like the squared 369
The soils I knew ran dirty. River sand 464
The solid letters of the world grew airy 489
The sound of clay being slapped, the shine of it, every now and 1189
The stable door was open, the upper half 532
The stripped and bitten flags 103
The sunlit basalt spondee of Fair Head 1182
The swell foams where they float and crawl 75
The tan clay between the stones in the foot of the hedge was cool 161
The teacher let some big boys out at two 458
The three-tongued glacier has begun to melt 617

The tightness and the nilness round that space 359
The timeless waves, bright, sifting, broken glass 42
The uprights are sharpen'd, pegged straight in the ground 60
The visible sea at a distance from the shore 447
The way we are living 230
The way you had to stand to swing the sledge 593
The white towelling bathrobe 291
The whole county apparently afloat 422
The whole place airier. Big summer trees 419
The wintry haw is burning out of season 360
'The wool trade' – the phrase 130
The work you're going to hear to-night 587
Their bonfire scorched his gable 105
Then all of a sudden there appears to me 500
Then at Christmas he'd return 1190
Then I entered a strongroom of vocabulary 463
Then I found a two-faced stone 112
There, in the corner, staring at his drink 39
There I was all right, the groom in the suit 509
There is a willow grows aslant a brook 514
There they were, as if our memory hatched them 217
There was a sunlit absence 173
There we were in the vaulted tunnel running 291
There's a shadow-boost, a giddy strange assistance 414
There's no heat on the bus, but the engine's running and 611
They are riding away from whatever might have been 380
They both needed to talk 483
They have grafted his nightmares 106
'They just kept turning up 175
They seem hundreds of years away. Breughel 174
They stood. And stood for something. Just by standing 527
They thought he was lost. For years they talked about it 161
They're busy in a high boat 85
Thigh-deep in sedge and marigolds 128
Things I saw best when light was rectangular 256
This evening the cuckoo and the corncrake 232
This morning from a dewy motorway 117
Those were the days 406
Those winter evenings we walked the strand 1192
Three marble holes thumbed in the concrete road 428
Threshed corn lay piled like grit of ivory 27
Thunderface. Not Zeus's ire, but hers 550
Thunderlight on the split logs: big raindrops 234
To be carried back to the shrine some dawn 297
To be marvellously yourself like the river water 560
To Blake and Andrew, Editors 257
To-night, a first movement, a pulse 197
To put a glass roof on the handball alley 431
To say 'oak groves' 1180
To win the hand of the princess 654
Tommy Evans must be sixty now as well. The last time 607
Tonight, my love, a first movement, a pulse 155

Towards Ireland a grey eye 675
Travelling south at dawn, going full out 437
Tufted cranium 9
Tunes from a tin whistle underground 600
Turning a corner, taking a hill 90

Uisce: water. And *fionn*: the water's clear 585
Unless his hair was fine-combed 87
Unseal the undisturbed 286
Unsettling silt 65
Up, black, striped and damasked like the chasuble 239
Up with the cock. The light. The early language 510
Upend the rain stick and what happens next 463
Upon soft ground I found a mortal church 20

Vowels ploughed into other: opened ground 231

Walking with you and another lady 240
Was a bright ritual 1177
Was it wind off the dumps 140
Wasps among sunlit whins. The confidence 264
Water-slicked hair already wafer-dry 638
We are prepared: we build our houses squat 44
We came upon him, stilled 300
We climbed the Capitol by moonlight, felt 443
We first drop anchor, beyond the pier 59
We had already left him. I walked the ice 246
We have no prairies 91
We lived deep in a land of optative moods 380
We look up at her 310
We marked the pitch: four jackets for four goalposts 405
We picked flints 133
We were all hard at it in the boat 567
We were busy in the fetid corner we christened Botany Bay 163
'We were killing pigs when the Americans arrived 594
We were wraiths in the afternoon 672
We'd be told, 'If you don't behave 603
WELCOME HOME YE LADS OF THE EIGHTH ARMY 167
Well, as Kavanagh said, we have lived 204
Weni, widi, wiki – the black gown 275
'We're not a mile off it,' I heard him say, with an *ought* 507
'What bloody man is that?' 'A drum, a drum!' 558
'What did Thought do?' 309
What has the end of an ancestral bed 21
What I loved about that much-snapped scarlet coat 542
What she remembers 139
What stays with me from my time in Santiago 580
What stays with me is the rich braid of his voice 505
What were the virtues of an eelskin? What 434
When all the others were away at Mass 371
When Cézanne died watching the empty door 353
When Francis preached love to the birds 45

When he died a congregation of owls 67
'When he jumps down out of a tree 287
When he said *musk* big generative 279
When he stands in the judgment place 366
When human beings found out about death 495
When I had spread it all on linen cloth 77
When I hoked there, I would find 359
When I imagine civil war 1179
When I landed in the republic of conscience 363
When I lie on the ground 174
When I looked down from the bridge 148
When I made the rush to throw salt 344
When I was a child I thought as a grown-up 1186
When the badger glimmered away 226
When the deaf phonetician spread his hand 495
When the lamp glowed 146
When the new house was nearly finished, soon after the stairs and 1191
When they said *Carrickfergus* I could hear 227
When we climbed the slopes of the cutting 308
When we left the bar at one in the morning 263
When you have nothing more to say, just drive 74
When you plunged 238
When you sat, far-eyed and cold, in the basalt throne 443
Where are you headed, Moeris? Into town? 544
Where does spirit live? Inside or outside 436
Where the flat water 527
Where the sally tree went pale in every breeze 241
Where the strange bird 1180
While the Constabulary covered the mob 207
White bone found 184
White bones that roving dogs had gnawed 276
Whitethorn, not blackthorn 511
Who carved on the butter-print's round open face 489
Who is Billy, what is he 634
Who is this coming to the ash-pit 646
Who rowed out between islands one evening 102
Why, when it was all over, did I hold on to them? 347
Willed down, waited for, in place at last and for good 416
Wind shakes the big poplar, quicksilvering 493
With a billhook 71
With cut-offs of black calico 675
Words are scarfing 109

Years and years ago, these sounds took sides 408
Yeats said, *To those who see spirits, human skin* 441
'Yes, pretty, *veh* pretty.' How many times 543
'Yes,' said the proconsul, replacing the scroll 627
You came to print your future after dark 1181
You can hardly call him a flat-earther since the roundness of it 517
You can still feel the community pack 75
You find anatomical plates 183
You never saw it used but still can hear 384

You sharpened the end of a sally rod, a foot to eighteen inches long,   520
You told me how cattle breasted the sound   99
You were one of those from the back of the north wind   565
You were the one for skylights. I opposed   420
You would hoist an old hat on the tines of a fork   306
Your mother walks light as an empty creel   79
Your songs, when you sing them with your two eyes closed   499
You're off, a pilgrim, in the age of steam   614

Index of Titles

Act of Union 197, 812
Actaeon 685, 1167
Advancement of Learning, An 27, 707
Aerodrome, The 597, 1101
After a Killing 217, 829
After Dark 587, 1094
After Liberation 465
Afterwards, An 236, 845
Aisling 197, 812
Aisling in the Burren, An 309, 883
Album 643, 1140
Alerted 341, 909
Alphabets 357, 919
Among the Whins 264, 859
Anahorish 119, 757
Anahorish 1944 594, 1099
Ancestral Photograph 31, 710
Anniversary Verse 265, 861
Antaeus 174, 801
Anything Can Happen 598, 1102
Aran 6, 695
Architect, An 496, 1032
Aries 51, 721
Arion 567, 1082
Arkansas 1187, 1202
Artist, An 346, 911
Ash Plant, The 411, 966
At a Potato Digging 34, 711
At Ardboe Point 81, 737
At Banagher 500, 1034
At the Water's Edge 219, 830
At the Wellhead 499, 1033
At Toomebridge 527, 1051
At Yeats's Grave 1177, 1195
Aubade 52, 722
Audenesque 563, 1078
Augean Stables, The 550, 1066
Augury 138, 769
August Night, An 412, 967
Away from it All 292, 871

Bachelor Deceased 64, 726
Backward Look, The 126, 762
Badgers, The 226, 836
Bait 84, 738
Baler, The 652, 1147

Ballad 169, 791
Ballynahinch Lake 541, 1061
Banks of a Canal 689, 1171
Bann Clay 91, 741
Bann Valley Eclogue 531, 1054
Baptism 110, 749
Barn, The 27, 707
Basket of Chestnuts, A 414, 968
Basket-Maker, The 60, 725
Basket-Maker's Song, The 60, 724
Bassae 510, 1042
Bat on the Road, A 306, 881
Beacons at Bealtaine 585, 1092
Bedside Reading 419, 974
Belderg 175, 802
Belfast Harp Festival 1792, The 157, 777
Bereaved, The 568, 1083
Betrothal of Cavehill, The 198, 812
Beyond Sargasso 83, 738
Big Wiper, The 583, 1091
Birch Grove, The 627, 1128
Birdwatcher 67, 726
Biretta, The 414, 968
Birl for Burns, A 637, 1133
Birthday Tribute to Marie Bullock 354, 914
Birthplace, The 303, 879
Black Walnuts 1192, 1204
Blackberry-Picking 28, 708
Blackbird of Glanmore, The 628, 1129
Blinker, The 111, 750
Blue 543, 1062
Boarders 611, 1114
Bodies and Souls 567, 1082
Bog Oak 118, 757
Bog Queen 187, 807
Bogland 91, 741
Boiling House, The 523, 1048
Bone Dreams 184, 806
Bookcase, The 556, 1072
Border Campaign, The 536, 1057
Boy Driving His Father to Confession 54, 723
Brancardier 614, 1118

Branded 161, 782
Bridge, The 559, 1074
Brigid's Girdle, A 465, 1008
Broagh 125, 761
Brocquy's *Táin*, Le 575, 1087
Brother Stalk 522, 1047
Butter-Print, The 489, 1025
Butts, The 646, 1142
Bye-Child 146, 773

Cairn-Maker 136, 767
Call, A 494, 1030
Cana Revisited 79, 735
Canopy 663, 1150
Cargo, The 63, 724
Carlo 508, 1040
Cart for Edward Gallagher, A 253, 856
Cassandra 481, 1021
Cassette, The 1190, 1204
Castalian Spring 550, 1067
Casting and Gathering 408, 964
Casualty 223, 835
Catechism, The 558, 1074
Cauled 161, 782
Cavafy: 'The rest I'll speak of to the ones below in Hades' 627, 1129
Ceili on the Deck 58, 724, 725
Centenary Stanza 638, 1133
Chair, Pocket Knife, Guitar 1189, 1203
Chairing Mary 624, 1126
Changes 304, 880
Chanson d'Aventure 648, 1142
Cheers 458, 1001
Chekhov on Sakhalin 293, 872
Chestnut Time 56, 724
'Chestnut was the whitest wood veneer' 1183, 1199
Child Lost 57, 724
Chow, A 606, 1111
Churning Day 29, 708
City, The 638, 1134
Clearances 370, 930
Cleric, The 342, 909
Clip, A 608, 1112
Cloistered 168, 791
Clonmany to Ahascragh 568, 1083
Clothes Shrine, The 541, 1062
Coat, A 507, 1039
Colly 560, 1075
Colum Cille Cecinit 674, 1158
Come to the Bower 187, 807
Comet at Lullwater, The 585, 1092

Confirmation Day 586, 1094
Conkers 549, 1065
Constable Calls, A 205, 819
Conway Stewart, The 645, 1141
Corncrake 56, 723
Cot, The 418, 971
Cow in Calf 38, 714
Craig's Dragoons 107, 748
Crossing, The 448, 996
Crossings 437, 988
Crowing Man 100, 746
Cutaways 635, 1133

Damson 472, 1013
Dawn 149, 774
Dawn Shoot 33, 711
Daylight Art, A 361, 923
Dealer, The 62, 724
Dealing Man, The 62, 724
Dearest Freshness, The 518, 1046
Death of a Naturalist 26, 706
Death of a Painter 669, 1154
Demobbed Bricklayer, The 313, 887
Derry Derry Down 653, 1148
Desfina 551, 1068
Digging 25, 705
Digging Skeleton, The 183, 805
Dirraghs, The 1180, 1197
Disappearing Island, The 383, 944
Discharged Soldier, The 164, 785
Discovery of the Eel, The 1183, 1199
District and Circle 600, 1105
Diviner, The 37, 713
Docker 39, 715
Dog Was Crying Tonight in Wicklow Also, A 495, 1031
'door was open and the house was dark, The' 680, 1162
Dream 71, 730
Dream of Jealousy, A 240, 848
Dream of Solstice, A 515, 1044
Drifting Off 340, 908
Drink of Water, A 220, 832
Driving in the Small Hours 66, 726
Dublin 4 387, 948

Early Purges, The 30, 709
Easter House, The 286, 864
Easter Son 14, 697
Education, An 1184, 1200
Edward Thomas on the Lagans Road 608, 1112

Eelworks 654, 1148
Electric Light 571, 1085
Elegy 230, 839
Elegy for a Postman 102, 746
Elegy for a Still-born Child 79, 736
Empty Surfboard on a Flat Sea, An 517, 1046
'enfant aux rochers, L'' 510, 1041
England's Difficulty 166, 788
Epithalamium, An 581, 1090
Errand, The 494, 1031
Essences 10, 696
Evening at Killard, An 99, 745
Evening Land, The 58, 724, 725
Expectant 276, 863
Exposure 208, 822

Fair 12, 696
Father of the Bride 110, 749
Fiddleheads 622, 1125
Field of Vision 412, 967
Field Work 241, 848
Fil súil nglais 675, 1159
Fireside 149, 774
First Calf 147, 773
First Flight, The 339, 908
First Gloss, The 337, 907
First Kingdom, The 339, 908
First Words, The 486, 1023
Fisher 13, 696
Five Derry Glosses 390, 949
Flight Path, The 475, 1015
Flourish for the Prince of Denmark, A 156, 777
Fodder 117, 756
Folk Singers, The 46, 719
Follower 31, 709
For a Young Nun 21, 699
For Alma Mater 578, 1089
[For Bernard and Jane McCabe] 357, 918
For David Hammond and Michael Longley 117, 756
For the Commander of the 'Eliza' 36, 712
Forge, The 73, 731
Fosterage 208, 821
Fosterling 426, 978
Found Prose 609, 1114
Fragment: 'Nairn in darkness and in light' 634, 1132
Fragment, The 560, 1076

Freedman 203, 817
Frogman 65, 726
From Cave Hill 98, 745
From the Canton of Expectation 380, 941
From the Frontier of Writing 359, 922
From the Land of the Unspoken 367, 928
From the Republic of Conscience 363, 925
Funeral Rites 176, 802

Gaeltacht, The 551, 1068
Gate 21, 699
Gifts of Rain 122, 760
Girls Bathing, Galway, 1965 75, 732
Given Note, The 87, 739
Glanmore Eclogue 547, 1064
Glanmore Revisited 417, 971
Glanmore Sonnets 231, 840
Going In 10, 696
Golden Bough, The 403, 958
Gone 71, 730
Good-night 147, 773
Grace Note for Michael, A 505, 1038
Granite Chip 295, 874
Grauballe Man, The 189, 808
Gravel Walks, The 486, 1023
Gravities 40, 715
Grief in North Antrim 1182, 1198
Grotus and Coventina 377, 937
Grove Hill 399, 953
Guttural Muse, The 228, 837

'Had I not been awake' 643, 1139
Hag, The 285, 864
Hagging Match, A 622, 1125
Hailstones 365, 926
Hank of Wool, A 254, 857
Harrow-Pin, The 603, 1108
Harvest Bow, The 244, 850
Haul, A 407, 964
Haw Lantern, The 360, 922
Hawthorns 1179, 1196
Hazel Stick for Catherine Ann, A 307, 882
He Remembers Lynchechaun 674, 1158
Hedge-School 161, 783
Helmet 598, 1103
Helping Sarah 624, 1126
Her Home 8, 695

Herbal, A 657, 1149
Hercules and Antaeus 198, 813
Hermit, The 342, 909
Hermit Songs 675, 1160
High Street, 1786 97, 744
High Summer 237, 845
His Dawn Vision 483, 1021
His Reverie of Water 485, 1022
Höfn 617, 1120
Holding Course 377, 938
Holdings, *from* 389, 948
Holly 346, 910
Home Fires 626, 1128
Home Help 624, 1126
Homecomings 240, 847
Honeymoon Flight 43, 717
Human Chain 649, 1144

Icon 95, 743
Idyll 96, 744
In a Field 687, 1170
In a Loaning 628, 1129
In a Yard 1180, 1196
In an Airport Coach 67, 726
In Bellaghy Graveyard 458, 1001
In Gallarus Oratory 75, 732
In Illo Tempore 347, 911
In Iowa 616, 1119
In Memoriam Francis Ledwidge 245, 851
In Memoriam: Robert Fitzgerald 369, 929
In Memoriam Sean Ó Riada 229, 838
In Memory of Bill Cole 577, 1088
In Small Townlands 46, 719
In the Afterlife 567, 1082
In the Attic 680, 1163
In the Beech 338, 908
In the Chestnut Tree 345, 910
In the Loft 1191, 1204
In Time 688, 1170
Incertus 170, 793
Indomitable Irishry, The 13, 697
Inisheer 59, 724, 725
Inquisition 170, 792
Intimidation 105, 747
Into Arcadia 549, 1065
Invocation, An 478, 1019
Iridescence, An 586, 1093
Iron Spike 296, 875
Is aire charaim Doire 675, 1159
Is scíth mo chrob ón scríbainn 674, 1158

January God 112, 750
John Field 157, 778
Journey Back, The 404, 962
July 166, 788

Keen for the Coins, A 578, 1089
Keeping Going 468, 1010
Kernes 165, 787
King of the Ditchbacks, The 315, 887
Kinship 192, 810
Kite for Aibhín, A 682, 1164
Kite for Michael and Christopher, A 308, 882
Known World 536, 1058

Lagans Road, The 609, 1114
Land 121, 760
Landfall, A 457, 1001
Last Camp 104, 747
Last Look (1968) 56, 724
Last Look (1984) 300, 877
Last Mummer, The 120, 759
Late in the Day 566, 1081
Late Paul Cézanne, The 353, 913
Latecomers, The 688, 1171
Lauds and Gauds for a Laureate 587, 1094
Lauds for Loretta 686, 1169
Leavings 243, 850
Lenten Stuff 353, 913
Lesson, The 559, 1075
Letter to an Editor 108, 748
'Lick the Pencil' 679, 1161
Lictor 100, 746
Lift, The 611, 1115
Lifting 85, 739
Lightenings 427, 979
Lighting Plot, A 256, 857
Lighting the Lamp 1177, 1195
'Like everybody else . . .' 614, 1117
Limbo 146, 773
Linen Town 131, 764
Lines to Myself 7, 695
Lint Water 20, 699
Little Canticles of Asturias, The 539, 1060
Loaning, The 312, 885
Loose Box, The 533, 1056
Lough Neagh Sequence, A 83, 738
Loughanure 670, 1154
Lovers on Aran 42, 716
Lullaby 63, 724

Lupins 527, 1052
Lustral Sonnet 419, 973

M. 495, 1031
MacKenna's Saturday Night 12, 696
Maighdean Mara 144, 772
Making Strange 302, 878
Man and Boy 409, 964
Marching Season, The 558, 1074
Markings 405, 962
Master, The 343, 909
May 148, 774
Medallion 95, 743
Michael 61, 724
Mid-Term Break 32, 711
Midnight 134, 765
Midnight Anvil 605, 1109
Migration, A 298, 876
Milk Factory, The 374, 935
Ministry of Fear, The 204, 818
Mint 466, 1009
Miracle 649, 1143
Mirror 1178, 1195
Mite-Box, A 650, 1144
Moling's Gloss 560, 1075
Montana 532, 1055
More River Rhymes 456, 1000
Mossbawn: Two Poems in Dedication 173, 800
Mother 78, 735
Mother of the Groom 139, 770
Moyulla 620, 1124
Mud Vision, The 382, 943
muse inspirant le poète, La 509, 1041
Museum Pieces 106, 748
Mycenae 511, 1042
Mycenae Lookout 480, 1021

Natura Naturans 522, 1047
Navvy 137, 768
Neddy 61, 724
Nerthus 136, 767
Nesting Ground 162, 783
New Life, A 155, 777
New Song, A 128, 763
New Worlds 387, 948
Night Drive 80, 736
Night Piece for Tom Flanagan, A 282, 863
Night-Piece 71, 729
Nights, The 483, 1021
Nights of '57 568, 1082

1946 313, 887
1973 418, 972
No Harm 522, 1047
No Man's Land 132, 765
No Sanctuary 133
Nod, The 608, 1112
Non-U 513, 1044
Nonce Words 612, 1116
Norman Simile, A 560, 1075
North 178, 803
Northern Hoard, A 132, 764
Nostalgia in the Afternoon 6, 695

Oarsmen's Song, The 59, 724 725
Ocean's Love to Ireland 196, 811
October Thought 5, 694
'Of all those starting out' 685, 1165
Offerings 97, 744
Old Icons, The 347, 911
Old Perfume Bottle 279
Old Pewter 296, 875
Old Refrain, An 650, 1145
Old Smoothing Iron 295, 874
Old Team, The 370, 930
Omen and Plan 1178, 1196
On His Work in the English Tongue 561, 1076
On Hogarth's Engraving 'Pit Ticket for the Royal Sport' 18, 698
On the Gift of a Fountain Pen 686, 1168
On the Road 348, 911
On the Spot 617, 1121
One Christmas Day in the Morning 607, 1111
1.1.87 412, 966
Open Letter, An 257, 858
Oracle 125, 761
Oral English 1181, 1198
Orange Drums, Tyrone, 1966 206, 820
Other Side, The 128, 763
Otter, The 238, 846
Otterboy 673, 1157
Our Lady of Guadalupe 514, 1044
Our Mystery 633, 1132
Out of Shot 599, 1103
Out of the Bag 528, 1053
Out of This World 614, 1117
Outlaw, The 72, 730
Oysters 217, 829

Parable Island 362, 924

Parking Lot 672, 1157
Party, The 559, 1074
Pastoral 276, 863
Patrick and Oisin 163, 784
Pattern, The 674, 1158
Paved Text, A 285, 864
Peacock's Feather, A 376, 936
Peninsula, The 74, 731
Perch 527, 1052
Personal Helicon 47, 720
Peter Street at Bankside 20, 699
Pewters 280
Pillowed Head, A 420, 975
Pit Stop Near Castletown 584, 1092
Pitchfork, The 413, 967
Plantation, The 89, 740
Planting the Alder 621, 1124
Plaster Cast 1190
Plasterseed 1189
Play Way, The 47, 719
Pleasures of the Day, The 213, 823
Poem 42, 717
Poet Crowned, The 158, 779
Poet to Blacksmith 604, 1109
'Poet's Chair' 490, 1026
Point, The 406, 963
Polder 241, 848
Polish Sleepers 594, 1099
Poor Man's Death 11, 696
Poor Women in a City Church 40, 715
Poplar, The 493, 1029
Postcard from Iceland, A 375, 936
Postcard from North Antrim, A 221, 834
Postscript 502, 1035
Postscript to St Lucia 519, 1046
Present from Mr Pause, A 521, 1047
Present from Old Ardboe, A 577, 1087
Pulse, The 407, 963
Punishment 190, 808
Pussy Willow 279
Pylos 550, 1066

Quitting Time 625, 1127

Race, The 1186, 1202
Rags 103, 746
Railway Children, The 308, 883
Rain Stick, The 463, 1006
Real Names, The 552, 1069
Reaping in Heat 5, 693

Red 542, 1062
Red, White and Blue 542, 1062
Relic of Memory 82, 737
Remembered Columns 489, 1025
Remembering Malibu 301, 877
Requiem for the Croppies 76, 733
Rescue, The 424, 977
Resin 388, 948
Retort 104, 747
Retrospect, A 422, 976
Return, The 86, 739
Ribbons 1185, 1201
Riddle, The 384, 944
Rilke: After the Fire 599, 1104
Rilke: The Apple Orchard 625, 1127
Rite of Spring 76, 733
Riverbank Field, The 664, 1151
Road to Derry, The 505, 1038
Rookery 51, 722
Roots 132, 765
Route 110 665, 1152
Royal Prospect, A 421, 975
Rubric 106, 747

Sabbath-Breakers, The 164, 786
Saint Francis and the Birds 45, 719
St Kevin and the Blackbird 474, 1015
Saint Patrick's Stone 19, 699
Sally Rod 520, 1047
Sally Rod, The 606, 1111
Salmon Fisher to the Salmon, The 73, 730
Sand Boom, The 314, 887
Sandpit, The 313, 887
Sandstone Keepsake 294, 873
Santiago de Compostela 580, 1090
Saw Music 615, 1119
Scaffolding 44, 718
Scene Shifts 418, 972
Schoolbag, The 417, 970
Scotch Fir in City Cemetery 9, 696
Scrabble 417, 971
Screenplay 516, 1045
Scribes, The 344, 910
Scullions 111, 750
Scuttle for Dorothy Wordsworth, A 626, 1128
Sectarian Alphabet 276, 863
Sectarian Latin 275, 862
Sectarian Water 275, 862
Seed Cutters, The 174, 800
Seeing the Sick 570, 1084

Seeing Things 410, 965
Senior Infants 606, 1111
September Song (1968) 98, 745
September Song (1977) 235, 844
Serenades 141, 770
Servant Boy 119, 758
Setting 85, 738
Settings 432, 984
Settle Bed, The 416, 969
Sharping Stone, The 496, 1032
['She taught me what her uncle once taught her'] 370, 930
Sheelagh na Gig 310, 885
Shelf Life (1983) 279, 863
Shelf Life (1984) 295, 874
Ship of Death, A 368, 928
Shiver, A 593, 1099
Shooting Script, A 380, 940
Shore Woman 143, 771
Shoreline 90, 741
Sibyl 218, 830
Sidhe 672, 1156
Sile na Gig 112, 750
Singer's House, The 227, 836
Singing School 203, 818
Sinking the Shaft 162, 783
Sister Clare 579, 1090
Skims and Glances 455, 1000
Skunk, The 239, 847
Skylight, The 420, 974
Slack 656, 1149
Slieve Gallon's Brae 109, 749
Sloe Gin 292, 871
Snapshot, A 579, 1089
Snowball, The 576, 1087
Snowshoe, A 297, 876
Sofa in the Forties, A 467, 1009
Soliloquy for an Old Resident 16, 698
Somnambulist 142, 771
Song 243, 849
Song of My Man-Alive 7, 695
Song of the Bullets, The 378, 938
Sonnets from Hellas 549, 1065
Sonnets from the Peloponnese 510, 1041
Sophoclean 583, 1091
Sounds of Rain, The 425, 977
South Derry Evening 55, 723
Spoonbait, The 369, 929
Squarings 442, 993
Sruth 569, 1083
Station Island 317, 889

Station Island III 277, 863
Station Island IV 280, 863
Stations of the West, The 169, 792
Stern 613, 1116
Stick, The 511, 1042
Stirling Stanzas, The 399, 953
Stone from Delphi 297, 876
Stone Grinder, The 361, 923
Stone Verdict, The 366, 927
Storm on the Island 44, 718
Stove Lid for W. H. Auden, A 626, 1128
Strand, The 498, 1033
Strand at Lough Beg, The 220, 832
Strand Hotel, The 388, 948
Strange Fruit 191, 809
Strange House, A 213, 823
Stump 133, 765
Such Men Are Dangerous 14, 697
Súgán 605, 1110
Suit, A (1997) 505, 1039
Suit, A (2001) 559, 1074
Summer 1969 207, 821
Summer Home 140, 770
Summer Night, A 263, 859
Summer of Lost Rachel, The 374, 935
Sunlight 173, 800
Survivor, The 57, 724
Swallow 1191, 1204
Sweeney as Lyre 1188, 1202
Sweeney Out-Takes 673, 1157
Sweeney Redivivus 337, 907
Sweeney's Returns 345, 910
Sweet William 164, 785
Sweetpea 309, 883
Swing, The 491, 1029
Synge on Aran 45, 718

Taking Stock 17, 698
Tall Dames 610, 1114
Tate's Avenue 622, 1125
Ten Glosses 558, 1073
Terminus 359, 921
Thatcher 74, 731
Thaw 51, 721
Their Brother 99, 745
Thimble, The 488, 1025
Third Degree 103, 747
Those Winter Evenings 1192, 1205
Three Drawings 406, 963
Three-Piece 505, 1039
Tie, A 506, 1039

Tinder 133, 765
To a Dutch Potter in Ireland 463, 1006
To George Seferis in the Underworld 602, 1106
To Mick Joyce in Heaven 595, 1100
To Pablo Neruda in Tamlaghtduff 623, 1125
To Sorley MacLean 453, 999
To the Shade of Zbigniew Herbert 565, 1079
Toast for Rand, A 633, 1131
Toilette, La 291, 870
Tollund 501, 1034
Tollund Man, The 135, 766
Tollund Man in Springtime, The 617, 1121
Toome 124, 761
Toome Road, The 219, 831
Toy for Catherine, A 214, 823
Tractors 9, 696
Traditions 127, 762
Transgression, A 458, 1002
Travel 150, 774
Trea 521, 1047
Tremor 287, 864
Trial Runs 167, 790
Triptych (1977) 217, 829
Triptych (2013) 1166
Triptych for the Easter Battlers 52, 722
Trout 38, 714
Turkeys Observed 37, 713
Turnip Man 97, 744
Turnip-Snedder, The 593, 1098
Turpin Song 535, 1057
Twice Shy 41, 716
Twilight, A 101, 746
Twins 1181, 1197
Two Lorries 470, 1012
Two Paintings by Le Douanier Rousseau 509, 1040
Two Quick Notes 366, 927
Two Stick Drawings 493, 1030

Ugolino 246, 852
Ulster Quatrains 275, 862
Ulster Twilight, An 305, 880
Unacknowledged Legislator's Dream, The 199, 813
Uncoupled 646, 1142
Underground, The 291, 870
Undine 77, 734

Unwinding 338, 908
Up the Shore 83, 738
Úrlár 518, 1046

Valediction 42, 716
Valedictory Verses 387, 947
Verses for a Fordham Commencement 267, 861
Veteran's Dream 137, 769
Victorian Guitar 80, 736
Viking Dublin: Trial Pieces 180, 804
Villanelle for an Anniversary 354, 913
Villanelle for Marie, A 255, 857
Villanelle of Northwest Orient Flight 4, The 454, 1000
Virgil: Eclogue IX 544, 1063
Vision 87, 739
Visitant 167, 789
Vitruviana 557, 1072
Voices from Lemnos: IV, *from* 395, 951

W. H. Auden, 1907–73 559, 1074
Waking Dream, A 344, 910
Walk, The 498, 1033
Wanderer, The 168, 790
Watchman's War, The 480, 1021
Waterbabies 163, 784
Watercolour 579, 1090
Waterfall 39, 714
Wedding Day 139, 769
Weighing In 473, 1014
Welfare State 11, 696
Well at New Place, The 256, 857
Westering 150, 774
What the Brick Keeps 315, 887
Whatever You Say Say Nothing 200, 814
Wheels within Wheels 424, 977
Whinlands 88, 740
Whirligig, The 1186, 1201
Whitby-sur-Moyola 487, 1024
White 542, 1062
White Nights 673, 1157
Who Is Billy? 634, 1132
Widgeon 310, 884
Wife's Tale, The 77, 734
Willow, Ophelia, Moyola 514, 1044
Winter's Tale, A 142, 771
Wishing Tree, The 375, 936
With Hindsight 639, 1135
Wolfe Tone 379, 940
Wood Road, The 651, 1146

Woodcut 109, 749
Wool Trade, The 130, 764
Wordsworth's Skates 603, 1108
Working the Head 1189, 1203
'Would They Had Stay'd' 565, 1080

Wraiths 672, 1156
Writer and Teacher 15, 697

Yank 101, 746
Young Bachelor 15, 698